FEDERAL PRACTICE TOOLS FROM WEST

Courtroom Handbook on Federal Evidence
Steven Goode and Olin Guy Wellborn III

Federal Civil Rules Handbook
Steven Baicker-McKee, William M. Janssen, and John B. Corr

Modern Scientific Evidence
David L. Faigman, David H. Kaye, Michael J. Saks and Joseph Sanders

Federal Jury Practice and Instructions
Kevin F. O'Malley, Jay E. Grenig and William C. Lee
[Instructions available in CD-ROM]

Federal Practice and Procedure
Charles Alan Wright, Arthur R. Miller, Mary Kay Kane,
Edward H. Cooper, Richard L. Marcus, Kenneth W. Graham,
Victor James Gold, Richard D. Freer, Patrick J. Schiltz, Vikram D. Amar,
Joan E. Steinman, Nancy J. King, Susan R. Klein and Michael H. Graham
[Also available in CD–ROM]

**Police Misconduct and Civil Rights:
Federal Jury Practice and Instructions**
Stephen Yagman and Harold S. Lewis, Jr.
[Includes Instructions on Disk]

West's Federal Administrative Practice
Federal Practice Experts

West's Federal Forms
Federal Practice Experts
[Also available in CD–ROM]

Federal Court of Appeals Manual
David G. Knibb

Federal Practice Deskbook
Charles Alan Wright and Mary Kay Kane

Handbook of Federal Evidence
Michael H. Graham

Treatise on Constitutional Law
Ronald D. Rotunda and John E. Nowak

Handbook of Federal Civil Discovery and Disclosure
Jay E. Grenig and Jeffrey S. Kinsler
[Includes Forms on Disk]

Annotated Manual for Complex Litigation
David F. Herr

Federal Rules of Evidence With Trial Objections
Charles B. Gibbons

FEDERAL PRACTICE TOOLS FROM WEST

THE JUDGE'S EVIDENCE BENCH BOOK
Leo H. Whinery

ANNOTATED REFERENCE MANUAL ON SCIENTIFIC EVIDENCE
Michael J. Saks, David L.Faigman, David H. Kaye and Joseph Sanders

---

Federal Case News

Federal Civil Judicial Procedure and Rules

Federal Sentencing Guidelines Manual

Manual for Complex Litigation

Reference Manual on Scientific Evidence

USCA

US Code Congressional and Administrative News

Westlaw®

West Books, CD–ROM Libraries, Disk Products and Westlaw
The Ultimate Research System

To order any of these Federal practice tools, call your West Representative or 1–800–328–9352.

A Student's Guide to the

FEDERAL RULES OF CIVIL PROCEDURE

Eighth Edition

By

STEVEN BAICKER-McKEE
Babst, Calland, Clements & Zomnir, P.C.

WILLIAM M. JANSSEN
Saul Ewing LLP

JOHN B. CORR
Professor of Law, American University
Washington College of Law

Mat #40368625

610 Opperman Drive
P.O. Box 64526
St. Paul, MN 55164–0526
1–800–328–9352

Printed in the United States of America

ISBN 0–314–16129–5

PREFACE TO THE 8TH EDITION OF THE STUDENT'S GUIDE

Like other areas of law, civil procedure experiences important changes from one year to the next. If nothing else occurs, it is a certainty that we will witness important change and development of case law governing our field of study. The past year has been no exception to that rule, but we have also seen a great deal more. This is the year that Congress resumed a central role in shaping the way civil procedure governs class actions. Indeed, the impact of new legislation on that important body of civil procedure can hardly be understated.

What's New in the Eighth Edition: By far the most important effect of Congress' work has been on class action issues relating to jurisdiction, removal, attorneys' fees, and settlement notification. A year ago it is not too much to say that most observers of civil procedure had been impressed with the scope of changes to Rule 23 (governing class actions) itself. At that time we had to report to our readers that the Rule had been altered in areas relating to the time of class certification and notification to class members. Additionally, entirely new subsections of Rule 23 were added that controlled appointment of class counsel and compensation to such attorneys. That was a great deal of change. But what came this year, in the same area of class actions, is probably even more important.

Working through legislation, Congress enacted changes to 28 U.S.C.A. § 1332 (governing diversity jurisdiction) that are intended to ease significantly the ability to file class actions based on state law in federal district courts. At the same time, Congress enacted § 1453, whose purpose, consistent with the amendment to § 1332, was to ease the way for removal to federal court of class actions that were originally filed in state court and which now met the new, more relaxed standards for federal subject matter jurisdiction.

Congress did not stop, however, with jurisdictional and removal issues. New legislation also addressed the issue of attorneys' compensation in important categories of class actions, as well as the issue of notification requirements when settlements are proposed. It may be too much to call some of these changes revolutionary, but it is certain that they will have a significant impact on the way in which class action lawsuits are prosecuted and even, in some cases whether they will be filed at all.

Notwithstanding these changes and others—changes that once again required that we provide close to 1,000 new citations to judicial authority interpreting the federal rules—the format of the Eighth Edition will be familiar to our readers from earlier editions. The heart of the *Student's Guide* begins with a reprint of the text of each Rule. The reprint is followed by a compact distillation of each Rule in the "Purpose and Scope" section. This section, in turn, is followed by a recap of each subpart to the Rule in the "Core Concept" description. A nationwide survey of the "Applications" of the Rule's subparts by the federal courts completes the discussion. Each "Application" is introduced with a bold-printed descriptive heading to allow the law student to identify quickly the points under discussion. The commentary ends with references to other research sources and finding aids.

PREFACE TO THE 8TH EDITION OF THE STUDENT'S GUIDE

When a law student graduates, the relationship with the *Student's Guide* may end. However, the authors of this text also write another study, the *Federal Civil Rules Handbook* (published annually by Thomson/West), which supplements the material contained in the *Student's Guide* with resources essential for civil practitioners, including the full text Advisory Committee Notes to the Rules, the Federal Rules of Evidence, and other helpful aids.

As in years past, we respectfully invite educators and students alike to get in touch with us with suggestions, observations, and criticisms. Veteran readers will recall that these ideas have frequently resulted in improvements to the *Student's Guide*. More such assistance will help maintain the book as an easy-to-use, premier resource that supplements casebooks and treatises on this vitally important subject.

THE AUTHORS

April 2005

THE AUTHORS

Steven Baicker–McKee is co-chair of the litigation group at Babst, Calland, Clements and Zomnir, a Professional Corporation, in Pittsburgh, Pennsylvania. His practice includes a wide variety of commercial litigation, with an emphasis on technology issues, contractual issues, toxic torts, products liability, and energy law.

Mr. Baicker-McKee received his B.A. from Yale University, then spent the next several years building fine furniture and custom cabinets in Charlottesville, Virginia before attending law school. Mr. Baicker-McKee received his J.D. from Marshall–Wythe School of Law, College of William and Mary, where he was on the Board of Editors of the *William and Mary Law Review*. He served a two-year clerkship with the Honorable Glenn E. Mencer of the United States District Court for the Western District of Pennsylvania, to whom he is forever indebted. Mr. Baicker-McKee's tenure as Judge Mencer's law clerk provided the inspiration for this book.

Mr. Baicker-McKee resides in Pittsburgh, Pennsylvania with his wife, Carol, and their three children, Kyle, Eric, and Sara. Their love and support were instrumental in the development of this book. Mr. Baicker-McKee is also grateful for the support of his parents, Joe and Macky Baicker.

John B. Corr is a Professor of Law at the American University, Washington College of Law, in Washington, D.C. As a specialist in civil procedure, conflict of laws, and bankruptcy, he has advised and consulted with private practitioners in a variety of litigation matters. The author of articles dealing with civil procedure and/or conflicts in a number of journals, Mr. Corr has also received numerous "outstanding professor" awards, based on student ballots.

As a member of the New York and District of Columbia Bars, Mr. Corr practiced in the litigation department of the Washington office of Fried, Frank, Harris, Shriver & Kampelman before he began a career in legal education.

Mr. Corr graduated from the Georgetown University Law Center, where he was an editor of the *Georgetown Law Journal*. Before receiving his J.D. degree, Mr. Corr earned M.A. and Ph.D. degrees in history. He also served for two years in the U.S. Army as a captain in military intelligence.

William M. Janssen is a litigation partner in the Philadelphia law firm of Saul Ewing LLP, and co-chair of the firm's LifeSciences practice. Mr. Janssen specializes in commercial litigation, with an emphasis on pharmaceutical and medical device defense, multilevel marketing defense, defense of educational institutions, and litigation under the federal anti-racketeering laws. For five academic years, 1991 through 1996, Mr. Janssen taught as an adjunct instructor at the Temple University School of Law, in addition to his law practice.

Mr. Janssen graduated from St. Joseph's University in Philadelphia and The American University, Washington College of Law, in Washington, D.C. He served as Executive Editor of the *American University Law Review* and as a member of the Moot Court Board. After law school, Mr. Janssen clerked for the Honorable James McGirr Kelly, on the United States District Court for the Eastern District of Pennsylvania, and for the Honorable Joseph F. Weis, Jr., on the United States Court of Appeals for the Third Circuit.

Mr. Janssen thanks his family and friends for teaching him that you have not truly lived until you've answered, for the thousandth time: "No, we're still not done with that book yet." Mr. Janssen dedicates this effort to his parents, Bill and Catherine, and to TMcP.

The authors welcome any comments, suggestions, or constructive criticisms of this book. Their telephone and telefax numbers and email addresses are provided below.

Steven Baicker-McKee
(412) 394–5499
(412) 394–6576 (fax)
sbaicker@bccz.com (email)

John B. Corr
(202) 274–4208
(202) 274–4130 (fax)
jbcorr@cox.net (email)

William M. Janssen
(215) 972–1967
(215) 972–7725 (fax)
wjanssen@saul.com (email)

TABLE OF CONTENTS

*

PART I

FEDERAL JURISDICTION AND VENUE—OVERVIEW

Table of Sections

A. FEDERAL JURISDICTION AND VENUE

§ 1.1 Introduction

Although the Federal Rules of Civil Procedure control many aspects of a civil suit in a district court, the Rules do not contain all the elements that must be satisfied before the suit can be prosecuted successfully. Of particular importance at the onset of litigation are the concepts of jurisdiction and venue. For the most part, these elements are not discussed in the Rules. In fact, Rule 82 provides that the Rules neither increase nor limit a district court's power and obligations in the areas of jurisdiction and venue. A claimant's failure to satisfy requirements of subject matter jurisdiction and venue, however, will usually assure failure in the suit.

Before a federal district court may hear a plaintiff's claim, it must satisfy three prerequisites. These are: (1) jurisdiction over persons or things (*i.e.*, the court's ability to drag an individual into its district); (2) subject matter jurisdiction (*i.e.*, the court's ability to hear a particular kind of claim);[1] and (3) venue.

1. *Ruhrgas AG v. Marathon Oil Co.*, 526 U.S. 574, 119 S.Ct. 1563, 143 L.Ed.2d 760 (1999) (while jurisdictional issues should generally be resolved before court addresses merits of a case, there is no rigid rule directing court to decide

Every cause of action sued upon in a case, irrespective of whether it is a count brought by the plaintiff, a counterclaim, crossclaim, or impleader, must satisfy one of the kinds of jurisdiction over persons or things, *as well as* some kind of subject matter jurisdiction. However, requirements of venue, discussed below, apply only to the claims brought by a plaintiff. If, upon appropriate notice to the court, it is found that any of these requirements are lacking, the court will not hear the case.

§ 1.2 Jurisdiction Over Persons or Things—Introduction

There are three kinds of jurisdiction over persons or things: personal jurisdiction (the normal form of action against an individual, company, or other entity, also known as *in personam* jurisdiction); quasi in rem jurisdiction (actions in the nature of attachment); and in rem jurisdiction (where an object or piece of land is the subject of the lawsuit). Every count in a case must satisfy one or another of these jurisdictional standards.[1] There is no requirement that a count satisfy more than one. However, in cases where one kind of jurisdiction over persons or things is uncertain, it would be a wise tactic to try to satisfy another kind as well. In certain factual settings there may also be advantages if one particular kind or other is achieved.

Important: In the area of jurisdiction over persons or things, it should be kept in mind that in many circumstances the power of a federal court to hear cases is closely analogous to the power of a state court in the state where the federal court sits. Thus, jurisdiction over persons or things should not pose many new problems for practicing attorneys already familiar with similar jurisdictional concepts in state courts.

Important: If jurisdiction over persons or things is absent, and the court also has no quasi in rem jurisdiction or in rem jurisdiction, the typical remedy is to dismiss the claim.[2]

ADDITIONAL RESEARCH REFERENCES

C.J.S. Federal Courts §§ 4(1)–6.

West's Key No. Digests, Federal Courts ⚷3–5.

§ 1.3 Jurisdiction Over Persons or Things—Requirements for Personal Jurisdiction

Two elements play important roles in determining the requirements for personal jurisdiction. These are notions of fair play, as developed under Due Process provisions of the Constitution, and state limitations on the authority of

questions of subject matter jurisdiction before deciding questions of personal jurisdiction).

1. *See, e.g., Youn v. Track, Inc.,* 324 F.3d 409, 417 (6th Cir.2003) ("The party seeking to assert personal jurisdiction bears the burden of demonstrating that such jurisdiction exists;" standard of proof is preponderance of evidence).

2. *See* Rule 12(b)(2)(authorizing dismissal for lack of personal jurisdiction); *See, e.g., Swaim v. Moltan Co.,* 73 F.3d 711, 718 (7th Cir.1996), *cert. denied,* 517 U.S. 1244, 116 S.Ct. 2499, 135 L.Ed.2d 191 (1996) ("If the district court finds itself without [personal] jurisdiction ... then it is obligated to dismiss the case because it has no authority over the defendant.").

the state courts to exercise personal jurisdiction. Fair play, or due process, divides into two components: an evaluation of the contacts that exist between the defendant and the state where the court sits; and an evaluation of the quality of notice of the suit that the defendant received.

§ 1.4 Jurisdiction Over Persons or Things—Requirements for Personal Jurisdiction—Due Process: Consent, In–State Service, or Minimum Contacts

CORE CONCEPT

Before a federal trial court may exert personal jurisdiction over a defendant, it must satisfy the due process standard of the 5th and 14th Amendments of the Constitution. This requirement must be met for each defendant.[1]

This requirement has meant primarily that the exercise of personal jurisdiction must not be fundamentally unfair to the defendant. The most common means of satisfying this fairness requirement are: (1) the defendant's consent to jurisdiction; (2) service of process on the defendant within the territorial confines of a state in which the district court sits; or (3) service of process on a non-consenting defendant not within a state, when such service is fair because the defendant has sufficient "contacts" with the state.

APPLICATIONS

Consent to Jurisdiction

If a party consents to jurisdiction, the Due Process requirement of fairness is satisfied. Consent may occur in a variety of ways. The following examples are typical of circumstances where persons may have consented to personal jurisdiction:

(1) *By Contract:* If the parties, through a contract or agreement prior to the initiation of litigation, consent to the jurisdiction of a court, such agreements will generally be enforced even if the chosen court might not otherwise have been able to sustain its jurisdiction.[2] Exceptions arise when there was substantially unequal bargaining power between the parties that gave one side an unfair advantage in choosing the jurisdiction, or there was the absence of *any* rational link between the court chosen and the parties or cause of action.[3]

1. *Cf., Rush v. Savchuk,* 444 U.S. 320, 332, 100 S.Ct. 571, 572, 62 L.Ed.2d 516 (1980) ("The requirements of *International Shoe* . . . must be met as to each defendant over whom a . . . court exercises jurisdiction." Acknowledging, however, that parties' relationships among themselves may be relevant to their relationships to the forum). *See also Patin v. Thoroughbred Power Boats, Inc.,* 294 F.3d 640, 653 (5th Cir.2002) (*Rush* "does not preclude us from imputing the jurisdictional contacts of a predecessor corporation to its successor corporation or individual alter ego.").

2. *National Equipment Rental v. Szukhent,* 375 U.S. 311, 315, 84 S.Ct. 411, 414, 11 L.Ed.2d 354 (1964). ("[I]t is settled. . . . that parties to a contract may agree in advance to submit to the jurisdiction of a given court.").

3. *See, e.g., Shell v. R.W. Sturge, Ltd.,* 55 F.3d 1227 (6th Cir.1995)(holding that forum selection clause is presumptively enforceable in the absence of fraud, overreaching, grave inconvenience, or violation of forum's public policy).

A related question that arises about forum selection clauses in contracts is whether such clauses may properly *exclude* the use of judicial fora not chosen in the clause (even if such courts could, in the absence of the clause, have exercised personal jurisdiction under, e.g., principles of minimum contacts, discussed elsewhere in this text), or whether forum selection clauses may only provide the potential to *expand* the available fora to include courts that might otherwise have not enjoyed jurisdiction over the parties. It is now settled that such clauses are to be construed according to standard principles of contract law, which may result–depending on the wording of specific clauses in individual cases–in either restriction or expansion of the available fora.[4]

(2) *Waiver:* A party who does not object to personal jurisdiction in a timely manner waives objections, and thereby consents.[5] In the federal courts, timely objections to personal jurisdiction are controlled by Rule 12(b)(2), (g), and (h)(1), and must be raised in the answer or before the answer is filed.

(3) *Counterclaims:* A plaintiff sued on a counterclaim may consent to personal jurisdiction on the counterclaim by filing the original complaint.[6] It is unclear if this consent to jurisdiction over the counterclaim is limited to countersuits closely related to plaintiff's original claims, or whether consent extends to unrelated counterclaims.[7]

On the other hand, most courts agree that if a defendant files *both* an objection to jurisdiction and a claim that is either a counterclaim, cross-claim, or third party impleader, the objection to jurisdiction is not waived[8]—provided that the new claim does not involve the joinder of new parties.[9] The conclusion is that

4. *See, e.g., Dunne v. Libbra,* 330 F.3d 1062, 1064 (8th Cir.2003).

5. *See, e.g., Preferred RX, Inc. v. American Prescription Plan, Inc.,* 46 F.3d 535 (6th Cir. 1995)(defendants objected to personal jurisdiction in their original answer; but when plaintiff filed amended complaint containing new count, defendants answered but did not challenge jurisdiction as to new count; held, as to new count, defendants waived defense of lack of personal jurisdiction).

6. *Adam v. Saenger,* 303 U.S. 59, 58 S.Ct. 454, 82 L.Ed. 649 (1938). (By suing, a plaintiff submits to the court's jurisdiction over counterclaims). *Cf., General Contracting & Trading Co. v. Interpole, Inc.,* 940 F.2d 20, 22 (1st Cir.1991) (third-party defendant in first suit filed second, related suit against original defendant in same court; held, by filing second suit, third-party defendant submitted to personal jurisdiction in first suit).

7. *But see, Threlkeld v. Tucker,* 496 F.2d 1101, 1103 (9th Cir.1974), *cert. denied,* 419 U.S. 1023, 95 S.Ct. 499, 42 L.Ed.2d 297 (1974)(action to enforce state court judgment; held, state court had jurisdiction to hear counterclaim because filing complaint meant plaintiff had submitted to jurisdiction as to *any* counterclaim. *See also Frank's Casing Crew & Rental Tools, Inc. v. PMR Technologies, Ltd.,* 292 F.3d 1363, 1372 (Fed.Cir.2002) ("Where . . . a defendant seeks to bring into the same action new claims against new parties, not arising out of the same transaction or occurrence, such action is not authorized by the joinder rules, and we think that such an attempted joinder constitutes a waiver as to the claims then pending in the action against the party seeking to add the additional claims.").

8. *Bayou Steel Corp. v. M/V Amstelvoorn,* 809 F.2d 1147, 1149 (5th Cir.1987) (not distinguishing between compulsory and permissive counterclaims; holding that view is majority position).

9. *See, e.g., Frank's Casing Crew & Rental Tools, Inc. v. PMR Technologies, Ltd.,* 292 F.3d 1363, 1372 (Fed.Cir.2002) (counterclaims, cross-claims and impleader actions against persons already parties do not, by themselves, constitute a waiver of properly raised objections to jurisdiction; different result if claims do not arise from original transaction or occurrence and are brought against new parties).

an objection to jurisdiction may be preserved if it is filed with a claim asserted against someone who is already a party.

It is unsettled whether filing an in rem action constitutes consent to personal jurisdiction to a counterclaim.[10]

(4) *Consent to Determine Jurisdiction:* Perhaps the most subtle form of consent occurs when a defendant objects to personal jurisdiction, claiming that sufficient links between the defendant and the court do not exist. In that circumstance, the defendant, though preserving the objection to jurisdiction, has consented for the limited purpose of allowing the court to determine whether personal jurisdiction exists.[11]

Transient Jurisdiction ("Tag" Jurisdiction)

A defendant served with process while physically present within a state is normally subject to the personal jurisdiction of the trial courts within that state. It is irrelevant whether the defendant lives within the state or was just passing through; personal jurisdiction is present in such cases simply because the defendant was properly served within the state.[12] One important exception to exercise of "tag" jurisdiction occurs when a defendant was either forced into a jurisdiction, or induced there by fraud. Enticing a defendant to come to a state for bogus reasons will vitiate personal jurisdiction.[13]

Minimum Contacts

A defendant served with process outside the territorial confines of the state where a court sits may nonetheless be subject to the personal jurisdiction of courts within that state. Personal jurisdiction may be sustained even if the defendant does not consent to jurisdiction. For such jurisdiction to be constitutional, the defendant has to have "con-

10. *Compare, United States v. One Lear Jet Aircraft,* 836 F.2d 1571, 1576–77 (11th Cir.1988) (en banc), *cert. denied,* 487 U.S. 1204, 108 S.Ct. 2844, 101 L.Ed.2d 881 (1988) (filing an in rem action does not usually equal consent to personal jurisdiction), *with United States v. 51 Pieces of Real Property, Roswell, New Mexico,* 17 F.3d 1306, 1313 (10th Cir.1994) (rejecting *One Lear Jet Aircraft*; concluding that government submits to personal jurisdiction upon filing forfeiture action).

11. *Insurance Corp. of Ireland v. Compagnie des Bauxites de Guinee,* 456 U.S. 694, 102 S.Ct. 2099, 72 L.Ed.2d 492 (1982). *See also Transaero, Inc. v. La Fuerza Aerea Boliviana,* 162 F.3d 724, 729 (2d Cir.1998), cert. denied 526 U.S. 1146, 119 S.Ct. 2022, 143 L.Ed.2d 1033 (1999) ("[W]hen a defendant appears and challenges jurisdiction, it agrees to be bound by the court's determination on the jurisdictional issue.").

12. *Burnham v. Superior Court,* 495 U.S. 604, 110 S.Ct. 2105, 109 L.Ed.2d 631 (1990) (plurality opinion). *See generally* Fed. R. Civ. P. 4(e)(2). *See also, Edelman v. Taittinger,* 295 F.3d 171 (2d Cir.2002) (tag jurisdiction that is constitutional under *Burnham,* supra, is *a fortiori* applicable to personal service of a discovery subpoena on a non-party); *First American Corp. v. Price Waterhouse LLP,* 154 F.3d 16, 20 (2d Cir. 1998) (subpoena served on non-party witness; "We are satisfied that in light of *Burnham* . . . the assertion of personal jurisdiction . . . based upon service [within a state] satisfies due process."); *Kadic v. Karadzic,* 70 F.3d 232, 247 (2d Cir.1995) ("Fed. R. Civ. P. 4(e)(2) specifically authorizes personal service of a summons and complaint upon an individual physically present within a judicial district of the United States, and such personal service comports with the requirements of due process for the assertion of personal jurisdiction." Citing *Burnham,* supra).

13. *See, e.g., Wyman v. Newhouse,* 93 F.2d 313 (2d Cir.1937), *cert. denied,* 303 U.S. 664, 58 S.Ct. 831, 82 L.Ed. 1122 (1938). *See also, Amusement Equipment, Inc. v. Mordelt,* 779 F.2d 264, 271 (5th Cir.1985)(where defendant's presence is obtained by fraud, service can be quashed).

tacts" with the state in which the court sits of such a quality and nature that exercise of personal jurisdiction would not offend "traditional notions of fair play and substantial justice." [14] It should be noted, however, that the "contacts" necessary to sustain personal jurisdiction need not always be physical contacts. In appropriate circumstances an intentional relationship with residents of a state can be a basis for sustaining personal jurisdiction.[15]

Once such minimum contacts have been identified, the court will then typically evaluate the reasonableness of an assertion of personal jurisdiction over the defendant. The following factors are often considered when a court is determining whether a defendant's contacts with a state are sufficient to sustain personal jurisdiction. There is no requirement that all these factors be satisfied before personal jurisdiction attaches. Moreover, other considerations, not yet identified, may arise and be more significant in the factual settings of other cases.[16]

(1) *Magnitude of Defendant's Contacts:* The greater the defendant's contacts with a state, the more likely it is that a court within that state will sustain personal jurisdiction.[17] Means of measuring magnitude may include the dollar value of defendant's activity or the nature and size of the wrong that defendant is alleged to have committed.

(2) *Purposefulness of Defendant's Contacts:* If a defendant has deliberately engaged in activity within a state, then such purposefulness may support a finding of jurisdiction.[18] Often facts exist where a

14. *International Shoe Co. v. Washington,* 326 U.S. 310, 66 S.Ct. 154, 90 L.Ed. 95 (1945). *Cf., ALS Scan, Inc. v. Digital Service Consultants, Inc.,* 293 F.3d 707, 711 (4th Cir.2002), *cert. denied,* 537 U.S. 1105, 123 S.Ct. 868, 154 L.Ed.2d 773 (2003) ("However minimal the burden of defending in a foreign tribunal, a defendant may not be called upon to do so unless he has had the 'minimal contacts' with that State that are a prerequisite to its exercise of power over him."); *IMO Industries, Inc. v. Kiekert AG,* 155 F.3d 254, 259 (3d Cir.1998) (where plaintiff has not met burden of demonstrating defendant's minimum contacts with forum, court need not reach question of whether exercise of jurisdiction would satisfy fair play and substantial justice).

15. *Burger King v. Rudzewicz,* 471 U.S. 462, 476, 105 S.Ct. 2174, 2184, 85 L.Ed.2d 528 (1985) ("So long as a commercial actor's efforts are 'purposefully directed' toward residents of another State, we have consistently rejected the notion that an absence of physical contacts can defeat personal jurisdiction there."). *See also, e.g., Oriental Trading Co. v. Firetti,* 236 F.3d 938, 943 (8th Cir.2001) (in fraud case, "numerous" telephone calls, faxes and invoices sent to forum state should have caused defendants to understand that injury from fraud would be felt in forum–held, absence of physical contacts with forum may not necessarily defeat personal jurisdiction).

16. *International Shoe Co. v. Washington,* 326 U.S. 310, 66 S.Ct. 154, 90 L.Ed. 95 (1945). *See also Asahi Metal Industry Co. v. Superior Court,* 480 U.S. 102, 113, 107 S.Ct. 1026, 1032, 94 L.Ed.2d 92 (1987) (plurality opinion) (to determine reasonableness, "[a] court must consider the burden on the defendant, the interests of the forum State, and the plaintiff's interest in obtaining relief. It must also weigh in its determination 'the interstate judicial system's interest in obtaining the most efficient resolution of controversies; and the shared interest of the several States in furthering fundamental substantive social policies.' ").

17. *See, e.g., Omeluk v. Langsten Slip & Batbyggeri A/S,* 52 F.3d 267, 270 (9th Cir. 1995)(if defendant's activities had been substantial, then jurisdiction would have been good even if activities had been unrelated to cause of action).

18. *Burger King v. Rudzewicz,* 471 U.S. 462, 474, 105 S.Ct. 2174, 2183, 85 L.Ed.2d 528 (1985)("the constitutional touchstone remains whether the defendant purposefully established minimum contacts in the forum state.").

defendant had no deliberate contact with a state, but could reasonably have foreseen that activities outside a state might have consequences within the state. Thus, selling products into an interstate "stream of commerce," with only an expectation that they will go to a particular state, may nevertheless cause the defendant reasonably to foresee that the products might enter the state and thereby give rise to a cause of action.[19] However, when the facts of a particular case will only support "specific jurisdiction" (if any jurisdiction at all), courts may require that the defendant's contacts with the forum state be more purposeful.[20]

(3) *Systematic and Continuous Nature of Defendant's Contacts:* The longer a defendant's contacts with a state endure, the greater the possibility that such contacts may be used to sustain personal jurisdiction.[21] Thus, a corporation doing substantial business within a state for a prolonged period of time will be more vulnerable to personal jurisdiction within that state.[22] Similarly, a defendant domiciled in a state is very likely to be vulnerable to suit in that state (even if process is served outside the state), because domicile almost always connotes a

19. *World–Wide Volkswagen Corp. v. Woodson*, 444 U.S. 286, 296, 100 S.Ct. 559, 567, 62 L.Ed.2d 490 (1980)(good jurisdiction over corporation that injects products into stream of commerce with expectation of sales in forum). *See also, e.g., Clune v. Alimak AB*, 233 F.3d 538, 542 (8th Cir.2000), *cert. denied*, 533 U.S. 929, 121 S.Ct. 2551, 150 L.Ed.2d 718 (2001) (noting that in *Asahi Metal Industry Co. v. Superior Court*, 480 U.S. 102, 107 S.Ct. 1026, 94 L.Ed.2d 92 (1987), five justices of Supreme Court rejected ruling that jurisdiction based on stream of commerce also requires purposeful contact).

20. *Quill Corp. v. North Dakota*, 504 U.S. 298, 112 S.Ct. 1904, 119 L.Ed.2d 91 (1992) (as long as "commercial actor's efforts are 'purposefully directed' toward residents of another State," mail and wire communications can satisfy requirements of personal jurisdiction, notwithstanding absence of physical contacts with State). *See, e.g., Inamed Corp. v. Kuzmak*, 249 F.3d 1356, 1360–61 (Fed.Cir.2001) (discussing three-part test: "(1) whether the defendant 'purposefully directed' its activities at residents of the forum; (2) whether the claim 'arises out of or relates to' the defendant's activities with the forum; and (3) whether assertion of personal jurisdiction is 'reasonable and fair;' " letter sent by defendant to plaintiff's lawyer in New York held to be purposeful contact with California forum because defendant intended plaintiff to receive letter, and plaintiff was in California; held, letter alone did not satisfy personal jurisdiction over defendant in California; but where defendant also negotiated license agreements with plaintiff, and received royalty payments from plaintiff (who remained in California), jurisdiction is satisfied; held irrelevant that defendant remained in New Jersey while conducting most negotiations); *Chew v. Dietrich*, 143 F.3d 24 (2d Cir.1998), *cert. denied*, 525 U.S. 948, 119 S.Ct. 373, 142 L.Ed.2d 308 (1998) (purposeful availment required for specific jurisdiction). *See also, Asahi Metal Industry Co. v. Superior Court*, 480 U.S. 102, 111, 107 S.Ct. 1026, 1032, 94 L.Ed.2d 92 (1987) (plurality opinion) (to satisfy due process, defendant's substantial connection with state must have been purposefully directed toward state; mere foreseeability of contact following injection of defendant's product into stream of commerce, without more, does not establish personal jurisdiction). *But see Kernan v. Kurz–Hastings, Inc.*, 175 F.3d 236 (2d Cir. 1999) (expressing doubt, but not deciding, whether finding of purposeful availment is prerequisite to assertion of specific jurisdiction).

21. *See, e.g., Omeluk v. Langsten Slip & Batbyggeri A/S*, 52 F.3d 267 (9th Cir. 1995)("systematic and continuous" contacts usually equals good jurisdiction). *Cf., Streber v. Hunter*, 221 F.3d 701, 718 (5th Cir.2000) (where defendant's contact with forum is not continuous, personal jurisdiction is satisfied only when defendant purposefully avails himself of protection of forum law through minimum contacts and where exercise of jurisdiction does not offend fair play and substantial justice).

22. *See also, e.g., Doe v. Unocal Corp.*, 248 F.3d 915, 925–28 (9th Cir.2001) (existence of parent-subsidiary relationship, by itself, does not establish personal jurisdiction over parent based on subsidiary's contacts with forum; instead, to be subject to jurisdiction based on subsidiary's contacts, subsidiary must be either alter ego of parent or agent of parent).

longstanding relationship with a state. Note, however, that a single contact for a short period of time may not be systematic or continuous, but could still sustain personal jurisdiction because the contact is large enough, purposeful enough, and sufficiently related to a cause of action so that the exercise of jurisdiction is not unfair.

(4) *Relation Between Defendant's Contacts and the Cause of Action:* If a defendant's contacts with a state have nothing to do with a cause of action, the burden of establishing personal jurisdiction based on such contacts will be more difficult to achieve.[23] If the contacts are closely related to the cause of action, it is more likely that jurisdiction based on such contacts will be upheld.[24]

(5) *Availability of Witnesses and Evidence:* If the plaintiff's choice of forum will make it burdensome or impossible for the defendant to produce relevant testimony and other evidence, personal jurisdiction will be more difficult to sustain.[25]

(6) *Forum Interest in a Suit:* Although not strictly a contact between a defendant and a state, the presence of a special state interest in a suit might help sustain personal jurisdiction.[26] A state's interest in title to land within its boundaries is such an interest.[27] In practice, however, special state interests are rarely identified, and even when identified, are not often significant in the weighing of factors of fairness.[28]

Jurisdictional Discovery

Sometimes a plaintiff will allege that the defendant has possession of facts demonstrating that the defendant has contacts with the state sufficient to support personal jurisdiction. In such circumstances a court may grant limited discovery to determine such jurisdictional facts. If such discovery is allowed, it will take place within the rules of discovery discussed elsewhere in this text and within any limits the court may impose.

Before authorizing such discovery, courts normally require that the plaintiff make a good faith showing that discovery might lead to facts demonstrating existence of personal jurisdiction over the defendant.[29]

23. *See, e.g., Glater v. Eli Lilly & Co.*, 744 F.2d 213, 216 (1st Cir.1984)(if suit is unrelated to defendant's instate activities, the standard for satisfying jurisdiction is "considerably more stringent").

24. *Cf., Inamed Corp. v. Kuzmak*, 249 F.3d 1356, 1362 (Fed.Cir.2001) ("arise out of or related to" standard "has not been clearly delineated by the Supreme Court").

25. *See, e.g., Terracom v. Valley National Bank*, 49 F.3d 555, 561 (9th Cir. 1995)(availability of witnesses and evidence should be weighed).

26. *Keeton v. Hustler Magazine, Inc.*, 465 U.S. 770, 776, 104 S.Ct. 1473, 1479, 79 L.Ed.2d 790 (1984) (fairness of jurisdiction depends partially on whether state has "legitimate interest" in requiring defendant to answer claim related to defendant's activities).

27. *Shaffer v. Heitner*, 433 U.S. 186, 206, 97 S.Ct. 2569, 2581, 53 L.Ed.2d 683 (1977)(state has interest in marketability of property within its borders that may help support some form of jurisdiction).

28. *See, e.g., Kulko v. Superior Court*, 436 U.S. 84, 98–101, 98 S.Ct. 1690, 1700–01, 56 L.Ed.2d 132 (1978)(state's "substantial interests" in care of children do not sustain jurisdiction; interest can be vindicated through existing interstate means of cooperation).

29. *Cf., e.g., Caribbean Broadcasting System, Ltd. v. Cable & Wireless PLC*, 148 F.3d 1080,

Specific Jurisdiction v. General Jurisdiction

Frequently courts use the terms "specific jurisdiction" and "general jurisdiction." These terms may appear daunting, but in fact they are merely explanations for the application of personal jurisdiction to different sets of facts.[30] "Specific jurisdiction" is generally used to indicate that a defendant's contacts with a state may not be large or systematic and continuous. However, the contact may still satisfy jurisdictional requirements if the contacts are related to the cause of action and purposeful, and jurisdiction based on the contacts is otherwise reasonable.[31] By contrast, "general jurisdiction" may be found where the defendant's contacts with the state are unrelated to the cause of action, but are substantial, systematic and continuous.[32] However, it should be

1089–90 (D.C.Cir.1998) (plaintiff's failure to make good faith showing justifies refusal to grant jurisdictional discovery). *See also Phoenix Consulting, Inc. v. Republic of Angola,* 216 F.3d 36, 40 (D.C.Cir.2000) (jurisdictional discovery should not be permitted if defendant has raised other procedural defenses, such as forum non conveniens or other jurisdictional issues).

30. *See generally, Helicopteros Nacionales de Colombia, S.A. v. Hall,* 466 U.S. 408, 414–15, 104 S.Ct. 1868, 1872, 80 L.Ed.2d 404 nn. 8–9 (1984)(identifying "specific" and "general" jurisdiction, and distinguishing them). *See also, e.g., ALS Scan, Inc. v. Digital Service Consultants, Inc.* 293 F.3d 707, 711 (4th Cir.2002), *cert. denied,* 537 U.S. 1105, 123 S.Ct. 868, 154 L.Ed.2d 773 (2003) (two approaches exist for *International Shoe*–"by finding specific jurisdiction based on conduct connected to the suit or by finding general jurisdiction"); *Alpine View Co. v. Atlas Copco, A.B.,* 205 F.3d 208, 215 (5th Cir. 2000), *cert. denied,* 537 U.S. 1105, 123 S.Ct. 868, 154 L.Ed.2d 773 (2003) (" 'Minimum contacts' can be established either through contacts sufficient to assert specific jurisdiction, or contacts sufficient to assert general jurisdiction.").

31. *See, e.g., Harris Rutsky & Co. Insurance Services v. Bell & Clements, Ltd.,* 328 F.3d 1122, 1129 (9th Cir.2003) (specific jurisdiction requires: purposeful contact; related to cause of action; and exercise of jurisdiction must be consistent with fair play and substantial justice); *Phillips Exeter Academy v. Howard Phillips Fund, Inc.,* 196 F.3d 284, 288 (1st Cir.1999) ("Short of general jurisdiction, a court may still hear a particular case if that case relates sufficiently to, or arises from, a significant subset of contacts between the defendant and the forum." Specific jurisdiction requires that court find that plaintiff has satisfied three elements: (1) "direct relationship" between cause of action and defendant's contacts; (2) contacts constitute "purposeful availment" of laws and benefits of forum state; and (3) overall fairness, on facts of particular case, of exercise of personal jurisdiction; however, while all three elements must be met, "the relative strength or weakness of the plaintiff's showing on the first two elements bears upon the third element"); *Mink v. AAAA Development, LLC,* 190 F.3d 333, 336 (5th Cir.1999) (same definition of specific jurisdiction). *Cf., Pennzoil Products Co. v. Colelli & Associates, Inc.,* 149 F.3d 197 (3d Cir.1998) (so holding; also explaining that two standards exist for specific jurisdiction, "the first mandatory and the second discretionary;" first standard looks at whether defendant had minimum contacts that should make defendant reasonably anticipate being forced to litigate in forum; second standard asks whether assertion of personal jurisdiction satisfies fair play and substantial justice).

32. *See, e.g., LSI Industries, Inc. v. Hubbell Lighting, Inc.,* 232 F.3d 1369, 1375 (Fed.Cir. 2000) (patent dispute; defendant is subject to jurisdiction where defendant nets several million dollars in annual sales within forum; general jurisdiction exists, notwithstanding fact that disputed product itself was not sold within forum); *Phillips Exeter Academy v. Howard Phillips Fund, Inc.,* 196 F.3d 284, 288 (1st Cir.1999) ("[A] defendant who has maintained a continuous and systematic linkage with the forum state brings himself within the general jurisdiction of that state's courts in respect to all matters, even those that are unrelated to the defendant's contacts with the forum."); *Mink v. AAAA Development, LLC,* 190 F.3d 333, 336 (5th Cir.1999) (similar definition of general jurisdiction). *But cf., Bancroft & Masters, Inc. v. Augusta National, Inc.,* 223 F.3d 1082, 1086 (9th Cir.2000) (for general jurisdiction, factors to consider include "whether the defendant makes sales, solicits or engages in business in the state, serves the state's markets, designates an agent for service of process, holds a license, or is incorporated there;" defendant who is registered or licensed

emphasized that when a plaintiff seeks to sustain a suit based on unrelated contacts, the contacts should indeed be substantial.[33]

ADDITIONAL RESEARCH REFERENCES

C.J.S. Constitutional Law §§ 1150, 1153; Federal Courts §§ 165(1)–190 et seq.

West's Key No. Digests, Constitutional Law ⚷305(4); Federal Courts ⚷76–76.35.

§ 1.5 Jurisdiction Over Persons or Things—Requirements for Personal Jurisdiction—State Limitations: Long–Arm Statutes

CORE CONCEPT

Before a federal trial court may exert its personal jurisdiction over an out-of-state, non-consenting defendant, the court must usually satisfy requirements laid down by the legislature of the state in which it sits. These requirements are found in the so-called "long-arm" statutes, which every state has enacted. Satisfying the long-arm requirements is a burden additional to the obligations of fairness imposed by the Constitution.[1]

The long-arm powers may not exceed the constitutional limits of due process, discussed above. In fact, some state long-arm statutes are drafted to allow trial courts to reach as far as due process will allow. However, it is possible that a state will choose not to permit an exercise of personal jurisdiction to the fullest extent permitted by the Constitution. In that circumstance, the court's ability to reach defendants outside the territory of the state may be constrained by the long-arm statute. These distinctions between the long-arm statutes of particular states require attorneys to consult, and become familiar with, the long-arm statutes of individual states relevant to their practices.

to do business, does not pay forum taxes or maintain forum bank accounts, does not advertise in forum, and whose website cannot be used to make purchases, is not subject to general jurisdiction; occasional unsolicited sales do not alter results, nor do license agreements with forum television networks and "a handful of [forum] vendors. These agreements constitute doing business with [the forum] but do not constitute doing business in [the forum].").

33. *See, e.g., Epps v. Stewart Information Services Corp.*, 327 F.3d 642, 648 (8th Cir.2003) (general jurisdiction requires systematic and continuous contacts, plus other enumerated factors of fairness); *ALS Scan, Inc. v. Digital Service Consultants, Inc.*, 293 F.3d 707, 712 (4th Cir.2002), *cert. denied*, 537 U.S. 1105, 123 S.Ct. 868, 154 L.Ed.2d 773 (2003) ("To establish general jurisdiction over the defendant, the defendant's activities in the State must have been 'continuous and systematic,' a more demanding standard than is necessary for establishing specific jurisdiction."); *Chaiken v. VV Publishing Corp.*, 119 F.3d 1018, 1028 (2d Cir.1997), *cert. denied*, 522 U.S. 1149, 118 S.Ct. 1169, 140 L.Ed.2d 179 (1998) (circulation of 183 copies of publication in state, creating annual gross revenues of $21,000, does not of itself satisfy general jurisdiction); *Nichols v. G.D. Searle & Co.*, 991 F.2d 1195, 1200 (4th Cir.1993)(held, unrelated advertising and solicitation insufficient for general jurisdiction; "broad constructions of general jurisdiction should be generally disfavored").

1. *See, e.g., GTE New Media Services, Inc. v. BellSouth Corp.*, 199 F.3d 1343, 1347 (D.C.Cir. 2000), *rejected*, 2002 WL 31261330 (E.D.Pa. 2002) (even if long-arm statute is satisfied, requirement of due process must still be met); *Wenz v. Memery Crystal*, 55 F.3d 1503 (10th Cir.1995)(for jurisdiction over nonresident defendant, court must examine both the state long-arm statute and issues of due process).

APPLICATIONS

Consent

Where a defendant has already consented to the personal jurisdiction of the court, the need for application of a long-arm statute is eliminated.[2]

Service Within a State

Long-arm statutes authorize exercise of personal jurisdiction beyond the boundaries of the state in which a court sits. Thus if a defendant is properly served with process within a state, the long-arm statute of that state will have no application.

Overlap With Due Process

The long-arm statutes of some states permit their courts to exercise personal jurisdiction over out-of-state defendants to the full extent of Due Process limitations of the Constitution.[3] In such states there is thus no need to make separate analyses to determine if both the constitutional requirements of fairness and long-arm requirements are satisfied: if due process is satisfied, so is the long-arm statute.[4] However, in states that do not permit exercise of personal jurisdiction to the fullest constitutional extent, it is necessary to make two different analyses. Jurisdiction must satisfy due process, and it must also fit within the statutory scheme of the long-arm statute.[5]

Example

The New York long-arm statute permits exercise of personal jurisdiction in New York courts over many out-of-state defendants who commit tortious acts outside the state which create injury within the state.[6] However, that authority explicitly excludes cases where defendants are accused of defamatory acts outside New York that cause injury within the state. Thus a federal court in New York could not use the New York long-arm statute to exercise personal jurisdiction over a defendant who was accused of defamation outside New York that caused injury within the state. This would be true even if the due

2. *See, e.g., General Contracting & Trading Co. v. Interpole, Inc.,* 940 F.2d 20, 22 (1st Cir. 1991) (long-arm analysis is unnecessary if defendant has submitted to personal jurisdiction); *Knowlton v. Allied Van Lines, Inc.,* 900 F.2d 1196, 1197–99 (8th Cir.1990) (existence of consent to jurisdiction, whether expressly or by waiver, eliminates need to satisfy state long-arm statute; appointment of agent to receive service of process is "[o]ne of the most solidly established ways of giving . . . consent").

3. *See, e.g.,* Rhode Island General Laws Annotated § 9–5–33(a). *See also, e.g., Pennzoil Products Co. v. Colelli & Associates, Inc.,* 149 F.3d 197, 200 (3d Cir.1998) ("We have acknowledged that the [long-arm] statute permits Pennsylvania courts to exercise personal jurisdiction over nonresident defendants 'to the constitutional limits of the Due Process Clause of the Fourteenth Amendment' ").

4. *See, e.g., Chan v. Society Expeditions, Inc.,* 39 F.3d 1398, 1405 (9th Cir.1994), *cert. denied,* 514 U.S. 1004, 115 S.Ct. 1314, 131 L.Ed.2d 196 (1995)(when long-arm statute is "coextensive" with due process, court needs to examine only the due process requirement).

5. *Cf., e.g., Bensusan Restaurant Corp. v. King,* 126 F.3d 25, 27 (2d Cir.1997) (failure to meet New York long-arm requirements makes due process analysis unnecessary).

6. New York Civil Practice Law and Rules 302(a)(3).

process requirements for personal jurisdiction, discussed above, were satisfied.

ADDITIONAL RESEARCH REFERENCES

C.J.S. Constitutional Law §§ 1150, 1153; Federal Courts §§ 165(1)–190 et seq.

West's Key No. Digests, Constitutional Law ⚿305(4); Federal Courts ⚿76–76.35.

§ 1.6 Jurisdiction Over Persons or Things—Requirements for Personal Jurisdiction—Notice

CORE CONCEPT

The notice requirement for personal jurisdiction overlaps substantially with the fairness requirements. Both "notice" and "minimum contacts" are requirements derived from the Due Process clauses of the Constitution. Even so, there are a few distinctions to be made between notice and minimum contacts. For example, if a defendant had elaborate contacts with a state, but was never notified of the pendency of a lawsuit, the defendant would never have a fair opportunity to present a defense. Thus, personal jurisdiction would be lacking—even though minimum contacts were present—because requirements of notice were not satisfied.[1]

APPLICATIONS

Due Process Standard

To satisfy Due Process requirements, notice to the defendant must be of a quality that is reasonably likely, in all the circumstances of the case, to apprise the defendant of the pending action and afford an opportunity to make a defense.[2] This standard is very fact-dependent.[3]

1. *Murphy Bros., Inc. v. Michetti Pipe Stringing, Inc.*, 526 U.S. 344, 350, 119 S.Ct. 1322, 1327, 143 L.Ed.2d 448 (1999) ("In the absence of service of process (or waiver of service by the defendant), a court ordinarily may not exercise power over a party the complaint names as a defendant."). *See, e.g., Peay v. BellSouth Medical Assistance Plan,* 205 F.3d 1206, 1209 (10th Cir. 2000) ("While service of process and personal jurisdiction both must be satisfied before a suit can proceed, they are distinct concepts that require separate inquiries.").

2. *Nelson v. Adams, USA, Inc.*, 529 U.S. 460, 467, 120 S.Ct. 1579, 1585, 146 L.Ed.2d 530 (2000) (amended complaint joining new party; held, where newly joined defendant is "adjudged liable the very first moment his personal liability was legally at issue" he is denied an opportunity to prepare a defense and is thereby denied due process).

3. *Mennonite Board of Missions v. Adams,* 462 U.S. 791, 799, 103 S.Ct. 2706, 2711, 77 L.Ed.2d 180 (1983) (heightened duty to provide notice where state knows of opponent's inexperience or incompetence). *See, e.g., Folger Adam Security, Inc. v. DeMatteis/MacGregor, JV,* 209 F.3d 252, 265 (3d Cir.2000) (notice of bankruptcy auction that provides sale of assets will be free and clear of "interests" is not adequate notice that affirmative defenses and contract defenses will be extinguished); *Petrovic v. Amoco Oil Co.,* 200 F.3d 1140, 1153 (8th Cir.1999) (notice of proposed settlement of class action under Rule 23(e) must have sufficient detail to permit estimate of potential costs and benefits "or at least whether additional investigation into the matter would be an efficient use of ... time"); *Lakeshore Broadcasting, Inc. v. FCC,* 199 F.3d 468, 474 (D.C.Cir.1999) (publication notice of regulations gave party that had initiated administrative process sufficient notice; distinguishing *Mullane v. Central Hanover Bank & Trust* as applying to parties who had no reason to know a judicial proceeding was pending).

Normally, notice by first-class mail is satisfactory for Due Process purposes[4] (*but see* Rule 4 for acceptable methods of service of original pleadings.) However, where the names or addresses of defendants are not known and cannot reasonably be known, little in the way of notice is required.[5]

Statutory Notice

In addition to satisfying constitutional requirements for notice, a party must also serve process in accordance with the statute or rule of procedure governing service in a particular court. For federal courts, Rule 4 governs service of process at the beginning of a suit. Rule 4 cannot establish standards for service that do not meet the constitutional requirements for notice. However, Rule 4 could prescribe requirements for service more rigorous than those required by the Constitution.

ADDITIONAL RESEARCH REFERENCES

C.J.S. Constitutional Law § 1154; Federal Courts §§ 165(1)–190 et seq.

West's Key No. Digests, Constitutional Law ⚷309; Federal Courts ⚷76–76.35.

§ 1.7 Jurisdiction Over Persons or Things—Requirements for Personal Jurisdiction—Special Considerations in Federal Court

CORE CONCEPT

In matters of jurisdiction over persons and things, federal courts generally behave in much the same way as state courts sitting in the same state:[1] the jurisdictional authority is much the same in the two systems. Rule 4(k), which generally governs the territorial limit of

4. *Robinson v. Hanrahan,* 409 U.S. 38, 93 S.Ct. 30, 34 L.Ed.2d 47 (1972) (mail service of notice of forfeiture to home address of party government knows to be incarcerated does not meet constitutional requirement). *See, e.g., United States v. One Toshiba Color Television,* 213 F.3d 147 (3d Cir.2000) (forfeiture case involving incarcerated party; held, while mailing is usually adequate notice, mailing is not "per se satisfaction of notice requirements"; noting differences among circuits, but holding that in providing mail service on prisoner held in state confinement, using proper address of jail, federal government need not prove actual notice; instead, government must demonstrate that methods of service used are reasonably calculated to result in actual notice). *But cf., United States v. Five Thousand Dollars in United States Currency,* 184 F.3d 958, 960 (8th Cir.1999) ("[I]f the government is incarcerating the property owner when it institutes forfeiture proceedings, we have consistently held that fundamental fairness requires that the property owner or his or her counsel receive actual notice of the forfeiture in time to decide whether to compel the government to proceed by judicial condemnation.").

5. *Mullane v. Central Hanover Bank & Trust Co.,* 339 U.S. 306, 70 S.Ct. 652, 94 L.Ed. 865 (1950).

1. *See, e.g., Ruiz de Molina v. Merritt & Furman Insurance Agency, Inc.,* 207 F.3d 1351, 1355 (11th Cir.2000) ("A federal court sitting in diversity may exercise jurisdiction over a nonresident defendant to the same extent as a court of that state."); *Access Telecom, Inc. v. MCI Telecommunications, Inc.,* 197 F.3d 694, 716 (5th Cir.1999) (same holding). *Cf., Deprenyl Animal Health, Inc. v. University of Toronto Innovations Foundation,* 297 F.3d 1343, 1350 (Fed.Cir.2002) (*International Shoe* applies to federal courts through Fifth Amendment as it applies to state courts through Fourteenth Amendment).

service of process from a federal court, makes that point explicitly. However, there are a few circumstances where a federal court may have a somewhat greater jurisdictional reach than its state counterpart. Rule 4(k) contains some of these exceptions. Others are creatures of Congressional legislation.

APPLICATIONS

Nationwide Personal Jurisdiction

For several federal causes of action, including suits under federal antitrust laws and the federal securities laws, Congress has authorized federal courts to exercise their personal jurisdiction throughout the United States. Thus, in hearing an antitrust claim filed in Baltimore, a federal court in Maryland has personal jurisdiction over a defendant in Hawaii, Puerto Rico, Alaska, or some other distant jurisdiction, even if it could not otherwise reach that defendant under the considerations mentioned earlier in this section on personal jurisdiction.[2] These statutes, while not rare, are generally the exceptions to the normal practice. When such statutes come into play, it is possible that the court will make a minimum contacts analysis that may differ somewhat from the concept developed for domestic defendants. In the first place, a court evaluating personal jurisdiction in a case involving a federal cause of action that authorized nationwide jurisdiction will be less concerned with issues of state/federal relationships and more concerned about the federal policies underlying the federal right that has been asserted by the plaintiff.[3] Secondly, it is uncertain whether, in making a minimum contact analysis in the context of nationwide personal jurisdiction, the court should examine only whether minimum contacts exist[4] or whether the court should also look to whether an exercise of jurisdiction reasonable in a particular district.[5]

For many other federal causes of action, such as civil rights claims or truth-in-lending cases, the more conventional forms of obtaining personal jurisdiction must be followed.

Important: Nationwide personal jurisdiction should not be equated with personal jurisdiction throughout the world. If the defendant in the antitrust action filed in Baltimore was in Brazil, the Congressional

2. *See, e.g.,* 15 U.S.C.A. § 22. *See also In re Federal Fountain, Inc.,* 165 F.3d 600, 601–02 (8th Cir.1999) (en banc) (where Congress has authorized personal jurisdiction nationwide and defendant is found within territory of United States, federal courts may exercise personal jurisdiction over defendant; concluding that "virtually every . . . court" has reached same conclusion). *But see Peay v. BellSouth Medical Assistance Plan,* 205 F.3d 1206, 1210 (10th Cir.2000) (acknowledging disagreement with *Federal Fountain*; citing other cases in conflict; concluding that even where Congress has authorized nationwide service, plaintiff's choice of forum must still be "fair and reasonable").

3. *See, e.g., Pinker v. Roche Holdings, Ltd.,* 292 F.3d 361 (3d Cir.2002).

4. *See, e.g., Securities Investor Protection Corp. v. Vigman,* 764 F.2d 1309, 1316 (9th Cir. 1985) (looking only to whether defendant has minimum contacts with United States as a whole; not concerned with any potential absence of contacts with particular federal district).

5. *See, e.g., Republic of Panama v. BCCI Holdings (Luxembourg), S.A.,* 119 F.3d 935, 945–46 (11th Cir.1997) (district court should weigh fairness to defendant in particular district against "federal interest involved in the litigation;" asserting that other circuits follow this approach).

grant of nationwide jurisdiction would not be effective to reach the Brazilian defendant. In such a circumstance the federal court would still have resort to the considerations of minimum contacts and either state long-arm statutes or the special provision of Rule 4(k)(2), discussed immediately below. But if those tools were insufficient then personal jurisdiction could not be sustained.

Special Considerations of Rule 4(k)

As is discussed elsewhere in this study, Rule 4(k) authorizes federal courts in certain circumstances to exercise personal jurisdiction over certain designated persons who may be served within 100 miles, measured in a straight line in any direction, from the federal courthouse. This Rule applies irrespective of how many state boundaries may intervene. Such designated persons include those who may be joined under the applicable state long-arm law, parties impleaded under Rule 14, parties joined under Rule 19, parties who can be served under federal statutory interpleader legislation, 28 U.S.C.A. § 1335, and parties subject to service authorized by any other applicable federal legislation. Note that Rule 4(k) does not provide the 100 mile bulge to plaintiffs seeking to initiate an action by serving a defendant.

This 100 mile rule applies only within the United States. A federal court in Detroit, Michigan, for example, could not use Rule 4(k) to serve a person in Windsor, Ontario, even though Windsor is much less than 100 miles from Detroit. If a federal court is located in the center of a state, more than 100 miles from its borders, Rule 4(k)'s 100–mile bulge has little utility. If, however, a federal court is located in a part of a state immediately adjacent to a neighboring state, Rule 4(k) may provide advantages not available in a state court.

Finally, Rule 4(k)(2) explicitly permits exercise of personal jurisdiction in federal causes of action where the defendant has sufficient contacts with the United States as a whole, but not with any particular state.[6]

ADDITIONAL RESEARCH REFERENCES

C.J.S. Constitutional Law § 1154; Federal Civil Procedure §§ 204–221 et seq., 486 et seq.; Federal Courts § 16 et seq.

West's Key No. Digests, Constitutional Law ⚷305; Federal Civil Procedure ⚷461–505; Federal Courts ⚷71.

6. *See also, e.g., Medical Mutual of Ohio v. deSoto,* 245 F.3d 561, 566–67 (6th Cir.2001) (in case brought under Employee Retirement Income and Security Act, 29 U.S.C.A. § 1132 provided nationwide personal jurisdiction; court, therefore, could look to defendant's contacts with entire country, rather than only forum state; rejecting contrary approach of requiring plaintiff to demonstrate that defendant had sufficient contacts with both United States as a whole and forum state). *But see Peay v. BellSouth Medical Assistance Plan,* 205 F.3d 1206, 1210–12 (10th Cir.2000) (29 U.S.C.A. § 1132 authorizes nationwide service of process, but requirement of personal jurisdiction requires separate due process analysis to determine whether plaintiff's choice of forum is fair and reasonable).

§ 1.8 Jurisdiction Over Persons or Things—Special Requirements for Quasi in Rem Jurisdiction

CORE CONCEPT

Quasi in rem jurisdiction is an alternative to personal jurisdiction. It is employed most commonly as a means of obtaining the presence of a defendant in a court by judicial attachment (i.e., seizure) of property belonging to the defendant. In order for the court to attach such property, the property must be located within the state in which the court sits.

APPLICATIONS

Prerequisites

A court may exercise quasi in rem jurisdiction when six elements are present: 1) thing of value; 2) territorial limit; 3) defendant's asset; 4) seizure or attachment; 5) notice; and 6) minimum contacts are satisfied. *All six* elements must be satisfied.[1]

(1) *Thing of Value:* Quasi in rem jurisdiction presupposes that the thing seized has value. Because a judgment in favor of a plaintiff will often be enforced through forced sale or forfeiture of the thing seized, quasi in rem jurisdiction would have little meaning if the asset had no value. Moreover, the value of the asset seized determines the monetary limit of the court's jurisdiction in quasi in rem cases.[2]

> ***Example:*** If a plaintiff's claim had a maximum value of one million dollars, that would normally be the amount for which the plaintiff would like to sue. If the court had personal jurisdiction over the defendant, normally the defendant would have potential liability (assuming a judgment for the plaintiff) up to the full amount of the claim. However, if the court's jurisdiction was based on quasi in rem jurisdiction, and the thing seized was a bank account with a value of $400,000, the limit of the court's quasi in rem jurisdiction would be $400,000—the value of the asset.[3] The plaintiff would retain a claim for $600,000, but normally could not prosecute it in that same court, unless additional assets could be seized, or jurisdiction could be established on the basis of personal jurisdiction.

Important: Although quasi in rem jurisdiction may sometimes be less advantageous from a plaintiff's point of view, historically it has also

1. *See, e.g., Winter Storm Shipping v. TPI,* 310 F.3d 263, 269 (2d Cir.2002), *cert. denied,* 539 U.S. 927, 123 S.Ct. 2578, 156 L.Ed.2d 605 (2003) (due process requirements for quasi in rem jurisdiction similar to those for personal jurisdiction). For a fuller discussion of the requirements for quasi in rem jurisdiction, *see Shaffer v. Heitner,* 433 U.S. 186, 97 S.Ct. 2569, 53 L.Ed.2d 683 (1977).

2. *Shaffer v. Heitner,* 433 U.S. 186, 207 n. 23, 97 S.Ct. 2569, 2581, n. 23, 53 L.Ed.2d 683 (1977) (liability in an in rem action is limited to the value of the property).

3. *Shaffer v. Heitner,* 433 U.S. 186, 209 n. 32, 97 S.Ct. 2569, 2582 n. 32, 53 L.Ed.2d 683 (1977)("the value of the property seized [serves] to limit the extent of possible liability."). *Cf., Teyseer Cement Co. v. Halla Maritime Corp.,* 794 F.2d 472, 477 (9th Cir.1986)(certain kinds of maritime jurisdiction are actually quasi in rem, "because any judgment rendered is limited to the value of the attached property").

posed dilemmas for defendants. Consider again the example mentioned above. If the plaintiff cannot obtain personal jurisdiction, the limit of the court's jurisdiction will be $400,000. An out-of-state defendant will have the choice of appearing in court to defend on the merits, or staying outside the state and defaulting. A decision to default obviously forfeits defenses on the merits. If the defendant appears, however, the plaintiff may be able to serve process in-state that will satisfy personal jurisdiction. The court could then hear plaintiff's claim for the full amount of $1,000,000. Thus defendant would be faced with the hard choice of defaulting on $400,000, or appearing and risking exposure for an additional $600,000. Some courts—but by no means all—resolved this dilemma by allowing defendant to make a "limited appearance," in which defendant could contest the merits of the quasi in rem claim ($400,000), but remain immune from service of process for personal jurisdiction while the $400,000 claim was litigated.[4] Nowadays the sixth requirement for quasi in rem jurisdiction, minimum contacts, has substantially eased this problem.

(2) *Territorial Requirement:* Courts exercising quasi in rem jurisdiction have a definite territorial limit to their jurisdiction. For quasi in rem jurisdiction to be sustained, the asset must be seized while it is within the territorial confines of the state in which the court sits.[5] Where the asset is something as tangible and immoveable as realty, the territorial requirement is not a substantial hurdle—if the land is within the state, the land is not going to change its location. More mobile assets, such as automobiles, present somewhat more significant problems because there is some risk that they will be moved before attachment can occur. The biggest questions of territoriality, however, arise when the asset is an intangible item. Things such as accounts receivable or stock ownership in a corporation certainly have value, but they have no definite situs comparable to that of land or automobiles. Courts have resolved these problems with rules arbitrary in their nature, but generally followed for lack of a better solution. Depending on the law of the state where a corporation is incorporated, for example, shares in a corporation are generally held to be located either where the certificate evidencing ownership is found, or in the state where the entity is incorporated.[6]

Important: Quasi in rem jurisdiction is always territorial in nature. Thus, there is no need to address long-arm statutes, because

4. *See, e.g., United States v. First Nat'l City Bank*, 379 U.S. 378, 390 n. 8, 85 S.Ct. 528, 535 n. 8, 13 L.Ed.2d 365 (1965)(noting split of authority on availability of limited appearance). *See also Shaffer v. Heitner*, 433 U.S. 186, 196 n. 12, 97 S.Ct. 2569, 2575 n. 12, 53 L.Ed.2d 683 (1977)(Delaware does not permit a limited appearance).

5. *See, e.g., Koken v. Viad Corp.*, 307 F.Supp.2d 650, 655 (E.D. Pa. 2004) ("If jurisdiction is based on the court's power over property within its territory, the action is in rem or quasi in rem."). *See also Glencore Grain Rotterdam B.V. v. Shivnath Rai Harnarain Co.*, 284 F.3d 1114, 1127 (9th Cir.2002) ("[T]he sine qua non of basing jurisdiction on a defendant's assets in the forum is the identification of [such an] asset.").

6. *See, e.g., Shaffer v. Heitner*, 433 U.S. 186, 191, 97 S.Ct. 2569, 2573, 53 L.Ed.2d 683 (1977)(Delaware law makes Delaware the situs of stock ownership in Delaware corporations).

such statutes are applicable only when the court is attempting to reach outside its own state's territory.[7]

(3) *Defendant's Asset:* Because the purpose of quasi in rem jurisdiction is to sue a particular defendant or group of defendants, it would make little sense if a suit against one person was sustained by seizure of the asset of another person, who was not a party and had no connection to the case. Certainly, in that case, the true defendant would have no incentive to appear in court, and the person whose property was seized would be entitled to retain the asset. Thus, the third requirement for quasi in rem jurisdiction is that the asset seized must at least arguably belong to the defendant. The defendant's title need not be absolutely clear, however. If the purpose of the plaintiff's suit is to resolve a dispute between the parties as to title in the asset that was seized, this requirement of quasi in rem jurisdiction is satisfied if the defendant merely claims the property or will claim the property.

(4) *Seizure or Attachment:* The court's quasi in rem jurisdiction cannot begin until the court has effective control of the asset. The nature of the seizure depends heavily on the nature of the property seized, but generally it is enough that the court has effectively interfered with the defendant's control, even if the court does not have actual possession. With land, for example, the court can simply order that title be frozen in the local records office pending the outcome of the suit. With stock shares, the same can be accomplished by ordering the appropriate authority to halt trading in the particular shares at issue. By contrast, if the asset was a rare diamond, or an automobile, the court might take physical custody of the property.

(5) *Notice:* As with personal jurisdiction, quasi in rem jurisdiction requires notice to the defendant that will satisfy both constitutional due process and the service of process requirements of Rule 4. Application of the due process requirement is similar to that imposed on personal jurisdiction, with allowance for the fact that quasi in rem cases may sometimes require less notice to the defendant. This may occur because sometimes the act of seizing a defendant's property may reasonably be assumed to notify a defendant of the pendency of the case.

(6) *Requirements of Fair Play: Minimum Contacts:* The due process requirement of "traditional notions of fair play and substantial justice" applies to quasi in rem jurisdiction. In practice, this means quasi in rem jurisdiction is likely to be sustained only in circumstances where the assets seized bear a substantial relation to the cause of action on which plaintiff is suing, or in circumstances where other facts suggest that exercise of quasi in rem jurisdiction would not be fundamentally unfair to defendant.[8] Both of those standards are highly fact-specific. An attorney uncertain whether, under due process, quasi in

7. *See, e.g., Newhard, Cook & Co. v. Inspired Life Ctrs., Inc.*, 895 F.2d 1226, 1228 n. 3 (8th Cir.1990)(if case is based on quasi in rem jurisdiction, long-arm requirements generally need not be satisfied).

8. *See, e.g., Louring v. Kuwait Boulder Shipping Co.*, 455 F.Supp. 630 (D.Conn. 1977)(permitting quasi in rem jurisdiction over assets of foreign defendant unrelated to cause of action; reasoning that United States plaintiffs should not be required to litigate their claims in foreign courts).

rem jurisdiction can be sustained, should research carefully the developing case law in this area.

Relation to Rule 4

Rule 4(n) limits the circumstances in which a federal court may assert quasi in rem or in rem jurisdiction, even if an assertion of such jurisdiction is constitutionally sound. Basically, there are two circumstances where a federal court may employ such jurisdiction. First, Rule 4(n) permits jurisdiction if a federal statute authorizes it. In that situation, notice to affected parties is governed by other applicable provisions of Rule 4, presumably including nationwide service when it is appropriate. Second, Rule 4(n) permits such jurisdiction even in the absence of a federal statute authorizing it, if the court is unable to obtain personal jurisdiction over the defendant(s). In that circumstance, Rule 4(n) provides that jurisdiction will be obtained according to the process of the state in which the district court sits.

Enforcing Judgments

It should be noted that the "minimum contacts" requirement for quasi in rem jurisdiction is applicable only in cases in which the plaintiff has brought a cause of action that will be litigated (assuming good jurisdiction) on the merits. By contrast, if the plaintiff has already won a judgment and seeks only to enforce the judgment against a defendant's assets, the requirement that the asset must have some relationship to the underlying litigation does not apply.[9] All the other elements, however, must still be met.

ADDITIONAL RESEARCH REFERENCES

C.J.S. Constitutional Law § 1139; Courts §§ 54–60; Federal Courts § 25(1, 2).

West's Key No. Digests, Constitutional Law ⚷305; Courts ⚷21; Federal Courts ⚷93.

§ 1.9 Jurisdiction Over Persons or Things—Requirements for in Rem Jurisdiction

CORE CONCEPT

As its name suggests, in rem jurisdiction is closely related to quasi in rem jurisdiction—so much so, in fact, that courts occasionally use the two terms interchangeably. The most important difference is that in rem jurisdiction usually involves trying title to property and, in theory, determining the rights of all people throughout the world in that property. Quasi in rem jurisdiction, by contrast, usually involves a much more discrete group of defendants, whose claims are usually far less theoretical. In practice, federal courts use in rem jurisdiction

9. *Shaffer v. Heitner*, 433 U.S. 186, 210 n. 36, 97 S.Ct. 2569, 2583, n. 36, 53 L.Ed.2d 683 (1977) ("Once it has been determined by a court of competent jurisdiction that the defendant is a debtor of the plaintiff, there would seem to be no unfairness in allowing an action to realize on that debt in a State where the defendant has property, whether or not that State would have jurisdiction to determine the existence of the debt as an original matter.").

infrequently. Those areas in which in rem jurisdiction may most often be employed are actions in admiralty, involving shipping on navigable waters where the vessel is seized as the basis of jurisdiction;[1] and condemnation of property that was the instrumentality of a crime, which the government now seeks to keep as its own.[2]

Important: If in rem jurisdiction is lacking, and the court also lacks personal jurisdiction and quasi in rem jurisdiction, the typical remedy is to dismiss the claim.

APPLICATIONS

Prerequisites: There are five prerequisites for a court to exercise in rem jurisdiction.

(1) *Thing of Value:* If the property whose title is at issue had no value, there would be little point to the litigation itself. As might be expected, this element of in rem jurisdiction is usually not difficult to satisfy.

(2) *Territorial Requirement:* Like quasi in rem jurisdiction, in rem jurisdiction is territorial in nature. The property must be located within the state in which the court sits at the onset of the action.

(3) *Seizure by the Court:* The court's in rem jurisdiction cannot begin until the court has effective control of the asset. The nature of the seizure depends heavily on the nature of the property seized, but generally it is enough that the court has effectively interfered with the defendant's control, even if the court does not have actual possession. With land, for example, the court can simply order that title be frozen in the local records office pending the outcome of the suit. With stock shares, the same can be accomplished by ordering the appropriate authority to halt trading in the particular shares at issue. By contrast, if the asset was a rare diamond, or an automobile, the marshal might take physical custody of the property.

(4) *Notice Requirement:* As with personal jurisdiction and quasi in rem jurisdiction, in rem jurisdiction requires notice to the defendant that will satisfy both due process and the service of process requirements of Rule 4. Otherwise, this is an area where in rem jurisdiction differs somewhat from quasi in rem jurisdiction. Because the nature of an in rem case—trying title as to potential claimants throughout the world—is much more diffuse than that of a typical quasi in rem case, notice that will satisfy constitutional requirements of due process will often be by publication in newspapers, etc., rather than some form of personal service on a defendant. In this area in rem requirements are probably substantially more relaxed than those of personal or quasi in

1. *See, e.g., The Belgenland,* 114 U.S. 355, 5 S.Ct. 860, 29 L.Ed. 152 (1885).

2. *See, e.g., United States v. United States Coin & Currency,* 401 U.S. 715, 91 S.Ct. 1041, 28 L.Ed.2d 434 (1971). *See also, United States v. One Parcel of Real Estate at 10380 SW 28th Street,* 214 F.3d 1291, 1294 (11th Cir.2000), *cert. denied,* 531 U.S. 969, 121 S.Ct. 406, 148 L.Ed.2d 313 (2000). ("The focus of an in rem narcotics forfeiture is not the guilt of any person or the attempt to punish a person, but the 'guilt' of the property, *i.e.,* whether the property had been used in connection with illicit drug activity."). *United States v. $506,231 in United States Currency,* 125 F.3d 442, 447 (7th Cir.1997) ("Civil forfeiture actions are in rem proceedings.").

rem jurisdiction. It is important to note, however, that if the identity and location of a particular claimant is known to the defendant, then the requirement of better notice, such as mail service, probably applies. Additionally, courts must satisfy their own rules on service, in addition to constitutional requirements. Under Rule 4(e)(2), governing in rem attachments, federal courts are authorized to use the service of process rules of the state in which they sit.

(5) *Requirements of Fair Play:* As with cases grounded upon personal jurisdiction or quasi in rem jurisdiction, cases founded on in rem jurisdiction must also satisfy requirements of due process.[3] Because in rem actions always involve suits closely related to the property seized, however, the fairness requirements of due process are usually met without difficulty.[4]

Relation to Rule 4

Rule 4(n) limits the circumstances in which a federal court may assert quasi in rem or in rem jurisdiction, even if an assertion of such jurisdiction is constitutionally sound. Basically, there are two circumstances where a federal court may employ such jurisdiction. First, Rule 4(n) permits jurisdiction if a federal statute authorizes it. In that situation, notice to affected parties is governed by other applicable provisions of Rule 4, presumably including nationwide service when it is appropriate. Second, Rule 4(n) permits such jurisdiction even in the absence of a federal statute authorizing it, if the court is unable to obtain personal jurisdiction over the defendant(s). In that circumstance, Rule 4(n) provides that jurisdiction will be obtained according to the process of the state in which the district court sits.

ADDITIONAL RESEARCH REFERENCES

C.J.S. Constitutional Law § 1139; Courts §§ 54–60; Federal Courts § 25(1, 2).

West's Key No. Digests, Constitutional Law ⚷305; Courts ⚷21; Federal Courts ⚷93.

§ 1.10 Subject Matter Jurisdiction in Federal District Courts—Introduction

Attorneys unfamiliar with federal trial courts often have substantial difficulty with two points about federal subject matter jurisdiction. First, federal courts are courts of *limited* subject matter jurisdiction, and thus will be unable to hear certain types of cases that could be brought routinely in a state trial court, which often enjoys a broader scope of subject matter jurisdiction. Second, the need to meet standards of federal subject matter jurisdiction is an *additional* requirement, separate from jurisdiction over persons and things, that must be

3. *See, e.g., Harrods Ltd. v. Sixty Internet Domain Names,* 302 F.3d 214, 224 (4th Cir.2002) (minimum contacts analysis of *International Shoe* also apply to in rem actions).

4. *See, e.g., Porsche Cars North America, Inc. v. Porsche.net,* 302 F.3d 248, 260 (4th Cir.2002) (in case based upon in rem jurisdiction, where property itself is cause of action, jurisdiction is good in state where property is located).

satisfied before a federal trial court will hear a case.[1] *Both* subject matter jurisdiction and jurisdiction over persons and things must be satisfied *as to each count in a case* before a federal court will hear a count.[2] Failure to satisfy either requirement as to any count creates a substantial risk that the count will be dismissed, even if other counts may proceed. These requirements apply irrespective of whether the count arises in plaintiff's complaint, a counterclaim, a crossclaim, an impleader, or under any other relevant rule.

Distinctions between jurisdiction over persons or things and subject matter jurisdiction are best understood by considering the limitations each kind of jurisdiction places on a federal court. Jurisdiction over persons or things defines the limits of a court's reach to take control of litigation affecting a specific person or piece of property. Subject matter jurisdiction, by contrast, limits the kind of cases a court may hear, irrespective of where the affected persons or pieces of property may be found. Thus, if a person is served with process within a state where a court sits, the personal jurisdiction of the court is probably satisfied. But if the cause of action is of a kind that a federal court cannot hear, the court would still lack subject matter jurisdiction and the case should be dismissed.

> ***Example:*** Subject to exceptions discussed below under supplemental jurisdiction, federal courts may not hear causes of action based on state law if the plaintiff and defendant are citizens of the same state. This particular difference between subject matter jurisdiction and jurisdiction over persons and things may be explained by the following case. If plaintiff and defendant are both citizens of New York, and if the cause of action is a tort under state law, personal jurisdiction will be satisfied if the defendant is served with process within New York. However, the federal court will not have subject matter jurisdiction because suits based on state law, where the parties are citizens of the same state, do not fall within any of the categories of suits a federal court can hear. Thus the case should be dismissed, even though personal jurisdiction is satisfactory.
>
> *Affirmative Duty to Plead Jurisdiction:* The burden of demonstrating that the requirements of federal subject matter jurisdiction are met rests on the party asserting the claim.[3]
>
> *Dismissal if Subject Matter Jurisdiction Absent:* As the foregoing example suggests, the standard remedy for failure to satisfy subject matter jurisdiction is dismissal of the claim.[4]

1. *See, e.g., Glencore Grain Rotterdam B.V. v. Shivnath Rai Harnarain Co.,* 284 F.3d 1114, 1128 (9th Cir.2002) (existence of subject matter jurisdiction, but not also personal jurisdiction, requires dismissal of case); *Southern Cross Overseas Agencies, Inc. v. Wah Kwong Shipping Group,* 181 F.3d 410, 413 (3d Cir.1999) (courts should decide jurisdiction first "and then address other issues only if there is jurisdiction").

2. *But cf., Goetzke v. Ferro Corp.,* 280 F.3d 766, 778–79 (7th Cir.2002) (state statute providing that claim may be heard only by administrative board may operate to strip state courts of jurisdiction, but not federal courts; if jurisdiction meets standards set by Congress, state law cannot bar federal district court's jurisdiction).

3. *Merrell Dow Pharmaceuticals, Inc. v. Thompson,* 478 U.S. 804, 810 n. 6, 106 S.Ct. 3229, 3233 n. 6, 92 L.Ed.2d 650 (1986) ("[J]urisdiction may not be sustained on a theory that the plaintiff has not advanced."). *See Leipzig v. AIG Life Insurance Co.,* 362 F.3d 406, 410 (7th Cir. 2004). *See also* Fed.R.Civ.P. Form 2 (indicating that subject matter jurisdiction should be alleged in complaint).

Consent: Unlike personal jurisdiction, subject matter jurisdiction cannot be obtained through consent of the parties.[5] The rationale is that limits on a federal district court's subject matter jurisdiction are grounded in a proper balance of federal and state judicial power, and it is not the prerogative of the parties to enter into agreements that have the effect of upsetting that balance. Moreover, because the parties cannot by consent confer subject matter jurisdiction on the court,[6] Rule 12(h) provides no time limit on objections to subject matter jurisdiction. Instead, Rule 12(h)(3) stipulates that objections to subject matter jurisdiction can be raised "[w]henever" they appear, and that the court can act on motion of either party or on its own motion.[7]

Comparison with Quasi in Rem Jurisdiction: Quasi in rem jurisdiction and subject matter jurisdiction are separate and distinct concepts. Quasi in rem jurisdiction permits a court to exercise power over a defendant, because the court has control of property belonging to the defendant. Subject matter jurisdiction defines the kind of cases the court may hear. In a case where the plaintiff and defendant were both New York citizens, for example, a federal court in California might have quasi in rem jurisdiction if it attached property in California belonging to defendant. If the cause of action was based on state law, however, subject matter jurisdiction would be lacking because the parties were not of diverse citizenship.

The three kinds of federal subject matter jurisdiction most frequently encountered are: (1) federal question jurisdiction; (2) jurisdiction based on diversity of citizenship; and (3) supplemental jurisdiction.

§ 1.11 Subject Matter Jurisdiction in Federal District Courts—Federal Question Jurisdiction

CORE CONCEPT

Congress authorized jurisdiction in federal district courts "of all civil actions arising under the Constitution, laws, or treaties of the

4. *Steel Co. v. Citizens for a Better Environment,* 523 U.S. 83, 118 S.Ct. 1003, 140 L.Ed.2d 210 (1998) (first responsibility of court is to determine jurisdiction; if jurisdiction is lacking, court should dismiss without addressing merits); *Louisville & Nashville R.R. Co. v. Mottley,* 211 U.S. 149, 29 S.Ct. 42, 53 L.Ed. 126 (1908).

5. *Capron v. Van Noorden,* 6 U.S. (2 Cranch) 126, 126, 2 L.Ed. 229 (1804). *See also, Smith v. Ashland, Inc.,* 250 F.3d 1167 (8th Cir.2001) (subject matter jurisdiction cannot be conferred on court by consent of parties; however, parties may stipulate to fact of diversity based on citizenship of party).

6. *See, e.g., Tamiami Partners, Ltd. v. Miccosukee Tribe of Indians,* 177 F.3d 1212, 1222 (11th Cir.1999), *cert. denied,* 529 U.S. 1018, 120 S.Ct. 1419, 146 L.Ed.2d 311 (2000) ("It is well-settled that parties cannot create subject matter jurisdiction by agreement.").

7. *Bender v. Williamsport Area School District,* 475 U.S. 534, 541, 106 S.Ct. 1326, 1331, 89 L.Ed.2d 501 (1986) ("[E]very federal appellate court has a special obligation 'to satisfy itself not only of its own jurisdiction, but also that of the lower courts in a case under review,' even though the parties are prepared to concede it."). *See, e.g., Fax Telecommunicaciones, Inc. v. AT & T,* 138 F.3d 479, 485 (2d Cir.1998) ("[W]e have an obligation to determine *sua sponte* whether the district court had jurisdiction to hear the case."); *State Farm Mutual Automobile Ins. Co. v. Powell,* 87 F.3d 93 (3d Cir.1996)(permitting challenge to diversity jurisdiction, notwithstanding that issue was raised only in appellate court).

United States." 28 U.S.C.A. § 1331.[1] In addition, Congress has enacted specific statutes authorizing federal district courts to hear causes of action relating to certain areas of federal law. For example, 28 U.S.C.A. § 1337 authorizes federal courts to hear civil actions arising under federal laws regulating commerce. In the same fashion, 28 U.S.C.A. § 1338 provides subject matter jurisdiction over claims arising under federal patent law, and 28 U.S.C.A. § 1343 authorizes a federal court to hear claims alleging violations of federally guaranteed civil rights.

APPLICATIONS

28 U.S.C.A. § 1331 and Specific Jurisdictional Statutes

The substantial overlap between the broad jurisdictional grant of § 1331 and the more discrete grants mentioned above does not necessarily make the specific jurisdictional statutes superfluous. For example, 28 U.S.C.A. § 1333, conferring subject matter jurisdiction over admiralty claims, preempts § 1331 when the case arises in admiralty. Thus the plaintiff must sue under § 1333, not § 1331,[2] and that has several important consequences.

(1) *Exclusive Subject Matter Jurisdiction:* Under § 1333, the jurisdiction of the federal district court is *exclusive,* i.e., the claim cannot be brought in a state court. Exclusive subject matter jurisdiction is characteristic of many of the specific jurisdictional statutes like § 1333. Federal jurisdiction under § 1331, by contrast, is usually concurrent with that of state courts, which means the claims could have been filed *either* in federal court *or* in state court.[3] It is settled that if a federal cause of action is silent as to whether it lies within exclusive federal jurisdiction, or instead is subject to the concurrent jurisdiction of federal and state trial courts, the jurisdiction is concurrent–not exclusive.[4]

(2) *Limitations in Specific Statute:* If a cause of action must be filed under a specific jurisdictional statute like § 1333, the limitations associated with that cause of action attach to the filing. In admiralty cases, for example, there is no right to a jury trial. Under § 1331, jury

1. *See also Up State Federal Credit Union v. Walker,* 198 F.3d 372, 375 n. 4 (2d Cir.1999) (contract disputes with federal government are controlled by federal common law and are thus federal questions within meaning of § 1331); *Sam L. Majors Jewelers v. ABX, Inc.,* 117 F.3d 922, 926 (5th Cir.1997) (§ 1331 also provides jurisdictional foundation for cases arising under federal common law).

2. *See, e.g., New York State Waterways Ass'n v. Diamond,* 469 F.2d 419 (2d Cir.1972). *See also Shalala v. Illinois Council on Long Term Care, Inc.,* 529 U.S. 1, 4, 120 S.Ct. 1084, 1089, 146 L.Ed.2d 1 (2000) (most claims under Medicare Act cannot invoke federal question jurisdiction under § 1331; such claims are usually consigned by statute to a special administrative review process); *International Science and Technology Institute, Inc. v. Inacom Communications, Inc.,* 106 F.3d 1146, 1154 (4th Cir.1997) ("It is clear ... that § 1331 is a general federal-question statute, which gives the district courts original jurisdiction unless a specific statute assigns jurisdiction elsewhere.").

3. *Grubb v. Public Utilities Comm'n of Ohio,* 281 U.S. 470, 50 S.Ct. 374, 74 L.Ed. 972 (1930).

4. *Tafflin v. Levitt,* 493 U.S. 455, 458–59, 110 S.Ct. 792, 794–95, 107 L.Ed.2d 887 (1990) (presumption is in favor of concurrent jurisdiction, not exclusive jurisdiction).

trials are available as they would be under the more general constraints of the Seventh Amendment to the Constitution.[5]

Additionally, if other federal law precludes a court's use of § 1331 to obtain jurisdiction over a case, § 1331 is simply not available as a source of jurisdiction.[6]

(3) *Absence of Specific Statute:* For many federal causes of action, the only statute authorizing enforcement in a federal court is 28 U.S.C.A. § 1331.[7] That is, many federal causes of action do not enjoy their own specific grant of jurisdiction, equivalent to those of §§ 1333, 1337, 1338, and 1343.

(4) *Suits Based on Treaties:* 28 U.S.C.A. § 1331 is the only provision authorizing subject matter jurisdiction in a federal district court to enforce a cause of action arising under "treaties of the United States."

Well–Pleaded Complaint Rule

In general, subject matter jurisdiction based on a federal question requires that the federal question must appear on a fair reading of a well-pleaded complaint.[8] Federal questions raised in the answer do not create jurisdiction. The significance of the rule is to restrict substantially federal question jurisdiction. It is always possible, and often happens, that important federal questions will arise on the defendant's side of the case, *i.e.,* as a federal defense to a state cause of action. Such defenses, though otherwise appropriate, and perhaps even central to the merits of a case, will not confer federal question jurisdiction on a federal district court[9]—not because there is no federal question, but

5. *See also, e.g., McCarthy v. Apfel,* 221 F.3d 1119, 1123 (9th Cir.2000), *cert. denied,* 532 U.S. 923, 121 S.Ct. 1361, 149 L.Ed.2d 290 (2001) (jurisdiction based on 42 U.S.C.A. § 405(g) of Social Security Act, rather than on 28 U.S.C.A. § 1331, would alter, *inter alia,* standard of proof from preponderance of evidence (§ 1331) to substantial evidence (§ 405(g))).

6. *Your Home Visiting Nurse Servs., Inc. v. Shalala,* 525 U.S. 449, 456, 119 S.Ct. 930, 933, 142 L.Ed.2d 919 (1999) (citing 42 U.S.C.A. § 405(h), providing that "no action against ... the [Secretary] or any officer or employee thereof shall be brought under section 1331 ... of title 28 to recover on any claim under" the Medicare Act). *See also, e.g., GTE North, Inc. v. Strand,* 209 F.3d 909, 916 (6th Cir.2000) (subject matter jurisdiction under § 1331 requires showing that cause of action arose under federal law *and* that § 1331 is not preempted by a more specific statute that strips district courts of subject matter jurisdiction).

7. *Cf., Verizon Maryland, Inc. v. Global Naps, Inc.,* 377 F.3d 355 (4th Cir. 2004) ("When a 'case's resolution depends on resolution of a federal question sufficiently substantial to arise under federal law within the meaning of 28 U.S.C. § 1331,' there is § 1331 jurisdiction even though the relevant statute does not explicitly or implicitly provide for a cause of action.").

8. *Cf., Duke Power Co. v. Carolina Environmental Study Group, Inc.,* 438 U.S. 59, 98 S.Ct. 2620, 57 L.Ed.2d 595 (1978) (test is not whether plaintiff can actually recover on cause of action; test is whether allegation of federal cause of action is patently without merit and thereby deserves dismissal); *Perpetual Securities, Inc. v. Tang,* 290 F.3d 132, 136–37 (2d Cir.2002) (allegation of federal question must be colorable; mere allegation of federal question, without more, "will not automatically confer federal question jurisdiction"); *Harris v. Owens,* 264 F.3d 1282, 1289 (10th Cir.2001), *cert. denied,* 535 U.S. 1097, 122 S.Ct. 2294, 152 L.Ed.2d 1052 (2002) ("If the federal claim is not wholly frivolous, it suffices to establish federal jurisdiction even if it ultimately is rejected on the merits.").

9. *See, e.g., Penobscot Nation v. Georgia–Pacific Corp.,* 254 F.3d 317 (1st Cir.2001), *cert. denied,* 534 U.S. 1127, 122 S.Ct. 1064, 151 L.Ed.2d 968 (2002) (fact that case involves federal issue does not, of itself, satisfy § 1331; Supreme Court "has, for some time, required that it be apparent from the fact of the plaintiff's complaint either that a cause of action arise

because the federal question arises only in a defense and not in a well-pleaded complaint.[10]

It should be noted that the term "well pleaded complaint" is a term of art and does not require the plaintiff to plead with any particular special skill. For purposes of federal question jurisdiction under § 1331 it is only necessary that the facts alleged in the complaint establish a cause of action arising under the Constitution, law or treaties of the United States.[11]

"Arising Under" Federal Law

Often it is clear on the face of the complaint that a cause of action arises under federal law. However, in some close cases nominally involving state law, the precise definition of what causes of action arise under the laws of the United States can be a bit slippery. Nevertheless, three elements appear necessary before a federal question may be found embedded in a complaint in a state law case. These elements require a claim of a federal right that: 1) involves "a substantial question of federal law; 2) is framed in terms of state law; and 3) requires interpretation of federal law to resolve the case." [12]

under federal law . . . or at least (in some cases) that a traditional state-law cause of action (e.g., a tort or contract claim) present an important federal issue;" also noting that second alternative is very narrow exception); *Gritchen v. Collier,* 254 F.3d 807 (9th Cir.2001) ("Simply raising a constitutional argument in defense of an action that is brought in state court does not open the federal forum."); *Iowa Management & Consultants, Inc. v. Sac & Fox Tribe,* 207 F.3d 488, 489 (8th Cir.2000) (plaintiff's anticipation that defendant will raise federal law as defense in contract litigation does not create federal question jurisdiction). *Cf., Transit Express, Inc. v. Ettinger,* 246 F.3d 1018, 1024 (7th Cir.2001) ("[T]he mere existence of a federal regulatory framework does not convey federal jurisdiction over contractual disputes between private parties that are ancillary to the governmental interest.").

10. *See, e.g., Metropolitan Life Ins. Co. v. Taylor,* 481 U.S. 58, 63, 107 S.Ct. 1542, 1546, 95 L.Ed.2d 55 (1987)("It is long settled law that a cause of action arises under federal law only when the plaintiff's well-pleaded complaint raises issues of federal law."). *See also Holmes Group, Inc. v. Vornado Air Circulation Systems, Inc.,* 535 U.S. 826, 122 S.Ct. 1889, 153 L.Ed.2d 13 (2002) (subject matter jurisdiction of Federal Circuit cannot be invoked when sole basis of such jurisdiction is a counterclaim, not a count in complaint; citing close analogy to well-pleaded complaint requirement of § 1331); *Louisville & Nashville R.R. Co. v. Mottley,* 211 U.S. 149, 29 S.Ct. 42, 53 L.Ed. 126 (1908); *Butero v. Royal Maccabees Life Ins. Co.,* 174 F.3d 1207, 1212 (11th Cir.1999) ("As an affirmative defense, [federal] preemption does not furnish federal subject-matter jurisdiction under 28 U.S.C. § 1331."). *Cf., Club Comanche, Inc. v. Government of Virgin Islands,* 278 F.3d 250, 260 (3d Cir.2002) (action to quiet title to land where defendant's claim to land is based on federal law does not satisfy federal question jurisdiction; noting, however, authority reaching opposite result if action is to remove cloud on title, not to quiet title); *McClelland v. Gronwaldt,* 155 F.3d 507, 512 (5th Cir.1998) (accepting general rule that federal preemption does not, of itself, create jurisdiction under § 1331; noting, however, that when federal law completely preempts an area, so that any "state" claim is actually a mislabeled federal claim, claim is a federal cause of action under § 1331; acknowledging that this principle of complete preemption has limited application).

11. *See, e.g., Radici v. Associated Insurance Companies, Blue Cross Blue Shield of Indiana,* 217 F.3d 737 (9th Cir.2000) (complaint erroneously asserted diversity jurisdiction; where court could clearly find federal question jurisdiction, error was insignificant). *See also Flowers v. First Hawaiian Bank,* 295 F.3d 966 (9th Cir.2002) ("An appropriate allegation that a claim arises 'under the Constitution, laws, or treaties of the United States,' 28 U.S.C. § 1331, is sufficient to vest a federal district court with jurisdiction to determine whether or not the claim actually does so arise, and if it does, to decide the issue the claim presents.").

12. *Grable & Sons Metal Products, Inc. v. Darue Engineering & Manufacturing,* 377 F.3d 592 (6th Cir. 2004) (noting general consensus

Congressionally Chartered Corporations

Most companies incorporated in the United States are created and organized under the law of a particular state. However, a small number of corporations are created through Congressional enactment. Such federally created corporations may sue or be sued under § 1331 without regard to whether claims at issue arise under federal or state law.[13]

Constitutional Torts

In a few unusual circumstances the Supreme Court has recognized a right to a private suit for a constitutional violation, notwithstanding that neither the relevant constitutional provision nor federal statutory law expressly recognizes such a right.[14] The authority to file such an implied constitutional tort in federal district court is derived from 28 U.S.C.A. § 1331.[15]

Refusing to Plead a Federal Claim: Complete Preemption

Ordinarily, the plaintiff has control of the counts in his complaint and may therefore avoid federal question jurisdiction simply by foregoing claims based on federal law.[16] However, in areas where federal law has completely preempted state law, a plaintiff cannot avoid the federal question by pleading only state law.[17] It should be noted, however, that assertion of federal question jurisdiction under this corollary to the well-pleaded complaint rule applies only where federal law has completely preempted an area.[18]

among circuits subject to only minor variances; collecting cases).

13. *Pacific Railroad Removal Cases,* 115 U.S. 1, 5 S.Ct. 1113, 29 L.Ed. 319 (1885). *See also, e.g., Aliotta v. National R.R. Passenger Corp.,* 315 F.3d 756, 758 n. 1 (7th Cir.2003) ("Federal question jurisdiction exists for congressionally incorporated corporations under 28 U.S.C.A. § 1331.").

14. *See, e.g., Bivens v. Six Unknown Federal Narcotics Agents,* 403 U.S. 388, 91 S.Ct. 1999, 29 L.Ed.2d 619 (1971) (federal officers' alleged violation of Fourth Amendment gives rise to private cause of action).

15. *Correctional Services Corp. v. Malesko,* 534 U.S. 61, 122 S.Ct. 515, 151 L.Ed.2d 456 (2001) (also citing Supreme Court cases creating private rights of action under Fifth and Eighth Amendments, as well as cases refusing to recognize additional rights; refusing to extend *Bivens* principles to permit suit for damages by halfway-house inmate against private defendants).

16. *Caterpillar, Inc. v. Williams,* 482 U.S. 386, 389, 107 S.Ct. 2425, 2427, 96 L.Ed.2d 318 (1987) (normally, non-diverse plaintiff who has federal cause of action but who prefers to avoid federal district court "may avoid federal jurisdiction by exclusive reliance on state law"); *The Fair v. Kohler Die & Specialty Co.,* 228 U.S. 22, 25, 33 S.Ct. 410, 411, 57 L.Ed. 716 (1913) ("[T]he party who brings a suit is master to decide what law he will rely upon.").

17 *Beneficial National Bank v. Anderson,* 539 U.S. 1, 8, 123 S.Ct. 2058, 2063, 156 L.Ed.2d 1 (2003) ("When the federal statute completely pre-empts the state-law cause of action, a claim which comes within the scope of that cause of action, even if pleaded in terms of state law, is in reality based on federal law."); *Avco Corp. v. Aero Lodge No. 735,* 390 U.S. 557, 88 S.Ct. 1235, 20 L.Ed.2d 126 (1968) (plaintiff sued union for breach of no-strike clause in contract; plaintiff did not assert applicable federal labor law; held, union could remove case to district court, because case was controlled by federal law notwithstanding plaintiff's plea of state law). *See also, Franchise Tax Bd. v. Construction Laborers Vacation Trust,* 463 U.S. 1, 103 S.Ct. 2841, 77 L.Ed.2d 420 (1983) ("[O]riginal federal jurisdiction is unavailable unless it appears that some substantial, disputed question of federal law is a necessary element of one of the well-pleaded state claims, or that one or the other claim is 'really' one of federal law.").

18. *Beneficial National Bank v. Anderson,* 539 U.S. 1, 7, 123 S.Ct. 2058, 2063, 156 L.Ed.2d 1 (2003) (test of complete preemption is whether federal statute "wholly displaces" otherwise rel-

Preemption as a Cause of Action

As is discussed immediately above, preemption is normally a defense available when a plaintiff has pleaded only state law claims and thereby tried to avoid applicable federal law. However, it is settled that the doctrine also permits a cause of action on grounds of preemption when the plaintiff seeks "to enjoin state officials from interfering with federal rights." [19]

State Claims That Depend on Federal Law

There is another narrow exception to the general rule that jurisdiction under § 1331 may be based only upon an allegation of a federal question in a well-pleaded complaint. Where the plaintiff's cause of action arises from state law, but depends for its resolution on "a substantial question of federal law," it is possible that a district court will have federal question jurisdiction under § 1331.[20] However, attorneys are cautioned that this is indeed a narrow exception to the general rule, extending the scope of jurisdiction under § 1331 only modestly.[21]

Declaratory Judgments

The well-pleaded complaint rule applies to declaratory judgments in the following fashion. For a declaratory judgment action to rest on federal question jurisdiction, the federal question must be found on the defendant's side of the case. In other words, federal question jurisdiction exists if, had the suit been brought as a conventional case, the pleading of the declaratory judgment defendant, as a conventional plaintiff, would have stated a federal question.[22]

evant state claims). *See, e.g., Plumbing Industry Bd. v. E.W. Howell Co.,* 126 F.3d 61, 66 (2d Cir.1997) ("Ordinarily, a claim of preemption is a defense to be raised in the defendant's answer, and thus cannot support jurisdiction . . . because it would not appear on the face of a well-pleaded complaint;" different result only when Congress completely preempts an area, so that "any civil complaint raising a state law claim in that area is of necessity so federal in character that it arises under federal law for purposes of 28 U.S.C. § 1331"). *See also, e.g.,* 42 U.S.C.A. § 2014(hh) (federal courts have exclusive jurisdiction over torts arising from nuclear accidents).

19. *Shaw v. Delta Air Lines, Inc.,* 463 U.S. 85, 96 n. 14, 103 S.Ct. 2890, 2899 n. 14, 77 L.Ed.2d 490 (1983).

20. *Franchise Tax Board v. Construction Laborers Vacation Trust,* 463 U.S. 1, 27–28, 103 S.Ct. 2841, 2856, 77 L.Ed.2d 420 (1983). *See also Verizon Maryland, Inc. v. Global Naps, Inc.,* 377 F.3d 355(4th Cir. 2004) ("When a 'case's resolution depends on resolution of a federal question sufficiently substantial to arise under federal law within the meaning of 28 U.S.C. § 1331,' there is § 1331 jurisdiction even though the relevant statute does not explicitly or implicitly provide for a cause of action.").

21. *Merrell Dow Pharmaceuticals, Inc. v. Thompson,* 478 U.S. 804, 813–14, 106 S.Ct. 3229, 3234, 92 L.Ed.2d 650 (1986) ("[T]he mere presence of a federal issue in a state cause of action does not automatically confer federal-question jurisdiction." Congressional determination that no federal remedy exists for violation of federal statute means that claimed violation of federal statute as element of state claim "is insufficiently 'substantial' to confer federal-question jurisdiction"). *But cf., Downey v. State Farm Fire & Casualty Co.,* 266 F.3d 675, 682 (7th Cir.2001) (insurance contract between private parties fell within § 1331 for two reasons: first, on particular facts of case it implicated provisions of federal flood control program; second, if private insurer did not pay, federal funds were at risk).

22. *Skelly Oil Co. v. Phillips Petroleum Co.,* 339 U.S. 667, 70 S.Ct. 876, 94 L.Ed. 1194 (1950) *See also, e.g., Heydon v. MediaOne of Southeast Michigan, Inc.,* 327 F.3d 466, 470 (6th Cir.2003) ("The Declaratory Judgment Act does not create an independent basis for federal subject matter

Weak Federal Claims: "Insubstantiality"

It is settled that the probability of defeat on the merits does not, by itself, strip a plaintiff's claim of federal question jurisdiction.[23] However, where a plaintiff files a claim that superficially appears to be a federal question but is actually only a "dressed up" state claim offered to satisfy federal question jurisdiction, the court may dismiss the claim. This "insubstantiality doctrine" is only employed rarely.[24]

Post-Filing Events

In general, jurisdiction is evaluated on the basis of facts as they existed at the time the complaint was filed. Events that occur subsequent to filing of the complaint normally have no bearing on the court's jurisdictional decision.[25]

Amount in Controversy

Unlike diversity jurisdiction, there is usually no requirement that federal question cases satisfy any specific dollar amount.[26] Thus, if a case arose under the federal civil rights laws, and the amount at issue was only ten dollars, the case would still qualify for federal subject matter jurisdiction.

Citizenship

Unlike diversity jurisdiction, the citizenship of parties in federal question cases has no relevance to subject matter jurisdiction. It is irrelevant, for example, if both the plaintiff and the defendant are citizens of the same foreign country, or if both the plaintiff and the defendant are citizens of the same American state.

jurisdiction."); *Columbia Gas Transmission Corp. v. Drain,* 237 F.3d 366, 370 (4th Cir.2001) ("One does need to understand ... that in a declaratory judgment action, the federal right litigated may belong to the declaratory judgment defendant rather than the declaratory judgment plaintiff."); *Northeast Illinois Regional Commuter Railroad Corp. v. Hoey Farina & Downes,* 212 F.3d 1010, 1014 (7th Cir.2000) ("[I]f the plaintiff cannot get into federal court by anticipating what amounts to a federal defense to a state-law cause of action, he also should not be able to use the Declaratory Judgment Act to do so by asserting what is really a preemptive federal defense as the basis of his complaint."); *State of Missouri ex rel. Missouri Highway & Transp. Comm'n v. Cuffley,* 112 F.3d 1332, 1335 (8th Cir.1997) (In a declaratory judgment suit, "we must consider whether a well-pleaded complaint in ... a traditional action would present a federal issue."). *But cf., Textron Lycoming Reciprocating Engine Division, Avco Corp. v. United Automobile, Aerospace and Agricultural Implement Workers of America,* 523 U.S. 653, 659–60, 118 S.Ct. 1626, 1630, 140 L.Ed.2d 863 (1998) ("No decision of this Court has squarely confronted and explicitly upheld federal-question jurisdiction on the basis of the anticipated claim against which the declaratory-judgment plaintiff presents a nonfederal defense;" suggesting application of *Skelly Oil* to such facts is unclear, but declining to decide issue).

23. *Bell v. Hood,* 327 U.S. 678, 66 S.Ct. 773, 90 L.Ed. 939 (1946).

24. *See, e.g., Dixon v. Coburg Dairy, Inc.,* 330 F.3d 250, 255–56 (4th Cir.2003) (noting that pretextual motive for miscast claim or patently insubstantial and frivolous claim is ground for invocation of rarely used doctrine).

25. *See, e.g., Sallen v. Corinthians Licenciamentos LTDA,* 273 F.3d 14, 23 (1st Cir.2001) (noting only very narrow exceptions to general rule).

26. *See, e.g., Bartels v. Alabama Commercial College, Inc.,* 54 F.3d 702, 708 (11th Cir. 1995)("Congress ... has ... eliminated the amount in controversy requirement for cases arising under federal law.").

ADDITIONAL RESEARCH REFERENCES

C.J.S. Federal Courts §§ 27–43 et seq.

West's Key No. Digests, Federal Courts ⚷161–247.

§ 1.12 Subject Matter Jurisdiction in Federal District Courts—Requirements for Diversity Jurisdiction

CORE CONCEPT

Subject matter jurisdiction based on diversity of citizenship permits a federal district court to hear state causes of action if two basic requirements are fulfilled: the plaintiff must be a citizen of a state or jurisdiction other than that in which the defendant is a citizen; and the amount in controversy must exceed $75,000, exclusive of interest and costs.[1] Such claims are within the concurrent jurisdiction of federal courts, which means that they can be filed in either state court or federal court. Between twenty and twenty-five percent of the cases in federal court are founded on diversity jurisdiction, but a larger percentage of jurisdictional difficulties arise in this area.

APPLICATIONS

Diverse Citizenship

28 U.S.C.A. § 1332 describes four different circumstances that satisfy diversity of citizenship:

(1) when the plaintiff is a citizen of an American state other than that of which the defendant is a citizen;

(2) when the parties on one side are citizens of American states, and the opposing parties are citizens or subjects of foreign states;[2]

(3) when the parties are citizens of different American states, and additional parties are citizens or subjects of foreign states;[3] and

(4) when a foreign state is a plaintiff suing citizens of American states.

Citizenship of an Individual

For purposes of diversity jurisdiction, 28 U.S.C.A. § 1332(a) defines citizenship for an individual in an American state as domicile in the state.[4] Domicile normally requires that the individual has both a

1. 28 U.S.C.A. § 1332.

2. *Cf., Iraola & CIA, S.A. v. Kimberly–Clark Corp.*, 232 F.3d 854, 859 (11th Cir.2000) (citizens of American states on one side of case may themselves be citizens of various American states; rejecting argument that § 1332(a)(2) requires American citizens to be citizens of only one American state).

3. Under this provision it appears settled that citizens or subjects of foreign states may be "additional parties" on both sides of a case. *See, e.g., Dresser Indus., Inc. v. Underwriters at Lloyd's of London*, 106 F.3d 494, 497-98 (3d Cir.1997) (so holding; citing other authority).

4. *See, e.g., Denlinger v. Brennan*, 87 F.3d 214, 216 (7th Cir.1996)(" 'Citizenship' for purposes of § 1332 means domicile rather than resi-

physical presence in the state and an intent to reside in the state indefinitely.[5] 28 U.S.C.A. § 1332(a) also provides specifically that an alien permanently residing in the United States is, for diversity purposes, a "citizen" of the American state where the alien is domiciled.[6]

Corporate Citizenship

28 U.S.C.A. § 1332(c) provides that for diversity purposes a corporation is a citizen both of the state where it is incorporated and the state in which it has its principal place of business. If a corporation is incorporated in more than one state, then it is a citizen of every state where incorporated.[7] However, a corporation will have only one principal place of business.[8] Thus, depending on the particular facts of incorporation and location of business operations, a corporation may be a citizen of one, two, or even more jurisdictions for diversity purposes.[9] The lower federal courts have developed two distinct approaches to defining "principal place of business": the location of the corporation's headquarters (i.e., its corporate nerve center) [10] or the place where the bulk of the corporation's assets may be found.[11] More recently courts

dence."). *Cf., Tylka v. Gerber Products Co.,* 211 F.3d 445, 447 (7th Cir.2000), *cert. denied,* 531 U.S. 1002, 121 S.Ct. 504, 148 L.Ed.2d 473 (2000) (reference to parties' "residence," not citizenship, is "obvious shortcoming" that does not satisfy § 1332).

5. *See, e.g., Kanter v. Warner–Lambert Co.,* 265 F.3d 853, 857 (9th Cir.2001) (state citizenship is domicile, not mere residence; residence is only physical presence, while domicile is residence plus intention to make permanent abode); *Palazzo v. Corio,* 232 F.3d 38, 41 (2d Cir.2000) ("An individual's citizenship . . . is determined by his domicile;" a natural person "has but one domicile"); *Mas v. Perry,* 489 F.2d 1396, 1399 (5th Cir.1974) *cert. denied,* 419 U.S. 842, 95 S.Ct. 74, 42 L.Ed.2d 70 (1974)(noting twin requirements of physical presence and intent). *See also Mitchell v. Brown & Williamson Tobacco Corp.,* 294 F.3d 1309, 1314 (11th Cir.2002) (incarcerated party is citizen of state in which he was domiciled at time of imprisonment, not state in which he is held); *McCormick v. Aderholt,* 293 F.3d 1254, 1257–58 (11th Cir.2002) (change of domicile requires, concurrently, physical presence at new domicile and intention to reside there indefinitely).

6. *See, e.g., Saadeh v. Farouki,* 107 F.3d 52, 58 (D.C.Cir.1997).

7. *See, e.g., Freeman v. Northwest Acceptance Corp.,* 754 F.2d 553, 558 (5th Cir.1985)(if parent and subsidiary are treated as a single corporation, then all states of incorporation are states in which the corporation is a citizen). *Cf., Wild v. Subscription Plus, Inc.,* 292 F.3d 526, 528–29 (7th Cir.2002), *cert. denied,* 537 U.S. 1045, 123 S.Ct. 619, 154 L.Ed.2d 517 (2002) (held, where corporate charter is revoked at time of filing but was later restored, revocation does not affect corporation's status for diversity purposes; noting that state law permitted corporation to sue and be sued in its own name until corporation was actually dissolved). *But see Universal Licensing Corp. v. Paola del Lungo, S.p.A.,* 293 F.3d 579, 581 (2d Cir.2002) (corporation "could not be considered to be incorporated in a state that had revoked its corporate charter").

8. *Cf., Cincinnati Insurance Co. v. Eastern Atlantic Insurance Co.,* 260 F.3d 742, 747 (7th Cir.2001) (noting with some irritation that doing business is not the same as the rule that corporate citizenship may rest upon corporation's principal place of business).

9. *See, e.g., Union Pacific Railroad Co. v. 174 Acres of Land Located in Crittenden County,* 193 F.3d 944, 946 (8th Cir.1999) (for purposes of diversity it is "long recognized that a corporation can be incorporated in more than one State"). *Cf., Firstar Bank, N.A. v. Faul,* 253 F.3d 982 (7th Cir.2001) (for diversity purposes a national chartered bank is located in its principal place of business and in the state listed on its organizational certificate).

10. *See, e.g., Metropolitan Life Ins. Co. v. Estate of Cammon,* 929 F.2d 1220, 1222 (7th Cir.1991). (applying "nerve center" approach).

11. *See, e.g., Kelly v. United States Steel Corp.,* 284 F.2d 850 (3d Cir.1960). (looking to center of production or service activities). *Cf., Gadlin v. Sybron International Corp.,* 222 F.3d 797, 800 (10th Cir.2000) (affirming Colorado as principal place of business where president of corporation lived in California, but 36 of 46

have sometimes combined both tests into a "total activity" test to find the principal place of business.[12]

Important: If a corporation has citizenship in more than one jurisdiction, the opposing party must be diverse from *all* the citizenships, or diversity is not established.[13]

Corporations No Longer Doing Business

In unusual cases it may occur that a corporation has *no* place of business at the time a lawsuit is filed. This situation can occur when a corporation remains incorporated but is simply not presently doing any business. Two differing approaches have been developed to deal with that situation. The first looks to the corporation's most recent place of business to help determine citizenship.[14] The second approach concludes that because a corporation ceased operations before the lawsuit was filed, it has no place of business for purposes of diversity jurisdiction.[15]

There is also some uncertainty as to the threshold issue of the kinds of facts necessary to establish whether a corporation has actually ceased business operations.[16] This entire area obviously requires that attorneys consult the local practice.

Unincorporated Associations

For diversity purposes, unincorporated associations such as partnerships, joint ventures, and labor unions are treated as citizens of every state in which one or more of their members is a citizen.[17] Thus,

employees worked in Colorado and manufacturing, production, and distribution facilities were in Colorado).

12. *See, e.g., United Computer Systems, Inc. v. AT & T Corp.*, 298 F.3d 756 (9th Cir.2002) (principal place of business "is determined by the following two-part inquiry: (1) in what state does a 'substantial predominance' of corporate activity take place? or (2) if the corporation's activities are not predominant in a single state, then the principal place of business is where the majority of its executives and administrative functions are performed"); *Harris v. Black Clawson Co.*, 961 F.2d 547, 549 (5th Cir. 1992)(balancing both earlier tests to determine principal place of business). *See also Peterson v. Cooley*, 142 F.3d 181, 184 (4th Cir.1998) (noting approval of both tests in Fourth Circuit and endorsing "neither to the exclusion of the other"). It should be noted that when an American corporation's principal place of business is found in a foreign country, there is authority holding that the corporation is a citizen of its (American) state of incorporation only, and that the "place of business" standard therefore does not apply at all. *See, e.g., Torres v. Southern Peru Copper Corp.*, 113 F.3d 540 (5th Cir.1997).

13. *See, e.g., Hall v. Rental Assocs., Inc.*, 833 F.2d 370 (D.C.Cir.1987)(plaintiff must be diverse from both corporate citizenships).

14. *See, e.g., Harris v. Black Clawson Co.*, 961 F.2d 547, 551 (5th Cir.1992) (state where corporation last conducted business is relevant to inquiry); *William Passalacqua Builders, Inc. v. Resnick Developers South, Inc.*, 933 F.2d 131, 141 (2d Cir.1991) (diversity includes state where party "last transacted business").

15. *See, e.g., Midlantic National Bank v. Hansen*, 48 F.3d 693, 696 (3d Cir.1995), *cert. dismissed*, 515 U.S. 1184, 116 S.Ct. 32, 132 L.Ed.2d 914 (1995) (inactive corporation has no principal place of business and therefore is citizen of state of incorporation).

16. *See, e.g., Grand Union Supermarkets of the Virgin Islands v. H.E. Lockhart Management*, 316 F.3d 408, 409–11 (3d Cir.2003) ("corporate trappings," such as paying franchise taxes, filing corporate reports, or the qualifications required to potentially conduct business in the future are not enough if company is not entering contracts, hiring employees, making sales, maintaining an address, possessing office equipment or owning property; "[A] corporation must actually conduct business for it to have a principal place of business.").

17. *Carden v. Arkoma Associates*, 494 U.S. 185, 195–96, 110 S.Ct. 1015, 1021, 108 L.Ed.2d 157 (1990) (in diversity cases a limited partnership has the citizenship of every general partner

for very large unincorporated entities, such as national labor unions with members in every state, diversity of citizenship is unlikely to exist between the labor union and its opponent in a lawsuit.[18]

Exception: When the case involves class litigation, a recent amendment to 28 U.S.C.A. § 1332 will produce a different result than was available under established case law. In the future, for class actions, the citizenship of an unincorporated association shall be both the state where it has its principal place of business and the state under whose laws it is organized.[19]

"Stateless" Foreign Persons and Corporations

Section 1332(a)(2) confers diversity jurisdiction in suits between citizens of an American state and citizens or subjects of foreign states (assuming that the amount-in-controversy requirement is also satisfied). However, some parties, who are clearly not citizens of any American state, also may not enjoy the status of citizens of foreign states because they are citizens of some sort of governmental unit that does not possess the elements of sovereignty. Until recently there was substantial disagreement as to whether corporations who are not citizens of American states and do not enjoy full citizen status under a foreign sovereign could nevertheless be citizens or subjects of a foreign state for purposes of § 1332(a)(2). The disagreement is now resolved. Such a corporation is now treated as a citizen or subject of a foreign sovereign for purposes of diversity.[20]

Foreign Citizens Suing One Another

28 U.S.C.A. § 1332 contains no provision authorizing citizens or subjects of one foreign state to sue citizens or subjects of another foreign state in diversity. Thus if a subject of Great Britain sought to use a federal district court to sue a citizen of Brazil on a state cause of action, diversity jurisdiction would not exist, unless an additional party was a citizen of an American state.[21]

and limited partner). *See, e.g., American Vantage Companies, Inc. v. Table Mountain Rancheria,* 292 F.3d 1091, 1093 (9th Cir.2002) ("[A]n unincorporated Indian tribe . . . is not a 'citizen' of a state within the meaning of the federal diversity statute . . . and thus cannot sue or be sued in diversity."); *Riley v. Merrill Lynch, Pierce, Fenner & Smith, Inc.,* 292 F.3d 1334 (11th Cir. 2002), *cert. denied,* 537 U.S. 950, 123 S.Ct. 395, 154 L.Ed.2d 296 (2002) (business trust has citizenship of all its shareholders); *Ninigret Development Corp. v. Narragansett Indian Wetuomuck Housing Authority,* 207 F.3d 21, 27 (1st Cir. 2000) (Indian tribes are not citizens of any state; for diversity purposes they are "analogous to a stateless person;" presence of Indian tribe destroys diversity, "notwithstanding the joinder of other diverse parties"). *Cantor Fitzgerald, L.P. v. Peaslee,* 88 F.3d 152 n. 1 (2d Cir. 1996)(Partnerships "take the citizenship of each of their respective partners.").

18. *See, e.g., Belle View Apartments v. Realty Refund Trust,* 602 F.2d 668 (4th Cir.1979). (diversity fails because citizenships of unincorporated associations' memberships overlap).

19. 28 U.S.C.A. § 1332(d)(10).

20. *JPMorgan Chase Bank v. Traffic Stream (BVI) Infrastructure Limited,* 536 U.S. 88, 122 S.Ct. 2054, 153 L.Ed.2d 95 (2002) (British Virgin Islands corporation may appropriately be a citizen of United Kingdom for diversity purposes; issue is governed by construction of § 1332, not foreign law (although in instant case foreign law and § 1332 are harmonious); held, corporation may be a citizen of United Kingdom notwithstanding that it is organized under law of British Overseas Territory, not law of Britain itself).

21. *See, e.g., MCC-Marble Ceramic Ctr., Inc. v. Ceramica Nuova d'Agostino, S.p.A.,* 144 F.3d 1384 n. 15 (11th Cir.1998), *cert. denied,* 526 U.S. 1087, 119 S.Ct. 1496, 143 L.Ed.2d 650 (1999).

District of Columbia, Puerto Rico, and U.S. Territories

For purposes of diversity jurisdiction, 28 U.S.C.A. § 1332(d) treats jurisdictions such as the District of Columbia, Puerto Rico, the Virgin Islands, Guam, etc., as American states. Thus, persons domiciled in those jurisdictions will typically be treated as citizens of those "states" for diversity purposes.[22]

U.S. Citizens Domiciled in Foreign Countries

Americans domiciled abroad are obviously not domiciled in an American state. Thus, they cannot be citizens of an American state for diversity purposes. At the same time, American citizens domiciled abroad are not citizens or subjects of the foreign countries in which they reside. Thus they do not qualify for diversity jurisdiction as citizens or subjects of foreign states. The result, anomalous as it may seem, is that American citizens domiciled abroad do not qualify for diversity jurisdiction under any of the four categories of 28 U.S.C.A. § 1332, and thus may not sue or be sued in a federal district court on the basis of diversity jurisdiction.[23]

Note, however, that such persons may qualify for federal court if the cause of action rests on a federal question, discussed above. It is also possible that such persons may sue or be sued in federal court if they fit within the description of supplemental jurisdiction, discussed below.

Timing of Citizenship

The parties must be diverse at the time the suit is filed.[24] It is irrelevant that the parties may not have been diverse at the time the

(Section 1332 provides "no statutory grant for suits between aliens unless a citizen of a State is present."). *See also, Franceskin v. Credit Suisse,* 214 F.3d 253 (2d Cir.2000) (if plaintiff is citizen of a foreign country and defendant is incorporated in a different foreign country but maintains principal place of business in United States, diversity is still lacking). *Cf. Dresser Indus., Inc. v. Underwriters at Lloyd's of London,* 106 F.3d 494, 497–98 (3d Cir.1997) (if foreign subjects are only additional parties to suit between citizens of different American states, diversity jurisdiction may be satisfied). *But see Universal Licensing Corp. v. Paola del Lungo, S.p.A.,* 293 F.3d 579, 581 (2d Cir.2002) ("[D]iversity is lacking ... where the only parties are foreign entities, or where on one side there are citizens and aliens and on the opposite side there are only aliens.").

22. *See, e.g., Brown v. Francis,* 75 F.3d 860, 865 (3d Cir.1996)(for purposes of diversity jurisdiction, Virgin Islands is a state). *But cf., Barwood, Inc. v. District of Columbia,* 202 F.3d 290, 292 (D.C.Cir.2000) (District of Columbia is treated as a state under § 1332, but it is "not a citizen of a state (or of itself)"; thus, where District of Columbia is a defendant, there is no diversity).

23. *See, e.g., Coury v. Prot,* 85 F.3d 244, 248 (5th Cir.1996) ("An American national, living abroad, cannot sue or be sued in federal court under diversity jurisdiction ... unless that party is a citizen, *i.e.* domiciled, in a particular state of the United States."); *Cresswell v. Sullivan & Cromwell,* 922 F.2d 60, 68–69 (2d Cir.1990), *cert. denied,* 505 U.S. 1222, 112 S.Ct. 3036, 120 L.Ed.2d 905 (1992) (noting failure of diversity where some plaintiffs and several partners of defendant law firm were United States citizens domiciled abroad); *Sadat v. Mertes,* 615 F.2d 1176, 1183 (7th Cir.1980)(An American citizen's domicile abroad does not thereby make him a citizen of a foreign state.).

24. *Grupo Dataflux v. Atlas Global Group, L.P.,* 541 U.S. 567, 124 S.Ct. 1920, 158 L.Ed.2d 866 (2004) (party's post-filing change in citizenship cannot cure lack of subject matter jurisdiction that existed at time of filing); *Dole Food Co. v. Patrickson,* 538 U.S. 468, 477, 123 S.Ct. 1655, 1662, 155 L.Ed.2d 643 (2003) ("It is well settled ... that federal-diversity jurisdiction depends on

cause of action arose,[25] or that a party diverse at the time of filing acquires a non-diverse citizenship in the course of the lawsuit.[26] Thus, if a citizen of New York seeks to sue another New York citizen in federal district court over a state cause of action, the plaintiff could create diversity of citizenship by making a genuine change of domicile from New York to another jurisdiction prior to filing suit. Conversely, if the parties are diverse when the suit is filed, a subsequent change of domicile will not *defeat* diversity, either.

It should be noted that recent Congressional amendments to 28 U.S.C.A. § 1332, governing diversity jurisdiction, have tended to adopt the existing case law approach to the timing of diversity jurisdiction.[27]

Complete Diversity

To satisfy diversity jurisdiction, *all* plaintiffs must have citizenship different from that of *all* defendants.[28] There is no requirement that plaintiffs have citizenships different from one another, or that defendants have citizenships different from each other. Thus if a plaintiff was a citizen of Ohio, diversity jurisdiction would fail if any defendant was also a citizen of Ohio. However, if five plaintiffs were citizens of Ohio, diversity jurisdiction could still exist if all defendants were citizens of states other than Ohio.

the citizenship of the parties at the time suit is filed."). *But see Wild v. Subscription Plus, Inc.,* 292 F.3d 526, 528 (7th Cir.2002), *cert. denied,* 537 U.S. 1045, 123 S.Ct. 619, 154 L.Ed.2d 517 (2002) (held, where corporate charter is revoked at time of filing but was later restored, revocation does not affect corporation's status for diversity purpose; noting that state law permitted corporation to sue and be sued in its own name until corporation was actually dissolved; citing this circumstances as exception to general rule); *Soberay Machine & Equipment Co. v. MRF Ltd.,* 181 F.3d 759, 763 (6th Cir.1999) ("Although we agree that a party may not create diversity by dropping a nondiverse and indispensable party, we note that it is appropriate to drop a nondiverse and dispensable party from litigation in order to achieve diversity.").

25. *See, e.g., Associated Ins. Management Corp. v. Arkansas General Agency, Inc.,* 149 F.3d 794 (8th Cir.1998) ("[W]e determine diversity of citizenship at the time an action is filed; . . . the district court cannot retroactively create diversity jurisdiction if it did not exist when the complaint was filed."). *Rodriguez–Diaz v. Sierra–Martinez,* 853 F.2d 1027, 1029 (1st Cir.1988)("It is the domicile at the time suit is filed which controls, and the fact that the plaintiff has changed his domicile with the purpose of bringing a diversity action in federal court is irrelevant."). *See also Hartford Insurance Group v. Lou–Con, Inc.,* 293 F.3d 908 (5th Cir.2002) (facts underlying jurisdictional amount are judged as of filing complaint).

26. *See, e.g., Bank One, Texas, N.A. v. Montle,* 964 F.2d 48, 49 (1st Cir.1992)("Domicile is determined as of the time the suit is filed, and once diversity jurisdiction is established, it is not lost by a later change in domicile."). *But cf., Dominium Austin Partners, L.L.C. v. Emerson,* 248 F.3d 720, 725 (8th Cir.2001) (subject matter jurisdiction is usually evaluated at commencement of action; exception exists where nondiverse but indispensable party is later joined under Rule 19).

27. 28 U.S.C.A. § 1332(d)(7) (citizenship in most class actions to be determined as of date of filing original or amended complaint or, if case did not originally qualify for federal subject matter jurisdiction, as of date federal subject matter jurisdiction might have existed).

28. *Strawbridge v. Curtiss,* 7 U.S. (3 Cranch) 267, 267, 2 L.Ed. 435 (1806). *See also Lee v. American National Insurance Co.,* 260 F.3d 997, 1004 (9th Cir.2001), *cert. denied,* 535 U.S. 928, 122 S.Ct. 1299, 152 L.Ed.2d 211 (2002) (for two hundred years diversity statute has required that "each plaintiff must be diverse from each defendant").

Diversity Jurisdiction in Class Actions

Congress has recently enacted major changes in the requirements for diversity jurisdiction in most cases involving class actions governed by Rule 23.[29] These changes are fairly complex, but their net effect will sometimes be to ease substantially the requirements for diversity jurisdiction in class actions from what had been the established requirements for such jurisdiction in class lawsuits. The changes, to be incorporated as an amendment to 28 U.S.C.A. § 1332,[30] provide that diversity jurisdiction shall be satisfied when the following new requirements are met. First, the amount in controversy requirement for diversity class actions will be satisfied when the amount in controversy exceeds $5,000,000, exclusive of interest and costs. This amount in controversy need not be satisfied by every single individual member of the class. Instead, the individual claims of the class members will be aggregated to determine if the amount in controversy has been satisfied.[31] Second, diversity jurisdiction in class actions now requires that one of three other requirements is met. Diversity is satisfied if, in addition to meeting the amount in controversy requirement: (a) any member of a class of plaintiffs is a citizen of an American state different from the American state of citizenship of any defendant; (b) any member of a class of plaintiffs is a foreign state or a citizen or subject of a foreign state and any defendant is a citizen of an American state; or (c) any member of a class of plaintiffs is a citizen of an American state and any defendant is a foreign state or a citizen or subject of a foreign state. It is worth noting that *all* class actions based on diversity must satisfy the amount in controversy requirement. However, the additional requirement for diverse citizenship can be met by satisfying *any* of the three foregoing descriptions of diverse citizenship.[32]

Declining Diversity Jurisdiction in Class Actions

Notwithstanding the possibility that a class action has met the requirements for diversity jurisdiction discussed immediately above, the recent amendments to § 1332 also provide federal district courts with some substantial opportunities to refrain from hearing such a class lawsuit. The first of these, governed by new § 1332(d)(3), provides the court with discretion to decline to exercise diversity jurisdiction when two requirements are met and some other prudential considerations are weighed. The first of the two requirements is that more than one-third and less than two-thirds of the total membership of a plaintiff class is comprised of citizens of the state in which the action was originally filed. The second requirement is that the "primary" defendants are citizens of the state in which the action was originally filed.[33] In addition to the existence of those two requirements the court must also weigh the following factors:

29. *See* Fed.R.Civ.P. 23.

30. As amended, the provision that is currently designated as § 1332(d) is renamed § 1332(e). A new provision, governing jurisdiction in class actions, is inserted as 28 U.S.C.A. § 1332(d).

31. 28 U.S.C.A. § 1332(d)(6).

32. 28 U.S.C.A. § 1332(d)(2).

33. 28 U.S.C.A. § 1332(d)(3).

(a) whether the claims in question involve matters of national or interstate interest;

(b) whether the claims will be controlled by the law of the state where the case was originally filed or by the law of another state or states;

(c) whether the plaintiffs have, through artful pleading, sought to avoid federal subject matter jurisdiction;

(d) whether the action was filed in a court with a clear relationship with the plaintiffs, the underlying events, or the defendants;

(e) whether the number of class plaintiffs are citizens of the state in which the case was filed is substantially larger than the number of plaintiffs from any other state, and the citizenship of other plaintiffs is dispersed among a significant variety of other states; and

(f) whether during the three years prior to filing the instant action, some other class action has been filed asserting similar claims, without regard to whether the claims were asserted on behalf of the identical plaintiffs.[34]

Moreover, while § 1332(d)(3) provides the court with discretion to refuse to exercise diversity jurisdiction in class actions, § 1332(d)(4) identifies factual situations in which the court must decline to exercise jurisdiction. Specifically, § 1332(d)(4) directs the court to decline jurisdiction when three requirements are met. First, more than two-thirds of the class members of a plaintiff class are citizens of the state in which the case was originally filed. Second, one or more defendants from whom the class seeks substantial relief and whose conduct allegedly forms a significant basis for the class claims is a citizen of the state in which the case was originally filed. Third, the principal injuries pleaded by the class or any related conduct were incurred in the state in which the action was originally filed, and either of two other elements are met: in the preceding three years prior to the instant action, no similar allegations have been filed against any of the same defendants by the same or other plaintiffs; or, both two-thirds or more of the class plaintiffs and the primary defendants are citizens of the state in which the action was originally filed.[35]

Class Actions Unaffected by Amendments

Notwithstanding the broad scope of the recent amendment to § 1332, certain fairly narrow categories of class actions are expressly excluded from the scope of the new provisions. Specifically, amended § 1332 does not apply to any class action in which the primary defendants are "States, State officials, or other governmental entities against whom the district court may be foreclosed from ordering relief." [36] Thus, for example, a suit against a state that was barred by the Eleventh Amendment of the Constitution[37] if it had been brought by an individual plaintiff does not somehow acquire subject matter jurisdic-

34 Id.

35 28 U.S.C.A. § 1332(d)(4).

36 28 U.S.C.A. § 1332(d)(5)(A).

37 U.S. Const., Amend. 11.

tion because it has been brought by a class of plaintiffs pursuant to new § 1332. Additionally, the amendments to § 1332 may not be used to satisfy diversity jurisdiction when the aggregate number of class plaintiffs is less than 100.[38] It may conceivably still be possible to satisfy diversity jurisdiction over classes that are comprised of less than 100 plaintiffs using the old rules for diversity in class lawsuits established by the Supreme Court. These old rules are discussed at greater length in the treatment of Federal Rule of Civil Procedure 23 (governing class actions) elsewhere in this book. It may also be, however, that the courts will take a hint from Congress and simply refuse to certify class lawsuits where the number of plaintiffs is less than 100. The question of the numerosity requirement for class certification is also discussed in the treatment of Rule 23.

Finally, the amended version of § 1332 does not apply to class actions that rest "solely" upon a claim arising under certain federal securities laws, the laws of a state involving the internal affairs of corporations or other business entities (provided that the corporation or entity is incorporate or organized in that state), or laws that relate to rights and duties, including fiduciary duties, created by any security or the federal Securities Act of 1933.[39] Where parties may seek to files such cases on the basis of diversity jurisdiction, presumably the older case law requirements for diversity jurisdiction—with citizenship evaluated based on the citizenship of the class representatives only,[40] but amount in controversy based on the need of each member of the class individually to satisfy the jurisdictional amount[41]—will still apply.

Exceptions for Domestic Relations and Probate Cases

Although § 1332 is silent on the issue, federal courts routinely do not exercise diversity jurisdiction over cases in which divorce, child custody or matters of probate are at issue.[42] However, these exceptions to the application of diversity jurisdiction are construed narrowly. Thus, if a case involved a dispute over property arising out of a divorce decree previously granted, the federal court might hear the case if the requirements of diversity jurisdiction were otherwise satisfied.[43]

38. 28 U.S.C.A. § 1332(d)(5)(B).

39. 28 U.S.C.A. § 1332(d)(9).

40. *Supreme Tribe of Ben Hur v. Cauble,* 255 U.S. 356, 41 S.Ct. 338, 65 L.Ed. 673 (1921).

41. *Zahn v. International Paper Co.,* 414 U.S. 291, 94 S.Ct. 505, 38 L.Ed.2d 511 (1973).

42. *Markham v. Allen,* 326 U.S. 490, 494, 66 S.Ct. 296, 298, 90 L.Ed. 256 (1946) ("[A] federal court has no jurisdiction to probate a will or administer an estate;" but the district court may hear a suit against an estate, provided it is only to establish the claim against the estate and does not interfere with the probate court's jurisdiction or proceedings). *See also Moser v. Pollin,* 294 F.3d 335, 338 (2d Cir.2002) (probate matter is outside scope of diversity jurisdiction in either of two circumstances: when district court is asked "to directly probate a will or administer an estate;" or when hearing the action would cause district court to interfere with probate proceedings, disrupt state jurisdiction of probate court, or take control of property that was controlled by probate court).

43. *Ankenbrandt v. Richards,* 504 U.S. 689, 112 S.Ct. 2206, 119 L.Ed.2d 468 (1992) (domestic relations exception only prevents issuing divorce, alimony, or child custody decrees). *See, e.g., Rash v. Rash,* 173 F.3d 1376 (11th Cir. 1999), *cert. denied* 528 U.S. 1077, 120 S.Ct. 793, 145 L.Ed.2d 669 (2000) (rule of refusing jurisdiction is not absolute and is narrowly confined; court will not adjudicate parties' "domestic affairs," but will resolve dispute over assets).

Insurance Companies and Direct Action Suits

A few states permit plaintiffs in tort actions to sue the defendant's insurance company directly, rather than proceeding first against the alleged tortfeasor. 28 U.S.C.A. § 1332(c)(1) takes account of that circumstance, providing that in such cases insurance companies will be treated as citizens of the state where the alleged tortfeasors have citizenship, in addition to the states where the insurance company has citizenship. When applicable, the practical effect of this provision is to reduce somewhat a plaintiff's possibilities for obtaining diversity jurisdiction.

It should be noted that attribution of an insured's citizenship to the insured's own insuror applies only to circumstances where a plaintiff has a claim against the insured that may also properly be asserted against the insuror without necessarily first joining or suing the insured.[44] If the suit is a dispute between the insuror and the insured, conventional standards of diversity jurisdiction apply.[45]

Decedents, Infants, and Incompetents

28 U.S.C.A. § 1332(c)(2) provides that, for diversity purposes, parties acting as representatives of decedents' estates, infants, or incompetent persons shall be deemed to take the citizenship of the estate or persons whom they represent.[46] 28 U.S.C.A. § 1332(c)(2) was enacted to preclude creation of diversity in such cases simply by appointing a representative of different citizenship than the party the representative opposes.

Collusive Invocation of Diversity Jurisdiction

The diversity provisions of 28 U.S.C.A. § 1332 are modified by 28 U.S.C.A. § 1359, governing collusive invocation of jurisdiction. Section 1359 provides that if a party, "by assignment or otherwise," has been "improperly or collusively . . . joined" to invoke jurisdiction, the federal district court will not have jurisdiction. Section 1359 prohibits invocation of diversity jurisdiction where a corporation, not diverse from the defendant, assigned its cause of action to another person for the primary purpose of creating diversity. This rule applies even if the assignment itself is lawful and valid under state law.[47] However, it is still reasonable to assume that an assignment lawful under state law, and made primarily for purposes other than to create diversity, may surmount this obstacle.[48]

44. *See, e.g., Searles v. Cincinnati Ins. Co.,* 998 F.2d 728, 729 (9th Cir.1993) (so holding).

45. *See, e.g., Clark v. Chubb Group of Insurance Cos.,* 337 F.3d 687 (6th Cir.2003) (Ohio insured sued insurer that was citizen of state other than Ohio; held, standard requirements for diversity apply because suit was not direct action suit governed by § 1332(c)(1)).

46. *See, e.g., PaineWebber, Inc. v. Cohen,* 276 F.3d 197, 201 (6th Cir.2001), *cert. denied,* 537 U.S. 815, 123 S.Ct. 83, 154 L.Ed.2d 19 (2002) (for diversity purposes § 1332(c)(2) makes representatives of decedent's estate citizen of same state as decedent); *Long v. Sasser,* 91 F.3d 645, 647 (4th Cir.1996) (same).

47. *Kramer v. Caribbean Mills, Inc.,* 394 U.S. 823, 827, 89 S.Ct. 1487, 1490, 23 L.Ed.2d 9 (1969). (legality of assignment under state law does not necessarily equate to validity for purposes of federal jurisdiction).

48. *Cf. Yokeno v. Mafnas,* 973 F.2d 803, 811 (9th Cir.1992)(even if jurisdictional motive is apparent, assignment may create jurisdiction if

Fraudulent Joinder and Removal

Fraudulent joinder occurs when a plaintiff who has sued in state court joins a nondiverse defendant against whom the plaintiff obviously has no cause of action under settled law. The purpose of such joinder, of course, is to prevent removal of the real case, against a diverse defendant, to federal district court. When the true defendant nevertheless files a removal petition, the court, upon identifying a fraudulent joinder of the nondiverse defendant, will deny a motion to remand and retain jurisdiction over the removed case.[49]

Amount in Controversy

Diversity jurisdiction requires not only that the parties be citizens of different states or countries, but also that the matter in controversy exceed $75,000, exclusive of interest and costs.[50] The time at which the amount in controversy is measured is the date that the suit is filed. Later events that may reduce the amount recoverable do not nullify diversity jurisdiction that was proper at the time of filing.[51]

"Legal Certainty" Test

In the ordinary case, determination of the amount in controversy is made by reference to plaintiff's prayer for relief. Unliquidated claims for more than $75,000 will normally be taken at face value as satisfying the amount in controversy requirement.[52] Only in the unusual case,

independent business motive is "sufficiently compelling").

49. *Morris v. Princess Cruises, Inc.*, 236 F.3d 1061, 1067–68 (9th Cir.2001).

50. *See, e.g., State Farm Mutual Automobile Ins. Co. v. Powell,* 87 F.3d 93 (3d Cir. 1996)(amount in controversy not satisfied by pleading exact amount identified in § 1332; amount pleaded must *exceed* amount identified in § 1332). *Cf., Missouri State Life Insurance Co. v. Jones,* 290 U.S. 199, 202, 54 S.Ct. 133, 134, 78 L.Ed. 267, 269 (1933) (attorney's fees may be counted toward amount in controversy when prevailing party may collect them as part of damages per, e.g., state statute; held, state characterization of such fees as "costs" is irrelevant to diversity jurisdiction). *See, e.g., Manguno v. Prudential Property & Casualty Insurance Co.,* 276 F.3d 720, 723 (5th Cir.2002) ("If a state statute provides for attorney's fees, such fees are included as part of the amount in controversy."). *But see Martin v. Franklin National Corp.,* 251 F.3d 1284 (10th Cir.2001) ("[A]ttorneys fees cannot be aggregated for purposes of diversity jurisdiction."); *Spielman v. Genzyme Corp.,* 251 F.3d 1 (1st Cir.2001) (denying aggregation of attorney's fees even where state statute authorizes such fees).

51. *See, e.g., Hart v. Schering–Plough Corp.,* 253 F.3d 272 (7th Cir.2001) ("The amount in controversy is whatever is required to satisfy the plaintiff's demand in full, on the date suit began;" issue of $90,000 annual salary does not satisfy amount in controversy because defendant had paid plaintiff more than $17,000 in severance payments prior to suit); *Wolde–Meskel v. Vocational Instruction Project Community Servs., Inc.,* 166 F.3d 59, 62 (2d Cir.1999) (defendant obtained summary judgment on one count, resulting in decline in amount in controversy; held, trial court retained jurisdiction over other counts because once jurisdiction is obtained, a change in domicile or amount in controversy does not oust court's jurisdiction; summarizing cases and citing contrary minority view).

52. *See, e.g., Zunamon v. Brown,* 418 F.2d 883, 885 (8th Cir.1969)(Plaintiff's claim ordinarily decides amount in controversy.). *See also, Mitchell v. Brown & Williamson Tobacco Corp.,* 294 F.3d 1309, 1315 (11th Cir.2002) (where plaintiff filed in state court and defendant removed, plaintiff's allegation of damages in state court that satisfy amount in controversy requirement should have "strong presumption" that pleading does not allege large amount simply to satisfy diversity); *Cohn v. Petsmart, Inc.,* 281 F.3d 837, 840 (9th Cir.2002) ("A settlement letter is relevant evidence of the amount in controversy if that appears to reflect a reasonable estimate of the plaintiff's claim."); *Neuma, Inc. v. AMP, Inc.,* 259 F.3d 864, 881 (7th Cir. 2001) (amount in controversy satisfied by "good

where it is certain—based on the liquidated nature of the claim, the manifestly frivolous nature of the prayer for relief, or an existing statutory limitation on damages recoverable—that the plaintiff cannot possibly recover the jurisdictional amount, will the court disregard the plaintiff's prayer.[53]

If the amount in controversy is at issue, it is normally the plaintiff's burden to demonstrate that the requirement is met. An exception arises when a plaintiff originally files suit in state court and the defendant successfully removes the case to federal court. In that circumstance, if it is unclear whether the plaintiff's state claim met the amount in controversy requirement, the burden of proving the existence of the jurisdictional amount is shifted to the defendant who removed.[54]

Recovery of Less than $75,000

If a plaintiff initially seeks more than $75,000, but ultimately recovers less than that amount, 28 U.S.C.A. § 1332(b) provides that the court may deny recovery of costs to the plaintiff, and may assess costs against the plaintiff.[55] The calculation of the plaintiff's recovery under § 1332(b) is made solely on the basis of awards to plaintiff, and does not include deductions for the defendant's successful claims against the

faith, minimally reasonable" assertion of requisite amount or more); *United States Fire Insurance Co. v. Villegas,* 242 F.3d 279, 284 (5th Cir.2001) (if applicable law permits recovery of punitive damages, good-faith pleading of such damages may be included in determination of amount in controversy, notwithstanding that jury ultimately did not award such damages); *Massachusetts Casualty Ins. Co. v. Harmon,* 88 F.3d 415 (6th Cir.1996)(where validity of disability insurance policy is at issue, assessment of amount in controversy may include future potential benefits). *But cf., Middleton v. City of Blue Springs,* 145 F.3d 993 (8th Cir.1998) (if amount in controversy is challenged by opponent or court, claimant must prove amount by preponderance of evidence; court must dismiss if it concludes to legal certainty that claimant cannot recover required amount); *Larkin v. Brown,* 41 F.3d 387, 388 (8th Cir.1994)(if claim for punitive damages is necessary to satisfy amount in controversy requirement, the claim should get closer scrutiny than claim for compensatory damages.).

53. *See, e.g., Chase Manhattan Bank, N.A. v. American Nat'l Bank & Trust Co. of Chicago,* 93 F.3d 1064, 1070 (2d Cir.1996) (where plaintiff suffered no damages, there is "a legal certainty" that jurisdictional amount is not satisfied); *Burns v. Anderson,* 502 F.2d 970, 972 (5th Cir. 1974)(broken thumb with no lingering pain or disability; only modest lost wages; held, jurisdictional amount not satisfied).

54. *See, e.g., Smith v. American General Life & Accident Insurance Co.,* 337 F.3d 888 (7th Cir.2003) (explaining general rule, but noting exception applies in removal cases because plaintiff is unlikely to have fabricated an amount in controversy when plaintiff originally filed in state court). *See generally Kokkonen v. Guardian Life Insurance Co. of America,* 511 U.S. 375, 377, 114 S.Ct. 1673, 1675, 128 L.Ed.2d 391 (1994) ("[T]he burden of establishing [subject matter jurisdiction] rests upon the party asserting jurisdiction."). *See also TIG Insurance Co. v. Reliable Research Co.,* 334 F.3d 630 (7th Cir.2003) (intervening plaintiff bears burden of establishing subject matter jurisdiction).

55. *See, e.g., Pratt Central Park Ltd. Partnership v. Dames & Moore, Inc.,* 60 F.3d 350, 351 (7th Cir.1995)("The penalty for recovering less than [the jurisdictional amount] is the denial of costs ... not the loss of the whole judgment."). *Cf. Herremans v. Carrera Designs, Inc.,* 157 F.3d 1118, 1121 (7th Cir.1998) (no dismissal for failure to win more than amount in controversy; "The test for whether a case satisfies the amount in controversy requirement is whether the complaint makes a good-faith claim for the amount, ... not whether the plaintiff is actually entitled to such an amount. Otherwise every diversity case that a plaintiff lost on the merits would be dismissed for lack of federal jurisdiction, allowing the plaintiff to start over in state court.").

plaintiff. The court's authority under § 1332(b) is discretionary.[56] Moreover, "costs" do not include recovery of attorney fees.

Jurisdictional Amount in Equity Cases

Because suits seeking equitable relief are grounded in an allegation that traditional money damages are an inadequate remedy, federal courts have had to adjust the more-than $75,000 requirement to the peculiarities of such cases. Perhaps the most common approach is to try to measure the amount in controversy in equity cases by the value of the right the plaintiff seeks to enforce.[57] A similar approach is to measure the amount in controversy by the value of vindication to the plaintiff.[58] A less favored approach is to measure the amount in controversy by the costs of compliance a defendant will face.[59] As these constructions suggest, there are a variety of techniques for attempting the evaluation, and lower courts enjoy substantial discretion in how they make their determinations.

> ***Example:*** Assume a plaintiff owns a small plot of land worth less than $75,000 immediately below a large dam owned by the defendant. If the defendant intends to release water held by the dam, it may not do damage worth more than $75,000 to the plaintiff's property. Measuring the amount in controversy by the value to the plaintiff of an injunction preventing the release would therefore not satisfy the amount in controversy. However, the cost to the defendant of not releasing the water might be considerably more than $75,000. If so, measuring the amount in controversy by the cost to defendant of complying with the injunction would satisfy the jurisdictional requirement.

Aggregation of Claims

If a plaintiff has more than one claim against a defendant, but no single claim exceeds $75,000 in value, questions arise as to whether the plaintiff may add the value of the claims together to satisfy the amount in controversy requirement. Case law indicates that a single plaintiff may aggregate claims against a single defendant, no matter how dissim-

56. *See, e.g., Coventry Sewage Assocs. v. Dworkin Realty Co.,* 71 F.3d 1, 8 n. 6 (1st Cir.1995)("The determination of whether or not to impose such cost sanctions is, of course, within the sound discretion of the district court.").

57. *Glenwood Light & Water Co. v. Mutual Light, Heat & Power Co.,* 239 U.S. 121, 36 S.Ct. 30, 60 L.Ed. 174 (1915). *See also Hartford Insurance Group v. Lou–Con Inc.,* 293 F.3d 908, 911 (5th Cir.2002) (in declaratory judgment action over validity of insurance policy, amount in controversy is usually measured by limits of policy; however, if issue is applicability of policy to particular occurrence, amount in controversy is usually not policy limit, but value of claim underlying the particular dispute).

58. *See, e.g., Cohen v. Office Depot, Inc.,* 204 F.3d 1069, 1077 (11th Cir.2000), *cert. denied,* 531 U.S. 957, 121 S.Ct. 381, 148 L.Ed.2d 294 (2000)("When a plaintiff seeks injunctive or declaratory relief, the amount in controversy is the monetary value of the object of the litigation from the plaintiff's perspective.").

59. *See, e.g., Justice v. Atchison, Topeka & Santa Fe Ry. Co.,* 927 F.2d 503, 505 (10th Cir. 1991)(looking to defendant's cost of compliance; noting authority for looking either to cost to defendant or value to plaintiff). *But see McCauley v. Ford Motor Co.,* 264 F.3d 952, 960–61 (9th Cir.2001), *cert. granted in part,* 534 U.S. 1126, 122 S.Ct. 1063, 151 L.Ed.2d 966 (2002) (refusing to measure jurisdictional amount by cost to defendant of complying with injunction).

ilar the claims may be.[60] However, if each claim is merely an alternative theory for which only one recovery would be permitted, only the amount of that potential recovery may be considered when calculating the amount in controversy.

When multiple parties are involved, the case law is less liberal. It appears that two or more plaintiffs can add their claims together to satisfy the jurisdictional amount only if the claims are truly joint.[61] For example, if two plaintiffs each owned, as joint tenants, half of an automobile worth $80,000, and the suit alleged that the defendant had destroyed the automobile completely, the plaintiffs could probably add their individual $40,000 claims to satisfy the jurisdictional amount. But if the allegations were that the two plaintiffs each suffered $40,000 in personal injuries at the hands of the defendant, aggregation would not be permitted because the claims would be seen as distinct—even if the injuries occurred in the same accident.[62]

The precedent in cases where a single plaintiff seeks to sue more than one defendant follows a similar pattern. Aggregation is permitted only if the claims against the defendants involve joint liability.[63]

ADDITIONAL RESEARCH REFERENCES

C.J.S. Federal Courts §§ 44–73 et seq.

West's Key No. Digests, Federal Courts ⚷261–319.

60. *See, e.g., Werwinski v. Ford Motor Co.,* 286 F.3d 661, 666 (3d Cir.2002) ("Only claims, whether related or unrelated, of a single plaintiff against a single defendant may be aggregated."); *Galt G/S v. JSS Scandinavia,* 142 F.3d 1150 (9th Cir.1998) (upholding aggregation of statutorily authorized attorneys' fees with principal claim); *Klepper v. First American Bank,* 916 F.2d 337, 341 (6th Cir.1990) ("It is well established that claims [brought by a single plaintiff against a single defendant] can be aggregated to satisfy the jurisdictional amount requirement."); *But see In re Abbott Laboratories,* 51 F.3d 524, 529 (5th Cir.1995) (Congressional enactment of supplemental jurisdiction, 28 U.S.C.A. § 1367, obviated need for each plaintiff to satisfy independently the requisite amount in controversy in class actions).

61. *See, e.g., Snyder v. Harris,* 394 U.S. 332, 334, 89 S.Ct. 1053, 1056, 22 L.Ed.2d 319 (1969)(allowing multiple plaintiffs to aggregate where they have "common and undivided interest"). *But cf. Ard v. Transcontinental Gas Pipe Line Corp.,* 138 F.3d 596 (5th Cir.1998) (acknowledging differences among appellate courts; holding that, generally, several plaintiffs may not aggregate their individual claims for punitive damages).

62. *See also Martin v. Franklin National Corp.,* 251 F.3d 1284 (10th Cir.2001) ("[P]unitive damages may not ordinarily be aggregated and attributed in total to each member of a putative class for purposes of satisfying diversity jurisdiction."); *Spielman v. Genzyme Corp.,* 251 F.3d 1 (1st Cir.2001) (denying aggregation of attorney's fees even where state statute authorizes such fees). *Cf., e.g., Mehlenbacher v. Akzo Nobel Salt, Inc.,* 216 F.3d 291 (2d Cir.2000) (claims are separate and distinct where plaintiffs "seek recovery for their losses as individuals only, and not collectively"; thus no aggregation permitted in instant case); *Meritcare, Inc. v. St. Paul Mercury Ins. Co.,* 166 F.3d 214, 218 (3d Cir.1999) (plaintiffs claimed losses on similar insurance policies covering a single event; denying aggregation when "the plaintiffs have a community of interest, but fall short of establishing a single title or right in which they have a common and undivided interest").

63. *See, e.g., Jewell v. Grain Dealers Mutual Ins. Co.,* 290 F.2d 11, 13 (5th Cir. 1961)(Permitting aggregation against multiple defendants only where they are jointly liable to plaintiff).

§ 1.13 Subject Matter Jurisdiction in Federal District Courts—Requirements for Supplemental Jurisdiction

CORE CONCEPT

Supplemental jurisdiction, authorized by Congress at 28 U.S.C.A. § 1367, is the means by which parties may add state law counts in a federal court case, even though the state law counts could not have been brought by themselves because they cannot satisfy the requirements of either federal question or diversity jurisdiction.

Example: Suppose that a New York plaintiff had two causes of action against a New York defendant: one arising under federal antitrust law, the other under state law. Federal antitrust claims are within the exclusive subject matter jurisdiction of federal district courts. The state claim, by contrast, does not qualify for diversity jurisdiction because both parties are New York citizens. Thus the plaintiff in a situation such as this might theoretically have to prosecute two separate suits, one in federal court and the other in state court, and incur all the extra expenditures in time and money such suits would entail for both the parties and the taxpayers. Supplemental jurisdiction is intended to reduce such diseconomies, and at the same time limit damage to federalism by limiting the circumstances in which nondiverse state claims may be prosecuted in federal district courts.

NOTE: 28 U.S.C.A. § 1367, governing supplemental jurisdiction only became effective in December 1990. Prior to that date the area was governed by two closely related doctrines of case law: pendent jurisdiction and ancillary jurisdiction. In creating supplemental jurisdiction, Congress combined much of those two doctrines.[1] However, Congress also overruled some previously existing features of the case law, so that judicial precedent prior to December 1990 should be approached with care.

APPLICATIONS

Prerequisite for Supplemental Jurisdiction

As its name suggests, supplemental jurisdiction is not an independent basis for satisfying requirements of federal subject matter jurisdiction in the same way as federal question jurisdiction or diversity jurisdiction. Instead, counts based on supplemental jurisdiction must be able to attach themselves to some other count already properly present in the lawsuit. Thus, before supplemental jurisdiction can be invoked, there must already exist at least one count that can satisfy federal subject matter jurisdiction through either, e.g., federal question jurisdiction, diversity jurisdiction, or a suit where the United States is a party.[2]

1. *Peacock v. Thomas,* 516 U.S. 349, 355 n. 5, 116 S.Ct. 862, 867 n. 5, 133 L.Ed.2d 817 (1996).

2. 28 U.S.C.A. § 1367(a). *See also, e.g., Herman Family Revocable Trust v. Teddy Bear,* 254 F.3d 802 (9th Cir.2001) ("[W]here there is no underlying original federal subject matter jurisdiction, the court has no authority to adjudicate supplemental claims under § 1367."); *Nowak v. Ironworkers Local 6 Pension Fund,* 81 F.3d 1182, 1187 (2d Cir.1996)(A court "cannot exer-

Same Case or Controversy

28 U.S.C.A. § 1367(a) establishes that supplemental jurisdiction will be effective, if at all, only over non-diverse state claims that "form part of the same case or controversy" as another count or counts in the action. This requirement confirms the need for at least one count in the case that can independently satisfy one of the kinds of federal subject matter jurisdiction discussed above. It goes further than that, however, in requiring some relationship between the supplemental count and the counts that already satisfy jurisdiction.[3] The pre–1990 case law concentrated on how much similarity existed between the witnesses and evidence relevant to the respective counts. Where substantial similarity existed, the court's power to hear non-diverse state claims could probably be established. Cases applying the "same case or controversy" standard of § 1367 are likely to employ much the same approach to determining whether the non-diverse state counts are sufficiently related to the other counts to satisfy supplemental jurisdiction.[4]

Joined or Intervening Parties

28 U.S.C.A. § 1367(a) specifically provides that in appropriate circumstances supplemental jurisdiction may be extended to include counts involving joined or intervening parties.[5] This provision overrides prior case law holding that courts could not extend their ancillary jurisdiction to persons not already parties to the case.[6] However, this provision is limited somewhat by § 1367(b), discussed below.

cise supplemental jurisdiction unless there is first a proper basis for original federal jurisdiction.").

3. *See, e.g., Ammerman v. Sween,* 54 F.3d 423, 424 (7th Cir.1995) ("A loose factual connection between the claims" may satisfy the requirements of same case or controversy.). *But see Serrano–Moran v. Grau–Gaztambide,* 195 F.3d 68, 69 (1st Cir.1999) (civil rights claim against police officers accused of beating deceased does not share common nucleus of facts with supplemental claim of malpractice against medical defendants).

4. *See, e.g., Tamiami Partners, Ltd. v. Miccosukee Tribe of Indians of Florida,* 177 F.3d 1212 (11th Cir.1999), *cert. denied* 529 U.S. 1018, 120 S.Ct. 1419, 146 L.Ed.2d 311 (2000) (all claims arose from defendant's actions relating to underlying agreement; holding requirement for commonality satisfied even though success of federal claims did not depend on success of state claims); *see also 3D Systems, Inc. v. Aarotech Laboratories, Inc.,* 160 F.3d 1373, 1377 (Fed.Cir. 1998) (state claims of trade libel and unfair competition are "hand-in-hand" with federal claims of patent infringement when all claims arise out of defendant's sales activity for certain products in California); *Itar-Tass Russian News Agency v. Russian Kurier, Inc.,* 140 F.3d 442, 445–48 (2d Cir.1998) (state law motion for fees for plaintiff's attorney and expert witness are supplemental to underlying federal copyright claims). *Cf., Southwestern Bell Telephone Co. v. Brooks Fiber Communications of Oklahoma, Inc.,* 235 F.3d 493, 498 (10th Cir.2000) (in addition to review for compliance with federal law, district court may use § 1367(a) to review state administrative agency's decision for compliance with state law).

5. *See, e.g., Ciambriello v. County of Nassau,* 292 F.3d 307, 325 (2d Cir.2002) (federal claims against one defendant (but not others) dismissed; but state claims against defendant who obtained dismissal of federal claim remain in federal court under § 1367(a)); *Tamiami Partners, Ltd. v. Miccosukee Tribe of Indians of Florida,* 177 F.3d 1212, 1223–24 (11th Cir.1999), *cert. denied,* 529 U.S. 1018, 120 S.Ct. 1419, 146 L.Ed.2d 311 (2000) ("[T]he parties to the federal and supplemental claims need not be identical in order for supplemental jurisdiction to lie.").

6. *See, e.g., Abbott Laboratories, Inc. v. CVS Pharmacy, Inc.,* 290 F.3d 854, 858 (7th Cir.2002) ("Ever since 28 U.S.C. § 1367(a) overturned [prior case law], the supplemental jurisdiction has been capacious enough to include claims by or against third parties.").

Nondiverse Pendent Parties and Claims

Closely related to some of the issues addressed by § 1367(b) is the question of nondiverse pendent parties. Prior to enactment of § 1367, it was fairly well settled that simply because one plaintiff could assert diversity jurisdiction, a nondiverse plaintiff could not attach a state claim to the first plaintiff's diverse count. That result applied even if the two claims were closely related. Now, however, some courts have permitted application of § 1367 to sustain the nondiverse plaintiff's claim.[7] Whether this result is correct is uncertain. Moreover, the issue remains an unsettled difference among the courts, and will require further development.[8]

Sua Sponte Application

It is settled that federal courts may dismiss a case for lack of subject matter jurisdiction even when the parties have not raised the issue.[9] However, when a party asserting a nondiverse claim has not attempted to invoke supplemental jurisdiction, there is uncertainty as to whether courts should invoke such jurisdiction *sua sponte*.[10] Attorneys are encouraged to investigate the local practice.

Restrictions on Supplemental Jurisdiction

28 U.S.C.A. § 1367(b) probably eliminates the use of supplemental jurisdiction when certain facts are present. Thus, even if a non-diverse state count meets the "same case or controversy" requirement of § 1367(a), it may still not qualify for supplemental jurisdiction. This possibility occurs when the counts already satisfying federal subject

7. *See, e.g., Jones v. Ford Motor Credit Co.,* 358 F.3d 205, 212–13 (2d Cir. 2004) (no longer requiring nondiverse permissive counterclaims to satisfy original subject matter jurisdiction); *Allapattah Services, Inc. v. Exxon Corp.,* 333 F.3d 1248, 1254 (11th Cir.2003) (§ 1367 clearly and unambiguously "provides district courts with the authority in diversity class actions to exercise supplemental jurisdiction over the claims of class members who do not meet the minimum amount in controversy as long as the district court has original jurisdiction over the claims of at least one of the class representatives"); *In re Abbott Laboratories, Bristol–Meyers Squibb Co.,* 51 F.3d 524, 527–29 (5th Cir. 1995)(permitting pendent party jurisdiction over state claim of less than the required jurisdictional amount). *But see Estate of Harshman v. Jackson Hole Mountain Resort Corp.,* 379 F.3d 1161 (10th Cir. 2004) ("District courts do not otherwise have jurisdiction to hear pendent state law claims but for their intertwinement with claims over which they have original jurisdiction."); *Leonhardt v. Western Sugar Co.,* 160 F.3d 631, 632 (10th Cir.1998) (refusing to extend supplemental jurisdiction to situation in which a single plaintiff satisfies amount in controversy, but other plaintiffs do not meet jurisdictional amount; rejecting *Abbot Laboratories, supra,* and *Stromberg Metal Works, infra*).

8. *See, e.g., Stromberg Metal Works, Inc. v. Press Mechanical, Inc.,* 77 F.3d 928, 930 (7th Cir.1996)(following *Abbott Laboratories, supra,* but noting contrary conclusions in many district courts).

9. *See, e.g., Pennsylvania Nurses Ass'n v. Pennsylvania State Education Ass'n,* 90 F.3d 797, 801 (3d Cir.1996) *cert. denied,* 519 U.S. 1110, 117 S.Ct. 947, 136 L.Ed.2d 835 (1997) ("[W]e must consider the jurisdictional question even where the parties are prepared to concede it.").

10. *Compare, e.g., United States ex rel. Ramseyer v. Century Healthcare Corp.,* 90 F.3d 1514 n. 8 (10th Cir.1996)(declining to invoke supplemental jurisdiction where plaintiff failed to assert it in complaint), *with Rodriguez v. Doral Mortgage Corp.,* 57 F.3d 1168 (1st Cir. 1995)(holding that federal court, with proper notice to parties, may invoke supplemental jurisdiction on its own initiative over previously unpleaded nondiverse state claim that court identified for parties).

matter jurisdiction are based solely on diversity jurisdiction under § 1332 and either of two other elements are present:

(1) the non-diverse counts are claims by plaintiffs[11] in the original action against persons made parties under Rule 14 (impleader), Rule 19 (joinder), Rule 20 (permissive joinder), or Rule 24 (intervention);[12] *or*

(2) the non-diverse counts are claims by persons who entered the case as plaintiffs under either Rule 19 (joinder) or Rule 24 (intervention).

The exceptions in 28 U.S.C.A. § 1367(b) are a legislative adoption of existing case law. An example may demonstrate their operation.

Example: If a plaintiff wanted to sue two defendants on a tort claim, but only one of the defendants was of citizenship diverse from that of the plaintiff, a claim against both defendants could not be filed in federal court. Instead, the plaintiff might sue only the diverse defendant, in which case (assuming other requirements of jurisdiction are satisfied), the federal court could hear the claim. In those circumstances it would often be predictable that the diverse defendant would use Rule 14 to implead the non-diverse defendant. Now that the non-diverse defendant is in the case, the plaintiff might seek to bring a new count against the non-diverse defendant. Requirements of § 1367(a) would be satisfied, because the count against the non-diverse defendant certainly forms part of the same case or controversy as the original count against the diverse defendant. Notice, however, what the effective result is, if this "supplemental" count against the non-diverse defendant is allowed. The plaintiff, by anticipating the impleader, will have achieved suit in federal district court against both defendants—even though diversity jurisdiction would have failed if plaintiff had sought to sue them both directly. However, § 1367(b) prohibits the plaintiff from using supplemental jurisdiction to sue a party joined under Rule 14. In fact, § 1367(b) usually precludes use of supplemental jurisdiction by a plaintiff if the original basis of federal subject matter jurisdiction is diversity jurisdiction under § 1332.

NOTE: Note that 28 U.S.C.A. § 1367(b) restricts a plaintiff's use of supplemental jurisdiction only when the original cause of action is based upon diversity jurisdiction under § 1332. If the original basis for federal jurisdiction is a federal question, under § 1331, the restrictions

11. *But cf., United Capitol Ins. Co. v. Kapiloff,* 155 F.3d 488 (4th Cir.1998) (defendants in declaratory judgment action sought to use supplemental jurisdiction to join nondiverse parties on counterclaim; held, § 1367(b) does not bar such joinder).

12. *See, e.g., Ryan ex rel. Ryan v. Schneider National Carriers, Inc.,* 263 F.3d 816, 820 (8th Cir.2001) (per curiam) (diversity claims by several plaintiffs; cross-claim by some plaintiffs against another plaintiff, who was not diverse from them; held, § 1367(b) does not prevent use of supplemental jurisdiction over cross-claim because original plaintiff sued on cross-claim was not made party by other plaintiffs under any of Rules 14, 19, 20 or 24); *Burka v. Aetna Life Ins. Co.,* 87 F.3d 478 n. 4 (D.C.Cir.1996)(noting that § 1367(b) does not prevent use of supplemental jurisdiction over claims against parties added pursuant to Rule 25(c)).

imposed by § 1367(b) on the use of supplemental jurisdiction simply do not apply.

Court's Discretion

Even if supplemental jurisdiction exists under 28 U.S.C.A. § 1367(a) and (b), § 1367(c) provides the court with substantial discretion to refuse to hear the supplemental counts.[13] When a district court dismisses state counts under any provision of § 1367(c), it will typically do so without prejudice to any re-filing of those counts in state court.[14]

The four circumstances in which a federal court might choose to dismiss a count that otherwise qualifies for supplemental jurisdiction are:

(1) *Difficult Questions of State Law:* This provision of 28 U.S.C.A. § 1367(c)(1) codifies the common sense precedent permitting district courts to dismiss a non-diverse state count if it is clear state courts would be better able to untangle the uncertain questions of state law. However, it is likely that federal courts will employ § 1367(c)(1) only in unusual cases involving the greatest difficulty in applying state law.[15]

(2) *Non–Diverse State Claim Predominates:* The court may decline to exercise supplemental jurisdiction when the non-diverse state claim predominates over the claims which formed the original basis of the court's subject matter jurisdiction.[16] Such cases are probably fairly unusual.

13. *See, e.g., Saglioccolo v. Eagle Ins. Co.,* 112 F.3d 226, 233 (6th Cir.1997) ("[T]he presence of supplemental jurisdiction does not mean that the district court must entertain this claim."). *Cf., International Association of Firefighters of St. Louis, Local 2665 v. City of Ferguson,* 283 F.3d 969, 976 (8th Cir.2002), *cert. denied,* 537 U.S. 1105, 123 S.Ct. 868, 154 L.Ed.2d 773 (2003) ("The District Court would always be free, of course, to proceed to the merits of the state claim, in its discretion, even if one of the conditions in 28 U.S.C. § 1367(c) for dismissal of the state claim had been satisfied."); *Acri v. Varian Associates, Inc.,* 114 F.3d 999, 1000 (9th Cir.1997) (en banc) (when district court has jurisdiction under § 1367(a), there is no obligation on the court to make a sua sponte analysis under § 1367(c) when no party sought such an analysis). *But cf. Southern Council of Industrial Workers v. Ford,* 83 F.3d 966, 969 (8th Cir.1996)("Where original jurisdiction exists, exercise of supplemental jurisdiction over all adequately related claims is mandatory, absent certain exceptions."). *See also, Seabrook v. Jacobson,* 153 F.3d 70 (2d Cir.1998) (nondiverse state claims satisfied requirements of § 1367(a); nevertheless, where federal claims were dismissed, district court abused discretion by exercising supplemental jurisdiction to retain state claims).

14. *See, e.g., Scott v. Clay County,* 205 F.3d 867, 880 (6th Cir.2000), *cert. denied,* 531 U.S. 874, 121 S.Ct. 179, 148 L.Ed.2d 123, (2000) (district court has discretion to dismiss without prejudice or to hear the claims); *Horton v. Board of County Commissioners of Flagler County,* 202 F.3d 1297, 1300 n. 3 (11th Cir.2000) (if district court dismisses under § 1367(c) plaintiff can refile in state court); *Bass v. Parkwood Hospital,* 180 F.3d 234, 236 (5th Cir.1999) ("When a court dismisses all federal claims before trial, the general rule is to dismiss any pendent claims. . . . However, the dismissal of the pendent claims should expressly be without prejudice so that the plaintiff may refile his claims in the appropriate state court.").

15. *See, e.g., Houlton Citizens' Coalition v. Town of Houlton,* 175 F.3d 178 (1st Cir.1999) (federal claims resolved before trial; state claim was both difficult and novel question; held, district court should dismiss state claim without prejudice); *Edmondson & Gallagher v. Alban Towers Tenants Ass'n,* 48 F.3d 1260 (D.C.Cir. 1995)(justifying refusal to hear state claims because the applicable law has been the subject of conflicting decisions).

16. *See, e.g., Diven v. Amalgamated Transit Union Int'l,* 38 F.3d 598, 602 (D.C.Cir. 1994)(apparent primacy of state claim indicated

(3) *Original Counts Dismissed:* Sometimes the court may decline to exercise supplemental jurisdiction when it has already dismissed the claims over which it has federal question or diversity jurisdiction.[17] Whether the court "may" dismiss, or "must" dismiss, the supplemental claims depends heavily on the reasoning that underlies the dismissal of the claims that asserted original subject matter jurisdiction. If the basis for dismissal of those claims is a finding that the court lacked original jurisdiction, the supplemental claims must be dismissed.[18] If, on the other hand, the basis for dismissal of the supplemental claims relates to the merits, the district court may have discretion to retain the supplemental claims under § 1367(c).[19]

Courts applying § 1367(c) also give substantial weight to the point in the case at which dismissal on the merits occurred. If the federal court was able to dismiss the federal question or diversity claims at the outset of the case, it would probably be appropriate to dismiss the supplemental claims immediately (or remand to state court if the case reached federal court through the process of removal).[20] If, however, the federal court proceeded through much of the

by weakness of federal claim—"even before discovery"). *Cf., San Pedro Hotel Co. v. City of Los Angeles,* 159 F.3d 470, 478 (9th Cir.1998) (if court dismisses under § 1367(c)(2), failure to state reasons for doing so is not abuse of discretion; nevertheless, suggesting that courts should provide explanation, and noting that statement of reasons is required for dismissal under § 1367(c)(4)).

17. *See, e.g., Roche v. John Hancock Mutual Life Ins. Co.,* 81 F.3d 249, 256-57 (1st Cir.1996) (identifying factors of "comity, judicial economy, convenience, fairness, and the like" in deciding whether to dismiss under § 1367(c)(3)). *But cf., Goodson v. City of Corpus Christi,* 202 F.3d 730, 741 (5th Cir.2000) (if district court erroneously dismisses claims that enjoyed original jurisdiction, it is abuse of discretion to dismiss state claims on ground that original jurisdiction is lacking).

18. *See, e.g., Ward v. Alternative Health Delivery Systems, Inc.,* 261 F.3d 624, 626 (6th Cir. 2001) ("If [the district court] dismisses the claims within its original jurisdiction for lack of subject matter jurisdiction ... it *must* remand the remaining claims." [italics in original]); *Pinney Dock & Transport Co. v. Penn Central Corp.,* 196 F.3d 617, 621 (6th Cir.1999) (if dismissal of counts alleging original jurisdiction occurs under Rule 12(b)(1) (failure of subject matter jurisdiction), dismissal of supplemental claim "must occur;" if dismissal of original jurisdiction counts occurs under Rule 12(b)(6) (failure to state a claim for which relief may be granted), a " 'strong presumption' " favors dismissal of supplemental claim); *Scarfo v. Ginsberg,* 175 F.3d 957 (11th Cir.1999), *cert. denied,* 529 U.S. 1003, 120 S.Ct. 1267, 146 L.Ed.2d 217 (2000) ("The federal courts of appeals ... have uniformly held that once the district court determines that subject matter jurisdiction over a plaintiff's federal claims does not exist, courts must dismiss a plaintiff's [nondiverse] state law claims.").

19. *See, e.g., Herman Family Revocable Trust v. Teddy Bear,* 254 F.3d 802 (9th Cir.2001) ("A dismissal on the merits is different from a dismissal on jurisdictional grounds. If the district court dismisses all federal claims on the merits, it has discretion under § 1367(c) to adjudicate the remaining claims; if the court dismisses for lack of subject matter jurisdiction, it has no discretion and must dismiss all claims.")

20. *Carnegie-Mellon University v. Cohill,* 484 U.S. 343, 350 n. 7, 108 S.Ct. 614, 614 n. 7, 98 L.Ed.2d 720 (1988) (noting absence of inflexible or mandatory rule, but "[i]n the usual case in which all federal-law claims are eliminated before trial, the balance of the factors to be considered under [supplemental jurisdiction]–judicial economy, convenience, fairness, and comity–will point toward declining to exercise jurisdiction over the remaining state-law claims"). *See, e.g., O'Connor v. Commonwealth Gas Co.,* 251 F.3d 262 (1st Cir.2001) ("Courts generally decline to exercise supplemental jurisdiction over state claims if the federal predicate is dismissed early in the litigation."); *Hedges v. Musco,* 204 F.3d 109, 123 (3d Cir.2000) (where claim that was basis for original jurisdiction is dismissed before trial, district court " 'must decline to decide [supplemental claims] unless consideration of judicial economy, convenience, and fairness to the parties provide an affirmative justification for doing so' "); *Annulli v. Panikkar,* 200 F.3d 189, 202–03 (3d Cir.1999) (no abuse of discretion to dismiss state claims even though federal claims

litigation and had informed itself of the merits of the supplemental claims, then dismissal of the other claims would probably not justify dismissing the supplemental claims.[21]

(4) *Other Exceptional Circumstances:* This provision of 28 U.S.C.A. § 1367(c) obviously provides the court with discretion in circumstances not anticipated by Congress.[22]

Important: It is important to note that if a non-diverse state claim fails to qualify for supplemental jurisdiction and is dismissed (or remanded to state court) by the court, the dismissal has no consequence for claims that qualify for the court's jurisdiction. Those latter claims may continue to be prosecuted.[23] It is possible, however, that for reasons of economy a claimant may choose to dismiss the qualifying claims and prosecute those claims, along with the dismissed claims, in state court.

were on "eve of trial" when defendant filed motion for summary judgment; although federal court was site of two years of litigation, fifteen pages of court docket, 1,800 pages of depositions, and 2,800 pages of discovery documents, plaintiff could still use evidence in state court; moreover, plaintiff assumed risk of dismissal of state claims when plaintiff filed in federal court and invoked § 1367). *But cf., Blakely v. United States,* 276 F.3d 853, 863 (6th Cir.2002) (pretrial dismissal of claims supporting original jurisdiction should generally result in remand, but "that rule is not absolute").

21. *See, e.g., Tomaiolo v. Mallinoff,* 281 F.3d 1, 11 (1st Cir.2002) (retention of state claims was not abuse of discretion when "[t]he litigation was far advanced, the court had before it cross-motions for summary judgment, discovery had closed, [the plaintiff] had filed her sixth amended complaint, and all claims arose from the same core of facts"); *Miller Aviation v. Milwaukee County Board of Supervisors,* 273 F.3d 722, 731–32 (7th Cir.2001) (abuse of discretion to dismiss state count when previous disposition of federal claim left nothing of state claim for state court to decide, or when substantial investment of judicial resources have already been expended and dismissal would therefore produce judicial efficiency). *Mizuna, Ltd. v. Crossland Fed. Savings Bank,* 90 F.3d 650 (2d Cir. 1996)(claim supporting original jurisdiction voluntarily dismissed; held, because court had properly acquired original jurisdiction, it enjoyed discretion to retain supplemental jurisdiction over related nondiverse claims; discretion to retain supplemental counts properly exercised where "three judicial officers had already expended substantial resources ... over a year's time"); *Metropolitan Wholesale Supply, Inc. v. M/V Royal Rainbow,* 12 F.3d 58, 61 (5th Cir. 1994)(federal counts already resolved; but court, having before it all facts as to non-diverse state claim, may decide that count).

22. *See, e.g., Gregory v. Shelby County,* 220 F.3d 433, 446 (6th Cir.2000) (where state law provides that cause of action against state officer in his official capacity is within "exclusive original jurisdiction" of state trial court, state legislature's "clear preference" to have such claims tried in state court is exceptional circumstance within scope of § 1367(c)(4)); *Birchem v. Knights of Columbus,* 116 F.3d 310 n. 3 (8th Cir.1997) (if plaintiff, who is entitled to jury trial, seeks to join federal claims with state claims, but state cause of action places burden of proof on defendant, trial court should consider dismissing state claim under § 1367(c)(4)); *Hays County Guardian v. Supple,* 969 F.2d 111 (5th Cir.1992), *cert. denied,* 506 U.S. 1087, 113 S.Ct. 1067, 122 L.Ed.2d 371 (1993) (finding exceptional circumstances and compelling reasons where adjudicating state claims in federal court would parallel adjudication of identical claims in state court). *Cf., Treglia v. Town of Manlius,* 313 F.3d 713, 723 (2d Cir.2002) (court has discretion to decline supplemental jurisdiction only if reason is based on at least one of four enumerated categories in § 1367(c)); *Executive Software North America, Inc. v. U.S. District Court,* 24 F.3d 1545, 1557 (9th Cir.1994) (if court dismisses under § 1367(c)(4), it must identify the circumstances the court found "exceptional").

23. *See, e.g., In re City of Mobile,* 75 F.3d 605, 607–08 (11th Cir.1996)(although properly remanding nondiverse counts to state court, district court has no authority under § 1367(c) to remand counts within its original subject matter jurisdiction).

Statutes of Limitations

28 U.S.C.A. § 1367(d) provides that actions filed in federal court under § 1367(a), and subsequently dismissed, will usually not be barred by a statute of limitations because of time lost in federal court.[24] Section 1367(d) accomplishes this end by tolling statutes of limitations while the claim is pending, and by providing a period of at least 30 days after dismissal in which the claim may be refiled in state court. Moreover, § 1367(d) provides that if state law will allow more than 30 days in which to refile, the claimant will enjoy the benefit of the longer period.[25] Section 1367(d) is a most unusual provision, in that it is a circumstance where federal law extends a state statute of limitations for a claim that arises under state law. However, it is now settled that the provision is constitutional.[26]

Tolling Other Claims

If a claim filed under 28 U.S.C.A. § 1367(a) is dismissed by the federal court, it is possible the claimant will want to dismiss other claims that qualify for federal subject matter jurisdiction, so that the entire case may be refiled in state court. To permit such a possibility free of the bar of statutes of limitations, § 1367(d)'s tolling provisions also extend to claims voluntarily dismissed in the aftermath of a denial of supplemental jurisdiction to one claim.

"State" Defined

28 U.S.C.A. § 1367(e) provides that whenever the term "State" is used in § 1367, it shall also include the District of Columbia, Puerto Rico, and United States Territories.

ADDITIONAL RESEARCH REFERENCES

C.J.S. Federal Courts §§ 11–26 et seq.

West's Key No. Digests, Federal Courts ⚷14–25.

§ 1.14 Venue

CORE CONCEPT

The requirement of venue sets the appropriate federal districts in which a particular case should be heard. Requirements to satisfy venue are additional to the jurisdictional prerequisites. Thus, even if a plaintiff satisfied both kinds of jurisdiction, the case might still be

24. *But cf., Raygor v. Regents of the University of Minnesota,* 534 U.S. 533, 122 S.Ct. 999, 152 L.Ed.2d 27 (2002) (when state claims asserted under § 1367 are dismissed on Eleventh Amendment grounds, § 1367(d) does not toll statute of limitations for such claims against non-consenting defendants).

25. *Myers v. County of Lake,* 30 F.3d 847, 848 (7th Cir.1994), *cert. denied,* 513 U.S. 1058, 115 S.Ct. 666, 130 L.Ed.2d 600 (1994)(§ 1367(d) "removes the principal reason for retaining a case in federal court when the federal claim belatedly disappears.").

26. *Jinks v. Richland County,* 538 U.S. 456, 123 S.Ct. 1667, 155 L.Ed.2d 631 (2003).

dismissed if venue was lacking.[1] State courts are also subject to the venue requirements established by their respective legislatures, and such requirements may differ significantly from the federal venue statutes. For federal courts, however, the only venue requirements that must be met are those enacted by Congress.

For certain specific causes of action, Congress has enacted special venue statutes. For example, venue in civil suits arising under the federal copyright laws is controlled by 28 U.S.C.A. § 1400. Similarly, venue in a stockholder's derivative suit is controlled by 28 U.S.C.A. § 1401. When a cause of action arises within those particular areas of law, the case law indicates that the ability of a plaintiff to choose between general venue provisions and more specific provisions depends on whether Congress intended to make the more specific provision the exclusive source of venue.[2] In the absence of a special venue provision, venue for diversity suits and federal questions is controlled by § 1391.

APPLICATIONS

Venue Generally

Section 1391 restricts the choice of federal district court in which a plaintiff may sue to those districts that Congress deems fair. This assessment of fairness is sometimes quite distinct from the concepts of constitutional fairness discussed under jurisdiction over persons or things. Thus, it is possible that a federal district court might have satisfactory personal jurisdiction over a defendant, but the action could still be dismissed for failure to meet venue requirements. For example, a defendant might be served with process within the state where the federal court sits, which would normally satisfy personal jurisdiction, but requirements of § 1391 might still not be met. In that sense, venue can be an additional trap for the unwary plaintiff.

Considerations of the relative merits of venue requirements aside, § 1391 can influence significantly the suitability of the particular federal district court a plaintiff has chosen. For that reason alone, the technical elements of venue are also important to successful prosecutions and defenses of civil claims in federal court.

NOTE: 28 U.S.C.A. §§ 1391(a) and (b) were substantially rewritten in December 1990. Section 1391(c) was also substantially rewritten shortly before that. These and other changes in § 1391 make some, but not all, of the older case law on venue unreliable.

1. *Cf., e.g., United States ex rel. Rudick v. Laird,* 412 F.2d 16, 20 (2d Cir.1969), *cert. denied,* 396 U.S. 918, 90 S.Ct. 244, 24 L.Ed.2d 197 (1969) ("[J]urisdiction must first be found over the subject matter and the persons involved in the cause before the question of venue can be properly reached.").

2. *See, e.g., Textile Unlimited v. A .. BMH & Co.,* 240 F.3d 781 (9th Cir.2001) (where venue provision of Federal Arbitration Act, 9 U.S.C.A. § 1 et seq., are permissive, they supplement § 1391 and do not supplant it); *Delong Equip. Co. v. Washington Mills Abrasive Co.,* 840 F.2d 843, 855 (11th Cir.1988), *cert. denied,* 494 U.S. 1081, 110 S.Ct. 1813, 108 L.Ed.2d 943 (1990)(when venue is satisfied under general venue statute, no need to look at venue under Clayton Act (*i.e.,* antitrust law)). *But see Garus v. Rose Acre Farms, Inc.,* 839 F.Supp. 563, 566 (N.D.Ind.1993)(Title VII civil rights claims have their own venue provisions, which displace general venue statute).

Federal Judicial Districts

State borders matter significantly in questions of jurisdiction. For venue questions, however, the important boundary is that which exists between federal judicial districts. In smaller states, the entire state may be a single district. In Rhode Island, for example, the United States District Court for the District of Rhode Island is the only federal district court within the state. Larger states may have as many as four federal judicial districts within them. New York, for example has four judicial districts: the Eastern, Western, Southern, and Northern Districts.

NOTE: It is also possible that a federal judicial district will break itself down into still smaller components. For example, the United States District Court for the Eastern District of Virginia is one of two federal district courts within Virginia. The Eastern District, in turn, is subdivided into four divisions: the Alexandria Division; the Norfolk Division; the Richmond Division; and the Newport News Division. Local rules of a federal district court might supplement venue statutes by requiring that a case be filed not only within the proper judicial district, but also within the appropriate division within that district.[3]

Residence Requirements

Reference is frequently made throughout 28 U.S.C.A. § 1391 to judicial districts in which a defendant resides. Although the case law is not unanimous, it appears that "residence," when applied to venue requirements, is similar to the jurisdictional concepts of "citizenship" and "domicile". Though natural persons may have several houses scattered around the country, only one is a domicile, which confers state citizenship for diversity purposes. Probably only one is a residence, for venue purposes.[4]

Counterclaims and Crossclaims

Generally speaking, only plaintiffs have the burden of satisfying requirements of venue. Counterclaims, crossclaims, and similar actions normally do not raise venue questions.[5] This distinction is a significant departure from jurisdictional requirements, discussed above, for which every count in a case must satisfy some form of both jurisdiction over persons or things and subject matter jurisdiction.

Consent to Venue

If parties consent to personal jurisdiction in a particular district or state, it appears settled that they also consent to venue there.[6] More-

3. *See, e.g., Garus v. Rose Acre Farms, Inc.,* 839 F.Supp. 563, 566 n. 2 (N.D.Ind.1993)(noting that local rule divides division into subdivision for venue purposes).

4. *See, e.g., Manley v. Engram,* 755 F.2d 1463, 1466 (11th Cir.1985)("mere residence" in a state does not equal venue; "rather, it is the individual's 'permanent' residence—*i.e.,* his domicile that is the benchmark for determining proper venue").

5. *See, e.g., Bredberg v. Long,* 778 F.2d 1285, 1288 (8th Cir.1985)(where venue is proper as to plaintiff's claims, it is improbable that an objection to venue will be heard as to counterclaims or cross-claims).

6. *See, e.g., Doctor's Assocs., Inc. v. Stuart,* 85 F.3d 975 (2d Cir.1996)(party may consent to venue by consenting to personal jurisdiction).

over, if the plaintiff files suit in a federal judicial district where venue is improper, the court may still hear that case if the defendant does not object to venue.[7] Rule 12(g) and (h), governing timing and waiver of certain motions to dismiss, identify the time frame in which a defendant must either raise objections to venue or forego them.[8]

Venue and Removal

If a claim is removed from a state court to a federal district court, § 1391 does not apply. Thus, a removed claim is treated somewhat differently than a case originally filed in federal court.[9] However, a party who sought removal of a claim does not thereby waive a challenge to the state court's venue. That challenge is preserved and may be raised in federal court.[10] Another way of understanding the interplay of these two points is to recognize that for a removed claim the applicable venue standard is that which governed the state court in which the claim was originally filed.

Remedy

If the court, on timely objection of a party, finds venue to be deficient, the court may dismiss the action, allowing plaintiff to refile the claim elsewhere if the action is not otherwise barred.[11] This can raise significant statutes of limitations problems for a plaintiff. With limitations periods in mind, Congress enacted 28 U.S.C.A. § 1406, which allows a federal district court, on finding venue to be faulty, to *transfer* a cause of action to a judicial district or division where venue is proper. The court's discretion to employ this remedy is broad, constrained only by "the interest of justice." The practical consequence of transfer is that the court need not dismiss the action—which means the plaintiff will not run afoul of statutes of limitations.[12]

Venue in Diversity Cases

28 U.S.C.A. § 1391(a) provides three opportunities for venue in cases where subject matter jurisdiction is based solely on diversity of

7. *See, e.g., Leroy v. Great Western United Corp.*, 443 U.S. 173, 99 S.Ct. 2710, 61 L.Ed.2d 464 (1979)(both personal jurisdiction and venue may be waived). *See also Tri-State Employment Services, Inc. v. Mountbatten Surety Co.*, 295 F.3d 256, 260 n. 2 (2d Cir.2002) (defendant's failure to raise venue means defendant has waived issue); *King v. Russell*, 963 F.2d 1301 (9th Cir.1992) (per curiam), *cert. denied*, 507 U.S. 913, 113 S.Ct. 1263, 122 L.Ed.2d 660 (1993)(improper venue waived if defendant does not object to venue while raising other Rule 12 issues).

8. *But see Costlow v. Weeks*, 790 F.2d 1486, 1488 (9th Cir.1986)(where defendant has made no appearance whatever, court may dismiss for lack of venue *sua sponte*).

9. *See, e.g., PT United Can Co. v. Crown Cork & Seal Co.*, 138 F.3d 65, 72 (2d Cir.1998) (In a removed case "one may not challenge venue in the district court as of right, according to that court's venue rules, as if the case had been originally brought there."). *See generally Polizzi v. Cowles Magazines, Inc.*, 345 U.S. 663, 665, 73 S.Ct. 900, 902, 97 L.Ed. 1331 (1953) ("[T]he venue of removed actions is governed by ... § 1441(a) [the federal removal statute]."),

10. *See, e.g., PT United Can Co. v. Crown Cork & Seal Co.*, 138 F.3d 65, 73 (2d Cir.1998) (so holding; citing *Polizzi, supra*).

11. *Polizzi v. Cowles Magazines*, 345 U.S. 663, 73 S.Ct. 900, 97 L.Ed. 1331 (1953).

12. *See, e.g., Smith v. Thompson*, 685 F.Supp. 177 (N.D.Ill.1988) (where pro se inmate files in an improper venue, this court usually transfers in preference to a dismissal).

citizenship. Subject to some qualifications on the third option discussed below, the plaintiff may file in any of the following districts,[13] as tactics in a particular suit may require:

(1) *Where Defendants Reside:* in any judicial district where a single defendant resides, provided that all defendants reside in the same state;[14]

(2) *Where Substantial Events or Omissions Occurred:* in any judicial district where a substantial part of the relevant events occurred,[15] or where a substantial part of the property that gave rise to the action is found, such as a district in which damage occurred in a tort case, or where performance was to have occurred in a contract action.[16] It should be noted that in making this assessment, courts generally consider acts of both the plaintiff and the defendant.[17] Section 1391(a)(2)'s provision for venue where property is located is a reference to attachments of property in quasi in rem actions as well as the location of property disputed in a case of personal jurisdiction;[18] or

(3) *Where Any Defendant is Subject to Personal Jurisdiction:* in any judicial district in which any defendant is subject to personal jurisdiction at the time a suit is filed. Note that for purposes of § 1391(a)(3), personal jurisdiction is measured by the boundaries of a federal judicial district. Thus, in states which have more than one federal judicial district, § 1391(a)(3) may be used to satisfy venue requirements only when a defendant is subject to personal jurisdiction in that portion of the state which comprises the federal judicial district. It should be noted that § 1391(a)(3) may only be employed if a party is unable to satisfy venue requirements under either § 1391(a)(1) or (a)(2). If either of those options are available, the party may not employ § 1391(a)(3).

13. *See, e.g., Willis v. Caterpillar, Inc.,* 199 F.3d 902, 905 (7th Cir.1999) (venue proper either in district where defendant resides or where allegedly defective forklift was manufactured).

14. *See, e.g., Willis v. Caterpillar, Inc.,* 199 F.3d 902, 905 (7th Cir.1999) (principle place of business of sole defendant, a corporation, satisfies § 1391); *Manley v. Engram,* 755 F.2d 1463, 1466 (11th Cir.1985)(for purposes of venue, for natural persons, "residence" means "domicile").

15. *See, e.g., Uffner v. La Reunion Francaise, S.A.,* 244 F.3d 38, 42 (1st Cir.2001) (when events underlying claim occurred in different places, "venue may be proper in any number of districts;" but when single event supports allegation of venue in particular district, event must be substantial); *Setco Enters. Corp. v. Robbins,* 19 F.3d 1278 (8th Cir.1994)(issue is not whether other judicial districts had more significant contacts; issue is only whether district chosen by plaintiff had "a substantial connection" to the cause of action).

16. *See, e.g., Voest-Alpine Trading USA Corp. v. Bank of China,* 288 F.3d 262, 265 (5th Cir.2002) (dispute over validity of letter of credit that was issued in China; held, good venue in Houston (Southern District of Texas) where: letter was partially negotiated in Houston; letter was accepted in Houston; letter was presented to correspondent bank in Houston; and payment was to be made to correspondent bank in Houston); *Ciena Corp. v. Jarrard,* 203 F.3d 312, 318 (4th Cir.2000) (trade secrets case; venue appropriate in district where defendant was trained and employed by plaintiff and where alleged damage to plaintiff might occur).

17. *See, e.g., Uffner v. La Reunion Francaise, S.A.,* 244 F.3d 38, 43 n. 6 (1st Cir.2001) (collecting cases and adopting majority view). *But see Woodke v. Dahm,* 70 F.3d 983, 985 (8th Cir. 1995) (only location of defendant's activities is relevant; location of plaintiff's contacts held irrelevant).

18. *See, Cottman Transmission Sys., Inc. v. Martino,* 36 F.3d 291 (3d Cir.1994)(contacts must be "substantial").

28 U.S.C.A. § 1391(a) and Other Venue Statutes

Section 1391(a) controls venue for cases whose subject matter jurisdiction is based solely on diversity jurisdiction "except as otherwise provided by law." Thus, it defers explicitly to the provisions of other, more specific, venue statutes such as 28 U.S.C.A. § 1401, governing shareholder's derivative actions. In theory, that deference may afford a plaintiff greater venue opportunities under the provisions of the more specific venue statute. Generally, however, the current version of § 1391(a) provides the broadest opportunities for venue selection, and the more specific venue provisions, such as § 1401, tend to be more restrictive. Whether a litigant may employ the venue opportunities of § 1391 depends on whether Congress enacted a special venue provision and provided for its exclusive use.[19]

Cases Not Based Solely on Diversity

28 U.S.C.A. § 1391(b) controls when subject matter jurisdiction is not based solely on diversity of citizenship. Like § 1391(a), § 1391(b) provides three opportunities for venue. The first two of these are identical to their counterparts in § 1391(a). Until recently, the third contained several subtle differences, whose significance was unclear. However, all but one of these differences have now been eliminated. Thus, § 1391(a)(3) is now identical to § 1391(b)(3), with one exception. Where § 1391(a)(3) refers to "a judicial district in which any defendant is subject to personal jurisdiction at the time the action is commenced," § 1391(b)(3) refers to "a judicial district in which any defendant may be found." It appears that the legislative drafters intended no significant distinction between these two phrases, but obviously some uncertainty remains. The provisions of § 1391(b) are as follows:

(1) *Where Defendants Reside:* in any judicial district where a single defendant resides, provided that all defendants reside within the same state;[20]

(2) *Where Substantial Events or Omissions Occurred:* in any judicial district where a substantial part of the relevant events occurred, or where a substantial part of the property that gave rise to the action is found, such as a district in which damage occurred in a tort case,[21] or where performance was to have occurred in a contract action. Section 1391(b)(2)'s provision for venue where property is located is a reference to attachments of property in quasi in rem actions as well as the location of property disputed in a case of personal jurisdiction; or

19. *Compare, e.g., Garus v. Rose Acre Farms, Inc.*, 839 F.Supp. 563, 566 (N.D.Ind.1993)(Title VII civil rights claims have their own venue provisions, which displace general venue statute) *with, e.g., Urrutia v. Harrisburg County Police Department,* 91 F.3d 451, 462 (3d Cir.1996) ("[42 U.S.C. §] 1983 contains no special venue provision. ... Therefore, the general venue provisions of 28 U.S.C. § 1391 apply.").

20. *See, e.g., Manley v. Engram*, 755 F.2d 1463, 1466 (11th Cir.1985)(for purposes of venue, "residence" for natural persons means "domicile.").

21. *See, e.g., Friedman v. Revenue Management of New York, Inc.*, 38 F.3d 668, 671 (2d Cir.1994)(defendant is New York corporation, servicing New York hospitals, collecting from New York debtors, employs New York law firm, and sues in New York; but no good venue where alleged acts of commingling, mismanagement and fraud related to assets, books and records that are in Illinois).

(3) *Where Any Defendant May Be Found:* in any judicial district in which a single defendant may be found, "if there is no district in which the action may otherwise be brought." The liberal reach of § 1391(b)(3) can be deceptive, for this third option can only be employed "if there is no district in which the action may otherwise be brought." This means § 1391(b)(3) cannot be used as a first resort. Instead, a plaintiff seeking venue in cases not founded solely on diversity must use either § 1391(b)(1) or (b)(2) if they are available. Only if venue *fails* under *both* those provisions may plaintiff seek the benefit of § 1391(b)(3). Thus the practical utility of (b)(3), while potentially significant as a device for saving venue, is still substantially less than might appear at first glance.

28 U.S.C.A. § 1391(b) and Other Venue Statutes

Section 1391(b), like its counterpart in Section 1391(a), also permits use of more specific venue statutes if they are available to the plaintiff for a given cause of action. Given the fairly broad provisions of § 1391(b), however, there may be little benefit from using other, more specific venue statutes. Whether special venue statutes displace § 1391 depends on whether Congress made the particular venue statute at issue the exclusive source of venue for that particular cause of action.[22]

Residence for Corporations

28 U.S.C.A. § 1391(c) establishes the standards of residence for corporations for purposes of venue. This is a complicated provision, but if properly understood it can substantially expand opportunities for satisfying venue when a corporation is a defendant. To understand § 1391(c), it is best to break this provision into three component parts.

(1) *Corporate Venue Based on Personal Jurisdiction:* Corporations are deemed to be residents of any judicial district in which they would be subject to personal jurisdiction at the time an action is commenced.[23]

(2) *Multi–District States:* If a state has more than one judicial district, corporations are residents only of the judicial districts within the state in which they would be subject to personal jurisdiction, if the judicial district was a separate state.[24] Thus, while a corporation's contacts in one judicial district of a multi-district state might create personal jurisdiction over the corporation in all judicial districts in that state, the corporation's activity might satisfy venue only in the judicial district in which its contacts occurred.

(3) *Corporate Activities Dispersed Throughout a Multi–District State:* The third layer of § 1391(c) arises from the possibility that in a state with multiple federal districts, a corporation might have sufficient

22. *See, e.g., Garus v. Rose Acre Farms, Inc.,* 839 F.Supp. 563, 566 (N.D.Ind.1993) (Title VII civil rights claims have their own venue provisions, which displace § 1391).

23. *See, e.g., Waeltz v. Delta Pilots Retirement Plan,* 301 F.3d 804, 809 (7th Cir.2002) (for purposes of § 1391(c), residence is tested by amenability to personal jurisdiction); *Jumara v. State Farm Ins. Co.,* 55 F.3d 873 (3d Cir. 1995)(venue proper in judicial district where corporate defendant transacts business, signed contract, and where cause of action arose).

24. *See, e.g., id.*

contacts with the state as a whole to satisfy personal jurisdiction; but the contacts could be sufficiently dispersed among the judicial districts so that, if each of the districts was a "state," personal jurisdiction could not be achieved in any of them. In that case neither the first nor second provisions within § 1391(c) would give the corporation residence in any of the judicial districts of that state. Section 1391(c) deals with this possibility by providing that if it arises, a corporation is deemed to reside in the judicial district with which the corporation has "the most significant contacts."

NOTE: The complexities of venue should not be allowed to obscure the fact that for purposes of venue, as it relates to corporations, the important element is "residence," not domicile or citizenship. This is an important difference from venue for natural persons, where residence usually arises from domicile.[25] Thus, while 28 U.S.C.A. § 1391(c) bears some facial similarity to the statute governing diversity citizenship for corporations, the results of these two rules can be quite different. For example, assume that General Motors, a large company, is for diversity purposes a citizen of Delaware (place of incorporation) and of Michigan (principal place of business). This would mean that for a party to sue General Motors on a state claim in federal court on the basis of diversity of citizenship, the plaintiff would have to be a citizen of some state (or foreign country) other than Delaware and Michigan. For venue, however, the fact that General Motors is a large company doing business in many judicial districts means, first, that General Motors is probably subject to personal jurisdiction in all of those districts. That means, in turn, that General Motors has residence in many judicial districts, and venue may be appropriate in all of them. Thus the company's widespread business activity makes it subject to personal jurisdiction, as well as venue, in many places. But for purposes of diversity jurisdiction, it is a citizen of only two states, affording plaintiffs from other states and foreign countries substantial opportunities to sue in federal court on state claims involving more than $75,000. As these examples indicate, the interplay of venue, subject matter jurisdiction, and jurisdiction over persons or things can create major complexities for plaintiffs, as well as important opportunities for defendants to oppose plaintiff's initial choice of forum.

Unincorporated Associations

For venue purposes, the case law treats partnerships, sole proprietorships, and other unincorporated associations in much the same manner as corporations, so that unincorporated associations are probably deemed to reside in every judicial district where they are subject to personal jurisdiction, according to the same threefold analysis of 28 U.S.C.A. § 1391(c).[26]

25. *See Manley v. Engram*, 755 F.2d 1463, 1466 (11th Cir.1985)(for purposes of venue, "residence" for natural persons mean "domicile.").

26. *Denver & Rio Grande Western R.R. Co. v. Brotherhood of Railroad Trainmen*, 387 U.S. 556, 87 S.Ct. 1746, 18 L.Ed.2d 954 (1967)(multi-state unincorporated association has residence, for venue purposes, wherever it does business).

Aliens

Section 1391(d) provides that aliens may be sued in any judicial district. Case law suggests that this provision applies equally to alien corporations as well as alien natural persons,[27] so venue requirements for most alien defendants are not difficult to satisfy. It is uncertain whether a non–U.S. citizen domiciled in an American state (and therefore a citizen of that state for diversity purposes, under 28 U.S.C.A. § 1332(a)), is an "alien" for purposes of § 1391(d). Assuming such a person is not an alien, § 1391(d) would have no application in a suit where that person was the defendant. Thus ordinary requirements for venue, found in § 1391(a) and (b), would have to be satisfied.

The United States

Section 1391(e) expands venue possibilities if the United States, a federal agency, or a federal officer acting in an official capacity is a defendant. These provisions apply to the governmental defendant only. A separate basis for venue must be found as to other defendants. The three venue possibilities available under § 1391(e) are:

(1) *A Single Defendant's Residence:* in a judicial district where a single defendant in the action resides. It is important to note that the United States, its agencies or officers can thereby be sued in a judicial district where some other defendant resides.[28] That would be true even if the federal officer, for example, did not reside in that district and did no business there; or

(2) *Location of Events or Property:* in a judicial district where "a substantial part of the events or omissions giving rise to the claim occurred, or a substantial part of property that is the subject of the action is situated;"[29] or

(3) *Plaintiff's Residence:* in a judicial district where the plaintiff resides, provided that the cause of action does not involve real property.[30] Section 1391(e)(3), in particular, is a major expansion of venue opportunities for suits against the United States and its agents.

It is important to note that a plaintiff may obtain the benefit of 28 U.S.C.A. § 1391(e) even if the suit also contains additional, non-federal defendants. In fact, the presence of non-federal defendants, and the use of their residences, creates the foundation for using § 1391(e)(1) to satisfy venue as to the United States, its agencies, and officers in judicial districts where venue as to the governmental defendant would not otherwise be possible.

27. *See, e.g., Go–Video, Inc. v. Akai Elec. Co., Ltd.,* 885 F.2d 1406, 1413 (9th Cir. 1989)(permitting use of § 1391(d) to establish venue in suit against foreign corporations).

28. *See also Bartman v. Cheney,* 827 F.Supp. 1, 3 (D.D.C.1993)(residence for federal officer or agency exists in any district where defendant performs "significant amount" of official duties).

29. *See, e.g., Andrean v. Secretary of United States Army,* 840 F.Supp. 1414, 1422 (D.Kan. 1993)(for purposes of § 1391(e)(2), court is not restricted to only events or activities involving named defendant; court may examine "all" events that gave rise to claim).

30. *See, e.g., Immigrant Assistance Project of the Los Angeles County Federation of Labor v. Immigration & Naturalization Service,* 306 F.3d 842, 868 (9th Cir.2002).

NOTE: The additional venue possibilities of § 1391(e) are available *only against federal defendants in a case.*[31] Section 1391(e) specifically provides that if non-federal parties are also defendants, venue as to them must be satisfied under § 1391(a) or (b), or some other specific venue statute. Thus, § 1391(e) may permit a plaintiff to satisfy venue as to a federal officer in a judicial district where venue would not be available as to the federal defendant under § 1391(a) or (b), but as to non-federal defendants the normal requirements of other venue provisions would apply.

Nationwide Personal Jurisdiction Over Federal Agencies and Officers

To ensure that the broad venue authority of § 1391(e) is not nullified by problems of personal jurisdiction, § 1391(e) also provides that the federal district court shall be able, by certified mail, to obtain personal jurisdiction over federal agencies and officers not found within the state in which the court sits.

Personal Suits Against Federal Officers

The venue opportunities provided by 28 U.S.C.A. § 1391(e) as to federal officers are available only when the officers are sued in their official capacities. If they are sued personally for money damages, § 1391(e) is not applicable.[32] In such circumstances the provisions of § 1391(a) or (b), or some other more specific venue statute, would control.

Suits Against Foreign Countries

Section 1391(f) prescribes the venue when foreign countries, or their agencies, are defendants. Four possibilities for venue exist, depending on whether suit is against the foreign sovereign itself, its agency, or its shipping or cargo. These possibilities are:

(1) *Location of Events or Property:* in a judicial district where a substantial portion of the events giving rise to the claim occurred,[33] or where a substantial part of property that is the subject of the claim is located.

(2) *Location of Vessel or Cargo:* in any judicial district where a vessel or cargo belonging to a foreign state is located. This venue possibility is available only if the claim arose under 28 U.S.C.A. § 1605(b), governing suits in admiralty against foreign states; or

(3) *Location of Agency That is Doing Business:* if the defendant is an agency or instrumentality of the foreign state, as described in 28

31. *See, e.g., King v. Russell,* 963 F.2d 1301, 1303 (9th Cir.1992), *cert. denied,* 507 U.S. 913, 113 S.Ct. 1263, 122 L.Ed.2d 660 (1993)(§ 1391(e) "only applies to suits against officers of the executive branch").

32. *Stafford v. Briggs,* 444 U.S. 527, 100 S.Ct. 774, 63 L.Ed.2d 1 (1980)(§ 1391(e) unavailable where suit is for money damages against federal employees individually).

33. *See, e.g., U.S. Titan, Inc. v. Guangzhou Zhen Hua Shipping Co.,* 241 F.3d 135, 153–54 (2d Cir.2001) (noting parallel language of § 1391(b)(2) and (f)(1); requirement of substantial events satisfied by fact that defendant directed relevant communications to plaintiff in form district).

U.S.C.A. § 1603(b), in any judicial district in which the agency is licensed to do business or doing business. It is important to note that privately owned non-American corporations do not fit within the description of a foreign state's instrumentality as defined by § 1603(b). For § 1603(b) to apply, the foreign state itself, not merely its citizens, must be the majority owner of an instrumentality;[34] or

(4) *Venue in the District of Columbia:* if the defendant is a foreign state itself, or a political subdivision of a foreign state, venue may be satisfied in the United States District Court for the District of Columbia.

Sovereign Immunity

Nothing in § 1391(f) waives whatever immunity a foreign state, or its agencies or instrumentalities, may have. Instead, § 1391(f) provides venue possibilities only on the assumption that the suit is otherwise permitted by law, and that immunities either do not apply or have been waived for the purposes of the suit.

ADDITIONAL RESEARCH REFERENCES

C.J.S. Federal Courts §§ 16–21 et seq., 165–190 et seq.

West's Key No. Digests, Federal Courts ⚷71–157.

§ 1.15 Forum Non Conveniens

CORE CONCEPT

The forum non conveniens doctrine provides that a court selected by the claimant will not hear a cause of action if the court is an "inappropriate" forum. A trial court enjoys substantial discretion to determine whether it is an appropriate forum for a case, but that discretion is qualified by some important requirements, discussed below, that must be satisfied before a court's determination receives such deference.

APPLICATIONS

Relationship to Jurisdiction and Venue

Forum non conveniens shares some characteristics with jurisdiction and venue, but operates independently of those requirements. Thus, even if a plaintiff has chosen a court that enjoys: personal jurisdiction or quasi in rem jurisdiction over the defendant; subject matter jurisdiction over the kind of case at issue; and satisfactory venue, the court may refuse to hear the case if it determines that the court is an inappropriate forum.[1] At the same time, the court will typically not

34. *See, e.g., Transaero, Inc. v. La Fuerza Aerea Boliviana,* 30 F.3d 148, 152 (D.C.Cir. 1994), *cert. denied,* 513 U.S. 1150, 115 S.Ct. 1101, 130 L.Ed.2d 1068 (1995)(limiting venue under § 1391(f)(3) to commercial enterprise that is agent or instrumentality of foreign state).

1. *See, e.g., Wiwa v. Royal Dutch Petroleum Co.,* 226 F.3d 88, 100 (2d Cir. 2000) (forum non

address the question of forum non conveniens until it first determines whether requirements of jurisdiction and venue are satisfied.[2]

Timing

In the ordinary course of events a motion to dismiss under the doctrine of forum non conveniens or a motion to transfer a case under 28 U.S.C.A. § 1404 (discussed below) will normally be made early in the litigation. A motion made after judgment will not be granted.[3]

Moreover, even a motion made earlier in a case is substantially less likely to prevail on appeal once the case has proceeded through trial to judgment.[4]

Forum Selection Clauses

In circumstances where the parties have agreed in advance to a forum selection clause, that choice of forum will normally be resistant an attack on grounds of forum non conveniens.[5] Other factors of public and private interest may still be examined, but they will normally not prevail over an otherwise valid forum selection clause.[6]

Requirement of an Adequate Alternative Forum

An important limit on a trial court's discretion to dismiss a case on forum non conveniens grounds arises from the requirement that, before the court employs its discretion in the matter, it must first determine

conveniens is "a discretionary device permitting a court in rare instances to dismiss claims even if the court is a permissible venue with proper jurisdiction over the claim.").

2. *Gulf Oil Corp. v. Gilbert,* 330 U.S. 501, 504, 67 S.Ct. 839, 840, 91 L.Ed. 1055 (1947) ("[T]he doctrine of forum non conveniens can never apply if there is absence of jurisdiction or venue."); *Baris v. Sulpicio Lines, Inc.,* 932 F.2d 1540, 1542 (5th Cir.1991), *cert. denied,* 502 U.S. 963, 112 S.Ct. 430, 116 L.Ed.2d 449 (1991) (court should typically address issue of forum non conveniens only after determining that jurisdiction exists). *See also Albion v. YMCA Camp Letts,* 171 F.3d 1, 2 (1st Cir.1999) (transfer under 28 U.S.C.A. § 1404 also inappropriate where court lacked personal jurisdiction over defendant). *But see In re Papandreou,* 139 F.3d 247 (D.C.Cir.1998) (in some cases dismissal on grounds of forum non conveniens may not require court to address issues of jurisdiction first).

3. *See, e.g., Ortiz v. Gaston County Dyeing Machine Co.,* 277 F.3d 594, 597–98 (1st Cir. 2002) ("Once the court entered judgment ... it was too late to request a transfer.").

4. *See, e.g., Zelinski v. Columbia 300, Inc.,* 335 F.3d 633, ___ (7th Cir.2003) (once trial was finished, public interest in favor of not moving case may arise from policy of not wasting judicial resources already expended on case); *McLennan v. American Eurocopter Corp., Inc.,* 245 F.3d 403, 423–24 (5th Cir.2001) (when case is tried to conclusion, denial of motion is strengthened; to prevail on appeal, moving party must show "great prejudice").

5. *Stewart Organization, Inc. v. Ricoh Corp.,* 487 U.S. 22, 29, 108 S.Ct. 2239, 2243, 101 L.Ed.2d 22 (1988) ("The presence of a forum-selection clause ... will be a significant factor that figures centrally in the district court's calculus."). *See, e.g., P & S Business Machines, Inc. v. Canon USA, Inc.,* 331 F.3d 804, 807–08 (11th Cir.2003) (choice made in forum selection clause will rarely be disturbed).

6. *See, e.g., Bonny v. Society of Lloyd's,* 3 F.3d 156, 160 n. 11 (7th Cir.1993), *cert. denied,* 510 U.S. 1113, 114 S.Ct. 1057, 127 L.Ed.2d 378 (1994) ("[A] party's financial status at any given time in the course of litigation cannot be the basis for enforcing or not enforcing a valid forum selection clause."); *Moses v. Business Card Express, Inc.,* 929 F.2d 1131, 1138–39 (6th Cir. 1991), *cert. denied,* 502 U.S. 821, 112 S.Ct. 81, 116 L.Ed.2d 54 (1991) (economic disparity between parties and one party's claim of financial hardship cannot overcome valid forum selection clause).

that an adequate alternative forum exists.[7] The defendant has the burden of demonstrating the availability of such a forum.[8] Even if the plaintiff's choice of forum seems strained, that choice will not be overruled (assuming no problems with jurisdiction and venue) until the trial court makes that determination.[9] If there is no other such forum, the court will retain the case.

Evaluating the adequacy of an alternative forum requires a determination as to whether the defendants are subject to service of process in the alternative forum, and whether the alternative forum will hear the case. For other American jurisdictions this analysis tends to focus on the question of jurisdiction over the defendant.[10] If there is some question about jurisdiction in the proposed alternative forum, a defendant can usually eliminate the issue by stipulating to jurisdiction in that forum.[11]

7. *See, e.g., DiRienzo v. Philip Services Corp.*, 294 F.3d 21, 28 (2d Cir.2002), *cert. denied*, 537 U.S. 1028, 123 S.Ct. 556, 154 L.Ed.2d 442 (2002) ("A forum non conveniens motion cannot be granted absent an adequate alternative forum."); *Iragorri v. International Elevator, Inc.*, 203 F.3d 8, 13 (1st Cir.2000) (district court should determine adequacy of alternative forum before weighing factors of private and public interest).

8. *See, e.g., Jones v. GNC Franchising, Inc.*, 211 F.3d 495, 499 n. 22 (9th Cir.2000), *cert. denied*, 531 U.S. 928, 121 S.Ct. 307, 148 L.Ed.2d 246 (2000), (defendant has burden of proving existence of adequate alternative forum); *Gschwind v. Cessna Aircraft Co.*, 161 F.3d 602, 606 (10th Cir.1998), *cert. denied*, 526 U.S. 1112, 119 S.Ct. 1755, 143 L.Ed.2d 787 (1999) ("Plaintiff correctly notes that the defendant bears the burden of proving that an adequate alternative forum exists.").

9. *Piper Aircraft Co. v. Reyno*, 454 U.S. 235, 255 n. 22, 102 S.Ct. 252, 265, 70 L.Ed.2d 419 (1981) ("At the outset of any forum non conveniens inquiry, the court must determine whether there exists an alternative forum."). *See also Alpine View Co. v. Atlas Copco AB*, 205 F.3d 208, 221 (5th Cir.2000) ("A court facing a motion to dismiss for forum non conveniens must first assess whether an alternative forum is both available and adequate."); *Boosey & Hawkes Music Publishers, Ltd. v. Walt Disney Co.*, 145 F.3d 481 (2d Cir.1998) (failure to consider whether issues are justiciable in at least one alternative forum mandates reversal of dismissal).

10. *Piper Aircraft Co. v. Reyno*, 454 U.S. 235, 255 n. 22, 102 S.Ct. 252, 265, 70 L.Ed.2d 419 (1981) ("Ordinarily, this requirement [of an adequate alternative forum] will be satisfied when the defendant is 'amenable to process' in the other jurisdiction.").

11. *See, e.g., Monegro v. Rosa*, 211 F.3d 509, 514 (9th Cir.2000), *cert. denied*, 531 U.S. 1112, 121 S.Ct. 857, 148 L.Ed.2d 771 (2001)(abuse of discretion where, *inter alia*, district court did not condition dismissal on defendant's participation in judicial proceedings in Dominican Republic; case also had significant relation with plaintiff's chosen forum and evidence was at least as likely to be available in United States); *Gschwind v. Cessna Aircraft Co.*, 161 F.3d 602, 606 (10th Cir.1998), *cert. denied*, 526 U.S. 1112, 119 S.Ct. 1755, 143 L.Ed.2d 787 (1999) ("Defendants agreed to be subject to suit in France. That concession is generally enough to make the alternative forum available."). *Cf., Jota v. Texaco, Inc.*, 157 F.3d 153, 159 (2d Cir.1998) ("[D]ismissal for forum non conveniens is not appropriate, at least absent a commitment by [defendant] to submit to the jurisdiction of the Ecuadoran courts for purposes of this action"). *See also Alpine View Co. v. Atlas Copco, AB*, 205 F.3d 208, 221 (5th Cir.2000) (foreign court is available if " 'entire case and all parties' " are subject to its jurisdiction); *Reid–Walen v. Hansen*, 933 F.2d 1390, 1393 n. 2 (8th Cir.1991) (case involved more than one defendant; "An alternative forum is available if ***all*** parties are amenable to process and come within the jurisdiction of the forum." [emphasis added]). *But cf., Wild v. Subscription Plus, Inc.*, 292 F.3d 526, 531 (7th Cir.2002) ("[T]here is no absolute bar to the transfer of a multidefendant suit to a district in which one of the defendants cannot be served." Treating § 1404 as closely analogous to § 1406 for this purpose); *In re Papandreou*, 139 F.3d 247, 256 n. 6 (D.C.Cir.1998) (dicta; if district court dismisses case, involving possible foreign sovereign immunity issues, on grounds of forum non conveniens, dismissal should not "be subject to conditions, *e.g.*, a condition that defendants promise to submit to the jurisdiction of another

However, if the proposed alternative forum is found in another country, the trial court hearing the forum non conveniens motion will, in addition to questions of jurisdiction and service of process, also examine whether the foreign court has the capacity to provide an adequate remedy.[12] In extreme cases, there may also be questions about the integrity of a particular foreign court.[13] When the court believes that another forum would be more appropriate but still retains some concern over whether a case will actually be heard in the foreign court, the appropriate practice is to include a clause in the dismissal order providing that parties may return to the dismissing court to resume their case.[14]

The probability that a foreign court will not apply American substantive law is usually not weighed heavily in determining the adequacy of an alternative forum.[15] However, the result may be different in cases

court, for exaction of such a condition would appear inescapably to constitute an exercise of jurisdiction").

12. *See, e.g., Nemariam v. Federal Democratic Republic of Ethiopia,* 315 F.3d 390, 394 (D.C.Cir.2003) (alleged alternative forum is inadequate where foreign tribunal cannot make award directly to plaintiff, and government that would be claimant in place of plaintiff has no duty to send any award to her); *Gonzalez v. Chrysler Corp.,* 301 F.3d 377, 382 (5th Cir.2002), *cert. denied,* 538 U.S. 1012, 123 S.Ct. 1928, 155 L.Ed.2d 848 (2003) (Mexico's low cap on tort damages does not make Mexico an inappropriate forum); *Leon v. Millon Air, Inc.,* 251 F.3d 1305, 1311 (11th Cir.2001) ("Courts have been strict about requiring that defendants demonstrate that the alternative forum offers at least some relief."); *Satz v. McDonnell Douglas Corp.,* 244 F.3d 1279, 1283 (11th Cir.2001) ("An adequate forum need not be a perfect forum;" concerns about filing fees, lack of discovery, and delay do not automatically render foreign forum inadequate; noting that, in instant case, defendant agreed to use of discovery rules of American federal courts); *DiRienzo v. Philip Services Corp.,* 232 F.3d 49, 58 (2d Cir.2000) (procedural differences, such as possibility that foreign court will not certify a class action, do not make foreign forum inadequate); *Alpine View Co. v. Atlas Copco AB,* 205 F.3d 208, 221 (5th Cir.2000) (foreign court is available when " 'entire case and all parties' " are subject to its jurisdiction; it is adequate where parties " 'will not be deprived of all remedies or treated unfairly' "; availability of United States procedure in foreign court is not dispositive); *El–Fadl v. Central Bank of Jordan,* 75 F.3d 668, 678 (D.C.Cir.1996) (Jordanian courts unsuitable in part because recently enacted Jordanian law immunized defendants from liability for actions in question).

13. *See, e.g., BP Chemicals, Ltd. v. Jiangsu Sopo Corp.,* 285 F.3d 677, 688 (8th Cir.2002), *cert. denied,* 537 U.S. 942, 123 S.Ct. 343, 154 L.Ed.2d 250 (2002) ("[P]roper resolution of the forum non conveniens argument will depend heavily upon whether [plaintiff] could receive a fair hearing in the Chinese courts."). *Cf., Monegasque de Reassurances S.A.M. v. Nak Naftogaz of Ukraine,* 311 F.3d 488, 499 (2d Cir.2002) ("We have been reluctant to find foreign courts 'corrupt' or 'biased.' "); *Leon v. Millon Air, Inc.,* 251 F.3d 1305 (11th Cir.2001) (plaintiff's assertion that foreign court is too corrupt to be fair usually does not prevail; significant evidence of severe problems of partiality or years of delay needed to upset presumption that foreign forum is adequate); *Iragorri v. International Elevator, Inc.,* 203 F.3d 8, 13 (1st Cir.2000) (notwithstanding State Department advisory on danger of traveling in Columbia, native Columbians who are naturalized United States citizens face less danger and are more familiar with culture and language of Columbia than other Americans).

14. *See, e.g., Vasquez v. Bridgestone/Firestone, Inc.,* 325 F.3d 665, 675 (5th Cir.2003) (if foreign forum may not be open or defendant may not submit to jurisdiction there, it is abuse of discretion to fail to include "return jurisdiction" clause in dismissal order; remedy for such abuse of discretion is to remand to insert clause); *Ford v. Brown,* 319 F.3d 1302, 1311 (11th Cir.2003) (approving dismissal that is conditioned on defendant's waiver of jurisdiction and limitations defenses in foreign forum and willingness of foreign court to hear case).

15. *Piper Aircraft Co. v. Reyno,* 454 U.S. 235, 247, 102 S.Ct. 252, 261, 70 L.Ed.2d 419 (1981) ("The possibility of a change in substantive law should ordinarily not be given conclusive or even substantial weight in the forum non conveniens inquiry."). *See, e.g., Dickson Marine, Inc. v. Pan-*

where distinctions in procedural law preclude a reasonable opportunity for the plaintiff to present a case.[16]

Deference to Plaintiff's Choice of Forum: Exceptions and Modification

Normally, the court will give substantial deference to a plaintiff's choice of forum.[17] Thus, for a defendant to prevail on a forum non conveniens motion, the defendant must demonstrate that the plaintiff's choice of forum was significantly inappropriate, notwithstanding the existence of satisfactory jurisdiction and venue. As applied to the facts of particular cases, this deference means that when the court is weighing the public and private interests discussed below, the plaintiff's choice of forum will not be defeated by a mere preponderance of interests favoring dismissal. In fact, in most cases the forum non conveniens motion will not be granted unless the weighing factors discussed below "weigh heavily in favor of trial in the alternative forum."[18] In all cases the trial court's discretion in weighing factors may not be used to nullify the deference to which a plaintiff's choice of

alpina, Inc., 179 F.3d 331, 342 (5th Cir.1999) ("[D]ifferences in substantive law should not be given conclusive weight in a forum non conveniens inquiry."). *Cf., Boosey & Hawkes Music Publishers, Ltd. v. Walt Disney Co.*, 145 F.3d 481, 492 (2d Cir.1998) (noting that refusal to dismiss case on grounds of forum non conveniens will require trial court to apply foreign law, but also noting that "[w]hile reluctance to apply foreign law is a valid factor favoring dismissal, ... standing alone it does not justify dismissal.").

16. *See, e.g., Lacey v. Cessna Aircraft Co.*, 932 F.2d 170, 185 n. 12 (3d Cir.1991) (Canadian forum inadequate because plaintiff would face "serious impediments" to obtaining sources of proof). *But see Alpha Therapeutic Corp. v. Nippon Hoso Kyokai*, 199 F.3d 1078, 1090 (9th Cir. 1999) (fact that Japan's civil procedure rules "are not friendly to plaintiffs" did not by itself make erroneous district court's finding that Japan was adequate alternative forum); *Alfadda v. Fenn*, 159 F.3d 41, 48 (2d Cir.1998) (inability of plaintiff to use materials obtained through U.S. discovery in a French court is a relevant factor, but not necessarily dispositive).

17. *Koster v. (American) Lumbermens Mutual Casualty Co.*, 330 U.S. 518, 524, 67 S.Ct. 828, 831, 91 L.Ed. 1067 (1947) (plaintiff's choice of forum gets great deference when suit is in plaintiff's home forum); *Gulf Oil Corp. v. Gilbert*, 330 U.S. 501, 508, 67 S.Ct. 839, 843, 91 L.Ed. 1055 (1947) ("[U]nless the balance is strongly in favor of the defendant, the plaintiff's choice of forum should rarely be disturbed."). *See also Iragorri v. United Technologies Corp.*, 274 F.3d 65, 71–72 (2d Cir.2001) (noting sliding scale of deference involving several factors, but beginning with high deference for plaintiff's choice of home forum and sliding to less deference for foreign plaintiff; "the more it appear that a domestic or foreign plaintiff's choice of forum has been dictated by reasons that the law recognizes as valid, the greater the deference that will be given to the plaintiff's forum choice"); *Nowak v. Tak How Investments, Ltd.*, 94 F.3d 708, 719 (1st Cir.1996), *cert. denied*, 520 U.S. 1155, 117 S.Ct. 1333, 137 L.Ed.2d 493 (1997) ("We have emphasized that the doctrine of forum non conveniens is used to avoid 'serious unfairness' and that a plaintiff's choice of a forum will be disturbed only rarely."). Moreover, in a case where the plaintiff is a United States citizen and one or more defendants are non-Americans, the plaintiff's decision to sue in a judicial district other than the one in which the plaintiff resides does not nullify the deference to which the plaintiff's choice is entitled. *See, e.g., Wiwa v. Royal Dutch Petroleum Co.*, 226 F.3d 88, 103 (2d Cir.2000), *cert. denied*, 532 U.S. 941, 121 S.Ct. 1402, 149 L.Ed.2d 345 (2001) ("The benefit for a U.S. resident plaintiff of suing in a U.S. forum is not limited to suits in the very district where the plaintiff resides, especially considering that the defendant may not be amenable to suit in the plaintiff's district of residence."); *Reid–Walen v. Hansen*, 933 F.2d 1390, 1394 (8th Cir.1991) (assuming plaintiff has not selected the forum to harass or vex the defendant, "the 'home' forum for the plaintiff is any federal district in the United States, not the particular district where the plaintiff lives").

18. *R. Maganlal & Co. v. M.G. Chemical Co.*, 942 F.2d 164, 167 (2d Cir.1991).

forum is entitled.[19]

Exception: Non-American Plaintiffs: In federal courts it is settled that American plaintiffs receive substantially more deference in their choices of fora than do non-American plaintiffs.[20] However, "less deference" is not the same as no deference at all, and a foreign plaintiff's choice of forum is still entitled to some respect.[21]

Exception: Certain Declaratory Judgment Plaintiffs: If the plaintiff who has chosen the forum has sought relief in the form of a declaratory judgment, with a "bad faith" motive of taking advantage of the true plaintiff in a race to the forum, it appears that the declaratory judgment plaintiff's choice of forum is not entitled any deference.[22]

Modification: Corporate Plaintiffs in International Business: If the plaintiff is an American corporation with substantial experience in international business transactions and is suing on a cause of action that arose outside the United States, it appears that such a plaintiff will receive less deference than would, *e.g.,* an individual American plaintiff suing on a personal injury incurred while on vacation outside the United States.[23]

Weighing Factors: Judicial Discretion

Once a trial court has identified an adequate alternative forum in which the defendants will be subject to jurisdiction, it is authorized to weigh the important factors of public and private interest in determining whether to grant a defendant's forum non conveniens motion. In

19. *See also DiRienzo v. Philip Services Corp.,* 232 F.3d 49, 60 (2d Cir.2000) (presumption in favor of home forum not weakened by fact that case is class action; acknowledging, however, that such weakening exists in shareholder's derivative suit, per *Koster v. (American) Lumbermens Mutual Casualty Co.,* 330 U.S. 518, 525, 67 S.Ct. 828, 832, 91 L.Ed. 1067 (1947)); *Wiwa v. Royal Dutch Petroleum Co.,* 226 F.3d 88, 101 (2d Cir.2000), *cert. denied,* 532 U.S. 941, 121 S.Ct. 1402, 149 L.Ed.2d 345 (2001) (deference to plaintiff's choice of forum "increases as the plaintiff's ties to the forum increase"); *Guidi v. Inter-Continental Hotels Corp.,* 224 F.3d 142 (2d Cir.2000) (failure to give American plaintiffs choice of forum "significant deference" is "unsound").

20. *Piper Aircraft Co. v. Reyno,* 454 U.S. 235, 256, 102 S.Ct. 252, 266, 70 L.Ed.2d 419 (1981) ("Because the central purpose of any forum non conveniens inquiry is to ensure that the trial is convenient, a foreign plaintiff's choice deserves less deference.").

21. *See, e.g., Lacey v. Cessna Aircraft Co.,* 862 F.2d 38, 45–46 (3d Cir.1988) (Less deference for foreign plaintiffs "is 'not an invitation to accord a foreign plaintiff's selection of an American forum no deference.' ").

22. *See, e.g., Hyatt Inaternational Corp. v. Coco,* 302 F.3d 707, 718 (7th Cir.2002) (plaintiff's choice of forum normally gets deference, but "[w]e have wariness at the prospect of 'a suit for declaratory judgment aimed solely at wrestling the choice of forum from the natural plaintiff.' "); *NSI Corp. v. Showco, Inc.,* 843 F.Supp. 642, 645 (D.Ore.1994) (using declaratory judgment proceeding to obtain unfair advantage in choice of forum is ground for dismissal).

23. *See, e.g., Pollux Holding Ltd. v. Chase Manhattan Bank,* 329 F.3d 64, 70–71 (2d Cir. 2003), *cert. denied,* ___ U.S. ___, 124 S.Ct. 1145, 157 L.Ed.2d 1041 (2004) (corporations with status of United States citizen residing abroad receives deference only to extent that corporations have significant connections with forum; otherwise, corporations get less deference); *Guidi v. Inter-Continental Hotels Corp.,* 224 F.3d 142 (2d Cir.2000) (because plaintiffs are "ordinary American citizens," they face significant inconvenience in litigating in Egypt; corporate defendant with principal place of business in forum faces no comparable hardship in defending in United States); *Kamel v. Hill-Rom Co., Inc.,* 108 F.3d 799, 804 (7th Cir.1997) (suggesting that sophisticated American corporate plaintiff suing on foreign cause of action receives "somewhat discounted" deference).

doing so, the court enjoys significant discretion that will not lightly be overturned on appeal, including the power to impose conditions on its decisions.[24] However, failure to weigh all the factors of public or private interest that arise in a particular case may be abuse of discretion.[25]

Public Interest Factors

The public interest factors may differ somewhat from one case to another, but it is settled that they include: "(1) having local disputes settled locally; (2) avoiding problems of applying foreign law; and (3) avoiding burdening jurors with cases that have no impact on their community."[26] In some cases there may also be questions about the enforceability of a judgment that the court would render if it retained the case.

Local Disputes: The desire to settle local disputes locally (or, alternatively, the desire to avoid imposing distant disputes on a local court) takes into account questions such as local court congestion or burdens on jurors.[27]

Application of Foreign Law: Courts may be reluctant to take cases in which they will be obligated to apply the law of another jurisdiction. However, in a weighing of factors related to forum non conveniens, this consideration normally carries only limited weight.[28]

Burdening Jurors with Cases of No Local Interest: This factor contains two parts: whether local citizens should have to carry the burden of trying a case unrelated to their community; and whether the

24. *See, e.g., Bank of Credit and Commerce International (Overseas) Ltd. v. State Bank of Pakistan,* 273 F.3d 241, 244–48 (2d Cir.2001) (in granting motion, court has discretion to require party prevailing on motion to: waive statute of limitation defense; agree that if opponent obtains final judgment on in foreign court, it may be enforced elsewhere; and to waive forum non conveniens defense if foreign court refused to hear case on statute of limitations grounds).

25. *See, e.g.,EFCO Corp. v. Aluma Systems USA, Inc.,* 268 F.3d 601, 603 (8th Cir.2001) ("Abuse of discretion occurs when the district court does not hold the defendants to their burden of persuasion on all the elements of the forum non conveniens analysis, fails to consider the relevant public and private interest factors established in *Piper Aircraft* ... or clearly errs in weighing the *Piper Aircraft* factors."); *Dickson Marine, Inc. v. Panalpina, Inc.,* 179 F.3d 331, 341 (5th Cir.1999) ("[A] district court abuses its discretion when it grants a motion to dismiss without oral or written reasons or when it fails to address and balance the relevant principles and factors."); *Reid–Walen v. Hansen,* 933 F.2d 1390, 1393 (8th Cir.1991) ("An abuse of discretion may occur when the district court fails to consider one or more of the important private or public interest factors, does not hold the defendants to their burden of persuasion on all elements of the forum non conveniens analysis, or has clearly erred in weighing the factors the court must consider.").

26. *Alfadda v. Fenn,* 159 F.3d 41, 46 (2d Cir.1998) (citing *Piper Aircraft* and *Gulf Oil*). *See also Zelinski v. Columbia 300, Inc.,* 335 F.3d 633, ___ (7th Cir.2003) (once trial was finished, public interest in favor of not moving case may arise from policy of not wasting judicial resources already expended on case).

27. *Gulf Oil Corp. v. Gilbert,* 330 U.S. 501, 67 S.Ct. 839, 91 L.Ed. 1055 (1947). *But cf., Guidi v. Inter–Continental Hotels Corp.,* 224 F.3d 142 (2d Cir.2000) (district court's finding that it is " 'heavily overburdened' " is of "little or no significance" where all judicial vacancies have recently been filled; moreover, while the existence of related litigation in another forum may sometimes justify dismissal so that judicial efficiency is served by permitting consolidation of cases, this consideration usually arises only when the parties in both lawsuits are substantially identical).

28. *See, e.g., Boosey & Hawkes Music Publishers, Ltd. v. Walt Disney Co.,* 145 F.3d 481, 492 (2d Cir.1998) (by itself, burden of applying foreign law does not justify dismissal).

citizenry of another area has a greater interest in the outcome of a case.[29]

Enforceability of a Judgment: If enforcement of a prospective judgment could require further litigation outside the United States, the court may weigh that factor in determining whether the case should be heard in the United States in the first instance.[30] This consideration would carry particular weight if there was a significant possibility that the judgment would be unenforceable, thus potentially reducing the American judicial proceeding to a waste of time and judicial resources. However, this "enforceability" factor normally plays no role in forum non conveniens determinations if enforcement will occur in the United States, because the Full Faith and Credit clause of the Constitution generally requires an American court to enforce the final judgment of another American court.

Public Policy: In unusual cases, courts may retain a particular lawsuit because public policy favors an American forum for such a suit.[31]

Private Interest Factors

Private interest factors include: "(1) ease of access to evidence; (2) the cost for witnesses to attend trial; (3) the availability of compulsory process; and (4) other factors that might shorten trial or make it less expensive."[32] For the most part, these factors revolve around the impact of forum selection on the ability of parties to prove their case. If a plaintiff's choice of forum–or the defendant's proposed alternative–substantially affects a party's ability to put forward witnesses and evidence, the court will be inclined to weigh that consideration heavily.[33]

29. *Gulf Oil Corp. v. Gilbert,* 330 U.S. 501, 67 S.Ct. 839, 91 L.Ed. 1055 (1947). *But cf., P & S Business Machines, Inc. v. Canon USA, Inc.,* 331 F.3d 804, 808 (11th Cir.2003) (docket congestion is an appropriate consideration, but "case law does not suggest that docket congestion is, by itself, a dispositive factor").

30. *Gulf Oil Corp. v. Gilbert,* 330 U.S. 501, 67 S.Ct. 839, 91 L.Ed. 1055 (1947).

31. *See, e.g., DiRienzo v. Philip Services Corp.,* 294 F.3d 21, 29–31 (2d Cir.2002), *cert. denied,* 537 U.S. 1028, 123 S.Ct. 556, 154 L.Ed.2d 442 (2002) (private interest factors: documents in Canada, but no particular problems of transport; most witnesses in Canada, but all within a few hours of New York forum by automobile and air travel; some third-party witnesses in Canada cannot be forced to testify in New York, but videotaped depositions arranged through letters rogatory may be suitable substitute; public interest factors: most tend not to weigh heavily on instant facts, but United States has strong interest in hearing cases arising under federal securities laws, and this factor strongly supports plaintiff's choice of forum); *Wiwa v. Royal Dutch Petroleum Co.,* 226 F.3d 88, 105 (2d Cir.2000), *cert. denied,* 532 U.S. 941, 121 S.Ct. 1402, 149 L.Ed.2d 345 (2001) (federal law reflects policy in favor of hearing claims of torture under color of foreign law).

32. *Alfadda v. Fenn,* 159 F.3d 41, 46 (2d Cir.1998) (citing *Piper Aircraft* and *Gulf Oil*). *See also Leon v. Millon Air, Inc.,* 251 F.3d 1305 (11th Cir.2001) (private interest factors generally considered more significant than public factors, but both kinds of facts should be weighed); *Guidi v. Inter–Continental Hotels Corp.,* 224 F.3d 142 (2d Cir.2000) (abuse of discretion for district court not to consider emotional burden of litigating in Egypt, where plaintiffs or their relatives were attacked by terrorists and where plaintiffs justifiably fear for their safety).

33. *Piper Aircraft Co. v. Reyno,* 454 U.S. 235, 102 S.Ct. 252, 70 L.Ed.2d 419 (1981) (large proportion of relevant evidence in foreign country is factor weighing in favor of dismissal). *See also, e.g., Alpine View Co. v. Atlas Copco AB,* 205 F.3d 208, 222 (5th Cir.2000) (upholding district

Application of Doctrine *Sua Sponte*

Normally, a forum non conveniens issue is raised by a party. At the same time, parties are free to waive the issue, and such waiver may occur in a variety of circumstances.[34] However, a party's decision to waive the issue is subject to the court's authority to raise the issue *sua sponte*.[35] For example, the court might do so if the convenience of non-party witnesses was an important issue.

Transfer

Congress has provided a special remedy for forum non conveniens cases. 28 U.S.C.A. § 1404 provides that a federal court that is an inappropriate forum may *transfer* the case to another federal district court in which the case "might have been brought."[36] Because a transferred case is not dismissed, transfer creates no statute of limitations problems.[37] Transfer is now the standard remedy in cases where it can be applied.[38]

Limits on Transfer

Federal district courts may use § 1404 only to transfer cases to other federal district courts. If a federal court recognizes that the appropriate forum for an action is outside the United States, the only remedy available is dismissal of the action, with permission to the plaintiff to file the cause of action elsewhere.[39] This remedy can create

court's assessment of private factors where no witness was identified in United States who would be needed for "general discovery" and documents existed mostly outside United States; private interest factors favor dismissal sufficiently so that circuit court need not address factors of public interest). *But see DiRienzo v. Philip Services Corp.,* 294 F.3d 21 (2d Cir.2002), *cert. denied,* 537 U.S. 1028, 123 S.Ct. 556, 154 L.Ed.2d 442 (2002) (private interest factors: documents in Canada, but no particular problems of transport; most witnesses in Canada, but all within a few hours of New York forum by automobile and air travel; some third-party witnesses in Canada cannot be forced to testify in New York, but videotaped depositions arranged through letters rogatory may be suitable substitute; public interest factors: most tend not to weigh heavily on instant facts, but United States has strong interest in hearing cases arising under federal securities laws, and this factor strongly supports plaintiff's choice of forum).

34. *See, e.g., Corporacion Mexicana de Servicios Maritimos, S.A. de C.V. v. M/T Respect,* 89 F.3d 650, 656 n. 1 (9th Cir.1996)(by intervening, party waived forum non conveniens); *Heller Fin., Inc. v. Midwhey Powder Co.,* 883 F.2d 1286, 1293 (7th Cir.1989)(valid forum-selection clause waives defense of forum non conveniens).

35. *See, e.g., Corporacion Mexicana de Servicios Maritimos, S.A. de C.V. v. M/T Respect,* 89 F.3d 650, 656 n. 1 (9th Cir.1996).

36. *But cf., Wild v. Subscription Plus, Inc.,* 292 F.3d 526, 531 (7th Cir.2002), *cert. denied,* 537 U.S. 1045, 123 S.Ct. 619, 154 L.Ed.2d 517 (2002) ("[T]here is no absolute bar to the transfer of a multidefendant suit to a district in which one of the defendants cannot be served." Treating § 1404 as closely analogous to § 1406 for this purpose).

37. *Ferens v. John Deere Co.,* 494 U.S. 516, 110 S.Ct. 1274, 108 L.Ed.2d 443 (1990)(transfer to state where applicable statute of limitations will bar suit has no ill consequence for suit, because statute of limitations of transferor jurisdiction remains in effect).

38. *Quackenbush v. Allstate Ins. Co.,* 517 U.S. 706, 116 S.Ct. 1712, 135 L.Ed.2d 1 (1996)(for federal courts, transfer pursuant to § 1404 is preferred remedy for problems arising from forum non conveniens; dismissal appropriate "only in 'cases where the alternative forum is abroad' "). *See, e.g., Monegro v. Rosa,* 211 F.3d 509, 512 (9th Cir.2000), *cert. denied,* 531 U.S. 1112, 121 S.Ct. 857, 148 L.Ed.2d 771 (2001) (§ 1404(a) applicable when alternative forum is within United States).

39. *See, e.g., Piper Aircraft Co. v. Reyno,* 454 U.S. 235, 102 S.Ct. 252, 70 L.Ed.2d 419 (1981).

practical problems for plaintiffs, so courts often condition a grant of a defendant's motion to dismiss for forum non conveniens on understandings that the defendant will submit to jurisdiction in another country and will not challenge the suit on statute of limitations grounds.[40]

ADDITIONAL RESEARCH REFERENCES

C.J.S. Federal Courts §§ 10(1) et seq.

West's Key No. Digests, Federal Courts ⚷45.

§ 1.16 Removal

Removal permits a defendant to move a case from a state trial court to a federal district court. The process is controlled by federal law.

CORE CONCEPT

28 U.S.C.A. § 1441 identifies most of the kinds of lawsuits that may be removed from a state court to federal district court. These include most diversity suits, most federal question suits, non-diverse state claims which are joined with federal questions, and suits against foreign states.[1] Section 1441 also contains a provision permitting removal even in circumstances where a state court lacked jurisdiction over the case when it was originally filed.

APPLICATIONS

Removal Statutes

The most important removal provisions are 28 U.S.C.A. § 1441 (governing removal for diversity cases, most federal questions, and non-diverse claims joined with federal questions), 28 U.S.C.A. § 1446 (establishing the procedure for accomplishing removal), and § 1447 (governing procedure after removal). Specific statutes provide for removal in particular circumstances, such as suits against federal officers or agencies (28 U.S.C.A. §§ 1442, 1442a, and 1444), and suits where a defendant might not be able to assert a federal civil right in a state court (28 U.S.C.A. § 1443). Additionally, 28 U.S.C.A. § 1445 provides that certain kinds of cases (*e.g.,* suits against railroads under the Federal Employers' Liability Act and suits arising under state workers' compensation laws) may not be removed. Finally, 28 U.S.C.A. §§ 1447–49 establish the procedures a court will follow after a case has been removed.

40. *See, e.g., Leon v. Millon Air, Inc.,* 251 F.3d 1305 (11th Cir.2001) (affirming dismissal, subject to following conditions: (1) admission of liability for damage caused by plane crash; (2) acceptance of service of process and jurisdiction in appropriate foreign court; (3) waiver of statute of limitations; (4) payment of final judgments of foreign court; and (5) case may be reinstated if foreign court rejects jurisdiction).

1. *Cf. City of Chicago v. International College of Surgeons,* 522 U.S. 156, 163, 118 S.Ct. 523, 529, 139 L.Ed.2d 525 (1997) ("The propriety of removal . . . depends on whether the case originally could have been filed in federal court.").

Exceptions to § 1441(a)

Section 1441(a) provides that the general right of removal is subject to such exceptions as Congress may create.[2] Congress has preserved some exceptions in 28 U.S.C.A. § 1445, such as cases arising under state workers' compensation statutes.

Jurisdictional Requirement

Removal is permissible only when at least one claim filed by the plaintiff falls within the original subject matter jurisdiction of the federal district court.[3]

Removal from State Court Only

For removal to be effective under § 1441, the case must have been in state court at the time the removal petition was filed. Section 1441 provides no authority to remove a case from a state administrative agency to a federal district court.[4]

Defendant's Right

Section 1441(a) restricts the right of removal to parties who are defendants to the plaintiff's case in chief. The majority view appears to be that defendants on counterclaims, crossclaims, or third-party impleaders have no right to remove cases from state court.[5] However,

2. *Breuer v. Jim's Concrete of Brevard, Inc.,* 538 U.S. 691, 123 S.Ct. 1882, 155 L.Ed.2d 923 (2003) (if federal subject matter jurisdiction is satisfied, statutory prohibition against removal must be express). *Cf., e.g., Nevada v. Hicks,* 533 U.S. 353, 121 S.Ct. 2304, 150 L.Ed.2d 398 (2001) (federal civil rights claims governed by 42 U.S.C.A. § 1983 may not be filed in tribal courts, partly because § 1441 does not authorize removal of federal claims from such courts; only claims in state courts might qualify for removal under § 1441).

3. *Jefferson County, Alabama v. Acker,* 527 U.S. 423, 430, 119 S.Ct. 2069, 2074, 144 L.Ed.2d 408 (1999) ("It is the general rule that an action may be removed from state court to federal court only if a federal district court would have original jurisdiction over the claim in suit."). *See, e.g., Carpenter v. Wichita Falls Indep't Sch. Dist.,* 44 F.3d 362, 365 (5th Cir.1995)(noting that propriety of removal depends on existence of original jurisdiction of federal courts). *Cf. Wisconsin Dept. of Corrections v. Schacht,* 524 U.S. 381, 118 S.Ct. 2047, 141 L.Ed.2d 364 (1998) (presence of one claim that is barred by Eleventh Amendment immunity does not prevent removal of other claims that meet jurisdictional requirements). *See also Barbers, Hairstyling for Men & Women, Inc. v. Bishop,* 132 F.3d 1203, 1204 (7th Cir.1997) (noting that plaintiffs prevented removal of state claims by seeking relief in an amount that was $50 less than the jurisdictional requirement for diversity); *Duncan v. Stuetzle,* 76 F.3d 1480, 1485 (9th Cir.1996) (nondiverse plaintiff may defeat removal by foregoing federal claim and pleading only state claims). *But cf., Marcus v. AT&T Corp.,* 138 F.3d 46, 52–53 (2d Cir.1998) (where federal law has completely preempted an area, plaintiff cannot defeat removal by pleading state claims, because those claims are really federal in nature). *See also Wellness Community-Nat'l v. Wellness House,* 70 F.3d 46, 50 (7th Cir.1995) (after case is removed, diversity jurisdiction cannot be defeated by amending claim to seek less than jurisdictional amount).

4. *See, e.g., Oregon Bureau of Labor & Industries ex rel. Richardson v. U.S. West Communications, Inc.,* 288 F.3d 414, 415 (9th Cir.2002) ("§ 1441(a) authorizes removal only from a 'state court,'" not an administrative agency).

5. *See, e.g., First National Bank of Pulaski v. Curry,* 301 F.3d 456, 461 (6th Cir.2002) ("[N]either § 1441(a) nor § 1441(c) provides third-party defendants with the right to remove a case to federal court."); *Lewis v. Windsor Door Co.,* 926 F.2d 729, 733 (8th Cir.1991)(removal cannot be based on third-party claim that may be within original jurisdiction of federal court); *Thomas v. Shelton,* 740 F.2d 478, 487–88 (7th Cir.1984) (third party defendants may not remove). *But see In re Wilson Indus., Inc.,* 886 F.2d 93, 96 (5th Cir.1989)(removal "can be based on a third-

these defendants may find claims affecting them removed if a defendant on an original count files a notice of removal. This possibility is discussed below, under *Joinder of "Non–Removable" Claims.* Further, if the basis of removal is a third-party claim against a foreign state, § 1441(d) (governing removal of claims against foreign states) will permit removal, notwithstanding the different result reached in cases governed by § 1441(a) or (b).[6]

Unanimous Consent

Although nowhere stated in the removal statutes, case law has established that an action generally cannot be removed to federal district court unless *all* defendants join in the notice of removal.[7] Thus, if two defendants are sued on a single count that might qualify for removal, but only one seeks to remove, the case is not eligible for removal.

It should be noted that Congress recently enacted 28 U.S.C.A. § 1453, governing removal of class actions from state court to federal district court. One of the provisions of new § 1453 eliminates the case law requirement for unanimous consent among the defendants before removal is possible. Instead, § 1453 provides that in cases involving class actions eligible for removal, *any* defendant may seek removal "without consent of all defendants."[8]

party claim where a separate and independent controversy is stated"; apparent minority view).

6. *See, e.g., Davis v. McCourt,* 226 F.3d 506 (6th Cir.2000) (collecting cases; also noting that entire lawsuit, not merely third-party complaint against foreign entity, is removed).

7. *Chicago, Rock Island and Pacific Railway Co. v. Martin,* 178 U.S. 245, 248, 20 S.Ct. 854, 855, 44 L.Ed. 1055 (1900) ("[I]t was well settled that a removal could not be effected unless all the parties on the same side of the controversy united in the petition."). *See, e.g., McMahon v. Bunn–O–Matic Corp.,* 150 F.3d 651 (7th Cir. 1998) (noting requirement that all defendants must sign removal notice); *Henry v. Independent American Savings Ass'n,* 857 F.2d 995, 999 (5th Cir.1988). ("Although failure of all defendants to join is usually a bar to removal, if one defendant's removal petition is premised on removable claims 'separate and independent' from the claims brought against other defendants, consent of the other defendants is not required."); *Pecherski v. General Motors Corp.,* 636 F.2d 1156, 1161 (8th Cir.1981) (subject to some exceptions for nominal parties or parties never served with process, "a Jane Doe case may not be removed until the plaintiff files an amendment in state court substituting the names of real parties and the defendant seeking removal thereafter establishes diversity of citizenship between the plaintiff and all named defendants."). *But cf., Vasquez v. North County Transit District,* 292 F.3d 1049 (9th Cir.2002) (removal is "procedurally defective" when some defendants do not join removal–but defect was waived by failure to make timely motion to remand); *Akin v. Ashland Chemical Co.,* 156 F.3d 1030, 1034 (10th Cir.1998), *cert. denied,* 526 U.S. 1112, 119 S.Ct. 1756, 143 L.Ed.2d 788 (1999) (under 28 U.S.C.A. § 1442(a), requirement for unanimous consent to removal does not apply to United States as a defendant or to federal officers sued for actions taken under color of federal office); *Lewis v. Rego Co.,* 757 F.2d 66, 68 (3d Cir.1985) (removing defendants file petition before nonresident defendants had been served with process; held, removal petition may still be effective, provided that petition explains that defendants who did not join petition were not yet served in state proceeding; when such defendants are finally served, 28 U.S.C.A. § 1448 may permit such defendants to challenge removal).

8. 28 U.S.C.A. § 1453(b). It should be noted that the exceptions created by § 1453 for class actions are themselves subject to an exception. Specifically, § 1453(d) provides that § 1453 is inapplicable to any class action "solely" involving: (1) a claim concerning a covered security under certain federal securities laws; (2) a claim relating to the internal affairs or governance of a corporation or other business entity arising under the laws of the state that incorporated or organized the enterprise; or (3) a claim relating

Geography of Removal

Cases removed from state court are removed to the federal court of the district (or division) that includes the location in which the state court sits.[9] Thus, a case removed from a Pennsylvania state trial court in Harrisburg, Pennsylvania would be sent to the United States District Court for the Middle District of Pennsylvania, the federal district court that includes Harrisburg.

Fictitious Names Disregarded

When determining whether the federal court has diversity jurisdiction over a removed case, § 1441(a) provides that if state procedure allows suits against defendants under fictitious names (*e.g.* General Motors v. John Doe, Mary Roe, and Jane Coe), the citizenship of such defendants will be disregarded.[10]

Federal Question Cases

Section 1441(b) authorizes a defendant to remove any cause of action based upon the Constitution, laws or treaties of the United States, if the federal court has original jurisdiction over the claim.[11] 28 U.S.C.A. § 1445(a) creates an exception to this general right of removal by prohibiting removal of suits against railroads based upon the Federal Employers' Liability Act.

Diversity Cases

Section 1441(b) also authorizes removal of cases where the parties meet requirements of diversity jurisdiction, subject to one significant exception. If any defendant sued on a diversity count is a citizen of the state in which the claim was filed, that count is not eligible for removal to federal district court.[12]

to the rights and duties, including fiduciary duties, created by the Securities Act of 1933.

9. 28 U.S.C.A. § 1441(a). *See, e.g., Kerobo v. Southwestern Clean Fuels, Corp.,* 285 F.3d 531, 534 (6th Cir.2002) (removal from state court within area embraced by Eastern District of Michigan could only be to Eastern District of Michigan). *But cf. Peterson v. BMI Refractories,* 124 F.3d 1386, 1394 (11th Cir.1997) (removal to "wrong" district court is procedural error that is waivable; issue is not jurisdictional in nature).

10. *See, e.g., Howell v. Tribune Entertainment Co.,* 106 F.3d 215, 218 (7th Cir.1997) ("[N]aming a John Doe defendant will not defeat the named defendants' right to remove a diversity case if their citizenship is diverse from that of the plaintiffs.").

11. *Rivet v. Regions Bank of Louisiana,* 522 U.S. 470, 118 S.Ct. 921, 139 L.Ed.2d 912 (1998) (basis for removal of federal question claim must appear on face of well-pleaded complaint; "a defendant cannot remove on the basis of a federal defense," *e.g.,* res judicata). *But cf., Romero v. International Terminal Operating Co.,* 358 U.S. 354, 368–69, 79 S.Ct. 468, 478, 3 L.Ed.2d 368 (1959) (admiralty case filed in state court may not be removed to federal court as federal question; thus, if removal was possible at all, it would have to rest on some other ground, e.g., diversity jurisdiction).

12. *See, e.g., Tillman v. R.J. Reynolds Tobacco,* 253 F.3d 1302 (11th Cir.2001) ("no defendant can be a citizen of the state in which the action was brought;" one narrow exception arises if a defendant is such a citizen but "there is no possibility that the plaintiff can establish any cause of action against that defendant;" in that circumstance, court may dismiss that defendant and retain diversity jurisdiction); *Coury v. Prot,* 85 F.3d 244 (5th Cir.1996)("[A] defendant may not remove a state action to federal court if a defendant is a citizen of the state in which the action is filed."). *But cf. McCall v. Scott,* 239 F.3d 808, 813 n. 2 (6th Cir.2001) ("[T]he inclusion of an unserved resident defendant in the

Congress recently enacted § 1453, which eliminated the applicability of this exception to removal of cases that are class actions. For such class actions, the exception contained in § 1441(b) is replaced by an express provision making removal possible "without regard to whether any defendant is a citizen of the State in which the action is brought." [13]

It should also be noted that removal cannot be defeated simply by joining defendants with no real interest in the claim. In such cases of "fraudulent joinder," the court will dismiss the unnecessary parties and uphold removal.[14]

Fraudulent Joinder

It is possible that a plaintiff will join a nondiverse defendant for the purpose of preventing removal of an otherwise diverse claim. Such a tactic is permissible if there is a legitimate basis for the joinder. It is not always easy to identify the standard for fraudulent joinder.[15] However, if there is no colorable basis for the claim against the nondiverse defendant, federal case law provides that the court will disregard the nondiverse defendant when ruling on a motion for remand to state court.[16] Fraudulent joinder may also be found when a plaintiff engages in "outright fraud" in pleading jurisdictional allegations.[17] A third type of fraudulent joinder may arise when the plaintiff joins a nondiverse defendant who has no joint, several or alternative liability with a diverse defendant, and there is no connection between the claims against the diverse and nondiverse defendants.[18]

Forum Selection Clauses

If the parties have an enforceable agreement that any dispute between them is to be heard in state court, an otherwise removable claim will be remanded to state court.[19]

action does not defeat removal."); *Blackburn v. United Parcel Service, Inc.,* 179 F.3d 81 n. 3 (3d Cir.1999) (suit against defendant in defendant's home state court that would meet requirements for diversity jurisdiction is nevertheless not eligible for removal; however, defect is waivable under 28 U.S.C.A. § 1447(c) if not raised within 30 days of filing of notice of removal).

13. 28 U.S.C.A. § 1453(b). It should be noted that the exceptions created by § 1453 for class actions are themselves subject to an exception. Specifically, § 1453(d) provides that § 1453 is inapplicable to any class action "solely" involving: (1) a claim concerning a covered security under certain federal securities laws; (2) a claim relating to the internal affairs or governance of a corporation or other business entity arising under the laws of the state that incorporated or organized the enterprise; or (3) a claim relating to the rights and duties, including fiduciary duties, created by the Securities Act of 1933.

14. *See e.g., Pampillonia v. RJR Nabisco, Inc.,* 138 F.3d 459, 461 (2d Cir.1998) (so holding; but noting that defendant bears heavy burden of proof on "fraudulent joinder").

15. *See, e.g., Travis v. Irby,* 326 F.3d 644, 647 (5th Cir.2003) ("Neither our circuit nor other circuits have been clear in describing the fraudulent joinder standard;" collecting cases).

16. *See, e.g., Jerome–Duncan, Inc. v. Auto-By-Tel, L.L.C.,* 176 F.3d 904 (6th Cir.1999).

17. *See, e.g., Triggs v. John Crump Toyota, Inc.,* 154 F.3d 1284, 1287 (11th Cir.1998).

18. *See, e.g., Tapscott v. MS Dealer Service Corp.,* 77 F.3d 1353, 1360 (11th Cir.1996).

19. *See, e.g., Florida Polk County v. Prison Health Servs., Inc.,* 170 F.3d 1081 (11th Cir. 1999) (applying principles of contract law to determine whether to enforce forum selection clause). *But cf., Kerobo v. Southwestern Clean Fuels, Corp.,* 285 F.3d 531, 534–35 (6th Cir. 2002) (suit in Michigan state court; parties had forum selection clause choosing California venue; held, such a clause could not prevent removal to Michigan federal court).

Joinder of "Non–Removable" Claims

Section 1441(c) governs circumstances in which many counts, including counts removable under § 1441(b) and counts that do not qualify for removal under that section, are filed in the same case. If at least one separate and independent count would qualify for federal question jurisdiction, then § 1441(c) provides that a notice of removal will cause *all* counts in the case to be removed to federal district court.[20] Removal of the entire case includes removal of counterclaims, cross-claims, and claims against third parties.

By contrast, there is no authority in § 1441(c), or anywhere else in § 1441, to remove nondiverse state claims to federal court when the basis for removal is a diverse count. Little or no authority exists on the topic, but it appears that in such circumstances the diverse claim may be removed under § 1441(b), and the nondiverse claims must remain in state court.

A possible way around this situation in some circumstances might be for the defendant to remove the diverse claim to federal court. Then, with the case pending in federal court, the defendant might file a nondiverse counterclaim (nondiverse, e.g., because it does not meet the amount in controversy) and try to sustain the federal court's supplemental jurisdiction over the nondiverse claim under 28 U.S.C.A. § 1367.

Discretion to Retain/Remand Claims

Once a multi-count case has been removed to federal district court in the manner provided by § 1441(c), the court has discretion to retain jurisdiction over the "non-removable" counts.[21] A court will retain those non-removable counts which form part of the same case or controversy as the count(s) which qualified for removal in their own right.[22] If the court chooses not to retain the non-removable counts,

20. *See, e.g., Gaming Corp. of America v. Dorsey & Whitney,* 88 F.3d 536 (8th Cir. 1996)("[T]he presence of even one federal claim gives the defendant the right to remove the entire case to federal court."). *But see Reed v. Heil Co.,* 206 F.3d 1055, 1058 (11th Cir.2000) (noting that some claims, such as those governed by § 1445(c) (barring removal of claims arising under workers' compensation laws), cannot be removed even if basis for removal is other claims falling within court's federal question jurisdiction); *In re City of Mobile,* 75 F.3d 605 (11th Cir.1996) (single accident, giving rise to both state and federal claims, does not create "separate and independent" claims within meaning of § 1441(c)).

21. *See, e.g., Justice v. Atchison, Topeka and Santa Fe Railway Co.,* 927 F.2d 503, 504 (10th Cir.1991)(remand of non-diverse state claims is within court's discretion). *But cf., Ward v. Alternative Health Delivery Systems, Inc.,* 261 F.3d 624, 626 (6th Cir.2001) (acknowledging that district court normally has discretion to remand; but "[i]f it dismisses the claim within its original jurisdiction for lack of subject matter jurisdiction . . . it *must* remand the remaining claims" [italics in original]).

22. *See, e.g., Smith v. Amedisys, Inc.,* 298 F.3d 434 (5th Cir.2002) (state and federal claims involved common allegations of sexual harassment, discrimination, and retaliation; held, district court had no discretion to remand); *Anderson v. Red River Waterway Commission,* 231 F.3d 211, 214 (5th Cir.2000) (where liability of third-party defendant is based on same operative facts as claim against defendant/third-party plaintiff, there is no separate and independent claim and district court must retain such claim). *Metro Ford Truck Sales, Inc. v. Ford Motor Co.,* 145 F.3d 320, 327 (5th Cir.1998), *cert. denied,* 525 U.S. 1068, 119 S.Ct. 798, 142 L.Ed.2d 660 (1999) ("[F]or remand to be proper, the claim remanded must be (1) a separate and independent claim or cause of action; (2) joined with a

the appropriate remedy is to remand those counts to the state court from which they were removed.[23]

Additionally, there is a modest trend in courts to permit remand under § 1441(c) of both federal and state claims if the state claims predominate.[24] Whether this view of a court's authority under § 1441(c) will prevail is currently uncertain.[25]

Suits Against Foreign States

Section 1441(d) authorizes removal of suits filed in state court against foreign countries or their agents,[26] without regard to whether the suit was based on a federal question or state law.[27]

This right to remove applies without regard to the amount in controversy, and permits removal even after the time limits of § 1446(b) have expired–at least when the party seeking removal can show cause.[28]

Foreign States—Jury Trials

In any suit where removal was based upon § 1441(d), the court must try the case without a jury.

Time

If a defendant seeks removal because a suit is against a foreign country, § 1441(d) authorizes the court to extend the provisions in § 1446(b) that normally govern time limits for filing a removal notice. However, extensions are granted only "for cause shown."

federal question; (3) otherwise non-removable; and (4) a matter in which state law predominates.").

23. *See, e.g., Ondis v. Barrows*, 538 F.2d 904, 908 (1st Cir.1976)(dismissal is inappropriate; remand is the appropriate remedy).

24. *See, e.g., Wirtz Corp. v. United Distillers & Vintners North America, Inc.*, 224 F.3d 708, 713 (7th Cir.2000) (state interest in administration of alcoholic beverage program outweighs diversity jurisdiction; reversing denial of motion to remand); *Eastus v. Blue Bell Creameries, L.P.*, 97 F.3d 100, 106 (5th Cir.1996) (collecting cases, so holding). *See Metro Ford Truck Sales, Inc. v. Ford Motor Co.*, 145 F.3d 320 (5th Cir.1998), *cert. denied*, 525 U.S. 1068, 119 S.Ct. 798, 142 L.Ed.2d 660 (1999) (permitting remand of federal claims within concurrent jurisdiction of federal and state courts; noting different result if federal court's jurisdiction is exclusive).

25. *See generally Gaming Corp. of America v. Dorsey & Whitney*, 88 F.3d 536, 542 (8th Cir. 1996) ("A district court has no discretion to remand a claim that states a federal question.").

26. *Dole Food Co. v. Patrickson*, 538 U.S. 468, 477, 123 S.Ct. 1655, 1662, 155 L.Ed.2d 643 (2003) (for a corporation to remove on ground it is instrumentality of foreign state, the foreign state must own a majority of the corporation's shares; mere control of corporation is not enough; such majority ownership must exist at time lawsuit is filed).

27. *See, e.g., Hanil Bank v. PT. Bank Negara Indonesia*, 148 F.3d 127 (2d Cir.1998)(noting removal of breach of contract claim against bank owned by Indonesian government). *See also Davis v. McCourt*, 226 F.3d 506 (6th Cir.2000) (noting that § 1441(d) authorizes removal even where count against foreign entity is third-party complaint; further, where removal occurs under § 1441(d), entire lawsuit, not merely third-party complaint against foreign entity, is removed); *Alonzi v. Budget Const. Co.*, 55 F.3d 331, 332–33 (7th Cir.1995)(noting that § 1441(d) allows removal by foreign states; also noting that under majority view, § 1441(d) permits removal of entire case, including otherwise non-removable claims against citizens of American states; but also citing contrary authority).

28. *See, e.g., Suter v. Munich Reinsurance Co.*, 223 F.3d 150, 156 (3d Cir.2000) (removal outside time limits of § 1446(b) permitted "for cause shown").

State Court Jurisdiction

Section 1441(e) permits a federal district court to hear a removed case even if the state court in which the case was originally filed lacked jurisdiction.[29] Section 1441(e) was added in December 1990, and renders obsolete prior case law on the matter. However, nothing in § 1441(e) excuses a federal court from its own obligation to satisfy federal jurisdictional requirements, which generally means that at least one count in the removed case must satisfy requirements for federal question jurisdiction or diversity jurisdiction.[30]

Venue

Section 1441(e), governing the authority of a federal court to retain a case where a state court lacked jurisdiction, does not address the additional question of venue. However, case law indicates that while a removed claim does not have to satisfy the federal venue statute, 28 U.S.C.A. § 1391, it must have satisfied the venue rules governing the state court from which it was removed.[31]

ADDITIONAL RESEARCH REFERENCES

C.J.S. Removal of Causes §§ 1–46 et seq., 52–101 et seq., 126–171 et seq., 177–226 et seq., 235–275 et seq., 297–310 et seq.

West's Key No. Digests, Removal of Cases ⚷1–120.

§ 1.17 Removal Procedure

CORE CONCEPT

Defendants eligible for removal from state court to federal district court should file a notice of removal with the appropriate federal court[1] within 30 days of receipt of the plaintiff's original pleading. Filing the notice automatically removes the case from the jurisdiction of the state court, and the federal court will make decisions as to how the case will thereafter be processed. If the federal court determines that removal

29. *See, e.g., In re Brand Name Prescription Drugs Antitrust Litig.,* 123 F.3d 599, 611 (7th Cir.1997), *cert. denied,* 522 U.S. 1153, 118 S.Ct. 1178, 140 L.Ed.2d 186 (1998) (case is removable even where state court could not hear it because case is within exclusive federal jurisdiction).

30. *See, e.g., In re CSX Transp., Inc.,* 151 F.3d 164 (4th Cir.1998), *cert. denied,* 525 U.S. 1019, 119 S.Ct. 547, 142 L.Ed.2d 455 (1998) ("While state court jurisdiction is not ordinarily a prerequisite for removability . . . jurisdiction in the district court is.").

31. *See, e.g., PT United Can Co. v. Crown Cork & Seal Co.,* 138 F.3d 65, 72 (2d Cir.1998) (so holding; citing other cases). *But see Hollis v. Florida State University,* 259 F.3d 1295, 1296 (11th Cir.2001) ("We conclude that state-law venue deficiencies cannot be the basis for dismissal of a removed action because 28 U.S.C. § 1441(e) . . . abrogated the theory of derivative jurisdiction. Upon removal the question of venue is governed by federal law, not state law, and under § 1441(a) a properly removed action necessarily fixes venue in the district where the state court action was pending." Suggesting that if defendant dislikes federal venue, motion to transfer to another division or district is appropriate).

1. *See, e.g., Global Satellite Communication Co. v. Starmill U.K. Ltd.,* 378 F.3d 1269 (11th Cir. 2004) (appropriate court is district court in district and division where case is pending).

was erroneous, the remedy is remand to the state court from which the case was originally removed.

APPLICATIONS

Contents of Notice

The notice of removal should contain a concise statement of the grounds upon which removal is based. The notice should be accompanied by copies of "all process, pleadings, and orders served upon" the defendant seeking removal.[2]

Filing Equals Removal

Removal occurs as soon as the defendant files an appropriate notice of removal with the federal district court.[3] The federal court may then make decisions on the sustainability of the removal.

Rule 11

Section 1446(a) explicitly provides that notices of removal are subject to the provisions of Rule 11, which permits the court to impose sanctions for inappropriate pleadings and motions. However, there is no rule prohibiting a party from filing more than one petition for removal, provided that each petition meets the requirements of Rule 11 and is timely.[4]

Time

In general, a defendant eligible for removal has 30 days from receipt of the plaintiff's initial pleading[5] to file a notice of removal.[6] In

2. *See, e.g., L & O Partnership No. 2 v. Aetna Casualty & Surety Co.,* 761 F.Supp. 549 (N.D.Ill. 1991). *Cf., Usatorres v. Marina Mercante Nicaraguenses, S.A.,* 768 F.2d 1285, 1286 (11th Cir. 1985)(defendant filed motion to dismiss in state court, then filed removal petition; held, defendant had no duty to file copy of motion to dismiss with removal petition, because motion was not "served upon" defendant within meaning of § 1446(a)). *See also Asociacion Nacional de Pescadores a Pequena Escala O Artesanales de Colombia v. Dow Quimica de Colombia, S.A.,* 988 F.2d 559, 565 (5th Cir.1993), *cert. denied,* 510 U.S. 1041, 114 S.Ct. 685, 126 L.Ed.2d 653 (1994)(removal petitions are more persuasive when defendant has, *inter alia,* jurisdictional facts at hand.).

3. *See, e.g., Speiser, Krause & Madole P.C. v. Ortiz,* 271 F.3d 884, 887 (9th Cir.2001) (removal is automatic upon proper filing and service of papers; thereafter, case is controlled by rules of federal district court); *Yarnevic v. Brink's, Inc.,* 102 F.3d 753, 754 (4th Cir.1996) ("A proper filing of a notice of removal immediately strips the state court of its jurisdiction.").

4. *See, e.g., Benson v. SI Handling Systems, Inc.,* 188 F.3d 780, 782 (7th Cir.1999) ("Nothing in § 1446 forecloses multiple petitions for removal." Rejecting per se rule that a party may seek removal only once).

5. *But see Gillis v. State of Louisiana,* 294 F.3d 755 (5th Cir.2002) (all defendants must consent within 30 days; but where defendant organization did not formally consent within that period because its meeting to consent occurred later, prior informally authorized consent would be ratified after passage of 30 days; held, in this exceptional circumstance, removal was effective notwithstanding formal lack of timeliness); *Delgado v. Shell Oil Co.,* 231 F.3d 165, 177 (5th Cir.2000), *cert. denied,* 532 U.S. 972, 121 S.Ct. 1603, 149 L.Ed.2d 470 (2001) (formal service of process "is not an absolute prerequisite to removal;" requirement exists that suit be commenced before removal, but defendant need only have receipt of a document, through service or otherwise, that case is eligible for removal; distinguishing *Murphy Brothers, supra*); *Addo v. Globe Life and Accident Insurance Co.,* 230 F.3d 759, 761–62 (5th Cir.2000) (post-complaint letter containing terms of settlement may be "other paper" within meaning of § 1446(b)).

cases involving multiple defendants, of course, it is possible and even likely that different defendants will be served with process on different days. That situation raises the possibility that one or more defendants might be served more than thirty days after other defendants have been served. The question that results is how to identify the appropriate point at which to measure the start of the running of the thirty days provided in § 1446. Appellate courts generally take two approaches to the issue. Some courts hold that the time begins to run when the first defendant is served.[7] Other decisions measure the time as beginning when the last defendant is served.[8] The issue has not been resolved by the Supreme Court, so at this time attorneys must consult local precedent.

"After–Acquired" Eligibility for Removal

If a case does not qualify for removal at the time of receipt of the original process on a defendant, the defendant will have 30 days to file a notice of removal from the time an amended pleading motion, order, or other paper giving notice of eligibility for removal is served.[9] However, if the basis for removal is subject matter jurisdiction based on diversity of citizenship, the period of time for "after-acquired" eligibility will normally be no more than one year after the initiation of the lawsuit.[10]

6. *Murphy Bros., Inc. v. Michetti Pipe Stringing, Inc.*, 526 U.S. 344, 119 S.Ct. 1322, 143 L.Ed.2d 448 (1999) (30 days begins to run when defendant receives either service of summons and complaint together, or receipt of complaint after service of summons; mere receipt of complaint without formal service does not start running of time; in instant case, defendant had received "courtesy copy" of complaint by fax, but 30 day time limit did not begin to run until later service).

7. *See, e.g., Getty Oil Corp. v. Insurance Co. of North America*, 841 F.2d 1254, 1262–63 (5th Cir. 1988) (in case involving multiple defendants, 30 day time limit begins to run from service of summons and complaint on first defendant served; only "exceptional circumstances" may alter this approach).

8. *See, e.g., United Computer Systems, Inc. v. AT & T Corp.*, 298 F.3d 756 (9th Cir. 2002) (lengthy discussion of "first served" rule and "last served" rule, with numerous case cites; adopting "last served" rule); *Marano Enterprises of Kansas v. Z–Teca Restaurants*, 254 F.3d 753 (8th Cir. 2001) (in case involving multiple defendants, each defendant is entitled to 30 days from service of that particular defendant). *See also Boyd v. Phoenix Funding Corp.*, 366 F.3d 524, 530–31 (7th Cir. 2004) (reporting divergence of opinion in leading treatises; holding that in situation where defendants have assigned liability to another entity "the removal statutes do not permit defendants deliberately to manipulate assignments so that the 30–day time limit found in § 1446(b) can be avoided").

9. *See, e.g., Peters v. Lincoln Electric Co.*, 285 F.3d 456, 466 (6th Cir.2002) (adopting majority rule that plaintiff's response to deposition questions may constitute an "other paper" for purposes of § 1446(b)); *Green v. R.J. Reynolds Tobacco Co.*, 274 F.3d 263, 266 (5th Cir.2001) (appellate decision in unrelated but similar case can be "order" for purposes of triggering application of second paragraph of § 1446(b); collecting cases, acknowledging that holding is minority view); *Huffman v. Saul Holdings Limited Partnership*, 194 F.3d 1072, 1078–79 (10th Cir. 1999) (adopting majority rule that for purpose of § 1446(b) a discovery deposition is treated as equivalent to receipt of "an actual written document"; combination of "petition setting out the factual premise of plaintiff's lawsuit; financial documents produced in discovery; and, most importantly, the voluntary and unequivocal testimony of [one plaintiff] that plaintiffs were seeking $300,000 in damages" gave defendant notice–no later than date of plaintiff's deposition testimony–that jurisdictional amount was satisfied); *S.W.S. Erectors, Inc. v. Infax, Inc.*, 72 F.3d 489, 494 (5th Cir.1996)(§ 1446(b) permits removal more than 30 days after service of process on defendant only in circumstances where plaintiff's "voluntary act" created right to removal; right to removal cannot be created by judicial act, such as issuance of order).

10. *Cf., e.g., In re Burns & Wilcox, Ltd.*, 54 F.3d 475, 476 n. 4 (8th Cir.1995)(noting that diversity case may not be removed if one year has elapsed since commencement of suit; but

However, in unusual cases where it would be inequitable to apply the time limit strictly, it is apparently possible to obtain an extension of time in which to seek removal.[11] It should also be noted that the time limit for § 1446(b) can be enlarged for good cause shown in cases controlled by § 1441(d) (governing removal of suits against foreign states).[12]

Congress recently enacted § 1453, which eliminated the one year time limit for removal of cases based on "after-acquired" diversity jurisdiction if the case is a class action.[13] Thus, while it is still necessary for a defendant seeking removal to do so within 30 days of notice of eligibility of removal, there is no requirement in class action lawsuits for such a defendant to have sought removal within the one year period for seeking removal in non-class action suits that are based on diversity.

Criminal Matters

Removal is also available for a narrow range of criminal actions. Section 1446(c) governs procedure in such matters, but has no relevance to removal in civil cases.

Notification to State Court and Other Parties

Section 1446(d) requires that the defendants seeking removal "promptly" notify the state court and other parties, through filing and service of copies of the notice of removal.

State Court Jurisdiction

Section 1446(d) also directs the state court, upon receipt of notice of removal, to take no further action in a removed case. The state court may only re-acquire jurisdiction if the federal court remands one or more counts.[14]

issue waived when claimant failed to raise it). *But cf. Brown v. Tokio Marine & Fire Insurance Co.*, 284 F.3d 871, 872 (8th Cir.2002), *cert. denied*, 537 U.S. 826, 123 S.Ct. 115, 154 L.Ed.2d 37 (2002) (one-year limitation does not apply to cases eligible for removal when they were filed); *Brierly v. Alusuisse Flexible Packaging, Inc.*, 184 F.3d 527 (6th Cir.1999), *cert. denied*, 528 U.S. 1076, 120 S.Ct. 790, 145 L.Ed.2d 667 (2000) (plaintiff sued two defendants on state diversity claim; after lengthy delay, second defendant was finally served; thereupon both defendants sought removal; because of delay in service of second defendant, more than one year passed before both defendants sought removal together; held, one year time limit is inapplicable to cases that were removable from their inception; time limit "applies only to those [diversity cases] that were not initially removable").

11. *See, e.g., Tedford v. Warner–Lambert Co.*, 327 F.3d 423, 428–29 (5th Cir.2003) (plaintiff's inequitable forum manipulation justifies extension of time; but noting that equitable exception is subject of substantial disagreement among various district courts).

12. *See, e.g., EIE Guam Corp. v. Long Term Credit Bank of Japan, Ltd.*, 322 F.3d 635, 649 (9th Cir.2003).

13. 28 U.S.C.A. § 1453(b). It should be noted that the exceptions created by § 1453 for class actions are themselves subject to an exception. Specifically, § 1453(d) provides that § 1453 is inapplicable to any class action "solely" involving: (1) a claim concerning a covered security under certain federal securities laws; (2) a claim relating to the internal affairs or governance of a corporation or other business entity arising under the laws of the state that incorporated or organized the enterprise; or (3) a claim relating to the rights and duties, including fiduciary duties, created by the Securities Act of 1933.

14. *See, e.g., California v. United States*, 215 F.3d 1005 (9th Cir.2000) ("The removal of an action to federal court necessarily divests state and local courts of their jurisdiction over a par-

Bond, Rule 11 and Sanctions

Until 1991, § 1446 required that a defendant seeking removal post a bond to cover the plaintiff's costs if the federal court determined that removal was inappropriate. Congress amended the removal statutes in 1991 to remove that requirement, and case law addressing the issue of bonds is obsolete. However, there are still two provisions that may provide reimbursement to a plaintiff whose case has been wrongly removed. Section 1446(a) explicitly provides that notices of removal are subject to the provisions of Federal Rule of Civil Procedure 11, which permits the court to impose sanctions for inappropriate pleadings and motions. Additionally, 28 U.S.C.A. § 1447(c) authorizes a district court that has decided to remand a case to impose costs and actual expenses, "including attorney fees," as part of an order remanding a case to a state court.[15]

Remedy for Inappropriate Removal

If the federal court determines that removal was inappropriate, it may remand part or all of the case to the state court. Dismissal is *not* an appropriate remedy.[16]

ADDITIONAL RESEARCH REFERENCES

C.J.S. Removal of Causes §§ 8, 182–230 et seq., 235–275 et seq., 297–310 et seq.

West's Key No. Digests, Removal of Cases ⚷77–120.

§ 1.17a Procedure After Removal

CORE CONCEPT

Once a case has been removed to a federal district court, 28 U.S.C.A. §§ 1447–49 provide much of the direction for decisions that the court may be required to make in the initial processing of the removed case. The areas governed by these sections include: authority

ticular dispute."); *Kansas Public Employees Retirement Sys. v. Reimer & Koger Assocs., Inc.*, 77 F.3d 1063, 1069 (8th Cir.1996), *cert. denied*, 519 U.S. 948, 117 S.Ct. 359, 136 L.Ed.2d 250 (1996) (§ 1446(d) is "express authorization to stay state court proceedings"). *But see Lawrence v. Chancery Court of Tennessee*, 188 F.3d 687, 693 (6th Cir.1999) (§ 1446(d) does not prohibit state court from taking "ministerial steps that do not affect the adjudication of the parties' dispute," such as collection of accrued costs from state-court party who signed cost bond).

15. *See, e.g., Maguire Oil Co. v. City of Houston*, 143 F.3d 205, 207 (5th Cir.1998).

16. *See, e.g., University of South Alabama v. American Tobacco Co.*, 168 F.3d 405, 411 (11th Cir.1999) ("[A] federal court must remand for lack of subject matter jurisdiction notwithstanding the presence of other motions pending before the court."); *Ondis v. Barrows*, 538 F.2d 904, 908 (1st Cir.1976) (dismissal is inappropriate; remand is appropriate remedy). *See also, Glover v. Midland Mortgage Co. of Oklahoma*, 228 B.R. 293, 294 n. 1 (N.D.Ala.1998) (comparing Federal Rule of Civil Procedure 12(h)(3) and 28 U.S.C.A. § 1447(c); noting that when jurisdiction is lacking in a case originally filed in federal district court, Rule 12 requires dismissal; however, in case removed to federal district court, failure of jurisdiction produces remand to state court where case was originally filed, as directed by 28 U.S.C.A. § 1447). *But cf. Caterpillar, Inc. v. Lewis*, 519 U.S. 61, 77, 117 S.Ct. 467, 477, 136 L.Ed.2d 437 (1996) (if district court denies motion to remand removed case, and denial of motion is subsequently found to be error on appeal, "the judgment must be vacated").

to issue orders and process; acquisition of the record of the case during the period that the case was in state court; timing of remand motions; appeals of remand decisions; and joinder after removal.

APPLICATIONS

Authority to Issue Orders and Process

Section 1447(a) supplies the district court with authority to issue orders and process necessary to bring parties within the jurisdiction of the court. This authority is supplemental to process that may already have been served under the authority of the state court before the case was removed. Section 1447(a) has been the source of very few reported decisions in the past two decades.

Obtaining Case Record

Section 1447(b) authorizes the district court to obtain all records of a removed case in either of two ways. The court may require the party who sought removal to provide such copies, or the court may, through writ of certiorari to the state court, obtain the records directly. If the district court chooses to impose the burden on the party who sought removal, a party's failure to comply may be a consideration in a decision to remand the case to state court.[1]

Timing of Motion to Remand

Section 1447(c) provides two different time limits on motions to remand cases to state court. If the ground for remand is any basis other than the federal court's lack of subject matter jurisdiction, a party seeking remand must file an appropriate motion within 30 days of the date of the petition to remove required by § 1446(a).[2] However, if the basis for seeking remand is an allegation that the federal court lacks subject matter jurisdiction over the case, § 1447(c) provides that the motion to remand may be made at any time prior to final judgment in the case.[3]

Remand *Sua Sponte*

If the federal district court notices its own lack of subject matter jurisdiction, § 1447(c) provides that the court need not wait for a motion to remand from a party. Instead, the court can and must

1. *See, e.g., Patel v. Moore,* 968 F.Supp. 587, 591 (D.Kan.1997) ("[C]ompliance with section 1446(a) does not satisfy the additional requirement authorized by section 1447(b).").

2. *See, e.g., Vasquez v. North County Transit District,* 292 F.3d 1049 (9th Cir.2002) (failure to make timely objection to erroneously removed workers' compensation claim waives right to remand); *Handelsman v. Bedford Village Associates, L.P.,* 213 F.3d 48, 50 n. 2 (2d Cir.2000) (procedural defect–in case based on diversity jurisdiction, defendant was citizen of forum state–was waived when plaintiff failed to object within 30 days of removal).

3. *Wisconsin Dep't of Corrections v. Schacht,* 524 U.S. 381, 391, 118 S.Ct. 2047, 2054, 141 L.Ed.2d 364 (1998) ("[Section 1447(c)] differentiates between removals that are defective because of lack of subject matter jurisdiction and removals that are defective for some other reason, *e.g.,* because the removal took place after relevant time limits had expired. For the latter kind of case, there must be a motion to remand no later than 30 days after the filing of the removal notice. . . .For the former kind of case, remand may take place without such a motion and at any time.").

remand the case on its own initiative. Such action must be taken if the court notices its lack of subject matter jurisdiction at any time prior to final judgment.[4]

However, if the basis for remand is not a lack of subject matter jurisdiction but only a procedural defect, it is error for the district court to remand *sua sponte*.[5]

Section 1447(c) and Non–Jurisdictional Grounds for Remand

Although lack of subject matter jurisdiction is probably the most common reason alleged for seeking remand, a number of other possibilities exist. Because these other possible grounds for remand do not address the district court's subject matter jurisdiction, motions for remand on these grounds may fall within the 30 day time limit established by § 1447(c).[6]

An example of such a ground is failure to comply with the time limits of § 1446(b), which mandates that a petition for removal must be filed within 30 days of receipt of the "pleading, motion, order or other paper" which put the defendant on notice that the case is removable. Additionally, § 1446(b) requires that if the original basis for subject matter jurisdiction is diversity of citizenship under 28 U.S.C.A. § 1332, no petition for removal is allowable if it is filed more than one year after commencement of the action. If the party seeking removal did not comply with either of these time limits when they are applicable, there is authority that the opposing party's motion to remand must be filed within the 30 day limit imposed by § 1447(c).[7]

Less certain is whether an objection to removal because one of the defendants on a state claim was a citizen of the state in which the case was filed falls within the time limit of § 1447(c). On the one hand, if the parties are diverse from one another and the amount in controversy was satisfied, the federal court would have had subject matter jurisdiction over any case originally filed in the district court. On the other hand, removal is prohibited notwithstanding the presence of diversity jurisdiction if a defendant is sued in the defendant's home state court (§ 1441(b)).[8]

4. *Id.* (Whenever the district court concludes that it lacks subject matter jurisdiction, "remand may take place without . . . a motion and at any time.").

5. *See, e.g., In re FMC Corp. Packaging Systems Division,* 208 F.3d 445, 451 (3d Cir.2000) (citing other circuit courts).

6. *Id.* (when removal is defective on grounds other than lack of subject matter jurisdiction, motion to remand must be made within 30 day time limit of § 1447(c)).

7. *See, e.g., Huffman v. Saul Holdings Limited Partnership,* 183 F.3d 1180, n. 3 (10th Cir. 1999) (although time limits of § 1446 are mandatory, defect may be waived by failing to file motion to remand within time limit of § 1447(c)).

8. *Compare, e.g., Handelsman v. Bedford Village Associates, L.P.,* 213 F.3d 48, 50 n. 2 (2d Cir.2000) (erroneous removal of case based on diversity jurisdiction where defendant was citizen of forum state; held, error was procedural defect, waived when plaintiff failed to object within 30 days of removal); *Blackburn v. United Parcel Serv., Inc.,* 179 F.3d 81 n. 3 (3d Cir.1999) (although complete diversity existed in case, removal was inappropriate because one defendant was a citizen of state in which case was filed; however, defect in removal waived when motion to remand was not made within 30 days, as provided in § 1447(c)) *with, e.g., Hurt v. Dow Chemical Co.,* 963 F.2d 1142, 1145 (8th Cir. 1992) (original jurisdiction present if plaintiff has originally filed in federal court; however,

It should also be noted that although § 1447(c) itself is held to specify only two grounds for remand (lack of subject matter jurisdiction and defects in removal procedure),[9] other grounds for remand may exist, such as an exercise of the district court's discretion to abstain from deciding a question.[10] Such grounds are certainly not jurisdictional and they also do not necessarily indicate a defect in removal procedure. In that sense, they are not specified by § 1447(c), and it is unclear whether they are subject to the 30 day time limit § 1447(c) provides for filing remand motions on grounds other than jurisdiction. However, as is discussed further below, the fact that these grounds are not specified in § 1447(c) has an impact on the ability of a party to seek review of a district court's decision to remand on such grounds.

Discretion to Impose Costs and Fees

As is discussed above, § 1446(a) imposes the signature requirements of Federal Rule of Civil Procedure 11 to notices of removal. Additionally, § 1447(c) expressly authorizes the district court, when remanding a case, to impose costs and actual expenses, "including attorney fees," where such action would be appropriate.[11]

removal authority was lacking under § 1441(b); held, plaintiff did not waive objection to removal by waiting more than 30 days to file motion to remand, because lack of removal authority under § 1441(b) should be treated as jurisdictional defect). *See also Williams v. AC Spark Plugs Division of General Motors Corp.*, 985 F.2d 783, 787 (5th Cir.1993) (removal of workers' compensation case in violation of 28 U.S.C.A. § 1445(c) is equivalent to "procedural defect" within meaning of § 1447(c) and is therefore not subject to 30 day time limit of § 1447(c)).

9. *Quackenbush v. Allstate Ins. Co.*, 517 U.S. 706, 712, 116 S.Ct. 1712, 1718, 135 L.Ed.2d 1 (1996) (section 1447(c) specifies only two grounds for remand; however, other grounds not specified in § 1447(c) may conceivably arise).

10. As an example, consider the effect of 28 U.S.C.A. § 1441(c). Section 1441(c) provides that if the basis for removal of a case is the presence of a separate and independent federal question, as defined in 28 U.S.C.A. § 1331, the entire case, including "otherwise non-removable claims" may be removed at the same time. Presumably these non-removable claims would typically be claims where diversity jurisdiction was lacking or, perhaps, situations in which the parties were diverse but the defendant had been sued in a state court of a state in which the defendant is a citizen. Section 1441(c) provides not only that such claims may be removed, but also that the district court shall decide whether to retain or remand such "non-removable" claims in which state law predominates. The meaning of § 1441(c), when considered in light of § 1447(c), is that certain claims may be remanded to state court even when there was no defect in removal procedure and the requirement of federal subject matter jurisdiction is satisfied (assuming, *e.g.*, that non-diverse state claims fall within the supplemental jurisdiction of the district court under 28 U.S.C.A. § 1367). A district court's decision to remand non-diverse supplemental claims is not subject to the ban on judicial review established by § 1447(d), *see, e.g., Eastus v. Blue Bell Creameries, L.P.*, 97 F.3d 100, 103 (5th Cir.1996) (§ 1447(d) does not bar review of remand based on district court's discretionary authority under § 1441(c)), but it is unclear whether the time limit of § 1447(c) is applicable to a motion to remand on such discretionary grounds.

11. *See, e.g., Garbie v. DaimlerChrysler Corp.*, 211 F.3d 407, 410–11 (7th Cir.2000) (bad faith is not a necessary element of § 1447(c), though bad faith in defendant's removal petition may strengthen the position of plaintiff seeking reimbursement; moreover, such reimbursement may include expenses on appeal); *Balcorta v. Twentieth Century–Fox Film Corp.*, 208 F.3d 1102, 1105–06 n. 6 (9th Cir.2000) (award of attorney's fees for erroneous removal is permissible simply because removal "was wrong as a matter of law"; no need to find bad faith by defendant; also, fact that removal was "fairly supportable" is no defense to imposition of fees, although district court has discretion not to award fees in such circumstances). *But see Waste Control Specialists, LLC v. Envirocare of Texas, Inc.*, 207 F.3d 225, 225 (5th Cir.2000), *cert. denied*, 531 U.S. 956, 121 S.Ct. 377, 148 L.Ed.2d 291 (2000) (standard for attorney's fees under § 1447(c) is whether removal was "objectively

Notice of Remand: Termination of Federal Jurisdiction

When the district court decides to remand a case to state court, § 1447(c) directs the clerk of court to send a certified copy of the notice of remand to the clerk of the relevant state court. This mailing has significance beyond its value as notification to the state court. In addition to fulfilling the purpose of notice, it is generally held that mailing of the notice of remand divests the federal district court of its jurisdiction over the case.[12] At that point, jurisdiction has been returned to the state court.

Appeal or Reconsideration of Remand Order

Section 1447(d) governs the circumstances in which a district court's decision to remand a case to state court may be reviewed, either by that court or upon appeal. It will probably come as a significant surprise to many attorneys to learn that, subject to fairly narrow exceptions, remand orders are not reviewable by any court whatsoever.[13] In fact, § 1447(d) provides that subject to an exception, once remand orders are certified to the appropriate state court, they "are not reviewable on appeal or otherwise." The "or otherwise" provision has been construed to mean that even the district court may not look again at a final remand order, because the effect of entering the order (as is discussed immediately above) divests the district court of jurisdiction.[14]

reasonable"). *Cf., e.g., Wisconsin v. Hotline Industries, Inc.,* 236 F.3d 363, 364 (7th Cir.2000) (recovery for expenditures on salaried government attorneys is limited to "actual outlays," not prevailing market rates for private attorneys); *Maguire Oil Co. v. City of Houston,* 143 F.3d 205, 209 (5th Cir.1998) (discretion to impose sanctions under § 1447(c) for inappropriate removal should take into account any responsibility plaintiff may bear for case's period of time in district court). *But see Circle Industries, USA, Inc. v. Parke Construction Group, Inc.,* 183 F.3d 105, 109 (2d Cir.1999), *cert. denied,* 528 U.S. 1062, 120 S.Ct. 616, 145 L.Ed.2d 510 (1999) (§ 1447(c) does not authorize award of fees if defendant successfully opposes remand; fee award possible under § 1447(c) only if remand granted).

12. *See, e.g., Arnold v. Garlock, Inc.,* 278 F.3d 426, 438 (5th Cir.2001) ("Once the remand order is certified and mailed ... the matter remanded is removed from federal jurisdiction."); *McClelland v. Gronwaldt,* 155 F.3d 507, 513 n. 15 (5th Cir.1998).

13. *See, e.g., Smith v. American States Preferred Insurance Co.,* 249 F.3d 812, 813 (8th Cir.2001) ("The remand order must stand whether it is erroneous or not."); *Snodgrass v. Provident Life & Accident Ins. Co.,* 147 F.3d 1163, 1165 (9th Cir.1998) ("Ordinarily, a district court's order remanding a case to the state court in which it was originally filed is not reviewable."). *See also Horton v. Board of County Commissioners of Flagler County,* 202 F.3d 1297, 1302 (11th Cir.2000) (believing that district court erred in remanding case to state court on ripeness or exhaustion grounds, but noting that § 1447(d) precludes review of remand; expressly acknowledging that appellate court's view is therefore dicta). *See also Things Remembered, Inc. v. Petrarca,* 516 U.S. 124, 116 S.Ct. 494, 133 L.Ed.2d 461 (1995) (§ 1447(d)'s proscription on review also applies to bankruptcy cases; holding § 1447(d) applicable to 28 U.S.C.A. § 1452, governing remand of federal bankruptcy case to state court). *But see Xiong v. Minnesota,* 195 F.3d 424, 426 (8th Cir.1999) (district court ignored clear circuit court precedent in remanding on ground of lack of jurisdiction; thus, "there was simply no jurisdictional question" to be resolved in district court, and circuit court could hear appeal of remand). *Cf., Bauer v. Transitional School District of St. Louis,* 255 F.3d 478 (8th Cir.2001) (confining *Xiong, supra,* to situations in which "a district court patently ignores governing precedent").

14. *See, e.g., Doe v. American Red Cross,* 14 F.3d 196, 199 (3d Cir.1993) ("Courts have construed Section 1447(d) as prohibiting appeals of remand orders as well as reviews by district courts of their own remands based on the same grounds as the initial removals."); *Seedman v. United States District Court for the Central District of California,* 837 F.2d 413, 414 (9th Cir.

Further, if this prohibition on review of a certified remand order is applicable, it usually acts as a bar to a second effort at removal by the same parties on similar grounds.[15]

Exceptions to § 1447(d)

The impact of the prohibition in § 1447(d) on review of a certified remand order is difficult to overstate. Moreover, the exceptions to the general rule of § 1447(d) are varied.[16] The most important of these exceptions are discussed immediately below.

(1) *Statutory Exception:* Section 1447(d) expressly provides that if the original ground for removal was found in § 1443 (removal of civil rights cases), the prohibition on review of the remand order found in § 1447(d) does not apply.[17]

(2) *Remand Not Based on § 1447(c):* Section 1447(c), discussed above, identifies two grounds for remanding removed cases: defects in removal procedure, and lack of federal subject matter jurisdiction.[18] It appears settled that when the district court has remanded a case based on either of these grounds, § 1447(d) prohibits review of the decision.[19] However, when the ground

1988) (per curiam) (Section 1447(d) "has been universally construed to preclude not only appellate review but also reconsideration by the district court. Once a district court certifies a remand order to state court it is divested of jurisdiction and can take no further action on the case."). This result still applies in the context of statutes of limitations. *Jinks v. Richland County,* 538 U.S. 456, 123 S.Ct. 1667, 155 L.Ed.2d 631 (2003) (dicta) ("For *Erie* purposes ... statutes of limitation are treated as substantive;" citing *Guaranty Trust*). *But see Roe v. O'Donohue,* 38 F.3d 298, 301 (7th Cir.1994) (noting that Northern District of Illinois "automatically delays remands to afford time for reconsideration").

15. *See, e.g., Hunt v. Acromed Corp.,* 961 F.2d 1079, 1081 (3d Cir.1992) (court may not reconsider remand through device of second removal effort based on same reasoning as original removal effort). *But cf., Benson v. SI Handling Systems, Inc.,* 188 F.3d 780, 783 (7th Cir.1999) (second effort to remove not prohibited if allegations of jurisdictional facts had changed after initial remand).

16. *See generally Adkins v. Illinois Central Railroad Co.,* 326 F.3d 828, 831 (7th Cir.2003) ("The naïve reader might think that [§ 1447(d)] meant no appellate consideration by appeal, by writ of mandamus, or by any other device that lawyers might serve up, but that reader would be wrong.").

17. *See, e.g., First Union Mortgage Corp. v. Smith,* 229 F.3d 992, 994 (10th Cir.2000) (remand where removal was based on § 1443 does not fit within scope of § 1447(d) and may therefore be reviewed by circuit court). *Cf., Borneman v. United States,* 213 F.3d 819, 826 (4th Cir. 2000), *cert. denied,* 531 U.S. 1070, 121 S.Ct. 759, 148 L.Ed.2d 661 (2001) (§ 1447(d) does not bar review of remand order where removal occurred after Attorney General certified, pursuant to 28 U.S.C.A. § 2679(d)(2), that government employee's action fell within scope of employment; "more specific statute" such as § 2679(d)(2) creates exception to § 1447(d)).

18. *Quackenbush v. Allstate Ins. Co.,* 517 U.S. 706, 712, 116 S.Ct. 1712, 1718, 135 L.Ed.2d 1 (1996).

19. *See, e.g., Webb v. B.C. Rogers Poultry, Inc.,* 174 F.3d 697, 700 (5th Cir.1999), *cert. denied,* 528 U.S. 964, 120 S.Ct. 399, 145 L.Ed.2d 311 (1999) ("[I]n 28 U.S.C. § 1447(d), Congress denied us jurisdiction over remands pursuant to 28 U.S.C. § 1447(c), which requires a district court to remand if it lacks subject matter jurisdiction or if the removal was defective."). *But see Heaton v. Monogram Credit Card Bank of Georgia,* 297 F.3d 416 (5th Cir.2002) (remand based on lack of jurisdiction is normally not appealable, but 12 U.S.C. § 1819(b)(2)(C) creates exception to § 1447(d) for Federal Deposit Insurance Corporation); *Poore v. American–Amicable Life Insurance Co.,* 218 F.3d 1287, 1291 (11th Cir.2000) (notwithstanding § 1447(d), finding of lack of subject matter jurisdiction was reviewable where district court exceeded its authority by erroneously relying on post-removal amendment to complaint); *Carr v. American Red Cross,* 17 F.3d 671, 680 (3d Cir.1994) (district court dis-

for remand falls outside the scope of §§ 1443 and 1447(c), review of the remand decision is possible either in the district court that granted it or upon appellate review.[20] Examples of such grounds for remand that have been subjected to review include: a district court's decision to abstain from deciding state questions;[21] a *sua sponte* remand by the district court based only on a procedural defect in removal (not a defect in subject matter jurisdiction);[22] a remand based on the discretionary jurisdiction of the Declaratory Judgment Act;[23] a magistrate judge's remand order;[24] a remand based on the district court's discretionary authority under § 1441(c);[25] a remand based not upon jurisdiction as it existed at the time of removal, but upon some event relating to jurisdiction that arose after removal had occurred;[26] a discretionary remand of claims within a district

missed cross-claim against one defendant and remanded remainder of case on jurisdictional grounds; held, bar to appellate review of jurisdictionally motivated remand did not apply because district court's dismissal of cross-claim meant that cross-claim would not be heard in state court; thus, where that order triggered the removal, both the dismissal and the remand must be subject to appellate review).

20. *Quackenbush v. Allstate Ins. Co.,* 517 U.S. 706, 712, 116 S.Ct. 1712, 1718, 135 L.Ed.2d 1 (1996). *See also, e.g., City of Tucson v. U.S. West Communications, Inc.,* 284 F.3d 1128, 1131 (9th Cir.2002) ("[I]t is clear that non-jurisdictional, discretionary remands are not barred from appellate review."); *In re CSX Transp., Inc.,* 151 F.3d 164, 167 (4th Cir.), *cert. denied,* 525 U.S. 1019, 119 S.Ct. 547, 142 L.Ed.2d 455 (1998) (citing Supreme Court holding that "§ 1447(d) only restricted appellate review of remand orders based on § 1447(c)–a provision addressing remands where a removal was improvident or the district court was without subject matter jurisdiction"); *Snodgrass v. Provident Life & Accident Ins. Co.,* 147 F.3d 1163, 1165 (9th Cir.1998) ("'Exceptional' remand orders, entered pursuant to some doctrine or authority other than § 1447(c), are not subject to § 1447(d)'s prohibition.").

21. *See, e.g., Carvel v. Thomas & Agnes Carvel Foundation,* 188 F.3d 83, 86 (2d Cir.1999) (remand on grounds of abstention based on comity among courts is reviewable, because issues are not jurisdictional); *Webb v. B.C. Rogers Poultry, Inc.,* 174 F.3d 697, 700 (5th Cir.), *cert. denied,* 528 U.S. 964, 120 S.Ct. 399, 145 L.Ed.2d 311 (1999) (§ 1447(d) has no impact on appellate court's authority to review district court's possible abuse of discretion in remanding on abstention grounds).

22. *See, e.g., Whole Health Chiropractic & Wellness, Inc. v. Humana Medical Plan, Inc.,* 254 F.3d 1317 (11th Cir.2001) (noting that all circuits addressing this issue agree).

23. *See, e.g., Snodgrass v. Provident Life & Accident Ins. Co.,* 147 F.3d 1163, 1165 (9th Cir. 1998). *See also Long v. Bando Manufacturing of America, Inc.,* 201 F.3d 754, 758 (6th Cir.2000) (remand of claims within supplemental jurisdiction of district court was within discretion of court and was therefore not jurisdictional; thus, remand was reviewable); *Xiong v. Minnesota,* 195 F.3d 424, 426 (8th Cir.1999) (district court ignored clear circuit court precedent in remanding on ground of lack of jurisdiction; thus, "there was simply no jurisdictional question" to be resolved in district court, and circuit court could hear appeal of remand).

24. *See, e.g., Vogel v. U.S. Office Products Co.,* 258 F.3d 509, 517–18 (6th Cir.2001) (remand order is dispositive matter, which magistrate judge cannot enter; instead, magistrate judge must submit findings and recommendations to district judge for review and approval; thus, § 1447(d)'s prohibition on appellate review of remand order does not apply to magistrate judge's attempted remand order, which itself is invalid and subject to review by both district court and appellate court; noting some disagreement, collecting cases).

25. *See, e.g., Niehaus v. Greyhound Lines, Inc.,* 173 F.3d 1207, 1210 (9th Cir.), *cert. denied,* 528 U.S. 986, 120 S.Ct. 445, 145 L.Ed.2d 362 (1999) (asserting authority to review district court's remand of pendant state claims); *Eastus v. Blue Bell Creameries, L.P.,* 97 F.3d 100, 103 (5th Cir.1996).

26. *See, e.g., First National Bank of Pulaski v. Curry,* 301 F.3d 456, 460 (6th Cir.2002) ("[A] remand order is reviewable . . . when the district court concludes that the action was properly removed but that the court lost subject matter

court's supplemental jurisdiction under 28 U.S.C.A. § 1367(c);[27] situations where the Supreme Court has clarified a party's right to remove in the period between the original remand decision and a party's second attempt to remove;[28] circumstances in which, if a federal court did not review an order that determines a claim for attorney fees, no court would be able to review it because the state court would lack jurisdiction to do so;[29] a remand based on defendants' waiver of their arbitration rights;[30] an erroneous holding that multiple efforts to remove are barred even where changed allegations of fact demonstrate that subject matter jurisdiction is now satisfied;[31] a remand order issued after the district judge erroneously refused to recuse himself;[32] and a remand granted as enforcement of a valid forum selection clause.[33] Finally, the circuit court may properly look at the "objective merits" of the remand order to determine the appropriateness of an award of costs and fees under § 1447(c).[34] As these examples indicate, however, the

jurisdiction at some point post-removal;" citing example of remand of state claims after federal claims were dismissed in case based on federal question jurisdiction).

27. *See, e.g., Green v. Ameritrade, Inc.,* 279 F.3d 590, 595 (8th Cir.2002) (remand based on § 1367(c) is appealable); *In re U.S. Healthcare, Inc.,* 193 F.3d 151, 158–59 (3d Cir.1999), *cert. denied,* 530 U.S. 1242, 120 S.Ct. 2687, 147 L.Ed.2d 960 (2000) (remand of supplemental claims under discretionary provision of 28 U.S.C.A. § 1367(c)(3) is reviewable; contrary result if remand had been ordered under § 1447(c)). *But see Heaton v. Monogram Credit Card Bank of Georgia,* 231 F.3d 994, 997 (5th Cir.2000), *cert. denied,* 533 U.S. 915, 121 S.Ct. 2520, 150 L.Ed.2d 693 (2001) (party's allegation that true basis for remand was § 1367(c)(3), not district court's stated reason that subject matter jurisdiction was lacking, is not reviewable).

28. *See, e.g., Doe v. American Red Cross,* 14 F.3d 196 (3d Cir.1993) (Red Cross had attempted to remove, but district court remanded; after Supreme Court upheld right of Red Cross to remove in unrelated case, appellate court approved second effort at removal in instant case).

29. *See, e.g., Garbie v. DaimlerChrysler Corp.,* 211 F.3d 407, 409 (7th Cir.2000) (award of attorney's fees for wrongful removal is "independently appealable order"); *K.V. Mart Co. v. United Food & Commercial Workers Int'l Union, Local 324,* 173 F.3d 1221, 1223 (9th Cir.), *cert. denied,* 528 U.S. 872, 120 S.Ct. 176, 145 L.Ed.2d 148 (1999).

30. *See, e.g., Restoration Preservation Masonry, Inc. v. Grove Europe, Ltd.,* 325 F.3d 54, 59 (1st Cir.2003) (appellate court is not engaging in prohibited review of jurisdictional issue where its review of waiver of arbitration may be made separately from jurisdiction).

31. *See, e.g., Benson v. SI Handling Systems, Inc.,* 188 F.3d 780, 783 (7th Cir.1999) (§ 1447(d) does not bar review of remand of second effort to remove–on second effort district court acknowledged that subject matter jurisdiction was now satisfied, but remanded on ground that multiple efforts to remove are not permitted).

32. *See, e.g., Republic of Panama v. American Tobacco Co., Inc.,* 217 F.3d 343, 345–46 (5th Cir.2000) (remand order that was issued after district judge denied recusal motion may technically be insulated from review by § 1447(d); however, when recusal was appropriate, erroneous failure to recuse means that all orders issued after that failure should be vacated; in such circumstances, vacating remand order is " 'ministerial task' unrelated to the remand itself, and thus not prohibited by § 1447(d)").

33. *See, e.g., Global Satellite Communication Co. v. Starmill U.K. Ltd.,* 378 F.3d 1269 (11th Cir. 2004) ("§ 1447(d) does not bar review of remand order based upon a forum selection clause"); *Autoridad de Energia Electrica de Puerto Rico V. Ericsson, Inc.,* 201 F.3d 15, 16 (1st Cir.2000).

34. *See, e.g., Dahl v. Rosenfeld,* 316 F.3d 1074, 1079 (9th Cir.2003) (although remand was error that cannot be reversed, award of attorneys' fees based on such error is reviewable and may be reversed); *Roxbury Condominium Assocation, Inc. v. Anthony S. Cupo Agency,* 316 F.3d 224, 227 (3d Cir.2003) (when court examines attorney's fees, it may not reverse remand order but it may evaluate merits of order to help

exceptions to the general rule that remand orders are not reviewable are themselves fairly limited. In particular, remands on the grounds of defects in removal procedure or lack of subject matter jurisdiction remain almost entirely beyond the scope of any review, even if they are mixed with considerations that appear to fall outside the scope of the prohibition of § 1447(d).[35]

It should be noted that *denial* of remand does not implicate § 1447(d). Thus, such a denial is reviewable on appeal.[36]

New Exception: Appeal of Grant or Denial of Remand in Class Action Cases

Congress recently created an exception to the general rule that, pursuant to § 1447(d), remand of a case removed from state court is not appealable. Pursuant to 28 U.S.C.A. § 1453(c), in a case involving class action litigation, district court decisions granting or denying remand may be appealed to the appropriate court of appeals. Such an appeal must be made within seven days of entry of the original order.[37]

The appellate court must decide such an appeal within 60 days of the filing of the appeal,[38] unless one of two circumstances arises. First, the time may be extended for any amount of time if all parties consent to the extension.[39] Alternatively, the time may be extended for up to ten days, for good cause shown.[40] If the appellate court does not act within the specified time limits, including any applicable extensions, the appeal is automatically denied.[41]

Joinder After Removal

If a district court retains jurisdiction of a removed case, § 1447(e) vests the court with considerable discretion to determine whether to permit joinder of additional parties. This discretion includes authority to join parties whose participation in the case destroys subject matter jurisdiction.[42] However, if such non-diverse parties are joined, the court

determine whether fee award is appropriate); *Stuart v. UNUM Life Insurance Co. of America,* 217 F.3d 1145, 1148 (9th Cir.2000) (acknowledging, however, that remand order itself may not be reviewed with any view to reversing it).

35. *See, e.g., Yakama Indian Nation v. State of Washington Department of Revenue,* 176 F.3d 1241 (9th Cir.1999), *cert. denied,* 528 U.S. 1116, 120 S.Ct. 935, 145 L.Ed.2d 813 (2000) (treating remand order based primarily, but not entirely, on jurisdictional issues as not reviewable). *But cf. In re U.S. Healthcare,* 159 F.3d 142, 146 (3d Cir.1998) (where magistrate judge issues remand order and lacks authority to do so under § 1447(c), prohibitions on review under § 1447(d) do not apply).

36. *See, e.g., Bracken v. Matgouranis,* 296 F.3d 160 (3d Cir.2002) ("[A]ppellate review of District Court orders denying remand is not prohibited.").

37. 28 U.S.C.A. § 1453(c)(1). It should be noted that the exceptions created by § 1453 are themselves subject to an exception. Specifically, § 1453(d) provides that § 1453 is inapplicable to any class action "solely" involving: (1) a claim concerning a covered security under certain federal securities laws; (2) a claim relating to the internal affairs or governance of a corporation or other business entity arising under the laws of the state that incorporated or organized the enterprise; or (3) a claim relating to the rights and duties, including fiduciary duties, created by the Securities Act of 1933.

38. 28 U.S.C.A. § 1453(c)(2).

39. 28 U.S.C.A. § 1453(c)(3)(A).

40. 28 U.S.C.A. § 1453(c)(3)(B).

41. 28 U.S.C.A. § 1453(c)(4).

42. *Cf., Kabakjian v. United States,* 267 F.3d 208, 212 (3d Cir.2001) (§ 1447(e) is exception to

must remand the case to state court. In other words, the district court has discretion to refuse to join parties whose presence destroys subject matter jurisdiction.[43] If, on the other hand, such parties are joined, the court may not retain the case, and must remand because it lacks jurisdiction.[44]

Appellate Review of Remand Pursuant to § 1447(e)

As has been discussed earlier, § 1447(d) often prevents appellate review of a district court's decision under § 1447(c) to remand a case to state court based on lack of subject matter jurisdiction. A question that remains is whether a remand order pursuant to § 1447(e) is subject to the same limitations on review. To this date it appears that a § 1447(e) decision to remand based on lack of subject matter jurisdiction is similarly non-reviewable.[45] It should be noted, however, that when a district court decides to retain a case and *not* remand under § 1447(e), that decision is reviewable.[46]

Serving Defendants After Removal Has Occurred

It is possible that in a case involving several defendants, the first defendant served with process will be eligible to petition for removal. Such a defendant might promptly seek removal in order to avoid the time limit on removal petitions (30 days from service) established in § 1446. That might mean that some defendants remain unserved after removal. To correct that situation, 28 U.S.C.A. § 1448 addresses two points. First, § 1448 expressly authorizes the district court to permit

general rule, particularly applicable to diversity cases, that jurisdiction is determined at time of filing); *Ryan ex rel. Ryan v. Schneider National Carriers, Inc.,* 263 F.3d 816, 819 (8th Cir.2001) ("In the case of a removed action diversity must exist both when the state petition is filed and when the petition for removal is filed.").

43. *See, e.g., Mayes v. Rapoport,* 198 F.3d 457, 462 (4th Cir.1999) (where plaintiff joined new non-diverse defendant without leave of court (using provision of Rule 15(a) permitting plaintiff one amended complaint as of right), district court still retains authority under § 1447(e) to reject joinder of new defendant; where purpose of joinder is to defeat diversity jurisdiction, decision to reject joinder is within court's discretion); *Newcombe v. Adolf Coors Co.,* 157 F.3d 686, 691 (9th Cir.1998) (affirming district court's decision not to join non-diverse party under § 1447(e)).

44. *See, e.g., Mayes v. Rapoport,* 198 F.3d 457, 461 (4th Cir.1999) ("[T]he statute does not allow a district court to retain jurisdiction once it permits a nondiverse defendant to be joined in the case."); *Ingram v. CSX Transp., Inc.,* 146 F.3d 858, 863 (11th Cir.1998) ("Because § 1447(e) was applicable here, the district court was left with only two options: (1) deny joinder; or (2) permit joinder and remand [the] case to state court. The district court chose to permit the diversity-destroying joinder and, as a result, it should have remanded this action to [state] court.").

45. *See, e.g., Stevens v. Brink's Home Security, Inc.,* 378 F.3d 944 (9th Cir. 2004) (applying proscription of § 1447(d) to remand under § 1447(e)); *In re Florida Wire and Cable Co.,* 102 F.3d 866, 868–69 (7th Cir. 1996) (no jurisdiction to review, by mandamus or otherwise); *Washington Suburban Sanitary Commissiion v. CRS/Sirrine, Inc.,* 917 F.2d 834, 836 n. 5 (4th Cir. 1990) (remand under § 1447(e) should be treated similarly to remand under § 1447(c)–no appellate review of remand based on lack of subject matter jurisdiction).

46. *See, e.g., Ingram v. CSX Transportation, Inc.,* 146 F.3d 858, 863 (11th Cir. 1998) ("Because § 1447(e) was applicable here, the district court was left with only two options: (1) deny joinder; or (2) permit joinder and remand [the] case to state court. The district court chose to permit the diversity-destroying joinder and, as a result, it should have remanded this action to [state] court."). *Cf., Roche v. Lincoln Property Co.,* 373 F.3d 610, 613 (4th Cir. 2004) (denial of remand is reviewed *de novo*).

completion of service initiated in the state proceeding or to issue its own service on unserved defendants.[47] Second, once such defendants have been served, § 1448 permits them to make a decision either to challenge the removal by seeking remand or to accept the removal that has already occurred.[48] In establishing this potential right for later-served defendants to seek remand or removal, § 1448 does not affect in any way whatever rights a plaintiff might have to file a motion to remand.[49]

Failure of State Court to Supply Record

In the unusual circumstance where a state court does not supply the federal court with the record of proceedings that occurred before the case was removed, 28 U.S.C.A. § 1449 provides the district court with authority to re-create the record "by affidavit or otherwise." Such authority under § 1449 exists only where the state court's failure to provide the record is inappropriate. If, for example, the party seeking use of the record failed to pay appropriate legal fees to the state court, a district court would not have authority under § 1449 to re-create the record. Section 1449 has not been the subject of significant reported precedent in the past two decades.

47. *Murphy Bros., Inc. v. Michetti Pipe Stringing, Inc.,* 526 U.S. 344, 354, 119 S.Ct. 1322, 1329, 143 L.Ed.2d 448, n. 6 (1999) ("[Section 1448] allows the plaintiff to serve an unserved defendant or to perfect flawed service once the action has been removed.").

48. *Id.* (second paragraph of § 1448 "explicitly reserves the unserved defendant's right to take action (move to remand) after service is perfected"). *See also, e.g., McKinney v. Board of Trustees of Mayland Community College,* 955 F.2d 924, 926 n. 3 (4th Cir.1992) (if second defendant is served more than 30 days after first defendant is served, the first defendant can file for, and obtain, removal, and the second defendant can use authority of § 1448 to seek remand); *Getty Oil Corp. v. Insurance Co. of North America,* 841 F.2d 1254, 1263 (5th Cir.1988) ("[I]f a removal petition is filed by a served defendant and another defendant is served after the case is thus removed, the latter defendant may still either accept the removal or exercise its right to choose the state forum by making a motion to remand.").

49. *See, e.g., Lewis v. Rego Co.,* 757 F.2d 66, 69 (3d Cir.1985) ("The right which the statute gives to such a defendant to move to remand the case confers no rights upon a plaintiff.").

*

PART II

The *Erie* Doctrine

I. THE PROBLEM

Federal district courts are sometimes called upon to hear state law disputes—that is, disputes arising under a state's constitution, statutes, or common law, rather than under federal law. The two most frequent circumstances when federal courts hear state disputes arise when the court's jurisdiction is based on diversity of citizenship[1] or supplemental jurisdiction.[2] When a federal court is confronted with a state law dispute, what substantive law should it apply: federal law or state law? In adjudicating state law disputes, should federal or state procedural rules apply? Efforts to determine when federal or state substantive or procedural law applies have bewitched federal courts almost since the founding of the Republic.

Questions of the subject matter jurisdiction of federal district courts over state causes of action (that is, when federal courts are even entitled to hear state claims) are difficult enough in their own right. However, even after jurisdictional questions are resolved, a party's ability to file a state cause of action in a federal district court gives rise to another set of difficult questions, going to the law that the court should apply to the state claim. As will become evident below, the answers to such questions are still a source of some uncertainty. For that reason alone, it is important not to make the investigation of this problem more difficult than it needs to be.

With that consideration in mind, it should be clear at the outset that the question of identifying the appropriate law a federal district court should apply to a state cause of action is not a matter of jurisdiction. Generally, before a court reaches this question, usually it will have addressed and resolved jurisdictional issues in the case. In other words, if the court lacks jurisdiction to hear the case, normally it will dismiss the action. When that happens, the court need not concern itself with identifying the law that would apply if the court could hear the case. Therefore, the court usually will address questions of the appropriate law to apply to a case only after determining that the court has jurisdiction to hear the claims.[3]

II. THE RULES OF DECISION ACT: *SWIFT V. TYSON*[4]

More than 200 years ago Congress addressed the question of the law that should apply when a federal court, exercising its diversity jurisdiction, heard a state claim. Through the Rules of Decision Act,[5] Congress directed that in such cases, federal trial courts should apply applicable state law.

1. 28 U.S.C.A. § 1332.

2. 28 U.S.C.A. § 1367.

3. It sometimes happens that a court may take an objection to its jurisdiction under advisement and render a decision only after hearing other portions of the case. This approach is an exception to the more typical practice. Moreover, it means that at least tentatively the court has assumed that it possesses jurisdiction to hear the case, subject to the possibility of a different decision later.

4. 41 U.S. (16 Pet.), 1, 10 L.Ed. 865 (1842).

5. 28 U.S.C.A. § 1652.

The Rules of Decision Act might have seemed to close the matter, but instead the Act proved to be only the opening chapter in a continuing legal saga. The next event was the decision of the Supreme Court in *Swift v. Tyson*. The most important result of *Swift* was a construction of the Rules of Decision Act that seemed to strain the letter of the law. In essence, the Supreme Court held that when federal trial courts heard most state claims under their diversity jurisdiction, they would not be bound by otherwise applicable state common law. Instead, the federal courts would be free to develop, case by case, their own precedent (federal general common law) on matters that, at first glance, would seem to have been reserved to the states.[6]

Swift made two important exceptions to the general rule that federal courts hearing diversity cases need not defer to state law. First, where state legislatures had enacted statutes, the statutes controlled (not federal common law). Second, if the matter before the court related to issues of real property, state law controlled even if the state law was not in a statute but was developed as common law.[7] Otherwise, federal common law—more precisely, federal general common law, as this particular body of law came to be called—applied, even where it was different from the common law that a state court hearing the same case might have applied.

The policy behind *Swift* was driven primarily by a desire to create a body of common law that would apply in a more or less uniform fashion across all the states. The Supreme Court hoped that as federal courts developed federal general common law, it would not only be uniform in all the states, but would also serve as a model common law for the states to adopt. In what way federal general common law would help unite the various state judicial systems with each other and with the federal judiciary.

III. CRITICISMS OF *SWIFT*

The *Swift* doctrine lived a long time, but it appears never to have enjoyed the success that the Supreme Court envisioned. Over a period of decades, the scope of the exceptions to the use of federal general common law—particularly the exception for matters relating to real estate and other local questions—remained a source of great uncertainty.[8] Even more important, the Supreme Court's expectation that state courts would adjust their common law to conform to federal general common law was never substantially fulfilled.[9]

The failure to build a uniform body of common law addressing state law questions led to one practice that the Supreme Court later found especially undesirable. In the numerous circumstances in which individual state courts adhered to their own common law that produced different litigation results than that produced by federal general common law, lawyers filing claims could often choose between the more favorable of two bodies of law for their clients. For example, if the cause of action arose under state law, and the case could be filed in either a federal court under diversity jurisdiction or in a state court, wise

6. *Swift*, 41 U.S. at 12–13.

7. *Id.* at 18.

8. *Erie R.R. Co. v. Tompkins*, 304 U.S. 64, 73, 58 S.Ct. 817, 820, 82 L.Ed. 1188 (1938) (The "impossibility of discerning a satisfactory line of demarcation between the province of general law and that of local law developed a new well of uncertainties.").

9. *Id.* (noting "persistence" of state courts in developing their own unique common law).

lawyers would examine both federal general common law and state common law, and choose the court that used the law most favorable to their particular clients.

This practice of forum shopping could also arise in contexts outside the area of the current discussion, but it was clear that *Swift* had opened up an additional range of possibilities for forum shopping. The practice of using *Swift* to shop for the best available law was, of course, an opportunity for plaintiffs (who normally make the first choice of court by filing a case there), but less so for parties who had to defend against claims.

Ultimately, concerns about forum shopping and other perceived shortcomings of *Swift* caused the Supreme Court to re-examine the foundations of its own approach. When it did so, the result was to abolish the entrenched doctrine of *Swift* and replace it with a very different approach.

IV. THE NEW AGE: *ERIE R.R. CO. v. TOMPKINS*[10]

The current approach to identifying the proper law to apply to a state cause of action in a federal court[11] is based on the *Erie* doctrine. *Erie* rests on two important premises: (1) a claimant should not be encouraged to shop for a federal forum because doing so might result in application of federal law that would affect the outcome of the case; and (2) federal courts hearing state claims lack Constitutional authority to create common law independent of the law that state courts would apply to those claims. Thus, the established approach prior to *Erie*, which permitted federal courts to create so-called "federal general common law" that might be at odds with state law, was unconstitutional.

The case arose out of an injury that Tompkins suffered while walking alongside a railroad track. When Tompkins sued, the possibility of recovery rested on a determination of his legal status while he was walking on what was clearly railroad property. Under state common law, Tompkins was a trespasser, to whom the railroad owed at most a minimal duty of care. If state law was applied, Tompkins was entitled to no damages. Federal general common law, developed prior to *Erie*, offered the plaintiff greater possibilities. By placing less emphasis on Tompkins' status as an individual not invited onto railroad property, and more emphasis on the railroad's duty of care to individuals who were on its property, federal general common law afforded Tompkins substantial possibilities for a sizeable award of damages.[12]

However, when the Supreme Court got the case, it abolished the body of law that existed prior to *Erie*. At one stroke the Court overruled older precedent and held that in the future there would be no federal general common law. Instead,

10. 304 U.S. 64, 58 S.Ct. 817, 82 L.Ed. 1188 (1938).

11. It should be noted that while the original *Erie* doctrine developed in the context of cases based on the diversity jurisdiction of federal district courts, it appears now to be applied also to cases in which district courts have supplemental jurisdiction over non-diverse state claims. *Felder v. Casey,* 487 U.S. 131, 151, 108 S.Ct. 2302, 2313, 101 L.Ed.2d 123 (1988) (*Erie* also applies to claims based on predecessors to supplemental jurisdiction). *See, e.g., Lytle v. City of Haysville, Kansas,* 138 F.3d 857, 868 (10th Cir. 1998) ("When examining jurisdiction over [supplemental] state claims, we must apply the substantive law of the forum state and reach the same decision we believe the state's highest court would, just as we would if our jurisdiction rested on diversity of citizenship.").

12. *Id.* at 68, 79, 58 S.Ct. at 818, 823.

federal trial courts hearing diversity cases were directed to apply the same state law that a state court hearing the same case would have used.[13]

Part of the impact was immediate and lasting. Federal courts would, in the future, defer to state common law as well as to state statutes. If this rule had been in effect at the time that Tompkins was injured, his lawyer would have known that state law, identifying Tompkins as a trespasser, would have given him little in the way of a claim against the railroad. That result—the federal court's use of state law to determine if the plaintiff has a cognizable cause of action, and to determine if any applicable substantive defenses block the suit—continues to be the law of *Erie* to the present day.

Abolition of federal general common law also meant that the Constitutional concern that the Court expressed in *Erie* was resolved. Recognition of the requirement to apply state substantive law meant that the Constitutionally questionable practice of creating a body of federal substantive law in competition with state law was at an end.

Finally, the temptation to engage in forum shopping was reduced, though not eliminated. Once federal general common law was no more, lawyers lost an important reason to file in federal district courts (*i.e.,* to get different substantive law than a state court would apply). The transformation was radical and, in some respects, complete.

But some new and knotty problems emerged in the wake of *Erie*. It is those problems which continue to cluster around the *Erie* doctrine to the current day, and which are the subject of the remainder of this section.

V. SUBSTANCE v. PROCEDURE: *GUARANTY TRUST CO. v. YORK*[14]

A clue to the central problem arising in the aftermath of *Erie* can be found in a concurring opinion. One justice agreed with the central holding of *Erie, i.e.,* that federal general common law should be abolished and that federal district courts should apply state substantive law. At the same time, he also commented that it was obvious federal courts would remain free to apply their own procedural law—even in diversity cases.[15] But what seemed obvious at the time the Court decided *Erie* proved to be somewhat less clear as additional time passed.

Courts have long identified differences between substantive law and procedural law. Usually substantive law is described as the law that determines whether a party has a claim cognizable in a court, and whether the defendant has a legal defense that bars such a claim on the merits. For example, if a plaintiff sued on a claim of negligence, most states would permit recovery only if the plaintiff could demonstrate that: (1) the defendant owed the plaintiff a duty of care; (2) the defendant breached that duty; and (3) the breach proximately caused injury to the plaintiff or damage to the plaintiff's property. Those are the

13. *Id.* at 79, 58 S.Ct. at 823.

14. 326 U.S. 99, 65 S.Ct. 1464, 89 L.Ed. 2079 (1945).

15. *Erie,* 304 U.S. at 90, 58 S.Ct. at 828 (Reed, J., concurring) ("No one doubts federal power over procedure."). The passage of time, however, has demonstrated that Justice Reed's optimism about the primacy of federal procedure should be approached with care. *See Jinks v. Richland County,* 538 U.S. 456, 123 S.Ct. 1667, 155 L.Ed.2d 631 (2003) (implying that courts cannot always easily untangle the relationship between substance and procedure, no matter what the purpose may be for trying to do so).

substantive elements of the tort of negligence.[16] In a state that recognized the defense of contributory negligence, a defendant could defeat the claim by demonstrating that the plaintiff had been contributorily negligent in the event that led to the plaintiff's injury. This assertion of contributory negligence is a substantive defense.

By contrast, procedural law does not address whether the plaintiff has a cause of action or whether the defendant necessarily has a defense. Instead, procedure governs the way in which both plaintiff and defendant must present their sides of the case to the court. At its simplest level, procedural law will control the length of paper on which pleadings must be filed (*e.g.*, letter size or legal size) or whether the complaint may be written out by hand. More complex problems arise over procedure regulating the joining of additional parties, the conduct of discovery, or the admissibility of evidence. These procedural rules help direct the course of a lawsuit and, pragmatically, can often determine the outcome of a case. At the same time, they do not directly address the substantive legal standard a plaintiff must meet in order to demonstrate negligence to the satisfaction of the court.

In the context of the *Erie* doctrine, the ability of federal courts to apply their own procedure (or not) remains the central unresolved question that *Erie* produced. On the one hand, there is no serious question about the Constitutional authority of federal courts and Congress to create procedural law that governs federal courts. In that sense, the decision of a federal district court to apply its own procedure to a case involving a state cause of action does not raise the same Constitutional doubts that application of federal general common law had raised in the era prior to *Erie*.

At the same time, in many cases procedure can alter the outcome of a case as surely as substantive law. For example, a case can easily be lost when a party is unprepared to cross-examine effectively an opponent's expert. In some states, preparation to cross-examine an expert is impaired by rules of procedure limiting or prohibiting deposition of opposing experts. By contrast, Federal Rule of Civil Procedure 26 generally permits such depositions. Therefore, to the extent that a federal court's procedure might be different than that of a state court, lawyers might still choose to file cases in federal court (when, *e.g.*, diversity requirements are satisfied) in order to obtain the benefit of federal procedure. Potential problems of forum shopping thus remain when federal courts are able to apply their own procedure.

After *Erie*, the Supreme Court returned to the problem of determining when, if at all, federal courts may use their own procedure in diversity cases. One of the most important early decisions was *Guaranty Trust Co. v. York*,[17] in which the Court had to choose between application of a federal doctrine limiting the time in which a case had to be filed or a state statute of limitations that set a different time limit. Under the state statute, the plaintiff's claim was barred. Under the federal doctrine, the plaintiff's case could proceed.

In its own way, *Guaranty Trust* was more difficult than *Erie*. *Guaranty Trust* involved an arguably procedural issue, and there could be no question that

16. These elements may be stated somewhat differently in different states, but the basic requirements are usually very similar.

17. 326 U.S. 99, 65 S.Ct. 1464, 89 L.Ed. 2079 (1945).

federal courts are authorized to apply their own procedure in many of the cases they hear. For example, when a cause of action arises out of federal law, a federal court must have procedure with which to process the case. The federal court cannot be bound to the application of the procedure of the state in which the federal court sits, because that would mean the procedure applied to federal questions would differ from one state to another. The result would be an unacceptable lack of uniformity in the way federal claims were heard across the United States. Additionally, the Court could not simply order lower federal courts to apply federal procedure when hearing federal claims and state procedure when hearing state claims. In the first place, that approach would require federal judges to learn, and apply, two different bodies of procedure on a regular basis. Secondly, when cases appeared on the federal docket involving both federal and state claims, an attempt to apply federal procedure to federal claims and state procedure to state claims might often produce unacceptable confusion. Consider, for example, what would happen if federal rules of evidence treated a piece of testimony as inadmissible, while state rules of evidence would admit the testimony.

Guaranty Trust took a tentative step toward resolving the problem by directing federal courts to use state procedure whenever the choice of procedure would determine the outcome of the case. As applied to the facts of *Guaranty Trust,* this approach meant that the federal court should use the state statute of limitations.[18] The reasoning was that under the state rule, the plaintiff's claim was time barred. Application of the federal limitation period would permit the plaintiff to pursue the claim. While it was still possible that the plaintiff might lose the case on the merits, the difference between certain defeat for the plaintiff under the state law and a possibility of victory under the federal law is a sufficient difference in outcome to justify barring the use of federal procedure.

VI. CONTINUING DEVELOPMENT: SOURCES OF FEDERAL PROCEDURE

The underpinning of the decision in *Guaranty Trust* was a concern that a sufficiently large potential difference in outcome caused by the application of federal procedure would create unacceptable levels of forum shopping of the kind that *Erie* originally sought to prevent. This linkage between outcome determination and forum shopping was an important step in extending the *Erie* doctrine to procedural issues as well as matters of substantive law. However, at the same time, an emphasis on "outcome determination" as the basis for choosing between federal procedure and state procedure can easily be an overly broad assessment. In a given case, even the most modest differences in procedure, *e.g.,* page limitations in different courts on the length of briefs, can produce a significantly different outcome. For example, conforming to such page limitations might force an attorney to abandon arguments of potential value. Moreover, because sensible lawyers will litigate only issues that could have a bearing on the outcome of a case, a test that considered only outcome determination might require application of state procedure for almost every state claim filed in federal court—including claims filed in conjunction with federal causes of action.

18. This result still applies in the context of statutes of limitations. *Jinks v. Richland County,* 538 U.S. 456, 123 S.Ct. 1667, 155 L.Ed.2d 631 (2003) (dicta) ("For *Erie* purposes . . . statutes of limitation are treated as substantive;" citing *Guaranty Trust*).

For that reason, the continuing evolution of the *Erie* doctrine has included the identification of other factors to weigh in a determination as to the applicability of state or federal procedure. Perhaps the most significant factor identified in later cases is the importance of identifying the source of the federal procedure that is arguably applicable to a state cause of action. Over time, the Supreme Court has addressed the relationship of *Erie* to three different sources of federal procedure somewhat differently, as follows.

A. Federal Case Law Procedure.

In instances where the pertinent federal procedure develops through case law, and not through statutes or rules, the choice between federal and state procedure depends heavily on a weighing of interests. In *Byrd v. Blue Ridge Rural Electric Cooperative, Inc.,*[19] a worker's compensation case, one key issue was whether the injured plaintiff was an employee, for purposes of the worker's compensation statute, of the defendant. A second issue, and the one that raised the *Erie* question, was whether the jury or the judge should decide the plaintiff's employment relationship (if any) with the defendant. Under state procedure the judge was authorized to make that decision, while the established federal practice was to leave the question to the jury.

The Supreme Court acknowledged that if the only *Erie* measurement was outcome determination, identification of the proper role of judge and jury might well require application of state procedure. However, the Court concluded that other factors, in addition to outcome determination, were also relevant to the case. In particular, the Court extended the *Erie* analysis to include consideration of the competing state and federal interests in applying state and federal procedure, respectively. These considerations, along with an evaluation of the possibility that application of federal procedure might significantly affect the outcome of the case, were to be weighed to determine whether state or federal procedure should control.[20] In other words, a strong state interest in application of state procedure weighs in favor of applying state procedure, while a weak state interest reduces the argument for using state procedure. A strong federal interest in applying federal procedure supports use of federal procedure, while a weak federal interest reduces the argument for using federal procedure. And if the use of federal procedure might significantly affect the outcome of the case, such a prospect argues in favor of using state procedure.[21]

A major difficulty in applying *Byrd* arises when the court tries to identify state and federal interests and to weigh their relative importance in a particular case. Additionally, an assessment of the impact that application of federal procedure might have on the outcome of a case can also be uncertain.[22] The only

19. 356 U.S. 525, 78 S.Ct. 893, 2 L.Ed.2d 953 (1958).

20. *Id.* at 533–539, 78 S.Ct. at 899–902.

21. *Id.* at 539, 78 S.Ct. at 902.

22. *Id.* (noting uncertainty of effect of difference between judge and jury on outcome of case). *See also, e.g., Esfeld v. Costa Crociere, S.P.A.,* 289 F.3d 1300, 1306–09 (11th Cir.2002) (noting that "vast majority" of federal appellate courts use federal law of forum non conveniens; holding that while forum non conveniens will often be outcome-determinative, federal interest in controlling its own process in a way that is uniform across the country outweighed the outcome-determinative factor; holding that federal law of forum non conveniens should control; citing other cases). It is probably worth noting that *Esfeld* used a modified version of *Byrd,* because the *Esfeld* court appeared not to have factored in the potential significance of the state's interest in application of state law on forum non conveniens.

way attorneys can approach this question is to research the policies behind the competing state and federal procedures and then see how those policies measure up against one another.[23] For assessing prospects of outcome determination, the inquiry is more nearly a pragmatic evaluation of the way in which application of federal procedure might affect the course of the litigation.

The weighing analysis developed in *Byrd* is still used today for one category of procedural questions arising under *Erie*. When the federal procedure potentially applicable to a case is procedure developed by judicial practice (*i.e.,* case law procedure), courts typically weigh the three factors identifies in *Byrd*: (1) relative strength of state interests behind state procedure; (2) relative strength of federal interests behind federal procedure; and (3) likelihood that application of federal procedure will significantly alter the outcome of the case.[24]

B. Rules Enabling Act:[25] Federal Rules of Procedure.

Case law is not the only source of federal procedure. In fact, only a few years before the Supreme Court decided *Erie,* Congress enacted legislation creating a process by which federal rules of procedure could be enacted without necessarily involving direct participation in each rule by Congress. The Rules Enabling Act was the source of, *inter alia,* the current Federal Rules of Civil Procedure, which are so important to the processing of civil cases in federal courts.

Interplay between the *Erie* doctrine and federal rules developed under the authority of the Rules Enabling Act was inevitable. For example, in a case where state procedure required a plaintiff to post a bond before proceeding with a suit, but Federal Rule of Civil Procedure 23.1 required no bond, the Court had to decide whether the state bond requirement prevailed over a federal rule that otherwise appeared to be relevant to the case.[26] In another case, state procedure provided that an applicable statute of limitations continued to run after a case was filed with the court until the defendant was served. By contrast, Federal Rule of Civil Procedure 3 provides that a federal case is "commenced" by filing a complaint with the federal district court. A possible construction of Rule 3 is

23. This suggestion is not meant to indicate that thorough research alone will yield an answer upon which diligent attorneys may confidently rely. Indeed, continuing developments in the Supreme Court indicate that *Byrd* does not identify a single true path with the clarity and precision of a laser. In *Gasperini v. Center for Humanities, Inc.,* 518 U.S. 415, 116 S.Ct. 2211, 135 L.Ed.2d 659 (1996), a jury awarded a large verdict to the plaintiff. Under New York law, a state appellate court has authority to order a new trial when the jury's verdict "deviates materially" from reasonable compensation. Federal procedure differs from that standard in two important respects. First, a federal district judge normally has less discretion to modify a jury's verdict than the New York law allows. Second, New York vests this power in an appellate court. By contrast, the Seventh Amendment to the United States constitution normally imposes much stricter limits on the authority of federal appellate courts to modify jury verdicts.

The Supreme Court grappled with this cluster of problems in the following manner. First, in diversity cases federal district courts–not circuit courts–will apply the New York statute's standard for modifying jury verdicts. This practice, of course, is not directly consistent with the New York mandate to provide such review in appellate courts. Second, in a bow to the Seventh Amendment, federal circuit courts will review the district court's application of the New York law under the existing federal standard for circuit courts, *i.e.,* an abuse of discretion.

24. It should be noted that the *Byrd* analysis does not assess directly the possible impact that application of state procedure will have on the outcome of a case.

25. 28 U.S.C.A. § 2072.

26. *Cohen v. Beneficial Industrial Loan Corp.,* 337 U.S. 541, 69 S.Ct. 1221, 93 L.Ed. 1528 (1949).

that once the case is filed, the statute of limitations is tolled. The case before the Supreme Court was one in which the plaintiff had filed the complaint in federal district court before the statute of limitations had expired, but service of process on the defendant did not occur until after the statute of limitations would have expired.[27] Under state procedure, therefore, the plaintiff's suit was untimely. Under the apparent literal language of Federal Rule 3, the plaintiff's filing was timely, and the case could proceed.

In both cases, the Supreme Court concluded that the applicable procedure was state procedure, but the reasoning was insufficiently persuasive to lay to rest concerns about the impact of the *Erie* doctrine on cases involving rules of procedure developed under the authority of the Rules Enabling Act. Some, but by no means all, of this uneasiness was laid to rest when the Supreme Court decided *Hanna v. Plumer*.[28]

In *Hanna* a plaintiff served the defendant by leaving a copy of the summons and complaint with the defendant's spouse at the defendant's residence. This was lawful service under Federal Rule of Civil Procedure 4. However, under state procedure, service was not satisfactory unless the defendant was served personally. The Supreme Court re-examined its growing body of precedent under the *Erie* doctrine and concluded that service was satisfactory because Rule 4 applied, not the state procedure.[29]

The reasoning of the Court's majority was that the relation of *Erie* to the Rules Enabling Act required a two-step analysis of the possible application of a federal rule of civil procedure to a state cause of action. The first step was to determine if the rule at issue could lawfully be made. Because the Rules Enabling Act only permitted creation of federal rules which were purely procedural, and which did not alter substantive rights, the first inquiry was to determine if the rule in question in a particular case was procedural. In the case at bar Rule 4, governing the means of making service of process on a defendant, affected no substantive rights and clearly passed this "pure procedure" requirement.

The second step was to determine if the federal rule (such as Rule 4) could be harmonized with state procedure, or whether the federal and state procedures were locked in conflict. The Court explained that if the two could be harmonized because, *e.g.*, they did not address the same concerns, no choice between them was necessary. However, if they actually collided, then a federal rule of civil procedure lawfully created under the Rules Enabling Act should be applied over the state procedure.[30]

The literal rule of *Hanna* appears to be that if a federal rule of civil procedure is a lawful exercise of rule-making power under the Rules Enabling Act, and the rule conflicts directly with state procedure, the federal rule applies. That approach appears to leave little room for considerations of outcome determination, which had been so important to the Supreme Court in both *Erie* and *Guaranty Trust*. However, an important concurring opinion in *Hanna* helps

27. *Ragan v. Merchants Transfer & Warehouse Co.,* 337 U.S. 530, 69 S.Ct. 1233, 93 L.Ed. 1520 (1949).

28. 380 U.S. 460, 85 S.Ct. 1136, 14 L.Ed.2d 8 (1965).

29. *Id.* at 462, 85 S.Ct. at 1140.

30. *Id.* at 468, 85 S.Ct. at 1143.

explain the interplay between the federal rules of civil procedure and concerns about outcome determination under *Erie*.

While agreeing with the result in *Hanna* (application of Rule 4 over conflicting state procedure), Justice Harlan added that a determination of the applicability of a federal rule to a case arising under state law should also take into account whether the possible application of federal procedure would have influenced an attorney's decision to choose the federal court in order to avoid the application of state procedure.[31] Where such a decision might reasonably have been made, and where the application of federal procedure would impinge on a significant state policy, Justice Harlan believed the state procedure should apply—even if, under the majority's test, state procedure conflicted with a valid federal rule of procedure.[32] When applied, Justice Harlan's approach refined the "outcome-determinative" test for procedure that had been so important at least since *Guaranty Trust*. In essence, Justice Harlan avoided the possibility that a difference in procedure could always determine the outcome by concentrating his analysis on the estimated importance of procedure at the time an attorney was choosing the court in which the case would be heard. Put another way, if a reasonable attorney, upon noticing that federal procedure offered a significant advantage not available under state procedure, would choose the federal court in order to obtain the benefit of federal procedure, the federal procedure would be sufficiently outcome determinative to justify displacing it with state procedure. While Justice Harlan made these observations in the context of federal rules of procedure, they appear to have applicability also to the circumstances governed by *Byrd, i.e.,* situations in which federal procedure arising purely from case law may conflict with state procedure.

Understanding *Hanna* can be difficult enough. However, the difficulty is sometimes compounded when *Hanna* is applied in particular cases. In *Walker v. Armco Steel Corp.,*[33] for example, the Supreme Court returned to a question it had originally addressed a generation earlier. *Walker* involved a plaintiff who had sued on a state claim in federal district court. The claim was filed before the statute of limitations expired, but the complaint was not served on the defendant until after the statute would have expired. Applicable state law provided that the statute continued to run until service on the defendant. The plaintiff argued that Federal Rule of Civil Procedure 3, describing an action as "commenced" when filed with the district court, meant that the statute of limitations was tolled by the plaintiff's timely filing with the clerk's office.

Walker was a reprise of *Ragan v. Merchants Transfer & Warehouse Co.,*[34] in which the Court had held that state procedure controlled, and Rule 3 did not apply.[35] Many observers believed that the intervening decision in *Hanna* had nullified the result in *Ragan*. A unanimous Supreme Court, applying *Hanna*, concluded otherwise. The Court recognized that under the *Hanna* analysis, Rule 3 was a lawful rule of procedure, enacted within the authority of the Rules Enabling Act. However, the Court also concluded that Rule 3, at least in diversity cases, was not intended to toll state statutes of limitations. The Court

31. *Id.* at 474, 85 S.Ct. at 1146 (Harlan, J., concurring).

32. *Id.*

33. 446 U.S. 740, 100 S.Ct. 1978, 64 L.Ed.2d 659 (1980).

34. 337 U.S. 530, 69 S.Ct. 1233, 93 L.Ed. 1520 (1949).

35. *See supra,* notes 24–25 and accompanying text.

was a bit vague as to the precise purpose of Rule 3 when state claims were before a federal district court.[36] However, its conclusion was that state procedure for tolling a statute of limitation (service on the defendant) controlled because there was "no direct conflict" between the state law and Rule 3.[37] Thus, the requirement of *Hanna* that, before a lawful federal rule can apply to a diversity case it must first be in direct conflict with state procedure was not met, and state law applied.

Walker suggests that there can be grave uncertainty as to the circumstances when a federal rule conflicts to a substantial degree with state procedure. To that extent, *Walker* casts doubt on the predictability of the *Hanna* test as it applies to cases concerning the applicability of federal rules of procedure enacted under the Rules Enabling Act. The Supreme Court appears to be sensitive to this problem, and in the aftermath of *Walker* the Court emphasized that the analysis enunciated in *Hanna* continues to govern in most circumstances.[38] Nevertheless, *Walker* serves as a caution to attorneys that, before assuming a federal rule of procedure displaces state procedure, one must first establish not only that the federal rule is authorized by the Rules Enabling Act, but also that the federal rule truly clashes with otherwise applicable state procedure.

C. Procedure Enacted Directly by Congress.

Although Congress enacted the Rules Enabling Act to authorize a process for creating rules of procedure in which Congress itself did not have to be actively involved, Congress has also created other important procedural provisions independent of the Rules Enabling Act. These provisions are codified at Title 28 of the United States Code.

When one of these statutory procedures is arguably applicable in a diversity case, considerations related to *Erie* arise again. In this circumstance, as with case law controlled by *Byrd* or rules of procedure controlled by *Hanna*, the federal district court must decide whether federal statutory procedure may be applied, or whether it must defer to state procedure. The Supreme Court addressed this question in *Stewart Organization, Inc. v. Ricoh Corp.*[39] *Stewart* addressed whether a motion to transfer a case pursuant to a contractual forum selection clause was enforceable under 28 U.S.C.A. § 1404(a) or unenforceable because state procedure disfavored such clauses.

The Supreme Court held that the standards for transfer of venue under the federal statute controlled. In a straightforward opinion the Court concluded that federal courts are bound to apply procedure enacted by Congress, provided only that Congress was within its Constitutional authority and that the statute was relevant to the issue before the district court.[40] *Stewart* may have left some modest room for questioning when an attorney can be certain that the federal statutory procedure controls. However, it appears that this question can be

36. *Walker,* 446 U.S. at 750, 100 S.Ct. at 1985 ("Rule 3 governs the date from which various timing requirements of the Federal Rules begin to run, but does not affect state statutes of limitations.").

37. *Id.* at 751, 100 S.Ct. at 1986.

38. *See, e.g., Burlington Northern Railway Co. v. Woods,* 480 U.S. 1, 107 S.Ct. 967, 94 L.Ed.2d 1 (1987) (applying *Hanna* test, finding Federal Rule of Appellate Procedure 38 applicable in place of state procedure).

39. 487 U.S. 22, 108 S.Ct. 2239, 101 L.Ed.2d 22 (1988).

40. *Id.* at 26, 108 S.Ct. at 2242.

answered with somewhat more confidence than the question posed by *Hanna* when a federal rule is at issue, *i.e.*, does the rule conflict sufficiently with state procedure?

VII. IDENTIFYING STATE LAW

In cases where a federal district court recognizes that it is obligated to apply state law on an issue, a question remains as to how to identify the state law. Of course, if the relevant state supreme court has addressed the matter clearly, its word on state law is normally final. The question becomes more difficult, however, if state law is not entirely clear.[41]

Federal judges hear many cases where state law is implicated. However, they still lack the experience with state law that state judges will typically have. Moreover, when a state judge decides a difficult question of state law, a party has the ability to seek review of that decision by state appellate judges, who presumably are also familiar with state law. By contrast, if a federal district judge applies state law in a potentially erroneous way, the challenge to that decision is heard by other federal judges. Those federal appellate judges, in turn, may not even be from the state whose law is at issue.

To address the problems raised by this situation, three distinct approaches have evolved. The first is simply to recognize that difficult questions of state law are best handled in the state court system, and to abstain from deciding the case. This approach has the advantage of ensuring that a decision will not be made by a federal court. However, it imposes on the parties all the delay and additional expense involved in re-starting the case in state court. For this reason and others, federal courts have not employed the abstention option frequently.[42]

The second option is to certify the difficult question to the high court of the state whose law is at issue. In states whose legislatures have enacted certification legislation, federal courts may apply to state supreme courts for resolution of difficult questions of state law. Certification carries with it the prospect of a definitive answer to a hard question, but its promise has always been limited by some real-world obstacles. In the first place, certification is expensive for litigants, involving a possible need to brief and argue an issue before yet another court. Second, certification is almost certain to produce delay in obtaining a final judgment in the federal case, for the federal litigation must be held in abeyance pending the decision in the state supreme court.[43] Finally, a certification statute does not necessarily require a state supreme court to answer a question from a federal court. In circumstances where state high courts already feel themselves overburdened by their own dockets, it is sometimes possible that in the end no answer will be forthcoming. A more frustrating conclusion to a search for a solution to a hard question can hardly be imagined. Thus, while certification is used more frequently than abstention, it has been much less than a universal solution to the problem of getting a good answer to a hard question of state law.

41. *West v. AT & T Co.,* 311 U.S. 223, 236, 61 S.Ct. 179, 183, 85 L.Ed. 139 (1940) ("The highest court of the state is the final arbiter of what is state law." Citing *Erie*. Possible exception if state supreme court has made clear its previous view has changed.).

42. *Meredith v. City of Winter Haven,* 320 U.S. 228, 234, 64 S.Ct. 7, 11, 88 L.Ed. 9 (1943) (abstention should be employed only in "exceptional circumstances").

43. *See, e.g., West American Ins. Co. v. Bank of Isle of Wight,* 673 F.Supp. 760, 764 (E.D.Va. 1987) (certification imposes on time and resources of both state supreme court and parties).

The third option available to federal courts is the course followed most frequently. Federal courts simply address the difficult question directly, and try to resolve it themselves with the tools available. To undertake this effort, federal courts look to a variety of sources, including: analogous decisions by the state high court; reported decisions from lower state courts;[44] trends in neighboring states; and even "scholarly treatises, the Restatement of Law, and germane law review articles."[45] This approach has the greatest potential for producing analyses of state law that are later established to be incorrect.[46] At the same time, it provides the best answer a federal court can achieve without forcing the parties into the delay and expense that may attend abstention or certification.

VIII. THE JOB IS NOT DONE

As difficult as it may be to follow the evolution of the *Erie* doctrine on these pages, the reader should understand that *Erie* and some related issues have still other ramifications. Many of these questions are outside the scope of the current discussion, but their importance in cases where they arise cannot be overstated. Consider, for example, the following two issues.

A. Using the Law the State Court Would Use.

The heart of *Erie* is a rule directing federal district courts to apply the substantive law that a state court would use. In *Erie* itself, application of that rule meant that a federal district court sitting in New York would apply the same substantive law that a New York state trial court would use.

That application may seem straightforward enough, but it contains a subtle distinction. *Erie* does not direct a federal district court sitting in New York to use New York substantive law in every single case controlled by *Erie*. Instead, it directs the federal district court to defer to the state courts in two different ways: first, to use the same substantive law that the state court would use; and second, to use the same system for determining which state's substantive law the state court would actually apply. The second point is complicated, but can be seen more clearly using *Erie* itself as an example.

The injury to Tompkins that gave rise to the *Erie* case occurred in Pennsylvania. The lawsuit was heard in a federal district court in New York. If the case had been heard in a state court in New York, the state court would have had to decide whether to use New York substantive law (the law of the state where the case was heard), Pennsylvania substantive law (the law of the state where the incident took place), or the substantive law of some other state. On the facts of *Erie,* it was clear at the time the case was heard that a New York state court would have applied the substantive law of Pennsylvania on the ground that the

44. *See, e.g., State Farm Mutual Automobile Insurance Co. v. Pate,* 275 F.3d 666, 669 (7th Cir.2001) ("When the state Supreme Court has not decided the issue, the rulings of the state intermediate appellate courts must be accorded great weight, unless there are persuasive indications that the state's highest court would decide the case differently.").

45. *McKenna v. Ortho Pharmaceutical Corp.,* 622 F.2d 657, 662 (3d Cir.), *cert. denied,* 449 U.S. 976, 101 S.Ct. 387, 66 L.Ed.2d 237 (1980).

46. *See, e.g., Rotella v. Pederson,* 144 F.3d 892 (5th Cir.1998) (referring to this process as requiring the court to make an "*Erie* guess"). *See also Calbillo v. Cavender Oldsmobile, Inc.,* 288 F.3d 721, 729 (5th Cir.2002) (when making *Erie* guess, court may not decide as it thinks best; instead, court must do what it believes state supreme court would do).

accident giving rise to the suit occurred in Pennsylvania.[47] Because a New York court would have used Pennsylvania law, the duty of the federal district court in New York under the *Erie* doctrine—to apply the same law that a state court would use—was also to use Pennsylvania law.

An entire body of law (called either "conflict of laws" or "choice of law") is devoted to determining when a state trial court should use its own law or the law of another state. While the study of conflict of laws is not immediately within the scope of *Erie,* it is probably apparent how important conflict of laws can be for cases to which the *Erie* doctrine applies.

B. A Residue of Federal Common Law.

Although *Erie* abolished federal general common law, another form of federal common law continues to exist on the margin of *Erie*. The Supreme Court has held that such common law may apply to cases nominally involving state law, but in which the United States has such a strong interest in a uniform body of law applied across the country that *Erie* must defer to other considerations. It should be emphasized that the federal common law at issue is not the kind of federal general common law that the older rule of *Swift v. Tyson* imposed on most state causes of action in federal courts. At the same time, this surviving body of federal common law can be substantive law, notwithstanding *Erie.* For example, in *Clearfield Trust Co. v. United States,*[48] the Supreme Court concluded that federal law controlled whether the federal government was liable to an innocent party that had cashed a stolen federal payroll check. The need for uniform treatment of federal checks throughout the country was held to require the application of federal common law on this substantive issue.[49]

The number of circumstances in which federal common law may, notwithstanding *Erie,* displace state substantive law is uncertain but probably quite limited.[50] In any event, the question arises only infrequently, and is therefore not central to an understanding of the problems raised more frequently by *Erie.* However, in the occasional case where precedent like *Clearfield Trust* may displace *Erie,* an awareness of the continuing vitality of this pocket of surviving federal common law can be crucial.

IX. SUMMARY

The following summary addresses the central points of *Erie.* If a reader appreciates the reasoning underlying these summary points, the reader will probably have a working understanding of this challenging doctrine.

47. This point was so thoroughly settled at the time of *Erie* that the discussion of applicable law centered solely on whether federal general common law or Pennsylvania law controlled the case. There was, in short, no suggestion that a federal district court in New York would apply New York substantive law to the facts of *Erie.* That same result might not be quite as clear today, but it was eminently clear when *Erie* was decided.

48. 318 U.S. 363, 63 S.Ct. 573, 87 L.Ed. 838 (1943).

49. *Id.* at 365, 63 S.Ct. at 575.

50. *See, e.g., Bank of America Nat'l Trust & Savings Ass'n v. Parnell,* 352 U.S. 29, 77 S.Ct. 119, 1 L.Ed.2d 93 (1956) (applying state law to determine who had burden of proof on issue of defendants' good faith; refusing to extend rule of *Clearfield Trust). See also United States v. City of Las Cruces,* 289 F.3d 1170, 1186 (10th Cir. 2002) ("The reluctance to create common law is a core feature of federal court jurisprudence.").

A. *Erie* resolved that federal courts hearing most state causes of action will apply state substantive law.

B. *Erie's* impact on the possible application of federal procedure in diversity cases is more complicated. It is clear that *Guaranty Trust* was an important starting point for this matter, but over time more sophisticated approaches have developed. In particular, determining whether federal or state procedure applies depends heavily on the source from which federal procedure emanates.[51]

1. If the source of federal procedure is federal case law, *Byrd v. Blue Ridge Rural Electric Co-op., Inc.* provides the analytical framework. *Byrd* requires identification and weighing of the purpose behind the state's procedure, the purpose behind federal procedure, and the prospect that application of federal procedure might encourage litigants to shop for the federal forum in order to obtain a more favorable outcome.
2. If the source of federal procedure is one of the Federal Rules of Civil Procedure, or another rule promulgated under the Rules Enabling Act (or a case construing such a rule), *Hanna v. Plumer* provides the framework. First, it will be important to determine if the rule at issue is a lawful rule of procedure within the scope of the Rules Enabling Act. Second, if the rule is legitimately procedural, it will be necessary to determine if the rule conflicts with otherwise applicable state procedure, or if it is possible to harmonize the rule with state procedure. If federal and state procedure conflict, federal law will apply. However, there remains the question as to whether the federal law actually conflicts with state procedure. Additionally, there is uncertainty as to whether federal procedure will apply if a litigant chose the federal court in order to obtain a more favorable outcome in the case through application of the federal rule.
3. If the source of federal procedure is Title 28 of the United States Code, *Stewart Organization, Inc. v. Ricoh Corp.* directs the application of federal procedure if: (1) the federal statute is on point, and; (2) is a Constitutional exercise of power by Congress.

C. If the federal district court decides that it should apply state law (whether substantive or procedural), but the state law to be applied is uncertain, the court may have three options to consider: (1) abstain from deciding the issue; (2) certify the question to the state supreme court, if a certification statute is available; or (3) attempt, from available sources, to predict how the state supreme court would have decided the matter.

51. The source of state procedure, it should be noted, is not relevant.

*

PART III

RES JUDICATA AND COLLATERAL ESTOPPEL

I. Introduction

A. Generally

Res judicata and collateral estoppel are related doctrines that address the consequences of an entry of judgment in one lawsuit on subsequent cases that are related to the original case. Subject to some important exceptions, these judicial doctrines establish the rule that once a case has reached a final judgment, many claims or issues related to that case should be treated as finally decided, once and for all. Thus, if res judicata applies to a case, a plaintiff who lost a lawsuit will often be precluded from raising claims which were raised (or perhaps, which could have been raised) in that lawsuit. In a roughly analogous way, collateral estoppel provides that once an issue has been decided in litigation, that issue may be treated as decided—without further proof—in any subsequent litigation in which the issue is relevant.

The policies behind these related doctrines are judicial economy and finality in litigation. At the same time, when these doctrines are potentially applicable to a case they can create the possibility of substantial risk or opportunity for opposing parties. For example, under the doctrine of res judicata, a plaintiff who has several related claims against the same defendant may often find it necessary to raise both claims in the same litigation, or risk foregoing any claims that are not asserted.

B. Case Law Doctrine

Res judicata and collateral estoppel owe their existence almost entirely to development in the courts. Legislative influence on these doctrines is limited, and constitutional considerations arise only in circumstances where res judicata or collateral estoppel might have the potential to limit the due process right of an interested party to a fair hearing. Thus, if res judicata was applied to preclude a claim by a party that had not yet had a fair opportunity to be heard in court, it is possible that res judicata would run afoul of due process and the claim would have to be heard.[1] The due process limitation on these doctrines is therefore important. However, as is discussed below, due process can sometimes be satisfied even in circumstances where an interested person was not, literally, a party to a case.

Because res judicata and collateral estoppel are not constitutional in nature, the influence of the Supreme Court on these doctrines is somewhat limited. The Court can and does establish the standards for these two doctrines when they are used in federal courts, but the states are free to accept or reject federal views

1. *See, e.g., South Central Bell Tel. Co. v. Alabama,* 526 U.S. 160, 168, 119 S.Ct. 1180, 1185, 143 L.Ed.2d 258 (1999) (due process prevents application of res judicata to bar litigation by parties who did not participate in prior action, either personally, through concept of privity, or through membership in a class).

of these doctrines. Supreme Court cases may therefore be an important source of influence on the application of res judicata or collateral estoppel in state courts, but such decisions are not necessarily the final word.[2]

C. Basic Terminology

Two basic areas of terminology can produce some confusion in application of these doctrines, but the confusion can be clarified without difficulty. The first source of confusion arises from the fact that some older cases apply the term "res judicata" indiscriminately to circumstances involving either res judicata or collateral estoppel. The doctrines certainly share some common attributes, but they are also different enough to deserve the distinctive names that have come to be applied to them. Thus, when using an older case that describes what appears to be an application of collateral estoppel as "res judicata," a reader should simply be cautioned to remember the now generally discarded habit of using "res judicata" as an umbrella term covering both doctrines.[3]

The second source of confusion may arise from more recent efforts to replace the terms "res judicata" and "collateral estoppel" with labels that are more descriptive of what the underlying doctrines try to do. Thus, "res judicata" is sometimes described as "claim preclusion," and "collateral estoppel" may be called "issue preclusion."[4] Reception of these newer terms has been mixed over the past generation or so of judicial decisions, but enough cases use the terms so that a reader must be familiar with them. However, for purposes of reducing confusion in this section, the terms "res judicata" and "collateral estoppel" will be used exclusively.

These two areas are not the only sources of difficulty with terms that attach to the two doctrines. Case law developments in collateral estoppel, especially, have produced a few terms that will be discussed in greater detail below.

II. Res Judicata

A. Elements

Before a court will apply res judicata to a claim, ordinarily three elements must be satisfied. First, there must have been prior litigation in which "identical" claims were raised, or at least could have been raised. Second, the parties in the second litigation must be "identical" in some manner to the parties in the

2. Because state courts often develop their own case law in this area, federal courts hearing diversity claims must sometimes determine whether to apply state procedure or federal procedure. In other words, federal courts must make an analysis under the rule of *Erie v. Tompkins,* discussed in Part II. As a general rule, federal courts have concluded that where state and federal views of res judicata differ, state views should be applied in a diversity case. See, e.g., *Xantech Corp. v. Ramco Indus., Inc.,* 159 F.3d 1089, 1092 (7th Cir.1998) ("[W]e look to the law of Indiana in this diversity action to determine whether the claims that [the plaintiff] makes in this suit are barred on res judicata grounds.").

3. *Migra v. Warren City Sch. Dist. Bd. of Educ.,* 465 U.S. 75, 77 n. 1, 104 S.Ct. 892, 894 n. 1, 79 L.Ed.2d 56 (1984) (noting older practice of using res judicata as term describing both res judicata and collateral estoppel; also noting Court's more recent tendency to apply label of res judicata only to matters of claim preclusion).

4. *See, e.g., id. (using "claim preclusion"* in case addressing principals of res judicata, as means of distinguishing res judicata from collateral estoppel). *See also Baker v. General Motors Corp.,* 522 U.S. 222, 223 n. 5, 118 S.Ct. 657, 664, 139 L.Ed.2d 580 (1998).

original litigation. Third, there must have been a final judgment on the merits in the original litigation.[1]

As may already be obvious, these three seemingly straightforward requirements contain within them some important ambiguities, which will be examined in turn. Immediately before doing so, however, it would be useful to keep in mind an underlying feature of res judicata that is also a useful means of spotting potential res judicata issues. Res judicata may potentially apply to a case only in circumstances where that case bears some relationship to a prior lawsuit that has already been decided. In the absence of previous litigation, a court in a pending case would have no prior decision to which to refer. Thus, while the existence of prior litigation does not necessarily establish the existence of res judicata questions, the absence of prior litigation means there is no possibility of res judicata problems in a pending case.

1. "Identical Claims"; Same Transaction or Occurrence

If the claims at issue in pending litigation bear no relationship to claims that were raised in prior litigation, the instant claims will not be barred by res judicata. For example, if a plaintiff now suing a defendant on a contract claim that arose six weeks ago had previously brought a lawsuit against the same defendant for an utterly unrelated claim that occurred a decade before the breach claim arose, the claims in the two cases would not be identical and res judicata would not be applied. However, if a plaintiff had two claims against a defendant arising out of the same event—and had previously sued on one claim, but not the other—there is a substantial possibility that the requirement for identical claims would be satisfied. Thus, if the defendant was a state police officer who allegedly beat and injured a citizen for motives arising from religious bias, the plaintiff might have at least two civil causes of actions against the police officer, such as: (1) a federal civil rights claim under 42 U.S.C.A. § 1983 (deprivation of a federal civil right by a person acting under color of state law); and (2) a state law claim of battery. If we assume that the plaintiff sued on the state battery claim in previous litigation, and then tried to sue on the federal claim in the pending litigation, it is likely that the requirement of "identical" claims between the two lawsuits would be satisfied.

It is important to note that the claims need not be literally identical to satisfy this requirement for res judicata. In the example above, the federal claim shares much in common with the state claim that was previously litigated, but to prevail on the merits of the federal claim the plaintiff would have to demonstrate additional evidence not necessary to win on the state lawsuit. For the state battery claim, the plaintiff would have to demonstrate only the elements of the common law tort of battery. However, for the federal cause of action, the plaintiff would also have to demonstrate that the defendant was acting under color of state law (*i.e.,* a police officer) and that there was some intent to violate the plaintiff's federal civil rights (religious discrimination). These elements would be additional to the requirements for common law battery, and in a particular case they might require proof that the plaintiff does not possess. In

1. *Cromwell v. County of Sac,* 94 U.S. (4 Otto) 351, 352–53, 24 L.Ed. 195 (1876), *cert. denied,* 435 U.S. 933, 98 S.Ct. 1508, 55 L.Ed.2d 530 (1978) (identifying elements to be satisfied in first action before res judicata will bar a subsequent lawsuit).

that sense, the two claims in the example are not literally "identical," because they rest on distinct theories of recovery.

Courts once struggled to develop rules to determine when two claims share enough in common to satisfy the requirement that the claims are "identical" for purposes of res judicata. However, many years ago most courts abandoned the notion that claims based on the same facts, but different theories of recovery, were insufficiently "identical" to satisfy this requirement. Today, most courts have accepted the proposition that two claims are "identical" if their "underlying facts are 'related in time, space, origin, or motivation, whether they form a convenient trial unit, and whether their treatment as a unit conforms to the parties' expectations or business understanding or usage.' "[2] Put another way, the claim in the second suit is sufficiently "identical" to the claim that was or could have been litigated in the first suit if both claims share a common "nucleus of operative fact."[3] This language shares much in common with judicial commentary about the requirement in supplemental jurisdiction, 28 U.S.C.A. § 1367(a), for the "same case or controversy."[4] It is also related to the idea in Federal Rule of Civil Procedure 13(a) that counterclaims may be compulsory if they arise out of the same "transaction or occurrence" as the opposing party's claim.[5]

Applying this transactional test to the claims in the case involving the alleged beating inflicted by the police officer, most courts would almost certainly conclude that the state battery claims and the federal civil rights claim share enough common features to satisfy this requirement of "identical" claims for res judicata. The primary reason courts would likely reach that conclusion is that the two claims, though based on somewhat differing legal theories, arose from the same occurrence, at the same time, and would require substantially overlapping items of proof.[6]

At the same time, the transactional test for "identical" claims should not be pushed too far. If the transactions or events at issue took place at significantly different points in time, claims arising from those different times will generally not be treated as "identical."[7] Thus, in a circumstance where ship pilots had

2. *Interoceanica Corp. v. Sound Pilots, Inc.*, 107 F.3d 86, 90 (2d Cir.1997) (quoting Restatement (Second) of Judgments § 24(b) (1982)).

3. *Apparel Art Int'l, Inc. v. Amertex Enters., Ltd.*, 48 F.3d 576, 583 (1st Cir.1995) ("Under this approach, a cause of action is defined as a set of facts which can be characterized as a single transaction or a series of related transactions."). *See also, e.g., Lane v. Peterson*, 899 F.2d 737, 742 (8th Cir.1990), *cert. denied*, 498 U.S. 823, 111 S.Ct. 74, 112 L.Ed.2d 48 (1990) (standard for measuring same cause of action is whether both claims derive from "same nucleus of operative facts").

4. *See, e.g., United Mine Workers of America v. Gibbs*, 383 U.S. 715, 86 S.Ct. 1130, 16 L.Ed.2d 218 (1966) (developing the concept of "common nucleus of operative fact" in the context of judicial predecessor of supplemental jurisdiction).

5. Fed.R.Civ.P. 13(a). *See also, e.g.*, Fed. R.Civ.P. 15(c)(2) (permitting relation back of amended pleading if, inter alia, "the claim or defense asserted in the amended pleading arose out of the conduct, transaction, or occurrence set forth or attempted to be set forth in the original pleading"); Fed.R.Civ.P. 20(a) (permitting joinder of parties as plaintiffs if, inter alia, their claims arise from "the same transaction, occurrence, or series of transactions or occurrences").

6. *See, e.g., National Labor Relations Bd. v. United Technologies Corp.*, 706 F.2d 1254, 1260 (2d Cir.1983) (for res judicata, test is whether "same evidence is needed to support both claims, and [whether] the facts essential to the second were present in the first").

7. *See, e.g., Securities & Exchange Comm'n v. First Jersey Securities, Inc.*, 101 F.3d 1450, 1464 (2d Cir.1996), *cert. denied*, 522 U.S. 812, 118 S.Ct. 57, 139 L.Ed.2d 21 (1997) ("If the

sued to recover fees owed by a shipping company under a state statute, the judgment in that case would not preclude subsequent claims for fees arising from voyages that had not yet taken place at the time of the first litigation.[8]

2. "Identical" Parties; Privity

The second requirement for res judicata is that the parties in the second action must be identical to the parties in the first action, or in privity with parties in the first action. Thus, if two pedestrians walking along a sidewalk were injured by a motorist whose automobile went out of control and struck them, the outcome of a suit involving only the first pedestrian as a plaintiff would not be a bar to a second and independent suit by the second pedestrian. Even though the claims of both pedestrians arose from the same occurrence, the obvious difference between the parties would preclude application of res judicata.

For purposes of this second requirement for res judicata, parties who are literally the same persons or business entities are clearly "identical." The question that may arise, however, is whether persons who are different but who share a common interest may be treated as "identical." The issue raised here is a concept of privity of interest between two distinct individuals or business entities.

In general, there are several circumstances in which someone not literally a party to the first action may nevertheless be treated as in privity with a person or entity that was a party: (1) where the nonparty succeeded to the interest of a party, for example, by purchasing whatever interest the party may have had after completion of the first litigation; (2) where the nonparty, though technically not participating in the first suit, nevertheless controlled one party's litigation in that suit—where, for example, the nonparty is an insurance company for a party; (3) where the nonparty shares a property interest with the party;[9] (4) where the party and nonparty have an agent-principal relationship; or (5) where the party otherwise "adequately represented" the interest of the nonparty.[10]

These categories may superficially appear straightforward. However, it appears that privity is applied only after careful scrutiny of the nuances of particular cases, and perhaps not always with consistency. For example, where one entity holds a twenty percent interest in another entity's lawsuit, the two interests were deemed "completely identical" with one another and the entities were held to be in privity.[11] However, defendants sued individually may not be in privity with their employers.[12] A general rule is that while privity may in some

second litigation involved different transactions, and especially subsequent transactions, there generally is no claim preclusion;" presence of same parties or even overlapping facts need not be dispositive to prove "identical" claims).

8. *See, e.g., Interoceanica Corp. v. Sound Pilots, Inc.*, 107 F.3d 86, 91 (2d Cir.1997) ("While the subsequent voyages represent wrongs that are the 'same' in legal theory, they are not related in time, space, or origin to the wrongs litigated [earlier].").

9. *See, e.g., Hart v. Yamaha–Parts Distrib., Inc.*, 787 F.2d 1468, 1472 (11th Cir.1986) (citing these examples). *See also, e.g., Nero v. Ferris*, 222 Va. 807, 813, 284 S.E.2d 828, 831 (1981) ("[P]rivity generally involves a party so identical in interest with another that he represents the same legal right [but making this determination requires] a careful examination into the circumstances of each case.").

10. *Howell Hydrocarbons, Inc. v. Adams*, 897 F.2d 183, 188 (5th Cir.1990).

11. *Virginia Surety Co. v. Northrop Grumman Corp.*, 144 F.3d 1243, 1247 (9th Cir.1998).

12. *See, e.g., Willner v. Budig*, 848 F.2d 1032, 1034 (10th Cir.1988) ("Res judicata does not bar [plaintiff's] claims against the defendants in their individual capacities because the

circumstances substitute adequately for the requirement that the parties in both lawsuits be identical, there should be no assumption that a court will support an assertion of privity without a careful examination of the facts underlying the assertion.

It should be noted that in this requirement of identical parties (or privity), the doctrine of res judicata differs in an important respect from case law addressing the doctrine of collateral estoppel. As is discussed later in this analysis, courts do not invariably require that the parties be identical before applying collateral estoppel to issues in a case. However, this distinction comes with several important qualifications, which are addressed under the discussion of collateral estoppel.

3. Final Judgment "On the Merits"

The third and final prerequisite for application of res judicata is the requirement that the first litigation has proceeded to a final judgment on the merits of the case. When considering application of this prerequisite there are two points to keep in mind. First, not all judicial decisions are "final." Second, not all final judgments are based on the merits of the case.

It is generally well settled that when a trial judge enters judgment, so that the parties are now in a position to enforce or appeal the judgment, finality has been achieved and this element of res judicata has been satisfied.[13] By contrast, one apparently obvious example of litigation that does not constitute a final judgment arises when the parties settle their case. A settlement that does not involve action by the court does not constitute a judgment. The result may be different, however, if the parties seek to have their settlement entered by the court as a judgment or decree. Such action may convert a settlement into a final judgment, which therefore may qualify as res judicata for subsequent litigation.[14]

Res judicata also may not apply to situations in which a judge makes an important decision which is, nevertheless, less than a final judgment. For example, in a case in which plaintiffs seek certification of their lawsuit as a class action, denial of such certification may not necessarily be a final judgment, even though the reality of the situation is that denial of class status is often a punishing blow to the parties seeking certification.[15]

defendants are not in privity with the University."); *Headley v. Bacon,* 828 F.2d 1272, 1277–79 (8th Cir.1987) (distinguishing privity between principal and agent from privity between a governmental entity and officials sued in their individual capacities).

13. *Clay v. United States,* 537 U.S. 522, 123 S.Ct. 1072, 1076, 155 L.Ed.2d 88 (2032) ("[A] federal judgment becomes final for appellate review and claim preclusion purposes when the district court disassociates itself from the case, leaving nothing to be done at the court of first instance save execution of the judgment.").

14. *See, e.g., Richardson v. Alabama State Bd. of Educ.,* 935 F.2d 1240, 1244 (11th Cir. 1991) ("We specifically have held that res judicata applies to Title VII consent decrees."). *But cf. Keith v. Aldridge,* 900 F.2d 736, 740 (4th Cir. 1990), *cert. denied,* 498 U.S. 900, 111 S.Ct. 257, 112 L.Ed.2d 215 (1990) (where parties consent to resolution of one portion of a case but expressly reserve right to continue litigating other claims, res judicata will not block continuation of unresolved litigation).

15. *See, e.g., In re General Motors Corp. Pick–Up Truck Fuel Tank Prods. Liability Litig.,* 134 F.3d 133, 146 (3d Cir.1998) ("Denial of class certification is not a 'judgment' for the purposes of the Anti–Injunction Act while the underlying litigation remains pending."). *But cf. In re Varat Enters., Inc.,* 81 F.3d 1310, 1315 (4th Cir.1996) (bankruptcy court's order confirming debtor's plan of reorganization "is treated as a final judgment with res judicata effect").

For res judicata to apply, a judgment must also be on the merits of a case. Litigation that goes through to a jury verdict obviously meets this requirement. However, the applicability of res judicata to litigation terminated under, for example, a subsection of Federal Rule of Civil Procedure 12(b) may depend on both the particular subsection employed as well as the facts of a particular case. In general, cases dismissed for failure to state a claim for which relief may be granted—e.g., Rule 12(b)(6)—are judgments on the merits for purposes of res judicata.[16] By contrast, cases dismissed on jurisdictional grounds, such as Rule 12(b)(1) (lack of subject matter jurisdiction) have res judicata effect only to the extent that the jurisdictional issue is foreclosed. If the claimant subsequently files a second suit alleging a different theory of recovery, or files in a different, appropriate forum, the original dismissal will normally not block the second suit because the jurisdictional dismissal was not on the merits of the case.[17]

B. Res Judicata—Scope

When it is applicable to a case, res judicata bars re-litigation of claims which have previously been litigated—or which could have been litigated in a prior lawsuit. This scope of res judicata differs significantly from the requirement for collateral estoppel, because collateral estoppel applies only to claims which were actually litigated—not claims that could have been litigated but were not.

When applied to claims that were not actually raised, but which could have been raised, the scope of res judicata is rather broad. Thus, where a police officer allegedly attacked and beat a citizen in circumstances that give rise to both a state battery claim and a federal civil rights claim, a plaintiff's decision to sue only on the state claim may preclude assertion of the federal claim at a later date. Provided that the federal claim and the state claim could have been raised concurrently in the court in which the plaintiff filed and provided that the other elements of res judicata are satisfied, the claim not raised would be barred because it could have been raised.[1] This corollary of res judicata should strongly encourage attorneys to consider carefully all their potential theories of recovery in the first litigation.

By contrast, if a claim could not have been raised in the first lawsuit, assertion of that claim in later litigation is not barred by collateral estoppel. Thus, if the first court lacked jurisdiction to hear a particular kind of claim, that claim may be asserted later in a court of competent jurisdiction.[2] This circumstance may most commonly arise when a plaintiff has both a state cause of action and a federal claim which is within the exclusive subject matter jurisdic-

16. *Federated Dep't Stores, Inc. v. Moitie,* 452 U.S. 394, 399 n. 3, 101 S.Ct. 2424, 2428 n. 3, 69 L.Ed.2d 103 (1981)(dismissal under Rule 12(b)(6) is final judgment for purposes of res judicata). *Cf., Manufacturers Hanover Trust Co. v. United States,* 399 U.S. 392, 481, 90 S.Ct. 2054, 2104, 26 L.Ed.2d 691 (1970) (failure to appeal adverse decision makes that decision a matter of res judicata).

17. *Semtek International Inc. v. Lockheed Martin Corp.,* 531 U.S. 497, 121 S.Ct. 1021, 149 L.Ed.2d 32 (2001) (judgment "on the merits" does not always trigger application of claim preclusion in subsequent lawsuit). *See, e.g., Costner v. URS Consultants, Inc.,* 153 F.3d 667, 673 (8th Cir.1998) (distinguishing between application of res judicata for jurisdictional issue in first case and inapplicability of res judicata to different theory of recovery, even where second suit arises from same facts as first claim).

1. *Cromwell v. County of Sac,* 94 U.S. (4 Otto) 351, 352–53, 24 L.Ed.195 (1876) (when applicable, res judicata bars claims actually raised and which might have been raised).

2. *Crossroads Cogeneration Corp. v. Orange & Rockland Utilities, Inc.,* 159 F.3d 129 (3d Cir.1998).

tion of a federal court. If the plaintiff files first in a state court, the outcome of that case will not serve as a bar, under res judicata, to a subsequent filing on the federal claim in a federal court. However, if the plaintiff filed first in a federal district court which had jurisdiction (either diversity or supplemental jurisdiction) over the state claim, failure to file both claims at once would probably create a situation in which the unasserted claim will be barred in later litigation.

C. Res Judicata—Counterclaims: Rule 13(a)

In the federal system, res judicata is not generally applied to potential counterclaims by defendants. Thus, when a defendant does not assert counterclaims, res judicata does not bar their assertion in subsequent litigation. However, the fact that the case law doctrine of res judicata is generally inapplicable to potential counterclaims in federal court does not mean defendants are free to raise or withhold all of their counterclaims. Instead, Federal Rule of Civil Procedure 13(a) provides that counterclaims deemed "compulsory" must be asserted.[1] Failure to do so usually results in judicial refusal to hear the claim in subsequent litigation.[2]

Some state court systems have no compulsory counterclaim rule comparable to Rule 13(a). In such states, the use of collateral estoppel to bar a claim that was not raised as a counterclaim in prior litigation may vary significantly from the federal practice.

D. Res Judicata—Affirmative Defense: Rule 8(c)

In the federal system, res judicata is specifically listed within Federal Rule of Civil Procedure 8(c) as an affirmative defense. That means a defendant seeking to use res judicata to preclude a plaintiff's claim must affirmatively raise the defense. Subject to some important exceptions, failure to raise the defense means that it is waived.[1]

E. Res Judicata—Relationship to Full Faith and Credit

Full faith and credit is a constitutional provision[1] controlling the circumstances when courts of one state must enforce the judicial decisions of another state. This constitutional provision relies on res judicata in the following manner. If the res judicata doctrine of the state in which a judgment was rendered would require other courts in that same state to treat the judgment as final and preclusive, full faith and credit will generally require the courts of other states to give the same effect to the judgement as would be given in the state that rendered the judgment. Analogous rules usually require federal courts to give similar deference to the final judgments of state courts of competent jurisdiction.[2]

1. *See generally*, Fed.R.Civ.P. 13(a).

2. *See, e.g., New York Life Ins. Co. v. Deshotel*, 142 F.3d 873, 882 (5th Cir.1998) ("It is well settled that a failure to plead a compulsory counterclaim bars a party from bringing a later independent action on that claim.").

1. See, e.g., *McKinnon v. Kwong Wah Restaurant*, 83 F.3d 498, 505 (1st Cir.1996) ("To avoid waiver, a defendant must assert all affirmative defenses in the answer."). *But cf. Jakobsen v. Massachusetts Port Authority*, 520 F.2d 810, 813 (1st Cir.1975) (no waiver where failure to plead affirmative defense does not unfairly prejudice opposing party).

1. U.S. Const. Art. IV § 1.

2. *Durfee v. Duke*, 375 U.S. 106, 84 S.Ct. 242, 11 L.Ed.2d 186 (1963) (where Nebraska had considered, inter alia, jurisdictional issues and would treat the judgment as res judicata, federal district court in Missouri had duty under full

III. Collateral Estoppel

A. Elements

As will be explained in greater detail below, the requirements for the application of collateral estoppel (or "issue preclusion")[1] vary more significantly among the jurisdictions than does the application of res judicata. Nevertheless, there are several requirements for collateral estoppel that are applied fairly consistently throughout the United States. First, there must have been a prior litigation in which the identical issue was before the court.[2] Second, the issue must have been actually litigated in the first judicial proceeding.[3] Third, the issue must necessarily have been decided in a case in which a final judgment was entered.[4]

On the surface there is an apparent overlap between the requirements for collateral estoppel and the requirements, discussed earlier, for res judicata. However, while there is reason to recognize the two bodies of case law as related, the similarities can easily be overstated, with resulting unfavorable consequences. As is explained immediately below, some of the superficial similarities actually conceal differences between res judicata and collateral estoppel that can affect the outcome of a particular case.

1. Identical Issues

The standard for determining whether, for purposes of applying collateral estoppel, an issue in a prior lawsuit is the same as an issue in pending litigation is very different from the standard for identical claims in matters of res judicata. As discussed earlier, most courts conclude that two claims are identical for purposes of res judicata if they arise from the same transaction or occurrence. By contrast, in determining whether two issues are identical, most courts require that the issues track each other more closely than that. However, once such a substantial amount of similarity is identified, it is unimportant whether claims in one case bear any significant relationship to claims in another case.[5]

faith and credit provisions to give the same effect to judgement as Nebraska would give it). *See also, e.g., Community Bank of Homestead v. Torcise*, 162 F.3d 1084 n. 5 (11th Cir.1998) ("Under the Full Faith and Credit Act, 28 U.S.C. § 1738 (1994), state court judgments are to be given the same preclusive effect in federal court that they would have in the state in which judgment was rendered.").

1. *See, e.g., Dodd v. Hood River County*, 136 F.3d 1219, 1224 (9th Cir.1998), *cert. denied*, 525 U.S. 923, 119 S.Ct. 278, 142 L.Ed.2d 229 (1998) (acknowledging that most courts still use "collateral estoppel" as appropriate term, but noting that the Ninth Circuit prefers to use "issue preclusion").

2. See, e.g., *United States v. Shanbaum*, 10 F.3d 305, 311 (5th Cir.1994) ("[T]he issue under consideration in a subsequent action must be identical to the issue litigated in a prior action.").

3. *Regions Hosp. v. Shalala*, 522 U.S. 448, 461, 118 S.Ct. 909, 918, 139 L.Ed.2d 895 (1998) ("Absent actual and adversarial litigation ... principles of issue preclusion do not hold fast.").

4. *Cf., Arizona v. California*, 530 U.S. 392, 120 S.Ct. 2304, 147 L.Ed.2d 374 (2000) ("[S]ettlements ordinarily occasion no issue preclusion ... unless it is clear ... that the parties intend their agreement to have such an effect."). *See, e.g., Murdock v. Ute Indian Tribe of Uintah and Ouray Reservation*, 975 F.2d 683, 687 (10th Cir. 1992), *cert. denied*, 507 U.S. 1042, 113 S.Ct. 1879, 123 L.Ed.2d 497 (1993) (to apply collateral estoppel, "the prior action [must have] finally adjudicated on the merits").

5. *United States v. Shanbaum*, 10 F.3d 305, 311 (5th Cir.1994) ("[U]nder issue preclusion, unlike claim preclusion, the subject matter of the later suit need not have any relationship to the subject matter of the prior suit.").

2. Actually, Vigorously Litigated

The requirement in collateral estoppel for actual litigation of an issue in a prior proceeding differs in at least two important respects from the possibility under res judicata that claims which were not litigated, but which could have been litigated, may be barred in later litigation. First, it is settled that collateral estoppel will not bar litigation of any issue that was not actually raised in a prior proceeding, regardless of whether the issue could have been raised. For example, in a breach of contract suit, it is possible that a defendant would make a tactical decision not to raise questions about whether the contract was unenforceable for a failure of consideration. If the plaintiff sued to enforce another obligation on the contract that only became due after the first suit was resolved, collateral estoppel would not prevent the defendant from raising the consideration simply because it could have been (but was not) raised in the first litigation. An even simpler example would arise if, in the first suit, the defendant chose to default and not enter any defense. The plaintiff would thereby win, but when the second cause of action arose all issues about consideration would still be available for the defendant to raise.[6]

Similarly, for collateral estoppel to apply an issue must have been litigated with some vigor. Thus, if an issue was raised in a passing way but did not engage the attention of the litigants significantly, the issue may not be estopped in later litigation because it was not litigated vigorously. To permit collateral estoppel to apply to issues raised in such a casual manner, perhaps because their importance to subsequent litigation was not yet foreseen, would produce unfair surprise for litigants.[7] It might also force needless complexity on the first litigation, as parties jockeyed to ensure that they would not be estopped collaterally in subsequent litigation.

3. Necessarily Decided on the Merits

This requirement has two parts, and courts sometimes treat them as distinct requirements. However, a decision to do so does not alter the analysis of this standard.

The first part of this requirement is that for collateral estoppel to apply, the issue decided in the first suit must have been decided in a way that is consistent with the judgment in the first suit. Thus, in the contract example used above, assume that the defendant was not found liable in the first suit because the plaintiff was found to have been in breach. If the jury also found that the consideration underlying the contract was good consideration, that finding would, in a literal sense, be unnecessary to the judgment that vindicated the defendant. Thus, if the same contract later gave rise to another cause of action not available at the time of the first lawsuit, the defendant would not be

6. *Cromwell v. County of Sac,* 94 U.S. (4 Otto) 351, 356–57, 24 L.Ed. 195 (1876) (default judgments not eligible for collateral estoppel).

7. Id. at 356 ("Various considerations, other than the actual merits, may govern a party in bringing forward grounds of recovery or defence in one action, which may not exist in another action upon a different demand, such as the smallness of the amount or the value of the property in controversy, the difficulty of obtaining the necessary evidence, the expense of the litigation, and his own situation at the time."). *But cf. Community Bank of Homestead v. Torcise,* 162 F.3d 1084 (11th Cir.1998) (observing that this requirement does not examine the quality or quantity of evidence or argument presented, only that fair opportunity to present the issue arose in a context where party understood potential adverse consequences).

precluded from asserting lack of consideration as a defense. Keep in mind, of course, that permission to relitigate the issue does not mean the defendant will prevail on the consideration issue. Refusal to apply collateral estoppel does not, of itself, guarantee victory for anyone. Instead, it only provides that the issue will be fought over again.

Similarly, if a jury finds for a plaintiff without explaining which of two distinct grounds (or both) is the basis for the verdict, a defendant retains the right to challenge those same grounds if they arise as issues in subsequent litigation.[8] Conversely, if a jury expressly finds for a plaintiff on two distinct grounds, both of which were vigorously litigated and which were decided in the plaintiff's favor, both may be treated as eligible for collateral estoppel in subsequent lawsuits.[9]

The second part of this requirement is that collateral estoppel applies only to issues resolved in cases decided on the merits.[10] Often, this will mean that cases which were dismissed on, for example, jurisdictional grounds will not develop issues in ways that qualify for collateral estoppel in subsequent cases. However, if the issues for which collateral estoppel treatment is sought are the procedural issues on which the original case was actually decided, then the requirement that the prior judgment "on the merits" is satisfied, at least for the procedural issues.[11]

B. Elements—Mutuality v. Nonmutual Estoppel

As discussed previously under the law of res judicata, there is a requirement that the parties in the second suit must be identical to (or in privity with) parties in the first suit before any claims may be precluded. At one time, a similar requirement of identical parties also applied to situations involving collateral estoppel. In the context of collateral estoppel, this requirement has been referred to as the "mutuality requirement,"[1] meaning that estoppel could not apply unless it applied mutually to all parties in a lawsuit. However, that requirement has experienced substantial erosion over the past half century. Today most jurisdictions (but not all)[2] have substantially abandoned this requirement.

8. *Cf., e.g., In re Caton,* 157 F.3d 1026, 1029 (5th Cir.1998), *cert. denied,* 526 U.S. 1068, 119 S.Ct. 1462, 143 L.Ed.2d 547 (1999) ("We only require that the record introduced have sufficient detail to allow the use of collateral estoppel.").

9. *But cf., National Satellite Sports, Inc. v. Eliadis, Inc.,* 253 F.3d 900, 909–10 (6th Cir. 2001), *cert. denied,* 534 U.S. 1156, 122 S.Ct. 1127, 151 L.Ed.2d 1019 (2002) (if prior decision involved resolution of two issues, either of which could have supported prior decision, prior judgment is not conclusive as to either issue standing alone; collecting substantial authority on both sides of question).

10. *Arizona v. California,* 530 U.S. 392, 120 S.Ct. 2304, 147 L.Ed.2d 374 (2000) (noting that while settlement entered by court as judgment can have res judicata effect, such a settlement normally does not have collateral estoppel effect).

11. *See, e.g., Transaero, Inc. v. La Fuerza Aerea Boliviana,* 162 F.3d 724, 731 (2d Cir. 1998), *cert. denied,* 526 U.S. 1146, 119 S.Ct. 2022, 143 L.Ed.2d 1033 (1999) ("[T]he service of process and personal jurisdiction issues were necessary to support the D.C. Circuit's final judgment—indeed, these issues were the subject of that judgment.").

1. *See, e.g., Blonder–Tongue Laboratories, Inc. v. University of Illinois Foundation,* 402 U.S. 313, 91 S.Ct. 1434, 28 L.Ed.2d 788 (1971).

2. *See, e.g., State Farm Fire & Casualty Co. v. Mabry,* 255 Va. 286, 289, 497 S.E.2d 844, 846 (1998) (imposing requirement that parties in current litigation be identical with parties in prior litigation or in privity with such parties). It should also be noted that collateral estoppel may

The replacement for the mutuality requirement—the requirement that parties in the second suit be identical to or in privity with parties in the first suit—is an assessment of fairness that, when satisfied, is ground for permitting application of nonmutual collateral estoppel.

The terminology of this area of the law of collateral estoppel can be awkward and initially difficult to grasp. However, because courts tend to use the terms that have been created for this area, it is essential that they be understood before proceeding any further. First, to repeat, a "mutuality" requirement means merely that a court will not apply collateral estoppel unless the parties in the second action are identical to (or in privity with) the parties in the original case. Second, when a court says it follows an approach of "nonmutuality," the court merely means that it may not always impose a requirement that the parties in the second lawsuit be identical to the parties in the first suit. Thus, subject to the requirements discussed below, an application of "nonmutual" collateral estoppel means that the court found collateral estoppel appropriate even though the parties in both suits were not identical. Third, "defensive" nonmutual collateral estoppel means that the court is being asked to apply collateral estoppel in a circumstance where the defendant in the second lawsuit is trying to use nonmutual collateral estoppel defensively—as a shield—to ward off the plaintiff's attack. Fourth, "offensive" nonmutual collateral estoppel means that the court is being asked to apply collateral estoppel to prevent a defendant from raising an issue that was (allegedly) litigated in a prior lawsuit. Thus, the plaintiff is trying to use nonmutual collateral estoppel as a sword, to strike down a defense raised by a defendant. The distinction between defensive and offensive nonmutual collateral estoppel is important, because it is distinctly possible that the requirements for defensive nonmutual collateral estoppel might be less difficult to meet than the requirements for offensive nonmutual collateral estoppel.

1. Defensive Nonmutual Collateral Estoppel

Suppose a plaintiff sues a defendant for patent infringement. Suppose further that the essence of the defense is that the patent on which the plaintiff's claim is based is not a valid patent. If the defendant wins the case on that ground, the matter is obviously res judicata between the two parties. But if the plaintiff later files a second lawsuit, against a different defendant, asserting that the same patent was infringed, it is clear that the parties in the second suit are not identical with the parties in the first suit. Additionally, it will often be true that the defendant in the second suit will not be in privity with the defendant in the first suit. In those circumstances, if the mutuality requirement is imposed, the plaintiff will not be estopped from asserting (in the second suit) the validity of the patent that was found to be invalid in the first suit. This is inefficient for the courts, and also creates the possibility that a finding of a valid patent in the second suit will create an unacceptable situation for other parties trying to discern the validity of the patent. Thus, the majority of judicial systems facing such problems now permit a party in the position of the defendant in the second suit to assert the defense of collateral estoppel, provided only that the plaintiff

be invoked against the federal government when the United States is a party to litigation and the elements of collateral estoppel (including requirements of mutuality) are established. *United States v. Stauffer Chemical Co.,* 464 U.S. 165, 104 S.Ct. 575, 78 L.Ed.2d 388 (1984). However, it is also settled that nonmutual collateral estoppel may not be invoked against the federal government. *United States v. Mendoza,* 464 U.S. 154, 104 S.Ct. 568, 78 L.Ed.2d 379 (1984).

had a full and fair opportunity to litigate the patent validity issue in the first lawsuit.[3]

2. Offensive Nonmutual Collateral Estoppel

A more problematic use of nonmutual collateral estoppel arises when a party seeks to use the rule as more than a defense to an action. In a well known case decided by the Supreme Court,[4] the defendants had previously been sued by the Securities and Exchange Commission for making false proxy statements. The Commission sought an injunction, and the defendants lost that lawsuit. Subsequently a class of shareholders sued the defendants on the same grounds and sought collateral estoppel for the previous court's finding that the proxy statements had been false and misleading. In contrast to defensive nonmutual collateral estoppel, where collateral estoppel is used as a shield to ward off a subsequent claim by a plaintiff who had lost a prior lawsuit, this case was an attempt to use the defendants' prior loss as a sword with which to produce a second unfavorable result for those defendants.

The Supreme Court concluded that, at least sometimes, nonmutual collateral estoppel could be used offensively as well as defensively. However, for collateral estoppel to be applied offensively, the Court directed lower federal courts to examine all the circumstances of a case to ensure that application of collateral estoppel is fair. Specifically, the Court suggested that lower courts examine: (1) whether the plaintiff seeking offensive nonmutual collateral estoppel could have participated in the previous suit; (2) whether the defendant had a fair chance to litigate the issue with knowledge of the fact that the same issue might arise in subsequent litigation; (3) whether the judgment in the litigation for which collateral estoppel is sought was inconsistent with results in any litigation which had taken place still earlier;[5] and (4) whether, in the previous suit, procedural limitations had prevented the defendant from offering some evidence or otherwise defending himself in ways now open in the later litigation.[6]

3. Nonmutuality and the United States

Although the United States is as vulnerable as any party to the application of collateral estoppel when the requirement of mutuality is satisfied, it is settled

3. *See, e.g., Blonder–Tongue Laboratories, Inc. v. University of Illinois Foundation,* 402 U.S. 313, 91 S.Ct. 1434, 28 L.Ed.2d 788 (1971).

4. *Parklane Hosiery Co. v. Shore,* 439 U.S. 322, 99 S.Ct. 645, 58 L.Ed.2d 552 (1979).

5. An example of how this situation could occur arises if one posits a one-car automobile accident in which three passengers in the car are injured. If the first passenger sues the driver and alleges that the driver was intoxicated at the time of the accident, the driver might win by introducing into evidence a police report showing that the driver was free of intoxicants. That finding, of course, would not bind the two passengers who had not yet sued. If the second passenger then sued, making the same allegation about intoxication, that passenger might win by demonstrating that the police test for intoxicants in the driver's blood was administered improperly. Thus, if the third passenger waited to sue until he/she was sufficiently healed to participate actively in a lawsuit, offensive nonmutual collateral estoppel might apply to the victory of the second passenger over the driver. Given the fact that the driver had both a prior victory and a prior defeat on the issue of intoxication, it might seem unfair to treat the issue as estopped against the driver in the third lawsuit. Thus, the Supreme Court's approach suggests that in such circumstances no party should be able to claim estoppel, and the parties in the third suit should relitigate the issue of intoxication again.

6. *Parklane Hosiery Co. v. Shore,* 439 U.S. 322, 99 S.Ct. 645, 58 L.Ed.2d 552 (1979).

that nonmutual collateral estoppel (defensive or offensive) may not be applied against the United States.[7]

C. Application to Issues of Law and Fact

Older cases expressed doubt that collateral estoppel was applicable to issues of law as well as fact. While some jurisdictions may still follow that rule, the clear trend in most circumstances is to apply collateral estoppel to issues of both law and fact.[1]

D. Exceptions to Collateral Estoppel

Even in situations where all the requirements of collateral estoppel are satisfied, it is still possible that additional considerations may make application of estoppel unfair in a particular case. For example, as has already been discussed above, courts are reluctant to impose collateral estoppel in circumstances where the affected party might not reasonably have appreciated the risk of collateral estoppel in subsequent cases. Additionally, if the law or facts of a situation undergo material change between the first lawsuit and the second one, it might be unfair to impose collateral estoppel on issues decided in the first suit.[1]

E. Collateral Estoppel—Affirmative Defense: Rule 8(c)

Collateral estoppel, like res judicata, is listed as an affirmative defense under Federal Rule of Civil Procedure 8(c).[1] In theory, affirmative defenses must be raised or waived.[2] However, if a party is seeking to apply nonmutual collateral estoppel offensively, so as to preclude a defendant from relitigating an issue previously decided, such use of collateral estoppel is obviously not a "defense" to a claim and therefore raises no issues that would be governed by Rule 8(c).

F. Relationship to Full Faith and Credit

The command that courts of one jurisdiction must give full faith and credit[1] to the judgments of another jurisdiction applies to matters of collateral estoppel. Thus, if the courts of a jurisdiction where a case was decided would treat an issue in that case as controlled by collateral estoppel, other courts have a duty to

7. *United States v. Mendoza,* 464 U.S. 154, 162, 104 S.Ct. 568, 573, 78 L.Ed.2d 379 (1984).

1. *Montana v. United States,* 440 U.S. 147, 162, 99 S.Ct. 970, 978, 59 L.Ed.2d 210 (1979) (normal rules of collateral estoppel apply to questions of law, provided that both lawsuits involve substantially related claims).

1. *Montana v. United States,* 440 U.S. 147, 159, 99 S.Ct. 970, 976, 59 L.Ed.2d 210 (1979) ("[C]hanges in facts essential to a judgment will render collateral estoppel inapplicable in a subsequent action raising the same issues."); *Commissioner v. Sunnen,* 333 U.S. 591, 601, 68 S.Ct. 715, 721, 92 L.Ed. 898 (1948) (collateral estoppel inapplicable where relevant law changed between first and second proceeding). *But cf. Hickerson v. City of New York,* 146 F.3d 99, 105 (2d Cir.1998), *cert. denied,* 525 U.S. 1067, 119 S.Ct. 795, 142 L.Ed.2d 658 (1999) (failure to offer evidence already available in first suit is not a defense to collateral estoppel in second suit).

1. *See also Blonder–Tongue Laboratories, Inc. v. University of Illinois Foundation,* 402 U.S. 313, 91 S.Ct. 1434, 28 L.Ed.2d 788 (1971).

2. *But cf., e.g., Petrocelli v. Daniel Woodhead Co.,* 993 F.2d 27, 29 n. 1 (3d Cir.1993) (affirmative defense not raised in original pleading is not waived if it can be properly raised under Rule 15, governing amendments to pleadings).

1. U.S. Const. Art. IV § 1. See also, 28 U.S.C.A. § 1738.

give the issue the same status of collateral estoppel as would be accorded by the court that decided the case.[2]

2. *See, e.g., Community Bank of Homestead v. Torcise,* 162 F.3d 1084, 1087 n. 5 (11th Cir. 1998) (noting obligation to use Florida standard for collateral estoppel because prior judgment was rendered in Florida).

*

PART IV

FEDERAL RULES OF CIVIL PROCEDURE WITH COMMENTARY

Rules Effective September 16, 1938

Including Amendments Effective December 1, 2004

Research Note

Rule requirements, case law applications, commentary, and references to treatises and law reviews are available in Wright, Miller, et al., Federal Practice and Procedure, *Volumes 4 to 20.*

Use WESTLAW®*to find cases citing or applying rules.* WESTLAW *may also be used to search for terms in court rules or to update court rules. See the US–RULES and US–ORDERS SCOPE screens for detailed descriptive information and search tips.*

Table of Rules

IV. PARTIES

VIII. PROVISIONAL AND FINAL REMEDIES

IX. SPECIAL PROCEEDINGS

APPENDIX OF FORMS

[The Appendix of Forms is reproduced in Part V, below.]

I. SCOPE OF RULES—ONE FORM OF ACTION

RULE 1

SCOPE AND PURPOSE OF RULES

These rules govern the procedure in the United States district courts in all suits of a civil nature whether cognizable as cases at law or in equity or in admiralty, with the exceptions stated in Rule 81. They shall be construed and administered to secure the just, speedy, and inexpensive determination of every action.

[Amended December 29, 1948, effective October 20, 1949; February 28, 1966, effective July 1, 1966; April 22, 1993, effective December 1, 1993.]

AUTHORS' COMMENTARY ON RULE 1

PURPOSE AND SCOPE

The Federal Rules generally apply to all civil actions in the district courts of the United States. Federal courts, and the attorneys who appear before them, are required to construe and administer the Rules in a manner that achieves the just, speedy, and inexpensive determination of each civil action.

APPLICATIONS

Creation, Status, and Validity of the Federal Rules

Under the authority vested by the Rules Enabling Act of 1934,[1] the United States Supreme Court promulgated the original Federal Rules of Civil Procedure in December 1937. The original Rules became effective in September 1938, and have been amended on numerous occasions since. The Rules have the force and effect of law. They superseded inconsistent statutes enacted prior to their effective date.

With the exceptions noted below, the Rules define the procedures for all civil actions proceeding in the District Courts of the United States. Unless a Rule requires or permits the application of State procedure, the federal courts do not apply State procedural laws, procedural rules, or procedural decisions.[2]

Although prescribed by the Supreme Court, a Federal Rule may be challenged as inconsistent with the rulemaking power delegated by Congress to the Supreme Court under the Rules Enabling Act.[3] To date, however, no Rule has been declared invalid.

1. Act of June 19, 1934, ch. 651, 48 Stat. 1064, codified in current form at 28 U.S.C.A. §§ 2071–77.

2. *See E.E.O.C. v. HBE Corp.*, 135 F.3d 543, 551 (8th Cir.1998) (federal rules apply to all civil actions tried in federal court, and control over conflicting State law).

3. *See Mississippi Publishing Corp. v. Murphree*, 326 U.S. 438, 444, 66 S.Ct. 242, 246, 90 L.Ed. 185 (1946)("The fact that this Court pro-

The Advisory Committee and Its Committee Notes

To help draft the original Federal Rules, the Supreme Court appointed an Advisory Committee on Rules comprising a panel of attorneys and law professors. This consultative tradition continues today, in the form of the Judicial Conference of the United States' Advisory Committee on Civil Rules, which investigates and recommends amendments to the Federal Rules. The members of the Advisory Committee have included federal and State judges, practicing attorneys, law professors, and Department of Justice representatives.[4]

Both the original Advisory Committee and its successors have published "Notes" as an aid in construing and interpreting the particular purpose and intent of each Rule and its amendments. The Committee Notes are only guides; the Notes neither are a part of the Rules nor have they been approved by the Supreme Court. However, in practice, the Notes have assumed the force of a veritable legislative history to the Rules and their amendments. The Notes can be cited as formidable (though non-binding) authority for construing the Rules.[5]

Where the Rules Apply

Rule 1 implements Article 3, Section 2 of the Constitution which extends the judicial power of the United States "to all Cases, in Law and Equity, arising under this Constitution, the Laws of the United States, and [its] Treaties . . . [and] to all Cases of admiralty and maritime Jurisdiction."[6] The Rules apply to all "district courts" of the United States. By special congressional enactments, the Rules have been extended to the United States District Court for the District of Columbia,[7] and to the territorial and insular courts of Guam,[8] the Northern Mariana Islands,[9] Puerto Rico,[10] and the Virgin Islands.[11] Because it is not a "district court", the Rules do not apply to the United States Tax Court.[12]

mulgated the rules as formulated and recommended by the Advisory Committee does not foreclose consideration of their validity, meaning or consistency").

4. The procedure for amending the Federal Rules is more specifically described in Part I of this text.

5. A discussion of the history behind and the legal effect of the Advisory Committee Notes, the collected case law discussing the interpretative value and weight of the Notes, and the full text of the original and amending Notes appears in Part VII of this text.

6. *See Vodusek v. Bayliner Marine Corp.*, 71 F.3d 148, 153 n. 2 (4th Cir.1995) (citing U.S. Const. art. 3, § 2).

7. *See* 28 U.S.C.A. § 88 (officially confirming that the District of Columbia is a judicial district of the United States). *See also* Rule 81(e) (applying law of District of Columbia, where appropriate, when word "state" is used).

8. *See* 48 U.S.C.A. § 1424 (creating district court of Guam and vesting it with the jurisdiction of a district court of the United States).

9. *See* 48 U.S.C.A. §§ 1821 & 1822 (creating district court of the Northern Mariana Islands and vesting it with the jurisdiction of a district court of the United States).

10. *See* 28 U.S.C.A. § 119 (creating Puerto Rico as a judicial district).

11. *See* 48 U.S.C.A. §§ 1611 & 1612 (creating district court of the Virgin Islands and vesting it with the jurisdiction of a district court of the United States).

12. *See Michaels v. Commissioner*, 144 F.3d 495, 497 (7th Cir.1998) (commenting that although the Rules are not binding on the Tax Court, they "provide a source of persuasive authority to that court in filling any gaps in its own rules of procedure"); *Smith v. Commissioner*, 926 F.2d 1470, 1478 (6th Cir.1991) (same); *Scherping v. Commissioner*, 747 F.2d 478, 480

Civil Rules and the Courts of Appeals

By their terms the Federal Rules of Civil Procedure apply only to the federal District Courts. However, the policies that underlie the Rules may apply equally to the Courts of Appeals.[13]

Specialized Proceedings

The Rules set the procedure in district courts "in all suits of a civil nature".[14] However, Rule 1 cross-references to Rule 81, which sets forth a list of specialized proceedings to which the Rules do *not* apply.[15] Under Rule 81, for example, the Federal Rules apply in bankruptcy proceedings, but only to the extent prescribed by the Federal Rules of Bankruptcy Procedure.[16] Although the Rules apply generally to admiralty proceedings,[17] they do *not* apply to prize proceedings in admiralty.[18] The Rules also do *not* alter certain existing statutory review procedures, such as those prescribed for reviewing orders of the Secretary of Agriculture, the Secretary of the Interior, or petroleum control boards,[19] or the existing procedures to enforce orders of the National Labor Relations Board,[20] although such proceedings must conform to the Rules as "far as applicable". Likewise, certain "summary proceedings", expressly authorized by statute, are not necessarily governed by the Rules.[21] Nor do the Rules apply in administrative proceedings or in disciplinary or disbarment proceedings.

The Rules, however, do apply to other specialized proceedings, such as certain arbitration proceedings[22] and proceedings for admission to citizenship, habeas corpus, and *quo warranto*,[23] but only to the extent Congress has not framed alternative procedural rules for those contexts.

The Rules also apply generally to de novo immigration proceedings,[24] civil contempt proceedings (when the original proceeding was governed by the Rules), civil actions for forfeiture and penalty actions

(8th Cir.1984) (noting that Tax Court operates under its own Rules of Practice and Procedure). *See generally* 26 U.S.C.A. § 7453 (authorizing promulgation of Tax Court Rules of Practice & Procedure); Tax Ct. R. 1(b) (providing that "These Rules shall be construed to secure the just, speedy, and inexpensive determination of every case").

13. *See Newman–Green, Inc. v. Alfonzo–Larrain*, 490 U.S. 826, 832, 109 S.Ct. 2218, 2223, 104 L.Ed.2d 893 (1989); *Wilson v. Maritime Overseas Corp.*, 150 F.3d 1 (1st Cir.1998); *Balgowan v. New Jersey*, 115 F.3d 214 (3d Cir. 1997).

14. *See* Rule 1.

15. Rule 81 was amended in 2001 to omit references that had formerly excluded the Rules from Copyright cases and from mental health proceedings in the United States District Court for the District of Columbia. With the abrogation of the separate Copyright Rules, the Rules now apply in copyright cases, and because Congress has now transferred such proceedings to local courts in the District of Columbia, the mental health proceedings provision was eliminated as superfluous.

16. *See* Rule 81(a)(1).

17. *See* Rule 1.

18. *See* Rule 81(a)(1).

19. *See* Rule 81(a)(4).

20. *See* Rule 81(a)(5).

21. *See SEC v. McCarthy*, 322 F.3d 650, 655–59 (9th Cir.2003) (recognizing exception for "summary proceedings" expressly authorized by statute, such as Securities Exchange Act which grants district courts jurisdiction to enforce SEC orders).

22. *See* Rule 81(a)(3).

23. *See* Rule 81(a)(2).

24. *See Alvear v. Kirk*, 87 F.Supp.2d 1241, 1243 (D.N.M.2000) (holding that Rules 12 and 56 governed de novo immigration proceedings pursuant to 8 U.S.C. § 1421(c)).

by the United States,[25] patent cases, removed cases,[26] civil actions in which the United States or one of its officers or agencies is a party,[27] and proceedings to compel compliance with a subpoena to testify or to produce documents, as issued by an officer or agency of the United States pursuant to federal statute.[28]

"Just", "Speedy", and "Inexpensive" Mandate

Aside from defining when the Rules apply, Rule 1 also fixes the objectives of the Federal Rules: they are to be construed and administered so as to achieve the "just, speedy, and inexpensive determination of every action". Often cited, these goals have been heralded by the Supreme Court as "the touchstones of federal procedure".[29] The 1993 amendments to Rule 1 emphasized the District Court's affirmative duty to exercise the procedural authority the Rules bestow so as to ensure that civil litigation in the federal courts is resolved fairly and without undue cost or delay.[30] This affirmative duty is shared by practicing attorneys, as officers of the court.[31] To realize Rule 1's goals of "just, speedy, and inexpensive" determinations of federal cases, the parties must work diligently to follow the Rules and the courts must resolutely enforce the Rules, otherwise the Rules—and the laudable objectives they seek—will become illusory.[32]

The courts have quoted these touchstones, typically in combination with other Rules, as authority for their constructions and interpretations of a Rule. Indeed, Rule 1 has been cited as authority for preventing a litigant from flouting the "spirit" of the Rules, even where the litigant's conduct might otherwise comport with the Rule's literal

25. *Cf. United States v. Mosavi*, 138 F.3d 1365 (11th Cir.1998) (Federal Rules of Civil Procedure do not apply to criminal forfeitures).

26. *See* Rule 81(c).

27. The Rules were not designed to extend the jurisdiction of the federal courts. Consequently, the Rules' references to procedures for suing or being sued by the United States does not constitute a waiver of sovereign immunity.

28. *See* Rule 81(a)(3).

29. *Brown Shoe Co. v. United States*, 370 U.S. 294, 306, 82 S.Ct. 1502, 1513, 8 L.Ed.2d 510 (1962). *See In re Bayer AG*, 146 F.3d 188, 189 (3d Cir.1998) (commenting that the Rules and Rule 1's touchstones "initiated a revolution in the litigation process in the federal courts in this country" and, ultimately, influenced foreign litigation as well).

30. *See* Rule 1 advisory committee notes 1993. *See also Active Prods. Corp. v. A.H. Choitz & Co.*, 163 F.R.D. 274, 277–78 (N.D.Ind. 1995) (citing amended language of Rule as authority for employing a panel of special masters and an electronic filing, docketing, and service system to assist in the administration of complex, multi-party environmental litigation); *Johnson v. Board of County Comm'rs for County of Fremont*, 868 F.Supp. 1226 (D.Colo. 1994)(commenting that public interest demands a seemly and efficient use of judicial resources to achieve Rule 1 goals, and courts are thus obligated to raise perceived dangers to these objectives even if parties do not).

31. *See Reebok Int'l v. Sebelen*, 959 F.Supp. 553, 558 n. 1 (D.P.R.1997) (citing Herman Melville's fable, *Bartleby the Scrivener*, as a valuable reminder that "the lawyer's role extends beyond filing motions and be an unquestioning mouthpiece for his client. His role is to engage in the adversarial process in good faith and in accordance with" the precepts of Rule 1); *Hill v. MacMillan McGraw–Hill Sch. Publishing Co.*, No. C–93–20824, 1995 WL 317054 (N.D.Cal. 1995) (noting that litigants have obligation to court to refrain from conduct that frustrates the aims of Rule 1), *appeal dismissed*, 102 F.3d 422 (9th Cir.1996).

32. *See Mused v. United States Dep't of Agriculture Food & Nutrition Serv.*, 169 F.R.D. 28, 35 (W.D.N.Y.1996).

meaning.[33]

Examples of the courts' reliance on Rule 1 to achieve these objectives are legion. For instance, the Supreme Court cited Rule 1's mandate to justify a broadening of the long-cramped reach of the summary judgment rule.[34] The Supreme Court also mentioned the Rule 1 mandate in rejecting an overly technical interpretation of pleading procedure, noting that, led by Rule 1, the Rules "reject the approach that pleading is a game of skill in which one misstep by counsel may be decisive to the outcome and accept the principle that the purpose of pleading is to facilitate a proper decision on the merits."[35]

Courts of Appeals have quoted the touchstones to guide the interpretations of other Federal Rules,[36] to criticize a trial court's delay in issuing its findings of fact and conclusions of law,[37] to approve a trial court's immediate, oral announcement of its findings of fact,[38] to forbid parties from "ambushing" a trial court by ignoring conflict-of-law objections until after they learn whether they've won or lost at trial,[39] to deny a perceived "end-run" around the statutory prohibition against a *pro se* representation of a corporate party,[40] to affirm a trial court's discretionary refusal to reconsider and vacate its earlier summary judgment ruling,[41] to justify the imposition of sanctions for discovery abuses,[42] to overturn a trial court's decision to admit into evidence a

33. *See United States v. High Country Broadcasting Co.*, 3 F.3d 1244, 1245 (9th Cir. 1993), *cert. denied*, 513 U.S. 826, 115 S.Ct. 93, 130 L.Ed.2d 44 (1994). *But see Central States, Southeast & Southwest Areas Pension Fund v. Central Cartage Co.*, 69 F.3d 1312, 1314–15 (7th Cir.1995) (cautioning that "the need to consider the objectives in Fed.R.Civ.P. 1 when construing all of the rules does not justify disregarding limitations explicitly built into them"), *cert. denied*, 517 U.S. 1134, 116 S.Ct. 1419, 134 L.Ed.2d 544 (1996).

34. *See Celotex Corp. v. Catrett*, 477 U.S. 317, 327, 106 S.Ct. 2548, 2555, 91 L.Ed.2d 265 (1986)(commenting how summary judgment constitutes an integral role in implementing the Federal Rules' task of a just, speedy, and inexpensive resolution of litigation).

35. *See Conley v. Gibson*, 355 U.S. 41, 48, 78 S.Ct. 99, 103, 2 L.Ed.2d 80 (1957). *See also Foman v. Davis*, 371 U.S. 178, 181–82, 83 S.Ct. 227, 230 (1962) (same quotation).

36. *See Transamerica Occidental Life Ins. Co. v. Aviation Office of America, Inc.*, 292 F.3d 384, 389 (3d Cir.2002) (citing Rule 1 in concluding that policy underlying Rule 13(a) is "judicial economy"); *In re Grand Jury*, 286 F.3d 153, 159 (3d Cir.2002) (citing Rule 1 in explaining that Rule 26(c) protective orders are intended to "secure the just, speedy, and inexpensive determination" of civil trials by "encouraging full disclosure of all evidence that might conceivably be relevant").

37. *See Ashelman v. Wawrzaszek*, 111 F.3d 674, 675 n. 3 (9th Cir.1997) (chastising trial court's five year delay in issuing findings and conclusions, noting that the just, speedy, and inexpensive resolution of every action is "the first principle of the Federal Rules of Civil Procedure" and "should not be forgotten, as it apparently was here").

38. *See Lansford-Coaldale Joint Water Auth. v. Tonolli Corp.*, 4 F.3d 1209, 1214–15 (3d Cir. 1993).

39. *See Celle v. Filipino Reporter Enters. Inc.*, 209 F.3d 163, 175–76 (2d Cir.2000) (such ruling "would permit a losing party to lead a trial court into error and then to profit on appeal from the misguidance").

40. *See United States v. High Country Broadcasting Co.*, 3 F.3d 1244, 1245 (9th Cir. 1993)(per curiam) *cert. denied*, 513 U.S. 826, 115 S.Ct. 93, 130 L.Ed.2d 44 (1994).

41. *See Calpetco 1981 v. Marshall Exploration, Inc.*, 989 F.2d 1408, 1415 (5th Cir. 1993)(citing Rule 1 to hold that, on applications for reconsideration, trial court must have "considerable discretion in determining when enough is enough").

42. *See Malautea v. Suzuki Motor Co.*, 987 F.2d 1536, 1546 (11th Cir.1993), *cert. denied*, 510 U.S. 863, 114 S.Ct. 181, 126 L.Ed.2d 140 (1993).

previously undisclosed surveillance videotape,[43] to overrule a rigid, prior precedent commanding that the trial court always grant a plaintiff one chance to amend a dismissed complaint even where no such leave had ever been sought,[44] to excuse the failure to file a motion for judgment as a matter of law before submission to the jury where such a filing would have violated the law-of-the-case doctrine,[45] and to affirm a judgment instead of remanding for a subsequent amendment to a party's complaint.[46] The Rule 1 mandates have also been cited as support for the conclusion that a federal district's local rules on proper forms for filed documents are not jurisdictional, and do not justify a prejudicial dismissal.[47]

The District Courts, too, have cited Rule 1's touchstone mandate as support for various rulings. For example, federal trial judges have cited this mandate in regulating "Rambo"-style litigation tactics,[48] in decrying misbehavior by counsel,[49] in imposing Rule 11 actions for pleading falsely,[50] in permanently enjoining a plaintiff from filing frivolous complaints and seeking further *in forma pauperis* status,[51] in fining a non-appearing attorney for the monetary value of lost federal court trial time,[52] in refusing to assess against "impoverished" plaintiffs the fees charged by defendants' experts for appearing at a deposition taken by plaintiffs' counsel,[53] in issuing discovery orders,[54] in permitting a defen-

43. *See Chiasson v. Zapata Gulf Marine Corp.*, 988 F.2d 513, 518 n. 10 (5th Cir. 1993)(noting that non-disclosure thwarted Rule 1's policies because it eliminated an opportunity for a pretrial settlement), *cert. denied*, 511 U.S. 1029, 114 S.Ct. 1536, 128 L.Ed.2d 189 (1994).

44. *See Wagner v. Daewoo Heavy Indus. America Corp.*, 314 F.3d 541, 542–43 (11th Cir. 2002) (overruling prior rule).

45. *See Kerman v. City of New York*, 374 F.3d 93, 118–19 (2d Cir. 2004) ("Such a motion would invite the trial court to commit error" and, if wrongly granted, "a new trial ... would be required—hardly a just, speedy, or inexpensive course").

46. *See Boston & Maine Corp. v. Town of Hampton*, 987 F.2d 855, 867 (1st Cir.1993).

47. *See Ordonez v. Johnson*, 254 F.3d 814, 816 (9th Cir.2001) (treating such technical local rules as jurisdictional "would conflict with the mandate of Federal Rule of Civil Procedure 1 to provide a just and speedy determination of every action").

48. *See In re Amezaga*, 195 B.R. 221 (Bkrtcy. D.P.R.1996) (noting that "Rambo Litigation" is not tolerated by the Court because, although it may project zealous advocacy, it does not promote Rule 1's goals of a just, speedy, and inexpensive determination of every action); *Applied Telematics, Inc. v. Sprint Corp.*, No. 94–CV–4603, 1995 WL 79237 (E.D.Pa.1995)(decrying counsel's "Rambo Litigation" deposition defense tactics as failing to promote goals of Rule 1).

49. *See Nissan Motor Co. v. Nissan Computer Corp.*, 180 F.Supp.2d 1089, 1096 (C.D.Cal. 2002) (holding that counsel's conduct in threatening to record, or actually recording, conversations with opposing counsel "interferes with the just and speedy determination of this action").

50. *See Young v. City of Providence*, 301 F.Supp.2d 187, 197 (D.R.I. 2004).

51. *See Hill v. Gates*, 940 F.Supp. 108 (M.D.Pa.1996) (filing of frivolous complaints containing offensive and derogatory material justified a permanent injunction against future such filings and a requirement that plaintiff pay filing fees).

52. *See Specialized Plating, Inc. v. Federal Envtl. Servs., Inc.*, 975 F.Supp. 397 (D.Mass. 1997).

53. *See Reed v. Binder*, 165 F.R.D. 424, 427–28 (D.N.J.1996) (citing Rule 1, and concluding that "the imposing economic obstacle facing these plaintiffs seeking redress for the death of their wife and mother ... requires that these costs be shifted to the defendants").

54. *See Jackson v. County of Sacramento*, 175 F.R.D. 653, 658 (E.D.Cal.1997) (citing Rule to limit scope of discovery); *Zapata v. IBP, Inc.*, 160 F.R.D. 625, 628 (D.Kan.1995)(ruling that general, blanket protective order barring parties in one case from sharing discovery with litigants

dant to file a "renewed" motion for summary judgment,[55] in denying a late intervention motion,[56] in excusing the need for a full *Daubert* evidentiary hearing on an expert's reliability,[57] in limiting the number of expert witnesses,[58] in embracing the videotaping of discovery depositions,[59] and in otherwise generally controlling pretrial conduct.[60]

ADDITIONAL RESEARCH REFERENCES

Wright & Miller, *Federal Practice and Procedure* §§ 1011–1040.

C.J.S. Federal Civil Procedure §§ 5 et seq.; Federal Courts § 284.

West's Key No. Digests, Federal Civil Procedure ⚷21, 31–44; Federal Courts ⚷522.

in another case (where that same discovery would have been allowed) "would hardly accord with the purpose of the rules set forth in Fed. R.Civ.P. 1"); *Johns Hopkins Univ. v. Cellpro*, 160 F.R.D. 30 (D.Del.1995)(citing Rule 1's goals as justification for refusing to stay certain discovery until after one component of trial was completed); *Agostino Ferrari, S.p.A. v. Antonacci*, 858 F.Supp. 478 (E.D.Pa.1994)(denying reopening of discovery and concomitant lengthening of litigation as injuring public's interest in Rule 1 goals).

55. *See Fleischer v. Resolution Trust Corp.*, 882 F.Supp. 1010 (D.Kan.1995)(noting that "renewed" motion represented the most efficient vehicle for resolving certain issues).

56. *See Coburn v. DaimlerChrysler Servs. N.A.*, L.L.C., 218 F.R.D. 607, 610–11 (N.D. Ill. 2003).

57. *See Lanni v. New Jersey*, 177 F.R.D. 295, 303 (D.N.J.1998).

58. *See Planned Parenthood of Central N.J. v. Verniero*, 22 F.Supp.2d 331, 339 (D.N.J.1998).

59. *See Fanelli v. Centenary Coll.*, 211 F.R.D. 268, 271 (D.N.J.2002) (because it may foster careful assessment of the strengths and weaknesses of trial testimony of witnesses (including how a jury might view that testimony), videotaped discovery depositions may lead to more prompt settlements).

60. *See Myers v. County of Orange*, 870 F.Supp. 555 (S.D.N.Y.1994) (in ruling on summary judgment motion, court refused to consider informal comments by counsel during off-the-record pretrial conferences because to consider such comments would have a chilling effect on the open discussions necessary to promote Rule 1 objectives).

RULE 2

ONE FORM OF ACTION

There shall be one form of action to be known as "civil action".

AUTHORS' COMMENTARY ON RULE 2

PURPOSE AND SCOPE

The Rules have merged the law and equity sides of the federal courts, providing a single procedural framework for all claims and defenses. All relief may now be obtained in the same action, whether the case seeks legal remedies, equitable remedies, or both.

APPLICATIONS

Civil Action Defined

For civil claims, the Rules establish only one form of proceeding, known as a "civil action". This term refers to the entire civil proceeding, including all component "claims" and "cases" within that proceeding.[1] Thus, for example, a party may not remove to federal court only a portion of lawsuit filed in State court.[2]

Equity Principles Applicable

Although the Rules have fused law and equity into a single procedural framework, the federal courts still apply equity principles in appropriate cases.[3]

1. *See Nolan v. Boeing Co.*, 919 F.2d 1058, 1066 (5th Cir.1990)(ruling that "case" and "action" refer to the same thing—the entirety of a civil proceeding, including third party claims), *cert. denied*, 499 U.S. 962, 111 S.Ct. 1587, 113 L.Ed.2d 651 (1991). *See also Fogg v. Ashcroft*, 254 F.3d 103, 107 (D.C.Cir.2001) (citing Rule 2 as support for holding that statutory cap on damages in "an action brought" under the Civil Rights of Act of 1964 applies to entire lawsuit, not just to individual claims within lawsuit); *Hudson v. Reno*, 130 F.3d 1193, 1199 (6th Cir. 1997) (same); *In re Hinote*, 179 F.R.D. 335 (S.D.Ala.1998); (State court petition filed to obtain pre-commencement discovery in likely ERISA case was not removable because it was not commenced by the filing of a complaint and, thus, was not a "civil action" within the meaning of Rule 2).

2. *See, e.g., Clark Const. Group, Inc. v. Hellmuth, Obata & Kassabaum, Inc.*, 286 F.Supp.2d 1348, 1348–52 (M.D.Fla. 2003) (litigant's attempt to remove less than whole civil action, and "unilaterally sever ... claims and remove only part of the State Court Action", was foreclosed by Rules and deprived Court of subject matter jurisdiction).

3. *See Stainback v. Mo Hock Ke Lok Po*, 336 U.S. 368, 382 n. 26, 69 S.Ct. 606, 614 n. 26, 93 L.Ed. 741 (1949)(noting that Rules' merger of law and equity did not affect the substantive principles of equity); *In re U.S. Brass Corp.*, 110 F.3d 1261, 1267 (7th Cir.1997) (commenting that since law and equity were merged in the federal courts, judges have freely imported equitable defenses into suits at law).

Determining Form of Action

Although the federal courts no longer recognize a distinction in procedure between cases on the "law-side" and cases in "equity",[4] this distinction still persists in some limited contexts in which the federal courts may yet be called upon to discern the substantive "form" of the litigation (*i.e.*, legal or equitable).[5] This inquiry may arise when the court has to decide whether a litigant enjoys a right to a trial by jury,[6] or when, in diversity cases, the controlling State law retains the law / equity distinction as to such substantive issues as the applicable statute of limitations.

Joinder of All Claims and Defenses

Without a separate law-side and equity-side to the federal courts, a party may now join all claims and defenses (legal and equitable) against all opposing parties in one action.[7] Note, however, that the Rules and certain judiciary title statutes may limit such joinder.[8]

Complete Relief

When granting final judgment, a court may grant all the relief to which a party is entitled (legal and equitable), regardless of the relief demanded in the pleadings.[9] Note, however, that many judicial districts require parties to list in a pretrial memorandum the specific relief they intend to seek and, thereafter, to remain bound by that listing at trial.[10]

ADDITIONAL RESEARCH REFERENCES

Wright & Miller, *Federal Practice and Procedure* §§ 1041–1050.

C.J.S. Federal Civil Procedure §§ 4, 37 et seq.

West's Key No. Digests, Federal Civil Procedure ⚷5–7, 71–73, 81–86.

4. *See Cablevision of Midwest, Inc. v. City of Brunswick*, 117 F.Supp.2d 658, 661 (N.D. Ohio 2000) (noting that purpose of Rule 2 "was to abolish the distinction between actions at law and suits in equity, and thereby to simplify procedure in the federal courts").

5. *See Burlington N. R.R. Co. v. Nebraska Pub. Power Dist.*, 931 F.Supp. 1470, 1479 (D.Neb.1996).

6. *See Wooddell v. International Bhd. of Elec. Workers, Local 71*, 502 U.S. 93, 97, 112 S.Ct. 494, 497, 116 L.Ed.2d 419 (1991)(to decide whether a particular lawsuit would resolve "legal" rights, and thus entitle the litigants to a trial by jury, the courts: (1) compare the action to 18th Century claims brought in English courts prior to the merger of law and equity; and (2) determine whether the remedy sought is legal or equitable in nature). *See also* Rule 38 (discussing effect of action "in equity" in assessing a party's Seventh Amendment right to a jury trial).

7. *See United States ex rel. Rahman v. Oncology Assocs., P.C.*, 198 F.3d 502, 508–09 (4th Cir.1999) (citing Rule 2 as support for the proposition that mandamus relief can be sought in same lawsuit that involved other, unrelated relief because "the modern trend in civil pleading has been to encourage that all claims for relief be brought in a single suit").

8. *See, e.g.*, 28 U.S.C.A. § 1367 (enumerating the federal court's supplemental jurisdiction over state law claims); Rule 18 (joinder of claims and remedies); Rule 19 (joinder of parties).

9. *See* Rule 54(c).

10. *See, e.g.*, E.D. Pa. Loc. R. 16.1(c)(3) & (d)(2)(b)(3) (requiring party seeking relief to identify the precise monetary and non-monetary relief requested).

II. COMMENCEMENT OF ACTION; SERVICE OF PROCESS, PLEADINGS, MOTIONS AND ORDERS

RULE 3

COMMENCEMENT OF ACTION

A civil action is commenced by filing a complaint with the court.

AUTHORS' COMMENTARY ON RULE 3

PURPOSE AND SCOPE

A civil action is commenced under Rule 3 on the date on which a complaint is filed, *not* the date of service. This dating function is important for many purposes, including the tolling of the statute of limitations in federal question cases. Note, however, that Rule 3 may be supplanted in diversity cases by State commencement statutes and, where they exist, by contrary federal statutes in other cases.

NOTE: Plaintiffs only receive the benefit of this Rule if they serve the summons and the complaint on the defendant within 120 days after commencement or have good cause for not doing so.[1]

APPLICATIONS

Action "Commences" When Complaint is Filed

An action becomes "pending" when the complaint is delivered for filing to a court officer authorized to receive it.[2] Prior to filing, the federal district court lacks authority to act in the dispute.[3]

Service Generally Not Required for Action to "Commence"

Service of process is generally not required for the lawsuit to "commence". So long as service is completed within 120 days after the complaint is filed with the court, the litigants become "plaintiff" and "defendant" when the complaint is filed, not when it is served.[4]

1. *See* Rule 4(m).

2. *See United States v. $8,221,877.16 in U.S. Currency*, 330 F.3d 141, 159 (3d Cir.2003) (noting that the word "commence" is term of art with only one unambiguous meaning—it does not "encompass broad concepts, but rather requires 'invocation of the judicial process' "). *See also Local Union No. 38, Sheet Metal Workers' Int'l v. Pelella*, 350 F.3d 73, 82 (2d Cir. 2003) (an action is instituted in federal court "a plaintiff files a complaint as that constitutes the first step invoking the judicial process"), *cert. denied*, ___ U.S. ___, 124 S.Ct. 2821, 159 L.Ed.2d 248 (2004).

3. *But see* Rule 27 (permitting depositions before complaint is filed).

4. *See Howell by Goerdt v. Tribune Entertainment Co.*, 106 F.3d 215, 217 (7th Cir.1997). *See also Clay v. United States*, 199 F.3d 876, 880

"Commencement" is Provisional—Action Dismissed in 120 Days Without Service

Although an action becomes "pending" when the complaint is delivered for filing, Rule 4(m) authorizes the district court to dismiss the action, without prejudice, if service of both the summons and the complaint is not made within 120 days of commencement (unless good cause is shown why service was not accomplished during that period).[5]

Uses of Rule 3's Dating Function

Rule 3's function of "dating" the commencement of a lawsuit as of the day the complaint is filed with the court is useful in many contexts. This dating function may be used to evaluate:

- The timeliness of the action, under the applicable statute of limitations and/or laches (see discussions below);
- Ripeness;
- Personal Jurisdiction, which generally vests at the time an action is commenced;[6]
- Diversity Jurisdiction, which also generally vests at the time an action is commenced;[7]
- Venue, which likewise is generally assessed as of the date the action is commenced;
- Procedural Timing Deadlines, such as the earliest moment for propounding discovery and filing summary judgment motions;
- Competing Jurisdiction Issues, when complaints involving the same parties and issues are filed in two different courts and the law provides that the first court to obtain jurisdiction should proceed and the second court should dismiss the case or abstain from exercising jurisdiction;
- Litigation of Claims Accruing After the Filing of the Complaint, where new claims usually cannot be litigated in the same case absent an amendment to the complaint;[8] and

(6th Cir.1999) ("A person becomes 'a party' only by beginning a lawsuit, Fed. R. Civ. P. 3, or by being joined as a party after a suit has been instituted").

5. *See* Rule 4(m). Note, however, that Rule 4(m) does not apply to service within a foreign country, *see* Fed. R. Civ. P. 4(m)(referencing Rule 4(f)); or to service upon a foreign state and its political subdivisions, agencies, and instrumentalities, *see* Fed. R. Civ. P. 4(m)(referencing Rule 4(j)(1)).

6. *See Burnham v. Superior Court of California*, 495 U.S. 604, 110 S.Ct. 2105, 109 L.Ed.2d 631 (1990) (holding that court had personal jurisdiction over nonresident defendant who was served with process while temporarily in forum State for purposes unrelated to lawsuit). *But see United States v. Certain Real & Personal Property Belonging to Hayes*, 943 F.2d 1292 (11th Cir. 1991) (court's in rem jurisdiction depends upon court's continued control over property; if property is sold or removed from the court's jurisdiction, the forum is divested of jurisdiction).

7. *See Freeport–McMoRan, Inc. v. K N Energy, Inc.*, 498 U.S. 426, 428, 111 S.Ct. 858, 859, 112 L.Ed.2d 951 (1991) (if diversity jurisdiction exists at the time the lawsuit is filed, jurisdiction will not be divested by subsequent events). *Cf. Stevens v. Nichols*, 130 U.S. 230, 231–32, 9 S.Ct. 518, 518–19, 32 L.Ed. 914 (1889) (case may be removed to federal court only if diversity exists both at the time the action is commenced and at the time removal is sought).

8. *See* Rule 15. *See also Altseimer v. Bell Helicopter Textron Inc.*, 919 F.Supp. 340, 342–43 (E.D.Cal.1996) (citing Rule 3's "commence-

- Compulsory Counterclaims, which must be filed or are deemed waived unless they are already the subject of another "pending" action.

"Commencement" in Federal Question Jurisdiction Cases

Ordinarily, in cases involving federal question jurisdiction, Rule 3 will govern when a lawsuit "commences" and will, typically, serve to toll the statute of limitations upon the filing of the complaint.[9] One exception exists–where the federal question is based on a statute that, itself, contains a separate "commencement" provision, the terms of that statute will control. In neither event will State law apply to the issue of "commencement". Even where the federal law lacks a specific statute of limitations, and the applicable limitations period is "borrowed" either from another federal law[10] or from State law,[11] Rule 3's commencement function will govern, and the filing of the complaint will generally toll the limitations period.

"Commencement" in Diversity Jurisdiction Cases

In diversity cases, Rule 3 will apply for the purposes of evaluating uniquely federal issues, such as the presence or absence of diverse citizenship and the computation of time under the Federal Rules.

However, Rule 3 will not always toll the applicable State law statute of limitations upon the mere filing of a diversity complaint. The *Erie* doctrine [12] compels that, where State law provides a contrary tolling requirement or tolling limitation, Rule 3 cannot be permitted to give the State law cause of action a longer life in a federal court than it would otherwise have in the State courts.[13] Thus, if, for example, under State law, the limitations period would not be tolled until service is accomplished, Rule 3 will not act to toll the limitations period merely upon filing.[14] Similarly, where State law requires the issuance of a summons before the applicable statute of limitations is tolled, the

ment" dating function in refusing to apply new federal statute to existing civil action, where new Act expressly did not apply to lawsuits "commenced" before the date of the Act's enactment).

9. *See Henderson v. United States*, 517 U.S. 654, 657 n.2, 116 S.Ct. 1638, 1641 n.2, 134 L.Ed.2d 880 (1996). *See also Iran Air v. Kugelman*, 996 F.2d 1253, 1257 (D.C.Cir.1993) (applying Rule 3 to toll statute of limitations on federally-created right even though service not accomplished until after period had expired).

10. *See West v. Conrail*, 481 U.S. 35, 107 S.Ct. 1538, 95 L.Ed.2d 32 (1987) (in action under Railway Labor Act, which lacked specific statute of limitations or commencement period, Rule 3 tolled the applicable statute of limitations upon filing).

11. *See Sain v. City of Bend*, 309 F.3d 1134, 1135–38 (9th Cir.2002) (joining other federal circuits in ruling that Rule 3 provides tolling function for limitations period borrowed from State law in Section 1983 case); *Moore v. Indiana*, 999 F.2d 1125, 1129–30 (7th Cir.1993) (same).

12. *Erie R.R. Co. v. Tompkins*, 304 U.S. 64, 58 S.Ct. 817, 82 L.Ed. 1188 (1938). Generally, the *Erie* doctrine obligates the federal courts to apply State law as the substantive law of decision in diversity cases.

13. *See Walker v. Armco Steel Corp.*, 446 U.S. 740, 100 S.Ct. 1978, 64 L.Ed.2d 659 (1980)(holding that Oklahoma law, which tolls the statute of limitations only upon service, will supersede Rule 3's tolling effect); *Ragan v. Merchants Transfer & Warehouse Co.*, 337 U.S. 530, 69 S.Ct. 1233, 93 L.Ed. 1520 (1949)(same, under Kansas law).

14. *See Henderson v. United States*, 517 U.S. 654, 657 n. 2, 116 S.Ct. 1638, 1641 n. 2, 134 L.Ed.2d 880 (1996) (commenting that in a federal-court action upon a right created by State law, the plaintiff must serve process before the statute of limitations has expired, if the law of that

federal courts will honor that requirement: until the summons is issued, the limitations period will continue to run.[15]

"Commencement" in Supplemental Jurisdiction Cases

Where a complaint, invoking the federal courts' supplemental jurisdiction, pleads both federal claims and State law claims, the courts will follow the same rules as they do in diversity cases. Rule 3 will not give a State law cause of action longer life in a federal forum than that same cause of action would enjoy in State court.[16]

Commencement and Amended Complaints

Because an amended complaint often cannot be filed until leave of court has first been granted,[17] many courts have ruled that the amended complaint is deemed filed, for "commencement" and statute of limitations purposes, as of the date that the motion for leave to amend is filed.[18] Practitioners should rely on this principle with great care, however. Whether this treatment applies to all cases (or just those where an earlier amendment was made impossible by circumstances), whether this treatment applies where the motion neither attaches the proposed amended complaint nor properly describes it, and whether this treatment has any effect where the leave is denied, are each unclear.

Unique Prerequisites for Commencement

Certain federal statutes contain special prerequisites for commencing a civil action, such as receiving a right-to-sue letter or exhausting

State so requires); *Walker v. Armco Steel Corp.*, 446 U.S. 740, 100 S.Ct. 1978, 64 L.Ed.2d 659 (1980) (holding that Oklahoma law, which tolls the statute of limitations only upon service, supersedes Rule 3's tolling effect); *Ragan v. Merchants Transfer & Warehouse Co.*, 337 U.S. 530, 69 S.Ct. 1233, 93 L.Ed. 1520 (1949) (same conclusion under Kansas law); *Larsen v. Mayo Med. Ctr.*, 218 F.3d 863 (8th Cir.2000), *cert. denied*, 531 U.S. 1036, 121 S.Ct. 625, 148 L.Ed.2d 534 (2000) (holding that Minnesota's commencement rule applies, which dates commencement by service); *Habermehl v. Potter*, 153 F.3d 1137, 1139 (10th Cir.1998) (ruling that case was time-barred under Wyoming law, where limitations periods are only tolled 60 days for service, and service was not completed until 107 days after filing); *Jenkins v. City of Topeka*, 136 F.3d 1274, 1275 (10th Cir.1998) (under Kansas law, plaintiff could rely on filing date as "commencement" only if service was complete within 90 days of filing, thereafter "commencement" would occur on date of actual service). *But cf. Hart v. Bates*, 897 F.Supp. 710 (E.D.N.Y.1995) (applying federal, rather than Pennsylvania, time limitation for proper service of process where Pennsylvania did not condition the "commencement" of a civil action upon effective service, and did not deem service as integral to the tolling of its statute of limitations).

15. *See Eades v. Clark Distrib. Co.*, 70 F.3d 441 (6th Cir.1995), *cert. denied*, 517 U.S. 1157, 116 S.Ct. 1545, 134 L.Ed.2d 649 (1996).

16. *See Anderson v. Unisys Corp.*, 47 F.3d 302, 309 (8th Cir.1995) (affirming dismissal of State law claims where, under Minnesota law, an action is not "commenced" until the initial process is served), *cert. denied*, 516 U.S. 913, 116 S.Ct. 299, 133 L.Ed.2d 205 (1995); *Appletree Square I, Ltd. v. W.R. Grace & Co.*, 29 F.3d 1283, 1286 (8th Cir.1994)(same).

17. *See* Rule 15.

18. *See, e.g., Mayes v. AT & T Info. Sys.*, 867 F.2d 1172, 1173 (8th Cir.1989); *Koch v. Shell Oil Co.*, 8 F.Supp.2d 1264, 1267–68 (D.Kan.1998); *Massachusetts Pub. Interest Research Group v. ICI Americas Inc.*, 777 F.Supp. 1032, 1036 (D.Mass.1991); *Wallace v. Sherwin Williams Co.*, 720 F.Supp. 158, 158–60 (D.Kan.1988). *See also Nett v. Bellucci*, 437 Mass. 630, 630–47, 774 N.E.2d 130, 130–42 (2002) (on certified question from the First Circuit Court of Appeals, citing cases, and extensively discussing "commencement" effect of motion for leave to amend); *Children's Store v. Cody Enterps.*, 154 Vt. 634, 640–42, 580 A.2d 1206, 1209–11 (1990) (same effect).

administrative remedies.[19] Thus, merely filing a complaint pursuant to Rule 3 might not toll the statute of limitations if such prerequisites are not met. Particular statutes should be consulted carefully for such prerequisites.

Filing By Mail

The "mailbox" rule generally will not apply in Rule 3 circumstances. If original papers are mailed to the Clerk's Office for filing, filing is only complete—and the lawsuit only "commences"—upon the Clerk's receipt of the complaint.[20]

Filing After Business Hours

Rule 77 prescribes that the District Courts are "always open". Accordingly, a complaint will ordinarily be deemed to be filed as of the time it was delivered to the Clerk's Office, even if delivered after the Clerk's business hours.[21]

Filing Fees

The federal courts are divided over whether the payment of filing fees is required prior to commencing an action (and tolling the limitations period).[22] To avoid any risk on this point, fees should be paid properly at the time the complaint is delivered to the court.

Pauper and Prisoner Plaintiffs

The federal courts have an *in forma pauperis* procedure for plaintiffs who lack the ability to pay filing fees. A plaintiff proposing to proceed *in forma pauperis* can toll the statute of limitations by filing a proper motion for leave to proceed *in forma pauperis.*[23] However, if the petition to proceed *in forma pauperis* is denied, the plaintiff must promptly pay the court filing fees or risk losing the limitations period tolling benefit of having "commenced" the lawsuit.[24]

19. *See, e.g., Truitt v. County of Wayne*, 148 F.3d 644 (6th Cir.1998) (discussing EEOC right-to-sue letter procedure).

20. *See McIntosh v. Antonino*, 71 F.3d 29, 36–37 (1st Cir.1995); *Cooper v. City of Ashland*, 871 F.2d 104, 105 (9th Cir.1989).

21. *See Turner v. City of Newport*, 887 F.Supp. 149 (E.D.Ky.1995) (holding that complaint was timely filed when delivered to the Clerk's post office box, after the office had closed, on last day before statute of limitations ran).

22. *Compare Robinson v. America's Best Contacts & Eyeglasses*, 876 F.2d 596 (7th Cir. 1989)(in Rule 4 context, construing local court rule to require payment of fee as prerequisite for filing) *with McDowell v. Delaware State Police*, 88 F.3d 188, 191 (3d Cir.1996) (filing fee is not jurisdictional; although complaint is not deemed to be formally filed until fee is paid, it is constructively filed when the Clerk receives it, so long as the plaintiff ultimately pays the fee or is granted leave to proceed *in forma pauperis*); *Cintron v. Union Pac. R. Co.*, 813 F.2d 917, 920–21 (9th Cir.1987)(filing fee is not jurisdictional); *Rodgers on Behalf of Jones v. Bowen*, 790 F.2d 1550 (11th Cir.1986)(holding that dismissal was inappropriate sanction for non-payment of filing fees); *Wrenn v. American Cast Iron Pipe Co.*, 575 F.2d 544, 547 (5th Cir.1978)(timely payment of filing fee is not a jurisdictional prerequisite).

23. *See Powell v. Jacor Communications Corporate*, 320 F.3d 599, 602–03 (6th Cir.2003) (ruling that complaint, which would have been timely filed under Kentucky law had the acceptance of the complaint not been delayed by the *in forma pauperis* petition, was deemed timely filed under Rule 3).

24. *See Truitt v. County of Wayne*, 148 F.3d 644 (6th Cir.1998) (pauper litigant must pay filing fee within applicable limitations period, as tolled during the pendency of the *in forma pau-*

In complaints prepared by *pro se* prisoner plaintiffs, the courts have generally followed a variation of the "mailbox" rule that deems a lawsuit as "commenced" upon delivery of the complaint to the prison officials.[25]

Plaintiff Must Prosecute

Once a plaintiff files the complaint, the plaintiff must prosecute the action with due diligence. Rule 3 does not relieve plaintiffs of their obligation to prosecute the complaint after filing. The court may dismiss any action for lack of due diligence in proceeding with the lawsuit.[26]

ADDITIONAL RESEARCH REFERENCES

Wright & Miller, *Federal Practice and Procedure* §§ 1051–57.

C.J.S. Federal Civil Procedure § 3.

West's Key No. Digests, Federal Civil Procedure ⚷4.

peris application); *Williams-Guice v. Board of Educ. of Chicago*, 45 F.3d 161 (7th Cir.1995) (limitations period resumes running once *in forma pauperis* application is denied); *Jarrett v. U.S. Sprint Communications Co.*, 22 F.3d 256 (10th Cir.1994) (same), *cert. denied*, 513 U.S. 951, 115 S.Ct. 368, 130 L.Ed.2d 320 (1994).

25. *See Cooper v. Brookshire*, 70 F.3d 377 (5th Cir.1995); *Dory v. Ryan*, 999 F.2d 679 (2d Cir.1993); *Garvey v. Vaughn*, 993 F.2d 776 (11th Cir.1993); *Lewis v. Richmond City Police Dep't*, 947 F.2d 733 (4th Cir.1991). *Cf. Houston v. Lack*, 487 U.S. 266, 108 S.Ct. 2379, 101 L.Ed.2d 245 (1988)(holding that notice of appeal is "filed" within the meaning of the Federal Rules of Appellate Procedure when delivered by a *pro se* prisoner to the prison authorities); Fed. R.App.P. 4(c)(same). *But see Jackson v. Nicoletti*, 875 F.Supp. 1107 (E.D.Pa.1994)(after recounting six reasons for refusing to extend the Supreme Court's *Houston v. Lack* appeal-period mailbox rule to assessing "commencement" of a *pro se* prisoner's lawsuit under Rule 3, the district court dismissed the lawsuit as time-barred where the complaint was not delivered to the clerk of court within two years after the prisoner's claim accrued).

26. *See* Rule 41(b).

RULE 4

SUMMONS

(a) Form. The summons shall be signed by the clerk, bear the seal of the court, identify the court and the parties, be directed to the defendant, and state the name and address of the plaintiff's attorney or, if unrepresented, of the plaintiff. It shall also state the time within which the defendant must appear and defend, and notify the defendant that failure to do so will result in a judgment by default against the defendant for the relief demanded in the complaint. The court may allow a summons to be amended.

(b) Issuance. Upon or after filing the complaint, the plaintiff may present a summons to the clerk for signature and seal. If the summons is in proper form, the clerk shall sign, seal, and issue it to the plaintiff for service on the defendant. A summons, or a copy of the summons if addressed to multiple defendants, shall be issued for each defendant to be served.

(c) Service With Complaint; by Whom Made.

(1) A summons shall be served together with a copy of the complaint. The plaintiff is responsible for service of a summons and complaint within the time allowed under subdivision (m) and shall furnish the person effecting service with the necessary copies of the summons and complaint.

(2) Service may be effected by any person who is not a party and who is at least 18 years of age. At the request of the plaintiff, however, the court may direct that service be effected by a United States marshal, deputy United States marshal, or other person or officer specially appointed by the court for that purpose. Such an appointment must be made when the plaintiff is authorized to proceed in forma pauperis pursuant to 28 U.S.C. § 1915 or is authorized to proceed as a seaman under 28 U.S.C. § 1916.

(d) Waiver of Service; Duty to Save Costs of Service; Request to Waive.

(1) A defendant who waives service of a summons does not thereby waive any objection to the venue or to the jurisdiction of the court over the person of the defendant.

(2) An individual, corporation, or association that is subject to service under subdivision (e), (f), or (h) and that receives notice of an action in the manner provided in this paragraph has a duty to avoid unnecessary costs of serving the summons. To avoid costs,

the plaintiff may notify such a defendant of the commencement of the action and request that the defendant waive service of a summons. The notice and request

(A) shall be in writing and shall be addressed directly to the defendant, if an individual, or else to an officer or managing or general agent (or other agent authorized by appointment or law to receive service of process) of a defendant subject to service under subdivision (h);

(B) shall be dispatched through first-class mail or other reliable means;

(C) shall be accompanied by a copy of the complaint and shall identify the court in which it has been filed;

(D) shall inform the defendant, by means of a text prescribed in an official form promulgated pursuant to Rule 84, of the consequences of compliance and of a failure to comply with the request;

(E) shall set forth the date on which the request is sent;

(F) shall allow the defendant a reasonable time to return the waiver, which shall be at least 30 days from the date on which the request is sent, or 60 days from that date if the defendant is addressed outside any judicial district of the United States; and

(G) shall provide the defendant with an extra copy of the notice and request, as well as a prepaid means of compliance in writing.

If a defendant located within the United States fails to comply with a request for waiver made by a plaintiff located within the United States, the court shall impose the costs subsequently incurred in effecting service on the defendant unless good cause for the failure be shown.

(3) A defendant that, before being served with process, timely returns a waiver so requested is not required to serve an answer to the complaint until 60 days after the date on which the request for waiver of service was sent, or 90 days after that date if the defendant was addressed outside any judicial district of the United States.

(4) When the plaintiff files a waiver of service with the court, the action shall proceed, except as provided in paragraph (3), as if a

summons and complaint had been served at the time of filing the waiver, and no proof of service shall be required.

(5) The costs to be imposed on a defendant under paragraph (2) for failure to comply with a request to waive service of a summons shall include the costs subsequently incurred in effecting service under subdivision (e), (f), or (h), together with the costs, including a reasonable attorney's fee, of any motion required to collect the costs of service.

(e) Service Upon Individuals Within a Judicial District of the United States. Unless otherwise provided by federal law, service upon an individual from whom a waiver has not been obtained and filed, other than an infant or an incompetent person, may be effected in any judicial district of the United States:

(1) pursuant to the law of the state in which the district court is located, or in which service is effected, for the service of a summons upon the defendant in an action brought in the courts of general jurisdiction of the State; or

(2) by delivering a copy of the summons and of the complaint to the individual personally or by leaving copies thereof at the individual's dwelling house or usual place of abode with some person of suitable age and discretion then residing therein or by delivering a copy of the summons and of the complaint to an agent authorized by appointment or by law to receive service of process.

(f) Service Upon Individuals in a Foreign Country. Unless otherwise provided by federal law, service upon an individual from whom a waiver has not been obtained and filed, other than an infant or an incompetent person, may be effected in a place not within any judicial district of the United States:

(1) by any internationally agreed means reasonably calculated to give notice, such as those means authorized by the Hague Convention on the Service Abroad of Judicial and Extrajudicial Documents; or

(2) if there is no internationally agreed means of service or the applicable international agreement allows other means of service, provided that service is reasonably calculated to give notice:

(A) in the manner prescribed by the law of the foreign country for service in that country in an action in any of its courts of general jurisdiction; or

(B) as directed by the foreign authority in response to a letter rogatory or letter of request; or

(C) unless prohibited by the law of the foreign country, by

(i) delivery to the individual personally of a copy of the summons and the complaint; or

(ii) any form of mail requiring a signed receipt, to be addressed and dispatched by the clerk of the court to the party to be served; or

(3) by other means not prohibited by international agreement as may be directed by the court.

(g) Service Upon Infants and Incompetent Persons. Service upon an infant or an incompetent person in a judicial district of the United States shall be effected in the manner prescribed by the law of the state in which the service is made for the service of summons or other like process upon any such defendant in an action brought in the courts of general jurisdiction of that state. Service upon an infant or an incompetent person in a place not within any judicial district of the United States shall be effected in the manner prescribed by paragraph (2)(A) or (2)(B) of subdivision (f) or by such means as the court may direct.

(h) Service Upon Corporations and Associations. Unless otherwise provided by federal law, service upon a domestic or foreign corporation or upon a partnership or other unincorporated association that is subject to suit under a common name, and from which a waiver of service has not been obtained and filed, shall be effected:

(1) in a judicial district of the United States in the manner prescribed for individuals by subdivision (e)(1), or by delivering a copy of the summons and of the complaint to an officer, a managing or general agent, or to any other agent authorized by appointment or by law to receive service of process and, if the agent is one authorized by statute to receive service and the statute so requires, by also mailing a copy to the defendant, or

(2) in a place not within any judicial district of the United States in any manner prescribed for individuals by subdivision (f) except personal delivery as provided in paragraph (2)(C)(i) thereof.

(i) Serving the United States, Its Agencies, Corporations, Officers, or Employees.

(1) Service upon the United States shall be effected

(A) by delivering a copy of the summons and of the complaint to the United States attorney for the district in which the action is brought or to an assistant United States attorney or clerical employee designated by the United States attorney in a writing filed with the clerk of the court or by sending a copy of the summons and of the complaint by registered or certified mail addressed to the civil process clerk at the office of the United States attorney and

(B) by also sending a copy of the summons and of the complaint by registered or certified mail to the Attorney General of the United States at Washington, District of Columbia, and

(C) in any action attacking the validity of an order of an officer or agency of the United States not made a party, by also sending a copy of the summons and of the complaint by registered or certified mail to the officer or agency.

(2)(A) Service on an agency or corporation of the United States, or an officer or employee of the United States sued only in an official capacity, is effected by serving the United States in the manner prescribed by Rule 4(i)(1) and by also sending a copy of the summons and complaint by registered or certified mail to the officer, employee, agency, or corporation.

(B) Service on an officer or employee of the United States sued in an individual capacity for acts or omissions occurring in connection with the performance of duties on behalf of the United States—whether or not the officer or employee is sued also in an official capacity—is effected by serving the United States in the manner prescribed by Rule 4(i)(1) and by serving the officer or employee in the manner prescribed by Rule 4 (e), (f), or (g).

(3) The court shall allow a reasonable time to serve process under Rule 4(i) for the purpose of curing the failure to serve:

(A) all persons required to be served in an action governed by Rule 4(i)(2)(A), if the plaintiff has served either the United States attorney or the Attorney General of the United States, or

(B) the United States in an action governed by Rule 4(i)(2)(B), if the plaintiff has served an officer or employee of the United States sued in an individual capacity.

(j) Service Upon Foreign, State, or Local Governments.

(1) Service upon a foreign state or a political subdivision, agency, or instrumentality thereof shall be effected pursuant to 28 U.S.C. § 1608.

(2) Service upon a state, municipal corporation, or other governmental organization subject to suit shall be effected by delivering a copy of the summons and of the complaint to its chief executive officer or by serving the summons and complaint in the manner prescribed by the law of that state for the service of summons or other like process upon any such defendant.

(k) Territorial Limits of Effective Service.

(1) Service of a summons or filing a waiver of service is effective to establish jurisdiction over the person of a defendant

(A) who could be subjected to the jurisdiction of a court of general jurisdiction in the state in which the district court is located, or

(B) who is a party joined under Rule 14 or Rule 19 and is served at a place within a judicial district of the United States and not more than 100 miles from the place from which the summons issues, or

(C) who is subject to the federal interpleader jurisdiction under 28 U.S.C. § 1335, or

(D) when authorized by a statute of the United States.

(2) If the exercise of jurisdiction is consistent with the Constitution and laws of the United States, serving a summons or filing a waiver of service is also effective, with respect to claims arising under federal law, to establish personal jurisdiction over the person of any defendant who is not subject to the jurisdiction of the courts of general jurisdiction of any state.

(*l*) Proof of Service. If service is not waived, the person effecting service shall make proof thereof to the court. If service is made by a person other than a United States marshal or deputy United States marshal, the person shall make affidavit thereof. Proof of service in a place not within any judicial district of the United States shall, if effected under paragraph (1) of subdivision (f), be made pursuant to the applicable treaty or convention, and shall, if effected under paragraph (2) or (3) thereof, include a receipt signed by the addressee or other evidence of delivery to the addressee satisfactory to the court. Failure to make proof of service does not affect the validity of the service. The court may allow proof of service to be amended.

(m) Time Limit for Service. If service of the summons and complaint is not made upon a defendant within 120 days after the filing of the complaint, the court, upon motion or on its own initiative after notice to the plaintiff, shall dismiss the action without prejudice as to that defendant or direct that service be effected within a specified time; provided that if the plaintiff shows good cause for the failure, the court shall extend the time for service for an appropriate period. This subdivision does not apply to service in a foreign country pursuant to subdivision (f) or (j)(1).

(n) Seizure of Property; Service of Summons Not Feasible.

(1) If a statute of the United States so provides, the court may assert jurisdiction over property. Notice to claimants of the property shall then be sent in the manner provided by the statute or by service of a summons under this rule.

(2) Upon a showing that personal jurisdiction over a defendant cannot, in the district where the action is brought, be obtained with reasonable efforts by service of summons in any manner authorized by this rule, the court may assert jurisdiction over any of the defendant's assets found within the district by seizing the assets under the circumstances and in the manner provided by the law of the state in which the district court is located.

[Amended January 21, 1963, effective July 1, 1963; February 28, 1966, effective July 1, 1966; April 29, 1980, effective August 1, 1980; amended by Pub.L. 97-462, § 2, January 12, 1983, 96 Stat. 2527, effective 45 days after January 12, 1983; amended March 2, 1987, effective August 1, 1987; April 22, 1993, effective December 1, 1993; April 17, 2000, effective December 1, 2000.]

AUTHORS' COMMENTARY ON RULE 4

PURPOSE AND SCOPE

Rule 4 sets forth the procedure for notifying defendants that a federal civil lawsuit has been filed against them. This procedure requires that the defendants be served with "original process"—a copy of a summons and complaint. Rule 4 does *not* address whether a defendant is amenable to service of process within the particular judicial district, or whether service on a defendant is consistent with the Due Process Clause of the United States Constitution. Instead, Rule 4 simply sets forth the procedure for serving the summons and complaint, *assuming* the defendant can be served properly and constitutionally.

GOAL OF RULE 4

The central function of service of process under Rule 4 is to provide notice that a legal action has been filed, and to provide this notice in such a manner and at such a time that the defending party will have a fair opportunity to answer the pleading and raise defenses and objections.[1] Service and the provisions of Rule 4 are distinct from the question of the court's jurisdiction either to entertain the subject matter of the dispute or to render a judgment against a particular person or entity.[2]

"Actual Notice" Alone Is *Not* Enough: Although one of the goals of service of process is to make the defendants aware that a lawsuit has been filed against them, simply demonstrating that the defendant has received actual notice of the lawsuit is not enough—Rule 4's formal requirements for proper service must also be satisfied.[3]

DISTINCTIONS BETWEEN SERVICE, JURISDICTION, AND VENUE

Rule 4 does not determine whether the district court enjoys subject matter jurisdiction in a lawsuit or personal jurisdiction over the named defendant. Rule 4 also does not gauge whether venue is proper in a particular judicial district. These questions must be addressed and resolved before the lawsuit is filed, and before Rule 4 is consulted in determining how to serve process. These topics are discussed in greater detail in Part II of this text (General Concepts In Federal Practice). A brief summary of these topics follows.

Subject Matter Jurisdiction. Federal courts are courts of limited jurisdiction. The district courts are authorized to hear disputes over "federal questions," such as those involving federal laws or the United States Constitution, admiralty, bankruptcy, patents, copyrights, and postal matters. *See* 28 U.S.C.A. §§ 1331, 1333–67. The district courts may also hear "diversity jurisdiction" disputes: where the amount in controversy—exclusive of interest and costs—exceeds $75,000, and the dispute is between citizens of different States, or between American citizens and foreign nationals or a foreign country. *See* 28 U.S.C.A. § 1332. In those instances where a district court possesses federal subject matter jurisdiction over certain claims, the trial court is entitled to exercise its "supplemental jurisdiction" over other claims that, although not federal question or diversity claims, are nevertheless so related to the existing claims that they form part of the same Article III case or controversy. *See* 28 U.S.C. § 1367. The federal courts' subject matter jurisdiction is discussed in more detail in Part II of this text, §§ 2.10–2.13.

Personal Jurisdiction. Like all courts, federal courts may exercise personal (or "in personam") jurisdiction over a defendant only when the defendant is amenable to suit and when the Constitution's Due Process Clause permits the lawsuit to go forward. Amenability to suit

1. *See Henderson v. United States*, 517 U.S. 654, 672, 116 S.Ct. 1638, 1648, 134 L.Ed.2d 880 (1996).

2. *See Henderson v. United States*, 517 U.S. 654, 670, 116 S.Ct. 1638, 1647, 134 L.Ed.2d 880 (1996).

3. *See Bridgeport Music, Inc. v. Rhyme Syndicate Music*, 376 F.3d 615, 623 (6th Cir. 2004); *Ayres v. Jacobs & Crumplar, P.A.*, 99 F.3d 565, 567–68 (3d Cir.1996); *Way v. Mueller Brass Co.*, 840 F.2d 303, 306 (5th Cir.1988). *See also Prewitt Enters. v. Organization of Petroleum Exporting Countries*, 353 F.3d 916, 924 n.14 (11th Cir. 2003) (noting that although "receipt of actual notice is an important factor in considering whether service of process is adequate . . . actual notice alone . . . [is] not enough to allow the court personal jurisdiction over the defendant").

is determined by State statute in diversity cases and by either federal or State statute in federal question cases. In addition, the constitutional Due Process limitations require that "traditional notions of fair play and substantial justice" not be offended by forcing the defendant to travel to the plaintiff's chosen forum and defend a lawsuit there.[4] Of necessity, this assessment is made on the basis of the particular facts in an individual case. The federal courts alternatively may exercise "in rem" or "quasi in rem" jurisdiction over a defendant's property when permitted by State law and the Due Process Clause. The federal courts' personal, in rem, and quasi in rem jurisdiction is discussed in more detail in Part II of this text, §§ 2.2–2.9.

Venue. Finally, a particular district court may hear a lawsuit only if "venue" is proper—where the judicial district is a logical, convenient site to decide the dispute. *See* 28 U.S.C.A. §§ 1391–1412. Federal statutes control what constitutes proper venue in a particular case. The proper venue in the federal courts is discussed in more detail in Part II of this text, § 2.14.

Summary. Each of these three characteristics—subject matter jurisdiction, personal jurisdiction, and venue—must be present before a defendant can be served properly with a summons and complaint. The practitioner must remember that Rule 4 does *not* address whether these three characteristics are present, but only guides the procedural means for serving process. Service (or waiver of service) is, however, a prerequisite to the district court's exercise of personal jurisdiction over any defendant.[5]

IMMUNITY FROM SERVICE OF PROCESS

In certain circumstances, a defendant who might otherwise be properly served with a summons and complaint may be deemed to be "immune" from service. Immunity from service is governed by federal case law, and exists where the due administration of justice demands it.[6] Whether to confer the immunity is vested in the discretion of the district court; the purpose of the immunity is *not* primarily to protect the defendant seeking to avoid service, but instead to aid the court in its judicial administration.[7] The courts have held that persons are generally immune from service when they are present in the jurisdiction to attend court, give a deposition, or conduct settlement discussions in connection with another, unrelated lawsuit, or when they enter the jurisdiction to participate in a legislative or administrative hearing process.[8] This immunity generally encompasses not only the time when

4. *See International Shoe Co. v. Washington,* 326 U.S. 310, 316, 66 S.Ct. 154, 158, 90 L.Ed. 95 (1945).

5. *See Omni Capital Int'l v. Rudolf Wolff & Co.,* 484 U.S. 97, 103, 108 S.Ct. 404, 409, 98 L.Ed.2d 415 (1987).

6. *See Stewart v. Ramsay,* 242 U.S. 128, 37 S.Ct. 44, 61 L.Ed. 192 (1916). *See also ARW Exploration Corp. v. Aguirre,* 45 F.3d 1455 (10th Cir.1995)(noting that immunity from service is a procedural, not substantive, rule, and *Erie* concerns do not dictate that State law apply).

7. *See Northern Light Tech., Inc. v. Northern Lights Club,* 236 F.3d 57, 62 (1st Cir.2001), *cert. denied,* 533 U.S. 911, 121 S.Ct. 2263, 150 L.Ed.2d 247 (2001).

8. *See Lamb v. Schmitt,* 285 U.S. 222, 52 S.Ct. 317, 76 L.Ed. 720 (1932); *Page Co. v. Macdonald,* 261 U.S. 446, 43 S.Ct. 416, 67 L.Ed. 737 (1923).

the person is actually present in court or attending other formal proceedings, but also typically extends for a reasonable period before and after the proceedings to allow the person to enter and then freely leave the jurisdiction.[9]

Persons may also be immune from service when they are lured by fraud or trickery into the jurisdiction by the plaintiff who then attempts to serve them with a summons and complaint.[10] Indeed, some courts have even adopted a bright line rule for in-State negotiations: these courts hold that when a plaintiff invites a defendant to enter the foreign jurisdiction for settlement discussions, the plaintiff may not, during those discussions, serve the defendant with process unless the defendant is either cautioned that she may be served while present or, after having entered the jurisdiction, she is first given an opportunity to depart immediately after the discussions fail.[11]

This immunity, however, can be waived. A defendant who fails to timely assert immunity may be deemed to have waived it.[12] Likewise, a defendant who is immune for the purposes of attending court or a deposition may waive the immunity by arriving in the jurisdiction prematurely, by conducting other business while in the jurisdiction, or by failing to leave the jurisdiction promptly.[13] One ruling has even suggested that a defendant–already named and served with process–might not enjoy immunity if he enters the forum to attend proceedings in his case as a "spectator" (and was not required to appear).[14] In addition, this service immunity may not apply where the defendant is served with process in conjunction with the same case, or a case arising out of or involving the same subject matter, as the one in which the defendant is present in the forum attending at the time of service.[15]

CASES REMOVED TO FEDERAL COURT

Once a case has been removed from State court to federal court, service of process can be completed (or, if defective, new process can

9. *See Cabiri v. Assasie–Gyimah*, 921 F.Supp. 1189, 1193 (S.D.N.Y.1996).

10. *See May Dep't Stores v. Wilansky*, 900 F.Supp. 1154, 1163–64 (E.D.Mo.1995); *Henkel Corp. v. Degremont, S.A.*, 136 F.R.D. 88, 91 (E.D.Pa.1991).

11. *See May Dep't Stores v. Wilansky*, 900 F.Supp. 1154, 1164–65 (E.D.Mo.1995) (collecting cases).

12. *See Republic Productions, Inc. v. American Fed'n of Musicians of U.S. & Canada*, 173 F.Supp. 330 (S.D.N.Y.1959).

13. *See Uniroyal, Inc. v. Sperberg*, 63 F.R.D. 55 (S.D.N.Y.1973) (applying the "dual purpose rule", which forfeits service immunity when a person, present in a foreign jurisdiction for the purpose of the administration of justice, engages in unrelated business dealings or social activity while present in the foreign jurisdiction). *Cf. Fun–Damental Too, Ltd. v. Hwung*, 1997 WL 289712, at *2–*3 (S.D.N.Y.1997) (immunity not waived where nonresident defendant traveled to the forum for a deposition and, on the night before his deposition, visited a showroom for one hour and had dinner; such activities were "trivial and insubstantial").

14. *See Northern Light Tech., Inc. v. Northern Lights Club*, 236 F.3d 57, 63 (1st Cir.2001), *cert. denied*, 533 U.S. 911, 121 S.Ct. 2263, 150 L.Ed.2d 247 (2001).

15. *See ARW Exploration Corp. v. Aguirre*, 45 F.3d 1455 (10th Cir.1995); *Sullivan v. Sullivan*, 2003 WL 22218166, at *1 (D.Conn. Sept. 23, 2003); *Cabiri v. Assasie–Gyimah*, 921 F.Supp. 1189 (S.D.N.Y.1996); *In re Aluminum Phosphide Antitrust Litig.*, 160 F.R.D. 629 (D.Kan. 1995).

issue) as though the lawsuit had been filed originally in federal court.[16] Prior to removal, the applicable State laws will typically govern the propriety of service and process; following removal, the federal Rules will govern.[17]

SERVICE "OTHERWISE PROVIDED BY FEDERAL LAW"

Congress has, on occasion, accompanied its lawmaking with specific service of process provisions. When such particular service means are, in that way, "otherwise provided by federal law", service of process on individuals, corporations, associations, and other non-governmental entities can ordinarily be accomplished by effecting service in accordance with the specific statutory directive.[18]

- *Multiparty, Multiforum Jurisdiction Statute:* Where federal jurisdiction is based, in whole or in part, upon the federal multiparty, multijurisdictional statute,[19] service can be made at any place within the United States or, if otherwise permitted by law, anywhere outside the United States.[20]

SERVING AMENDED COMPLAINTS

Generally, amended complaints are served under Rule 5, and the rigors of proper Rule 4 service are not implicated.[21] However, Rule 4 service could nevertheless still be required for the amended complaint if the claims contained there differ significantly from those in the original pleading, if circumstances persuade the court that Rule 5 service on the attorney is unlikely to ensure notice to the party, if extraterritorial service was made originally and the amendment contains claims unrelated to the original dispute, or if the precepts of Due Process otherwise require it.[22]

BURDEN OF PROOF

The party attempting service bears the burden of establishing that the service is proper.[23]

16. *See* 28 U.S.C.A. § 1448.

17. *See Norsyn, Inc. v. Desai*, 351 F.3d 825, 829 n.4 (8th Cir. 2003) (federal service rules apply only when attempted service is accomplished after removal; before that, State rules apply).

18. *See* Rule 4(e) (permitting service on individuals within the United States in accordance with means "otherwise provided by federal law"); Rule 4(f) (same, for individuals in a foreign country); Rule 4(h) (same, for corporations and associations). *But see* Rule 4(g) (service on infants and incompetents contains no such "otherwise provided by federal law" provision); Rule 4(i) (same, for United States, its agencies, corporations, officers, or employees); Rule 4(j) (same, for foreign, state, or local governments).

19. *See* 28 U.S.C.A. § 1369.

20. *See* 28 U.S.C.A. § 1697.

21. *See Mach v. Florida Casino Cruise, Inc.*, 187 F.R.D. 15, 17 (D.Mass.1999).

22. *See Beckham v. Grand Affair of North Carolina, Inc.*, 671 F.Supp. 415, 418 (W.D.N.C. 1987). *See also* Authors' Commentary to Rule 5(b) ("**New Claims Against Existing Parties**").

23. *See Grand Entertainment Group, Ltd. v. Star Media Sales, Inc.*, 988 F.2d 476, 488 (3d Cir.1993); *Aetna Business Credit, Inc. v. Universal Decor & Interior Design, Inc.*, 635 F.2d 434, 435 (5th Cir.1981); *Commer v. McEntee*, 283 F.Supp.2d 993, 997 (S.D.N.Y. 2003).

RULE 4(a). FORM OF SUMMONS

CORE CONCEPT

The form of a federal summons is the same in all federal cases. The earlier practice of permitting the use of State forms of summons has been abandoned. A standardized federal summons form has been approved by the United States Supreme Court.[24] The summons must:

- *Issue from the Clerk:* The summons must be issued by the clerk of court, and must bear the court's seal and the clerk's signature.
- *Identify the Case:* The summons must also identify the district court, name the parties to the lawsuit, and list the name and address of plaintiff or plaintiff's attorney.
- *Directed to the Defendant:* The summons must be directed specifically to the defendant.
- *Time to Appear:* The summons must state the time within which the defendant must appear and defend.
- *Warn Against Default:* The summons must caution the defendant that a failure to appear and defend will result in the entry of a default judgment for the relief requested in the complaint.

APPLICATIONS

Purpose of Summons

The purpose of the summons is to alert the defendant that a lawsuit is pending against him and that he has a limited time in which to respond. The summons is not required to advise the defendant of every conceivable response he could make to the lawsuit.[25]

Form of Summons Liberally Examined

If the summons omits one of the requirements for proper form, but otherwise generally complies with the Rule's requirements, the court may choose not to dismiss the lawsuit but instead may permit an amendment to the summons or grant some other cure.[26] Where the summons more fundamentally fails to comply with the Rule, the court may enter a dismissal.[27]

24. *See* Form 1 ("Summons"), included with the Appendix of Forms as reprinted in this text.

25. *See Frye v. Bowman, Heintz, Boscia, Vician, P.C.*, 193 F.Supp.2d 1070, 1080 (S.D.Ind. 2002) (noting the "inherent difficulties in attempting to provide all potentially helpful information in a summons", the court wrote that it "would hardly seem practical to attach to a summons a copy of the Federal Rules of Civil Procedure and portions of the United States Code").

26. *See Wortham v. American Family Ins. Co.*, No. C01–2067, 2002 WL 31128057, at *2–3 (N.D. Iowa 2002) (dismissal denied, and leave to amend summons granted, where only one defendant's name appeared on summons, although other defendants were clearly identified in caption of both summons and complaint); *George W. v. United States Dep't of Educ.*, 149 F.Supp.2d 1195, 1200–02 (E.D.Cal.2000) (noting that Rule 4 is "flexible" and "should be liberally construed so long as a party receives sufficient notice of the complaint"); *GMAC Mortg. Corp. v. Weisman*, 1997 WL 83416, at *2 (S.D.N.Y.1997) (although summons failed to state the time for response, because defendant did not immediately object to the defect and even reached stipulation on time for response, court would not dismiss the complaint).

27. *See Schroeder v. Kochanowski*, 311 F.Supp.2d 1241, 1256 (D.Kan. 2004) (dismissal granted where served summons was copy, lacking court seal, and omitted plaintiff's name and address).

RULE 4(b). ISSUANCE OF SUMMONS

CORE CONCEPT

Once the complaint is filed, the plaintiff is responsible for preparing the summons in an appropriate form, and submitting it to the clerk of court for signing and sealing. If the plaintiff's summons is proper, the clerk will sign and seal the form, and issue it to the plaintiff for service. Copies of the summons must be issued for each defendant.

APPLICATIONS

Form of Summons Liberally Examined

Courts liberally construe the issuance requirements of Rule 4(b). If the summons is sufficiently accurate to provide proper notice, and any alleged defect in form has not prejudiced the defendant, a defect in the form of summons as issued will be discounted as harmless and the plaintiff will be afforded an opportunity to amend the summons to cure the error.[28]

Photocopies of Summons in Multi–Defendant Cases

An original summons–containing a raised seal-of-the-court and a pen-signed signature of the clerk–may not be necessary in cases involving multiple defendants. In such cases, copies of the original summons (that bear the name of the served defendant) may be used.[29]

RULE 4(c). SERVICE OF COMPLAINT; BY WHOM MADE

CORE CONCEPT

A summons and complaint are served together. The plaintiff is responsible for effective service. A U.S. Marshal will serve process only if ordered to do so by the court.

APPLICATIONS

Plaintiff Selects the Process Server

Except in certain cases, such as those involving pauper plaintiffs or seamen plaintiffs, the plaintiff generally is responsible for selecting an appropriate person to serve all defendants with copies of the summons and complaint. Typically, the plaintiff appoints a commercial process server who accomplishes the service task for a fee.[30]

Service by Adult Non–Party

Any person over the age of 18 who is not a party to the lawsuit may personally serve original service. Because they are "parties" to the

28. *See Time Prods. v. J. Tiras Classic Handbags, Inc.*, 1994 WL 363930 (S.D.N.Y. 1994).

29. *See New York Transp., Inc. v. Naples Transp., Inc.*, 116 F.Supp.2d 382, 386 (E.D.N.Y. 2000).

30. *See Byrd v. Stone*, 94 F.3d 217, 219 (6th Cir.1996).

lawsuit, plaintiffs may not serve process themselves.[31]

Service by U.S. Marshal or Others Specially Appointed

The court, upon a plaintiff's request, may direct that the United States Marshal or some other specially-appointed person serve process. Such court-appointed service is required, however, in the cases of pauper plaintiffs[32] or seamen plaintiffs.[33] If such an appointment is made, and as long as the plaintiff was entitled to Marshal service in the first instance, and cooperated with the Marshal in accomplishing service, the plaintiff is permitted to rely on the Marshal to complete service.[34]

Service Must Occur *After* the Complaint is Filed

Service is not effective unless the complaint that is served has first been filed with the court. Thus, the practice of informally presenting an adversary with a copy of a complaint before it is filed with the clerk of court will not satisfy the requirements for service of process under Rule 4.[35]

RULE 4(d). WAIVER OF SERVICE; DUTY TO SAVE COSTS OF SERVICE

CORE CONCEPT

A defendant is duty-bound to avoid the unnecessary costs of formal personal service of process, or risk being taxed with the costs of service and associated attorney's fees. Rule 4 now enforces this duty through the waiver-of-service procedure of Rule 4(d).

APPLICATIONS

Precaution In Citing Earlier Cases

Prior to 1993, Rule 4 permitted "service by mail" in limited circumstances. With the 1993 amendments to Rule 4, this "service by mail" provision was replaced with the current waiver of service procedure of Rule 4(d). Case authority under the former service-by-mail

31. *See Walker v. University of Colorado Bd. of Regents*, 139 F.3d 913 (10th Cir.1998) (Table; text available on Westlaw at 1998 WL 67321, at **1) (although disfavored, the Tenth Circuit permits this opinion to be cited if it has persuasive value on a material issue and copies are supplied to the court) (holding that plaintiff's attempt to effect service of process himself was not effective); *Boltes v. Entex*, 158 F.R.D. 110 (S.D.Tex. 1994)(commenting that plaintiff, as a party, is expressly prohibited from serving process upon a defendant).

32. 28 U.S.C.A. § 1915(c). *See Lindsey v. United States R.R. Retirement Bd.*, 101 F.3d 444, 447–48 (5th Cir.1996); *Byrd v. Stone*, 94 F.3d 217, 219 (6th Cir.1996).

33. 28 U.S.C.A. § 1916.

34. *See Olsen v. Mapes*, 333 F.3d 1199, 1204–05 (10th Cir.2003) (finding that plaintiffs were not culpable for failing to comply with Rules or court orders when they relied on Marshal to complete service); *Thompson v. Maldonado*, 309 F.3d 107, 109 n.2 (2d Cir.2002) (noting that *in forma pauperis* plaintiffs may use Marshals to effect service).

35. *See J.O. Alvarez, Inc. v. Rainbow Textiles, Inc.*, 168 F.R.D. 201 (S.D.Tex.1996) (default judgment not proper against defendants who failed to answer a complaint that was served before it was filed; defendants' actual or constructive notice of lawsuit does not satisfy the Rule 4 service requirements).

procedure cautioned against construing the mail service Rule in so literal a manner that it could promote "sandbagging" or "blindsiding" an opponent into overlooking or misinterpreting the type of service of process that was being attempted.[36] The current waiver-of-service provision, with its prerequisite of a formal and executed acknowledgement form, is designed to cure the risks inherent in practice under the former Rule.

Certain Defendants Exempt From Rule

The waiver-of-service procedure applies to all defendants *except*: (1) the United States as defendant;[37] (2) agencies, corporations, or officers[38] of the United States as defendants; (3) other governments and government-related entities as defendants;[39] (4) infant defendants; and (5) incompetent defendants.[40] Note, however, that although federal workers are exempt from the waiver of service provisions when sued in their official capacities, they are *not* exempt when sued as individuals.[41]

Applies to Defendants Outside the United States, But Without Penalties

Although Rule 4 generally emphasizes a strong preference for proceeding under international service treaty agreements (such as the Hague Service Convention), the waiver-of-service procedure is intended to permit waiver of service by foreign (non-governmental) defendants because of the cost savings to both plaintiff and defendant.[42]

Note, however, that the penalties for refusing to waive formal service of process do *not* apply to foreign defendants.[43]

36. *See Carimi v. Royal Carribean Cruise Line, Inc.*, 959 F.2d 1344,1348 (5th Cir.1992) (commenting that service-by-mail provisions were intended to provide a convenient way to eliminate the costly and time consuming traditional methods of service, but "being a less dependable and less formal alternative to conventional service and citation, [the old service-by-mail Rule] must be construed strictly as must all rules in derogation of the norm.").

37. *See Robinson v. Turner*, 886 F.Supp. 1460, 1465 n. 5 (S.D.Ind.1995)(commenting that unreliability caused United States and its facilities to be exempted from Rule 4(d) waiver provisions).

38. *See Emuchay v. Catron*, 2000 WL 303223, at *2 (D.Conn.2000) (confirming that Rule does not authorize waiver of service in lawsuits against federal employees sued in their official capacities).

39. *See Mosley v. Douglas County Correctional Ctr.*, 192 F.R.D. 282, 283 (D.Neb.2000) (waiver of service provision does not apply to municipal corporations, thus District of Columbia not subject to the procedure).

40. *See* Rule 4(d)(2).

41. *See Mosley v. Douglas County Correctional Ctr.*, 192 F.R.D. 282, 283 (D.Neb.2000). *See also* Rule 4(i)(2)(B) (noting that federal officers and employees sued in their individual capacity are served in the manners prescribed by Rule 4(e), (f), or (g)). *See also* Rule 4(i)(2)(B) advisory committee notes to 2000 amendments ("Invocation of the individual service provisions of subdivisions (e), (f), and (g) invokes also the waiver-of-service provisions of subdivision (d)").

42. *See* Rule 4(d) advisory committee rule (noting specifically the cost-saving nature of the waiver procedure for defendants who otherwise would be served under an international service of process convention, which costs might include "the sometimes substantial expense of translation that may be wholly unnecessary for defendants fluent in English").

43. *See* Rule 4(d)(2). *See also Quilling v. Shaw*, 2001 WL 611147, at *1 (N.D. Tex.2001) (cost provisions of Rule 4(d) do not apply to defendants located outside United States). Note that at least one district court has rejected the argument that a foreign defendant should be considered "located" in the United States within the meaning of Rule 4(d) when that defendant has such significant contacts with the forum that it is susceptible to personal jurisdiction in the United States. *See Hoffman–La Roche, Inc. v. Invamed, Inc.*, 183 F.R.D. 157 (D.N.J.1998).

Venue and Jurisdiction Defenses Preserved

A defendant who waives formal service of process does not lose the right to contest venue and jurisdiction.[44] The defendant does, however, waive any objection to service and to the form of process.

Incentives for Waiving

By agreeing to waive formal service of process, a defendant's time for responding to the complaint is tripled—from 20 days (following personal service) to 60 days (following request for waiver).[45] For defendants who are addressed outside the United States, the extension is even longer: a defendant addressed outside the United States who agrees to waive formal service has 90 days to respond to the complaint.[46]

Penalties for Not Waiving

The Rule 4(d) waiver provision does *not* discharge a plaintiff's obligation to complete service of process. If a plaintiff requests waiver, but the defendant ignores the request or otherwise refuses to waive, the plaintiff must then proceed with formal service of process in accordance with Rule 4(e), (f), or (h).[47] However, if the defendant lacks "good cause" for refusing to waive service, the court must tax costs against the defendant.[48] These costs include the expenses incurred in formally serving process on the defendant, as well as a reasonable attorney's fee for any motion practice required to collect those service costs.[49] Before any costs and attorney's fees will be taxed, the prescribed time for the defendant to waive service must first have expired.[50]

"Good Cause" Defined: The Advisory Committee comments that the necessary "good cause" for refusing to waive formal service of process should be rare. This "good cause" test is not satisfied by a belief that the claim is unjust[51] or that the court lacks jurisdiction,

44. *See* Rule 4(d)(1).

45. *See* Rule 4(d)(3). One district court has extended the 60–day period to 63 days, citing the 3–day service-by-mail provision of Fed. R. Civ. P. 6(e). *See Petrousky v. Civil Air Patrol, Inc.*, 1998 WL 213726, at *1 (N.D.N.Y.1998).

46. *See* Rule 4(d)(3).

47. *See O.J. Distrib., Inc. v. Hornell Brewing Co.*, 340 F.3d 345, 354 (6th Cir.2003) (noting that actual service is required, if defendant fails to return signed waiver of service form); *Boley v. Kaymark*, 123 F.3d 756, 757 (3d Cir.1997) (same), *cert. denied*, 522 U.S. 1109, 118 S.Ct. 1038, 140 L.Ed.2d 104 (1998); *Mathon v. Marine Midland Bank, N.A.*, 875 F.Supp. 986 (E.D.N.Y. 1995)(same).

48. *See United States v. Butterfield*, 91 F.Supp.2d 704, 706 (D.Vt.2000) (granting to federal government reimbursement of costs associated with service where waiver was not provided and no good cause existed); *Mathon v. Marine Midland Bank, N.A.*, 875 F.Supp. 986 (E.D.N.Y. 1995)(observing that effect of Rule 4(d) is to shift the cost of service to a defendant who refuses to agree to waive formal service).

49. *See* Rule 4(d)(2) & (d)(5). *See Graves v. Church of Lord Jesus Christ of Apostalic Faith, Inc.*, 2003 WL 21659168, at *1 (E.D.Pa.2003) (awarding plaintiff $1,520, representing costs for process server, courier, and photocopying, and then expenses (including reasonable attorney's fee) to collect those costs from defendant); *United States v. First Midwest Bank*, 1995 WL 447762 (N.D.Ill.1995)(awarding service costs and $1,047.42 in motion preparation fee against defendant who knew of pending lawsuit, but refused to cooperate in facilitating service).

50. *See* Rule 4(d)(5) advisory committee note.

51. *See Morales v. SI Diamond Tech., Inc.*, 1999 WL 144469, at *2 (S.D.N.Y.1999) (defendants' belief that the complaint lacks merit and

or by counsel's claim that he or she was busy or otherwise preoccupied.[52] However, non-receipt of the waiver request,[53] a failure to otherwise comply with all the prerequisites of Rule 4(d),[54] a good faith belief that, as a matter of law, the waiver-of-service provisions would not apply,[55] an illiteracy in English, or defects in waiver form would likely satisfy the "good cause" test.[56]

Waiver Procedure

The waiver-of-service procedure is triggered when (but only when) a plaintiff formally requests a defendant to waive formal service of process. A failure to meet—literally—each of these prerequisites may result in defective service[57] and/or a refusal by the court to impose the penalties for a refusal to waive service.[58]

desire to increase plaintiff's costs do not constitute "good cause" for refusing to waive).

52. *See D'Agostine v. United Hosp. Supply Corp.*, 1996 WL 417266, at *5 (E.D.Pa.1996) (rejecting "good cause" claim premised upon defendants' counsel's assertion that he failed to return an executed waiver because "he was in the process of relocating his practice and was in the middle of various litigations ... A busy schedule hardly constitutes good cause for failing to comply with the Federal Rules of Civil Procedure.").

53. *See Hausmann v. Roscher*, 2001 WL 115462, at *2 (E.D.Pa.2001) (physically absent from residence is "good cause"). *But see Double S Truck Line, Inc. v. Frozen Food Exp.*, 171 F.R.D. 251, 253–54 (D.Minn.1997) (service costs were taxed against defendant, notwithstanding defendant's claim that it did not receive sufficient time to respond to waiver form; form had been delivered to defendant's agent but was delayed in reaching defendant because agent lacked defendant's current, accurate address).

54. *See McGann v. New York*, 77 F.3d 672 (2d Cir.1996) (waiver-of-service procedure not effective where plaintiff failed to include acknowledgement form along with the mailed summons and complaint); *Perez v. County of Westchester*, 83 F.Supp.2d 435, 441 (S.D.N.Y.2000) (denying reimbursement of costs of personal service and motion fees, notwithstanding defendants' refusal to waive personal service, where notice and request were not addressed directly to the defendant, was not accompanied by a copy of the complaint, and lacked a prepaid means for compliance in writing); *Steinberg v. Quintet Publ'g Ltd.*, 1999 WL 459809, at *2 (S.D.N.Y. 1999) (assessing no costs because waiver request form defectively failed to name an officer or managing agent of the defendant); *Mason Tenders Dist. Council Pension Fund v. Messera*, 1997 WL 221200, at *6 (S.D.N.Y.1997) (no costs taxed where plaintiffs sent acknowledgement form with self-addressed return envelope, but did not stamp the return envelope); *Spivey v. Board of Church Extension & Home Mission of Church of God*, 160 F.R.D. 660 (M.D.Fla. 1995)(refusing to award costs where waiver form was sent errantly addressed to "Edwin Ross" rather than "R. Edward Ross", and was mailed to corporate defendant generally, rather than addressed to an officer or managing general agent of the corporation).

55. *See Mosley v. Douglas County Correctional Ctr.*, 192 F.R.D. 282, 283 (D.Neb.2000) (finding good cause for failure to waive service because no legal authority addressed whether employees of a municipal corporation were susceptible to this procedure).

56. *See* Rule 4(d)(2)(B) advisory committee note.

57. *See Larsen v. Mayo Medical Ctr.*, 218 F.3d 863 (8th Cir.2000) (where Rule 4(d) provisions not complied with strictly, waiver-of-service procedure not complied with and personal service must be obtained), *cert. denied*, 531 U.S. 1036, 121 S.Ct. 625, 148 L.Ed.2d 534 (2000); *McGann v. New York*, 77 F.3d 672 (2d Cir.1996) (waiver-of-service procedure not effective where plaintiff failed to include acknowledgement form along with the mailed summons and complaint).

58. *See Green v. Benden*, 2000 WL 1468764, at *6 (N.D.Ill.2000) (service costs denied where waiver request failed to contain copies of commencement notice, request for waiver, or prepaid means of compliance), *aff'd in part, vac'd in part on other grounds*, 281 F.3d 661 (7th Cir. 2002); *Perez v. County of Westchester*, 83 F.Supp.2d 435, 441 (S.D.N.Y.2000) (denying reimbursement of costs of personal service and motion fees, where notice and request were not addressed directly to the defendant, was not accompanied by a copy of the complaint, and lacked a prepaid means for compliance in writing).

The waiver-of-service procedure follows:

(1) *Request For Waiver:* The plaintiff formally requests a defendant to waive formal service of process. The request must:

- Be in writing; [59]
- Conform to the federal "Notice & Request For Waiver" form, which will list: (a) the date on which the plaintiff's request was sent; (b) the date by which the defendant's waiver is due; (c) the identity of the court; and (d) the consequences of both waiver and a refusal to waive;[60]
- Contain a copy of the complaint; [61]
- Contain an additional copy of the Notice form[62] and a prepaid means for the defendant to respond[63] (prudent counsel should also include a "Waiver of Service of Summons" form, conforming to the federal model, on which the defendants can certify their waiver);[64]
- Be sent by first-class mail or by "other reliable means", including private hand delivery and facsimile transmission;[65] and

  Note: If electronic means are used for requesting a waiver, the plaintiff should maintain proof of transmission.

- Be addressed directly to the individual defendant or, if the defendant is a corporation or association, to the individual subject to, or authorized to accept, service.[66]

59. *See* Rule 4(d)(2)(A).

60. *See* Rule 4(d)(2)(A)-(F). *See also* Form 1A ("Notice Of Lawsuit And Request For Waiver Of Service Of Summons"), included with the Appendix to Forms as reprinted in this text. *Compare McGann v. New York*, 77 F.3d 672 (2d Cir.1996) (waiver-of-service procedure not effective where plaintiff failed to include an acknowledgment form along with the mailed summons and complaint) *with Trevino v. D.H. Kim Enters.*, 168 F.R.D. 181, 182–83 (D.Md.1996) (service not defective where plaintiffs did not use the official Notice form, but did advise defendants of consequences of compliance and noncompliance) *and Dymits v. American Brands, Inc.*, 1996 WL 751111, at *15 (N.D.Cal.1996) (finding that plaintiff "substantially complied" with waiver procedures, even though plaintiff omitted a small portion of the official form warning).

61. *See* Rule 4(d)(2)(C).

62. *See Dymits v. American Brands, Inc.*, 1996 WL 751111, at *15 (N.D.Cal.1996) (finding that plaintiff "substantially complied" with waiver procedures, even though plaintiff failed to include 2 copies of the waiver form with the service waiver package and omitted a small portion of the official form warning).

63. *See* Rule 4(d)(2)(G). *See also Mason Tenders Dist. Council Pension Fund v. Messera*, 1997 WL 221200, at *6 (S.D.N.Y.1997) (waiver-of-service procedure found to be defective where plaintiffs sent to defendant the acknowledgement form with self-addressed return envelope, but failed to stamp the return envelope).

64. *See* Form 1B ("Waiver Of Service Of Summons"), included with the Appendix to Forms as reprinted in this text.

65. *See* Rule 4(d)(2)(B). *See also* Rule 4(d)(2)(B) advisory committee note (describing availability of and procedure for electronic communications, such as facsimile transmission).

66. *See* Rule 4(d)(2)(A). *See also Spivey v. Board of Church Extension & Home Mission of Church of God*, 160 F.R.D. 660 (M.D.Fla. 1995)(to comply with Rule 4(d) waiver procedure, waiver form must be accurately addressed to individual defendants and must be addressed to an authorized agent of corporate defendants).

Note: Merely mailing "blind" to a business address will not constitute proper delivery.

(2) *Response Time:* After the request is sent, the defendant must be given at least 30 days (60 days if outside the United States) to respond by returning the waiver.[67]

120–Day Warning: Rule 4(m)'s 120–day period for completing service continues to run while the waiver-of-service request is outstanding. This 120–day period does *not* toll while the defendant considers whether to waive.[68] Either waiver of service or, alternatively, formal service must be accomplished within the 120–day period.[69] In addition, in some jurisdictions, the statutes of limitation are not tolled in diversity or supplemental jurisdiction cases until actual service is made. Thus, in such jurisdictions, this waiver-of-service procedure should not be used if the limitations period is close to expiring.

(3) *Date of Service:* If the defendant agrees to waive service by returning the waiver, the date of service is deemed to be the date the plaintiff files the waiver form with the court.[70]

Motion to Recover Service Expenses

Where a defendant refuses, without good cause, to waive formal service of process, a motion to collect the costs and expenses of actual service can be filed promptly after the actual service is completed. The plaintiff need not wait until the bill of costs is submitted at the end of the case to recover these expenses.[71] These expenses may include a reasonable attorney's fee for prosecuting the motion to collect costs, but may *not* include any attorney's fee associated with arranging for formal service after the defendant's refusal to waive.[72]

The reported practice under Rule 4(d) suggests that courts are scrutinizing carefully the requested fees and costs to ensure against overreaching by counsel in their requests for reimbursement.[73]

67. *See* Rule 4(d)(2)(F).

68. *See* Rule 4(d)(4) advisory committee note to 1993 amendment.

69. *See Chicago Dist. Council & Carpenters Pension Fund v. Wright Erectors, Inc.*, 1994 WL 592068 (N.D.Ill.1994).

70. *See* Rule 4(d)(4).

71. *See Double S Truck Line, Inc. v. Frozen Food Exp.*, 171 F.R.D. 251, 253–54 (D.Minn. 1997).

72. *See Graves v. Church of Lord Jesus Christ of Apostalic Faith, Inc.*, 2003 WL 21659168, at *1 (E.D.Pa.2003) (denying plaintiff's request for reimbursement for attorney's fees spent arranging formal service on defendant after waiver was refused); *Morales v. SI Diamond Tech., Inc.*, 1999 WL 144469, at *3 (S.D.N.Y.1999)(same).

73. *See, e.g., Ahern v. Northern Tech. Int'l Corp.*, 206 F.Supp.2d 418, 422 (W.D.N.Y.2002) (finding request for $1,845 in attorney's fees "unreasonable", and granting a reduced fee award of $80 instead); *Donaghue v. CT Holdings, Inc.*, 2001 WL 1543816, at *1 (S.D.N.Y. 2001) (granting motion, and awarding plaintiff reasonably fee of $406.25 for the preparation, service, and filing of motion, and costs of $140.00 for effecting service).

U.S. Marshal's Use of Waiver-of-Service Procedure

When the Rules authorize service by the U.S. Marshal, the Marshal may mail the waiver-of-service forms to the defendants, prior to attempting to serve process personally.[74]

RULE 4(e). SERVICE UPON INDIVIDUALS WITHIN A JUDICIAL DISTRICT OF THE UNITED STATES

CORE CONCEPT

Original process may be served upon any competent, adult individual found within the United States in the following manners:

(1) ***Specific Federal Law***: In any manner specifically authorized by federal law for such service, where Congress has determined that a particular type of service is necessary or proper;[75] or

(2) ***Waiver***: Under the waiver-of-service provisions of Rule 4(d); or

(3) ***State Law***: In the manner authorized by the State in which the district court sits, or by the State in which the service is to be accomplished; or

(4) ***Personal Service***: By personally delivering the summons and complaint to the individual being served; or

(5) ***Left at Dwelling House***: By leaving the summons and complaint at the individual's dwelling house or usual place of abode with a person of suitable age and discretion residing there; or

(6) ***Agent***: By delivering the summons and complaint to an agent appointed by the individual to receive service, or to an agent authorized by law to receive service.

Service Upon Individuals, Generally

This Rule applies whenever service is made upon individual persons. Thus, the individual service Rule will govern when the served defendant is the unincorporated business trade name by which a natural individual conducts his or her business.[76]

APPLICATIONS

Service by Personal Delivery

Personal delivery may not always require that the recipient walk away from the encounter holding the summons and complaint. The

74. *See Hairston v. Falano*, 1999 WL 412440, at *3 (N.D.Ill.1999); *Rose v. Garbs*, 1999 WL 299892, at *3 (N.D.Ill.1999); *Johnson v. Quinn*, 1999 WL 116222, at *5 (N.D.Ill.1999).

75. *See, e.g., Green v. William Mason & Co.*, 996 F.Supp. 394, 395–96 (D.N.J.1998) (noting that ERISA contains just such a jurisdictional provision, permitting breach of fiduciary duty claims to be served in any district court where the defendants reside or may be found) (citing 29 U.S.C.A. § 1132(e)(2)).

76. *See, e.g., Bridgeport Music, Inc. v. Rhyme Syndicate Music*, 376 F.3d 615, 624–25 (6th Cir. 2004) ("Service on Carrumba Music, the d/b/a for Jorge Hinojosa, is governed by Fed.R.Civ.P. 4(e), the provision for service of process on individuals").

service documents must be "tendered" to the recipient. Thereafter, once the recipient is physically confronted with service, and refuses to take personal possession of the service documents, service by personal delivery may still, under certain circumstances, be accomplished by leaving the documents near the recipient (such as on a nearby table or on the floor near the person).[77]

Service on Non–Resident Individual's Agent

A non-resident person, not otherwise present in the forum, may be served properly with process by serving that individual's agent for service. The recipient "agent", however, must be authorized to accept service either by appointment or by operation of law.[78] Some States have provided, by statute, that service on non-residents (who are otherwise amenable to jurisdiction within the State) may be accomplished by serving the secretary of State or some similar State law official; in such States, service in this manner may be appropriate service under federal law as well.[79]

Service on Individual's Attorney

Service upon an individual is proper by serving the individual's attorney *only* when the attorney has been specifically authorized to accept service on the individual's behalf.[80]

Service at Individual's Dwelling House

An individual can be served with process by delivering the summons and complaint to a "person of suitable age and discretion" residing at the defendant's dwelling house or usual place of abode. In such cases, the process need not be handed directly to the served defendant.[81] Moreover, the recipient need not necessarily be an adult, so long as the court reaches the case-by-case, fact-specific determination

77. *See Novak v. World Bank*, 703 F.2d 1305, 1310 n.14 (D.C.Cir.1983) ("When a person refuses to accept service, service may be effected by leaving the papers at a location, such as on a table or on the floor, near that person"); *Republic Credit Corp. I v. Rance*, 172 F.Supp.2d 1178, 1181 (S.D. Iowa 2001) (NO. 4–01–CV–90032) (service effected by leaving summons and complaint at front gate, when process server encountered defendant, advised defendant of service papers, and defendant turned and entered residence without speaking; "This Court has no interest in forcing process servers to chase down defendants and jam court papers into their hands in order to effect personal service, as depicted on television").

78. *See Silvious v. Pharaon*, 54 F.3d 697, 701–02 (11th Cir.1995). *Compare Nazareth Nat'l Bank & Trust Co. v. E.A. Int'l Trust*, 1999 WL 549036, at *2 (W.D.Pa.1999) (holding service proper because return of service showed that summons and complaint "were left with a specified security guard at defendant's residence who was 'instructed by [defendant] to accept service' ") *with Staudinger v. Hoelscher, Inc.*, 166 F.Supp.2d 1335, 1339 (D.Kan.2001) (holding service improper where no authority offered to establish that plant manager (on whom service was made) was authorized by virtue of that position to accept service for president and owner of plant).

79. *See, e.g., Goktepe v. Lawrence*, 220 F.R.D. 8, 8–12 (D.Conn. 2004) (Connecticut statute); *Gyadu v. Hartford Ins. Co.*, 283 F.Supp.2d 740, 745–46 (D.Conn. 2003) (same).

80. *See Guess ?, Inc. v. Chang*, 163 F.R.D. 505, 507–08 (N.D.Ill.1995).

81. *See Limon–Hernandez v. Lumbreras*, 171 F.R.D. 271 (D.Or.1997).

that the recipient was of "suitable age and discretion". Nevertheless, the recipient ordinarily must be "residing" at the home;[82] service upon a non-resident maid or landlady might be ineffective.[83]

Traveling Defendants: A traveling defendant's "usual place of abode" is likely to include either the place where she is actually living at the time of service or the place she recognizes as her legal residence, even if business takes her away on a regular basis.[84]

Transient Defendants: Service at a "dwelling house" or "usual place of abode" may not always be an available option. In certain circumstances, there may be no acceptable "dwelling house" service location for transient defendants, such as those living aboard ships or those who are homeless, living on the streets or in shelters.[85]

Hotels and Motels: In certain circumstances, particularly during long, extended stays, service can be appropriate at a hotel or motel where the defendant is residing.[86]

State Law Service Generally

The Rules permit service in any manner authorized by *either* the State in which the district court sits *or* the State in which the service is to be accomplished.[87] If service is accomplished in accordance with either of those State service laws, Rule 4(e) is satisfied.[88]

82. *See Srein v. Silverman*, 2001 WL 366620, at *2 (E.D.Pa.2001) (dwelling-house service only complete when papers left with person who actually resides at defendant's home, not merely present at the time of service).

83. *Compare Franklin America, Inc. v. Franklin Cast Prods., Inc.,* 94 F.R.D. 645 (E.D.Mich.1982)(service on part-time housekeeper deemed insufficient) *with Barclays Bank of New York v. Goldman,* 517 F.Supp. 403 (S.D.N.Y.1981)(service on resident maid deemed sufficient). *See also Jaffe & Asher v. Van Brunt,* 158 F.R.D. 278 (S.D.N.Y.1994)(although defendant was not staying at his parents' home when service was made there, service ruled proper where defendant resided at that address when in the area, maintained private bedroom, clothes, phone line, and fax there, received mail there (which mother forwarded to him), and represented to plaintiff that this was his residence); *TRW, Inc. v. Derbyshire,* 157 F.R.D. 59 (D.Colo. 1994)(holding that service on defendant's mother, at address defendant represented to be his current forwarding address, was proper).

84. *See S.E.C. v. Marino*, 29 Fed.Appx. 538, 540–41 (10th Cir.2002) (citation restricted—not selected for publication in Federal Reporter) (finding service proper because, even though defendant's vocation took him on extended trips abroad, he maintained his home and family in service location).

85. *See Cox v. Quigley*, 141 F.R.D. 222 (D.Me.1992)(young college graduate, who left home and was serving on board a ship, had no "dwelling house" or "usual place of abode", other than his ship); *see id.* at 226 ("The last shelter at which a homeless person slept will often not furnish reasonable assurance that process will reach the defendant. For such defendants service at the dwelling house or place of abode is unavailable; personal service may be a plaintiff's only option then, no matter how difficult").

86. *See Howard Johnson Int'l, Inc. v. Wang,* 7 F.Supp.2d 336 (S.D.N.Y.1998) (finding hotel to be defendant's dwelling place or usual place of abode).

87. *See* Rule 4(e).

88. *See Webster Indus., Inc. v. Northwood Doors, Inc.,* 244 F.Supp.2d 998, 1005–06 (N.D. Iowa 2003) (noting that if service is proper under the rules of one qualifying state, court need not consider law of other qualifying State, nor conduct any "choice of law" analysis).

State Law Service–Serving at Place of Business

The Federal Rules do *not* specifically authorize serving individuals by leaving a copy of the summons and complaint at the individual's regular place of business.[89] This type of service is, nevertheless, often still available to the plaintiff because many States authorize service at business addresses.[90]

RULE 4(f). SERVICE UPON INDIVIDUALS IN A FOREIGN COUNTRY

CORE CONCEPT

Original process may be served upon any competent, adult defendant outside the United States, who is both amenable to service and subject to the court's personal jurisdiction, as follows:

(1) ***Specific Federal Law***: In any manner specifically authorized by federal law for such service, where Congress has determined that a particular type of service is necessary or proper; or

(2) ***Waiver***: Under the waiver-of-service provisions of Rule 4(d), if not prohibited by the law of the foreign country of service;[91] or

(3) ***International Agreement***: Where Congress has not established otherwise, and where the waiver-of-service provisions either are prohibited by foreign law or are not honored by an executed acknowledgement of service, service may be completed in any internationally agreed upon manner that is reasonably calculated to give notice, such as the *Hague Convention on the Service Abroad of Judicial and Extrajudicial Documents in Civil or Commercial Matters*;[92] or

(4) ***Court Order***: In any other manner directed by the court, so long as the chosen method is not prohibited by international agreement.

If no international agreement exists, or if the agreement permits service by other means, then original process may be served upon any competent, adult defendant outside the United States, who is both amenable to service and subject to the court's personal jurisdiction, as follows:

(5) ***Foreign Law***: In the manner prescribed by the law of the foreign country; or

(6) ***Letters Rogatory***: In the manner directed in response to a letter rogatory or letter of request; or

89. *See Melkaz Int'l Inc. v. Flavor Innovation Inc.*, 167 F.R.D. 634 (E.D.N.Y.1996). *See also Boateng v. Inter American Univ. of P.R.*, 188 F.R.D. 26 (D.P.R.1999) (holding that place of employment is not "dwelling place" or "usual place of abode").

90. *See* Rule 4(e)(1).

91. *See R. Griggs Group Ltd. v. Filanto Spa*, 920 F.Supp. 1100, 1103 (D.Nev.1996).

92. Nov. 15, 1965, 20 U.S.T. 361, T.I.A.S. No. 6638, 658 U.N.T.S. 163. The text of the Convention on the Service Abroad of Judicial and Extrajudicial Documents in Civil or Commercial Matters is reprinted in the Supplement to 28 U.S.C.A. following Rule 4 (WESTLAW: USCA database, **ci(frcp/2 4) & treaties**).

(7) ***Personal Service / Mail Delivery***: Unless prohibited by the foreign country's law: (a) by personally delivering the summons and complaint to the individual defendant, or (b) by the clerk of court mailing process in a manner requiring a signed receipt; or

(8) ***Court Order***: In any other manner directed by the court, so long as the chosen method is not prohibited by international agreement.

APPLICATIONS

Hague Service Is Required, If Available

The Supreme Court has ruled that service in accordance with the Hague Service Convention is mandatory, wherever that Convention applies.[93] Note, however, that the substantial majority of foreign Nations are *not* signatories to the Hague Service Convention.[94] Note also, that there is a division among the courts as to whether the Hague Service Convention authorizes original service of process by mail.[95] Consequently, practitioners should take special care to research well the construction of the Hague Service Convention applicable to their litigation.

Internationally Agreed Upon Service

Process served pursuant to an international agreement must comport with all specific, peculiar requirements imposed by the host country, such as the translation of process into the local language.[96]

Applies to Foreign Service, Not to Foreign Citizens

The provisions of Rule 4(f) are not triggered merely because the defendant is a citizen of a foreign country. Foreign nationals living, traveling, or conducting business within the United States generally may be served with process domestically under Rule 4(e), just as any other individual may. Instead, Rule 4(f) is triggered only when the

93. *See Volkswagenwerk Aktiengesellschaft v. Schlunk*, 486 U.S. 694, 108 S.Ct. 2104, 100 L.Ed.2d 722 (1988). *See also Marcantonio v. Primorsk Shipping Corp.*, 206 F.Supp.2d 54, 57 (D.Mass.2002) (Rule 4(f) requires the use of the Hague Convention provisions when Convention is in effect); *In re CINAR Corp. Secs. Litig.*, 186 F.Supp.2d 279, 303–04 (E.D.N.Y.2002) (same); *Taft v. Moreau*, 177 F.R.D. 201, 203 (D.Vt.1997) (same). *Cf. Brown v. Bandai America, Inc.*, 2002 WL 1285265, at *3 (N.D.Tex.2002) (because Japan is signatory to Hague Convention, court must determine whether defendant was properly served in accordance with Convention requirements).

94. *See Mayoral–Amy v. BHI Corp.*, 180 F.R.D. 456, 459 n. 3 (S.D.Fla.1998).

95. *See generally Nuovo Pignone, SpA v. STORMAN ASIA M/V*, 310 F.3d 374, 383–85 (5th Cir.2002) (collecting cases reaching differing constructions of Hague Service Convention's "postal channels" language in Article 10(a)).

96. *See Friedman v. Israel Labour Party*, 1997 WL 379181 (E.D.Pa.1997) (holding service improper on Israeli defendant where plaintiff failed to send complaint directly to Israeli Director of Courts, as Israel required in its adoption of the Hague Service Convention); *Pennsylvania Orthopedic Ass'n v. Mercedes–Benz A.G.*, 160 F.R.D. 58 (E.D.Pa.1995)(ruling that service attempted under the Hague Convention on a German corporate defendant was ineffective because the complaint had not been translated into German).

defendant—whether an American national or a citizen of another country—is served outside the United States.[97]

Service on United States Agent

When formally serving an individual located in a foreign country, a plaintiff has two options. First, the individual may be served personally in the foreign country, pursuant to the various provisions of this Rule 4(f). Second, the individual may be served by serving process within the United States on the individual's authorized agent (if one exists), pursuant to Rule 4(e).[98]

"Court–Ordered" Type of Service, Generally

So long as the method of service is not prohibited by "international agreement", the plaintiff can request and the district court can order a means of service specifically tailored to achieve service upon individuals in a foreign country.[99]

This type of "court-ordered" service has been particularly useful to the courts when encountering elusive international defendants, especially those striving to evade service of process.[100] Few restrictions exist on the district court's creativity in crafting an alternate means of service. So long as the alternative service is (1) ordered by the court, (2) not prohibited by applicable international agreement, and (3) reasonably calculated, under the circumstances, to apprise the defendant of the pendency of the action and afford an opportunity to respond, the courts enjoy wide discretion.[101] Indeed, at least one court has confirmed that this "court-ordered" service option may even be employed where service could otherwise be accomplished through the various options set forth in Rule 4(f)(2).[102] The "court-ordered" service option has been applied by the courts to authorize service by publication, ordinary mail, mail to a last known address, delivery to certain members of the defendant's family, delivery to the defendant's attorney, and telex.[103]

97. *See Stars' Desert Inn Hotel & Country Club, Inc. v. Hwang*, 105 F.3d 521, 524 (9th Cir.1997).

98. *See Silvious v. Pharaon*, 54 F.3d 697 (11th Cir.1995)(per curiam).

99. *See Forum Fin. Group, LLC v. President, Fellows of Harvard College*, 199 F.R.D. 22, 23–24 (D.Me.2001) (authorizing service upon foreign defendant by certified mail sent to his American attorney).

100. *See Rio Properties, Inc. v. Rio Int'l Interlink*, 284 F.3d 1007, 1018 (9th Cir.2002) (justifying alternate service because plaintiff was "faced with an international e-business scofflaw, playing hide-and-seek with the federal court"). *See also Smith v. Islamic Emirate of Afghanistan*, 2001 WL 1658211, at *3 (S.D.N.Y.2001) (permitting alternative service on Osama Bin Laden and Al Qaeda terrorist network).

101. *See Rio Properties, Inc. v. Rio Int'l Interlink*, 284 F.3d 1007, 1014–18 (9th Cir.2002) (discussing analysis for crafting alternative service under Rule 4(f)). *But see id.* at 1014 (briefly discussing controversy over whether court's discretion to craft alternative service includes methods in violation of foreign country's internal laws).

102. *See Rio Properties, Inc. v. Rio Int'l Interlink*, 284 F.3d 1007, 1014–15 (9th Cir.2002) (expressly rejecting argument that Rule creates "a hierarchy of preferred methods of service of process" that first requires failed service under each of the Rule 4(f)(2) options before resorting to court-ordered service).

103. *See Rio Properties, Inc. v. Rio Int'l Interlink*, 284 F.3d 1007, 1016 (9th Cir.2002) (listing alternate service authorizations by other courts, and granting alternative service on local affiliate, on American attorney consulted by defendant, and by e-mail). *See also United States v. Padilla*, 2002 WL 471838, at *1 (E.D.Cal.2002) (authorizing United States to serve defendant by

"Court-Ordered" Service by E-Mail

Recently, and cautiously, courts have, on occasion, ordered alternate service of process by electronic mail (e-mail) in cases involving international defendants with a known e-mail address, engaged in internet activities, and attempting to evade service by other means.[104] Noting the many complications with e-mail service (*e.g.*, an inability to confirm actual receipt of an e-mail message, system compatibility issues, possible failure of attachments (such as exhibits) to transmit, be received, or be "opened" in comprehensible form, etc.), courts have granted e-mail service upon a proper balancing, on a case-by-case basis, of these limitations against the corresponding benefits of such service in particular circumstances.[105]

Return of Service

Once service abroad is complete, the proof of service can be made in the manner provided by Rule 4(*l*), by the law of the foreign country, or by order of court. If service was accomplished by mail, the proof of service shall include a signed return receipt.

Effect of Foreign Service

Foreign countries are not parties to the Constitution's Full Faith and Credit Clause, and thus the enforcement abroad of a judgment entered by an American federal court is dependent on comity and international treaties. Moreover, in certain foreign countries, failure to adhere to the host nation's service regulations could even subject the unwary process server to criminal penalties.[106]

RULE 4(g). SERVICE UPON INFANTS AND INCOMPETENT PERSONS

CORE CONCEPT

Original process may be served upon any infant or incompetent person in the following manners:

personally delivering a copy of summons and complaint to both defendant's daughter and defendant's attorney, currently representing defendant in another matter, with letter requesting that recipients forward the summons and complaint to defendant, and offering to send copies directly to defendant's residence if the recipient provides the government with defendant's address); *Smith v. Islamic Emirate of Afghanistan*, 2001 WL 1658211, at *3 (S.D.N.Y.2001) (permitting alternative service on Osama Bin Laden and Al Qaeda terrorist network by publication in Afghani newspapers, Pakistani newspaper where Bin Laden published his Fatwahs, and broadcast advertising on local television networks).

104. *See Rio Properties, Inc. v. Rio Int'l Interlink*, 284 F.3d 1007, 1017–18 (9th Cir.2002) (listing alternate service authorizations by other courts, and granting alternative service on local affiliate, on American attorney consulted by defendant, and by e-mail).

105. *See Rio Properties, Inc. v. Rio Int'l Interlink*, 284 F.3d 1007, 1017–18 (9th Cir.2002) (discussing e-mail option, and finding that e-mail service was perhaps most likely method to notify defendant of summons and complaint).

106. *See Volkswagenwerk Aktiengesellschaft v. Schlunk*, 486 U.S. 694, 108 S.Ct. 2104, 100 L.Ed.2d 722 (1988)(commenting on possible adverse consequences of failing to comply with applicable international treaties). *See generally* Joseph F. Weis, Jr., *The Federal Rules and the Hague Conventions: Concerns of Conformity and Comity*, 50 U. Pitt. L. Rev. 903 (1989).

- *Service in the United States:* In any manner authorized for the service of process on infants or incompetent persons by the State in which service is to be made.
- *Service Outside the United States:* In any manner: (1) prescribed by the law of the foreign country, (2) directed in response to a letter rogatory or letter of request; or (3) by such other means as the court may direct.

APPLICATIONS

State Law Dictates Proper Service

For service of process to be effective upon a minor or incompetent person, the service must comply with the requirements for such service as promulgated by the State in which service is attempted.[107]

RULE 4(h). SERVICE UPON CORPORATIONS AND ASSOCIATIONS

CORE CONCEPT

Original process may be served upon any domestic or foreign corporation, partnership, or unincorporated association subject to suit under a common name, in the following manners:

(1) ***Specific Federal Law***: In any manner specifically authorized by federal law for such service, where Congress has determined that a particular type of service is necessary or proper; or

(2) ***Waiver***: Under the waiver-of-service provisions of Rule 4(d); or

(3) ***SERVICE IN THE UNITED STATES***:

(a) ***State Law***: In the manner authorized by the State in which the district court sits, or by the State in which the service is to be accomplished; or

(b) ***Officer, Managing Agent, or General Agent***: By delivering the summons and complaint to an officer, managing agent, or general agent;[108] or

107. *See Seibels, Bruce & Co. v. Nicke*, 168 F.R.D. 542, 545 (M.D.N.C.1996) (mailing complaint to minor's last place of residence was defective service because Indiana law required service on both minor and the minor's custodial parent).

108. *Cf. Ayres v. Jacobs & Crumplar, P.A.*, 99 F.3d 565, 567–68 (3d Cir.1996) (service upon "office manager" was insufficient service under Rule 4(h)); *Adams v. AlliedSignal General Aviation Avionics*, 74 F.3d 882, 885 (8th Cir.1996) (service upon officer of a subsidiary does not satisfy Rule 4(h) service on the parent corporation, absent probative evidence that the subsidiary and the parent are not independently operated); *Baade v. Price*, 175 F.R.D. 403, 405 (D.D.C.1997) (holding that generally person served must have "some measure of discretion in operating some phase of the defendant's business or in the management of a given office", must have "such status that common sense would expect the recipient to see that the summons promptly gets into the hands of the appropriate personnel", and must be working for the company at the time of service); *Romand v. Zimmerman*, 881 F.Supp. 806 (N.D.N.Y. 1995)(holding that service on chairperson of board of trustees was insufficient service under Rule 4(h)).

(c) ***Agent***: By delivering the summons and complaint to an agent appointed to receive service or authorized by law to receive service;[109] and if required by statute, by also mailing the summons and complaint to the defendant; or

(4) ***SERVICE OUTSIDE THE UNITED STATES***:

In any manner provided for service upon individuals in a foreign country, except personal service.[110]

APPLICATIONS

Service on Domestic Corporation's Officer, Manager, or General Agent

To effectively serve a corporation through an officer, manager, or general agent, the summons and complaint must be served on that person. Simply addressing the mail to the corporation generally, or to its legal department, will generally not suffice.[111] Whether a particular person qualifies as an officer, managing agent, or general agent of a corporation or association is determined on the basis of the particular facts presented.[112]

Service at Domestic Corporate Headquarters

The Federal Rules do *not* specifically authorize service by leaving a copy of the summons and complaint with a person of suitable age and discretion at the corporation's headquarters.[113] This type of service, however, may still be permitted. Rule 4(h) authorizes service in the federal courts in any manner permitted by the forum's State law.[114]

Service on Foreign Corporation

Proper service on a foreign corporation or association is governed by the foreign service on individuals rule, Rule 4(f). Failure to comply

109. *Cf. Schollenberger v. Sears, Roebuck & Co.*, 876 F.Supp. 153 (E.D.Mich.1995)(ruling that delivery to defendant's insurance claims representative was not sufficient service).

110. *See* Rule 4(f); *but see* Rule 4(f)(2)(C)(i)(no personal service).

111. *See Larsen v. Mayo Medical Ctr.*, 218 F.3d 863 (8th Cir.2000), *cert. denied*, 531 U.S. 1036, 121 S.Ct. 625, 148 L.Ed.2d 534 (2000) (holding that papers mailed to "Medical/Legal Department, Mayo Clinic" was ineffective service under Rule 4(h)).

112. *See, e.g., Battie v. Freeman Decorating*, 2001 WL 1345927, at *1 (E.D.La.2001) (commenting the delivery of summons and complaint to corporation's receptionist is sufficient service); *Reed v. Weeks Marine, Inc.*, 166 F.Supp.2d 1052, 1056 (E.D.Pa.2001) (same); *Estates of Ungar ex rel. Strachman v. Palestinian Auth.*, 153 F.Supp.2d 76, 89–91 (D.R.I.2001) (in lawsuit against Palestinian authority and PLO, court held that service on general or managing agent accomplished when process was delivered to Chief PA and PLO Representative in the United States and to PLO's Deputy Permanent Observer to the United Nations).

113. *See Melkaz Int'l Inc. v. Flavor Innovation Inc.*, 167 F.R.D. 634 (E.D.N.Y.1996). *See also Dailey v. R & J Commercial Contracting*, 2002 WL 484988, at *3 (S.D.Ohio 2002) ("When a corporation holds itself out to the public as receiving mail at a particular address, it must take some minimal steps to insure that when certified mail service is directed to that address, it receives actual notice, and its failure to do so cannot be attributed to the plaintiff, who is entitled to rely upon the address in requesting certified mail service"); *Battie v. Freeman Decorating*, 2001 WL 1345927, at *1 (E.D.La.2001) (commenting the delivery of summons and complaint to corporation's receptionist is sufficient service); *Reed v. Weeks Marine, Inc.*, 166 F.Supp.2d 1052, 1056 (E.D.Pa.2001) (same).

114. *See* Rule 4(h)(1) (incorporating Rule 4(e)(1)).

with those provisions will render the service ineffective.[115]

RULE 4(i). SERVICE UPON THE UNITED STATES, ITS AGENCIES, CORPORATIONS, AND OFFICERS

CORE CONCEPT

To properly serve the United States, its agencies, corporations, or officers with original process, the summons and complaint must be served at several different locations. This multiple service obligation is mandatory, not discretionary.

APPLICATIONS

The United States as Defendant

Original process must be served upon the United States as follows:

(1) ***United States Attorney***: By *either* (a) personally delivering the summons and complaint to the United States Attorney for the judicial district in which the action is brought, or her designee, *or* (b) sending the summons and complaint by registered or certified mail to the civil process clerk at the office of the United States Attorney; *and*

(2) ***Attorney General***: By *also* sending a copy of the summons and complaint by registered or certified mail to the United States Attorney General in Washington, D.C.; *and*

(3) ***Federal Officer or Agency***: In lawsuits attacking the validity of an order of a non-party officer or agency of the United States, by *also* sending a copy of the summons and complaint by registered or certified mail to such officer or agency.

Federal Officers, Agencies, or Corporations as Defendants

Original process may be served upon an officer, agency, or corporation of the United States as follows:

(1) ***United States***: By serving the United States (see above); *and*

(2) ***Federal Officer, Agency, or Corporation***: By also sending a copy of the summons and complaint by registered or certified mail to the federal officer, agency, or corporation named as a defendant.[116]

Suing Federal Officers/Employees in their Individual Capacities

In certain instances, federal officers and employees may be sued in their individual—rather than official—capacities.[117] In such cases, the type of service required will depend on the allegations of the pleading:

115. *See Emery v. Wood Indus., Inc.*, 2001 WL 274747, at **2–3 (D.N.H.2001) (hand-delivery of complaint and summons to Assistant Manager for Public Relations in Taiwan failed to comply with procedures authorized by Rule 4).

116. *See* Rule 4(i)(2)(A). *See also Cleveland v. Williams*, 874 F.Supp. 270 (E.D.Cal. 1994)(where United States was not also served in lawsuit against IRS agents sued in their official capacities, complaint was dismissed as to all defendants).

117. *See Bivens v. Six Unknown Named Agents of Fed. Bureau of Narcotics*, 403 U.S. 388, 91 S.Ct. 1999, 29 L.Ed.2d 619 (1971) (per-

- *On-the-Job Claims:* If the federal officers or employees are sued in their individual capacities for acts or omissions occurring in connection with the performance of their federal duties, then proper service requires (1) service upon the United States *and* (2) service upon the officer or employee under Rule 4(e), (f), or (g).[118]
- *Claims Unrelated to the Job:* If the federal officers or employees are sued in their individual capacities for any other acts or omissions (that is, for conduct unrelated to the performance of their federal duties), then proper service requires only service under Rule 4(e), (f), or (g). Service on the United States is not required.[119]

These procedures apply to former federal officers and employees, as well as current personnel.[120]

If the plaintiff intends to sue the federal officials in *both* their individual and official capacities, the plaintiff must: (1) individually serve the officials under Rule 4(e), (f), or (g); *and*(2) serve the United States as well under Rule 4(i).[121] The plaintiff generally does not need to serve the official twice personally, however (*i.e.*, one service for each capacity).[122]

Careful! Name the Correct Federal Defendant

Practitioners should take special care while consulting the applicable substantive law to ensure that the proper defendant is named. A lawsuit may be dismissed if the practitioner mistakenly names a federal officer or agency as a defendant when the proper defendant is the United States, or mistakenly names the United States as a defendant when the proper defendant is a federal agency or officer, or mistakenly names federal officers as defendants in their official rather than individual capacities.[123]

mitting action for money damages against federal officers acting under color of their official authority for injuries caused by the officers' unconstitutional conduct).

118. *See* Rule 4(i)(2)(B).

119. *See* Rule 4(i)(2)(B) advisory committee note to 2000 amendments ("Many actions are brought against individual federal officers or employees of the United States for acts or omissions that have no connection whatever to their government roles. There is no reason to require service on the United States in these actions").

120. *See* Rule 4(i)(2)(B) advisory committee notes to 2000 amendments (noting that an action against former federal personnel "is covered by paragraph (2)(B) in the same way as an action against a present officer or employee").

121. *See McCaslin v. Cornhusker State Indus.*, 952 F.Supp. 652, 658–59 (D.Neb.1996) (construing Rule 4(j), holding that service delivered directly to government employees conferred jurisdiction over them only in their individual capacities; to sue the government itself, service on the chief executive officer or the State attorney general's office was required).

122. *See* Rule 4(i)(2) advisory committee notes to 2000 amendments (commenting that amendments are intended "to ensure that no one would read the seemingly independent provisions of paragraphs 2(A) and 2(B) to mean that service must be made twice both on the United States and on the United States employee when the employee is sued in both official and individual capacities"). *See also Buttler v. Keller*, 169 F.R.D. 9, 10 (N.D.N.Y.1996) (under applicable State law, a single service upon an individual, named in both his individual and representative capacities, suffices to confer jurisdiction).

123. *See, e.g.,* 28 U.S.C.A. § 2671 (under Federal Torts Claims Act, actions to recover for the torts of a federal agency must name the United States as a defendant).

Curing Incomplete Service on Federal Defendants

In view of the complexity of these multiple service obligations, Rule 4(i) establishes a "cure" for incomplete service in cases requiring service on multiple officers, agencies, or federal corporations. So long as either the United States Attorney or the Attorney General has been properly served in such cases, the court must allow a plaintiff a reasonable period of time to fulfill the multiple service obligations at all other locations.[124]

"Cure" is Opportunity for Extension, Not an Excuse of Obligation: The "cure" provision in Rule 4(i) does not authorize the courts to excuse or forgive incomplete service on the United States. To the contrary, the "cure" provision only authorizes an extension of time to complete the plaintiff's obligations–the full, required service under Rule 4(i) must still be achieved.[125]

"Cure" in Federal Agency, Corporation, & Official Capacity Lawsuits: If the plaintiff succeeds in serving either the United States Attorney or the Attorney General in a lawsuit asserting Rule 4(i)(2)(A) claims (claims against a federal agency or corporation, or official capacity claims against federal officers of employees), but the plaintiff neglects to serve other required parties, the courts will allow the plaintiff a "reasonable time" to perfect proper service.[126] Note, however, that this "cure" provision applies *only* when proper service has already been achieved on the United States Attorney or the Attorney General.[127]

"Cure" in On-the-Job Individual Capacity Lawsuits: In a lawsuit against federal officers or employees sued for Rule 4(i)(2)(B) claims (individual capacity, "on-the-job" claims), a plaintiff who successfully serves the officer or employee will be granted a "reasonable time" to serve the United States as well.[128]

"Cure" Not General Extension of Time: The "cure" is not triggered unless effective service is first accomplished upon the United States Attorney or the Attorney General.[129] Similarly, the extension is not unlimited; the "cure" must be accomplished within

124. Rule 4(i)(3).

125. *See McMasters v. United States*, 260 F.3d 814, 817–18 (7th Cir.2001), *cert. denied*, 535 U.S. 1112, 122 S.Ct. 2327, 153 L.Ed.2d 158 (2002).

126. *See* Rule 4(i)(3)(A).

127. *But see Gargano v. I.R.S.*, 207 F.R.D. 22, 23 (D.Mass.2002) (commenting that some courts, confronted by a failure to serve the U.S. Attorney or Attorney General, "see room for a grant of equitable relief where overly strict adherence to the literal wording of the Rule appears to elevate form over substance", and have applied a four-part analysis that could grant such relief where: (1) all necessary governmental parties have actual notice of the lawsuit; (2) the government has suffered no prejudice from the service defect; (3) the plaintiff had a justifiable excuse for the failure to make proper service; and (4) the plaintiff would be severely prejudiced by a dismissal).

128. *See* Rule 4(i)(3)(B).

129. *See Parham v. Lamar*, 1 F.Supp.2d 1457 (M.D.Fla.1998) (Court refuses cure period where plaintiff failed to properly serve either the United States Attorney General or the local United States Attorney); *T & S Rentals v. United States*, 164 F.R.D. 422, 425–26 (N.D.W.Va. 1996) (same).

a "reasonable time" after service is made on the United States Attorney or the Attorney General.[130]

RULE 4(j). SERVICE UPON FOREIGN, STATE, OR LOCAL GOVERNMENTS

CORE CONCEPT

Original process may be served upon a foreign, State, or local government as follows:

- ***On Foreign Governments, their political subdivisions, agencies, or instrumentalities:*** Service must be accomplished in accordance with the federal Foreign Sovereign Immunities Act, 28 U.S.C.A. § 1608, which permits service in the following order of preference:
  - **On Foreign Governments:**
    (1) ***Agreed-Method:*** In any manner arranged between the plaintiff and the foreign State, but if not then:
    (2) ***International Agreement:*** In accordance with an applicable international treaty or convention, such as the *Hague Convention on the Service Abroad of Judicial and Extrajudicial Documents in Civil or Commercial Matters,*[131] but if not then:
    (3) ***Ministry of Foreign Affairs:*** By the clerk of court mailing a copy of the summons and complaint and a notice of suit, along with translations thereof, in a manner requiring a signed receipt, to the head of the ministry of foreign affairs, but if such service is not available within 30 days, then:
    (4) ***Special Consular Services:*** By the clerk of court mailing a copy of the summons and complaint and a notice of suit, along with translations thereof, in a manner requiring a signed receipt, to the United States Director of Special Consular Services, for transmittal to the foreign State through diplomatic channels.
  - **On Foreign Agencies or Instrumentalities:**

130. *See Tuke v. United States*, 76 F.3d 155, 158 (7th Cir.1996) (cure not reasonable where plaintiff failed to serve "for months" and, after being notified by the United States of the deficiency, failed to act promptly or properly); *Mused v. United States Dep't of Agriculture Food & Nutrition Serv.*, 169 F.R.D. 28, 35–36 (W.D.N.Y.1996) (cure not reasonable where plaintiff waited nearly a year to cure service defect). *See also Mused v. United States Dep't of Agriculture Food & Nutrition Serv.*, 169 F.R.D. 28, 36 n. 7 (W.D.N.Y.1996) (rejecting argument that duration of defect be marked from date defect was "discovered", rather than when defect actually occurred).

131. Nov. 15, 1965, 20 U.S.T. 361, T.I.A.S. No. 6638, 658 U.N.T.S. 163. The text of the Convention on the Service Abroad of Judicial and Extrajudicial Documents in Civil or Commercial Matters is reprinted in the Supplement to 28 U.S.C.A. following Fed.R.Civ.P. 4 (WESTLAW: USCA database, **ci(frcp/2 4) & treaties).**

(1) ***Agreed–Method:*** By serving process in any manner arranged between the plaintiff and the foreign agency or instrumentality,[132] but if not then:

(2) ***Agent or International Agreement***: *Either* (a) by delivering process to an officer, managing agent, or general agent of the foreign agency or instrumentality, or to an agent appointed by the foreign agent or instrumentality to receive service of process or authorized by law to receive such service; *or* (b) by serving process in accordance with an applicable international treaty or convention, such as the *Hague Convention on the Service Abroad of Judicial and Extrajudicial Documents in Civil or Commercial Matters,*[133] but if not then:

(3) ***Letter Rogatory, Clerk Mailing, or Court Order***: In one of the following manners: (a) by delivering process (together with a translation thereof) as directed in response to a letter rogatory or letter of request; *or* (b) by the clerk of court mailing process (along with translations thereof) in a manner requiring a signed receipt, to the agency or instrumentality; *or* (c) by order of court consistent with the law of the place where service is to be accomplished.

- ***On States, Municipal Corporations, and Other Governmental Organizations:*** A State, municipal corporation, or other governmental organization may be served with process:

  (1) ***Chief Executive Officer:*** By personally delivering the summons and complaint to the chief executive officer of the State, municipal corporation, or governmental organization;[134] or

  (2) ***State Law:*** By serving the summons and complaint in the manner authorized by the State in which the service is to be accomplished.

  Note: The Eleventh Amendment to the United States Constitution restricts the authority of the

132. *See In re Arbitration Between Trans Chemical Ltd. & China Nat'l Mach. Import & Export Corp.*, 978 F.Supp. 266 (S.D.Tex.1997) (service upon foreign agency was proper because it was made in accordance with the terms of the contract between the agency and the plaintiff).

133. Nov. 15, 1965, 20 U.S.T. 361, T.I.A.S. No. 6638, 658 U.N.T.S. 163. The text of the Convention on the Service Abroad of Judicial and Extrajudicial Documents in Civil or Commercial Matters is reprinted in the Supplement to 28 U.S.C.A. following Fed.R.Civ.P. 4 (WESTLAW: USCA database, **ci(frcp/2 4) & treaties).**

134. *See Coleman v. Milwaukee Bd. of Sch. Dirs.*, 290 F.3d 932, 933–34 (7th Cir.2002) (where school board had no "chief executive officer", only option for plaintiff was to serve as prescribed by State law); *McCaslin v. Cornhusker State Indus.*, 952 F.Supp. 652, 658–59 (D.Neb. 1996) (holding that service delivered directly to government employees conferred jurisdiction over them only in their individual capacities; to sue the government itself, service on the chief executive officer or the State attorney general's office was required).

federal courts to hear lawsuits against States.[135] Additionally, individual State and municipal sovereign immunity laws limit the federal courts' ability to enter awards against States, municipalities, and governmental entities.

RULE 4(k). TERRITORIAL LIMITS OF EFFECTIVE SERVICE

CORE CONCEPT

Service of a summons and complaint is effective to confer personal, or *in personam*, jurisdiction over any defendant amenable to service under the forum State's long-arm statute, under the federal interpleader statute,[136] or under other federal long-arm statutes. Additionally, persons or entities joined to the lawsuit as third-parties, necessary parties, or indispensable parties may be served with original process anywhere in the "bulge" region—within 100 miles of the place from where the summons issued (whether within or outside the State). Finally, service may also confer personal jurisdiction over a defendant who is not subject to the jurisdiction of any particular State.

APPLICATIONS

Exercise of Federal Personal Jurisdiction

Absent a waiver of formal service, the federal courts may generally exercise personal jurisdiction over the following categories of parties who are either served with process:

- *State Long–Arm Statutes:* Defendants who are amenable to suit in the State where the district court is sitting in accordance with the provisions of that State's long-arm statute; [137]
- *100 Mile "Bulge" Rule:* Defendants joined as third-parties, necessary parties, or indispensable parties and who are served within 100 miles of the place where the summons issues; [138]

  Note: The bulge rule does *not* apply to service on the original parties to the lawsuit, nor does it constrict the range for service when a State or federal statute authorizes broader (or unlimited) service of process.
- *Federal Interpleader Statute:* Parties of completely diverse citizenship who are claiming title to assets of $500

135. *See Pennhurst State Sch. & Hosp. v. Halderman,* 465 U.S. 89, 104 S.Ct. 900, 79 L.Ed.2d 67 (1984)(noting that Eleventh Amendment prevents federal courts from hearing suits for damages filed by citizens against States, unless the defending State first consents). *See also Florida Dep't of State v. Treasure Salvors, Inc.,* 458 U.S. 670, 102 S.Ct. 3304, 73 L.Ed.2d 1057 (1982)(confirming that Eleventh Amendment extends to bar suits by citizens against their own State of residence, in the absence of that State's consent to suit).

136. 28 U.S.C.A. § 1335.

137. Rule 4(k)(1)(A). *See ePlus Tech., Inc. v. Aboud,* 313 F.3d 166, 176 (4th Cir.2002); *United States v. Botefuhr,* 309 F.3d 1263, 1271 (10th Cir.2002); *Bank Brussels Lambert v. Fiddler Gonzalez & Rodriguez,* 305 F.3d 120, 124 (2d Cir.2002).

138. Rule 4(k)(1)(B).

or more, which assets have been deposited into the registry of the district court;[139] and

- *Federal Long–Arm Statutes:* Defendants who are amenable to suit in the district court pursuant to a federal statute providing for national or worldwide service of process.[140]

Jurisdiction Over No–State–Resident

The federal courts also have personal jurisdiction over defendants who are not residents of the United States, but who have sufficient contacts with the United States as a Nation to warrant the application of federal law, yet who lack sufficient contacts with any single, particular State to support personal jurisdiction under State law long-arm statutes.[141]

Prerequisites for Asserting No–State–Resident Jurisdiction

To qualify for this type of national-contacts service of process, three conditions are first required:[142]

(1) Federal Claims: Plaintiff's claims against the No–State–Resident defendant must arise under federal law;[143]

(2) No Conventional Jurisdiction Possible: The defendant is beyond the jurisdictional reach of any individual State court and no situation-specific federal statute applies to confer jurisdiction;[144]

139. Rule 4(k)(1)(C).

140. Rule 4(k)(1)(D). *See SEC v. Carrillo*, 115 F.3d 1540 (11th Cir.1997) (where federal statute authorizes nationwide or worldwide service, the requisite "minimum contacts" analysis tests for contacts with the United States as a Nation).

141. *See* Rule 4(k)(2). *See also Omni Capital Int'l v. Rudolf Wolff & Co.*, 484 U.S. 97, 111, 108 S.Ct. 404, 413, 98 L.Ed.2d 415 (1987)(defendant had sufficient contacts to satisfy constitutional due process concerns, but insufficient contacts to fall within narrower State long-arm statute); *Eskofot A/S v. E.I. Du Pont De Nemours & Co.*, 872 F.Supp. 81 (S.D.N.Y. 1995)(holding that federal courts may exercise this jurisdiction over non-State defendants only where the defendants have sufficient contacts with United States generally so that due process concerns are not offended, such as where the defendants transact business in the United States, perform an act within the United States, or have an effect in the United States by an act done elsewhere).

142. *See Glencore Grain Rotterdam B.V. v. Shivnath Rai Harnarain Co.*, 284 F.3d 1114, 1126 (9th Cir.2002) (listing elements); *Base Metal Trading, Ltd. v. OJSC "Novokuznetsky Aluminum Factory"*, 283 F.3d 208, 215 (4th Cir. 2002) (same), *cert. denied*, 537 U.S. 822, 123 S.Ct. 101, 154 L.Ed.2d 30 (2002); *Consolidated Dev't Corp. v. Sherritt, Inc.*, 216 F.3d 1286, 1291 (11th Cir.2000) (same), *cert. denied*, 534 U.S. 827, 122 S.Ct. 68, 151 L.Ed.2d 34 (2001); *United States v. Swiss American Bank, Ltd.*, 191 F.3d 30, 38 (1st Cir.1999) (same).

143. *See World Tanker Carriers Corp. v. M/V Ya Mawlaya*, 99 F.3d 717, 720–23 (5th Cir.1996) (in admiralty case, holding that federal court may exercise jurisdiction over foreign defendants for claims arising under federal law when the defendants have sufficient contacts with the country as a whole); *United States v. Offshore Marine Ltd.*, 179 F.R.D. 156, 158–60 (D.Vi.1998) (Rule 4(k)(2) applies to admiralty cases); *West Africa Trading & Shipping Co. v. London Int'l Group*, 968 F.Supp. 996 (D.N.J.1997) (same); *Eskofot A/S v. E.I. Du Pont De Nemours & Co.*, 872 F.Supp. 81 (S.D.N.Y.1995).

144. *See United States v. Swiss American Bank, Ltd.*, 191 F.3d 30, 38 (1st Cir.1999); *See World Tanker Carriers Corp. v. M/V Ya Mawlaya*, 99 F.3d 717, 720 (5th Cir.1996); *In re Telectronics Pacing Sys.*, 953 F.Supp. 909, 914 (S.D.Ohio 1997) (Rule unavailable where case arises under State law); *Aerogroup Int'l, Inc. v. Marlboro Footworks, Ltd.*, 956 F.Supp. 427, 434 (S.D.N.Y.1996) (Rule requires that defendant not be subject to jurisdiction of courts of any one State).

(3) Exercise of Personal Jurisdiction is Constitutional: The exercise of personal jurisdiction over the defendant would not offend the Constitution or other federal law.[145] Ordinarily, this will require that the defendants' contacts with the Nation generally (1) must relate to the plaintiff's cause of action or have given rise to it, (2) must involve some act whereby the defendant purposefully avails itself of the privilege of conducting activities within the forum, and (3) must be such that defendant should reasonably have anticipated being haled into court there.[146] In conducting this constitutional inquiry, courts may apply the familiar "general" and "specific" jurisdictional concepts used in the traditional due process analysis.[147]

Burden of Proof in No–State–Resident Cases

The plaintiff bears the burden of establishing that the prerequisites exist for Rule 4(k)(2) national-contacts service.[148] To satisfy this burden, one court requires that the plaintiff make three prima facie showings and one certification: (1) that the claim arises under federal law, (2) that personal jurisdiction is not available under any situation-specific federal statute, (3) that the defendant's contacts with the Nation generally comport with the Constitution's requirements; and (4) that the plaintiff certify, based on information readily available to the plaintiff and counsel, that the defendant is not subject to the jurisdiction of any particular State's court. The plaintiffs may be granted limited jurisdictional discovery to help them carry this burden.[149]

145. *See Dardana Ltd. v. Yuganskneftegaz,* 317 F.3d 202, 207 (2d Cir.2003); *Associated Transport Line, Inc. v. Productos Fitosanitarios,* 197 F.3d 1070, 1074 (11th Cir.1999).

146. *See Associated Transport Line, Inc. v. Productos Fitosanitarios,* 197 F.3d 1070, 1074 (11th Cir.1999). *Cf. Consolidated Dev't Corp. v. Sherritt, Inc.,* 216 F.3d 1286 (11th Cir.2000) (holding that personal jurisdiction will not lie where foreign corporation, that does not engage in general business in the forum, simply negotiates a contract there or has a subsidiary that markets defendant's products), *cert. denied,* 534 U.S. 827, 122 S.Ct. 68, 151 L.Ed.2d 34 (2001).

147. *See Submersible Sys., Inc. v. Perforadora Central, S.A. de C.V.,* 249 F.3d 413, 420–21 (5th Cir.2001); *BP Chemicals Ltd. v. Formosa Chemical & Fibre Corp.,* 229 F.3d 254, 258–63 (3d Cir.2000); *Consolidated Dev't Corp. v. Sherritt, Inc.,* 216 F.3d 1286, 1291–94 (11th Cir. 2000), *cert. denied,* 534 U.S. 827, 122 S.Ct. 68, 151 L.Ed.2d 34 (2001). *See also Base Metal Trading, Ltd. v. OJSC "Novokuznetsky Aluminum Factory",* 283 F.3d 208, 216 (4th Cir.2002) (rejecting Rule 4(k)(2) jurisdiction because alleged contacts with United States "appear sparse and limited to a few shipments of aluminum arriving in American ports", and refusing to commit "the limited resources of the federal courts ... [to] resolving disputes between two foreign corporations with little or no connection to our country"), *cert. denied,* 537 U.S. 822, 123 S.Ct. 101, 154 L.Ed.2d 30 (2002).

148. *See United States v. Swiss American Bank, Ltd.,* 191 F.3d 30, 38 (1st Cir.1999). *See also United States v. Offshore Marine Ltd.,* 179 F.R.D. 156, 160 (D.Vi.1998). *See also ISI Int'l, Inc. v. Borden Ladner Gervais LLP,* 256 F.3d 548, 552 (7th Cir.2001) (endorsing burden-shift view and thus concluding that "constitutional analysis for each of the 50 states is eminently avoidable by allocating burdens sensibly": thus, "[a] defendant who wants to preclude use of Rule 4(k)(2) has only to name some other state in which the suit could proceed").

149. *See Toys "R" Us, Inc. v. Step Two, S.A.,* 318 F.3d 446, 458 (3d Cir.2003) (allowing jurisdictional discovery on limited issue of defendant's business activities in United States, including business plans, marketing strategies, sales, and other commercial interactions); *Dardana Ltd. v. Yuganskneftegaz,* 317 F.3d 202, 208 (2d Cir.2003) (remanding for discovery).

If the plaintiff makes these showings, the burden shifts to the defendant to come forward with evidence that, if credited, would show that jurisdiction would be proper in some State. If the defendant fails to carry this burden, the factfinder can infer that no State enjoys personal jurisdiction. If, however, the defendant carries this burden, the inference drops from the case. Thereafter, the plaintiff may (a) seek a transfer to a State where proper jurisdiction exists, (b) discontinue the lawsuit and re-file it, or (c) challenge the defendant's assertions.[150]

This burden-shifting technique invests the defendant with the ability to "knock out" Rule 4(k)(2) by actually consenting to personal jurisdiction in some other State. Conversely, failing to so consent will permit the federal courts to proceed with the Rule 4(k)(2) analysis without the accompanying burden of a 50–State constitutional analysis.[151]

RULE 4(*l*). PROOF OF SERVICE

CORE CONCEPT

Where formal service has not been waived, the process server must present proof of service to the court.

APPLICATIONS

Nature of Proof

The proof of service should contain sufficient facts to confirm that valid service has been accomplished (*e.g.*, the dwelling place where process was left, the name of the receiving agent or corporate officer). Where service was made by someone other than a United States Marshal, an affidavit of service is required.

Service Outside the United States

If service is made under treaty or other international agreement, proof of service must be in accordance with that treaty or agreement. If service is made in any other manner, proof of service must include a receipt signed by the addressee or other satisfactory evidence of delivery.

150. *See United States v. Swiss American Bank, Ltd.*, 191 F.3d 30, 38 (1st Cir.1999). *See also ISI Int'l, Inc. v. Borden Ladner Gervais LLP*, 256 F.3d 548, 552 (7th Cir.2001) (endorsing burden-shift view and thus concluding that "constitutional analysis for each of the 50 states is eminently avoidable by allocating burdens sensibly": thus, "[a] defendant who wants to preclude use of Rule 4(k)(2) has only to name some other state in which the suit could proceed").

151. *See ISI Int'l, Inc. v. Borden Ladner Gervais LLP*, 256 F.3d 548, 552 (7th Cir.2001) ("This procedure makes it unnecessary to traipse through the 50 states, asking whether each could entertain the suit"). *Accord Adams v. Unione Mediterranea Di Sicurta*, 364 F.3d 646, 651 (5th Cir. 2004) (agreeing that "a piecemeal analysis of the existence vel non of jurisdiction in all fifty states is not necessary. Rather, so long as a defendant does not concede to jurisdiction in another state, a court may use 4(k)(2) to confer jurisdiction").

Failure to Present Proof of Service

So long as the plaintiff demonstrates that the defendant was properly served, the process server's technical failure to present proof of service will not affect the validity of the service.

Amendment to Proof of Service

Where an amendment would cure the defect in the proof of service, the courts generally will grant leave to so amend.[152]

RULE 4(m). TIME LIMIT FOR SERVICE

CORE CONCEPT

A summons and complaint must be served within 120 days after the complaint is filed. However, if the plaintiff is able to show "good cause" why process could not be served within those 120 days, the district court must extend the time for service. If "good cause" is not shown, the district court must either dismiss the lawsuit without prejudice or, in its discretion, direct that service be accomplished within a specified time.

APPLICATIONS

"Good Cause" Defined

The plaintiff bears the burden of proving that "good cause" exists to excuse a delay in service of process.[153] Whether "good cause" exists is a matter committed to the sound discretion of the trial court.[154] Minimally, good cause requires a showing of excusable neglect: good faith and a reasonable basis, beyond the plaintiff's control, for failing to comply with the Rules.[155] This standard is ordinarily applied narrowly to protect only those litigants who have exercised meticulous care in

152. *See Nolan v. City of Yonkers*, 168 F.R.D. 140, 143 (S.D.N.Y.1996) (noting that request to amend proof of service should rarely be refused, and then granting leave to do so).

153. *See Habib v. General Motors Corp.*, 15 F.3d 72, 73 (6th Cir.1994); *Friedman v. Estate of Presser*, 929 F.2d 1151, 1157 (6th Cir.1991); *Zermeno v. McDonnell Douglas Corp.*, 246 F.Supp.2d 646, 666 (S.D.Tex.2003).

154. *See Byrd v. Stone*, 94 F.3d 217, 219 (6th Cir.1996).

155. *See Adams v. AlliedSignal General Aviation Avionics*, 74 F.3d 882, 887 (8th Cir.1996). *See also Coleman v. Milwaukee Bd. of Sch. Dirs.*, 290 F.3d 932, 934 (7th Cir.2002) (good cause requires showing valid reason for delay, such as defendant attempting to evade service); *In re Sheehan*, 253 F.3d 507, 512 (9th Cir.2001) (to qualify for "good cause", plaintiff may be required to show that (a) defendant received actual notice of the lawsuit; (b) defendant would not suffer prejudice; and (c) plaintiff would be severely prejudiced if lawsuit were dismissed); *De Tie v. Orange County*, 152 F.3d 1109 (9th Cir. 1998) (pending bankruptcy stay of service of process qualified as "good cause"); *Matasareanu v. Williams*, 183 F.R.D. 242, 246 (C.D.Cal.1998) (ill health may constitute "good cause", depending on the factual showing made); *Howard v. Klynveld Peat Marwick Goerdeler*, 977 F.Supp. 654, 658 (S.D.N.Y.1997) (ordinarily, "good cause" is found in only exceptional circumstances, where the failure to timely serve process was caused by circumstances beyond plaintiff's control), *aff'd*, 173 F.3d 844 (2d Cir.1999) (Table); *Gambino v. Village of Oakbrook*, 164 F.R.D. 271, 274 (M.D.Fla.1995) (noting that, although the Rules do not define "good cause", the courts look to circumstances beyond plaintiff's control, "such as sudden illness, natural catastrophe, or evasion of service of process" to test for good cause).

attempting to complete service.[156] As one court has aptly warned: "The lesson to the federal plaintiff's lawyer is not to take any chances. Treat the 120 days with the respect reserved for a time bomb."[157]

"Good Cause" and U.S. Marshal Service Delays

Ordinarily, *pro se* litigants for whom the United States Marshal's Service may be directed to serve process will be granted a "good cause" extension of the 120–day period where a delay in service is attributable to the Marshal's Service.[158]

Effect of Showing "Good Cause"

Under old Rule 4 (prior to the 1993 Amendments),[159] unless the plaintiff could demonstrate "good cause" for failing to serve process within 120 days of filing, the district court had no alternative but to dismiss the lawsuit without prejudice. New Rule 4(m) changed this practice in 1993.[160] Since the amendment, the courts have distinguished between justifiable delay ("good cause") and excusable neglect.[161] As to the former (justifiable delay), the district court *must* grant a plaintiff an

156. *See Despain v. Salt Lake Area Metro Gang Unit*, 13 F.3d 1436, 1438 (10th Cir.1994). *Accord Hamilton v. Endell*, 981 F.2d 1062, 1065 (9th Cir.1992) (commenting that "good cause" standard is applied in only limited circumstances, and that inadvertent error or ignorance of governing rules will not excuse a failure to timely serve process). *Compare Despain v. Salt Lake Area Metro Gang Unit*, 13 F.3d 1436, 1438 (10th Cir.1994)(neither mere absence of prejudice nor mistake of counsel constitutes "good cause") *and Powell v. Starwalt*, 866 F.2d 964 (7th Cir.1989)(noting that attorney inadvertence will not constitute "good cause") *and Feingold v. Hankin*, 269 F.Supp.2d 268, 276 (S.D.N.Y. 2003) (attorney's ignorance of rules, inadvertence, neglect, or mistake are not good cause) *and Matasareanu v. Williams*, 183 F.R.D. 242, 246 (C.D.Cal.1998) (noting that lack of legal training and attorney guidance does not constitute "good cause") *and Braithwaite v. Johns Hopkins Hosp.*, 160 F.R.D. 75 (D.Md. 1995)(holding that delay resulting from the psychological distress caused by the murder of plaintiff's only daughter during 120–day service period did not constitute "good cause") *with Habib v. General Motors Corp.*, 15 F.3d 72, 73 (6th Cir.1994)(*pro se* litigant's medical conditions, combined with diligent efforts to complete service, satisfies "good cause" test).

157. *Braxton v. United States*, 817 F.2d 238, 241 (3d Cir.1987)(quoting *Siegel, Practice Commentary on Amendment of Federal Rule 4 (Eff. Feb. 26, 1983) with Special Statute of Limitations Precautions*, 96 F.R.D. 88, 103 (1983)).

158. *See Graham v. Satkoski*, 51 F.3d 710 (7th Cir.1995) (if Marshals Service should have been able to obtain new address for defendants with reasonable efforts, but failed to do so, "good cause" exists to extend time); *Dumaguin v. Secretary of Health & Human Servs.*, 28 F.3d 1218 (D.C.Cir.1994) (Marshal's failure to serve United States Attorney with *in forma pauperis* complaint was "good cause" to extend time), *cert. denied*, 516 U.S. 827, 116 S.Ct. 94, 133 L.Ed.2d 50 (1995); *Scott v. Reno*, 902 F.Supp. 1190, 1196 n. 4 (C.D.Cal.1995) (commenting that indigent plaintiffs cannot be penalized for the United States Marshals failure to serve process as ordered); *Stoenescu v. Jablonsky*, 162 F.R.D. 268, 270 (S.D.N.Y.1995) (noting that failure of the Marshals Service to properly complete service qualifies as "good cause" under Rule 4(m)).

159. The prior practice, former Rule 4(j), provided: "If a service of the summons and complaint is not made upon a defendant within 120 days after the filing of the complaint and the party on whose behalf such service was required cannot show good cause why such service was not made within that period, the action shall be dismissed as to that defendant without prejudice upon the court's own initiative with notice to such party or upon motion".

160. Courts have given the revised Rule 4(m) practice retroactive effect. *See Espinoza v. United States*, 52 F.3d 838 (10th Cir.1995); *Petrucelli v. Bohringer & Ratzinger*, 46 F.3d 1298 (3d Cir.1995).

161. *See Coleman v. Milwaukee Bd. of Sch. Dirs.*, 290 F.3d 932, 934 (7th Cir.2002).

extension for "an appropriate period" when good cause is shown.[162] When good cause is not shown, the district court has the option of either dismissing the lawsuit without prejudice or, in the exercise of its discretion, excusing the delay by issuing an order that directs that service be completed within a specified addition period of time.[163]

Permissive Extensions

In those instances where "good cause" is not shown, the decision whether to dismiss or grant a further extension is committed to the district court's discretion.[164] In considering whether to exercise this discretion, the court will examine whether the applicable statute of limitations would bar a re-filing, whether the failure to timely serve was due to a difficulty in serving government officials, whether the offending party is proceeding *pro se*, whether the unserved defendant has been evading service or concealing a defect in service, and whether service was eventually accomplished and, if so, how far beyond the 120–day period actual, effective service occurred.[165] The courts of appeals review such decisions under an abuse of discretion standard, and can be expected to most often affirm any reasoned and principled decision by the trial court.[166]

Note: Although the effect of the statute of limitations may be considered by the court in evaluating whether to grant a permissive extension,[167] this does not mean that "good cause" will automati-

162. *See Boley v. Kaymark*, 123 F.3d 756, 758 (3d Cir.1997) (confirming that if good cause exists, extension must be granted), *cert. denied*, 522 U.S. 1109, 118 S.Ct. 1038, 140 L.Ed.2d 104 (1998).

163. *See Panaras v. Liquid Carbonic Indus. Corp.*, 94 F.3d 338, 340 (7th Cir.1996) (noting that 1993 Amendments broadened prior practice); *Thompson v. Brown*, 91 F.3d 20, 21 (5th Cir.1996) (same); *Adams v. AlliedSignal General Aviation Avionics*, 74 F.3d 882, 887 (8th Cir. 1996) (same); *Espinoza v. United States*, 52 F.3d 838 (10th Cir.1995) (same); *Board of Trustees of Trucking Employees of North Jersey Welfare Fund v. Canny*, 876 F.Supp. 14 (N.D.N.Y. 1995)(commenting that 1993 Amendments authorized court to relieve plaintiff of mandatory consequences of former Rule 4(j)). *But see Mendez v. Elliot*, 45 F.3d 75 (4th Cir.1995)(relying on former Rule 4(j), and without commenting on broadened language under 1993 Amendments, the court held that district court lacks discretion if "good cause" is not shown).

164. *See Petrucelli v. Bohringer & Ratzinger*, 46 F.3d 1298 (3d Cir.1995). *See also Momah v. Albert Einstein Medical Ctr.*, 158 F.R.D. 66 (E.D.Pa.1994)(refusing to exercise discretion to grant permissive extension where "good cause" was not shown, plaintiff delayed until the 120th day to begin service, service was not accomplished until the 121st day, the defendant had not attempted to evade service, and the statute of limitations had not expired).

165. *See Espinoza v. United States*, 52 F.3d 838 (10th Cir.1995)(listing factors for consideration in granting permissive extensions); *Petrucelli v. Bohringer & Ratzinger*, 46 F.3d 1298 (3d Cir.1995)(same); *Goodstein v. Bombardier Capital, Inc.*, 167 F.R.D. 662, 666 (D.Vt.1996) (same).

166. *See Coleman v. Milwaukee Bd. of Sch. Dirs.*, 290 F.3d 932, 934 (7th Cir.2002) (affirming denial of permissive extension under abuse of discretion standard, notwithstanding that "most district judges probably would exercise lenity and allow a late service" in similar cases where actual harm is not shown, where defendant likely received timely actual notice of the lawsuit, and where dismissal would bar a re-filing because the limitations period has expired); *Hason v. Medical Bd. of Cal.*, 279 F.3d 1167, 1174 (9th Cir.2002) (applying abuse of discretion standard to affirm denial of leave to serve outside 120 days), *cert. dismissed*, 538 U.S. 958, 123 S.Ct. 1779, 155 L.Ed.2d 508 (2003).

167. *See Mann v. American Airlines*, 324 F.3d 1088, 1090–91 (9th Cir.2003) (noting that district court still has discretion to grant permissive extension, even where limitations period would otherwise bar a re-filing of the case).

cally exist whenever a dismissal would result in a time-bar.[168] Instead, the district court must assess whether other criteria, in addition to time-bar, warrant the permissive extension.

Dismissal Without Prejudice

Dismissals under this Rule for failure to timely serve process are made without prejudice.[169] If, however, a re-filed complaint would be beyond the applicable statute of limitations, the Rule 4(m) dismissal "without prejudice" will not act to defeat an affirmative defense asserting time-bar.[170]

Substantive State Law Rules Can Undercut The 120–Day Period

This 120–day period is simply a creation of federal procedural rules—it merely acts to preserve, from dismissal, a federal complaint for 120 days so as to facilitate service of process. Under the *Erie* doctrine, however, the federal courts are obligated to apply State substantive law to State causes of action that are pending in federal court under diversity or supplemental jurisdiction. The substantive laws of some States provide that merely filing a complaint does not toll the applicable statutes of limitations. In those instances, Rule 4(m) will not prevent a cause of action from becoming time-barred during the 120–day service period, if State law would so dictate.[171]

Defendants Can Waive 120–Day Service Period

Although Rule 4(m) contains mandatory-sounding dismissal language, defendants may still waive the 120–day period by filing an omnibus Rule 12 motion and omitting from that motion the claim that

168. *See Boley v. Kaymark*, 123 F.3d 756, 759 (3d Cir.1997) (concluding that the running of a limitations period "is a factor supporting the discretionary granting of an extension of time to make service under Rule 4(m)," but noting that "it is not a factor that standing alone supports a finding of prejudice to the defendant"), *cert. denied*, 522 U.S. 1109, 118 S.Ct. 1038, 140 L.Ed.2d 104 (1998); *Petrucelli v. Bohringer & Ratzinger*, 46 F.3d 1298 (3d Cir. 1995)("We caution against such a myopic reading"). *See also Panaras v. Liquid Carbonic Indus. Corp.*, 94 F.3d 338, 340 (7th Cir.1996) (holding that the running of the statute of limitations does not require that a district court extend the time for service of process); *Gowan v. Teamsters Union*, 170 F.R.D. 356, 361 (S.D.N.Y. 1997) (noting that time-bar may justify relief from Rule 4(m), but an extension is such cases is not guaranteed).

169. *See Bann v. Ingram Micro, Inc.*, 108 F.3d 625, 626 (5th Cir.1997) (commenting that dismissals with prejudice cannot be based on Rule 4(m)'s 120–day requirement); *Hunt v. Smith*, 67 F.Supp.2d 675, 685 (E.D.Tex.1999) (noting that Rule 4(m) dismissals are without prejudice).

170. *See Conover v. Lein*, 87 F.3d 905, 908–09 (7th Cir.1996) (commenting that dismissals "without prejudice" under Rule 4(m) are not necessarily dismissals "without consequence," if the pertinent statutes of limitations have run); *Hawkins v. McHugh*, 46 F.3d 10 (5th Cir. 1995)(applying Louisiana law and holding that dismissal under this Rule does not interrupt prescription or toll the prescription period).

171. *See Torre v. Brickey*, 278 F.3d 917, 919–20 (9th Cir.2002) (holding that Rule 4(m) did not preserve claims for 120–day period where substantive law of forum State, Oregon, does not toll statute of limitations until service is effected); *Larsen v. Mayo Med. Ctr.*, 218 F.3d 863 (8th Cir.2000) (same, under Minnesota law), *cert. denied*, 531 U.S. 1036, 121 S.Ct. 625, 148 L.Ed.2d 534 (2000); *Habermehl v. Potter*, 153 F.3d 1137, 1139 (10th Cir.1998) (same, under Wyoming law). *See also* Authors' Commentary to Rule 3 ("Diversity Jurisdiction Cases" and "Supplemental Jurisdiction Cases").

process was served beyond Rule 4(m)'s 120–day time period.[172]

Sua Sponte Dismissals

When service has not been effected within the 120–day period, the action may be dismissed upon motion, or upon the court's own initiative.[173] Such *sua sponte* dismissals under Rule 4(m) require prior "notice to the plaintiff".[174]

Time Limitation Does Not Apply to Foreign Service

The 120–day service rule does not apply to service within a foreign country,[175] or to service upon a foreign state and its political subdivisions, agencies, and instrumentalities.[176] However, some courts have conditioned this foreign service "exemption" upon a showing that good faith attempts were made to serve within the 120–day period; if no such attempts were made, these courts hold that the exemption will not apply and the passage of 120 days can justify a dismissal.[177]

New 120–Day Period For Newly Added Parties

When a complaint is amended to add new parties, the plaintiff is given 120 days from the date of amendment to serve the new defendants.[178]

In Forma Pauperis Motions and 120–Day Period

Because the statute of limitations is ordinarily tolled during the pendency of a motion for leave to proceed *in forma pauperis*, the Rule 4(m) 120–day period for service will not begin to run until the com-

172. *See McCurdy v. American Bd. of Plastic Surgery*, 157 F.3d 191, 195 (3d Cir.1998) (citing cases).

173. *See* Rule 4(m).

174. *See Thompson v. Maldonado*, 309 F.3d 107, 110 (2d Cir.2002) (vacating *sua sponte* dismissal because court had not given plaintiff prior notice of the intent to dismiss under Rule 4(m)). *Cf. TIG Ins. Co. v. 2200 M St., LLC.*, 216 F.R.D. 2, 3 (D.D.C.2003) (dismissing action *sua sponte* under Rule 4(m) where plaintiff failed to respond to court's prior notice by "show-cause" order).

175. *See* Fed.R.Civ.P. 4(m)(referencing Fed. R. Civ. P. 4(f))(providing for service upon individuals in foreign countries). *See Goodstein v. Bombardier Capital, Inc.*, 167 F.R.D. 662, 665–66 (D.Vt.1996) (holding that Rule 4(m)'s timeliness requirement is only excused where service is attempted in a foreign country); *Sang Young Kim v. Frank Mohn A/S*, 909 F.Supp. 474, 479–80 (S.D.Tex.1995) (noting that exclusion of foreign service from the 120–day limit "helps to counterbalance the complex and time-consuming nature of foreign service of process"); *Pennsylvania Orthopedic Ass'n v. Mercedes–Benz A.G.*, 160 F.R.D. 58 (E.D.Pa.1995)(commenting that, to compensate for the possibility of very complex and time-consuming service, Rule 4(m) acts to remove all deadlines for serving a complaint in a foreign country).

176. *See* Fed.R.Civ.P. 4(m)(referencing Fed. R.Civ.P. 4(j)(1)) (providing for service upon foreign States and their political subdivisions, agencies, and instrumentalities).

177. *See Thayer v. Dial Indus. Sales, Inc.*, 85 F.Supp.2d 263, 266 n. 1 (S.D.N.Y.2000) (holding that because plaintiff never attempted to complete service and the 120–day period expired, the claims will be dismissed for failure to prosecute). *See also Montalbano v. Easco Hand Tools, Inc.*, 766 F.2d 737, 740 (2d Cir.1985) (same holding, construing former Rule 4(j) (predecessor to Rule 4(m))).

178. *See City of Merced v. Fields*, 997 F.Supp. 1326, 1338 (E.D.Cal.1998); *Del Raine v. Carlson*, 153 F.R.D. 622, 628 (S.D.Ill.1994), *rev'd in part on other grounds*, 77 F.3d 484 (7th Cir.1996) (Table).

plaint is stamped "filed" (either when the *in forma pauperis* motion is granted without a fee or the filing fee is actually paid).[179]

RULE 4(n). SEIZURE OF PROPERTY; SERVICE OF SUMMONS NOT FEASIBLE

CORE CONCEPT

If authorized by federal statute, the district court may exercise jurisdiction over property. Moreover, if personal jurisdiction over a particular defendant is not possible, the district court may exercise jurisdiction over that defendant's property by seizing the property as permitted under State law.

APPLICATIONS

Effect

A judgment in a quasi-in-rem or in-rem lawsuit acts only upon the seized property; it has no *in personam* effect. Thus, a plaintiff cannot enforce a quasi-in-rem or in-rem judgment against property of the defendant located outside the forum State.[180]

Amount in Controversy

A quasi-in-rem or in-rem action only permits execution of the seized property; the courts, however, are divided on the proper method for computing the amount in controversy—either by the value of the seized property or the sum stated in the complaint's demand clause.[181]

Note: If the plaintiff's claim exceeds the value of seized property, the plaintiff is free to sue elsewhere for the remaining, unrecovered amount of the claim.

Due Process

Just as in the personal jurisdiction context, a federal court can hear a quasi-in-rem action only if the Due Process "traditional notions of fair play and substantial justice" test is satisfied.[182]

ADDITIONAL RESEARCH REFERENCES

Wright & Miller, *Federal Practice and Procedure* §§ 1061–1137.

C.J.S. Federal Civil Procedure §§ 187–223.

West's Key No. Digests, Federal Civil Procedure ⚷403, 404, 411–427, 441–446, 461–505, 511–518, 531–540.

179. *See Scary v. Philadelphia Gas Works*, 202 F.R.D. 148 (E.D.Pa.2001).

180. *See Sara Lee Corp. v. Gregg*, No. 1:02CV00195, 2002 WL 1925703, at *2 (M.D.N.C.2002) (noting that quasi in rem jurisdiction over defendant's property is limited to the property located within forum). The effect of quasi-in-rem and in-rem actions are discussed in greater depth in Part II of this text, §§ 2.8–2.9.

181. *See Great American Ins. Co. v. Louis Lesser Enters., Inc.*, 353 F.2d 997 (8th Cir. 1965)(noting disagreement among courts).

182. *See Shaffer v. Heitner*, 433 U.S. 186, 97 S.Ct. 2569, 53 L.Ed.2d 683 (1977).

RULE 4.1

SERVICE OF OTHER PROCESS

(a) Generally. Process other than a summons as provided in Rule 4 or subpoena as provided in Rule 45 shall be served by a United States marshal, a deputy United States marshal, or a person specially appointed for that purpose, who shall make proof of service as provided in Rule 4(*l*). The process may be served anywhere within the territorial limits of the state in which the district court is located, and, when authorized by a statute of the United States, beyond the territorial limits of that state.

(b) Enforcement of Orders: Commitment for Civil Contempt. An order of civil commitment of a person held to be in contempt of a decree or injunction issued to enforce the laws of the United States may be served and enforced in any district. Other orders in civil contempt proceedings shall be served in the state in which the court issuing the order to be enforced is located or elsewhere within the United States if not more than 100 miles from the place at which the order to be enforced was issued.

[Adopted April 22, 1993, effective December 1, 1993.]

AUTHORS' COMMENTARY ON RULE 4.1

PURPOSE AND SCOPE

Rule 4.1 sets the procedure for service of types of process other than a civil summons or a subpoena. Such process is served either by the United States Marshal or by an individual specially appointed by the court.

APPLICATIONS

What Is "Other" Process

The procedures for service of a civil summons and complaint or a subpoena are defined elsewhere in the Rules.[1] Similarly, once initial process is served, the service of all subsequent papers is prescribed by Rule 5. Rule 4.1 is intended to establish the procedure for service of process in all other cases, such as in the case of execution orders and orders of civil commitment.[2]

1. *See* Rule 4 (procedure for serving summons and complaint); Rule 45 (procedure for serving subpoena).

2. *See Schneider v. National R.R. Passenger Corp.*, 72 F.3d 17 (2d Cir.1995) (applying Rule 4.1 to execution orders); *Federal Trade Comm'n v. Verity Int'l, Ltd.*, 140 F.Supp.2d 313, 318

This Rule does *not* apply to civil contempt orders intended to enforce non-federally created rights, such as contempt orders issued in a diversity proceeding where the substantive rights in dispute arise under State law.[3] The Rule also does *not* apply to orders of criminal commitment.

Process Server

"Other" process must be served either by the United States Marshal, a deputy Marshal, or some other person specially appointed for the purpose by the court. Service performed by anyone else is defective.[4] To date, the only case law exception to this requirement appears in the context of process to enforce a judgment for the payment of money. Such enforcement proceedings are governed in the Federal Rules by Rule 69(a), which provides that the "procedure on execution" must follow State practice. At least one court has held that, notwithstanding the broad, general language of Rule 4.1, the provisions of Rule 69(a) compel that State practice govern the service of process in such execution proceedings.[5]

Limits of Service

"Other" process may be served either within the State in which the district court is sitting or as otherwise provided by federal statute.[6] An order of civil commitment, however, may be served and enforced in any federal district. All other civil contempt orders may be served either within the State in which the district court is sitting or within 100 miles of the place where the order was issued.

Proof of Service

The process server—the Marshal, deputy Marshal, or specially appointed person—must file a proof of service with the court as provided in Rule 4(*l*).[7]

(S.D.N.Y.2001) (applying Rule 4.1 to civil commitment order which directed that defendants, who had willfully disobeyed court order, were to be arrested and detained if they enter the United States, until such time as they complied with court order); *Spectacular Venture, L.P. v. World Star Int'l, Inc.*, 927 F.Supp. 683 (S.D.N.Y.1996) (applying Rule 4.1 to civil contempt orders).

3. *See Spectacular Venture, L.P. v. World Star Int'l, Inc.*, 927 F.Supp. 683 (S.D.N.Y.1996) (holding that, in a diversity case, contempt of federal orders issued under the Judicial Code and Rules of Civil Procedure is not contempt of "laws of the United States" and, thus, the provisions of Rule 4.1 would not apply).

4. *See Schneider v. National R.R. Passenger Corp.*, 72 F.3d 17 (2d Cir.1995) (State sheriff who had "seized" Amtrak locomotives in the course of executing upon a $1.8 million plaintiff's personal injury judgment was not a Marshal, deputy Marshal, or specially appointed process server, and thus process was defective under Rule 4.1 and the sheriff was not entitled to his service fee for executing upon the trains).

5. *See Apostolic Pentecostal Church v. Colbert*, 169 F.3d 409, 414 (6th Cir.1999).

6. *See Hoult v. Hoult*, 373 F.3d 47, 53 (1st Cir. 2004).

7. *See* Rule 4.1(a).

RULE 5

SERVING AND FILING PLEADINGS AND OTHER PAPERS

(a) Service: When Required. Except as otherwise provided in these rules, every order required by its terms to be served, every pleading subsequent to the original complaint unless the court otherwise orders because of numerous defendants, every paper relating to discovery required to be served upon a party unless the court otherwise orders, every written motion other than one which may be heard ex parte, and every written notice, appearance, demand, offer of judgment, designation of record on appeal, and similar paper shall be served upon each of the parties. No service need be made on parties in default for failure to appear except that pleadings asserting new or additional claims for relief against them shall be served upon them in the manner provided for service of summons in Rule 4.

In an action begun by seizure of property, in which no person need be or is named as defendant, any service required to be made prior to the filing of an answer, claim, or appearance shall be made upon the person having custody or possession of the property at the time of its seizure.

(b) Making Service.

(1) Service under Rules 5(a) and 77(d) on a party represented by an attorney is made on the attorney unless the court orders service on the party.

(2) Service under Rule 5(a) is made by:

(A) Delivering a copy to the person served by:

(i) handing it to the person;

(ii) leaving it at the person's office with a clerk or other person in charge, or if no one is in charge leaving it in a conspicuous place in the office; or

(iii) if the person has no office or the office is closed, leaving it at the person's dwelling house or usual place of abode with someone of suitable age and discretion residing there.

(B) Mailing a copy to the last known address of the person served. Service by mail is complete on mailing.

(C) If the person served has no known address, leaving a copy with the clerk of court.

(D) Delivering a copy by any other means, including electronic means, consented to in writing by the person served. Service by electronic means is complete on transmission; service by other consented means is complete when the person making service delivers the copy to the agency designated to make delivery. If authorized by local rule, a party may make service under this subparagraph (D) through the court's transmission facilities.

(3) Service by electronic means under Rule 5(b)(2)(D) is not effective if the party making service learns that the attempted service did not reach the person to be served.

(c) Same: Numerous Defendants. In any action in which there are unusually large numbers of defendants, the court, upon motion or of its own initiative, may order that service of the pleadings of the defendants and replies thereto need not be made as between the defendants and that any cross-claim, counterclaim, or matter constituting an avoidance or affirmative defense contained therein shall be deemed to be denied or avoided by all other parties and that the filing of any such pleading and service thereof upon the plaintiff constitutes due notice of it to the parties. A copy of every such order shall be served upon the parties in such manner and form as the court directs.

(d) Filing; Certificate of Service. All papers after the complaint required to be served upon a party, together with a certificate of service, must be filed with the court within a reasonable time after service, but disclosures under Rule 26(a)(1) or (2) and the following discovery requests and responses must not be filed until they are used in the proceeding or the court orders filing: (i) depositions, (ii) interrogatories, (iii) requests for documents or to permit entry upon land, and (iv) requests for admission.

(e) Filing With the Court Defined. The filing of papers with the court as required by these rules shall be made by filing them with the clerk of the court, except that the judge may permit the papers to be filed with the judge, in which event the judge shall note thereon the filing date and forthwith transmit them to the office of the clerk. A court may, by local rule, permit papers to be filed, signed, or verified by electronic means that are consistent with technical standards, if any, that the Judicial Conference of the

United States establishes. A paper filed by electronic means in compliance with a local rule constitutes a written paper for the purpose of applying these rules. The clerk shall not refuse to accept for filing any paper presented for that purpose solely because it is not presented in proper form as required by these rules or any local rules or practices.

[Amended January 21, 1963, effective July 1, 1963; March 30, 1970, effective July 1, 1970; April 29, 1980, effective August 1, 1980; March 2, 1987, effective August 1, 1987; April 30, 1991, effective December 1, 1991; April 22, 1993, effective December 1, 1993; April 23, 1996, effective December 1, 1996; April 17, 2000, effective December 1, 2000; April 23, 2001, effective December 1, 2001.]

AUTHORS' COMMENTARY ON RULE 5

PURPOSE AND SCOPE

Rule 5 sets forth the general filing requirements for all pleadings and other papers, and the general service requirements for all pleadings and other papers *except* the complaint (Rule 4 governs the service of the complaint). The provisions of Rule 5 are designed to achieve two objectives: to ensure that each party to a civil action obtains a copy of all documents formally used in prosecuting and defending the case, and to create a rationally-assembled record with the clerk of court.

This is a general service and filing rule. Other Rules establish separate requirements crafted for particular circumstances (*e.g.,* Rule 45(b), governing service of subpoenas). Likewise, many federal district courts have developed specific local service and filing requirements that supplement the provisions of Rule 5. Practitioners should *always* check the other Rules and the district's local rules to ensure that they understand how the requirements of Rule 5 may have been supplemented in their courts.

RULE 5(a). SERVICE REQUIRED

CORE CONCEPT

Unless such service is specifically excused by the Court, every party who has entered an appearance must be served with a copy of the following:

- *All Pleadings After the Complaint,* generally including amended complaints[1] (the original complaint and summons must be served in accordance with Rule 4);
- *All Discovery Papers;*
- *All Written Motions* (except *ex parte* motions);

1. *See Mach v. Florida Casino Cruise, Inc.,* 187 F.R.D. 15, 17 (D.Mass.1999). *But see* Authors' Commentary to Rule 5(b) ("**New Claims Against Existing Parties**") (noting instances where amended complaints might have to be served under Rule 4).

- *All Orders required by their terms to be served* (*i.e.*, Rule 77(d) notices of entry of orders); and
- *All Other Appropriate Legal Papers* (such as written notices, appearances, demands, offers of judgment,[2] designations of record on appeal, and similar papers).

APPLICATIONS

Broadly Construed

Rule 5 is interpreted expansively to apply to nearly all court papers (*e.g.*, affidavits in support of motions must be served under Rule 5).

Unserved Pleadings and Papers

Unserved pleadings and other papers may be found to lack any legal force and effect, until service is accomplished. For example, amended complaints that are not served (even if they are filed with the clerk of court) may be deemed to have not superseded the original complaint.[3] However, when a party is not served, but receives actual notice of the document and is not prejudiced by the lack of service, the document may still be accepted as effective.[4]

Exceptions

Rule 5 does *not* apply to the service of:

- Original complaints (controlled by Rule 4);
- *Ex parte* motions;
- Pleadings between numerous defendants (when service is excused by court order under Rule 5(c)); or
- As provided otherwise in the Rules (*i.e.*, Rule 45(b) subpoena requirements).

Appearance Required

A party who has not entered an appearance generally need not be served with court papers. However, if a later pleading asserts a new or additional claim against a party, the party must be served with that document in accordance with Rule 4.[5]

2. *See Magnuson v. Video Yesteryear*, 85 F.3d 1424, 1429 (9th Cir.1996) (service of Rule 68 offers must comply with Rule 5).

3. *See International Controls Corp. v. Vesco*, 556 F.2d 665, 669 (2d Cir.1977)(amended complaint remains inchoate until served under Rule 5(a)), *cert. denied*, 434 U.S. 1014, 98 S.Ct. 730, 54 L.Ed.2d 758 (1978).

4. *See McKinnie v. Roadway Express, Inc.*, 341 F.3d 554, 557–59 (6th Cir.2003) (holding that where party is not properly served with summary judgment motion, but yet has actual notice of the motion prior to disposition, a court's decision to grant the motion will not be reversed on appeal for this reason unless the affected party demonstrates a genuine issue of material fact that would defeat summary judgment).

5. *See Waters v. Farmers Texas County Mutual Ins. Co.*, 9 F.3d 397, 399 (5th Cir. 1993)(holding that Rule 5 service was not effective because crossclaim created a new and additional claim against the crossclaim defendant, requiring service under Rule 4). *See also* Rule 71A(f)(in federal condemnation proceedings, a notice of amended pleading must be served on all parties, irrespective of whether they have filed a formal entry of appearance).

Seizure Actions

Actions begun by the seizure of property (arrest, attachment, garnishment) are subject to Rule 5. In these cases, any paper required to be served before filing an answer, claim, or appearance must be served on the person with custody or possession of the property at the time of seizure.

RULE 5(b). METHOD OF SERVICE

CORE CONCEPT

Service is ordinarily made on each party's attorney, not on the party directly. Service may be accomplished in several ways:

SERVICE BY PERSONAL DELIVERY:

(1) ***Hand Delivery***: The served document is handed either to the attorney or, if unrepresented or if the court orders otherwise, to the party; *or*

(2) ***Office***: The served document is left at the recipient's office with the person "in charge" of the office or, if no one is "in charge" of the office, at the recipient's office in a conspicuous place; *or*

(3) ***Home***: If hand delivery and office service are unavailable, the served document may be left at the recipient's residence with a person of suitable age and discretion residing there.

SERVICE BY MAIL:

Last Known Address: The served document is mailed to the recipient's last known address.

SERVICE BY OTHER AGREED MEANS:

Electronic Transmission or Otherwise: The served document is delivered or transmitted by "any other means" to which the person served has agreed, in writing.

SERVICE WHERE NO ADDRESS IS KNOWN:

Clerk of Court: If the recipient's last known address is unavailable, the served document may be left with the clerk of court.

APPLICATIONS

Service on Attorney, Not Party

Pleadings and other papers generally must be served on the party's attorney, and not on the party directly. However, service may be made on the party directly if a specific Rule so requires, if the party is unrepresented, or if the court so requires.

Parties Represented by Multiple Attorneys

Service is complete upon serving one attorney for each represented party. If a party is represented by multiple counsel, multiple service is ordinarily not required.[6]

New Claims Against New Parties

Pleadings asserting claims against new parties (*e.g.*, third-party claims) must be served in accordance with Rule 4.

New Claims Against Existing Parties

Pleadings asserting new claims against existing parties must be served in accordance with Rule 4, if:

- The new claims differ significantly from those in the original pleading; [7]
- Circumstances persuade the court that service on the attorney is unlikely to ensure notice to the party;
- Extraterritorial service of process was used in the original pleading and a new claim is unrelated to the initial claim; or
- Due Process requires Rule 4 service (*i.e.*, federal jurisdiction was premised on a particular injury-causing event, and the complaint was amended to assert an unrelated claim which could not otherwise be brought in that district).

Service by Mail

Service by mail is complete at the moment a properly posted envelope is deposited with the Post Office.[8] The Post Office's failure to postmark the envelope on the day of deposit does not alter this effect.[9] Non-receipt or non-acceptance usually does not affect the validity of service.[10]

- Notices of Removal can be served by mail.
- *Note:* Rule 6(e) gives the recipient of mailed service 3 extra days to respond. Accordingly, if a quick response is preferred, personal service will eliminate this additional 3 day response period.

Service By Electronic Transmission And By "Other Means"

Service by electronic transmission or by some other means may be made, but only if the person served has expressly consented to such

6. *See Buchanan v. Sherrill*, 51 F.3d 227, 228 (10th Cir.1995); *Daniel Int'l Corp. v. Fischbach & Moore, Inc.*, 916 F.2d 1061, 1063 (5th Cir. 1990); *United States v. Schooner Windspirit*, 161 F.R.D. 321, 323 (D.Vi.1995).

7. *See Beckham v. Grand Affair of North Carolina, Inc.*, 671 F.Supp. 415, 418 (W.D.N.C. 1987)(holding that amended complaint containing new theory of liability should be served on defendant pursuant to Rule 4, rather than on the defendant's appearing attorney as per Rule 5).

8. *See* Rule 5(b)(2)(B). *See also United States v. Clingman*, 288 F.3d 1183, 1185 (10th Cir. 2002); *United States v. Novaton*, 271 F.3d 968, 1015–16 (11th Cir.2001), *cert. denied*, 535 U.S. 1120, 122 S.Ct. 2345, 153 L.Ed.2d 173 (2002); *Greene v. WCI Holdings Corp.*, 136 F.3d 313, 315 (2d Cir.1998), *cert. denied*, 525 U.S. 983, 119 S.Ct. 448, 142 L.Ed.2d 402 (1998); *United States v. Kennedy*, 133 F.3d 53, 59 (D.C.Cir.1998), *cert. denied*, 525 U.S. 911, 119 S.Ct. 255, 142 L.Ed.2d 210 (1998); *Rivera v. M/T Fossarina*, 840 F.2d 152, 155 (1st Cir.1988) (same effect).

9. *See Larez v. Holcomb*, 16 F.3d 1513, 1515 n. 1 (9th Cir.1994)(noting that document placed in the mail on the last day for service was timely served, even though Post Office did not postmark the envelope until the next day).

10. *Dunlap v. Transamerica Occidental Life Ins. Co.*, 858 F.2d 629 (11th Cir.1988).

service. The consent must be in writing; consent may not be implied from conduct (such as an e-mail address on a defendant's letterhead).[11] Thus, service by facsimile remains ineffective, absent this written consent.[12]

Electronic Transmission: When consent has been obtained, service by electronic transmission (including both direct transmission of the document and transmission of a notice that the document is available through a certain electronic link) is deemed complete upon transmission.[13] (Each district may, by local rule, authorize the making of such transmissions from common court facilities.[14]) Parties are "encouraged" by the Advisory Committee to reach specific agreement on the specific scope of the written consent, including (1) the name of the person to whom service should be made, (2) the appropriate address (facsimile number, e-mail address, etc.) for such service, (3) the format to be used for attachments, and (4) the duration of the consent.[15]

Failed Transmission: If the serving party learns, after the electronic transmission is attempted, that the transmission failed and did not reach the person to be served, the service is not considered effective.[16] Such a transmission failure can be a mechanical one (*e.g.*, an "incomplete" or "failed" fax message) or one relating to a change in the recipient's profile (*e.g.*, original counsel consents to the District's electronic filing service, but a change in counsel renders this consent ineffective).[17]

Service By "Other Means": Service by some "other means", consented to by the recipient, is deemed complete when the person making the service delivers the document to the entity engaged to make the delivery.[18]

Private Overnight Courier Services

Private overnight courier services (such as FedEx) are not the Post Office, and they do not provide "mail" service. Thus, handing legal papers to a private courier service might not constitute "service by mail" under Rule 5(b)(2)(B), and therefore might not entitle the sender to completed service upon mailing. Rather, service by a courier service is more likely to be deemed personal service, complete only upon the courier's delivery of the document to the ultimate recipient.[19] If, howev-

11. *See* Rule 5(b)(2)(D). *See also* Rule 5(b)(2)(D) advisory committee note to 2001 amendments.

12. *See Magnuson v. Video Yesteryear*, 85 F.3d 1424, 1430 (9th Cir.1996); *United States v. Galiczynski*, 44 F.Supp.2d 707, 713 (E.D.Pa. 1999); *Erbacci, Cerone & Moriarty, Ltd. v. United States*, 166 F.R.D. 298, 303 (S.D.N.Y.1996).

13. *See* Rule 5(b)(2)(D). *See also* Rule 5(b)(2)(D) advisory committee note to 2001 amendments.

14. *See* Rule 5(b)(2)(D).

15. *See* Rule 5(b)(2)(D) advisory committee note to 2001 amendments.

16. *See* Rule 5(b)(2)(E).

17. *See McKinnie v. Roadway Express, Inc.*, 341 F.3d 554, 557 (6th Cir. 2003).

18. *See* Rule 5(b)(2)(D).

19. *See Transco Leasing Corp. v. United States*, 992 F.2d 552, 554 n. 2 (5th Cir. 1993)(commenting, without deciding, that service by overnight courier might not qualify as service by mail under Rule 5). *Compare Schudel v. General Elec. Co.*, 120 F.3d 991 (9th Cir.

er, service by private overnight courier has been consented to, it will qualify as effective service by "other means".[20]

Service At Home

Service can be accomplished at the recipient's home, if hand delivery or office service are unavailable.[21] Presumably, this Rule will be interpreted by the courts in the same manner as Rule 4. Thus, the recipient of service need not necessarily be an adult, so long as the court reaches the case-by-case factual determination that the recipient is of "suitable age and discretion". Generally, service must be made on a person "residing" at the home; service on a maid, a landlady, or some other non-resident might be ineffective.[22]

Prisoner Plaintiffs

For documents served by *pro se* prisoners, the courts generally recognize a "mailbox" rule that deems documents as served upon delivery of those documents to the prison officials.[23]

RULE 5(c). SERVICE ON NUMEROUS DEFENDANTS

CORE CONCEPT

Where an unusually large number of defendants are sued, the court may order that the defendants need not serve every other defendant with pleadings and responses, and that cross-claims, counterclaims, and affirmative defenses are deemed automatically denied or avoided as between the numerous defendants.

1997) (noting that personal delivery or delivery to U.S. Postal Service could have satisfied service requirement, delivery to Federal Express did not), *cert. denied*, 523 U.S. 1094, 118 S.Ct. 1560–61, 140 L.Ed.2d 792 (1998) *and Magnuson v. Video Yesteryear*, 85 F.3d 1424, 1430–31 (9th Cir.1996) (holding that delivery by Federal Express is not "mail", noting that drafters in 1937—working in an "era that predates modern overnight delivery services"—could not have intended to authorize service by private delivery services) *and Audio Enters. v. B & W Loudspeakers of America*, 957 F.2d 406, 409 (7th Cir.1992) (noting that Federal Express is not first class mail within the meaning of Rule 4) *and Prince v. Poulos*, 876 F.2d 30, 32 n. 1 (5th Cir.1989)(in construing Federal Rule of Appellate Procedure 25, the court held that Federal Express is not a "public authority" and is not a form of "mail") and *Chudasama v. Mazda Motor Corp.*, 1995 WL 641984, at *16 n. 20 (M.D.Ga. 1995) (holding that service by private courier is not complete under Rule until the paper is handed to counsel or delivered to counsel's office), *vacated on other grounds*, 123 F.3d 1353 (11th Cir.1997) *and Edmond v. United States Postal Serv.*, 727 F.Supp. 7 (D.D.C.1989) (holding that service via Federal Express was effective when delivered to litigant's home); *aff'd in part and reversed in part on other grounds*, 949 F.2d 415 (D.C.Cir.1991) *with United States v. Certain Real Property & Premises Known as 63–29 Trimble Rd., Woodside, N.Y.*, 812 F.Supp. 332, 334 (E.D.N.Y.1992) (service via Federal Express "mail" is valid because Rule 5(b) does not require that "mailing" occur through the United States Postal Service).

20. *See* Rule 5(b)(2)(D).

21. *See* Rule 5(b)(2)(A)(iii).

22. *See* Rule 4(e).

23. *See Schroeder v. McDonald*, 55 F.3d 454 (9th Cir.1995)(noting that incarcerated *pro se* litigants effect service under Rule 5(b) by submitting their documents to prison authorities); *cf.* Fed.R.App.P. 4(c)(document deemed "filed" by prisoner when deposited into prison's internal mail system).

APPLICATIONS

Court Order

Rule 5(c) is seldom used, and is effective only on court order. The court's enabling order must be served on all parties.

Plaintiff Must Be Served

Rule 5(c) does not excuse service on the plaintiff of all papers.

Court Filing Still Required

Rule 5(c) also does not excuse the pleader's obligation to *file* the pleading with the Court.[24]

Only Pleadings/Responses

This limitation applies only to pleadings and responses; all papers other than pleadings and responses must be served.

Defendants Only

If the action involves a large number of plaintiffs (*e.g.*, a mass tort case), service must still be made on each plaintiff.

RULE 5(d). FILING WITH THE COURT

CORE CONCEPT

Any paper required to be served must also be filed with the court within a reasonable time after service. Along with any such paper, the party must also include a certificate of service.

APPLICATIONS

"Reasonable" Time Defined

Whether the time between service and filing is "reasonable" is a matter left to the discretion of the district court.[25] Consequently, practitioners should err on the side of caution and file their papers simultaneously with service, or as soon thereafter as possible.

Certificate of Service

A party's certificate of service should identify the document served, the date of service, and the manner of delivery.[26] Nevertheless, because the principal purpose of a certificate of service is to verify for the court that proper service has been accomplished, the court will likely not

24. *See United States v. Atlas Lederer Co.*, 282 F.Supp.2d 687, 701–03 (S.D.Ohio 2001).

25. *See Chesson v. Jaquez*, 986 F.2d 363, 365 (10th Cir.1993)(holding that filing within six days after service is "reasonable", particularly because a weekend fell within that period); *Biocore Medical Techs., Inc. v. Khosrowshahi*, 181 F.R.D. 660, 668 (D.Kan.1998) (noting that courts have decided that documents filed up to six days after service are filed within a "reasonable time" under Rule 5(d); holding that filing almost two months after service is not "reasonable"); *Ives v. Guilford Mills, Inc.*, 3 F.Supp.2d 191, 194 (N.D.N.Y.1998) (finding three weeks reasonable under the circumstances).

26. *See Golden v. McCaughtry*, 915 F.Supp. 77, 79 (E.D.Wis.1995) (noting certificate of service filing obligation).

invalidate a legal filing that lacks a certificate of service, so long as proper service is not contested.[27]

Other Rules

Certain Rules and the district's local rules may prescribe specific service/filing guidelines (*e.g.,* Rule 65(b) provides that temporary restraining orders must be filed "forthwith"). Consult the specific Rule and the applicable local rules.

Discovery Papers

The widespread proliferation of local rules establishing, on a district-by-district basis, whether discovery materials should be filed with the clerk's office is addressed in Rule 5(d). In order to conserve the physical resources of the clerk's office and federal courthouses, discovery requests and discovery responses are *not* to be filed with the court unless and until (a) they are actually "used" in court proceedings or (b) the trial court so orders.[28] This prohibition applies to deposition notices and objections, interrogatories and their objections and responses, requests for documents and their objections and responses, requests to permit entry upon land and their objections and responses, and request for admission and their objections and responses.[29] Local rules that prescribe different filing requirements are superseded and invalidated in favor of this uniform, national approach.[30]

The phrase "used in the proceeding" is to be interpreted broadly to include those discovery materials used in connection with motions, pretrial conferences, and otherwise.[31] However, a party who "uses" discovery materials while interrogating witnesses during depositions need not file those materials with the court.[32] Moreover, if a party "uses" only a portion of a voluminous discovery document, only the "used" portion need be filed with the court (although any other party would be free to file other relevant portions used).[33]

RULE 5(e). METHOD OF FILING

CORE CONCEPT

Papers are to be filed with the clerk of court, unless the court permits filing with the judge personally. Where so provided by proper

27. *See Russell v. City of Milwaukee*, 338 F.3d 662, 665–67 (7th Cir.2003) (finding that failure to include certificate of service with suggestion of death did not defeat court's finding that service had, in fact, been made); *Ives v. Guilford Mills, Inc.*, 3 F.Supp.2d 191 (N.D.N.Y. 1998) (concluding that an invalidation under such circumstances "would seem to serve no purpose except to fruitlessly extend the length of this litigation").

28. *See* Rule 5(d) (as amended Dec. 1, 2000). *See also* Rule 5(d) advisory committee note to 2000 amendments (discussing resource conservation objective).

29. *See* Rule 5(d) advisory committee note to 2000 amendments.

30. *See* Rule 5(d) advisory committee note to 2000 amendments.

31. *See* Rule 5(d) advisory committee note to 2000 amendments.

32. *See* Rule 5(d) advisory committee note to 2000 amendments.

33. *See* Rule 5(d) advisory committee note to 2000 amendments.

local rules (but *only* where so provided), papers may be filed by electronic means, including by facsimile transmission. The clerk of court may not refuse to accept a paper for filing simply because the paper does not conform to these Rules or the district's local rules.

APPLICATIONS

Document Itself Must Be Filed

A document will not be deemed "filed" unless it is separately and formally filed with the court. Thus, attaching a document as an exhibit to another paper will not constitute a "filing" of the attachment.[34]

Possession by Clerk

Documents are only filed when placed in the clerk's possession.[35] Thus, leaving a document lying against the clerk's office door or slipping a document underneath the clerk's office door will generally *not* be considered an effective filing until the day the clerk actually receives the document. However, placing a document in a box designated by the clerk as an after-hours depository should constitute effective filing as of the time of deposit.[36]

Filing by Mail

Because documents are only deemed to be filed when they come into the clerk's possession, a document will not be deemed "filed" when it is placed in the United States Mail, addressed to the clerk. Instead, mailed documents are "filed" on the date they are actually received by the clerk.[37]

Filing With the Judge

Where the judge so permits, papers may be "filed" with the judge directly, after which the judge is required to transmit the papers "forthwith" to the clerk's office.[38]

34. *See Orsini v. Kugel*, 9 F.3d 1042, 1045 (2d Cir.1993)(holding that a stipulation had not been "filed" merely because it was attached as an exhibit to another court paper).

35. *See McIntosh v. Antonino*, 71 F.3d 29, 36–37 (1st Cir. 1995); *Flying Cross Check, L.L.C. v. Central Hockey League, Inc.*, 153 F.Supp.2d 1253, 1257 (D.Kan. 2001); *Central States, Southeast & Southwest Areas Pension Fund v. Paramount Liquor Co.*, 34 F.Supp.2d 1092, 1094 (N.D.Ill.1999).

36. *See* Rule 77(a) ("District Courts Always Open"). *See also Greenwood v. State of New York, Office of Mental Health*, 842 F.2d 636 (2d Cir.1988)(document placed in night depository box operated by Clerk's Office, and bearing date/time stamp imprinted on document by device also operated by Clerk's Office, was deemed to have been "filed" as of the date and time stamped on document); *Turner v. City of Newport*, 887 F.Supp. 149 (E.D.Ky.1995) (holding that complaint was timely filed when placed in the Clerk's post office box at 11:30 p.m. on the final day of the statute of limitations).

37. *McIntosh v. Antonino*, 71 F.3d 29, 36–37 (1st Cir.1995).

38. *See Life Ins. Co. of North America v. Von Valtier*, 116 F.3d 279, 282–83 (7th Cir.1997) (disapproving of trial judge's delay in transmitting motion to the clerk's office, noting that "the system will break down unless the judge scrupulously follows the directions to note the date and transmit the documents immediately to the clerk. Less than perfect adherence to these instructions will mean that actual filing dates will become as uncertain as the former dates of service were, and something as important as the jurisdictional time limit for taking an appeal will once again be subject to factual disputes").

Fees

It is unresolved whether filing is effective prior to the payment of any applicable filing fees. Thus, prudence dictates that all filing fees be paid at the time a document is filed with the court.

Filing by Electronic Means, Including Facsimile Transmission

Electronic filing is *not* permitted in every district, although the Rules permit each court, on a district-by-district basis, to provide for such filing in their local rules. Consequently, each district's local rules must be consulted. Attempting to file by facsimile or by other electronic means in a district that has not adopted such a procedure will not constitute effective, or timely, filing.[39]

Rule 5(e) also allows each judicial district to permit, under its local rules, the electronic filing, signing, or verifying of documents. A document properly filed electronically, in accordance with local rules, qualifies as a "written paper" within the meaning of the Rules.

Prisoner Plaintiffs

As with service under Rule 5(b), a *pro se* prisoner's papers are usually deemed "filed" under Rule 5(e) upon delivery of those documents to the prison officials.[40]

Refusal to File

Although the clerk of court may not refuse to file a paper that does not conform to the Federal Rules or the district's local rules, the clerk may advise the filing party or attorney of the paper's deficiencies. The task of enforcing rules concerning procedure and form are, therefore, reserved exclusively for the district judge.[41] However, a local rule may instruct the clerk to inform the court of the paper's defect.

ADDITIONAL RESOURCE SOURCES

Wright & Miller, *Federal Practice and Procedure* §§ 1141–53.

C.J.S. Federal Civil Procedure §§ 261, 349.

West's Key No. Digests, Federal Civil Procedure ⚷664, 665.

39. *See McIntosh v. Antonino*, 71 F.3d 29, 34–35 (1st Cir.1995) (litigant's claim that a facsimile "filing" was effective, when such filing was not expressly authorized under the local rules, "is whistling past the graveyard"—without a local rule permitting such transmissions, "facsimile filings in a federal court are dead on arrival"); *In re Fisherman's Wharf Fillet, Inc.*, 83 F.Supp.2d 651, 657 (E.D.Va.1999) (absent local rule permitting such filings, facsimile transmission "filings" are "deemed null and of no legal effect"); *Johnson v. United Steel Workers of America*, 172 F.R.D. 185, 187 n. 5 (W.D.Va.1997) (refusing to consider faxed copy of affidavit because it was a facsimile copy, not an original, and no local rule permitted filing of facsimile papers in lieu of originals).

40. *See Cooper v. Brookshire*, 70 F.3d 377 (5th Cir.1995); *Dory v. Ryan*, 999 F.2d 679 (2d Cir.1993), *modified on other grounds* 25 F.3d 81 (2d Cir.1994); *Garvey v. Vaughn*, 993 F.2d 776 (11th Cir.1993). *Cf. Houston v. Lack*, 487 U.S. 266, 108 S.Ct. 2379, 101 L.Ed.2d 245 (1988)(holding that a *pro se* prisoner's notice of appeal was "filed" within the meaning of the Federal Rules of Appellate Procedure when the notice was delivered to the prison authorities).

41. *See Jones v. Warden of Stateville Correctional Ctr.*, 918 F.Supp. 1142, 1151 (N.D.Ill. 1995).

RULE 6

TIME

(a) Computation. In computing any period of time prescribed or allowed by these rules, by the local rules of any district court, by order of court, or by any applicable statute, the day of the act, event, or default from which the designated period of time begins to run shall not be included. The last day of the period so computed shall be included, unless it is a Saturday, a Sunday, or a legal holiday, or, when the act to be done is the filing of a paper in court, a day on which weather or other conditions have made the office of the clerk of the district court inaccessible, in which event the period runs until the end of the next day which is not one of the aforementioned days. When the period of time prescribed or allowed is less than 11 days, intermediate Saturdays, Sundays, and legal holidays shall be excluded in the computation. As used in this rule and in Rule 77(c), "legal holiday" includes New Year's Day, Birthday of Martin Luther King, Jr., Washington's Birthday, Memorial Day, Independence Day, Labor Day, Columbus Day, Veterans Day, Thanksgiving Day, Christmas Day, and any other day appointed as a holiday by the President or the Congress of the United States, or by the state in which the district court is held.

(b) Enlargement. When by these rules or by a notice given thereunder or by order of court an act is required or allowed to be done at or within a specified time, the court for cause shown may at any time in its discretion (1) with or without motion or notice order the period enlarged if request therefor is made before the expiration of the period originally prescribed or as extended by a previous order, or (2) upon motion made after the expiration of the specified period permit the act to be done where the failure to act was the result of excusable neglect; but it may not extend the time for taking any action under Rules 50(b) and (c)(2), 52(b), 59(b), (d) and (e), and 60(b), except to the extent and under the conditions stated in them.

(c) [Rescinded].[1]

(d) For Motions—Affidavits. A written motion, other than one which may be heard ex parte, and notice of the hearing thereof shall be served not later than 5 days before the time specified for the hearing, unless a different period is fixed by these rules or by

1. Rule 6(c) was rescinded in 1966 when Congress directed that the district courts shall not hold formal court terms. Rule 6(c) had provided that the computation of time under the Federal Rules was unaffected by the expiration of court terms.

order of the court. Such an order may for cause shown be made on ex parte application. When a motion is supported by affidavit, the affidavit shall be served with the motion; and, except as otherwise provided in Rule 59(c), opposing affidavits may be served not later than 1 day before the hearing, unless the court permits them to be served at some other time.

(e) Additional Time After Service Under Rule 5(b)(2)(B), (C), or (D). Whenever a party has the right or is required to do some act or take some proceedings within a prescribed period after the service of a notice or other paper upon the party and the notice or paper is served upon the party under Rule 5(b)(2)(B), (C), or (D), 3 days shall be added to the prescribed period.

[Amended effective March 19, 1948; July 1, 1963; July 1, 1966; July 1, 1968; July 1, 1971; August 1, 1983; August 1, 1985; August 1, 1987; December 1, 1999; April 23, 2001, effective December 1, 2001.]

AUTHORS' COMMENTARY ON RULE 6

PURPOSE AND SCOPE

Rule 6 sets the procedure for computing the passage of time under the Rules. Although other, substantive Rules define the length of allowable time for such acts as answering pleadings or filing motions, Rule 6 dictates how those defined time periods are to be calculated. Rule 6 also authorizes the district court to enlarge the time periods fixed in the Rules.

A perpetual calendar can be found in Part XI of this text.

RULE 6(a). COMPUTATION OF TIME

CORE CONCEPT

None of the time periods established in the Rules may end on a Saturday, Sunday, or legal holiday. In addition, if a Rule requires the filing of legal papers with the clerk of court, the applicable time period also may not end on a day when weather or other conditions make the clerk's office inaccessible. When a defined time period ends on such days, the time period is deemed extended until the end of the next day that is not a Saturday, Sunday, legal holiday, or inclement weather day.

Moreover, when a time period fixed in the Rules is less than 11 days, intermediate Saturdays, Sundays, and legal holidays are excluded when computing the passage of time.

APPLICATIONS

When Counting Begins

The computation of time periods set in the Rules begin on the day *after* the triggering act, event, or default occurs. For example, Rule 12(a)(1)(A) requires a defendant to serve an answer within 20 days of service of process. If the defendant is served with process on February 1, the 20-day answering period begins to run on February 2.

When Counting Ends

If the defined time period would expire on a Saturday, Sunday, or legal holiday, the time period is deemed extended to the next day that is not a Saturday, Sunday, or legal holiday. Thus, in the example above, if the 20th day after service (February 21) is a Saturday, February 22 is a Sunday, and February 23 is Washington's Birthday, the defendant's answering date would be deemed extended until February 24.

There are twelve legal holidays:

1. New Year's Day
2. Birthday of Dr. Martin Luther King, Jr.
3. Washington's Birthday
4. Memorial Day
5. Independence Day
6. Labor Day
7. Columbus Day
8. Veterans Day
9. Thanksgiving
10. Christmas Day
11. Any other day designated as a legal holiday by the President or Congress
12. Any other day designated as a holiday by the State in which the court sits

"Any Other" Holiday

In addition to the Rule's delineated list of federal holidays, time periods are also extended on other days "appointed as a holiday by the President or the Congress . . . or by the state in which the district court is held." Such "other holidays" have been designated and recognized by the forum courts.[2] Consistently with the Rule, qualifying time periods are extended past state holidays, even when the federal courts are otherwise open on those days.[3] In determining whether a particular

2. *See, e.g., Reyes–Cardona v. J.C. Penney Co.*, 690 F.2d 1 (1st Cir.1982) (legal holiday in Puerto Rico honoring Eugenio Maria de Hostos was properly excluded from computation of time under Rule 6(a)).

3. *See Seacor v. Secretary of Dep't of Health & Human Servs.*, 34 Fed.Cl. 141, 143–44 (1995) (Massachusetts State holiday, "Patriot's Day", was excluded properly from computation of time even though federal court was open and filing could have been made on that date).

holiday qualifies under this Rule, the courts recognize that the Rule provides "reasonable flexibility" in the measurement of time periods, and is intended to abate the "hardship" of permitting "days of rest to shorten already tight deadlines".[4] Days when the clerk's office is declared closed by the Chief Judge might not, however qualify for this extension.[5] By its terms, the Rule allows for extensions granted by the President, Congress, and the State–less formal, District-specific "holidays" are not encompassed in the Rule.

Extended Dates for Filing When Courthouse Inaccessible

When the defined time period sets the date for filing a paper in court, the time period is deemed extended past any day on which weather or other conditions make the office of the clerk inaccessible. The clerk's office has been deemed "inaccessible" when inclement weather forces it to close,[6] when local weather conditions near the courthouse make travelling to the clerk's office dangerous, difficult, or impossible,[7] or when other circumstances make the courthouse inaccessible as a practical matter.[8]

Time Periods Less than 11 Days

When the defined time period is less than 11 days, intermediate Saturdays, Sundays, and legal holidays are not counted.[9] For example, if judgment in a lawsuit was entered on Friday, February 10, the parties would have 10 days under Rule 59 to move for a new trial. This 10-day period would begin on Monday, February 13 and expire on Monday, February 27, since intermediate Saturdays (February 11, 18, 25), Sundays (February 12, 19, 26), and legal holidays (*e.g.*, Washington's Birthday—February 20) would not be counted.

4. *See Mashpee Wampanoag Tribal Council, Inc. v. Norton*, 336 F.3d 1094, 1098–99 (D.C.Cir. 2003) (recognizing Christmas Eve 2001 as qualifying holiday for federal litigators, where President gave all Executive Branch employees that day off).

5. *See Garcia–Velazquez v. Frito Lay Snacks Caribbean*, 358 F.3d 6, 9–11 (1st Cir. 2004) (New Year's Eve not excluded, even though Chief Judge declared clerk's office closed); *In re Cascade Oil Co.*, 848 F.2d 1062, 1064 (10th Cir. 1988) (day after Thanksgiving not excluded, same reasoning); *Kirby v. General Elec. Co.*, 2000 WL 33917974, at *2 (W.D.N.C. Feb. 9, 2000) (Christmas Eve and New Year's Eve not excluded, same reasoning), *aff'd*, 20 Fed.Appx. 167, 2001 WL 1187957 (4th Cir. 2001) (per curiam).

6. *See Telephone & Data Sys., Inc. v. Amcell F Atlantic City, Inc.*, 20 F.3d 501 (D.C.Cir. 1994)(clerk's office is "inaccessible" within the meaning of Rule 6(a) when inclement weather forces office to close, notwithstanding that clerk's office's 24–hour "drop box" was still available).

7. The courthouse need not be physically closed in order for the clerk's office to be deemed "inaccessible". *See U.S. Leather, Inc. v. H & W Partnership*, 60 F.3d 222 (5th Cir.1995)("An ice storm that temporarily knocks out an area's power and telephone service and makes travelling dangerous, difficult or impossible, thereby rendering the federal courthouse inaccessible to those in the area of the courthouse, is enough to come within Rule 6(a)'s weather exception").

8. *See Latham v. Dominick's Finer Foods*, 149 F.3d 673 (7th Cir.1998) (holding that district court was "inaccessible as a practical matter without heroic measures" on December 26, 1997 because chief judge ordered the court closed, in recognition of President's executive order closing executive branch of federal government on that day).

9. *See Union Nat'l Bank v. Lamb*, 337 U.S. 38, 69 S.Ct. 911, 93 L.Ed. 1190 (1949)(observing that Rule 6(a) provides that an act which must, by statute, be performed within a prescribed period of time may be performed a day later when the time period ends on a Sunday).

No Effect on Dates Certain

When the court sets a "date certain" for an act or a filing, Rule 6(a) will *not* extend that date if it falls on a Saturday, Sunday, or holiday.[10]

Effect on Rule 23(f) Applications

Rule 23(f) permits a court of appeals to allow an appeal from a grant or denial of class action certification if an application is made for the appeal within ten days of the trial court's order. Rule 6 applies to such applications.[11]

Effect on Time Periods Set by Private Contracts

Ordinarily, the computation procedures embodied in Rule 6 do *not* apply to time periods set in private contracts.[12]

Effect on Federal Statutes of Limitation

The federal courts are divided on whether these time computation methods apply to federal statutes of limitation.[13] Congress may, of course, fix a different method for time computation applicable to particular statutes.[14]

Effect on Other Federal Statutes

Noting the broadly encompassing language of Rule 6(a),[15] at least one court has adopted as a general policy, guided by perceived legisla-

10. *See Fleischhauer v. Feltner*, 3 F.3d 148, 151 (6th Cir.1993)(holding that Rule 6's counting procedures will not apply where court fixes a date certain that happens to be a Saturday).

11. *See Beck v. Boeing Co.*, 320 F.3d 1021, 1021–23 (9th Cir.2003); *In re Veneman*, 309 F.3d 789, 793 (D.C.Cir.2002); *In re Sumitomo Copper Litig.*, 262 F.3d 134, 137 n.1 (2d Cir.2001); *Lienhart v. Dryvit Sys.*, 255 F.3d 138, 142 n.1 (4th Cir.2001); *Shin v. Cobb County Bd. of Educ.*, 248 F.3d 1061, 1065 (11th Cir.2001); *Blair v. Equifax Check Servs.*, 181 F.3d 832, 837 (7th Cir.1999).

12. *See J. Aron & Co. v. S/S Olga Jacob*, 527 F.2d 416, 417 (5th Cir.1976).

13. *See Bartlik v. United States Dep't of Labor, Tenn. Valley Auth.*, 62 F.3d 163 (6th Cir. 1995) (en banc) (majority view: holding that computational extensions under Rule 6(a) do not enlarge a court's jurisdiction, and thus petition for review of agency decision due on Saturday, Sunday, federal holiday, or courthouse-inaccessible day is timely if filed on the next day courthouse is open for business). *Compare Moore v. Campbell*, 344 F.3d 1313, 1319–20 (11th Cir. 2003) (applying Rule 6(a) to federal statute of limitations), *cert. denied*, 540 U.S. 1180, 124 S.Ct. 1417, 158 L.Ed.2d 83 (2004) *and Sain v. City of Bend*, 309 F.3d 1134, 1136–38 (9th Cir. 2002) (same) *and Reid v. Universal Maritime Serv. Corp.*, 41 F.3d 200 (4th Cir. 1994) (same) *and Newell v. Hanks*, 283 F.3d 827, 833 (7th Cir. 2002) (same) *and Flanagan v. Johnson*, 154 F.3d 196, 201–02 (5th Cir.1998) (same) *and Merriweather v. City of Memphis*, 107 F.3d 396, 398 n. 2 (6th Cir.1997) (same) *and Frey v. Woodard*, 748 F.2d 173 (3d Cir.1984)(same) *with Scanio v. United States*, 37 F.3d 858, 860–61 (2d Cir.1994) (minority view: rejecting argument that Rule 6(a) applies to expand time for filing habeas motion, and holding that final filing day is not extended when statutory last day is a Saturday, Sunday, holiday, or a day on which the clerk's office is inaccessible). *See also Union Nat'l Bank v. Lamb*, 337 U.S. 38, 40–41, 69 S.Ct. 911, 912–13, 93 L.Ed. 1190 (1949) (holding that a petition for review of State supreme court decision filed on Monday—the ninety-first day of the statutory ninety-day filing period, was timely filed: "[s]ince [Rule 6(a)] had the concurrence of Congress and since no contrary policy is expressed in the statute governing this review, we think that the considerations of liberality and leniency which find expression in Rule 6(a) are equally applicable").

14. *See FDIC v. Enventure V*, 77 F.3d 123, 125–26 (5th Cir.1996) (Rule 6(a) counting procedure does not apply when Congress' statute of limitations expressly states otherwise).

15. *See* Rule 6(a) ("In computing *any* period of time prescribed or allowed *by these rules, by the local rules of any district court, by order of*

tive intent, to apply the Rule to every federal statute enacted or amended after the adoption of the Rule, unless the statute at issue itself conveys a contrary drafting intention.[16]

Effect on State Statutes of Limitation

In diversity cases, the federal courts typically apply the time computation methods set by State law.[17] If, however, the applicable State law is silent on the computation question, the courts may apply Rule 6.

RULE 6(b). ENLARGEMENT

CORE CONCEPT

The district courts may enlarge the time periods fixed in the Rules.

APPLICATIONS

No Stipulations

The parties cannot unilaterally enlarge the time periods set in the Rules by simply stipulating to the extension.[18] Court approval of the stipulated enlargement is required.[19]

Enlargements Before the Time Period Expires

If the enlargement request is made *before* [20] the time period expires, the district court, in its discretion, may grant an enlargement "for cause shown".[21] Neither notice to the adversary nor a formal motion is required by the Rule, although applicable local rules may establish a more specific enlargement procedure. Pre-expiration enlargements are granted routinely if they are sought in good faith and do not prejudice the adversary.

Enlargements After the Time Period Expires

If the enlargement request is made *after* the time period expires, the district court's discretion is more restricted. The district court may grant such post-expiration enlargements if: (1) cause is shown, *and* (2) the failure to act was the result of excusable neglect. The courts have tested carefully a litigant's claim of excusable neglect; unfamiliarity with the Rules or a crowded professional schedule will not constitute

court, or by any applicable statute...") (emphasis added).

16. *See American Canoe Ass'n v. City of Attalla*, 363 F.3d 1085, 1086 (11th Cir. 2004).

17. *See Walker v. Armco Steel Corp.*, 446 U.S. 740, 100 S.Ct. 1978, 64 L.Ed.2d 659 (1980).

18. *See Orange Theatre Corp. v. Rayherstz Amusement Corp.*, 130 F.2d 185 (3d Cir.1942).

19. *See Gray v. Lewis & Clark Expeditions, Inc.*, 12 F.Supp.2d 993 (D.Neb.1998); *Allstate Ins. Co. v. Administratia Asigurarilor De Stat*, 163 F.R.D. 196, 199 (S.D.N.Y.1995); *Keller v. District Lodge No. 19, Int'l Ass'n of Machinists & Aerospace Workers*, 882 F.Supp. 560, 564 n. 3 (S.D.W.Va.1995), *aff'd*, 92 F.3d 1179 (4th Cir. 1996) (Table).

20. *See Hetzel v. Bethlehem Steel Corp.*, 50 F.3d 360, 367 (5th Cir.1995)(observing that district courts are granted "broad discretion" under Rule 6(b) to expand filing deadlines).

21. *See Lujan v. National Wildlife Fed'n*, 497 U.S. 871, 896, 110 S.Ct. 3177, 3192, 111 L.Ed.2d 695 (1990) (noting that cause must be shown before an enlargement of time is granted).

excusable neglect.[22] As one court has written: "When parties wait until the last minute to comply with a deadline, they are playing with fire."[23]

The Supreme Court has noted that "excusable neglect" is a "somewhat elastic concept", not limited exclusively to omissions caused by circumstances outside the moving party's control, but which must be assessed in view of all relevant circumstances surrounding the omission.[24] The Justices have labeled this "excusable neglect" hurdle as the "greatest" substantive obstacle of all.[25] In testing whether the neglect was excusable, the courts consider:

1. The prejudice to the opponent;
2. The length of the delay and its potential impact on the course of the judicial proceedings;
3. The causes for the delay, and whether those causes were within the reasonable control of the moving party;
4. The moving party's good faith;
5. Whether the omission reflected professional incompetence, such as an ignorance of the procedural rules;
6. Whether the omission reflected an easily manufactured excuse that the court could not verify;
7. Whether the moving party had failed to provide for a consequence that was readily foreseeable; and
8. Whether the omission constituted a complete lack of diligence.[26]

Significantly, the fact that the error lies with the attorney, and not with the attorney's client, is *not* dispositive on whether "excusable neglect" exists. Clients will be held responsible for the omissions of their attorneys, even if the clients are not otherwise culpable for the error.[27] Moreover, courts are reluctant to approve enlargements of time

22. *See Committee For Idaho's High Desert, Inc. v. Yost*, 92 F.3d 814 (9th Cir.1996) (ruling that ignorance of an amendment to a Rule could not constitute excusable neglect); *Marane, Inc. v. McDonald's Corp.*, 755 F.2d 106 (7th Cir. 1985).

23. *Spears v. City of Indianapolis*, 74 F.3d 153, 157 (7th Cir.1996).

24. *See Pioneer Investment Servs. Co. v. Brunswick Assocs. Ltd. Partnership*, 507 U.S. 380, 390–95, 113 S.Ct. 1489, 1496–98, 123 L.Ed.2d 74 (1993)(construing excusable neglect in the context of Bankruptcy Rule 9006(b), which was patterned after Rule 6(b)).

25. *Lujan v. National Wildlife Federation*, 497 U.S. 871, 897, 110 S.Ct. 3177, 3193, 111 L.Ed.2d 695 (1990).

26. *See Pioneer Investment Servs. Co. v. Brunswick Assocs. Ltd. Partnership*, 507 U.S. 380, 390–95, 113 S.Ct. 1489, 1496–98, 123 L.Ed.2d 74 (1993)(applying concept in bankruptcy rules context); *Dominic v. Hess Oil V.I. Corp.*, 841 F.2d 513, 516–17 (3d Cir.1988) (applying concept in late service of process context). *See also In re Painewebber Limited Partnerships Litig.*, 147 F.3d 132 (2d Cir.1998) (although litigant's seven-month period of hospitalization might excuse failure to submit timely class action opt-out request during that period, ten-month delay after discharge from hospital was not excused).

27. *See Allen v. Murph*, 194 F.3d 722, 724 (6th Cir.1999) (discussing client-responsibility issue, and finding no excusable neglect where counsel tried the case and knew deadline for moving for an award of counsel fees, but instead left for vacation without discussing the issue with his clients or arranging for another attorney to direct the case in his absence).

after prior extensions have been granted and ignored.[28]

No Enlargements

With one judicially-created exception,[29] Rule 6(b) prohibits the district court from extending the following time periods: [30]

(1) Time for seeking a judgment as a matter of law, under Rules 50(b) or 50(c)(2);

(2) Time for requesting an amendment or expansion of the court's findings in a non-jury case, under Rule 52(b);

(3) Time for granting a new trial or proposing to alter or amend the judgment, under Rule 59(b), (d), or (e); and

(4) Time for requesting relief from judgment, under Rule 60(b).

In these instances, the Rules' time periods are jurisdictional; a party's failure to act within the designated period deprives the district court of its power of enlargement.[31]

Other Enlargement Rules

Several other Rules authorize the district court to grant enlargements of time in particular circumstances.[32] Both Rule 6 and the specifically applicable enlargement Rule should be consulted.

28. *See Spears v. City of Indianapolis*, 74 F.3d 153 (7th Cir.1996) (finding no abuse of discretion where the district court refused to grant a 24–hour extension, after having previously granted several, earlier extensions); *McIntosh v. Antonino*, 71 F.3d 29 (1st Cir.1995) (finding no abuse of discretion in court's "exasperated denial" of a third extension).

29. The Seventh Circuit Court of Appeals has adopted a "unique circumstances" exception to these Rule prohibitions. Under this exception, if the district court grants (albeit improperly) an enlargement of time under one of the Rules that cannot be enlarged, the court's order will be allowed so long as the party seeking the enlargement can prove that she acted belatedly in reliance on the legal effect of the improper court order. *Eady v. Foerder,* 381 F.2d 980 (7th Cir.1967). *Accord Miller v. Maxwell's Internat'l Inc.*, 991 F.2d 583, 585 (9th Cir.1993)(discussing twin elements of "unique circumstances" exception: (1) the trial court took action that gave the parties good reason to believe that an appeal deadline had been extended, and (2) the time period for appealing had not yet lapsed at the time the court acted), *cert. denied* 510 U.S. 1109, 114 S.Ct. 1049, 127 L.Ed.2d 372 (1994). *See Varhol v. National R.R. Passenger Corp.*, 909 F.2d 1557 (7th Cir.1990)(by equally divided en banc court, the Seventh Circuit Court of Appeals refused to overrule the *Eady* decision). *See generally Pickering v. Provost*, 1993 WL 389293 (W.D.N.Y.1993)(surveying current state of "unique circumstances" exception).

30. Although not listed specifically as a non-extending Rule, the courts have construed Rule 71A as prohibiting the district court from enlarging the time to answer in a condemnation proceeding.

31. *See Browder v. Director, Dep't of Corrections*, 434 U.S. 257, 261–62 n. 5, 98 S.Ct. 556, 559–60 n. 5, 54 L.Ed.2d 521 (1978)(commenting that Rule 59(b) motions for new trial, Rule 52(b) motions to amend findings, and Rule 59(e) motions to alter or amend a judgment may not be enlarged); *Rodick v. City of Schenectady*, 1 F.3d 1341, 1346 (2d Cir.1993) (noting jurisdictional nature of time periods).

32. *See, e.g.,* Rule 4(m)(enlargements to serve summons and complaint); Rule 30(d)(2)(enlargements for oral depositions); Rule 31(a)(4)(enlargements for depositions on written interrogatories); Rule 33(b)(3)(enlargements to answer interrogatories); Rule 34(b) (enlargements to respond to production requests); Rule 36(a) (enlargements to answer requests for admission); Rule 39(b)(enlargements to demand jury trial); Rule 59(c)(enlargements to submit affidavits in opposition to new trial motion).

Time Periods Set by Statute

The court may only enlarge time periods set in the Rules or by court order. The court generally may not enlarge statutory time periods unless otherwise authorized to do so.[33]

Scope of Enlargement

The language of a party's proposed enlargement order should be chosen carefully. An order enlarging the time for a defendant to "answer" the complaint does not necessarily enlarge the time for "moving" to dismiss the complaint. Therefore, broad language is advised: *e.g.*, requesting an enlargement to "answer, move, or otherwise plead".

RULE 6(d). FOR MOTIONS—AFFIDAVITS

CORE CONCEPT

A written motion and notice of hearing must be served on the non-moving party not later than 5 days before a motion hearing date, unless the district court specifies otherwise.

APPLICATIONS

Motion Days

This 5–day notice procedure applies to those district courts with "motion days" or the equivalent (where all motions are heard orally). The Rule provides that the non-moving party must be served with notice of all motions within 5 days of the hearing day, unless the court directs otherwise.[34]

Saturdays/Sundays/Legal Holidays Excluded

The 5–day notice period is computed in accordance with Rule 6(a), with intermediate Saturdays, Sundays, and Legal Holidays excluded from the 5–day period.

Special Notice Rules

Some Rules contain specific notice requirements, such as Rule 56(c)'s provision that summary judgment motions be served within 10 days of a hearing or Rule 65(b)'s provision that motions to dissolve a temporary restraining order be served within 2 days of a hearing. In these unusual instances, the special notice requirements supplant Rule 6(d)'s notice period.

33. *See Kreutzer v. Bowersox*, 231 F.3d 460, 463 n.2 (8th Cir.2000) ("Rule 6(b), by its own terms, only applies to time limits set by the Federal Rules of Civil Procedure, or to limits set by the court. . . . It cannot be used to extend a statutory limit."), *cert. denied*, 534 U.S 863, 122 S.Ct. 145, 151 L.Ed.2d 97 (2001). *But see* **Authors' Commentary** to Rule 6(a), *supra*, "Effect on Federal Statutes of Limitation" and "Effect on State Statutes of Limitation" (discussion regarding application of Rule 6(a)'s time computation procedures to federal and State statutes of limitation).

34. *See Stewart Title Guaranty Co. v. Cadle Co.*, 74 F.3d 835, 837 n. 1 (7th Cir.1996) (noting that judicial district adopted a different schedule by local rule, permitting written motions to be filed just two days before hearing).

Special Timing When Court Directs Otherwise

The 5–day notice requirement is a rule of general application. It is subject to change by court order when circumstances warrant a different time period.[35]

Motion Affidavits

When a motion is supported with affidavits, the supporting affidavits must be served simultaneously with the motion. When an opposition to a motion is supported with affidavits, the opposing affidavits must be served not less than 1 day before the hearing. These service requirements do not apply to affidavits submitted in support of reply briefs.[36] The district court may modify these service requirements.[37]

Exception: Affidavits opposing a motion for new trial must be served within 10 days after service of the motion, unless an additional period of time not to exceed 20 days is permitted by stipulation or court order.[38]

RULE 6(e). ADDITIONAL TIME AFTER SERVICE BY MAIL

CORE CONCEPT

Whenever a Rule permits an act to be accomplished within a certain time after "service", an extra 3 days will be added to the response time if the service was made through the mails.

APPLICATIONS

Purpose

Rule 5(b)(2)(B) permits service of certain legal papers by mail and, with the consent of the recipient, by electronic transmission or other delivery method. Such service is complete at the time of mailing, transmission, or presentation to the delivery service–completed service does *not* await actual receipt. To compensate for the time lapse caused by mailing, Rule 6(e) assumes that postal deliveries will typically arrive at their destinations within 3 days of mailing.[39] Similarly, when service is made by electronic transmission or other means, this additional 3–day

35. *See Ciena Corp. v. Jarrard*, 203 F.3d 312, 319–20 (4th Cir.2000) (permitting different time periods in the context of interlocutory injunctions).

36. *See McGinnis v. Southeast Anesthesia Assocs., P.A.*, 161 F.R.D. 41 (W.D.N.C. 1995)(ruling that affidavits submitted with reply brief during a motion to dismiss briefing were not governed by Rule 6(d)). Note, however, that such affidavits must still be filed simultaneously with the reply brief. *Id. See also Kershner v. Norton*, 2003 WL 21960605, at *1–2 (D.D.C. 2003) (no error in relying on affidavit submitted simultaneously with reply to motion to transfer); *Ironworkers Dist. Council of Pac. Northwest v. George Sollit Corp.*, 2002 WL 31545972, at *5 (W.D.Wash.2002) (court will not strike reply affidavits when filed simultaneously with reply and do not prejudice adversary).

37. *See Orsi v. Kirkwood*, 999 F.2d 86, 91–92 (4th Cir.1993)(noting that although the district court may enlarge the time period of Rule 6(d), such enlargements should generally be granted only if cause or excusable neglect is shown).

38. *See* Rule 59(c).

39. *See Sherlock v. Montefiore Medical Ctr.*, 84 F.3d 522, 525–26 (2d Cir.1996) (noting "assumption" that mailed documents are received 3 days after mailing).

period is also added to offset possible transmission or delivery delays.[40]

Exception: Three days are not added in those instances when the defined time period begins to run only upon actual receipt.[41]

Applies to "Service" Deadlines Only

This 3–day extension applies only to responses due within a certain time after "service" of a preceding document.

No 3-Day Extension to "Filing" Deadlines

There is *no* 3–day extension when responses are due within a prescribed time after the "filing" of a document, even if that document is subsequently served through the mails (or through the special, service-by-consent means provided in Rule 5(b)(2)(D)).[42] Nor is a 3–day extension self-acquired by the act of mailing a document that must otherwise be filed by a particular date.[43]

No 3–Day Extension to "Receipt"–Based Deadlines

There generally is also *no* 3-day extension where responses are due within a prescribed period after actual "receipt" of a document, even though the received document was served through the mails (or through the special, service-by-consent means provided in Rule 5(b)(2)(D)).[44] However, a party may receive additional "mail" time when a party receives notice that the delivery of a letter was attempted, unsuccessfully, and is now ready to be picked up. In such cases, the courts may choose to extend the time period so as to allow that party a few extra days to retrieve the letter.[45]

No 3–Day Extension for Certain Rules

For Rule 6(b)'s list of jurisdictional time periods, the clerk's mailing of an order or filing will not activate Rule 6(e)'s 3–day enlargement provision.[46]

40. *See* Rule 6(e). *See also* Rule 6(e) advisory committee note to 2001 amendments (noting that electronic transmission is not always instantaneous, and may not arrive in a readable format, causing further delays).

41. *See Mosel v. Hills Dep't Store, Inc.*, 789 F.2d 251 (3d Cir.1986).

42. *See Jackson v. Crosby*, 375 F.3d 1291, 1293 n.5 (11th Cir. 2004) (3–day extension does not apply where document must be delivered within prescribed period from entry, not from service); *Rouse v. Lee*, 339 F.3d 238, 245–46 (4th Cir. 2003) (same), *cert. denied*, ___ U.S. ___, 124 S.Ct. 1605, 158 L.Ed.2d 248 (2004); *Pavone v. Mississippi Riverboat Amusement Corp.*, 52 F.3d 560 (5th Cir.1995)(same); *Sea-Land Serv., Inc. v. Barry*, 41 F.3d 903 (3d Cir.1994)(same).

43. *See Johnson v. McBride*, 381 F.3d 587 (7th Cir. 2004).

44. *See Begay v. St. Joseph's Indian Sch.*, 922 F.Supp. 270, 272–73 (D.S.D.1996) (Rule 6(e) does not provide an additional 3-days for responses to mailed right-to-sue letter, where response period begins to run only from date of receipt of the letter).

45. *See Zillyette v. Capital One Fin. Corp.*, 179 F.3d 1337, 1341–42 (11th Cir.1999); *Sousa v. N.L.R.B.*, 817 F.2d 10, 11 (2d Cir.1987).

46. *See Albright v. Virtue*, 273 F.3d 564, 570–71 (3d Cir.2001) (motions for reconsideration under Rule 59(e) cannot be enlarged by Rule 6(e)); *Parker v. Board of Public Utilities of Kansas City*, 77 F.3d 1289, 1291 (10th Cir.1996) (same); *Cavaliere v. Allstate Ins. Co.*, 996 F.2d 1111 (11th Cir.1993)(same).

No 3–Day Extension to Most Statutes of Limitation

The prevailing view among the courts is that the 3–day extension period does not apply to extend statutes of limitation.[47]

Applies to No–Known–Address Service

The 3–day extension also applies in those cases where, aware of a defendant's last known address, the serving party delivers the documents to the clerk of court.[48]

11 Day or Greater Time Periods

If an act required to be accomplished in 11 days or longer is performed by mail, (or through the special, service-by-consent means provided in Rule 5(b)(2)(D)), 3 days are added to the end of the defined time period.

Less Than 11 Day Time Periods

If an act required to be accomplished in less than 11 days is performed by mail, (or through the special, service-by-consent means provided in Rule 5(b)(2)(D)), the method for including the added 3 days is unclear. (Time periods of less than 11 days are counted specially: these time periods exclude intervening Saturdays, Sundays, and legal holidays.[49])

Some courts believe that the only way to ensure that the parties receive the full benefit of the 3–day mail extension is to add the 3–days at the end of the computation. Thus, if a party serves a legal document by mail to which the adversary must respond within 10 days, the 10–day period is counted off first (excluding Saturdays, Sundays, and legal holidays), and then the 3 extra days are added (with the due date extended further to the next business day, if the 3–day period expires on a Saturday, Sunday, or legal holiday).[50]

Note, however, that some commentators hold the contrary view—that the additional 3 days are counted first, and then the 10–day period is counted off. Thus, if a party serves a legal paper by mail on Friday, February 10 to which an adversary must respond within 10 days, the response must be served no later than Tuesday, February 28: Friday, February 10 is not counted because it is the date of service; three *calendar* days are counted next (thus, Saturday, Sunday, and Monday, Feb. 11–13); lastly, ten days are counted, excluding Saturdays (Feb. 18 & 25), Sundays (Feb. 19 & 26), and legal holidays (Monday, Feb. 27).[51]

47. *See Donovan v. Maine*, 276 F.3d 87, 91 (1st Cir.2002) (noting prevailing view); *Berman v. United States*, 264 F.3d 16, 19 (1st Cir.2001) (same).

48. *See* Rule 6(e); *see also* Rule 5(b)(2)(C). *See also* Rule 6(e) advisory committee note to 2001 amendments.

49. *See* Rule 6(a).

50. *See Treanor v. MCI Telecommunications Corp.*, 150 F.3d 916, 918–19 (8th Cir.1998); *Lerro v. Quaker Oats Co.*, 84 F.3d 239, 242 (7th Cir.1996); *CNPq-Conselho Nacional de Desenvolvimento Cientifico e Technologico v. Inter–Trade, Inc.*, 50 F.3d 56, 58 (D.C.Cir.1995); *Tushner v. United States Dist. Ct. for Central Dist. of Cal.*, 829 F.2d 853, 855 (9th Cir.1987).

51. *See* Wright & Miller, *Federal Practice & Procedure* § 1171. *See also United States v. Bondurant*, 1999 WL 357920, at *1 (W.D.N.C.1999); *Mullins v. Hinkle*, 953 F.Supp. 744, 747–48

There does, however, appear to be general agreement that Rule 6(a) and Rule 6(e) should never be applied in such a way that a 10–day period (in which intervening Saturdays, Sundays, and legal holidays are excluded) is itself converted into an 11–day-or-more period (in which intervening Saturdays, Sundays, and legal holidays *are* counted) by virtue of the added 3–days. Such a reading would defeat the very objectives of Rule 6(e). The purpose of the 3–day added period is to attempt to ensure that the responding party is afforded the same amount of response time, whether service results in immediate receipt (through hand delivery) or is delayed a few days (by postal delivery).[52]

> *Note:* This 3–day period is not, itself, a "period of time" subject to Rule 6(a). Consequently, the 3–day extension is not further expanded if the 3 days include intervening Saturdays, Sundays, holidays, or weather inaccessible days.[53]

Additional 3–Day Period Applies to Objections to Magistrate Judge Rulings

A district judge may direct a magistrate judge to consider and decide nondispositive pretrial matters, and to consider and submit a recommendation on dispositive motions.[54] The parties, thereafter, have 10 days from service to file objections to the magistrate judge's order or recommendation.[55] If the magistrate judge's order or recommendation is served upon the parties by mail, the additional 3–day period of Rule 6(e) applies to extend this 10–day objection period.[56]

ADDITIONAL RESEARCH REFERENCES

Wright & Miller, *Federal Practice and Procedure* §§ 1161–71.

C.J.S. Federal Civil Procedure §§ 194, 250, 302, 331, 354–369, 394–436, 569, 571, 701, 732, 764–789 et seq., 933–934; Time §§ 2–17 et seq.

West's Key No. Digests, Federal Civil Procedure ⚷417, 624, 734–735, 824, 865, 868, 923, 956, 1033, 1051, 1143, 1342–1343, 1612, 1679–1680, 1701–1705, 1991–1998; Time ⚷2–15.

(S.D.W.Va.1997). *But see CNPq–Conselho Nacional de Desenvolvimento Cientifico e Technologico v. Inter–Trade, Inc.*, 50 F.3d 56 (D.C.Cir. 1995)(counting 3–day extension by adding it to the end of the computed time period).

52. *See Lerro v. Quaker Oats Co.*, 84 F.3d 239, 242 (7th Cir.1996).

53. *See CNPq–Conselho Nacional de Desenvolvimento Cientifico e Technologico v. Inter–Trade, Inc.*, 50 F.3d 56 (D.C.Cir.1995). *See also Ramsdell v. Bowles*, 64 F.3d 5, 8 n. 1 (1st Cir.1995), *cert. denied*, 516 U.S. 1113, 116 S.Ct. 913, 133 L.Ed.2d 844 (1996) (noting District of Maine's local rule which excludes intervening weekends and holidays from ten-day period, but not from three-day mailing period).

54. *See* 28 U.S.C. § 636(b)(1); Fed. R. Civ. P. 72(a)-(b).

55. *See* 28 U.S.C. § 636(b)(1); Fed. R. Civ. P. 72(a)-(b).

56. *See* Rule 72(b) advisory committee's note 1983 Addition; *Vanderberg v. Donaldson*, 259 F.3d 1321, 1325 (11th Cir.2001), *cert. denied*, 535 U.S. 976, 122 S.Ct. 1449, 152 L.Ed.2d 391 (2002); *Lerro v. Quaker Oats Co.*, 84 F.3d 239, 241–42 (7th Cir.1996); *Glendora v. Marshall*, 947 F.Supp. 707, 722 (S.D.N.Y.1996), *aff'd*, 129 F.3d 113 (2d Cir.1997), *cert. denied*, 522 U.S. 1059, 118 S.Ct. 717, 139 L.Ed.2d 657 (1998).

III. PLEADINGS AND MOTIONS

RULE 7

PLEADINGS ALLOWED; FORM OF MOTIONS

(a) Pleadings. There shall be a complaint and an answer; a reply to a counterclaim denominated as such; an answer to a cross-claim, if the answer contains a cross-claim; a third-party complaint, if a person who was not an original party is summoned under the provisions of Rule 14; and a third-party answer, if a third-party complaint is served. No other pleading shall be allowed, except that the court may order a reply to an answer or a third-party answer.

(b) Motions and Other Papers.

(1) An application to the court for an order shall be by motion which, unless made during a hearing or trial, shall be made in writing, shall state with particularity the grounds therefor, and shall set forth the relief or order sought. The requirement of writing is fulfilled if the motion is stated in a written notice of the hearing of the motion.

(2) The rules applicable to captions and other matters of form of pleadings apply to all motions and other papers provided for by these rules.

(3) All motions shall be signed in accordance with Rule 11.

(c) Demurrers, Pleas, etc., Abolished. Demurrers, pleas, and exceptions for insufficiency of a pleading shall not be used.

[Amended effective March 19, 1948; July 1, 1963; August 1, 1983.]

AUTHORS' COMMENTARY ON RULE 7

PURPOSE AND SCOPE

Rule 7 lists the pleadings permitted in federal court, and sets forth the general requirements for the form of motions. The provisions of this Rule are often supplemented extensively by local rules, which practitioners should consult carefully.

RULE 7(a). PLEADINGS PERMITTED AND REPLIES

CORE CONCEPT

Rule 7(a) lists the six types of pleadings that may be filed in federal court: (1) a complaint; (2) an answer; (3) a reply to a counterclaim, if the counterclaim is so denominated; (4) an answer to any cross-claim; (5) a third-party complaint; and (6) a third-party answer. In addition to these six pleadings, the court may, in its discretion, order a reply to either an answer or a third-party answer.

APPLICATIONS

Not Pleadings

The list in Rule 7(a) is exhaustive.[1] Consequently, the following documents—which do not appear in the Rule 7(a) list—are *not* "pleadings": a writ, a motion to dismiss,[2] a motion for summary judgment,[3] a motion for sanctions,[4] a response to a motion, a "suggestion" under Rule 12(h)(3) of a lack of subject matter jurisdiction, a brief or memorandum,[5] discovery papers,[6] a notice of appeal,[7] affidavits,[8] filings in a condemnation proceeding, and special pre-answer "reports" required of defendants in certain cases, such as prisoner civil rights lawsuits.[9]

Definitions

(1) *Complaint:* A complaint is the document that sets forth either the initial plaintiff's claim for relief or a third-party plaintiff's claim for relief.

(2) *Answer:* An answer is the document that sets forth a defendant's opposition to a complaint, a cross-claim, or a third-party complaint.[10]

(3) *Counterclaim:* A counterclaim is the document that sets forth a defendant's or third-party defendant's claims against the original plaintiff or third-party plaintiff.

1. *See Yuhasz v. Brush Wellman, Inc.*, 341 F.3d 559, 569 (6th Cir.2003) (Rule 7 provides exhaustive list of pleadings).

2. *See Tahoe–Sierra Preservation Council, Inc. v. Tahoe Reg'l Planning Agency*, 216 F.3d 764, 788 (9th Cir.2000); *Maldonado v. Dominguez*, 137 F.3d 1, 11 n. 8 (1st Cir.1998); *Mellon Bank, N.A. v. Ternisky*, 999 F.2d 791, 795 (4th Cir.1993); *United States v. Snider*, 779 F.2d 1151, 1155 (6th Cir.1985).

3. *See Principal Health Care of Louisiana, Inc. v. Lewer Agency, Inc.*, 38 F.3d 240, 244 (5th Cir.1994); *Trotter v. Jack Anderson Enters.*, 818 F.2d 431, 436 & 436 n. 23 (5th Cir.1987).

4. *See Phinney v. Paulshock*, 181 F.R.D. 185 (D.N.H.1998).

5. *See Bush v. Barnett Bank*, 916 F.Supp. 1244, 1249 (M.D.Fla.1996); *International Longshoremen's Ass'n, S.S. Clerks Local 1624 v. Virginia Int'l Terminals, Inc.*, 904 F.Supp. 500, 504 (E.D.Va.1995).

6. *See Carlson v. Reed*, 249 F.3d 876, 878 n.1 (9th Cir.2001) (noting that interrogatories are not pleadings).

7. *See Adkins v. Safeway, Inc.*, 985 F.2d 1101, 1102 (D.C.Cir.1993).

8. *See International Longshoremen's Ass'n, S.S. Clerks Local 1624 v. Virginia Int'l Terminals, Inc.*, 904 F.Supp. 500, 504 (E.D.Va.1995).

9. *See Burns v. Lawther*, 53 F.3d 1237 (11th Cir.1995) (in prisoner civil rights case, special, pre-answer reports filed by defendants as requested by magistrate judge did not constitute "pleadings" within the meaning of Rule 7(a)).

10. *See LeBoeuf, Lamb, Greene & MacRae, L.L.P. v. Worsham*, 185 F.3d 61, 66–67 (2d Cir. 1999) (noting that responsive pleading (an answer) is required to a complaint).

(4) *Cross-claim:* A cross-claim is the document that sets forth one defendant's claims against one or more co-defendants. In many cases, defendants cross-claim against one another for indemnification or contribution. Note that answers to cross-claims are "pleadings", but the cross-claims themselves (which ordinarily are contained in a defendant's answer to the original complaint) are not considered "pleadings".[11]

(5) *Reply:* A reply is the pleading by which a party responds to an answer or to a counterclaim. Rule 7(a) permits replies to counterclaims without leave of court. Replies to answers are only permitted if the court so directs.[12]

> *Note:* Practitioners may encounter answers that include an averment designated as a "counterclaim" but which, in reality, is actually only an affirmative defense. Although responses are only required to bona fide counterclaims, practitioners should reply to all labeled "counterclaims"—whether they appear facially proper or not—to avoid any risk that the averments of the "counterclaim" might be deemed admitted.

Motion to Permit or Compel a Reply

Although otherwise not required, replies to an answer may be permitted or compelled by the court. To be granted leave to make such a filing, or to compel such a filing by another litigant, the moving party must make a clear and convincing showing that substantial reason or necessity or extraordinary circumstances require a reply.[13] Courts may permit or compel a reply to an answer for several reasons: when a type of new matter is pleaded in the answer that might affect the outcome of the trial or might otherwise greatly broaden the issues in the case, when the information sought through the reply cannot be acquired through discovery, when a misdesignated affirmative defense must be answered or clarified, or when the case otherwise should not proceed without a reply.

> *Note:* More recently, courts have required that plaintiffs in federal civil rights cases file specific and particularized replies when the defendants are public officials and assert qualified immunity as an affirmative defense.[14]

11. *See In re Cessna Distributorship Antitrust Litig.*, 532 F.2d 64, 67 (8th Cir.1976).

12. *See, e.g., Mihos v. Swift*, 358 F.3d 91, 106 (1st Cir. 2004) (noting court's discretion to permit reply to answer); *United States v. Shanbaum,* 10 F.3d 305, 312 n. 4 (5th Cir.1994)(court's discretion to permit reply to affirmative defense).

13. *See Moviecolor Ltd. v. Eastman Kodak Co.*, 24 F.R.D. 325 (S.D.N.Y.1959).

14. *See Crawford–El v. Britton*, 523 U.S. 574, 118 S.Ct. 1584, 140 L.Ed.2d 759 (1998) (commenting that trial court may order a reply to an answer that asserts a public official's qualified immunity, to protect the substance of the defense by compelling the plaintiff to aver some "specific, nonconclusory factual allegations" that demonstrate improper motive); *Reyes v. Sazan*, 168 F.3d 158, 161 (5th Cir.1999) (commenting that trial courts, when faced with sparse details of claimed wrongdoing alleged against public officials, should routinely require plaintiffs to file a reply under Rule 7(a) to qualified immunity defenses).

RULE 7(b). MOTIONS AND OTHER PAPERS

CORE CONCEPT

Rule 7(b) sets the procedures for motion practice in the federal courts, and requires that all motions be signed in accordance with Rule 11.

APPLICATIONS

Motion Defined

A motion is an application to the court, usually submitted in writing, that requests an order.[15]

WARNING: Consult the Local Rules

Nearly every district has promulgated local rules governing motion practice before their courts and, in some instances, individual judges have issued "standing orders" for their Chambers or case-specific orders regulating such particulars as the time for and method of responding to motions, page limitations for motions and responses, the proper form for such filings, the acceptability of "reply briefs", chambers' policies on courtesy copies for the judge, the number of motion copies that must be submitted, and the scheduling of oral arguments. Practitioners should always consult the local rules of court and chambers' standing orders to locate any unique procedures for motion practice within a specific district.

Rules Governing Pleading Forms Also Apply to Motions

The Rules that govern the styling of captions and the form of pleadings also apply to motions.[16]

Formal Requirements for Motions

All motions must be in writing, unless they are presented during a hearing or trial. A written "notice of hearing" on the motion will satisfy this requirement.

Form: Written motions must comply with the requirements of Rule 10—they must include a caption listing the name of the court, the title of the action, the docket number, and the title of the motion.

Contents: Written motions must set forth "with particularity" the grounds for the relief the motion requests. The purpose of this "particularity" requirement is to provide both the court and the adversary with ample notice of the grounds supporting the motion and the specific relief requested, so that the court may fully comprehend the request and the adversary can have a meaningful

15. *See In re Vogel Van & Storage, Inc.*, 59 F.3d 9, 12 (2d Cir.1995).

16. This directive is not a license for creative lawyering designed to evade either the requirements of other Rules or the express instructions of the court. *See Swanson v. United States Forest Serv.*, 87 F.3d 339, 345 (9th Cir.1996) (when court denied counsel the right to file an overlength motion brief, counsel could not escape this ruling by relying on Rule 7(b)(2) to justify the "incorporation by reference" under Rule 10(c) of an additional 69 pages of argument contained in earlier filings).

opportunity to respond.[17] Although "ritualistic detail" is not required,[18] the courts look for "reasonable particularity" in assessing whether this requirement is satisfied,[19] and will examine a supporting brief or memoranda in making this evaluation.[20] The courts will decide challenges to a motion's particularity by evaluating whether any party is prejudiced by the motion's form and whether the court can discern the motion's basis and rule upon it fairly.[21] If the motion fails to satisfy the particularity requirement, it may be dismissed.[22]

Motions to Amend: When a party submits a motion to amend, the particularity requirement of Rule 7(b) may require the party to attach to the motion a copy of the proposed amended pleading, unless the motion sets forth the substance of or otherwise adequately describes the contemplated revision.[23] Informal amendment requests—unaccompanied by the proposed amended pleading itself or a summary of its substance—do not conform to Rule 7(b) and may be refused by the trial court for that reason.[24]

Supporting Memorandum or Brief: Rule 7 does not expressly require a party to submit a supporting memorandum or brief along with motions or oppositions to motions. Note, however, that many districts have promulgated local rules requiring supporting memoranda, and providing that a motion lacking such support may be dismissed.

17. *See Kelly v. Moore*, 376 F.3d 481, 484 (5th Cir. 2004); *Andreas v. Volkswagen of America, Inc.*, 336 F.3d 789, 793 (8th Cir.2003); *Calderon v. Kansas Dep't of Social & Rehab. Servs.*, 181 F.3d 1180, 1186 (10th Cir.1999); *Cambridge Plating Co. v. Napco, Inc.*, 85 F.3d 752, 760 (1st Cir.1996); *Lac Du Flambeau Band of Lake Superior Chippewa Indians v. Wisconsin*, 957 F.2d 515, 516 (7th Cir.1992), *cert. denied*, 506 U.S. 829, 113 S.Ct. 91, 121 L.Ed.2d 53 (1992); *Registration Control Sys. v. Compusystems, Inc.*, 922 F.2d 805, 807 (Fed.Cir.1990). *See also Goodman v. 1973 26 Foot Trojan Vessel, Arkansas Registration No. AR1439SN*, 859 F.2d 71, 74 (8th Cir.1988)(commenting that requirement protects district courts from becoming subject to reversal on rulings where courts lacked benefit of argument from opposing counsel, and affords opposing parties notice of opponents' positions).

18. *See Kelly v. Moore*, 376 F.3d 481, 484 (5th Cir. 2004).

19. *See Talano v. Northwestern Med. Faculty Found., Inc.*, 273 F.3d 757, 760 (7th Cir.2001); *Registration Control Sys. v. Compusystems, Inc.*, 922 F.2d 805, 807 (Fed.Cir.1990).

20. *See Lac Du Flambeau Band of Lake Superior Chippewa Indians v. Wisconsin*, 957 F.2d 515, 516 (7th Cir.1992)(simultaneously filed brief satisfied Rule 7(b)'s particularity requirement), *cert. denied*, 506 U.S. 829, 113 S.Ct. 91, 121 L.Ed.2d 53 (1992).

21. *See Cambridge Plating Co. v. Napco, Inc.*, 85 F.3d 752, 760 (1st Cir.1996).

22. *See Butler v. Coral Volkswagen, Inc.*, 804 F.2d 612, 614–15 (11th Cir.1986)(commenting that failure to specify particular grounds can result in denial of a new trial motion). *Cf. Hopkins v. Bowen*, 850 F.2d 417, 420 (8th Cir. 1988)(memorandum in support of summary judgment considered a "motion" for summary judgment where it described particular grounds for the motion, prayed for specific relief, provided the opponent sufficient opportunity to respond, and caused no prejudice).

23. *See Long v. Satz*, 181 F.3d 1275 (11th Cir.1999); *Moore v. Indiana*, 999 F.2d 1125, 1131 (7th Cir.1993); *Wolgin v. Simon*, 722 F.2d 389, 394 (8th Cir.1983); *AT & T Corp. v. American Cash Card Corp.*, 184 F.R.D. 515, 520–21 (S.D.N.Y.1999).

24. *See PR Diamonds, Inc. v. Chandler*, 364 F.3d 671, 699–700 (6th Cir. 2004); *Calderon v. Kansas Dep't of Social & Rehab. Servs.*, 181 F.3d 1180, 1186 (10th Cir.1999); *Posner v. Essex Ins. Co.*, 178 F.3d 1209, 1222 (11th Cir.1999).

Form of Order: Many districts also have local rules obligating the moving party to attach a form of order to the motion which, if signed and entered, would grant the relief requested in the motion. Similarly, the party opposing a motion may be required to attach a form of order which would deny the requested relief.

Attaching Affidavits and Other Exhibits: A party may support a motion with affidavits or other materials. Practitioners are cautioned, however, that such attachments can have substantial procedural consequences.[25]

Signing: The written motion must be signed in accordance with Rule 11 by the party's counsel or, if unrepresented, by the party herself. If the motion is not signed after the omission is called to the attention of the party or her counsel, the court may strike the document.

Service: A signed copy of the motion or "notice of hearing" must be served upon counsel for represented parties or, if unrepresented, upon the party herself. Unless the court directs otherwise, service must be accomplished not later than 5 days prior to the hearing on the motion.[26]

Certificate of Service: The motion must contain a certificate of service verifying that the document was served.[27]

Filing: The written motion or "notice of hearing" must be filed within a reasonable time after service.[28] Note, however, that local rules may prescribe other, supplemental filing requirements.

Opposing Written Motions

Rule 7 contains no requirement that an opponent file an "answer" to any motion and, absent local rule requirements to the contrary, a motion can be opposed solely by filing a brief or memorandum. The form, signing, filing, and service requirements for motions are generally applicable to oppositions as well.

Withdrawing Written Motions

A written motion should ordinarily be withdrawn with the same formality with which it was filed. Consequently, written motions should be withdrawn in writing.[29]

Hearings and Arguments on Written Motions

The court may, in its discretion, schedule a motion for a hearing or oral argument. Neither is expressly required under the Rules, although local rule provisions may specify additional hearing and argument

25. *See, e.g.,* Rule 12(b)(if matters outside the pleadings are presented to, and considered by, the court on a Rule 12(b)(6) motion to dismiss, court must convert motion into Rule 56 motion for summary judgment); Rule 12(c)(same, in context of motion for judgment on the pleadings).

26. *See* Rule 5 and Rule 6(d).

27. *See* Rule 5(d).

28. *See* Rule 5(d).

29. *See United Coin Meter Co. v. Seaboard Coastline RR.*, 705 F.2d 839, 843 (6th Cir.1983).

requirements. Hearings held *ex parte* (without notice to the opponent) are generally discouraged and are permitted only in exceptional circumstances, such as applications for temporary restraining orders.[30]

Oral Motions

Oral motions may be made, so long as they are raised in open court at a hearing or trial.[31] This presentation will satisfy the writing requirement of Rule 7 if the oral motion is transcribed or otherwise recorded.[32] This "writing" requirement for oral motions functions to ensure that the motion is accurately memorialized and that both the court and the opponent have sufficient opportunity to prepare for the motion.[33]

Amendments to Motions

A party may seek leave to amend a motion. Leave is generally granted if the amendment is sought before the opponent has filed the opposition memorandum or brief, before the court has entertained oral argument, and before a ruling has been issued. Motions are amended, rather than just refiled, where a new, replacement motion would be improper or out of time.[34]

RULE 7(c). DEMURRERS, PLEAS, AND EXCEPTIONS FOR INSUFFICIENCY ARE ABOLISHED

CORE CONCEPT

The Rules have abolished historical forms of motions, such as demurrers, pleas, and exceptions.[35]

ADDITIONAL RESEARCH REFERENCES

Wright & Miller, *Federal Practice and Procedure* §§ 1181–1200.

C.J.S. Federal Civil Procedure §§ 124, 247–280 et seq., 301–319 et seq., 363–375 et seq.

West's Key No. Digests, Federal Civil Procedure ⚷295, 621–665, 671–680, 731–745, 771–786, 903, 921–928.

30. *See* Rule 65(b).

31. *See Meriwether v. Coughlin*, 879 F.2d 1037, 1042 (2d Cir.1989)(noting that, because oral motion was asserted in open court, written document not required). *See also Kerry Steel, Inc. v. Paragon Indus., Inc.*, 106 F.3d 147, 154 (6th Cir.1997) (noting that Rules allow motions at hearings, and refusing to hold as significant the attorney's omission of the utterance: "I move").

32. *See Atchison, Topeka & Santa Fe Ry. Co. v. California State Bd. of Equalization*, 102 F.3d 425, 427 (9th Cir.1996); *People of Illinois ex rel. Hartigan v. Peters*, 871 F.2d 1336, 1341 (7th Cir.1989).

33. *See Taragan v. Eli Lilly & Co.*, 838 F.2d 1337, 1340–41 (D.C.Cir.1988)(requirement of adequate opportunity to prepare and respond satisfied by oral motions if they are germane to hearing or trial).

34. *See, e.g.*, Rule 12(g) and 12(h)(providing that defenses of improper personal jurisdiction, lack of venue, insufficient process, or inadequate service of process are deemed waived if not asserted in original Rule 12(b) motion).

35. *See, e.g.*, *Transamerica Ins. Co. v. Avenell*, 66 F.3d 715, 720 (5th Cir.1995) (Rules abolished the archaic, common law plea in abatement, replacing it with a motion to dismiss).

RULE 7.1

DISCLOSURE STATEMENT

(a) Who Must File: Nongovernmental Corporate Party. A nongovernmental corporate party to an action or proceeding in a district court must file two copies of a statement that identifies any parent corporation and any publicly held corporation that owns 10% or more of its stock or states that there is no such corporation.

(b) Time for Filing; Supplemental Filing. A party must:

(1) file the Rule 7.1(a) statement with its first appearance, pleading, petition, motion, response, or other request addressed to the court, and

(2) promptly file a supplemental statement upon any change in the information that the statement requires.

[Added April 29, 2002, effective December 1, 2002.]

AUTHORS' COMMENTARY ON RULE 7.1

PURPOSE AND SCOPE

Rule 7.1 was added to the Federal Rules in 2002 to help assist district judges in making properly informed decisions on whether certain financial interests require their disqualification in particular cases.

CORE CONCEPT

Rule 7.1 is modeled after Rule 26.1 of the Federal Rules of Appellate Procedure,[1] and requires specific financial disclosures by all nongovernmental corporate parties to an action or proceeding in district court.[2] The Rule is intended to provide the appropriate level and volume of financial disclosures necessary to allow for properly informed disqualification decisions in those circumstances where automatic financial interest disqualification is compelled.[3]

1. *See* Rule 7.1 advisory committee note to 2002 amendments. *See also* Fed. R. App. P. 26.1 (setting forth filing requirements for "Corporate Disclosure Statements").

2. Rule 7.1(a).

3. *See* Rule 7.1 advisory committee note to 2002 amendments (explaining that Rule strikes balance between requiring adequate amount of financial information and more detailed disclosures that "will be difficult", would unnecessarily "place a burden on the parties and on the courts", and "create a risk that a judge will overlook the one bit of information that might require disqualification, and also may create a risk that unnecessary disqualifications will be made rather than attempt to unravel a potentially difficult question"). *See also Gebhart v. Raytheon Aircraft Co.*, 2004 WL 1212047, at *2 n.13 (D.Kan. May 25, 2004) (Statement is required "so that the assigned judge can ascertain wheth-

APPLICATIONS

Automatic Financial Interest Disqualifications

Rule 7.1 was not designed to cover all circumstances that might call for a district judge's disqualification.[4] Instead, the information compelled by Rule 7.1 reflects the financial interest standard for automatic disqualification under the Code of Conduct for United States Judges.[5]

Disclosure Procedures

The disclosure obligation applies to non-governmental corporate litigants. Such parties must file with the court a written statement that either (1) identifies each parent corporation and publicly held corporation owning 10% or more of their stock, *or* (2) states that no such corporation exists.[6] Two copies of the statement must be filed.[7] The filing must be made when the party files its first appearance, pleading, petition, motion, response, or other request addressed to the court.[8]

Supplementing the Statement

Parties are also obligated under the Rule to "promptly" file a supplemental statement when any change in the required information occurs.[9]

More Extensive Financial Disclosures Required by Local Rules

The drafters of Rule 7.1 expressly noted that local rules may require additional disclosures (and those regional experiences along with advances in electronic technology may one day justify additional National disclosures and an amendment to this Rule).[10]

Collateral Effects of Statement

Although court decisions construing this newly promulgated Rule are few, early indications are that the Statement will not readily be used for purposes other than those for which it was intended. For example, one court has ruled that the Statement does not operate as a substitution of parties or an amendment to a complaint.[11]

er he or she has a financial interest in the party or associated entities, which would require recusal").

4. *See* Rule 7.1 advisory committee note to 2002 amendments.

5. *See* Rule 7.1 advisory committee note to 2002 amendments. *See also* Code of Conduct for United States Judges at Canon 3C(1)(c) ("A judge shall disqualify himself or herself in a proceeding in which the judge's impartiality might reasonably be questioned, including but not limited to instances in which . . . (c) the judge knows that the judge, individually or as a fiduciary, or the judge's spouse or minor child residing in the judge's household, has a financial interest in the subject matter in controversy or in a party to the proceeding, or any other interest that could be affected substantially by the outcome of the proceeding").

6. *See* Rule 7.1(a).

7. *See* Rule 7.1(a).

8. *See* Rule 7.1(b)(1).

9. *See* Rule 7.1(b)(2).

10. *See* Rule 7.1 advisory committee note to 2002 amendments.

11. *See Gebhart v. Raytheon Aircraft Co.*, 2004 WL 1212047, at *2 (D.Kan. May 25, 2004).

RULE 8

GENERAL RULES OF PLEADING

(a) Claims for Relief. A pleading which sets forth a claim for relief, whether an original claim, counterclaim, cross-claim, or third-party claim, shall contain (1) a short and plain statement of the grounds upon which the court's jurisdiction depends, unless the court already has jurisdiction and the claim needs no new grounds of jurisdiction to support it, (2) a short and plain statement of the claim showing that the pleader is entitled to relief, and (3) a demand for judgment for the relief the pleader seeks. Relief in the alternative or of several different types may be demanded.

(b) Defenses; Form of Denials. A party shall state in short and plain terms the party's defenses to each claim asserted and shall admit or deny the averments upon which the adverse party relies. If a party is without knowledge or information sufficient to form a belief as to the truth of an averment, the party shall so state and this has the effect of a denial. Denials shall fairly meet the substance of the averments denied. When a pleader intends in good faith to deny only a part or a qualification of an averment, the pleader shall specify so much of it as is true and material and shall deny only the remainder. Unless the pleader intends in good faith to controvert all the averments of the preceding pleading, the pleader may make denials as specific denials of designated averments or paragraphs or may generally deny all the averments except such designated averments or paragraphs as the pleader expressly admits; but, when the pleader does so intend to controvert all its averments, including averments of the grounds upon which the court's jurisdiction depends, the pleader may do so by general denial subject to the obligations set forth in Rule 11.

(c) Affirmative Defenses. In pleading to a preceding pleading, a party shall set forth affirmatively accord and satisfaction, arbitration and award, assumption of risk, contributory negligence, discharge in bankruptcy, duress, estoppel, failure of consideration, fraud, illegality, injury by fellow servant, laches, license, payment, release, res judicata, statute of frauds, statute of limitations, waiver, and any other matter constituting an avoidance or affirmative defense. When a party has mistakenly designated a defense as a counterclaim or a counterclaim as a defense, the court on terms, if justice so requires, shall treat the pleading as if there had been a proper designation.

(d) Effect of Failure to Deny. Averments in a pleading to which a responsive pleading is required, other than those as to the amount of damage, are admitted when not denied in the responsive pleading. Averments in a pleading to which no responsive pleading is required or permitted shall be taken as denied or avoided.

(e) Pleading to Be Concise and Direct; Consistency.

(1) Each averment of a pleading shall be simple, concise, and direct. No technical forms of pleadings or motions are required.

(2) A party may set forth two or more statements of a claim or defense alternately or hypothetically, either in one count or defense or in separate counts or defenses. When two or more statements are made in the alternative and one of them if made independently would be sufficient, the pleading is not made insufficient by the insufficiency of one or more of the alternative statements. A party may also state as many separate claims or defenses as the party has regardless of consistency and whether based on legal, equitable, or maritime grounds. All statements shall be made subject to the obligations set forth in Rule 11.

(f) Construction of Pleadings. All pleadings shall be so construed as to do substantial justice.

[Amended effective July 1, 1966; August 1, 1987.]

AUTHORS' COMMENTARY ON RULE 8

PURPOSE AND SCOPE

Rule 8 establishes the "notice" pleading protocol for the federal courts. It sets the requirements for pleading claims and defenses, and outlines both the procedures for proper denials and the consequences for failing to deny. Rule 8 entitles pleaders to allege claims or defenses alternatively, hypothetically, or inconsistently—provided the pleading complies with the requirements of Rule 11. In federal court, pleadings are construed liberally so as to accomplish substantial justice.

RULE 8(a). CLAIMS FOR RELIEF

CORE CONCEPT

In a "short" and "plain" statement, a party asserting a claim must include: (1) the grounds upon which the court's jurisdiction rests; (2) a statement of a claim which, if accepted as true, would entitle the pleader to relief; and (3) a demand for relief.

APPLICATIONS

Element 1: Grounds for Jurisdiction

A party filing a claim in a complaint, counterclaim, cross-claim, or third party complaint must state in short and plain terms the basis for the court's subject matter jurisdiction for each count.[1]

• *Diversity Jurisdiction:* When jurisdiction is based on diversity of citizenship,[2] the plaintiff must allege: (1) the citizenship of each party (for individuals, their State of citizenship; for corporations, their State of incorporation *and* their principal place of business); and (2) that the amount in controversy—exclusive of interest and costs—exceeds $75,000.

• *Federal Question Jurisdiction:* When jurisdiction is based on the presence of a federal question,[3] the claimant must identify the Constitutional provisions, laws, or treaties that create such jurisdiction.

• *Admiralty Jurisdiction:* A claim that has both an admiralty or maritime basis for jurisdiction and another basis for jurisdiction may be brought under either the federal court's specific admiralty jurisdiction or ordinary jurisdiction. A party wishing to proceed under the rules governing admiralty or maritime claims must include a statement in the complaint that the action is an admiralty or maritime claim within the meaning of Rule 9(h).[4]

• *Supplemental Jurisdiction:* When diversity, federal question, or admiralty/maritime jurisdiction exists as to one or more claims in the complaint, the pleader may litigate other, non-federal claims in the same case so long as the non-federal claims are so related to the federal claims that they form part of the same "case or controversy".[5]

• *Personal ("In Personam") Jurisdiction:* Ordinarily, plaintiffs need not allege personal jurisdiction in their complaint; Rule 8(a) requires only that subject matter jurisdiction be alleged.[6]

Element 2: Short and Plain Statement of the Claim

The Rules impose a relatively lenient obligation upon pleaders in federal court. Litigants are generally[7] required to satisfy only "notice"

1. For a discussion of jurisdiction in the federal courts, see §§ 2.1—2.13 of this text. *See McNutt v. General Motors Acceptance Corp.*, 298 U.S. 178, 189, 56 S.Ct. 780, 785, 80 L.Ed. 1135 (1936) (commenting that pleader "must allege in his pleading the facts essential to show jurisdiction"); *United States v. Bustillos*, 31 F.3d 931, 933 (10th Cir.1994) (noting that party seeking to invoke the jurisdiction of a federal court must affirmatively allege facts supporting jurisdiction and, if challenged, bear the burden of proving that).

2. 28 U.S.C.A. § 1332.

3. 28 U.S.C.A. § 1331.

4. 28 U.S.C.A. § 1333.

5. 28 U.S.C.A. § 1367.

6. *See Caribbean Broad. Sys., Ltd. v. Cable & Wireless P.L.C.*, 148 F.3d 1080, 1090 (D.C.Cir. 1998) (commenting that, because lack of personal jurisdiction is an affirmative defense, pleader's complaint was not required to make specific personal jurisdiction allegations). *See also Purdue Research Found. v. Sanofi–Synthelabo, S.A.*, 338 F.3d 773, 781–82 (7th Cir.2003) (noting that federal complaints need not set forth facts alleging personal jurisdiction); *Gray v. Lewis & Clark Expeditions, Inc.*, 12 F.Supp.2d 993 (D.Neb. 1998).

7. Note, however, that this generally applicable "notice" pleading standard does *not* apply in certain particular contexts. *See* Rule 9.

pleading obligations–that is, they must provide their opponent with fair notice of their claim and the grounds upon which that claim rests.[8] A pleader generally meets this obligation by notifying the opponent of the claim and proposed relief to such a degree that the opponent is able to formulate a response.[9] In this respect, federal court practice differs from the more elaborate and demanding responsibilities imposed by many State courts in "fact" pleading jurisdictions.[10] A pleader does *not* have to set forth legal theories,[11] and pleading an incorrect legal theory is not necessarily fatal.[12] But the pleading must contain either direct or inferential allegations from which each of the material elements necessary to support a recovery under some cognizable legal theory can be discerned.[13] The simplified federal "notice" pleading standard depends upon the discovery rules and summary judgment practice to define the disputed facts in the case and remove unmeritorious claims.[14] In its liberality, Rule 8's "notice" pleading standard thus erects a powerful presumption against dismissing pleadings as deficient.[15]

• *Pleading With Extra Factual Detail:* Pleadings may sometimes contain a level of factual detail beyond that required under "notice" pleading standards.[16] The wisdom of pleading in detail is widely debated among practitioners. Some favor detailed pleadings as tactically wise because they may offer the trial judge a favorable early impression of the claim and incline the judge to belief in the pleader's ability to marshal a factual record to support it. Others disfavor detailed pleadings, satisfied that the "educating-the-judge" mission can be accomplished later in the case. In either event, detailed pleading is certainly a risky endeavor. It may offer an adversary too much detail too quickly,

8. *See Swierkiewicz v. Sorema N. A.*, 534 U.S. 506, 512, 122 S.Ct. 992, 998, 152 L.Ed.2d 1 (2002); *Conley v. Gibson*, 355 U.S. 41, 47, 78 S.Ct. 99, 102, 2 L.Ed.2d 80 (1957).

9. *See, e.g., Hamilton v. Allen–Bradley Co.*, 217 F.3d 1321 (11th Cir.2000) (short and plain statement of claim showing entitlement to relief is all that is required; "Detail is not the bedrock on which a proper complaint stands"); *Yamaguchi v. United States Dep't of Air Force*, 109 F.3d 1475, 1481 (9th Cir.1997) (federal courts' liberal pleading rules require only that complaint sufficiently establish a basis for judgment against defendant); *Atchinson v. District of Columbia*, 73 F.3d 418, 421–22 (D.C.Cir.1996) (complaint need not allege all that plaintiff must eventually prove); *Rodriguez v. Doral Mortg. Corp.*, 57 F.3d 1168, 1171 (1st Cir.1995) (court must protect "defendant's inalienable right to know in advance the nature of the cause of action being asserted against him.").

10. *See, e.g., Enron Oil Trading & Transp. Co. v. Walbrook Ins. Co.*, 132 F.3d 526, 529 (9th Cir.1997) (commenting that complaint need not allege evidentiary facts in support of its theory of recovery); *Palmer v. Board of Educ. of Community Unit Sch. Dist. 201–U*, 46 F.3d 682, 688 (7th Cir.1995)("Complaints need not plead facts.").

11. *See Crull v. GEM Ins. Co.*, 58 F.3d 1386 (9th Cir.1995).

12. *See Williams v. Seniff*, 342 F.3d 774 (7th Cir.2003).

13. *See Roe v. Aware Woman Center for Choice, Inc.*, 253 F.3d 678, 683–84 (11th Cir. 2001), *cert. denied*, 534 U.S. 1129, 122 S.Ct. 1067, 151 L.Ed.2d 970 (2002).

14. *See Swierkiewicz v. Sorema N. A.*, 534 U.S. 506, 512, 122 S.Ct. 992, 998, 152 L.Ed.2d 1 (2002).

15. *See Gilligan v. Jamco Dev't Corp.*, 108 F.3d 246, 249 (9th Cir.1997). *See also Swierkiewicz v. Sorema N. A.*, 534 U.S. 506, 514, 122 S.Ct. 992, 999, 152 L.Ed.2d 1 (2002) ("The liberal notice pleading of Rule 8(a) is the starting point of a simplified pleading system, which was adopted to focus litigation on the merits of a claim").

16. *See, e.g., Chaveriat v. Williams Pipe Line Co.*, 11 F.3d 1420, 1430 (7th Cir.1993)(noting increasing trend toward greater specificity in complaints).

presenting the formidable danger that the very detail offered so gratuitiously could be quoted in a pre-answer Rule 12 challenge to the complaint to defeat the lawsuit.[17] Moreover, detail in a pleading harnesses the attorney by allowing very little room to maneuver if other facts come to light through discovery or otherwise. In extreme, aggravated circumstances, excessively verbose claims for relief may even be subject to dismissal.[18] Although more austere than fact-pleading jurisdictions, federal notice pleading still requires a comprehensible presentation, "so that judges and adverse parties need not try to fish a gold coin from a bucket of mud".[19]

• *Relying On Federal Forms:* Rule 84 provides that the federal form models contained in the Appendix of Forms[20] are sufficient to meet the "notice" pleading requirements of Rule 8.[21]

• *Case Law Exceptions:* Although courts occasionally have tried to impose more elaborate pleading standards in certain categories of cases, it now appears settled that the only permissible exceptions to the "notice" pleading standard of Rule 8(a) are those contained in other Rules themselves.[22]

17. *See, e.g., Sparrow v. United Air Lines, Inc.*, 216 F.3d 1111, 1116 (D.C.Cir.2000) ("In some cases, it is possible for a plaintiff to plead too much: that is, to plead himself out of court by alleging facts that render success on the merits impossible"); *Barry Aviation Inc. v. Land O'Lakes Municipal Airport Comm'n*, 377 F.3d 682 (7th Cir. 2004) (noting that litigant "may plead itself out of court by alleging (and thus admitting) the ingredients of a defense") (citation omitted); *Jackson v. Marion County*, 66 F.3d 151, 153–54 (7th Cir.1995) (noting that plaintiffs can plead themselves out of court by alleging facts showing they have no claim, even though they were not required to allege those facts in first instance; "[w]e have expressed our puzzlement that lawyers insist on risking dismissal by filing prolix complaints").

18. *See, e.g., United States ex rel. Garst v. Lockheed–Martin Corp.*, 328 F.3d 374, 378 (7th Cir.2003) (finding no error when trial judge, after "wading through" four complaints and an ensuing statement, properly dismissed plaintiff's "distended" 400–paragraph, 155–page pleading accompanied by 99 attachments), *cert. denied,* 540 U.S. 968, 124 S.Ct. 450, 157 L.Ed.2d 313 (2003); *Magluta v. Samples*, 256 F.3d 1282, 1284 (11th Cir.2001) (vacating judgment and directing that plaintiff replead because 58–page, group-pleaded "complaint is a quintessential 'shotgun' pleading of the kind we have condemned repeatedly" where "any allegations that are material are buried beneath innumerable pages of rambling irrelevancies"); *Kuehl v. Federal Deposit Ins. Corp.,* 8 F.3d 905 (1st Cir.1993), *cert. denied*, 511 U.S. 1034, 114 S.Ct. 1545, 128 L.Ed.2d 196 (1994) (dismissing 43–page, 358–paragraph complaint that did not meet rule 8(a) requirement for concise statement; plaintiffs had a chance to amend original complaint, filed in state court prior to removal to federal court, and did not make changes sufficient to satisfy the court).

19. *See United States ex rel. Garst v. Lockheed–Martin Corp.*, 328 F.3d 374, 378 (7th Cir. 2003), *cert. denied*, 540 U.S. 968, 124 S.Ct. 450, 157 L.Ed.2d 313 (2003).

20. Fed.R.Civ.P. App. Forms 1–18. (reprinted in Part IV of this text).

21. *See* Rule 84 (noting that Appendix forms are "sufficient under the rules" and are "intended to indicate the simplicity and brevity of statement which the rules contemplate"). *See also Swierkiewicz v. Sorema N. A.*, 534 U.S. 506, 512 n.4, 122 S.Ct. 992, 998 n.4, 152 L.Ed.2d 1 (2002) (same).

22. *See, e.g., Swierkiewicz v. Sorema N. A.*, 534 U.S. 506, 512–15, 122 S.Ct. 992, 152 L.Ed.2d 1 (2002) (no enhanced "prima facie case of discrimination" standard required in employment discrimination cases); *Leatherman v. Tarrant County Narcotics Intelligence & Coordination Unit,* 507 U.S. 163, 113 S.Ct. 1160, 122 L.Ed.2d 517 (1993)(no "heightened pleading standard" in civil rights cases filed under 42 U.S.C.A. § 1983). *See also Educadores Puertorriquenos en Accion v. Hernandez*, 367 F.3d 61, 67 (1st Cir. 2004) ("All civil rights actions are subject to Rule 8(a)'s notice pleading regime").

• *Rule 9 Exceptions:* The liberal notice pleading standard of Rule 8 is tempered by Rule 9, which provides that certain categories of allegations must be pleaded with specificity.[23] Moreover, where those special categories are inseparably intertwined with the essential allegations of other elements of a claim, those elements might be held to the "particularity" requirement as well.[24]

• *RICO Case Statements:* Many Districts now require that pleaders alleging violations of the federal Racketeer Influenced and Corrupt Organizations Act ("RICO") submit "RICO Case Statements", using a template prepared by the District, to flesh out the factual predicates and legal theory underlying such claims.[25] Such Statements have been approved, unless they would obligate the pleader to allege more information than Rule 8(a) and Rule 9(b) would otherwise require.[26]

• *Pleading in Anticipation of Defenses:* Ordinarily, a pleader need not anticipate defenses, nor preemptively include averments to "plead around" an expected defense.[27]

Element 3: Demand for Judgment

The claimant must make a demand for judgment that identifies the remedies desired and the parties against whom relief is sought.[28] A party is not required to plead a specific sum certain in the demand.

• *Diversity of Citizenship Cases:* In cases based upon diversity of citizenship jurisdiction, a claimant must demand an amount in excess of $75,000, exclusive of interests and costs.[29]

23. *See Eternity Global Master Fund Ltd. v. Morgan Guar. Trust Co. of N.Y.*, 375 F.3d 168, 177 (2d Cir. 2004) (liberal notice pleading provides standard for judging complaints, except in claims for fraud and mistake, which Rule 9(b) requires be pleaded with particularity).*But see, e.g., Vicom, Inc. v. Harbridge Merchant Servs., Inc.*, 20 F.3d 771, 776 (7th Cir.1994)("[T]he particularity demands of pleading fraud under Rule 9(b) in no way negate the commands of Rule 8.").

24. *See Lachmund v. ADM Investor Servs., Inc.*, 191 F.3d 777 (7th Cir.1999) (holding that general allegations of agency do not suffice where the substantive fraud allegations offered by plaintiff are necessary to establish the agency relationship).

25. *See Northland Ins. Co. v. Shell Oil Co.*, 930 F.Supp. 1069, 1074 (D.N.J.1996). Where claims are asserted under the federal Racketeer Influenced and Corrupt Organizations Act ("RICO"), 18 U.S.C.A. §§ 1961–68, many judicial districts now require, by Standing Order, chambers policy, or otherwise, that the pleader answer a series of questions that supplement the RICO allegations of the complaint. *See, e.g.*, S.D. Cal. Rule 11.1; W.D. N.Y. Rule 5.1; *National Org. for Women, Inc. v. Scheidler*, 510 U.S. 249, 249, 114 S.Ct. 798, 800, 127 L.Ed.2d 99 (1994)(noting local rule in force in Northern District of Illinois); *O'Ferral v. Trebol Motors Corp.*, 45 F.3d 561, 562 (1st Cir.1995) (same, District of Puerto Rico); *Frank v. D'Ambrosi*, 4 F.3d 1378, 1381 (6th Cir.1993)(same, Northern District of Ohio); *Boogaerts v. Bank of Bradley*, 961 F.2d 765, 767 n. 3 (8th Cir.1992)(same, Western District of Arkansas). This pleading obligation is especially important where the facts noted in the RICO Case Statement are deemed to be pleading averments, properly considered in ruling upon a motion to dismiss. *See Glessner v. Kenny*, 952 F.2d 702, 712 n. 9 (3d Cir. 1991)(collecting cases so holding).

26. *See Wagh v. Metris Direct, Inc.*, 363 F.3d 821, 826–28 (9th Cir. 2003), *cert. denied*, ___ U.S. ___, 124 S.Ct. 2176, 158 L.Ed.2d 733 (2004).

27. *See Barry Aviation Inc. v. Land O'Lakes Municipal Airport Comm'n*, 377 F.3d 682 (7th Cir. 2004); *United States v. Northern Trust Co.*, 372 F.3d 886, 888 (7th Cir. 2004).

28. *See, e.g., Goldsmith v. City of Atmore*, 996 F.2d 1155, 1161 (11th Cir. 1993)(requirement of demand for judgment easily met by identifying requested remedies and parties from whom remedies are sought).

29. *See St. Paul Mercury Indemnity Co. v. Red Cab Co.*, 303 U.S. 283, 58 S.Ct. 586, 82 L.Ed. 845 (1938); *Mitchell v. American Tobacco Co.*, 28 F.R.D. 315 (M.D.Pa.1961).

• *Federal Question Cases:* In cases where jurisdiction is based upon a federal question, a claimant is not required to demand a certain minimum amount to obtain federal jurisdiction as required in cases based upon diversity jurisdiction.

• *Pleading Damages Claim:* Although pleaders are not required to do more than state "the relief the pleader seeks", the Rules *do* require pleaders to identify the type of relief they seek.[30] Thus, a pleading for equitable relief that does not include a demand for damages might not permit the pleader to later insist upon a damages award.[31]

• *Pleading Unliquidated Damages:* By local rule, certain Districts expressly forbid a plaintiff to plead a specific sum of unliquidated damages; instead, the pleader in those jurisdictions is permitted only to demand unliquidated damages generally.[32] Practitioners should consult their own local rules on this point.

• *Equitable and Declaratory Relief:* A party seeking equitable relief must plead the specific act to be prohibited or compelled. A party seeking declaratory relief must plead the specific declaration sought.

• *Special Damages:* A claimant must plead special damages with specificity, as provided by Rule 9(g).

• *Default Judgment:* In cases of default judgment, a claimant is limited to the specific amount of the demand, as provided by Rule 54(c).

• *Jury Demand:* A jury demand may be part of the original pleading. Rule 38 controls the circumstances in which a party may request trial by jury.

• *Alternative, Hypothetical, and Cumulative Demands:* A party may assert all demands for legal or equitable relief alternatively, hypothetically, and/or cumulatively. Rule 8 protects a party's right to plead inconsistently; under this Rule, portions of a pleading cannot be offered as admissions against other portions containing inconsistent or alternative averments.[33]

30. *See* Rule 8(a)(3). *See also Seven Words LLC v. Network Solutions*, 260 F.3d 1089, 1098 (9th Cir.2001) ("Surely a simple request 'for damages' would satisfy the notice requirement without imposing any undue burden on the drafter").

31. *See Seven Words LLC v. Network Solutions*, 260 F.3d 1089, 1098 (9th Cir.2001) (where damages claim was made years into litigation, after various representations that only declaratory and injunctive relief was sought, after a motion to dismiss, and only days before oral argument on appeal, court joins other Courts of Appeals in declining to read a damages claim into complaint as improper under Rule 8(a)).

32. *See, e.g.*, D. Del. Loc. R. 9.4 ("A pleading which sets forth a claim for relief in the nature of unliquidated money damages shall state in the ad damnum clause a demand specifying the nature of the damages claimed, e.g., "compensatory," "punitive," or both, but shall not claim any specific sum"); D. N.J. Loc. R. 8.1 ("A pleading which sets forth a claim for relief in the nature of unliquidated money damages shall state in the ad damnum clause a demand for damages generally without specifying the amount"); E.D. Pa. Loc. R. 5.1.1 ("No pleading asserting a claim for unliquidated damages shall contain any allegation as to the specific dollar amount claimed"); M.D. Pa. Loc. R. 8.1 ("The demand for judgment . . . shall not claim any specific sum where unliquidated damages are involved"); W.D. Pa. Loc. R. 8.1 ("any pleading demanding general damages unliquidated in amount shall, without claiming any specific sum, set forth only that money damages are claimed").

33. *See Rodriguez-Suris v. Montesinos*, 123 F.3d 10, 20 (1st Cir.1997); *Independent Enters. Inc. v. Pittsburgh Water & Sewer Auth.*, 103 F.3d 1165, 1175 (3d Cir.1997); *Henry v. Daytop Vil-*

Rule 8's Rules Supplant Inconsistent State Rules

Some States impose by statute specialized pleading obligations for the courts in their jurisdiction. Where such pleading provisions conflict with Rule 8, those inconsistent State requirements will not apply in the federal courts of that State.[34]

RULE 8(b). DEFENSES; FORM OF DENIALS

CORE CONCEPT

A party may respond to a pleader's allegations with an admission, a specific denial, a general denial, or a denial based upon insufficient information.

APPLICATIONS

"Notice" Pleading

Rule 8(b) contemplates that denials, like claims for relief under Rule 8(a), may be short and concise.[35]

Responsive Pleading Options

By its terms, Rule 8(b) offers the responsive pleader only three options: (1) admit, (2) deny, or (3) deemed deny, because the pleader lacks the knowledge or information necessary to respond.[36] The Rules do not appear to approve or permit other types of responses, and choosing to answer in other ways is a dangerous practice. Because an averment in a pleading that is not properly denied is deemed to be admitted,[37] failing to properly counter-plead could be catastrophic. One court has gone to great lengths to caution responsive pleaders away from antiquated (and perhaps now meaningless) pleading practices, such as "denied as a conclusion of law",[38] no response is required

lage, Inc., 42 F.3d 89, 95 (2d Cir.1994); *McCalden v. California Library Ass'n*, 955 F.2d 1214, 1219 (9th Cir.1990), *cert. denied*, 504 U.S. 957, 112 S.Ct. 2306, 119 L.Ed.2d 227 (1992).

34. *See Cohen v. Office Depot, Inc.*, 184 F.3d 1292 (11th Cir.1999) (finding that Florida statute, which requires plaintiffs to obtain leave from court before including punitive damages prayer, "conflicted" with Rule 8's requirement of concise statement identifying pleader's remedies; because federal rule occupied field in this regard, Florida statute could not apply to federal district court), *opinion vacated in part*, 204 F.3d 1069 (11th Cir.2000) (Rule 8(a) discussion expressly reaffirmed), *cert. denied*, 531 U.S. 957, 121 S.Ct. 381, 148 L.Ed.2d 294 (2000).

35. *See, e.g., Home Ins. Co. v. Matthews*, 998 F.2d 305, 309 (5th Cir.1993)(differentiating defenses under Rule 8(b) from the somewhat higher standard of pleading that may be required for affirmative defenses under Rule 8(c)).

36. *See In re TCW/Camil Holding L.L.C.*, 2004 WL 1151562, at *5 (D.Del. May 12, 2004).

37. *See* Rule 8(d).

38. *See Gracedale Sports & Entertainment, Inc. v. Ticket Inlet, LLC*, 1999 WL 618991 (N.D.Ill.1999) (refusing to answer "legal conclusions" "flies in the face of the established doctrine that legal conclusions are a proper part of federal pleading, to which Rule 8(b) also compels a response"); *Saldana v. Riddle*, 1998 WL 373413 (N.D.Ill.1998) (dismissing as "nonsense" the responsive pleader's claim that legal conclusions need not be admitted or denied); *Pessler v. CBS, Inc./WBBM–TV*, 1998 WL 246138 (N.D.Ill. 1998) (commenting that "Rule 8(b) does not confer on any pleader a right of self-determination as to any allegation that the pleader believes does not require a response"); *Ponce v. Sheahan*, 1997 WL 798784 (N.D.Ill.1997) (Rule 8(b) "requires a defendant to respond to all allegations in a complaint" and "creates no exception for so-called 'legal conclusions' "). *See also Neitzke v. Williams*, 490 U.S. 319, 324, 109 S.Ct. 1827, 1831, 104 L.Ed.2d 338 (1989) (ob-

because the written document "speaks for itself",[39] or neither admitted nor denied, but "strict proof" is demanded at trial.[40] Finding such pleading responses to be inconsistent with Rule 8(b), this court has ordered a re-pleading with specific instructions to counsel *not* to bill the client for "correcting" the "counsel's errors"[41] and, in some instances, has even deemed paragraphs containing such responses to be admissions, binding the party throughout the trial.[42]

Specific Denial

A specific denial specifically denies a particular paragraph or portion of a claim. The most common denial is the specific denial.

General Denial

A party makes a general denial by denying each and every averment of the pleading.

Qualified General Denial

A party may also assert a qualified general denial when the party wishes to deny all of the averments in the complaint except certain specific averments.

Special Matters

Rule 9 requires that certain matters be denied specifically, such as the capacity of a party to sue or be sued, the legal existence of a party, the authority of a party to sue or be sued in a representative capacity, the occurrence or performance of conditions precedent, the issuance of a judgment, or the legality of a document or act.[43]

Fairly Meeting the Substance of the Averment

In a denial, the responding party must fairly meet the substance of the averment. Denials may include legal conclusions or evidence, and a party may deny portions of an averment and admit others.

serving that federal civil complaints "contain[] ... both factual allegations and legal conclusions").

39. *See Chicago Dist. Council of Carpenters Pension Fund v. Balmoral Racing Club, Inc.*, 2000 WL 876921, at *1 (N.D.Ill.2000)(deriding "speaks for itself" responses, commenting that "[t]his Court has been attempting to listen to such written materials for years (in the forlorn hope that one will indeed give voice)—but until some such writing does break its silence, this Court will continue to require pleaders to employ one of the three alternatives that are permitted by Rule 8(b)"); *Central States, Southeast & Southwest Areas Pension Fund v. Pilger Transp. Servs., L.L.C.*, 1997 WL 656209 (N.D.Ill. 1997) (same holding).

40. *See Gracedale Sports & Entertainment, Inc. v. Ticket Inlet, LLC*, 1999 WL 618991 (N.D.Ill.1999) (noting that demand for "strict proof" is meaningless); *King Vision Pay Per View, Ltd. v. J.C. Dimitri's Restaurant, Inc.*, 180 F.R.D. 332 (N.D.Ill.1998) (commenting that under Rule 8(d), defendant was not entitled to respond that averments where "[n]either admit[ted] nor den[ied]" but instead that "strict proof thereof" was demanded).

41. *See Bobbitt v. Freeman Cos.*, 2000 WL 1131948, at *1–*2 & *2 n. 2 (N.D.Ill.2000); *Chicago Dist. Council of Carpenters Pension Fund v. Balmoral Racing Club, Inc.*, 2000 WL 876921 (N.D.Ill.2000) (same).

42. *See King Vision Pay Per View, Ltd. v. J.C. Dimitri's Restaurant, Inc.*, 180 F.R.D. 332 (N.D.Ill.1998) (deeming "strict proof" paragraphs to be admitted, and commenting that "this action will proceed on that basis") (Shadur, J.).

43. *See* Rule 9(a), (c), (d), & (e).

Denials Based Upon Lack of Knowledge or Information

(1) *Substance:* A party may plead based upon lack of knowledge or information. But to do so, the party must plead *both* lack of knowledge *and* lack of information.[44] A party may assert lack of information when the information exists but is difficult to uncover, such as information that must be uncovered through an accounting. A party pleading lack of knowledge and information is also bound by the obligation of honesty in pleading; an allegation that is obviously within the responding party's knowledge or information cannot be avoided, and averring lack of knowledge or information in such circumstances may have the unintended effect of *admitting* the allegation.[45]

(2) *Duty of Investigation:* A party denying based upon a lack of knowledge or information has the duty to reasonably investigate whether the information exists and how difficult it would be to find.

(3) *Treatment:* A pleading based upon a lack of knowledge or information is not an admission of the adverse party's averments.

RULE 8(c). AFFIRMATIVE DEFENSES

CORE CONCEPT

An affirmative defense is any *fact* asserted by the respondent that vitiates the opposing party's claim. Rule 8(c) provides for the pleading of affirmative defenses and provides that misdesignated counterclaims will be deemed affirmative defenses.[46]

In theory, a party must raise all affirmative defenses as affirmative defenses or they are waived.[47] In practice, courts may not invoke this approach if the result would be unduly harsh.[48]

APPLICATIONS

Definition

An affirmative defense is an assertion by the defendant of new facts or arguments that, if true, would defeat plaintiff's claim, even if all plaintiff allegations were presumed correct.[49] A defense is an affirmative

44. *See Bobbitt v. Freeman Cos.*, 2000 WL 1131948, at *1 (N.D.Ill.2000).

45. *See In re TCW/Camil Holding L.L.C.*, 2004 WL 1151562, at *5 (D.Del. May 12, 2004).

46. *See also, Hatco Corp. v. W.R. Grace & Co.*, 59 F.3d 400, 411 n. 8 (3d Cir.1995)(noting that defense improperly pleaded as counterclaim should simply be treated as if properly pleaded, citing Rule 8(c)).

47. *See, e.g., McKinnon v. Kwong Wah Restaurant*, 83 F.3d 498, 505 (1st Cir.1996) (commenting that to avoid a waiver, defendants must assert all of their affirmative defenses in the answer), *cert. denied*, 525 U.S. 964, 119 S.Ct. 408, 142 L.Ed.2d 331 (1998); *Williams v. Ashland Engineering Co.*, 45 F.3d 588, 593 (1st Cir.1995), *cert. denied,* 516 U.S. 807, 116 S.Ct. 51, 133 L.Ed.2d 16 (1995) ("generally speaking, a party must set forth all affirmative defenses in the pleadings, on pain of possible forfeiture.").

48. *See, e.g., Petrocelli v. Daniel Woodhead Co.,* 993 F.2d 27, 29 n. 1 (3d Cir. 1993)(affirmative defense not raised in original pleading is not waived if it can be properly raised under Rule 15, governing amendments to pleadings); *Allied Chemical Corp. v. Mackay,* 695 F.2d 854, 855–56 (5th Cir.1983)("Where the matter is raised in the trial court in a manner that does not result in unfair surprise ... technical failure to comply precisely with Rule 8(c) is not fatal.").

49. *See Emergency One, Inc. v. American Fire Eagle Engine Co.*, 332 F.3d 264, 271 (4th

one if the defendant bears the burden of proving it or if it does not controvert the plaintiff's proofs.[50]

Enumerated Affirmative Defenses

Rule 8(c) contains a *non-exhaustive* list of defenses that must be pleaded affirmatively: accord and satisfaction, arbitration and award, assumption of risk, contributory negligence, discharge in bankruptcy, duress, estoppel, failure of consideration, fraud, illegality, injury by fellow servant, laches, license, payment, release, res judicata, statute of frauds, statute of limitations, and waiver.

Unenumerated Affirmative Defenses

In addition to the matters enumerated as affirmative defenses, parties are generally required under Rule 8(c) to plead as affirmative defenses any new factual matter that would come as a surprise at trial.[51] To determine whether a defense qualifies as an unenumerated "residual" affirmative defense, the courts check the logical relationship between the defense and the cause of action, and decide whether a failure to timely plead the defense could cause unfair surprise.[52] The courts may also consult the applicable State law to determine which party bears the burden of proving the defense and, thus, whether the defense is an "affirmative" one or not.[53]

Pleading Affirmative Defenses

Affirmative defenses should be asserted in the answer or responsive pleading. The obligation to plead affirmative defenses is designed to ensure that the plaintiff receives both appropriate notice of the defense and an opportunity to rebut it.[54] Thus, courts require that when pleading affirmative defenses, parties have a duty to provide reasonable notice of the defense to opposing parties, in a manner similar to the requirement Rule 8(a) imposes on claims for relief. A party should plead affirmative defenses in separate paragraphs and label each paragraph as an affirmative defense, as provided in Rule 8(e).

Cir.2003); *Saks v. Franklin Covey Co.*, 316 F.3d 337, 350 (2d Cir.2003).

50. *See Brunswick Leasing Corp. v. Wisconsin Cent., Ltd.*, 136 F.3d 521, 530 (7th Cir.1998).

51. *See, e.g., Frederick v. Kirby Tankships, Inc.*, 205 F.3d 1277, 1286–87 (11th Cir.2000) (failure to mitigate is affirmative defense), *cert. denied*, 531 U.S. 813, 121 S.Ct. 46, 148 L.Ed.2d 16 (2000); *Brinkley v. Harbour Recreation Club*, 180 F.3d 598, 612 (4th Cir.1999) ("factor-other-than-sex" defense to Equal Pay Act claims is affirmative defense); *Ringuette v. City of Fall River*, 146 F.3d 1 (1st Cir.1998) (qualified immunity is an affirmative defense);*Gray v. Bicknell*, 86 F.3d 1472, 1480 (8th Cir.1996) (merger is an affirmative defense); *Federal Deposit Ins. Corp. v. Calhoun*, 34 F.3d 1291, 1299 (5th Cir. 1994)("ratification" is an affirmative defense recognized by State law); *Union Mut. Life Ins. Co. v. Chrysler Corp.*, 793 F.2d 1, 13 (1st Cir. 1986) ("novation" is an affirmative defense); *Red Deer v. Cherokee County, Iowa*, 183 F.R.D. 642 (N.D.Iowa 1999) ("after-acquired evidence" is an affirmative defense).

52. *See Oden v. Oktibbeha County*, 246 F.3d 458, 467 (5th Cir.2001), *cert. denied*, 534 U.S. 948, 122 S.Ct. 341, & 342, 151 L.Ed.2d 258 (2001).

53. *See Brunswick Leasing Corp. v. Wisconsin Cent., Ltd.*, 136 F.3d 521, 530 (7th Cir.1998).

54. *See Huss v. King Co.*, 338 F.3d 647, 651–52 (6th Cir.2003) , *cert. denied,* 541 U.S. 1015, 124 S.Ct. 2080, 158 L.Ed.2d 629 (2004); *Davignon v. Clemmey*, 322 F.3d 1, 15 (1st Cir.2003); *Saks v. Franklin Covey Co.*, 316 F.3d 337, 350 (2d Cir.2003); *Robinson v. Johnson*, 313 F.3d 128, 134–35 (3d Cir.2002), *petition for cert. pending*, No. 02–9087 (U.S. Feb. 14, 2003).

Burden of Proof

The party raising an affirmative defense has the burden of proving it.[55]

No Pleading in Response to Affirmative Defenses

All affirmative defenses are automatically denied as provided by Rule 8(d), and therefore require no response.[56]

Special Matters

When asserting an affirmative defense that contains special matters, such as the capacity of a party to sue or be sued, fraud or mistake, the performance of conditions precedent, the authority of a party to sue or be sued in a representative capacity, the legal existence of a party, the legality of an official document or act, or the issuance of a judgment, the party should plead with particularity, as provided in Rule 9.[57]

Misdesignated Affirmative Defenses

Misdesignated counterclaims will be deemed affirmative defenses. Affirmative defenses labeled as denials will be treated as affirmative defenses and will not be deemed waived where their proper assertion will promote a disposition of the case on the merits and will not prejudice the adverse parties.[58]

Waiver

An affirmative defense that is not pleaded may be deemed waived.[59] Waiver might not be found, however, where the defense is later pleaded–without undue delay or prejudice to the opponent–or where a timely assertion is prevented because the predicates for the defense had not yet arisen by the time the answer was filed.[60] Moreover, where the plaintiff receives sufficient actual notice of the affirmative defense by some method other than a pleading *and* is not prejudiced in the process, a failure to plead the affirmative defense may be excused.[61] Thus, for example, in an appropriate case, an affirmative defense asserted for the first time by motion for summary judgment may be considered by the

55. *See, e.g., F.T.C. v. National Bus. Consultants, Inc.*, 376 F.3d 317, 322 (5th Cir. 2004); *Gonzalez-Gonzalez v. United States*, 257 F.3d 31, (1st Cir.2001); *Bridgestone/Firestone Research, Inc. v. Automobile Club De L'Ouest De La France*, 245 F.3d 1359, 1361 (Fed.Cir.2001); *Continental Airlines, Inc. v. Intra Brokers, Inc.*, 24 F.3d 1099, 1103 (9th Cir.1994).

56. *See* Rule 8(d) ("Averments in a pleading to which no responsive pleading is required or permitted shall be taken as denied or avoided"); Rule 7(a) (absent court order, no counter-pleading to an answer (where affirmative defenses are ordinarily contained) is permitted).

57. *See* Rule 9(a), (c), (d), & (e).

58. *See Reiter v. Cooper*, 507 U.S. 258, 113 S.Ct. 1213, 122 L.Ed.2d 604 (1993). *See also Giles v. General Elec. Co.*, 245 F.3d 474, 491–92 (5th Cir.2001) (affirmative defense not waived if asserted "at a pragmatically sufficient time" and did not prejudice the opponent).

59. *See, e.g., Horton v. Potter*, 369 F.3d 906, 911–12 (6th Cir. 2004); *Davignon v. Clemmey*, 322 F.3d 1, 15 (1st Cir.2003).

60. *See Davignon v. Clemmey*, 322 F.3d 1, 15 (1st Cir.2003).

61. *See Huss v. King Co.*, 338 F.3d 647 (6th Cir.2003), *cert. denied*, 541 U.S. 1015, 124 S.Ct. 2080, 158 L.Ed.2d 629 (2004) *See also Jakobsen v. Massachusetts Port Auth.*, 520 F.2d 810, 813 (1st Cir.1975) (no waiver where failure to plead affirmative defense did not cause unfair prejudice).

court a motion to amend the defendant's answer, which would prevent waiver.[62] Notwithstanding this possible liberality, the trial court enjoys broad discretion, and its decision will likely not be disturbed unless it is completely unreasonable.[63] In exercising their discretion, the courts remain vigilant to protect the plaintiff against being "ambushed" by an unpleaded affirmative defense–a naked "failure-to-state-a-claim" defense, therefore, is unlikely to be considered by the court a preservation of an otherwise unpleaded affirmative defense.[64]

Raising Affirmative Defenses *Sua Sponte*

Some courts have held that certain defenses–such as *res judicata* and collateral estoppel–may, in certain instances, be raised by the court *sua sponte*, even when they had not been properly pleaded, mindful of the strong public interest in conserving scarce judicial resources by avoiding improper relitigations.[65]

RULE 8(d). EFFECT OF FAILURE TO DENY

CORE CONCEPT

If a response is required, a party failing to respond is deemed to have admitted all averments, except the amount of damages. This consequence applies equally to replies to counterclaims and court-ordered replies. Conversely, if a response is not required, a party is deemed to have denied all averments.[66]

APPLICATIONS

Affirmative Defenses

Affirmative defenses are automatically denied and do not need to be answered, unless required by court order.[67]

Improper Responses: Denying an Averment as a "Conclusion of Law", Refusing to Plead and Demanding "Strict Proof", Declaring that Documents "Speak For Themselves"

As noted earlier, Rule 8(b) offers the responsive pleader only three options: (1) admit, (2) deny, or (3) deny through an inability to respond due to lack of knowledge or information. An averment in a pleading that is not denied properly is deemed admitted.[68] Responding to a pleading by refusing to answer because the averment is a "conclusion of law", because the averment concerns a written document that "speaks

62. *See Anthony v. City of New York*, 339 F.3d 129, n.5 (2d Cir.2003).

63. *See Castro v. Chicago Housing Auth.*, 360 F.3d 721, 735 (7th Cir. 2004).

64. *See Saks v. Franklin Covey Co.*, 316 F.3d 337, 350 (2d Cir.2003).

65. *See Curry v. City of Syracuse*, 316 F.3d 324, 330 (2d Cir.2003).

66. *See, e.g., Schultea v. Wood*, 47 F.3d 1427, 1433 (5th Cir.1995) ("[A]llegations in a pleading for which no response is required are deemed denied.").

67. *See* Rule 8(d) ("Averments in a pleading to which no responsive pleading is required or permitted shall be taken as denied or avoided"); Rule 7(a) (absent court order, no counter-pleading to an answer (where affirmative defenses are ordinarily contained) is permitted).

68. *See* Rule 8(d).

for itself", or because "strict proof" is demanded at time of trial exposes the responding party to having the averments deemed admitted by the court.[69]

Fifth Amendment

Where an answer would subject a party to criminal charges or be used as evidence or a link in the evidence in a criminal proceeding, the pleader may refuse to answer by claiming the privilege to be free from self-incrimination, founded in the Fifth Amendment to the United States Constitution.[70]

RULE 8(e). PLEADING TO BE CONCISE AND DIRECT: CONSISTENCY

CORE CONCEPT

Parties should plead claims or defenses in a simple, direct, and concise manner consistent with the notice pleading standard of Rule 8(a). No technical pleading forms are necessary. Parties should set forth the averments in general terms and should omit evidentiary material.

APPLICATIONS

Improper Pleadings

Although liberally construed, when pleadings are not simple, concise, and direct, but instead are so convoluted and difficult to understand that it is impossible to assess whether the pleader has alleged a meritorious claim, the trial court may either grant a motion to dismiss for violating Rule 8 or, alternatively, grant a motion for a more definite statement.[71]

Incorporation by Reference

A party may adopt by reference paragraphs of previous counts rather than repleading each alternative or hypothetical claim or defense, as provided by Rule 10(c).

Alternative, Hypothetical, And Inconsistent Pleading Permitted

Statements of claims or defenses may be asserted in the alternative, hypothetically, and even inconsistently.[72] However, pleaders are ex-

69. *See King Vision Pay Per View, Ltd. v. J.C. Dimitri's Restaurant, Inc.*, 180 F.R.D. 332 (N.D.Ill.1998) (deeming "strict proof" paragraphs to be admitted, and commenting that "this action will proceed on that basis") (Shadur, J.).

70. *See, e.g., LaSalle Bank Lake View v. Seguban,* 54 F.3d 387, 389–91 (7th Cir. 1995)(complaint cannot be deemed admitted when defendant invokes Fifth Amendment; complainant must produce evidence to support allegations); *Industrial Indemnity Co. v. Niebling,* 844 F.Supp. 1374, 1376 (D.Ariz. 1994)(proper invocation of Fifth Amendment avoids invocation of Rule 8(d)).

71. *See Hassek v. Simmons*, 2003 WL 22416698, at *1 (N.D.Cal. 2003). *See also Desardouin v. United Parcel Serv., Inc.*, 285 F.Supp.2d 153, 157 (D.Conn. 2003) (noting that dismissal is permitted where complaint "is so confused, ambiguous, vague, or otherwise unintelligible that its true substance, if any, is well disguised").

72. *See* Rule 8(e)(2). *See also Cleveland v. Policy Mgmt. Sys. Corp.*, 526 U.S. 795, 805, 119

pressly reminded by Rule 8(e) that all pleaded statements–including alternative, hypothetical, and inconsistent ones–are still subject to the obligations of Rule 11.[73] Moreover, the court must be able to readily identify claims or defenses that are pleaded alternatively, hypothetically, or inconsistently. Although no "magic words" are required, it must be reasonably obvious from the pleading itself that these types of claims or defenses are being asserted.[74] While separate inconsistent *claims* and *defenses* are permitted under the Rules, the factual allegations *within* each claim or defense cannot be inconsistent with the alleged right of recovery, or else the claim or defense could defeat itself.[75]

Inconsistent Pleadings As Admissions Against the Pleader

Because Rule 8(e) protects a party's right to plead inconsistent claims and defenses, statements made in claims or defenses cannot generally be offered as admissions against other claims or defenses within the same pleading that contain inconsistent or alternative averments.[76] However, unequivocal averments of fact, made *within* a particular claim or defense and not inconsistently pleaded, may constitute judicial admissions that conclusively bind the pleader throughout the litigation.[77] Additionally, if the positions taken by the pleader are accepted by the court, the pleader may be foreclosed by judicial estoppel from taking an inconsistent, contrary position in later proceedings.[78]

S.Ct. 1597, 1603, 143 L.Ed.2d 966 (1999) ("Our ordinary Rules recognize that a person may not be sure in advance upon which legal theory she will succeed, and so permit parties to 'set forth two or more statements of a claim or defense alternately or hypothetically,' and to 'state as many separate claims or defenses as the party has regardless of consistency' ").

73. *See* Rule 8(e)(2). *See also American Int'l Adjustment Co. v. Galvin*, 86 F.3d 1455, 1461 (7th Cir. 1996) (commenting that "a pleader may assert contradictory statements of fact only when legitimately in doubt about the facts in question").

74. *See Holman v. Indiana*, 211 F.3d 399, 407 (7th Cir.2000) ("While the [pleaders] need not use particular words to plead in the alternative, they must use a formulation from which it can be reasonably inferred that this is what they were doing"), *cert. denied*, 531 U.S. 880, 121 S.Ct. 191, 148 L.Ed.2d 132 (2000).

75. *See In re Livent, Inc. Noteholders Sec. Litig.*, 151 F.Supp.2d 371 (S.D.N.Y.2001) (commenting that Rule 8(e) does not "grant[] plaintiffs license to plead inconsistent assertions of facts within the allegations that serve as the factual predicates for an independent, unitary claim. Internally conflicting factual assertions that constitute integral components of a claim must be distinguished from a permissible alternative statement embodying a theory of a whole sufficient claim.") (citation omitted).

76. *See Rodriguez-Suris v. Montesinos*, 123 F.3d 10, 20 (1st Cir.1997); *Independent Enters. Inc. v. Pittsburgh Water & Sewer Auth.*, 103 F.3d 1165, 1175 (3d Cir.1997); *Henry v. Daytop Village, Inc.*, 42 F.3d 89, 95 (2d Cir.1994); *McCalden v. California Library Ass'n*, 955 F.2d 1214, 1219 (9th Cir.1990), *cert. denied*, 504 U.S. 957, 112 S.Ct. 2306, 119 L.Ed.2d 227 (1992). *See also American Int'l Adjustment Co. v. Galvin*, 86 F.3d 1455, 1460 (7th Cir.1996) (noting that, in pleading context, Rules abolish doctrine of election of remedies).

77. *See Astroworks, Inc. v. Astroexhibit, Inc.*, 257 F.Supp.2d 609, 615 n.10 (S.D.N.Y.2003); *Friedmann v. United States*, 107 F.Supp.2d 502, 510–11 (D.N.J.2000).

78. *Cf. Montrose Medical Group Participating Savings Plan v. Bulger*, 243 F.3d 773, 782 (3d Cir.2001) (judicial estoppel will not apply to the assertion of contrary positions in different proceedings when the initial claim was never accepted or adopted by the court).

RULE 8(f). CONSTRUCTION OF PLEADINGS

CORE CONCEPT

As long as the pleading provides the adverse party with proper notice of the claim or defense, courts will not construe the pleading hypertechnically.

All Pleadings Construed Liberally

The "fundamental tenor of the Rules is one of liberality rather than technicality."[79] Because Rule 8(f) requires the courts to construe pleadings "as to do justice", all pleadings are construed liberally.[80] Consequently, courts will not rely solely on the labels used by the pleader to describe claims or defenses, but may reach deeper and seek out the true substance of the allegations.[81] Where those allegations, so construed, would state a cognizable claim or defense, the requirements of Rule 8 are satisfied.

APPLICATIONS

Inferring Types of Relief Not Actually Demanded

Although liberally construed, a pleading will not be construed in a manner that would entitle the pleader to seek a type of relief not concisely demanded in the allegations, particularly where such a construction would prejudice an opponent.[82]

Pleadings Drafted by Laypersons

Courts generally apply less stringent standards to pleadings drafted by laypersons, such as *pro se habeas corpus* petitions and social security applications.[83]

ADDITIONAL RESEARCH REFERENCES

Wright & Miller, *Federal Practice and Procedure* §§ 1201–1290.

C.J.S. Federal Civil Procedure §§ 252–280 et seq., 301–308.

West's Key No. Digests, Federal Civil Procedure ⚿631–653, 654–657, 671–680, 731–745, 751–759.

79. *See Minger v. Green*, 239 F.3d 793, 799 (6th Cir.2001).

80. *See, e.g., Rodriguez v. Doral Mortg. Corp.*, 57 F.3d 1168, 1171 (1st Cir.1995) (noting that while courts construe pleadings generously, defendants enjoy right to know in advance the nature of the claims asserted against them); *Brinson v. Linda Rose Joint Venture*, 53 F.3d 1044, 1049 (9th Cir.1995)("Rule 8(f) . . . requires a liberal reading of complaints.").

81. *See Mead Corp. v. ABB Power Generation, Inc.*, 319 F.3d 790, 795 (6th Cir.2003) (noting that courts do "not rely solely on labels", but "probe deeper and examine the substance of the complaint"). *See also Minger v. Green*, 239 F.3d 793, 799 (6th Cir.2001) (construing claim labeled as "negligent misrepresentation" (which would have been barred by discretionary function doctrine) as one for intentional misrepresentation (which could go forward)).

82. *See Seven Words LLC v. Network Solutions*, 260 F.3d 1089, 1098 (9th Cir.2001) (where damages claim was made years into litigation, after various representations that only declaratory and injunctive relief was sought, after a motion to dismiss, and only days before oral argument on appeal, court joins other Courts of Appeals in declining to read a damages claim into complaint).

83. *See Hughes v. Rowe*, 449 U.S. 5, 101 S.Ct. 173, 66 L.Ed.2d 163 (1980), *cert. denied*, 528 U.S. 1155, 120 S.Ct. 1162, 145 L.Ed.2d 1073 (2000); *Haines v. Kerner*, 404 U.S. 519, 92 S.Ct. 594, 30 L.Ed.2d 652 (1972).

RULE 9

PLEADING SPECIAL MATTERS

(a) Capacity. It is not necessary to aver the capacity of a party to sue or be sued or the authority of a party to sue or be sued in a representative capacity or the legal existence of an organized association of persons that is made a party, except to the extent required to show the jurisdiction of the court. When a party desires to raise an issue as to the legal existence of any party or the capacity of any party to sue or be sued or the authority of a party to sue or be sued in a representative capacity, the party desiring to raise the issue shall do so by specific negative averment, which shall include such supporting particulars as are peculiarly within the pleader's knowledge.

(b) Fraud, Mistake, Condition of the Mind. In all averments of fraud or mistake, the circumstances constituting fraud or mistake shall be stated with particularity. Malice, intent, knowledge, and other condition of mind of a person may be averred generally.

(c) Conditions Precedent. In pleading the performance or occurrence of conditions precedent, it is sufficient to aver generally that all conditions precedent have been performed or have occurred. A denial of performance or occurrence shall be specifically and with particularity.

(d) Official Document or Act. In pleading an official document or official act it is sufficient to aver that the document was issued or the act done in compliance with law.

(e) Judgment. In pleading a judgment or decision of a domestic or foreign court, judicial or quasi-judicial tribunal, or of a board or officer, it is sufficient to aver the judgment or decision without setting forth matter showing jurisdiction to render it.

(f) Time and Place. For the purpose of testing the sufficiency of a pleading, averments of time and place are material and shall be considered like all other averments of material matter.

(g) Special Damage. When items of special damage are claimed, they shall be specifically stated.

(h) Admiralty and Maritime Claims. A pleading or count setting forth a claim for relief within the admiralty and maritime jurisdiction that is also within the jurisdiction of the district court on some other ground may contain a statement identifying the claim as an admiralty or maritime claim for the purposes of Rules 14(c), 38(e), 82, and the Supplemental Rules for Certain Admiralty and Maritime Claims. If the claim is cognizable only in admiralty, it is an admiralty or maritime claim for those purposes whether so identified or not. The amendment of a pleading to add or withdraw an identifying statement is governed by the principles of Rule 15. A case that includes an admiralty or maritime claim within this subdivision is an admiralty case within 28 U.S.C. § 1292(a)(3).

[Amended effective July 1, 1966; July 1, 1968; July 1, 1970; August 1, 1987, April 11, 1997, effective December 1, 1997.]

AUTHORS' COMMENTARY ON RULE 9

PURPOSE AND SCOPE

Special requirements apply for pleading capacity, fraud, mistake, conditions precedent, official documents or acts, judgments, time and place, special damages, and admiralty and maritime claims. Those special requirements are set out in Rule 9.

RULE 9(a). CAPACITY

CORE CONCEPT

Unless necessary to establish the court's subject matter jurisdiction over the dispute, a pleading need not aver capacity. A defendant may challenge the plaintiff's capacity, but must do so by specific negative averment in a responsive pleading or motion.

APPLICATIONS

Pleading Capacity When Jurisdictional

Unless it is necessary to establish the jurisdiction of the federal courts, a party's capacity need not be pleaded. When necessary to establish jurisdiction, however, the party's capacity must be averred.[1]

Procedure For Challenging Capacity

Ordinarily, a litigant seeking to challenge (a) a party's legal existence, (b) a party's capacity to sue or be sued, or (c) a party's authority to sue or be sued in a representative capacity must raise the issue by "specific negative averment" in a responsive pleading or pre-answer

1. *See Moore v. City of Harriman*, 272 F.3d 769, 772–74 (6th Cir.2001) (noting division among appellate courts as to whether, given limitations of Eleventh Amendment, a Section 1983 defendant's "capacity" must be formally alleged in the complaint, and ruling that such capacity may be pleaded or, in certain circumstances, discerned under "course of proceedings" test), *cert. denied*, 536 U.S. 922, 122 S.Ct. 2586, 153 L.Ed.2d 776 (2002).

motion.[2] This "specific negative averment" must, additionally, include all specific facts that are "peculiarly within the pleader's knowledge".[3] Parties have successfully asserted lack of capacity by a motion to dismiss under Rule 12(b)(6), a motion for judgment on the pleadings under Rule 12(c), a motion for summary judgment under Rule 56, and at trial by a motion to dismiss when evidence is presented demonstrating a lack of capacity.[4]

Waiver By Failing To Raise Lack Of Capacity

The defense of lack of capacity may be waived if it is not timely and specifically asserted by the party challenging it.[5] Waiver might not occur, however, where the defect in a party's capacity is affirmatively apparent from the face of the complaint, and a "specific negative averment" to challenge capacity is found to be unnecessary.[6] Similarly, when capacity is jurisdictional (*i.e.,* such as when suing the United States or when relevant to a party's citizenship for diversity jurisdiction), a party may assert the lack of capacity to vitiate subject matter jurisdiction *at any time*, as provided by Rule 12(h)(3), or the court may raise the issue *sua sponte*.[7]

RULE 9(b). FRAUD, MISTAKE, CONDITION OF MIND

CORE CONCEPT

A party must plead fraud and mistake with particularity, but may plead malice, intent, knowledge, and other conditions of mind generally.

APPLICATIONS

Goal of Pleading With Particularity

Some claims—like fraud—may have an *in terrorem* or stigmatizing effect on defendants and their reputations.[8] Requiring that such claims

2. *See* Rule 9(a). *See also Federal Deposit Ins. Corp. v. Calhoun*, 34 F.3d 1291, 1299 (5th Cir.1994); *Brown v. Williamson*, 134 F.Supp.2d 1286, 1291 (M.D.Ala.2001).

3. *See* Rule 9(a).

4. *See e.g., Cooper v. Wal–Mart Stores, Inc.*, 959 F.Supp. 964, 966 n. 2 (C.D.Ill.1997) (commenting that case law supports notion that capacity issues under Rule 17(b) may be raised by motion to dismiss).

5. *See, e.g., De Saracho v. Custom Food Machinery, Inc.*, 206 F.3d 874, 878 (9th Cir.2000), *cert. denied*, 531 U.S. 876, 121 S.Ct. 183, 148 L.Ed.2d 126 (2000) (No. 00–10); *Swaim v. Moltan Co.*, 73 F.3d 711, 718 (7th Cir.1996), *cert. denied*, 517 U.S. 1244, 116 S.Ct. 2499, 135 L.Ed.2d 191 (1996); *FDIC v. Calhoun*, 34 F.3d 1291, 1299 (5th Cir.1994); *Howerton v. Designer Homes by Georges, Inc.*, 950 F.2d 281, 283 (5th Cir.1992); *Wagner Furniture Interiors, Inc. v. Kemner's Georgetown Manor, Inc.*, 929 F.2d 343, 345 (7th Cir.1991).

6. *See Brown v. Williamson*, 134 F.Supp.2d 1286, 1291 (M.D.Ala.2001).

7. *See E.R. Squibb & Sons, Inc. v. Accident & Cas. Ins. Co.*, 160 F.3d 925, 935–36 (2d Cir. 1998) (if party with capacity defense is strategically not asserting it in order to preserve federal jurisdiction, court may assess the capacity of the parties *sua sponte*).

8. *See Vess v. Ciba–Geigy Corp. USA*, 317 F.3d 1097, 1104 (9th Cir.2003) (noting that Rule 9(b)'s heightened pleading requirements comports with goal of protecting defendants from reputational harm); *Schaller Tel. Co. v. Golden Sky Sys., Inc.*, 298 F.3d 736, 745 (8th Cir.2002) (noting higher degree of notice pleading in fraud cases due to potentially damaging allegations of immoral and criminal behavior); *Ziemba v. Cascade Int'l, Inc.*, 256 F.3d 1194, 1202 (11th Cir. 2001) (noting important purpose served by particularity rule in fraud actions to alert defendants to precise misconduct alleged to protect

be pleaded with particularity (1) ensures that the defendants have fair notice of the plaintiff's claim, (2) helps safeguard the defendants against spurious accusations, and the resulting reputational harm, (3) reduces the possibility that a meritless fraud claim can remain in the case, by ensuring that the full and complete factual allegation is not postponed until discovery, and (4) protects defendants against "strike" suits.[9]

Fraud

A party must plead each of the elements of fraud with particularity.[10] When pleading fraud the claimant must allege more than mere conclusory allegations of fraud or the technical elements of fraud.[11] The added pleading burden varies somewhat from circuit to circuit, and claim to claim. The typical common law elements of fraud are: (1) false representation or omission of material fact; (2) knowledge of or belief in its falsity by person making it; (3) belief in its truth by receiver of statement; (4) intent that statement will be acted upon; and (5) detrimental reliance by the person who was deceived.[12]

- *Claims "Grounded" in Fraud:* The "particularity" requirement of Rule 9(b) applies not only to claims expressly denominated as "fraud" allegations, but also to claims that are "grounded" in fraud or that "sound" in fraud.[13]

- *Federal Statutory Fraud Claims:* Generally, the "particularity" requirement of Rule 9(b) also applies to federal statutory fraud claims as well as federal common law fraud claims.[14] However, the issue of precisely how this Rule (and its interpretative precedent) interrelates

against spurious charges of immoral or fraudulent behavior); *Payton v. Rush–Presbyterian–St. Luke's Medical Ctr.*, 184 F.3d 623 (7th Cir.1999) (enhanced pleading standard for fraud is justified by the great harm a fraud claim can cause to business reputation).

9. *See In re Rockefeller Ctr. Props., Inc. Secs. Litig.*, 311 F.3d 198, 216 (3d Cir.2002); *Schaller Tel. Co. v. Golden Sky Sys., Inc.*, 298 F.3d 736, 745 (8th Cir.2002); *Harrison v. Westinghouse Savannah River Co.*, 176 F.3d 776, 784 (4th Cir.1999); *Campaniello Imports, Ltd. v. Saporiti Italia S.p.A.*, 117 F.3d 655 (2d Cir.1997); *Brooks v. Blue Cross & Blue Shield of Florida, Inc.*, 116 F.3d 1364, 1370–71 (11th Cir.1997); *Suna v. Bailey Corp.*, 107 F.3d 64, 68 (1st Cir.1997); *Harsco Corp. v. Segui*, 91 F.3d 337, 347 (2d Cir.1996).

10. *See, e.g., Shushany v. Allwaste, Inc.*, 992 F.2d 517, 521 (5th Cir.1993).

11. *See Schaller Tel. Co. v. Golden Sky Sys., Inc.*, 298 F.3d 736, 745 (8th Cir.2002); *In re Burlington Coat Factory Sec. Litig.*, 114 F.3d 1410, 1418 (3d Cir.1997); *Suna v. Bailey Corp.*, 107 F.3d 64, 68 (1st Cir.1997); *Chill v. General Elec. Co.*, 101 F.3d 263, 267 (2d Cir.1996).

12. *See, e.g., In re Rockefeller Ctr. Props., Inc. Secs. Litig.*, 311 F.3d 198, 216 (3d Cir.2002); *In re Burlington Coat Factory Sec. Litig.*, 114 F.3d 1410, (3d Cir.1997); *Williams v. WMX Technologies, Inc.*, 112 F.3d 175, 177 (5th Cir. 1997), *cert. denied*, 522 U.S. 966, 118 S.Ct. 412, 139 L.Ed.2d 315 (1997); *In re Westinghouse Sec. Litig.*, 90 F.3d 696, 710 (3d Cir.1996).

13. *See Vess v. Ciba–Geigy Corp. USA*, 317 F.3d 1097, 1103–04 (9th Cir.2003).

14. *See, e.g., Abrams v. Baker Hughes Inc.*, 292 F.3d 424, 430 (5th Cir.2002) (applies in Private Securities Litigation Reform Act claims); *United States ex rel. Clausen v. Laboratory Corp. of America, Inc.*, 290 F.3d 1301, 1308–09 (11th Cir.2002) (applies in False Claims Act lawsuits), *cert. denied*, 537 U.S. 1105, 123 S.Ct. 870, 154 L.Ed.2d 774 (2003); *United States ex rel. Totten v. Bombardier Corp.*, 286 F.3d 542, 551–52 (D.C.Cir.2002) (same); *Warden v. McLelland*, 288 F.3d 105, 114 (3d Cir.2002) (applies in mail/wire fraud RICO cases); *In re Burlington Coat Factory Sec. Litig.*, 114 F.3d 1410, 1417 (3d Cir.1997) (particularity requirement applies in federal securities fraud cases); *Williams v. WMX Techs., Inc.*, 112 F.3d 175, 177 (5th Cir.1997) (applies to securities fraud and RICO claims), *cert. denied*, 522 U.S. 966, 118 S.Ct. 412, 139 L.Ed.2d 315 (1997).

with a particular federal statute (such as the Private Securities Litigation Reform Act[15]) remains a not fully resolved question.[16]

- *State Law Fraud Claims:* The "particularity" requirement applies to both federal and State-law fraud claims.[17]

Mistake

A party must also plead mistake with particularity. When pleading mistake with particularity, the pleader should state what the parties intended and identify the mistaken result.

Amount of Particularity Required

The amount of particularity or specificity required for pleading fraud or mistake will differ from case to case,[18] but generally depends upon the amount of access the pleader has to the specific facts,[19] considering the complexity of the claim, the relationship of the parties, the context in which the alleged fraud or mistake occurs,[20] and the amount of specificity necessary for the adverse party to prepare a responsive pleading.[21] The particularity requirement of Rule 9 is not,

15. *See* 15 U.S.C.A. § 78u–4(b)(2) ("In any private action arising under this chapter in which the plaintiff may recover money damages only on proof that the defendant acted with a particular state of mind, the complaint shall, with respect to each act or omission alleged to violate this chapter, state with particularity facts giving rise to a strong inference that the defendant acted with the required state of mind").

16. *Compare In re K-tel Int'l, Inc. Secs. Litig.*, 300 F.3d 881, 889 (8th Cir.2002) (PSLRA "embodies the pleading requirement" of Rule 9(b)) *and ABC Arbitrage Plaintiffs Group v. Tchuruk*, 291 F.3d 336, 349 (5th Cir.2002) (Rule 9(b) particularity requirement sets "the same standard" required by the PSLRA) *with Adams v. Kinder Morgan, Inc.*, 340 F.3d 1083, 1096 (10th Cir.2003) (PSLRA imposed more stringent requirement for pleading scienter than had Rule 9(b)) *and No. 84 Employer–Teamster Joint Council Pension Trust Fund v. America West Holding Corp.*, 320 F.3d 920, 931 (9th Cir.2003), *petition for cert. filed*, 72 U.S.L.W. 3148 (U.S. Aug. 14, 2003) (No. 03–250) (same) *and In re Rockefeller Ctr. Props., Inc. Sec. Litig.*, 311 F.3d 198, 217 (3d Cir.2002) (same). *See also Rosenzweig v. Azurix Corp.*, 332 F.3d 854, 866 (5th Cir.2003) (noting that PSLRA, "at a minimum", incorporates Rule 9(b)'s particularity requirement).

17. *See Vess v. Ciba–Geigy Corp. USA*, 317 F.3d 1097, 1102–03 (9th Cir.2003); *Williams v. WMX Technologies, Inc.*, 112 F.3d 175, 177 (5th Cir.1997) (finding "no principled reason" why State law fraud claims should escape pleading requirements of federal rules), *cert. denied*, 522 U.S. 966, 118 S.Ct. 412, 139 L.Ed.2d 315 (1997).

18. *See Benchmark Elec., Inc. v. J.M. Huber Corp.*, 343 F.3d 719, 724 (5th Cir.2003), *modified on other grounds*, 355 F.3d 356 (5th Cir.2003).

19. *See, e.g., In re Rockefeller Ctr. Props., Inc. Secs. Litig.*, 311 F.3d 198, 216 (3d Cir. 2002) (noting that rigidity of pleading requirements may be relaxed in situations where requisite factual information is peculiarly within defendant's knowledge or control); *Devaney v. Chester*, 813 F.2d 566, 569 (2d Cir.1987) ("[W]e recognize that the degree of particularity required should be determined in light of such circumstances as whether the plaintiff has had an opportunity to take discovery of those who may possess knowledge of the pertinent facts.").

20. *See, e.g., In re Craftmatic Sec. Litig. v. Kraftsow*, 890 F.2d 628, 645 (3d Cir.1989)("[I]n the case of corporate fraud, plaintiff cannot be expected to have personal knowledge of the details of corporate internal affairs."). *See also In re GlenFed, Inc. Sec. Litig.*, 60 F.3d 591 (9th Cir.1995)("In cases of corporate fraud where the false and misleading information is conveyed in prospectuses, registration statements, annual reports, press releases, or other 'group-published information,' it is reasonable to presume that these are collective actions of the officers. [Thus,] a plaintiff fulfills the particularity requirement of Rule 9(b) by pleading the misrepresentations with particularity and where possible the roles of the individual defendants in the misrepresentations.").

21. *See Dudley v. Southeastern Factor & Finance Corp.*, 446 F.2d 303 (5th Cir.1971), *cert. denied*, 404 U.S. 858, 92 S.Ct. 109, 30 L.Ed.2d 101.

however, intended to abrogate or mute the Rule 8 "notice" pleading standard that applies in federal courts, and the two Rules must be read in harmony with one another.[22] Plaintiffs are still obligated to plead only notice of a fraud or mistake claim; Rule 9(b) simply compels a higher degree of notice.[23] Thus, Rule 9(b) generally requires the pleader to fill-in "the first paragraph of any newspaper story"—the "who, what, when, where, and how" of the alleged scheme.[24] In the context of fraud claims, many courts require the pleader to allege (1) the time, place, and contents of the false representations or omissions, and explain how they were fraudulent, (2) the identity of the person making the misrepresentations, (3) how the misrepresentations misled the plaintiff, and (4) what the speaker gained from the fraud.[25]

Pleading on Information and Belief

The rigors of Rule 9(b) do not necessarily foreclose pleading upon information and belief, although such pleading is still subject to the Rule's particularity requirements and, further, the pleader generally must aver the facts upon which the information and belief rests.[26]

Exception to Particularity Requirement

If the facts necessary to plead fraud or mistake are peculiarly within the defendant's knowledge, courts may relax the particularity requirement of Rule 9(b) in favor of permitting discovery to proceed.[27]

22. *See Schaller Tel. Co. v. Golden Sky Sys., Inc.*, 298 F.3d 736, 745 (8th Cir.2002); *Ziemba v. Cascade Int'l, Inc.*, 256 F.3d 1194, 1202 (11th Cir.2001).

23. *See Schaller Tel. Co. v. Golden Sky Sys., Inc.*, 298 F.3d 736, 746 (8th Cir.2002).

24. *See In re Alpharma Inc. Secs. Litig.*, 372 F.3d 137, 148 (3d Cir. 2004); *Alternative Sys. Concepts, Inc. v. Synopsys, Inc.*, 374 F.3d 23, 29 (1st Cir. 2004); *United States ex rel. Doe v. Dow Chem. Co.*, 343 F.3d 325, 328 (5th Cir. 2003); *DiLeo v. Ernst & Young*, 901 F.2d 624, 627 (7th Cir.1990), *cert. denied*, 498 U.S. 941, 111 S.Ct. 347, 112 L.Ed.2d 312 (1990).

25. *See, e.g., Yuhasz v. Brush Wellman, Inc.*, 341 F.3d 559, 563 (6th Cir.2003) (must allege time, place, content of alleged misrepresentation, fraudulent scheme, fraudulent intent, and resulting injury); *Benchmark Elec., Inc. v. J.M. Huber Corp.*, 343 F.3d 719, 724 (5th Cir.2003), *modified on other grounds*, 355 F.3d 356 (5th Cir.2003) (must allege "the particulars" of time, place, contents of misrepresentations, identity of speaker, and what was obtained thereby); *Arruda v. Sears, Roebuck & Co.*, 310 F.3d 13, 18–19 (1st Cir.2002) (requiring time, place, and content of alleged misrepresentations); *Schaller Tel. Co. v. Golden Sky Sys., Inc.*, 298 F.3d 736, 746 (8th Cir.2002) (requiring time, place, and contents, speaker identity, and object obtained); *Board of Trustees of Teamsters Local 863 Pension Fund v. Foodtown, Inc.*, 296 F.3d 164, 172 n.10 (3d Cir. 2002) (requiring precise allegations of date, time, and place, or alternatively some other "measure of substantiation"); *Ziemba v. Cascade Int'l, Inc.*, 256 F.3d 1194, 1202 (11th Cir.2001) (requiring specification of statements or omissions, the time and place of each state, the speaker, a description of how they misled the claimant, and what defendants obtained as a consequence); *Koehler v. Bank of Bermuda (New York) Ltd.*, 209 F.3d 130, 136 (2d Cir.2000), *amended*, 229 F.3d 424 (2d Cir.2000) (requiring allegations to specify the precise fraudulent statements, the speaker, where and when the statements were made, and why the statements were fraudulent); *Koch v. Koch Indus., Inc.*, 203 F.3d 1202, 1236 (10th Cir.2000) (requiring complaint to state the time, place, and contents of the false representation, the speaker, and the consequences of the fraud), *cert. denied*, 531 U.S. 926, 121 S.Ct. 302, 148 L.Ed.2d 242 (2000); *Firestone v. Firestone*, 76 F.3d 1205, 1211 (D.C.Cir.1996).

26. *See United States ex rel. Karvelas v. Melrose–Wakefield Hosp.*, 360 F.3d 220, 226 (1st Cir. 2004), *petition for cert. pending*, No. 03–1901 (U.S. June 22, 2004).

27. *See, e.g., In re Rockefeller Ctr. Props., Inc. Secs. Litig.*, 311 F.3d 198, 216 (3d Cir.2002) (noting that rigidity of pleading requirements may be relaxed in situations where requisite

Although the rigors of Rule 9(b) may be relaxed by these courts, they are not ignored altogether: the pleader must still plead an adequate factual premise for concluding that the fraud claim is a plausible one.[28] Other courts hold otherwise, refusing to relax the requirements of Rule 9(b) even where the facts lie exclusively within the defendant's knowledge.[29] Whether this relaxation is even permitted in the context of certain federal statutory fraud claims remains an unresolved question.[30]

Malice, Intent, Knowledge, and Condition of Mind

A party may allege malice, intent, knowledge, and condition of mind generally, as with any ordinary allegation under Rule 8.[31]

Pleading Tensions Between Fraud and Intent

There is some internal tension between Rule 9(b)'s requirement that fraud—including the fraud element of intent—be pleaded with particularity, and Rule 9(b)'s provision that intent itself may be pleaded generally. Courts usually resolve this apparent inconsistency by requiring that when the claim is based upon allegations of fraud, the party has a duty to follow the requirement to plead fraud with some degree of particularity, and intent generally.[32] Nevertheless, many courts require

factual information is peculiarly within defendant's knowledge or control); *Corley v. Rosewood Care Ctr., Inc.*, 142 F.3d 1041, 1051 (7th Cir. 1998) (commenting that particularity requirement "must be relaxed where the plaintiff lacks access to all facts necessary to detail his claim"); *In re Burlington Coat Factory Sec. Litig.*, 114 F.3d 1410, 1418 (3d Cir.1997) (noting that courts should be sensitive to risk that strict application of particularity rule prior to discovery could permit sophisticated defrauders to conceal their fraud); *Tuchman v. DSC Communications Corp.*, 14 F.3d 1061, 1068 (5th Cir. 1994)(accord, but noting that exception is not a "license to base claims of fraud on speculation and conclusory allegations"). *See also United States ex rel. Karvelas v. Melrose–Wakefield Hosp.*, 360 F.3d 220, 228–29 (1st Cir. 2004), *petition for cert. pending*, No. 03–1901 (U.S. June 22, 2004) (noting "relaxation" as permitting a general pleading originally, which must later be amended, following discovery, with particulars); *Katz v. Household Int'l, Inc.*, 91 F.3d 1036 (7th Cir.1996)("We acknowledge that Rule 9(b) does not require plaintiffs to plead facts to which they lack access prior to discovery").

28. *See In re Rockefeller Ctr. Props., Inc. Secs. Litig.*, 311 F.3d 198, 216 (3d Cir.2002) (noting that even where defendant retains control over information flow, "boilerplate and conclusory allegations" are not sufficient, and the pleaders must still include "factual allegations that make their theoretically viable claim plausible").

29. *See, e.g., Koch v. Koch Indus., Inc.*, 203 F.3d 1202, 1237 (10th Cir.2000) (explaining that prior precedent did not relax Rule 9(b)'s particularity requirements when the fraud facts are within an opponent's knowledge and control; however, those facts can be premised on information and belief), *cert. denied*, 531 U.S. 926, 121 S.Ct. 302, 148 L.Ed.2d 242 (2000); *Greebel v. FTP Software, Inc.*, 194 F.3d 185, 193 (1st Cir. 1999) (holding that even when allegations are premised on information and belief, the facts supporting that belief must be set forth in the complaint).

30. *See* Federal Statutory Fraud Claims discussion above.

31. *See Wight v. Bankamerica Corp.*, 219 F.3d 79 (2d Cir.2000) (although actual fraud must be alleged with particularity, the intent of the perpetrator need not be alleged with specificity). *But see Johnson v. Waddell & Reed, Inc.*, 74 F.3d 147, 150 (7th Cir.1996)("At least some facts need to be pled under Rule 9(b) to show why this breach of contract is also a malicious tort.").

32. *See, e.g., Wight v. Bankamerica Corp.*, 219 F.3d 79 (2d Cir.2000) (although actual fraud must be alleged with particularity, the intent of the perpetrator need not be alleged with specificity); *In re GlenFed, Inc., Sec. Litig.*, 42 F.3d 1541 (9th Cir.1994)(en banc)(same result; rejecting contrary precedent). *See also Chill v. General Elec. Co.*, 101 F.3d 263, 267 (2d Cir.1996) (commenting that speaker's intent need not be pleaded with specificity because plaintiff realistically

that the pleaded facts must give rise to a "strong inference of fraudulent intent".[33]

Group Pleading

The particularized pleading requirement is designed to notify each defendant of his, her, or its purported role in the alleged misconduct. Lumping multiple defendants together in a group pleading (*e.g.*, "defendants misled the plaintiff by stating ...") defeats this notice objective and, thus, may be found to be improper under Rule 9(b).[34]

Counterclaims and Affirmative Defenses

When asserting fraud or mistake in counterclaims or affirmative defenses, the pleader must assert fraud or mistake there with particularity.

Non-Party Fraud or Mistake

It has been held that where fraud or mistake was caused by non-parties[35] or when alleging that non-parties were defrauded,[36] a party may plead fraud or mistake more generally.

Opposing an Insufficiently Particular Pleading

A party may oppose a pleading that fails to plead fraud or mistake with particularity by asserting a Rule 12(e) motion for a more definite statement,[37] a Rule 12(f) motion to strike, or a Rule 12(b) motion to dismiss.[38] Often, parties assert these motions in the alternative.

Granting Leave to Amend

Where a complaint is dismissed for failing to allege with particulari-

cannot be held to allege a defendant's actual state of mind).

33. *See Campaniello Imports, Ltd. v. Saporiti Italia S.p.A.*, 117 F.3d 655 (2d Cir.1997); *In re Burlington Coat Factory Sec. Litig.*, 114 F.3d 1410, 1418 (3d Cir.1997) (quoting authority, that requisite inference of fraud may be shown either (a) by alleging facts to show that defendants had both motive and opportunity to commit fraud, or (b) by alleging facts that constitute strong circumstantial evidence of conscious misbehavior or recklessness); *Suna v. Bailey Corp.*, 107 F.3d 64, 68 (1st Cir.1997); *Chill v. General Elec. Co.*, 101 F.3d 263, 267 (2d Cir.1996); *DiLeo v. Ernst & Young*, 901 F.2d 624, 629 (7th Cir.1990), *cert. denied*, 498 U.S. 941, 111 S.Ct. 347, 112 L.Ed.2d 312 (1990). *But see In re GlenFed, Inc. Sec. Litig.*, 42 F.3d 1541, 1545–47 (9th Cir.1994) (in banc) (rejecting such requirement, holding that plaintiff need not alleged facts from which intent to commit fraud may be inferred).

34. *See Brooks v. Blue Cross & Blue Shield of Florida, Inc.*, 116 F.3d 1364, 1381 (11th Cir. 1997); *Vicom, Inc. v. Harbridge Merchant Servs., Inc.*, 20 F.3d 771, 777–78 (7th Cir.1994); *Mills v. Polar Molecular Corp.*, 12 F.3d 1170, 1175 (2d Cir.1993). *But see Phillips v. Scientific–Atlanta, Inc.*, 374 F.3d 1015, 1018–19 (11th Cir. 2004) (noting permissive "group pleading doctrine" in securities cases, which allows presumption of group responsibility for statements and omissions).

35. *See, e.g., Uni*Quality, Inc. v. Infotronx, Inc.*, 974 F.2d 918, 923 (7th Cir.1992) "([W]here a plaintiff is alleging fraud against a third party, less detail may be required.").

36. *See, e.g., Segal v. Gordon*, 467 F.2d 602, 607 (2d Cir.1972) ("when the pleader is asserting that third persons have been defrauded, he may be unable to detail the claim and less specificity should be required.").

37. *See, e.g., Coffey v. Foamex L.P.*, 2 F.3d 157, 162 (6th Cir.1993)(approving use of Rule 12(e) to force correction of complaint defective under Rule 9(b)).

38. *See, e.g., Kowal v. MCI Communications Corp.*, 16 F.3d 1271, 1279 (D.C.Cir. 1994)(affirming dismissal under Rule 12(b)(6) for failure to meet requirements of Rule 9(b)).

ty, leave to amend should generally be granted freely.[39] Leave to amend may be denied, however, where an amendment is "futile" and could never offer the particularity necessary under Rule 9.[40]

RULE 9(c). CONDITIONS PRECEDENT

CORE CONCEPT

Where applicable to the cause of action pleaded (such as in contract cases and in certain exhaustion contexts), a plaintiff may aver *generally* that all conditions precedent have been performed or have occurred. Conversely, a reply alleging that a requisite condition precedent has *not* been performed or has not occurred must be set forth *specifically* and with particularity.

APPLICATION

Applies to Both Contractual And Statutory Conditions Precedent

The pleading practice set forth in Rule 9(c) for conditions precedent applies whether the conditions precedent are contractual or statutory in nature.[41]

Rule Sets Procedure Only

Rule 9(c) does *not* require the conditions precedent be alleged; rather, the Rule simply provides the procedure for doing so.[42]

General Allegations Sufficient To Plead Conditions Precedent

The complaint does not need to allege in detail how each condition was performed; the allegations are sufficient if they aver generally that all conditions precedent have been performed[43] and plead facts from which an inference arises that all conditions precedent have been met.[44]

Specific Allegations Necessary To Challenge Conditions Precedent

Where a defendant seeks to challenge a plaintiff's allegation that a condition precedent has been fulfilled, the denial must be pleaded with specificity and particularity. Once the issue is joined in this way, the burden returns to plaintiff to prove that the condition precedent contested by the defendant has been met.[45]

39. *See United States ex rel. Willard v. Humana Health Plan of Texas Inc.*, 336 F.3d 375, 387 (5th Cir.2003); *Koehler v. Bank of Bermuda (New York) Ltd.*, 209 F.3d 130, 138 (2d Cir. 2000), *amended*, 229 F.3d 424 (2d Cir.2000); *In re Burlington Coat Factory Sec. Litig.*, 114 F.3d 1410, 1435 (3d Cir.1997).

40. *See Chill v. General Elec. Co.*, 101 F.3d 263, 271–72 (2d Cir.1996).

41. *See Walton v. Nalco Chem. Co.*, 272 F.3d 13, 21 n.13 (1st Cir.2001).

42. *See Kiernan v. Zurich Cos.*, 150 F.3d 1120, 1123–24 (9th Cir.1998).

43. *See, e.g., Wyatt v. Terhune*, 315 F.3d 1108, 1118 n.12 (9th Cir.2003), *cert. denied*, ___ U.S. ___, 124 S.Ct. 50, 157 L.Ed.2d 23 (2003); *Walton v. Nalco Chem. Co.*, 272 F.3d 13, 22 (1st Cir.2001); *Anderson v. United Tele. Co.*, 933 F.2d 1500, 1505 (10th Cir.1991), *cert. denied*, 502 U.S. 940, 112 S.Ct. 375, 116 L.Ed.2d 327 (1991); *Peterson v. Brownlee*, 314 F.Supp.2d 1150, 1153 (D.Kan. 2004).

44. *See Floorcoverings, Int'l, Ltd v. Swan*, 2000 WL 528480, at *4 (N.D.Ill.2000).

45. *See Hill v. Citibank Corp.*, 312 F.Supp.2d 464, 473–74 (S.D.N.Y. 2004); *Richey v. City of Lilburn*, 127 F.Supp.2d 1250, 1257 (N.D.Ga. 1999).

RULE 9(d). OFFICIAL DOCUMENT OR ACT

CORE CONCEPT

A party asserting the existence or legality of an official document need only assert that the official document was issued or the official act was performed legally. Conversely, a party opposing the official document or act must specifically assert the defect in the official document or the illegality of the official act.

RULE 9(e). JUDGMENT

CORE CONCEPT

When pleading the issuance of a judgment, a party need not set forth matter showing the jurisdiction of the tribunal issuing the judgment.

APPLICATION

Pleading Issuance of Judgment

When pleading the issuance of a judgment or a decision of any court, judicial or quasi-judicial tribunal, board, or officer, a party should specifically identify the judicial body issuing the judgment, the date of the judgment, the parties participating in the proceeding, and the character or effect of the judgment. A party challenging the judgment in the answer must specifically state the defect in the judgment, and cannot deny generally.

RULE 9(f). TIME AND PLACE

CORE CONCEPT

Time and space averments are material allegations and can, if appropriate, support a dismissal of a claim or defense.

APPLICATION

Specificity *Not* Required, But If Made, Averments Are Material

Rule 9(f) does *not* require that averments of time and place be pleaded specifically. What Rule 9(f) does is confirm that averments of time and place are material and can be considered in testing the sufficiency of a pleading. Thus, if the averments of time and place establish an obvious defense (such as time-bar), the inclusion of those averments can support a dismissal.[46]

46. *See Rosen ex rel. Egghead.Com, Inc. v. Brookhaven Capital Mgmt., Co.*, 179 F.Supp.2d 330, 334 (S.D.N.Y.2002) (noting that Rule does not obligate pleader to specifically allege time and place, "it merely states the significance of these allegations when they are actually interposed"); *Jairett v. First Montauk Secs. Corp.*, 203 F.R.D. 181 (E.D.Pa.2001) ("By 'material,' Rule 9(f) means such allegations are significant in that any difficulties with the allegations may cause immediate loss of a claim or defense. Thus, a date used by a claimant in pleading a claim for relief may trigger a dismissal if the statute of

RULE 9(g). SPECIAL DAMAGES

CORE CONCEPT

Special damages must be pleaded with particularity.

APPLICATIONS

Defined

Identifying special damages (which must be specially pleaded) is not always clear.[47] Generally, special damages are those damages that are proximately caused by the defendant's alleged wrongdoing, but which were unforeseeable or which might not come to the defendant's attention unless pleaded with specificity.[48] Emotional distress damages,[49] attorney's fees,[50] punitive damages,[51] defamation damages,[52] and damages flowing from trade disparagement[53] are examples of special damages that must be pleaded with specificity.

Specificity

A party should allege special damages by alleging actual damages with particularity and averring how those damages were the natural and direct result of the defendant's conduct.[54] A pleading is sufficiently specific if the opposing party can respond to the allegations of special damages.[55] This obligation is not "reducible to formula", and will depend on the nature of the claim at issue, the alleged injury, and the causal connection between the two.[56] Ordinarily, pleading an estimate of the final lost dollar amounts will be unnecessary.[57]

Consequences of Failing to Plead Special Damages

A party's failure to plead special damages with specificity may bar

limitations is shown to have run") (citation omitted).

47. *See 44 Liquormart, Inc. v. Rhode Island*, 940 F.Supp. 437, 438–39 (D.R.I.1996).

48. *See, e.g., LINC Fin. Corp. v. Onwuteaka*, 129 F.3d 917, 922 (7th Cir.1997) (noting that special damages "are damages that are unusual for the type of claim in question—that are not the natural damages associated with such a claim"); *V.I.M. Recyclers, L.P. v. Magner*, 271 F.Supp.2d 1072, 1074 (N.D.Ill.2003) (same).

49. *See Botosan v. Fitzhugh*, 13 F.Supp.2d 1047, 1053 (S.D.Cal.1998).

50. *See, e.g., United Indus., Inc. v. Simon–Hartley, Ltd.*, 91 F.3d 762 (5th Cir.1996); *Botosan v. Fitzhugh*, 13 F.Supp.2d 1047, 1053 (S.D.Cal.1998); *44 Liquormart, Inc. v. Rhode Island*, 940 F.Supp. 437, 439 (D.R.I.1996).

51. *See Teel v. United Technologies Pratt & Whitney*, 953 F.Supp. 1534, 1537 (S.D.Fla.1997).

52. *See Muzikowski v. Paramount Pictures Corp.*, 322 F.3d 918, 924–27 (7th Cir. 2003).

53. *See KBT Corp., Inc. v. Ceridian Corp.*, 966 F.Supp. 369 (E.D.Pa.1997).

54. *See Browning v. Clinton*, 292 F.3d 235, 245–46 (D.C.Cir.2002).

55. *See, e.g., Matos v. Ashford Presbyterian Community Hosp., Inc.*, 4 F.3d 47, 52 (1st Cir. 1993)("We believe the purpose [of Rule 9(g)] is to give notice; the more natural are the damages, the less the pleading is needed."); *Italiano v. Jones Chemicals, Inc.*, 908 F.Supp. 904, 907 (M.D.Fla.1995) (commenting that Rule 9(g) requires nothing more than specific statement permitting defendants to prepare responsive pleading and begin their defense).

56. *See Marseilles Hydro Power, LLC. v. Marseilles Land & Water Co.*, 2003 WL 259142, at *6 (N.D.Ill.2003).

57. *See Marseilles Hydro Power, LLC. v. Marseilles Land & Water Co.*, 2003 WL 259142, at *6 (N.D.Ill.2003).

that party's recovery for special damages.[58] Vague, conclusory catch-all allegations (such as "including but not limited to") are likely to be insufficient under Rule 9(g).[59] However, since there is no timing requirement in the Rule, a party can seek leave from the court to amend to include further items of special damages in the pleading.[60]

RULE 9(h). ADMIRALTY AND MARITIME CLAIMS

CORE CONCEPT

Special rules apply to admiralty and maritime claims.[61] When the plaintiff asserts an admiralty or maritime claim, the plaintiff[62] should identify in the complaint that the case is one in admiralty. When a party asserts a claim containing an admiralty claim and another basis of subject matter jurisdiction, the party may designate whether the claim is premised on admiralty jurisdiction or on another basis of subject matter jurisdiction.[63]

APPLICATIONS

Significance of Election: No Jury Trial in Admiralty

Ordinarily, choosing to proceed in admiralty means that the claims in the case are decided by the court, and not by a jury.[64]

Type of Designation Required

To invoke the federal courts' admiralty jurisdiction, a plaintiff must include an affirmative statement in the pleadings identifying the proceeding as an admiralty or maritime claim.[65] Failing to so identify the

58. *See, e.g., United Indus., Inc. v. Simon-Hartley, Ltd.*, 91 F.3d 762, 764 (5th Cir.1996) (failure to plead attorney's fees waives the right to collect them); *44 Liquormart, Inc. v. Rhode Island*, 940 F.Supp. 437, 439 (D.R.I.1996) (noting that court properly bars items of special damages that were not pleaded specifically pled). *Woodmont Corp. v. Rockwood Ctr. Partnership*, 811 F.Supp. 1478, 1484 (D.Kan.1993)(if complaint is not amended to reflect special damages, court is free to dismiss the case).

59. *See Marseilles Hydro Power, LLC. v. Marseilles Land & Water Co.*, 2003 WL 259142, at *6 (N.D.Ill.2003) (holding that court would not require answer to such "including but not limited to" allegation, and would not permit an unpleaded damages item to reach trial).

60. *See Jones v. Krautheim*, 208 F.Supp.2d 1173, 1178 (D.Colo.2002).

61. The full text of the *Supplemental Rules For Certain Admiralty And Maritime Claims* appears at the end of Part III of this text.

62. *See, e.g., Lewis v. United States*, 816 F.Supp. 1097, 1100–01 (E.D.Va.1993)(in appropriate cases, choice of invoking Rule 9(h) rests with plaintiff—who thereby may alter certain features of litigation, including availability of jury trial).

63. *See, e.g., Murphy v. Florida Keys Elec. Co-op. Ass'n*, 329 F.3d 1311, 1319 (11th Cir. 2003) (when claim has multiple jurisdictional bases, pleading may contain statement identifying claim as one in admiralty or maritime law); *Fedorczyk v. Caribbean Cruise Lines, Ltd.*, 82 F.3d 69, 73 (3d Cir.1996)(so holding; additionally, noting that plaintiff invoking admiralty jurisdiction must affirmatively identify claim in pleading as "admiralty or maritime claim").

64. *See Wingerter v. Chester Quarry Co.*, 185 F.3d 657 (7th Cir.1998); *Concordia Co. v. Panek*, 115 F.3d 67, 70–71 (1st Cir.1997); *Canal Barge Co. v. Commonwealth Edison Co.*, 2002 WL 206054, at *4 (N.D.Ill.2002); *Gaines v. Ampro Fisheries, Inc.*, 836 F.Supp. 347, 348–49 (E.D.Va. 1993). *But cf. Miles v. M/V HANSA CALEDONIA*, 245 F.Supp.2d 1261, 1263 (S.D.Ga.2002) (noting that Circuits differ on question of whether jury trials are permitted where plaintiff asserts both admiralty and diversity jurisdiction).

65. *See Fedorczyk v. Caribbean Cruise Lines, Ltd.*, 82 F.3d 69, 73 (3d Cir.1996).

claim means that it is not one.[66] However, a plaintiff need not specifically incant a citation to Rule 9(h), although that is certainly the preferred practice; instead, a simple statement asserting claims in admiralty or maritime law is sufficient.[67] The absence of a jury demand is one indication that the party intends to proceed in admiralty.[68]

Appellate Review

Admiralty claims enjoy a right of immediate interlocutory appeal, including admiralty claims contained in cases having non-admiralty claims as well.[69]

ADDITIONAL RESEARCH REFERENCES

Wright & Miller, *Federal Practice and Procedure* §§ 1291–1320.

C.J.S. Federal Civil Procedure §§ 252–257 et seq.

West's Key No. Digests, Federal Civil Procedure ⚷633–651.

66. *See Murphy v. Florida Keys Elec. Co-op. Ass'n*, 329 F.3d 1311, 1319 (11th Cir.2003).

67. *See Foulk v. Donjon Marine Co.*, 144 F.3d 252, 256 (3d Cir.1998) (noting that direct citation to Rule 9(h) is unambiguous and may be preferable, but it is not required); *Concordia Co. v. Panek*, 115 F.3d 67, 72 (1st Cir.1997) (although preferred technique is to expressly invoke Rule 9(h), including the phrase "In Admiralty" in the caption, with no accompanying demand for a jury trial, found sufficient); *Rosales v. Bouchard Coastwise Mgmt. Corp.*, 2004 WL 1146953, at *1 (E.D.La. 2004) (same effect).

68. *See Concordia Co. v. Panek*, 115 F.3d 67, 72 (1st Cir.1997).

69. *See* 28 U.S.C.A. § 1292(a)(3).

RULE 10

FORM OF PLEADINGS

(a) Caption; Names of Parties. Every pleading shall contain a caption setting forth the name of the court, the title of the action, the file number, and a designation as in Rule 7(a). In the complaint the title of the action shall include the names of all the parties, but in other pleadings it is sufficient to state the name of the first party on each side with an appropriate indication of other parties.

(b) Paragraphs; Separate Statements. All averments of claim or defense shall be made in numbered paragraphs, the contents of each of which shall be limited as far as practicable to a statement of a single set of circumstances; and a paragraph may be referred to by number in all succeeding pleadings. Each claim founded upon a separate transaction or occurrence and each defense other than denials shall be stated in a separate count or defense whenever a separation facilitates the clear presentation of the matters set forth.

(c) Adoption by Reference; Exhibits. Statements in a pleading may be adopted by reference in a different part of the same pleading or in another pleading or in any motion. A copy of any written instrument which is an exhibit to a pleading is a part thereof for all purposes.

AUTHORS' COMMENTARY ON RULE 10

PURPOSE AND SCOPE

Rule 10 establishes the form generally required for pleadings and motions. Pleadings and motions must contain a caption. Claims and defenses must be set forth in numbered paragraphs, with each paragraph limited to a single set of circumstances. Separate counts must be pleaded for each claim or defense premised on a separate transaction or occurrence. Earlier paragraphs may be adopted by reference to avoid repetition, and exhibits may be attached to pleadings.

RULE 10(a). CAPTION; NAMES OF PARTIES

CORE CONCEPT

Every pleading and motion must contain a caption. In the original complaint, the names of all parties must be listed in the caption. For later pleadings (except notices of appeal), listing the first named party is sufficient.

APPLICATIONS

Contents of Caption

Captions must contain: (a) the name of the court; (b) the title of the action (including all party names); (c) the docket number; and (d) the document's designation (*e.g.*, complaint, answer, reply to counterclaim).

Party Names

The title of a lawsuit properly includes the names of all parties, and these names must be listed in the original complaint.[1] Ordinarily, persons and entities not listed in the original complaint's caption are not parties to the lawsuit.[2] In all pleadings subsequent to the complaint, however, the court and the parties may shorten the caption to include only the names of the first plaintiff, the first defendant, and (where necessary) an indication that others are parties to the case (*e.g.*, "et al.").[3]

Warning for Notices of Appeal: The parties to an appeal must be individually named. Omitting party names with the use of "et al." or similar phrases may be fatally deficient. The courts of appeals may disregard these shortened phrases and may accept the appeal *only* as to those parties individually named in the notice of appeal or those parties who make their intent to appeal objectively clear.[4]

Actual Names: The caption must state the parties' actual names. Descriptive titles will only be deemed appropriate where they clearly identify the party.[5]

1. *Cf. Ferdik v. Bonzelet*, 963 F.2d 1258, (9th Cir.1992)(striking original complaint that listed parties-defendant as "et al."), *cert. denied*, 506 U.S. 915, 113 S.Ct. 321, 121 L.Ed.2d 242 (1992).

2. *See W.N.J. v. Yocom*, 257 F.3d 1171, 1172 (10th Cir.2001) (federal courts lack jurisdiction over unnamed parties since a case has not been commenced with respect to them); *Ahmed v. Goldberg*, 2001 WL 1842398, at *3 n.7 (D.N.Mar. I.2001) (because claimant not identified in complaint, and without class action status, court lacked jurisdiction to hear unnamed claimant's case); *Seeney v. Kavitski*, 1995 WL 314735 at *2, n. 3 (E.D.Pa.1995)(noting that person is not a defendant in the case where the person's name does not appear in the caption).

3. *See Spivey v. Board of Church Extension & Home Mission of Church of God*, 160 F.R.D. 660, 662 n. 3 (M.D.Fla.1995)(requesting counsel to use short form captioning of case in all future court documents).

4. *See* Fed.R.App.P. 3(c)(modifying *Torres v. Oakland Scavenger Co.*, 487 U.S. 312, 108 S.Ct. 2405, 101 L.Ed.2d 285 (1988)(holding that use of "et al." phrase did not constitute an effective appeal as to parties not specifically named)).

5. *See Mitchell v. Maynard*, 80 F.3d 1433, 1441 (10th Cir.1996) (commenting that a party not properly named in caption may still be deemed in the case if the allegations in the text of the complaint make plain that the party is intended as a defendant, although simply mentioning the party's name in a brief will not suffice). *Compare OTR Drivers at Topeka Frito–Lay, Inc.'s Distrib. Ctr. v. Frito–Lay, Inc.*, 988 F.2d 1059 (10th Cir.1993)("Over–The–Road Drivers" was insufficient identification of plaintiffs in the lawsuit) *with Dean v. Barber*, 951 F.2d 1210 (11th Cir.1992)(naming "Chief Deputy of County Jail" was sufficient identification of defendant) *and English v. Cowell*, 969 F.2d 465 (7th Cir.1992)(use of alleged pseudonym permitted where party may have legally changed name to adopt pseudonym and where no claim of confusion or prejudice was asserted).

Fictitious Names: In very unusual circumstances, a court may grant parties leave to identify themselves throughout the lawsuit by a fictitious name or pseudonym (*e.g.* "Jane Doe").[6] Such permission is extraordinary and conflicts with the public's right to open access to the judiciary, and is therefore typically denied in all but a few rare, exceptional cases.[7] Pseudonym litigation may be granted, for example, in those unusual cases that involve highly personal matters, true risks of physical harm, or where the injury sought to be avoided through the litigation would be suffered merely by the disclosure of the party's identity. In assessing whether pseudonym litigation should be permitted, the courts consider many factors, including whether the anonymous plaintiffs are challenging governmental activity, whether pressing the lawsuit will compel the plaintiffs to reveal highly intimate information or disclose an intention or desire to engage in illegal activity, and whether a child plaintiff is involved.[8] The courts may also examine whether disclosure of identities would create a risk of retaliatory physical or mental harm.[9] To proceed by pseudonym, the party must petition the court for permission.[10] Permission, if granted, may be accompanied by a requirement that the true names of the parties be disclosed to the defendants and the court, although the names would remain sealed to the general public.[11] More narrowly, a party may temporarily

6. *See Barth v. Kaye*, 178 F.R.D. 371, 376 (N.D.N.Y.1998) (party must request right to proceed under fictitious name, and court has discretion to grant or deny it).

7. *See M.M. v. Zavaras*, 139 F.3d 798 (10th Cir.1998) (denying leave because adversaries already knew plaintiff's identity and because public has right to know full circumstances of the case); *Doe v. Frank*, 951 F.2d 320 (11th Cir. 1992)(noting that "[l]awsuits are public events"); *Rowe v. Burton*, 884 F.Supp. 1372 (D.Alaska 1994)(commenting that courts are reluctant to grant pseudonym litigation because access to judicial proceedings is believed to improve the integrity and quality of justice). *See also Barth v. Kaye*, 178 F.R.D. 371, 376–77 (N.D.N.Y.1998) (denying request where plaintiff failed to make adequate showing of need, and citing public's right of access to the courts); *Doe v. Bell Atlantic Bus. Sys. Servs., Inc.*, 162 F.R.D. 418 (D.Mass.1995)(denying pseudonym status to alleged victim of sexual harassment who claimed her traditional Chinese family would react negatively if the allegations became public, noting that "[i]n the civil context, the plaintiff instigates the action, and, except in the most exceptional circumstances, must be prepared to proceed on the public record"). *But see Roe v. Aware Woman Center for Choice, Inc.*, 253 F.3d 678, 684–85 (11th Cir.2001) (reversing trial court's refusal to permit pseudonym litigation in abortion case), *cert. denied*, 534 U.S. 1129, 122 S.Ct. 1067, 151 L.Ed.2d 970 (2002).

8. *See Doe v. Porter*, 370 F.3d 558, 560 (6th Cir. 2004); *W.N.J. v. Yocom*, 257 F.3d 1171 (10th Cir.2001); *Roe v. Aware Woman Center for Choice, Inc.*, 253 F.3d 678, 684–85 (11th Cir. 2001), *cert. denied*, 534 U.S. 1129, 122 S.Ct. 1067, 151 L.Ed.2d 970 (2002); *Does I thru XXIII v. Advanced Textile Corp.*, 214 F.3d 1058, 1068 (9th Cir.2000); *Doe v. Stegall*, 653 F.2d 180, 185 (5th Cir.1981); *EW v. New York Blood Ctr.*, 213 F.R.D. 108, 111 (E.D.N.Y.2003); *Javier H. v. Garcia–Botello*, 211 F.R.D. 194, 195–96 (W.D.N.Y.2002). *See also Heather K. v. City of Mallard*, 887 F.Supp. 1249 (N.D.Iowa 1995) (noting that pseudonym litigation has been permitted in cases involving abortion, birth control, welfare cases involving illegitimate children, and homosexuality).

9. *See Does I thru XXIII v. Advanced Textile Corp.*, 214 F.3d 1058, 1068 (9th Cir.2000) (in retaliation-case petitions, district court should weigh (1) severity of threatened harm, (2) reasonableness of fear of harm, (3) plaintiff's vulnerability to harm, (4) prejudice, at each stage of the proceedings, to the defendants and how that prejudice could be mitigated, and (5) whether public's interest would be best served by requiring disclosure of identities).

10. *See W.N.J. v. Yocom*, 257 F.3d 1171 (10th Cir.2001).

11. *See W.N.J. v. Yocom*, 257 F.3d 1171 (10th Cir.2001).

identify an opponent with a fictional name so long as the identities of the opponents are clear and their actual names will be uncovered through discovery.[12]

Alterations to the Caption

As noted above, Rule 10(a) specifically encourages parties and the court to shorten the case caption in all documents subsequent to the complaint by listing only the first named plaintiff and defendant. Other immaterial alterations to the caption, such as changes in capitalization, fonts, or type faces, likewise are generally not improper and will not require remedy by the court.[13]

RULE 10(b). PARAGRAPHS; SEPARATE STATEMENTS

CORE CONCEPT

Pleadings should contain separately-numbered paragraphs, each of which, to the extent practicable, should contain a single set of circumstances. Pleadings should contain separate counts for claims arising from different transactions or occurrences. Defenses (other than denials) should be set forth in separate counts as well. In all other instances, separate counts are permitted, though not required.

APPLICATIONS

Paragraphing a Pleading's Facts

As far as practicable, a party should set forth each distinct allegation of fact in a separate paragraph, and each paragraph should be numbered.[14] The purpose of Rule 10(b) is to require the drafting of a pleading that is easily understood by both the opponent and the court.[15]

"Group" Pleading

"Group" pleading allegations (*e.g.*, accusing the "defendants" generally of engaging in certain misconduct, without particularizing which defendant committed what act) are generally inappropriate. Such "group" pleading techniques defeat the clarity objectives of the separate-paragraph requirement by failing to specify what each party is alleged to have done wrong.[16]

12. *See Dean v. Barber*, 951 F.2d 1210 (11th Cir.1992).

13. *See Jaeger v. Dubuque County*, 880 F.Supp. 640 (N.D.Iowa 1995) (finding no Rule 10 violation by capitalization of party names or other alterations of fonts, type faces, ink types, printer types, or printing methods).

14. *See Politico v. Promus Hotels, Inc.*, 184 F.R.D. 232, 234 (E.D.N.Y.1999) (as far as possible, complaint should avoid multiple allegations per paragraph); *Bieros v. Nicola*, 851 F.Supp. 683 (E.D.Pa.1994)(commenting that each factual allegation should be pleaded in a separate paragraph).

15. *See RTC v. Hess*, 820 F.Supp. 1359, 1371 (D.Utah 1993). *See also O'Donnell v. Elgin, J. & E. Ry.*, 338 U.S. 384, 392, 70 S.Ct. 200, 205, 94 L.Ed. 187 (1949)(chastising that "the unfortunately prolonged course" of the jury trial was due, in part, to counsel's failure to separate issues in counsel's pleading, preparation, and thinking).

16. *See Veltmann v. Walpole Pharmacy, Inc.*, 928 F.Supp. 1161, 1164 (M.D.Fla.1996) (pleading was insufficient where complaint made general allegations against all named defendants, making it impossible to determine which defendant committed which alleged act); *Gen-Probe, Inc. v.*

Pleading in Separate Counts

A party may include in a single count all theories of recovery, so long as those theories are all premised on the same facts.[17] The better practice, however, is to plead distinct claims and theories in separate counts.[18] In any event, where the claims and theories rest on different facts [19] or where clarity otherwise requires it,[20] distinct claims and theories must be pleaded in separate counts.[21] In those circumstances, separate counts help to ensure that the pleadings achieve their goals of framing the issues and providing a platform for informed pretrial proceedings and the effective management of discovery.[22] The paragraphing and separate counts practice also enables a court to grant dispositive relief with respect to an entire count, and not just part of one.[23]

Remedy by Motion Practice

When a party's pleading provides insufficient notice of the claims because of its confusing structure, the absence of numbered paragraphs, or the improper combination of multiple claims in a single count, the opposing party may move for a more definite statement or to strike the pleading.[24] Such a motion must be made before filing a response. The typical remedy granted by the court is an order directing the party to

Amoco Corp., 926 F.Supp. 948, 962 (S.D.Cal. 1996) (noting that Rule 10(b) requires each court to identify which averments relate to which claims and to which defendants). *See also Magluta v. Samples*, 256 F.3d 1282, 1284 (11th Cir.2001) (vacating judgment and directing that plaintiff replead because 58–page, group-pleaded "complaint is a quintessential 'shotgun' pleading of the kind we have condemned repeatedly"). *Cf. In re GlenFed, Inc. Sec. Litig.*, 60 F.3d 591, 592–93 (9th Cir.1995) (noting that "group" pleading might be appropriate if complaint alleged that outside directors either participated in day-to-day activities of business, or had special relationship with business, such as participating in preparing or communicating group information).

17. *See Lamar Adver. of Mobile, Inc. v. City of Lakeland*, 980 F.Supp. 1455, 1458 (M.D.Fla. 1997) (holding that Rule 10(b) is inapplicable to multiple claims arising out of single transaction); *FDIC v. Miller*, 781 F.Supp. 1271 (N.D.Ill. 1991); *Sherman v. Johnson & Towers Baltimore, Inc.*, 760 F.Supp. 499 (D.Md.1990).

18. *See Stone Mountain Game Ranch, Inc. v. Hunt*, 746 F.2d 761, 763 n. 1 (11th Cir. 1984)(noting that it is improper to mix legal theories and allegations of damages in a single count); *Selep v. City of Chicago*, 842 F.Supp. 1068 (N.D.Ill.1993)(noting that multiple claims in a single count is not condoned).

19. *See RTC v. Hess*, 820 F.Supp. 1359 (D.Utah 1993)(granting motion for more definite statement where multiple transactions were included within a single count).

20. *See Dodge v. Susquehanna Univ.*, 796 F.Supp. 829 (M.D.Pa.1992)(because failure to separate into distinct counts gave defendant the impression that no breach of contract claim was being pressed, the belatedly asserted breach of contract theory was dismissed from the complaint); *Gilbert v. Feld*, 788 F.Supp. 854 (E.D.Pa.1992)(separate counts not required where such practice would not enhance the clarity of the presentation of an already clear pleading). *See also Pelletier v. Zweifel*, 921 F.2d 1465, 1479 n. 29 (11th Cir.1991), *cert. denied,* 502 U.S. 855, 112 S.Ct. 167, 116 L.Ed.2d 131 (1991)(claim of pendent State law cause of action discounted where no separate count was pleaded).

21. *See Bautista v. Los Angeles County*, 216 F.3d 837, 840–41 (9th Cir.2000).

22. *See Bautista v. Los Angeles County*, 216 F.3d 837, 840–41 (9th Cir.2000).

23. *See Savin v. Robinson*, 2001 WL 1191192, at *1 (N.D.Ill.2001).

24. *See Gonzales v. Wing*, 167 F.R.D. 352, 354–355 (N.D.N.Y.1996) (dismissing plaintiff's 287–page, numberless complaint because it presented a "far too ... heavy burden" upon the defendants to frame a comprehensive defense and provided the court with no meaningful basis to assess the claims' sufficiency).

replead, or a dismissal without prejudice and with leave to amend within a short period of time.[25]

RULE 10(c). ADOPTION BY REFERENCE; EXHIBITS

CORE CONCEPT

A party may adopt by reference statements from the same pleading, or from a different pleading or motion filed in the same case. A party may also attach exhibits or writings to the pleading, thereby making the exhibits part of the pleading for all purposes.

APPLICATIONS

Adopting Paragraphs by Reference

By clearly identifying the adopted paragraphs, a party may incorporate by reference allegations made in an earlier portion of the same pleading. Parties frequently adopt such allegations in order to avoid repeating the same factual allegations in each count.

Adopting Documents or Pleadings by Reference

A party may adopt documents or pleadings (in whole or in part) by reference so long as the adopted document or pleading is expressly named. Generally, this practice is limited to documents and pleadings that are already before the court. Documents or pleadings filed in another lawsuit usually cannot be adopted by reference.

Attaching Exhibits

A party may (but is not required to) attach copies of "written instruments" as exhibits to a pleading. Generally, newspaper articles[26] and affidavits[27] do not qualify for attachment as exhibits. A videotape recording, however, may qualify.[28]

Attachments by Opponent: If the pleader does *not* attach, but instead merely refers to, a written instrument in the pleading, the opponent may usually still attach that instrument to the responsive pleading, so long as the instrument is referred to in the first pleading, is indisputably authentic, and is "central" to the pleader's claim.[29]

25. *See, e.g., Nicolaysen v. BP Amoco Chem. Co.*, 2002 WL 1060587 (E.D.Pa.2002); *Perez v. Radioshack Corp.*, 2002 WL 1335158 (S.D.Fla. 2002).

26. *See Perkins v. Silverstein*, 939 F.2d 463, 467 n. 2 (7th Cir.1991)(commenting that newspaper articles, commentaries, and editorial cartoons are not the type of documentary evidence or written instruments that Rule 10(c) contemplates).

27. *See Rose v. Bartle*, 871 F.2d 331, 339 n. 3 (3d Cir.1989)(noting that affidavits are not Rule 10(c) materials).

28. *See Howell by Goerdt v. Tribune Entertainment Co.*, 106 F.3d 215, 218–19 (7th Cir. 1997) (citing Rule 10(c) in treating videotape as "appended" to the complaint, where plaintiff's counsel urged the court to view it).

29. *See United States v. Ritchie*, 342 F.3d 903, 908 (9th Cir. 2003); *Beddall v. State Street Bank & Trust Co.*, 137 F.3d 12, 17 (1st Cir. 1998); *Weiner v. Klais & Co.*, 108 F.3d 86, 89 (6th Cir.1997).

Effect of Attaching Exhibits

Exhibits attached to a pleading are made a part of that pleading for all purposes.[30]

Possible Dismissal: In ruling on a motion to dismiss, the court may consider not only the textual averments of the pleading itself, but also the contents of all exhibits attached to the pleading.[31] Where an inconsistency exists between an attached document and any allegation in the pleading based on that document, the document controls.[32] Similarly, where an attached document reveals a "built-in" defense that precludes recovery as a matter of law, the court may recognize the defense and dismiss the action.[33]

"Vouching" Risk: By adopting by reference a portion of an attached document, the pleader does not necessarily "vouch" for the truth of all the contents of the document. The attached document will be read in conjunction with the pleading that adopts it. Thus, a defamation plaintiff may safely attach an allegedly libelous writing without being deemed to have admitted as true all the asserted libels contained in the writing, just as a commercial plaintiff, alleging the non-receipt of goods, may attach an allegedly forged receipt without admitting that the document truthfully recounts that the goods were received.[34] Likewise, an aggrieved litigant generally can safely attach a copy of an appealed-from opinion, order, or other ruling without being deemed to have thereby "vouched" for the very reasoning or result she is in the process of challenging.[35]

30. *See Verizon Md., Inc. v. Global Naps, Inc.*, 377 F.3d 355, 363 (4th Cir. 2004); *Sira v. Morton*, 380 F.3d 57 (2d Cir. 2004); *Witzke v. Femal*, 376 F.3d 744, 749 (7th Cir. 2004); *Nieman v. NLO, Inc.*, 108 F.3d 1546, 1555 (6th Cir.1997).

31. *See Witzke v. Femal*, 376 F.3d 744, 749 (7th Cir. 2004) (may be considered on motion to dismiss); *United States ex rel. Riley v. St. Luke's Episcopal Hosp.*, 355 F.3d 370, 375 (5th Cir. 2004); *Meehan v. United Consumers Club Franchising Corp.*, 312 F.3d 909, 913 (8th Cir.2002); *E.E.O.C. v. Staten Island Savings Bank*, 207 F.3d 144, 148 (2d Cir.2000); *Taylor v. Appleton*, 30 F.3d 1365, 1367 n. 3 (11th Cir.1994); *ALA, Inc. v. CCAIR, Inc.*, 29 F.3d 855 (3d Cir.1994).

32. *See ALA, Inc. v. CCAIR, Inc.*, 29 F.3d 855 (3d Cir.1994); *Fayetteville Investors v. Commercial Builders, Inc.*, 936 F.2d 1462 (4th Cir. 1991); *Banco del Estado v. Navistar Int'l Transp. Corp.*, 942 F.Supp. 1176, 1179 (N.D.Ill. 1996).

33. *See Hamilton v. O'Leary*, 976 F.2d 341 (7th Cir.1992).

34. *See Guzell v. Hiller*, 223 F.3d 518, 519 (7th Cir.2000) (giving examples); *Gant v. Wallingford Bd. of Educ.*, 69 F.3d 669, 674–75 (2d Cir.1995)(giving these examples).

35. In fact, one Court of Appeals harshly derided this sort of "vouching" argument as "beyond nonsensical" and "unworthy" of the attorneys who asserted it. *See Carroll v. Yates*, 362 F.3d 984, 986 (7th Cir. 2004) ("The logic of the ... argument is that an appellant, required by the appellate rules to append to his brief the decision of the district court or administrative agency that he is appealing, ... by doing so kills the appeal because appending amounts to vouching for the truth of the propositions in the appended decision. The argument if accepted would do wonders for our workload, but is beyond nonsensical and unworthy of the office of the Attorney General of Illinois."). The Court, then, directed the filing attorneys to show cause why they should not be sanctioned for briefing "frivolous argumentation". *Id.*

ADDITIONAL RESEARCH REFERENCES

Wright & Miller, *Federal Practice and Procedure* §§ 1321–1330.

C.J.S. Federal Civil Procedure § 251.

West's Key No. Digests, Federal Civil Procedure ⚷625–629.

RULE 11

SIGNING OF PLEADINGS, MOTIONS, AND OTHER PAPERS; REPRESENTATIONS TO COURT; SANCTIONS

(a) Signature. Every pleading, written motion, and other paper shall be signed by at least one attorney of record in the attorney's individual name, or, if the party is not represented by an attorney, shall be signed by the party. Each paper shall state the signer's address and telephone number, if any. Except when otherwise specifically provided by rule or statute, pleadings need not be verified or accompanied by affidavit. An unsigned paper shall be stricken unless omission of the signature is corrected promptly after being called to the attention of the attorney or party.

(b) Representations to Court. By presenting to the court (whether by signing, filing, submitting, or later advocating) a pleading, written motion, or other paper, an attorney or unrepresented party is certifying that to the best of the person's knowledge, information, and belief, formed after an inquiry reasonable under the circumstances,—

(1) it is not being presented for any improper purpose, such as to harass or to cause unnecessary delay or needless increase in the cost of litigation;

(2) the claims, defenses, and other legal contentions therein are warranted by existing law or by a nonfrivolous argument for the extension, modification, or reversal of existing law or the establishment of new law;

(3) the allegations and other factual contentions have evidentiary support or, if specifically so identified, are likely to have evidentiary support after a reasonable opportunity for further investigation or discovery; and

(4) the denials of factual contentions are warranted on the evidence or, if specifically so identified, are reasonably based on a lack of information or belief.

(c) Sanctions. If, after notice and a reasonable opportunity to respond, the court determines that subdivision (b) has been violated, the court may, subject to the conditions stated below, impose an appropriate sanction upon the attorneys, law firms, or parties that have violated subdivision (b) or are responsible for the violation.

(1) *How Initiated.*

(A) By Motion. A motion for sanctions under this rule shall be made separately from other motions or requests and shall describe the specific conduct alleged to violate subdivision (b). It shall be served as provided in Rule 5, but shall not be filed with or presented to the court unless, within 21 days after service of the motion (or such other period as the court may prescribe), the challenged paper, claim, defense, contention, allegation, or denial is not withdrawn or appropriately corrected. If warranted, the court may award to the party prevailing on the motion the reasonable expenses and attorney's fees incurred in presenting or opposing the motion. Absent exceptional circumstances, a law firm shall be held jointly responsible for violations committed by its partners, associates, and employees.

(B) On Court's Initiative. On its own initiative, the court may enter an order describing the specific conduct that appears to violate subdivision (b) and directing an attorney, law firm, or party to show cause why it has not violated subdivision (b) with respect thereto.

(2) *Nature of Sanction; Limitations.* A sanction imposed for violation of this rule shall be limited to what is sufficient to deter repetition of such conduct or comparable conduct by others similarly situated. Subject to the limitations in subparagraphs (A) and (B), the sanction may consist of, or include, directives of a nonmonetary nature, an order to pay a penalty into court, or, if imposed on motion and warranted for effective deterrence, an order directing payment to the movant of some or all of the reasonable attorneys' fees and other expenses incurred as a direct result of the violation.

(A) Monetary sanctions may not be awarded against a represented party for a violation of subdivision (b)(2).

(B) Monetary sanctions may not be awarded on the court's initiative unless the court issues its order to show cause before a voluntary dismissal or settlement of the claims made by or against the party which is, or whose attorneys are, to be sanctioned.

(3) *Order.* When imposing sanctions, the court shall describe the conduct determined to constitute a violation of this rule and explain the basis for the sanction imposed.

(d) Inapplicability to Discovery. Subdivisions (a) through (c) of this rule do not apply to disclosures and discovery requests, responses, objections, and motions that are subject to the provisions of Rules 26 through 37.

[Amended April 28, 1983, effective August 1, 1983; March 2, 1987, effective August 1, 1987; April 22, 1993, effective December 1, 1993.]

AUTHORS' COMMENTARY ON RULE 11

PURPOSE AND SCOPE

Rule 11 establishes the standards attorneys and parties must meet when filing pleadings, motions, or other documents in court. It also regulates the circumstances in which sanctions may be imposed if the standards of Rule 11 are not met.

NOTE: Rule 11 was changed significantly on December 1, 1993. Previous authority on Rule 11 should therefore be approached with great care. Moreover, because some cases continued to apply the old version of Rule 11 after that date, even decisions handed down after 1993 should be examined to determine which version of Rule 11 the court applied.[1]

RULE 11(a). SIGNATURE

CORE CONCEPT

Rule 11(a) requires that documents be signed by an attorney or (if there is no attorney) the party. It abolishes old verification requirements, unless they have been preserved by rule or statute.

APPLICATIONS

Scope

Rule 11 applies to every pleading, written motion, or other paper filed or served[2] in the course of litigation, as well as to advocacy of documents previously filed.[3] Rule 11 does not apply to misconduct

1. *See e.g., Jones v. International Riding Helmets, Ltd.*, 49 F.3d 692, 694 (11th Cir. 1995)(noting amendments to Rule 11, but applying version of Rule 11 in effect at time the events took place).

2. *See, e.g., Antonious v. Spalding & Evenflo Companies, Inc.*, 281 F.3d 1258, 1261 (Fed.Cir. 2002) (court ordered filing of document; through apparent inadvertence document was served but not filed; held, party which served offending document falls within scope of Rule 11 notwithstanding that document was never actually filed with court; acknowledging general principle that Rule 11 does not apply to documents not filed with court).

3. *See, e.g., In re Highgate Equities, Ltd.*, 279 F.3d 148, 153–54, 154 (2d Cir.2002) (bankruptcy case involving analogous Federal Rule of Bankruptcy Procedure 9011; Rule 11 generally applicable only to documents served or filed with court; letter sent to court but not filed is normally not within scope of Rule 11); *Legault v. Zambarano*, 105 F.3d 24, 27–28 (1st Cir.1997) (letter is within scope of Rule 11 only where

unrelated to signed motions, pleadings or other papers.[4] Rule 11 is also inapplicable to state-court filings.[5]

Rule 11 and Appellate Jurisdiction

In general, Rule 11 is applicable only to lawsuits in district courts. Federal Rule of Appellate Procedure 38 usually controls sanctions for groundless appeals to circuit courts.[6] However, an exception to that delineation of authority occurs when a party files a notice of appeal. In that circumstance it is Rule 11 that requires the appellant to sign the notice of appeal. Thus, a failure to sign the notice is an error, which may be correctable under Rule 11(a), and an appellate court does not lose jurisdiction of an appeal if the appellant corrects the original failure to sign.[7]

Administrative Litigation

Normally Rule 11 is not applicable in proceedings before administrative agencies. Application of Rule 11 occurs in such cases only when the case becomes a lawsuit in a federal court.[8]

letter was motion in disguise that was intended to affect judicial decision on such matter as whether to issue a preliminary injunction; acknowledging general rule that letter is outside scope of Rule 11); *O'Brien v. Alexander,* 101 F.3d 1479, 1489 (2d Cir.1996) (oral advocacy flowing directly from documents filed with court fall within scope of Rule 11; other oral statements are not controlled by Rule 11).

4. *See, e.g., Christian v. Mattell,* 286 F.3d 1118, 1130–1131 (9th Cir.2002) (Rule 11 inapplicable to discovery abuses or oral misrepresentations unrelated to document filings); *Loggerhead Turtle v. County Council of Volusia County, Florida,* 148 F.3d 1231, 1256 (11th Cir.1998), *cert. denied,* 526 U.S. 1081, 119 S.Ct. 1488, 143 L.Ed.2d 570 (1999) (Rule 11 applies only to court filings. "Assuming the author acts in good faith, an investigation preceding an intent to sue letter need not be as thorough as that leading up to the complaint."); *Milltex Industries Corp. v. Jacquard Lace Co., Ltd.,* 55 F.3d 34, 37 n. 5 (2d Cir.1995)(Rule 11 applicable only to circumstances involving pleadings, motions, or other papers; Rule 11 inapplicable to attorney's defiance of judicial order). *But see, Antonious v. Spalding & Evenflo Companies, Inc.,* 281 F.3d 1258, 1261 (Fed.Cir.2002) (court ordered filing of document; through apparent inadvertence document was served but not filed; held, party which served offending document falls within scope of Rule 11 notwithstanding that document was never actually filed with court; however, acknowledging general principle that Rule 11 does not apply to documents not filed with court). *Turner v. Sungard Business Systems, Inc.,* 91 F.3d 1418, 1421 (11th Cir.1996) (attorney whose only written document was notice of appearance was nevertheless subject to sanctions for later oral advocacy).

5. *See, e.g., Edwards v. General Motors Corp.,* 153 F.3d 242, 245 (5th Cir.1998) (Rule 11 inapplicable to filing made in state court before case was removed to federal court; sanctions may be imposed on post-removal filings; noting general agreement among circuit courts); *Bisciglia v. Kenosha Unified School District No. 1,* 45 F.3d 223, 226 (7th Cir.1995)(filing in state court not sanctionable under Rule 11).

6. *See, e.g., In re 60 East 80th Street Equities, Inc.,* 218 F.3d 109, 118–19 n. 3 (2d Cir.2000) (Rule 11 inapplicable to appellate litigation).

7. *Becker v. Montgomery,* 532 U.S. 757, 121 S.Ct. 1801, 149 L.Ed.2d 983 (2001) (distinguishing Rule 11 from jurisdictional requirements of Rules 3 and 4; also suggesting that appropriate means of adjusting signature requirement of Rule 11 "to keep pace with technological advances" is through process of rule amendment, not judicial decision).

8. *See, e.g., Santa Maria v. Pacific Bell,* 202 F.3d 1170, 1179 (9th Cir.2000) ("The obligations of Rule 11 extend only to suits filed in federal court, not to such administrative procedures as filing a charge with the EEOC. . . .In fact, the very nature of an EEOC charge makes this clear: the charge serves as an allegation of wrongdoing which the EEOC investigates to determine if it has merit.").

Documents Filed in State Court

If a document was filed when a case was pending in state court, Rule 11 cannot be used to sanction the signer of the document in federal district court. Thus, a failure to update or amend a state complaint, by itself, is not sanctionable in federal court.[9]

Party v. Attorney

Rule 11 does not authorize actions in favor of a party against the party's attorney.[10]

Pro se Litigants

Rule 11 applies to pro se litigants. Thus, a pro se litigant may be sanctioned for violating Rule 11. However, a party's pro se status is a factor that is weighed in determining whether the party's behavior was reasonable under the standard of Rule 11.[11]

Lack of Subject Matter Jurisdiction

Rule 11 applies even in cases where it is subsequently determined that the district court lacked subject matter jurisdiction.[12]

Voluntary Dismissal: Rule 41

It appears that a district court retains jurisdiction to impose Rule 11 sanctions even after a case has been voluntarily dismissed without prejudice under Rule 41.[13]

Signature of Attorney

If a party has retained counsel, at least one attorney must sign the document and provide the attorney's address and telephone number.[14]

9. *See, e.g., Bisciglia v. Kenosha Unified School District No. 1,* 45 F.3d 223, 226–27 (7th Cir.1995).

10. *See, e.g., Mark Industries, Ltd. v. Sea Captain's Choice, Inc.,* 50 F.3d 730 (9th Cir. 1995)(purpose of Rule 11 is to deter abuses that harm the opponent, not the client).

11. *See, e.g., Kennedy v. National Juvenile Detention Association,* 187 F.3d 690, 696 (7th Cir.1999), *cert. denied,* 528 U.S. 1159, 120 S.Ct. 1169, 145 L.Ed.2d 1079 (2000) (affirming conclusion that claim was not frivolous, "especially considering the plaintiff's lack of legal representation"); *Moore v. Time, Inc.,* 180 F.3d 463, 463 (2d Cir.), *cert. denied,* 528 U.S. 932, 120 S.Ct. 331, 145 L.Ed.2d 258 (1999) (per curiam) (affirming district court's denial of Rule 11 sanctions on attorney who appeared pro se where district court had reasoned that attorney was "not sophisticated"; however, also imposing sanctions under Federal Rule of Appellate Procedure 38 for frivolous appeal; attorney had received "clear warning" from district court and had previously brought other frivolous appeals to appellate court).

12. *Willy v. Coastal Corp.,* 503 U.S. 131, 112 S.Ct. 1076, 117 L.Ed.2d 280 (1992). *See also, e.g., Tropf v. Fidelity National Title Insurance Co.,* 289 F.3d 929, 938 (6th Cir.2002), *cert. denied,* 537 U.S. 1118, 123 S.Ct. 887, 154 L.Ed.2d 797 (2003) (citing *Willy,* supra; noting that sanctions in such circumstances do not violate Article III of Constitution); *Perpetual Securities, Inc. v. Tang,* 290 F.3d 132, 141 (2d Cir.2002) (same result); *Branson v. Nott,* 62 F.3d 287, 293 (9th Cir.1995), *cert. denied,* 516 U.S. 1009, 116 S.Ct. 565, 133 L.Ed.2d 491 (1995)(absence of subject matter jurisdiction does not preclude application of Rule 11 sanctions).

13. *See, e.g., Sequa Corp. v. Cooper,* 245 F.3d 1036, 1037 (8th Cir.2001) (also acknowledging some potentially contrary results in earlier cases).

14. *See, e.g., Duran v. Carris,* 238 F.3d 1268, 1271 (10th Cir.2001) (attorney's failure to disclose that brief submitted by allegedly pro se

Rule 11 requires that an individual attorney must sign the document. Under older law that is probably still good precedent, a signature that purports to be on behalf of an entire law firm does not satisfy the signature requirement of Rule 11.[15]

Signature of Party

A party must sign the document if the party is not represented by counsel.[16] The party must also provide an address and telephone number, if any. Although courts may be more lenient with pro se litigants, it should not be assumed that they are immune from Rule 11 sanctions.[17]

Verification and Affidavits

Rule 11 abolishes requirements of verification and affidavits for documents filed or served in the course of litigation, except where such a requirement is expressly preserved by another rule or statute.[18] The signature of a party or counsel is the substitute for prior verification practices. Continuing requirements for verification are most commonly encountered in suits at state law. Occasionally, however, a federal rule or statute may also require verification. For example, Rule 23.1, governing derivative actions by shareholders, requires verification of a plaintiff-shareholder's complaint.[19]

Failure to Sign

If a document subject to Rule 11 is not signed, the court has power to strike the document unless the proponent signs it promptly upon notification of the missing signature.[20]

RULE 11(b). REPRESENTATIONS TO COURT

CORE CONCEPT

Rule 11(b) establishes the standards that documents which are regulated by Rule 11 must meet. It also specifically provides that the standards are applicable to later advocacy of such documents, as well as to the initial submission of the documents.

party was actually ghostwritten by attorney, who did not enter appearance, is violation of Rule 11(a)).

15. *Pavelic & LeFlore v. Marvel Entertainment Group,* 493 U.S. 120, 110 S.Ct. 456, 107 L.Ed.2d 438 (1989).

16. *Cf., Business Guides v. Chromatic Communications Enterprises,* 498 U.S. 533, 111 S.Ct. 922, 112 L.Ed.2d 1140 (1991).

17. *Warren v. Guelker,* 29 F.3d 1386, 1390 (9th Cir.1994)(Rule 11 "explicitly applies to parties not represented by attorneys.").

18. *See, e.g., Frank R. Jelleff, Inc. v. Braden,* 233 F.2d 671, 674, 675 (D.C.Cir.1956)(subject to exceptions, Rule 11 eliminates the need for verification).

19. *See also, e.g.,* 15 U.S.C.A. § 78u–4 (requiring sworn certification by proposed class representative in cases within scope of Private Securities Litigation Reform Act of 1995).

20. *See, e.g., De Aza–Paez v. United States,* 343 F.3d 552, 552 (1st Cir. 2003) (per curiam) ("Rule 11(a) provides that an unsigned paper will not be stricken for lack of signature if it is corrected promptly"); *Kovilic Construction Co. v. Missbrenner,* 106 F.3d 768, 772 (7th Cir.1997) ("[D]ocuments should be struck only where the failure to sign severely prejudiced the opposing party.").

APPLICATIONS

Unsuccessful Pleadings and Motions

Under the previous version of Rule 11, a violation occurred only when a client or attorney engaged in improper behavior or failed to demonstrate due care. Thus, mere failure to prevail on a particular pleading or motion does not, of itself, establish a violation of Rule 11.[21] This standard will presumably carry over into the current version of Rule 11.

Claims Evaluated Individually

Although the literal language of Rule 11 might seem to address whether entire documents meet the Rule's requirements, it is settled that portions of a document might be in violation of Rule 11, notwithstanding that other portions of the same document are satisfactory.[22]

Improper Rule 11 Motions

Attorneys are cautioned that because Rule 11 violations may be raised by motions, such motions themselves are subject to review under Rule 11, and can be the subject of additional allegations of violations of Rule 11.[23]

Reasonable Inquiry

Rule 11(b) provides that persons who sign, file, submit or later advocate documents are certifying to the court that the document or advocacy is based upon the person's best knowledge, information or belief, which is in turn based upon an inquiry that was reasonable in the circumstances of the particular case.[24] This is a change in language

21. *See, e.g., Hartmarx Corp. v. Abboud,* 326 F.3d 862, 868 (7th Cir.2003) (reasonable position on close question under new rule is not sanctionable even if other position is superior); *Ford Motor Co. v. Summit Motor Products,* 930 F.2d 277, 289 (3d Cir.1991), *cert. denied sub nom., Altran Corp. v. Ford Motor Co.,* 502 U.S. 939, 112 S.Ct. 373, 116 L.Ed.2d 324 (1991)(if party's position is reasonable, a loss on the merits does not trigger Rule 11 sanctions).

22. *See, e.g., Perez v. Posse Comitatus,*373 F.3d 321 (2d Cir. 2004) ("A complaint challenged under Rule 11(b) is not ordinarily analyzed as an individual unit. ... [T]he fact that a claim is properly asserted against one defendant does not mean that the same claim may properly be asserted against a different defendant.").

23. *But see, Blue v. United States Department of the Army,* 914 F.2d 525, 548 (4th Cir. 1990), *cert. denied,* 499 U.S. 959, 111 S.Ct. 1580, 113 L.Ed.2d 645 (1991)("Litigants should be able to defend themselves from the imposition of sanctions without incurring further sanctions.").

24. *See, e.g., Belleville Catering Co. v. Champaign Market Place, L.L.C.,* 350 F.3d 691, 692–93 (7th Cir. 2003) (reliance on lease agreement's erroneous description of corporation as Missouri corporation does not meet requirement of reasonable inquiry; "counsel must secure jurisdictional details from original sources"); *Antonious v. Spalding & Evenflo Companies,* 275 F.3d 1066, 1072 (Fed.Cir.2002) ("Rule 11 requires that the attorney not rely solely on the client's claim interpretation, but instead perform an independent claim analysis."); *View Engineering, Inc. v. Robotic Vision Systems, Inc.,* 208 F.3d 981, 984–86 (Fed.Cir.2000) (upholding sanctions for patent infringement suit filed on basis of no facts; only basis for filing was belief of key person, which was in turn based on knowledge of company's own patents, opponent's advertising, and opponent's statements to customers; financial inability to purchase opponent's machine for inspection prior to lawsuit does not provide defense to sanctions; opponent's refusal to permit pre-litigation examination of its machine also irrelevant because opponent has no duty to permit such pre-litigation discovery); *Hernandez v. Joliet Police Department,* 197 F.3d 256, 264 (7th Cir.1999) (failure to perform basic legal research

from the previous Rule 11 standard, and is intended to lower the burden on the proponent of a document.[25] However, an attorney operates under a "continuous obligation to make inquiries."[26] Moreover, although the matter is still uncertain, the unwillingness of a party's opponent to cooperate in a pre-litigation examination of facts might not justify a party's failure to undertake a reasonable inquiry.[27]

Bad Faith

Rule 11(b)(1) provides that by presenting a document or arguing on its behalf, a person certifies that the document has no improper purpose, such as harassment[28] or undue delay or expense. This language carries over from the previous version of Rule 11, and is intended to regulate bad faith filings.[29] It should already be clear, of course, that while bad faith may indeed trigger sanctions under Rule 11, conduct that does not involve bad faith may also be sanctionable.[30]

to learn that suit against state's attorney's office was barred by 11th Amendment to federal constitution). *But see Commercial Cleaning Services, L.L.C. v. Colin Service Systems, Inc.*, 271 F.3d 374, 386 (2d Cir.2001) (error for district court not to provide sanctioned plaintiff with opportunity to conduct discovery to fill deficiencies in information; Rule 11(b) does not require plaintiff "to know at the time of pleading all facts necessary to establish the claim"); *Dubois v. United States Department of Agriculture,* 270 F.3d 77, 82 (1st Cir.2001) (duty to investigate need not be pursued until absolute certainty is achieved); *Garr v. U.S. Healthcare, Inc.*, 22 F.3d 1274, 1278 (3d Cir.1994) (the "obligation personally to comply with the requirements of Rule 11 clearly does not preclude the signer from any reliance on information from other persons"). *See also Circuit City Stores, Inc. v. Najd,* 294 F.3d 1104 (9th Cir.2002) (abuse of discretion to impose sanctions on party who would have prevailed, but for Supreme Court's intervening contrary decision in unrelated case while instant appeal was pending).

25. *Hadges v. Yonkers Racing Corp.*, 48 F.3d 1320, 1329–30 (2d Cir.1995)(amended Rule 11 permits attorney to rely on objectively reasonable representation of client; thus, duty of attorney to make inquiry is relaxed).

26. *Battles v. City of Ft. Myers,* 127 F.3d 1298, 1300 (11th Cir.1997) (failure to do so may be sanctionable if attorney advocates position that has become untenable).

27. *Compare View Engineering, Inc. v. Robotic Vision Systems, Inc.,* 208 F.3d 981, 986 (Fed.Cir.2000) (an opponent "is not required to allow pre-litigation discovery" and lack of such an opportunity is not a defense to sanctions for failure to make reasonable inquiry), *with Hoffmann–La Roche, Inc. v. Invamed, Inc.,* 213 F.3d 1359 (Fed.Cir.2000) (reasonable inquiry met where claimants sought information from opponent prior to litigation, but were rejected; opponent was bound by confidentiality agreement with third party, but had not sought any sort of release; opponent released samples of drug at issue, but claimants were unable to reverse engineer samples to determine if patent infringement had occurred).

28. *See, e.g., Whitehead v. Food Max of Mississippi, Inc.,* 332 F.3d 796 (5th Cir.2003), *cert. denied,* 540 U.S. 1047, 124 S.Ct. 807, 157 L.Ed.2d 694 (2003) (en banc) (even a nonfrivolous submission to court may be sanctionable when document was submitted for improper purpose; noting that excessive motions can constitute harassment, and even legitimate documents that also "use abusive language toward opposing counsel" can trigger sanction).

29. *See, e.g., American International Adjustment Co. v. Galvin,* 86 F.3d 1455 (7th Cir. 1996)("[A] pleader may assert contradictory statements of fact only when legitimately in doubt about the facts in question;" citing Rule 11). *But cf., In re Pennie & Edmonds, L.L.P.,* 323 F.3d 86, 87 (2d Cir.2003) (where court decides to impose sanctions sua sponte, law firm did not have benefit of "safe harbor" provision; thus sanctions were only appropriate for subjective bad faith, not for unreasonable but genuine subjective good faith).

30. *See, e.g., Sprewell v. Golden State Warriors,* 231 F.3d 520, 530 (9th Cir.2000) (noting circuit's practice of imposing sanctions against civil rights plaintiffs only in exceptional cases; however, filing amended complaint "that failed to ameliorate ... weaknesses inherent in ... original complaint" is example of exceptional cases); *Anjelino v. New York Times Co.,* 200 F.3d 73, 100 (3d Cir.1999) (Rule 11 does not require finding of bad faith).

Advocating Changes in Law

Rule 11(b)(2) provides that by presenting a document or arguing on its behalf, a person certifies that the arguments in the document are either justified by existing law or are "nonfrivolous" arguments for alteration in existing law.[31] Rule 11(b)(2) is a change from the previous version of Rule 11, and is intended to be a lesser burden on an advocate than the former standard of "good faith" arguments.[32]

Foundation for Factual Allegations

Rule 11(b)(3) requires persons alleging facts to do so with "evidentiary support" or, when specifically stated, to believe they can develop evidentiary support through further investigation. Rule 11(b)(3) thus establishes a lesser standard than the former requirement that allegations be "well grounded" in fact.[33]

Foundation for Denials

Rule 11(b)(4) requires denials of factual allegations to be warranted by the evidence unless a person specifically states that the denial is reasonably based upon a lack of information or on belief. Like Rule 11(b)(3), this provision also establishes a lesser standard than the former version of Rule 11.[34]

31. *See, e.g., Brunt v. Service Employees International Union,* 284 F.3d 715, 721 (7th Cir. 2002) (although parties' claims "were barred by existing Supreme Court and Seventh Circuit case law," district court could still properly find that complaint was not frivolous under rule 11); *In re Sargent,* 136 F.3d 349, 352 (4th Cir.1998), *cert.denied,* 525 U.S. 854, 119 S.Ct. 133, 142 L.Ed.2d 108 (1998) (standard of Rule 11(b)(2) is "objective reasonableness. . . .[P]ut differently, a legal position violates Rule 11 if it 'has absolutely no chance of success under the existing precedent.' "). *Cf., Hartmarx Corp. v. Abboud,* 326 F.3d 862, 868 (7th Cir.2003) (reasonable position on close question under new rule is not sanctionable even if other position is superior).

32. *See, e.g., Independent Lift Truck Builders Union v. NACCO Materials Handling Group, Inc.,* 202 F.3d 965, 968 (7th Cir.2000) (no sanction for advocating position in conflict with two controlling decisions where position was " 'not totally baseless' " and " 'had some logical and practical appeal' "); *Protective Life Insurance Co. v. Dignity Viatical Settlement Partners, L.P.,* 171 F.3d 52, 57 (1st Cir.1999) (party's attempt "to squeeze too much from [prior case law] . . . though aggressive, did not justify the imposition of Rule 11 sanctions;" using analogous case law as "building block" may not be persuasive to court, but can still be good faith). *But see, e.g., Margo v. Weiss,* 213 F.3d 55 (2d Cir.2000) (Rule 11(b)(2) "establishes an objective standard, intended to eliminate any 'empty-head pure-heart' justification for patently frivolous arguments").

33. *Rotella v. Wood,* 528 U.S. 549, 120 S.Ct. 1075, 145 L.Ed.2d 1047 (2000) (Rule 11(b)(3) provides flexibility by "allowing pleadings based on evidence reasonably anticipated after further investigation or discovery"). *See, e.g., Tennessee Valley Authority v. Whitman,* 336 F.3d 1236 n. 6 (11th Cir.2003) (when EPA files suit, it need not possess evidence sufficient for victory at trial; instead, it need only meet equivalent of "probable cause" standard of criminal law, and not even "more rigorous 'substantial evidence' " standard of administrative law); *O'Brien v. Alexander,* 101 F.3d 1479, 1489 (2d Cir.1996) ("[S]anctions may not be imposed unless a particular allegation is utterly lacking in support."). *But cf., Macken v. Jensen,* 333 F.3d 797 (7th Cir.2003) (Rule 11(b)(3) requires plaintiff "to establish evidentiary support [of amount in controversy], or at least a likelihood of obtaining that support, *before* filing suit in federal court.").

34. *But see, e.g., Attwood v. Singletary,* 105 F.3d 610, 613 (11th Cir.1997) (actions based on arguably good faith belief are sanctionable where party failed to make reasonable inquiry into accuracy of information).

RULE 11(c). SANCTIONS

CORE CONCEPT

Rule 11(c) regulates who may be sanctioned for violations of Rule 11(b), as well as how the sanction process may be initiated. Rule 11(c) also governs the extent and limitations of the court's sanctioning power.

APPLICATIONS

Applicability to Rule 11(a)

By its terms, Rule 11(c) applies only to violations of Rule 11(b), not Rule 11(a). It is unnecessary to apply Rule 11(c) to Rule 11(a) because the last sentence of Rule 11(a) contains its own sanction.

Persons Sanctioned

Rule 11(c) provides that in appropriate circumstances the court may sanction attorneys, law firms, or parties.[35] This is a change from the former provision, which was construed as not permitting sanctions against an entire law firm.

Sovereign Immunity

It appears that government attorneys and their clients are subject to sanctions, including monetary sanctions, notwithstanding considerations of sovereign immunity.[36]

Magistrate Judges

It appears that magistrate judges do not have independent authority to order sanctions under Rule 11.[37] However, the issue is sufficiently unsettled so that attorneys should investigate local practice.

Discretionary Sanctions

Rule 11(c) ordinarily permits the court to decide whether sanctions are appropriate.[38] Under the former provision, at least in theory,

35. *See, e.g., Union Planters Bank v. L & J Development Co.,* 115 F.3d 378, 384 (6th Cir. 1997) ("Rule 11 explicitly allows for the imposition of sanctions upon a party responsible for the rule's violation, provided that a represented party is not sanctioned for a violation of subsection (b)(2) involving unwarranted legal contentions.").

36. *See, e.g., Mattingly v. United States,* 939 F.2d 816, 817–18 (9th Cir.1991)(affirming monetary sanctions; held, government is not immune from Rule 11); *Adamson v. Bowen,* 855 F.2d 668, 672 (10th Cir.1988)(sovereign immunity does not bar monetary sanctions awarded under Rule 11); *cf., King v. Cooke,* 26 F.3d 720, 722 (7th Cir.1994), *cert. denied,* 514 U.S. 1023, 115 S.Ct. 1373, 131 L.Ed.2d 228 (1995)(noting with approval imposition of Rule 11 sanctions on Indiana Office of the Attorney General; however, no discussion of sovereign immunity).

37. *See, e.g., Rajaratnam v. Moyer,* 47 F.3d 922, 923 (7th Cir.1995)(Congress has restricted independent authority of magistrate judges to three areas, none of which includes Rule 11 matters); *Bennett v. General Caster Service of N. Gordon Company, Inc.,* 976 F.2d 995, 998 (6th Cir.1992)(magistrate judge may not order sanctions pursuant to Rule 11). *But see, Maisonville v. F2 America, Inc.,* 902 F.2d 746 (9th Cir.1990), *cert. denied,* 498 U.S. 1025, 111 S.Ct. 674, 112 L.Ed.2d 666 (1991)(permitting Rule 11 sanction by magistrate judge).

38. *See, e.g., Perez v. Posse Comitatus,* 373 F.3d 321 (2d Cir. 2004) (finding of Rule 11 violation still leaves district court with discretion whether to impose sanctions); *Silva v. Witschen,* 19 F.3d 725 (1st Cir.1994)(amended Rule 11 makes sanctions discretionary). *See also Salois v. Dime Savings Bank of New York, F.S.B.,* 128 F.3d 20, 28 (1st Cir.1997) ("Our review of denials of Rule 11 motions 'calls for somewhat more

sanctions were mandatory. Congress, of course, retains authority to reduce judicial discretion, and has occasionally done so.[39]

(1) HOW INITIATED

(A) BY MOTION

Specificity

Motions for sanctions under Rule 11(c) must be made separately from other motions [40] and must allege with specificity the alleged violation of Rule 11(b).

Service and Due Process

Rule 11(c)(1)(A) provides that motions for sanctions must be served as required under Rule 5. Of course, any entity who may be subjected to Rule 11 sanctions, whether on a party's motion or on the court's initiative, has a due process right to present a defense before any sanction is imposed.[41] In practice, the quality and nature of hearings is controlled by the specific factual circumstances in which the alleged Rule 11 violation occurs.[42]

restraint than review of positive actions imposing sanctions and shifting fees.' "). *But see Professional Management Associates, Inc. v. KPMG L.L.P.*, 345 F.3d 1030, 1033 (8th Cir. 2003), *cert. denied,* 540 U.S. 1162, 124 S.Ct. 1176, 157 L.Ed.2d 1207 (2004) ("[A] district court abuses its discretion by refusing to sanction a plaintiff and his counsel under Rule 11 for filing and maintaining a frivolous lawsuit when the plaintiff seeks to relitigate claims he had been denied leave to serve against the same defendant in an earlier lawsuit.").

39. *See, e.g., Simon DeBartolo Group, L.P. v. Richard E. Jacobs Group, Inc.,* 186 F.3d 157, 166–67 (2d Cir.1999) ("Ordinarily, courts are under no particular obligation to make findings with regard to the compliance of litigants and their counsel with Rule 11 or to impose sanctions once a violation is found." However, the Private Securities Litigation Reform Act of 1995 requires courts, at the conclusion of all private lawsuits arising under the Securities Exchange Act of 1934 to make specific findings as to compliance with Rule 11. If a violation occurs in such cases, the court has no discretion and must impose sanctions, which are rebuttably presumed to be attorneys' fees and other expenses incurred in the lawsuit. The standard for determining whether a Rule 11 violation has occurred, however, remains unchanged by this legislation). *See also Rombach v. Chang,* 355 F.3d 164, 178 (2d Cir. 2004) (PSLRA requires court to make findings as to each party's and attorney's compliance with every element of Rule 11(b); where violations are found, court must impose sanctions; no discretion, as is normally the case with Rule 11 issues).

40. *See, e.g., Perpetual Securities, Inc. v. Tang,* 290 F.3d 132, 142 (2d Cir.2002) (abuse of discretion to grant party's motion for sanctions which was not made separately, and was only included in memorandum addressing other issues before court); *Johnson v. Waddell and Reed, Inc.,* 74 F.3d 147, 150 (7th Cir.1996) (current version of Rule 11 requires "that a motion for sanctions . . . shall be made separately from other motions"). *But see Nisenbaum v. Milwaukee County,* 333 F.3d 804 (7th Cir.2003) (sending "letter" or "demand" to opposing party's lawyer instead of "motion" is nonetheless substantial compliance with Rule 11(c)(1)(A)).

41. *See, e.g., Perpetual Securities, Inc. v. Tang,* 290 F.3d 132, 141 n. 2 (2d Cir.2002) (whether on motion of party or on court's initiative, award of sanctions is inappropriate if party to be sanctioned has no opportunity to respond; when court initiates Rule 11 matter *sua sponte,* it must issue "show cause" order); *Vollmer v. Publishers Clearing House and Campus Subscriptions, Inc.,* 248 F.3d 698 (7th Cir.2001) (evidence of violation "must be stated with some specificity in the record" and there must be a full and fair opportunity to respond; also noting that court may consider past record of questionable conduct); *Tompkins v. Cyr,* 202 F.3d 770, 788 (5th Cir.2000) (where motion is served after trial had concluded, opponents of motion had no opportunity to defend or correct complaint).

42. *See, e.g., Spiller v. Ella Smithers Geriatric Center,* 919 F.2d 339, 346 (5th Cir.1990)(in Rule 11 cases, Due Process is usually satisfied if the accused has a chance to respond with a

"Safe Harbor"

Rule 11(c)(1)(A) does not permit sanctions motions to be filed with the court until 21 days after service of the motion, or within any other time frame the court provides.[43] If the document challenged by the sanctions motion is withdrawn or corrected within that time frame, the motion may not be filed with the court, and thus no sanctions will be imposed.[44]

Costs of Presenting or Opposing Sanctions Motion

Rule 11(c)(1)(A) provides the court with discretion to award costs, including attorney's fees, associated with presenting or opposing a sanctions motion.[45]

Law Firm's Liability: Presumptions

When a sanction is to be imposed, Rule 11(c)(1)(A) creates a strong presumption in favor of imposing it upon an entire law firm, in addition to whatever sanction may be imposed upon an individual attorney. This provision changes the old rule, which was construed to apply only to individual attorneys, not to their firms.

Standing: Non–Parties

In general, persons who are not parties to litigation have no standing to bring a Rule 11 motion.[46] Exceptions to that general rule arise in narrow circumstances where a non-party is affected directly by otherwise sanctionable conduct.[47]

brief); *Union Planters Bank v. L & J Development Co.*, 115 F.3d 378, 385 (6th Cir.1997) (evidentiary hearing not required where sanctioned parties had "ample" notice and "meaningful" opportunity to be heard).

43. *See, e.g., First Bank of Marietta v. Hartford Underwriters Insurance Co.*, 307 F.3d 501, 510–11 (6th Cir.2002) (Rule 11 sanction inapplicable where moving party did not comply with safe harbor provision); *Rector v. Approved Federal Savings Bank*, 265 F.3d 248, 252–53 (4th Cir.2001) (movant must serve Rule 11 motion at least 21 days before filing it with court; however, sanctioned party's failure to enter timely objection to movant's untimely service waives issue); *Hadges v. Yonkers Racing Corp.*, 48 F.3d 1320 (2d Cir.1995)(sanctions cannot be imposed on motion against party not afforded "safe harbor").

44. *Cf., e.g., Barber v. Miller*, 146 F.3d 707, 710–11 (9th Cir.1998) (motion served and filed after offending complaint was dismissed does not meet safe harbor requirement because no opportunity existed to withdraw complaint); *AeroTech, Inc. v. Estes*, 110 F.3d 1523 (10th Cir.1997) (where offending party dismissed its claim before Rule 11 motion was filed, sanctions were not possible because offending party had no opportunity to cure offense within time limit provided by safe harbor provision). *But see Truesdell v. Southern California Permanente Medical Group*, 293 F.3d 1146 (9th Cir.2002) (district court dismissed complaint, with leave to amend, on twentieth day after service of motion for sanctions; held, full 21–day period was provided because: (1) moving party had provided informal written notice of Rule 11 motion 27 days prior to actually filing motion; and (2) dismissal with leave to amend left offending party with additional time to withdraw complaint).

45. *See, e.g., Margolis v. Ryan*, 140 F.3d 850 (9th Cir.1998) (so noting; also observing that this provision alters earlier case law prohibiting award of fees and costs relating to filing sanctions motions).

46. *See, e.g., New York News, Inc. v. Kheel*, 972 F.2d 482, 488–89 (2d Cir.1992) (person who had not met intervention requirements of Rule 24 lacked standing to seek sanctions; moreover, such a person may not intervene solely to seek sanctions).

47. *See, e.g., Nyer v. Winterthur International*, 290 F.3d 456 (1st Cir.2002) (person not made party because judge reserved judgment on motion to amend complaint nevertheless had stand-

(B) ON COURT'S INITIATIVE

Show Cause Orders

When the court believes there may have been a violation of Rule 11(b), it may initiate the sanction process without waiting for a party to make a motion.[48] This is done by issuing an order directing the attorney, law firm, or party to show cause why it has not violated a provision of Rule 11(b). Rule 11(c)(1)(B) requires the court to identify the potentially offending conduct with reasonable specificity,[49] and guarantees an affected party both notice and an opportunity to defend against the proposed sanction.[50] Normally, a "show cause" order will be issued only in circumstances analogous to contempt of court.[51]

No Formal "Safe Harbor"

Rule 11(c)(1)(B) contains no explicit "safe harbor" provision such as is found in Rule 11(c)(1)(A), although the court in its discretion may afford an offending party substantial leeway.[52]

(2) NATURE OF SANCTION; LIMITATIONS

Policy of Deterrence

For the most part, sanctions for violations of Rule 11(b) are to be imposed primarily to deter similar violations by the offender or "others similarly situated." [53] This policy represents a substantial change from

ing to seek Rule 11 sanctions because he had to prepare possible defense against against pending amended complaint); *Greenberg v. Sala,* 822 F.2d 882 (9th Cir.1987) (individuals named in frivolous complaint, but not served, incurred costs and attorney fees and had Rule 11 standing); *Westmoreland v. CBS, Inc.,* 770 F.2d 1168 (D.C.Cir.1985) (non-party is entitled to Rule 11 after party's attorney commenced contempt proceedings against him).

48. *But cf., Perpetual Securities, Inc. v. Tang,* 290 F.3d 132, 141 n. 2 (2d Cir.2002) (when court initiates Rule 11 matter *sua sponte,* it must issue "show cause" order).

49. *See, e.g., Thornton v. General Motors Corp.,* 136 F.3d 450, 455 (5th Cir.1998) (per curiam) (order that does not identify specific offending conduct does not afford adequate notice and constitutes abuse of district court's discretion).

50. *See, e.g., Nuwesra v. Merrill Lynch, Fenner & Smith, Inc.,* 174 F.3d 87 (2d Cir.1999) (abuse of discretion to impose sanctions *sua sponte* without prior notice and opportunity to be heard); *Johnson v. Waddell & Reed, Inc.,* 74 F.3d 147, 151 (7th Cir.1996) (noting court's duty, when considering Rule 11 sanctions *sua sponte,* to identify offending contact specifically, and to provide adequate notice). *See also Dailey v. Vought Aircraft Co.,* 141 F.3d 224 (5th Cir. 1998) (hearing on sanction that takes place after sanction has already been imposed violates due process).

51. *See, e.g., Kaplan v. DaimlerChrysler, Inc.,* 331 F.3d 1251, 1255 (11th Cir.2003) (Because Rule 11(c)(1)(B) does not provide safe harbor, court must provide notice and opportunity to be heard and "a higher standard ('akin to contempt') than in the case of party-initiated sanctions.").

52. *See, e.g., Elliott v. Tilton,* 64 F.3d 213, 216 (5th Cir.1995) (noting contrast between "safe harbor" provision applicable when parties seek Rule 11 sanctions, and absence of "safe harbor" when court acts *sua sponte*). *See also In re Pennie & Edmonds, L.L.P.,* 323 F.3d 86, 87 (2d Cir.2003) (where court decides to impose sanctions sua sponte, law firm did not have benefit of "safe harbor" provision; thus sanctions were only appropriate for subjective bad faith, not for unreasonable but genuine good faith).

53. *See, e.g., Silva v. Witschen,* 19 F.3d 725 (1st Cir.1994)(under amended Rule 11, purpose is deterrence, not compensation of injured parties). *But cf., Union Planters Bank v. L & J Development Co.* 115 F.3d 378 (6th Cir.1997) (acknowledging general rule, but authorizing payment to injured party where sanctionable conduct was produced by bad motive).

previous versions of Rule 11, which included a substantially stronger interest in compensating parties who had been damaged by Rule 11 violations.[54]

Sanctions Available

Rule 11(c)(2) authorizes the court to issue nonmonetary orders,[55] to require payment of a penalty into court, to require payment of some or all of an opposing party's attorney's fees[56] and expenses, or any combination thereof.[57] Payment to an opposing party requires a motion by a party,[58] and is unlikely to occur unless the court believes such payment serves a deterrent purpose.[59] All of the monetary sanctions listed in Rule 11(c)(2) are subject to additional significant limitations, discussed below.

Calculating Attorney's Fees

If a sanction includes payment of an opposing party's attorney's fees or associated costs, courts generally use a "lodestar" method of calculating the appropriate amount. "The lodestar is determined by multiplying the number of hours reasonably expended by the reasonable hourly rate."[60] It should be noted, however, that the amount of fees

54. *But see* 15 U.S.C.A. § 78u–4 (subject to some exceptions, when party or attorney violates Rule 11(b) in litigation controlled by Private Securities Litigation Reform Act of 1995, there is a rebuttable presumption that appropriate sanction is reasonable attorney's fees and expenses directly resulting from violation). *See also Gurary v. Nu–Tech Bio-Med, Inc.,* 303 F.3d 212, 221–22 (2d Cir.2002), *cert. denied,* 538 U.S. 923, 123 S.Ct. 1583, 155 L.Ed.2d 314 (2003) (under P.S.L.R.A., substantial violation of Rule 11 requires sanction of repayment of full cost of violation to victim unless such a sanction would either be unreasonable burden or violation was de minimus; held, violation is not de minimus simply because offending complaint contains both frivolous and nonfrivolous allegations).

55. *See, e.g., Ortman v. Thomas,* 99 F.3d 807, 811 (6th Cir.1996) (rejecting permanent injunction on filing federal court lawsuit that arises out of claims alleged in, or underlying, case at bar; imposing, however, prefiling requirement mandating that, in future, sanctioned party would be required to satisfy magistrate judge that proposed claims were not frivolous or asserted for an improper purpose). *But see Tropf v. Fidelity National Title Insurance Co.,* 289 F.3d 929, 940–41 (6th Cir.2002), *cert. denied,* 537 U.S. 1118, 123 S.Ct. 887, 154 L.Ed.2d 797 (2003) (approving permanent injunction against future lawsuit arising out of claims underlying instant case; applying injunction to federal and state filings as well as administrative proceedings; distinguishing *Ortman,* supra); *Villar v. Crowley Maritime Corp.,* 990 F.2d 1489, 1498–99 (5th Cir.1993), *cert. denied,* 510 U.S. 1044, 114 S.Ct. 690, 126 L.Ed.2d 658 (1994) (permanent injunction against similar lawsuits in both federal and state court).

56. *But cf., Massengale v. Ray,* 267 F.3d 1298, 1302 (11th Cir.2001) (per curiam) (pro se litigant who is also a lawyer is not entitled to attorney's fees because pro se parties, by definition, have no such fees).

57. *See, e.g., Riccard v. Prudential Life Insurance Co. of America,* 307 F.3d 1277, 1295 (11th Cir.2002) (order enjoining new actions without first obtaining leave of court was reasonable where monetary sanction would not prevent further harassment of opposing party or clogging of judicial machinery).

58. *See, e.g., Methode Electronics, Inc. v. Adam Technologies, Inc.,* 371 F.3d 923, 926 (7th Cir. 2004) (if sanction is not imposed as result of motion by party but instead on court's initiative, attorney fees cannot be imposed); *Baffa v. Donaldson, Lufkin & Jenrette Securities Corp.,* 222 F.3d 52, 57 (2d Cir.2000) (attorneys' fees may be awarded only pursuant to motion; such fees may not be awarded by court on its own initiative).

59. *See, e.g., Barber v. Miller,* 146 F.3d 707 (9th Cir.1998) (if court initiates sanction, payment must be to court, not to party; payment to party appropriate only when sanction initiated by motion and only to serve deterrent purpose).

60. *View Engineering, Inc. v. Robotic Vision Systems, Inc.,* 208 F.3d 981, 987 n. 7 (Fed.Cir. 2000).

recoverable from the offending party is limited to fees "incurred as a direct result of the [violation]."[61] Fees for government attorneys are calculated on the same basis as prevailing rates in the private sector.[62]

Nonmonetary Sanctions

Under previous versions of Rule 11, nonmonetary sanctions included reprimands,[63] findings or dismissals unfavorable to the offender.[64] Presumably these are the kinds of nonmonetary sanctions available under the current version of Rule 11.[65]

Punitive Damages

The previous version of Rule 11 was construed to permit punitive damages when the court found that sanction appropriate. [66] It appears that under the current version of Rule 11, punitive damage payments to parties are inappropriate.

Financial Status of Offender

In assessing monetary sanctions, courts take into account the financial status of the offender. However, if the offender wants the court to know of the offender's limited ability to pay sanctions, the burden is on the offender to bring the relevant facts before the court.[67]

61. *Divane v. Krull Electric Co.,* 200 F.3d 1020, 1030 (7th Cir.1999) (error to impose all fees incurred in litigation where at least some of such expenses are unrelated to violations of Rule 11).

62. *See, e.g., Napier v. Thirty or More Unidentified Federal Agents, Employees or Officers,* 855 F.2d 1080, 1092–93 (3d Cir. 1988) (assistant United States attorney should be billed at appropriate market rate in private sector, even in the absence of a regular billing rate for government lawyers).

63. *See, e.g., In re Walter F. Kelly,* 808 F.2d 549 (7th Cir.1986).

64. *See, e.g., Hrobowski v. Commonwealth Edison Co.,* 203 F.3d 445, 448 (7th Cir.2000) ("[W]hile Rule 11 . . . does not mandate dismissal for false statements, the district court could do so if it deemed that [plaintiff's] deeds merited such a harsh punishment." Court could also choose a less severed sanction.); *Hatchet v. Nettles,* 201 F.3d 651, 654 (5th Cir.2000) ("Prisoners are reminded that false statements in their pleadings may result in sanctions against them . . . including dismissal with or without prejudice.").

65. *See, e.g., In the Matter of Dragoo,* 186 F.3d 614, 615–16 (5th Cir.1999) (husband and wife attorneys suspended from practice before bankruptcy court for four years; readmission conditioned upon (1) 15 hours of continuing legal education in consumer bankruptcy law, (2) submission of records of all grievance and malpractice claims brought against attorneys, and disposition of such claims, and (3) evidence of mental stability of husband, who had used depression as defense against Rule 11 sanctions; however, rejecting requirement that wife, who had indicated no mental instability, must also demonstrate mental stability). *But see, Hutchinson v. Pfeil,* 208 F.3d 1180, 1186 (10th Cir.2000) (sanctions should not be used to drive attorneys out of practice; when district court believes such remedies are appropriate, referral should be made to appropriate authorities who will ensure that attorneys receive due process); *Thornton v. General Motors Corp.,* 136 F.3d 450, 455 (5th Cir.1998) (suspension from practice before court is inappropriate sanction under Rule 11(c)(1)(B); "[W]hen a district court finds that a disciplinary sanction more severe than admonition, reprimand, or censure under Rule 11 is warranted, it should refer the matter to the appropriate disciplinary authorities.").

66. *See, e.g., Robeson Defense Committee v. Britt,* 132 F.R.D. 650 (E.D.N.C.1989), *affirmed in part, vacated in part on other grounds,* 914 F.2d 505 (4th Cir.1990), *cert. denied,* 499 U.S. 969, 111 S.Ct. 1607, 113 L.Ed.2d 669 (1991).

67. *See, e.g., Silva v. Witschen,* 19 F.3d 725 (1st Cir.1994)(if the offender presents no such facts, the court has no duty to inquire into them).

Alternative Remedies

Rule 11 is in addition to whatever remedies, such as censure or reprimand,[68] contempt, disciplinary complaints to a bar, Federal Rule of Appellate Procedure 38 (frivolous appeals), state claims such as abuse of process,[69] 28 U.S.C.A. § 1447(c) (expenses, including attorney's fees, for improper removal),[70] 28 U.S.C.A. § 1915(a) and (d)(frivolous filings *in forma pauperis*), and 28 U.S.C.A. § 1927 (unreasonable and vexatious multiplication of proceedings), the court or other persons may have.[71]

Duty to Mitigate

Under the previous version of Rule 11, a party seeking damages under Rule 11 must have made reasonable efforts to mitigate its losses.[72] Presumably that requirement carries over to the current Rule 11, at least as to those unusual circumstances where a party may be entitled to compensation for a violation.

(A)

Monetary Sanctions: Frivolous Arguments of Law

Rule 11(c)(2)(A) explicitly prohibits application of monetary sanctions against a represented party for violations of Rule 11(b)(2), governing requirements that arguments for changes in law be nonfrivolous.[73] Monetary sanctions obviously remain available against attorneys or non-represented parties who violate Rule 11(b)(2).

68. *See, e.g., Thomas v. Tenneco Packaging Co.,* 293 F.3d 1306 (11th Cir.2002) (per curiam) (separate from Rule 11, district court has inherent power to sanction attorney for documents that were rude and demeaning, with no purpose except harassment and intimidation of opposing counsel). *See also Miller v. Cardinale,* 361 F.3d 539, 548 (9th Cir. 2004) (noting that sanctions under court's inherent power require finding of bad faith, while imposition of Rule 11 sanctions "requires only a showing of objectively unreasonable conduct").

69. *See, e.g., U.S. Express Lines, Ltd. v. Higgins,* 281 F.3d 383, 393 (3d Cir.2002) (Federal Rules do not preempt abuse of process and similar state torts).

70. *See, e.g., Wisconsin v. Hotline Industries, Inc.,* 236 F.3d 363, 366 (7th Cir.2000) (§ 1447(c) is alternative to Rule 11, which " 'can be used to impose a more severe sanction when appropriate.' ").

71. *Clinton v. Jones,* 520 U.S. 681, 709 n. 42, 117 S.Ct. 1636, 1652 n. 42, 137 L.Ed.2d 945 (1997) (court may apply broad array of authority, including Rule 11, 28 U.S.C.A. § 1927, and/or its inherent powers). *See also Xantech Corp. v. Ramco Industries, Inc.,* 159 F.3d 1089, 1094 (7th Cir.1998) ("[F]ee requests made under Rule 11 do not pose a res judicata bar to subsequent actions for claims akin to malicious prosecution.").

72. *See, e.g., Pollution Control Industries of America, Inc. v. Van Gundy,* 21 F.3d 152, 156 (7th Cir.1994)(aggrieved party has duty to mitigate its costs "by resolving frivolous issues quickly and efficiently").

73. *See, e.g., Tropf v. Fidelity National Title Insurance Co.,* 289 F.3d 929, 939 (6th Cir.2002), *cert. denied,* 537 U.S. 1118, 123 S.Ct. 887, 154 L.Ed.2d 797 (2003) ("[M]onetary sanctions may not be imposed on represented parties for the violation of subsection (b)(2) involving unwarranted legal contentions."); *Gurary v. Winehouse,* 235 F.3d 792, 797 (2d Cir.2000), *cert. denied,* 534 U.S. 826, 122 S.Ct. 66, 151 L.Ed.2d 33 (2001). *See also Baffa v. Donaldson, Lufkin & Jenrette Securities Corp.,* 222 F.3d 52, 57 (2d Cir.2000) (order to represented party to pay attorney's fees for Rule 11(b)(2) violation is abuse of discretion because it contravenes prohibition on monetary sanctions against represented parties under Rule 11(c)(2)).

(B)

Court–Initiated Monetary Sanctions: Settlement

If the court seeks to impose monetary sanctions on its own initiative, it may not do so if its show cause order was not issued before the parties voluntarily dismissed or settled the claims. However, Rule 11(c)(2)(B) provides no similar protection if the case goes to judgment.

Motions for Sanctions: Timing

Under the previous version of Rule 11, courts generally required that motions for sanctions be filed as soon as practicable after the alleged violation has occurred.[74] That principle carries over to the current version of Rule 11. However, courts using the previous version were divided as to whether motions may be filed after the case has ended. Under the current version of Rule 11, it appears settled that a movant's duty to offer the offending party a "safe harbor" means that an injured party may not move for sanctions after a case has ended or the court has rejected the offending contention.[75]

(3) ORDER

Order Imposing Sanctions

Rule 11(c)(3) provides that if the court imposes sanctions, it will describe the offending conduct and explain the basis for the sanction the court imposed.[76]

74. *See, e.g., Hunter v. Earthgrains Co. Bakery,* 281 F.3d 144, 152 (4th Cir.2002) (delay of 14 months in moving for sanctions is unacceptable, even where opponent of sanctions has not alleged prejudice or lack of notice).

75. *See, e.g., Tompkins v. Cyr,* 202 F.3d 770, 787–88 (5th Cir.2000) (rejecting sanctions where Rule 11 motion was not filed until after conclusion of trial); *Ridder v. City of Springfield,* 109 F.3d 288 (6th Cir.1997), *cert. denied,* 522 U.S. 1046, 118 S.Ct. 687, 139 L.Ed.2d 634 (1998). *But cf., Divane v. Krull Electric Co.,* 200 F.3d 1020, 1025–26 (7th Cir.1999) (initial Rule 11 motion was premature, but gave clear notice to offending party that appropriateness of motion could not be determined until, after trial, lack of evidentiary support for offending claims might be clear; result was that trial court extended period of safe harbor for duration of trial; additionally appellate court notes that "Rule 11(c)(1)(A) does not specify any time period when a motion for sanctions must be filed, and we see no need to establish one. . . . By themselves, the purposes of Rule 11(c)(1)(A) do not justify a broad rule that sanctions cannot be imposed as a result of a motion properly submitted to the court after a judgment."). By contrast, when a court initiates a sanctions process by issuing a show cause order before a plaintiff voluntarily dismisses a case, the court retains power to impose sanctions even after dismissal. *Cooter & Gell v. Hartmarx Corp.,* 496 U.S. 384, 110 S.Ct. 2447, 110 L.Ed.2d 359 (1990). *But cf., Woodard v. STP Corp.,* 170 F.3d 1043, 1045 (11th Cir.1999) (held, error for court to enter order retaining jurisdiction to impose sanctions under Rule 11 if plaintiff's attorneys bring a subsequent lawsuit in another forum; held, only court hearing subsequent lawsuit could impose such sanctions).

76. *But cf., McLane, Graf, Raulerson & Middleton, P.A. v. Rechberger,* 280 F.3d 26, 44–45 (1st Cir.2002) (district court encouraged, but not required, to give reasons for denying sanctions); *Anderson v. Boston School Committee,* 105 F.3d 762, 769 (1st Cir.1997) (no requirement for explicit findings explaining denial of sanctions "where the record itself, evidence or colloquy, clearly indicates one or more sufficient supporting reasons. The occasional statements referring to an inflexible requirement for explicit findings in every case do not reflect our present considered judgment.").

Rule 11(d). INAPPLICABILITY TO DISCOVERY

CORE CONCEPT

Rules 26 through 37, governing the discovery process, control the circumstances when sanctions may be imposed for inappropriate behavior in discovery. For that reason, Rule 11(d) provides that Rule 11(a), (b) and (c) have no applicability to discovery issues.[77]

ADDITIONAL RESEARCH REFERENCES

Wright & Miller, *Federal Practice and Procedure* §§ 1331–39.

C.J.S. Federal Civil Procedure §§ 260.

West's Key No. Digests, Federal Civil Procedure ⇐660–661, 2750–2848.

77. *See, e.g., Patelco Credit Union v. Sahni*, 262 F.3d 897, 913 n. 15 (9th Cir.2001) ("Rule 11(d) specifically exempts discovery motions and objections from its procedural requirements."); *Baffa v. Donaldson, Lufkin & Jenrette Securities Corp.*, 222 F.3d 52, 57 (2d Cir.2000) (failure to answer interrogatories fully is not sanctionable under Rule 11).

RULE 12

DEFENSES AND OBJECTIONS—WHEN AND HOW PRESENTED—BY PLEADING OR MOTION—MOTION FOR JUDGMENT ON THE PLEADINGS

(a) When Presented.

(1) Unless a different time is prescribed in a statute of the United States, a defendant shall serve an answer

(A) within 20 days after being served with the summons and complaint, or

(B) if service of the summons has been timely waived on request under Rule 4(d), within 60 days after the date when the request for waiver was sent, or within 90 days after that date if the defendant was addressed outside any judicial district of the United States.

(2) A party served with a pleading stating a cross-claim against that party shall serve an answer thereto within 20 days after being served. The plaintiff shall serve a reply to a counterclaim in the answer within 20 days after service of the answer, or, if a reply is ordered by the court, within 20 days after service of the order, unless the order otherwise directs.

(3)(A) The United States, an agency of the United States, or an officer or employee of the United States sued in an official capacity, shall serve an answer to the complaint or cross-claim— or a reply to a counterclaim—within 60 days after the United States attorney is served with the pleading asserting the claim.

(B) An officer or employee of the United States sued in an individual capacity for acts or omissions occurring in connection with the performance of duties on behalf of the United States shall serve an answer to the complaint or cross-claim—or a reply to a counterclaim—within 60 days after service on the officer or employee, or service on the United States attorney, whichever is later.

(4) Unless a different time is fixed by court order, the service of a motion permitted under this rule alters these periods of time as follows:

(A) if the court denies the motion or postpones its disposition until the trial on the merits, the responsive pleading shall be served within 10 days after notice of the court's action; or

(B) if the court grants a motion for a more definite statement, the responsive pleading shall be served within 10 days after the service of the more definite statement.

(b) How Presented. Every defense, in law or fact, to a claim for relief in any pleading, whether a claim, counterclaim, cross-claim, or third-party claim, shall be asserted in the responsive pleading thereto if one is required, except that the following defenses may at the option of the pleader be made by motion: (1) lack of jurisdiction over the subject matter, (2) lack of jurisdiction over the person, (3) improper venue, (4) insufficiency of process, (5) insufficiency of service of process, (6) failure to state a claim upon which relief can be granted, (7) failure to join a party under Rule 19. A motion making any of these defenses shall be made before pleading if a further pleading is permitted. No defense or objection is waived by being joined with one or more other defenses or objections in a responsive pleading or motion. If a pleading sets forth a claim for relief to which the adverse party is not required to serve a responsive pleading, the adverse party may assert at the trial any defense in law or fact to that claim for relief. If, on a motion asserting the defense numbered (6) to dismiss for failure of the pleading to state a claim upon which relief can be granted, matters outside the pleading are presented to and not excluded by the court, the motion shall be treated as one for summary judgment and disposed of as provided in Rule 56, and all parties shall be given reasonable opportunity to present all material made pertinent to such a motion by Rule 56.

(c) Motion for Judgment on the Pleadings. After the pleadings are closed but within such time as not to delay the trial, any party may move for judgment on the pleadings. If, on a motion for judgment on the pleadings, matters outside the pleadings are presented to and not excluded by the court, the motion shall be treated as one for summary judgment and disposed of as provided in Rule 56, and all parties shall be given reasonable opportunity to present all material made pertinent to such a motion by Rule 56.

(d) Preliminary Hearings. The defenses specifically enumerated (1)–(7) in subdivision (b) of this rule, whether made in a pleading or by motion, and the motion for judgment mentioned in subdivision (c) of this rule shall be heard and determined before trial on application of any party, unless the court orders that the hearing and determination thereof be deferred until the trial.

(e) Motion for More Definite Statement. If a pleading to which a responsive pleading is permitted is so vague or ambiguous that a party cannot reasonably be required to frame a responsive pleading, the party may move for a more definite statement before interposing a responsive pleading. The motion shall point out the defects complained of and the details desired. If the motion is granted and the order of the court is not obeyed within 10 days after notice of the order or within such other time as the court may fix, the court may strike the pleading to which the motion was directed or make such order as it deems just.

(f) Motion to Strike. Upon motion made by a party before responding to a pleading or, if no responsive pleading is permitted by these rules, upon motion made by a party within 20 days after the service of the pleading upon the party or upon the court's own initiative at any time, the court may order stricken from any pleading any insufficient defense or any redundant, immaterial, impertinent, or scandalous matter.

(g) Consolidation of Defenses in Motion. A party who makes a motion under this rule may join with it any other motions herein provided for and then available to the party. If a party makes a motion under this rule but omits therefrom any defense or objection then available to the party which this rule permits to be raised by motion, the party shall not thereafter make a motion based on the defense or objection so omitted, except a motion as provided in subdivision (h)(2) hereof on any of the grounds there stated.

(h) Waiver or Preservation of Certain Defenses.

(1) A defense of lack of jurisdiction over the person, improper venue, insufficiency of process, or insufficiency of service of process is waived (A) if omitted from a motion in the circumstances described in subdivision (g), or (B) if it is neither made by motion under this rule nor included in a responsive pleading or an amendment thereof permitted by Rule 15(a) to be made as a matter of course.

(2) A defense of failure to state a claim upon which relief can be granted, a defense of failure to join a party indispensable under Rule 19, and an objection of failure to state a legal defense to a claim may be made in any pleading permitted or ordered under Rule 7(a), or by motion for judgment on the pleadings, or at the trial on the merits.

(3) Whenever it appears by suggestion of the parties or otherwise that the court lacks jurisdiction of the subject matter, the court shall dismiss the action.

[Amended December 27, 1946, effective March 19, 1948; January 21, 1963, effective July 1, 1963; February 28, 1966, effective July 1, 1966; March 2, 1987, effective August 1, 1987; April 22, 1993, effective December 1, 1993; April 17, 2000, December 1, 2000.]

AUTHORS' COMMENTARY ON RULE 12

PURPOSE AND SCOPE

Rule 12 fixes the time and procedures for serving responsive pleadings, for asserting factual and legal defenses and objections, and for making preliminary motions and motions for judgment on the pleadings.

Answers to complaints generally must be served within 20 days after service of process. If a defendant waives formal service of process, the answer is due within 60 days. Answers to cross-claims and replies to counterclaims must be served within 20 days of service. Longer periods apply to service made on the United States and federal employees or when service is made outside the country. These response periods may be modified by court-approved stipulation, by court order, or by the defendant's filing of a Rule 12 motion.

Parties generally should assert their defenses and objections in their first responsive pleadings. However, certain enumerated defenses and objections may, at the party's discretion, be raised earlier by motion. If the party chooses to file such a motion, the party must assert all enumerated defenses and objections in the same motion.

A failure to assert all defenses and objections in the responsive pleading, or alternatively, a failure to include all enumerated defenses and objections when making a Rule 12 motion, results in a waiver of certain unasserted defenses and objections.

RULE 12(a). TIME FOR SERVING RESPONSIVE PLEADINGS

CORE CONCEPT

Responsive pleadings generally must be filed within 20 days after service of the document to which they relate. If, however, the defendant waives formal service of process, the answer generally is due within 60 days after the plaintiff's request for waiver was sent.

APPLICATIONS

Answers and Replies

Unless a Rule 12 motion is filed, a party must serve an answer within 20 days after being served with a summons and complaint, or a cross-claim. A party must serve a reply within 20 days after being served with a counterclaim or a court order directing a reply.

Note: The time limitations set in this Rule run from the date of "service", not the date of "filing". Under Rule 5, a responsive pleading may be "filed" with the court either before service or within a reasonable time after service.

State Court Rules Do Not Apply

Unless, by a statute applicable to the particular lawsuit at issue, Congress has provided otherwise, the time for responding to a summons and complaint is set forth in Rule 12(a). The federal time periods apply even if the defendant is served pursuant to State law and the relevant State law would otherwise afford the defendant a longer time to reply.[1]

Exception When Formal Service of Process is Waived

The Rules encourage defendants to waive the requirement of formal service of process.[2] In return for waiving formal service, Rule 12(a)(1)(B) gives the defendant additional time to respond. If the request for waiver was mailed to a defendant within the United States, a defendant who waives formal service of process has 60 days from the date the request for waiver was sent in which to serve an answer. If the request was mailed to a defendant outside the United States, a defendant who waives service has 90 days from the date the request for waiver was sent in which to serve an answer. These provisions apply only to service of original process, and not to counterclaims or cross-claims.

Exception for United States and Federal Officers and Agencies

Responsive pleadings must be filed within 60 days by the United States, by its agencies, and by those federal officers and employees who are *either* sued in their "official" capacities or sued in their "individual" capacities for acts or omissions occurring in connection with the performance of their federal duties.[3] In "individual" capacity, "on-the-job" claim lawsuits against federal personnel, this 60–day period begins to run when the individual is served or when the United States Attorney is served, whichever is later.[4] In all other cases (lawsuits against the United States, a federal agency, or a federal officer or employee sued in an official capacity), the 60–day period begins to run when the United States Attorney is served.[5] This pleading timetable applies to both current and former federal officers and employees.[6]

Note: When a pleading names as defendants both a governmental party and a non-governmental party, only the governmental party has 60 days in which to serve a responsive pleading. The non-

1. *See Beller & Keller v. Tyler*, 120 F.3d 21 (2d Cir.1997).

2. *See* Rule 4(d).

3. *See* Rule 12(a)(3)(A)-(3)(B).

4. *See* Rule 12(a)(3)(B).

5. *See* Rule 12(a)(3)(A).

6. *See* Rule 12(a)(3) advisory committee notes to 2000 amendments.

governmental party's time for serving a responsive pleading remains 20 days.

Enlargement of Time by Court

The court may enlarge the time for serving responsive pleadings. Upon stipulation approved by the court, the parties can agree to an enlargement of time for serving responsive pleadings.

Tolling for Pending Motion

The service of a Rule 12 motion tolls the time for serving a responsive pleading. Note, however, that the service time is *not* tolled for every defendant, but only for those defendants who file Rule 12 motions.[7] Note also that this exception does *not* apply where the motion is a Rule 12(f) motion to strike.

- If the court denies a party's Rule 12 motion or postpones ruling on the Rule 12 motion until trial, the responsive pleading is due within 10 days after receiving "notice" of the court's order.[8]
- If the court grants a motion for a more definite statement under Rule 12(e), the responsive pleading is due within 10 days after service of the pleader's more definite statement.
- These 10–day time periods can be displaced by a different schedule set in the court's order on the Rule 12 motion.
- If service is made on a party by mail (or through the special, service-by-consent means provided in Rule 5(b)(2)(D)), these 10 day periods are extended by 3 extra days.[9]

Effect of Tolling for Pending, Partial Motion

The text of Rule 12 does not expressly state whether making a partial Rule 12 motion (*e.g.*, motion to dismiss counts I, III, and V) tolls the time for serving a responsive pleading to the unchallenged counts. The very substantial majority of the courts to have considered the question favor a complete tolling,[10] but a few courts and some practi-

7. *See Hanley v. Volpe*, 48 F.R.D. 387, 387–88 (E.D.Wis.1970).

8. Neither the Advisory Committee Notes nor published case law have expositively defined when a party is deemed to have received "notice" of such a court order within the meaning of Rule 12(a)(4)(A) (*e.g.*, when the order is docketed, when it arrives at counsel's office or the party's home, when counsel or the party actually sees it, etc.). The sparse case law references to this section either offer no substantive guidance at all or use language that appears directly inconsistent with the plain terms of the Rule itself. *See, e.g., United States v. $57,960.00 in U.S. Currency*, 58 F.Supp.2d 660 (D.S.C.1999) (citing Rule as requiring party to file an answer within 10 days "of being served" with the denial order); *Ziegler v. Ziegler*, 28 F.Supp.2d 601, 620 (E.D.Wash.1998) (citing Rules as requiring party to file an answer within 10 days "after receipt" of denial order); *United States v. Ware*, 172 F.R.D. 458, 459 (D.Kan.1997) (citing Rule as mandating that party file an answer within ten days "after the court's denial" of the motion); *Johnson-Medland v. Bethanna*, 1996 WL 612467, at *6 (E.D.Pa.1996) (citing Rule as requiring party to serve an answer within 10 days "of the date of this order").

9. *See* Rule 6(e).

10. *See Godlewski v. Affiliated Computer Servs., Inc.*, 210 F.R.D. 571, 572–73 (E.D.Va. 2002) (following majority approach, and holding that motion to dismiss suspends time for responding to all portions of complaint, even unchallenged ones); *Batdorf v. Trans Union*, 2000 WL 635455 (N.D.Cal.2000); *Finnegan v. University of Rochester Med. Ctr.*, 180 F.R.D. 247, 249–

tioner commentary prefer a requirement that the responding party serve an interim responsive pleading to the unchallenged counts.[11]

The apparent uniformity of the courts' rejection of this interim responsive pleading approach is noteworthy, and should give comfort to most practitioners (particularly those located in the growing number of jurisdictions where this approach has been affirmatively rejected). For those who need even greater certainty on the issue, practitioners might seek a stipulated extension of time from their opponents or file a motion for enlargement of time with the court.

Manipulative Motions

Courts will not tolerate the use of this Rule 12 tolling feature in attempts to frivolously manipulate the time period for responsive pleading. Thus, the pending-motion tolling rule will not apply where a motion for summary judgment is deliberately mislabeled as a Rule 12 motion solely to avoid the obligation to file an answer.[12]

RULE 12(b). DEFENSES AND OBJECTIONS

CORE CONCEPT

All legal and factual defenses to a claim for relief must be asserted in the responsive pleading to the claim. However, seven enumerated defenses may alternatively be asserted by motion served before the responsive pleading is due (normally 20 days from service of the initial pleading or 60 days with waiver of service).

50 (W.D.N.Y.1998); *Schwartz v. Berry College, Inc.*, 1997 WL 579166 (N.D.Ga.1997) (same); *Oil Express Nat'l, Inc. v. D'Alessandro*, 173 F.R.D. 219, 221 (N.D.Ill.1997); *Alex. Brown & Sons Inc. v. Marine Midland Banks, Inc.*, 1997 WL 97837 (S.D.N.Y.1997); *Porter v. United States Dep't of Army*, 1995 WL 461898 (N.D.Ill.1995), *aff'd*, 99 F.3d 1142 (7th Cir.1996) (Table), *cert. denied*, 520 U.S. 1129, 117 S.Ct. 1274, 137 L.Ed.2d 351 (1997); *Becker v. Fitzgerald*, 1995 WL 215143 (N.D.Ill.1995); *Circuit City Stores, Inc. v. Citgo Petroleum Corp.*, 1994 WL 483463 (E.D.Pa. 1994); *Rawson v. Royal Maccabees Life Ins. Co.*, 1994 WL 9638 (N.D.Ill.1994); *Brocksopp Eng'g, Inc. v. Bach–Simpson, Ltd.*, 136 F.R.D. 485, 486–87 (E.D.Wis.1991); *Ricciuti v. New York City Transit Auth.*, 1991 WL 221110 (S.D.N.Y.1991); *Baker v. Universal Die Casting, Inc.*, 725 F.Supp. 416, 420–21 (W.D.Ark.1989); *Business Incentives Co. v. Sony Corp. of America*, 397 F.Supp. 63 (S.D.N.Y.1975).

11. *See Gerlach v. Michigan Bell Tel. Co.*, 448 F.Supp. 1168 (E.D.Mich.1978)(holding that responsive pleading was required to unchallenged counts, refusing to enter default, but awarding plaintiffs attorney fees for filing for default). *See also Okaya (USA), Inc. v. United States*, 2003 WL 22284567, at *5 (CIT 2003) (noting that that motion to dismiss part of a complaint did not extend time to answer remainder). *See generally* Scott L. Cagan, *A "Partial" Motion to Dismiss Under Federal Rule of Civil Procedure 12: You Had Better Answer*, 39 Fed. B.J. 202 (1992)(advocating same result). *But see Tingley Sys., Inc. v. CSC Consulting, Inc.*, 152 F.Supp.2d 95, 122 (D.Mass.2001) (noting that "no court has relied on [*Gerlach*'s] reasoning or followed its ruling" and that "one court explicitly rejected its reasoning").

12. *See Ricke v. Armco, Inc.*, 158 F.R.D. 149 (D.Minn.1994)("Such an attempt to manipulate the Federal Rules of Civil Procedure should not be condoned or encouraged by the Court"). *See also RTC v. Ruggiero*, 994 F.2d 1221 (7th Cir. 1993)(holding that frivolous motion under Rule 12 buys the movant no additional time within which to serve a responsive pleading).

APPLICATIONS

Enumerated Defenses

As to the following seven defenses, a party may assert the defense either in the responsive pleading or by motion served before the responsive pleading is due:

- Lack of Subject Matter Jurisdiction, Rule 12(b)(1).
- Lack of Personal ("In Personam") Jurisdiction, Rule 12(b)(2).
- Improper Venue, Rule 12(b)(3).
- Insufficient Process, Rule 12(b)(4).
- Insufficient Service of Process, Rule 12(b)(5).
- Failure to State a Claim for which Relief Can Be Granted, Rule 12(b)(6).
- Failure to Join a Party Under Rule 19 (persons needed for just adjudication), Rule 12(b)(7).

Waived Defenses and Objections

If a party chooses to assert a Rule 12 motion, the party should join all Rule 12 defenses and objections in that motion. If the party makes a Rule 12 motion but omits a potential Rule 12 objection to (2) personal jurisdiction, (3) venue, (4) process, or (5) service, that objection is waived and cannot be asserted later in the responsive pleading or in a subsequent motion or trial objection.[13]

Time for Making Motion

A party who intends to assert a Rule 12 defense or objection in a motion must do so before the responsive pleading is due. This requires Rule 12 motions to be served generally within 20 days after service of the complaint, cross-claim, or counterclaim to which the motions are directed. A defendant who waives formal service of process is given 60 days in which to respond. The parties can, upon court approval, stipulate to an extension of time. Moreover, although the time for filing a Rule 12 motion is logistically tied to the time for filing an answer,[14] a delay in filing such a motion may, under certain circumstances, still be permitted.[15]

Note: In the unusual instance where a responsive pleading is not required (*e.g.*, counterclaim asserted in cross-claim answer, third-party answer, or intervention complaint answer), the responding party's defenses and objections can be asserted at trial.

13. *See* Rule 12(h).

14. By its terms, Rule 12(b) motions must "be made before pleading if a further pleading is permitted". *See* Rule 12(b). That pleading, in turn, must be made within the time prescribed in Rule 12(a)–20 days (when served domestically), 60 days (when service is waived or upon the United States), or 90 days (when served internationally) after service. *See* Rule 12(a).

15. *See Luv N' Care, Ltd. v. Babelito, S.A.*, 306 F.Supp.2d 468, 468–73 (S.D.N.Y. 2004) (ruling that motion was not waived where delay was explained by settlement discussions and certain service complications).

Amended Pleadings

When litigants amend their pleadings, the responding parties may withdraw their answers or replies, and replead. If an amendment adds new matter that gives rise to a new, previously inapplicable Rule 12 motion, the responding party may assert the new Rule 12 defense by motion or responsive pleading.

Note: An amendment does not give the responding party an entirely new opportunity to assert Rule 12 defenses. A possible Rule 12 defense that was not asserted to the original pleading (and, thus, was waived) cannot be asserted to the amended pleading unless it relates to new matter added by the amendment.[16]

Preliminary Motions Not Listed in Rule 12

Rule 12 does not provide an exhaustive list of all possible preliminary motions.[17] Motions for enlargements of time, to amend a pleading, to intervene, to substitute parties, or for the entering of a stay or an order commanding the posting of security, may all be raised as preliminary motions. The court's broad discretion and the federal policy against unwarranted, dilatory motions are the principal limitations on such unenumerated motions.

Form of Motion

Rule 12 provides only sparse guidance on the form and procedure for federal motion practice.[18] The other Rules provide very little additional detail. For example, Rule 7 requires that motions generally be in writing, be signed in accordance with Rule 11, include a caption, state with particularity the basis for the motion, and request specific relief.[19] Rule 5 requires that motions be served upon each party to the litigation.[20] Rule 78 provides for regularly and sufficiently frequent "motion days" for the hearing and disposition of motions, unless "local conditions" make such a practice impracticable.[21] Rule 78 also provides that the district court, by rule or order, may permit motions to be submitted and determined on the papers only, without oral argument.[22]

Most of the other details of federal motion practice and procedure are governed by local court rules.[23] Practitioners are strongly cautioned: these details often vary greatly from one judicial district to another. For example:

16. *See Sohns v. Dahl,* 392 F.Supp. 1208, 1220 n. 7 (W.D.Va.1975).

17. *See International Ass'n of Entrepreneurs of America v. Angoff,* 58 F.3d 1266, 1271 (8th Cir.1995)(commenting that although Rule 12(b) ostensibly enumerates available pre-answer motions, the district courts have discretion to permit other, unenumerated pre-answer motions), *cert. denied,* 516 U.S. 1072, 116 S.Ct. 774, 133 L.Ed.2d 726 (1996).

18. *See, e.g.,* Rule 12(b) (enumerating types of pre-answer motions; requiring motion before answer; permitting extrinsic materials to be submitted on converted motions).

19. *See* Rule 7(b)(1)-(b)(3).

20. *See* Rule 5(a).

21. *See* Rule 78.

22. *See* Rule 78.

23. *See* Rule 83(a) (authorizing districts to establish local rules of practice).

Pre-Filing Consultation: Some districts require that the moving party meet and confer with the adversary prior to filing any motion, and then certify—in a manner subjecting the movant to sanctions—that good faith attempts to resolve the motion before filing have failed.[24]

Form of Order Required: Some districts require that the moving party include with the motion a blank form of order which, if signed by the judge, would grant the relief that the movant requests.[25]

Legal Memorandum Required: Some districts require that a brief or legal memorandum accompany the motion.[26]

Page Limits: Many districts set formal page limits that must be followed strictly, unless leave of court is sought and granted for the filing of a longer document.[27]

Oral Argument: Some districts establish a formal procedure for seeking oral argument on a motion.[28]

Miscellaneous Requirements: Local rules provide a myriad of other requirements, varying from district to district. For example, some districts dictate the number of copies of each motion or memorandum that must be submitted.[29] Some districts require that the motion or memorandum begin with a formal statement of the exact legal question presented for the court's decision.[30] Other districts require that, under the signature line, attorneys identify themselves by attorney registration or identification numbers.[31]

Because these types of significant differences abound, practitioners must carefully consult their district's local rules before engaging in motion practice.

Time for / Form of Response to Motion

Likewise, the Federal Rules provide very little guidance on the practice and procedure for responding to motions. This detail is also

24. *See, e.g.*, D. Colo. Loc. R. 7.1.A. (pre-filing meet and confer duty); E.D. Mich. Loc. R. 7.1(a) (duty to seek concurrence in motion); D. Or. Loc. R. 7.1(a) (good faith certification requirement); M.D. Pa. Loc. R. 7.1 (certification of concurrence / non-concurrence obligation).

25. *See, e.g.*, D. Idaho Loc. R. 7.1(a)(3) (requiring proposed order under certain circumstances); E.D. Pa. Loc. R. 7.1(a) (every motion must be accompanied by form of order); W.D. Pa. Loc. R. 7.1(B) (motion improper if proposed order is not included); W.D. Tenn. Loc. R. 7.2(a)(1)(A) (all motions must be accompanied by form of order).

26. *See, e.g.*, E.D. Pa. Loc. R. 7.1(c); D.R.I. Loc. R. 12(a)(1); D.S.C. Loc. R. 7.04; D. Utah Loc. R. 202(a).

27. *See, e.g.*, M.D. Pa. Loc. R. 7.8 (requiring double-spaced briefs limited to 15 pages); D.S.C. Loc. R. 7.05(2) (35 page limit for initial brief); E.D. Tenn. Loc. R. 7.1(a) (25 page limit for initial brief).

28. *See, e.g.*, W.D. Mo. Loc. R. 7.1(g) (oral argument may be requested at conclusion of motion); D.S.D. Loc. R. 7.1 (request made either in conclusion of motion or by separate pleading); D. Utah Loc. R. 202(d) (oral argument only granted for "good cause shown").

29. *See, e.g.*, M.D. Pa. Loc. R. 7.5, 7.6, & 7.7 (requiring original and two copies of each memorandum).

30. *See, e.g.*, Or. Loc. R. 7.1(d); M.D. Pa. Loc. R. 7.8.

31. *See, e.g.*, S.D.N.Y. Loc. R. 11.1(b).

almost always governed by the district's local rules of practice, which may establish requirements regarding:

Time for Responding: Many districts require non-moving parties to file their opposition papers within a certain number of days after *either* the filing of or service of the motion.[32]

Forms of Order: Some districts require that the non-moving party include a form of order which, if signed by the judge, would deny or modify the relief sought in the pending motion.[33]

Page Limits: Many districts establish page limits for opposition papers.[34]

Reply Briefs: Some districts permit the moving party to file a reply brief, so long as the reply is filed within a prescribed period after filing or service of the opposition papers.[35] Local rules may also set reply brief page limits.[36]

Because these response provisions vary so greatly from judicial district to judicial district, non-moving parties must also take care to consult the district's local rules before responding to a pending motion.

Liberal Reading of Motions

Liberality applies to motions to dismiss. A motion to dismiss will not generally be rejected merely because it fails to specify which particular Rule it invokes.[37] Nevertheless, careful practitioners will ensure that the court is accurately focused on the precise nature of the motion's attack.

RULE 12(b)(1). DISMISSAL FOR LACK OF SUBJECT MATTER JURISDICTION

CORE CONCEPT

A case will be dismissed under this provision if the court lacks the statutory authority to hear and decide the dispute (*e.g.,* if there is no federal question at issue, if the parties are not completely diverse, or if the amount in controversy does not exceed $75,000).

32. *See, e.g.,* Alaska Loc. R. 7.1(c) (opposition due within 15 days after service of motion); D.S.C. Loc. R. 7.06 (opposition due within 15 days after motion is filed); E.D. Tenn. Loc. R. 7.1(a) (opposition to dispositive motion due within 20 days of service); E.D. Va. Loc. R. 7(E)(1) (opposition due within 11 days of service).

33. *See, e.g.,* E.D. Pa. Loc. R. 7.1(a); W.D. Tenn. Loc. R. 7.2(a)(2).

34. *See, e.g.,* D. Az. Loc. R. 1.10(e) (opposition brief limited to 15 pages); M.D. Fla. Loc. R. 3.01(c) (opposition brief limited to 20 pages); D. Vt. Loc. R. (a)(4) (opposition to dispositive motions limited to 25 pages); D. Wyo. Loc. R. 7.1(b)(2)(B) (same).

35. *See, e.g.,* D.S.C. Loc. R. 7.07 (reply briefs are "discouraged", but may be filed within 5 days after service of the opposition); N.D. Tex. Loc. R. 7.1(f) (reply briefs must be filed within 15 days after opposition is filed). *But see* M.D. Fla. Loc. R. 3.01(b) (no reply briefs permitted absent leave of court); D. Neb. Loc. R. 7.1(c) (same); D.N.H. Loc. R. 7.1(a)(4) (same).

36. *See, e.g.,* E.D. Mich. Loc. R. 7.1(d) (reply briefs limited to 5 pages); N.D. Tex. Loc. R. 7.2(c) (reply briefs limited to 10 pages); D. Utah Loc. R. 202(b)(2) (same).

37. *See Travel All Over the World, Inc. v. Kingdom of Saudi Arabia,* 73 F.3d 1423, 1429 (7th Cir.1996).

APPLICATIONS

Types of Challenges

A claim can be challenged under this provision both facially and substantively.[38] On a *facial* challenge, the defendant contests the adequacy of the language used in the pleading.[39] The pleader is required to formally aver the basis for jurisdiction in federal court; if the pleader fails to do so, the pleading can be dismissed.[40] On a *substantive* challenge, the defendant objects to the factual merits of the asserted federal jurisdiction.[41] In such a challenge, the pleading itself may have adequately alleged the presence of federal subject matter jurisdiction, but the actual facts and allegations before the court may belie that averment, confirming that federal jurisdiction is absent and, thus, compelling the case's dismissal.[42]

Timing

Challenges to subject matter jurisdiction may be raised at any time, by any party, or by the court.[43] Such challenges can even be raised after final judgment is entered.[44]

Waiver

A party cannot waive the requirement of subject matter jurisdiction,[45] nor can the parties consent to have a case heard in federal court

38. *See Gould Elecs. Inc. v. United States*, 220 F.3d 169 (3d Cir.2000) (discussing differences between facial and factual subject matter jurisdiction attacks). *See also White v. Lee*, 227 F.3d 1214, 1242 (9th Cir.2000); *Ruiz v. McDonnell*, 299 F.3d 1173, 1179 (10th Cir.2002), *cert. denied*, 538 U.S. 999, 123 S.Ct. 1908, 155 L.Ed.2d 826 (2003); *Robinson v. Government of Malaysia*, 269 F.3d 133, 140 (2d Cir.2001); *Scarfo v. Ginsberg*, 175 F.3d 957, 960–61 (11th Cir. 1999), *cert. denied*, 529 U.S. 1003, 120 S.Ct. 1267, 146 L.Ed.2d 217 (2000).

39. *See City of Albuquerque v. United States Dep't of Interior*, 379 F.3d 901 (10th Cir. 2004); *Savage v. Glendale Union High Sch.*, 343 F.3d 1036, 1039 n.2 (9th Cir. 2003), *cert. denied*, 541 U.S. 1009, 124 S.Ct. 2067, 158 L.Ed.2d 618 (2004); *Turicentro, S.A. v. American Airlines Inc.*, 303 F.3d 293, 300 n.4 (3d Cir.2002).

40. *See Gibbs v. Buck*, 307 U.S. 66, 59 S.Ct. 725, 83 L.Ed. 1111 (1939). *See also Valentin v. Hospital Bella Vista*, 254 F.3d 358, 363–64 (1st Cir.2001); *Scarfo v. Ginsberg*, 175 F.3d 957, 960–61 (11th Cir.1999), *cert. denied*, 529 U.S. 1003, 120 S.Ct. 1267, 146 L.Ed.2d 217 (2000).

41. *See City of Albuquerque v. United States Dep't of Interior*, 379 F.3d 901 (10th Cir. 2004); *Savage v. Glendale Union High Sch.*, 343 F.3d 1036, 1039 n.2 (9th Cir. 2003), *cert. denied*, 541 U.S. 1009, 124 S.Ct. 2067, 158 L.Ed.2d 618 (2004).

42. *See Gibbs v. Buck*, 307 U.S. 66, 59 S.Ct. 725, 83 L.Ed. 1111 (1939); *Scarfo v. Ginsberg*, 175 F.3d 957, 960–61 (11th Cir.1999), *cert. denied*, 529 U.S. 1003, 120 S.Ct. 1267, 146 L.Ed.2d 217 (2000); *United States v. North Carolina*, 180 F.3d 574, 580 (4th Cir.1999) *See also New Mexicans for Bill Richardson v. Gonzales*, 64 F.3d 1495, 1499 (10th Cir.1995); *Holt v. United States*, 46 F.3d 1000, 1003 (10th Cir.1995)(in resolving a substantive attack on subject matter jurisdiction, the district court will not assume the truthfulness of the complaint's allegations, and enjoys wide discretion to consider affidavits or other documents, or conduct a limited evidentiary hearing).

43. *See Nesbit v. Gears Unlimited, Inc.*, 347 F.3d 72, 76–77 (3d Cir. 2003), *cert. denied*, 541 U.S. 959, 124 S.Ct. 1714, 158 L.Ed.2d 400 (2004); *Emrich v. Touche Ross & Co.*, 846 F.2d 1190 (9th Cir.1988).

44. *See* Rule 60(b)(4).

45. *See Nesbit v. Gears Unlimited, Inc.*, 347 F.3d 72, 76–77 (3d Cir. 2003), *cert. denied*, 541 U.S. 959, 124 S.Ct. 1714, 158 L.Ed.2d 400 (2004); *Moodie v. Federal Reserve Bank of New York*, 58 F.3d 879, 882 (2d Cir.1995). *See also Boatmen's First Nat'l Bank of Kansas City v. Kansas Pub. Employees Retirement Sys.*, 57 F.3d 638, 640 n. 4 (8th Cir.1995)(noting that subject matter jurisdiction objections are not waived if not asserted

where subject matter jurisdiction is absent.[46]

Burden of Proof

When a defendant challenges subject matter jurisdiction, the plaintiff (as the party asserting the existence of jurisdiction) must bear the burden of establishing jurisdiction.[47] The plaintiff must carry this burden by a preponderance of the evidence.[48] The burden, however, is generally not a heavy one.[49] In federal question cases, the party must demonstrate a non-frivolous claim based on federal law,[50] and must meet all other statutory prerequisites for litigating the federal claim (such as exhaustion of administrative remedies and compliance with all claims-filing limitations and requirements).[51] In diversity cases, the

in the trial court, and courts of appeals are obligated to consider the issue *sua sponte*).

46. *See Neirbo Co. v. Bethlehem Shipbuilding Corp.,* 308 U.S. 165, 60 S.Ct. 153, 84 L.Ed. 167 (1939). *See also Laughlin v. Kmart Corp.*, 50 F.3d 871, 873 (10th Cir.1995)(commenting that subject matter jurisdiction cannot be conferred upon the district court by waived, consent, estoppel, or failure to challenge), *cert. denied*, 516 U.S. 863, 116 S.Ct. 174, 133 L.Ed.2d 114 (1995).

47. *See Thomson v. Gaskill,* 315 U.S. 442, 62 S.Ct. 673, 86 L.Ed. 951 (1942); *Lujan v. Defenders of Wildlife*, 504 U.S. 555, 561, 112 S.Ct. 2130, 2136, 119 L.Ed.2d 351 (1992); *APWU v. Potter*, 343 F.3d 619, 623 (2d Cir. 2003); *United Phosphorus, Ltd. v. Angus Chem. Co.*, 322 F.3d 942, 946 (7th Cir.2003), *cert. denied*, 540 U.S. 1003, 124 S.Ct. 533, 157 L.Ed.2d 408 (2003); *Toxgon Corp. v. BNFL, Inc.*, 312 F.3d 1379, 1383 (Fed. Cir.2002); *Michigan So. R.R. v. Branch & St. Joseph Counties Rail Users Ass'n*, 287 F.3d 568, 573 (6th Cir.2002); *Ramming v. United States*, 281 F.3d 158, 161 (5th Cir.2001), *cert. denied*, 536 U.S. 960, 122 S.Ct. 2665, 153 L.Ed.2d 839 (2002); *Tosco Corp. v. Communities for a Better Env't*, 236 F.3d 495, 499 (9th Cir.2001); *Gould Elecs. Inc. v. United States*, 220 F.3d 169 (3d Cir.2000).

48. *See APWU v. Potter*, 343 F.3d 619, 623 (2d Cir. 2003); *Toxgon Corp. v. BNFL, Inc.*, 312 F.3d 1379, 1383 (Fed.Cir.2002).

49. *See Garcia v. Copenhaver, Bell & Assocs.*, 104 F.3d 1256, 1260–61 (11th Cir.1997) (commenting that it is "extremely difficult" to dismiss a claim for lacking subject matter jurisdiction); *Musson Theatrical, Inc. v. Federal Express Corp.*, 89 F.3d 1244, 1248 (6th Cir.1996), *amended on denial of rehearing*, 1998 WL 117980 (6th Cir.1998) (commenting that plaintiff's burden to show federal question jurisdiction is not onerous). *See also Michigan So. R.R. v. Branch & St. Joseph Counties Rail Users Ass'n*, 287 F.3d 568, 573 (6th Cir.2002) (commenting that claim will generally survive motion to dismiss if plaintiff shows "any arguable basis in law" for claims alleged).

50. *See Neitzke v. Williams*, 490 U.S. 319, 327 n. 6, 109 S.Ct. 1827, 1832 n. 6, 104 L.Ed.2d 338 (1989)(noting that a patently insubstantial complaint may be dismissed for want of subject matter jurisdiction); *Hagans v. Lavine*, 415 U.S. 528, 536–37, 94 S.Ct. 1372, 1378–79, 39 L.Ed.2d 577 (1974) (commenting that federal courts lack power to hear cases otherwise within their jurisdiction but which are "so attenuated and unsubstantial" as to be clearly devoid of merit); *Bell v. Hood*, 327 U.S. 678, 682–83, 66 S.Ct. 773, 776, 90 L.Ed. 939 (1946)(observing that actions may sometimes be dismissed for lack of jurisdiction where the federal claim "clearly appears to be immaterial and made solely for the purpose of obtaining jurisdiction or where such a claim is wholly insubstantial and frivolous"); *Michigan So. R.R. v. Branch & St. Joseph Counties Rail Users Ass'n*, 287 F.3d 568, 573 (6th Cir.2002) (plaintiff must demonstrate that complaint alleges claim under federal law and that alleged claim is substantial). *See also Boock v. Shalala*, 48 F.3d 348, 353 (8th Cir.1995)(holding that federal claims, although "clearly meritless", were not so patently frivolous that they failed to confer subject matter jurisdiction); *Health Cost Controls v. Skinner*, 44 F.3d 535 (7th Cir.1995)(holding that subject matter dismissal is proper only where allegations are frivolous). Allegations that fail to meet the "frivolous" test warranting dismissal under Rule 12(b)(1) may nevertheless still be dismissed under Rule 12(b)(6) for failing to state a cognizable claim for relief. *See EEOC v. St. Francis Xavier Parochial Sch.*, 117 F.3d 621 (D.C.Cir.1997); *Janicki Logging Co. v. Mateer*, 42 F.3d 561 (9th Cir.1994).

51. *See Hart v. Department of Labor*, 116 F.3d 1338 (10th Cir.1997) (analyzing under Rule 12(b)(1) the defense that plaintiff failed to file timely claim with proper agency as required by

party must demonstrate complete diversity of citizenship[52] and a claim that in good faith exceeds $75,000, exclusive of interest and costs.[53] In all cases, the lawsuit must remain a live "case or controversy" subject to the federal courts' judicial power under Article III of the Constitution.[54]

Legal Test

In evaluating technical (or facial) subject matter jurisdiction attacks, the court ordinarily construes the complaint liberally, accepts all uncontroverted, well-pleaded factual allegations as true, and views all reasonable inferences in plaintiff's favor.[55] The court views the allegations as a whole; if a conclusory averment of subject matter jurisdiction is contradicted by other allegations in the pleading, the case may be dismissed.[56] Whether subject matter jurisdiction exists is tested as of the date the lawsuit was filed.[57]

Conversely, in the case of factual (or substantive) subject matter jurisdiction attacks, the court will *not* presume that plaintiff's factual allegations are true,[58] and will not accept conclusory allegations as true[59] but may instead weigh the evidence before it and find the facts, so long as this factfinding does not involve the merits of the dispute.[60]

the Federal Tort Claims Act). Whether the *Feres* doctrine applies (barring lawsuits against the United States where the alleged injury was incident to military service) is also tested under Rule 12(b)(1). *See Jackson v. United States*, 110 F.3d 1484, 1486 (9th Cir.1997).

52. *See City of Indianapolis v. Chase Nat'l Bank,* 314 U.S. 63, 62 S.Ct. 15, 86 L.Ed. 47 (1941).

53. *See St. Paul Mercury Indem. Co. v. Red Cab Co.,* 303 U.S. 283, 58 S.Ct. 586, 82 L.Ed. 845 (1938)(ruling that dismissal only proper where it appears, to a "legal certainty", that claim is truly for less than the jurisdictional amount); *NLFC, Inc. v. Devcom Mid–America, Inc.*, 45 F.3d 231, 237 (7th Cir.1995), *cert. denied*, 515 U.S. 1104, 115 S.Ct. 2249, 132 L.Ed.2d 257 (1995)(noting that amount in controversy alleged, in good faith, by plaintiff is decisive as to jurisdictional amount, unless it appears to a legal certainty that the true claim falls below the [then-applicable] $50,000 threshold).

54. *See Bateman v. City of West Bountiful*, 89 F.3d 704, 706 (10th Cir.1996)(ripeness challenges are examined under Rule 12(b)(1)); *Super Sack Mfg. Corp. v. Chase Packaging Corp.*, 57 F.3d 1054 (Fed.Cir.1995)(Rule 12(b)(1) motion granted where actual controversy had been removed and the remaining issues had been rendered moot).

55. *See Scheuer v. Rhodes,* 416 U.S. 232, 94 S.Ct. 1683, 40 L.Ed.2d 90 (1974); *City of Albuquerque v. United States Dep't of Interior*, 379 F.3d 901 (10th Cir. 2004); *Raila v. United States*, 355 F.3d 118, 119 (2d Cir. 2004); *Storm v. Storm*, 328 F.3d 941, 943 (7th Cir.2003); *Turicentro, S.A. v. American Airlines Inc.*, 303 F.3d 293, 300 & 300 n.4 (3d Cir.2002); *Michigan So. R.R. v. Branch & St. Joseph Counties Rail Users Ass'n*, 287 F.3d 568, 573 (6th Cir.2002); *McLachlan v. Bell*, 261 F.3d 908, 909 (9th Cir.2001); *Valentin v. Hospital Bella Vista*, 254 F.3d 358, 363–64 (1st Cir.2001). *See also Valhal Corp. v. Sullivan Assocs., Inc.*, 48 F.3d 760 (3d Cir. 1995)(observing that the threshold necessary to withstand Rule 12(b)(1) scrutiny is lower than that necessary to survive dismissal under Rule 12(b)(6)).

56. *See Gibbs v. Buck,* 307 U.S. 66, 59 S.Ct. 725, 83 L.Ed. 1111 (1939); *New Mexicans for Bill Richardson v. Gonzales*, 64 F.3d 1495, 1499 (10th Cir.1995).

57. *See Rosa v. Resolution Trust Corp.*, 938 F.2d 383, 392 n. 12 (3d Cir.1991), *cert. denied,* 502 U.S. 981, 112 S.Ct. 582, 116 L.Ed.2d 608 (1991).

58. *See Sizova v. National Inst. of Standards & Tech.*, 282 F.3d 1320, 1324 (10th Cir.2002); *White v. Lee*, 227 F.3d 1214, 1242 (9th Cir.2000); *Valentin v. Hospital Bella Vista*, 254 F.3d 358, 363–64 (1st Cir.2001).

59. *See Zappia Middle East Const. Co. v. Emirate of Abu Dhabi*, 215 F.3d 247, 253 (2d Cir.2000).

60. *See Nesbit v. Gears Unlimited, Inc.*, 347 F.3d 72, 77 (3d Cir. 2003) *cert. denied*, 541 U.S.

In doing so, the court enjoys broad discretion. The court may receive and consider extrinsic evidence.[61] The court must permit the pleader to respond with supporting evidence and, where necessary, may convene an evidentiary hearing or plenary trial to find the facts.[62] If the merits are implicated by the jurisdictional challenge, the court will treat the motion as any other substantive challenge to the merits of the dispute, constrained by the limitations of summary judgment practice and reserving the resolution of genuine issues of material fact for the ultimate factfinder.[63] Such a treatment is appropriate when the jurisdictional issue is so "intertwined" with the merits that the two cannot be separated.[64]

Allowing Jurisdictional Discovery

When a defendant moves to dismiss for lack of subject matter jurisdiction, discovery of the factual issues implicated by the motion may be permitted.[65] Although the trial judge enjoys broad discretion in resolving such motions, a refusal to grant jurisdictional discovery may constitute an abuse of discretion if it prejudices the plaintiff.[66]

959, 124 S.Ct. 1714, 158 L.Ed.2d 400 (2004); *APWU v. Potter*, 343 F.3d 619, 623 (2d Cir. 2003); *Grupo Dataflux v. Atlas Global Group, L.P.*, 541 U.S. 567, ___, 124 S.Ct. 1920, 1925, 158 L.Ed.2d 866 (2004); Conolly v. Taylor, 27 U.S. (2 Pet.) 556, 7 L.Ed. 518 (1829) (Marshall, C.J.); *Coalition for Underground Expansion v. Mineta*, 333 F.3d 193, 198 (D.C.Cir.2003); *United Phosphorus, Ltd. v. Angus Chem. Co.*, 322 F.3d 942, 946 (7th Cir.2003), *cert. denied*, 540 U.S. 1003, 124 S.Ct. 533, 157 L.Ed.2d 408 (2003); *Turicentro, S.A. v. American Airlines Inc.*, 303 F.3d 293, 300 n.4 (3d Cir.2002); *Sizova v. National Inst. of Standards & Tech.*, 282 F.3d 1320, 1324 (10th Cir.2002).

61. *See Skwira v. United States*, 344 F.3d 64, 71–72 (1st Cir. 2003), *cert. denied*, ___ U.S. ___, 124 S.Ct. 2836, 159 L.Ed.2d 267 (2004); *Savage v. Glendale Union High Sch.*, 343 F.3d 1036, 1039 n.2 (9th Cir. 2003), *cert. denied*, 541 U.S. 1009, 124 S.Ct. 2067, 158 L.Ed.2d 618 (2004); *Coalition for Underground Expansion v. Mineta*, 333 F.3d 193, 198 (D.C.Cir.2003); *Warren v. Fox Family Worldwide, Inc.*, 328 F.3d 1136, 1141 n.5 (9th Cir.2003); *United Phosphorus, Ltd. v. Angus Chem. Co.*, 322 F.3d 942, 946 (7th Cir.2003), *cert. denied*, 540 U.S. 1003, 124 S.Ct. 533, 157 L.Ed.2d 408 (2003); *Turicentro, S.A. v. American Airlines Inc.*, 303 F.3d 293, 300 n.4 (3d Cir. 2002); *Sizova v. National Inst. of Standards & Tech.*, 282 F.3d 1320, 1324 (10th Cir.2002).

62. *See Skwira v. United States*, 344 F.3d 64, 71–72 (1st Cir. 2003), *cert. denied*, ___ U.S. ___, 124 S.Ct. 2836, 159 L.Ed.2d 267 (2004); *Turicentro, S.A. v. American Airlines Inc.*, 303 F.3d 293, 300 n.4 (3d Cir.2002); *United Tribe of Shawnee Indians v. United States*, 253 F.3d 543, 546 (10th Cir.2001); *Zappia Middle East Const. Co. v. Emirate of Abu Dhabi*, 215 F.3d 247, 253 (2d Cir.2000).

63. *See Gonzalez v. United States*, 284 F.3d 281, 287 (1st Cir.2002); *Pringle v. United States*, 208 F.3d 1220, 1222 (10th Cir.2000); *United States v. North Carolina*, 180 F.3d 574, 580 (4th Cir.1999); *Garcia v. Copenhaver, Bell & Assocs.*, 104 F.3d 1256, 1260–61 (11th Cir.1997); *Metro Indus., Inc. v. Sammi Corp.*, 82 F.3d 839, 846 (9th Cir.1996), *cert. denied*, 519 U.S. 868, 117 S.Ct. 181, 136 L.Ed.2d 120 (1996); *LaSalle Nat'l Trust, N.A. v. ECM Motor Co.*, 76 F.3d 140, 144 (7th Cir.1996).

64. *See Gonzalez v. United States*, 284 F.3d 281, 287 (1st Cir.2002) (noting that jurisdictional issue is intertwined with merits where court's subject matter jurisdiction depends upon statute that governs substantive claims). *See also Warren v. Fox Family Worldwide, Inc.*, 328 F.3d 1136, 1139 (9th Cir.2003); *Sizova v. National Inst. of Standards & Tech.*, 282 F.3d 1320, 1324 (10th Cir.2002) (same).

65. *See Skwira v. United States*, 344 F.3d 64, 71–72 (1st Cir. 2003), *cert. denied*, ___ U.S. ___, 124 S.Ct. 2836, 159 L.Ed.2d 267 (2004); *Sizova v. National Inst. of Standards & Tech.*, 282 F.3d 1320, 1326 (10th Cir.2002).

66. *See Sizova v. National Inst. of Standards & Tech.*, 282 F.3d 1320, 1326 (10th Cir.2002) (noting that such prejudice exists if "pertinent facts bearing on the question of jurisdiction are

Remedy

Generally, the court will permit a party to amend unless it is clear that subject matter jurisdiction cannot be truthfully averred.[67]

Extrinsic Materials

In cases involving factual or substantive (rather than facial or technical) attacks to the court's subject matter jurisdiction, the parties may produce affidavits and other materials to support their positions on subject matter jurisdiction.[68] The court may also consider matters of public record.[69]

Ruling Deferred

Although the question of subject matter jurisdiction is resolved by the court, not the jury, the court may defer ruling on the challenge until after further materials are presented, after discovery is conducted, or after evidence is received at trial.[70] The court may *not*, however, defer ruling upon a subject matter jurisdictional challenge so as to rule instead upon a potentially simpler dispositive motion attacking the merits of the lawsuit.[71] Because the judicial power of the United States is limited, jurisdiction must be established as a threshold matter before any merits ruling is possible.

Prejudice on Dismissal

A dismissal for lack of subject matter jurisdiction is usually not a decision on the merits, and generally will not preclude the plaintiff from filing the claim in a court that may properly hear the dispute.[72]

controverted ... or where a more satisfactory showing of the facts is necessary").

67. *See Leaf v. Supreme Court of Wisconsin*, 979 F.2d 589, 595 (7th Cir.1992) (noting that leave to amend defective allegations of subject matter jurisdiction should be freely given), *cert. denied,* 508 U.S. 941, 113 S.Ct. 2417, 124 L.Ed.2d 639 (1993).

68. *See Savage v. Glendale Union High Sch.*, 343 F.3d 1036, 1039 n.2 (9th Cir. 2003), *cert. denied*, 541 U.S. 1009, 124 S.Ct. 2067, 158 L.Ed.2d 618 (2004); *Coalition for Underground Expansion v. Mineta*, 333 F.3d 193, 198 (D.C.Cir. 2003); *United Phosphorus, Ltd. v. Angus Chem. Co.*, 322 F.3d 942, 946 (7th Cir.2003), *cert. denied*, 540 U.S. 1003, 124 S.Ct. 533, 157 L.Ed.2d 408 (2003); *Turicentro, S.A. v. American Airlines Inc.*, 303 F.3d 293, 300 n.4 (3d Cir.2002); *Luckett v. Bure,* 290 F.3d 493, 496–97 (2d Cir.2002); *Valentin v. Hospital Bella Vista*, 254 F.3d 358, 363–64 (1st Cir.2001); *Pringle v. United States*, 208 F.3d 1220, 1222 (10th Cir.2000); *Scarfo v. Ginsberg*, 175 F.3d 957, 960–61 (11th Cir.1999), *cert. denied*, 529 U.S. 1003, 120 S.Ct. 1267, 146 L.Ed.2d 217 (2000).

69. *See White v. Lee*, 227 F.3d 1214, 1242 (9th Cir.2000).

70. *See Land v. Dollar,* 330 U.S. 731, 67 S.Ct. 1009, 91 L.Ed. 1209 (1947); *Valentin v. Hospital Bella Vista,* 254 F.3d 358, 364 n.3 (1st Cir.2001); *St. Clair v. City of Chico,* 880 F.2d 199 (9th Cir.1989), *cert. denied,* 493 U.S. 993, 110 S.Ct. 541, 107 L.Ed.2d 539 (1989).

71. *See Steel Co. v. Citizens for a Better Env't*, 523 U.S. 83, 118 S.Ct. 1003, 140 L.Ed.2d 210 (1998) (rejecting the so-called doctrine of "hypothetical" or "assumed" jurisdiction). But the Supreme Court has confirmed that there is no "unyielding hierarchy" *among* jurisdictional requirements, and courts are free to resolve *personal* jurisdiction challenges before reaching potentially more difficult questions of *subject* matter jurisdiction. *See also Ruhrgas AG v. Marathon Oil Co.*, 526 U.S. 574, 119 S.Ct. 1563, 143 L.Ed.2d 760 (1999); *Deniz v. Municipality of Guaynabo*, 285 F.3d 142, 149–50 (1st Cir. 2002); *Ramming v. United States*, 281 F.3d 158, 161 (5th Cir.2001), *cert. denied*, 536 U.S. 960, 122 S.Ct. 2665, 153 L.Ed.2d 839 (2002).

72. *See Mitchell v. Chapman*, 343 F.3d 811, 820 (6th Cir.2003), *cert. denied*, ___ U.S. ___, 124 S.Ct. 2908, 159 L.Ed.2d 813 (2004); *Ramming v. United States*, 281 F.3d 158, 161 (5th Cir.2001), *cert. denied*, 536 U.S. 960, 122 S.Ct.

Dismissal's Effect on Supplemental Jurisdiction Claims

If a lawsuit's federal claims are dismissed for lack of subject matter jurisdiction, then all supplemental jurisdiction claims must ordinarily be dismissed as well.[73]

Appealability

A dismissal premised upon a lack of subject matter jurisdiction is ordinarily considered a "final order", subject to immediate review by the court of appeals.[74] However, denying a motion to dismiss for lack of subject matter jurisdiction generally is interlocutory and not immediately appealable.[75]

RULE 12(b)(2). DISMISSAL FOR LACK OF PERSONAL JURISDICTION

CORE CONCEPT

A particular defendant may be dismissed from the lawsuit if that defendant or the dispute concerning that defendant lacks sufficient "contacts" with the forum for the court to exercise personal jurisdiction over the defendant and, thus, to require the defendant travel into the forum to defend the lawsuit.[76]

APPLICATIONS

Special Appearances

The Federal Rules have abandoned the concepts of "special" and "general" appearances.[77] Now, a defendant can assert jurisdictional

2665, 153 L.Ed.2d 839 (2002); *Leaf v. Supreme Court of Wisconsin*, 979 F.2d 589, 595 (7th Cir. 1992), *cert. denied,* 508 U.S. 941, 113 S.Ct. 2417, 124 L.Ed.2d 639 (1993); *Nowak v. Ironworkers Local 6 Pension Fund*, 81 F.3d 1182, 1188 (2d Cir.1996). *But cf. Frigard v. United States*, 862 F.2d 201 (9th Cir.1988)(noting that although Rule 12(b)(1) dismissals are ordinarily without prejudice to a re-filing in a court of competent jurisdiction, some dismissals (such as those premised on sovereign immunity) are absolute such that no court could hear the case and no re-drafting of the pleadings could cure the defect), *cert. denied*, 490 U.S. 1098, 109 S.Ct. 2448, 104 L.Ed.2d 1003 (1989).

73. *See Musson Theatrical, Inc. v. Federal Express Corp.*, 89 F.3d 1244, 1255 (6th Cir. 1996), *amended on denial of rehearing*, 1998 WL 117980 (6th Cir.1998) (dismissal under Rule 12(b)(1) presumes that no valid federal claim ever existed, thus defeating any supplemental jurisdiction over non-federal claims).

74. *See Carson Harbor Village Ltd. v. City of Carson*, 37 F.3d 468, 471 n. 3 (9th Cir.1994). Similarly, a dismissal "without prejudice" and with the right to file an amended complaint may be immediately appealable if the plaintiff elects not to amend and to stand on the dismissed complaint. *Id.*

75. *See Harrison v. Nissan Motor Corp.*, 111 F.3d 343, 347–48 (3d Cir.1997).

76. For a detailed discussion of personal jurisdiction, *see* Part II of this text, §§ 2.3–2.7.

77. *See Chase v. Pan-Pacific Broad., Inc.*, 750 F.2d 131 (D.C.Cir.1984); *Davenport v. Ralph N. Peters & Co.*, 386 F.2d 199, 204 (4th Cir. 1967); *DIRECTV, Inc. v. Meyers*, 214 F.R.D. 504, 507 n.1 (N.D.Iowa 2003); *Dunmars v. City of Chicago*, 22 F.Supp.2d 777, 783 n. 6 (N.D.Ill. 1998); *Johnson v. Board of County Comm'rs for County of Fremont*, 868 F.Supp. 1226, 1230 n. 2 (D.Colo.1994). *See also Orange Theatre Corp. v. Rayherstz Amusement Corp.*, 139 F.2d 871, 874 (3d Cir.1944)(writing that a defendant "is no longer required at the door of the federal courthouse to intone that ancient abracadabra of the law, de bene esse, in order by its magic power himself to remain outside even while he steps within"), *cert. denied,* 322 U.S. 740, 64 S.Ct. 1057, 88 L.Ed. 1573 (1944).

defenses, venue defenses, and even substantive defenses under Rule 12 without impliedly consenting to the court's personal jurisdiction.

In Rem and Quasi in Rem Actions

A party may use this Rule to challenge the court's in rem and quasi in rem jurisdiction, as well as its personal jurisdiction.[78]

Timing and Waiver

Challenges to personal jurisdiction are waived, unless raised by motion (if there is one) or in the responsive pleading.[79] Although the courts differ on the issue, the majority view holds that a defendant does not waive personal jurisdiction challenges by filing a responsive pleading that includes a claim for affirmative relief (*e.g.*, filing a counterclaim, cross-claim, or third-party claim), provided the defendant asserts a timely objection to jurisdiction.[80]

Sua Sponte Dismissals

In some circuits, a trial court may dismiss on its own initiative for lack of personal jurisdiction but, if it does so, the court of appeals will generally permit the plaintiffs to raise their arguments supporting personal jurisdiction (and even proffer new supporting evidence) for the first time on appeal.[81] Other circuits reject this approach, holding that personal jurisdiction is a defense that ordinarily must be raised by the affected parties or will be deemed waived. In those circuits, the trial court may not raise this issue *sua sponte*.[82]

Burden of Proof

The burden lies with the party invoking the court's jurisdiction to establish the existence of that jurisdiction.[83]

Types of Challenges

A defendant can challenge personal jurisdiction theoretically or factually.[84] Theoretical challenges contest the plaintiff's theory of juris-

78. *See Newhard, Cook & Co. v. Inspired Life Ctrs., Inc.*, 895 F.2d 1226, 1228 n. 2 (8th Cir.1990).

79. *See Porsche Cars North America, Inc. v. Porsche.Net*, 302 F.3d 248, 256 (4th Cir.2002); *Swaim v. Moltan Co.*, 73 F.3d 711, 718 (7th Cir.1996), *cert. denied*, 517 U.S. 1244, 116 S.Ct. 2499, 135 L.Ed.2d 191 (1996); *Preferred RX, Inc. v. American Prescription Plan, Inc.*, 46 F.3d 535, 550 (6th Cir.1995); *EF Operating Corp. v. American Buildings*, 993 F.2d 1046, 1048 (3d Cir.1993), *cert. denied*, 510 U.S. 868, 114 S.Ct. 193, 126 L.Ed.2d 151 (1993).

80. *See Bayou Steel Corp. v. M/V Amstelvoorn*, 809 F.2d 1147 (5th Cir.1987)(discussing divergent views, and adopting majority approach).

81. *See Buchanan v. Manley*, 145 F.3d 386, 388–89 (D.C.Cir.1998).

82. *See Uffner v. La Reunion Francaise, S.A.*, 244 F.3d 38, 40 (1st Cir.2001).

83. *See Schwarzenegger v. Fred Martin Motor Co.*, 374 F.3d 797, 800 (9th Cir. 2004); *Purdue Research Found. v. Sanofi–Synthelabo, S.A.*, 338 F.3d 773, 782 (7th Cir.2003); *In re Magnetic Audiotape Antitrust Litig.*, 334 F.3d 204, 206 (2d Cir.2003); *Epps v. Stewart Info. Servs. Corp.*, 327 F.3d 642, 646–47 (8th Cir.2003); *Revell v. Lidov*, 317 F.3d 467, 469 (5th Cir.2002); *Pinker v. Roche Holdings Ltd.*, 292 F.3d 361, 368 (3d Cir.2002); *OMI Holdings, Inc. v. Royal Ins. Co.*, 149 F.3d 1086 (10th Cir.1998); *Massachusetts Sch. of Law at Andover, Inc. v. American Bar Ass'n*, 142 F.3d 26, 34 (1st Cir.1998); *In re Celotex Corp.*, 124 F.3d 619, 628 (4th Cir.1997).

84. *See Credit Lyonnais Secs. (USA), Inc. v. Alcantara*, 183 F.3d 151, 153–54 (2d Cir.1999).

diction (*e.g.*, that the defendant subjected itself to jurisdiction in the forum by engaging in a particular set of actions). In testing theoretical challenges, the court will ordinarily (and provisionally) accept as true the plaintiff's rendition of the relevant disputed facts.[85] If the court determines that those facts, if proven to be true, would subject the defendant to personal jurisdiction in the forum, no hearing or factual resolution is required and the theoretical challenge fails.[86] Alternatively (or additionally), the defendant may challenge personal jurisdiction factually by disputing the facts the plaintiff has alleged. When jurisdiction is challenged factually, the court or the factfinder must resolve the factual dispute.[87]

Legal Test

The nature of the court's inquiry on a Rule 12(b)(2) challenge depends upon how the motion is supported.[88] If the motion rests upon the pleadings alone, or on affidavits and a cold record, the court will hold the plaintiff to merely a prima facie standard obligating the plaintiff to make a proffer which, if credited by the factfinder, would be sufficient to confer personal jurisdiction.[89] In this posture, the uncontroverted allegations in the complaint are accepted as true, and factual disputes are resolved in the pleader's favor.[90] Alternatively, in those

85. *See Electronics For Imaging, Inc. v. Coyle*, 340 F.3d 1344, 1349 (Fed.Cir.2003), *cert. denied*, 540 U.S. 1111, 124 S.Ct. 1085, 157 L.Ed.2d 899 (2004); *Purdue Research Found. v. Sanofi–Synthelabo, S.A.*, 338 F.3d 773, 782 (7th Cir.2003); *Epps v. Stewart Info. Servs. Corp.*, 327 F.3d 642, 646–47 (8th Cir.2003); *Revell v. Lidov*, 317 F.3d 467, 469 (5th Cir.2002); *Dole Food Co. v. Watts*, 303 F.3d 1104, 1108 (9th Cir.2002); *Pinker v. Roche Holdings Ltd.*, 292 F.3d 361, 368 (3d Cir.2002); *Daynard v. Ness, Motley, Loadholt, Richardson & Poole, P.A.*, 290 F.3d 42, 50–51 (1st Cir.2002), *cert. denied*, 537 U.S. 1029, 123 S.Ct. 558, 154 L.Ed.2d 444 (2002); *Distefano v. Carozzi North America, Inc.*, 286 F.3d 81, 84 (2d Cir.2001).

86. *See In re Magnetic Audiotape Antitrust Litig.*, 334 F.3d 204, 206 (2d Cir.2003); *Doe v. Unocal Corp.*, 248 F.3d 915, 921 (9th Cir.2001).

87. *See Credit Lyonnais Secs. (USA), Inc. v. Alcantara*, 183 F.3d 151, 153 (2d Cir.1999).

88. *See Foster–Miller, Inc. v. Babcock & Wilcox Canada*, 46 F.3d 138 (1st Cir. 1995)(discussing three levels of inquiry under Rule 12(b)(2)).

89. *See Schwarzenegger v. Fred Martin Motor Co.*, 374 F.3d 797, 800 (9th Cir. 2004); *Electronics For Imaging, Inc. v. Coyle*, 340 F.3d 1344, 1349 (Fed.Cir.2003), *cert. denied*, 540 U.S. 1111, 124 S.Ct. 1085, 157 L.Ed.2d 899 (2004); *Purdue Research Found. v. Sanofi–Synthelabo, S.A.*, 338 F.3d 773, 782 (7th Cir.2003); *Epps v. Stewart Info. Servs. Corp.*, 327 F.3d 642, 646–47 (8th Cir.2003); *Revell v. Lidov*, 317 F.3d 467, 469 (5th Cir.2002); *Daynard v. Ness, Motley, Loadholt, Richardson & Poole, P.A.*, 290 F.3d 42, 50–51 (1st Cir.2002), *cert. denied*, 537 U.S. 1029, 123 S.Ct. 558, 154 L.Ed.2d 444 (2002); *Distefano v. Carozzi North America, Inc.*, 286 F.3d 81, 84 (2d Cir.2001); *OMI Holdings, Inc. v. Royal Ins. Co.*, 149 F.3d 1086 (10th Cir.1998). *Cf. Nationwide Mutual Ins. Co. v. Tryg Int'l Ins. Co.*, 91 F.3d 790 (6th Cir.1996) (surmising, but not conclusively ruling, that Circuit would apply the prima facie inquiry in cases where trial judge permits limited discovery into the jurisdictional issue but does not convene an evidentiary hearing).

90. *See Schwarzenegger v. Fred Martin Motor Co.*, 374 F.3d 797, 800 (9th Cir. 2004); *Electronics For Imaging, Inc. v. Coyle*, 340 F.3d 1344, 1349 (Fed.Cir.2003), *cert. denied*, 540 U.S. 1111, 124 S.Ct. 1085, 157 L.Ed.2d 899 (2004); *Purdue Research Found. v. Sanofi–Synthelabo, S.A.*, 338 F.3d 773, 782–83 (7th Cir.2003); *Epps v. Stewart Info. Servs. Corp.*, 327 F.3d 642, 646–47 (8th Cir.2003); *Revell v. Lidov*, 317 F.3d 467, 469 (5th Cir.2002); *Kernan v. Kurz–Hastings, Inc.*, 175 F.3d 236, 240 (2d Cir.1999). *But cf. Massachusetts Sch. of Law at Andover, Inc. v. American Bar Ass'n*, 142 F.3d 26, 34 (1st Cir.

instances where the court finds it unfair to require a defendant to attend and participate in the trial prior to a conclusive ruling on personal jurisdiction, the court may convene an evidentiary hearing. In that case, the plaintiff will have to establish personal jurisdiction by a preponderance of the evidence.[91] Finally, the court might adopt a middle course, known as the "likelihood" standard, during which the court makes no conclusive ruling on personal jurisdiction, but requires the plaintiff to come forward with evidence showing a likelihood that personal jurisdiction exists.[92]

Extrinsic Materials

The parties may produce affidavits, interrogatories, depositions, oral testimony (if an evidentiary hearing is convened), and other materials to support their positions on personal jurisdiction.[93]

Ruling Deferred

The court may defer ruling on the challenge until after further materials are presented or after jurisdictional discovery is conducted.[94] But a court generally must resolve personal jurisdiction issues before reaching merits issues.[95]

Discretion to Permit Pre-Ruling Jurisdictional Discovery

Generally, discovery is available to aid the pleader in establishing the existence of personal jurisdiction.[96] Consequently, most courts may

1998) (cautioning that despite Rule 12(b)(2)'s liberal approach, "the law does not require us struthiously to 'credit conclusory allegations or draw farfetched inferences' ").

91. *See Purdue Research Found. v. Sanofi–Synthelabo, S.A.*, 338 F.3d 773, 782–83 (7th Cir. 2003); *Epps v. Stewart Info. Servs. Corp.*, 327 F.3d 642, 646–47 (8th Cir.2003); *Foster–Miller, Inc. v. Babcock & Wilcox Canada*, 46 F.3d 138 (1st Cir.1995); *Metropolitan Life Ins. Co. v. Robertson–Ceco Corp.*, 84 F.3d 560, 566–67 (2d Cir. 1996), *cert. denied* 519 U.S. 1006, 117 S.Ct. 508, 136 L.Ed.2d 398 (1996).

92. *See Foster–Miller, Inc. v. Babcock & Wilcox Canada*, 46 F.3d 138 (1st Cir.1995). *See also Purdue Research Found. v. Sanofi–Synthelabo, S.A.*, 338 F.3d 773, 782–83 (7th Cir.2003) (noting national precedent that once defendant submits affidavits or other evidence in opposition to jurisdiction, plaintiff must go beyond pleadings and submit affirmative evidence supporting jurisdiction).

93. *See Schwarzenegger v. Fred Martin Motor Co.*, 374 F.3d 797, 800 (9th Cir. 2004); *Purdue Research Found. v. Sanofi–Synthelabo, S.A.*, 338 F.3d 773, 782–83 (7th Cir.2003); *Revell v. Lidov*, 317 F.3d 467, 469 (5th Cir.2002); *Whitaker v. American Telecasting, Inc.*, 261 F.3d 196, 208 (2d Cir.2001).

94. *See Theunissen v. Matthews,* 935 F.2d 1454 (6th Cir.1991); *Data Disc, Inc. v. Systems Technology Assocs., Inc.*, 557 F.2d 1280 (9th Cir.1977); *Klockner–Pentaplast of America, Inc. v. Roth Display Corp.*, 860 F.Supp. 1119, 1121–22 (W.D.Va.1994)(holding that factually intensive inquiry into personal jurisdiction would be deferred until trial, because a jurisdictional ruling would translate into a ruling on the merits).

95. *See OMI Holdings, Inc. v. Royal Ins. Co.*, 149 F.3d 1086 (10th Cir.1998); *Republic of Panama v. BCCI Holdings (Luxembourg) S.A.*, 119 F.3d 935, 940 (11th Cir.1997); *Northwestern Nat'l Cas. Co. v. Global Moving & Storage Co.*, 533 F.2d 320, 323 (6th Cir.1976); *Arrowsmith v. United Press Int'l*, 320 F.2d 219, 221 (2d Cir. 1963). *See also Chudasama v. Mazda Motor Corp.*, 123 F.3d 1353, 1367–68 (11th Cir.1997) (commenting that motions to dismiss should be resolved before full discovery is permitted). *See generally Steel Co. v. Citizens for a Better Env't*, 523 U.S. 83, 118 S.Ct. 1003, 140 L.Ed.2d 210 (1998) (rejecting so-called "hypothetical" or "assumed" jurisdiction theory, and prohibiting federal courts from postponing subject matter jurisdiction challenge in preference to an easier, and also potentially dispositive, merits challenge). *But see Ruhrgas AG v. Marathon Oil Co.*, 526 U.S. 574, 119 S.Ct. 1563, 143 L.Ed.2d 760 (1999) (holding that there is no "unyielding hierarchy" *among* jurisdictional requirements, and courts are free to resolve simpler personal jurisdiction challenges before reaching potentially more difficult questions of subject matter jurisdiction).

96. *See Oppenheimer Fund, Inc. v. Sanders*, 437 U.S. 340, 351 n. 13, 98 S.Ct. 2380, 2389 n.

grant limited jurisdictional discovery before ruling on a Rule 12(b)(2) motion to dismiss for lack of personal jurisdiction.[97] Whether, and under what constraints, to permit jurisdictional discovery are matters typically reserved for the trial judge's discretion.[98] Jurisdictional discovery will generally be allowed where the material facts that bear on jurisdiction are controverted or where a more satisfactory development of those facts is necessary.[99] Conversely, such discovery may be properly refused when it is untimely sought,[100] where the request is improperly supported,[101] or when such discovery would be meaningless to the jurisdictional debate. Thus, jurisdictional discovery may be denied where the plaintiff's claim is "clearly frivolous"[102] or where the plaintiff lacks a good faith belief that such discovery could support the jurisdictional allegations.[103] Jurisdictional discovery is often dependent on the specific

13, 57 L.Ed.2d 253 (1978) ("discovery is ... available to ascertain the facts bearing on [jurisdictional] issues"). *See generally Doe v. Unocal Corp.*, 248 F.3d 915, 921 (9th Cir.2001); *Eaton v. Dorchester Dev't, Inc.*, 692 F.2d 727, 729 n. 7 (11th Cir.1982); Note, *The Use of Discovery to Obtain Jurisdictional Facts*, 59 Va. L. Rev. 533 (1973).

97. *See United States v. Swiss American Bank, Ltd.*, 274 F.3d 610, 625 (1st Cir.2001) (noting that a "timely and properly supported" motion for jurisdictional discovery "merits solicitous attention"). *See, e.g., GTE New Media Servs. Inc. v. BellSouth Corp.*, 199 F.3d 1343, 1351–52 (D.C.Cir.2000); *United States v. Swiss American Bank, Ltd.*, 191 F.3d 30, 45–46 (1st Cir.1999); *Massachusetts Sch. of Law at Andover, Inc. v. American Bar Ass'n*, 107 F.3d 1026, 1042 (3d Cir.1997), *cert. denied*, 522 U.S. 907, 118 S.Ct. 264, 139 L.Ed.2d 191 (1997); *Renner v. Lanard Toys Ltd.*, 33 F.3d 277, 283–84 (3d Cir. 1994); *Theunissen v. Matthews*, 935 F.2d 1454, 1465 (6th Cir.1991).

98. *See Laub v. United States Dep't of Interior*, 342 F.3d 1080, 1093 (9th Cir. 2003); *Carefirst of Md., Inc. v. Carefirst Pregnancy Ctrs., Inc.*, 334 F.3d 390, 402–03 (4th Cir. 2003); *United States v. Swiss American Bank, Ltd.*, 274 F.3d 610, 625 (1st Cir.2001); *Kelly v. Syria Shell Petroleum Dev't B.V.*, 213 F.3d 841, 855 (5th Cir.2000), *cert. denied*, 531 U.S. 979, 121 S.Ct. 426, 148 L.Ed.2d 435 (2000).

99. *See Laub v. United States Dep't of Interior*, 342 F.3d 1080, 1093 (9th Cir. 2003).

100. *See Massachusetts Sch. of Law at Andover, Inc. v. American Bar Ass'n*, 142 F.3d 26, 37 (1st Cir.1998) (refusing to consider jurisdictional discovery challenge on appeal where not raised below). *See also United States v. Swiss American Bank, Ltd.*, 274 F.3d 610, 625 (1st Cir.2001) (noting timely sought requirement); *Renner v. Lanard Toys Ltd.*, 33 F.3d 277, 283–84 (3d Cir. 1994) (although plaintiff had not made formal discovery requests, issue of jurisdictional discovery was, under the circumstances, adequately preserved in opposition briefing).

101. *See Carefirst of Md., Inc. v. Carefirst Pregnancy Ctrs., Inc.*, 334 F.3d 390, 402–03 (4th Cir. 2003) (denial of jurisdictional discovery proper where plaintiff "offers only speculation or conclusory assertions about contacts with a forum state"); *Terracom v. Valley Nat'l Bank*, 49 F.3d 555 (9th Cir.1995) (affirming denial of jurisdictional discovery where plaintiff failed to demonstrate how further discovery could establish jurisdiction). *Cf. United States v. Swiss American Bank, Ltd.*, 191 F.3d 30, 45–46 (1st Cir.1999) (holding that timely, properly supported motion for jurisdictional discovery "merits solicitous attention").

102. *See Massachusetts Sch. of Law at Andover, Inc. v. American Bar Ass'n*, 107 F.3d 1026, 1042 (3d Cir.1997) (holding that jurisdictional discovery should be permitted unless plaintiff's claim is "clearly frivolous"), *cert. denied*, 522 U.S. 907, 118 S.Ct. 264, 139 L.Ed.2d 191 (1997).

103. *See Caribbean Broad. Sys. v. Cable & Wireless P.L.C.*, 148 F.3d 1080, 1090 (D.C.Cir. 1998) (discussing good faith belief requirement); *Ellis v. Fortune Seas, Ltd.*, 175 F.R.D. 308, 312 (S.D.Ind.1997) (holding that "it is reasonable for a court ... to expect the plaintiff to show a colorable basis for jurisdiction before subjecting the defendant to intrusive and burdensome discovery"). *See also Kelly v. Syria Shell Petroleum Dev't B.V.*, 213 F.3d 841, 855–56 (5th Cir.2000) (holding that discovery may be denied where the discovery sought could not have added any significant facts), *cert. denied*, 531 U.S. 979, 121 S.Ct. 426, 148 L.Ed.2d 435 (2000); *Terracom v. Valley Nat'l Bank*, 49 F.3d 555 (9th Cir.1995)

circumstances presented. Thus, jurisdictional discovery into whether a corporate defendant is adequately "doing business" within the forum may be granted more liberally[104] than such discovery of an individual[105] or a foreign sovereign.[106]

Foreign Discovery: Generally, a party may–but is not necessarily obligated to–pursue foreign discovery through the Hague Evidence Convention.[107] When personal jurisdiction over the foreign party is contested, the courts are divided as to whether discovery can proceed simply under the Rules or whether Convention discovery is required until the question of jurisdiction is resolved.[108]

Prejudice on Dismissal

A dismissal for lack of personal jurisdiction generally does not preclude the plaintiff from refiling the lawsuit against the defendant in a forum where that defendant is amenable to jurisdiction.[109]

Appealability

A dismissal as to all defendants for lack of personal jurisdiction is generally considered an appealable "final order".[110]

RULE 12(b)(3). DISMISSAL FOR IMPROPER VENUE

CORE CONCEPT

A case will be dismissed or transferred if venue is improper or inconvenient in the chosen forum.

(affirming denial of jurisdictional discovery where plaintiff failed to demonstrate how further discovery could establish jurisdiction); *Hansen v. Neumueller GmbH*, 163 F.R.D. 471, 476 (D.Del.1995) (jurisdictional discovery denied where plaintiff responded to motion with complete absence of contrary facts); *Poe v. Babcock Int'l*, 662 F.Supp. 4, 7 (M.D.Pa.1985) (jurisdictional discovery denied where plaintiff responded to motion with "mere speculation"). *Cf. GTE New Media Servs. Inc. v. BellSouth Corp.*, 199 F.3d 1343, 1351–52 (D.C.Cir.2000) (jurisdictional discovery is justified if party demonstrates that discovery can supplement jurisdictional allegations).

104. *See Massachusetts Sch. of Law at Andover, Inc. v. American Bar Ass'n*, 107 F.3d 1026, 1042 (3d Cir.1997) (noting that jurisdictional discovery often relates to "doing business" inquiry), *cert. denied*, 522 U.S. 907, 118 S.Ct. 264, 139 L.Ed.2d 191 (1997).

105. *See Massachusetts Sch. of Law at Andover, Inc. v. American Bar Ass'n*, 107 F.3d 1026, 1042 (3d Cir.1997) (observing that presumption in favor of jurisdictional discovery is reduced when defendant is an individual), *cert. denied*, 522 U.S. 907, 118 S.Ct. 264, 139 L.Ed.2d 191 (1997).

106. *See Alpha Therapeutic Corp. v. Nippon Hoso Kyokai*, 199 F.3d 1078, 1087–88 (9th Cir. 1999) (discussing the circumspection under which jurisdictional discovery from foreign sovereign should be ordered).

107. Hague Convention on the Taking of Evidence Abroad in Civil or Commercial Matters, opened for signature, Mar. 18, 1970, 23 U.S.T. 2555, T.I.A.S. No. 7444, *reprinted in* 28 U.S.C. § 1781 Note. *See Societe Nationale Industrielle Aerospatiale v. United States Dist. Ct.*, 482 U.S. 522, 533–36, 107 S.Ct. 2542, 2550–51, 96 L.Ed.2d 461 (1987) (first resort to Convention discovery is not required).

108. *See In re Automotive Refinishing Paint Antitrust Litig.*, 358 F.3d 288, 299–305 (3d Cir. 2004) (ruling that Convention discovery is not required, but citing case law split).

109. *See Kendall v. Overseas Dev't Corp.*, 700 F.2d 536 (9th Cir.1983).

110. *See Carteret Savings Bank, FA v. Shushan*, 919 F.2d 225, 230 (3d Cir.1990)(noting that dismissal as to all defendants for lack of personal jurisdiction is appealable under the final order doctrine). *Cf. SEC v. Blazon Corp.*, 609 F.2d 960 (9th Cir.1979)(noting that denials of such motions are usually not appealable before the entry of the final judgment).

APPLICATIONS

Transfer

A request for a *transfer* of venue (rather than a *dismissal* for improper or inconvenient venue) is made under federal statute, not under Rule 12(b)(3).[111] However, if the trial court grants a Rule 12(b)(3) motion for improper venue, it enjoys the discretion, in lieu of a dismissal, to transfer the matter to a forum where venue is proper.[112]

Dismissal; Forum Non Conveniens

Rule 12(b)(3) is the proper mechanism for asserting that the action should be dismissed either for lack of proper venue, or under the common law doctrine of forum non conveniens,[113] pursuant to a forum selection clause (generally) or otherwise.[114]

Timing and Waiver

Venue challenges are waived unless raised by motion (if there is one) or in the responsive pleading.[115] Once the Rule 12 motion period and the responsive pleading time have passed, an otherwise "waived" venue defense cannot ordinarily be raised by the court on its own initiative.[116] A defaulting defendant, thus, generally is deemed to have waived any objections to venue.[117]

111. *See* 28 U.S.C.A. § 1404 (authorizing transfer to more convenient district); 28 U.S.C.A. § 1406 (authorizing transfer to proper district).

112. *See, e.g., Meteoro Amusement Corp. v. Six Flags*, 267 F.Supp.2d 263, 266 (N.D.N.Y. 2003); *Audi AG & Volkswagen of America, Inc. v. Izumi*, 204 F.Supp.2d 1014, 1017 (E.D.Mich. 2002); *Indymac Mortgage Holdings, Inc. v. Reyad*, 167 F.Supp.2d 222, 237 (D.Conn.2001).

113. *See Gulf Oil Corp. v. Gilbert,* 330 U.S. 501, 67 S.Ct. 839, 91 L.Ed. 1055 (1947).

114. *See Murphy v. Schneider Nat'l, Inc.*, 362 F.3d 1133, 1137 (9th Cir. 2004); *Continental Ins. Co. v. M/V ORSULA*, 354 F.3d 603, 606–07 (7th Cir. 2003); *K & V Scientific Co. v. Bayerische Motoren Werke Aktiengesellschaft ("BMW")*, 314 F.3d 494, 497 (10th Cir.2002). *But see Rainforest Cafe, Inc. v. EklecCo, L.L.C.*, 340 F.3d 544, 545 n.5 (8th Cir.2003) (noting division among Circuits on question of whether motion to dismiss on grounds of forum selection clause is properly brought under Rule12(b)(3) or Rule 12(b)(6)); *Kerobo v. Southwestern Clean Fuels, Corp.*, 285 F.3d 531, 534–36 (6th Cir. 2002) (same).

115. *See* Rule 12(h)(1); *Stjernholm v. Peterson*, 83 F.3d 347, 349 (10th Cir.1996) (noting that right to contest venue is waived if party fails to raise that defense either in responsive pleadings or Rule 12(b)(3) motion), *cert. denied*, 519 U.S. 930, 117 S.Ct. 301, 136 L.Ed.2d 219 (1996); *2215 Fifth Street Assocs. v. U Haul Int'l, Inc.*, 148 F.Supp.2d 50, 54 (D.D.C.2001) (same); *California Cas. & Fire Ins. Co. v. Brinkman*, 50 F.Supp.2d 1157 (D.Wyo.1999) (same). *See also Frietsch v. Refco, Inc.*, 56 F.3d 825, 830 (7th Cir.1995)(noting that venue objections must be asserted at the earliest possible opportunity).

116. *See Stjernholm v. Peterson*, 83 F.3d 347, 349 (10th Cir.1996) (noting that until defendants waive their venue defense, district courts may raise *sua sponte* defective venue, although the case may not be dismissed without affording the parties an opportunity to present their views on the question), *cert. denied* 519 U.S. 930, 117 S.Ct. 301, 136 L.Ed.2d 219 (1996). *See also Buchanan v. Manley*, 145 F.3d 386, 388–89 (D.C.Cir.1998) (to allow plaintiff to raise arguments supporting venue after a *sua sponte* dismissal by the trial court, court of appeals will permit plaintiffs to raise such arguments and proffer supporting evidence for the first time on appeal).

117. *See Union Planters Bank, N.A. v. EMC Mortg. Corp.*, 67 F.Supp.2d 915, 920 (W.D.Tenn. 1999).

Burden of Proof

The case law is fractured as to who bears the burden of proof on a Rule 12(b)(3) challenge.[118] One approach (evidently the substantial majority view) vests the plaintiff with the burden of proving that the chosen forum is proper;[119] the minority approach requires that the defendant, as the party challenging venue, bear this burden.[120]

Legal Test

The procedure for resolving a Rule 12(b)(3) motion is the same as the procedure used for testing challenges to personal jurisdiction.[121] Plaintiffs' well-pleaded factual allegations regarding venue will be accepted as true, all reasonable inferences from those allegations will be drawn in plaintiffs' favor, and factual conflicts will be resolved in plaintiffs' favor as well.[122] Legal conclusions need not be accepted as true, however.[123] The court may resolve the motion on the basis of the written submissions alone, or may convene an evidentiary hearing.[124] In the absence of an evidentiary hearing, a challenge to venue will be defeated if plaintiffs set forth sufficient facts which, if proven true, would confer venue.[125]

118. *See Beckley v. Auto Profit Masters, L.L.C.*, 266 F.Supp.2d 1001, 1003 (S.D.Iowa 2003) (noting division among the courts on burden in venue challenges); *McCaskey v. Continental Airlines, Inc.*, 133 F.Supp.2d 514, 522 (S.D.Tex.2001) (same); *Bacik v. Peek*, 888 F.Supp. 1405, 1412 (N.D.Ohio 1993) (same).

119. *See, e.g., Bartholomew v. Virginia Chiropractors Ass'n*, 612 F.2d 812 (4th Cir.1979), *cert. denied*, 446 U.S. 938, 100 S.Ct. 2158, 64 L.Ed.2d 791 (1980); *Cohen v. Newsweek, Inc.*, 312 F.2d 76, 78 (8th Cir.1963); *Wai v. Rainbow Holdings*, 315 F.Supp.2d 1261, 1268 (S.D.Fla. 2004); *Langton v. Cbeyond Communication, L.L.C.*, 282 F.Supp.2d 504, 508 (E.D.Tex. 2003); *Universal Premium Acceptance Corp. v. Oxford Bank & Trust*, 277 F.Supp.2d 1120, 1128 (D.Kan. 2003); *Greenblatt v. Gluck*, 265 F.Supp.2d 346, 352 (S.D.N.Y.2003); *Beckley v. Auto Profit Masters, L.L.C.*, 266 F.Supp.2d 1001, 1003 (S.D.Iowa 2003); *Meteoro Amusement Corp. v. Six Flags*, 267 F.Supp.2d 263, 266 (N.D.N.Y. 2003); *Interlease Aviation Investors II (Aloha) L.L.C. v. Vanguard Airlines, Inc.*, 262 F.Supp.2d 898, 913 (N.D.Ill.2003); *New Life Brokerage Servs. v. Cal–Surance Assocs.*, 222 F.Supp.2d 94, 97–98 (D.Me.2002); *Laserdynamics Inc. v. Acer America Corp.*, 209 F.R.D. 388, 390 (S.D.Tex. 2002); *Audi AG & Volkswagen of America, Inc. v. Izumi*, 204 F.Supp.2d 1014, 1017 (E.D.Mich. 2002); *Indymac Mortgage Holdings, Inc. v. Reyad*, 167 F.Supp.2d 222, 237 (D.Conn.2001).

120. *See Myers v. American Dental Ass'n*, 695 F.2d 716 (3d Cir.1982), *cert. denied*, 462 U.S. 1106, 103 S.Ct. 2453, 77 L.Ed.2d 1333 (1983); *International Truck & Engine Corp. v. Quintana*, 259 F.Supp.2d 553, 558 (N.D.Tex.2003).

121. *See Wai v. Rainbow Holdings*, 315 F.Supp.2d 1261, 1268 (S.D.Fla. 2004); *New Life Brokerage Servs. v. Cal–Surance Assocs.*, 222 F.Supp.2d 94, 98 (D.Me.2002); *M.K.C. Equip. Co. v. M.A.I.L. Code, Inc.*, 843 F.Supp. 679 (D.Kan. 1994).

122. *See Murphy v. Schneider Nat'l, Inc.*, 362 F.3d 1133, 1137 (9th Cir. 2004); *Wai v. Rainbow Holdings*, 315 F.Supp.2d 1261, 1268 (S.D.Fla. 2004); *Langton v. Cbeyond Communication, L.L.C.*, 282 F.Supp.2d 504, 508 (E.D.Tex. 2003); *Meteoro Amusement Corp. v. Six Flags*, 267 F.Supp.2d 263, 266 (N.D.N.Y.2003); *Interlease Aviation Investors II (Aloha) L.L.C. v. Vanguard Airlines, Inc.*, 262 F.Supp.2d 898, 913 (N.D.Ill.2003); *Quarles v. General Inv. & Dev't Co.*, 260 F.Supp.2d 1, 8 (D.D.C.2003); *Laserdynamics Inc. v. Acer America Corp.*, 209 F.R.D. 388, 390 (S.D.Tex.2002); *Audi AG & Volkswagen of America, Inc. v. Izumi*, 204 F.Supp.2d 1014, 1017 (E.D.Mich.2002); *Centerville ALF, Inc. v. Balanced Care Corp.*, 197 F.Supp.2d 1039, 1046 (S.D.Ohio 2002); *Indymac Mortgage Holdings, Inc. v. Reyad*, 167 F.Supp.2d 222, 237 (D.Conn. 2001).

123. *See Quarles v. General Inv. & Dev't Co.*, 260 F.Supp.2d 1, 8 (D.D.C.2003).

124. *See Centerville ALF, Inc. v. Balanced Care Corp.*, 197 F.Supp.2d 1039, 1046 (S.D.Ohio 2002).

125. *See Langton v. Cbeyond Communication, L.L.C.*, 282 F.Supp.2d 504, 508 (E.D.Tex.

Cases Involving Multiple Defendants And Multiple Claims

Where a case involves more than one defendant, or more than one claim against a defendant, venue must be proper as to each defendant and as to each claim.[126]

Extrinsic Materials

The parties may submit affidavits and other materials to support their positions on improper venue.[127]

Pre-Ruling Discovery

The court may permit limited discovery to aid in resolving the motion.[128]

Ruling Deferred

The court may defer ruling on a venue challenge pending further factual development.[129]

Prejudice on Dismissal

A dismissal for improper venue generally does not preclude the plaintiff from re-filing the claim in a forum where venue is proper.[130]

Appealability

Ordinarily, a dismissal for improper venue or forum non conveniens is immediately appealable as a "final order".[131] Conversely, a denial of a motion to dismiss for lack of venue or forum non conveniens is interlocutory and not immediately appealable.[132]

2003); *Darby v. United States Dep't of Energy*, 231 F.Supp.2d 274, 276–77 (D.D.C.2002); *McCaskey v. Continental Airlines, Inc.*, 133 F.Supp.2d 514, 522 (S.D.Tex.2001).

126. *See B-S Steel of Kansas, Inc. v. Texas Indus., Inc.*, 229 F.Supp.2d 1209, 1222–23 (D.Kan.2002); *McCaskey v. Continental Airlines, Inc.*, 133 F.Supp.2d 514, 522 (S.D.Tex.2001); *Centerville ALF, Inc. v. Balanced Care Corp.*, 197 F.Supp.2d 1039, 1046 (S.D.Ohio 2002).

127. *See Murphy v. Schneider Nat'l, Inc.*, 362 F.3d 1133, 1137 (9th Cir. 2004); *Wai v. Rainbow Holdings*, 315 F.Supp.2d 1261, 1268 (S.D.Fla. 2004); *Meteoro Amusement Corp. v. Six Flags*, 267 F.Supp.2d 263, 266 (N.D.N.Y.2003); *Travelers Cas. & Sur. Co. of America v. Telstar Const. Co.*, 252 F.Supp.2d 917, 922 (D.Ariz. 2003); *Audi AG & Volkswagen of America, Inc. v. Izumi*, 204 F.Supp.2d 1014, 1017 (E.D.Mich. 2002); *Centerville ALF, Inc. v. Balanced Care Corp.*, 197 F.Supp.2d 1039, 1046 (S.D.Ohio 2002); *Moore v. AT & T Latin America Corp.*, 177 F.Supp.2d 785, 788 (N.D.Ill.2001); *Indymac Mortgage Holdings, Inc. v. Reyad*, 167 F.Supp.2d 222, 237 (D.Conn.2001).

128. *See Centerville ALF, Inc. v. Balanced Care Corp.*, 197 F.Supp.2d 1039, 1046 (S.D.Ohio 2002).

129. *See Tenpenny v. United States*, 285 F.2d 213 (6th Cir.1960).

130. *See In re Hall, Bayoutree Assocs., Ltd.*, 939 F.2d 802, 804 (9th Cir.1991)(holding that although district court had discretion to either dismiss or transfer for improper venue, court erred in dismissing the case with prejudice; "A determination of improper venue does not go to the merits of the case and therefore must be without prejudice").

131. *See Young Props.Corp. v. United Equity Corp.*, 534 F.2d 847, 852 (9th Cir.1976)(noting general rule that order dismissing for improper venue or under the doctrine of forum non conveniens is final and appealable), *cert. denied*, 429 U.S. 830, 97 S.Ct. 90, 50 L.Ed.2d 94 (1976).

132. *See Hohn v. United States*, 524 U.S. 236, 248, 118 S.Ct. 1969, 1976, 141 L.Ed.2d 242 (1998); *Louisiana Ice Cream Distribs., Inc. v. Carvel Corp.*, 821 F.2d 1031, 1033 (5th Cir. 1987).

RULES 12(b)(4)–(5). DISMISSAL FOR (OR QUASHING OF) INSUFFICIENT PROCESS OR SERVICE

CORE CONCEPT

Process or service may be quashed or, in certain cases, the action dismissed if the process or the service is improper.[133]

APPLICATIONS

Insufficient Process—Rule 12(b)(4)

The process (summons and complaint) may be insufficient if the forms are technically deficient (*e.g.*, wrong name[134]) or not sealed by the clerk.[135] Because dismissals for defects in the forms of summons are generally disfavored, courts often overlook minor technical defects (particularly where they can be cured), unless the complaining party is able to demonstrate actual prejudice.[136]

Insufficient Service—Rule 12(b)(5)

Service of the process may be insufficient, for example, if the mode of delivery is invalid, if service is made improperly on an incompetent, a minor, or a non-agent,[137] or if delivery is either never accomplished or not accomplished within 120 days after commencement.[138]

Timing and Waiver

Service and process challenges are waived, unless raised by pre-answer motion (if there is one) or in the responsive pleading.[139] Thus, a defendant may not move for such a dismissal under these Rules *after*

133. *See Davies v. Jobs & Adverts Online, Gmbh*, 94 F.Supp.2d 719, 721 n. 5 (E.D.Va.2000) (noting difference between Rule 12(b)(4) (insufficient process) and Rule 12(b)(5) (insufficient service)).

134. *See Austin v. Spaulding*, 2001 WL 345602, at *2 (D.R.I.2001); *Ericson v. Pollack*, 110 F.Supp.2d 582, 584 (E.D.Mich.2000); *Richardson v. Alliance Tire & Rubber Co.*, 158 F.R.D. 475, 477 (D.Kan.1994); *Crane v. Battelle*, 127 F.R.D. 174 (S.D.Cal.1989).

135. *See Ayres v. Jacobs & Crumplar, P.A.*, 99 F.3d 565, 569 (3d Cir.1996).

136. *See U.S.A. Nutrasource, Inc. v. CNA Ins. Co.*, 140 F.Supp.2d 1049, 1052–53 (N.D.Cal. 2001) (refusing to dismiss where summons used service mark / tradename, rather than formal corporate name, where technical error caused no prejudice and where complaint could be amended to insert "doing-business-as" designation for clarity); *Louisiana Acorn Fair Housing v. Quarter House*, 952 F.Supp. 352, 355 (E.D.La.1997) (refusing to dismiss for insufficient process where summons served on "Quarter House Owners' Association" incorrectly identified the party as "Quarter House Homeowners Association, Inc.", absent showing that defendant did not receive notice or had suffered any prejudice from the technical error).

137. *See Schaeffer v. Village of Ossining*, 58 F.3d 48 (2d Cir.1995)(service quashed where process served on clerk not authorized to accept service on municipality defendant's behalf).

138. *See Richardson v. Alliance Tire & Rubber Co.*, 158 F.R.D. 475, 477 (D.Kan. 1994)(discussing distinction between Rule 12(b)(4) and Rule 12(b)(5) motions); *Crane v. Battelle*, 127 F.R.D. 174 (S.D.Cal.1989). *See also Austin v. Spaulding*, 2001 WL 345602, at **2–3 (D.R.I.2001); *Momah v. Albert Einstein Med. Ctr.*, 158 F.R.D. 66 (E.D.Pa.1994). Rule 12(b)(4) and Rule 12(b)(5) motions are often confused. Where this confusion does not prejudice the non-moving party, a mislabeling of such motions will be disregarded by the court. *See Richardson v. Alliance Tire & Rubber Co.*, 158 F.R.D. 475, 477–78 (D.Kan.1994).

139. *See Williams v. Jones*, 11 F.3d 247, 251 n. 4 (1st Cir.1993).

filing her answer[140] or *after* filing an earlier Rule 12 motion.[141] Such challenges also may not be raised by the court on its own. A defendant, of course, does *not* waive service and process objections by appearing in the case to object on those grounds.[142]

Waiting for Default to Raise Service Objections

Although defendants must raise their objections to process, service, and personal jurisdiction either in their omnibus Rule 12 motion or in their answer (if no Rule 12 motion is filed), these defenses are *not* waived where the failure of service is so complete that the defendants never even received actual notice of the unanswered pleading.[143] In such a case, the Constitutional protections of due process should permit the defendants to raise those objections in opposition to a motion for default. However, where a defendant receives actual notice of the pleading, decides that the process or service was improper, and then chooses not to assert these defenses by answer or motion (intending to press these objections in response to a later default motion), the defendant acts at her peril. There is case law precedent and commentary for the conclusion that this conduct may constitute a waiver of these defenses.[144]

Burden of Proof

The burden lies with the plaintiff to demonstrate sufficient process and service; when process or service is challenged, the plaintiff must make a prima facie showing that the court's personal jurisdiction is properly exercised.[145] The process server's return is prima facie evidence—but not conclusive proof—of good service.[146] Likewise, a conclu-

140. *See Green v. City of Bessemer*, 202 F.Supp.2d 1272, 1273–74 (N.D.Ala.2002) (finding Rule 12(b)(5) motion untimely because it was filed three days after party answered the complaint).

141. *See Chute v. Walker*, 281 F.3d 314, 319 (1st Cir.2002) (because defendant omitted Rule 12(b)(5) insufficiency of service defense from Rule 12(b)(6) motion to dismiss, insufficiency of service of process defense was waived).

142. *See Cataldo v. United States Dep't of Justice*, 2000 WL 760960, at *7 (D.Me.2000).

143. *See Corestates Leasing, Inc. v. Wright–Way Exp., Inc.*, 190 F.R.D. 356, 358 (E.D.Pa. 2000).

144. *See Corestates Leasing, Inc. v. Wright–Way Exp., Inc.*, 190 F.R.D. 356, 358 (E.D.Pa. 2000). *See also In re Worldwide Web Sys., Inc.*, 328 F.3d 1291, 1300 (11th Cir.2003) (service objection waived if Rule 60(b) "voidness" challenge to default judgment is made but claim of improper service is not "squarely raised"). *See also* 5A Charles Alan Wright & Arthur R. Miller, *Federal Practice & Procedure* § 1391, at 755–56 (1990) ("But when the party has received actual notice of the suit there is no due process problem in requiring him to object to the ineffective service within the period prescribed by Rule 12(h)(1) and the defense is one that he certainly can waive if he wishes to do so. This is because the defendant has failed to do what the rule says he must do if he is to avoid a waiver.").

145. *See Grand Entertainment Group, Ltd. v. Star Media Sales, Inc.*, 988 F.2d 476, 488 (3d Cir.1993); *McRae v. Rogosin Converters, Inc.*, 301 F.Supp.2d 471, 476 (M.D.N.C. 2004); *Baker v. Kingsley*, 294 F.Supp.2d 970, 980 (N.D.Ill. 2003); *Hilska v. Jones*, 217 F.R.D. 16, 20 (D.D.C. 2003); *Mende v. Milestone Tech., Inc.*, 269 F.Supp.2d 246, 251 (S.D.N.Y.2003); *Petsinger v. Pennsylvania Dep't of Transp.*, 211 F.Supp.2d 610, 610 (E.D.Pa.2002); *Preston v. State of New York*, 223 F.Supp.2d 452, 466 (S.D.N.Y.2002).

146. *See O'Brien v. R.J. O'Brien & Assocs., Inc.*, 998 F.2d 1394, 1398 (7th Cir.1993)(holding that signed return of service constitutes prima facie evidence of valid service that can be overcome by only "strong and convincing evidence"); *Oltremari v. Kansas Social & Rehabilitative Serv.*, 871 F.Supp. 1331, 1350 (D.Kan. 1994)(noting that once plaintiff files return of service, Rule 12(b)(5) dismissal requires strong

sory representation that the defendant was properly served will not overcome a defendant's sworn affidavit that she was not.[147]

Legal Test

A motion to dismiss under these Rules must be made with specificity, must describe any prejudice suffered by the defendant, and must detail the manner in which the process or service failed to meet the requirements of Rule 4.[148] The court will resolve disputed questions of fact by considering affidavits, depositions, and oral testimony received in connection with the motion.[149] In evaluating whether service has been effected, the courts may be more liberal where the defendant had actual notice of the lawsuit.[150]

Remedy

A party may request that the case be dismissed under this Rule or, alternatively, that service be quashed and re-attempted.[151] If service or process is found to be ineffective, the court has discretion to either dismiss or quash.[152] The courts will generally prefer to quash, rather than dismiss, where there is a reasonable prospect that the defendant can be properly served with sufficient process.[153] The courts will only dismiss when the failure of process or service prejudices the defendant

and convincing evidence that service was improper); *Blue Ocean Lines v. Universal Process Equip., Inc.*, 1993 WL 403961 at *4 n. 2 (S.D.N.Y.1993)(discussing evidentiary effect of private process server's return of service, noting that the return is not conclusive proof of good service but either creates a rebuttal presumption of good service or shifts the burden to the defendant to come forward with "strong and convincing evidence" that service failed).

147. *See Mende v. Milestone Tech., Inc.*, 269 F.Supp.2d 246, 251 (S.D.N.Y.2003).

148. *See O'Brien v. R.J. O'Brien & Assocs., Inc.*, 998 F.2d 1394, 1400 (7th Cir.1993)(holding that objections to the sufficiency of process must be specific and must identify how plaintiff failed to satisfy service); *Photolab Corp. v. Simplex Specialty Co.*, 806 F.2d 807, 810 (8th Cir. 1986)(same); *Berk v. City of New York*, 2001 WL 1029401, at *3 (S.D.N.Y.2001) (holding that motion must describe any prejudice to defendant, and set forth in detail manner in which service failed to satisfy Rule 4).

149. *See Travelers Cas. & Sur. Co. of America v. Telstar Const. Co.*, 252 F.Supp.2d 917, 923 (D.Ariz.2003); *Mende v. Milestone Tech., Inc.*, 269 F.Supp.2d 246, 251 (S.D.N.Y.2003).

150. *See Elkins v. Broome*, 213 F.R.D. 273, 275 (M.D.N.C.2003).

151. *See Boateng v. Inter American Univ. of P.R.*, 188 F.R.D. 26, 27 (D.P.R.1999) (holding that Rules offer trial court option of quashing deficient service); *R. Griggs Group Ltd. v. Filanto Spa*, 920 F.Supp. 1100, 1102 (D.Nev. 1996)(noting that federal courts possess the authority to quash improper service of process, rather than dismissing the complaint, even though the Rules technically do not provide for a "Motion to Quash").

152. *See Dimensional Communications, Inc. v. OZ Optics Ltd.*, 218 F.Supp.2d 653, 655 (D.N.J.2002).

153. *See Umbenhauer v. Woog*, 969 F.2d 25, 30–31 (3d Cir.1992)(noting that dismissal, rather than quashing, is inappropriate where there is a reasonable prospect for effective service); *Pell v. Azar Nut Co.*, 711 F.2d 949, 950 n. 2 (10th Cir.1983) (although courts should generally quash insufficient service and permit pleader another opportunity to serve properly, trial judges have broad discretion to dismiss if it is not likely that proper service can or will be accomplished); *Gartin v. Spyderco, Inc.*, 1997 WL 1037883, at *15 (D.Colo.1997) (same effect); *Dahl v. Kanawha Inv. Holding Co.*, 161 F.R.D. 673, 681 (N.D.Iowa 1995)(noting general rule that court will simply quash where the service is defective but curable, but will dismiss for improper service where further attempts at proper service would be futile); *Henkel Corp. v. Degremont, S.A.*, 136 F.R.D. 88 (E.D.Pa.1991).

or where proper service is unlikely to be accomplished.[154]

Extrinsic Materials

The parties may produce affidavits and other materials to support their positions on insufficient process or service.[155] The court may receive and consider such materials without converting the motion to dismiss into a motion for summary judgment.[156]

Prejudice on Dismissal

A dismissal for insufficient process or service is generally without prejudice and will not preclude the plaintiff from attempting to re-serve properly.[157]

RULE 12(b)(6). DISMISSAL FOR FAILURE TO STATE A CLAIM UPON WHICH RELIEF CAN BE GRANTED

CORE CONCEPT

A motion to dismiss for failure to state a claim is the descendant of the common law demurrer.[158] It tests the legal sufficiency of a party's claim for relief. The Rule's purpose is to permit trial courts to terminate lawsuits "that are fatally flawed in their legal premises and destined to fail, and thus to spare litigants the burdens of unnecessary pretrial and trial activity."[159]

APPLICATIONS

Legal Test

A claim may be dismissed either because it asserts a legal theory that is not cognizable as a matter of law or because it fails to allege

154. *See Gonzalez v. Ritz Carlton Hotel Co. of Puerto Rico*, 241 F.Supp.2d 142, 147–48 (D.P.R. 2003); *Oltremari v. Kansas Social & Rehabilitative Serv.*, 871 F.Supp. 1331, 1349 (D.Kan.1994); *Curcuruto v. Cheshire*, 864 F.Supp. 1410, 1411 (S.D.Ga.1994); *FDIC v. Swager*, 773 F.Supp. 1244 (D.Minn.1991).

155. *See Travelers Cas. & Sur. Co. of America v. Telstar Const. Co.*, 252 F.Supp.2d 917, 923 (D.Ariz.2003); *Mende v. Milestone Tech., Inc.*, 269 F.Supp.2d 246, 251 (S.D.N.Y.2003); *Bernard v. Husky Truck Stop*, 1994 WL 171732 (D.Kan. 1994).

156. *See BPA Int'l, Inc. v. Kingdom of Sweden*, 281 F.Supp.2d 73, 80 (D.D.C. 2003); *Travelers Cas. & Sur. Co. of America v. Telstar Const. Co.*, 252 F.Supp.2d 917, 923 (D.Ariz.2003). *But see Cubero Valderama v. Delta Air Lines, Inc.*, 931 F.Supp. 119, 120 (D.P.R.1996) (because court considered documents filed by party challenging service of process, it applied summary judgment standards to motion).

157. *See Umbenhauer v. Woog*, 969 F.2d 25, 30 n. 6 (3d Cir.1992); *Savior v. McGuire*, 2002 WL 1906023, at *2 n.2 (D.Minn.2002); *Malone v. Dallas City Manager's Office*, 2001 WL 910396, at *2 (N.D.Tex.2001). *But cf. Coffin v. Ingersoll*, 1993 WL 208806 at *5 n. 15 (E.D.Pa. 1993)(noting general rule that dismissal is without prejudice, but observing that where statute of limitations has lapsed, dismissal effectively bars plaintiff from court).

158. *See De Sole v. United States*, 947 F.2d 1169, 1178 n. 13 (4th Cir.1991); *Podell v. Citicorp Diners Club, Inc.*, 859 F.Supp. 701, 704 (S.D.N.Y.1994).

159. *Advanced Cardiovascular Sys., Inc. v. Scimed Life Sys., Inc.*, 988 F.2d 1157, 1160 (Fed. Cir.1993). *See Port Auth. of N.Y. & N.J. v. Arcadian Corp.*, 189 F.3d 305 (3d Cir.1999) (noting that Rule is designed to "screen out cases" where no remedy exists for the wrong alleged or where no relief could possibly be granted).

sufficient facts to support a cognizable legal claim.[160] When a claim is challenged under this Rule, the court presumes that all well-pleaded allegations are true, resolves all doubts and inferences in the pleader's favor, and views the pleading in the light most favorable to the non-moving party.[161]

In its liberality, the Rule erects a powerful presumption against dismissing pleadings for failing to state a cognizable claim for relief.[162] Such dismissals are disfavored and, in view of the Rules' "notice pleading" requirements, are not routinely granted.[163] A claim will only be dismissed under Rule 12(b)(6) if it appears beyond doubt that the pleader can prove no set of facts in support of the claim that would entitle the pleader to relief.[164] Thus, the pleader's stated legal theory and specific requests for relief are not necessarily dispositive in ruling on a Rule 12(b)(6) motion.[165] In fact, the complaint might not need to identify a particular legal theory at all.[166] A claim generally will not be dismissed, even though the asserted legal theories are not cognizable or the relief sought is unavailable, so long as other tenable legal claims are evident on the face of the complaint[167] or the pleader is otherwise entitled to any type of relief under another possible legal theory.[168]

160. *See SmileCare Dental Group v. Delta Dental Plan of Cal., Inc.*, 88 F.3d 780, 783 (9th Cir.1996), *cert. denied*, 519 U.S. 1028, 117 S.Ct. 583, 136 L.Ed.2d 513 (1996).

161. *See Albright v. Oliver*, 510 U.S. 266, 267, 114 S.Ct. 807, 810, 127 L.Ed.2d 114 (1994); *Scheuer v. Rhodes,* 416 U.S. 232, 94 S.Ct. 1683, 40 L.Ed.2d 90 (1974); *Ricco v. Potter*, 377 F.3d 599, 602 (6th Cir. 2004); *Carino v. Stefan*, 376 F.3d 156, 159 (3d Cir. 2004); *Dubbs v. Head Start, Inc.*, 336 F.3d 1194, 1201 (10th Cir.2003), *cert. denied*, 540 U.S. 1179, 124 S.Ct. 1411, 158 L.Ed.2d 79 (2004); *United States ex rel. Willard v. Humana Health Plan of Texas Inc.*, 336 F.3d 375, 379 (5th Cir.2003); *Thompson v. Illinois Dep't of Professional Regulation*, 300 F.3d 750, 753 (7th Cir.2002); *Gryl ex rel. Shire Pharms. Group PLC v. Shire Pharms. Group PLC*, 298 F.3d 136, 140 (2d Cir.2002), *cert. denied*, 537 U.S. 1191, 123 S.Ct. 1262, 154 L.Ed.2d 1024 (2003); *Schaller Tel. Co. v. Golden Sky Sys., Inc.*, 298 F.3d 736, 740 (8th Cir.2002); *Garrett v. Tandy Corp.*, 295 F.3d 94, 97 (1st Cir.2002); *Browning v. Clinton*, 292 F.3d 235, 242 (D.C.Cir. 2002).

162. *See Maez v. Mountain States Tel. & Tel., Inc.*, 54 F.3d 1488, 1496 (10th Cir.1995). *See also Strand v. Diversified Collection Serv., Inc.*, 380 F.3d 316 (8th Cir. 2004) (dismissal only when pleading shows, on its fact, "some insuperable bar to relief"); *Phonometrics, Inc. v. Hospitality Franchise Sys., Inc.*, 203 F.3d 790, 794 (Fed.Cir.2000) (noting that the complaint "contains enough detail to allow the defendants to answer. Rule 12(b)(6) requires no more.").

163. *See Gregson v. Zurich American Ins. Co.*, 322 F.3d 883, 885 (5th Cir.2003); *Morse v. Regents of Univ. of Colo.*, 154 F.3d 1124, 1127 (10th Cir.1998); *Rothner v. City of Chicago,* 929 F.2d 297 (7th Cir.1991); *Hall v. City of Santa Barbara*, 833 F.2d 1270, 1274 (9th Cir.1986), *cert. denied,* 485 U.S. 940, 108 S.Ct. 1120, 99 L.Ed.2d 281 (1988). *See also* Rule 8 (requiring only short, plain statement showing entitlement to relief); *Bennett v. Schmidt*, 153 F.3d 516, 518 (7th Cir.1998) (rejecting notion that complaints must recite all evidence needed to prevail at trial; instead, Rules make the complaint "just the starting point" and, rather than waiting until "plaintiff gets it just right", the court should keep the process moving, by requiring a more definite statement or inviting a motion for summary judgment—in a racial discrimination employment case, "I was turned down for a job because of my race" is all the complaint need say).

164. *Conley v. Gibson,* 355 U.S. 41, 78 S.Ct. 99, 2 L.Ed.2d 80 (1957). *See Hishon v. King & Spalding*, 467 U.S. 69, 73, 104 S.Ct. 2229, 2232, 81 L.Ed.2d 59 (1984).

165. *See Williams v. Seniff,* 342 F.3d 774, 792 (7th Cir.2003); *Barrett v. Tallon*, 30 F.3d 1296, 1299 (10th Cir.1994).

166. *See Williams v. Seniff,* 342 F.3d 774, 792 (7th Cir.2003).

167. *See Conley v. Gibson*, 355 U.S. 41, 45–46, 78 S.Ct. 99, 101–102, 2 L.Ed.2d 80 (1957)("a complaint should not be dismissed for failure to state a claim unless it appears beyond doubt that the plaintiff can prove no set of facts in support of his claim which would entitle him to relief"). *See also Barrett v. Tallon*, 30 F.3d 1296, 1299 (10th Cir.1994); *Mid America Title Co. v. Kirk*, 991 F.2d 417, 421 (7th Cir.1993), *cert. denied*, 510 U.S. 932, 114 S.Ct. 346, 126 L.Ed.2d 310 (1993).

168. *See Bowers v. Hardwick,* 478 U.S. 186, 106 S.Ct. 2841, 92 L.Ed.2d 140 (1986); *Figueroa*

In considering a Rule 12(b)(6) motion, the court will not decide the winners or losers in the case, or even examine the "believability" of the pleader's claims.[169] A claim will not be dismissed merely because the trial court doubts the pleader's allegations or suspects that the pleader will ultimately not prevail at trial.[170] The courts are especially hesitant to dismiss at the pleading stage those claims pressing novel legal theories, where the claims could be better examined following development of the facts through discovery,[171] or in peculiarly fact-intensive antitrust cases[172] and state-of-mind cases.[173]

Notwithstanding this generally liberal approach, a litigant's pleading obligations in the federal courts, while minimal, are not "toothless"; the pleader must still allege facts, either directly or inferentially, that satisfy each element required for a recovery under some actionable legal theory.[174] The court will *not* accept as true the pleader's bald assertions and legal conclusions, nor will the court draw unwarranted inferences to aid the pleader.[175] Unwarranted factual deductions, inferences, and

v. Rivera, 147 F.3d 77 (1st Cir.1998); *Carparts Distrib. Ctr. v. Automotive Wholesaler's Ass'n. of New England, Inc.*, 37 F.3d 12, 17 (1st Cir. 1994)("For purposes of Fed.R.Civ.P. 12(b)(6) , the possibility of a claim is enough to defeat dismissal").

169. *See Jacobson v. Hughes Aircraft Co.*, 105 F.3d 1288, 1292 (9th Cir.1997), *amended on other grounds*, 128 F.3d 1305 (9th Cir.1997), *rev'd on other grounds*, 525 U.S. 432, 119 S.Ct. 755, 142 L.Ed.2d 881 (1999).

170. *See Ideal Steel Supply Corp. v. Anza*, 373 F.3d 251, 264 (2d Cir. 2004); *Dubbs v. Head Start, Inc.*, 336 F.3d 1194, 1201 (10th Cir.2003), *cert. denied*, 540 U.S. 1179, 124 S.Ct. 1411, 158 L.Ed.2d 79 (2004); *Oatway v. American Int'l Group, Inc.*, 325 F.3d 184, 187 (3d Cir.2003); *Edwards v. City of Goldsboro*, 178 F.3d 231, 243–44 (4th Cir.1999). *See also Scheuer v. Rhodes*, 416 U.S. 232, 236, 94 S.Ct. 1683, 1686, 40 L.Ed.2d 90 (1974)("The issue is not whether a plaintiff will ultimately prevail but whether the claimant is entitled to offer evidence to support the claims"); *Moriarty v. Larry G. Lewis Funeral Directors Ltd.*, 150 F.3d 773, 777 (7th Cir.1998) (Rule does not allow judge to follow path "that seems 'most likely' on the basis of the complaint").

171. *See Baker v. Cuomo*, 58 F.3d 814, 818–19 (2d Cir.1995).

172. *See Dickson v. Microsoft Corp.*, 309 F.3d 193, 212 (4th Cir.2002) (recognizing that dismissal and other "summary procedures" should be applied "sparingly" in complicated antitrust litigation "where motive and intent play leading roles", but antitrust litigation does not have an exemption from Rule 12(b)(6) and plaintiff must allege facts supportive of each element of antitrust claim), *cert. denied*, 539 U.S. 953, 123 S.Ct. 2605, 156 L.Ed.2d 647 (2003).

173. *See Pryor v. National Collegiate Athletic Ass'n*, 288 F.3d 548, 565 (3d Cir.2002) (noting that "involving state of mind (e.g., intent) are often unsuitable for a Rule 12(b)(6) motion to dismiss").

174. *See Doyle v. Hasbro, Inc.*, 103 F.3d 186, 190 (1st Cir.1996) (commenting that pleading requirement, though low, "is real" and is "not entirely a toothless tiger"); *Educadores Puertorriquenos en Accion v. Hernandez*, 367 F.3d 61, 67–68 (1st Cir. 2004) (noting that notice pleading's "minimal requirements are not tantamount to nonexistent requirements"). *See also Dickson v. Microsoft Corp.*, 309 F.3d 193, 212 (4th Cir.2002), *cert. denied*, 539 U.S. 953, 123 S.Ct. 2605, 156 L.Ed.2d 647 (2003); *Advocacy Org. for Patients & Providers v. Auto Club Ins. Ass'n*, 176 F.3d 315, 319 (6th Cir.1999), *cert. denied*, 528 U.S. 871, 120 S.Ct. 172, 145 L.Ed.2d 145 (1999).

175. *See Aulson v. Blanchard*, 83 F.3d 1, 3 (1st Cir.1996)(commenting that Rule's deferential standard does not obligate a court "to swallow the plaintiff's invective hook, line, and sinker; bald assertions, unsupportable conclusions, periphrastic circumlocutions, and the like need not be credited"). *See also Alternative Sys. Concepts, Inc. v. Synopsys, Inc.*, 374 F.3d 23, 29 (1st Cir. 2004); *Campagna v. Massachusetts Dep't of*

legal conclusions "masquerading as facts" will not defeat a Rule 12(b)(6) motion.[176] The court may also refuse to accept as true factual averments discussed for the first time in a legal memorandum or brief which form no part of the official pleadings.[177] Moreover, commentators have observed that the courts tend to judge claims more harshly when they involve "disfavored" causes of action, such as malicious prosecution or defamation.[178]

"Clarifying" the Complaint with Briefs and Oral Argument

Although the factual averments in the *pleading* are deemed true on a motion to dismiss, the court may refuse to accept as true the pleader's statements made for the first time in a legal memorandum or brief that forms no part of the official pleadings.[179] However, the pleader's memorandum or brief can be used to "clarify" allegations of the pleading[180], as can statements made by the pleader during oral argument.[181]

Pleading in Anticipation of Affirmative Defenses

Ordinarily, plaintiffs need not anticipate the defendants' likely affirmative defenses, nor attempt, in the complaint, to preemptively "plead around" them.[182] Whether the complaint states a claim upon which relief can be granted is generally not dependent on whether the defendant has a defense.[183] Failure to "plead around" a likely affirmative defense is typically not a proper basis for dismissal.[184]

Envt'l Prot., 334 F.3d 150, 155 (1st Cir.2003); *Ruiz v. McDonnell*, 299 F.3d 1173, 1181 (10th Cir.2002), *cert. denied*, 538 U.S. 999, 123 S.Ct. 1908, 155 L.Ed.2d 826 (2003); *Browning v. Clinton*, 292 F.3d 235, 242 (D.C.Cir.2002); *Begala v. PNC Bank, Ohio, Nat'l Ass'n*, 214 F.3d 776, 779 (6th Cir.2000), *cert. denied*, 531 U.S. 1145, 121 S.Ct. 1082, 148 L.Ed.2d 958 (2001); *Edwards v. City of Goldsboro*, 178 F.3d 231, 243–44 (4th Cir.1999); *Advocacy Org. for Patients & Providers v. Auto Club Ins. Ass'n*, 176 F.3d 315, 319 (6th Cir.1999), *cert. denied*, 528 U.S. 871, 120 S.Ct. 172, 145 L.Ed.2d 145 (1999); *Judge v. City of Lowell*, 160 F.3d 67, 72 (1st Cir.1998); *Associated General Contractors of America v. Metropolitan Water Dist. of So. Calif.*, 159 F.3d 1178, 1181 (9th Cir.1998); *Morse v. Lower Merion Sch. Dist.*, 132 F.3d 902, 906 (3d Cir.1997); *Jefferson v. Lead Indus. Ass'n, Inc.*, 106 F.3d 1245, 1250 (5th Cir.1997); *Northern Trust Co. v. Peters*, 69 F.3d 123, 129 (7th Cir.1995).

176. *See Drs. Bethea, Moustoukas & Weaver LLC v. St. Paul Guardian Ins. Co.*, 376 F.3d 399, 403 (5th Cir. 2004); *Davila v. Delta Air Lines, Inc.*, 326 F.3d 1183, 1185 (11th Cir.2003), *cert. denied*, 540 U.S. 1016, 124 S.Ct. 568, 157 L.Ed.2d 430 (2003).

177. *See Henthorn v. Department of Navy*, 29 F.3d 682 (D.C.Cir.1994).

178. *See* 5A Charles A. Wright & Arthur R. Miller, *Federal Practice & Procedure* § 1357, at 359–60 (1990). In 1993, the Supreme Court rejected the practice of applying a "heightened pleading standard" to certain civil rights claims under 42 U.S.C.A. § 1983, holding that, with the exception of fraud, mistake, and certain conditions precedent governed expressly by Rule 9(b) and 9(c), the federal notice pleading standards apply universally. *See Leatherman v. Tarrant County Narcotics Intelligence & Coordination Unit*, 507 U.S. 163, 113 S.Ct. 1160, 122 L.Ed.2d 517 (1993). Consequently, courts may no longer have the ability to apply a stricter standard of review to malicious prosecution and defamation claims.

179. *See Henthorn v. Department of Navy*, 29 F.3d 682 (D.C.Cir.1994).

180. *See Pegram v. Herdrich*, 530 U.S. 211, 229, 120 S.Ct. 2143, 2155 n. 10, 147 L.Ed.2d 164 (2000).

181. *See Maio v. Aetna, Inc.*, 221 F.3d 472, 485 n. 12 (3d Cir.2000).

182. *See Xechem, Inc. v. Bristol–Myers Squibb Co.*, 372 F.3d 899, 901 (7th Cir. 2004); *Memphis, Tenn. Area Local, American Postal Workers Union v. City of Memphis*, 361 F.3d 898, 902 (6th Cir. 2004).

183. *See United States v. Northern Trust Co.*, 372 F.3d 886, 888 (7th Cir. 2004).

184. *See Xechem, Inc. v. Bristol–Myers Squibb Co.*, 372 F.3d 899, 901 (7th Cir. 2004).

"Built-In" Defenses

The court will dismiss for failing to state a claim where the face of the complaint reveals obvious, "built-in" affirmative defenses, such as statute of limitations, assumption of risk, or statute of frauds.[185] Similarly, the court may also dismiss under Rule 12(b)(6) where extrinsic materials (such as the complaint's exhibits and other materials properly considered by the court) reveal the same type of obvious, "built-in" defenses.[186]

Timing

The defense of failure to state a claim may be asserted at any time, even at trial.[187] Rule 12(b)(6) *motions* seeking dismissal of such claims, however, must ordinarily be filed before a responsive pleading is served. Once the pleadings are closed, the defense may be pressed on a Rule 12(c) motion for judgment on the pleadings or a Rule 56 motion for summary judgment.[188]

Waiver

A party generally does not waive the right to challenge a lawsuit for failing to state a claim.[189]

Burden of Proof

The burden lies with the moving party.[190] In fact, even a failure by the non-moving party to oppose the motion will not necessarily justify

185. *See Xechem, Inc. v. Bristol–Myers Squibb Co.*, 372 F.3d 899, 901 (7th Cir. 2004); *Brooks v. City of Winston–Salem*, 85 F.3d 178, 181 (4th Cir.1996); *Oshiver v. Levin, Fishbein, Sedran & Berman*, 38 F.3d 1380, 1384 n. 1 (3d Cir.1994); *Garrett v. Commonwealth Mortgage Corp.*, 938 F.2d 591 (5th Cir.1991). *See also Northern Trust Co. v. Peters*, 69 F.3d 123, 129 (7th Cir.1995) (noting that "[m]ore is not necessarily better under the Federal Rules", because parties can "allege" themselves out of court by unnecessarily averring facts that defeat their legal claims).

186. *See Thompson v. Illinois Dep't of Professional Regulation*, 300 F.3d 750, 754 (7th Cir.2002) ("where a plaintiff attaches documents and relies upon the documents to form the basis for a claim or part of a claim, dismissal is appropriate if the document negates the claim"); *Jacobsen v. Deseret Book Co.*, 287 F.3d 936, 941–42 (10th Cir.2002) (in deciding Rule 12(b)(6) motion in copyright cases, "the legal effect of the works are determined by the works themselves rather than by allegations in the complaint" if the works are attached as exhibits), *cert. denied*, 537 U.S. 1066, 123 S.Ct. 623, 154 L.Ed.2d 555 (2002). *See also* **Author's Commentary** to Rule 12(b)(6), *infra*, "Extrinsic Materials".

187. *See* Rule 12(h)(2).

188. *See Patel v. Contemporary Classics of Beverly Hills*, 259 F.3d 123, at 125–26 (2d Cir. 2001); *Turbe v. Government of Virgin Islands*, 938 F.2d 427, 428 (3d Cir.1991).

189. *See* Rule 12(h)(2). *See also McIntosh v. Antonino*, 71 F.3d 29, 38 (1st Cir.1995)(refusing to find waiver of statute of limitations defense, asserted as an affirmative defense, where defendant chose not to move for judgment earlier in the proceedings: "This assertion has no foothold in the law").

190. *See Ragin v. New York Times Co.*, 923 F.2d 995, 999 (2d Cir.1991), *cert. denied*, 502 U.S. 821, 112 S.Ct. 81, 116 L.Ed.2d 54 (1991); *Yeksigian v. Nappi*, 900 F.2d 101, 104–05 (7th Cir.1990); *Anyanwu v. Columbia Broad. Sys., Inc.*, 887 F.Supp. 690, 692 (S.D.N.Y. 1995)(observing that Rule 12(b)(6) imposes substantial proof burdens upon the movant). *See Brever v. Rockwell Int'l Corp.*, 40 F.3d 1119, 1125 (10th Cir.1994)(noting that Rules "erect a powerful presumption against rejecting plead-

an automatic dismissal (unless by local rule or court order a response is required on pain of dismissal).[191] The trial court must still determine whether a dismissal is appropriate.

Sua Sponte Motions

Provided it adopts a fair procedure for doing so, the trial court may, on its own initiative, dismiss a pleading for failing to state a claim upon which relief may be granted.[192] Such dismissals, however, are "strong medicine, and should be dispensed sparingly."[193] Generally, fair procedure requires that the trial court notify the plaintiffs of its intention to grant a *sua sponte* dismissal and permit them an opportunity to amend or otherwise respond.[194] Nevertheless, a *sua sponte* dismissal entered without forewarning to the plaintiff may still be affirmed if the pleading's allegations are "patently meritless" and without any hope of cure.[195].

Postponing Discovery

Some courts permit a postponement of discovery after a Rule 12(b)(6) motion is filed, and then continuing for so long as it remains pending.[196]

Pro Se Litigants

Courts are particularly cautious while inspecting pleadings prepared by plaintiffs who lack counsel and are proceeding *pro se*. Often inartful, and rarely composed to the standards expected of practicing attorneys, *pro se* pleadings are viewed with considerable liberality and are held to less stringent standards than those expected of pleadings drafted by lawyers.[197] Notwithstanding this liberality, unrepresented

ings for failure to state a claim")(citation omitted).

191. *See Pomerleau v. West Springfield Public Sch.*, 362 F.3d 143, 145 (1st Cir. 2004).

192. *See Lee v. City of Los Angeles*, 250 F.3d 668, 683 (9th Cir.2001); *Wyatt v. City of Boston*, 35 F.3d 13, 14–15 (1st Cir.1994); *Oatess v. Sobolevitch*, 914 F.2d 428, 430 n.5 (3d Cir.1990);*see also Ledford v. Sullivan*, 105 F.3d 354, 356 (7th Cir.1997) (*sua sponte* dismissals permitted if a sufficient basis for dismissal is apparent from the pleading); *Best v. Kelly*, 39 F.3d 328, 331 (D.C.Cir.1994) (noting that a complaint may be dismissed *sua sponte* under Rule 12(b)(6) where pleader cannot possibly win relief). *But cf. Blue Cross & Blue Shield of Alabama v. Sanders*, 138 F.3d 1347, 1354 (11th Cir.1998) (holding that because "failure to state a claim" is not a jurisdictional issue, court may not *sua sponte* decide the question unless plaintiff has preserved it); *Baker v. Cuomo*, 58 F.3d 814, 818 (2d Cir.1995) (commenting that *sua sponte* dismissals without service of process and a responsive filing by the opponent are disfavored).

193. *Chute v. Walker*, 281 F.3d 314, 319 (1st Cir.2002).

194. *See Chute v. Walker*, 281 F.3d 314, 319 (1st Cir.2002); *Lee v. City of Los Angeles*, 250 F.3d 668, 683 (9th Cir.2001).

195. *See Chute v. Walker*, 281 F.3d 314, 319 (1st Cir.2002) (commenting that *sua sponte* dismissal without notice may stand "[i]f it is crystal clear that the plaintiff cannot prevail and that amending the complaint would be futile").

196. *See Yuhasz v. Brush Wellman, Inc.*, 341 F.3d 559, 566 (6th Cir.2003) (noting that "very purpose" of Rule 12(b)(6) is to permit challenge to legal sufficiency of complaints without subjecting party to discovery); *Rutman Wine Co. v. E. & J. Gallo Winery*, 829 F.2d 729, 738 (9th Cir.1987) (same, and noting that it is "sounder practice to determine whether there is any reasonable likelihood that plaintiffs can construct a claim before forcing the parties to undergo the expense of discovery").

197. *See Haines v. Kerner*, 404 U.S. 519, 520–21, 92 S.Ct. 594, 595–96, 30 L.Ed.2d 652 (1972); *Calhoun v. Hargrove*, 312 F.3d 730, 733–34 (5th Cir.2002); *Smith v. Mensinger*, 293 F.3d 641, 647 (3d Cir.2002); *Chance v. Armstrong*, 143 F.3d 698, 701 (2d Cir.1998); *Ortez v. Wash-*

plaintiffs are not relieved of their obligation to allege sufficient facts to support a cognizable legal claim.[198] The court will dismiss a claim filed *in forma pauperis* if the claim is legally frivolous.[199]

Extrinsic Materials

The parties may produce affidavits and other materials either in support of or in opposition to a motion for failure to state a claim.[200] However, if the court, in its discretion,[201] considers such extrinsic evidence, the motion must be converted into a request for summary judgment under Rule 56.[202] The court must give all parties notice of such a conversion, and provide them with an opportunity both to be heard and to present further materials in support of their positions on the motion.[203] This required notice may be actual or constructive; in some instances, a litigant's act of submitting extrinsic materials may be considered notice enough.[204] Following conversion, the court is likely to permit the parties to engage in appropriate discovery before ruling on the converted motion.

The court may consider allegations contained in the complaint, exhibits attached to or otherwise incorporated in the complaint,[205]

ington County, 88 F.3d 804, 807 (9th Cir.1996); *Antonelli v. Sheahan*, 81 F.3d 1422, 1427 (7th Cir.1996).

198. *See Taylor v. Books A Million, Inc.*, 296 F.3d 376, 378 (5th Cir.2002), *cert. denied*, 537 U.S. 1200, 123 S.Ct. 1287, 154 L.Ed.2d 1041 (2003); *Riddle v. Mondragon*, 83 F.3d 1197, 1202 (10th Cir.1996).

199. *See* 28 U.S.C.A. § 1915(e)(2)(B); 28 U.S.C.A. § 1915A. *See also Neitzke v. Williams*, 490 U.S. 319, 109 S.Ct. 1827, 104 L.Ed.2d 338 (1989)(describing standards for dismissals of *in forma pauperis* pleadings as frivolous).

200. *See Ford Motor Co. v. Summit Motor Prods., Inc.*, 930 F.2d 277 (3d Cir.1991), *cert. denied*, 502 U.S. 939, 112 S.Ct. 373, 116 L.Ed.2d 324 (1991).

201. *See Pueschel v. United States*, 369 F.3d 345, 353 n.3 (4th Cir. 2004); *Stahl v. United States Dep't of Agric.*, 327 F.3d 697, 701 (8th Cir.2003); *Lybrook v. Members of Farmington Mun. Schs. Bd. of Educ.*, 232 F.3d 1334, 1341–42 (10th Cir.2000).

202. *See R.J. Corman Derailment Servs., LLC v. International Union of Operating Eng'rs, Local Union 150, AFL–CIO*, 335 F.3d 643, 647 (7th Cir.2003); *Pryor v. National Collegiate Athletic Ass'n.*, 288 F.3d 548, 560 (3d Cir.2002); *Trustmark Ins. Co. v. ESLU, Inc.*, 299 F.3d 1265, 1265 (11th Cir.2002); *Country Club Estates, L.L.C. v. Town of Loma Linda*, 213 F.3d 1001, 1005 (8th Cir.2000); *David v. City of Denver*, 101 F.3d 1344, 1352 (10th Cir.1996), *cert. denied*, 522 U.S. 858, 118 S.Ct. 157, 139 L.Ed.2d 102 (1997); *Anderson v. Angelone*, 86 F.3d 932, 934 (9th Cir.1996); *New York v. United States*, 942 F.2d 114 (2d Cir.1991), *aff'd in part and rev'd in part*, 505 U.S. 144, 112 S.Ct. 2408, 120 L.Ed.2d 120 (1992). *But cf. McNair v. Lend Lease Trucks, Inc.*, 62 F.3d 651, 656 (4th Cir. 1995)(conversion not required where trial court considers specific extrinsic evidence to which opposing party had opportunity to, and actually did, respond); *Terracom v. Valley Nat'l Bank*, 49 F.3d 555 (9th Cir.1995)(noting that because court made only "minor parenthetical observation" concerning an affidavit submitted by the parties, conversion was not required).

203. *See R.J. Corman Derailment Servs., LLC v. International Union of Operating Eng'rs, Local Union 150, AFL–CIO*, 335 F.3d 643, 647 (7th Cir.2003); *Trustmark Ins. Co. v. ESLU, Inc.*, 299 F.3d 1265, 1265 (11th Cir.2002); *Country Club Estates, L.L.C. v. Town of Loma Linda*, 213 F.3d 1001, 1005 (8th Cir.2000); *David v. City of Denver*, 101 F.3d 1344, 1352 (10th Cir. 1996), *cert. denied*, 522 U.S. 858, 118 S.Ct. 157, 139 L.Ed.2d 102 (1997).

204. *See Trustmark Ins. Co. v. ESLU, Inc.*, 299 F.3d 1265, 1267–68 (11th Cir.2002) (noting "limited exception" to notice rule where non-movant's knowledge is established by non-movant's own pleadings); *Country Club Estates, L.L.C. v. Town of Loma Linda*, 213 F.3d 1001, 1005 (8th Cir.2000); *David v. City of Denver*, 101 F.3d 1344, 1352 (10th Cir.1996) (collecting cases), *cert. denied*, 522 U.S. 858, 118 S.Ct. 157, 139 L.Ed.2d 102 (1997).

205. *See Witzke v. Femal*, 376 F.3d 744, 749 (7th Cir. 2004); *Blue Tree Hotels Inv. (Canada), Ltd. v. Starwood Hotels & Resorts Worldwide, Inc.*, 369 F.3d 212, 217 (2d Cir. 2004); *United*

matters of public record,[206] orders of record in the lawsuit,[207] and other materials subject to judicial notice, all without converting the motion to one for summary judgment.[208] In some instances, the courts may even properly consider case-specific documents that are not attached as exhibits to the complaint. For example, where a portion of a document is attached as an exhibit to the complaint, the court may consider other portions, not attached as exhibits, in ruling on the motion.[209] Moreover, many courts also permit the Rule 12(b)(6) consideration of "undisputably authentic documents", even though the documents were *not* attached to the complaint, so long as the authenticity of the documents is not challenged, the documents are attached to the motion to dismiss, and plaintiff's claims are premised upon the documents.[210]

Furthermore, even if extrinsic materials are improperly attached to a Rule 12(b)(6) motion to dismiss, a conversion to a summary judgment proceeding does not occur automatically.[211] The motion still need not be converted into a summary judgment proceeding if the district court does

States ex rel. Willard v. Humana Health Plan of Texas Inc., 336 F.3d 375, 379 (5th Cir.2003); *Pryor v. National Collegiate Athletic Ass'n*, 288 F.3d 548, 560 (3d Cir.2002).

206. *See New England Health Care Employees Pension Fund v. Ernst & Young, LLP*, 336 F.3d 495, 501 (6th Cir.2003), *cert. denied*, 540 U.S. 1183, 124 S.Ct. 1424, 158 L.Ed.2d 87 (2004); *Stahl v. United States Dep't of Agric.*, 327 F.3d 697, 701 (8th Cir.2003); *In re Colonial Mortgage Bankers Corp.*, 324 F.3d 12, 15 (1st Cir.2003); *Jefferson v. Lead Indus. Ass'n*, 106 F.3d 1245, 1250 n.14 (5th Cir.1997). *See also Blue Tree Hotels Inv. (Canada), Ltd. v. Starwood Hotels & Resorts Worldwide, Inc.*, 369 F.3d 212, 217 (2d Cir. 2004) (complaints filed in State court); *Bryant v. Avado Brands, Inc.*, 187 F.3d 1271, 1280 (11th Cir.1999) (public documents required to be (and actually) filed with SEC); *Southern Cross Overseas Agencies, Inc. v. Wah Kwong Shipping Group*, 181 F.3d 410, 426 (3d Cir.1999) (public records, including judicial proceedings); *Shaw v. Hahn*, 56 F.3d 1128, 1129 n.1 (9th Cir.1995) (public record including State administrative records used in collateral estoppel challenge), *cert. denied*, 516 U.S. 964, 116 S.Ct. 418, 133 L.E.2d 336 (1995); *Henson v. CSC Credit Servs.*, 29 F.3d 280, 284 (7th Cir.1994) (public court documents filed in earlier State court proceeding).

207. *See Oshiver v. Levin, Fishbein, Sedran & Berman*, 38 F.3d 1380, 1384 n.2 (3d Cir.1994).

208. *See United States ex rel. Willard v. Humana Health Plan of Texas Inc.*, 336 F.3d 375, 379 (5th Cir.2003); *New England Health Care Employees Pension Fund v. Ernst & Young, LLP*, 336 F.3d 495, 501 (6th Cir.2003), *cert. denied*, 540 U.S. 1183, 124 S.Ct. 1424, 158 L.Ed.2d 87 (2004).

209. *See Cooper v. Pickett*, 137 F.3d 616, 622–23 (9th Cir.1997); *In re Stac Elec. Sec. Litig.*, 89 F.3d 1399, 1405 n. 4 (9th Cir.1996), *cert. denied*, 520 U.S. 1103, 117 S.Ct. 1105, 137 L.Ed.2d 308 (1997).

210. *See MacArthur v. San Juan County*, 309 F.3d 1216, 1221 (10th Cir.2002) (even where documents are not attached to or incorporated by referenced in complaint, defendant may submit an "indisputably authentic copy" which court may consider in ruling if the documents are referred to in complaint and central to plaintiff's claim), *cert. denied*, 539 U.S. 902, 123 S.Ct. 2246, 156 L.Ed.2d 110 (2003); *Gryl ex rel. Shire Pharms. Group PLC v. Shire Pharms. Group PLC*, 298 F.3d 136, 140 (2d Cir.2002) (court may consider documents "whose terms and effect are relied upon by the plaintiff in drafting the complaint"), *cert. denied*, 537 U.S. 1191, 123 S.Ct. 1262, 154 L.Ed.2d 1024 (2003); *Pryor v. National Collegiate Athletic Ass'n*, 288 F.3d 548, 560 (3d Cir.2002) (court may consider extrinsic document if its contents are alleged in complaint and no one questions its authenticity); *Lee v. City of Los Angeles*, 250 F.3d 668, 688 (9th Cir.2001) (court may consider documents not physically attached to complaint if their authenticity is not contested and if the complaint "necessarily relies" on them); *Duferco Steel Inc. v. M/V Kalisti*, 121 F.3d 321, 324 n. 3 (7th Cir.1997) (commenting that documents "referred to in, but not attached to, a plaintiff's complaint that are central to its claim may be considered in ruling on a Rule 12(b)(6) motion if they are attached to the defendant's motion to dismiss").

211. *See Swedberg v. Marotzke*, 339 F.3d 1139, 1142–45 (9th Cir.2003); *Casazza v. Kiser*, 313 F.3d 414, 417–18 (8th Cir.2002).

not consider the materials in making its ruling[212] or if the materials are otherwise "irrelevant" to the court's resolution of the motion.[213]

Oral Argument

The trial judge may, but is not obligated to, convene oral argument on a Rule 12(b)(6) motion to dismiss.[214]

Ruling Deferred

Where circumstances persuade the court that claims should not be dismissed until further factual development is accomplished, the court may deny the Rule 12(b)(6) motion and revisit the merits of claims on a Rule 12(c) motion for judgment on the pleadings or a Rule 56 motion for summary judgment.[215]

Voluntary Dismissals While Motion is Pending

Plaintiffs may voluntarily dismiss a lawsuit at any time prior to the point where their adversaries serve an answer or a motion for summary judgment.[216] Consequently, plaintiffs are generally permitted to voluntarily dismiss their lawsuits during the pendency of a Rule 12(b)(6) motion to dismiss. This entitlement is *not* automatically lost when a defendant serves a motion to dismiss that is accompanied improperly by extrinsic materials (which could require that the motion be converted to a summary judgment proceeding); rather, until such a motion is formally converted by the court, the plaintiffs should still be permitted to voluntarily dismiss.[217]

212. *See Pueschel v. United States*, 369 F.3d 345, 353 n.3 (4th Cir. 2004); *Casazza v. Kiser*, 313 F.3d 414, 417–18 (8th Cir.2002); *Lybrook v. Members of Farmington Mun. Schs. Bd. of Educ.*, 232 F.3d 1334, 1341–42 (10th Cir.2000).

213. *See Stahl v. United States Dep't of Agriculture*, 327 F.3d 697, 701 (8th Cir.2003).

214. *See* Rule 78 ("To expedite its business, the court may make provision by rule or order for the submission and determination of motions without oral hearing upon brief written statements of reasons in support and opposition"); *Greene v. WCI Holdings Corp.*, 136 F.3d 313, 316 (2d Cir.1998) ("Every circuit to consider the issue has determined that the 'hearing' requirements of Rule 12 . . . do not mean that an oral hearing is necessary, but only require that a party be given the opportunity to present its views to the court"), *cert. denied*, 525 U.S. 983, 119 S.Ct. 448, 142 L.Ed.2d 402 (1998). *See also Pueschel v. United States*, 369 F.3d 345, 354 (4th Cir. 2004); *Cline v. Rogers*, 87 F.3d 176, 184 (6th Cir.1996), *cert. denied*, 519 U.S. 1008, 117 S.Ct. 510, 136 L.Ed.2d 400 (1996); *Riddle v. Mondragon*, 83 F.3d 1197, 1208 (10th Cir.1996).

215. *See Keys Jet Ski, Inc. v. Kays*, 893 F.2d 1225, 1230 (11th Cir.1990)(refusing to affirm district court's dismissal ruling in the absence of further factual development to support the claims); *Flue–Cured Tobacco Co–op. Stabilization Corp. v. United States EPA*, 857 F.Supp. 1137, 1145 (M.D.N.C.1994)(deferring determination of legal sufficiency of due process claim where adjudication on that issue can be more accurately accomplished after a factual record is developed); *Evello Investments, N.V. v. Printed Media Servs., Inc.*, 158 F.R.D. 172, 173 (D.Kan. 1994)(citing Rule 12(d), court elected to defer consideration of Rule 12(b)(6) motion in "highly contentious and complicated case" where dismissal motion hinged on "complicated factual and legal questions"). *But see First Commercial Trust Co., N.A. v. Colt's Mfg. Co.*, 77 F.3d 1081, 1083 n. 4 (8th Cir.1996)(noting that litigants have no entitlement to discovery in the absence of a plausible legal theory).

216. *See* Rule 41(a)(1)(i).

217. *See Swedberg v. Marotzke*, 339 F.3d 1139, 1142–45 (9th Cir.2003); *Finley Lines Joint Protective Bd. Unit 200 v. Norfolk So. Corp.*, 109 F.3d 993 (4th Cir.1997); *Aamot v. Kassel*, 1 F.3d 441 (6th Cir.1993).

Remedy and Amendments

The court will generally permit the pleader an opportunity to amend unless an amendment would be futile.[218] Even where the court doubts that the pleading defects can be overcome, the federal policy favoring decisions on the merits, rather than on technicalities, counsels in favor of permitting the plaintiff leave to amend and re-file the pleading at least once, unless the exercise is plainly futile.[219]

NOTE: A plaintiff who is otherwise entitled to file an amended complaint following a Rule 12(b)(6) dismissal may choose instead to stand on the original complaint and appeal the dismissal.[220]

Prejudice on Dismissal

Unless the ruling is premised on mere technical pleading defects or the court directs otherwise (or permits an amended pleading), a dismissal for failing to state a claim is deemed to be a ruling on the merits, and is accorded full res judicata effect.[221]

Appealability

Whether Rule 12(b)(6) rulings are immediately appealable presents complex issues that require careful study by practitioners. The general rule holds that a district court decision that grants a Rule 12(b)(6) motion is a "final order" within the meaning of 28 U.S.C. § 1291, from which an immediate appeal must be taken,[222] but a ruling that denies a Rule 12(b)(6) motion is interlocutory, and ordinarily is not immediately appealable.[223] Exceptions, however, are numerous. For example, deni-

218. *See Public Utility Dist. No. 1 v. IDACORP Inc.*, 379 F.3d 641 (9th Cir. 2004); *Alston v. Parker*, 363 F.3d 229, 235 (3d Cir. 2004); *Welch v. Laney*, 57 F.3d 1004, 1009 (11th Cir. 1995); *Perkins v. United States*, 55 F.3d 910, 917 (4th Cir.1995).

219. *See Ostrzenski v. Seigel*, 177 F.3d 245, 252–53 (4th Cir.1999).

220. *See Alston v. Parker*, 363 F.3d 229, 235 (3d Cir. 2004) ("If the plaintiff does not desire to amend, he may file an appropriate notice with the district court asserting his intent to stand on the complaint, at which time an order to dismiss the action would be appropriate"). *See also WMX Techs., Inc. v. Miller*, 104 F.3d 1133 (9th Cir.1997) (holding that plaintiff must obtain final judgment from district court before "standing" on original complaint and taking immediate appeal).

221. *See Federated Dep't Stores, Inc. v. Moitie*, 452 U.S. 394, 399 n. 3, 101 S.Ct. 2424, 2428 n. 3, 69 L.Ed.2d 103 (1981); *Davila v. Delta Air Lines, Inc.*, 326 F.3d 1183, 1189–90 (11th Cir. 2003), *cert. denied*, 540 U.S. 1016, 124 S.Ct. 568, 157 L.Ed.2d 430 (2003); *Stewart v. U.S. Bancorp*, 297 F.3d 953, 957 (9th Cir.2002); *Criales v. American Airlines, Inc.*, 105 F.3d 93, 97 (2d Cir.1997), *cert. denied*, 522 U.S. 906, 118 S.Ct. 264, 139 L.Ed.2d 190 (1997); *RMI Titanium Co. v. Westinghouse Elec. Corp.*, 78 F.3d 1125, 1134 (6th Cir.1996); *Best v. Kelly*, 39 F.3d 328, 331 (D.C.Cir.1994); *Randles v. Gregart*, 965 F.2d 90, 93 (6th Cir.1992); *Fayetteville Investors v. Commercial Builders, Inc.*, 936 F.2d 1462, 1471 (4th Cir.1991); *Lee v. Village of River Forest*, 936 F.2d 976, 981 (7th Cir.1991). *Cf. Davis v. Davis*, 526 F.2d 1286 (5th Cir.1976) (conversely, commenting that denial of Rule 12(b)(6) dismissal is not forecast of likely outcome of case). *But see Ostrzenski v. Seigel*, 177 F.3d 245, 252–53 (4th Cir.1999) (holding that dismissal under Rule 12(b)(6) generally is neither final nor a merits ruling).

222. *See ALA, Inc. v. CCAIR, Inc.*, 29 F.3d 855 (3d Cir.1994). *But see Eberhardt v. O'Malley*, 17 F.3d 1023, 1024 (7th Cir.1994)(order dismissing complaint "is not in itself a final, appealable judgment, since the plaintiff may be entitled to replead or be given leave to replead").

223. *See Hill v. City of New York*, 45 F.3d 653, 659 (2d Cir.1995)(denial not final order or immediately appealable); *Foster Wheeler Energy Corp. v. Metropolitan Knox Solid Waste Auth., Inc.*, 970 F.2d 199, 202 (6th Cir.1992)(same);

als of motions to dismiss that assert certain types of immunity issues have been deemed immediately appealable under the collateral order doctrine.[224] The question of appealability from Rule 12(b)(6) rulings, therefore, must be carefully researched within the context of the specific issues presented in the motion.

RULE 12(b)(7). DISMISSAL FOR FAILURE TO JOIN A RULE 19 PARTY

CORE CONCEPT

A case will be dismissed if there is an absent party under Rule 19, without whom complete relief cannot be granted or whose interest in the dispute is of such a nature that to proceed without that party could prejudice either that party or others.

APPLICATIONS

Legal Test

The courts are hesitant to dismiss for failure to join absent parties, and will not do so on a vague possibility that unjoined persons may have an interest in the litigation.[225] When a Rule 12(b)(7) motion is filed, the court will apply the standards of Rule 19(a) to determine whether joinder is essential and, if so, whether the factors of Rule 19(b) make dismissal appropriate.[226] The court will accept all of the pleader's well-pleaded factual allegations as true, and will draw all reasonable inferences in the pleader's favor.[227]

Timing and Waiver

An objection to the absence of a Rule 19 indispensable party may be asserted by motion filed before a responsive pleading, in the responsive pleading itself, by motion for judgment on the pleadings, or during the

Figueroa v. United States, 7 F.3d 1405, 1408 (9th Cir.1993)(same), *cert. denied*, 511 U.S. 1030, 114 S.Ct. 1537, 128 L.Ed.2d 190 (1994). *See also Bennett v. Pippin*, 74 F.3d 578, 585 (5th Cir. 1996), *cert. denied*, 519 U.S. 817, 117 S.Ct. 68, 136 L.Ed.2d 29 (1996)(holding that Rule 12(b)(6) motions to dismiss become moot after plaintiff prevails following a full trial on the merits; thereafter, any pleading defect may be cured by amendment).

224. *See, e.g., Puerto Rico Aqueduct & Sewer Auth. v. Metcalf & Eddy, Inc.*, 506 U.S. 139, 113 S.Ct. 684, 121 L.Ed.2d 605 (1993)(holding that denial of Eleventh Amendment immunity was immediately appealable collateral order); *Mitchell v. Forsyth*, 472 U.S. 511, 105 S.Ct. 2806, 86 L.Ed.2d 411 (1985)(holding that ruling denying qualified immunity was an immediately appealable collateral order); *Prager v. LaFaver*, 180 F.3d 1185, 1190 (10th Cir.1999) (same), *cert. denied*, 528 U.S. 967, 120 S.Ct. 405, 145 L.Ed.2d 315 (1999); *Jensen v. City of Oxnard*, 145 F.3d 1078, 1082 (9th Cir.1998) (same), *cert. denied*, 525 U.S. 1016, 119 S.Ct. 540, 142 L.Ed.2d 449 (1998).

225. *See Sever v. Glickman*, 298 F.Supp.2d 267, 275 (D.Conn. 2004); *Swartz v. Beach*, 229 F.Supp.2d 1239, 1250–51 (D.Wyo.2002).

226. *See HS Resources, Inc. v. Wingate*, 327 F.3d 432, 439 (5th Cir.2003); *Boulevard Bank Nat'l Ass'n v. Philips Med. Sys. Int'l B.V.*, 15 F.3d 1419, 1422 (7th Cir.1994); *Kansas City Royalty Co. v. Thoroughbred Assocs.*, 215 F.R.D. 628, 630 (D.Kan. 2003); *Ship Const. & Funding Servs. (USA), Inc. v. Star Cruises PLC*, 174 F.Supp.2d 1320, 1325 (S.D.Fla.2001); *Raytheon Co. v. Continental Cas. Co.*, 123 F.Supp.2d 22, 32 (D.Mass.2000).

227. *See Trademark Retail, Inc. v. Apple Glen Investors, LP*, 196 F.R.D. 535, 536 n.2 (N.D.Ind.2000).

trial on the merits.[228] One court, however, has held that the trial judge enjoys the discretion to reject such a motion as untimely, if the motion is found to have been submitted belatedly and for a litigant's own defensive purposes, rather than to protect the interests of the absent party.[229]

Sua Sponte Motions

Although the absence of a Rule 19 party is *not* a jurisdictional defect, the court may, on its own initiative, raise the absence of a Rule 19 party.

Burden of Proof

The burden lies with the person seeking the dismissal to demonstrate the "indispensable" nature of the absent party.[230]

Remedy

The court will, if possible, order that the absent party be joined in the lawsuit. If joinder is not possible, the court will consider whether in equity and good conscience the lawsuit should continue without the absent party.[231] Dismissals are disfavored, however.[232]

Extrinsic Materials

The parties may produce affidavits and other materials to support their positions on the absence of a Rule 19 party.[233] However, when matters outside the pleadings are submitted with the Rule 12(b)(7) motion to dismiss, the court may convert the filing into a motion for summary judgment, affording all parties notice of the conversion and the opportunity to file summary judgment oppositions.[234]

228. *See Legal Aid Society v. City of N.Y.*, 114 F.Supp.2d 204, 219 (S.D.N.Y.2000) (noting that failure to join indispensable party is not a "threshold defense"; instead, defendant may raise this challenge through end of trial).

229. *See Fireman's Fund Ins. Co. v. National Bank of Cooperatives*, 103 F.3d 888, 896 (9th Cir.1996).

230. *See Citizen Band Potawatomi Indian Tribe v. Collier*, 17 F.3d 1292, 1293 (10th Cir. 1994); *Ilan–Gat Engineers, Ltd. v. Antigua Int'l Bank,* 659 F.2d 234 (D.C.Cir.1981); *Sykes v. Hengel*, 220 F.R.D. 593, 595–96 (S.D.Iowa 2004); *Kansas City Royalty Co. v. Thoroughbred Assocs.*, 215 F.R.D. 628, 630 (D.Kan.2003); *Swartz v. Beach*, 229 F.Supp.2d 1239, 1250–51 (D.Wyo. 2002); *Ploog v. HomeSide Lending, Inc.*, 209 F.Supp.2d 863, 873 (N.D.Ill.2002); *Ship Const. & Funding Services (USA), Inc. v. Star Cruises PLC*, 174 F.Supp.2d 1320, 1325 (S.D.Fla.2001); *Raytheon Co. v. Continental Cas. Co.*, 123 F.Supp.2d 22, 32 (D.Mass.2000); *Rand v. Bath Iron Works Corp.*, 2000 WL 760730, at *2 (D.Me. 2000).

231. *See* Rule 19(b). *See also United States v. White*, 893 F.Supp. 1423 (C.D.Cal. 1995)(dismissal under Rule 12(b)(7) will be granted only where the unjoined party is "indispensable", and not just "necessary", and the party cannot otherwise be joined).

232. *See Gorsuch v. Fireman's Fund Ins. Co.*, 360 F.2d 23 (9th Cir.1966).

233. *See Davis Cos. v. Emerald Casino, Inc.*, 268 F.3d 477, 480 n.4 (7th Cir.2001); *Citizen Band Potawatomi Indian Tribe v. Collier*, 17 F.3d 1292, 1293 (10th Cir.1994); *Sykes v. Hengel*, 220 F.R.D. 593, 595–96 (S.D.Iowa 2004); *Kansas City Royalty Co. v. Thoroughbred Assocs.*, 215 F.R.D. 628, 630 (D.Kan.2003); *Swartz v. Beach*, 229 F.Supp.2d 1239, 1250–51 (D.Wyo. 2002); *Sierra Club v. Young Life Campaign, Inc.*, 176 F.Supp.2d 1070, 1076 (D.Colo.2001); *Rand v. Bath Iron Works Corp.*, 2000 WL 760730, at *2 (D.Me.2000).

234. *See Raytheon Co. v. Continental Cas. Co.*, 123 F.Supp.2d 22, 32 (D.Mass.2000); *Steward v. Gwaltney of Smithfield, Ltd.*, 954 F.Supp. 1118, 1121 (E.D.Va.1996), *aff'd*, 103 F.3d 120 (4th Cir.1996) (Table).

Ruling Deferred

The court may defer ruling on the challenge until after discovery is conducted.[235]

Prejudice on Dismissal

A dismissal for lack of a Rule 19 party is proper only when the defect cannot be cured.[236] Moreover, such a dismissal generally does not preclude the plaintiff from re-instituting the claim in a court that can join the "indispensable" absent party.[237]

Appealability

The district court's denial of a Rule 12(b)(7) motion is usually interlocutory and not immediately appealable.[238]

RULE 12(c). JUDGMENT ON THE PLEADINGS

CORE CONCEPT

After the pleadings are closed, a party may move for judgment on the pleadings if no material facts remain at issue and the parties' dispute can be resolved on both the pleadings and those facts of which the court can take judicial notice.

APPLICATIONS

Infrequently Used

Rule 12(c)'s usefulness has been displaced in many instances by the more familiar use of pre-answer Rule 12(b) motions to dismiss and post-answer Rule 56 motions for summary judgment.

Purpose

A motion for judgment on the pleadings may be used either to press Rule 12(b) defenses to the pleading's procedural defects or to seek a substantive disposition of the case on the basis of its underlying merits.[239]

Timing

A motion for judgment on the pleadings can be made any time after the pleadings are closed.[240] Such a motion need *not* await

235. *See Raytheon Co. v. Continental Cas. Co.*, 123 F.Supp.2d 22, 32 (D.Mass.2000); *Mije Assocs. v. Halliburton Servs.*, 552 F.Supp. 418 (S.D.N.Y.1982).

236. *See Sever v. Glickman*, 298 F.Supp.2d 267, 275 (D.Conn. 2004).

237. *See Dredge Corp. v. Penny*, 338 F.2d 456 (9th Cir.1964); *Raytheon Co. v. Continental Cas. Co.*, 123 F.Supp.2d 22, 33 n.9 (D.Mass. 2000). *See De Wit v. Firstar Corp.*, 879 F.Supp. 947, 992 (N.D.Iowa 1995)(dismissals with prejudice appropriate only where the court first orders joinder of the indispensable party and joinder is not accomplished).

238. *See PepsiCo. v. FTC*, 472 F.2d 179 (2d Cir.1972)(noting that general principle the denial of any motion to dismiss is not a "final order" is applicable to Rule 12(b)(7) rulings), *cert. denied*, 414 U.S. 876, 94 S.Ct. 44, 38 L.Ed.2d 122 (1973).

239. *See Alexander v. City of Chicago*, 994 F.2d 333 (7th Cir.1993).

240. *See Hughes v. Tobacco Inst., Inc.*, 278 F.3d 417, 420 (5th Cir.2001); *Republic Steel*

discovery.[241] A Rule 12(c) motion is premature if made before an answer is filed.[242] An unlabeled or mislabeled (Rule 12(b)(6)) motion to dismiss submitted after an answer is filed will be treated as a Rule 12(c) motion.[243] However, a motion filed too long after the pleadings are closed may be refused as untimely.[244].

Waiver

A motion for judgment on the pleadings cannot assert defenses and objections that a party has waived by failing to timely assert in a preliminary Rule 12(b) motion or in the responsive pleading.

Legal Test

A motion under Rule 12(c) is generally treated in the same manner as a Rule 12(b)(6) motion to dismiss.[245] The pleadings are construed liberally.[246] The court accepts all well-pleaded material allegations of the nonmoving party as true, and views all facts and inferences in a light most favorable to the pleader.[247] A pleading's legal conclusions, however, are not deemed admitted.[248] Likewise, unwarranted factual

Corp. v. Pennsylvania Eng'g Corp., 785 F.2d 174 (7th Cir.1986). *See also Warzon v. Drew*, 60 F.3d 1234, 1237 (7th Cir.1995)(where answer had already been filed, district court converted defendants' Rule 12(b)(6) motion for dismissal into a Rule 12(c) motion for judgment on the pleadings).

241. *See Carlson v. Reed*, 249 F.3d 876, 878 n.1 (9th Cir.2001) (rejecting as "frivolous" an argument that a Rule 12(c) motion was granted prematurely where discovery had not yet been completed).

242. *See Progressive Cas. Ins. Co. v. Estate of Crone*, 894 F.Supp. 383 (D.Kan.1995). However, the courts will generally treat premature, pre-answer Rule 12(c) motions as motions to dismiss under Rule 12(b)(6). *See also Warzon v. Drew*, 60 F.3d 1234 (7th Cir.1995); *Seber v. Unger*, 881 F.Supp. 323, 325 n. 2 (N.D.Ill.1995)(same). *But see Resolution Trust Corp. v. Wood*, 870 F.Supp. 797, 804 (W.D.Tenn.1994) (ruling that, even where pleadings were not yet closed at the time the motions were filed, court would nevertheless consider the pleadings where plaintiff does not object to the motions as premature).

243. *See Steele v. Federal Bureau of Prisons*, 355 F.3d 1204, 1212 n.4 (10th Cir. 2003).

244. *See* Rule 12(c) (motion must be made "[a]fter the pleadings are closed but within such time as not to delay the trial"). *See General Elec. Co. v. Sargent & Lundy*, 916 F.2d 1119, 1131 (6th Cir.1990)(reversing "timeliness" denial of Rule 12(c) motion where no allegation of prejudice was pressed and where the basis for any alleged prejudice was not articulated).

245. *See Guise v. BWM Mortg.*, 377 F.3d 795, 798 (7th Cir. 2004); *Mele v. Federal Reserve Bank*, 359 F.3d 251, 253 (3d Cir. 2004); *Oneida Indian Nation of New York v. City of Sherrill*, 337 F.3d 139, 152 (2d Cir.2003); *Ward v. Utah*, 321 F.3d 1263, 1266 (10th Cir.2003); *Brittan Communications Int'l Corp. v. Southwestern Bell Tel. Co.*, 313 F.3d 899, 904 (5th Cir.2002), *cert. denied*, 538 U.S. 1034, 123 S.Ct. 2091, 155 L.Ed.2d 1064 (2003).

246. *See Brittan Communications Int'l Corp. v. Southwestern Bell Tel. Co.*, 313 F.3d 899, 904 (5th Cir.2002), *cert. denied*, 538 U.S. 1034, 123 S.Ct. 2091, 155 L.Ed.2d 1064 (2003).

247. *See Smith v. City of Salem*, 378 F.3d 566 (6th Cir. 2004); *Guise v. BWM Mortg.*, 377 F.3d 795, 798 (7th Cir. 2004); *Mele v. Federal Reserve Bank*, 359 F.3d 251, 253 (3d Cir. 2004); *Deravin v. Kerik*, 335 F.3d 195, 200 (2d Cir. 2003); *Torbet v. United Airlines, Inc.*, 298 F.3d 1087, 1089 (9th Cir.2002); *Stewart v. Evans*, 275 F.3d 1126, 1132 (D.C.Cir.2002); *Hughes v. Tobacco Inst., Inc.*, 278 F.3d 417, 420 (5th Cir. 2001); *Ramirez v. Department of Corrections*, 222 F.3d 1238, 1240–41 (10th Cir.2000); *United States v. Any & All Radio Station Transmission Equip.*, 207 F.3d 458, 462 (8th Cir.2000), *cert. denied*, 531 U.S. 1071, 121 S.Ct. 761, 148 L.Ed.2d 663 (2001); *Feliciano v. State of R.I.*, 160 F.3d 780, 788 (1st Cir.1998); *Zeran v. America Online, Inc.*, 129 F.3d 327, 329 (4th Cir. 1997), *cert. denied*, 524 U.S. 937, 118 S.Ct. 2341, 141 L.Ed.2d 712 (1998).

248. *See Mixon v. Ohio*, 193 F.3d 389, 400 (6th Cir.1999); *Northern Ind. Gun & Outdoor Shows, Inc. v. City of South Bend*, 163 F.3d 449, 452 (7th Cir.1998) (commenting that court is not required to ignore facts in complaint that under-

inferences will not be drawn to aid the plaintiff.[249] A Rule 12(c) judgment will be granted if the pleadings demonstrate that the moving party is entitled to judgment as a matter of law.[250] If, however, a material issue of fact remains in dispute, the court must deny the Rule 12(c) motion.[251] Judgment on the pleadings is only warranted where it appears beyond doubt that the plaintiff will be unable to prove any facts to support the alleged claims for relief.[252] The pleader's choice of pleaded theories is not necessarily dispositive; the court will inquire whether relief for the pleader is possible under any set of facts that might be established consistent with the allegation.[253]

Note: A party who, for the purposes of Rule 12(c), presumes all of an opponent's well-pleaded facts as true, is not bound by any "admission" of this kind at trial. The party is free at trial to disprove or contradict the opponent's facts if the Rule 12(c) motion is denied.[254]

Civil Rights Cases

At least one court has held that the Rule 12(c) test is to be applied with "particular strictness" in cases involving federal civil rights claims.[255] In such cases, that court has characterized the pleading requirements as "very lenient, even de minimis".[256]

Extrinsic Materials

If the court, in its discretion, considers extrinsic evidence presented by the parties on a Rule 12(c) motion, the court must convert the

mine plaintiff's claim or to give weight to unsupported conclusions of law); *Republic Steel Corp. v. Pennsylvania Eng'g Corp.*, 785 F.2d 174, 178 n. 2 (7th Cir.1986)(noting that reasonable inferences are drawn in favor of nonmoving party, but legal characterizations pleader draws from pleaded facts do not bind the court).

249. *See Mixon v. Ohio*, 193 F.3d 389, 400 (6th Cir.1999).

250. *See United States v. Any & all Radio Station Transmission Equip.*, 207 F.3d 458, 462 (8th Cir.2000), *cert. denied*, 531 U.S. 1071, 121 S.Ct. 761, 148 L.Ed.2d 663 (2001); *Fajardo v. County of Los Angeles*, 179 F.3d 698, 699 (9th Cir.1999); *Nelson v. City of Irvine*, 143 F.3d 1196, 1200 (9th Cir.1998), *cert. denied*, 525 U.S. 981, 119 S.Ct. 444, 142 L.Ed.2d 399 (1998); *Burns Int'l Security Servs., Inc. v. International Union, United Plant Guard Workers of America*, 47 F.3d 14, 16 (2d Cir.1995); *New Zealand Lamb Co., Inc. v. United States*, 40 F.3d 377, 380 (Fed.Cir.1994).

251. *See Brittan Communications Int'l Corp. v. Southwestern Bell Tel. Co.*, 313 F.3d 899, 904 (5th Cir.2002), *cert. denied*, 538 U.S. 1034, 123 S.Ct. 2091, 155 L.Ed.2d 1064 (2003); *United States v. Any & all Radio Station Transmission Equip.*, 207 F.3d 458, 462 (8th Cir.2000), *cert. denied*, 531 U.S. 1071, 121 S.Ct. 761, 148 L.Ed.2d 663 (2001); *Gustafson v. Jones*, 117 F.3d 1015 (7th Cir.1997); *B.F. Goodrich v. Betkoski*, 99 F.3d 505, 530 (2d Cir.1996), *clarified*, 112 F.3d 88 (2d Cir.1997), *cert. denied*, 524 U.S. 926, 118 S.Ct. 2318, 141 L.Ed.2d 694 (1998); *Kruzits v. Okuma Machine Tool, Inc.*, 40 F.3d 52, 54 (3d Cir.1994). *United States v. Moriarty*, 8 F.3d 329, 332 (6th Cir.1993).

252. *See Guise v. BWM Mortg.*, 377 F.3d 795, 798 (7th Cir. 2004); *Mele v. Federal Reserve Bank*, 359 F.3d 251, 253 (3d Cir. 2004); *Oneida Indian Nation of New York v. City of Sherrill*, 337 F.3d 139, 152 (2d Cir.2003), *cert. granted*, ___ U.S. ___, 124 S.Ct. 2904, 159 L.Ed.2d 810 (2004); *Horsley v. Rivera*, 292 F.3d 695, 700 (11th Cir.2002); *Forseth v. Village of Sussex*, 199 F.3d 363, 368 (7th Cir.2000); *Mixon v. Ohio*, 193 F.3d 389, 400 (6th Cir.1999).

253. *See Smith v. City of Salem*, 378 F.3d 566 (6th Cir. 2004).

254. *See Wyman v. Wyman*, 109 F.2d 473 (9th Cir.1940).

255. *See Deravin v. Kerik*, 335 F.3d 195, 200 (2d Cir.2003); *Irish Lesbian & Gay Org. v. Giuliani*, 143 F.3d 638, 644 (2d Cir.1998).

256. *See Deravin v. Kerik*, 335 F.3d 195, 200 (2d Cir.2003).

motion into a request for summary judgment under Rule 56.[257] In this regard, the court generally applies the same "conversion" principles used to guide Rule 12(b)(6) motions for failure to state a cognizable claim.[258] The court must give all parties notice of such a conversion, and provide them with an opportunity to be heard and present further materials in support of their positions on the motion.[259] Constructive notice can suffice.[260] Courts have held that constructive notice exists where the conversion mandate is obvious–thus, a movant cannot complain of an unnoticed conversion if his own motion is accompanied by clearly extrinsic materials.[261] Similarly, the non-moving party will not be permitted to complain about an unnoticed conversion if she opposes the motion with extrinsic materials of her own.[262] Such a conversion is *not* required when the court considers documents attached as exhibits to the complaint, documents referred to in the complaint and central to the claim, and documents of which the court may take judicial notice.[263] Although a "written instrument" attached to a pleading becomes "a part thereof for all purposes",[264] a litigant cannot avoid this summary judgment conversion provision merely by attaching any random document to her answer–the attached document still can only be relied upon by the court on a Rule 12(c) motion if that document is both central to the plaintiff's claim and indisputably authentic.[265]

New Factual Allegations Asserted on Appeal

In unusual instances, the pleader may be able to raise new factual allegations in support of her pleading for the first time on appeal, provided those new allegations are consistent with her complaint.[266]

257. *See* Rule 12(c). *See also Sira v. Morton*, 380 F.3d 57 (2d Cir. 2004); *Olsen v. Idaho State Bd. of Med.*, 363 F.3d 916, 921–22 (9th Cir. 2004); *R.J. Corman Derailment Servs., LLC v. International Union of Operating Eng'rs, Local Union 150, AFL–CIO*, 335 F.3d 643, 647 (7th Cir.2003).

258. *See Rubert–Torres v. Hospital San Pablo, Inc.*, 205 F.3d 472, 475 (1st Cir.2000).

259. *See R.J. Corman Derailment Servs., LLC v. International Union of Operating Eng'rs, Local Union 150, AFL–CIO*, 335 F.3d 643, 647 (7th Cir.2003); *Rubert–Torres v. Hospital San Pablo, Inc.*, 205 F.3d 472, 475 (1st Cir.2000). *Baker v. Putnal*, 75 F.3d 190, 197 (5th Cir.1996); *Grimmett v. Brown*, 75 F.3d 506, 510 (9th Cir. 1996), *cert. dismissed as improvidently granted*, 519 U.S. 233, 117 S.Ct. 759, 136 L.Ed.2d 674 (1997); *Church v. General Motors Corp.*, 74 F.3d 795, 798 (7th Cir.1996); *Latecoere Int'l, Inc. v. United States Dep't of Navy*, 19 F.3d 1342, 1356 (11th Cir.1994). *But see Gagliardi v. Village of Pawling*, 18 F.3d 188 (2d Cir. 1994)(notwithstanding introduction of extrinsic evidence, conversion rule not relevant where motion decided solely on a review of the complaint).

260. *See Rubert–Torres v. Hospital San Pablo, Inc.*, 205 F.3d 472, 475–76 (1st Cir.2000).

261. *See Sira v. Morton*, 380 F.3d 57 (2d Cir. 2004); *Olsen v. Idaho State Bd. of Med.*, 363 F.3d 916, 921–22 (9th Cir. 2004); *Rubert-Torres v. Hospital San Pablo, Inc.*, 205 F.3d 472, 475–76 (1st Cir. 2000).

262. *See Gulf Coast Bank & Trust Co. v. Reder*, 355 F.3d 35, 38 (1st Cir. 2004);

263. *See Sira v. Morton*, 380 F.3d 57 (2d Cir. 2004); *Horsley v. Feldt*, 304 F.3d 1125, 1134–35 (11th Cir.2002); *Hatch v. TIG Ins. Co.*, 301 F.3d 915, 916 n.2 (8th Cir.2002).

264. *See* Rule 10(c).

265. *See Horsley v. Feldt*, 304 F.3d 1125, 1134–35 (11th Cir.2002) ("Otherwise, the conversion clause of Rule 12(c) would be too easily circumvented and disputed documents attached to an answer would have to be taken as true at the pleadings stage. The written instrument provision of Rule 10(c) does not require that.").

266. *See Guise v. BWM Mortg.*, 377 F.3d 795, 798 (7th Cir. 2004).

Remedy

If the Rule 12(c) motion is granted, the prevailing parties obtain a final judgment in their favor.[267]

Appealability

For the same reasons noted in Rule 12(b)(6)'s discussion of appealability, practitioners must proceed with care in analyzing whether an immediate appeal will lie from Rule 12(c) motions for judgment on the pleadings.[268] Generally, a decision granting such a motion is considered a "final order", and is immediately appealable, but a decision denying such a motion is ordinarily deemed "interlocutory" and must await a final disposition on the merits.[269]

RULE 12(d). PRELIMINARY HEARINGS

CORE CONCEPT

Unless the court orders that such motions are deferred until trial, a party may request the court to schedule Rule 12(b) and Rule 12(c) motions for a pretrial hearing and resolution.

APPLICATIONS

Rule 12(b) Defenses Asserted by Motion

When a Rule 12(b) defense or objection is asserted on a Rule 12(b) or Rule 12(c) motion, the moving papers themselves should include a "notice of hearing" or similar references following the practice dictated by the specific judicial district's local rules. As a matter of usual practice, the court will ordinarily resolve Rule 12(b) and Rule 12(c) motions by issuing a pretrial Memorandum and Order.

Rule 12(b) Defenses Asserted in Responsive Pleading Only

When a Rule 12(b) defense or objection is asserted only in the responsive pleading (*i.e.*, where no pre-answer Rule 12(b) motion for dismissal is filed), a Rule 12(d) application for preliminary hearing is necessary to obtain a pretrial determination from the court on those defenses and objections.[270]

When Pretrial Determinations are Appropriate

Notwithstanding the presence of a genuine factual dispute, the court may decide to make its own findings and resolve pretrial contests

267. *See Republic Steel Corp. v. Pennsylvania Eng'g Corp.*, 785 F.2d 174, 178 n. 2 (7th Cir.1986)(commenting that Rule 12(c) motions are directed towards obtaining final judgments on the merits).

268. *See* discussion of Appealability in Authors' Commentary to Rule 12(b)(6).

269. *See Paskvan v. City of Cleveland Civil Serv. Com'n*, 946 F.2d 1233 (6th Cir.1991). *But see Estate of Drayton v. Nelson*, 53 F.3d 165, 166 (7th Cir.1994)(holding that order granting judgment on the pleadings was not final, appealable order because the lawsuit remained pending against other defendants).

270. *See Rivera–Gomez v. de Castro*, 900 F.2d 1, 2 (1st Cir.1990) (Rule 12(d) is "perhaps too infrequently invoked and too often overlooked"; it can, in appropriate instances, "be an excellent device for conserving time, expenses, and scarce judicial resources by targeting early resolution of threshold issues").

challenging (1) the litigants' domiciles for diversity jurisdiction purposes, (2) the court's exercise of personal jurisdiction over a defendant, (3) a litigant's standing to press a claim, (4) the propriety of venue as laid, or (5) the assertion of claim preclusion defenses.[271] In deciding whether these types of issues should be determined preliminarily (or should, instead, await resolution at trial), the courts weigh the need to test these defenses and the litigants' interest in having the objections resolved promptly, against the expense and delay of a preliminary hearing, the court's difficulty in deciding the issues preliminarily, and the likelihood that the issues will become so interconnected with the merits that deferring them until trial would be preferable.[272]

Resolving Personal Jurisdiction Challenges

When the Rule 12(b)(2) defense of lack of personal jurisdiction is raised, the court has three options for resolving the motion:

(1) The court may hear and resolve the motion before trial, by applying the preponderance-of-the-evidence standard;

(2) The court may defer the motion until time of trial, provided the plaintiff has offered a prima facie showing of jurisdiction; or

(3) The court may apply an intermediate scrutiny in circumstances where it would be unfair to require a defendant to incur the expenses and burden of a trial on the merits in view of a substantial jurisdictional question. In those instances, the court will defer the motion until trial only if the plaintiff first demonstrates a likelihood that personal jurisdiction exists over the defendant.[273]

Ruling Deferred

This Rule confirms that a district court's *pretrial* review and disposition of Rule 12(b) defenses and Rule 12(c) motions is discretionary, not mandatory. In appropriate cases, involving peculiarly complicated factual and legal issues, or where further factual development is necessary, the court may defer resolving Rule 12(b) defenses until time of trial.[274]

Oral Argument and Hearing

The moving party is generally not *entitled* to oral argument or a hearing on the motion; whether to permit such argument or hearing is usually committed to the trial court's discretion.[275]

271. *See Cameron v. Children's Hosp. Med. Ctr.*, 131 F.3d 1167, 1170 (6th Cir.1997).

272. *See Cameron v. Children's Hosp. Med. Ctr.*, 131 F.3d 1167, 1170–71 (6th Cir.1997). *See also Cuoco v. United States Bureau of Prisons*, 2000 WL 347155, at *8 (S.D.N.Y.2000) (noting that Rule 12(d) request for the pretrial determination of a defense is not limited to only Rule 12(b) defenses, but is available for other types of defenses as well).

273. *See Foster–Miller, Inc. v. Babcock & Wilcox Canada*, 46 F.3d 138 (1st Cir.1995); *Boit v. Gar–Tec Prods., Inc.*, 967 F.2d 671 (1st Cir. 1992).

274. *See Evello Invs., N.V. v. Printed Media Servs., Inc.*, 158 F.R.D. 172, 173 (D.Kan.1994).

275. *See Greene v. WCI Holdings Corp.*, 136 F.3d 313, 316 (2d Cir.1998) ("Every circuit to consider the issue has determined that the 'hearing' requirements of Rule 12 ... do not mean

RULE 12(e). MOTION FOR MORE DEFINITE STATEMENT

CORE CONCEPT

If a pleading is so vague or ambiguous that a responsive pleading cannot be framed, the responding party need not serve a response, but may instead move the court for an order directing the pleader to serve a more definite statement.

APPLICATIONS

Distinct from Rule 12(b)(6) Motions

Motions to dismiss and motions for more definite statements are not interchangeable. A motion to dismiss under Rule 12(b)(6) attacks a pleading for failing to allege a cognizable legal theory eligible for some type of relief. In contrast, a Rule 12(e) motion for more definite statements attacks pleadings that do, in fact, state cognizable legal claims, but those pleadings are so unclear that drafting a response to them is impossible.[276] Where the defending party is unable to frame a fair response to a pleading because the pleading's meaning is unclear, the proper remedy is not a Rule 12(b) motion to dismiss but instead a motion for a more definite statement.[277]

Conversion: A motion to dismiss under Rule 12(b)(6) that, more correctly, is a motion for a more definite statement may be so converted by the court in its discretion.[278]

Disfavored Motion

The Rules require the pleader to serve only a short, plain statement showing an entitlement to relief.[279] Due to these liberal pleading requirements in federal court, motions for a more definite statement are disfavored and granted only sparingly.[280] They are not a substitute for discovery,[281] and ordinarily will not be granted where the informa-

that an oral hearing is necessary, but only require that a party be given the opportunity to present its views to the court"), *cert. denied*, 525 U.S. 983, 119 S.Ct. 448, 142 L.Ed.2d 402 (1998). *See also Pueschel v. United States*, 369 F.3d 345, 354 (4th Cir. 2004).

276. *See Humpherys v. Nager*, 962 F.Supp. 347, 352–53 (E.D.N.Y.1997).

277. *See American Nurses' Ass'n v. Illinois*, 783 F.2d 716, 725 (7th Cir.1986). *See also McClellon v. Lone Star Gas Co.*, 66 F.3d 98, 103 (5th Cir.1995)(vacating court's dismissal of deficient complaint, without first permitting the pleader an opportunity to replead).

278. *See Hall v. Tyco Int'l Ltd.*, 223 F.R.D. 219 (M.D.N.C. 2004).

279. *See* Rule 8.

280. *See Home & Nature Inc. v. Sherman Specialty Co.*, 322 F.Supp.2d 260, 265 (E.D.N.Y. 2004) ("discourage[d]"); *Peterson v. Brownlee*, 314 F.Supp.2d 1150, 1155–56 (D.Kan. 2004) ("disfavored"); *Ekberg v. Pennington*, 2002 WL 1611641, at *1 (E.D.La.2002) ("disfavored"); *Synagro-WWT, Inc. v. Rush Township*, 204 F.Supp.2d 827, 849 (M.D.Pa.2002) ("generally disfavored"); *DVI Business Credit Corp. v. Crowder*, 193 F.Supp.2d 1002, 1009 (S.D.Tex.2002) ("disfavored"); *Tinder v. Lewis County Nursing Home Dist.*, 207 F.Supp.2d 951, 960 (E.D.Mo. 2001) ("universally disfavored"); *Wallett v. Anderson*, 198 F.R.D. 20, 23 (D.Conn.2000) ("not favored"); *Eye Care Int'l, Inc. v. Underhill*, 92 F.Supp.2d 1310, 1316 (M.D.Fla.2000) ("not favored"); *Cellars v. Pacific Coast Packaging, Inc.*, 189 F.R.D. 575, 578 (N.D.Cal.1999) ("viewed with disfavor" and "rarely granted").

281. *See Hilska v. Jones*, 217 F.R.D. 16 (D.D.C.2003); *Tinder v. Lewis County Nursing Home Dist.*, 207 F.Supp.2d 951, 959–60 (E.D.Mo.

tion sought could be obtained in discovery.[282]

Legal Test

As a disfavored remedy, motions for a more definite statement will ordinarily only be granted where the pleading is "unintelligible": so hopelessly vague and ambiguous that a defendant cannot fairly be expected to frame a response or denial, at least not without risking prejudice.[283] Nevertheless, courts continue to grant these motions, even though disfavored, where the minimal federal "notice pleading" standards are not met.[284] Just as Rule 12(e) motions are not legitimate substitutes for discovery, discovery is not a fair substitute for proper notice pleading.[285] Both the court and the litigants are entitled to know, at the pleading stage, who is being sued, why, and for what.[286]

2001); *Davenport v. Rodriguez*, 147 F.Supp.2d 630, 639–40 (S.D.Tex.2001); *S.E.C. v. Saltzman*, 127 F.Supp.2d 660, 668 (E.D.Pa.2000); *Board of Trustees, Sheet Metal Workers' Nat'l Pension Fund v. Illinois Range, Inc.*, 186 F.R.D. 498 (N.D.Ill.1999); *Radisson Hotels Int'l, Inc. v. Westin Hotel Co.*, 931 F.Supp. 638, 644 (D.Minn. 1996); *Campbell v. Miller*, 836 F.Supp. 827, 832 (M.D.Fla.1993). *See also Eisenach v. Miller–Dwan Med. Ctr.*, 162 F.R.D. 346 (D.Minn. 1995)(commenting that with notice pleading, rubric, discovery obviates need for extended elaboration because discovery can be more efficient than detailed pleading in expediting the pretrial processing of lawsuits); *In re Triple Screw Marine Towing, Inc.*, 1994 WL 151101 at *2 (E.D.La.1994)(noting Rule's disfavor, and commenting that where discovery is underway, motion practice directed to the pleadings is of little value, and that the wiser approach is to allow discovery to unearth facts and then press with a Rule 56 motion for summary judgment).

282. *See Sheffield v. Orius Corp.*, 211 F.R.D. 411, 414–15 (D.Or.2002). *See also Cross Timbers Concerned Citizens v. Saginaw*, 991 F.Supp. 563, 572–73 (N.D.Tex.1997) (quoting Local Rule 12.1, which provides that "[e]xcept for motions complaining of failure to plead fraud or mistake with particularity pursuant to Fed.R.Civ.P. 9(b), a motion for more definite statement may only be filed where the information sought cannot be obtained by discovery").

283. *See Home & Nature Inc. v. Sherman Specialty Co.*, 322 F.Supp.2d 260, 265 (E.D.N.Y. 2004); *Thompson v. City of Shasta Lake*, 314 F.Supp.2d 1017, 1022 (E.D.Cal. 2004); *Hilska v. Jones*, 217 F.R.D. 16, 22 (D.D.C.2003); *Sheffield v. Orius Corp.*, 211 F.R.D. 411, 414–15 (D.Or. 2002); *Synagro-WWT, Inc. v. Rush Township*, 204 F.Supp.2d 827, 849 (M.D.Pa.2002); *DVI Business Credit Corp. v. Crowder*, 193 F.Supp.2d 1002, 1009 (S.D.Tex.2002); *Tinder v. Lewis County Nursing Home Dist.*, 207 F.Supp.2d 951, 959–60 (E.D.Mo.2001); *ESI, Inc. v. Coastal Corp.*, 61 F.Supp.2d 35, 68 (S.D.N.Y.1999); *S.E.C. v. Saltzman*, 127 F.Supp.2d 660, 668 (E.D.Pa.2000); *Wallett v. Anderson*, 198 F.R.D. 20, 23 (D.Conn.2000); *S.E.C. v. Digital Lightwave, Inc.*, 196 F.R.D. 698, 700 (M.D.Fla.2000); *Cellars v. Pacific Coast Packaging, Inc.*, 189 F.R.D. 575, 578 (N.D.Cal.1999).

284. *See Swierkiewicz v. Sorema N. A.*, 534 U.S. 506, 512, 122 S.Ct. 992, 998, 152 L.Ed.2d 1 (2002) (noting that if pleading "fails to specify the allegations in a manner that provides sufficient notice", defendant can move for more definite statement before responding).

285. *See Eisenach v. Miller–Dwan Med. Ctr.*, 162 F.R.D. 346, 348 (D.Minn.1995)("any current view that the deficiencies in pleading may be cured through liberalized discovery is at increasingly mounting odds with the public's dissatisfaction with exorbitantly expansive discovery, and the impact that the public outcry has had upon our discovery Rules").

286. *See McHenry v. Renne*, 84 F.3d 1172, 1179–80 (9th Cir.1996) (writing that "[p]rolix, confusing complaints such as the ones plaintiffs filed in this case impose unfair burdens on litigants and judges. As a practical matter, the judge and opposing counsel, in order to perform their responsibilities, cannot use a complaint such as the one plaintiffs filed, and must prepare outlines to determine who is being sued for what. Defendants are then put at risk that their outline differs from the judge's, that plaintiffs will surprise them with something new at trial which they reasonably did not understand to be in the case at all, and that res judicata effects of settlement or judgment will be different from what they reasonably expected. . . . The judge wastes half a day in chambers preparing the 'short and plain statement' which Rule 8 obligated plaintiffs to submit. He then

The decision to grant or deny a motion for a more definite statement is committed to the district court's sound discretion.[287]

When proper and appropriate, Rule 12(e) motions can seek more definite statements concerning the pleader's claim for relief, the court's jurisdiction, or the pleader's capacity to press the lawsuit.

- *Special Pleading Obligations:* The motion may be appropriate where the pleader fails to allege properly facts that must be specially pleaded, such as fraud, mistake, denial of performance or occurrence, and special damages.[288]
- *Threshold Defenses:* The motion may also be appropriate where the pleading fails to provide facts necessary to determine whether threshold defenses exist, such as statute of limitations (when claim arose) or statute of frauds (whether contract was written or oral, term for performance).[289]
- *RICO Case Statements*: Rule 12(e), among other Rules, has been cited as authority for compelling the filing of "RICO Case Statements", as now required in many judicial districts to flesh out the factual predicates and legal theory underlying federal civil racketeering claims.[290] Such Statements have been approved, unless they would obligate the pleader to allege more information than Rule 8(a) and Rule 9(b) would otherwise require.[291]

Burden of Proof

The burden lies with the moving party to demonstrate that the challenged pleading is too vague or ambiguous to permit a response. The moving party must identify the deficiencies in the pleading, list the details sought to be provided, and assert an inability to frame a response.[292]

must manage the litigation without knowing what claims are made against whom. This leads to discovery disputes and lengthy trials, prejudicing litigants in other case who follow the rules, as well as defendants in the case in which the prolix pleading is filed.").

287. *See Sheffield v. Orius Corp.*, 211 F.R.D. 411, 414 (D.Or.2002); *Ekberg v. Pennington*, 2002 WL 1611641, at *1 (E.D.La.2002); *DVI Business Credit Corp. v. Crowder*, 193 F.Supp.2d 1002, 1009 (S.D.Tex.2002); *Graham v. Prudential Home Mortg. Co.*, 186 F.R.D. 651 (D.Kan. 1999); *Tilley v. Allstate Ins. Co.*, 40 F.Supp.2d 809, 814 (S.D.W.Va.1999).

288. *See* Rule 9.

289. *See Rose v. Kinevan,* 115 F.R.D. 250 (D.Colo.1987).

290. *See Northland Ins. Co. v. Shell Oil Co.*, 930 F.Supp. 1069, 1074 (D.N.J.1996). Where claims are asserted under the federal Racketeer Influenced and Corrupt Organizations Act ("RICO"), 18 U.S.C.A. §§ 1961–68, many judicial districts now require, by Standing Order, chambers policy, or otherwise, that the pleader answer a series of questions that supplement the RICO allegations of the complaint. *See, e.g.*, S.D. Cal. Rule 11.1; W.D. N.Y. Rule 5.1; *National Org. for Women, Inc. v. Scheidler*, 510 U.S. 249, 249, 114 S.Ct. 798, 800, 127 L.Ed.2d 99 (1994)(noting local rule in force in Northern District of Illinois); *O'Ferral v. Trebol Motors Corp.*, 45 F.3d 561, 562 (1st Cir.1995) (same, District of Puerto Rico); *Frank v. D'Ambrosi*, 4 F.3d 1378, 1381 (6th Cir.1993) (same, Northern District of Ohio); *Boogaerts v. Bank of Bradley*, 961 F.2d 765, 767 n. 3 (8th Cir.1992)(same, Western District of Arkansas). This pleading obligation is especially important where the facts noted in the RICO Case Statement are deemed to be pleading averments, properly considered in ruling upon a motion to dismiss. *See Glessner v. Kenny*, 952 F.2d 702, 712 n. 9 (3d Cir.1991)(collecting cases so holding).

291. *See Wagh v. Metris Direct, Inc.*, 363 F.3d 821, 826–28 (9th Cir. 2003), *cert. denied*, ___ U.S. ___, 124 S.Ct. 2176, 158 L.Ed.2d 733 (2004).

292. *See Davenport v. Rodriguez*, 147 F.Supp.2d 630, 639–40 (S.D.Tex.2001); *Nebout*

Sua Sponte Motions

The district court may, on its own initiative, strike a deficient pleading and direct the pleader to file a more definite statement.[293]

Timing

Obviously, a motion for more definite statement must be filed before the party serves a response to the pleading claimed to be too vague or ambiguous.[294] Additionally, the moving party should appreciate the significance of moving for Rule 12(e) relief–once a Rule 12 motion is made, any waivable defense that could have been, but was not, joined in that Rule 12 motion may be lost.[295] To abate the harshness of this result, the court may permit the moving party to withdraw the Rule 12(e) motion for more definite statement so as to permit a larger Rule 12 filing.[296]

Tolling Effect

While the motion is pending, the party's time for serving a responsive pleading is tolled. Once the court rules on the motion, a new response time begins. If the motion is granted, the party must serve a responsive pleading within 10 days after the more definite statement is served or within such other time as the court may direct. If the motion is denied, the party must serve a responsive pleading within 10 days of the court's order.

Complying With Court's Order For More Definite Statement

To comply with a Rule 12(e) order for a more definite statement, the pleader must amend the pleading to add sufficient detail to satisfy the court and to meet the adversary's objections.[297] If the pleader fails to serve the more definite statement, or fails to do so within the designated time period, the court may strike the pleading or make such other order as it deems just.[298]

v. City of Hitchcock, *71 F.Supp.2d 702, 706 (S.D.Tex.1999).*

293. *See Cesnik v. Edgewood Baptist Church*, 88 F.3d 902, 907 n. 13 (11th Cir.1996), *cert. denied*, 519 U.S. 1110, 117 S.Ct. 946, 136 L.Ed.2d 834 (1997); *Fikes v. City of Daphne*, 79 F.3d 1079, 1083 n. 6 (11th Cir.1996).

294. *See Marx v. Gumbinner*, 855 F.2d 783, 792 (11th Cir.1988); *Santana Prods., Inc. v. Sylvester & Assocs., Ltd.*, 121 F.Supp.2d 729, 738 (E.D.N.Y.1999) (because Rule 12(e) motions must be presented before filing a responsive pleading, defendants' decision to file an answer precluded relief under motion); *Clark v. Associates Commercial Corp.*, 149 F.R.D. 629, 633 (D.Kan.1993) (same).

295. *See* Rules 12(g) & 12(h). *See also Caldwell–Baker Co. v. Southern Illinois Railcar Co.*, 225 F.Supp.2d 1243, 1259, (D.Kan.2002) (noting substantial number of courts that had ruled that a party moving for more definite statement may not later assert by motion another Rule 12(b) defense that was then available).

296. *See Caldwell–Baker Co. v. Southern Illinois Railcar Co.*, 225 F.Supp.2d 1243, 1259 (D.Kan.2002) (holding that party's withdrawal of Rule 12(e) motion abated possible waiver of motion to dismiss for lack of personal jurisdiction).

297. *See Sefton v. Jew*, 204 F.R.D. 104, 106 (W.D.Tex.2000).

298. *See Sefton v. Jew*, 204 F.R.D. 104, 106 (W.D.Tex.2000); *Iacampo v. Hasbro, Inc.*, 929 F.Supp. 562, 571 (D.R.I.1996).

RULE 12(f). MOTION TO STRIKE

CORE CONCEPT

On its own initiative or upon motion, the court may strike from a pleading any insufficient defense or any redundant, immaterial, impertinent, or scandalous matter. This motion is viewed with disfavor and is rarely granted.

APPLICATIONS

Purpose

Insufficient defenses and redundant, immaterial, impertinent, or scandalous matter are properly stricken from a pleading in order to avoid the time, effort, and expense necessary to litigate spurious issues.[299] Such motions may be granted when necessary to clean up the pleadings, streamline the litigation, or sidestep unnecessary efforts on immaterial issues.[300]

General Test

Motions to strike are disfavored by the courts.[301] In considering a motion to strike, courts will generally apply the same test used to determine a Rule 12(b)(6) motion[302]–the courts will deem as admitted all of the non-moving party's well-pleaded facts, draw all reasonable inferences in the pleader's favor, and resolve all doubts in favor of denying the motion to strike.[303] But the court will not accept as true

299. *See Fantasy, Inc. v. Fogerty*, 984 F.2d 1524, 1527 (9th Cir.1993), *rev'd on other grounds,* 510 U.S. 517, 114 S.Ct. 1023, 127 L.Ed.2d 455 (1994); *Cardinale v. La Petite Academy, Inc.*, 207 F.Supp.2d 1158, 1161–62 (D.Nev. 2002); *Sony Pictures Entertainment, Inc. v. Fireworks Entertainment Group, Inc.*, 156 F.Supp.2d 1148 (C.D.Cal.2001); *Chicago Sch. Reform Bd. of Trustees v. Substance, Inc.*, 79 F.Supp.2d 919, 930 (N.D.Ill.2000); *Bristol-Myers Squibb Co. v. IVAX Corp.*, 77 F.Supp.2d 606, 619 (D.N.J.2000); *Estee Lauder, Inc. v. Fragrance Counter, Inc.*, 189 F.R.D. 269, 272 (S.D.N.Y.1999); *Hardin v. American Elec. Power*, 188 F.R.D. 509, 511 (S.D.Ind.1999).

300. *See McInerney v. Moyer Lumber & Hardware, Inc.*, 244 F.Supp.2d 393, 402 (E.D.Pa. 2002).

301. *See Boreri v. Fiat S.p.A.*, 763 F.2d 17, 23 (1st Cir.1985) (commenting that motions to strike "are narrow in scope, disfavored in practice, and not calculated readily to invoke the court's discretion"); *E.E.O.C. v. Bay Ridge Toyota, Inc.*, 327 F.Supp.2d 167 (E.D.N.Y. 2004); *Association of American Med. Colleges v. Princeton Rev., Inc.*, 332 F.Supp.2d 11, 21–22 (D.D.C. 2004); *In re Complaint of J.A.R. Barge Lines, L.P.*, 307 F.Supp.2d 668, 670 (W.D.Pa. 2004); *United States v. Southern Cal. Edison Co.*, 300 F.Supp.2d 964, 973 (E.D.Cal. 2004); *Breedlove v. Cabou*, 296 F.Supp.2d 253, 274–75 (N.D.N.Y. 2003); *Germaine Music v. Universal Songs of Polygram*, 275 F.Supp.2d 1288, 1300 (D.Nev. 2003); *Wailua Assocs. v. Aetna Cas. & Sur. Co.*, 183 F.R.D. 550, 553–54 (D.Haw.1998).

302. *See Breedlove v. Cabou*, 296 F.Supp.2d 253, 274–75 (N.D.N.Y. 2003); *Solvent Chem. Co. ICC Indus., Inc. v. E.I. Dupont De Nemours & Co.*, 242 F.Supp.2d 196, 212 (W.D.N.Y.2002); *Siegel ex rel. Latham v. J & H Marsh & McLennon, Inc.*, 159 F.Supp.2d 1118, 1125 n.1 (N.D.Ill. 2001).

303. *See Von Grabe v. Sprint PCS*, 312 F.Supp.2d 1285, 1294 (S.D.Cal. 2003); *Microsoft Corp. v. Jesse's Computers & Repair, Inc.*, 211 F.R.D. 681, 683 (M.D.Fla.2002); *Rosales v. Citibank, Federal Sav. Bank*, 133 F.Supp.2d 1177, 1180 (N.D.Cal.2001); *Lazar v. Trans Union LLC*, 195 F.R.D. 665, 668 (C.D.Cal.2000); *Wailua Assocs. v. Aetna Cas. & Sur. Co.*, 183 F.R.D. 550, 553–54 (D.Haw.1998).

the non-moving party's conclusions of law.[304] If disputed questions of fact or law remain as to the challenged material or defense, the motion to strike must be denied.[305]

Burden of Proof

The burden lies with the party moving to strike.[306] The moving party must generally make at least two showings: first, the challenged allegations must be clearly unrelated to the pleader's claims,[307] *and*, second, the moving party must be prejudiced by permitting those allegations to remain in the pleading.[308] Prejudice exists when the contested allegation would confuse the issues or, by its length and complexity, would place an undue burden on the respondent, would confuse the issues, inject the possibility of unnecessarily extensive and burdensome discovery, improperly increase the time, expense, and complexity of the trial, or otherwise unduly burden the moving party.[309] The moving party must state the basis for the motion with particularity and identify specifically the relief sought.[310]

304. *See United States v. Rohm & Haas Co.*, 939 F.Supp. 1142, 1151 (D.N.J.1996).

305. *See Canadian St. Regis Band of Mohawk Indians v. New York*, 278 F.Supp.2d 313, 325 (N.D.N.Y.2003); *Graff v. Prime Retail, Inc.*, 172 F.Supp.2d 721, 731 (D.Md.2001); *Morell v. United States*, 185 F.R.D. 116, 117–18 (D.P.R. 1999); *Environ Prods., Inc. v. Total Containment, Inc.*, 951 F.Supp. 57, 59 (E.D.Pa.1996). *See also Bristol–Myers Squibb Co. v. IVAX Corp.*, 77 F.Supp.2d 606, 619 (D.N.J.2000) (commenting that motion should not be used as vehicle to determine disputed and substantial questions of law or fact).

306. *See Canadian St. Regis Band of Mohawk Indians v. New York*, 278 F.Supp.2d 313, 325 (N.D.N.Y.2003); *All America Ins. Co. v. Broeren Russo Const., Inc.*, 112 F.Supp.2d 723, 729 (C.D.Ill.2000); *Vakharia v. Little Co. of Mary Hosp. & Health Care Ctrs.*, 2 F.Supp.2d 1028 (N.D.Ill.1998).

307. *See McInerney v. Moyer Lumber & Hardware, Inc.*, 244 F.Supp.2d 393, 402 (E.D.Pa. 2002); *Hughes v. Amerada Hess Corp.*, 187 F.R.D. 682 (M.D.Fla.1999); *Porter v. International Bus. Machs. Corp.*, 21 F.Supp.2d 829, 831 (N.D.Ill.1998); *Larsen v. Senate of Pa.*, 955 F.Supp. 1549, 1582 (M.D.Pa.1997), *aff'd in part and rev'd in part on other grounds*, 154 F.3d 82 (3d Cir.1998), *cert. denied*, 525 U.S. 1144, 119 S.Ct. 1037, 143 L.Ed.2d 45 (1999); *Sierra Club v. Tri–State Generation & Transmission Ass'n*, 173 F.R.D. 275 (D.Colo.1997); *Government Guarantee Fund v. Hyatt Corp.*, 166 F.R.D. 321, 324 (D.Vi.1996), *aff'd*, 95 F.3d 291 (3d Cir.1996); *Velez v. Lisi*, 164 F.R.D. 165, 166–67 (S.D.N.Y. 1995).

308. *See Canadian St. Regis Band of Mohawk Indians v. New York*, 278 F.Supp.2d 313, 325 (N.D.N.Y.2003); *McInerney v. Moyer Lumber & Hardware, Inc.*, 244 F.Supp.2d 393, 402 (E.D.Pa.2002); *Connell v. City of New York*, 230 F.Supp.2d 432, 438 (S.D.N.Y.2002); *Bristol-Myers Squibb Co. v. IVAX Corp.*, 77 F.Supp.2d 606, 619 (D.N.J.2000); *Hughes v. Amerada Hess Corp.*, 187 F.R.D. 682 (M.D.Fla.1999); *Morell v. United States*, 185 F.R.D. 116, 117–18 (D.P.R. 1999); *Wailua Assocs. v. Aetna Cas. & Sur. Co.*, 183 F.R.D. 550, 553–54 (D.Haw.1998); *Ross-Simons of Warwick, Inc. v. Baccarat, Inc.*, 182 F.R.D. 386, 398 (D.R.I.1998); *Porter v. International Bus. Machs. Corp.*, 21 F.Supp.2d 829, 831 (N.D.Ill.1998); *Wine Markets Int'l, Inc. v. Bass*, 177 F.R.D. 128, 133 (E.D.N.Y.1998); *Government Guarantee Fund v. Hyatt Corp.*, 166 F.R.D. 321, 324 (D.V.I.1996), *aff'd*, 95 F.3d 291 (3d Cir. 1996); *FDIC v. Wise*, 758 F.Supp. 1414 (D.Colo. 1991). *But see Atlantic Richfield Co. v. Ramirez*, 176 F.3d 481 (9th Cir.1999) (Table) (Unpublished Opinion, text available in WestLaw No. 98–56372) (in non-precedential decision, Ninth Circuit Court of Appeals ruled that "prejudice" requirement does not appear in the text of Rule 12(f) and, therefore, should not be required of a movant).

309. *See Canadian St. Regis Band of Mohawk Indians v. New York*, 278 F.Supp.2d 313, 325 (N.D.N.Y.2003); *Hart v. Baca*, 204 F.R.D. 456, 457 (C.D.Cal.2001); *Anderson v. Board of Ed. of Chicago*, 169 F.Supp.2d 864, 867–68 (N.D.Ill.2001); *Estee Lauder, Inc. v. Fragrance Counter, Inc.*, 189 F.R.D. 269, 272 (S.D.N.Y. 1999).

310. *See Credit General Ins. Co. v. Midwest Indemnity Corp.*, 916 F.Supp. 766, 771 (N.D.Ill. 1996).

Test For Striking Defenses

A motion to strike is the pleader's parallel to a Rule 12(b)(6) motion to dismiss. The pleader can seek to use this Rule to strike an opponent's defense as legally insufficient.[311] The court may strike any defense that is legally insufficient under the controlling substantive law,[312] or that contains matters that would confuse the issues in the case.[313] An insufficient defense is one that is so impertinent and immaterial that no evidence in support of the allegation would be admissible.[314] The objective of such strikes is to eliminate irrelevant and frivolous defenses, the trial of which would otherwise unnecessarily waste time and money.[315] Thus, to strike a defense, the moving party must show (a) there is no question of fact or law which might allow the challenged defense to succeed, (b) it appears to a certainty that the defense will fail regardless of what evidence is marshalled to support it, and (c) prejudice if the defense remains in the case.[316] In conducting this analysis, the court will construe the pleadings liberally in the favor of the defendant (the non-moving party).[317] If an affirmative defense is stricken by the court, the pleader will generally be granted leave to file an amended answer unless the amendment would be futile.[318]

- *Strikes Involving Inference–Drawing*: Defenses will not be stricken on a motion to strike if the court would be required to draw factual inferences or decided disputed questions of fact.[319]

311. *See United States v. Winnebago Tribe of Nebraska*, 542 F.2d 1002, 1007 (8th Cir.1976); *Environ Prods., Inc. v. Total Containment, Inc.*, 951 F.Supp. 57, 59 (E.D.Pa.1996).

312. *See Owens v. UNUM Life Ins. Co.*, 285 F.Supp.2d 778, 780 (E.D.Tex. 2003) (whether defense is invalid, as a matter of law, depends on nature of claim and asserted defense).

313. *See Waste Management Holdings, Inc. v. Gilmore*, 252 F.3d 316, 347 (4th Cir.2001), *cert. denied*, 535 U.S. 904, 122 S.Ct. 1203, 152 L.Ed.2d 142 (2002); *Kaiser Aluminum & Chem. Sales, Inc. v. Avondale Shipyards, Inc.*, 677 F.2d 1045 (5th Cir.1982), *cert. denied*, 459 U.S. 1105, 103 S.Ct. 729, 74 L.Ed.2d 953 (1983); *Oneida Indian Nation of New York v. New York*, 194 F.Supp.2d 104, 117 (N.D.N.Y.2002); *Hart v. Baca*, 204 F.R.D. 456, 457 (C.D.Cal.2001); *Sayad v. Dura Pharms., Inc.*, 200 F.R.D. 419, 421 (N.D.Ill.2001).

314. *See Openshaw v. Cohen, Klingenstein & Marks, Inc.*, 320 F.Supp.2d 357, 364 (D.Md. 2004); *Microsoft Corp. v. Jesse's Computers & Repair, Inc.*, 211 F.R.D. 681, 683 (M.D.Fla.2002); *Etienne v. Wal–Mart Stores, Inc.*, 197 F.R.D. 217, 219–20 (D.Conn.2000); *United States v. Green*, 33 F.Supp.2d 203, 212 (W.D.N.Y.1998); *Hayes v. City of Des Plaines*, 182 F.R.D. 546, 549 (N.D.Ill. 1998); *Honeywell Consumer Prods., Inc. v. Windmere Corp.*, 993 F.Supp. 22, 24 (D.Mass.1998).

315. *See E.E.O.C. v. Bay Ridge Toyota, Inc.*, 327 F.Supp.2d 167 (E.D.N.Y. 2004); *Association of American Med. Colleges v. Princeton Rev., Inc.*, 332 F.Supp.2d 11, 21–22 (D.D.C. 2004); *In re Complaint of J.A.R. Barge Lines, L.P.*, 307 F.Supp.2d 668, 670 (W.D.Pa. 2004);

316. *See E.E.O.C. v. Bay Ridge Toyota, Inc.*, 327 F.Supp.2d 167 (E.D.N.Y. 2004); *Tompkins v. R.J. Reynolds Tobacco Co.*, 92 F.Supp.2d 70, 80 (N.D.N.Y.2000); *Resolution Trust Corp. v. Massachusetts Mut. Life Ins. Co.*, 93 F.Supp.2d 300, 303 (W.D.N.Y.2000); *Chicago Sch. Reform Bd. of Trustees v. Substance, Inc.*, 79 F.Supp.2d 919, 930 (N.D.Ill.2000); *Federal Deposit Ins. Corp. v. Ornstein*, 73 F.Supp.2d 277, 279 (E.D.N.Y.1999); *Estee Lauder, Inc. v. Fragrance Counter, Inc.*, 189 F.R.D. 269, 271–72 (S.D.N.Y.1999); *Johnson v. Chrysler Corp.*, 187 F.R.D. 440 (D.Me.1999); *MAN Roland Inc. v. Quantum Color Corp.*, 57 F.Supp.2d 576 (N.D.Ill.1999); *SEC v. McCaskey*, 56 F.Supp.2d 323 (S.D.N.Y.1999); *Morell v. United States*, 185 F.R.D. 116, 117–18 (D.P.R.1999); *FDIC v. Pelletreau & Pelletreau*, 965 F.Supp. 381 (E.D.N.Y.1997).

317. *See Tompkins v. R.J. Reynolds Tobacco Co.*, 92 F.Supp.2d 70, 80 (N.D.N.Y.2000); *Estee Lauder, Inc. v. Fragrance Counter, Inc.*, 189 F.R.D. 269, 271 (S.D.N.Y.1999).

318. *See United States v. Green*, 33 F.Supp.2d 203, 212 (W.D.N.Y.1998); *See United States v. 416.81 Acres of Land*, 514 F.2d 627 (7th Cir.1975).

319. *See Augustus v. Board of Public Instruction*, 306 F.2d 862 (5th Cir.1962); *Ammira-*

- *Strikes Involving Substantial and Disputed Questions:* Motions to strike are generally not intended to resolve substantial and disputed questions of law–legal issues on which courts are divided, confused or unsettled legal areas, or issues involving close or new questions of law.[320]
- *Strikes Before Discovery:* Although motions to strike must generally be filed before a responsive pleading is served, some courts have noted their reluctance to strike defenses where there has been "no significant discovery".[321]

Test For Striking Redundant, Immaterial, Impertinent, or Scandalous Matter

A motion to strike redundant, immaterial, impertinent, or scandalous matter is also viewed with disfavor as a time-waster.[322] The court will not strike such matter unless it bears no possible relation to the parties' dispute, or could confuse the issues.[323] Moreover, mere redundancy, immateriality, impertinence, or scandalousness is not sufficient to justify striking an allegation—the allegation must also be shown to be prejudicial to the moving party.[324] Thus, absent a "strong reason for so doing", courts will generally "not tamper with pleadings".[325] The

ti v. Bonati, 1994 WL 34175 at *1 (M.D.Fla. 1994).

320. *See Canadian St. Regis Band of Mohawk Indians v. New York*, 278 F.Supp.2d 313, 324 (N.D.N.Y.2003) (noting that, otherwise, courts would risk "offering an advisory opinion on an abstract and hypothetical set of facts"); *Solvent Chem. Co. ICC Indus., Inc. v. E.I. Dupont De Nemours & Co.*, 242 F.Supp.2d 196, 212 (W.D.N.Y.2002) (noting that defense must not present disputed and substantial questions of law).

321. *See Canadian St. Regis Band of Mohawk Indians v. New York*, 278 F.Supp.2d 313, 324–25 (N.D.N.Y.2003).

322. *See Germaine Music v. Universal Songs of Polygram*, 275 F.Supp.2d 1288, 1299–1300 (D.Nev.2003); *Rosales v. Citibank, Federal Sav. Bank*, 133 F.Supp.2d 1177, 1180 (N.D.Cal.2001); *WTM, Inc. v. Henneck*, 125 F.Supp.2d 864, 869 (N.D.Ill.2000); *Lazar v. Trans Union LLC*, 195 F.R.D. 665, 668 (C.D.Cal.2000); *Somerset Pharms., Inc. v. Kimball*, 168 F.R.D. 69, 71 (M.D.Fla.1996); *Citizens & Southern Sec. Corp. v. Braten*, 733 F.Supp. 655 (S.D.N.Y.1990).

323. *See Salahuddin v. Cuomo*, 861 F.2d 40, 42 (2d Cir.1988)(commenting that dismissals under Rule 12(f) are reserved for instances where the pleading "is so confused, ambiguous, vague, or otherwise unintelligible that its true substance, if any, is well disguised"); *Lipsky v. Commonwealth United Corp.*, 551 F.2d 887 (2d Cir.1976); *Anderson v. Board of Ed. of Chicago*, 169 F.Supp.2d 864, 867–68 (N.D.Ill.2001); *Kies v. City of Aurora*, 149 F.Supp.2d 421, 427 (N.D.Ill.2001); *Rosales v. Citibank, Federal Sav. Bank*, 133 F.Supp.2d 1177, 1180 (N.D.Cal.2001); *Bristol-Myers Squibb Co. v. IVAX Corp.*, 77 F.Supp.2d 606, 619 (D.N.J.2000); *In re Sunbeam Secs. Litig.*, 89 F.Supp.2d 1326, 1340 (S.D.Fla. 1999); *Seidel v. Lee*, 954 F.Supp. 810, 812 (D.Del.1996); *Somerset Pharms., Inc. v. Kimball*, 168 F.R.D. 69, 71 (M.D.Fla.1996); *Hartsell v. Duplex Prods., Inc.*, 895 F.Supp. 100 (W.D.N.C. 1995); *North Penn Transfer, Inc. v. Victaulic Co. of America*, 859 F.Supp. 154, 158–59 (E.D.Pa. 1994). *Cf. Delaware Health Care, Inc. v. MCD Holding Co.*, 893 F.Supp. 1279, 1291–92 (D.Del. 1995)(allegations that might create better understanding of plaintiff's claims or perform some other useful purpose in the dispute's just disposition will not be stricken).

324. *See Anderson v. Board of Ed. of Chicago*, 169 F.Supp.2d 864, 867–68 (N.D.Ill.2001); *Hardin v. American Elec. Power*, 188 F.R.D. 509, 511 (S.D.Ind.1999).

325. *See Lazar v. Trans Union LLC*, 195 F.R.D. 665, 668 (C.D.Cal.2000); *Lennon v. Seaman*, 63 F.Supp.2d 428, 447 (S.D.N.Y.1999).

court will also be disinclined to strike matter where the case will be tried without a jury.

If granted, the court's order will typically describe in detail the precise matter that must be stricken.[326]

- *Redundant Matter:* A redundant allegation is a needless repetition of other averments.[327]
- *Immaterial Matter:* Immaterial allegations are those that either bear no essential or important relationship to the pleader's claim for relief or contain a statement of unnecessary particulars.[328] Allegations are immaterial if no evidence to support them would be admissible at trial.[329]
- *Impertinent Matter:* An impertinent allegation is an averment that does not pertain to, or is unnecessary to, the issues in dispute. If the pleader would not be permitted to offer evidence at trial in support of the allegation, the allegation is likely impertinent.[330]
- *Scandalous Matter:* Scandalous matter does not merely offend someone's sensibilities; it must improperly cast a person or

326. *See Salahuddin v. Cuomo*, 861 F.2d 40, 43 (2d Cir.1988)(noting that court would strike only so much of pleading as is redundant or immaterial).

327. *See Germaine Music v. Universal Songs of Polygram*, 275 F.Supp.2d 1288, 1299 (D.Nev. 2003); *Dethmers Mfg. Co. v. Automatic Equip. Mfg. Co.*, 23 F.Supp.2d 974, 1008–09 (N.D.Iowa 1998) (mere duplicative remedies do not necessarily make claims "redundant" if those claims require proof of different elements, but claim that simply recasts same elements under the guise of different theory may be stricken as redundant), *appeal denied*, 185 F.3d 879 (Fed. Cir.1998) (Table); *Ross-Simons of Warwick, Inc. v. Baccarat, Inc.*, 182 F.R.D. 386, 398 (D.R.I. 1998); *Owens v. Blue Tee Corp.*, 177 F.R.D. 673, 678 (M.D.Ala.1998); *Environ Prods., Inc. v. Total Containment, Inc.*, 951 F.Supp. 57, 59 (E.D.Pa. 1996); *Resolution Trust Corp. v. Fiala*, 870 F.Supp. 962, 977 (E.D.Mo.1994); *Stewart v. Thomas*, 538 F.Supp. 891 (D.D.C.1982). *See also Sorosky v. Burroughs Corp.*, 826 F.2d 794, 802 (9th Cir.1987) (where no arguments were presented in support of theory, it was vulnerable to dismissal as redundant).

328. *See Fantasy, Inc. v. Fogerty*, 984 F.2d 1524, 1527 (9th Cir.1993), *rev'd on other grounds*, 510 U.S. 517, 114 S.Ct. 1023, 127 L.Ed.2d 455 (1994); *Germaine Music v. Universal Songs of Polygram*, 275 F.Supp.2d 1288, 1300 (D.Nev.2003); *Reyn's Pasta Bella, LLC v. Visa U.S.A.*, 259 F.Supp.2d 992, 1001–02 (N.D.Cal.2003); *In re 2TheMart.com, Inc. Secs. Litig.*, 114 F.Supp.2d 955, 965 (C.D.Cal.2000); *Wrench LLC v. Taco Bell Corp.*, 36 F.Supp.2d 787, 789 (W.D.Mich.1998); *Velez v. Lisi*, 164 F.R.D. 165, 166–67 (S.D.N.Y.1995); *Delaware Health Care, Inc. v. MCD Holding Co.*, 893 F.Supp. 1279 (D.Del.1995); *Resolution Trust Corp. v. Fiala*, 870 F.Supp. 962, 977 (E.D.Mo. 1994); *In re Crazy Eddie Sec. Litig.*, 747 F.Supp. 850 (E.D.N.Y.1990). *See Bureerong v. Uvawas*, 922 F.Supp. 1450, 1478 (C.D.Cal.1996)(striking Complaint's reference to "Slave Sweatshop"); *Helwig v. Kelsey-Hayes Co.*, 907 F.Supp. 253, 256 (E.D.Mich.1995)(commenting that immaterial matters include requests for relief that are unavailable under controlling law).

329. *See Lennon v. Seaman*, 63 F.Supp.2d 428, 446–47 (S.D.N.Y.1999).

330. *See Fantasy, Inc. v. Fogerty*, 984 F.2d 1524, 1527 (9th Cir.1993), *rev'd on other grounds*, 510 U.S. 517, 114 S.Ct. 1023, 127 L.Ed.2d 455 (1994); *Germaine Music v. Universal Songs of Polygram*, 275 F.Supp.2d 1288, 1300 (D.Nev.2003); *Reyn's Pasta Bella, LLC v. Visa U.S.A.*, 259 F.Supp.2d 992, 1001–02 (N.D.Cal.2003); *In re 2TheMart.com, Inc. Secs. Litig.*, 114 F.Supp.2d 955, 965 (C.D.Cal.2000); *Lennon v. Seaman*, 63 F.Supp.2d 428, 446–47 (S.D.N.Y.1999). *Wailua Assocs. v. Aetna Cas. & Sur. Co.*, 183 F.R.D. 550, 553–54 (D.Haw.1998); *Ali v. New York City Transit Auth.*, 176 F.R.D. 68, 70 (E.D.N.Y.1997); *Delaware Health Care, Inc. v. MCD Holding Co.*, 893 F.Supp. 1279 (D.Del.1995); *Resolution Trust Corp. v. Fiala*, 870 F.Supp. 962, 977 (E.D.Mo.1994).

entity in a derogatory light.[331] Moreover, such matter will not be stricken if it describes acts or events relevant to the parties' dispute, unless the descriptions contain unnecessary detail.[332]

Striking Prayers For Relief

The court may also use Rule 12(f) to strike prayers for relief where the damages or other relief sought are not recoverable as a matter of law.[333]

Striking Documents Other Than Pleadings

As defined in Rule 12(f), motions to strike are directed to "pleadings" only. Consequently, these motions are technically not available to strike material contained in motions, briefs, memoranda, or affidavits.[334] However, such motions may be treated by the court as an invitation to adjudicate the admissibility of certain material.[335]

331. *See Alvarado–Morales v. Digital Equip. Corp.*, 843 F.2d 613 (1st Cir.1988)(striking as "scandalous" references to "concentration camp", "brainwash", and "torture" which impugned the characters of the defendant); *Global View Ltd. Venture Capital v. Great Central Basin Exploration, L.L.C.*, 288 F.Supp.2d 473, 481 (S.D.N.Y. 2003) (striking reference to defendants as "unscrupulous, unprincipled con artists" since it "amounts to nothing more than name calling, and does not contribute to [the] ... substantive claims"); *Sierra Club v. Tri–State Generation & Transmission Ass'n*, 173 F.R.D. 275 (D.Colo.1997) (irrelevant allegations will be stricken as scandalous if they degrade the defendants' moral character, contain repulsive language, or detract from the court's dignity); *See also Germaine Music v. Universal Songs of Polygram*, 275 F.Supp.2d 1288, 1300 (D.Nev.2003); *Pigford v. Veneman*, 215 F.R.D. 2, 4 (D.D.C. 2003); *In re 2TheMart.com, Inc. Secs. Litig.*, 114 F.Supp.2d 955, 965 (C.D.Cal.2000); *Nault's Auto. Sales, Inc. v. American Honda Motor Co.*, 148 F.R.D. 25, 30 (D.N.H.1993).

332. *See Talbot v. Robert Matthews Distrib. Co.*, 961 F.2d 654, 664–65 (7th Cir.1992)(matter is "scandalous" only if it bears no possible relation to the controversy before the court); *Sierra Club v. Tri–State Generation & Transmission Ass'n*, 173 F.R.D. 275 (D.Colo.1997) (relevant allegations will be stricken as scandalous only if they meet the "scandalous" test and contain unnecessary detail); *Delaware Health Care, Inc. v. MCD Holding Co.*, 893 F.Supp. 1279 (D.Del. 1995)(defining "scandalous" allegations as matter bearing no possible relation to the dispute and which may cause prejudice to the movant).

333. *See Sony Pictures Entertainment, Inc. v. Fireworks Entertainment Group, Inc.*, 156 F.Supp.2d 1148 (C.D.Cal.2001); *Lazar v. Trans Union LLC*, 195 F.R.D. 665, 668 (C.D. Cal.2000).

334. *See Pilgrim v. Trustees of Tufts College*, 118 F.3d 864 (1st Cir.1997) (rules does not apply to motion papers or supporting affidavits); *United States v. Southern Cal. Edison Co.*, 300 F.Supp.2d 964, 973 (E.D.Cal. 2004) (applies only to pleadings); *Milk Drivers, Dairy & Ice Cream Employees, Laundry & Dry Cleaning Drivers, Clerical & Allied Workers v. Roberts Dairy*, 219 F.R.D. 151, 152–53 (S.D.Iowa 2003) (motion to strike motion for summary judgment is inappropriate); *Bovee v. Coopers & Lybrand, L.L.P.*, 216 F.R.D. 596 (S.D.Ohio 2003) (affidavits not subject to motion to strike); *VanDanacker v. Main Motor Sales Co.*, 109 F.Supp.2d 1045, 1047 (D.Minn.2000) (plaintiffs' opposition memorandum not subject to motion to strike); *Lowery v. Hoffman*, 188 F.R.D. 651, 653 (M.D.Ala.1999) (only pleadings can be stricken); *York v. Ferris State Univ.*, 36 F.Supp.2d 976, 980 (W.D.Mich. 1998) (affidavits are not pleadings and cannot be stricken under Rule 12(f); *Transamerica Leasing, Inc. v. La Republica de Venezuela*, 21 F.Supp.2d 47, 55–56 (D.D.C.1998) (declarations and exhibits to Rule 12(b) motion cannot be struck under Rule 12(f); *Phinney v. Paulshock*, 181 F.R.D. 185 (D.N.H.1998) (cannot "strike" a motion for sanctions), *aff'd*, 199 F.3d 1 (1st Cir.1999); *E.E.O.C. v. Admiral Maintenance Serv., L.P.*, 174 F.R.D. 643, 645–46 (N.D.Ill. 1997) (motion to strike cannot be used to strike a motion for summary judgment or supporting affidavit); *Morroni v. Gunderson*, 169 F.R.D. 168, 170 (M.D.Fla.1996) (motion to strike a motion is improper); *Cobb v. Monarch Fin. Corp.*, 913 F.Supp. 1164, 1181 (N.D.Ill.1995) (no authority for "striking" summary judgment motion); *International Longshoremen's Ass'n, S.S. Clerks Local 1624, AFL–CIO v. Virginia Int'l Terminals, Inc.*, 904 F.Supp. 500, 504 (E.D.Va. 1995) (motion not proper way to challenge reply brief and accompanying affidavits); *Manchester* Mfg. Acquisitions, Inc. v. Sears, Roebuck & Co., *909 F.Supp. 47, 55 (D.N.H.1995) (generally, motions are not subject to being stricken).*

335. *See United States v. Southern Cal. Edison Co.*, 300 F.Supp.2d 964, 973 (E.D.Cal. 2004).

Discretion of Trial Court

The decision to grant or deny a motion to strike is vested in the trial judge's sound discretion.[336]

Timing

A motion to strike must be made before a responsive pleading is served or, if no responsive pleading is required, within 20 days after service of the preceding pleading.[337] In view of the court's authority to strike on its own initiative, (*see* "*Sua Sponte* Strikes" below), this 20–day period is often not applied strictly when the proposal to strike has merit.[338]

Sua Sponte Strikes

At any time, the court may, on its own initiative, strike matter from a pleading.[339] Thus, the court may properly consider a party's untimely motion or "suggestion" under Rule 12(f) to strike matter from the pleading.[340]

336. *See Talbot v. Robert Matthews Distrib. Co.*, 961 F.2d 654, 665 (7th Cir.1992); *Association of American Med. Colleges v. Princeton Rev., Inc.*, 332 F.Supp.2d 11, 21–22 at *8 (D.D.C. 2004); *Pigford v. Veneman*, 215 F.R.D. 2, 4 (D.D.C.2003); *Morell v. United States*, 185 F.R.D. 116, 117–18 (D.P.R.1999; *Ross-Simons of Warwick, Inc. v. Baccarat, Inc.*, 182 F.R.D. 386, 398 (D.R.I.1998); *Vanderhurst v. Colorado Mountain College Dist.*, 16 F.Supp.2d 1297, 1303 (D.Colo. 1998); *Larsen v. Senate of Pa.*, 955 F.Supp. 1549, 1582 (M.D.Pa.1997), *aff'd in part and rev'd in part on other grounds*, 154 F.3d 82 (3d Cir.1998), *cert. denied*, 525 U.S. 1144, 119 S.Ct. 1037, 143 L.Ed.2d 45 (1999); *Johnson v. Metropolitan Sewer Dist.*, 926 F.Supp. 874, 875 (E.D.Mo.1996); *Credit General Ins. Co. v. Midwest Indemnity Corp.*, 916 F.Supp. 766, 771 (N.D.Ill.1996); *North Penn Transfer, Inc. v. Victaulic Co. of America*, 859 F.Supp. 154, 158–59 (E.D.Pa. 1994).

337. *See United States v. $38,000.00 Dollars in U.S. Currency*, 816 F.2d 1538, 1547 n. 20 (11th Cir.1987); *Culinary & Serv. Employees Union v. Hawaii Employee Benefit Admin., Inc.*, 688 F.2d 1228 (9th Cir.1982). *See also Circuit Sys., Inc. v. Mescalero Sales, Inc.*, 925 F.Supp. 546, 548 (N.D.Ill.1996)(motion made beyond 20–day period is untimely and subject to denial).

338. *See In re Complaint of Rationis Enters. of Panama*, 210 F.Supp.2d 421, 424–25 (S.D.N.Y. 2002) (noting that while rule requires motion to strikes to be filed within 20 days after service, court's power to strike on its own initiative permits consideration of untimely motions to strike); *Wine Markets Int'l, Inc. v. Bass*, 177 F.R.D. 128, 133 (E.D.N.Y.1998) (holding that court's discretion "renders the twenty (20) day rule 'essentially unimportant' ").

339. *See Calcutti v. SBU, Inc.*, 224 F.Supp.2d 691, 701 (S.D.N.Y.2002); *Wine Markets Int'l, Inc. v. Bass*, 177 F.R.D. 128, 133 (E.D.N.Y.1998); *Owens v. Blue Tee Corp.*, 177 F.R.D. 673, 678 (M.D.Ala.1998); *FDIC v. Collins*, 920 F.Supp. 30, 33 (D.Conn.1996); *In re Clearly Canadian Sec. Litig.*, 875 F.Supp. 1410, 1416 n. 5 (N.D.Cal. 1995); *FDIC v. Modular Homes, Inc.*, 859 F.Supp. 117, 120 (D.N.J.1994).

340. *See United States v. Lot 65 Pine Meadow*, 976 F.2d 1155, 1157 (8th Cir.1992); *In re Complaint of Rationis Enters. of Pananma*, 210 F.Supp.2d 421, 424–25 (S.D.N.Y.2002); *Chicago Sch. Reform Bd. of Trustees v. Substance, Inc.*, 79 F.Supp.2d 919, 929 (N.D.Ill.2000); *Federal Deposit Ins. Corp. v. Ornstein*, 73 F.Supp.2d 277, 280 n. 2 (E.D.N.Y.1999); *Estee Lauder, Inc. v. Fragrance Counter, Inc.*, 189 F.R.D. 269, 271 (S.D.N.Y.1999); *Food Lion, Inc. v. Capital Cities/ABC, Inc.*, 951 F.Supp. 1233, 1234 (M.D.N.C. 1996).

Extrinsic Materials

Generally, the court will not consider extrinsic materials on a motion to strike.[341] Instead, the grounds supporting the motion to strike must be readily apparent from the face of the pleadings themselves or from materials that may be judicially noticed.[342]

Prejudice on Dismissal

Where an allegation or defense is stricken as technically deficient, the dismissal is generally without prejudice to refile with a technically correct pleading.[343]

RULE 12(g). CONSOLIDATION OF DEFENSES

CORE CONCEPT

If a party chooses to make a motion under Rule 12, the party must include all Rule 12 defenses and objections then available in a single, omnibus motion. Rule 12(g) must be read in conjunction with Rule 12(h), concerning waiver and preservation of certain defenses.

APPLICATIONS

Objective—Avoiding Piecemeal Motions

The goal behind Rule 12(g) is to eliminate piecemeal motion practice. A party is not *required* to serve a Rule 12 motion. However, if the party chooses to do so, all Rule 12 defenses and objections must be brought to the court's attention at one time.[344] As to whatever defenses or objections are not asserted in the motion, the waiver principles of Rule 12(h) apply.

Successive Rule 12 Motions to Dismiss Generally Prohibited

The text of Rule 12(g) expressly excludes the defense of failure to

341. *See Diamond Scientific Co. v. Ambico, Inc.*, 848 F.2d 1220, 1226 (Fed.Cir.1988) (noting that although extrinsic materials are generally not considered on a motion to strike, they may be accepted by the court where they present uncontested factual matters), *cert. dismissed*, 487 U.S. 1265, 109 S.Ct. 28, 101 L.Ed.2d 978 (1988); *Oneida Indian Nation of New York v. New York*, 194 F.Supp.2d 104, 117 (N.D.N.Y. 2002); *Seibel v. Society Lease, Inc.* 969 F.Supp. 713 (M.D.Fla.1997); *United States v. Rohm & Haas Co.*, 939 F.Supp. 1142, 1151 (D.N.J.1996); *Environ Prods., Inc. v. Total Containment, Inc.*, 951 F.Supp. 57, 59 (E.D.Pa.1996); *Johnson v. Metropolitan Sewer Dist.*, 926 F.Supp. 874, 875 (E.D.Mo.1996); *Francosteel Corp. v. M.V. Pal Marinos*, 885 F.Supp. 86, 89 n. 2 (S.D.N.Y.1995); *D.S. America (East), Inc. v. Chromagrafx Imaging Sys., Inc.*, 873 F.Supp. 786, 797 (E.D.N.Y. 1995). *But see Fantasy, Inc. v. Fogerty*, 984 F.2d 1524, 1528–29 (9th Cir.1993)(in ruling on Rule 12(f) motion to strike, district court did not act improperly in considering materials of which it could take judicial notice, nor was submission of affidavits improper where court did not consider them), *rev'd on other grounds*, 510 U.S. 517, 114 S.Ct. 1023, 127 L.Ed.2d 455 (1994).

342. *See Wailua Assocs. v. Aetna Cas. & Sur. Co.*, 183 F.R.D. 550, 553–54 (D.Haw.1998).

343. *See D.S. America (East), Inc. v. Chromagrafx Imaging Sys., Inc.*, 873 F.Supp. 786, 798 (E.D.N.Y.1995).

344. *See McCurdy v. American Bd. of Plastic Surgery*, 157 F.3d 191, 194 (3d Cir.1998). *See also Skrtich v. Thornton*, 280 F.3d 1295, 1306 (11th Cir.2002) (affirming dismissal of untimely asserted qualified immunity defense because Rule 12(g) prohibits party from filing a second pre-answer motion to dismiss raising omitted defense that could have been presented in earlier motion).

state a claim from this piecemeal-motion bar.[345] Nevertheless, the courts have held that a defendant is generally precluded from filing successive motions to dismiss to raise arguments that the defendant could have raised, but did not, in the first motion.[346] This prohibition ordinarily applies even after an amended complaint is filed; if the basis for the motion to dismiss was available to the defendant at the time of the original complaint, the filing of an amended complaint will not trigger a new opportunity to assert the motion.[347] Although Rules 12(g) and 12(h)(2) specifically preserve a party's right to file a pre-answer motion to dismiss for failure to state a claim *and*, later, assert a failure to state a claim by motion for judgment on the pleadings or at trial, this right might not be unrestricted. There is some authority for supposing that a defendant may not be permitted to file a Rule 12(b) motion to dismiss for failure to state a claim, lose on the motion, and then file a Rule 12(c) motion for judgment on the pleadings that makes the very same arguments the court had just rejected.[348]

Exception–Prohibition Applies Only to Defenses "Then Available"

A party is required to assert in an omnibus motion only those defenses and objections "then available" to that party. Thus, if new defenses or objections are prompted by an amended pleading or a more definite statement, the responding party may generally file a new Rule 12 motion to assert defenses and objections to such newly introduced matter.[349] Similarly, parties may generally file a new Rule 12 motion if, while their case has been pending, a change in the law offers them a new legal defense or objection.[350] But parties must act promptly. An unnecessarily lengthy delay in asserting a latent Rule 12 objection may, itself, be deemed a waiver.[351]

345. *See* 12(g) (no subsequent Rule 12 motions permitted "except a motion as provided in subsection (h)(2) hereof on any of the grounds there stated"); Rule 12(h)(2) (permitting defense of failure to state a claim to "be made in any pleading permitted or ordered under Rule 7(a), or by motion for judgment on the pleadings, or at the trial on the merits").

346. *See 766347 Ontario Ltd. v. Zurich Capital Mkts., Inc.*, 274 F.Supp.2d 926, 930 (N.D.Ill. 2003); *Wafra Leasing Corp. 1999–A–1 v. Prime Capital Corp.*, 247 F.Supp.2d 987, 999 (N.D.Ill. 2002).

347. *See Albany Ins. Co. v. Almacenadora Somex*, 5 F.3d 907, 909 (5th Cir.1993); *766347 Ontario Ltd. v. Zurich Capital Mkts., Inc.*, 274 F.Supp.2d 926, 930 (N.D.Ill.2003); *Wafra Leasing Corp. 1999–A–1 v. Prime Capital Corp.*, 247 F.Supp.2d 987, 999 (N.D.Ill.2002).

348. *See Sprint Telephony PCS, L.P. v. County of San Diego*, 311 F.Supp.2d 898, 904–05 (S.D.Cal. 2004), *clarified on other grounds*, 2004 WL 859333 (S.D.Cal. Jan. 23, 2004) (although permitting Rule 12(c) motion asserting same arguments raised in earlier Rule 12(b)(6) motion, court noted the "tension" between Rule 12(g)'s consolidation policy and this sort of practice).

349. *See McCurdy v. American Bd. of Plastic Surgery*, 157 F.3d 191, 196 n. 1 (3d Cir.1998); *Goodstein v. Bombardier Capital, Inc.*, 167 F.R.D. 662, 665 (D.Vt.1996); *Chatman–Bey v. Thornburgh*, 864 F.2d 804 (D.C.Cir.1988); *Glater v. Eli Lilly & Co.*, 712 F.2d 735, 738–39 (1st Cir.1983).

350. *See Holzsager v. Valley Hosp.*, 646 F.2d 792, 796 (2d Cir.1981) (courts will not demand clairvoyance from litigants; parties not deemed to have waived defenses or objections not then known to them); *Engel v. CBS, Inc.*, 886 F.Supp. 728, 728–730 (C.D.Cal.1995)(holding that Rule 12(g) will not fault defendants for failing to press a defense they did not then know was available to them).

351. *See Overseas Partners, Inc. v. PROGEN Musavirlik ve Yonetim Hizmetleri, Ltd. Sikerti*, 15 F.Supp.2d 47 (D.D.C.1998) (holding that, although service objections were not "available" at the time a first motion to dismiss was filed, litigants delayed in raising the new defense and

Exception–No Unnecessary Delay

The prohibition on successive Rule 12 motions to dismiss is not absolute. Some courts have permitted such a practice where the second motion would not result in unnecessary delay, expense, or inconvenience, yet would allow a more expeditious resolution of the case.[352]

"Amending" a Rule 12 Motion

To avoid waiving Rule 12 defenses that were omitted inadvertently from a Rule 12 motion, parties may seek leave of court to "amend" or supplement their Rule 12 motions to include the omitted defenses or objections.[353] In considering such amendments, the court may examine whether the amendment request was filed before the Rule 12 motion was heard, the time interval between the original Rule 12 motion and the attempted correction, the moving party's good faith, and the likelihood that the omission was intentional and tactical, or merely inadvertent.[354]

Applies Only to Rule 12 Motions

This omnibus "consolidation" provision applies only to Rule 12 motions and only to defenses that may be asserted under Rule 12 (*e.g.*, lack of personal jurisdiction, improper venue, improper service). Affirmative defenses generally are not waived if asserted in the responsive pleading filed after a Rule 12 motion.[355] This Rule does not apply to motions allowed under other Rules.[356] Moreover, certain Rule 12 defenses and objections, even though not raised in the Rule 12 motion, are not deemed forever waived. Rule 12(h)(2) expressly preserves a pleader's right to assert in any pleading, in a Rule 12(c) motion, or at trial the defenses of (a) failure to state a claim upon which relief can be granted, (b) failure to join an indispensable party, and (c) failure to state a legal defense.[357]

this failure to promptly amend the motion constituted a waiver of the defense).

352. *See Muhammad v. Village of Bolingbrook*, 2004 WL 1557958, at *1 (N.D.Ill. July 8, 2004); *MCW, Inc. v. Badbusinessbureau.com, L.L.C.*, 2004 WL 833595, at *5–*6 (N.D.Tex. April 19, 2004).

353. *See Chatman–Bey v. Thornburgh*, 864 F.2d 804 (D.C.Cir.1988); *Glater v. Eli Lilly & Co.*, 712 F.2d 735, 738 (1st Cir.1983); *Gray v. Snow King Resort, Inc.*, 889 F.Supp. 1473 (D.Wyo.1995).

354. *See Nycal Corp. v. Inoco PLC*, 949 F.Supp. 1115, 1119–20 (S.D.N.Y.1997) (setting out considerations, and denying leave to supplement where the omission was found to be a deliberate intent to obtain a tactical advantage).

355. *See Parker v. United States*, 110 F.3d 678, 682 (9th Cir.1997). *See also Tahoe–Sierra Preservation Council, Inc. v. Tahoe Regional Planning Agency*, 992 F.Supp. 1218, 1225–26 (D.Nev.1998), *aff'd in part, rev'd in part*, 216 F.3d 764 (9th Cir.2000) (holding that omitting statute of limitations defense from pre-answer motion is not a waiver).

356. *See Aetna Life Ins. Co. v. Alla Med. Servs., Inc.*, 855 F.2d 1470 (9th Cir.1988); *Baranof Fisheries Ltd. Partnership v. Elsey*, 1996 WL 467323 (D.Or.1996) (Rule 12(g) consolidation rule did not apply where prior motion was a Rule 41 motion for voluntary dismissal, and not a Rule 12 motion).

357. *See* Rule 12(h)(2). *See also Vega v. State Univ. of New York Bd. of Trustees*, 2000 WL 381430, at *2 (S.D.N.Y.2000) (permitting successive Rule 12(b)(6) motions under circumstances); *United States ex rel. S. Prawer & Co. v. Verrill & Dana*, 962 F.Supp. 206, 209 n. 4 (D.Me.1997) (noting that Rule 12(b)(6) motions are not encompassed in Rule 12(g), and can be considered even after the Rule 12 motion is ruled upon). *But see Federal Express Corp. v. United States Postal Serv.*, 40 F.Supp.2d 943, 948 (W.D.Tenn.

Objections to Subject Matter Jurisdiction

Objections to subject matter jurisdiction concern the court's authority to hear and decide the case. Consequently, such objections cannot generally be lost through waiver.[358]

Effect of Same Counsel for Multiple Defendants

Where the same attorney represents multiple defendants and files a consolidated Rule 12(b) motion jointly on their behalf, there is some uncertainty as to the effect of the attorney's decision to assert certain Rule 12(b) defenses by motion as to some, but not all, defendants. One view, emphasizing the goal of avoiding the dilatory effect of successive Rule 12(b) motions, would preclude a later Rule 12(b) filing by the other defendants.[359] An opposing, more recent, and more authoritative (and perhaps better reasoned) view rejects this result, citing the absence of any such consolidated defendant provision in Rule 12(g).[360]

RULE 12(h). WAIVER AND PRESERVATION OF DEFENSES

CORE CONCEPT

Rule 12(h) sets forth the defenses and objections that are waived if not timely asserted, and lists the defenses and objections that are not waivable.

APPLICATIONS

Waived Defenses and Objections

Defenses and objections to personal jurisdiction (Rule 12(b)(2)), improper venue (Rule 12(b)(3)), insufficient process (Rule 12(b)(4)), and insufficient service (Rule 12(b)(5)), are waived unless they are:

- *Asserted By Motion*: In an omnibus Rule 12(b) motion, but only if one is filed, *or*
- *Asserted By Responsive Pleading:* If such an omnibus Rule 12(b) motion is not filed.[361]

Similarly, a defendant's denials to the pleader's factual allegations, as well as the defendants' affirmative defenses, are also waived if they are

1999) (although failure-to-state-a-claim is not a waived defense, Rule 12(g) precludes successive, pre-answer Rule 12(b)(6) motions); *see* Authors' Commentary to Rule 12(h).

358. *See* Rule 12(h)(3). *See also Williams v. Roche*, 2002 WL 1585568, at *4 (E.D.La.2002).

359. *See Church of Scientology v. Linberg*, 529 F.Supp. 945, 966–67 (C.D.Cal.1981).

360. *See Schnabel v. Lui*, 302 F.3d 1023, 1034 (9th Cir.2002).

361. *See, e.g., Taubman Co. v. Webfeats*, 319 F.3d 770, 773 (6th Cir.2003) (personal jurisdiction challenge waived if not raised in first responsive pleading); *Farm Credit Bank of Baltimore v. Ferrera–Goitia*, 316 F.3d 62, 68 (1st Cir.2003) (personal jurisdiction defense waived if not made by first-filed motion or included in initial responsive pleading); *Porsche Cars North America, Inc. v. Porsche.Net*, 302 F.3d 248, 256 (4th Cir.2002) (personal jurisdiction defense indubitably waived absent timely objection); *Posner v. Essex Ins. Co.*, 178 F.3d 1209, 1213 n. 4 (11th Cir.1999) (defendant waived personal jurisdiction challenge by omitting this defense from Rule 12(b) motion); *McCurdy v. American Bd. of Plastic Surgery*, 157 F.3d 191, 195 (3d Cir.1998) (untimely service waived if not raised timely); *Texas Municipal Power Agency v. EPA*, 89 F.3d 858, 867 (D.C.Cir.1996)(improper venue waived for failure to object).

not asserted in the responsive pleading.[362]

Purpose

Judicial economy underlies this waiver provision. Automatic waiver is designed to prevent the delaying effect of the piecemeal assertion of Rule 12 objections and defenses through multiple motions, and to permit the early dismissal of inappropriate claims before the court devotes unnecessary time and resources to adjudication.[363]

Waiver is Mandatory, Not Discretionary

The waiver provision of Rule 12(h) imposes a mandatory, not discretionary, obligation upon the district court.[364]

Avoiding Waiver by Seeking Leave to Amend

A party's failure to assert a timely factual denial or defense can be cured if the court grants the party leave to amend the pleading or Rule 12 motion.[365] Before granting leave to amend or supplement a Rule 12 motion, the court may examine whether the amendment request was filed before the Rule 12 motion was heard, the time interval between the original Rule 12 motion and the attempted correction, the moving party's good faith, and the likelihood that the omission was intentional and tactical, or merely inadvertent.[366]

Raising Defenses/Objections in Answer Only (Without Motion)

If the defendant elects *not* to file a Rule 12 motion, the waivable Rule 12 defenses and objections are preserved if included in the Answer.[367] However, in certain circumstances, a waiver may be implied by conduct that is deemed inconsistent with an intention to preserve a defense.[368]

Implied Waiver

The courts may, under certain circumstances, find that a party has waived personal jurisdiction, venue, insufficient process, or insufficient service of process, even though those defenses were set forth in a timely motion to dismiss or in a responsive pleading. For example, a defendant who asserts a timely but waivable Rule 12(b) defense, but then interposes an affirmative claim for relief (*e.g.*, a permissive counterclaim), may be deemed to have abandoned the waivable Rule 12 defens-

362. *See Pusey v. Dallas Corp.*, 938 F.2d 498 (4th Cir.1991).

363. *See Flory v. United States*, 79 F.3d 24, 25 (5th Cir.1996); *Schneider v. National R.R. Passenger Corp.*, 72 F.3d 17, 20 (2d Cir.1995).

364. *See Polaroid Corp. v. Feely*, 889 F.Supp. 21 (D.Mass.1995).

365. *See* Rule 15; *Gray v. Snow King Resort, Inc.*, 889 F.Supp. 1473 (D.Wyo.1995).

366. *See Nycal Corp. v. Inoco PLC*, 949 F.Supp. 1115, 1119–20 (S.D.N.Y.1997) (setting out considerations, and denying leave to supplement where the omission was found to be a deliberate intent to obtain a tactical advantage).

367. *See McIntosh v. Antonino*, 71 F.3d 29, 38 (1st Cir.1995)(statute of limitations defense is not waived even if no motion for judgment on that issue is filed, so long as the defense is preserved in the Answer);

368. *See* **Authors' Commentary** to Rule 12(h), *infra*, "Implied Waiver."

es.[369] The court may consider the party's act of pressing such an affirmative claim as inconsistent with an objection to jurisdiction, venue, process, or service.

Note: The case law is unclear on this issue. However, the developing trend seems to suggest that a party does *not* waive a properly, timely asserted objection to jurisdiction by pressing an affirmative claim for relief,[370] or by filing ancillary motions (*e.g.,* for stay or injunction pending appeal) premised on the asserted jurisdictional defense.[371] This trend construes such affirmative claims for relief as simply contingent on the court's denial of the party's jurisdictional objections.[372]

Similarly, a defendant who objects to personal jurisdiction, but then actively conducts discovery, submits motions for the court's ruling, participates in trial, and files post-trial motions may be deemed to have waived the jurisdictional objection.[373] This implied waiver effect is not limited only to defendants. A plaintiff, obviously, by the very act of suing, submits herself to the jurisdiction of the court for purposes of a defendant's counterclaims.[374]

Preserved Defenses and Objections

Defenses and objections to a failure to state a claim upon which relief can be granted (Rule 12(b)(6)), failure to join an indispensable party (Rule 12(b)(7)), and failure to state a legal defense (Rule 12(f)) are waived *only* if not asserted before the close of trial.[375] Thus, these defenses, though generally preserved throughout the lawsuit, may not be raised for the first time in post-trial motions or on appeal.[376]

369. *See Frank's Casing Crew & Rental Tools, Inc. v. PMR Tech., Ltd.*, 292 F.3d 1363, 1372 (Fed.Cir.2002) (holding that non-resident defendant in patent noninfringement declaratory judgment action waived personal jurisdiction objection when it filed class action counterclaim asserting unrelated infringements of patent by others).

370. *See PaineWebber Inc. v. Chase Manhattan Private Bank (Switzerland)*, 260 F.3d 453, 461 (5th Cir.2001) (filing of counterclaim, cross-claim, or third-party claim does not, without more, waive personal jurisdiction defense); *Kaplan v. First Options of Chicago, Inc.*, 19 F.3d 1503, 1520 (3d Cir.1994) (filing counterclaim does not waive objection to jurisdiction), *aff'd*, 514 U.S. 938, 115 S.Ct. 1920, 131 L.Ed.2d 985 (1995); *Bayou Steel Corp. v. M/V Amstelvoorn*, 809 F.2d 1147, 1149 (5th Cir.1987) (same). *See also Media Duplication Servs., Ltd. v. HDG Software, Inc.*, 928 F.2d 1228, 1233 & n. 2 (1st Cir.1991) (ineffective service of process defense was not waived where it was seasonably raised and consistently pressed, notwithstanding filing of counterclaim).

371. *See PaineWebber Inc. v. Chase Manhattan Private Bank (Switzerland)*, 260 F.3d 453, 461 (5th Cir.2001) (defendant who timely and properly asserted personal jurisdiction objection by motion, and engaged in no counterclaim or third-party practice, did not waive defense by filing motion for stay and injunction pending appeal premised on the jurisdictional defense).

372. *See Bayou Steel Corp. v. M/V Amstelvoorn*, 809 F.2d 1147, 1149 (5th Cir.1987) (discussing divergent views, and adopting majority approach).

373. *See White v. National Football League*, 41 F.3d 402, 407 (8th Cir.1994), *cert. denied*, 515 U.S. 1137, 115 S.Ct. 2569, 132 L.Ed.2d 821 (1995).

374. *See Adam v. Saenger*, 303 U.S. 59, 67–68, 58 S.Ct. 454, 458, 82 L.Ed. 649 (1938).

375. *See Eberhardt v. Integrated Design & Const., Inc.*, 167 F.3d 861, 870–71 (4th Cir.1999) (ruling that Rule 12(b)(6) defense is waived after completion of trial on the merits); *Romstadt v. Allstate Ins. Co.*, 59 F.3d 608, 610–11 (6th Cir. 1995)(failure to state a claim defense is protected from waiver through trial).

376. *Brown v. Trustees of Boston Univ.*, 891 F.2d 337 (1st Cir.1989), *cert. denied,* 496 U.S. 937, 110 S.Ct. 3217, 110 L.Ed.2d 664 (1990).

- *Only One Pre-Answer Rule 12(b)(6) Motion Permitted:* Although the Rule 12(b)(6) defense of failure to state a claim is generally not waived (so long as it is asserted before the time of trial), it ordinarily may not be asserted in multiple pre-answer motions. Some (but not all) courts have ruled that successive, pre-answer Rule 12(b)(6) motions are prohibited by Rule 12(g)'s requirement that all Rule 12 defenses (including failure to state a claim) be raised in a single, omnibus, pre-answer motion—if the party chooses to file a motion at all.[377]
- *Non-Waiver Applies to "Indispensable" Parties Only:* Rule 12(h) preserves only the defense of dismissal for failing to join an "indispensable" party. Where a party is necessary for proper adjudication under Rule 19, but can be joined as a party in the lawsuit, a motion for joinder may not be made if omitted from an omnibus Rule 12 motion or, alternatively, from the responsive pleading.[378]

Objections to Subject Matter Jurisdiction

Because objections to the court's subject matter jurisdiction concern the court's authority to hear and decide the parties' dispute, no one can waive such an objection, be estopped from raising the objection, or cure such a problem by consenting to jurisdiction where none exists.[379]

- *Asserted At Any Time:* Objections to subject matter jurisdiction may be made in the omnibus Rule 12 motion, in the responsive pleading, in subsequent pretrial motions, in a motion for relief from final judgment, or on appeal.[380] The objection, however, must be made while the case is still pending (*e.g.*, before trial, at trial, or on appeal); it cannot be raised for the first time as a

377. *See Swart v. Pitcher*, 9 F.3d 109 (6th Cir.1993) (Table) (Unpublished Opinion, text available on WestLaw, 1993 WL 406802) (citation restricted); *766347 Ontario Ltd. v. Zurich Capital Mkts., Inc.*, 274 F.Supp.2d 926, 930 (N.D.Ill.2003); *Federal Express Corp. v. United States Postal Serv.*, 40 F.Supp.2d 943, 948 (W.D.Tenn.1999). *But see Vega v. State Univ. of New York Bd. of Trustees*, 2000 WL 381430, at *2 (S.D.N.Y.2000) (permitting successive Rule 12(b)(6) motions under circumstances); *Campbell–El v. District of Columbia*, 881 F.Supp. 42, 43 (D.D.C.1995)(permitting second Rule 12(b)(6) motion in the exercise of court's sound discretion and in order to avoid undue delay).

378. *See Citibank, N.A. v. Oxford Properties & Fin. Ltd.*, 688 F.2d 1259 (9th Cir.1982).

379. *See* Rule 12(b)(1). *See also American Fiber & Finishing, Inc. v. Tyco Healthcare Group, LP*, 362 F.3d 136, 139 (1st Cir. 2004); *Taubman Co. v. Webfeats*, 319 F.3d 770, 773 (6th Cir.2003); *In re Stock Exchanges Options Trading Antitrust Litig.*, 317 F.3d 134, 151 (2d Cir. 2003); *United States v. Nye County*, 178 F.3d 1080, 1089 n. 12 (9th Cir.1999); *Mennen Co. v. Atlantic Mutual Ins. Co.*, 147 F.3d 287 (3d Cir. 1998); *Magee v. Exxon Corp.*, 135 F.3d 599, 601 (8th Cir.1998); *Coury v. Prot*, 85 F.3d 244, 248–49 (5th Cir.1996)(litigants cannot consent to subject matter jurisdiction, and its absence cannot be waived). *Cf. Moravian School Advisory Bd. v. Rawlins*, 70 F.3d 270 (3d Cir.1995)(where district court lacked subject matter jurisdiction to hear the case, it also lacked jurisdiction to transfer it; the only remedy for lack of subject matter jurisdiction is dismissal).

380. *See S.J. v. Hamilton County*, 374 F.3d 416, 418 n.1 (6th Cir. 2004); *American Fiber & Finishing, Inc. v. Tyco Healthcare Group, LP*, 362 F.3d 136, 139 (1st Cir. 2004); *Brown v. Philadelphia Housing Auth.*, 350 F.3d 338, 347 (3d Cir. 2003); *Coury v. Prot*, 85 F.3d 244, 248–49 (5th Cir.1996).

collateral attack on the earlier judgment.[381]

- *"Suggestions":* Although a motion to dismiss for lack of subject matter jurisdiction is procedurally untimely if filed after the pleadings are closed, the courts will typically treat such a belated motion as a "suggestion" to the court that it lacks subject matter jurisdiction, and will then proceed to consider it on its merits.[382]
- *Raised By Court:* The trial court or the court of appeals may raise an objection to subject matter jurisdiction on its own initiative.[383]

Waiting for Default to Raise Service Objections

Although defendants must raise their objections to process, service, and personal jurisdiction either in their omnibus Rule 12 motion or in their answer (if no Rule 12 motion is filed), these defenses are *not* waived where the failure of service is so complete that the defendants never even received actual notice of the unanswered pleading.[384] In such a case, the Constitutional protections of due process should permit the defendants to raise those objections in opposition to a motion for default. However, where a defendant receives actual notice of the pleading, decides that the process or service was improper, and then chooses not to assert these defenses by answer or motion (intending to press these objections in response to a later default motion), the defendant acts as her peril. There is case law precedent and commentary for the conclusion that this conduct may constitute a waiver of these defenses.[385]

ADDITIONAL RESEARCH REFERENCES

C.J.S. Federal Civil Procedure §§ 302, 376–409 et seq., 413–440 et seq., 796 et seq., 842 et seq.

West's Key No. Digests, Federal Civil Procedure ⚷734–735, 941–1020, 1031–1033, 1041–1068, 1101–1150, 1721–1842.

381. *See City of South Pasadena v. Mineta*, 284 F.3d 1154, 1156–57 (9th Cir.2002).

382. *See S.J. v. Hamilton County*, 374 F.3d 416, 418 n.1 (6th Cir. 2004).

383. *See Insurance Corp. of Ireland, Ltd. v. Compagnie des Bauxites de Guinee*, 456 U.S. 694, 704, 102 S.Ct. 2099, 2105, 72 L.Ed.2d 492 (1982); *See also Blue Cross & Blue Shield of Alabama v. Sanders*, 138 F.3d 1347, 1351–52 (11th Cir.1998); *Campanella v. Commerce Exchange Bank*, 137 F.3d 885, 890 (6th Cir.1998); *Magee v. Exxon Corp.*, 135 F.3d 599, 601 (8th Cir.1998); *Florio v. Olson*, 129 F.3d 678, 680 (1st Cir.1997); *Coury v. Prot*, 85 F.3d 244, 248–49 (5th Cir.1996)(absence of subject matter jurisdiction may be raised by any party or by the court); *Bueford v. RTC*, 991 F.2d 481, 485 (8th Cir. 1993). *See also Ward v. Brown*, 22 F.3d 516 (2d Cir.1994)("it has been the rule since nearly the inception of our republic that subject matter jurisdiction may be raised any time").

384. *See Corestates Leasing, Inc. v. Wright-Way Exp., Inc.*, 190 F.R.D. 356, 358 (E.D.Pa. 2000).

385. *See Corestates Leasing, Inc. v. Wright-Way Exp., Inc.*, 190 F.R.D. 356, 358 (E.D.Pa. 2000). *See also* 5A Charles Alan Wright & Arthur R. Miller, *Federal Practice & Procedure* § 1391, at 755–56 (1990) ("But when the party has received actual notice of the suit there is no due process problem in requiring him to object to the ineffective service within the period prescribed by Rule 12(h)(1) and the defense is one that he certainly can waive if he wishes to do so. This is because the defendant has failed to do what the rule says he must do if he is to avoid a waiver.").

RULE 13

COUNTERCLAIM AND CROSS-CLAIM

(a) Compulsory Counterclaims. A pleading shall state as a counterclaim any claim which at the time of serving the pleading the pleader has against any opposing party, if it arises out of the transaction or occurrence that is the subject matter of the opposing party's claim and does not require for its adjudication the presence of third parties of whom the court cannot acquire jurisdiction. But the pleader need not state the claim if (1) at the time the action was commenced the claim was the subject of another pending action, or (2) the opposing party brought suit upon the claim by attachment or other process by which the court did not acquire jurisdiction to render a personal judgment on that claim, and the pleader is not stating any counterclaim under this Rule 13.

(b) Permissive Counterclaims. A pleading may state as a counterclaim any claim against an opposing party not arising out of the transaction or occurrence that is the subject matter of the opposing party's claim.

(c) Counterclaim Exceeding Opposing Claim. A counterclaim may or may not diminish or defeat the recovery sought by the opposing party. It may claim relief exceeding in amount or different in kind from that sought in the pleading of the opposing party.

(d) Counterclaim Against the United States. These rules shall not be construed to enlarge beyond the limits now fixed by law the right to assert counterclaims or to claim credits against the United States or an officer or agency thereof.

(e) Counterclaim Maturing or Acquired After Pleading. A claim which either matured or was acquired by the pleader after serving a pleading may, with the permission of the court, be presented as a counterclaim by supplemental pleading.

(f) Omitted Counterclaim. When a pleader fails to set up a counterclaim through oversight, inadvertence, or excusable neglect, or when justice requires, the pleader may by leave of court set up the counterclaim by amendment.

(g) Cross–Claim Against Co-party. A pleading may state as a cross-claim any claim by one party against a co-party arising out of the transaction or occurrence that is the subject matter either of the original action or of a counterclaim therein or relating to any property that is the subject matter of the original action. Such cross-claim may include a claim that the party against whom it is asserted is or may be liable to the cross-claimant for all or part of a claim asserted in the action against the cross-claimant.

(h) Joinder of Additional Parties. Persons other than those made parties to the original action may be made parties to a counterclaim or cross-claim in accordance with the provisions of Rules 19 and 20.

(i) Separate Trials; Separate Judgments. If the court orders separate trials as provided in Rule 42(b), judgment on a counterclaim or cross-claim may be rendered in accordance with the terms of Rule 54(b) when the court has jurisdiction so to do, even if the claims of the opposing party have been dismissed or otherwise disposed of.

[Amended effective March 19, 1948; July 1, 1963; July 1, 1966; August 1, 1987.]

AUTHORS' COMMENTARY ON RULE 13

PURPOSE AND SCOPE

Rule 13 authorizes persons who are already parties to an action to assert counterclaims against an opposing party. The Rule distinguishes between counterclaims that must be raised in pending litigation, and counterclaims that may either be raised in the pending litigation or retained for subsequent litigation.[1] Rule 13 also controls the circumstances in which cross-claims against co-parties—*i.e.,* against persons who are aligned on the same side of the case as the cross-claimant—may be maintained in a pending action.

RULE 13(a). COMPULSORY COUNTERCLAIMS

CORE CONCEPT

Subject to some exceptions discussed below, compulsory counterclaims are those counterclaims arising from the same transaction or occurrence that gave rise to the plaintiff's complaint. Such counterclaims are so closely related to claims already raised by a plaintiff that they can be adjudicated in the same action without creating confusion for a trier of fact or undue prejudice to the plaintiff. Consequently, Rule 13(a) generally requires that compulsory counterclaims must be asserted in the pending litigation or they are waived.

1. *Cf., Tank Insulation International, Inc. v. Insultherm, Inc.,* 104 F.3d 83, 88 (5th Cir.1997), *cert. denied,* 522 U.S. 907, 118 S.Ct. 265, 139 L.Ed.2d 191 (1997)("[U]nder rule 13 a counterclaim is either compulsory or permissive—it cannot be both.").

APPLICATIONS

Procedure

Compulsory counterclaims are asserted by pleading them in the answer to a complaint or a reply to a previously asserted counterclaim.[2]

Same Transaction or Occurrence

Courts generally agree that this standard for identifying compulsory counterclaims should be construed liberally, so as to further the goal of judicial economy.[3] However, courts differ substantially in the way they actually apply the standard to specific facts. The broadest application of the same transaction or occurrence standard finds a compulsory counterclaim when there is any significant logical relationship between the plaintiff's claim and the counterclaim.[4] Thus, if a plaintiff sued on a contract, and the defendant had a counterclaim resting on an assertion that the contract was a violation of federal antitrust law, the "logical relationship" test would probably treat the counterclaim as compulsory.[5] Other, less broad, applications of the standard look to the degree of overlap in evidence between claim and counterclaim, and may require substantial overlap before a counterclaim is deemed compulsory.[6]

Exceptions to "Same Transaction" Standard

As stated immediately above, a counterclaim is not compulsory unless it arises from the same transaction or occurrence as one of the claims filed by an opposing party. However, the converse—that counterclaims arising from the same transaction or occurrence are compulsory—is not always true. Listed below are the circumstances in which a counterclaim need not be asserted even though it shares the same transaction or occurrence as a claim filed by an opposing party.[7]

2. *See, e.g., Shelter Mutual Insurance Co. v. Public Water Supply District No. 7 of Jefferson County, Missouri,* 747 F.2d 1195 (8th Cir.1984).

3. *See, e.g., Transamerica Occidental Life Insurance Co. v. Aviation Office of America, Inc.,* 292 F.3d 384, 390 (3d Cir.2002) ("[T]he objective of Rule 13(a) is to promote judicial economy, so the term 'transaction or occurrence' is construed generously to further this purpose.").

4. *See, e.g., Transamerica Occidental Life Insurance Co. v. Aviation Office of America, Inc.,* 292 F.3d 384, 389 (3d Cir.2002) ("The concept of a 'logical relationship' has been viewed liberally to promote judicial economy."). *But see, Whigham v. Beneficial Finance Co. of Fayetteville,* 599 F.2d 1322, 1324 (4th Cir.1979)(held, insufficient "logical relationship" between complaint under Truth in Lending Act and lender's counterclaim on the loan). *See also Consolidated Coal Co. v. United Mine Workers of America, District 12, Local Union 1545,* 213 F.3d 404 (7th Cir.2000) (labor-management disputes all arose out of same disagreement over staffing; all disputes submitted to different arbitrators; union sought to bar management from seeking enforcement of management victories in later arbitrations, arguing that union suit to enforce union victory in earlier arbitration required management to assert its arbitration victories as compulsory counterclaims; held, "while the seven arbitrations all arose out of the same transaction or occurrence, namely the staffing dispute, the two district court proceedings did not. They arose out of the arbitrations, which we deem to have been separate transactions or occurrences.").

5. *See, e.g., Great Lakes Rubber Corp. v. Herbert Cooper Co.,* 286 F.2d 631 (3d Cir.1961).

6. *See, e.g., Federman v. Empire Fire and Marine Insurance Co.,* 597 F.2d 798 (2d Cir. 1979); *Columbia Plaza Corp. v. Security National Bank,* 525 F.2d 620 (D.C.Cir.1975).

7. *See, e.g., Kane v. Magna Mixer Co.,* 71 F.3d 555, 561–62 (6th Cir.1995), *cert. denied,* 517 U.S. 1220, 116 S.Ct. 1848, 134 L.Ed.2d 949 (1996)("If the claim does arise out of the same

(1) *Exception: Immature Claims:* A counterclaim that does not mature until after the party has served a pleading is not a compulsory counterclaim, even if it arises from the same transaction or occurrence as a claim filed by an opposing party.[8] Rule 13(e) provides that such a claim may be asserted as a permissive counterclaim by filing a supplemental pleading, as provided by Rule 15(d), or it may be retained for future litigation, at the discretion of the party who holds the claim.

(2) *Exception: Rule 13(a) Inapplicable to Claims Until Service of Pleading:* Even if a counterclaim arises from the same transaction or occurrence as a plaintiff's claim, Rule 13(a) provides that it does not become a compulsory counterclaim until the time when the party holding the counterclaim is required to file a responsive pleading. Thus, if a defendant initially filed a motion to dismiss under Rule 12(b), that rule provides that no pleading need be filed until the court decides the Rule 12(b) motion. If the court granted the motion to dismiss, the defendant never had an obligation to file a responsive pleading. In that circumstance, any claim the defendant had against the plaintiff would not be deemed a compulsory counterclaim, and would be preserved for assertion in subsequent litigation. Similarly, if a plaintiff and defendant settle the plaintiff's claim before expiration of the time in which the defendant must answer, any counterclaim the defendant might have is not compulsory.[9]

(3) *Exception: Lack of Jurisdiction Over Third Parties:* If a counterclaim requires joinder of some additional person not subject to the court's jurisdiction, the counterclaim will not be deemed compulsory, irrespective of the amount of overlap it shares with the plaintiff's claim.[10]

(4) *Exception: Pending Lawsuits:* A counterclaim is not compulsory within the meaning of Rule 13(a) if it has already been sued upon in other litigation. Thus, if one person filed suit in a state court, and the opponent of that claim then sued in federal court, the original state claim would not be a compulsory counterclaim in federal court because it is already the subject of pending litigation.[11]

transaction or occurrence, it is not a permissive counterclaim, although ... it may not be required to be asserted.").

8. *See, e.g., Harbor Insurance Co. v. Continental Bank Corp.,* 922 F.2d 357, 360 (7th Cir. 1990)(counterclaim that did not exist when complaint was filed is not compulsory counterclaim).

9. *See, e.g., Bluegrass Hosiery, Inc. v. Speizman Industries, Inc.,* 214 F.3d 770 (6th Cir.2000) (permitting claims not raised as counterclaims in prior lawsuit in state court; claims not barred as compulsory counterclaims because prior suit was settled before party had a duty to file an answer; "Rule 13(a) ... only requires a compulsory counterclaim if the party who desires to assert a claim has served a pleading. ...In other words, Rule 13(a) does not apply unless there has been some form of pleading."); *Carteret Savings & Loan Association v. Jackson,* 812 F.2d 36, 38 (1st Cir.1987)(Rule 13(a) does not apply "if a pleading had never been required, as for example, if 'the time of serving, had never been reached.' ").

10. *See, e.g., Landmark Bank v. Machera,* 736 F.Supp. 375, 379 (D.Mass.1990)("Rule 13(a) specifically precludes compulsory counterclaims that require for adjudication the presence of third parties over whom 'the court cannot acquire jurisdiction.' ").

11. *See, e.g., In re Piper Aircraft Corp.,* 244 F.3d 1289, 1296 n. 3 (11th Cir.2001), *cert. denied,* 534 U.S. 827, 122 S.Ct. 66, 151 L.Ed.2d 33 (2001) (for a counterclaim to fit within this exception to the compulsory counterclaim requirement "Rule 13(a) literally requires that the [counterclaim] be pending before the other action was commenced"). *See also, United States v.*

(5) *Exception: Quasi in Rem/In Rem Jurisdiction:* Where the plaintiff's complaint rests on the court's quasi in rem or in rem jurisdiction, a counterclaim will not be compulsory,[12] so long as the defendant refrains from raising any counterclaims under Rule 13. If, however, the defendant raises a Rule 13 counterclaim, then all other counterclaims that fall within the same transaction or occurrence as the plaintiff's claim—and not exempted by other exceptions, discussed above—are compulsory counterclaims and must be asserted.

(6) *Exception: Injunction/Declaratory Judgment Actions:* In some circumstances, defendants who have been sued only on equity claims may not be required to assert claims for money damages as counterclaims.[13]

"Opposing Party": Successors in interest & Privity

When a party seeks to use Rule 13(a) to bar a claim in a later lawsuit because the claim should have been raised as a compulsory counterclaim against the plaintiff in the original litigation, a question may arise as to the applicability of the Rule when the party seeking to bar the claim shares a close identity with the original plaintiff but is not literally identical to that plaintiff. Precedent on the issue is not plentiful, but in general it appears that the term "opposing party" is read rather broadly. Thus, a party who is sufficiently closely related to a plaintiff who should have been sued on a compulsory counterclaim in previous litigation is entitled to raise Rule 13(a) as a defense when that counterclaim is finally raised in a subsequent lawsuit.[14]

Dico, Inc., 136 F.3d 572, 577 (8th Cir.1998) (pending administrative claim is not a compulsory counterclaim; "[Rule 13] does not require that the action be pending before another court, to the exclusion of an administrative tribunal of competent jurisdiction.").

12. *Baker v. Gold Seal Liquors,* 417 U.S. 467, 469, 94 S.Ct. 2504, 2506 n. 1, 41 L.Ed.2d 243 (1974)("The claim is not compulsory ... if the opposing party brought his suit by attachment or other process not resulting in personal jurisdiction but only in rem or quasi in rem jurisdiction.").

13. *See, e.g., United States v. Snider,* 779 F.2d 1151, 1156 (6th Cir.1985)(plaintiff sought only declaratory and injunctive relief; then sought preliminary injunction; court, pursuant to Rule 65, held trial on merits simultaneously with preliminary injunction hearing; held, defendant was not obligated to file counterclaim for money damages).

14. *See, e.g., Transamerica Occidental Life Insurance Co. v. Aviation Office of America, Inc.,* 292 F.3d 384, (3d Cir.2002) (successor in interest to party in prior litigation is "opposing party" under Rule 13(a) and therefore can raise bar to claim that should have been raised as counterclaim against predecessors in previously filed litigation); *Avemco Insurance Co. v. Cessna Aircraft Co.,* 11 F.3d 998, 1001 (10th Cir.1993) (airplane crash; first suit brought by one passenger against plane owner and pilot, but not insurer-subrogee; first suit was settled; second injured passenger then sued plane owner and pilot, as well as airplane manufacturer; manufacturer filed third-party complaint against insured for negligence in operation of plane; insured plane owner and pilot filed no counterclaim for contribution or indemnification for money paid in settlement of first claim; later, in third lawsuit, insurer of owner and pilot sought such indemnification from manufacturer, but was barred by Rule 13(a); court noted that insurer controlled defense of owner and pilot in both previous lawsuits and should have raised issues of contribution and indemnification); *Banco Nacional de Cuba v. First National Bank of New York,* 478 F.2d 191, 193 n. 1 (2d Cir.1973) (counterclaim against Republic of Cuba is proper, notwithstanding that named plaintiff is Cuban national bank; held, bank and government are one and the same and thus government is proper "opposing party" within scope of Rule 13(a)).

Subject Matter Jurisdiction

Compulsory counterclaims must satisfy subject matter jurisdiction. They do so by satisfying the requirements of either federal question jurisdiction or diversity jurisdiction, or by qualifying for supplemental jurisdiction. Because compulsory counterclaims must arise from the same transaction or occurrence as the plaintiff's claim, counterclaims that do not qualify for federal question jurisdiction or diversity jurisdiction nevertheless usually meet the requirements for supplemental jurisdiction.[15]

It should be noted that the party asserting a counterclaim must include an allegation of facts demonstrating that the requirement of subject matter jurisdiction is met.[16] Subject matter jurisdiction is discussed at Part II, §§ 2.10–2.13.

Personal Jurisdiction Over Plaintiffs

Assertion of a compulsory counterclaim usually involves very few problems with personal jurisdiction over the plaintiff. By instituting an action, a plaintiff is held to have consented to the court's jurisdiction to adjudicate related claims,[17] and by definition, a compulsory counterclaim is closely related to the plaintiff's claim. Consent to personal jurisdiction is discussed at § 2.4.

Venue

Most courts hold that compulsory counterclaims need not satisfy venue requirements.[18]

Failure to Assert a Compulsory Counterclaim

Defendants who do not assert compulsory counterclaims are usually barred from raising the counterclaims in subsequent litigation.[19] The

15. *Baker v. Gold Seal Liquors,* 417 U.S. 467, 94 S.Ct. 2504, 41 L.Ed.2d 243 (1974). *See, e.g., St. Jude Medical, Inc. v. Lifecare International, Inc.,* 250 F.3d 587 (8th Cir.2001) ("Because [defendant's] claims were compulsory counterclaims, there was supplemental jurisdiction to hear them in federal court."). *See also Columbia Gas Transmission Corp. v. Drain,* 191 F.3d 552, 559 (4th Cir.1999) (where party raised counterclaims only to comply with Rule 13(a), and otherwise vigorously and successfully challenged district court's subject matter jurisdiction over original complaint, justice requires adherence to counterclaimant's request to dismiss counterclaim without prejudice).

16. *McNutt v. General Motors Acceptance Corp.,* 298 U.S. 178, 189, 56 S.Ct. 780, 785, 80 L.Ed. 1135 (1936) ("[P]rerequisites to the exercise of jurisdiction . . . are conditions which must be met by the party who seeks the exercise of jurisdiction in his favor. He must allege in his pleading the facts essential to show jurisdiction."). *Cf., e.g., Martin v. Franklin Capital Corp.,* 251 F.3d 1284 (10th Cir.2001) (removal case; "As the parties invoking the federal court's jurisdiction in this case, defendants bear the burden of establishing that the requirements for the exercise of diversity jurisdiction are present.").

17. *Adam v. Saenger,* 303 U.S. 59, 58 S.Ct. 454, 82 L.Ed. 649 (1938), *cert. denied,* 487 U.S. 1204, 108 S.Ct. 2844, 101 L.Ed.2d 881 (1988). *See e.g., Schnabel v. Lui,* 302 F.3d 1023, 1037 (9th Cir.2002) ("[P]laintiffs who avail themselves of the district court consent to personal jurisdiction" over counterclaims.) *See also In re Charter Oak Associates,* 361 F.3d 760, 768 (2d Cir. 2004) (most circuits agree that state's decision to file bankruptcy claim is waiver of immunity as to compulsory counterclaims).

18. *See, e.g., Schoot v. United States,* 664 F.Supp. 293, 295 (N.D.Ill.1987)("[I]n the case of compulsory counterclaims, the venue statutes have been construed to apply only to the original claim, and not to the compulsory counterclaims.").

19. *Baker v. Gold Seal Liquors, Inc.,* 417 U.S. 467, 469 n. 1, 94 S.Ct. 2504, 2506, 41

harshness of this result is mitigated by Rule 13(f), authorizing the court to permit amended pleadings that include counterclaims, when the court believes such permission serves the interest of justice. Rule 13(a) is also limited by Rule 15(a), which permits a party to amend a pleading once as of right within certain designated time frames. Thus, a party who failed to include a compulsory counterclaim within an initial answer might be able to use Rule 15(a) to amend the answer of right or, if the time in which to amend of right has already passed, to seek leave of opposing counsel or leave of court to amend. However, once judgment is entered on a plaintiff's claim, compulsory counterclaims that were not raised are effectively barred, unless they can fit within the stricter standards of Rule 60(b), governing relief from judgments.

Exception: Class Actions

The normal requirement that a compulsory counterclaim must be timely raised is generally inapplicable to claims held by class action defendants.[20]

Mislabelled Counterclaims

Parties sometimes mistakenly identify counterclaims as cross-claims, and *vice versa*. They may also mislabel a counterclaim as a defense. Courts usually attach no significance to such errors, unless somehow they unfairly prejudice an opposing party.[21]

Statutes of Limitations

Courts are substantially divided as to the effect that a complaint has on statutes of limitations applicable to compulsory counterclaims. Most agree that if the counterclaim was still timely at the time the

L.Ed.2d 243 (1974) ("A counterclaim which is compulsory but is not brought is thereafter barred."). *See, e.g., Polymer Industrial Products Co. v. Bridgestone/Firestone, Inc.,* 347 F.3d 935, 938 (Fed. Cir. 2003) ("Rule 13(a) makes [a patent] infringement counterclaim to a declaratory judgment action for noninfringement compulsory"); *New York Life Insurance Co. v. Deshotel,* 142 F.3d 873, 882 (5th Cir.1998) ("It is well settled that a failure to plead a compulsory counterclaim bars a party from bringing a later independent action on that claim."). *But see Handy v. Shaw, Bransford, Veilleux & Roth,* 325 F.3d 346, 350–53 (D.C.Cir.2003) (practice of barring counterclaim in subsequent litigation "is usually applied in subsequent litigation on res judicata or collateral estoppel principles;" where district court has good subject matter jurisdiction, determination to proceed with claim not raised as counterclaim in previously filed lawsuit is matter of discretion which should take into account value of proceeding with related claims in one case and importance of exercising subject matter jurisdiction when it exists; held, where initial suit in state court had already been dismissed, no substantial proceedings had occurred in state court, and statute of limitations had in the meantime become a bar if instant litigation was dismissed, it is possible that district court should hear claim notwithstanding apparent mandate of Rule 13(a)).

20. *See, e.g., Allapattah Services, Inc. v. Exxon Corp.,* 333 F.3d 1248 n. 14 (11th Cir.2003) (normal practice is to wait until liability is established and individual class members file damage claims; at that point setoffs and counterclaims can properly be adjudicated on an individual basis).

21. *Reiter v. Cooper,* 507 U.S. 258, 262, 113 S.Ct. 1213, 1217, 122 L.Ed.2d 604 (1993)(holding that counterclaim mislabelled as defense should simply be treated as counterclaim).

complaint was filed, the limitation period on the counterclaim is tolled by the filing of the complaint.[22]

RULE 13(b). PERMISSIVE COUNTERCLAIMS

CORE CONCEPT

Permissive counterclaims include those counterclaims that do not arise out of the same transaction or occurrence as the opposing party's claim. Although not stated expressly in Rule 13(b), permissive counterclaims also include counterclaims arising out of the same transaction or occurrence as the opposing party's claims, but which fall within one or more of the exceptions to Rule 13(a) compulsory counterclaims, discussed above. Counterclaims denoted as permissive may be filed in the pending action, but they may also be asserted in a separate action. However, parties often encounter substantially greater difficulties with jurisdiction over permissive counterclaims than they normally encounter with compulsory counterclaims.

APPLICATIONS

Procedure

Permissive counterclaims are filed in answers to complaints or replies to counterclaims.[23]

Different Transaction or Occurrence

The standard for measuring whether a permissive counterclaim arises from a transaction or occurrence dissimilar from that underlying the complaint is the mirror image of the same transaction or occurrence test of compulsory counterclaims. For dissimilarity, courts usually look for the absence of a logical relationship between the complaint and counterclaim.[24] Thus, if a plaintiff sued on a contract, and the defendant had a counterclaim resting on a tort that had allegedly occurred at a different place and time, and had no relationship to the contract claim beyond the happenstance that the parties to both claims were identical, the counterclaim would probably be deemed permissive.

Subject Matter Jurisdiction

Permissive counterclaims must satisfy requirements for subject matter jurisdiction. Subject matter jurisdiction can be satisfied through any of three routes: federal question jurisdiction; diversity jurisdiction; or supplemental jurisdiction. However, as is discussed immediately below, it is uncertain whether supplemental jurisdiction is

22. *See, e.g., Kirkpatrick v. Lenoir County Board of Education,* 216 F.3d 380, 388 (4th Cir.2000) ("Because [plaintiffs] timely filed [their] actions, [defendant's] counterclaim relates back to the date of the original filing. Therefore, the counterclaim was timely regardless of whether the statute of limitations governing the matter was thirty days or three years.").

23. *See, e.g., Shelter Mutual Insurance Co. v. Public Water Supply District No. 7 of Jefferson County, Missouri,* 747 F.2d 1195 (8th Cir.1984).

24. *See, e.g., Warshawsky & Co. v. Arcata National Corp.,* 552 F.2d 1257, 1261 (7th Cir. 1977)("[A] counterclaim that has its roots in a separate transaction or occurrence is permissive.").

available in cases involving permissive counterclaims. Jurisdiction is discussed more elsewhere in this text.

(1) *Restrictions on Use of Supplemental Jurisdiction:* Generally, most permissive counterclaims do not arise from the same transaction or occurrence as the claim of the opposing party. Thus there is some question as to whether permissive counterclaims that do not meet the requirements for original subject matter jurisdiction (usually diversity or a federal question) and also do not arise from the same transaction or occurrence as the opponent's initial claims may either qualify for supplemental jurisdiction or may nevertheless be heard by a federal district court notwithstanding these deficiencies. The established view is that such permissive counterclaims cannot use supplemental jurisdiction. Therefore a lack of original subject matter jurisdiction would mandate dismissal of the claims.[25] A more recent view, however, is that the established view is either incorrect[26] or, if it was ever correct, enactment of 28 U.S.C.A. § 1367 (governing supplemental jurisdiction) renders it obsolete.[27] Resolution of this question will probably require a decision by the Supreme Court. In the meantime attorneys must consult local precedent. Section 1367 is discussed in greater detail elsewhere in this text.

(2) *Supplemental Jurisdiction: Exceptional Circumstances:* The foregoing discussion of uncertainty about the jurisdictional foundation of permissive counterclaims not arising from the same transaction or occurrence as the opponent's initial claims should not obscure one fact. Permissive counterclaims that arise from the same transaction or occurrence but which are not for some reason compulsory may nevertheless satisfy subject matter jurisdiction through the requirements of federal question jurisdiction, diversity jurisdiction, or supplemental jurisdiction.[28]

It should be noted that the party asserting a permissive counterclaim must include an allegation of facts demonstrating that the requirement of subject matter jurisdiction is met.[29]

25. *See, e.g., Oak Park Trust and Savings Bank v. Therkildsen,* 209 F.3d 648, 651 (7th Cir. 2000) (counterclaim arose from events unrelated to plaintiff's claim; "a permissive counterclaim ... is outside the supplemental jurisdiction ... and requires an independent basis of federal jurisdiction"); *Unique Concepts v. Manuel,* 930 F.2d 573, 574 (7th Cir. 1991) (compulsory counterclaims are eligible for supplemental jurisdiction, but permissive counterclaims "require their own jurisdictional basis").

26. *See, e.g., Jones v. Ford Motor Credit Co.,* 358 F.3d 205, 212–13 (2d Cir. 2004) ("[I]t is no longer sufficient for courts to assert, without any reason other than dicta or even holdings from the era of judge-created ancillary jurisdiction, that permissive counterclaims require independent jurisdiction.").

27. *See, e.g., Jones v. Ford Motor Credit Co.,* 358 F.3d 205, 213 (2d Cir. 2004) ("We share the view that section 1367 has displaced, rather than codified, whatever validity inhered in the earlier view that a permissive counterclaim requires independent jurisdiction (in the sense of federal question or diversity jurisdiction)."); *Channell v. Citicorp National Services, Inc.,* 89 F.3d 379, 385 (7th Cir. 1996) (holding that § 1367 broadened the power of courts to hear non-diverse permissive counterclaims that are based on state law).

28. *See, e.g., Leipzig v. AIG Life Insurance Co.,* 362 F.3d 406, 410 (7th Cir. 2004) ("Even a permissive counterclaim, if part of the same case or controversy, ... may be brought under the supplemental jurisdiction statute, 28 U.S.C. § 1367(a), without an independent basis of jurisdiction."); *Crosby Yacht Yard, Inc. v. Yacht "Chardonnay",* 164 F.R.D. 135 (D.Mass.1996) (permissive counterclaim arising from same case or controversy—but not compulsory for unrelated reasons—may nevertheless satisfy requirements for supplemental jurisdiction).

29. *McNutt v. General Motors Acceptance Corp.,* 298 U.S. 178, 189, 56 S.Ct. 780, 785, 80

Venue

It is unclear whether permissive counterclaims must satisfy venue requirements.[30]

Failure to Assert a Permissive Counterclaim

No sanction attaches if a party holding a permissive counterclaim chooses not to assert it in pending litigation. The claim is not treated as barred, and may be asserted at a later date.[31]

Mislabelled Counterclaims

Parties sometimes mistakenly identify counterclaims as cross-claims, and *vice versa*. They may also mislabel a counterclaim as a defense. Courts usually attach no significance to such errors, unless somehow they unfairly prejudice an opposing party.[32]

Statutes of Limitations

An opposing party's decision to file a claim does not toll the time in which a permissive counterclaim not arising from the same transaction or occurrence must be filed.[33]

Counterclaims Maturing After Pleading

Rule 13(b) should be read in conjunction with Rule 13(e), which provides that counterclaims maturing or acquired after pleading are permissive counterclaims that may be filed in the pending action, subject to the court's discretion.

Separate Trials

Permissive counterclaims not arising from the same transaction or occurrence as the opposing party's claim may contain substantial potential for confusing the trier of fact or delaying adjudication of the original claims. Thus, Rule 13(i) authorizes the court to order separate proceedings.

L.Ed. 1135 (1936) ("[P]rerequisites to the exercise of jurisdiction . . . are conditions which must be met by the party who seeks the exercise of jurisdiction in his favor. He must allege in his pleading the facts essential to show jurisdiction."). *Cf., e.g., Martin v. Franklin Capital Corp.,* 251 F.3d 1284 (10th Cir.2001) (removal case; "As the parties invoking the federal court's jurisdiction in this case, defendants bear the burden of establishing that the requirements for the exercise of diversity jurisdiction are present.").

30. *See, e.g., Hansen v. Shearson/American Express, Inc.,* 116 F.R.D. 246, 251 (E.D.Pa. 1987)(suggesting that "in some circumstances" permissive counterclaims must satisfy venue requirements; but rejecting challenge to venue in instant case).

31. *See, e.g., U.S. Philips Corp. v. Sears Roebuck & Co.,* 55 F.3d 592, 599 (Fed.Cir.1995), *cert. denied,* 516 U.S. 1010, 116 S.Ct. 567, 133 L.Ed.2d 492 (1995) (permissive counterclaim not asserted is not thereby barred in subsequent litigation).

32. *Reiter v. Cooper,* 507 U.S. 258, 262, 113 S.Ct. 1213, 1217, 122 L.Ed.2d 604 (1993)(holding that counterclaim mislabelled as defense should simply be treated as counterclaim).

33. *See, e.g., Employers Insurance of Wausau v. United States,* 764 F.2d 1572, 1576 (Fed.Cir. 1985)("[A] permissive counterclaim does not generate a . . . tolling period.").

RULE 13(c). COUNTERCLAIM EXCEEDING OPPOSING CLAIM

CORE CONCEPT

Rule 13(c) provides that: (1) counterclaims may be for any amount, irrespective of whether the amount sought in the counterclaim exceeds the amount sought in the other party's claim; and (2) counterclaims may seek kinds of relief not sought in the opposing party's claim. For example, if the opposing party's claim sought money damages only, the counterclaim could seek either money damages, equitable relief, or both money damages and equitable relief.

RULE 13(d). COUNTERCLAIMS AGAINST THE UNITED STATES

CORE CONCEPT

As a general rule, the United States and its officers and agencies are immune from suits in federal courts, unless the United States waives that sovereign immunity. Rule 13(d) expressly provides that the counterclaim provisions of Rule 13(a) and (b) do not alter the current law of sovereign immunity.[34]

APPLICATIONS

Waiver of Immunity

A decision by the United States to sue on a claim generally does not constitute a waiver of sovereign immunity as to counterclaims for amounts above those sums for which the United States is suing. This result applies even if the counterclaims arise from the same transaction or occurrence as the complaint brought by the United States.[35]

Setoffs

Some courts have permitted counterclaims against the United States where: the claim and counterclaim arise from the same transaction or occurrence; and the money sought is a setoff against the government's claim that will only reduce the government's recovery.[36]

RULE 13(e). COUNTERCLAIM MATURING OR ACQUIRED AFTER PLEADING

CORE CONCEPT

Rule 13(e) provides that if counterclaims mature or are acquired after a party has pleaded, the party may choose to assert them in a supplemental pleading, subject to the court's discretion.

34. *See, e.g., In the Matter of Armstrong,* 206 F.3d 465, 473 (5th Cir.2000) ("[T]he law is clear that a compulsory counterclaim shall not be used to expand claims against the United States beyond their limits as already established by law. See Fed.R.Civ.P. 13(d)."); *United States ex rel. Fallon v. Accudyne Corp.,* 921 F.Supp. 611 (W.D.Wis.1995)(limitations on waivers of sovereign immunity are enforceable against counterclaims; citing Rule 13(d)).

35. *See, e.g., United States v. Johnson,* 853 F.2d 619, 621 (8th Cir.1988)(so holding).

36. *See, e.g., United States v. Forma,* 42 F.3d 759, 765 (2d Cir.1994) (counterclaim permissible only to extent of reducing government's claim; barring affirmative relief).

APPLICATIONS

Procedure

A party seeking to assert a Rule 13(e) counterclaim must file a motion and supporting materials explaining the circumstances in which the counterclaim matured or was acquired.[37]

Party's Discretion

Rule 13(e) is permissive in nature, even if it arises from the same transaction or occurrence as the opposing party's claim. Thus, a party holding a counterclaim of the kind controlled by Rule 13(e) may assert it, subject to the court's permission, but is under no obligation to do so.

Judicial Discretion

If a party seeks to raise a Rule 13(e) counterclaim, the court retains discretion to refuse to hear the counterclaim in the pending action.[38] Generally, courts permit Rule 13(e) counterclaims where they will not confuse the trier of fact or where they will not unfairly prejudice other parties, particularly through excessively delaying the litigation.[39] Additionally, Rule 13(e) counterclaims that arise out of the same transaction or occurrence as the opposing party's claim are more likely to be heard in the pending litigation, than are claims that arise out of dissimilar transactions or occurrences.[40]

Jurisdiction

Rule 13(e) counterclaims must meet one of the bases of subject matter jurisdiction, such as federal question jurisdiction, diversity jurisdiction, or supplemental jurisdiction. If the Rule 13(e) counterclaim arises out of the same transaction or occurrence as the original claim, then it will likely satisfy supplemental jurisdiction. If not, the counterclaim will need an independent basis of jurisdiction. For a more detailed discussion of subject matter jurisdiction, see §§ 2.10–2.13.

Venue

There is no venue requirement for Rule 13(e) counterclaims.

RULE 13(f). OMITTED COUNTERCLAIM

CORE CONCEPT

Rule 13(f) permits assertion of counterclaims that were omitted through oversight, inadvertence, or excusable neglect, or that should be

37. *See, e.g., All West Pet Supply Co. v. Hill's Pet Products Division, Colgate–Palmolive Co.,* 152 F.R.D. 202, 204 (D.Kan.1993)(court has discretion to permit or reject supplemental counterclaim).

38. *See, e.g., id.*

39. *See, e.g., id.* (noting that in absence of factors indicating unfair prejudice to opponent, policy of liberally granting leave to file supplemental claims also applies to Rule 13(e) counterclaims).

40. *See, e.g., National Union Fire Insurance Co. of Pittsburgh v. Continental Illinois Corp.,* 113 F.R.D. 527, 530 (N.D.Ill.1986)("[W]hether the new counterclaim otherwise satisfies the Rule 13(a) requirements for a compulsory counterclaim bulks large in the exercise of the court's discretion.").

heard in the interest of justice. Rule 13(f) counterclaims are within the discretion of the court. Although counterclaims permitted under Rule 13(f) may be either permissive or compulsory, the most important effect of Rule 13(f) is to permit filing of compulsory counterclaims that might otherwise be barred.

APPLICATIONS

Procedure

A party seeking to file a counterclaim under Rule 13(f) should file a motion and supporting materials explaining the circumstances causing the delay as well as the reasons why it would now be just to permit the party to use Rule 13(f).[41]

Judicial Discretion

Courts generally permit assertion of counterclaims under Rule 13(f) in circumstances where the late filing does not unfairly prejudice an opposing party.[42]

Compulsory Counterclaims

Because they would be lost forever if not included, compulsory counterclaims are more likely to be permitted under Rule 13(f) than are permissive counterclaims. Permissive counterclaims may typically be sued upon in later suits, and are more likely to confuse the trier of fact if permitted in the pending litigation.[43]

RULE 13(g). CROSS–CLAIM AGAINST CO–PARTY

CORE CONCEPT

Rule 13(g) permits persons who are already parties to a suit to bring related claims against persons on the same side of the litigation. An essential difference between a cross-claim and a counterclaim is that cross-claims are suits against persons who had not, until the cross-claim was filed, been opponents of the person asserting the cross-claim.

41. *Pioneer Investment Services Co. v. Brunswick Associates Limited Partnership,* 507 U.S. 380, 392, n. 10, 113 S.Ct. 1489, 1497 n. 10, 123 L.Ed.2d 74 (1993)(noting that courts assess factors such as: good faith; extent of delay; and prejudice to opposing party).

42. *See, e.g., Fields v. Atchison, Topeka and Santa Fe Railway Co.,* 167 F.R.D. 462 (D.Kan. 1996)(factors to weigh in interest of justice under Rule 13(f) are: type of counterclaim; prejudice to opposing party; and delay of trial for additional discovery); *but see, Lone Star Steakhouse & Saloon, Inc. v. Alpha of Virginia, Inc.,* 43 F.3d 922, 940–41 (4th Cir.1995)(leave to file omitted counterclaim is normally granted freely when such leave is in the interest of justice; however, leave should not be granted when defendant had early information as to counterclaim, but waited nearly to the close of discovery to try to raise issue; delay and need for additional discovery would be unfair to opponent of proposed counterclaim). *See also, Triad Electric & Controls, Inc. v. Power Systems Engineering, Inc.,* 117 F.3d 180, 193–95 (5th Cir.1997) (Rule 13(f) affords court substantial discretion to add a counterclaim; but where counterclaim asserts fraud, particularity requirements of Rule 9(b) indicate that opponent of counterclaim cannot easily be assumed to have adequate notice of such a counterclaim unless Rule 9(b) is satisfied).

43. *See, e.g., Budd Co. v. Travelers Indemnity Co.,* 820 F.2d 787, 792 n. 3 (6th Cir. 1987)(counterclaims that are compulsory are treated more liberally under Rule 13(f)).

Counterclaims, by contrast, are suits against persons who have already sued the person asserting the counterclaim.

APPLICATIONS

Procedure

Cross-claims are typically raised in a responsive pleading.

Cross–Claims Are Always Permissive

Unlike compulsory counterclaims under Rule 13(a), Rule 13(g) does not create a category of compulsory cross-claims. Instead, under Rule 13(g), all cross-claims are permissive, and may therefore be asserted in the pending litigation or in a separate action.[44]

Same Transaction or Occurrence

Cross-claims must arise out of the same transaction or occurrence as the original action, or relate to the same property that is in dispute in the original action.[45] In this important sense cross-claims, though permissive, are fundamentally different from permissive counterclaims, which often arise from a transaction or occurrence that is different than the original action. The standard of same transaction or occurrence varies from court to court. The most liberal interpretation requires a logical relation between the cross-claim and the original action.[46] Other courts look to the degree of overlap between the evidence to be used in the cross-claim and the evidence relevant to the original action.[47]

Cross–Claims Against Co–Parties; Other Parties

Rule 13(g) provides that cross-claims may be brought only if at least one cross-claim defendant is a person already party to an action.[48] However, if a single cross-claim defendant is a party to the original action, additional persons may also be sued on the cross-claim, as provided by Rule 13(h)(discussed below).

44. *See, e.g., United States v. Confederate Acres Sanitary Sewage and Drainage System, Inc.,* 935 F.2d 796, 799 (6th Cir.1991)(Rule 13(g) makes cross-claims permissive). *But cf., Paramount Aviation Corp. v. Gruppo Agusta,* 178 F.3d 132 (3d Cir.1999), *cert. denied,* 528 U.S. 878, 120 S.Ct. 188, 145 L.Ed.2d 158 (1999) (observing that while cross-claims themselves are never compulsory, filing a cross-claim may make co-defendants into opposing parties, which might make a counterclaim on the cross-claim compulsory; not deciding, but suggesting that such counterclaims might never be compulsory if they were responses to cross-claims that merely sought contribution or indemnity).

45. *See, e.g., Federal Land Bank of St. Louis v. Cupples Brother,* 116 F.R.D. 63, 65 (E.D.Ark. 1987).

46. *See, e.g., Seattle Audubon Society v. Lyons,* 871 F.Supp. 1286, 1290 (W.D.Wash. 1994)(treating same transaction or occurrence as synonymous with "logical relationship" test).

47. *See, e.g., Danner v. Anskis,* 256 F.2d 123 (3d Cir.1958).

48. *See, e.g., In re Oil Spill by Amoco Cadiz off Coast of France on March 16, 1978,* 699 F.2d 909, 913 (7th Cir.1983), *cert. denied,* 464 U.S. 864, 104 S.Ct. 196, 78 L.Ed.2d 172 (1983)("[A] Rule 13(g) cross-claim will lie only against an existing defendant."); *Mauney v. Imperial Delivery Services, Inc.,* 865 F.Supp. 142, 153 (S.D.N.Y. 1994)(cross-claim cannot be filed against third-party defendant because cross-claims are filed between co-parties).

Comparison With Impleader

A key difference between Rule 13(g) and Rule 14 impleader is that Rule 13(g) requires that at least one cross-claim defendant be a party. Rule 14, by contrast, provides a means of joining persons who were not previously parties to a pending suit.[49]

Derivative Liability

A cross-claimant may seek either affirmative relief or compensation for any liability the cross-claimant may have as a result of claims already filed against the cross-claimant.

Subject Matter Jurisdiction

Cross-claims must meet the standards of either federal question jurisdiction, diversity jurisdiction, or supplemental jurisdiction. Moreover, the party asserting a counterclaim must include an allegation of facts demonstrating that the requirement of subject matter jurisdiction is met.[50] However, subject matter jurisdiction is usually not a problem with cross-claims; because Rule 13(g) requires that cross-claims arise out of the same transaction or occurrence as the original action, cross-claims that cannot meet the standards of federal question jurisdiction or diversity jurisdiction usually will nevertheless satisfy the requirements of supplemental jurisdiction.[51]

Personal Jurisdiction

Cross-claims must meet the requirements of personal jurisdiction. If the court in the original action has already acquired jurisdiction over the parties, it will normally also have jurisdiction over cross-claim defendants. If, however, jurisdiction is defective in the original action, it is possible that the cross-claim will suffer from similar jurisdictional defects. For a further discussion of jurisdiction over persons or things, see §§ 2.2–2.9.

Venue

Cross-claims need not satisfy venue requirements.[52]

49. *See, e.g., National Union Fire Insurance Co. of Pittsburgh v. Continental Illinois Corp.*, 658 F.Supp. 781, 794 (N.D.Ill.1987).

50. *McNutt v. General Motors Acceptance Corp.*, 298 U.S. 178, 189, 56 S.Ct. 780, 785, 80 L.Ed. 1135 (1936) ("[P]rerequisites to the exercise of jurisdiction ... are conditions which must be met by the party who seeks the exercise of jurisdiction in his favor. He must allege in his pleading the facts essential to show jurisdiction."). *Cf., e.g., Martin v. Franklin Capital corp.*, 251 F.3d 1284 (10th Cir.2001) (removal case; "As the parties invoking the federal court's jurisdiction in this case, defendants bear the burden of establishing that the requirements for the exercise of diversity jurisdiction are present.").

51. *See, e.g., Ryan ex rel. Ryan v. Schneider National Carriers, Inc.*, 263 F.3d 816, 819, 820 (8th Cir.2001) (per curiam) (addition of cross-claim against co-plaintiff that satisfies requirements of Rule 13(g) satisfies supplemental jurisdiction); *Meritor Savings Bank v. Camelback Canyon Investors*, 783 F.Supp. 455, 457 (D.Ariz. 1991)(permitting supplemental jurisdiction over cross-claim).

52. *See, e.g., Bredberg v. Long*, 778 F.2d 1285, 1288 (8th Cir.1985)(if venue is proper on original claims, there may be no venue objection to cross-claims).

Mislabelled Cross–Claims

Parties sometimes mistakenly identify cross-claims as counterclaims, and *vice versa.* Courts usually attach no significance to such errors, unless somehow they unfairly prejudice an opposing party.[53]

Statutes of Limitations: "Relation Back"

The precedent addressing whether statutes of limitations for cross-claims are tolled by the filing of the original action is unsettled, but some generalizations are possible. Cross-claims seeking "affirmative and independent relief" do not relate back to the original complaint. By contrast, cross-claims "in the nature of recoupment, indemnity, or contribution" will typically enjoy the benefit of relation back to the date of the filing of the original action.[54]

RULE 13(h). JOINDER OF ADDITIONAL PARTIES

CORE CONCEPT

Many times a counterclaim or cross-claim will require, for the just adjudication of the case, the joinder of persons who are not yet parties. Rule 13(h) expressly authorizes the use of Rules 19 and 20, governing joinder of persons, to achieve that end.

APPLICATIONS

Procedure

Although the law is not entirely settled, it appears that when counterclaimants or cross-claimants seek to join additional parties under Rule 13(h), they may simply make appropriate service on the parties to be joined and provide notice to those already parties. There appears to be no need to file a motion requesting leave to join the parties.[55]

Prerequisite of One Party

Rule 13(a), (b), and (g) provide that counterclaims and cross-claims cannot be sued upon unless at least one person being sued is already a party to the action. However, once one such person is sued on a counterclaim or cross-claim, Rule 13(h) permits joinder of other persons on that counterclaim or cross-claim, subject to the authority of Rules 19 and 20.[56]

53. *See, e.g., Schwab v. Erie Lackawanna Railroad Co.,* 438 F.2d 62, 64 (3d Cir. 1971)(mislabelling need not be fatal).

54. *See, e.g., Kansa Reinsurance Co. v. Congressional Mortgage Corp. of Texas,* 20 F.3d 1362, 1367–68 (5th Cir.1994), *cert. denied,* 526 U.S. 1158, 119 S.Ct. 2047, 144 L.Ed.2d 214 (1999)(making distinction between two categories of cross-claims; noting also that Rule 15(c), governing relation back of pleadings, does not automatically permit an untimely cross-claim to relate back simply because the cross-claim arose from the same transaction or occurrence).

55. *See, e.g., Northfield Insurance Co. v. Bender Shipbuilding & Repair Co.,* 122 F.R.D. 30 (S.D.Ala.1988)(1966 amendment to Rule 13(h) eliminated requirement to obtain judicial approval for joinder); *but see, Mountain States Sports, Inc. v. Sharman,* 353 F.Supp. 613, 618 (D.Utah 1972), *reversed on other grounds,* 548 F.2d 905 (10th Cir.1977) (general practice is to seek an order joining additional parties).

56. *See, e.g., Asset Allocation and Management Co. v. Western Employers Insurance Co.,* 892 F.2d 566, 574 (7th Cir.1989)(noting interplay of Rules 13(h) and 20).

Subject Matter Jurisdiction

Rule 13(h) claims must satisfy either federal question jurisdiction, diversity jurisdiction, or supplemental jurisdiction.[57] For a further discussion of subject matter jurisdiction, see §§ 2.10–2.13.

(1) *Claims by Original Plaintiff:* If the counterclaim or cross-claim is part of a case based solely on diversity of citizenship, and was filed by someone who was a plaintiff on the original claim, supplemental jurisdiction is not available as to new parties joined under either Rule 19 or Rule 20.[58]

(2) *Dissimilar Claims or Occurrences:* If a counterclaim does not arise from the same transaction or occurrence as the original action, Rule 13(h) may usually be employed only where the court has federal question jurisdiction or diversity jurisdiction over the counterclaim.[59] For a further discussion of subject matter jurisdiction, see §§ 2.10–2.13.

Personal Jurisdiction

Additional parties may be joined under Rule 13(h) only if they are subject to the jurisdiction of the court.[60] For a further discussion of personal jurisdiction, see §§ 2.3–2.7.

Venue

Venue requirements do not apply to counterclaims or cross-claims in which Rule 13(h) joinder is sought.[61]

RULE 13(i). SEPARATE TRIALS; SEPARATE JUDGMENTS

CORE CONCEPT

Because additional claims added to a case through Rule 13(a), (b), and (g) have substantial potential for confusing the trier of fact or delaying adjudication of the original claims, Rule 13(i) authorizes the court to hold separate hearings, as provided by Rule 42(b), and/or enter separate judgments, as provided by Rule 54(b).

APPLICATIONS

Judicial Discretion

Courts have substantial discretion to order separate trials and enter separate judgments, and the decision to process claims separately is not normally disturbed on appeal.[62]

57. *But see, Rayman v. Peoples Savings Corp.,* 735 F.Supp. 842, 854 (N.D.Ill.1990) (noting, however, that compulsory counterclaims or cross-claims will usually satisfy supplemental jurisdiction).

58. 28 U.S.C.A. § 1367(b).

59. *See, e.g., Federal Deposit Insurance Corp. v. La Rambla Shopping Center, Inc.,* 791 F.2d 215, 220 (1st Cir.1986) (noting that counterclaims arising from unrelated transactions do not usually qualify for supplemental jurisdiction, and must have independent basis for jurisdiction).

60. *See, e.g., Cordner v. Metropolitan Life Ins. Co.,* 234 F.Supp. 765, 769 (S.D.N.Y.1964) (Rule 13(h) requires jurisdiction over parties to be joined).

61. *See, e.g., Lesnik v. Public Industrials Corp.,* 144 F.2d 968, 977 (2d Cir.1944) (so holding).

62. *See, e.g., McLaughlin v. State Farm Mutual Automobile Insurance Co.,* 30 F.3d 861, 870

Jurisdiction

Rule 13(i) is subject to the prerequisite that the court have jurisdiction over the claims and parties before it.[63]

ADDITIONAL RESEARCH REFERENCES

Wright & Miller, *Federal Practice and Procedure* §§ 1401–37.

C.J.S. Federal Civil Procedure §§ 309–319 et seq.

West's Key No. Digests, Federal Civil Procedure ⚷771–786.

(7th Cir.1994), *cert. denied,* 513 U.S. 1149, 115 S.Ct. 1098, 130 L.Ed.2d 1066 (1995)(noting discretion of trial court in deciding whether to bifurcate trial).

63. *See, e.g., Chattanooga Corp. v. Klingler,* 621 F.Supp. 756 (E.D.Tenn.1985).

RULE 14

THIRD-PARTY PRACTICE

(a) When Defendant May Bring in Third Party. At any time after commencement of the action a defending party, as a third-party plaintiff, may cause a summons and complaint to be served upon a person not a party to the action who is or may be liable to the third-party plaintiff for all or part of the plaintiff's claim against the third-party plaintiff. The third-party plaintiff need not obtain leave to make the service if the third-party plaintiff files the third-party complaint not later than 10 days after serving the original answer. Otherwise the third-party plaintiff must obtain leave on motion upon notice to all parties to the action. The person served with the summons and third-party complaint, hereinafter called the third-party defendant, shall make any defenses to the third-party plaintiff's claim as provided in Rule 12 and any counterclaims against the third-party plaintiff and cross-claims against other third-party defendants as provided in Rule 13. The third-party defendant may assert against the plaintiff any defenses which the third-party plaintiff has to the plaintiff's claim. The third-party defendant may also assert any claim against the plaintiff arising out of the transaction or occurrence that is the subject matter of the plaintiff's claim against the third-party plaintiff. The plaintiff may assert any claim against the third-party defendant arising out of the transaction or occurrence that is the subject matter of the plaintiff's claim against the third-party plaintiff, and the third-party defendant thereupon shall assert any defenses as provided in Rule 12 and any counterclaims and cross-claims as provided in Rule 13. Any party may move to strike the third-party claim, or for its severance or separate trial. A third-party defendant may proceed under this rule against any person not a party to the action who is or may be liable to the third-party defendant for all or part of the claim made in the action against the third-party defendant. The third-party complaint, if within the admiralty and maritime jurisdiction, may be in rem against a vessel, cargo, or other property subject to admiralty or maritime process in rem, in which case references in this rule to the summons include the warrant of arrest, and references to the third-party plaintiff or defendant include, where appropriate, a person who asserts a right under Supplemental Rule C(6)(b)(i) in the property arrested.

(b) When Plaintiff May Bring in Third Party. When a counterclaim is asserted against a plaintiff, the plaintiff may cause a third party to be brought in under circumstances which under this rule would entitle a defendant to do so.

(c) Admiralty and Maritime Claims. When a plaintiff asserts an admiralty or maritime claim within the meaning of Rule 9(h), the defendant or person who asserts a right under Supplemental Rule C(6)(b)(i), as a third-party plaintiff, may bring in a third-party defendant who may be wholly or partly liable, either to the plaintiff or to the third-party plaintiff, by way of remedy over, contribution, or otherwise on account of the same transaction, occurrence, or series of transactions or occurrences. In such a case the third-party plaintiff may also demand judgment against the third-party defendant in favor of the plaintiff, in which event the third-party defendant shall make any defenses to the claim of the plaintiff as well as to that of the third-party plaintiff in the manner provided in Rule 12 and the action shall proceed as if the plaintiff had commenced it against the third-party defendant as well as the third-party plaintiff.

[Amended effective March 19, 1948; July 1, 1963; July 1, 1966; August 1, 1987; April 17, 2000, effective December 1, 2000.]

AUTHORS' COMMENTARY ON RULE 14

PURPOSE AND SCOPE

Rule 14 permits parties who are defending against claims to join other persons, not yet parties, who may be obligated to reimburse the party defending the claim for some or all of that party's liability. The decision to seek joinder, or to hold the claim for assertion in later litigation, belongs to the party defending on the claim: Rule 14 contains no requirement similar to Rule 13(a), which makes compulsory the assertion of certain counterclaims. Typically, a person is joined because that person, as a guarantor of some transaction, has an obligation to indemnify a party if the party is forced to pay on a claim. Third-party practice is also commonly employed when an alleged tortfeasor seeks contribution from others who may also be liable but whom the plaintiff has not sued. The Rule also describes the rights of persons who are joined as third-party defendants to claim and defend against the original plaintiffs and defendants, as well as to join still other persons who may be liable to the third parties.

NOTE: The labels necessitated by Rule 14 are superficially complex, but follow a consistent pattern. A party who seeks to join another person under Rule 14 is called a third-party plaintiff. The person joined is called a third-party defendant. Thus, if a defendant in a pending action sought to join someone not yet a party under Rule 14, the defendant would carry the additional title of third-party plaintiff, and the person joined would be a third-party defendant. If the third-party defendant sought, in turn, to join someone else, the person joined would be a fourth-party defendant, and the third-party defendant would carry the additional title of fourth-party plaintiff.

RULE 14(a). WHEN DEFENDANT MAY BRING IN THIRD PARTY

CORE CONCEPT

Rule 14(a) describes the power of defendants to implead third parties. The Rule also describes the defenses available to third-party defendants, as well as the circumstances in which third-party defendants may claim against plaintiffs and defendants. Finally, Rule 14(a) authorizes third-party defendants to implead potential fourth-party defendants who may be liable for some or all of any claim the third-party defendants might have to pay.

APPLICATIONS

Third–Party Plaintiff's Discretion

Where applicable, a party's right to implead under Rule 14 is optional. There is no obligation to implead third parties.[1]

Who May Be Impleaded

Only persons not already parties may be impleaded.[2] This provision of Rule 14 stands in contrast to provisions of Rule 13, governing counterclaims and cross-claims, in which at least one of the persons sued on a counterclaim or cross-claim must already be a party to the case.

Procedure

A third-party defendant is joined upon service of a proper summons and third-party complaint.[3] For purposes of impleader under Rule 14, Rule 4(k) permits service on a third-party defendant found within 100 miles of the place from where the summons issued–without regard to whether such service takes place within another state.[4] This is a small but sometimes crucial expansion of personal jurisdiction in the context of Rule 14.

Time; Leave of Court

Rule 14(a) permits service of a third-party complaint "at any time." However, a party may file a third-party complaint without obtaining

1. *See, e.g., Fernandez v. Corporacion Insular De Seguros,* 79 F.3d 207 (1st Cir.1996)(no obligation to implead; decision to forego impleader does not require instruction that jury is authorized to draw adverse inference).

2. *See, e.g., Mauney v. Imperial Delivery Services, Inc.,* 865 F.Supp. 142, 153 (S.D.N.Y. 1994)(under Rule 14, third-party suit cannot be filed against a third-party defendant who is already a party).

3. *See, e.g., Jackson v. Southeastern Pennsylvania Transportation Authority,* 727 F.Supp. 965, 966 (E.D.Pa.1990)(by its terms, Rule 14(a) authorizes service of third-party complaints).

4. Fed.R.Civ.P. 4(k).

leave of court only in the ten-day period following that party's service of an answer to a claim.[5] Thereafter, a third-party complaint may be filed only upon motion, served on all parties, and after obtaining leave of court.[6] Generally, courts permit assertion of impleader claims unless they are raised so late in a pending suit that they unreasonably prejudice persons who are already parties.[7]

Relationship to Pending Claims

Rule 14(a) explicitly provides that claims against third-party defendants must relate to claims pending against the third-party plaintiff and must depend in some degree on the outcome of the original action. Rule 14(a) provides no authorization to assert claims against third-party plaintiffs that are unrelated to claims already pending.[8]

Affirmative Relief; Derivative Liability and Rule 18

Although Rule 14(a)'s literal language might seem to limit third-party practice to claims for reimbursement or compensation,[9] a minority of courts have used Rule 18(a), governing joinder of claims, to permit third-party claims even when the amount sought is greater than that for which the third-party plaintiff might be liable on the original claim.[10] However, it appears settled that once a party is properly impleaded under Rule 14, that party may also be sued for affirmative relief under Rule 18.[11]

Defenses Available

Third-party defendants are entitled to raise their own defenses against the third-party plaintiff. The explicit language of Rule 14(a)

5. *See, e.g., Smith v. Local 819 I.B.T. Pension Plan,* 291 F.3d 236 n. 2 (2d Cir.2002) (defendant's third-party complaint filed within ten days of serving answer, so no need to obtain leave of court).

6. *See, e.g., Raytheon Aircraft Credit Corp. v. Pal Air International, Inc.,* 923 F.Supp. 1408 (D.Kan.1996)(no obligation to obtain leave of court when impleader is brought within 10 days of answer).

7. *See, e.g., New York v. Solvent Chemical Co.,* 875 F.Supp. 1015 (W.D.N.Y.1995)(impleader allowed more than 10 years after original complaint was filed; case was still in discovery, and third-party defendant still had good opportunity to prepare case). *See also Marseilles Hydro Power, L.L.C. v. Marseilles Land and Water Co.,* 299 F.3d 643, 650 (7th Cir.2002) (suit filed in February; counterclaim and third-party complaint filed in June; held, "clearly wrong" for district court to assert that third-party plaintiff waited too long to file third-party complaint; "We cannot for the life of us see what procedural economy could be gained by forcing [third-party plaintiff] to sue [third-party defendant] in a separate action or how the plaintiff could be prejudiced.").

8. *See, e.g., United States v. Olavarrieta,* 812 F.2d 640, 643 (11th Cir.1987), *cert. denied,* 484 U.S. 851, 108 S.Ct. 152, 98 L.Ed.2d 107 (1987) (Rule 14 requires that outcome of impleader must at least partly depend on outcome of original suit; "Rule 14(a) does not allow the defendant to assert a separate and independent claim even though the claim arises out of the same general set of facts as the main claim.").

9. *See, e.g., Federal Deposit Insurance Corp. v. Bathgate,* 27 F.3d 850, 872 (3d Cir.1994) (limiting Rule 14(a) to claims based on derivative liability).

10. *See, e.g., King Fisher Marine Service, Inc. v. 21st Phoenix Corp.,* 893 F.2d 1155, 1158 (10th Cir.1990), *cert. denied,* 496 U.S. 912, 110 S.Ct. 2603, 110 L.Ed.2d 283 (1990) (permitting joinder of unrelated third-party claims, provided that jurisdiction and Rule 14 are already satisfied).

11. *Id.*

also authorizes third-party defendants to assert defenses that the third-party plaintiff may have against the original claim.[12]

Counterclaims by Third–Party Defendants

Rule 14(a) authorizes third-party defendants to file claims against third-party plaintiffs,[13] consistent with the requirements of Rule 13. Applying Rule 13 to such claims means that, when the counterclaims satisfy the requirements of Rule 13(a), governing compulsory counterclaims, they must be filed in the pending action or they are waived.

Cross–Claims by Third–Party Defendants

If more than one third-party defendant has been impleaded, Rule 14(a) authorizes the third-party defendants to file claims against one another, subject to the requirements of Rule 13. Because Rule 13(g) is permissive, such claims may be filed or may be retained for subsequent litigation. Additionally, because Rule 13(g) only permits cross-claims that arise out of the same transaction or occurrence as the original claims, third-party claims must relate to the transaction or occurrence underlying the original claims by the third-party plaintiff.

Claims Against Plaintiffs

Rule 14(a) permits a third-party defendant to make claims against an original plaintiff that arise out of the same transaction or occurrence as the claims originally filed by the plaintiff. Such claims are permissive, in that they may either be raised or retained for subsequent litigation. Note, however, that if an original plaintiff has already sued the third-party defendant in the litigation, the third-party defendant's claims against the plaintiff may be compulsory counterclaims subject to Rule 13(a). In such a circumstance, a third-party defendant's claims against a plaintiff are not permissive. Counterclaims against plaintiffs are discussed below.

Plaintiffs' Claims Against Third–Party Defendants

Rule 14(a) also permits plaintiffs to sue persons joined as third-party defendants, provided that the claim arises out of the same transaction or occurrence as the original claims against the defendants.[14] The language of Rule 14(a) makes clear that assertion of such claims is discretionary, and a plaintiff may choose to retain the claims for subsequent litigation.[15]

12. Fed.R.Civ.P. 14(a).

13. *Cf., Thomas v. Barton Lodge II, Ltd.*, 174 F.3d 636 (5th Cir.1999) (observing that some courts prohibit third-party defendants' suits against original defendants who are not third-party plaintiffs; concluding that such prohibitions are erroneous, and permitting such claims).

14. *United States ex rel. S. Prawer & Co. v. Fleet Bank of Maine*, 24 F.3d 320, 328 (1st Cir.1994) (Rule 14(a) requires that plaintiff's claim against third-party defendant arose from same transaction or occurrence as claim against original defendant). *Cf., Project Hope v. M/V Ibn Sina*, 250 F.3d 67 (2d Cir.2001) (apparent dicta; if third-party defendant "is effectively on notice that it will be held liable on the plaintiff's claims and the two proceed against one another in an adverse manner," plaintiff need not formally amend complaint to include causes of action against impleaded party).

15. *See, e.g., Atchison, Topeka and Santa Fe Railway Co. v. Hercules, Inc.*, 146 F.3d 1071, 1073 (9th Cir.1998) ("Rule 14 makes claims by a

Third–Party Defendants' Counterclaims Against Plaintiffs

If a plaintiff sues a third-party defendant, any counterclaims the third-party defendant may have are governed by Rule 13.

Third–Party Defendants' Cross–Claims Upon Suit by Plaintiffs

Just as Rule 14(a) permits third-party defendants to cross-claim against one another after being joined by a third-party plaintiff, the Rule also permits third-party defendants to cross-claim against one another if one or more third-party defendant is sued by a plaintiff. Rule 14(a) expressly provides that such cross-claims are regulated by Rule 13.

Severance; Separate Trials

Third-party practice has obvious potential for complexity and for confusing a trier of fact. Rule 14(a) therefore provides that *any* party to the litigation may move to strike or sever the claims. Courts have substantial discretion when deciding such motions.[16]

Fourth–Party Practice

Rule 14(a) grants third-party defendants the same power to implead as is enjoyed by the defendants. Thus, third-party defendants may join persons not yet parties who may be liable to the third-party defendants for part or all of the liability the third-party defendants may have to the third-party plaintiffs.

Rights of Fourth–Party Defendants

Although not explicitly addressed in Rule 14(a), it seems settled that fourth-party defendants enjoy all the rights and authority the Rule provides to third-party defendants, including availability of defenses, counterclaims, cross-claims, and impleader of additional persons.[17]

Admiralty and Maritime Cases; In Rem Jurisdiction

Rule 14(a) provides that third-party complaints arising under the admiralty jurisdiction of the court may be in rem actions against maritime property. In such cases, the summons used in conventional litigation may be supplanted by admiralty process, and the terminology for third-party plaintiffs and defendants may conform to admiralty practice.

Subject Matter Jurisdiction

Every third-party claim must fall within at least one of the forms of subject matter jurisdiction: *e.g.*, federal question jurisdiction; diversity jurisdiction; or supplemental jurisdiction. Because third-party claims

plaintiff against a third-party defendant permissive, not compulsory.").

16. *See, e.g., Williams v. Ford Motor Credit Co.*, 627 F.2d 158 (8th Cir.1980)(noting that trial court has substantial, but not unlimited, discretion to dismiss a third-party complaint).

17. *See, e.g., Garnay, Inc. v. M/V Lindo Maersk*, 816 F.Supp. 888 (S.D.N.Y.1993) (processing fourth-party complaint under same jurisdictional standards as any third-party complaint).

of necessity are closely related to the original claims between the plaintiff and defendant, subject matter jurisdiction can usually be obtained under supplemental jurisdiction even in the absence of federal question jurisdiction or diversity jurisdiction.[18] However, an important exception to that generalization exists when the third-party claim is asserted by a plaintiff. 28 U.S.C.A. § 1367(b), governing restrictions on supplemental jurisdiction, expressly provides that when the original claims in the case are based solely on diversity jurisdiction, suits by plaintiffs against persons made parties under Rule 14 may not be founded on supplemental jurisdiction.[19] For a further discussion of subject matter jurisdiction, see §§ 2.10–2.13.

Personal Jurisdiction; Service of Process

Every third-party claim must also satisfy requirements of jurisdiction over persons and things.[20] For a further discussion of such jurisdiction, see §§ 2.2–2.9. For service of process on parties joined under Rule 14, a special provision in Rule 4(k)(1)(B) provides a sometimes useful extension of normal limits on service.[21] Rule 4 is discussed elsewhere in this text.

Venue

Requirements of venue do not apply to claims asserted under Rule 14.[22]

RULE 14(b). WHEN PLAINTIFF MAY BRING IN THIRD PARTY

CORE CONCEPT

Rule 14(b) provides that if a plaintiff is the subject of a counterclaim, the 0plaintiff may join third parties who may be liable for part or all of that claim, in the same manner that Rule 14(a) authorizes defendants to join third parties.

18. *See, e.g., Grimes v. Mazda North American Operations,* 355 F.3d 566, 572 (6th Cir. 2004) (third-party claim for contribution falls within scope of supplemental jurisdiction if "common nucleus" requirement is met); *LaSalle National Trust, N.A. v. Schaffner,* 818 F.Supp. 1161, 1164–65 (N.D.Ill.1993)(observing that when requirements of Rule 14(a) are met, requirements of § 1367 will also typically be satisfied). *See also Spring City Corp. v. American Buildings Co.,* 193 F.3d 165, 169 (3d Cir.1999) ("[A] third-party defendant joined under [Rule 14] does not become a defendant as against the original plaintiff, so that federal jurisdiction is not destroyed where those parties are citizens of the same state.").

19. *See, e.g., Grimes v. Mazda North American Operations,* 355 F.3d 566, 572 (§ 1367(b) is intended to prevent original plaintiffs, "but not defendants or third parties – from circumventing the requirements of diversity"); *Herrick Co. v. SCS Communications, Inc.,* 251 F.3d 315 n. 7 (2d Cir.2001) (generally in diversity cases, there is "no supplemental jurisdiction over claims by plaintiffs against persons made parties under Fed. R. Civ. P. 14"). *But see Ryan ex rel. Ryan v. Schneider National Carriers, Inc.,* 263 F.3d 816, 820 (8th Cir.2001) (permitting supplemental jurisdiction over third-party complaint brought by some plaintiffs against co-plaintiff; holding that co-plaintiff was not made party by other plaintiffs under, *inter alia,* Rule 20).

20. *See, e.g., Rodd v. Region Construction Co.,* 783 F.2d 89 (7th Cir.1986).

21. *See, e.g., ESAB Group v. Centricut, Inc.,* 126 F.3d 617, 622 (4th Cir.1997), *cert. denied,* 523 U.S. 1048, 118 S.Ct. 1364, 140 L.Ed.2d 513 (1998) (so noting).

22. *See, e.g., Gundle Lining Construction Corp. v. Adams County Asphalt, Inc.,* 85 F.3d 201 (5th Cir.1996)(Rule 14 claims are not subject to venue requirements).

APPLICATIONS

Plaintiff as Counterclaim Defendant

A plaintiff may not join persons under Rule 14 until the plaintiff has been sued on a counterclaim, and then only on third-party claims related to the counterclaim. Thus, if a plaintiff sued a defendant on a single count, and the defendant counterclaimed on an unrelated count, the plaintiff would be entitled to employ Rule 14 to implead third-party defendants.[23]

Applicability of Rule 14(a) to Plaintiff's Third–Party Claims

Once a plaintiff has been served with a counterclaim, Rule 14(b) provides that the plaintiff may employ third-party practice as to that counterclaim in the same manner that Rule 14(a) makes third-party practice available to a defendant.[24]

Subject Matter Jurisdiction; Restraints on Supplemental Jurisdiction

If the original cause of action in the case is based solely on diversity of citizenship, a plaintiff's third-party claims must satisfy either federal question jurisdiction or diversity jurisdiction. Title 28 U.S.C.A. § 1367(b), governing restraints on the use of supplemental jurisdiction, expressly provides that the court has no supplemental jurisdiction over claims by plaintiffs against persons made parties under Rule 14.[25] For a further discussion of subject matter jurisdiction, see §§ 2.10–2.13.

Personal Jurisdiction

A plaintiff's third-party claims must satisfy requirements of jurisdiction over persons and things. For a further discussion of such jurisdiction, see §§ 2.2–2.9.

RULE 14(c). ADMIRALTY AND MARITIME CLAIMS

CORE CONCEPT

Rule 14(c) provides that when the original cause of action arose under the court's admiralty jurisdiction, the defendant may join third persons by alleging either that: they are liable to reimburse the defendant for some or all of the defendant's liability, or that the third persons are liable directly to the plaintiff. This expands the general practice of impleader under Rule 14(a), where a defendant may implead only to establish that the person joined is liable to the defendant, and may not implead by alleging that the person to be joined is liable directly to the plaintiff.[26] The practical result of this feature of Rule

23. *See, e.g., Chase Manhattan Bank, N.A. v. Aldridge,* 906 F.Supp. 866, 867 (S.D.N.Y.1995) (once plaintiff is sued on a counterclaim, Rule 14(b) affords plaintiff same impleader powers provided to defendant by Rule 14(a)).

24. *See, e.g., Powell, Inc. v. Abney,* 83 F.R.D. 482, 485 (S.D.Tex.1979)("Rule 14(b) . . . places a plaintiff in the same position as a defendant under Rule 14(a) when a counterclaim is filed.").

25. *See, e.g., Guaranteed Systems, Inc. v. American National Can Co.,* 842 F.Supp. 855 (M.D.N.C.1994)(clear language of § 1367(b) prohibits use of supplemental jurisdiction by plaintiff, where original suit is based on diversity).

26. *See, e.g., Spring City Corp. v. American Buildings Co.,* 193 F.3d 165, 169 (3d Cir.1999) ("[A] third-party defendant joined under [Rule

14(c) is that the third person becomes a co-defendant in the original action, rather than a third-party defendant.[27]

APPLICATIONS

Demand for Judgment

In order to designate an impleaded third-party defendant as a defendant to the plaintiff's original complaint, the literal language of Rule 14(c) appears to require that the third-party complaint "demand judgment against the third-party defendant in favor of the plaintiff." The precise meaning of this language is not entirely free from doubt. However, while there is some authority indicating that the third-party complaint must specifically demand judgment in that precise way, the greater weight of authority is that the requirement of Rule 14(c) should be liberally construed. Thus, clear language intending to implead third-party defendants as co-defendants to the original complaint satisfies the requirement of Rule 14(c).[28]

Applicability of Rule 14(a)

Beyond the special provision of Rule 14(c) that may make the third party a co-defendant, Rule 14(c) impleader actions generally proceed as though controlled by relevant provisions of Rule 14(a).[29]

Prerequisite of Rule 9(h)

By its terms, Rule 14(c) is available only when the plaintiff has asserted a claim "within the meaning of Rule 9(h)."[30]

14(a)] does not become a defendant as against the original plaintiff.").

27. *See, e.g., LeBlanc v. Cleveland,* 198 F.3d 353, 355 (2d Cir.1999) ("Pursuant to Rule 14(c) ... third-party complaints allowed the case to proceed as if [plaintiffs] had sued [the impleaded third party] as well as [the original defendants]."); *Galt G/S v. Hapag–Lloyd AG,* 60 F.3d 1370, 1374 n. 2 (9th Cir.1995)(noting distinction between Rule 14(a) and (c)). *But see Texaco Exploration and Production Co. v. AmClyde Engineered Products Co.,* 243 F.3d 906, 910 (5th Cir.2001) (statutory right to enforce contractual arbitration provision overrides liberal joinder provision of Rule 14(c) when the two provisions are in conflict).

28. *See, e.g., Royal Insurance Co. of America v. Southwest Marine,* 194 F.3d 1009, 1018 (9th Cir.1999) (collecting cases; also noting that while third-party complaints in instant case did not specifically demand judgment against third parties in favor of plaintiff, both complaints made specific and repeated references to Rule 14(c) and to defendants' alleged liability to plaintiff).

29. *See, e.g., Rosario v. American Export–Isbrandtsen Lines,* 531 F.2d 1227, 1231–32 (3d Cir.1976), *cert. denied sub nom., Rosario v. United States,* 429 U.S. 857, 97 S.Ct. 156, 50 L.Ed.2d 135 (1976) (noting that apart from special provision, Rule 14(c) does not operate exclusive of Rule 14(a)). *See also Greenwell v. Aztar Indiana Gaming Corp.,* 268 F.3d 486, 493–94 (7th Cir. 2001), *cert. denied,* 535 U.S. 1034, 122 S.Ct. 1790, 152 L.Ed.2d 649 (2002) (if plaintiff does not choose to notify opponent and court that plaintiff chooses to prosecute a claim as an admiralty claim that qualifies for both admiralty jurisdiction and ordinary civil jurisdiction, case will proceed under ordinary civil rules, and special admiralty provisions will not apply). *Royal Insurance Co. of America v. Southwest Marine,* 194 F.3d 1009, 1019 (9th Cir.1999) (once a direct relationship exists between plaintiff and third-party defendants pursuant to Rule 14(c), plaintiff must assert its claims directly against the third-party defendants and they must answer the complaint; however, where third-party defendants have sufficient notice of lawsuit from original complaint, plaintiff had no duty to amend original complaint to assert claim against them).

30. *See, e.g., Foulk v. Donjon Marine Co.,* 144 F.3d 252 (3d Cir.1998).

Subject Matter Jurisdiction

Persons impleaded under the special provision of Rule 14(c) will generally be subject to the admiralty jurisdiction of the court.[31]

Personal Jurisdiction

Persons impleaded under Rule 14(c) must be within either the personal jurisdiction, quasi in rem jurisdiction, or in rem jurisdiction of the court. Because in rem jurisdiction is generally available in admiralty practice, however, jurisdictional requirements may usually be satisfied without difficulty.

Venue

Venue requirements do not generally apply to claims asserted under Rule 14.[32]

ADDITIONAL RESEARCH REFERENCES

Wright & Miller, *Federal Practice and Procedure* §§ 1441–65.

C.J.S. Federal Civil Procedure §§ 117–126 et seq., 318.

West's Key No. Digests, Federal Civil Procedure ⚷281–293.

31. *See, e.g., Harrison v. Glendel Drilling Co.,* 679 F.Supp. 1413, 1417 (W.D.La.1988)(Rule 14(c) can be invoked only in admiralty cases).

32. *See, e.g., Gundle Lining Construction Corp. v. Adams County Asphalt, Inc.,* 85 F.3d 201 (5th Cir.1996)(Rule 14 claims are not subject to venue requirements).

RULE 15

AMENDED AND SUPPLEMENTAL PLEADINGS

(a) Amendments. A party may amend the party's pleading once as a matter of course at any time before a responsive pleading is served or, if the pleading is one to which no responsive pleading is permitted and the action has not been placed upon the trial calendar, the party may so amend it at any time within 20 days after it is served. Otherwise a party may amend the party's pleading only by leave of court or by written consent of the adverse party; and leave shall be freely given when justice so requires. A party shall plead in response to an amended pleading within the time remaining for response to the original pleading or within 10 days after service of the amended pleading, whichever period may be the longer, unless the court otherwise orders.

(b) Amendments to Conform to the Evidence. When issues not raised by the pleadings are tried by express or implied consent of the parties, they shall be treated in all respects as if they had been raised in the pleadings. Such amendment of the pleadings as may be necessary to cause them to conform to the evidence and to raise these issues may be made upon motion of any party at any time, even after judgment; but failure so to amend does not affect the result of the trial of these issues. If evidence is objected to at the trial on the ground that it is not within the issues made by the pleadings, the court may allow the pleadings to be amended and shall do so freely when the presentation of the merits of the action will be subserved thereby and the objecting party fails to satisfy the court that the admission of such evidence would prejudice the party in maintaining the party's action or defense upon the merits. The court may grant a continuance to enable the objecting party to meet such evidence.

(c) Relation Back of Amendments. An amendment of a pleading relates back to the date of the original pleading when

(1) relation back is permitted by the law that provides the statute of limitations applicable to the action, or

(2) the claim or defense asserted in the amended pleading arose out of the conduct, transaction, or occurrence set forth or attempted to be set forth in the original pleading, or

(3) the amendment changes the party or the naming of the party against whom a claim is asserted if the foregoing provision (2) is satisfied and, within the period provided by Rule 4(m) for

service of the summons and complaint, the party to be brought in by amendment (A) has received such notice of the institution of the action that the party will not be prejudiced in maintaining a defense on the merits, and (B) knew or should have known that, but for a mistake concerning the identity of the proper party, the action would have been brought against the party.

The delivery or mailing of process to the United States Attorney, or United States Attorney's designee, or the Attorney General of the United States, or an agency or officer who would have been a proper defendant if named, satisfies the requirement of subparagraphs (A) and (B) of this paragraph (3) with respect to the United States or any agency or officer thereof to be brought into the action as a defendant.

(d) Supplemental Pleadings. Upon motion of a party the court may, upon reasonable notice and upon such terms as are just, permit the party to serve a supplemental pleading setting forth transactions or occurrences or events which have happened since the date of the pleading sought to be supplemented. Permission may be granted even though the original pleading is defective in its statement of a claim for relief or defense. If the court deems it advisable that the adverse party plead to the supplemental pleading, it shall so order, specifying the time therefor.

[Amended January 21, 1963, effective July 1, 1963; February 28, 1966, effective July 1, 1966; March 2, 1987, effective August 1, 1987; April 30, 1991, effective December 1, 1991; amended by Pub.L. 102–198, § 11, December 9, 1991, 105 Stat. 1626; amended April 22, 1993, effective December 1, 1993.]

AUTHORS' COMMENTARY ON RULE 15

PURPOSE AND SCOPE

Rule 15 governs the circumstances in which parties who have already pleaded in a case will be permitted to amend such pleadings. The Rule also provides the circumstances in which parties will be allowed to file new pleadings describing events that have occurred since the original pleadings were filed.

RULE 15(a). AMENDMENTS

CORE CONCEPT

Rule 15(a) provides an automatic right to amend pleadings a single time before a response is filed or, if no response is required, within 20 days after the original pleading to be amended was served, provided that the case has not been placed on the court's trial calendar. Otherwise, a party must seek leave of court or permission of the opposing party to amend pleadings. The Rule also governs time limits in which a party served with an amended pleading must file a responsive pleading to the amendment.

NOTE: On some occasions an amended pleading may be feasible under Rule 15(a), but the effects of the pleading will be restricted by Rule 15(c). Rule 15(c) determines whether an amended pleading will be treated as though it was filed on the date of the original pleading or on the date of filing. When the timing of a pleading (particularly a claim for relief) is at issue, attorneys should consult both Rule 15(a) and Rule 15(c).

APPLICATIONS

Amendment of Right

A party may amend a pleading without leave of court or consent of opposing parties *once,* under either of two circumstances. First, a pleading may be amended of right if the amendment is filed before receipt of a responsive pleading to the earlier, unamended version of the pleading.[1] Alternatively, if the pleading to be amended is one requiring no responsive pleading, and the action has not yet been placed on the court's trial calendar, Rule 15(a) expressly provides for an amendment of right if the amendment is filed within 20 days after service of the previous version of the pleading.

Motions and Rule 15(a)

Motions are not pleadings, as Rule 7(a) and (b) makes clear. A motion filed in opposition to a pleading is therefore not a responsive pleading within the meaning of Rule 15(a). Thus, if a plaintiff's complaint was opposed only by a Rule 12(b)(6) motion to dismiss for failure to state a claim for which relief may be granted, the plaintiff could amend the complaint as of right because the complaint had not yet evoked a responsive pleading.[2]

1. *See, e.g., Thompson v. Carter,* 284 F.3d 411, 415 n. 2 (2d Cir.2002) (motion to dismiss is not a responsive pleading and therefore does not, in the absence of a responsive pleading, terminate a plaintiff's right to amend a complaint); *Washington v. New York City Board of Estimate,* 709 F.2d 792, 795 (2d Cir.1983), *cert. denied,* 464 U.S. 1013, 104 S.Ct. 537, 78 L.Ed.2d 717 (1983)(when defendant has not yet answered complaint, plaintiff's first amendment of complaint is as of right). *But see, Duda v. Board of Education of Franklin Park Public School District No. 84,* 133 F.3d 1054, 1057 (7th Cir.1998) (court may reject even an amendment filed prior to receipt of responsive pleading if "examination of the proposed complaint makes clear that it does not cure the deficiencies of the original pleading and the amended complaint is doomed not to survive a motion to dismiss").

2. *See, e.g., Shaver v. Operating Engineers Local 428 Pension Trust Fund,* 332 F.3d 1198 (9th Cir.2003) (motion to dismiss not responsive pleading; thus plaintiff retained "absolute right" to amend complaint); *Bowden v. United States,* 176 F.3d 552 (D.C.Cir.1999) (alternative motions to dismiss and for summary judgment are not responsive pleadings and therefore do not nullify plaintiff's right to amend); *Domino Sugar Corp. v. Sugar Workers Local Union 392,* 10 F.3d 1064, 1068 n. 1 (4th Cir.1993), *cert. denied,* 522 U.S. 912, 118 S.Ct. 295, 139 L.Ed.2d 227 (1997)(motion to dismiss is not a responsive pleading; thus if defendant has not filed a responsive pleading, plaintiff may still amend once as of right).

Cases Removed from State Court: 28 U.S.C. § 1447(e)

Section 1447(e) of Title 28 of the United States Code provides that if, after a case is removed, a plaintiff seeks to join non-diverse defendants whose joinder would destroy diversity, the district may permit or deny joinder. If joinder is denied, the court continues to have jurisdiction over the case. However, if joinder is permitted, diversity jurisdiction no longer exists and (in the absence of some other basis for subject matter jurisdiction) the court must then remand the case to state court.

That situation gets more complicated if, after removal but before a responsive pleading has been filed, a plaintiff exercises the right to amend a pleading and join a non-diverse defendant under Rule 15(a) without needing leave of court. If Rule 15(a) could be used in that manner, it would undermine the district court's discretion under § 1447(e) to retain the removed case by denying joinder. Courts have resolved this conflict by concluding that they have authority to deny joinder under Rule 15(a), notwithstanding the plaintiff's apparent right under that Rule.[3]

Removal and § 1447(e) are discussed at greater length elsewhere in this text.

Rights of Joined Parties

If a party is joined though an amended pleading permitted under Rule 15, that party normally enjoys a minimum of 10 days from the date of service of the amended pleading to respond to it.[4] Rule 15(a) expressly provides the district court with authority to modify that time limit.

Termination of Right to Amend

Many courts hold that once the court has entered an order of final judgment, a party's ability to amend of right terminates.[5] Thus if the

3. *See, e.g., Mayes v. Rapoport,* 198 F.3d 457, 461 n. 11 (4th Cir.1999) ("[A] district court has the authority to reject a post-removal joinder that implicates 28 U.S.C. § 1447(e), even if the joinder was without leave of court.").

4. *Nelson v. Adams, USA, Inc.*, 529 U.S. 460, 465, 120 S.Ct. 1579, 1584, 146 L.Ed.2d 530 (2000) ("This opportunity to respond, fundamental to due process, is the echo of the opportunity to respond to original pleadings secured by Rule 12." Held, where grant of leave to amend occurred simultaneously with entry of judgment against joined party, due process has been denied).

5. *Ahmed v. Dragovich,* 297 F.3d 201 (3d Cir.2002) (once final judgment is entered, Rule 15 is inapplicable unless a party obtains relief under Rule 59 or Rule 60; unless judgment is set aside, party cannot use Rule 15 to amend); *Dwares v. City of New York,* 985 F.2d 94, 101 (2d Cir.1993)(right to amend "did not survive the entry of final judgment"). *Cf., Morse v. McWhorter,* 290 F.3d 795, 799 (6th Cir.2002) ("Where a timely motion to amend judgment is filed under Rule 59(e), the Rule 15 and Rule 59 inquiries turn on the same factors."). *But cf., Camp v. Gregory,* 67 F.3d 1286 (7th Cir.1995), *cert. denied,* 517 U.S. 1244, 116 S.Ct. 2498, 135 L.Ed.2d 190 (1996)(if complaint is dismissed but judgment is not yet entered, Rule 15(a) may still be available); *see also, Whitaker v. City of Houston,* 963 F.2d 831, 835 (5th Cir.1992)(if complaint is dismissed but court has not indicated that dismissal is with prejudice, or that an amendment is futile, plaintiff loses right to amend, but may be permitted to amend with leave of court.); *Diersen v. Chicago Car Exchange,* 110 F.3d 481, 488 n. 6 (7th Cir.1997), *cert. denied* 522 U.S. 868, 118 S.Ct. 178, 139 L.Ed.2d 119 (1997) (to obtain such leave, party should first move to have judgment set aside or vacated under Rule 59 or 60).

court grants a motion to dismiss, and enters judgment, the dismissed party's right to amend expires.[6]

Motions to Amend: Particularity and Rule 7(b)

When a party submits a motion to amend, the particularity requirement of Rule 7(b) may require the party to attach to the motion a copy of the proposed amended pleading, unless the motion adequately describes the contemplated revision.[7]

Multiple Opposing Parties

If some opposing parties have already filed responsive pleadings and others have not, courts generally hold that the original pleading may be amended as of right, at least as to those parties that have not yet pleaded.[8]

Relation to Joinder Rules

It should be noted that when a party seeks to amend a complaint under Rule 15(a) to join additional claims or parties, the joinder will not be permitted simply because the requirements of Rule 15 have been met. In addition, the applicable joinder rules must also be satisfied.[9]

Relation to Rule 41(a)

When a party moves to amend a complaint to dismiss one of its pending counts, that motion may be made pursuant to either Rule 15(a) or Rule 41(a)(2). Such a dismissal is ordinarily granted without prejudice to a possible subsequent refiling of the dismissed count.[10]

6. *See, e.g., Lewis v. Fresne,* 252 F.3d 352 (5th Cir.2001) (noting termination of right to amend; also noting that leave to amend may still be available, but court has substantial discretion to refuse leave). *But see generally Pure Country, Inc. v. Sigma Chi Fraternity,* 312 F.3d 952, 956 (8th Cir.2002) ("[S]eeking leave to amend does not, by itself, invoke the district court's discretionary authority to deny leave if the amendment would otherwise fall within the purview of the first sentence of rule 15(a) [governing a party's right to amend]").

7. *See, e.g., Moore v. Indiana,* 999 F.2d 1125, 1131 (7th Cir.1993) (noting that courts may require submission of copy of proposed amended complaint, and commenting that motion alone might be adequate if it places adversary on proper notice of amendment's content); *Wolgin v. Simon,* 722 F.2d 389, 394 (8th Cir.1983) (commenting that Rule 7(b)'s particularity requirement is satisfied by accompanying motion for leave to amend with copy of proposed amendment). *See also Long v. Satz,* 181 F.3d 1275, 1279 (11th Cir.1999) (plaintiff did not file motion for leave to amend; request for leave to amend was found only in memorandum opposing defendant's motion to dismiss; held, district court could properly deny leave to amend for failure to request leave properly).

8. *See, e.g., Barksdale v. King,* 699 F.2d 744 (5th Cir.1983)(plaintiff retains right to amend against defendant who filed motion to dismiss but not a responsive pleading; held, right to amend lost only as to codefendant who filed responsive pleading).

9. *See, e.g., Hinson v. Norwest Financial South Carolina, Inc.,* 239 F.3d 611, 618 (4th Cir.2001) (joinder of additional plaintiffs triggers application of Rule 20 requirements).

10. *See, e.g., Jet, Inc. v. Sewage Aeration Systems,* 223 F.3d 1360, 1364 (Fed.Cir.2000) (in case at bar the Rules are "functionally interchangeable," although Rule 15(a) is preferred; moreover, dismissal is typically without prejudice). *Cf., Klay v. United Healthgroup, Inc.,* 376 F.3d 1092 (11th Cir. 2004) (plaintiff who wishes to dispose of only part of a claim should normally cite Rule 15; Rule 41(a) should normally be used to dismiss an entire action; under either Rule, dismissal is normally without prejudice).

Relation With Rule 81(c)

If a case is removed from state court, it is possible that a party will be ordered under Rule 81(c) to file a repleading that conforms to federal practice. Generally, such a mandated repleading will not deprive a party of a one-time right to amend that may be available under Rule 15(a).[11]

Adverse Party's Consent

If a party's proposed amendment falls outside the time limits described above, it is often practical to ask the opposing party to consent to the amendment. When their duties to their own clients are not at issue, attorneys often cooperate in such matters as a matter of professional courtesy, and/or because they recognize that withholding consent will only force the party trying to amend to seek leave of court. If the opposing party consents to an amendment, there is no need to obtain court approval.[12] Rule 15(a) requires that consent of other parties be in writing,[13] which is usually filed with the court in the form of a praecipe.

Leave of Court

If a proposed amendment cannot be filed as of right, and the opposing party will not consent, a motion may be filed with the court seeking leave to amend. In that circumstance, permission to amend rests within the discretion of the court. However, Rule 15(a) directs the court to grant leave to amend "when justice so requires," and in practice the burden is usually on the party opposing the amendment to demonstrate why the amendment should not be permitted.[14] Moreover,

11. *See, e.g., Kuehl v. Federal Deposit Insurance Corp.*, 8 F.3d 905, 907 (1st Cir.1993) *cert. denied,* 511 U.S. 1034, 114 S.Ct. 1545, 128 L.Ed.2d 196 (1994)(but where party engages in dilatory conduct in meeting Rule 81(c) requirements, Rule 15(a) right to amend may be treated as exhausted).

12. *See, e.g., American States Insurance Co. v. Dastar Corp.*, 318 F.3d 881, 888 (9th Cir.2003) (parties who consent to amendment need not obtain court's approval).

13. *But cf., Mooney v. City of New York,* 219 F.3d 123 (2d Cir.2000), *cert. denied*, 531 U.S. 1145, 121 S.Ct. 1083, 148 L.Ed.2d 958 (2001) (plaintiff's response on merits to defense raised on motion rather than by responsive pleading is construed "as an implied grant of leave to amend the answer").

14. *Foman v. Davis,* 371 U.S. 178, 83 S.Ct. 227, 9 L.Ed.2d 222 (1962). *See, e.g., Lyn-Lea Travel Corp. v. American Airlines, Inc.*, 283 F.3d 282, 286 (5th Cir.2002), *cert. denied,* 537 U.S. 1044, 123 S.Ct. 659, 154 L.Ed.2d 516 (2002) (no error to permit defendants' amended pleadings to raise affirmative defense of preemption when new issue is question of law based on undisputed facts in instant case; also noting that no new discovery was necessary in this case); *Laurie v. Alabama Court of Criminal Appeals,* 256 F.3d 1266, 1274 (11th Cir.2001) ("There must be a substantial reason to deny a motion to amend."); *Bryant v. DuPree,* 252 F.3d 1161 (11th Cir.2001) (plaintiffs' previous amendment, filed as of right under Rule 15(a), should not be counted as a prior opportunity to amend with leave of court when defendants later file a motion to dismiss); *Pangburn v. Culbertson,* 200 F.3d 65, 70 (2d Cir.1999) (liberal approach to leave to amend "applies with particular force to pro se litigants"); *Martin's Herend Imports, Inc. v. Diamond & Gem Trading United States of America Co.,* 195 F.3d 765, 770 (5th Cir.1999) (Rule 15(a) " 'evinces a bias in favor of granting leave to amend.' "). *See also Rose v. Hartford Underwriters Insurance Co.,* 203 F.3d 417, 420 (6th Cir.2000) (marginal entry order denying leave to amend, without explanation, is abuse of discretion; but error is harmless if amendment would be futile; proposed amendment is futile if it cannot withstand motion to dismiss under Rule 12(b)(6)); *Firestone v. Firestone,* 76 F.3d 1205,

at least some courts hold that where a complaint's deficiency could be cured by an amendment, leave to amend must be given–and where a party has not sought such leave, district courts are expected to notify parties of the opportunity to amend within whatever time limits are appropriate.[15]

Requirement to Submit Proposed Amendment

A party seeking leave to amend must, inter alia, submit a proposed amendment to the court.[16]

Termination of Leave to Amend; Rule 59

Some courts hold that once a case has been dismissed–with or without prejudice–leave to file subsequent amendments to pleadings lapses. The situation may change if a plaintiff can meet the requirements of Rule 59(e) (governing motions to alter or amend judgments).[17] Otherwise, only if a district court dismisses without prejudice *and* expressly grants leave to amend will the possibility of amending a pleading still exist.[18] However, at least one circuit court treats dismissal

1209 (D.C.Cir.1996)(per curiam)(criticizing district court's "complete failure" to explain grounds for denying leave to amend); *Viernow v. Euripides Development Corp.,* 157 F.3d 785, 799 (10th Cir.1998) (court is required to offer reason for denying leave to amend, but error is harmless if reason is obvious). *But see, Miller v. Champion Enterprises, Inc.,* 346 F.3d 660, 690 (6th Cir. 2003) (in cases involving Private Securities Litigation Reform Act, 15 U.S.C.A. § 78u–4(b)(2) and (3), heightened pleading requirements of that law restrict liberal amendment standard of Rule 15(a); thus, failure to allege fraud with particularity may result in dismissal rather than leave to amend); *Lans v. Digital Equipment Corp.,* 2 F.3d 1320 (Fed.Cir.2001) (patent infringement case; no abuse of discretion in denying permission to amend when plaintiff/inventor had assigned patent to wholly owned company; original lack of standing in assignor meant there was no action to amend); *Lake v. Arnold,* 232 F.3d 360, 374 (3d Cir.2000) (failure to provide draft amended complaint to district court is ground for denying leave to amend even where court did not provide reasons for denial); *Doe v. Howe Military School,* 227 F.3d 981, 989 (7th Cir.2000) (proper exercise of discretion to deny motion to amend where plaintiffs did not state specifically what amended pleadings would allege; motion to amend or supplement complaint is held to higher standard of specificity than original complaint); *Glatt v. Chicago Park District,* 87 F.3d 190 (7th Cir.1996)(it is within court's discretion to require substantiation of proposed amended or supplemental complaint (unlike original complaint), to ensure that motive is not simply to harass opponent).

15. *Shane v. Fauver,* 213 F.3d 113 (3d Cir. 2000). *Cf., Lopez v. Smith,* 203 F.3d 1122, 1130 (9th Cir.2000) (leave to amend should be granted–even if not requested–unless district court determines that amendment is futile).

16. *See, e.g., Spadafore v. Gardner,* 330 F.3d 849, 853 (6th Cir.2003) (otherwise court is unable to determine whether to grant leave to amend); *Meehan v. United Consumers Club Franchising Corp.,* 312 F.3d 909, 913–14 (8th Cir.2002) (no abuse of discretion to deny leave to amend when party fails to make motion to amend and to submit proposed amended complaint).

17. *See, e.g., Ciralsky v. CIA,* 355 F.3d 661, 672 (D.C. Cir. 2004) (once judgment is entered, ability to amend is terminated unless party can re-open judgment pursuant to Rule 59(e)).

18. *Mirpuri v. ACT Manufacturing, Inc.,* 212 F.3d 624 (1st Cir.2000). *See also Rodriguez v. United States,* 286 F.3d 972, 980 (7th Cir.2002), *cert. denied,* 537 U.S. 938, 123 S.Ct. 46, 154 L.Ed.2d 242 (2002) (after judgment is entered, presumption in favor of leave to amend is inapplicable, and party must pursue relief under Rule 59 or Rule 60); *Building Industry Association of Superior California v. Norton,* 247 F.3d 1241, 1245 (D.C.Cir.2001), *cert. denied,* 534 U.S. 1108, 122 S.Ct. 913, 151 L.Ed.2d 879 (2002) ("Ordinarily post-judgment amendment of a complaint under Rule 15(a) requires reopening of the judgment pursuant to Rule 59(e) or 60(b)."); *Vielma v. Eureka Co.,* 218 F.3d 458, 468 (5th Cir.2000) (after grant of summary judgment, leave to amend complaint "can only occur once the judgment itself is vacated under Fed. R. Civ. P. 59 or 60.").

without prejudice, by itself, as an opportunity to amend a defective pleading.[19] Attorneys are advised to consult the local precedent.

Rule 16 and Case Management

While, as a general rule, leave to amend may be granted freely in the interest of justice, the likelihood of obtaining permission to amend diminishes drastically after the court enters a scheduling order (with deadlines for amendments).[20] The same is true when the court enters a pretrial order limiting trial issues.[21] The converse, however, is probably not true. That is, compliance with a court order's time limits for filing motions to amend does not thereby enhance the probability that the motion will be granted.

Standard of Discretion

Generally, leave to amend is granted unless a weighing of several factors suggests that leave would be inappropriate.[22] In particular, if leave to amend is denied, it will often occur because an amendment

19. *Borelli v. City of Reading,* 532 F.2d 950, 951 (3d Cir.1976) (per curiam) ("Although the district court did not mention amendment, an implicit invitation to amplify the complaint is found in the phrase 'without prejudice.' " Also encouraging district courts to state expressly whether party has leave to amend).

20. *See, e.g., O'Connell v. Hyatt Hotels of Puerto Rico,* 357 F.3d 152, 154–55 (1st Cir. 2004) ("good cause" standard of Rule 16(b) is "more stringent" than standard of Rule 15(a); bad faith and unfair prejudice considerations of Rule 15 may still be considered, but Rule 16 emphasizes evaluation of a party's diligence in seeking the amendment); *Leary v. Daeschner,* 349 F.3d 888, 909 (6th Cir. 2003) (once deadline for scheduling order has passed, requirement for good cause under Rule 16(b) must be satisfied; but district court must also evaluate potential of prejudice to opposing party); *Grochowski v. Phoenix Construction,* 318 F.3d 80, 86 (2d Cir.2003) (after entry of scheduling order, the lenient standard of Rule 15(a) must be balanced against more rigorous "good cause" requirement of rule 16(b)). *But cf., Clark v. Martinez,* 295 F.3d 809 (8th Cir.2002) ("[W]hen an issue is tried by consent [pursuant to Rule 15(b), discussed infra], it becomes of little moment whether it was encompassed in the pretrial order."); *Papio Keno Club, Inc. v. City of Papillion,* 262 F.3d 725, 729 (8th Cir.2001) (noting that pretrial orders should be 'construed liberally' to include theories that might fit within order; also holding that notwithstanding pretrial order, issue tried with consent of parties may properly be heard).

21. *See, e.g., In re Milk Products Antitrust Litigation,* 195 F.3d 430, 437 (8th Cir.1999), *cert. denied sub nom., Rainy Lake One Stop, Inc. v. Marigold Foods, Inc.,* 529 U.S. 1038, 120 S.Ct. 1534, 146 L.Ed.2d 348 (2000) ("When the district court has filed a Rule 16 pretrial scheduling order, it may properly require that good cause be shown for leave to file an amended pleading that is substantially out of time under that order."). *Byrd v. Guess,* 137 F.3d 1126, 1131–32 (9th Cir.1998), *cert. denied,* 525 U.S. 963, 119 S.Ct. 405, 142 L.Ed.2d 329 (1998) ("Once the district court enters a scheduling order setting forth a deadline for the amendment of pleadings, modifications are allowed only upon showing of 'good cause.' ... And once a pretrial order has been entered pursuant to rule 16(e) setting forth the parties and issues for trial, modifications are allowed 'only to prevent manifest injustice.' ").

22. *See, e.g., Jackson v. Rockford Housing Authority,* 213 F.3d 389 (7th Cir.2000) ("The general rule that amendment is allowed absent undue surprise or prejudice to the plaintiff is widely adhered to by our sister courts of appeals."); *Lowrey v. Texas A & M University System,* 117 F.3d 242 (5th Cir.1997) (Rule 15(a) creates "strong presumption" in favor of permitting amendment); *DCD Programs, Ltd. v. Leighton,* 833 F.2d 183, 186 (9th Cir.1987), *cert. granted, judgment vac'd,* 492 U.S. 914, 109 S.Ct. 3236, 106 L.Ed.2d 584 (1989)(weighing "bad faith, undue delay, prejudice to the opposing party, and futility of the amendment"). *Cf., United States ex rel. Lee v. SmithKline Beecham, Inc.,* 245 F.3d 1048, 1052 (9th Cir.2001) (citing same factors, but noting they do not get equal weight; futility of amendment, by itself, can be ground for denying leave to amend).

would create unfair prejudice to another party.[23] Prejudice is most commonly found when there has been substantial unjustified delay in moving to amend that creates an unfair disadvantage for an opposing party.[24] By contrast, no unfair prejudice exists simply because a party has to defend against new or better pleaded claims.[25] However, while Rule 15(a) imposes no time limits on motions for leave to amend pleadings, substantial unexplained and unjustified delays in seeking leave to amend generally reduce the prospects for obtaining leave to amend.[26]

23. *See, e.g., Eminence Capital, L.L.C. v. Aspeon, Inc.,* 316 F.3d 1048, 1052 (9th Cir.2003) ("[I]t is the consideration of prejudice to the opposing party that carries the greatest weight."). *See also Thornton v. McClatchy Newspapers, Inc.,* 261 F.3d 789, 799 (9th Cir.2001) (finding of bad faith in party's history of dilatory tactics and "doubtful value of proposed amendment" may also justify denial of leave to amend). *Cf., SCS Communications, Inc. v. Herrick Co.,* 360 F.3d 329, 345 (2d Cir. 2004) (abuse of discretion to grant leave to amend without examining possible prejudice to opponent). *But see Kenda Corp. v. Pot O' Gold Money Leagues, Inc.,* 329 F.3d 216, 232 (1st Cir.2003) (absence of prejudice to nonmoving party is not always dispositive of issue; court may consider other factors and still deny motion to amend; failure to explain lengthy delay in making motion to amend can be fatal to proposed amendment).

24. *See, e.g., Jin v. Metropolitan Life Insurance Co.,* 295 F.3d 335 (2d Cir.2002) (no abuse of discretion to find undue delay in filing motion to amend over four years after original filing; more than three years after close of discovery; and nearly three months after ruling on summary judgment motions); *United States ex rel. Bernard v. Casino Magic Corp.,* 293 F.3d 419 (8th Cir. 2002) (no abuse of discretion to deny leave to amend "two and a half years into the litigation," especially when plaintiff can obtain desired information without joining company as party); *Campania Management Co. v. Rooks, Pitts & Poust,* 290 F.3d 843, 848 (7th Cir.2002) (proper denial of leave to amend when defendant failed to act with diligence and proposed amended answer "would have injected a new issue into the case on the eve of trial"); *Walton v. Nalco Chemical Co.,* 272 F.3d 13, 19–20 (1st Cir.2001) (affirming denial of motion to amend that was made eight months after date in scheduling order; six months after close of discovery; and one week prior to scheduled start of trial); *Owens Corning v. National Union Fire Insurance Co.,* 257 F.3d 484, 496–97 (6th Cir.2001) (unfair prejudice when amendments "suddenly appear" as opponent "was preparing to litigate the remaining issues by motion for summary judgment"); *Monahan v. New York City Department of Corrections,* 214 F.3d 275 n. 3 (2d Cir.2000) (Prejudice may be found where a new claim or defense would " '(i) require the opponent to expend significant additional resources to conduct discovery and prepare for trial; (ii) significantly delay the resolution of the dispute; or (iii) prevent the plaintiff from bringing a timely action in another jurisdiction.' "); *Rhodes v. Amarillo Hospital District,* 654 F.2d 1148, 1154 (5th Cir.1981) (undue delay where motion to amend was filed 30 months after filing original complaint and three weeks before trial, "where the only apparent reason for the delay was the plaintiff's retention of a new attorney"). *But compare Dennis v. Dillard Department Stores, Inc.,* 207 F.3d 523, 526 (8th Cir.2000) (discovery had closed, but no unfair prejudice to opposing party where three months remained before trial date which could be used to reopen limited discovery–and district court could impose costs of new discovery on party seeking amendment), *and Bowles v. Reade,* 198 F.3d 752, 758 (9th Cir.1999) ("Undue delay by itself . . . is insufficient to justify denying a motion to amend." Such delay justifies denial of leave to amend only when accompanied by unfair prejudice, bad faith, or futility), *with Jennings v. BIC Corp.* 181 F.3d 1250, 1258 (11th Cir.1999) ("The U.S. Supreme Court has held that undue delay is an adequate basis for denying leave to amend.").

25. *See, e.g., Popp Telcom, Inc. v. American Sharecom, Inc.,* 210 F.3d 928, 943 (8th Cir.2000) ("The inclusion of a claim based on facts already known or available to both sides does not prejudice the non-moving party."); *Busam Motor Sales v. Ford Motor Co.,* 203 F.2d 469, 472 (6th Cir.1953)(Rule 15 amendment is not barred simply because it raises new issue of law).

26. *Zenith Radio Corp. v. Hazeltine Research, Inc.,* 401 U.S. 321, 91 S.Ct. 795, 28 L.Ed.2d 77 (1971). *See also, Wade v. Knoxville Utilities Board,* 259 F.3d 452, 459 (6th Cir.2001) ("When amendment is sought at a late stage in the litigation, there is an increased burden to show justification for failing to move earlier."); *In re Burlington Coat Factory Securities Litigation,* 114 F.3d 1410, 1434 (3d Cir.1997) (also

Abuse of Discretion

Failure by the district court to explain its reasons for denying leave to amend may by itself be abuse of the court's discretion, unless the reason for the court's decision is apparent on the record.[27]

Futile Amendments

Amended pleadings that would clearly not prevail or improve the position of a party will be rejected.[28] For example, if the proposed amendment would not survive a motion to dismiss, it will be rejected.[29]

citing bad faith and "dilatory motive" as grounds for denying leave to amend). *See, e.g., Edwards v. City of Goldsboro,* 178 F.3d 231 (4th Cir.1999) ("Delay alone is an insufficient reason to deny leave to amend. ...Rather, the delay must be accompanied by prejudice, bad faith, or futility."); *and Harrison v. Rubin,* 174 F.3d 249 (D.C.Cir.1999) (undue delay where plaintiff sought to change factual allegations is ground for denying leave to amend; but where "amendment would do no more than clarify legal theories or make corrections" undue delay without prejudice to opposing party does not justify denial of leave to amend); *Viernow v. Euripides Development Corp.,* 157 F.3d 785, 799 (10th Cir. 1998) (untimeliness alone is insufficient ground to deny leave to amend). *See generally, Loggerhead Turtle v. County Council of Volusia County, Florida,* 148 F.3d 1231, 1257 (11th Cir.1998), *cert. denied,* 526 U.S. 1081, 119 S.Ct. 1488, 143 L.Ed.2d 570 (1999) (finding error in denial of leave to amend; "Any amendment to an original pleading necessarily involves some additional expense to the opposing party.").

27. *Foman v. Davis,* 371 U.S. 178, 182, 83 S.Ct. 227, 230, 9 L.Ed.2d 222 (1962). *Cf., HDM Flugservice GmbH v. Parker Hannifin Co.,* 332 F.3d 1025 (6th Cir.2003) (abuse of discretion to fail to state basis for denial of leave to amend or to fail to consider competing interests of parties and likelihood of prejudice to opponent); *Grayson v. Mayview State Hospital,* 293 F.3d 103 (3d Cir.2002) (moreover, when plaintiff does not seek leave to amend deficient complaint after defendant has moved to dismiss, court must inform plaintiff of leave to amend and provide time to do so; however, court has no such duty if amendment would be futile or inequitable).

28. *Foman v. Davis,* 371 U.S. 178, 83 S.Ct. 227, 9 L.Ed.2d 222 (1962); *Jefferson County School District No. R-1 v. Moody's Investor's Services, Inc.,* 175 F.3d 848 (10th Cir.1999) ("[T]he district court may deny leave to amend where amendment would be futile."); *Wisdom v. First Midwest Bank of Polar Bluff,* 167 F.3d 402, 409 (8th Cir.1999) ("[P]arties should not be allowed to amend their complaint without showing how the complaint could be amended to save the meritless claim."). *But see, Van Le v. Five Fathoms, Inc.,* 792 F.Supp. 372 (D.N.J. 1992)(opponent of proposed amendment carries burden of clearly establishing futility).

29. *See, e.g., Rodriguez v. United States,* 286 F.3d 972, 980 (7th Cir.2002), *cert. denied,* 537 U.S. 938, 123 S.Ct. 46, 154 L.Ed.2d 242 (2002) ("A district court may properly deny a motion to amend as futile if the proposed amendment would be barred by the statute of limitations."); *Rose v. Hartford Underwriters Insurance Co.,* 203 F.3d 417, 420 (6th Cir.2000) (proposed amendment is futile if it cannot withstand motion to dismiss under Rule 12(b)(6)); *Newland v. Dalton,* 81 F.3d 904, 907 (9th Cir. 1996)("[D]istrict courts need not accommodate futile amendments."); *Bailey v. Sullivan,* 885 F.2d 52, 59 (3d Cir.1989)("No purpose would be served by allowing [an] amendment to the complaint to add a challenge which would be dismissed."). *Cf., Kropelnicki v. Siegel,* 290 F.3d 118, 130 (2d Cir.2002) (proper denial of leave to amend where proposed complaint added no new facts or allegations that would alter district court's earlier conclusion that plaintiff lacked standing to sue); *Roskam Baking Co., Inc. v. Lanham Machinery Co.,* 288 F.3d 895, 906 (6th Cir.2002) (proper denial of leave to amend if party fails to provide court with substance of proposed amendment so that court could evaluate it); *Diesel "Repower," Inc. v. Islander Investments, Ltd.,* 271 F.3d 1318, 1322 (11th Cir.2001) (if amendment is futile, it is irrelevant that movant sought to amend in a timely manner and opposing party suffered no prejudice). *But cf., Wight v. Bankamerica Corp.,* 219 F.3d 79 (2d Cir.2000) (amended fraud complaint not futile where plaintiff could plead circumstances of

Imposition of Costs

Rule 15 does not address issues of costs arising from amended pleadings. However, it appears settled that, as a condition of granting leave to amend, a court may require an amending party to pay the opponent's costs caused by the amendment.[30]

Effect of Amendment

If an amendment is appropriate under Rule 15(a), it displaces the earlier pleading to which it is directed.[31] If a party filing an amendment wishes to preserve some portions of the original pleading, the party should incorporate those portions by specific reference in the amended pleading.

Responding to Amended Pleadings

Rule 15(a) provides that if the pleading amended is one to which a responsive pleading is appropriate, the opposing party will have either the time remaining before a response to the unamended version was due, or ten days—whichever is longer—in which to respond. However, the court has authority to alter those time limits as may be appropriate in the circumstances of the case.

Relationship to Rule 15(b)

Technically, a motion for leave of court to amend a pleading may be made at any time under Rule 15(a). However, if a suit has advanced to trial or post-trial motions, Rule 15(b), pertaining to amendments to conform to the evidence, is probably a more appropriate vehicle for amendments to pleadings. However, the difference between Rule 15(a) and (b) is not a bright line, and generally courts are liberal in granting permission for substantive amendments under either provision provided that no unfair prejudice thereby accrues to other parties.[32]

RULE 15(b). AMENDMENTS TO CONFORM TO THE EVIDENCE

CORE CONCEPT

Rule 15(b) permits amendments to pleadings in two circumstances. The first situation arises when an issue not raised in the original pleadings is tried[33] by consent of the parties. The second occurs when

fraud with particularity; intent of defendant need be stated only generally).

30. *See, e.g., General Signal Corp. v. MCI Telecommunications Corp.,* 66 F.3d 1500, 1514 (9th Cir.1995), *cert. denied,* 516 U.S. 1146, 116 S.Ct. 1017, 134 L.Ed.2d 97 (1996)(so noting, and citing other authority).

31. *See, e.g., King v. Dogan,* 31 F.3d 344, 346 (5th Cir.1994)("An amended complaint supercedes the original complaint and renders it of no legal effect unless the amended complaint specifically refers to and adopts or incorporates by reference the earlier pleading.").

32. *Compare Bank v. Pitt,* 928 F.2d 1108 (11th Cir.1991)(applying Rule 15(a) standards to amending dismissed complaint) *with United States for Use and Benefit of Seminole Sheet Metal Co. v. SCI, Inc.,* 828 F.2d 671 (11th Cir. 1987)(applying Rule 15(b) standards to amending dismissed complaint).

33. *Cf., Marsh v. Butler County, Alabama,* 268 F.3d 1014, 1024 n. 4 (11th Cir.2001) (al-

an issue not raised in the pleadings is objected to, but the proposed amendment will either not create unfair prejudice, or such prejudice as may result can be cured by other judicial action.

APPLICATIONS

Timing; Relationship to Rule 15(a)

Motions to amend under Rule 15(b) may theoretically be made at any time. The language of the Rule, however, speaks to matters raised at trial, suggesting that the Rule should not generally be used at early stages of litigation.[34] Instead, early in the litigation it is more appropriate to seek to amend a pleading under the authority of Rule 15(a). Generally speaking, motions to amend under Rule 15(b) are made at trial or in the immediate aftermath of a trial.[35]

Relationship to Rule 15(c)

If a new claim is asserted through a pleading amended pursuant to Rule 15(b), there may still be questions about the timeliness of the claim. While Rule 15(b) may permit the amended pleading, Rule 15(c) controls whether the amended pleading is deemed to have been filed on the date of the original pleading or the date of the amendment. The distinction is significant when questions of statutes of limitations are raised.

Claims for Relief

Rule 15(b) may be employed to assert claims for affirmative relief, even after a trial is ended. Thus, for example, a counterclaim may be asserted through a Rule 15(b) amendment where the evidence on the counterclaim was heard at trial.[36]

Failure to Object

Rule 15(b) provides that an opposing party's consent to an amendment may be express or implied.[37] Thus, the court may find that

though Rule 15(b) discusses cases that have been "tried" by consent, "we accept Rule 15(b) as a guide–by way of analogy, at the appellate level–for cases never tried, but litigated on motions").

34. *See, e.g., Gold v. Local 7 United Food and Commercial Workers Union*, 159 F.3d 1307, 1309 n. 3 (10th Cir.1998) ("Rule 15(b) seems a totally inappropriate vehicle for a motion to amend prior to trial.").

35. *Cf., Banks v. Dretke*, 540 U.S. 668, ___, 124 S.Ct. 1256, 1280, 157 L.Ed.2d 1166 (2004) (Rule 15(b) may be applicable to habeas corpus evidentiary hearing where opponent gave "any sort of consent" and had a fair opportunity to present contrary evidence).

36. *See, e.g., In re Meyertech Corp.*, 831 F.2d 410, 421 (3d Cir.1987)(approving use of Rule 15(b) to raise a counterclaim).

37. *See, e.g., United States ex rel. Modern Electric, Inc. v. Ideal Electronic Security Co.*, 81 F.3d 240 (D.C.Cir.1996)(noting that express or implied consent is "a condition for treating unpled issues as though they were raised in the pleadings"); *Rodriguez v. Doral Mortgage Corp.*, 57 F.3d 1168, 1172 (1st Cir.1995) (implied consent may be found where claim not mentioned in complaint is addressed "by means of a sufficiently pointed interrogatory answer or in a pretrial memorandum" to which opponent responds by engaging claim or by " 'silent acquiescence;' " alternatively, " 'consent to the trial of an issue may be implied if, during the trial, a party acquiesces in the introduction of evidence which is relevant only to that issue' "). *But see Koch v. Koch Industries, Inc.*, 203 F.3d 1202, 1217 (10th Cir.2000)), *cert. denied,* 531 U.S. 926, 121 S.Ct. 302, 148 L.Ed.2d 242 (2000) (no implied consent

parties who fail to object to the litigation of matters not within the four corners of the original pleadings have impliedly consented to adjudication of those matters.[38] In those circumstances, the court will permit an amended pleading that reflects the issues actually litigated.

Failure to File an Amended Pleading; Motions to Amend

Rule 15(b) expressly provides that if parties are found to have consented to litigation of issues outside the original pleadings, there is no requirement that a formal amended pleading be filed. Instead, the result in the case will stand, irrespective of the presence or absence of amendments.[39]

However, if an opposing party makes a proper objection to evidence going to a new claim, the party seeking relief under Rule 15(b) must make an appropriate motion to amend.[40]

Amendments Over Objections to Evidence

If a party objects to the use of evidence on the ground that it does not address issues raised in the original pleadings, Rule 15(b) authorizes the court to allow amendments that encompass such evidence.[41] Such

to new issue where testimony was relevant to issues already at trial.

38. *See, e.g., Eich v. Board of Regents for Central Missouri State University,* 350 F.3d 752, 762 (8th Cir. 2003) (failure to object to jury instructions on economic damages mean issue was tried by consent); *Moncrief v. Williston Basin Interstate Pipeline Co.,* 174 F.3d 1150, 1162 (10th Cir.1999) ("Implied consent cannot be based upon the introduction of evidence that is relevant to an issue already in the case when there is no indication that the party presenting the case when there is no indication that the party presenting the evidence intended to raise a new issue."); *Kenda Corp. v. Pot O' Gold Money Leagues, Inc.,* 329 F.3d 216, 232 (1st Cir.2003) (evidence directly relevant to pleaded issue cannot be used to imply consent to litigation of non-pleaded issue); *Kovacevich v. Kent State University,* 224 F.3d 806, 831 (6th Cir.2000) (" 'Implied consent' " requires considerable litigation of a matter–" 'it must appear that the parties understood the evidence to be aimed at the unpleaded issue.' "); *Viernow v. Euripides Development Corp.,* 157 F.3d 785, 790 n. 9 (10th Cir. 1998) ("Issues raised for the first time in a plaintiff's response to a motion for summary judgment may be considered a request to amend the complaint pursuant to Fed.R.Civ.P. 15."); *Moody v. FMC Corp.,* 995 F.2d 63, 66 (5th Cir.1993)(if evidence in support of amended pleading is also relevant to issues already pleaded in the case, opposing party could not reasonably have notice of new issue, and therefore could not have consented to amended pleading). *But see IES Industries, Inc. v. United States,* 349 F.3d 574, 579 (8th Cir. 2003) ("It is axiomatic that evidence bearing on both claims and the defenses to those claims may well overlap in a given case. Such an inevitability does not foreclose amendment under Rule 15(b).").

39. *See, e.g., People for the Ethical Treatment of Animals v. Doughney,* 263 F.3d 359, 367 (4th Cir.2001) ("Even without a formal amendment, 'a district court may amend the pleadings merely by entering findings on the unpleaded issues.' "); *Southwestern Stationery and Bank Supply, Inc. v. Harris Corp.,* 624 F.2d 168, 171 (10th Cir. 1980) ("When evidence is not objected to, a formal amendment to the pleadings is normally not necessary."). *See also, Creative Demos, Inc. v. Wal–Mart Stores, Inc.,* 142 F.3d 367, 371–72 (7th Cir.1998) (approving district court's amendment to conform to "what the parties were arguing about at trial, although they did not use the magic words"). *But see United States v. Davis,* 261 F.3d 1, 59 (1st Cir.2001) ("Where the party seeking amendment of the pleadings has shown no justification for its delay in doing so, we have affirmed the trial court's ruling to deny the amendment.").

40. *See, e.g., Green Country Food Market, Inc. v. Bottling Group, L.L.C.,* 371 F.3d 1275 , 1281 (10th Cir. 2004) (where proper objection was made but advocate of amendment made no motion, "the lack of prejudice to a party does not provide a basis for amendment.").

41. *Cf., Moncrief v. Williston Basin Interstate Pipeline Co.,* 174 F.3d 1150 (10th Cir.1999) (after objection has been made and ruled on, party seeking amendment under Rule 15(b) must

amendments may be permitted on either of two grounds: the absence of unfair prejudice to the objecting party,[42] or the ability of the court to cure such prejudice.[43]

Grounds for Denying Rule 15(b) Amendments

Courts deny Rule 15(b) amendments on any of four grounds: bad faith; undue delay; unfair prejudice to an opponent; or futility of a proposed amendment.[44]

Unfair Prejudice

Determinations of unfair prejudice are highly fact specific. The most likely circumstance in which such prejudice will be found occurs when the objecting party is surprised by the evidence and has no reasonable opportunity to meet it.[45]

Curing Unfair Prejudice

If the source of unfair prejudice is surprise, courts may attempt to cure the problem by using their authority under Rule 15(b) to grant a continuance, so that the objecting party can prepare for the new evidence.[46] Such an order may include re-opening opportunities for discovery.

Resisting Rule 15(b) Motions to Amend

An attorney seeking to resist introduction of new issues at trial that are outside the original pleadings is substantially handicapped by

make motion to amend; court cannot make amendment *sua sponte*).

42. *See, e.g., New York State Electric & Gas Corp. v. Secretary of Labor,* 88 F.3d 98 (2d Cir. 1996)("In assessing whether the pleadings should conform to the proof, the pivotal question is whether prejudice would result.").

43. *See, e.g., Green Country Food Market, Inc. v. Bottling Group, L.L.C.,* 371 F.3d 1275, 1280 (10th Cir. 2004) ("The court may grant a continuance to enable the objecting party to meet such evidence.").

44. *See, e.g., FilmTec Corp. v. Hydranautics,* 67 F.3d 931, 935 (Fed.Cir.1995), *cert. denied,* 519 U.S. 814, 117 S.Ct. 62, 136 L.Ed.2d 24 (1996)(listing grounds). *But cf., Kenda Corp. v. Pot O' Gold Money Leagues, Inc.,* 329 F.3d 216, 232 (1st Cir. 2003) (absence of prejudice to nonmoving party is not always dispositive of issue; court may consider other factors and still deny motion to amend; failure to explain lengthy delay in making motion to amend can be fatal to proposed amendment).

45. *See, e.g., Walton v. Nalco Chemical Co.,* 272 F.3d 13, 20 (1st Cir.2001) (implied consent found only if there is acquiescence to introduction of evidence relevant only to proposed new issue; if evidence also addresses existing issues, there is no implied consent); *Deere & Co. v. Johnson,* 271 F.3d 613, 622 (5th Cir.2001) (same reasoning; also noting that jury's verdict form never mentioned new theory, which is something to which advocate of new theory would have objected if it believed both parties had implicitly accepted new theory); *Gussack Realty Co. v. Xerox Corp.,* 224 F.3d 85, 94 (2d Cir.2000) ("Generally, introducing new claims for liability on the last day of the trial will prejudice the defendant;" prejudice found where plaintiffs moved to amend pleadings at close of their evidence after district court dismissed their nuisance claim); *United States v. Banks,* 115 F.3d 916, 918 (11th Cir.), *cert. denied,* 522 U.S. 1075, 118 S.Ct. 852, 139 L.Ed.2d 752 (1998)(unfair prejudice can be lack of notice to opposing party or some other denial of a fair opportunity to defend).

46. *See, e.g., Menendez v. Perishable Distributors, Inc.,* 763 F.2d 1374, 1379 (11th Cir. 1985)(approving amendment, but noting need to give opponent opportunity to collect evidence). *But cf., Kenda Corp. v. Pot O' Gold Money Leagues, Inc.,* 329 F.3d 216, 232 (1st Cir.2003) (absence of prejudice to nonmoving party is not always dispositive of issue; court may consider other factors and still deny motion to amend; failure to explain lengthy delay in making mo-

the liberal approach of Rule 15(b) to intra-trial and post-trial amendments. If no challenge to the new issues is made, the attorney will often be deemed to have consented to the insertion of the new issues at trial.[47] If an objection is made, the attorney may be granted only the limited relief of a continuance. It is an unusual circumstance when claims, issues, or evidence relevant to a case is precluded from the trial entirely because its admission, through an amended pleading, creates incurable, unfair prejudice.[48] Such cases occur most commonly where a party seeks to amend after judgment has been entered.[49]

Relation to Rule 16

Rule 16 governs pre-trial conferences, including, *inter alia,* determination of issues that will be omitted from the trial. However, if an issue omitted under Rule 16 is actually tried, and if the issue arose with the express or implied consent of the parties pursuant to Rule 15(b), then the issue is properly before the court. In other words, in that circumstance Rule 15(b) governs.[50]

Relation to Rule 56

Rule 15(b) questions usually arise in situations where a case has gone to trial and a dispute has arisen as to whether an issue or claim has been "tried by express or implied consent." Whether the principles underlying Rule 15(b) apply to cases decided on summary judgment, pursuant to Rule 56, appears to be an open question. Attorneys are advised to consult local precedent.[51]

tion to amend can be fatal to proposed amendment).

47. *See, e.g., Winger v. Winger,* 82 F.3d 140 (7th Cir.1996)(failure to object, along with other factors, "demonstrates that the issue was tried by implied consent"); *Kirkland v. District of Columbia,* 70 F.3d 629, 633 (D.C.Cir.1995) ("Trial of the issue without objection normally is enough to satisfy the Rule 15(b) requirement."). *Cf., Ale v. Tennessee Valley Authority,* 269 F.3d 680, 693 (6th Cir.2001) (acknowledging that opponent may not have impliedly consented to litigate new issue during liability phase of trial; holding nevertheless that no prejudice arose from amended complaint because court told opposing party it "would have ample opportunity to respond to this issue during the damages phase of the trial"); *Estate of Dietrich v. Burrows,* 167 F.3d 1007, 1013 (6th Cir.1999) (amended complaint never filed with court but nevertheless accepted because, *inter alia,* defendants "treated the amendment as filed by specifically asking the district court to grant ... summary judgment on the [amended] claim").

48. *But see Pinkley, Inc. v. City of Frederick, Maryland,* 191 F.3d 394, 401 (4th Cir.1999), *cert. denied,* 528 U.S. 1155, 120 S.Ct. 1161, 145 L.Ed.2d 1072 (2000) (amendment improper under rule 15(b) "where the defendant never conceded implicitly or explicitly that a conversion claim was at issue").

49. *See, e.g., DCPB, Inc. v. City of Lebanon,* 957 F.2d 913, 917–18 (1st Cir.1992)(where plaintiff, without good cause, did not raise claim until after judgment, court should deny "injection of new and different theory of liability at the very stroke of midnight"); *but cf., Pulla v. Amoco Oil Co.,* 72 F.3d 648, 658 (8th Cir.1995)(where evidence on new claim also related to original claim, amendment can be denied because defendant lacked notice).

50. *See, e.g., Clark v. Martinez,* 295 F.3d 809 (8th Cir.2002) ("[W]hen an issue is tried by consent [pursuant to Rule 15(b), discussed infra], it becomes of little moment whether it was encompassed in the pretrial order."); *Kirkland v. District of Columbia,* 70 F.3d 629, 633–34 (D.C.Cir.1995)(noting that if Rule 16 controlled, amendment by implied consent under Rule 15(b) would be "dead letter").

51. *See, e.g., Independent Petroleum Association of America v. Babbit,* 235 F.3d 588, 596 (D.C.Cir.2001) ("It is an open question whether the Federal Rules permit parties to impliedly consent to 'try' issues not raised in their pleadings through summary judgment motions;" citing cases). *See also Eddy v. Virgin Islands Water and Power Authority,* 256 F.3d 204, 209 (3d

RULE 15(c). RELATION BACK OF AMENDMENTS

CORE CONCEPT

Assuming that an amended pleading will be permitted under the standards of either Rule 15(a) or (b), Rule 15(c) governs the circumstances in which the amendment will be treated as though it was filed on the date of the original pleading. This determination is highly relevant to the applicability of statutes of limitations to claims raised or parties joined in amended pleadings.

NOTE: Rule 15(c) was changed in December 1991, making many previous decisions unreliable precedent. In particular, new Rule 15(c) is an express rejection of *Schiavone v. Fortune,* 477 U.S. 21, 106 S.Ct. 2379, 91 L.Ed.2d 18 (1986).

APPLICATIONS

Prerequisite of Right to Amend

Rule 15(c) deals only with whether an amendment will be treated as though it was filed at an earlier date rather than the actual date of filing—whether the amendment, in the words of Rule 15(c), "relates back" to the date the original pleading was filed. Before such relation back is contemplated, however, the proponent of the amended pleading must first persuade the court that an amended pleading should be permitted at all. The standards governing authority to file an amended pleading are discussed in Rule 15(a) and (b).[52]

Right to Amend Not Restricted to "Pleadings"

Although Rule 15(c) itself refers only to amendments of pleadings, it is also appropriately applied to amendments of some other documents filed in district court.[53]

Relation Back Permitted

Rule 15(c) permits an amended pleading to relate back to the date of the original pleading in any of three circumstances: (1) when the statute of limitations governing the cause of action permits relation back; (2) when the claim or defense in the amended pleading arose

Cir.2001) (suggesting disapproval of raising affirmative defense for first time in motion for summary judgment, but permitting such amendment if opponent is not prejudiced); *Whitaker v. T.J. Snow Co.,* 151 F.3d 661, 663 (7th Cir.1998) ("Because both parties squarely addressed the strict liability theory in their summary judgment briefs, the complaint was constructively amended to include that claim.").

52. *See, e.g., Ellzey v. United States,* 324 F.3d 521, 527 (7th Cir.2003) (before relation back occurs, proposed "amendment still must be appropriate under the criteria of Rule 15(a)"); *Caban–Wheeler v. Elsea,* 71 F.3d 837, 841 (11th Cir.1996) (noting difference in standards between permission to amend complaint and whether amended claim should relate back to original complaint). *See also Henderson v. Bolanda,* 253 F.3d 928 (7th Cir.2001) ("[I]n order to benefit from Rule 15(c)'s relation back doctrine, the original complaint must have been timely filed.").

53. *Scarborough v. Principi,* 541 U.S. 401, 124 S.Ct. 1856, 1867–68, 158 L.Ed.2d 674 (2004) (applying Rule 15(c) to application for award of attorney fees; noting previous decisions to apply Rule 15 to notice of appeal and EEOC discrimination charge).

from the same transaction or occurrence as that set forth in the original pleading; or (3) when a new party is joined and it is not unfair, as defined in Rule 15(c), for the claim against that party to be treated as if it was raised on the date the original pleading was filed. Each of these circumstances is discussed in greater detail below.

Statutes of Limitations

Rule 15(c)(1) provides that if the statute of limitations governing a particular cause of action permits relation back of amended pleadings, relation back is permitted. The purpose of Rule 15(c)(1) is to ensure that the Rule is not used to contravene statutes of limitations specifically permitting relation back, if a statute is more generous to the amended pleading. Rule 15(c)(1) defers to a statute of limitations only if the statute is more generous on relation back. By its own terms, Rule 15(c)(1) does not apply if the statute is more restrictive. In that circumstance the provisions of Rule 15(c)(2) or (3) would determine whether an amended pleading would relate back.

Same Transaction or Occurrence

Rule 15(c)(2) permits an amended pleading to relate back if the amended claim or defense arose out of the same transaction or occurrence as the original pleading. The standard of "same transaction or occurrence" varies substantially within the circuits, with the broadest description encompassing all events that bear a logical relationship to the original transaction.[54] Other courts look to the degree of overlap of evidence between the occurrences raised in the amended pleading and the original pleading.[55] This provision of Rule 15(c) did not change substantially in 1991, and many older cases applying the "same transaction or occurrence" standard are probably still reliable precedent.

It should be noted that this standard is measured by the facts pleaded. It does not depend on the legal theory offered. Thus, an amendment may relate back notwithstanding that the proffered amendment offers a new legal theory.[56]

54. *See, e.g., Wilson v. Fairchild Republic Co.,* 143 F.3d 733, 738 (2d Cir.1998) ("The pertinent inquiry ... is whether the original complaint gave the defendant fair notice of the newly alleged claims."); *Alpern v. UtiliCorp United, Inc.,* 84 F.3d 1525, 1543 (8th Cir.1996)("The basic inquiry is whether the amended complaint is related to the general fact situation alleged in the original pleading."). *See generally, Miller v. American Heavy Lift Shipping,* 231 F.3d 242, 249–50 (6th Cir.2000) (injury claims amended to include exposure to benzene in addition to original claim of exposure to asbestos arises from same transaction or occurrence where other allegations of employment and negligence remained unchanged); *Stevelman v. Alias Research, Inc.,* 174 F.3d 79 (2d Cir.1999) (new allegations added specificity but did not add new counts; held, "same transaction" requirement clearly satisfied; "Where no new cause of action is alleged, as here, this Court liberally grants relation back under Rule 15(c).").

55. *See, e.g., Martell v. Trilogy Limited,* 872 F.2d 322, 325 (9th Cir.1989)(noting that original and amended pleadings share "a common nucleus of operative facts"). *But see Massachusetts Bay Transportation Authority v. United States,* 254 F.3d 1367, 1380 (Fed.Cir.2001) (original complaint for damage to property did not include allegation of damage to terazzo floor; thus clam for damage to terrazo floor did not arise from same occurrence as required by Rule 15(c)(2); apparent dicta, however, because statute of limitations had not yet run and requirements of Rule 15(c)(2) were therefore irrelevant).

56. *See, e.g., Maegdlin v. International Association of Machinists and Aerospace Workers,* 309 F.3d 1051, 1053 (8th Cir.2002).

Amendments That Add a Party or Change a Party's Name

To obtain the benefits of relation back when a new party is named[57] or a party's name is changed, the amended pleading must satisfy the elements of Rule 15(c)(3): (1) it must arise from the same transaction or occurrence as the original pleading, as provided by Rule 15(c)(2); and (2) within the 120–day period after filing of the original pleading that Rule 4(m) provides for service of process, the party named in the amended pleading must have both received sufficient notice of the pendency of the action so as not to be prejudiced in preparing a defense, and have known or should have known that but for a mistake of identity the party would have been named in the original pleading. The first element—same transaction or occurrence—follows the discussion of Rule 15(c)(2), above. The other element has two parts—fair notice and awareness of a mistake in identity—that are explained immediately below. In addition to the requirement of same transaction or occurrence, *both* fair notice and awareness of a mistake concerning identity, must be satisfied before an amended pleading may relate back under Rule 15(c)(3).

(1) *Notice:* The kind of notice Rule 15(c)(3) requires is that which, in the particular circumstances of a case, ensures that the party joined is not unfairly prejudiced by an amended pleading that relates back to an earlier date.[58] If a party to be joined in an amended complaint learned of a suit within the 120–day period provided by Rule 4(m) for service of the original complaint, and that party's opportunity to prepare a defense was not hindered by the time lag between the original pleading and the amended pleading, Rule 15(c)(3)'s requirement of notice generally would be satisfied.[59] For example, corporations in a parent-subsidiary relationship with an entity sued in the original complaint would probably be held to have notice of the original action.[60] Similarly, if the proposed change merely corrects a "misnomer," the complaint may relate back.[61] However, where the original complaint

57. *See, e.g., Gallas v. Supreme Court of Pennsylvania,* 211 F.3d 760, 777 (3d Cir.2000) (replacing "John Doe" with real name of party changes a party within meaning of Rule 15(c)(3)). *See also Moore v. City of Harriman,* 272 F.3d 769, 774 (6th Cir.2001), *cert. denied,* 536 U.S. 922, 122 S.Ct. 2586, 153 L.Ed.2d 776 (2002) (applying Rule 15(c)(3), rather than Rule 15(c)(2), to permit plaintiff to amend complaint to clarify that same defendants were being sued in their personal capacities).

58. *See, e.g., Garvin v. City of Philadelphia,* 354 F.3d 215, 222 (3d Cir. 2003) (prejudice is that which might be caused, for lack of notice, by difficulty in gathering evidence and preparing defense in case that became stale).

59. *See, e.g., Singletary v. Pennsylvania Department of Corrections,* 266 F.3d 186, 189 (3d Cir.2001) (in absence of actual notice to potential new party, identifying two means of imputing notice received by original defendants to party sought to be added: (1) through sharing same attorney; or (2) identity of interest between original parties and party sought to be added). *Cf., e.g., Atchinson v. District of Columbia,* 73 F.3d 418, 427 (D.C.Cir.1996)(noting, *inter alia,* prejudice because individual defendant would probably have adopted different discovery and defense tactics if he had received adequate notice of claim of his individual liability).

60. *See, e.g., Andrews v. Lakeshore Rehabilitation Hospital,* 140 F.3d 1405, 1408 n. 5 (11th Cir.1998) (if subsidiary had notice of suit, parent holding 100% of subsidiary "is deemed to have had notice"); *G.F. Co. v. Pan Ocean Shipping Co.,* 23 F.3d 1498, 1503 (9th Cir.1994)(original defendant was claims agent for new party and both parties shared the same attorney; held, good notice to new party).

61. *See, e.g., Datskow v. Teledyne, Inc.,* 899 F.2d 1298, 1301–02 (2d Cir.1990) (complaint properly served, but correct name of defendant

cited only aliases of police officer defendants and not their actual names, the issue of notice is a more serious problem.[62] Finally, a person who had not been named as a defendant in the original complaint, but who was impleaded under Rule 14 by the original defendant, would probably be held to have had fair notice under Rule 15(c)(3), if the impleader was served on that person within the 120–day period provided by Rule 4(m).

(2) *Knowledge of Mistaken Identity*: Before an amended pleading may relate back under Rule 15(c)(3), the proponent of the pleading must also establish that within the 120–day period provided by Rule 4(m) the person to be joined knew, or should have known, that the person would have been sued under the original pleading but for some mistake in identity. Thus, if a subsidiary corporation was sued when the claim should have been against its parent, and was served within the period provided by Rule 4(m), the parent might be charged with timely knowledge of the fact that the proper defendant should have been the parent.[63] With natural persons, the requirement may be satisfied when the name of the proper defendant is similar to the name of the person originally designated as a defendant, *and* the proper defendant knew of the mistake within the time limit established by Rule 4(m).[64]

Rule 15(c)(3); Requirement of "Mistake"

Relation back under Rule 15(c)(3) is permitted only if the party joined by amendment knew or should have known that it would have been sued originally but for a mistake. It is unclear whether the mistake may be one of either fact or law,[65] but in other respects this requirement has been construed rather strictly. Thus if the party seeking to amend made no mistake, relation back is not permitted under Rule 15(c)(3).[66]

was "Teledyne Industries, Inc.;" held, defendant had adequate notice of suit and thus "case may be categorized as one of mislabeling").

62. *See, e.g., Eison v. McCoy,* 146 F.3d 468 (7th Cir.1998) (complaint's listing of "T.C., Cronie, Pac Man, and Crater Face" does not provide notice where police department has more than 17,000 employees). *But cf., Moore v. City of Harriman,* 272 F.3d 769, 774 (6th Cir.2001), *cert. denied,* 536 U.S. 922, 122 S.Ct. 2586, 153 L.Ed.2d 776 (2002) (police officers sued on state tort claims as well as federal civil rights claims have "clear notice" from state claims and federal claim under 42 U.S.C.A. § 1983 that "they faced individual liability of some sort").

63. *See, e.g., Peterson v. Sealed Air Corp.,* 902 F.2d 1232 (7th Cir.1990)(service was on agent of both parent and subsidiary).

64. *See, e.g., Brown v. Shaner,* 172 F.3d 927, 933 (6th Cir.1999), *cert. denied,* 528 U.S. 966, 120 S.Ct. 403, 145 L.Ed.2d 314 (1999) (police officers sued in civil rights case; plaintiff's complaint identified individual wrongful acts but did not state whether defendants were sued in their official capacity or individually; held, failure to identify allegation of individual liability satisfies "mistake" requirement, and defendants should have known that but for mistake they were being sued individually).

65. *Compare, e.g., Woods v. Indiana University—Purdue University at Indianapolis,* 996 F.2d 880, 887 (7th Cir.1993) (indicating that mistake may be of fact or law), *with Rendall–Speranza v. Nassim,* 107 F.3d 913, 918 (D.C.Cir. 1997) (amendment permitted, if at all, only for mistake of fact).

66. *See, e.g., Garrett v. Fleming,* 362 F.3d 692 (10th Cir. 2004) (lack of knowledge of relationship between entities does not satisfy requirement of error as to identity of proper party); *Worthington v. Wilson,* 8 F.3d 1253, 1256–57 (7th Cir.1993)(lack of knowledge as to joined party's identity does not satisfy "mistake" requirement of Rule 15(c)(3)); *see also, Louisiana–*

Relation to Laches

Laches is a case law doctrine that may be raised by a defendant where the plaintiff unreasonably delays in bringing a lawsuit, and thereby unfairly harms the defendant. Rule 15(c) governs circumstances where application of the Rule might avoid unfairness arising from strict application of a statute of limitations. Because laches applies, if at all, only in the absence of a relevant statute of limitations, Rule 15 "has no controlling force where ... a defendant's remedy is provided by the equitable doctrine of laches." [67]

Rule 17: Amendments Changing or Adding Plaintiffs

Rule 15(c)(3) discusses adding parties who are the subject of claims. Its applicability when the proposed amendment seeks to add a plaintiff is not entirely clear. On the one hand, there is precedent citing language in the Advisory Committee Notes to Rule 15(c) indicating that Rule 15(c) also governs that circumstance.[68] At the same time, Rule 17(a), governing requirements to prosecute a case in the name of the real party in interest, expressly provides that joinder or substitution of the real party in interest automatically relates back to the original filing date, apparently without regard to the requirements of Rule 15. Although the matter is not free of doubt, it appears that in such circumstances Rule 17(a), and not Rule 15, should control.[69]

Pacific Corp. v. ASARCO, Inc., *5 F.3d 431, 434 (9th Cir.1993)(mistake in choosing who is vulnerable to suit does not meet mistake of identity requirement of Rule 15(c)(3))*. But see, G.F. Co. v. Pan Ocean Shipping Co., *23 F.3d 1498, 1503 (9th Cir.1994) (held, requirement of mistake satisfied where named defendant is agent of true defendant, and where plaintiff's attorney swears in affidavit that initial failure to sue proper plaintiff was inadvertent);* Brown v. Shaner, *172 F.3d 927, 933 (6th Cir.1999),* cert. denied, *528 U.S. 966, 120 S.Ct. 403, 145 L.Ed.2d 315 (1999) (police officers sued in civil rights case; plaintiff's complaint identified individual wrongful acts but did not state whether defendants were sued in their official capacity or individually; held, failure to identify allegation of individual liability satisfies "mistake" requirement).* See also, Alston v. Parker, *363 F.3d 229, 236 (3d Cir.),* cert. denied, *541 U.S. 996, 124 S.Ct. 2003, 158 L.Ed.2d 506 (2004) (considering possibility that civil rights plaintiffs may have unusual problem of not knowing precisely who "relevant actors" were, and should therefore perhaps have access to "some initial discovery");* Woods v. Indiana University—Purdue University at Indianapolis, *996 F.2d 880, 887 (7th Cir.1993)(suit originally named police department rather than individual officers; held, police should have known that police department had sovereign immunity, and thus should have known of mistake; relation back permitted).* But cf., King v. One Unknown Federal Correction Officer, *201 F.3d 910, 914 (7th Cir.2000) ("[T]he mistake requirement is independent from whether the purported substitute party knew that the action would be brought against him.");* Singletary v. Pennsylvania Department of Corrections, *266 F.3d 186, 201 (3d Cir. 2001) (questioning majority view; suggesting but not deciding that lack of knowledge of defendant's identity should be treated as "mistake" for purpose of Rule 15(c))..*

67. *Brzozowski v. Correctional Physician Services, Inc.,* 360 F.3d 173, 182 (3d Cir. 2004).

68. *See, e.g., McCabe v. Trombley,* 867 F.Supp. 120, 127 n. 7 (N.D.N.Y.1994)(citing Advisory Committee notes for application of Rule 15(c) to situations where a party seeks to add a plaintiff). *See also Immigrant Assistance Project of the L.A. County Federation of Labor v. Immigration and Naturalization Service,* 306 F.3d 842, 857 (9th Cir.2002) (relation back should be measured by whether: (1) defendant already had notice of claim of new plaintiff; (2) presence of new plaintiff creates unfair prejudice for defendant; and (3) new plaintiff shares identity of interest with original plaintiff); *Young v. LePone,* 305 F.3d 1, 14 (1st Cir.2002) (Rule 15(c)(3) "can be applied to amendments that change the identity of plaintiffs").

69. *See, e.g., Scheufler v. General Host Corp.,* 126 F.3d 1261, 1271 (10th Cir.1997) (noting uncertainty; applying relation-back provisions of Rule 17(a)). *But cf., Cliff v. Payco General Amer-*

Commencement and Amended Complaints

Because an amended complaint often cannot be filed until leave of court has first been granted,[70] many courts have ruled that the amended complaint is deemed filed, for "commencement" and statute of limitations purposes, as of the date that the motion for leave to amend is filed.[71] Practitioners should rely on this principle with great care, however. Whether this treatment applies to all cases (or just those where an earlier amendment was made impossible by circumstances), whether this treatment applies where the motion neither attaches the proposed amended complaint nor properly describes it, and whether this treatment has any effect where the leave is denied, are each unclear.

Relation Back Against the United States

When the United States is a defendant, Rule 15(c)(3) provides that the requirements of timely notice of the action and knowledge of a mistake in identity, discussed immediately above, are satisfied if the original pleading was served on the United States Attorney (or designee), the Attorney General, or an agency or officer who would have been a proper defendant if named in the original complaint.[72] This express provision cuts through much of what might otherwise have been substantial technical obstacles to use of relation back against the United States under Rule 15(c)(3).[73] However, even when the United States is a defendant, the amended pleading must still arise out of the same transaction or occurrence as the original pleading, and service of the original pleading upon the federal officers identified above must occur within the 120–day period provided by Rule 4(m).

RULE 15(d). SUPPLEMENTAL PLEADINGS

CORE CONCEPT

Rule 15(d) governs circumstances in which parties are permitted to supplement previous pleadings to encompass events that have occurred since the earlier pleadings were filed.

APPLICATIONS

Leave of Court

There is no unqualified right to file a supplemental pleading.[74] Authority to file a supplemental pleading is obtained by filing a mo-

ican Credits, Inc., 363 F.3d 1113, 1132 (11th Cir. 2004) (concluding that use of Rule 15(c)(3) "rests on solid ground;" no discussion of Rule 17).

70. *See* Rule 15.

71. *See, e.g., Mayes v. AT & T Information Sys.*, 867 F.2d 1172, 1173 (8th Cir.1989).

72. *See, e.g., Roman v. Townsend,* 224 F.3d 24, 28 (1st Cir.2000).

73. *See, e.g., Delgado–Brunet v. Clark,* 93 F.3d 339, 344 (7th Cir.1996) (so noting; but also noting that notice to government officers who are sued personally cannot be inferred from service on another government officer).

74. *See, e.g., Zenith Radio Corp. v. Hazeltine Research, Inc.,* 401 U.S. 321, 91 S.Ct. 795, 28 L.Ed.2d 77 (1971). *See, e.g., Weeks v. New York,* 273 F.3d 76, 88 (2d Cir.2001) (acknowledging that supplemental pleadings that have a relationship with originally pleading are normally freely permitted, but holding that denial of supplemental pleading motion is within district

tion.[75] Courts grant such leave when the supplemental pleadings will not unfairly prejudice other parties.[76]

Party's Discretion

Supplemental pleadings are optional. Thus, if a party acquires a claim as a result of facts arising after the original pleading was filed, and the requirements of Rule 15(d) are satisfied, there is an opportunity but not a duty to file a supplemental claim.[77]

Same Transaction or Occurrence

If the issues addressed in a proposed supplemental pleading are related to the transaction or occurrence that gave rise to the original pleadings, and no other considerations of fairness weigh against hearing the supplemental pleading, courts generally permit the supplemental pleading.[78] A supplemental pleading may be permitted even if it arises from a separate transaction, but totally unrelated supplemental pleadings are disfavored.[79]

Relation to Rule 15(a)

Judicial decisions to grant or deny Rule 15(d) motions to supplement pleadings are generally based on the same factors of fairness courts weigh when considering motions to amend pleadings under Rule 15(a).[80]

court's discretion–even when opposing counsel does not object–when motion was presented to court on Friday preceding beginning of Monday trial and "the granting of the motion would potentially have entailed an amended pre-trial order, additional documents and additional witnesses (with any associated evidentiary issues), additional briefing, an expanded jury charge, and a longer trial than anticipated"). *Cf., Burns v. Exxon Corp.*, 158 F.3d 336, 343 (5th Cir.1998) ("While the text of Rule 15(a) provides that leave should be freely granted, the text of Rule 15(d) does not similarly provide." Also noting that plaintiffs had failed to allege that an event had occurred since filing of complaint).

75. *See, e.g., Bornholdt v. Brady,* 869 F.2d 57, 68 (2d Cir.1989) (noting that Rule 15(d) requires a motion). *But see Cabrera v. City of Huntington Park,* 159 F.3d 374, 382 (9th Cir. 1998) (per curiam) (Plaintiff's "failure formally to plead a malicious prosecution claim either in an amended or supplemental pleading does not preclude the district court from considering the claim.").

76. *See, e.g., Quaratino v. Tiffany & Co.,* 71 F.3d 58, 66 (2d Cir.1995)("Leave is normally granted, especially when the opposing party is not prejudiced."). *See also Glatt v. Chicago Park District,* 87 F.3d 190, 194 (7th Cir.1996) (motion to amend or supplement original complaint is held to higher standard of specificity than original complaint).

77. *See, e.g., Lundquist v. Rice Memorial Hospital,* 238 F.3d 975, 977 (8th Cir.2001) (decision not to file supplemental claim does not prevent assertion of that claim in later separate proceeding; doctrine of res judicata does not apply).

78. *See, e.g., Keith v. Volpe,* 858 F.2d 467, 473 (9th Cir.1988), *cert. denied sub nom., City of Hawthorne v. Wright,* 493 U.S. 813, 110 S.Ct. 61, 107 L.Ed.2d 28 (1989)(noting that use of Rule 15(d) is "favored"). *See also Weeks v. New York,* 273 F.3d 76, 88 (2d Cir.2001) (although other factors may be crucial, "[t]he threshhold consideration ... is whether 'the supplemental facts connect [the supplemental pleadings] to the original pleadings' ").

79. *See, e.g., Id.* at 474 (noting that Rule 15(d) does not require "same transaction," but does require "some relationship").

80. *See, e.g., Klos v. Haskell,* 835 F.Supp. 710, 715 (W.D.N.Y.1993), *affirmed,* 48 F.3d 81 (2d Cir.1995)(Rule 15(a) and (d) share same standard); *See also, Glatt v. Chicago Park District,* 87 F.3d 190 (7th Cir.1996)(under both Rule 15(a) and (d), court has authority to require substantiation of proposed amended or supplemental complaint, to ensure that motive is not simply to harass opponent).

Time to File

Rule 15(d) contains no restriction on the time in which a supplemental pleading may be filed. However, the court may consider inappropriate delay in attempting to assert supplemental claims as grounds for refusing to grant permission to file the supplemental pleading.[81] Additionally, a supplemental pleading is normally inappropriate if it attempts to introduce a new and distinct cause of action after the original case has gone to final judgment.[82]

Scope of Supplemental Pleadings

Supplemental pleadings should be restricted to events occurring since initiation of the suit. If the issues raised predate the original pleadings, supplemental pleadings are not the appropriate mechanism for raising them. Instead, a party should consider amending the original pleadings, pursuant to Rule 15(a) or (b).[83]

Intervening Judicial Decisions

It appears that intervening judicial decisions that change the applicable law are not the sort of "occurrences or events" that might implicate Rule 15(d).[84]

Additional Parties

In general, supplemental pleadings may join additional parties, subject to the normal requirements of jurisdiction. However, where such joinder might confuse the trier of fact or unduly distract attention from the original claims, proposals to add new parties may reduce the prospects for obtaining permission from the court to file a supplemental pleading.[85]

Relationship to Original Pleadings

Unlike amended pleadings, supplemental pleadings do not displace the original pleadings. Thus, there is no necessity to incorporate portions of the original pleadings in a supplemental pleading simply to preserve the original pleadings. However, it may often be convenient to

81. *See, e.g., Quaratino v. Tiffany & Co.,* 71 F.3d 58, 66 (2d Cir.1995)(undue delay may be ground for denying supplemental pleading).

82. *See, e.g., Planned Parenthood of Southern Arizona v. Neely,* 130 F.3d 400, 402–03 (9th Cir.1997) (per curiam) (final judgment divested district court of jurisdiction; noting possible exception in circumstances where district court retained jurisdiction or where plaintiff's supplemental allegation is that defendant was attempting to thwart original judgment; held, normal remedy after judgment is entered is to bring the "supplemental" allegations in a separate lawsuit).

83. *See, e.g., Flaherty v. Lang,* 199 F.3d 607, 613 n. 3 (2d Cir.1999) (Rule 15(d) applies to events that arise subsequent to a pleading; Rule 15(a) applies to efforts to replead facts that occurred prior to original pleadings.); *Federal Deposit Insurance Corp. v. Knostman,* 966 F.2d 1133, 1138 (7th Cir.1992)(identifying distinction between subdivisions of Rule 15).

84. *See, e.g., United States v. Hicks,* 283 F.3d 380, 385 (D.C.Cir.2002) (Rule 15(d) is addressed to relevant new facts, not changes in law).

85. *See, e.g., Albrecht v. Long Island Railroad,* 134 F.R.D. 40, 41 (E.D.N.Y.1991) (rejecting Rule 15(d) motion because new assertions of unrelated claims may confuse trier of fact). *See also, Planned Parenthood of Southern Arizona v. Neely,* 130 F.3d 400, 402 (9th Cir.1997) (supplemental pleading cannot be used to introduce new and distinct claim).

incorporate portions of original pleadings and thereby avoid possible duplication.

Mislabelled Pleadings

If a party inadvertently mislabels a supplemental pleading as an amended pleading, the court will disregard the error if it does not unfairly prejudice an opposing party.[86]

Defective Original Pleadings

Rule 15(d) explicitly provides that defects in the original pleadings have no effect on a party's ability to file a supplemental pleading. Thus, even an uncorrectable defect in the original pleading, requiring dismissal of the counts that pleading contains, does not necessarily bar filing of a supplemental pleading, if the supplemental pleading itself is free from substantial defects.

Responses to Supplemental Pleadings

Rule 15(d) does not create either a right or duty to respond to a supplemental pleading. Instead, the Rule vests the court with authority to order a response when appropriate in the circumstances of a case. Typically, an opportunity to respond will be permitted when the supplemental pleading asserts a new cause of action.

Relation Back of Supplemental Pleadings

Because supplemental pleadings address only events that have occurred since the original pleadings were filed, no question normally arises as to whether supplemental pleadings relate back to the date the original pleadings were filed. However, where relation back is important to the supplemental pleadings, courts tend to apply the standards of Rule 15(c) to determine whether relation back should be permitted.[87]

ADDITIONAL RESEARCH REFERENCES

Wright & Miller, *Federal Practice and Procedure* §§ 1471–1510.

C.J.S. Federal Civil Procedure §§ 322–356 et seq.

West's Key No. Digests, Federal Civil Procedure ⚷821–853, 861–871.

86. *See, e.g., Cabrera v. City of Huntington Park,* 159 F.3d 374, 382 (9th Cir.1998) (per curiam) (erroneously characterizing supplemental pleading as amended pleading is immaterial).

87. *See, e.g., Federal Deposit Insurance Corp. v. Knostman,* 966 F.2d 1133, 1138 (7th Cir. 1992)(using standards of Rule 15(c)).

RULE 16

PRETRIAL CONFERENCES; SCHEDULING; MANAGEMENT

(a) Pretrial Conferences; Objectives. In any action, the court may in its discretion direct the attorneys for the parties and any unrepresented parties to appear before it for a conference or conferences before trial for such purposes as

(1) expediting the disposition of the action;

(2) establishing early and continuing control so that the case will not be protracted because of lack of management;

(3) discouraging wasteful pretrial activities;

(4) improving the quality of the trial through more thorough preparation; and

(5) facilitating the settlement of the case.

(b) Scheduling and Planning. Except in categories of actions exempted by district court rule as inappropriate, the district judge, or a magistrate judge when authorized by district court rule, shall, after receiving the report from the parties under Rule 26(f) or after consulting with the attorneys for the parties and any unrepresented parties by a scheduling conference, telephone, mail, or other suitable means, enter a scheduling order that limits the time

(1) to join other parties and to amend the pleadings;

(2) to file motions; and

(3) to complete discovery.

The scheduling order may also include

(4) modifications of the times for disclosures under Rules 26(a) and 26(e)(1) and of the extent of discovery to be permitted;

(5) the date or dates for conferences before trial, a final pretrial conference, and trial; and

(6) any other matters appropriate in the circumstances of the case.

The order shall issue as soon as practicable but in any event within 90 days after the appearance of a defendant and within 120 days after the complaint has been served on a defendant. A schedule shall not be modified except upon a showing of good cause and by leave of the district judge or, when authorized by local rule, by a magistrate judge.

(c) Subjects for Consideration at Pretrial Conferences. At any conference under this rule consideration may be given, and the court may take appropriate action, with respect to

(1) the formulation and simplification of the issues, including the elimination of frivolous claims or defenses;

(2) the necessity or desirability of amendments to the pleadings;

(3) the possibility of obtaining admissions of fact and of documents which will avoid unnecessary proof, stipulations regarding the authenticity of documents, and advance rulings from the court on the admissibility of evidence;

(4) the avoidance of unnecessary proof and of cumulative evidence, and limitations or restrictions on the use of testimony under Rule 702 of the Federal Rules of Evidence;

(5) the appropriateness and timing of summary adjudication under Rule 56;

(6) the control and scheduling of discovery, including orders affecting disclosures and discovery pursuant to Rule 26 and Rules 29 through 37;

(7) the identification of witnesses and documents, the need and schedule for filing and exchanging pretrial briefs, and the date or dates for further conferences and for trial;

(8) the advisability of referring matters to a magistrate judge or master;

(9) settlement and the use of special procedures to assist in resolving the dispute when authorized by statute or local rule;

(10) the form and substance of the pretrial order;

(11) the disposition of pending motions;

(12) the need for adopting special procedures for managing potentially difficult or protracted actions that may involve complex issues, multiple parties, difficult legal questions, or unusual proof problems;

(13) an order for a separate trial pursuant to Rule 42(b) with respect to a claim, counterclaim, cross-claim, or third-party claim, or with respect to any particular issue in the case;

(14) an order directing a party or parties to present evidence early in the trial with respect to a manageable issue that could, on the evidence, be the basis for a judgment as a matter of law under Rule 50(a) or a judgment on partial findings under Rule 52(c);

(15) an order establishing a reasonable limit on the time allowed for presenting evidence; and

(16) such other matters as may facilitate the just, speedy, and inexpensive disposition of the action.

At least one of the attorneys for each party participating in any conference before trial shall have authority to enter into stipulations and to make admissions regarding all matters that the participants may reasonably anticipate may be discussed. If appropriate, the court may require that a party or its representative be present or reasonably available by telephone in order to consider possible settlement of the dispute.

(d) Final Pretrial Conference. Any final pretrial conference shall be held as close to the time of trial as reasonable under the circumstances. The participants at any such conference shall formulate a plan for trial, including a program for facilitating the admission of evidence. The conference shall be attended by at least one of the attorneys who will conduct the trial for each of the parties and by any unrepresented parties.

(e) Pretrial Orders. After any conference held pursuant to this rule, an order shall be entered reciting the action taken. This order shall control the subsequent course of the action unless modified by a subsequent order. The order following a final pretrial conference shall be modified only to prevent manifest injustice.

(f) Sanctions. If a party or party's attorney fails to obey a scheduling or pretrial order, or if no appearance is made on behalf of a party at a scheduling or pretrial conference, or if a party or party's attorney is substantially unprepared to participate in the conference, or if a party or party's attorney fails to participate in good faith, the judge, upon motion or the judge's own initiative, may make such orders with regard thereto as are just, and among others any of the orders provided in Rule 37(b)(2)(B), (C), (D). In lieu of or in addition to any other sanction, the judge shall require the party or the attorney representing the party or both to pay the reasonable expenses incurred because of any noncompliance with this rule, including attorney's fees, unless the judge finds that the noncompliance was substantially justified or that other circumstances make an award of expenses unjust.

[Amended April 28, 1983, effective August 1, 1983; March 2, 1987, effective August 1, 1987; April 22, 1993, effective December 1, 1993.]

AUTHORS' COMMENTARY ON RULE 16

PURPOSE AND SCOPE

Rule 16 authorizes the district court to convene pretrial conferences with the purpose of processing a case efficiently. While the court has discretion to hold such pretrial conferences, Rule 16 *requires* the court to issue a scheduling order setting procedures for discovery and trial, unless the case falls into a category which the court, by local rule, has exempted from the requirement for a scheduling order. Further, if a pretrial conference is held, Rule 16 also requires the court to issue a pretrial order after such a pretrial conference detailing the action at the conference and establishing the course of action to be followed. The order is binding unless subsequently modified by the court.

NOTE: Rule 16, particularly Rule 16(b) and (c), were amended substantially in December, 1993. Cases decided before that date should therefore be used with care.

RULE 16(a). PRETRIAL CONFERENCE; OBJECTIVES

CORE CONCEPT

Rule 16(a) outlines the parameters and objectives for the court's pretrial conferences with the parties. When preparing for a pretrial conference, the litigants should consult both Rule 16(c) and the local rules concerning the subjects to be discussed at a pretrial conference.

APPLICATIONS

Pretrial Conferences

(1) *Initial or First Conference:* The court may convene the first pretrial conference as soon as all of the parties have been served with the complaint. Typically, the court will delay the pretrial conference until after an answer is filed or preliminary motions to dismiss are resolved. The first pretrial conference permits the parties to familiarize the court with the issues in the case and to propose a discovery schedule. After the conference, the court will issue an order detailing the decisions reached and action taken. Typically, the initial conference will address issues of scope and timing of discovery, filing of parties' pretrial narrative statements, the timing for filing of motions, alternative dispute resolution, and possibly an anticipated date for trial.

(2) *Subsequent and Final Pretrial Conferences:* Ordinarily, the court holds a final pretrial conference after the close of discovery, after

ruling on dispositive pretrial motions and after the filing of the pretrial narrative statements.[1] At this conference, the court sets a trial date, seeks to further clarify the issues, discusses any extraneous matters, sets a schedule for any remaining motions, and encourages settlement discussions.

(3) *Other Pretrial Conferences:* Local rule may require the court to hold one pretrial conference, but the court may hold as many pretrial conferences as it deems necessary to apprise the court of the progress of the case.

Pretrial Orders

The court is required to issue a pretrial order detailing the action taken at any pretrial conference conducted pursuant to Rule 16, as provided by Rule 16(e).

Who Must Attend

Rule 16(a) authorizes the court to order attorneys and unrepresented parties to attend pretrial conferences,[2] and makes no reference to represented parties. Courts have held that represented parties (in contrast to their attorneys) may also be directed to attend.[3] Additionally, at least one court has held that the judge must also attend, and cannot delegate that function to a law clerk.[4]

Motion for Pretrial Conference

Generally, the court will set the time for pretrial conferences. However, the parties may seek a pretrial conference either by informal request or by motion.[5] The court has discretion to order additional pretrial conferences.

RULE 16(b). SCHEDULING AND PLANNING

CORE CONCEPT

After receiving the discovery report required under Rule 26(f) or after conducting a scheduling conference under Rule 16(a), the court will issue a scheduling order setting timetables for pretrial matters. This scheduling order must be issued within 90 days after the appearance of a defendant and within 120 days of the service of the com-

1. *But see Mizwicki v. Helwig*, 196 F.3d 828, 833 (7th Cir.1999) (there is no requirement that the court conduct a final pretrial conference).

2. *Royal Palace Hotel Associates, Inc. v. International Resort Classics, Inc.*, 178 F.R.D. 595, 597 (M.D.Fla.1998) (local rule requiring attendance of lead trial counsel is enforceable).

3. *See, e.g., In the Matter of Sargeant Farms, Inc.*, 224 B.R. 842, 845 (Bkrtcy.M.D.Fla.1998) (requiring party representative with settlement authority to attend Rule 16 conference); *G. Heileman Brewing Co. v. Joseph Oat Corp.*, 871 F.2d 648, 650–53 (7th Cir.1989)(en banc)("mere absence of language in the federal rules specifically authorizing or describing a particular judicial procedure should not, and does not, give rise to a negative implication of prohibition").

4. *Connolly v. National School Bus Service, Inc.*, 177 F.3d 593 (7th Cir.1999).

5. *See, e.g., DiDomenico v. New York Life Insurance Co.*, 837 F.Supp. 1203, 1206 (M.D.Fla. 1993)(motion for a conference under Rule 16(a)).

plaint.[6] The district judge may prepare the scheduling order or may refer this task to a magistrate judge.

APPLICATIONS

Mandatory Topics

Rule 16(b) requires the court's order to include time limits for: joining parties[7] and amending pleadings;[8] filing motions;[9] and completing discovery.[10]

Optional Topics

At the court's discretion, the scheduling order may also include: modifications of time limits for disclosures under Rule 26(a) and (e)(1) and of the amount of discovery parties shall be permitted; dates for pretrial conferences and for trial; and other matters the court deems appropriate.[11]

Modification of Scheduling Order Deadlines

For good cause shown,[12] the court may grant a motion modifying or enlarging the deadlines in the scheduling order.[13]

RULE 16(c). SUBJECTS FOR CONSIDERATION AT PRETRIAL CONFERENCES

CORE CONCEPT

Rule 16(c) contains a list of topics that the court may consider at Rule 16 conferences. Rule 16(c) also allows for the consideration of any other matters that may facilitate the "just, speedy, and inexpensive disposition of the action."

6. *O'Connell v. Hyatt Hotels of Puerto Rico*, 357 F.3d 152, 154 (1st Cir. 2004).

7. Howell v. Standard Motor Products, Inc., 2001 WL 196969 (N.D.Tex.2001).

8. *O'Connell v. Hyatt Hotels of Puerto Rico*, 357 F.3d 152, 154 (1st Cir. 2004) (the purpose of limiting the period for amending the pleadings is to assure that at some point both the parties and the pleadings will be fixed); *Sosa v. Airprint Systems, Inc.*, 133 F.3d 1417, 1418 (11th Cir. 1998).

9. *Rosario-Diaz v. Gonzalez*, 140 F.3d 312 (1st Cir.1998)(Rule 16 mandates that the court set a deadline for pretrial motions); *Lozada v. Dale Baker Oldsmobile, Inc.*, 145 F.Supp.2d 878 (W.D.Mich.2001).

10. *Suntrust Bank v. Blue Water Fiber*, L.P., 210 F.R.D. 196, 199 (E.D.Mich.2002). *But see Dodson v. Runyon*, 86 F.3d 37, 41 (2d Cir.1996), *cert. denied*, 520 U.S. 1156, 117 S.Ct. 1337, 137 L.Ed.2d 496 (1997) (explaining that a judge's failure to enter a scheduling order does not relieve counsel of the duty to his client to move forward with litigation).

11. *Does I thru XXIII v. Advanced Textile Corp.*, 214 F.3d 1058, 1068 (9th Cir.2000) (the court may use its powers under Rule 16 to address a party's need for anonymity).

12. *Leary v. Daeschner*, 349 F.3d 888, 906 (6th Cir. 2003) (a court choosing to modify the schedule upon a showing of good cause may do so only if the schedule cannot reasonably be met despite the diligence of the party seeking the extension); *Zivkovic v. Southern California Edison Co.*, 302 F.3d 1080, (9th Cir.2002) (the pretrial schedule may be modified if it cannot reasonably be met despite the diligence of the party seeking the extension); *Bradford v. DANA Corp.*, 249 F.3d 807 (8th Cir.2001).

13. *See, e.g., O'Connell v. Hyatt Hotels of Puerto Rico*, 357 F.3d 152, 154 (1st Cir. 2004) (Rule 16(b)'s "good cause" standard, rather than Rule 15(a)'s "freely given" standard, governs motions to amend filed after scheduling order deadlines); *Parker v. Columbia Pictures Industries*, 204 F.3d 326, 339–40 (2d Cir.2000).

APPLICATIONS

Topics for Conferences

During a pretrial conference, the court may seek to define and simplify the contested facts, theories, and issues,[14] eliminate frivolous claims or defenses,[15] determine whether an amendment of the pleadings is necessary, address disclosure and discovery issues, seek the admission or denial of facts or documents, make advance rulings on the admissibility of evidence[16] and the appropriateness of expert witnesses, require parties to file lists identifying witnesses[17] and documents, entertain requests to limit witnesses,[18] govern the order of proof at trial,[19] and discuss pretrial narrative statements, pending motions, stipulations limiting the issues for trial,[20] and scheduling matters. The court may consider stays, consolidations, or separate trials.[21] The court may also require parties to schedule presentation of evidence so that, if judgment as a matter of law or judgment on partial findings is appropriate, the court may reach those questions early in the trial. The court will also likely pursue the potential for settlement.[22] At the pretrial conference in a non-jury case, the court may decide to refer certain matters to another district judge, a magistrate judge, or a master.

Authority of Representatives

At the appropriate pretrial conference, which is usually the final pretrial conference, an attorney or party representative with the authority to enter stipulations and make admissions (not settlement) must be present. Rule 16(c) also authorizes the court, if appropriate, to require that an attorney or party representative with authority to settle the case be present or available by telephone.

14. *Castillo v. Norton*, 219 F.R.D. 155, 163 (D.Ariz. 2003).

15. *Chavez v. Illinois State Police*, 251 F.3d 612 (7th Cir.2001); *Rogan v. Menino*, 175 F.3d 75 (1st Cir.1999), *cert. denied*, 528 U.S. 1062, 120 S.Ct. 616, 145 L.Ed.2d 511 (1999) (the court cannot ignore the procedural safeguards of summary judgment under Rule 56 by dismissing defendants at the pretrial conference); *In re HealthSouth Corp.*, 308 F.Supp.2d 1253 (N.D.Ala. 2004) (a groundless contention without support in the facts or the law need not be heard in the district court).

16. *Tucker v. Ohtsu Tire & Rubber Co. Ltd.*, 49 F.Supp.2d 456 (D.Md.1999) (motions in limine may be presented at pretrial conferences);

17. *Hollander v. Sandoz Pharmaceuticals Corp.*, 289 F.3d 1193 (10th Cir.2002), *cert. denied*, 537 U.S. 1088, 123 S.Ct. 697, 154 L.Ed.2d 632 (2002).

18. *Planned Parenthood of Central New Jersey v. Verniero*, 22 F.Supp.2d 331, 339 (D.N.J. 1998).

19. *Dick v. Dep't of Veterans Affairs*, 290 F.3d 1356 (Fed.Cir.2002).

20. *United States v. One 48 Ft. White Colored Sailboat Named "Libertine"*, 24 F.Supp.2d 174, 178 (D.Puerto Rico 1998) (stipulations at a Rule 16 conference are enforceable); *Briggs v. Dalkon Shield Claimants Trust*, 174 F.R.D. 369, 373 (D.Md.1997) (stating that the trial court may have "authority to order one party to accept a stipulation offered by the opposing party.").

21. *Dick v. Dep't of Veterans Affairs*, 290 F.3d 1356 (Fed.Cir.2002).

22. *Sloan v. State Farm Mut. Auto. Ins. Co.*, 360 F.3d 1220, 1227 (10th Cir. 2004) (while settlement is an appropriate topic for a pretrial conference, some cases cannot be settled and the parties' desire for a trial must be respected); *In re Atlantic Pipe Corp.*, 304 F.3d 135, 143 (1st Cir.2002) (discussing the use of required mediation).

Memorializing Pretrial Conference

A court reporter generally will be present whenever the court expects to discuss and rule on issues at pretrial conference. In unusual circumstances, parties may bring their own stenographers if the court does not order a court reporter.

Settlement

It has been held that the court may order parties to attend a conference where settlement will be discussed[23] but may not coerce those parties into settlement.[24] However, a bankruptcy court may bar non-settling parties from bringing contribution claims against settling parties in an effort to facilitate a settlement.[25]

Rulings on Motions

At the pretrial conference, the court may rule on discovery motions, jurisdictional challenges, Rule 12(b) defenses preserved under Rule 12(g) and 12(h), other Rule 12 motions if those motions were not decided previously, motions for summary judgment,[26] or motions in limine.[27]

Binding Effect of Statements at Pretrial Conference

A party is held at trial to admissions and stipulations made at a pretrial conference. However, the court may permit a party in certain circumstances to withdraw its stipulations.

Pretrial Memorandum or Narrative Statement

(1) *Time:* At the first pretrial conference and in its scheduling order the court will usually provide a date on which the parties must file a pretrial memorandum or pretrial narrative statement. The court usually orders the plaintiff's pretrial narrative statement to be filed several weeks after the close of discovery and the defendant's pretrial narrative statement several weeks after the filing of the plaintiff's statement.

(2) *Contents:* Local rule or court order will define the information parties are required to include in their pretrial narrative statements. Ordinarily, the parties must state their legal theories or defenses, provide a list of witnesses and documents to be presented at trial, detail the intended use of expert witnesses, and describe any exceptional legal or evidentiary questions that will be asserted at trial.

23. *In Re Patenaude*, 210 F.3d 135, 144 (3d Cir.2000), *cert. denied*, 531 U.S. 1011, 121 S.Ct. 565, 148 L.Ed.2d 484 (2000).

24. *Goss Graphics Systems, Inc. v. DEV Industries, Inc.*, 267 F.3d 624, 627 (7th Cir.2001).

25. *Matter of Munford, Inc.*, 97 F.3d 449, 455 (11th Cir.1996).

26. *Pine Ridge Coal Company v. Local 8377, United Mine Workers of America*, 187 F.3d 415, 419 (4th Cir.1999); *but see Rogan v. Menino*, 175 F.3d 75, 80 (1st Cir.1999) (court may not deprive a party of the procedural protections of Rule 56 by granting summary judgment under Rule 16), *cert. denied*, 528 U.S. 1062, 120 S.Ct. 616, 145 L.Ed.2d 511 (1999).

27. *Tucker v. Ohtsu Tire & Rubber Co., Ltd.*, 49 F.Supp.2d 456, 462–63 (D.Md.1999) (motions in limine may be presented at pretrial conferences).

(3) *Effect and Amendment of:* The pretrial narrative statements are generally binding on the parties at trial, and failure to raise a legal issue may constitute waiver of that issue.[28] However, the court may permit the amendment of a pretrial narrative statement to include evidence not available at the time of filing the statement or for other legitimate reasons.[29]

(4) *Failure to File:* When a party fails to file a pretrial narrative statement required by local rule or court order, the court may impose sanctions under Rule 16(f).

RULE 16(d). FINAL PRETRIAL CONFERENCE

CORE CONCEPT

The court will usually conduct the final pretrial conference after the pretrial narrative statements have been filed and as close to trial as possible. At the final pretrial conference, the court will make a schedule for any remaining motions and set a trial date. An attorney who will conduct the trial or an unrepresented party must attend the conference with the authority to enter stipulations and make admissions (not settlement).

RULE 16(e). PRETRIAL ORDERS

CORE CONCEPT

Rule 16(e) requires the court to issue a pretrial order memorializing the action taken at any pretrial conference.[30] Once a pretrial order has been entered,[31] it supercedes all pleadings and controls the subsequent course of the case.[32] A pretrial order may include amendments to the pleadings,[33] stipulations, a statement of the issues for trial, the defenses available, the date for the filing of pretrial narrative statements, evidentiary or witness lists, and the date set for trial. The court may order a party to draft the order on the court's behalf.

APPLICATIONS

Pretrial Order Binding on Parties

All matters mentioned in the pretrial order are binding on the

28. *See McLean Contracting Co. v. Waterman Steamship Corp.*, 277 F.3d 477 (4th Cir.2002); *Olsen v. American Steamship Co.*, 176 F.3d 891 (6th Cir.1999).

29. *Payne v. S.S. Nabob*, 302 F.2d 803, 807 (3d Cir.1962), *cert. denied,* 371 U.S. 870, 83 S.Ct. 136, 9 L.Ed.2d 107 (1962).

30. *Athridge v. Rivas*, 141 F.3d 357, 362 n. 3 (D.C.Cir.1998).

31. *Wall v. County of Orange*, 364 F.3d 1107, 1111 (9th Cir. 2004) (a pretrial order that was lodged but not entered is not controlling).

32. *Hamburger v. State Farm Mut. Auto. Ins. Co.*, 361 F.3d 875, 887 (5th Cir. 2004); *Miller v. Pfizer Inc.*, 196 F.Supp.2d 1095 (D.Kan.2002).

33. *Deere v. Goodyear Tire and Rubber Co.*, 175 F.R.D. 157, 164–65 (N.D.N.Y.1997); *but see Wilson v. Muckala*, 303 F.3d 1207, 1215 (10th Cir.2002) (amendment to pleading not necessary if issue is addressed in a pretrial order, because the pretrial order supersedes the pleadings).

parties at trial.[34] Evidence or legal theories that are not at least implicitly raised in the pretrial order will be barred at trial.[35] Pretrial orders may not, however, be binding in retrials of the matter[36] or in subsequent litigation.[37] Because the purpose of Rule 16 is to clarify the real nature of the dispute, a claim or theory not raised in the pretrial order should not be considered by the factfinder.[38] The court may impose sanctions under Rule 16(f) for a party's failure to comply with the order.

Objection to Pretrial Order and Preservation of Right to Appeal

In order to preserve a party's rights on appeal, a party should object to a pretrial order at the time it is issued or at the commencement of trial by asserting a motion to amend the order.

Modification of Pretrial Order

Where its modification will not unduly prejudice the opposing party, the court has discretion to modify a pretrial order to prevent manifest injustice.[39] The court may also modify a pretrial order when evidence not raised in the pretrial statement is discovered after the pretrial order has been issued,[40] or is introduced at trial.[41]

Appeal of Pretrial Order

Prior to the entry of judgment, a party has no right to a direct appeal from a pretrial order.[42] Ultimately, the pretrial order will be reviewed for abuse of discretion.[43]

RULE 16(f). SANCTIONS

CORE CONCEPT

34. *Kay-Cee Enterprises, Inc. v. Amoco Oil Co.*, 45 F.Supp.2d 840 (D.Kan.1999) ("The pretrial order supersedes the pleadings and controls the subsequent course of the litigation.").

35. *DP Aviation v. Smiths Industries Aerospace and Defense Systems Ltd.*, 268 F.3d 829, 841 (9th Cir.2001).

36. *Johns Hopkins University v. Cellpro, Inc.*, 152 F.3d 1342, 1357 (Fed.Cir.1998) (rulings in pretrial order are controlling at trial, but may not control the scope of a retrial).

37. *Atchison, Topeka and Santa Fe Railway Co. v. Hercules Inc.*, 146 F.3d 1071, 1074 (9th Cir.1998) (pretrial order limiting joinder of additional parties did not preclude a separate action against such additional parties).

38. *Kona Technology Corp. v. Southern Pacific Transp. Co.*, 225 F.3d 595, 604 (5th Cir. 2000) (if a claim or issue is omitted from the pretrial order, it is waived, even if it appeared in the complaint); *Elvis Presley Enterprises, Inc. v. Capece*, 141 F.3d 188, 206 (5th Cir.1998).

39. *In re Olshan*, 356 F.3d 1078, 1085 (9th Cir. 2004); *In the Matter of: El Paso Refinery, L P*, 171 F.3d 249, 255 (5th Cir.1999) (trial court has broad discretion in determining whether a pretrial order should be modified); *Byrd v. Guess*, 137 F.3d 1126, 1131 (9th Cir.1998), *cert. denied*, 525 U.S. 963, 119 S.Ct. 405, 142 L.Ed.2d 329 (1998) (setting forth a four-part test for determination of whether to modify pretrial order).

40. *Ross v. Garner Printing Co.*, 285 F.3d 1106, 1114 (8th Cir.2002).

41. *See United Phosphorus, Ltd. v. Midland Fumigant, Inc.*, 205 F.3d 1219, 1236 (10th Cir. 2000).

42. *Bradley v. Milliken*, 468 F.2d 902 (6th Cir.1972), *cert. denied*, 409 U.S. 844, 93 S.Ct. 45, 34 L.Ed.2d 83 (1972).

43. *Koch v. Koch Industries, Inc.*, 203 F.3d 1202, 1222 (10th Cir.2000), *cert. denied*, 531 U.S. 926, 121 S.Ct. 302, 148 L.Ed.2d 242 (2000); *Gorlikowski v. Tolbert*, 52 F.3d 1439 (7th Cir. 1995).

Upon motion or on the court's own initiative, the court will impose sanctions to force parties to comply with scheduling and pretrial orders and to compensate parties for expenses caused by an opposing party's noncompliance.[44] Sanctions may also attach to incorrect or incomplete pretrial statements,[45] or the failure to participate in a settlement conference in good faith.[46]

APPLICATIONS

Procedural and Substantive Errors

When a party commits a procedural error, courts generally will not impose sanctions that compromise the merits of the case.[47] Instead the court should impose costs and fees.[48] When a party commits a substantive error the court may impose sanctions which compromise the merits of a party's case.[49]

Sanctions Imposed on Party's Motion

A party may file a motion for sanctions when a party or a party's attorney does not obey a scheduling[50] or pretrial order, when a party does not appear at a pretrial conference,[51] when a party is unprepared at a pretrial conference, or when a party does not act in good faith at a pretrial conference. The motion should be asserted as soon as possible after the sanctionable activity. Unless made during a hearing or trial, a party must file a written motion stating the reasons for the sanctions with particularity and the relief or order sought.

Sanctions Imposed Sua Sponte

When the court seeks to impose sanctions on its own initiative, the court must first provide notice and an opportunity to be heard to the sanctionable party.[52]

44. *Garlepied v. Main,* 2001 WL 305264 (E.D.La.2001).

45. *Bronk v. Ineichen,* 54 F.3d 425 (7th Cir. 1995)(excluding testimony of witness not named in pretrial statement).

46. *Smith v. Northwest Financial Acceptance, Inc.,* 129 F.3d 1408, 1419 (10th Cir.1997); *Landmark Legal Foundation v. E.P.A.,* 272 F.Supp.2d 70, 88 (D.D.C. 2003) (Rule 16(f) sanctions apply only to actions related to pretrial conferences and orders, not to other potential violations).

47. *Rice v. City of Chicago,* 333 F.3d 780, 786 (7th Cir. 2003) (a judge should consider punishing the lawyer through sanctions rather than the plaintiff through dismissal of the suit); *John v. Louisiana,* 828 F.2d 1129 (5th Cir.1987).

48. *Sanders v. Union Pacific Railroad Co.,* 154 F.3d 1037, 1042 (9th Cir.1998) (imposing monetary sanctions on attorney can appropriately punish the one responsible for the harm), *rehearing granted, opinion withdrawn,* 179 F.3d 1244 (9th Cir.1999).

49. *See, e.g., Lucien v. Breweur,* 9 F.3d 26, 29 (7th Cir.1993)(willful failure to attend final pretrial conference can be cause for dismissal with prejudice). *But see, Ball v. City of Chicago,* 2 F.3d 752, 758 (7th Cir.1993)(punishing a lawyer through monetary sanctions preferable to punishing plaintiff through dismissal when fault lies with lawyer).

50. *Lucas Automotive Engineering, Inc. v. Bridgestone/Firestone, Inc.,* 275 F.3d 762 (9th Cir.2001) (sanctioning a party for failing to appear for a scheduled mediation); *Engineered Products Co. v. Donaldson Co., Inc.,* 313 F.Supp.2d 951 (2004) (sanctions imposed for failure to meet deadline for expert reports).

51. *Templet v. HydroChem Inc.,* 367 F.3d 473, 481 (5th Cir. 2004); *Lititz Mutual Ins. Co. v. Royal Ins. Co. Of America,* 58 F.Supp.2d 1287, 1292 (D.Kan.1999).

52. *Ford v. Alfaro,* 785 F.2d 835 (9th Cir. 1986); *Newton v. A.C. & S., Inc.,* 918 F.2d 1121 (3d Cir.1990).

Purposes of Sanctions

Sanctions may be assessed to punish for improper conduct,[53] for purposes of deterrence, or to compensate the party injured by the improper conduct.[54]

Finding of Sanctionable Activity

The court will examine the record and any materials submitted by the parties. The court must make a specific finding of sanctionable activity. When it finds that a party has committed sanctionable activities, the court has discretion to impose sanctions, even in the absence of bad faith.[55] The court will not impose sanctions when the party can substantially justify its violation[56] or where the award of expenses would be unjust.

(1) *Against Whom:* The court may impose sanctions against the party and/or any attorney of the party.[57] Where a represented party has no knowledge of the sanctionable activity, the court may order sanctions against the attorney alone and preclude reimbursement from the client.

(2) *Notice and Hearing:* Before imposing sanctions, the court must provide the alleged sanctionable party with notice and an opportunity to be heard either orally or in writing.[58]

Nature of Sanctions

The court will design a sanction that appropriately matches the violation.[59] The court can impose any sanctions it deems appropriate,[60] including but not limited to the following:[61]

(1) *Discovery Sanctions:* Rule 16(f) incorporates the discovery sanctions found in Rule 37(b)(2)(B), (C),[62] and (D), such as refusing to allow a party to support or oppose designated claims or defenses, striking pleadings or parts thereof, precluding witnesses not properly disclosed,[63] or treating the conduct as contempt of court.[64]

53. *United States v. Samaniego*, 345 F.3d 1280, 1284 (11th Cir. 2003).

54. *See, e.g., Media Duplication Services, Ltd. v. HDG Software, Inc.*, 928 F.2d 1228, 1242 (1st Cir.1991) (court may consider deterrence when assessing sanctions under Rule 16(f)); *Royal Palace Hotel Assoc., Inc. v. International Resort Classics, Inc.*, 178 F.R.D. 588, 591 (M.D.Fla. 1997).

55. *Rice v. Barnes*, 201 F.R.D. 549, 551 (M.D.Ala.2001) (the court does not need to find that the violation was willful); *Martin Family Trust v. Heco/Nostalgia Enterprises Co.*, 186 F.R.D. 601, 604 (E.D.Cal.1999).

56. *Firefighter's Institute for Racial Equality ex rel. Anderson v. City of St. Louis*, 220 F.3d 898, 902 (8th Cir.2000), *cert. denied*, 532 U.S. 921, 121 S.Ct. 1359, 149 L.Ed.2d 288 (2001).

57. *Nick v. Morgan's Foods, Inc.*, 270 F.3d 590, 597 (8th Cir.2001); *Republic of the Philippines v. Westinghouse Electric Corp.*, 43 F.3d 65 (3d Cir.1994).

58. *Ford v. Alfaro,* 785 F.2d 835 (9th Cir. 1986).

59. *Republic of the Philippines v. Westinghouse Electric Corp.*, 43 F.3d 65 (3d Cir.1994); *Smith v. Rowe*, 761 F.2d 360 (7th Cir.1985).

60. *Young v. Gordon*, 330 F.3d 76 (1st Cir. 2003).

61. *Nick v. Morgan's Foods, Inc.*, 270 F.3d 590, 595–96 (8th Cir.2001).

62. *Ray v. Eyster*, 132 F.3d 152, 154 n. 2 (3d Cir.1997).

63. *Potomac Electric Power Co. v. Electric Motor Supply, Inc.*, 190 F.R.D. 372 (D.Md.1999) (setting forth factors for determining whether to exclude a witness); *Trost v. Trek Bicycle Corp.*, 162 F.3d 1004, 1008 (8th Cir.1998) (court may exclude untimely expert evidence because failure

64. See note 64 on page 411.

(2) *Reasonable Expenses:* The court must require the sanctionable person to pay reasonable expenses,[65] including attorney fees caused by noncompliance with Rule 16, unless the court finds that the noncompliance was "substantially justified" or that an award of expenses would be "unjust."[66] These expenses may be the only sanctions ordered or in addition to another sanction.

(3) *Court Costs:* The court may impose court costs on a party who causes court expense by the sanctionable activities.

(4) *Fines and Disciplinary Action:* In lieu of or in addition to other sanctions, the court may impose a fine[67] upon or seek disciplinary action against the sanctionable party.[68]

(5) Dismissal: The court may even dismiss a case[69] or enter default judgment[70] for failure to obey pretrial orders. However, a trial court must apply lesser sanctions than dismissal except in an extreme situation were there is a clear record of delay or disobedience.[71] Some pertinent factors considered by the courts are the severity of the violation, the legitimacy of the party's excuse, repetition of violations, the deliberateness of the misconduct, mitigating excuses, prejudice to the court or opponent, and the adequacy of lesser sanctions.[72]

Appeal

An order imposing sanctions for failing to obey a Rule 16 scheduling or pretrial order is appealable only after final judgment has been entered in the underlying action.[73] "A district court's imposition of sanctions will be upheld unless an abuse of discretion or clearly erroneous."[74]

to disclose timely was neither harmless nor substantially justified); *but see Lory v. General Electric Co.*, 179 F.R.D. 86, 89 (N.D.N.Y.1998) (exclusion of expert witness too severe a sanction where late disclosure was sole transgression and did not prejudice the defendant).

64. *Trilogy Communications, Inc. v. Times Fiber Communications, Inc.*, 109 F.3d 739, 745 (Fed.Cir.1997) (striking expert's reports from record when submitted after due date); *Bronk v. Ineichen*, 54 F.3d 425 (7th Cir.1995)(excluding testimony of witness not named in pretrial statement); *Hathcock v. Navistar International Transportation Corp.*, 53 F.3d 36 (4th Cir.1995)(default can be appropriate sanction for failure to obey a scheduling order).

65. *See Former Employees of Tyco Electronics, Fiber Optics Div. v. U.S. Dept. of Labor*, 259 F.Supp.2d 1246 (CIT 2003) (attorney fees can be reduced even if reasonable for the tasks at issue); *Lithuanian Commerce Corp. v. Sara Lee Hosiery*, 177 F.R.D. 205, 214–15 (D.N.J.1997) (reasonableness is to be determined outside of opposing party's actual expenses).

66. *Richardson v. Nassau County*, 184 F.R.D. 497 (E.D.N.Y.1999).

67. *Nick v. Morgan's Foods, Inc.*, 270 F.3d 590, 595–96 (8th Cir.2001).

68. *See Legault v. Zambarano*, 105 F.3d 24, 28–29 (1st Cir.1997).

69. *Hernandez v. Conriv Realty Assoc.*, 182 F.3d 121 (2d Cir.1999) (court must have subject matter jurisdiction to enter dismissal).

70. *DIRECTV, Inc. v. Huynh*, 318 F.Supp.2d 1122 (M.D.Ala. 2004)

71. *Tower Ventures, Inc. v. City of Westfield*, 296 F.3d 43, 45–46 (1st Cir.2002) (court may impose dismissal of action as a sanction for violation of court orders without consideration of lesser sanctions because disobedience of court orders constitutes extreme conduct).

72. *Gripe v. City of Enid, Okl.*, 312 F.3d 1184, 1188 (10th Cir.2002); *Robson v. Hallenbeck*, 81 F.3d 1, 2 (1st Cir.1996).

73. *Cato v. Fresno City*, 220 F.3d 1073, 1074 (9th Cir.2000).

74. *United States v. Samaniego*, 345 F.3d 1280, 1284 (11th Cir. 2003); *Young v. Gordon*, 330 F.3d 76 (1st Cir.2003); *Spain v. Board of*

Educ. of Meridian Community Unit School Dist. No. 101, 214 F.3d 925 (7th Cir.2000); *Olcott v. Delaware Flood Company*, 76 F.3d 1538, 1556 (10th Cir.1996).

ADDITIONAL RESEARCH REFERENCES

Wright & Miller, *Federal Practice and Procedure* §§ 1521–1540.

C.J.S. Federal Civil Procedure §§ 905–914.

West's Key No. Digests, Federal Civil Procedure ⚷1921–1943.

IV. PARTIES

RULE 17

PARTIES PLAINTIFF AND DEFENDANT; CAPACITY

(a) Real Party in Interest. Every action shall be prosecuted in the name of the real party in interest. An executor, administrator, guardian, bailee, trustee of an express trust, a party with whom or in whose name a contract has been made for the benefit of another, or a party authorized by statute may sue in that person's own name without joining the party for whose benefit the action is brought; and when a statute of the United States so provides, an action for the use or benefit of another shall be brought in the name of the United States. No action shall be dismissed on the ground that it is not prosecuted in the name of the real party in interest until a reasonable time has been allowed after objection for ratification of commencement of the action by, or joinder or substitution of, the real party in interest; and such ratification, joinder, or substitution shall have the same effect as if the action had been commenced in the name of the real party in interest.

(b) Capacity to Sue or Be Sued. The capacity of an individual, other than one acting in a representative capacity, to sue or be sued shall be determined by the law of the individual's domicile. The capacity of a corporation to sue or be sued shall be determined by the law under which it was organized. In all other cases capacity to sue or be sued shall be determined by the law of the state in which the district court is held, except (1) that a partnership or other unincorporated association, which has no such capacity by the law of such state, may sue or be sued in its common name for the purpose of enforcing for or against it a substantive right existing under the Constitution or laws of the United States, and (2) that the capacity of a receiver appointed by a court of the United States to sue or be sued in a court of the United States is governed by Title 28, U.S.C. §§ 754 and 959(a).

(c) Infants or Incompetent Persons. Whenever an infant or incompetent person has a representative, such as a general guardian, committee, conservator, or other like fiduciary, the representative may sue or defend on behalf of the infant or incompetent person. An infant or incompetent person who does not have a duly appointed representative may sue by a next friend or by a guardian ad litem. The court shall appoint a guardian ad litem for an infant or incompetent person not otherwise represented in an action or shall make such other order as it deems proper for the protection of the infant or incompetent person.

[Amended effective March 19, 1948; October 20, 1949; July 1, 1966; August 1, 1987; August 1, 1988; November 18, 1988.]

AUTHORS' COMMENTARY ON RULE 17

PURPOSE AND SCOPE

Rule 17 controls the determination of who may prosecute an action, or defend against one, in federal court. The standards are mandatory, but they can usually be satisfied without fundamentally altering the litigation.

RULE 17(a). REAL PARTY IN INTEREST

CORE CONCEPT

The only parties on whose behalf suits may be initiated are those persons whose interests will be materially affected by the outcome.[1] Such persons should be the named plaintiffs, except that Rule 17(a) permits certain exceptions. This requirement is imposed on plaintiffs so that defendants will only have to face one suit over the same interest.[2]

APPLICATIONS

Naming the Interested Party

Subject to exceptions discussed below, the suit must be commenced not only on behalf of the real party in interest but also in the name of the real party in interest. Thus, the real party in interest generally must be named in the caption.[3]

Raising a Rule 17 Defense

The manner in which a party may invoke Rule 17(a) is not clear.[4] Some courts indicate that the appropriate way to raise Rule 17 is

1. *See, e.g., United HealthCare Corp. v. American Trade Insurance Co.,* 88 F.3d 563, 569 (8th Cir.1996)(Rule 17(a) "requires that the party who brings an action actually possess, under the substantive law, the right sought to be enforced.").

2. *See, e.g., Marina Management Services, Inc. v. Vessel My Girls,* 202 F.3d 315, 318 (D.C.Cir.2000), *cert. denied,* 531 U.S. 985, 121 S.Ct. 441, 148 L.Ed.2d 446 (2000) ("Rule 17(a) protects a defendant against a subsequent claim for the same debt underlying a previously entered judgment.").

3. *See, e.g., Green v. Daimler Benz, AG,* 157 F.R.D. 340, 344 (E.D.Pa.1994)(ordering change in caption after substituting party).

4. *See, e.g., Whelan v. Abell,* 953 F.2d 663, 672 n. 7 (D.C.Cir.1992) ("We note that the question of how a Rule 17(a) defense is raised (as a

through a pleading,[5] while other authority indicates it might be the appropriate subject of a motion.[6] Attorneys are encouraged to examine carefully the local practice.

Invoking Rule 17(a) Sua Sponte

Most courts hold that the district court, as well as the parties, may raise a Rule 17(a) issue.[7]

Timing; Waiver

Rule 17(a) does not provide an express time limit within which an objection must be made. However, if the objection is not made with reasonable promptness, in the circumstances of a particular case, it is waived.[8]

Exceptions to Naming Interested Party

Rule 17(a) explicitly exempts certain categories of persons from the general principal that the named party be the real party in interest. The most important of these enumerated exceptions are executors, administrators, guardians, trustees,[9] persons who have made contracts on behalf of third parties,[10] and circumstances where a statute authorizes suit in the name of a representative party.[11]

12(b)(6) motion or as a Rule 8(c) affirmative defense) remains unsettled.").

5. *See, e.g., Weissman v. Weener,* 12 F.3d 84, 85 (7th Cir.1993) (citing older authority indicating that preferred method is by raising Rule 17 in a defendant's answer); *Howerton v. Designer Homes by Georges, Inc.,* 950 F.2d 281, 283 (5th Cir.1992) ("The issue of capacity is subject to waiver if not specifically raised by negative averment.").

6. *Cf., e.g., Lans v. Digital Equipment Corp.,* 252 F.3d 1320 (Fed.Cir.2001) (affirming grant of defendant's motion for summary judgment on ground of lack of Rule 17–related standing; affirming denial of plaintiff's motion to use Rules 15 and 17 to substitute a person who allegedly satisfied standing requirement).

7. *See, e.g., Weissman v. Weener,* 12 F.3d 84 (7th Cir.1993)(no recent decisions overrule district courts that invoke Rule 17(a) *sua sponte*).

8. *See, e.g., Rogers v. Samedan Oil Corp.,* 308 F.3d 477, 483 (5th Cir.2002) ("[T]he defense is waived when it is not timely asserted."); *International Meat Traders, Inc. v. H & M Food Systems,* 70 F.3d 836, 840 (5th Cir.1995) ("Raising this defense for the first time on a motion for judgment as a matter of law, at the close of all evidence, offends the Rule where it is not to be used as a trial-by-ambush tactic."); *Allegheny International, Inc. v. Allegheny Ludlum Steel Corp.,* 40 F.3d 1416, 1431 (3d Cir.1994) (approving denial of Rule 17 defense where party did not raise issue with reasonable promptness); *First Union Discount Brokerage Services, Inc. v. Milos,* 997 F.2d 835, 842 n. 12 (11th Cir.1993) (collecting precedent in some circuits requiring timely assertion of Rule 17 issue).

9. *See, e.g., Wieburg v. GTE Southwest, Inc.,* 272 F.3d 302, 306 (5th Cir.2001) (plaintiff was fired by employer, giving rise to possible age and sex discrimination claims; after firing but before initiating civil lawsuit, plaintiff filed for bankruptcy; held, plaintiff's bankruptcy filing meant civil claims were property of bankruptcy estate and plaintiff lacked standing to pursue claims; bankruptcy trustee is real party in interest); *Lenon v. St. Paul Mercury Insurance Co.,* 136 F.3d 1365, 1370 n. 2 (10th Cir.1998) (per curiam) (noting that trustee of express trust is real party in interest for purposes of Rule 17(a)).

10. *See, e.g., Local 538 United Brotherhood of Carpenters and Joiners of America v. United States Fidelity and Guaranty Co.,* 70 F.3d 741, 743 (2d Cir.1995)(noting general principle that named party to contract may sue in own name without joining third-party beneficiary; but refusing to extend Rule 17(a) to permit labor union to sue employer on behalf of welfare fund without first joining the fund).

11. *See, e.g., United States ex rel. Long v. SCS Business & Technical Institute, Inc.,* 173 F.3d 870 (D.C.Cir.1999), *cert. denied* 530 U.S. 1202, 120 S.Ct. 2194, 147 L.Ed.2d 231 (2000)(in *qui tam* action under False Claims Act, 31 U.S.C.A. § 3730(b) provides that both the Unit-

Subject Matter Jurisdiction

Rule 17(a) has some similarity with the requirements for diversity jurisdiction found in 28 U.S.C.A. § 1332. However, the two requirements can also diverge significantly from one another, with important consequences.[12] For example, Rule 17(a) permits, *inter alia,* an executor of a decedent's estate to be a real party in interest. However, such a person's status as a real party in interest under Rule 17(a) does not mean that person's citizenship is used for purposes of establishing diversity jurisdiction under 28 U.S.C.A. § 1332. Instead, § 1332(c)(2) provides that for purposes of diversity jurisdiction in an action brought on behalf of a decedent, infant, or incompetent person, the relevant citizenship is that of the deceased, infant, or incompetent person. Thus, under Rule 17(a) the executor may initiate the suit, but diversity is dependent on the citizenship of the represented person.[13]

Suits in the Name of the United States

If a statute allows the United States to sue on behalf of a real party in interest, Rule 17(a) also permits the United States to be the named plaintiff.

Relation to Rule 25(c)

Both Rules 17 and 25 govern who should be a party to a suit. However, Rule 17 applies to transfers of interest prior to initiation of the suit, while Rule 25(c) controls transfers occurring after the suit is filed.[14]

Remedy

The preferred remedy is to allow the party an opportunity to amend so that the action can thereafter be prosecuted by the real party in interest.[15] Dismissal is a disfavored remedy for violation of the

ed States and the relator are real parties in interest). *Cf., Femedeer v. Haun,* 227 F.3d 1244, 1246 (10th Cir.2000) (acknowledging possibility that some exceptional circumstances may require anonymity in unusual cases, but holding that previously convicted sex offender who is challenging state law requiring his registration as a sex offender must sue under his real name). *Marina Management Services, Inc. v. Vessel My Girls,* 202 F.3d 315, 318 (D.C.Cir.2000), *cert. denied,* 531 U.S. 985, 121 S.Ct. 441, 148 L.Ed.2d 446 (2000) (noting lack of judicial consensus as to whether "an agent authorized to sue based solely on a power of attorney is a real party in interest under Rule 17(a)").

12. *Navarro Savings Association v. Lee,* 446 U.S. 458, 463 n. 9, 100 S.Ct. 1779, 1783 n. 9, 64 L.Ed.2d 425 (1980) ("There is a 'rough symmetry' between the 'real party in interest' standard of Rule 17(a) and the rule that diversity jurisdiction depends upon the citizenship of real parties to the controversy. But the two rules serve different purposes and need not produce identical outcomes in all cases. . . . In appropriate circumstances, for example, a labor union may file suit in its own name as a real party in interest under Rule 17(a). To establish diversity, however, the union must rely upon the citizenship of each of its members.").

13. *See, e.g., Airlines Reporting Corp. v. S and N Travel, Inc.,* 58 F.3d 857, 862 n. 4 (2d Cir.1995).

14. *See, e.g., FDIC v. Deglau,* 207 F.3d 153, 159 (3d Cir.2000) (Rule 17(a) governs who may bring a suit at time of filing; thus it considers transfers of interest that occur prior to filing; however, once case is filed, the impact of a post-filing transfer is governed by Rule 25(c)); *Barker v. Jackson National Life Insurance Co.,* 163 F.R.D. 364, 365 (N.D.Fla.1995)(explaining distinction between Rules).

15. *See, e.g., Esposito v. United States,* 368 F.3d 1271, 1272 (10th Cir. 2004) (party bringing action is entitled, after objections, to reasonable

requirement to name the real party in interest as plaintiff.[16] Before a court grants a motion to dismiss, it must allow a real party in interest a reasonable opportunity to correct the defect by joining the action, or, if permitted as an exception to Rule 17(a), to ratify continuation of the action in the name of the original plaintiff. If the real party in interest takes such action, it is effective as if the joinder or ratification had occurred at the onset of the litigation.[17]

Relation to Rule 15

If an existing party must be replaced for failure to meet the requirements of rule 17, the real party in interest would normally join the litigation through the amendment process of rule 15.[18]

RULE 17(b). CAPACITY TO SUE OR BE SUED

CORE CONCEPT

This provision chooses the law that will govern the capacity of a person to prosecute or defend a suit in federal court.

APPLICATIONS

Natural Persons

For individuals, the law which determines their capacity to sue or be sued is the law of their domicile.[19] Domicile is generally defined as the jurisdiction where a person has established a physical presence and has the intent to remain for an indefinite period.[20] Thus, a person's home is generally that person's domicile. For many persons, the state of domicile will not be the same state in which the case is heard.

time to substitute real party in interest; such a right requires only that party's original mistake was "honest"); *Dunmore v. United States,* 358 F.3d 1107, 1112 (9th Cir. 2004) (purpose behind allowing plaintiff to cure defect without dismissal is to prevent plaintiff from being time-barred for "understandable mistake").

16. *See, e.g., Wieburg v. GTE Southwest, Inc.,* 272 F.3d 302, 308–09 (5th Cir.2001) (where plaintiff lacks standing because civil causes of action are property of plaintiff's bankruptcy estate, case should not be dismissed until bankruptcy trustee has opportunity to substitute himself for plaintiff); *Intown Properties Management, Inc. v. Wheaton Van Lines, Inc.,* 271 F.3d 164, 170 (4th Cir.2001) (Rule 17 expressly provides that case shall not be dismissed until real party in interest has reasonable opportunity to join litigation). *But see Consul General of Republic of Indonesia v. Bill's Rentals, Inc.,* 330 F.3d 1041, 1047–48 (8th Cir.2003) (dismissal with prejudice appropriate when Consul General did not act to cure defect within 18 months).

17. *See, e.g., O'Hara v. District No. 1–PCD, MEBA, AFL–CIO,* 56 F.3d 1514, 1519 (D.C.Cir. 1995)("substitution of real party in interest for party prosecuting a suit has same effect as if action had been commenced in the name of real party in interest"). *See also, Scheufler v. General Host Corp.,* 126 F.3d 1261, 1270 (10th Cir.1997) (when parties are joined as real parties in interest under Rule 17(a), joinder falls under "mandatory relation-back" authority of rule 17(a) and is not governed by Rule 15(c); thus claims of such parties automatically relate back to commencement of litigation).

18. *See, e.g., Intown Properties Management, Inc. v. Wheaton Van Lines, Inc.,* 271 F.3d 164, 170 (4th Cir.2001) (Rule 17 expressly provides that case shall not be dismissed until real party in interest has reasonable opportunity to join litigation). *See also* Advisory Committee Note to Rule 15 (1966).

19. *See, e.g., Johns v. County of San Diego,* 114 F.3d 874 (9th Cir.1997) (so holding).

20. *See, e.g., Stifel v. Hopkins,* 477 F.2d 1116, 1120 (6th Cir.1973) (using definition and discussing relationship to Rule 17(b)).

Particularly in diversity cases, at least one party will be domiciled outside the state where the case is heard.

Natural Persons as Representatives of Others

Natural persons suing on behalf of another, such as guardians or executors of estates, are governed by the law of the state in which the court sits.[21]

Pro Se Litigants

While a non-attorney parent may bring an action on behalf of a child, such a parent must be represented by an attorney.[22]

Corporations

The capacity of a corporation to sue or be sued is governed by the law of the jurisdiction in which the corporation is incorporated.[23]

Unincorporated Associations

If the cause of action is based on a federal question, Rule 17(b) provides that unincorporated associations have capacity to sue or be sued.[24]

Receivers

Rule 17(b) provides that the capacity of receivers appointed by a federal court to litigate in a federal court is governed by 28 U.S.C.A. §§ 754 (appointment of receivers in different federal judicial districts) and 959(a)(suits against receivers).

Capacity in All Other Cases

Notwithstanding the numerous specific provisions for capacity in Rule 17(b), there are other circumstances not addressed by those provisions. For example, when a partnership or other unincorporated association sues, or is sued, on a state cause of action in federal court, the law governing capacity is that of the state in which the court sits.[25]

21. *See, e.g., Maroni v. Pemi–Baker Regional School District,* 346 F.3d 247, 249 n. 2 (1st Cir. 2003) ("State law is used to determine the age of majority," citing Rule 17(b)); *Gibbs v. Carnival Cruise Lines,* 314 F.3d 125, 135 (3d Cir.2002) (state law controls whether representative has been duly appointed to litigate on behalf of infant); *Davis v. Piper Aircraft Corp.,* 615 F.2d 606, 609 (4th Cir.1980), *cert. dismissed,* 448 U.S. 911, 101 S.Ct. 25, 65 L.Ed.2d 1141 (1980)(citing Rule 17(b); state law controls capacity to bring wrongful death suit).

22. *See, e.g., Cheung v. Youth Orchestra Foundation of Buffalo, Inc.,* 906 F.2d 59, 61 (2d Cir.1990) ("The choice to appear pro se is not a true choice for minors who under state law, see Fed.R.Civ.P. 17(b), cannot determine their own legal actions.").

23. *See, e.g., Citizens Electric Corp. v. Bituminous Fire & Marine Insurance Co.,* 68 F.3d 1016, 1019 (7th Cir.1995)(approving application of state law under Rule 17(b)).

24. *See, e.g., Curley v. Brignoli, Curley & Roberts Associates,* 915 F.2d 81, 87 (2d Cir.1990), *cert. denied,* 499 U.S. 955, 111 S.Ct. 1430, 113 L.Ed.2d 484 (1991)(observing that Rule 17(b) grants "association capacity in federal question cases".)

25. *See, e.g., Kauffman v. Anglo–American School of Sofia,* 28 F.3d 1223, 1225 (D.C.Cir. 1994)(cause of action based on state law means capacity of unincorporated association is also based on state law). *See also Streit v. County of Los Angeles,* 236 F.3d 552, 565 (9th Cir.2001), *cert. denied,* 534 U.S. 823, 122 S.Ct. 59, 151 L.Ed.2d 27 (2001) (in federal civil rights suit

Capacity Distinguished From Real Party in Interest

There are two important differences between capacity (Rule 17(b)) and real parties in interest (Rule 17(a)) and the concerns they address. The first is that satisfying real party in interest requirements is the duty of those who file claims, most typically plaintiffs. Capacity, by contrast, measures the ability of both plaintiffs and defendants to participate in a suit, even if the defendant has not filed a counterclaim or a crossclaim. The second difference is in the concepts underlying the respective provisions of Rule 17. Individuals may, because they are individuals, have capacity to sue. Capacity alone, however, does not permit those individuals to initiate a suit or to defend one. Unless they also have a material interest in the outcome of a cause of action, they may not bring a suit (or defend against a suit) because they are not also the real parties in interest.[26] Thus, to bring a suit, a party must have both "capacity," under the applicable law chosen by Rule 17(b), as well as a real stake in the outcome, as defined by Rule 17(a). To be sued, a defendant need only satisfy the law of capacity selected by Rule 17(b).

RULE 17(c). INFANTS OR INCOMPETENT PERSONS

CORE CONCEPT

This portion of Rule 17 controls the manner in which infants and other persons unable to represent their own interests will be represented in suits in federal court. The provisions apply irrespective of whether the infant or incompetent person is participating in the suit as a plaintiff or defendant.

APPLICATIONS

Infants and Incompetents Already Represented

Where persons unable to care for their own interests already have others charged with the duty to care for them outside of litigation, such as guardians, Rule 17(c) grants such guardians authority to sue on behalf of the persons in their care.[27]

against county sheriff's department, Rule 17(b) deferred to state law to determine capacity of defendant to be sued).

26. *See, e.g., Lans v. Digital Equipment Corp.*, 252 F.3d 1320 (Fed.Cir.2001) (no right to amend complaint to name proper plaintiff where currently named plaintiff lacked standing to sue; original misrepresentation was apparently intentional).

27. *Cf., Gonzalez v. Reno*, 212 F.3d 1338 (11th Cir.2000), *cert. denied*, 530 U.S. 1270, 120 S.Ct. 2737, 147 L.Ed.2d 1001 (2000) (where child-plaintiff is "ably represented" by next friend, court need not appoint guardian ad litem); *Neilson v. Colgate–Palmolive Co.*, 199 F.3d 642, 650 (2d Cir.1999) ("[O]nly one party may act in a representative capacity with respect to an infant or incompetent who comes before the court."); *In re Kjellsen*, 53 F.3d 944 (8th Cir. 1995)(when incompetent person already has a guardian, Rule 17(c) does not authorize suit by another person). *See generally, In the Matter of Chicago, Rock Island and Pacific Railroad Co.*, 788 F.2d 1280, 1282 (7th Cir.1986) (in circumstances where an infant or incompetent person is only a potential party, or whose interest is already represented, court has no duty to appoint a guardian ad litem, but may do so at its discretion; but if interest is not represented adequately, court has duty to appoint a representative).

Infants and Incompetents Not Already Represented

Where persons unable to care for their own interests are not already within the legal authority of others, they may be represented in litigation by persons chosen to protect their interests. The court has power to appoint such guardians *ad litem* (persons who will represent the interest of others in litigation),[28] and to make other orders consistent with the best interests of infants and incompetents in litigation.[29]

In the absence of "actual documentation or testimony by a mental health professional, a court of record, or a relevant public agency," the district court has no duty to make a sua sponte inquiry into a pro se party's lack of mental capacity.[30]

Incompetence: Delay of Trial

A criminal defendant who suffers from significant mental impairment may be entitled to a delay in trial proceedings until the impairment eases. However, in civil litigation mental incompetence may not have the same result. Instead, the court may employ Rule 17(c) to appoint a guardian ad litem.[31]

Authority of Representative

When a representative is appointed under Rule 17(c), that person has most of the authority that a competent client would have. However, Rule 17(c) does not give the appointed person the right to serve as legal counsel for the infant or incompetent person.[32]

ADDITIONAL RESEARCH REFERENCES

Wright & Miller, *Federal Practice and Procedure* §§ 1541–73.

C.J.S. Federal Civil Procedure §§ 46–62 et seq.

West's Key No. Digests, Federal Civil Procedure ⚷111–116, 131–149.

28. *See, e.g., Gibbs v. Carnival Cruise Lines,* 314 F.3d 125, 135–36 (3d Cir.2002) (where infant is unrepresented, Rule 17(c) authorizes court to appoint guardian ad litem; unlike Rule 17(b), Rule 17(c) does not defer to state standards for appointment; instead Rule 17(c) directs court to look to best interests of infant); *T.W. v. Brophy,* 124 F.3d 893, 895 (7th Cir.1997) ("next friend" usually appointed for plaintiff, while guardian ad litem usually appointed for defendant; but terms are not controlling).

29. *See, e.g., Krain v. Smallwood,* 880 F.2d 1119, 1121 (9th Cir.1989), *cert. denied,* 502 U.S. 820, 112 S.Ct. 78, 116 L.Ed.2d 52 (1991)(if infant or incompetent is unrepresented, "the court should not enter . . . a judgment on the merits without complying with Rule 17(c)"). *See also, Wenger v. Canastota Central School District,* 146 F.3d 123 (2d Cir.1998), *cert. denied,* 526 U.S. 1025, 119 S.Ct. 1267, 143 L.Ed.2d 363 (1999) (under Rule 17(c) court may act *sua sponte* to protect interests of infants and incompetent persons).

30. *See, e.g., Ferrelli v. River Manor Health Care Center,* 323 F.3d 196, 202 (2d Cir.2003), *cert. denied,* 540 U.S. 1195, 124 S.Ct. 1448, 158 L.Ed.2d 107 (2004) ("bizarre behavior" by itself does not require examination of competence).

31. *See, e.g., United States v. Mandycz,* 351 F.3d 222, 225 n. 1 (6th Cir. 2003) (explaining application of Rule 17(c); "a civil defendant's mental incompetence does not trigger an abatement of trial as it does in the criminal context").

32. *See, e.g., Devine v. Indian River County School Board,* 121 F.3d 576, 581 (11th Cir.1997), *cert. denied,* 522 U.S. 1110, 118 S.Ct. 1040, 140 L.Ed.2d 106 (1998) (Rule 17(c) "permits authorized representatives, including parents, to sue on behalf of minors, but does not confer any right upon such representatives to serve as legal counsel.").

RULE 18

JOINDER OF CLAIMS AND REMEDIES

(a) Joinder of Claims. A party asserting a claim to relief as an original claim, counterclaim, cross-claim, or third-party claim, may join, either as independent or as alternate claims, as many claims, legal, equitable, or maritime, as the party has against an opposing party.

(b) Joinder of Remedies; Fraudulent Conveyances. Whenever a claim is one heretofore cognizable only after another claim has been prosecuted to a conclusion, the two claims may be joined in a single action; but the court shall grant relief in that action only in accordance with the relative substantive rights of the parties. In particular, a plaintiff may state a claim for money and a claim to have set aside a conveyance fraudulent as to that plaintiff, without first having obtained a judgment establishing the claim for money.

[Amended effective July 1, 1966; August 1, 1987.]

AUTHORS' COMMENTARY ON RULE 18

PURPOSE AND SCOPE

Rule 18 permits claimants to bring all claims they may have against persons already parties to a case, notwithstanding the fact that the claims may be unrelated to one another.

RULE 18(a). JOINDER OF CLAIMS

CORE CONCEPT

Rule 18(a) abolishes prohibitions against bringing unrelated claims against the same defendant(s) in a single action. The origin of the claims, whether equitable, legal, or originating in admiralty, is irrelevant to the right to plead claims in a single action.[1]

APPLICATIONS

Parties Who May Join Claims

The right to join claims is available to any claimant who is a party to the case, irrespective of whether the claims filed will be counter-

1. *See, e.g., Dodoo v. Seagate Technology, Inc.*, 235 F.3d 522, 529 (10th Cir.2000) (joinder of claims is "common and preferred method"); *Vodusek v. Bayliner Marine Corp.*, 71 F.3d 148, 154 (4th Cir.1995)(Rule 18 permits "joinder of claims at law, in equity, and in admiralty").

claims, crossclaims, third-party claims, or original claims filed by the plaintiff.[2]

Rule 18(a) is Permissive, Not Compulsory

A party choosing not to bring unrelated claims is free to file them in separate actions.[3] This assumes the claim is not otherwise barred by considerations such as a statute of limitations.

NOTE: Notwithstanding the permissive nature of Rule 18(a), there may be problems in subsequent litigation if the claims not filed in the initial litigation were related to the claims actually raised. In that circumstance, suits filed later may be subject to the bar of res judicata or collateral estoppel.

Separate Trials

Notwithstanding the liberal nature of this joinder provision, the trial court may still exercise its discretion to order separate trials on different claims pursuant to Rule 42(b).[4]

Relation to Rule 14

Rule 18 provides that a party properly asserting a third-party claim may join all claims that party has against a third-party defendant. However, it is still true that Rule 14, governing third-party practice, must first be applied to determine whether a third-party claim is permitted. If one of the claims does not meet the requirements of Rule 14, *e.g.,* if none of the asserted third-party claims relate to the claims against the third-party plaintiff, then impleader is not permissible. In that circumstance, there can be no joinder of third-party claims pursuant to Rule 18.[5]

Relation to Rule 15

Rule 18 identifies the circumstances in which a party may, in the party's original pleading, join more than one claim against other parties. However, if an additional claim is asserted after an original claim has been filed, the additional claim must also meet the requirements of Rule 15, governing amendments to pleadings.[6]

2. *See, e.g., First National Bank of Cincinnati v. Pepper,* 454 F.2d 626, 635 (2d Cir. 1972)(party asserting cross-claim that meets requirements of Rule 13(g) may also join unrelated claims pursuant to Rule 18(a)).

3. *See, e.g., Perkins v. Board of Trustees of the University of Illinois,* 116 F.3d 235 (7th Cir.1997) ("Rule 18(a) permits rather than compels the joinder of distinct claims against one adversary.")

4. *See, e.g., Parmer v. National Cash Register Co.,* 503 F.2d 275, 277 (6th Cir.1974)(per curiam)(separation is within trial court's discretion).

5. *See, e.g., Lehman v. Revolution Portfolio, L.L.C.,* 166 F.3d 389, 394 (1st Cir.1999) (once defendant, in role of third-party plaintiff, properly impleaded a third-party defendant, Rule 18(a) permits joinder of all claims that third-party plaintiff has against third-party defendant); *Tietz v. Blackner,* 157 F.R.D. 510, 512 (D.Utah 1994) ("Rule 18(a) would apply only after a suitable joinder under Rule 14 has been allowed.").

6. *See, e.g., Mackensworth v. S.S. American Merchant,* 28 F.3d 246, 251 (2d Cir.1994)(adding claim to existing complaint requires compliance with Rule 15; Rule 18 "deals only with pleading requirements").

Jurisdiction and Venue

Joinder under Rule 18(a) is subject to requirements of jurisdiction and venue. Thus, Rule 18(a) permits joinder of claims only where the claims independently satisfy such requirements.[7] For a further discussion of jurisdiction and venue, *see* §§ 2.1–2.14.

Joinder of Parties

Rule 18(a) authorizes only joinder of claims, not the addition of parties. If joining a particular claim also requires joining additional parties, such parties may be added only as permitted under other applicable Rules. *See* Rule 20, concerning joinder of parties.

RULE 18(b). JOINDER OF REMEDIES; FRAUDULENT CONVEYANCES

CORE CONCEPT

This portion of Rule 18 permits joining two claims in a single action, even if the situation is one in which the court must decide the first claim before the second claim can be determined. For example, a plaintiff may sue on a personal injury, and add a count accusing a defendant of fraudulently transferring assets to the defendant's spouse as a means of frustrating enforcement of a judgment the plaintiff might obtain.

APPLICATION

Timing

In the example cited above, a plaintiff can present evidence on both claims at the same time, even though recovery on the allegation of fraudulent conveyance would first require that the defendant be held liable on the personal injury claim.[8]

NOTE: Rule 18(b) may afford a plaintiff substantial opportunity to gain advantage with a jury by using evidence of a fraudulent conveyance to color the jury's view of the personal injury claim. In theory, the court's authority under Rule 42(b) to separate the claims is a safeguard against the risk of such inappropriate prejudice to the defendant. In practice, the need to separate the claims may not be sufficiently obvious at the outset of the trial, when Rule 42(b) is most likely to be employed.

7. *See, e.g., King Fisher Marine Service, Inc. v. 21st Phoenix Corp.,* 893 F.2d 1155, 1158 n. 2 (10th Cir.1990), *cert. denied,* 496 U.S. 912, 110 S.Ct. 2603, 110 L.Ed.2d 283 (1990)("[A] court may decide claims joined under Rule 18(a) only if independent jurisdiction and venue requirements are satisfied."). It should be noted that where two counts are sufficiently related, courts may use supplemental jurisdiction as an "independent" source of subject matter jurisdiction. *See, e.g., Kunkel v. Topmaster International, Inc.,* 906 F.2d 693, 697 n. 1 (Fed.Cir.1990)(so holding).

8. *See, e.g., Huntress v. Huntress' Estate,* 235 F.2d 205, 207–08 (7th Cir.1956)(noting that Rule 18(b) permits joinder of such counts).

ADDITIONAL RESEARCH REFERENCES

Wright & Miller, *Federal Practice and Procedure* §§ 1581–94.

C.J.S. Federal Civil Procedure §§ 40–41, 301; Fraudulent Conveyances §§ 331, 494.

West's Key No. Digests, Federal Civil Procedure ⚷81–86, 733; Fraudulent Conveyances ⚷241(2).

RULE 19

JOINDER OF PERSONS NEEDED FOR JUST ADJUDICATION

(a) Persons to Be Joined if Feasible. A person who is subject to service of process and whose joinder will not deprive the court of jurisdiction over the subject matter of the action shall be joined as a party in the action if (1) in the person's absence complete relief cannot be accorded among those already parties, or (2) the person claims an interest relating to the subject of the action and is so situated that the disposition of the action in the person's absence may (i) as a practical matter impair or impede the person's ability to protect that interest or (ii) leave any of the persons already parties subject to a substantial risk of incurring double, multiple, or otherwise inconsistent obligations by reason of the claimed interest. If the person has not been so joined, the court shall order that the person be made a party. If the person should join as a plaintiff but refuses to do so, the person may be made a defendant, or, in a proper case, an involuntary plaintiff. If the joined party objects to venue and joinder of that party would render the venue of the action improper, that party shall be dismissed from the action.

(b) Determination by Court Whenever Joinder Not Feasible. If a person as described in subdivision (a)(1)–(2) hereof cannot be made a party, the court shall determine whether in equity and good conscience the action should proceed among the parties before it, or should be dismissed, the absent person being thus regarded as indispensable. The factors to be considered by the court include: first, to what extent a judgment rendered in the person's absence might be prejudicial to the person or those already parties; second, the extent to which, by protective provisions in the judgment, by the shaping of relief, or other measures, the prejudice can be lessened or avoided; third, whether a judgment rendered in the person's absence will be adequate; fourth, whether the plaintiff will have an adequate remedy if the action is dismissed for nonjoinder.

(c) Pleading Reasons for Nonjoinder. A pleading asserting a claim for relief shall state the names, if known to the pleader, of any persons as described in subdivision (a)(1)–(2) hereof who are not joined, and the reasons why they are not joined.

(d) Exception of Class Actions. This rule is subject to the provisions of Rule 23.

[Amended effective July 1, 1966; August 1, 1987.]

AUTHORS' COMMENTARY ON RULE 19

PURPOSE AND SCOPE

Rule 19 addresses distinct but related questions concerning joinder of parties. Rule 19(a) describes when a court should order the joinder of a person who is not yet a party to the case. If such a person should be joined, the court will then evaluate whether, under principles of jurisdiction and venue, the person can be joined.[1] If joinder is not feasible, Rule 19(b) addresses whether the court should dismiss the case or continue without that person. Application of Rule 19 typically arises when a defendant makes a motion to dismiss the action under Rule 12(b)(7), alleging that the plaintiff failed to join a person whose presence is "indispensable" to the action.

AMENDMENT OF RULE

This Rule was substantially rewritten in 1966. Judicial decisions that predate 1966 should be cited with great care, if at all.

> **NOTE:** More than most Rules, the application of Rule 19 is highly fact specific.[2] Thus, when the court addresses questions of impairment of interest, the court will examine both legal and actual, real-world, impairment.

RULE 19(a). PERSONS TO BE JOINED IF FEASIBLE

CORE CONCEPT

> When feasible, persons should be joined when their absence will either materially reduce the likelihood that the court can provide justice for those already parties or be detrimental to the non-parties themselves.[3]

1. *See, e.g., Keweenaw Bay Indian Community v. State of Michigan,* 11 F.3d 1341, 1347 (6th Cir.1993)(describing Rule 19 as a "three-step" analysis, including the jurisdiction/venue analysis).

2. *See, e.g., Gonzalez v. Metropolitan Transportation Authority,* 174 F.3d 1016, 1019 (9th Cir.1999) ("Whether a party is necessary and indispensable is a pragmatic and equitable judgment, not a jurisdictional one."); *United States ex rel. Hall v. Tribal Development Corp.,* 100 F.3d 476, 481 (7th Cir.1996) (Rule 19 analysis is pragmatic and fact specific).

3. *See, e.g., Hammond v. Clayton,* 83 F.3d 191, 195 (7th Cir.1996) ("Rule 19 is designed to protect the interests of absent persons, as well as those already before the court, from duplicative litigation, inconsistent judicial determinations, or other practical impairment of their legal interests.").

APPLICATIONS

Joinder of Parties Necessary

The court may join necessary parties in the following cases:[4]

(1) The court may order joinder of a person in whose absence complete relief cannot be granted to those already parties to the case.[5] For example, when an Indian group sues a state for exclusive fishing rights, and does not join other competing Indian groups, the state is denied complete relief.[6]

(2) The court may order joinder of a party whose interest[7] may be impaired either practically or legally.[8] For example, when a plaintiff seeks to recover from a limited fund controlled by the defendant, and a non-party has a claim against the fund, the court may join the non-party so as to protect that person's possibility of sharing in the fund

4. *Cf., Johnson v. Smithsonian Institution,* 189 F.3d 180, 188 (2d Cir.1999) (error to find party necessary under Rule 19(a) because in party's absence district court " 'could not begin to determine whether [that party] unlawfully retained pieces of ... art in 1946, or which pieces of the art were kept, or how [others] came to learn of this tortious act.' ... The question of whether or not an entity or individual should be a party to an action is something quite different from the questions and problems associated with obtaining evidence from such an entity or individual." The need to obtain evidence is not a factor under Rule 19(a)).

5. *See, e.g., Disabled Rights Action Committee v. Las Vegas Events, Inc.,* 375 F.3d 861 (9th Cir. 2004) (party is "necessary" if in its absence meaningful relief cannot be afforded to those who are already joined, thus risking multiple lawsuits on same issue).

6. *See, e.g., Citizen Potawatomi Nation v. Norton,* 248 F.3d 993, 998 (10th Cir.2001), *opinion modified on reh'g,* 257 F.3d 1158 (10th Cir. 2001) (Rule 19(a) does not require possession of "actual" interest, but only a claimed interest where the claim is not "patently frivolous"). *See also Dawavendewa v. Salt River Project Agriculture Improvement & Power District,* 276 F.3d 1150, 1153 (9th Cir.2002) (plaintiff cannot get complete relief by obtaining injunction barring enforcement of lease provision giving preferential hiring to Navajo tribe; suit against tribe was barred by tribal sovereign immunity, and in absence of tribe, result of suit would bind only plaintiff and defendant (which has lease with tribe), but not tribe); *Manybeads v. United States,* 209 F.3d 1164, 1165 (9th Cir.2000), *cert. denied,* 532 U.S. 966, 121 S.Ct. 1504, 149 L.Ed.2d 388 (2001) (plaintiff cannot be provided complete relief without damage to prior settlement with rival Indian tribe; held, rival tribe is necessary party under Rule 19(a)(1)); *Keweenaw Bay Indian Community v. State of Michigan,* 11 F.3d 1341, 1345 (6th Cir.1993)(so holding). *But see, Angst v. Royal Maccabees Life Insurance Co.,* 77 F.3d 701, 705 (3d Cir.1996)(risk that successful party in instant lawsuit might face challenge to rights by receiver in later suit does not equal a lack of complete relief).

7. *Cf., National Union Fire Insurance Co. of Pittsburgh v. Rite Aid of South Carolina, Inc.,* 210 F.3d 246, 250–51 (4th Cir.2000) ("A court should hesitate to conclude ... that a litigant can serve as a proxy for an absent party unless the interests of the two are identical.").

8. *See, e.g., Davis v. United States,* 192 F.3d 951, 958 (10th Cir.1999) ("Rule 19 ... does not require the absent party to actually possess an interest; it only requires the movant to show that the absent party 'claims an interest relating to the subject of the action.' "); *Laker Airways, Inc. v. British Airways, PLC,* 182 F.3d 843, 847–48 (11th Cir.1999) (outside entity has interest in case where court must pass on neutrality of its behavior, because finding of failure of neutrality might affect British government's view of entity's legal obligation to behave in a neutral manner). *International Paper Co. v. Denkmann Associates,* 116 F.3d 134, 137 (5th Cir.1997) (party held indispensable where it owned parcels of land "interspersed" among land parcels held by other party—adjudication of some parcels will be affected by other land). *But see, Rishell v. Jane Phillips Episcopal Memorial Medical Center,* 94 F.3d 1407, 1411 (10th Cir.1996), *cert. denied,* 520 U.S. 1166, 117 S.Ct. 1427, 137 L.Ed.2d 536 (1997) (non-party husband's loss of consortium dependent on outcome of wife's right to recover on injury claim; but husband's interest is adequately represented by wife's guardian).

before it is exhausted.[9]

(3) Where several persons have overlapping interests in a defendant's property, the court may order their joinder to preclude the possibility of inconsistent obligations. For example, if a tenant seeks an injunction to enforce a lease against a landlord, complications can arise if the property is also subject to a potentially conflicting lease held by another person. In that circumstance, joinder of the second tenant will prevent the risk that the landlord will be subject to inconsistent duties to the two tenants.[10]

(4) As a general rule, courts construing contracts require that parties to the contract be joined.[11]

9. *See, e.g., In re Torcise,* 116 F.3d 860, 865 (11th Cir.1997) ("It is well established under Rule 19 that all claimants to a fund must be joined to determine the disposition of that fund."); *Angst v. Royal Maccabees Life Insurance Co.,* 77 F.3d 701, 705 (3d Cir.1996)(where defendant insurance company is sued in both state and federal court and will have to pay into escrow account for same policy in two cases, plaintiff in state suit should be joined under Rule 19(a)(2)(ii)). *But see HS Resources, Inc. v. Wingate,* 327 F.3d 432, 439 (5th Cir.2003) (in dispute over landowner's right to royalty payments on natural gas well, case between instant landowner and gas company could be decided without joinder of other landowners whose leases were not affected); *State of Washington v. Daley,* 173 F.3d 1158 (9th Cir.1999) (held, absent party need not be joined as necessary party if current party will adequately represent absent party's interest; adequate representation found where: (1) absent party and current party share similar interests; (2) current party will raise all appropriate issues; and (3) absent party will not add any important element to litigation). *Cf., Dawavendewa v. Salt River Project Agriculture Improvement & Power District,* 276 F.3d 1150, 1156–57 (9th Cir.2002) (action to set aside lease or contract threatens non-party's interest in lease, thereby raising Rule 19(a)(2)); *National Union Fire Insurance Co. of Pittsburgh v. Rite Aid of South Carolina, Inc.,* 210 F.3d 246, 252 (4th Cir.2000) ("[A] contracting party is the paradigm of an indispensable party."). *See also United States v. Bowen,* 172 F.3d 682, 689 (9th Cir.1999) (if absent party knows of litigation and does not claim a legally protected interest, joinder is unnecessary).

10. *See, e.g., Helzberg's Diamond Shops, Inc. v. Valley West Des Moines Shopping Center, Inc.,* 564 F.2d 816 (8th Cir.1977). *See also, Dawavendewa v. Salt River Project Agriculture Improvement & Power District,* 276 F.3d 1150, 1157–58 (9th Cir.2002) (absence of Navajo tribe, due to tribal sovereign immunity, leaves defendant, who is contracting party with tribe on lease that is challenged by plaintiff, vulnerable to later suit by tribe to enforce agreement); *National Union Fire Insurance Co. of Pittsburgh v. Rite Aid of South Carolina, Inc.,* 210 F.3d 246, 252 (4th Cir.2000) ("[A] contracting party is the paradigm of an indispensable party."). *But cf., Bassett v. Mashantucket Pequot Tribe,* 204 F.3d 343, 358–60 (2d Cir.2000) (in suit for copyright infringement and tort, plaintiff need not sue all defendants; thus, a defendant immune from suit is not indispensable; not deciding on indispensability of person who was party to contract action, but noting that such a person might be indispensable in action on contract); *Temple v. Synthes Corp., Ltd.,* 498 U.S. 5, 7, 111 S.Ct. 315, 316, 112 L.Ed.2d 263 (1990) (per curiam) ("It has long been the rule that it is not necessary for all joint tortfeasors to be named as defendants in a single lawsuit."); *Delgado v. Plaza Las Americas, Inc.,* 139 F.3d 1 (1st Cir.1998) (per curiam) (defendant was sued in two different courts over liability relating to rape; parent of rape victim sued for parent's emotional anguish in instant case, while daughter sued as victim of rape herself in a different court; held, Rule 19(a)(2)(ii) does not make daughter a necessary party in parent's lawsuit; requirement of Rule 19(a)(2)(ii) is for finding of inconsistent obligations–*i.e.,* inability of defendant to comply with one court's order without breaching another court's order; inconsistent adjudications, where defendant wins one suit and loses another arising from the same incident, do not trigger applicability of Rule 19(a)(2)(ii)).

11. *See, e.g., Dawavendewa v. Salt River Project Agriculture Improvement & Power District,* 276 F.3d 1150, 1156–57 (9th Cir.2002) (action to set aside lease or contract threatens non-party's interest in lease, thereby raising Rule 19(a)(2)); *Harris Trust and Savings Bank v. Energy Assets International Corp.,* 124 F.R.D. 115, 117 (E.D.La.1989)("[W]here interpretation of a contract is involved, parties to that contract must be joined."). *But cf., Extra Equipamentos e Exporta-*

Procedure

Only a party may make a Rule 19 motion.[12] In the ordinary course of events, use of Rule 19 is triggered when a claimant has not joined everyone potentially affected by a claim. The party claimed against may then file a motion to dismiss the claim under Rule 12(b)(7), governing dismissals for failure to join a person who should be a party.[13] To determine whether the motion should be granted, the court will apply the standards of Rule 19. Typically, the court will either: (1) order the person joined, and deny the motion to dismiss; (2) refuse to order joinder, and deny the motion to dismiss; or (3) acknowledge that the person crucial to the action cannot (for reasons of jurisdiction or venue) be joined, and grant the motion to dismiss.

Service on Non-parties

If the court determines that a person should be joined in pending litigation, it will direct that service be made upon that person.[14] It should be noted that such service may properly employ the "bulge" provision of Rule 4(k), permitting service within 100 miles of the place where the service issued without regard to normal limitations that may be imposed by state law.[15]

Time

Rule 19 contains no express time limit within which a party seeking joinder must file a motion. However, undue delay in filing can be grounds for denying a motion,[16] particularly if absent persons will not be prejudiced by nonjoinder.[17]

cao Ltda. v. Case Corp., 361 F.3d 359, 363–64 (7th Cir. 2004) (litigation over settlement agreement may not require presence of corporate subsidiary whose parent is already a party and whose parent is sole owner of subsidiary; in such a circumstance the "complete identity" of interest between parent and subsidiary means absence of subsidiary may not be harmful to subsidiary); *Davis Companies v. Emerald Casino, Inc.*, 268 F.3d 477, 482–83 (7th Cir.2001) (if absent party has separate and independent contract with a party, which did not implicate issues raised in separate contract dispute between those already parties, there is no need to join absent party).

12. *See, e.g., Arrow v. Gambler's Supply, Inc.*, 55 F.3d 407, 409 (8th Cir.1995)(while non-parties may not make motions under Rule 19, "a court may sua sponte join a party for good cause"). *See also Sac and Fox Nation of Missouri v. Pierce*, 213 F.3d 566 n. 11 (10th Cir. 2000), *cert. denied*, 531 U.S. 1144, 121 S.Ct. 1078, 148 L.Ed.2d 955 (2000) (raising joinder question sua sponte).

13. *See, e.g., HS Resources, Inc. v. Wingate*, 327 F.3d 432, 438–39 (5th Cir.2003) (describing relationship of rule 12(b)(7) to Rule 19).

14. *See, e.g., PaineWebber, Inc. v. Cohen*, 276 F.3d 197, 200 (6th Cir.2001), *cert. denied*, 537 U.S. 815, 123 S.Ct. 83, 154 L.Ed.2d 19 (2002) ("If the party is deemed necessary for the reasons enumerated in Rule 19(a), the court must next consider whether the party is subject to personal jurisdiction and can be joined without eliminating the basis for subject matter jurisdiction.").

15. Fed.R.Civ.P. 4(k). *See also Quinones v. Pennsylvania General Insurance Co.*, 804 F.2d 1167, 1173–74 (10th Cir.1986) (minimum contacts in bulge area made person amenable to service of process therein).

16. *See, e.g., Northeast Drilling, Inc. v. Inner Space Services, Inc.*, 243 F.3d 25, 36–37 (1st Cir.2001) (affirming denial of joinder when motion was made "well after" time limit set in scheduling order, with no explanation for delay); *Gil Enterprises, Inc. v. Delvy*, 79 F.3d 241, 247 (2d Cir.1996)(citing excessive delay in raising Rule 19 issue as ground to deny motion).

17. *See, e.g., Sierra Club v. Hathaway*, 579 F.2d 1162, 1166 (9th Cir.1978)(because absent persons were not prejudiced by judgment, parties' failure to raise Rule 19 issue did not undermine judgment).

Joinder of Plaintiffs

When a person should join as a plaintiff but refuses to do so, the court may join the person as an involuntary plaintiff or even a defendant.[18]

Joinder in Diversity Cases

In diversity cases joining an additional party may adversely affect jurisdiction. Courts have limited ability to avoid the problem, depending on whether the person to be joined should be joined as a plaintiff or a defendant. If the person to be joined could be made either an involuntary plaintiff or a defendant, the court may preserve jurisdiction simply by aligning the joined person in a way that maintains diversity.[19] However, if the person can only be joined as a defendant, and that joinder would destroy diversity, the court has no room to maneuver. In this situation, the court must apply Rule 19(b) to determine whether to proceed without the non-joined party.[20]

Venue

Joined persons retain the right to object to venue within the time frame provided in Rule 12(h)(1), governing preservation of certain defenses. When venue is inappropriate, the court must deny the motion to join a party. In that circumstance the court must consult Rule 19(b) to determine whether to proceed without the non-joined party. For a further discussion of venue, *see* § 2.14.

RULE 19(b). DETERMINATION BY COURT WHENEVER JOINDER NOT FEASIBLE

CORE CONCEPT

Rule 19(b) governs whether the court should proceed without persons who should be joined, but who cannot be joined because their joinder would defeat jurisdiction or venue. The court has substantial discretion to determine, under the considerations listed in Rule 19(b), whether to continue the litigation without the person or to dismiss the action because an indispensable party cannot be joined.[21]

18. *Independent Wireless Telegraph Co. v. Radio Corp. of America,* 269 U.S. 459, 46 S.Ct. 166, 70 L.Ed. 357 (1926); *but see, Eikel v. States Marine Lines, Inc.*, 473 F.2d 959, 962 (5th Cir. 1973)("involuntary" plaintiffs should not be joined freely; such joinder should occur only in unusual cases where the person has an obligation to participate).

19. *Koster v. (American) Lumbermens Mutual Casualty Co.,* 330 U.S. 518, 67 S.Ct. 828, 91 L.Ed. 1067 (1947). *Cf., Mayes v. Rapoport,* 198 F.3d 457, 462 (4th Cir.1999) (in cases removed from state court, 28 U.S.C. § 1447(e) provides district courts with considerable discretion to permit or deny post-removal joinder; however, if court permits joinder of non-diverse party and thereby destroys diversity jurisdiction, § 1447(e) requires court to remand case to state court; in any event, decision to permit or deny joinder in such removed cases is not controlled by Rule 19).

20. *Cf., Cobb v. Delta Exports, Inc.,* 186 F.3d 675, 677 (5th Cir.1999) ("[P]ost-removal joinder of non-diverse defendants pursuant to [Rule 19] destroys diversity for jurisdictional purposes and requires remand, even when the newly joined defendants are not indispensable.").

21. *See, e.g., Soberay Machine & Equipment Co. v. MRF Limited, Inc.,* 181 F.3d 759, 765 (6th Cir.1999) (determination under Rule 19(b) should be made on case by case assessment;

NOTE: In most cases under Rule 19(b) the court attempts to continue the suit rather than dismiss it.[22] Thus a defendant who has filed a motion under Rule 12(b)(7) should contemplate ways to reach a compromise with the court and opposing counsel that continues the suit on terms more favorable to the defendant. Shaping appropriate remedies is one area that might offer particularly good prospects for such terms.

APPLICATIONS

Relation to Rule 19(a)

If joinder is not required under Rule 19(a), the court will proceed without joinder. In such cases, the court does not have to evaluate the applicability of Rule 19(b).[23]

Who May Raise Rule 19(b)

The parties may raise Rule 19 issues. Additionally, the court may raise Rule 19(b) issues *sua sponte*.[24]

Relative Weight of Factors in Rule 19(b)

The considerations listed in Rule 19(b) are factors to be weighed, so that in a given case one might be more important than others.[25] The list is not one where every consideration must be satisfied before dismissal is ordered, or before the case may proceed.[26] Additionally, it is possible that in a particular case other factors not listed in Rule 19(b) could be important.[27]

Factors

(1) *Adverse Consequences of Proceeding Without a Person:* The court will examine whether adverse consequences such as legal or

"there is no prescribed formula for determining whether a party is indispensable").

22. *See, e.g., Teamsters Local Union No. 171 v. Keal Driveway Co.,* 173 F.3d 915, 918 (4th Cir.1999) ("Dismissal of a case is a drastic remedy ... which should be employed only sparingly."). *Jaser v. New York Property Insurance Underwriting Association,* 815 F.2d 240, 242 (2d Cir.1987)("[V]ery few cases should be terminated due to the absence of nondiverse parties unless there has been a reasoned determination that their nonjoinder makes just resolution of the action impossible.").

23. *See, e.g., Snap–On Tools Corp. v. Mason,* 18 F.3d 1261, 1267 (5th Cir.1994)(no need to apply Rule 19(b) standards when joinder is not mandated under Rule 19(a)).

24. *See, e.g., Manning v. Energy Conversion Devices, Inc.,* 13 F.3d 606, 609 (2d Cir. 1994)(even if parties make no Rule 19(a) objections, the court is "obliged" to raise Rule 19(b) issues if they are present).

25. *See, e.g., Delgado v. Plaza Las Americas, Inc.,* 139 F.3d 1 (1st Cir.1998) (referring to elements of Rule 19(b) as "gestalt factors").

26. *See, e.g., Universal Reinsurance Co. v. St. Paul Fire & Marine Insurance Co.,* 312 F.3d 82, 88–89 (2d Cir.2002) ("Rule 19(b) ... does not require that every factor support the district court's determination."); *Rhone-Poulenc, Inc. v. International Insurance Co.,* 71 F.3d 1299, 1301 (7th Cir.1995)("Rule 19(b) sets forth a standard, not a rigid rule."); *Glenny v. American Metal Climax, Inc.,* 494 F.2d 651, 653 (10th Cir. 1974)(each factor should be evaluated for its significance in the particular case).

27. *See, e.g., Gardiner v. Virgin Islands Water & Power Authority,* 145 F.3d 635, 640 (3d Cir.1998) (listed factors "are not exhaustive, but they are the most important considerations"). *Cf., Davis v. United States,* 192 F.3d 951, 960 (10th Cir.1999) (inability of court to join Indian tribe shielded by sovereign immunity may also be weighed, but presence of this additional factor does not eliminate application of factors listed in Rule 19(b)).

practical damage may result by proceeding without a party.[28] For example, persons already parties may be damaged if the suit creates the potential for inconsistent judgments discussed in Rule 19(a).[29] Similarly, a person not joined may be harmed if the suit proceeds to judgment and exhausts a fund from which compensation might otherwise have been anticipated.[30] Finally, if there is a risk of collateral estoppel for the absent person, that factor weighs in favor of dismissing the action.[31] By contrast, if a potential party shows no interest in a case, its interests probably are not significantly affected by the outcome of the case.[32]

If the interest at risk is that of the absent party, and that interest is adequately represented by someone already in the case, it is possible that a court will consider the risk of impairment to be nullified.[33] However, courts are cautious in reaching the conclusion that an interest is adequately represented by existing parties.[34]

(2) *Avoiding Adverse Consequences:* The second consideration directs the court to determine if means are available to the court for minimizing potential damage. When applying this factor, the court should make a fact-specific analysis. For example, as illustrated in the discussion of Rule 19(a), if a tenant sought injunctive relief against a

28. *Cf., HB General Corp. v. Manchester Partners, L.P.,* 95 F.3d 1185, 1193 (3d Cir.1996) (if all partners are parties, partnership itself may not be indispensable because its interests are represented adequately).

29. *See, e.g., Helzberg's Diamond Shops, Inc. v. Valley West Des Moines Shopping Center, Inc.,* 564 F.2d 816 (8th Cir.1977). *See also Estate of Alvarez v. Donaldson Co.,* 213 F.3d 993 (7th Cir.2000) (finding prejudice to plaintiff by proceeding in case without absent persons where, after potential favorable judgment, plaintiff would have to sue absent persons in state court); *National Union Fire Insurance Co. of Pittsburgh v. Rite Aid of South Carolina, Inc.,* 210 F.3d 246, 252 (4th Cir.2000) (first factor of Rule 19(b) "addresses many of the same concerns as Rule 19(a)(2)").

30. *See, e.g., In re Torcise,* 116 F.3d 860, 865 (11th Cir.1997) ("It is well established under Rule 19 that all claimants to a fund must be joined to determine the disposition of that fund.").

31. *See, e.g., Schulman v. J.P. Morgan Investment Management, Inc.,* 35 F.3d 799, 806 (3d Cir.1994)("Prejudice under Rule 19(b) . . . implicates principles of collateral estoppel.").

32. *See, e.g., Gardiner v. Virgin Islands Water & Power Authority,* 145 F.3d 635 (3d Cir. 1998) (so holding; moreover, a party's right to contribution or indemnity from a person not joined "does not render that absentee indispensable"). *But cf., Tell v. Trustees of Dartmouth College,* 145 F.3d 417 (1st Cir.1998) (fact that potential party is silent does not mean it does not claim an interest; language of Rule 19 merely means potential party "appears to have such an interest;" however, it is a different situation where potential party disclaimed an interest).

33. *See, e.g., Dainippon Screen Manufacturing Co. v. CFMT, Inc.,* 142 F.3d 1266 (Fed.Cir. 1998) (presence of parent corporation in suit assures adequate representation of absent subsidiary).

34. *See, e.g., Tell v. Trustees of Dartmouth College,* 145 F.3d 417 (1st Cir.1998) ("[W]ithout a perfect identity of interests, a court must be very cautious in concluding that a litigant will serve as a proxy for an absent party."). *See also Citizen Potawatomi Nation v. Norton,* 248 F.3d 993, 999 (10th Cir.2001), *opinion modified on reh'g,* 257 F.3d 1158 (10th Cir.2001) (where some tribes will win and others will lose in litigation, federal government's presence in suit cannot adequately represent interests of all tribes). *But cf., Dixon v. Edwards,* 290 F.3d 699, 714 (4th Cir.2002) (plaintiff faces no substantial risk of inconsistent obligation because, *inter alia,* non-parties support plaintiff's case and have stated that plaintiff represents overlapping interests they share with plaintiff); *Kansas v. United States,* 249 F.3d 1213 (10th Cir.2001) (when interests of existing defendants are "substantially similar, if not identical," to absent party, potential for prejudice to absent party is "largely nonexistent").

landlord, and the tenant agreed to a damage remedy rather than an injunction, the risk to the landlord of mutually inconsistent injunctions is minimized, and the case may be allowed to proceed.[35]

(3) *Adequacy of a Judgment:* This consideration addresses "adequacy" primarily from the point of view of the public interest in efficient and final disposition of legal disputes. Thus a judgment in a person's absence that will leave related claims by or against that person undecided, may be deemed an "inadequate" judgment.[36]

(4) *Availability of Another Forum:* The court will examine whether another forum is available in which the claimant may sue existing defendants as well as the person who cannot be joined.[37] When another forum is not available to the claimant, the court in most cases will proceed with the action.[38]

35. *See also Jota v. Texaco, Inc.,* 157 F.3d 153, 162 (2d Cir.1998) (absent party asserted sovereign immunity; without absent party, some aspects of equitable relief, such as environmental cleanup of polluted area, would be impossible; but dismissal was error because current defendant could provide all of legal relief and some of equitable relief plaintiff demanded; thus, relief could be shaped to diminish prejudice caused by inability to join absent party). *But see Laker Airways, Inc. v. British Airways, PLC,* 182 F.3d 843, 849 (11th Cir.1999) (although plaintiff no longer seeks injunctive relief, prejudice to absent entity would still be significant because finding in favor of plaintiff would still require court to find that absent entity acted improperly, which might damage that entity's relationship with British government).

36. *Provident Tradesmens Bank & Trust Co. v. Patterson,* 390 U.S. 102, 88 S.Ct. 733, 19 L.Ed.2d 936 (1968). *See, e.g., Estate of Alvarez v. Donaldson Co.,* 213 F.3d 993 (7th Cir.2000) (judgment is inadequate when plaintiff would have to relitigate in state court to recover against absent persons). *But see Universal Reinsurance Co. v. St. Paul Fire & Marine Insurance Co.,* 312 F.3d 82, 89–90 (2d Cir.2002) (party had already won on merits; thus judgment can be "adequate" because resolution of issue on merits means time and expense of trying issues has already been expended); *Sac and Fox Nation of Missouri v. Pierce,* 213 F.3d 566 n. 11 (10th Cir.), *cert. denied,* 531 U.S. 1144, 121 S.Ct. 1078, 148 L.Ed.2d 955 (2000) (where joinder is addressed for first time on appeal, "the preference for joinder . . . on efficiency grounds has all but disappeared at this late date"; thus, possibility that judgment in case will not settle whole controversy is not compelling).

37. *Cf., City of Marietta v. CSX Transportation, Inc.,* 196 F.3d 1300, 1307 (11th Cir.1999) (where case has been pending for three years, and remand to state court would cause more delay, court may take such facts into account in determining whether plaintiff's possible alternative form is truly adequate); *Laker Airways, Inc. v. British Airways, PLC,* 182 F.3d 843, 849 (11th Cir.1999) (plaintiff has adequate remedy in right to file complaints with administrative agencies of United States or British governments).

38. *Cf., e.g., Estate of Alvarez v. Donaldson Co.,* 213 F.3d 993 (7th Cir.2000) (dismissal appropriate in part because plaintiff can sue all parties in state court); *Angst v. Royal Maccabees Life Insurance Co.,* 77 F.3d 701, 706 (3d Cir. 1996)(because plaintiff may assert claims in pending state action, case should be dismissed). *Virginia Electric and Power Co. v. Westinghouse Electric Corp.,* 485 F.2d 78 (4th Cir.1973), *cert. denied,* 415 U.S. 935, 94 S.Ct. 1450, 39 L.Ed.2d 493 (1974); *but compare, Manybeads v. United States,* 209 F.3d 1164, 1166 (9th Cir.2000), *cert. denied,* 532 U.S. 966, 121 S.Ct. 1504, 149 L.Ed.2d 388 (2001) (where first three factors of Rule 19(b) weigh against continuing case, fact that plaintiff will have no other forum in which to pursue First Amendment claim does not prevent dismissal when continuation of case would cause "a sovereign, not a party to the case, [to] suffer substantially from [plaintiff's] vindication"); *Guerrero v. Clinton,* 157 F.3d 1190 (9th Cir.1998) (plaintiff's interest in litigation outweighed by Indian tribe's interest in sovereign immunity; dismissal appropriate even where plaintiff has no other forum), *with Dawavendewa v. Salt River Project Agriculture Improvement & Power District,* 276 F.3d 1150, 1161 (9th Cir.2002) ("If no alternative forum exists, we

Public Interest Exception

In some cases where a public right is to be litigated, but some persons indispensable under Rule 19 cannot be joined, courts have fashioned a "public interest exception" to Rule 19. When applicable, this exception means that such absent persons are not deemed indispensable, without regard to whatever a Rule 19 analysis might have concluded. The scope of this exception seems unclear, and attorneys are advised to consult local precedent.[39]

Failure to Intervene

If a person who would practically be affected by a judgment nevertheless refuses to intervene, it might seem that a court would not weigh that person's interests as heavily. However, in some circumstances it appears that the interests of such a person may still be taken into account in determining whether to proceed in the person's absence.[40]

Effect of Dismissal: Relation to Rule 41(b)

Rule 41 governs the effects of dismissals. In cases that have been dismissed for failure to join a party under Rule 19, Rule 41(b) provides that the dismissal is without prejudice to re-filing unless the order of dismissal provides otherwise.[41]

RULE 19(c). PLEADING REASONS FOR NONJOINDER

CORE CONCEPT

Rule 19(c) places an affirmative duty on parties seeking relief to identify in their pleadings potentially interested persons who have not been joined. A court may use such information to notify these persons, so that they may join on their own initiative.

APPLICATIONS

Motions to Dismiss

The defendant may use the names provided by the plaintiff as a basis for a motion to dismiss the action for failure to join necessary

should be 'extra cautious' before dismissing the suit." Concluding, however, that instant case should be dismissed).

39. *See, e.g., Kickapoo Tribe v. Babbitt,* 43 F.3d 1491, 1500 (D.C.Cir.1995) (explaining exception, collecting cases addressing it). *Cf., Kettle Range Conservation Group v. United States Bureau of Land Management,* 150 F.3d 1083, 1087 (9th Cir.1998) (exception applicable, if at all, where absent parties' private interests will not be destroyed by continuation of litigation).

40. *See, e.g., Kickapoo Tribe of Indians of the Kickapoo Reservation v. Babbitt,* 43 F.3d 1491, 1497 (D.C.Cir.1995)("Failure to intervene is not a component of the prejudice analysis where intervention would require the absent party to waive sovereign immunity."). *But see, Thunder Basin Coal Co. v. Southwestern Public Service Co.,* 104 F.3d 1205, 1208 (10th Cir.1997) ("We specifically hold that an entity or individual subject to impleader under Fed. R. Civ. P. 14 and entitled to intervene under Fed. R. Civ. P. 24 is never an indispensable party." But the court did not decide whether availability of impleader or intervention, "standing alone," makes a party not indispensable.).

41. *O'Rourke Brothers, Inc. v. Nesbitt Burns, Inc.,* 201 F.3d 948, 950 (7th Cir.2000).

parties under Rule 12(b)(7). In addition, defendants may make similar use of any such knowledge they possess independently of the pleadings.

RULE 19(d). EXCEPTION OF CLASS ACTIONS

CORE CONCEPT

When Rule 19 and Rule 23, governing class actions, both apply to a case, and they are in conflict, Rule 23 controls.

ADDITIONAL RESEARCH REFERENCES

Wright & Miller, *Federal Practice and Procedure* §§ 1601–26.

C.J.S. Federal Civil Procedure §§ 95–112 et seq.

West's Key No. Digests, Federal Civil Procedure ⚷201–233.

RULE 20

PERMISSIVE JOINDER OF PARTIES

(a) Permissive Joinder. All persons may join in one action as plaintiffs if they assert any right to relief jointly, severally, or in the alternative in respect of or arising out of the same transaction, occurrence, or series of transactions or occurrences and if any question of law or fact common to all these persons will arise in the action. All persons (and any vessel, cargo or other property subject to admiralty process in rem) may be joined in one action as defendants if there is asserted against them jointly, severally, or in the alternative, any right to relief in respect of or arising out of the same transaction, occurrence, or series of transactions or occurrences and if any question of law or fact common to all defendants will arise in the action. A plaintiff or defendant need not be interested in obtaining or defending against all the relief demanded. Judgment may be given for one or more of the plaintiffs according to their respective rights to relief, and against one or more defendants according to their respective liabilities.

(b) Separate Trials. The court may make such orders as will prevent a party from being embarrassed, delayed, or put to expense by the inclusion of a party against whom the party asserts no claim and who asserts no claim against the party, and may order separate trials or make other orders to prevent delay or prejudice.

[Amended effective July 1, 1966; August 1, 1987.]

AUTHORS' COMMENTARY ON RULE 20

PURPOSE AND SCOPE

Rule 20 describes the circumstances in which a plaintiff may join with other plaintiffs against a single defendant, or join several defendants in a single action. It is permissive only, allowing joinder in many situations, but not requiring it.[1] However, if plaintiffs do not voluntarily join, the court retains discretion to consolidate actions that were brought separately under Rule 42(a). Rule 20 also gives the court authority to sever claims for separate trials against parties already joined. In addition, Rule 21 provides that a court may, in appropriate circumstances, dismiss parties joined under Rule 20.

---

1. *See, e.g., Applewhite v. Reichhold Chemicals, Inc.*, 67 F.3d 571, 574 (5th Cir.1995)(Rule 20(a) is a plaintiff's option, once requirements are met).

RULE 20(a). PERMISSIVE JOINDER

CORE CONCEPT

Joinder of parties is generally encouraged in the interest of judicial economy, subject to fulfillment of two prerequisites: the persons who join as plaintiffs or who are joined as defendants must be interested in claims that arise out of the same transaction or occurrence, or series of transactions or occurrences; and all the parties joined must share in common at least one question of law or fact.[2]

APPLICATIONS

"Same Transaction or Occurrence" Test

The courts have adopted various standards for determining whether a claim arises out of the same transaction or occurrence. The assessment is very specific to the facts of the particular case, but in general this requirement is satisfied if there is a substantial logical relationship between the transactions or occurrences at issue.[3]

Common Question of Fact or Law

Rule 20(a) requires only that the joined parties share a single common question of fact or law. There is no requirement that the actions involving various parties overlap with one another to any greater degree.[4]

Denial of Joinder

Rule 20(a) is intended to afford broad opportunities for joinder of parties who have—or are the subject of—substantially related claims.

2. *See, e.g., A.M. Alexander v. Fulton County, Georgia,* 207 F.3d 1303, 1323 (11th Cir.2000) (identifying both requirements).

3. *See, e.g., Mosley v. General Motors Corp.,* 497 F.2d 1330, 1333 (8th Cir.1974); ("[A]ll reasonably related claims for relief by or against different parties [should] be tried in a single proceeding."). *See also A.M. Alexander v. Fulton County, Georgia,* 207 F.3d 1303, 1323 (11th Cir. 2000) (noting that courts use precedent construing rule 13(a) to determine existence of "same transaction or occurrence" under Rule 20(a)); *Blesedell v. Mobil Oil Co.,* 708 F.Supp. 1408, 1422 (S.D.N.Y.1989) ("A company-wide policy purportedly designed to discriminate against females in employment arises out of the same series of transactions or occurrences."). *But see Coughlin v. Rogers,* 130 F.3d 1348, 1350 (9th Cir.1997) (approving holding that transactions are dissimilar where plaintiffs sue alleging unreasonable delay in processing petitions relating to immigration status; noting that allegation of general delay does not of itself create common transaction or occurrence where delays are of different length, with different causes; "Moreover, Plaintiffs do not allege that their claims arise out of a systematic pattern of events and, therefore, arise from the same transaction or occurrence;" also, there is no allegation of a "common policy" at issue); *Saval v. BL Ltd.,* 710 F.2d 1027, 1031 (4th Cir.1983)(joinder properly denied when plaintiffs suing on breach of warranty claims relating to defective automobiles each purchased individual cars separately; moreover, cars had different driving records and service histories).

4. *See, e.g., Dougherty v. Mieczkowski,* 661 F.Supp. 267, 278 (D.Del.1987)("By its terms, Rule 20(a) only requires a single basis for commonality, in either law or fact, for the joinder to be acceptable."). *But see, Coughlin v. Rogers,* 130 F.3d 1348, 1350–51 (9th Cir.1997) (approving holding that no common question exists simply because all claims arise under same general law; noting that each claim is discrete on facts, standards, and procedures).

However, the trial court retains substantial discretion to deny joinder in circumstances where joinder might produce jury confusion or undue delay in resolving a case.[5]

Admiralty Actions

Under Rule 20(a) a party may join parties, vessels, and other property subject to admiralty jurisdiction (typically, admiralty actions are not based on personal jurisdiction over a vessel's owner, but upon the court's jurisdiction over the vessel, which is normally exercised when the vessel is served within the territorial confines of the jurisdiction in which the court sits).

Prisoners' Lawsuits

When a prison inmate files a civil suit *in forma pauperis,* the Prison Litigation Reform Act requires, *inter alia,* the prisoner to pay the full filing fee.[6] The effect of this legislation when multiple inmates seek to join their claims under Rule 20 is to require each such plaintiff to file a separate complaint and to pay separately the full filing fee, rather than pro-rate a single filing fee among all the plaintiffs. To the extent that joinder of multiple plaintiffs is permitted under Rule 20, the question that arises in inmate cases is whether such plaintiffs may file together and pay only a single fee. The appellate courts have so far reached different results on this issue.[7]

Complete Relief Unnecessary

Joinder of parties is feasible even if the court may not grant complete relief to each plaintiff or defendant. Thus, it is possible that two plaintiffs would join in a suit, even if the court could anticipate at the time of joinder that the judgment, if favorable, will satisfy the claim of one plaintiff completely, but will leave the other plaintiff with only partial satisfaction.[8]

Right to Relief Still Judged Separately

Notwithstanding joinder, parties still receive judgment according to the respective merits of their individual cases. Though important, this

5. *See, e.g., Chavez v. Illinois State Police,* 251 F.3d 612 (7th Cir.2001) (affirming denial of rule 20 joinder when discovery had already been terminated two years earlier and defendants would be unfairly prejudiced by need to reopen discovery); *Thompson v. Boggs,* 33 F.3d 847, 858 (7th Cir.1994), *cert. denied,* 514 U.S. 1063, 115 S.Ct. 1692, 131 L.Ed.2d 556 (1995)(in civil rights case against police officer, joinder of second party properly denied where the following factors would create jury confusion; the two alleged incidents were separated by two years; the injury claims were separate and distinct; and the second complaint would require joinder of additional police officers as defendants).

6. 28 U.S.C.A. § 1915(b). *See, e.g., Abdul–Akbar v. McKelvie,* 239 F.3d 307, 331 (3d Cir. 2001), *cert. denied,* 533 U.S. 953, 121 S.Ct. 2600, 150 L.Ed.2d 757 (2001) (legislative intent was to deter frivolous prisoner litigation).

7. *See Hubbard v. Haley,* 262 F.3d 1194, 1198 (11th Cir.2001), *cert. denied,* 534 U.S. 1136, 122 S.Ct. 1083, 151 L.Ed.2d 983 (2001) (28 U.S.C.A. § 1915(b)(1) requires each inmate to pay a full filing fee and, if relevant, a full appellate filing fee). *But see Talley–Bey v. Knebl,* 168 F.3d 884, 887 (6th Cir.1999) (permitting prorated assessment of fees).

8. *See, e.g., Triggs v. John Crump Toyota, Inc.,* 154 F.3d 1284, 1290 (11th Cir.1998) ("[T]he express language of Rule 20 indicates that all plaintiffs need not seek relief against all defendants.").

concept means no more than this: the victory of one of the joined parties in a case does not necessarily guarantee victory (or defeat) to another joined party.[9]

Jurisdiction: Relation to 28 U.S.C. § 1367

The supplemental jurisdiction of district courts is governed by 28 U.S.C. § 1367. In general, § 1367(a) authorizes courts to exercise supplemental jurisdiction over non-diverse state claims that arise from the same case or controversy as other claims that satisfy the original subject matter jurisdiction of district courts. However, § 1367(b) and (c) create some exceptions to the application of § 1367(a). In particular, § 1367(b) prohibits exercise of supplemental jurisdiction when: (1) the basis for original jurisdiction is diversity; (2) the supplemental claim is asserted by a plaintiff; and (3) the person who is the target of the claim was joined under, *inter alia,* Rule 20. One line of cases has construed these principles to require an independent evaluation of Rule 20 and § 1367(b), respectively.[10] However, another line of reasoning concludes that at least in some circumstances plaintiffs who satisfy the joinder requirements of Rule 20 also qualify for supplemental jurisdiction under § 1367.[11] Attorneys are therefore advised to consult the local precedent. Supplemental jurisdiction is discussed at greater length elsewhere in this text.

Relation to Rule 15

Rule 15 generally governs the circumstances when a party may amend a pleading, including amendments to add new parties. However, because Rule 20 also regulates whether parties may be joined, a proposed amended pleading to add a party must meet the requirements of both Rules 15 and 20.[12]

Compare With Rule 18

Though Rule 20(a) is quite liberal in permitting joinder of parties, it is still somewhat more restrictive than Rule 18, which governs joinder of *claims* by a single plaintiff against a single defendant. Rule 18 does

9. *See, e.g., Id. at* 1288 ("[T]he fact that a great many members of the putative plaintiff class can seek no relief against one of the defendants . . . would be no obstacle to the permissive joinder of [that defendant] under Rule 20."). *Cf., United States v. Real Property Known as 22249 Dolorosa St.,* 190 F.3d 977, 982 (9th Cir.1999) (claims in forfeiture proceeding joined under Rule 20; held, where government won most claims but lost others, government's liability for attorneys' fees in unsuccessful case cannot be shielded by fact that government prevailed on related claims; government liability for each forfeiture claim must be decided separately).

10. *See, e.g., Smith v. GTE Corp.,* 236 F.3d 1292, 1310 (11th Cir. 2001) (although Rule 20 may permit plaintiffs to join their claims, the issue of whether parties may aggregate their claims to satisfy the required jurisdictional amount in a diversity case is an entirely separate matter); *Meritcare, Inc. v. St. Paul Mercury Insurance Co.,* 166 F.3d 214, 216 (3d Cir. 1999) (each co-plaintiff must independently satisfy amount in controversy requirement).

11. *See, e.g., Stromberg Metal Works, Inc. v. Press Mechanical, Inc.,* 77 F.3d 928, 932 (7th Cir. 1996) (where one plaintiff satisfies amount in controversy requirement, other plaintiffs may use § 1367 to join transactionally related claims; but suggesting opposite result if issue involves claims against co-defendants).

12. *See, e.g., Hinson v. Norwest Financial South Carolina, Inc.,* 239 F.3d 611, 618 (4th Cir.2001).

not require that the claims arise from a common transaction or occurrence, and the claims need not share even a single question of law or fact in common.[13]

RULE 20(b). SEPARATE TRIALS

CORE CONCEPT

Although Rule 20(a) may permit plaintiffs to join together, or to join several defendants together, the court retains discretion to order separate trials or other proceedings if necessary in the interest of justice.

APPLICATIONS

Embarrassment, Expense, or Delay

Primary factors considered by the court in determining whether to order separate trials are unreasonable embarrassment, expense or delay. These broad standards afford the trial court significant discretion in determining whether to separate the parties.

Source of Embarrassment, Expense or Delay

Rule 20(b) appears to permit relief in the form of separate trials if the source of the embarrassment, expense, or delay is someone not adverse to the affected party. It does not apply to circumstances where a party's embarrassment is produced by addition of an adverse party. In actuality, this distinction is not a substantial impingement on a court's discretion to separate. The rule's language is construed to be broad enough to permit separation when injustice would occur.[14] Moreover, the court has discretion to order separate proceedings of any claim in the interest of justice or convenience under Rules 21 and 42(b).

ADDITIONAL RESEARCH REFERENCES

Wright & Miller, *Federal Practice and Procedure* §§ 1651–60.

C.J.S. Federal Civil Procedure §§ 94–116, 318, 917, 918.

West's Key No. Digests, Federal Civil Procedure 🔑241–267, 1956.

13. *See, e.g., Intercon Research Associates, Ltd. v. Dresser Industries, Inc.*, 696 F.2d 53, 57 (7th Cir.1982)("[J]oinder of claims under Rule 18 becomes relevant only after the requirements of Rule 20 . . . has [sic] been met.").

14. *See, e.g., Coleman v. Quaker Oats Co.*, 232 F.3d 1271, 1296 (9th Cir.2000), *cert. denied*, 533 U.S. 950, 121 S.Ct. 2592, 150 L.Ed.2d 751 (2001) (although joinder was proper under Rule 20(a), separate trials under Rule 20(b) were also appropriate where ten plaintiffs, alleging age discrimination, might have confused jury as to individual facts; defendant would also have faced risk of prejudice from having "all ten plaintiffs testify in one trial"); *Avitia v. Metropolitan Club of Chicago, Inc.*, 49 F.3d 1219, 1224 (7th Cir. 1995)(Rule 20(b) permits court to weigh embarrassment to defendant from multiple claims of labor law violations, against cost to other parties and to courts of having more than one trial; denying motion for separate trials).

RULE 21

MISJOINDER AND NON–JOINDER OF PARTIES

Misjoinder of parties is not ground for dismissal of an action. Parties may be dropped or added by order of the court on motion of any party or of its own initiative at any stage of the action and on such terms as are just. Any claim against a party may be severed and proceeded with separately.

AUTHORS' COMMENTARY ON RULE 21

PURPOSE AND SCOPE

Rule 21 contains the remedy for misjoinder or nonjoinder that violates other Rules governing multiparty litigation. It ensures that inappropriate joinder of a party, or failure to join a party that should have been joined, need not result in dismissal of the action. It also provides the court with discretion to sever claims against a party for separate trials, or to order separate trials for joined parties, even if the joinder was otherwise appropriate.

APPLICATIONS

What Constitutes Inappropriate Joinder

Joinder may be inappropriate for a variety of reasons, including situations in which joinder of parties produces defects in jurisdiction or venue.[1] Additionally, joinder that does not meet the requirements of Rule 20(a) is inappropriate, and may necessitate the use of Rule 21.[2]

Inappropriate Joinder: Consequences

The consequence of an inappropriate joinder need not be dismissal of the entire action. Instead, the court will order the inappropriately joined party dismissed, so that the remainder of the action may continue.[3]

1. *See, e.g., Whitaker v. American Telecasting, Inc.*, 261 F.3d 196, 206–07 (2d Cir.2001) (approving use of rule 21 to dismiss non-diverse defendant who had no real connection to litigation).

2. *Jonas v. Conrath*, 149 F.R.D. 520, 523 (S.D.W.Va.1993)("[P]arties are misjoined when they fail to satisfy either of the preconditions for permissive joinder . . . set forth in Rule 20(a).").

3. *Newman-Green, Inc. v. Alfonzo–Larrain*, 490 U.S. 826, 832, 109 S.Ct. 2218, 2222, 104 L.Ed.2d 893 (1989) ("[I]t is well settled that Rule 21 invests district courts with authority to allow a dispensable nondiverse party to be dropped at any time, even after judgment has been rendered;" suggesting that federal appellate courts have similar authority). *See, e.g., CGB Occupational Therapy, Inc. v. RHA Health Services, Inc.*, 357 F.3d 375, 382 (3d Cir. 2004) ("[I]t is well settled that courts, both district and circuit alike, have the power under Fed. R.Civ.P. 21 to dismiss dispensable parties to the suit in order to preserve diversity"). *But cf., Elmore v. Henderson*, 227 F.3d 1009, 1012 (7th Cir.2000) (where party was inappropriately

Failure to Join

If a party should have been joined but was not, the court will simply order appropriate service of process.[4]

Relationship to Rule 15

If parties seek to add a party under Rule 21, courts use the standard of Rule 15, governing amendments to pleadings, to determine whether to allow the addition.[5]

Relation to Rule 19; Diversity Jurisdiction

The authority of a district court to protect its diversity jurisdiction by dismissing a party under Rule 21 is subject to the restriction of Rule 19, which requires the presence of parties deemed indispensable to the action. In practice, that relationship means that if an indispensable party is also not diverse, the court cannot simply dismiss the party but must consider dismissing the action under Rule 19.[6]

Relation to Rule 25

Rule 25 governs substitution of parties in any of the specific sections addressed by that Rule. By contrast, Rule 21 governs substitution "in the discretion of the court in situations not covered by Rule 25."[7]

Relation to Rule 42(b)

When a claim is severed under Rule 21, it ceases to be part of the same suit.[8] By contrast, if an issue is separated under Rule 42(b), it will be tried separately but remain part of the same lawsuit. The most important result of this distinction is that severed proceedings under Rule 21 become final as each proceeding goes to judgment, and may be appealed individually. Separate trials under Rule 42(b), by contrast, are typically *not* ready for appeal until all claims and issues are decided.[9]

joined, Rule 21 permits district court to sever that party and hear that case separately rather than dismiss it, if dismissal would produce harsh result under applicable statute of limitations). *See also Max v. McLaughlin,* ___ F.3d ___ (5th Cir. 2004) (Rule 21 permits dismissal of misjoined parties, but not misjoined properties).

4. *See, e.g., Teamsters Local Union No. 116 v. Fargo–Moorhead Automobile Dealers Ass'n,* 620 F.2d 204 (8th Cir.1980).

5. *See, e.g., Frank v. U.S. West, Inc.*, 3 F.3d 1357, 1365 (10th Cir.1993)("A motion to add a party is governed by [Rule] 15(a)."); *see, also, United States ex rel. Precision Co. v. Koch Industries, Inc.,* 31 F.3d 1015, 1018 (10th Cir. 1994)(citing *Frank* for applicability of Rule 15(a), rather than Rule 21, when a party seeks to add a party through an amendment as of right). *Cf., Soberay Machine & Equipment Co. v. MRF Ltd.,* 181 F.3d 759, 763 (6th Cir.1999) ("[I]t makes no difference whether Rule 15 or Rule 21 is used to retain federal diversity jurisdiction over a case.").

6. *See, e.g., Kirkland v. Legion Insurance Co.*, 343 F.3d 1135, 1142 (9th Cir. 2003).

7. *Mathis v. Bess,* 761 F.Supp. 1023, 1026 (S.D.N.Y.1991), *opinion modified on denial of reargument*, 763 F.Supp. 58 (D.N.Y.1991).

8. *See, e.g., Rice v. Sunrise Express, Inc.*, 209 F.3d 1008, 1013 (7th Cir.2000), *cert. denied*, 531 U.S. 1012, 121 S.Ct. 567, 148 L.Ed.2d 486 (2000) ("Under Rule 21 . . . severance creates two separate actions where previously there was but one.").

9. *See, e.g., Acevedo–Garcia v. Monroig,* 351 F.3d 547, 559–60 (1st Cir. 2003) (observing that courts sometimes confuse the two rules; noting that important practical difference is that under Rule 21 a judgment entered is final and appeal-

Timing

The court may order dismissal or the addition of a party at any time in the action, subject only to the need to protect all parties from unfair prejudice.[10]

Motion

Adding or dropping a party may be done upon motion of someone already a party, or upon the court's own initiative.[11]

Preserving Diversity Jurisdiction

Even where a party is appropriately joined, circumstances can arise where the court can apply Rule 21 to drop a party. A notable example arises when a court dismisses a nondiverse party in order to obtain diversity jurisdiction over the remaining parties.[12]

Severance of Claims or Parties

Even if parties or claims have been appropriately joined, the court may nonetheless use this Rule to order separate trials in the interest of justice.[13]

able without regard to whether other severed portions of original case have proceeded to judgment; under Rule 42(b), however, separate trials do not usually become appealable until all of the trials have been decided); *Rice v. Sunrise Express, Inc.,* 209 F.3d 1008, 1013 (7th Cir.), *cert. denied,* 531 U.S. 1012, 121 S.Ct. 567, 148 L.Ed.2d 486 (2000) ("Under Rule 21 ... severance creates two separate actions where previously there was but one"); *White v. ABCO Engineering Corp.,* 199 F.3d 140, 145 n. 6 (3d Cir. 1999) (same analysis).

10. *Newman-Green, Inc. v. Alfonzo–Larrain,* 490 U.S. 826, 832, 109 S.Ct. 2218, 2223, 104 L.Ed.2d 893 (1989) ("It is well-settled that Rule 21 invests district courts with authority to allow a dispensable nondiverse party to be dropped at any time [to preserve diversity jurisdiction], even after judgment has been rendered." However, while appellate courts also possess such authority, they should probably exercise it much more sparingly.). *See also, e.g., California Credit Union League v. City of Anaheim,* 190 F.3d 997, 999 (9th Cir.1999), *cert. denied,* 528 U.S. 1154, 120 S.Ct. 1159, 145 L.Ed.2d 1071 (2000) (Rule 21 may permit joinder on appeal "when the party seeking joinder requests the same remedy as the original party and offers the same reasons for that remedy, and earlier joinder would not have affected the course of the litigation."); *Galt G/S v. JSS Scandinavia,* 142 F.3d 1150, 1154 (9th Cir.1998) ("Rule 21 specifically allows for the dismissal of parties at any stage of the action. There is no requirement that diversity exist at the time of the filing of the complaint.").

11. *See, e.g., Delgado v. Plaza Las Americas, Inc.,* 139 F.3d 1 (1st Cir.1998) (court may raise nonjoinder *sua sponte*).

12. *See, e.g., Newman-Green, Inc. v. Alfonzo–Larrain,* 490 U.S. 826, 832–33, 109 S.Ct. 2218, 2222–23, 104 L.Ed.2d 893 (1989) (Rule 21 permits dismissal of "dispensable" non-diverse defendants to cure jurisdictional defects; such dismissal can occur "even after judgment" and even by appellate court). *See, e.g., Fielder v. Credit Acceptance Corp.,* 188 F.3d 1031, 1039 (8th Cir.1999) ("Rule 21 is often used to allow federal courts to escape a multi-party jurisdictional quandry."); *Tuck v. United Services Automobile Association,* 859 F.2d 842, 845 (10th Cir. 1988), *cert. denied,* 489 U.S. 1080, 109 S.Ct. 1534, 103 L.Ed.2d 839 (1989)(so noting, provided that the party dismissed is not indispensable under Rule 19).

13. *See, e.g., Rice v. Sunrise Express, Inc.,* 209 F.3d 1008, 1016 (7th Cir.2000), *cert. denied,* 531 U.S. 1012, 121 S.Ct. 567, 148 L.Ed.2d 486 (2000) (noting district courts' "broad discretion" under Rule 21; "[a]s long as there is a discrete and separate claim, the district court may exercise its discretion and sever it"); *Old Colony Ventures I, Inc. v. SMWNPF Holdings, Inc.,* 918 F.Supp. 343 (D.Kan.1996)(in employing Rule 21, court should consider convenience of parties, avoidance of prejudice, and judicial efficiency.). *See also In re High Fructose Corn Syrup Antitrust Litigation,* 361 F.3d 439, 441 (7th Cir. 2004) (in the course of applying Rule 21, district court has authority to empanel separate juries in appropriate circumstances).

ADDITIONAL RESEARCH REFERENCES

Wright & Miller, *Federal Practice and Procedure* §§ 1681–89.

C.J.S. Federal Civil Procedure §§ 117–126 et seq., 171–177 et seq., 318, 343, 803–809.

West's Key No. Digests, Federal Civil Procedure ⚿281–297, 384–386, 387–388, 1747–1750.

RULE 22

INTERPLEADER

(1) Persons having claims against the plaintiff may be joined as defendants and required to interplead when their claims are such that the plaintiff is or may be exposed to double or multiple liability. It is not ground for objection to the joinder that the claims of the several claimants or the titles on which their claims depend do not have a common origin or are not identical but are adverse to and independent of one another, or that the plaintiff avers that the plaintiff is not liable in whole or in part to any or all of the claimants. A defendant exposed to similar liability may obtain such interpleader by way of cross-claim or counterclaim. The provisions of this rule supplement and do not in any way limit the joinder of parties permitted in Rule 20.

(2) The remedy herein provided is in addition to and in no way supersedes or limits the remedy provided by Title 28, U.S.C., §§ 1335, 1397, and 2361. Actions under those provisions shall be conducted in accordance with these rules.

[Amended effective October 20, 1949; August 1, 1987.]

AUTHORS' COMMENTARY ON RULE 22

PURPOSE AND SCOPE

Rule 22 permits a person who may be subject to multiple liability by claimants with overlapping or inconsistent claims to interplead or join such claimants as defendants in a single action. In the ordinary procedure, once claimants are joined they will compete with one another to establish the validity and priority of their claims against the interpleader plaintiff.

CORE CONCEPT

Interpleader complements liberal joinder of parties under Rule 20 by allowing a stakeholder to join multiple, mutually inconsistent claims of various parties, and thereby determine rights in the asset (the "stake") in a single proceeding.

NOTE: Rule 22 interpleader is not the only kind of federal interpleader available. Statutory interpleader, found at 28 U.S.C.A. §§ 1335, 1397, and 2361, discussed below, is at least as important a source of interpleader authority as Rule 22. Although the two kinds of interpleader may often be employed in the same action, the differing characteristics of the two interpleaders sometimes make one more desirable, or available when the other is unavailable. Thus, both versions should be considered when contemplating an interpleader action.

APPLICATIONS

Stakeholder as Claimant

The interpleader plaintiff may also be a claimant, as for example where a limited insurance fund is subject to claims exceeding the value of the fund. The insurance company may in appropriate circumstances be permitted to initiate the interpleader action, and then to participate as a claimant, if it contends that the other claims against the insurance fund are without merit.[1]

Claims Against the Stake

The only requirement under Rule 22 is that the interpleader plaintiff plead that the competing claims are at least partly inconsistent with one another, *e.g.,* where the claims against a fund exceed the value of the fund.[2] Interpleader actions need not be based on identical competing claims, or claims with a common origin, nor must the claims be totally incompatible with one another. In establishing this standard, Rule 22 eases significantly the requirements previously imposed on common law interpleader actions.

Defendants May Employ Interpleader

Sometimes a stakeholder will already have been sued by a claimant, but other claimants are not parties to the action. In such circumstances the stakeholder is entitled to initiate the interpleader action through a counterclaim or cross-claim, and then join the other claimants in the action.[3]

Subject Matter Jurisdiction

This Rule does not create jurisdiction in interpleader actions. Instead, it only authorizes interpleader *if* jurisdictional requirements in

1. *Cf., Nationwide Mutual Fire Insurance Co. v. Eason,* 736 F.2d 130, 133 (4th Cir. 1984)(stakeholder is "not precluded" from making a claim on the asset).

2. *See, e.g., Rhoades v. Casey,* 196 F.3d 592, 600 n. 8 (5th Cir.1999), *cert. denied,* 531 U.S. 924, 121 S.Ct. 298, 148 L.Ed.2d 240 (2000) ("A prerequisite to filing an interpleader action is that there must be a single, identifiable, fund."). *Pan American Fire & Casualty Co. v. Revere,* 188 F.Supp. 474 (E.D.La.1960)(adversity requirement satisfied if claims against stake amount to more than stakeholder's maximum liability); *see also, Hussain v. Boston Old Colony Insurance Co.,* 311 F.3d 623, 634 n. 40 (5th Cir.2002) ("[I]t is well settle that claims to the stake need not be mutually exclusive. ... We and other courts have also found that adversity of claims is also satisfied when additional claims to a fund are derivative of one particular claimant's right to the fund."); *Hebel v. Ebersole,* 543 F.2d 14, 17 (7th Cir.1976)(adversity requirement satisfied by "the risk of a double payment on single liability;" additional independent stakeholder liability does not defeat right to relief through interpleader).

3. *Grubbs v. General Electric Credit Corp.,* 405 U.S. 699, 92 S.Ct. 1344, 31 L.Ed.2d 612 (1972). *See also Hussain v. Boston Old Colony Insurance Co.,* 311 F.3d 623, 633 n. 39 (5th Cir.2002) (substance of pleading and nexus to existing parties predominates over nominal label on pleading).

the federal courts are met. Federal subject matter jurisdiction is still required.[4] If the underlying cause of action is a federal question, subject matter jurisdiction for an interpleader is usually satisfied without difficulty. More commonly, however, the interpleader will arise from a state cause of action, and then the standard requirements for diversity jurisdiction must also be satisfied. The citizenship of the stakeholder must be diverse from that of the claimants, and the amount in controversy must exceed $75,000. The claimants need not be diverse among themselves.[5]

Personal Jurisdiction

Interpleader actions are actions against individuals, not against the asset, and so must satisfy requirements of personal jurisdiction. This means that service of process on claimants must satisfy Rule 4 service requirements as well as constitutional Due Process protections discussed in the section on personal jurisdiction.[6]

Venue Requirements

Rule 22 interpleader actions are subject to the general venue requirements contained in 28 U.S.C.A. § 1391.[7] These requirements are discussed in § 2.14.

Disinterested Stakeholders: Attorney's Fees

It appears settled that a disinterested stakeholder is entitled to recover attorney's fees.[8]

Payment into Court: Relation to Rule 67

Rule 22 does not require that the stakeholder turn the asset in

4. *See, e.g., Aetna Life Insurance Co. v. Bayona,* 223 F.3d 1030, 1033 (9th Cir.2000) ("Rule 22 interpleader is only a procedural device ... –the rule does not convey [sic] jurisdiction on the courts"); *Commercial National Bank of Chicago v. Demos,* 18 F.3d 485, 487 (7th Cir.1994)("Rule 22(1) provides a procedural framework for interpleader actions, but it does not confer subject matter jurisdiction.").

5. *See, e.g., Hussain v. Boston Old Colony Insurance Co.,* 311 F.3d 623, 635 n. 46 (5th Cir.2002) (diversity met when amount in controversy is satisfied and stakeholder is diverse from all claimants "even if citizenship of the claimants is not diverse"); *State Street Bank & Trust Co. v. Denman Tire Corp.,* 240 F.3d 83, 89 n. 4 (1st Cir.2001) (statutory interpleader not available in diversity case "because the potential claimants are not diverse;" only Rule 22 is available); *Franceskin v. Credit Suisse,* 214 F.3d 253 (2d Cir.2000) (for Rule 22, diverse citizenship is satisfied if stakeholder is diverse from every claimant; thus, where stakeholder and claimants are all aliens, diversity requirement as defined by 28 U.S.C. § 1332 is not met; requirement of diversity for statutory interpleader is that two or more claimants must be diverse from one another; where all claimants are citizens of Argentina, this requirement is not met); *Commercial Union Insurance Co. v. United States,* 999 F.2d 581, 584 (D.C.Cir.1993)(Rule 22 looks to diversity between stakeholder and claimants; in contrast, statutory interpleader looks to diversity between claimants).

6. *See, e.g., Metropolitan Life Insurance Co. v. Chase,* 294 F.2d 500, 502 (3d Cir. 1961)(interpleader under Rule 22 requires personal jurisdiction over the claimants).

7. *See, e.g., Leader National Insurance Co. v. Shaw,* 901 F.Supp. 316, 320 (W.D.Okl.1995)("In cases of 'Rule' interpleader, venue is determined by reference to ... § 1391.").

8. *See, e.g., Perkins State Bank v. Connolly,* 632 F.2d 1306, 1311 (5th Cir.1980)("[C]osts and attorney's fees are generally awarded by federal courts to the plaintiff who initiates the interpleader as a mere stakeholder.").

dispute over to the custody of the court.[9] However, in practice, payment into court occurs in many Rule 22 cases.[10] It should be noted that Rule 67 authorizes a party, with leave of court, to pay a sum of money in dispute into court pending the outcome of the case. Rule 67 is sometimes the mechanism cited for payment of the stake into court in Rule 22 cases.[11]

Inconsistent Actions

Rule 22 interpleader contains no authority for the court to enjoin individual actions brought by claimants against the stakeholder in state courts. This is one of the important disadvantages of Rule 22 interpleader,[12] as compared with statutory interpleader, discussed immediately below.

Saving Clause

Rule 22 explicitly states that interpleader under the Rule exists alongside and complements, rather than supercedes, statutory interpleader, discussed below.

ADDITIONAL RESEARCH REFERENCES

Wright & Miller, *Federal Practice and Procedure* §§ 1701–21.

STATUTORY INTERPLEADER

PURPOSE AND SCOPE

The sections of 28 U.S.C.A. that together comprise the federal interpleader statute share much in common with Rule 22. Like the Rule, the interpleader statute permits a stakeholder plaintiff to file an action against two or more adverse claimants to a stake that the plaintiff holds.[13] Once joined, the statute

9. *See, e.g., Central Bank of Tampa v. United States,* 838 F.Supp. 564, 566 (M.D.Fla. 1993)(Rule 22 interpleaders do not require payment into court).

10. *See, e.g., In the Matter of Bohart,* 743 F.2d 313, 317 (5th Cir.1984)(in Rule 22 case, stakeholder turned fund over to court); *Kurland v. United States,* 919 F.Supp. 419 (M.D.Fla. 1996)(noting that Rule 22 does not require payment into court, but ordering such payment with consent of all parties).

11. *See, e.g., Southtrust Bank of Florida, N.A. v. Wilson,* 971 F.Supp. 539, 542 (M.D.Fla. 1997) (using Rule 67 in a Rule 22 interpleader case).

12. If the Rule 22 interpleader action has gone to judgment, a district court has authority to issue an injunction to protect the integrity of the judgment. *See, e.g., New York Life Insurance Co. v. Deshotel,* 142 F.3d 873 (5th Cir.1998) (if judgment has been entered in interpleader case, court may act under authority of All Writs Statute, 28 U.S.C.A. § 1651, to prevent relitigation of issues precluded by res judicata or collateral estoppel; injunction applies to other federal proceedings). This authority, however, falls short of the authority federal courts enjoy in statutory interpleader cases to enjoin litigation that may compete with a pending interpleader action. This distinction is discussed again under statutory interpleader, below.

13. *Cf., Airborne Freight Corp. v. United States,* 195 F.3d 238, 240 (5th Cir.1999) ("central prerequisite" for interpleader is that the "plaintiff-stakeholder runs the risk–but for determination in interpleader–of multiple liability when several claimants assert rights to a single stake"); *Minnesota Mutual Life Insurance Co. v. Ensley,* 174 F.3d 977 (9th Cir.1999) (held, it is not necessary, prior to initiation of the inter-

also contemplates that the claimants will then litigate against one another to determine the best disposition of the stake. However, the federal statute differs significantly from Rule 22 in a number of important respects. Thus there may be circumstances where both sources of interpleader authority should be employed, or where only one source and not the other will suffice.

The three specific sections of 28 U.S.C.A. that govern statutory interpleader are §§ 1335, 1397, and 2361. Section 1335 establishes the elements of a statutory interpleader action. Section 1397 establishes the special venue provisions governing statutory interpleader. Section 2361 establishes the broad personal jurisdiction of a court hearing an interpleader action, and also authorizes the court to enjoin other federal or state judicial actions that may interfere with the interpleader.

---

28 U.S.C.A. § 1335. INTERPLEADER

CORE CONCEPT

The interpleader statute allows a stakeholder to join multiple, mutually inconsistent claims of various parties, and thereby determine rights in the asset (the "stake") in a single proceeding.[14]

APPLICATIONS

Stakeholder as Claimant

The interpleader plaintiff may also be a claimant,[15] as is the case with Rule 22 interpleader.

Claims Need Not Be Identical

Like Rule 22, the federal interpleader statute requires that the interpleader plaintiff plead that the claims are independent of, and at least partly inconsistent with, one another, *e.g.*, where the claims against a fund exceed the value of the fund. Interpleader actions need not be based on identical competing claims, or claims with a common origin, nor must the claims be totally incompatible with one another.[16] These provisions are similar to those contained in Rule 22 interpleader.

Defendants May Employ Interpleader

Unlike Rule 22, the federal interpleader statute contains no *explicit* authority for defendants to initiate interpleader actions through a counterclaim or crossclaim. However, it appears settled that defen-

pleader action, that more than one claimant has actually filed on the stake; "The court's jurisdiction under the interpleader statute extends to potential, as well as actual, claims.").

14. *See, e.g., Rhoades v. Casey,* 196 F.3d 592, 600 n. 8 (5th Cir.1999), *cert. denied,* 531 U.S. 924, 121 S.Ct. 298, 148 L.Ed.2d 240 (2000) ("A prerequisite to filing an interpleader action is that there must be a single, identifiable, fund.").

15. *State Farm Fire & Casualty Co. v. Tashire,* 386 U.S. 523, 533, 87 S.Ct. 1199, 1205, 18 L.Ed.2d 270 n. 9 (1967)(stakeholder need not be a disinterested party).

16. *See, e.g., Metropolitan Property & Casualty Insurance Co. v. Shan Trac, Inc.,* 324 F.3d 20, 23 (1st Cir.2003) (state law duty of insurers to settle legitimate claims promptly in good faith creates potential obligation greater than value of stake; thus there "may" be sufficiently adverse claims within the meaning of § 1335); *Abex Corp. v. ABC Rail Corp.,* 158 F.R.D. 75, 76 (W.D.Pa.1994) (citing requirement that conflicting claims need only be adverse to one another).

dants may employ the interpleader statute in a manner parallel to that explicitly authorized by Rule 22.[17]

Subject Matter Jurisdiction

As with Rule 22, a federal court must have subject matter jurisdiction before it can hear interpleader claims. However, the requirements for subject matter jurisdiction in statutory interpleader are considerably more relaxed when compared to those which Rule 22 actions must satisfy. In diversity cases, statutory interpleader actions satisfy subject matter jurisdiction if the stake at issue is worth $500 or more,[18] and if the citizenship of only one of the claimants is diverse from that of any other claimant (not including the stakeholder).[19] If federal subject matter jurisdiction is based upon the presence of a federal question, the requirements are the same as those for Rule 22 actions, or for any other federal question sued upon in a federal court.

Payment Into Court

The interpleader statute requires that the plaintiff deposit the asset at issue with the court. This requirement is relaxed only if the plaintiff provides a bond in an amount subject to the court's discretion.[20] There is no similar explicit requirement for a bond in a Rule 22 action, but courts often require similar performance by plaintiffs in Rule 22 cases anyway.

28 U.S.C.A. § 1397. INTERPLEADER

CORE CONCEPT

Section 1397 provides that venue in a statutory interpleader action may be found in any judicial district in which one of the claimants

17. *See, e.g., Ellis National Bank of Jacksonville v. Irving Trust Co.*, 786 F.2d 466, 467 (2d Cir.1986)(noting without comment use of statutory interpleader as a counterclaim).

18. *See, e.g., NYLife Distributors, Inc. v. Adherence Group, Inc.*, 72 F.3d 371, 374 (3d Cir.1995), *cert. denied*, 517 U.S. 1209, 116 S.Ct. 1826, 134 L.Ed.2d 931 (1996)(noting $500 requirement).

19. *See, e.g., State Street Bank & Trust Co. v. Denman Tire Corp.*, 240 F.3d 83, 89 n. 4 (1st Cir.2001) (statutory interpleader not available in diversity case "because the potential claimants are not diverse;" only Rule 22 is available); *Franceskin v. Credit Suisse*, 214 F.3d 253 (2d Cir.2000) (requirement of diversity for statutory interpleader is that two or more claimants must be diverse from one another; where all claimants are citizens of Argentina, this requirement is not met; for Rule 22, diverse citizenship is satisfied if stakeholder is diverse from every claimant; thus, where stakeholder and claimants are all aliens, diversity requirement as defined by 28 U.S.C. § 1332 is not met); *Commercial Union Insurance v. United States,* 999 F.2d 581, 584 (D.C.Cir.1993)(for diversity in statutory interpleader cases, the focus is on diversity of claimant-defendants; citizenship of stakeholder is irrelevant in statutory interpleader).

20. *See e.g., United States Fire Insurance Co. v. Asbestospray, Inc.*, 182 F.3d 201, 210 (3d Cir. 1999) ("A proper deposit or bond is a jurisdictional prerequisite to bringing an interpleader [under § 1335]. The stakeholder invoking interpleader must deposit the largest amount for which it may be liable in view of the subject matter of the controversy." However, the amount to be deposited or bonded is measured by the realistic scope of the interpleader, not an "uncritical" assessment of "the highest amount claimed by the adverse claimants."). *Cf., Gaines v. Sunray Oil Co.*, 539 F.2d 1136, 1141 (8th Cir.1976)("The subject matter of an interpleader action is defined by the fund deposited by the stakeholder."); *see also, Prudential Insurance Co. of America v. Bank of Commerce*, 857 F.Supp. 62, 64 (D.Kan.1994)(when plaintiff seeks to post bond "the bond . . . should contain an obligor other than plaintiff as surety").

resides.[21] This requirement differs from the traditional federal court venue requirements for Rule 22 interpleader. *See* 28 U.S.C.A. § 1391.

28 U.S.C.A. § 2361. PROCESS AND PROCEDURE

CORE CONCEPT

Section 2361 provides substantially expanded personal jurisdiction over the claimants. These powers often provide the plaintiff with a major advantage over analogous provisions governing Rule 22 actions. Section 2361 also authorizes the district court to enter final judgment discharging the stakeholder from further liability, thereby making the injunction permanent.[22]

APPLICATIONS

Process and Personal Jurisdiction

Statutory interpleader provides for nationwide personal jurisdiction and service of process.[23] Rule 22 actions, by contrast, must satisfy standard requirements for personal jurisdiction and service of process.

Injunctive Powers

In statutory interpleader cases, the federal court has authority to enjoin other federal or state proceedings that may affect the assets that are the subject of the interpleader action.[24] No comparable authority exists in Rule 22 actions.[25]

21. *See, e.g., Nevada v. Pioneer Companies, Inc.,* 245 F.Supp.2d 1120, 1125 (D.Nev.2003).

22. *Advantage Title Agency, Inc. v. Rosen,* 297 F.Supp.2d 536, 539 (E.D.N.Y. 2003).

23. *See, e.g., Rhoades v. Casey,* 196 F.3d 592, 600 (5th Cir.1999), *cert. denied,* 531 U.S. 924, 121 S.Ct. 298, 148 L.Ed.2d 240 (2000) ("[T]he district court may also enter an order restraining the claimants from instituting any proceeding affective property until further order of the court."); *NYLife Distributors, Inc. v. Adherence Group, Inc.,* 72 F.3d 371, 375 (3d Cir.1995), *cert. denied,* 517 U.S. 1209, 116 S.Ct. 1826, 134 L.Ed.2d 931 (1996)(noting availability of nationwide service on all claimants); *Carolina Casualty Insurance Co. v. Mares,* 826 F.Supp. 149, 154 (E.D.Va.1993)(nationwide service of process under § 2361 available only in statutory interpleader actions).

24. *But cf., United States Fire Insurance Co. v. Asbestospray, Inc.,* 182 F.3d 201, 211 (3d Cir. 1999) (injunction extends only to portion of fund that is subject matter of interpleader action; injunction does not extend to portions beyond reach of interpleader dispute; moreover, district courts should ensure that parallel proceedings in state court that pre-date interpleader action are treated with deference, especially if state actions have resulted in judgments "or settlements in principle"). *See, e.g., NYLife Distributors, Inc. v. Adherence Group, Inc.,* 72 F.3d 371, 375 (3d Cir.1995), *cert. denied,* 517 U.S. 1209, 116 S.Ct. 1826, 134 L.Ed.2d 931 (1996)(noting injunctive power under § 2361). *Estrella v. V & G Management Corp.,* 158 F.R.D. 575, 578 (D.N.J. 1994)(noting that 28 U.S.C.A. § 2361 provides an "automatic stay" on related state claims).

25. *Cf., New York Life Insurance Co. v. Deshotel,* 142 F.3d 873 (5th Cir.1998) (All Writs Statute, 28 U.S.C.A. § 1651, authorizes district court, after entry of judgment in Rule 22 action, to enter injunction against proceedings in other federal courts that would relitigate issues precluded by judgment). Note, however, that injunctive authority here applies only to cases decided, not to pending cases; to that extent the injunctive authority that a court enjoys under statutory interpleader is much broader, including both pre-judgment and post-judgment orders. *See, e.g., General Electric Capital Assurance v. Van Norman,* 209 F.Supp.2d 668, 670 (S.D.Tex.2002) (judicial authority under § 2361 includes power to enter appropriate orders to ensure that judgments can be enforced).

ADDITIONAL RESEARCH REFERENCES

Wright & Miller, *Federal Practice and Procedure* §§ 1701–21.

C.J.S. Interpleader §§ 2–52, 53–57.

West's Key No. Digests, Interpleader ⚷1–43.

RULE 23

CLASS ACTIONS

(a) Prerequisites to a Class Action. One or more members of a class may sue or be sued as representative parties on behalf of all only if (1) the class is so numerous that joinder of all members is impracticable, (2) there are questions of law or fact common to the class, (3) the claims or defenses of the representative parties are typical of the claims or defenses of the class, and (4) the representative parties will fairly and adequately protect the interests of the class.

(b) Class Actions Maintainable. An action may be maintained as a class action if the prerequisites of subdivision (a) are satisfied, and in addition:

(1) the prosecution of separate actions by or against individual members of the class would create a risk of

(A) inconsistent or varying adjudications with respect to individual members of the class which would establish incompatible standards of conduct for the party opposing the class, or

(B) adjudications with respect to individual members of the class which would as a practical matter be dispositive of the interests of the other members not parties to the adjudications or substantially impair or impede their ability to protect their interests; or

(2) the party opposing the class has acted or refused to act on grounds generally applicable to the class, thereby making appropriate final injunctive relief or corresponding declaratory relief with respect to the class as a whole; or

(3) the court finds that the questions of law or fact common to the members of the class predominate over any questions affecting only individual members, and that a class action is superior to other available methods for the fair and efficient adjudication of the controversy. The matters pertinent to the findings include: (A) the interest of members of the class in individually controlling the prosecution or defense of separate actions; (B) the extent and nature of any litigation concerning the controversy already commenced by or against members of the class; (C) the desirability or undesirability of concentrating the litigation of the claims in the particular forum; (D) the difficulties likely to be encountered in the management of a class action.

(c) Determining by Order Whether to Certify a Class Action; Appointing Class Counsel; Notice and Membership in Class; Judgment; Multiple Classes and Subclasses.

(1)(A) When a person sues or is sued as a representative of a class, the court must—at an early practicable time—determine by order whether to certify the action as a class action.

(B) An order certifying a class action must define the class and the class claims, issues, or defenses, and must appoint class counsel under Rule 23(g).

(C) An order under Rule 23(c)(1) may be altered or amended before final judgment.

(2)(A) For any class certified under Rule 23(b)(1) or (2), the court may direct appropriate notice to the class.

(B) For any class certified under Rule 23(b)(3), the court must direct to class members the best notice practicable under the circumstances, including individual notice to all members who can be identified through reasonable effort. The notice must concisely and clearly state in plain, easily understood language:

- the nature of the action,
- the definition of the class certified,
- the class claims, issues, or defenses,
- that a class member may enter an appearance through counsel if the member so desires,
- that the court will exclude from the class any member who requests exclusion, stating when and how members may elect to be excluded, and
- the binding effect of a class judgment on class members under Rule 23(c)(3).

(3) The judgment in an action maintained as a class action under subdivision (b)(1) or (b)(2), whether or not favorable to the class, shall include and describe those whom the court finds to be members of the class. The judgment in an action maintained as a class action under subdivision (b)(3), whether or not favorable to the class, shall include and specify or describe those to whom the notice provided in subdivision (c)(2) was directed, and who have not requested exclusion, and whom the court finds to be members of the class.

(4) When appropriate (A) an action may be brought or maintained as a class action with respect to particular issues, or (B) a class may be divided into subclasses and each subclass treated as a class, and the provisions of this rule shall then be construed and applied accordingly.

(d) Orders in Conduct of Actions. In the conduct of actions to which this rule applies, the court may make appropriate orders: (1) determining the course of proceedings or prescribing measures to prevent undue repetition or complication in the presentation of evidence or argument; (2) requiring, for the protection of the members of the class or otherwise for the fair conduct of the action, that notice be given in such manner as the court may direct to some or all of the members of any step in the action, or of the proposed extent of the judgment, or of the opportunity of members to signify whether they consider the representation fair and adequate, to intervene and present claims or defenses, or otherwise to come into the action; (3) imposing conditions on the representative parties or on intervenors; (4) requiring that the pleadings be amended to eliminate therefrom allegations as to representation of absent persons, and that the action proceed accordingly; (5) dealing with similar procedural matters. The orders may be combined with an order under Rule 16, and may be altered or amended as may be desirable from time to time.

(e) Settlement, Voluntary Dismissal, or Compromise.

(1)(A) The court must approve any settlement, voluntary dismissal, or compromise of the claims, issues, or defenses of a certified class.

(B) The court must direct notice in a reasonable manner to all class members who would be bound by a proposed settlement, voluntary dismissal, or compromise.

(C) The court may approve a settlement, voluntary dismissal, or compromise that would bind class members only after a hearing and on finding that the settlement, voluntary dismissal, or compromise is fair, reasonable, and adequate.

(2) The parties seeking approval of a settlement, voluntary dismissal, or compromise under Rule 23(e)(1) must file a statement identifying any agreement made in connection with the proposed settlement, voluntary dismissal, or compromise.

(3) In an action previously certified as a class action under Rule 23(b)(3), the court may refuse to approve a settlement unless

it affords a new opportunity to request exclusion to individual class members who had an earlier opportunity to request exclusion but did not do so.

(4)(A) Any class member may object to a proposed settlement, voluntary dismissal, or compromise that requires court approval under Rule 23(e)(1)(A).

(B) An objection made under Rule 23(e)(4)(A) may be withdrawn only with the court's approval.

(f) Appeals. A court of appeals may in its discretion permit an appeal from an order of a district court granting or denying class action certification under this rule if application is made to it within ten days after entry of the order. An appeal does not stay proceedings in the district court unless the district judge or the court of appeals so orders.

(g) Class Counsel.

(1) Appointing Class Counsel.

(A) Unless a statute provides otherwise, a court that certifies a class must appoint class counsel.

(B) An attorney appointed to serve as class counsel must fairly and adequately represent the interests of the class.

(C) In appointing class counsel, the court

(i) must consider:

- the work counsel has done in identifying or investigating potential claims in the action,

- counsel's experience in handling class actions, other complex litigation,

and claims of the type asserted in the action,

- counsel's knowledge of the applicable law, and

- the resources counsel will commit to representing the class;

(ii) may consider any other matter pertinent to counsel's ability to fairly and adequately represent the interests of the class;

(iii) may direct potential class counsel to provide information on any subject pertinent to the appointment and to propose terms for attorney fees and nontaxable costs; and

(iv) may make further orders in connection with the appointment.

(2) Appointment Procedure.

(A) The court may designate interim counsel to act on behalf of the putative class before determining whether to certify the action as a class action.

(B) When there is one applicant for appointment as class counsel, the court may appoint that applicant only if the applicant is adequate under Rule 23(g)(1)(B) and (C). If more than one adequate applicant seeks appointment as class counsel, the court must appoint the applicant best able to represent the interests of the class.

(C) The order appointing class counsel may include provisions about the award of attorney fees or nontaxable costs under Rule 23(h).

(h) Attorney Fees Award. In an action certified as a class action, the court may award reasonable attorney fees and nontaxable costs authorized by law or by agreement of the parties as follows:

(1) Motion for Award of Attorney Fees. A claim for an award of attorney fees and nontaxable costs must be made by motion under Rule 54(d)(2), subject to the provisions of this subdivision, at a time set by the court. Notice of the motion must be served on all parties and, for motions by class counsel, directed to class members in a reasonable manner.

(2) Objections to Motion. A class member, or a party from whom payment is sought, may object to the motion.

(3) Hearing and Findings. The court may hold a hearing and must find the facts and state its conclusions of law on the motion under Rule 52(a).

(4) Reference to Special Master or Magistrate Judge. The court may refer issues related to the amount of the award to a special master or to a magistrate judge as provided in Rule 54(d)(2)(D).

[Amended effective July 1, 1966; August 1, 1987; April 24, 1998, effective December 1, 1998; March 27, 2003, effective December 1, 2003.]

AUTHORS' COMMENTARY ON RULE 23

PURPOSE AND SCOPE

Rule 23 governs joinder of parties in situations where the number of parties is sufficiently large so that it is impractical or inefficient for the parties to pursue their claims individually. Class actions are distinct from typical joinder situations in both the number of litigants involved and in the manner in which most class members participate in the case. Rule 23 contemplates that the class of litigants will be represented both by counsel and by "class representatives," *i.e.*, active members of the class who make many decisions for the entire class. Because there is potential for abusing the large number of class members who are not representatives and who therefore do not participate fully in many decisions, the court is charged with the obligation to monitor carefully important steps in the litigation process, such as approval of class litigation at the onset and potential settlements at the end. Class actions also present special problems of case management for the courts, so Rule 23 provides the trial judge with substantial additional authority to supervise progress in the case.

RULE 23(a). PREREQUISITES TO A CLASS ACTION

CORE CONCEPT

The specialized purpose of class actions—handling large numbers of litigants through class representatives—makes necessary a series of requirements intended to ensure that the opportunity to bring a class action is not misused or abused. Two of these requirements have developed in case law. Others are listed in Rule 23(a). *All* requirements, whether in Rule 23(a) or developed in case law, must be satisfied before the court will certify a case as a class action.[1]

NOTE: In addition to the requirements of case law and Rule 23(a), a class action will not be certified unless it fits within some provision of Rule 23(b) as well. Class actions must also meet the requirements of both personal jurisdiction and federal subject matter jurisdiction, and these requirements apply somewhat differently to class actions. Thus, while Rule 23(a) must be satisfied, meeting the requirements of Rule 23(a) alone will not produce a court-certified class action. With the exception of Rule 23(b), discussed separately, the additional prerequisites not mentioned in Rule 23(a), including case law requirements, venue and special questions of jurisdiction, are discussed immediately below. Additionally, it should be understood that even if a proposed class meets all the requirements mentioned above, the district court may still retain discretion not to certify the class action.

APPLICATIONS

Burden of Proof

It is settled that the party seeking certification has the burden of

1. *See, e.g., Berger v. Compaq Computer Corp.*, 257 F.3d 475, 481 (5th Cir.2001) ("[T]he party seeking certification bears the burden of establishing that *all* requirements of rule 23(a) have been satisfied.").

proving that the requirements for class certification are satisfied.[2]

Case Law Requirements for a Class

(1) *Class Must Be Logical:* Before a class is certified, the court must be satisfied that the litigants who are to be joined as a group actually comprise a class. The definition of a class is not entirely clear. It is clear, however, that the class must be sufficiently describable so that the court can contemplate with some confidence who is, and who is not, a member of the class.[3] Merely because the actual identities of the individuals are unknown does not prevent a class certification. However, the class' description must not be so vague as to make membership in the class meaningless. A class made up of "all females in the world," for example, would not be certified. A class of all American citizens who support national health insurance is also probably not certifiable, not because their identities are unknown, but because there is no way to ascertain with confidence what "support national health insurance" means, nor any reason to believe personal views on national health insurance will not change.[4] On the other hand, a class of all females who suffered, or may suffer, through past use of a defectively designed or manufactured birth control device is certifiable as a class action.

(2) *Representative Must Be a Member of the Class:* At least initially, the class representative must be a member of the class.[5] The purpose of this requirement is part of the courts' determination that class representatives will reflect the interests of the class. If a class representative was once a member but ceases to be a member of the

2. *See, e.g., Zinser v. Accufix Research Institute, Inc.,* 253 F.3d 1180 (9th Cir.2001), *opinion amended and superseded on denial of reh'g,* 273 F.3d 1266 (9th Cir.2001) (party seeking class certification bears burden of satisfying requirements of Rule 23(a) and (b)).

3. *See, e.g., Tefel v. Reno,* 180 F.3d 1286, 1304 (11th Cir.1999), *cert. denied,* 530 U.S. 1228, 120 S.Ct. 2657, 147 L.Ed.2d 272 (2000) (class that includes both aliens who had unsuccessfully applied for suspension of deportation and aliens who have never applied is "overly broad"); *Berman v. Narragansett Racing Ass'n,* 414 F.2d 311, 317 (1st Cir.1969), *cert. denied,* 396 U.S. 1037, 90 S.Ct. 682, 24 L.Ed.2d 681 (1970)("amorphously defined" class should not be certified; but class of racing horse owners who win purses is adequately defined); *see also, Simer v. Rios,* 661 F.2d 655, 669 (7th Cir.1981), *cert. denied,* 456 U.S. 917, 102 S.Ct. 1773, 72 L.Ed.2d 177 (1982)("It is axiomatic that for a class action to be certified a 'class' must exist."). *Cf., Mullen v. Treasure Chest Casino, LLC,* 186 F.3d 620, 624 n. 1 (5th Cir.1999), *cert. denied,* 528 U.S. 1159, 120 S.Ct. 1169, 145 L.Ed.2d 1078 (2000) (class of employees alleging illness caused by defective ventilation system is not deficient because allegation of defective system or injury from it has yet to be proven on merits).

4. *See, e.g., Simmons v. Poe,* 47 F.3d 1370, 1381–82 (4th Cir.1995)(approving denial of class certification for "all African-American males residing in Virginia"). *But cf., Hilao v. Estate of Marcos,* 103 F.3d 767, 774 (9th Cir.1996) (affirming certification of all "Philippines citizens who were (or whose decedents were) tortured, summarily executed, or 'disappeared' while in military custody during a 14–year period;" class totalled approximately 10,000 people).

5. *See, e.g., Holmes v. Pension Plan of Bethlehem Steel Corp.,* 213 F.3d 124, 135 (3d Cir. 2000) ("[A] plaintiff who lacks the personalized, redressable injury required for standing to assert claims on his own behalf would also lack standing to assert claims on behalf of a class."); *Great Rivers Cooperative of Southeastern Iowa v. Farmland Industries, Inc.,* 120 F.3d 893, 899 (8th Cir.1997) ("Inherent in Rule 23 is the requirement that the class representatives be members of the class."). *East Texas Motor Freight System, Inc. v. Rodriguez,* 431 U.S. 395, 403, 97 S.Ct. 1891, 1896, 52 L.Ed.2d 453 (1977)(error to certify class where named representatives are not members of class).

class, the proper remedy is to select a new, suitable member of the class as a replacement representative.[6]

Defendant Classes

Most class actions comprise litigation in which a large number of plaintiffs sue a single defendant or a small group of defendants. However, in unusual cases it is possible for a plaintiff to initiate a class action in which the class is made up of defendants.[7] Such classes may encounter greater problems with certification, in part because they are "initiated by those opposed to the interests of the class." [8]

Settlement Classes

It appears settled that a class may be certified for purposes of settlement only. However, it is also settled that certification of such classes must fully satisfy the relevant requirements of Rule 23.[9]

Rule 23(a) Requirements for a Class

(1) *Numerosity:* Rule 23(a)(1) requires that the class membership be sufficiently large to warrant a class action because the alternative of joinder is "impracticable".[10] There is no threshold number of class members guaranteed to satisfy the "numerosity" requirement of Rule

6. *See, e.g., Holmes v. Pension Plan of Bethlehem Steel Corp.,* 213 F.3d 124, 135–36 (3d Cir.2000) (if class representative has "live claim" at time of motion for class certification, "neither a pending motion nor a certified class action need be dismissed if his individual claim subsequently becomes moot"; but if claim became moot prior to motion for class certification, motion will be denied and case will be dismissed); *Hardy v. City Optical, Inc.*, 39 F.3d 765, 770 (7th Cir.1994)(party dismissed "can no longer be the class representative"). *But see Kifer v. Ellsworth,* 346 F.3d 1155, 1156 (7th Cir. 2003) (initially, class representative was prison inmate who was subsequently released from jail; because class sought prospective relief through an injunction, class representative's personal claim had therefore become moot; "but the mooting of the class representative's personal claim does not bar him from continuing to represent the class, . . . as otherwise defendants might delay the grant of relief in class actions indefinitely by buying off the class representatives in succession.").

7. *See, e.g., Ameritech Benefit Plan Committee v. Communication Workers of America,* 220 F.3d 814, 819 (7th Cir.2000), *cert. denied,* 531 U.S. 1127, 121 S.Ct. 883, 148 L.Ed.2d 791 (2001).

8. *Id.* (indicating potential problems with any defendant class not initiated under due process protections of Rule 23(b)(3)).

9. *Amchem Products, Inc. v. Windsor,* 521 U.S. 591, 117 S.Ct. 2231, 138 L.Ed.2d 689 (1997) (certification of settlement class requires "heightened attention" of trial court; affirming denial of certification for failure to satisfy Rule 23(a)(4) and (b)(3); but noting that consideration of trial management is irrelevant to settlement class; also holding that court's authority to approve settlement under Rule 23(e) does not authorize court to disregard requirements of Rule 23(a) and (b)). *See also, Ortiz v. Fibreboard Corp.,* 527 U.S. 815, 119 S.Ct. 2295, 144 L.Ed.2d 715 (1999) (holding that ruling of *Amchem* requiring settlement classes for which certification is sought under rule 23(b)(3) to meet requirements of Rule 23(a) applies equally to settlement classes for which certification is sought under Rule 23(b)(1)(B)).

10. *See, e.g., Mullen v. Treasure Chest Casino, LLC,* 186 F.3d 620, 624 (5th Cir.1999), *cert. denied,* 528 U.S. 1159, 120 S.Ct. 1169, 145 L.Ed.2d 1078 (2000) (class of 100 to 150 members sufficient; additional factors supporting finding of adequate numerosity are reluctance of current employees to sue individually for fear of retaliation and possibility that transient nature of employment in gambling business would tend to make joinder difficult because members of potential class would tend to disperse geographically); *Robidoux v. Celani,* 987 F.2d 931, 935 (2d Cir.1993)(emphasizing that for certification, joinder need only be impracticable, not necessarily impossible).

23(a).[11] A class comprised of many hundreds, or thousands, of members will likely meet this test.[12] Classes of ten litigants or less will almost certainly not meet this test,[13] and will instead be consigned to joinder of parties under Rule 20. When the number of members falls between, approximately, twenty-five and one hundred, the probability of meeting the numerosity requirement varies from one judicial district to another.[14]

(2) *Common Questions of Law or Fact:* Rule 23(a)(2) requires the existence of common questions of law or fact among the class members before the case will be certified as a class action. To satisfy the requirement of Rule 23(a)(2), the common questions need not predominate. Courts generally have a liberal attitude toward this requirement, and close questions as to the existence of sufficient commonality tend to be resolved in favor of finding common questions.[15] In class actions

11. *See, e.g., Bittinger v. Tecumseh Products Co.,* 123 F.3d 877, 884 n. 1 (6th Cir.1997) (noting that Rule 23(a)(1) is not a "strict numerical test;" holding, however, that where class comprises over 1,100 persons, suggestion that joinder is not impractical is "frivolous"); *Robidoux v. Celani,* 987 F.2d 931, 935 (2d Cir.1993) (numerosity does not require exact estimate of class size, but only a reasonable estimate).

12. *See, e.g., Bacon v. Honda of America Manufacturing, Inc.,* 370 F.3d 565, 570 (6th Cir. 2004) ("There is no automatic cut-off point at which the number of plaintiffs makes joinder impracticable, [but] sheer number of potential litigants in a class, especially if it is more than several hundred, can be the only factor needed to satisfy Rule 23(a)(1).").

13. *General Telephone Co. of the Northwest, Inc. v. Equal Employment Opportunity Commission,* 446 U.S. 318, 330, 100 S.Ct. 1698, 1706, 64 L.Ed.2d 319 (1980) (classes of 15 members will often be too small). *See, e.g., National Association of Government Employees v. City Public Service Board of San Antonio,* 40 F.3d 698, 715 (5th Cir.1994)(affirming that class of 11 members does not satisfy requirement of numerosity). *But cf., Grant v. Sullivan,* 131 F.R.D. 436, 446 (M.D.Pa.1990)(approving certification of class of 14 members).

14. *See, e.g., Stewart v. Abraham,* 275 F.3d 220, 226–27 (3d Cir.2001), *cert. denied,* 536 U.S. 958, 122 S.Ct. 2661, 153 L.Ed.2d 836 (2002) (no minimum number required but more than 40 is generally sufficient). *But see Hernandez v. Alexander,* 152 F.R.D. 192 (D.Nev.1993)(class of 52 too small where proponents of class did not demonstrate any unusual difficulties with joinder).

15. *See, e.g., Stewart v. Abraham,* 275 F.3d 220, 227 (3d Cir.2001), *cert. denied,* 536 U.S. 958, 122 S.Ct. 2661, 153 L.Ed.2d 836 (2002) (commonality can be satisfied if class representatives share a single question of fact or law with class members); *Armstrong v. Davis,* 275 F.3d 849, 868 (9th Cir.2001), *cert. denied,* 537 U.S. 812, 123 S.Ct. 72, 154 L.Ed.2d 14 (2002) ("[I]n a civil–rights suit ... commonality is satisfied where the lawsuit challenges a system-wide practice or policy that affects all of the putative class members." Rejecting significance of such individual factors as, e.g., hearing disability and learning disability); *Mullen v. Treasure Chest Casino, LLC,* 186 F.3d 620, 625 (5th Cir.1999), *cert. denied,* 528 U.S. 1159, 120 S.Ct. 1169, 145 L.Ed.2d 1078 (2000) ("The test of commonality is not demanding." Held, sufficient commonality in allegations of: protection by same federal law; negligence of defendant in ignoring safety hazards; and unseaworthiness of vessel; indeed, each allegation is sufficient to satisfy requirement. "It is therefore irrelevant whether the class members uniformly allege damages from second-hand smoke."); *Keele v. Wexler,* 149 F.3d 589, 594 (7th Cir.1998) (common nucleus of operative fact will satisfy requirement of Rule 23(a)(2); moreover, "factual variations among class members' grievances do not defeat a class action"); *Hanlon v. Chrysler Corp.,* 150 F.3d 1011 (9th Cir.1998) (requirements of Rule 23(a)(2) are "minimal"); *Lightbourn v. County of El Paso,* 118 F.3d 421, 426 (5th Cir.1997), *cert. denied,* 522 U.S. 1052, 118 S.Ct. 700, 139 L.Ed.2d 643 (1998) ("The commonality test is met when there is at least one issue, the resolution of which will affect all or a significant number of the putative class members."); *Baby Neal v. Casey,* 43 F.3d 48, 56 (3d Cir.1994) ("Commonality and typicality are broadly defined and tend to merge." Nevertheless, commonality addresses the suitability of a class action, and typicality goes to suitability of plaintiff.). *But see, Tefel v. Reno,* 180 F.3d

involving fraud, however, there can be some tension between this fairly generous approach to commonality for purposes of Rule 23(a)(2) and the more stringent requirements for pleading fraud with particularity under Rule 9(b). In securities cases it was settled until recently that the plaintiff could properly plead a generalized rebuttable presumption of fraud. However, in securities cases controlled by the Private Securities Litigation Reform Act of 1995,[16] it is now settled that a plaintiff seeking to serve as a class representative must plead with particularity sufficient to satisfy the requirements of Rule 9(b).[17] result is reached in cases where the plaintiff's degree of reliance on the alleged fraudulent statements varies significantly. In such cases, the particularity requirements of Rule 9(b) will probably be imposed and it will be difficult to establish that the requirement of Rule 23(a)(2) for commonality has been met.[18]

NOTE: Although Rule 23(a) may be satisfied even if the common questions of law or fact do not predominate in the case, a class seeking certification under Rule 23(b)(3) must nevertheless include common questions of law or fact that *do* predominate over other questions. The interplay between Rule 23(a) and Rule 23(b) is discussed further below.

(3) *Class Representatives' Claims Must Be Typical:* Rule 23(a)(3) requires that the claims of class representatives be typical of the class as a whole, not merely some portion thereof.[19] Generally the class representatives need not have claims identical in all respects with those of other members of the class.[20] Substantial commonality appears to be

1286, 1304 (11th Cir.1999), *cert. denied,* 530 U.S. 1228, 120 S.Ct. 2657, 147 L.Ed.2d 272 (2000) (insufficient commonality where significant differences exist in laws applicable to various sub-groups of aliens who may be subject to deportation); *Simmons v. Poe,* 47 F.3d 1370 (4th Cir.1995)(no common questions of law or fact where class representative—unlike most of class—fits within factual questions in case).

16. 15 U.S.C.A. § 78u.

17. *See, e.g., Berger v. Compaq Computer Corp.,* 257 F.3d 475, 478 n. 3 (5th Cir.2001) (explaining statutory requirement to plead scienter with particularity).

18. *See, e.g., Broussard v. Meineke Discount Muffler Shops, Inc.,* 155 F.3d 331, 340–41 (4th Cir.1998) (where members of class claimed fraud based on both uniform documents and non-standard oral statements made to individual plaintiffs, requirement of commonality under rule 23(a)(2) is not met).

19. *See, e.g., Rector v. City & County of Denver,* 348 F.3d 935, 950 (10th Cir. 2003) ("By definition, class representatives who do not have Article III standing to pursue the class claims fail to meet the typicality requirements of Rule 23."); *Schachner v. Blue Cross and Blue Shield of Ohio,* 77 F.3d 889, 896 n. 8 (6th Cir.1996), *cert. denied,* 519 U.S. 865, 117 S.Ct. 173, 136 L.Ed.2d 114 (1996)(representative holding federal claim does not adequately represent certain class members who hold only state claims). *See also Wooden v. Board of Regents,* 247 F.3d 1262, 1287 (11th Cir.2001) ("It should be obvious that there cannot be adequate typicality between a class and a named representative unless the named representative has individual standing to raise the legal claims of the class").

20. *See, e.g., Lightbourn v. County of El Paso,* 118 F.3d 421, 426 (5th Cir.1997), *cert. denied,* 522 U.S. 1052, 118 S.Ct. 700, 139 L.Ed.2d 643 (1998) ("The test for typicality, like the test for commonality, is not demanding."); *Paxton v. Union National Bank,* 688 F.2d 552, 561 (8th Cir.1982), *cert. denied,* 460 U.S. 1083, 103 S.Ct. 1772, 76 L.Ed.2d 345 (1983)("The Rule does not require that every question of law or fact be common to every member of the class."); *Appleyard v. Wallace,* 754 F.2d 955, 958 (11th Cir.1985) ("strong similarity of legal theories" may satisfy Rule 23(a)(2), even where substantial factual differences exist). *Cf., Cornett v. Donovan,* 51 F.3d 894, 897 n. 2 (9th Cir.1995), *cert. denied,* 518 U.S. 1033, 116 S.Ct. 2580, 135 L.Ed.2d 1095 (1996) (because claims of class representatives must be typical of class, class lacks standing if representatives lack standing).

sufficient, even if differences among the claims, *e.g.*, issues of damages, also exist.[21] This requirement is intended to ensure that class representatives will represent the best interests of class members who take a less active part in managing the litigation. It also overlaps considerably the case law requirement that class representatives be members of the class.[22]

(4) *Representatives Must Fairly Protect the Class:* Because class actions vest authority over the interests of passive members of the class in the hands of class activists, Rule 23(a)(4) requires the court to ensure that class representatives will be individuals who will meet those responsibilities fully. There is no "bright line" establishing when Rule 23(a)(4) is satisfied. Nevertheless, courts tend to be particularly sensitive to this requirement.[23] Potential conflicts of interest may disqualify applicants,[24] as can a suggestion that the proposed class representative

21. *See, e.g., Ball v. Union Carbide Corp.*, 376 F.3d 554 (6th Cir. 2004) (requirements of Rule 23(a)(2) and (3) "tend to merge"); *Mullen v. Treasure Chest Casino, LLC,* 186 F.3d 620, 625 (5th Cir.1999), *cert. denied,* 528 U.S. 1159, 120 S.Ct. 1169, 145 L.Ed.2d 1078 (2000) ("Like commonality, the test for typicality is not demanding."); *Alpern v. UtiliCorp United, Inc.,* 84 F.3d 1525, 1540 (8th Cir.1996)("Factual variations in the individual claims will not normally preclude class certification if the claim arises from the same event or course of conduct as the class claims, and gives rise to the same legal or remedial theory." Variations in damages do not necessarily undermine typicality.). *But see Stirman v. Exxon Corp.,* 280 F.3d 554, 562 (5th Cir.2002) (although typicality is not normally a demanding text, finding insufficient typicality where class is based on implied lease covenant, and leases vary between market-value leases and proceeds leases under one state's law, and other states have even greater range of differences in law); *Piazza v. Ebsco Industries, Inc.,* 273 F.3d 1341, 1347 (11th Cir.2001) ("Without individual standing to raise a legal claim, a named representative does not have the requisite typicality to raise the same claim on behalf of a class. . . . It is by now clear that a class representative whose claim is time-barred cannot assert the claim on behalf of the class."); *Armstrong v. Davis,* 275 F.3d 849, 868–69 (9th Cir.2001), *cert. denied,* 537 U.S. 812, 123 S.Ct. 72, 154 L.Ed.2d 14 (2002) (typicality satisfied by comparing type of injury alleged by named plaintiff with injuries of other class members; injuries must be similar but need not be identical; but class representatives should include parties who together have suffered the entire range of injuries alleged, from kidney disability to hearing impairment). *See also United States Parole Commission v. Geraghty,* 445 U.S. 388, 404, 100 S.Ct. 1202, 1212, 63 L.Ed.2d 479 (1980) (at time of class certification, class representatives must have standing; but subsequent mootness of individual claims of class representatives does not make class action moot–"even though class certification has been denied"); *Martens v. Thomann,* 273 F.3d 159, 173 (2d Cir.2001) (class representative still has fiduciary duty to class notwithstanding that class representative's individual claim subsequently became moot). *But cf., Johnson v. Board of Regents, University of Georgia,* 263 F.3d 1234, 1268 (11th Cir.2001) (distinguishing case in which plaintiff lacked standing at time of complaint and time of class certification; in such cases, plaintiff cannot represent class).

22. *See, e.g., Robinson v. Sheriff of Cook County,* 167 F.3d 1155, 1157 (7th Cir.1999), *cert. denied*, 528 U.S. 824, 120 S.Ct. 71, 145 L.Ed.2d 60 (1999) (Rule 23(a)(3) "is really an aspect of [Rule 23(a)(2)]; if [the representative's] claim is atypical, he is not likely to be an adequate representative.").

23. *See, e.g., Stirman v. Exxon Corp.,* 280 F.3d 554, 563 (5th Cir.2002) (error not to examine adequacy of class representatives as well as counsel; questioning adequacy of class representatives where leases may be dissimilar to those of class; and where representative may have waived statute of limitations issue unimportant to her individually but potentially significant to others in class; noting, inter alia, that adequacy of class representative often overlaps typicality requirement). *Cf., Dechert v. Cadle Co.,* 333 F.3d 801 (7th Cir.2003) (bankruptcy trustee is not per se unsuitable as class representative, but trustee's duty to protect interest of bankruptcy creditors may often conflict with interest of class members).

24. *Ortiz v. Fibreboard Corp.,* 527 U.S. 815, 119 S.Ct. 2295, 144 L.Ed.2d 715 (1999) (class

lacks integrity.[25] If in the course of litigation the trial court finds that class representatives previously approved have become inadequate, the court retains authority to order appointment of new representatives.[26]

(5) *Adequacy of Counsel:* Rule 23(a)(4) contains no express language addressing the issue of whether it authorizes the court to examine the ability of the class' legal counsel to represent the class. Nevertheless, courts have heretofore routinely cited Rule 23(a)(4) for their authority to examine the ability of the class' legal counsel to represent the class. With the introduction of Rule 23(g) in 2003, however, it is no longer necessary for courts to rely on Rule 23(a)(4) for supervision of class counsel. Instead, Rule 23(g) expressly grants a district court the right and responsibility to appoint suitable counsel. Until enough time has elapsed to permit the courts to develop their authority and duties under Rule 23(g), it is likely that much of the case law originally developed under the authority of Rule 23(a)(4) will continue to guide courts in this work. Rule 23(g) is discussed at greater length elsewhere in this text.

(6) *The "Most Sophisticated" Investor:* When a class action also falls within the scope of the Private Securities Litigation Reform Act of 1995[27] the court is obligated to appoint as lead plaintiff the "most adequate plaintiff." Such a person is identified as that member of the class who is most capable of representing the class. This requirement, however, has been held not to require that the chosen person possess unique advantages of experience, expertise, wealth or intellect.[28]

comprised of holders of both present and future tort claims should be divided into subclasses with different counsel for each subclass; failure to provide different counsel means requirements of Rule 23(a)(4) are not met). *See, e.g., London v. Wal–Mart Stores, Inc.,* 340 F.3d 1246, 1255–56 (11th Cir. 2003) (personal friendship between class representative and lawyer, plus fact that class representative had been lawyer's stockbroker and might resume that role in future, meant class representative "cannot fairly and adequately represent the class"); *Pickett v. Iowa Beef Processors,* 209 F.3d 1276, 1280–81 (11th Cir. 2000) (acknowledging that requirements of rule 23(a)(4) can be satisfied unless conflict "is a fundamental one, going to the specific issues in controversy"; finding such conflict where plaintiffs are challenging contracts and marketing agreements that harmed some class members but benefited others). *Cf., Fymbo v. State Farm Fire and Casualty Co.,* 213 F.3d 1320 (10th Cir.2000) (where class members each have "a sufficiently large stake to be able to litigate" separately, that factor weighs against certifying class). *Mullen v. Treasure Chest Casino, LLC,* 186 F.3d 620, 625–26 (5th Cir.1999), *cert. denied,* 528 U.S. 1159, 120 S.Ct. 1169, 145 L.Ed.2d 1078 (2000) (Rule 23(a)(4) satisfied where class representatives' interests are identical to class, leaving no basis for significant conflict of interest, and where attorneys have extensive experience in class actions and relevant federal law; variance in proof of causation and damages between class members who smoke and others who don't "does not affect the alignment of their interests").

25. *See, e.g., Savino v. Computer Credit, Inc.,* 164 F.3d 81, 87 (2d Cir.1998) ("To judge the adequacy of representation, courts may consider the honesty and trustworthiness of the named plaintiff.").

26. *See, e.g., Swanson v. Wabash,* 577 F.Supp. 1308, 1326 (N.D.Ill.1983)(citing cases).

27. 15 U.S.C.A. § 78u–4(a)(3)(B).

28. *Berger v. Compaq Computer Corp.,* 279 F.3d 313 (5th Cir.2002). *See also Herrgott v. United States District Court for the Northern District of California,* 306 F.3d 726, 729 (9th Cir.2002) (party with largest financial stake in litigation presumptively is most adequate party and, assuming requirements of Rule 23 are met, will typically be lead plaintiff).

General Considerations

(1) *Diversity Suits:* Congress recently changed the requirements for diversity jurisdiction in most class actions. The effect of these changes, discussed in greater detail under the topic of subject matter jurisdiction elsewhere in this book, is to ease somewhat the requirements for diversity jurisdiction in many cases involving class litigation. However, the new requirements are rather complex and should be studied carefully before concluding that diversity jurisdiction can be satisfied in a particular case. Moreover, as is also discussed under the treatment of diversity jurisdiction earlier in this book, there are still some fairly narrow categories of class actions that are not governed by the recent legislative enactments. Those cases will presumably still be governed by the case law requirements for diversity that now no longer apply to most class actions. Those older case law requirements provide that diversity of citizenship is satisfied if class representatives are diverse from the party opposing the class,[29] but the amount in controversy requirement is satisfied only if every member of the class individually satisfies the jurisdictional amount. Thus, each class member of such classes must have a claim for more than $75,000, exclusive of interest and costs.[30]

(2) *Scope:* The new requirements for diversity jurisdiction in class actions, discussed here and elsewhere in this book under diversity jurisdiction, are applicable to "any class action before or after the entry of a class certification order by the court with respect to that action." [31] Thus, there should be no situation in which proponents of a class must meet the more standard elements of diversity jurisdiction prior to certification, and then meet different standards subsequent to certification.

(3) *Federal Question Suits:* Federal courts have subject matter jurisdiction over class actions involving federal questions in the same manner as conventional litigation.

(4) *Personal Jurisdiction:* Jurisdiction over a defendant in a class action is obtained in the same manner, and subject to the same requirements, as jurisdiction over any defendant in conventional litigation. The same is true for personal jurisdiction over a class of defendants, *i.e.,* each individual must be subject to the jurisdiction of the court before that individual is subject to the judgment. For a class of plaintiffs, however, class members may be included in the suit even if they have no link with the state where the case is being heard. This holding applies only to cases where members of the plaintiff class were afforded an opportunity to drop out of the class early in the litigation, and chose not to do so.[32] The Supreme Court has not yet ruled on a circumstance where members of a plaintiff class have no contact with the state in which the case is being heard, *and* had no opportunity to drop out of the suit.

29. *Supreme Tribe of Ben Hur v. Cauble,* 255 U.S. 356, 41 S.Ct. 338, 65 L.Ed. 673 (1921).

30. *Zahn v. International Paper Co.,* 414 U.S. 291, 94 S.Ct. 338, 38 L.Ed.2d 511 (1973).

31. 28 U.S.C.A. § 1332(d)(8).

32. *Phillips Petroleum Co. v. Shutts,* 472 U.S. 797, 105 S.Ct. 2965, 86 L.Ed.2d 628 (1985).

(5) *Venue:* Venue in class actions does not generally differ from venue in conventional litigation. One potential exception should be noted. If venue is based on the residence of the class, the residences of the class representatives are examined, not those of the entire class.[33]

(6) *Choice of Law:* In class actions based on state law, the court can only apply the law of a jurisdiction that has a sufficient relationship with an individual litigant. Thus individual litigants from states other than the forum may be entitled to have the law of some other state applied to their claims. In a class action, therefore, it is possible that the court may have to apply the laws of a variety of states to different class members.[34]

(7) *Defendant Classes:* Most class action cases are suits in which the class is the plaintiff. However, it is possible that a class may be a defendant.[35] In that unusual circumstance, the provisions of Rule 23 apply in much the same fashion as they apply to plaintiff classes, with only a few differences. One difference is that members of a defendant class are entitled to constitutional protections of notice, as well as any protections provided within Rule 23. This difference tends to have little practical impact, however, because class representatives are obligated to protect the interests of passive class members, including appropriate notice, discussed elsewhere. A more significant potential distinction between a plaintiff class and a defendant class is heightened concern to ensure that the representatives of a defendant class adequately represent the interests of the class. The concern is greater with defendant classes because, at least initially, the representatives of a defendant class are chosen by the plaintiff who is suing the class.

(8) *Statutory Restrictions on Class Actions:* Congress has authority to restrict the ability of parties to litigate by means of a class action. However, it has done so only rarely.[36]

Certification and the Merits

The question whether a district court may properly consider the merits of the case when deciding a certification motion is not fully resolved. One line of cases cites Supreme Court authority for the proposition that the merits should not be consulted.[37] However, there is

33. *See, e.g., Appleton Electric Co. v. Advance–United Expressways,* 494 F.2d 126, 140 (7th Cir.1974)(looking only to venue of named representatives).

34. *Phillips Petroleum Co. v. Shutts,* 472 U.S. 797, 105 S.Ct. 2965, 86 L.Ed.2d 628 (1985).

35. *See, e.g., Consolidated Rail Corp. v. Town of Hyde Park,* 47 F.3d 473 (2d Cir.1995), *cert. denied,* 515 U.S. 1122, 115 S.Ct. 2277, 132 L.Ed.2d 281 (1995) (approving a defendant class and noting Rule 23 "does not require a willing representative, merely an adequate one").

36. *See, e.g., American Immigration Lawyers Association v. Reno,* 199 F.3d 1352 (D.C.Cir. 2000) (noting that in cases where aliens are removed from United States under Illegal Immigration Reform and Immigrant Responsibility Act of 1996, 8 U.S.C. § 1252(e)(1)(B) provides that Rule 23 cannot be used to bring a class action challenging the act; only individual aliens subject to summary removal procedures may challenge the act).

37. *Eisen v. Carlisle & Jacquelin,* 417 U.S. 156, 177, 94 S.Ct. 2140, 2152, 40 L.Ed.2d 732 (1974) ("We find nothing in either the language or history of Rule 23 that gives a court any authority to conduct a preliminary inquiry into the merits of a suit in order to determine whether it may be maintained as a class action."). *See also Lienhart v. Dryvit Systems, Inc.,* 255 F.3d 138, 143 n. 2 (4th Cir.2001) (merits should not

significant authority, also drawing upon Supreme Court precedent, permitting and even encouraging use of the merits to make the certification decision.[38] Until the matter is finally resolved, attorneys will be required to consult local precedent.

It should be noted, however, that there is clear agreement authorizing dismissal of a case without deciding a motion for certification because the plaintiff cannot, e.g., state a cognizable claim or satisfy jurisdiction. In such circumstances the dismissal may address some feature of the merits of the case but does not address certification at all.[39]

Statutes of Limitation: Equitable Tolling

In a case based on federal question jurisdiction, it is settled that institution of the class action tolls applicable statutes of limitations for the class.[40] The statute remains in suspension until the district court denies certification.[41] If the statute resumes running, it does so from the

be consulted when deciding certification; however, merits may be considered when appellate court decides whether to permit appeal under Rule 23(f)); *Caridad v. Metro–North Commuter Railroad,* 191 F.3d 283, 291–92 (2d Cir.1999), *cert. denied,* 529 U.S. 1107, 120 S.Ct. 1959, 146 L.Ed.2d 791 (2000) ("[A] motion for class certification is not an occasion for examination of the merits of the case." Although statistical data presented by proponent of class certification may ultimately prove unpersuasive on merits of case, it may still satisfactorily demonstrate common questions of fact under Rule 23(a)(2)); *Valentino v. Carter–Wallace, Inc.,* 97 F.3d 1227, 1232 (9th Cir.1996) (merits are not part of analysis required for class certification); *Blackie v. Barrack,* 524 F.2d 891, 901 (9th Cir.1975), *cert. denied,* 429 U.S. 816, 97 S.Ct. 57, 50 L.Ed.2d 75 (1976) (possibility that plaintiff will later fail on merits is not "a basis for declining to certify a class").

38. *General Telephone Co. of Southwest v. Falcon,* 457 U.S. 147, 160, 102 S.Ct. 2364, 2372, 72 L.Ed.2d 740 (1982) ("[S]ometimes it may be necessary for the court to probe behind the pleadings before coming to rest on the certification question."); *Coopers & Lybrand v. Livesay,* 437 U.S. 463, 469 n. 12, 98 S.Ct. 2454, 2458 n. 12, 57 L.Ed.2d 351 (1978) (determination of class action may be " 'intimately involved with the merits of the claim' "). *See also, Newton v. Merrill Lynch, Pierce, Fenner & Smith, Inc.,* 259 F.3d 154, 166–68 (3d Cir.2001) (*Eisen* should be taken in context; noting more qualified language of *Coopers & Lybrand,* supra; "[A] preliminary inquiry into the merits is sometimes necessary to determine whether the alleged claims can be properly resolved as a class action."); *Castano v. American Tobacco Co.,* 84 F.3d 734 (5th Cir. 1996) (citing *Rhone-Poulenc,* infra, with apparent approval); *In the Matter of Rhone–Poulenc Rorer, Inc.,* 51 F.3d 1293, 1299 (7th Cir.1995), *cert. denied,* 516 U.S. 867, 116 S.Ct. 184, 133 L.Ed.2d 122 (1995) (likelihood that plaintiffs will lose should be weighed in determining whether to certify class).

39. *See, e.g., Boulware v. Crossland Mortgage Corp.,* 291 F.3d 261, 268 n. 4 (4th Cir.2002) ("Because [plaintiff] failed to state a claim as the purported named plaintiff, and because all other similarly situated plaintiffs would likewise fail to state a claim, the district court necessarily acted within its discretion in denying class certification."); *Curtin v. United Airlines, Inc.,* 275 F.3d 88, 92 (D.C. Cir.2001) (approving resolution of straightforward summary judgment motion without addressing more difficult and unnecessary question of class certification). *Cf., Todd v. Exxon Corp.* 275 F.3d 191, 202 n. 5 (2d Cir.2001) ("[D]ifficulty meeting the predominance and typicality requirements for Rule 23 certification . . . does not indicate that plaintiff fails to state a claim upon which relief can be granted.").

40. *American Pipe & Construction Co. v. Utah,* 414 U.S. 538, 550–51, 94 S.Ct. 756, 764–65, 38 L.Ed.2d 713 (1974).

41. *See, e.g., Hemenway v. Peabody Coal Co.,* 159 F.3d 255, 265 (7th Cir.1998) ("[C]ases have confirmed that time begins immediately, rather than after final judgment or decision on appeal."); *Armstrong v. Martin Marietta Corp.,* 138 F.3d 1374, 1378 (11th Cir.1998) (en banc), *cert. denied,* 525 U.S. 1019, 119 S.Ct. 545, 142 L.Ed.2d 453 (1998) (denial by district court resumes running of statute of limitations). *Cf., Culver v. City of Milwaukee,* 277 F.3d 908, 913–14 (7th Cir.2002) (although instant case was properly decertified and individual claim dismissed, error not to provide class members with

point at which it was tolled.[42] This protection applies to parties who subsequently seek to intervene in the suit after certification has been denied.[43] Further, if the class was certified under Rule 23(b)(3) and some members of the class exercise their right to opt out of the class under Rule 23(c)(2), the statute remains tolled as to those individuals until they exercise the right to opt out.[44] This protection applies even to members of the class who were unaware of the pendency of the class litigation.[45] Finally, equitable tolling applies to "all members of the putative class until class certification has been denied."[46]

It should be noted that this doctrine of equitable tolling, though applicable to cases based on federal question jurisdiction, applies to class actions arising from state claims only when state law also provides for equitable tolling. Courts reach this conclusion through application of the *Erie* doctrine,[47] discussed elsewhere in this text.

RULE 23(b). CLASS ACTIONS MAINTAINABLE

CORE CONCEPT

Before a class action will be certified, all the requirements of case law, jurisdiction, and Rule 23(a) must be satisfied. In addition, a class will not be certified unless it also fits within one of the types of classes described in Rule 23(b).[48] Unlike the requirement that all elements of Rule 23(a) be satisfied, however, Rule 23(b) is satisfied if only one of the kinds of classes described is present.

NOTE: Although a class may be certified if it fits within only one of the Rule 23(b) categories, there are sometimes advantages to fitting within more than one of the categories. This analysis is discussed more fully immediately below and under Rule 23(c).

APPLICATIONS

Risk of Incompatible Duties for Class Opponent

A class will be certified if the opposing party will otherwise be at risk of being subjected to incompatible duties.[49] Rule 23(b)(1)(A) was

notice of proposed dismissal under Rule 23(e) so they could, as appropriate, prevent resumption of running and expiration of statute of limitations that had been tolled while class action was pending).

42. *American Pipe & Construction Co. v. Utah,* 414 U.S. 538, 542–43, 94 S.Ct. 756, 760–61, 38 L.Ed.2d 713 (1974) (class action filed eleven days before running of statute; six months later certification was denied; held, individual claims filed eight days after entry of order denying class status were timely).

43. *Id. at* 553.

44. *Id. at* 550–51 (statute begins to run against individuals at time they opt out).

45. *Id. at* 551.

46. *Crown, Cork & Seal Co. v. Parker,* 462 U.S. 345, 354, 103 S.Ct. 2392, 2397, 76 L.Ed.2d 628 (1983) (expanding *American Pipe* to apply to plaintiffs who file separate suits, not just those who intervene in the original suit).

47. *See, e.g., Wade v. Danek Medical, Inc.,* 182 F.3d 281, 286–87 (4th Cir.1999) (under principles of *Erie*, state law controls; in instant case, Virginia does not provide for equitable tolling).

48. *See, e.g., Parke v. First Reliance Standard Life Insurance Co.,* 368 F.3d 999, 1004 (8th Cir. 2004) (advocate of class must satisfy all four requirements of Rule 23(a) plus one requirement of Rule 23(b)).

49. *Cf., Weinman v. Fidelity Capital Appreciation Fund,* 354 F.3d 1246, 1263–64 (10th Cir. 2004) ("A widely recognized limitation on

invoked when the class opponent was sued by employees who, in the absence of a class action, might have obtained employment benefits for themselves that were inconsistent with the employer's obligations to other employees.[50]

Risk of Practical Impairment of Non–Parties' Interests

Rule 23(b)(1)(B) permits certification of a class if piecemeal litigation involving individual class members may as a practical matter produce injustice for class members who are not parties to the individual litigation.[51] One of the most common applications of Rule 23(b)(1)(B) occurs when numerous claimants may seek relief from a limited fund and, in the absence of class certification, individual lawsuits might deplete the fund before all worthy claimants had a chance to obtain some share of the fund.[52] However, to obtain certification under Rule 23(b)(1)(B) in such circumstances, it is settled that the "limited" fund must be "limited by more than the agreement of the parties."[53]

"Incompatible Duties" Contrasted with "Risk of Practical Impairment"

Rule 23(b)(1)(A), establishing the "incompatible duties" standard, has the primary purpose of protecting the opponent of the class from the possibility of inconsistent obligations. In a situation where Rule

(b)(1)(A) certification requires that there be 'more than the mere possibility that inconsistent judgments and resolution of identical questions of law would result if numerous actions are conducted instead of one class action;' " mere fact that class opponent might win some individual cases and lose others does not meet requirements of Rule 23(b)(1)(A)).

50. *Mungin v. Florida East Coast Railway Co.,* 318 F.Supp. 720 (M.D.Fla.1970), *affirmed,* 441 F.2d 728 (5th Cir.1971), *cert. denied sub nom., Howard v. Florida East Coast Railway Co.,* 404 U.S. 897, 92 S.Ct. 203, 30 L.Ed.2d 175 (1971). *See also Zinser v. Accufix Research Institute, Inc.,* 253 F.3d 1180 (9th Cir.2001), *opinion amended and superseded on denial of reh'g,* 273 F.3d 1266 (9th Cir.2001) (where possible relief is a fund, which would be created by defendant, to pay for future medical monitoring of plaintiffs, relief sought is primarily monetary damages–not relief that imposes inconsistent obligations on defendant–and therefore case is not suitable for certification under Rule 23(b)(1)(A)).

51. *See, e.g., Weinman v. Fidelity Capital Appreciation Fund,* 354 F.3d 1246, 1264 (10th Cir. 2004) (Rule 23(b)(1)(B) is satisfied when resolution of first individual case could be dispositive of factual and legal issues that would resolve subsequent individual cases before those litigants had a chance to pursue their claims); *McDonnell Douglas Corp. v. United States District Court for the Central District of California,* 523 F.2d 1083 (9th Cir.1975), *cert. denied sub nom., Flanagan v. McDonnell Douglas Corp.,* 425 U.S. 911, 96 S.Ct. 1506, 47 L.Ed.2d 761 (1976)(class certification appropriate to ensure "equitable distribution of the refund program"). *But cf., Tilley v. TJX Companies, Inc.,* 345 F.3d 34, 42 (1st Cir. 2003) (certification under Rule 23(b)(1)(B) "cannot rest solely on an anticipated stare decisis effect").

52. *See, e.g., Trautz v. Weisman,* 846 F.Supp. 1160 (S.D.N.Y.1994) (classic Rule 23(b)(1)(B) case occurs when multiple claims of individuals exceed value of limited fund, and early individual suits would exhaust fund before later-filing claimants can share).

53. *Ortiz v. Fibreboard Corp.,* 527 U.S. 815, 119 S.Ct. 2295, 144 L.Ed.2d 715 (1999) (error for district court to treat fund as limited only because parties agreed to limit claims to specified amount; before certifying class under Rule 23(b)(1)(B) district court should have examined grand total of funds actually available in event of success by plaintiffs; additionally, Supreme Court refuses to decide "whether Rule 23(b)(1)(B) may ever be used to aggregate individual tort claims"). *See also Zinser v. Accufix Research Institute, Inc.,* 253 F.3d 1180 (9th Cir. 2001), *opinion amended and superseded on denial of reh'g,* 273 F.3d 1266 (9th Cir.2001) (for certification under Rule 23(b)(1)(B) plaintiffs must prove that fund is actually limited to amount less than that for which defendant might be liable).

23(b)(1)(A) is suitable, there is less concern about the potential class members, because even if no class is certified individual members of the class can still bring their claims individually without loss to themselves. In a Rule 23(b)(1)(B) situation involving potential "practical impairment," however, failure to certify a class creates the probability that individual members will not be able to share recovery in limited resources in a proportional manner, fair to all.

Classes Seeking Final Equitable Relief

Rule 23(b)(2) permits certification of class actions where the primary relief sought is equitable in nature. There are two elements to satisfy before a class may be certified under Rule 23(b)(2): the class must share a general claim against the non-class party; and the class must seek either final injunctive or declaratory relief. Race and gender discrimination class actions, seeking an alteration in the future behavior of the opponent of the class, are typical of the class actions certified under Rule 23(b)(2).[54]

Obtaining Damages in "Equity" Class Actions Classes

Certification of a class under Rule 23(b)(2) requires that the relief sought in the case is primarily equitable in nature. However, there is no prohibition on adding pleas for damages in a (b)(2) class. Thus it is not necessarily disabling to a Rule 23(b)(2) certification if the suit, in addition to seeking final equitable relief, also seeks damages.[55] The key to obtaining certification under Rule 23(b)(2) is the court's determination of the relative importance of the equitable relief to the damages sought.[56] This distinction is explained in greater detail immediately below.

54. *See, e.g., Comer v. Cisneros,* 37 F.3d 775, 796 (2d Cir.1994)("[p]attern of racial discrimination cases for injunctions against state or local officials are the 'paradigm' of [Rule 23(b)(2)] cases." [sic]). *Cf., Washington v. CSC Credit Services, Inc.,* 199 F.3d 263, 267 (5th Cir.2000), *cert. denied,* 530 U.S. 1261, 120 S.Ct. 2718, 147 L.Ed.2d 983 (2000) (if underlying law does not permit injunctive relief, class cannot be certified under Rule 23(b)(2)).

55. *See, e.g., Robinson v. Metro–North Commuter Railroad Co.,* 267 F.3d 147, 164 (2d Cir. 2001), *cert. denied,* 535 U.S. 951, 122 S.Ct. 1349, 152 L.Ed.2d 251 (2002) (rejecting "incidental damages" approach; adopting an "ad hoc" approach based on facts of particular cases, with view to determining whether value of potential injunctive or declaratory relief is predominant; such determination requires deciding whether reasonable plaintiffs, in absence of any monetary relief, would still bring suit to obtain equitable relief; and equitable relief would be necessary and appropriate if plaintiff prevailed on merits); *Kanter v. Warner–Lambert Co.,* 265 F.3d 853, 860 (9th Cir.2001) ("In Rule 23(b)(2) cases, monetary damages requests are generally allowable only if they are merely incidental to the litigation."); *James v. City of Dallas, Texas,* 254 F.3d 551 (5th Cir.2001), *cert. denied,* 534 U.S. 1113, 122 S.Ct. 919, 151 L.Ed.2d 884 (2002) (class certification under Rule 23(b)(2) means "[p]laintiffs must demonstrate that their class action suit seeks predominantly injunctive relief rather than monetary damages"); *Probe v. State Teachers' Retirement System,* 780 F.2d 776, 780 (9th Cir.1986), *cert. denied,* 476 U.S. 1170, 106 S.Ct. 2891, 90 L.Ed.2d 978 (1986)(class certified under Rule 23(b)(2) may also seek "incidental" money damages). *But see, Ticor Title Insurance Co. v. Brown,* 511 U.S. 117, 119, 114 S.Ct. 1359, 1361, 128 L.Ed.2d 33 (1994) (per curiam) (suggesting in dicta the "substantial possibility" that classes seeking money damages can only be certified under Rule 23(b)(3)).

56. *See, e.g., Jefferson v. Ingersoll International, Inc.,* 195 F.3d 894, 896 (7th Cir.1999) (use of Rule 23(b)(2) in cases involving damages is permissible only where predominant relief is an injunction or declaration, and damages are incidental to such equitable relief; incidental damages arise from wrong to class as a whole,

NOTE: If damages are more important in the case than equitable remedies, it is likely that the suit will be certified under some provision other than Rule 23(b)(2) or not certified at all.[57] Alternatively, if a class is certified based on the predominance of common legal or factual questions under Rule 23(b)(3), substantial difficulties could follow. Rule 23(b)(3) class representatives may be burdened with substantial expenses in notifying other class members of the litigation.[58] Thus in seeking damages in a Rule 23(b)(2) class, the benefits of obtaining damages should be weighed against the possibility that the case might be certified under Rule 23(b)(3). If notification expenses in a particular case are likely to be substantial, it might be prudent to consider whether the class should seek damages at all.[59] Notification duties for a Rule 23(b)(3) class are discussed in Rule 23(c)(2), below. For other notification obligations the court may impose, see Rule 23(d)(2) and (e).

Rule 23(b)(2) and Jury Trials

The Seventh Amendment to the United States Constitution normally provides a right to trial by jury in federal district courts in civil litigation where money damages are sought.[60] At the same time, in class actions certified under Rule 23(b)(2), the case must be based primarily on equitable claims, which do not normally qualify to be heard by a jury. When the Rule 23(b)(2) class action also contains a plea for money

not from circumstances that require fact finding on individual class members' cases); *Boughton v. Cotter Corp.*, 65 F.3d 823, 827 (10th Cir. 1995)(where relief sought is primarily money, Rule 23(b)(2) class is inappropriate). *See also Lemon v. International Union of Operating Engineers, Local No. 139, AFL–CIO*, 216 F.3d 577 (7th Cir.2000) (where compensatory damages would require examination of each individual's magnitude of injury, and punitive damages would require finding that defendant was recklessly indifferent to each plaintiff's federal rights, damages are not "incidental" within meaning of Rule 23(b)(2)).

57. *See, e.g., Jefferson v. Ingersoll International, Inc.*, 195 F.3d 894, 898–99 (7th Cir.1999) (three options for cases involving damages that are not certifiable under Rule 23(b)(2): (1) certification under Rule 23(b)(3); (2) "divided certification," meaning a Rule 23(b)(2) class for portion of case requiring equitable relief and a Rule 23(b)(3) class for portion requiring damages; or (3) certification of entire action under Rule 23(b)(2), but with provision, pursuant to Rule 23(d)(2) and (5), that individual class members will receive personal notice and opportunity to opt out); *Allison v. Citgo Petroleum Corp.*, 151 F.3d 402 (5th Cir.1998) (denying Rule 23(b)(2) because equitable remedies do not outweigh importance of money damages; holding that key to determination of "predomination" issue is whether request for monetary relief makes class so disparate in makeup that notice and opt-out provisions are necessary). *But see Berger v. Xerox Corp. Retirement Income Guarantee Plan*, 338 F.3d 755 (7th Cir.2003) (declaratory judgment actions are usually preludes to requests for other relief (injunctive or monetary); likelihood that successful litigants may subsequently seek damages is not, of itself, fatal to effort to obtain certification under Rule 23(b)(2)).

58. *See also Bratcher v. National Standard Life Insurance Co.*, 365 F.3d 408, 417 (5th Cir. 2004) ("[D]ue process requires the provision of notice where a rule 23(b)(2) class seeks monetary damages."); *Jefferson v. Ingersoll International, Inc.*, 195 F.3d 894, 896–97 (7th Cir.1999) (judgments and settlements in cases certified under rule 23(b)(2) are more susceptible to collateral attack by class members than cases controlled by rule 23(b)(3); defendants who need finality prefer Rule 23(b)(3), whose provisions for notice and opt out make judgments and settlements less vulnerable to collateral attacks).

59. *Cf., Allen v. International Truck & Engine Corp.*, 358 F.3d 469, 470 (7th Cir. 2004) (suggesting that when case involving both equitable relief and money damages is certified under Rule 23(b)(2), notice and right to opt out may still be required for damages issues).

60. *Beacon Theatres, Inc. v. Westover*, 359 U.S. 500, 510, 79 S.Ct. 948, 956, 3 L.Ed.2d 988 (1959).

damages, the combination of circumstances might seem to create a problem. However, the solution appears to be readily available. In such cases, issues relating to damages alone or to both damages and equitable relief may require trial by jury, but issues going to the equitable claims alone should be heard by the judge.[61]

Predominance of Common Legal or Factual Questions

The final possibility for certifying a class action is a determination that the questions of law or fact common to the members of the class predominate over other questions. Rule 23(b)(3) certification is often a last resort for litigants who cannot be certified under any other portion of Rule 23(b).[62] Two special requirements exist for Rule 23(b)(3) classes. Both must be satisfied to achieve certification under Rule 23(b)(3). First among these is the requirement that common questions *predominate* over individual interests.[63] As can be seen from cites

61. *Allen v. International Truck & Engine Corp.*, 358 F.3d 469, 471 (7th Cir. 2004).

62. *See, e.g., DeBoer v. Mellon Mortgage Co.*, 64 F.3d 1171, 1175 (8th Cir.1995), *cert. denied*, 517 U.S. 1156, 116 S.Ct. 1544, 134 L.Ed.2d 648 (1996)(where certification is appropriate under either Rule 23(b)(1) or (2), certification under Rule 23(b)(3) is inappropriate).

63. *Amchem Products, Inc. v. Windsor*, 521 U.S. 591, 623, 117 S.Ct. 2231, 2250, 138 L.Ed.2d 689 (1997) (predominance issues require a "close look" at, among other factors, "difficulties likely to be encountered in the management of a class action;" predominance not satisfied if there are a number of significant questions peculiar to different categories within class or to individuals within class; exposure to different asbestos products, at different times, in different ways, for different periods of time, with differing results ranging from no injury through only symptoms of injury to grave illnesses of several different kinds, all complicated by differences in cigarette use among class members where use of cigarettes complicates injury, defeats allegation of predominance). *Tardiff v. Knox County*, 365 F.3d 1, 5 (county policy of strip searching most or all categories of persons arrested satisfies "predominance," notwithstanding differences between cases of individual persons within those categories); *Stirman v. Exxon Corp.*, 280 F.3d 554, 564 (5th Cir.2002) ("[S]ignificant variations in state law . . . defeat predominance."); *Johnston v. HBO Film Management, Inc.*, 265 F.3d 178, 190 (3d Cir.2001) ("[I]t has become well-settled that, as a general rule, an action based substantially on oral rather than written communications is inappropriate for treatment as a class action."); *Szabo v. Bridgeport Machines, Inc.*, 249 F.3d 672, 674 (7th Cir.2001), *cert. denied*, 534 U.S. 951, 122 S.Ct. 348, 151 L.Ed.2d 263 (2001) ("A nationwide class in what is fundamentally a breach of warranty action, coupled with a claim of fraud, poses serious problems about choice of law, the manageability of the suit, and thus the propriety of class certification;" noting differences in substantive laws of states, plus issues of who made fraudulent statements, where they were made, and on whose behalf); *Bolin v. Sears, Roebuck & Co.*, 231 F.3d 970, 978–79 (5th Cir.2000) (civil RICO claim cannot be certified as class action where individual reliance is an issue); *Nagel v. ADM Investor Services, Inc.*, 217 F.3d 436 (7th Cir.2000) (allegations of fraud tend to be "plaintiff-specific," and therefore issues common to class tend not to predominate over issues of interest to individuals); *Rutstein v. Avis Rent–A–Car Systems, Inc.*, 211 F.3d 1228 (11th Cir.2000), *cert. denied*, 532 U.S. 919, 121 S.Ct. 1354, 149 L.Ed.2d 285 (2001) (in non-employment discrimination case, each plaintiff must establish: (1) membership in racial minority; (2) intent to discriminate on basis of race; and (3) discrimination that fell within scope of activity prohibited by relevant statute; held, determination of intent to discriminate on basis of race is highly fact specific, including not only defendant's general policy, but also whether individual plaintiffs were denied benefits, whether independent legitimate reasons (such as age or financial status of individual plaintiffs) for defendant's behavior existed; held, where liability rests upon individualized determinations, common questions do not predominate as required by Rule 23(b)(3)); *Castano v. American Tobacco Co.*, 84 F.3d 734, 745 (5th Cir. 1996)("[A] fraud class action cannot be certified when individual reliance will be an issue;" moreover, where laws of different states will apply to different class members, "variations in state law may swamp any common issues and defeat predominance"). *Compare, e.g., Waste Management Holdings, Inc. v. Mowbray*, 208

contained in the immediately preceding footnote, resolution of the "predominance" analysis rests heavily on the facts of particular cases.[64] There is also an important unresolved question as to whose version of the "facts"–plaintiff's or defendant's–courts should use when addressing the predominance problem. On this particular point the cases are significantly divided, and attorneys are compelled to consult the local precedent.[65]

In other Rule 23(b) classes, by contrast, there is only the requirement, stated in Rule 23(a)(2), that common questions of law or fact exist among the class members, with no requirement that the common questions predominate.[66]

Certification Requirements for Classes Where Common Questions Predominate: Superiority

The second requirement for certification under Rule 23(b)(3) is a finding that a class action is the superior means of adjudicating the controversy. In reaching that determination, a court is required to make four findings described in Rule 23(b)(3). The court may also address other issues that, in particular cases, are relevant to determining whether certification of a class action is the best way to process a case.[67] The court's determination of those points will ordinarily be dispositive of a Rule 23(b)(3) class certification. It should be noted that while the court is required to make findings on the four points listed, there is no requirement that before a class is certified, all four findings

F.3d 288, 295–96 (1st Cir.2000) (on the one hand, in a securities context, fraud on the market "may be particularly well-suited for class treatment"; additionally individualized effects of statutes of limitations should be considered in Rule 23(b)(3) evaluations, but variations in such statutes need not be a per se disqualifier of class certification), *with Broussard v. Meineke Discount Muffler Shops, Inc.,* 155 F.3d 331, 340–43 (4th Cir.1998) (non-uniform oral representations to class members, differences in equitable tolling of statute of limitations for different class members, and differences in calculation of lost profits, all demonstrate that even the minimal requirement of commonality under rule 23(a)(2) is not satisfied). *See also, Mullen v. Treasure Chest Casino, LLC,* 186 F.3d 620, 626–27 (5th Cir. 1999), *cert. denied,* 528 U.S. 1159, 120 S.Ct. 1169, 145 L.Ed.2d 1078 (2000) (common issues of negligence and seaworthiness of vessel are "pivotal"; case invokes only federal law, so no choice of law issues; non-common issue of causation of illness will be left to second phase of litigation involving individual trials; held, requirement of predominance is satisfied).

64. *See also Tardiff v. Knox County,* 365 F.3d 1, 4 (1st Cir. 2004) (noting that in the context of class actions relating to strip searches of arrested persons, lower courts have reached opposite conclusions on questions of predominance).

65. *Id.* ("It is sometimes taken for granted that the complaint's allegations are necessarily controlling; but class action machinery is expensive and in our view a court has the power to test disputed premises early on if and when the class action would be proper on one premise but not another;" collecting various appellate decisions on point).

66. *Amchem Products, Inc. v. Windsor,* 521 U.S. 591, 623, 117 S.Ct. 2231, 2250, 138 L.Ed.2d 689 (1997) (for purposes of Rule 23(b)(3), predominance requirement is "far more demanding" than commonality requirement of Rule 23(a)). *See, e.g., Hanlon v. Chrysler Corp.,* 150 F.3d 1011 (9th Cir.1998) ("The commonality preconditions of Rule 23(a)(2) are less rigorous than the companion requirements of Rule 23(b)(3)."). *See also, Walters v. Reno,* 145 F.3d 1032 (9th Cir.1998), *cert. denied,* 526 U.S. 1003, 119 S.Ct. 1140, 143 L.Ed.2d 208 (1999) (no requirement under Rule 23(b)(2) that common issues predominate).

67. *See, e.g., Castano v. American Tobacco Co.,* 84 F.3d 734 (5th Cir.1996)(court may consider whether class action will preserve judicial resources). *See also, Hanlon v. Chrysler Corp.,* 150 F.3d 1011, 1022–23 (9th Cir.1998) (individual suits would be ineffective for members of potential class).

must be resolved in favor of certification. Instead, the court has discretion to weigh its findings in determining whether class certification is the superior method of litigating the controversy.

(1) *Rule 23(b)(3)(A)—Individual Interests in Separate Actions:* The court will evaluate the desire, if any, of individual litigants to pursue their own separate actions, and the net balance of interests between such individuals and the class as a whole.[68] Because individual litigants who feel the need to control their own cases may exercise their right under Rule 23(c) to "opt out" of a Rule 23(b)(3) class, it is usually possible to certify the class and still accommodate most of the needs of such individuals. Harmonizing individual interests with class certification would be more difficult if it was likely that so many individuals would opt out that the "class" no longer represented the bulk of its potential members. In that circumstance, the evidence of such strong interest in individual litigation would argue strongly against certifying a Rule 23(b)(3) class.

(2) *Rule 23(b)(3)(B)—Pending Litigation:* The court will also consider the effects of any other pending litigation on the proposed class action. If individual class members have already begun to pursue their own cases, it may be difficult to justify certification of a Rule 23(b)(3) class on grounds of judicial economy.[69] Indeed, it is possible that such pending litigation will reach judgment before the class action, and many of the contested issues in the class action might then be resolved through application of principles of stare decisis or collateral estoppel.

(3) *Rule 23(b)(3)(C)—Progress in Class Litigation:* If the court hearing the class action has already invested enough resources in the case so that dismissal or refusal to certify the action would be inefficient, a strong argument exists in favor of certifying the class so that the action can be concentrated in the chosen forum.[70]

(4) *Rule 23(b)(3)(C)—Geography:* Another consideration that may bear on the wisdom of proceeding with the class action in the chosen forum is geography. If the case is being heard in an area of the country

68. *See, e.g., Zinser v. Accufix Research Institute, Inc.*, 253 F.3d 1180 (9th Cir.2001), *opinion amended and superseded on denial of reh'g*, 273 F.3d 1266 (9th Cir.2001) ("Where damages suffered by each putative class member are not large, this factor weighs in favor of certifying a class action;" holding claims in excess of $50,000 each–the jurisdictional amount then in effect for diversity cases–tends to undermine somewhat an allegation that the claims are small); *In re Northern District of California Dalkon Shield IUD Products Liability Litigation*, 693 F.2d 847, 856 (9th Cir.1982), *cert. denied,* 459 U.S. 1171, 103 S.Ct. 817, 74 L.Ed.2d 1015 (1983)(where class members have a strong interest in individual suits, court should incline toward refusal to certify). *See also, Heaven v. Trust Company Bank,* 118 F.3d 735, 738 (11th Cir.1997) (counterclaims against individual class members is a factor to consider in evaluating whether, under Rule 23(b)(3)(A), individual members might have interest in controlling their own cases).

69. *See, e.g., City of Inglewood v. City of Los Angeles*, 451 F.2d 948, 952 n. 4 (9th Cir. 1971)(directing that if party seeks a Rule 23(b)(3) class, "the court should note the fact that some 2,350 members of the class are already involved in suits against the same defendant"). *But cf., Hanlon v. Chrysler Corp.*, 150 F.3d 1011 (9th Cir.1998) (no bar to class certification where only a few pending lawsuits may be difficult to merge into class action).

70. *Cf., e.g., In re Mid-Atlantic Toyota Antitrust Litigation*, 564 F.Supp. 1379, 1391 (D.Md. 1983)("The fact that the panel on multi-district litigation has transferred all actions [to the court] indicates the desirability [of the forum].")

where the class or the evidence is concentrated, this may be an argument for continuing in the chosen forum.[71]

(5) *Rule 23(b)(3)(D)—Difficulties in Managing a Class Action:* Courts can refuse to certify if too many administrative difficulties exist in class actions. In exercising this discretion, courts consider a wide variety of factors affecting ease of administration of a case. Examples of problems in managing a class include internal disputes within a class and problems of notification of class members[72], as well as the impact that state law variations can have on management in a multi-state case.[73]

Affirmative Defenses

The "predominance" requirement is obviously a substantial obstacle to class certification under Rule 23(b)(3). However, it appears settled that a defendant's possible affirmative defenses against claims by individual class members will not, of themselves, prevent the parties seeking class certification from meeting the requirement.[74]

RULE 23(c). DETERMINATION BY ORDER WHETHER CLASS ACTION TO BE MAINTAINED; NOTICE; JUDGMENT; ACTIONS CONDUCTED PARTIALLY AS CLASS ACTIONS

CORE CONCEPT

Rules 23(a) and (b) contain most of the requirements that must be satisfied before a class may be certified. Rule 23(c), by contrast,

71. *See, e.g., Zinser v. Accufix Research Institute, Inc.,* 253 F.3d 1180 (9th Cir.2001), *opinion amended and superseded on denial of reh'g,* 273 F.3d 1266 (9th Cir.2001) (where potential plaintiffs, witnesses and evidence are spread across country, it is undesirable to concentrate litigation in instant forum unless plaintiff can demonstrate adequate justification); *Langley v. Coughlin,* 715 F.Supp. 522, 561 (S.D.N.Y.1989) (location of "most relevant evidence" in forum is factor favoring certification under Rule 23(b)(3)(C)).

72. *See, e.g., Zinser v. Accufix Research Institute, Inc.,* 253 F.3d 1180 (9th Cir.2001), *opinion amended and superseded on denial of reh'g,* 273 F.3d 1266 (9th Cir.2001) (where pacemaker leads were implanted in different patients by different doctors in different states, producing different injuries at different times, there are too many individual issues and case management would be too difficult, notwithstanding common nucleus of facts about defendant's conduct); *Simer v. Rios,* 661 F.2d 655, 678 (7th Cir.1981), *cert. denied sub nom., Simer v. United States,* 456 U.S. 917, 102 S.Ct. 1773, 72 L.Ed.2d 177 (1982)(proper to consider problems of notifying class members in deciding whether to certify class). *But cf., Williams v. Chartwell Financial Services, Ltd.,* 204 F.3d 748, 760 (7th Cir.2000) (possible need for subclasses, by itself, is insufficient ground for denying certification because a class action would be unmanageable).

73. *See, e.g., Castano v. American Tobacco Co.,* 84 F.3d 734 (5th Cir.1996)(so holding). *See also, Heaven v. Trust Company Bank,* 118 F.3d 735, 738 (11th Cir.1997) (counterclaims against individual members of class with potential liability greater than original claims might create case management problems under Rule 23(b)(3)(D)). *But cf., Mullen v. Treasure Chest Casino, LLC,* 186 F.3d 620, 627 (5th Cir.1999), *cert. denied,* 528 U.S. 1159, 120 S.Ct. 1169, 145 L.Ed.2d 1078 (2000) (superiority requirement satisfied by: lack of complex choice-of-law or *Erie* problems; modest number of class members ("hundreds instead of millions"); bifurcated-trial plan; and likelihood that trial would focus on second-hand smoke as both result of poor ventilation and cause of illnesses).

74. *See, e.g., Smilow v. Southwestern Bell Mobile Systems, Inc.,* 323 F.3d 32, 39–40 (1st Cir.2003).

concentrates on the procedure and timing of motions to certify and the process to be followed once a decision to certify has been made.

APPLICATIONS

Motion or Court Initiative

A party may seek certification by motion, or the court may on its own initiative make the certification decision.[75]

"Implied" Classes

Rule 23(c)(1), by its express terms, appears to require that the district court "must" determine whether a class should be certified. However, there is authority that a court's failure to make a formal certification ruling does not mean the case at bar cannot be a class action. If the elements required for class certification are satisfied, an "implied" class may exist notwithstanding a lack of formal certification by the district court.[76]

Timing

Rule 23(c) provides no rigid timetable for resolving the certification issue, but the preference among the courts is to make the decision courts are directed to make the decision "at an early practicable time."[77]

75. *See, e.g., McGowan v. Faulkner Concrete Pipe Co.,* 659 F.2d 554 (5th Cir.1981)(trial court has duty to decide suitability of class action, even if no party makes a motion).

76. *See, e.g., Doe v. Bush,* 261 F.3d 1037, 1048–49 (11th Cir.2001), *cert. denied,* 534 U.S. 1104, 122 S.Ct. 903, 151 L.Ed.2d 872 (2002) ("[T]he fact that the district court failed to properly certify a class does not necessarily establish that no class exists, or that the defendants cannot be held in contempt for failing to provide class-wide relief." Plaintiffs filed certification motion in timely manner, but district court did not act; however, district court referred to plaintiffs as class and defendants behaved as opponents of class); *Navarro-Ayala v. Hernandez–Colon,* 951 F.2d 1325, 1333 (1st Cir. 1991) (no notice ever provided to class members, but "because this case was instituted by a complaint seeking class relief, implicitly granted class relief, and was conducted for years as a de facto class, it should and may be recognized as such"). *But see Brown v. Philadelphia Housing Authority,* 350 F.3d 338, 344 (3d Cir. 2003) (rejecting doctrine of implied class certification); *Martinez–Mendoza v. Champion International Corp.,* 340 F.3d 1200 n. 37 (11th Cir.2003) (Rule 23(c)(1) requires courts to determine independently whether case should be class action, even where no party seeks a ruling on class certification); *Davis v. Hutchins,* 321 F.3d 641, 648 (7th Cir.2003) ("Class damages cannot be awarded if no class is certified.").

77. *See, e.g., Kerkhof v. MCI Worldcom, Inc.,* 282 F.3d 44, 55 (1st Cir.2002) (post-judgment certification should usually be discouraged because it "would frustrate the opt-out mechanisms for Rule 23(b)(3) classes provided in Rules 23(c)(2) and (c)(3), which were intended to avoid situations in which class members could choose to join only when judgment favored the class"; also, "a delay in adding class allegations deprives a defendant of fair warning as to the true stakes and, by eliminating mutuality, leaves the defendant liable on class claims (if he loses the summary judgment motion) without protecting him (if he wins)"); *Grandson v. University of Minnesota,* 272 F.3d 568, 574 (8th Cir.2001), *cert. denied,* 535 U.S. 1054, 122 S.Ct. 1910, 152 L.Ed.2d 820 (2002) (failure to seek class certification before expiration of deadline for such motions (in this case, fifteen months after complaint was filed) and failure to seek extension of time constitute grounds for striking class allegations); *Prado-Steiman v. Bush,* 221 F.3d 1266, 1273 (11th Cir.2000) ("Rule 23 contemplates that the class certification decision will be made prior to the close of discovery."); *In re Philip Morris, Inc.,* 214 F.3d 132 (2d Cir.2000) (per curiam) (district court does not have "unfettered discretion" to delay decision on class certification; usually decision will be made somewhere

Conditional Certification

In the past Rule 23(c)(1) permitted the court to make certification conditional upon later developments in the case. Even if the court had not expressly reserved the power, it retained authority to amend its order as events require.[78] However, Rule 23(c)(1) was amended in 2003 to remove the language authorizing conditional certification. Instead, courts are encouraged to withhold certification until the requirements of Rule 23 are met. At the same time, courts are given latitude to make a decision on certification at all times up to the time of final judgment.[79]

Notice

As amended in 2003, Rule 23(c)(2) establishes various notice options and/or requirements for cases certified under Rule 23. For classes certified pursuant to Rule 23(b)(1) or (2), Rule 23(c)(2)(A) authorizes – but does not require – the district court to order notice to such classes. This authority is intended to supplement the court's already existing power under Rule 23(d)(2) to issue notice in some circumstances to class members.[80] This change in Rule 23(c)(2) leaves unaltered the assumption that courts will be cautious in their use of notice to Rule 23(b)(1) and (2) classes so as, *inter alia,* not to burden the class representatives with unnecessary costs of notice.[81]

between end of pleadings and end of discovery (depending on facts of individual cases), but only rarely should decision be delayed until after hearing on merits); *Navarro–Ayala v. Hernandez–Colon,* 951 F.2d 1325, 1334 (1st Cir. 1991)("egregious omission" for court not to move quickly on issue of class certification); *Peritz v. Liberty Loan Corp.,* 523 F.2d 349, 353 (7th Cir.1975) ("[A]mended Rule 23 requires class certification prior to a determination on the merits."). *But cf., Miami University Wrestling Club v. Miami University,* 302 F.3d 608, 616 (6th Cir.2002) ("We have consistently held that a district court is not required to rule on a motion for class certification before ruling on the merits of the case."); *Postow v. OBA Federal Savings & Loan Association,* 627 F.2d 1370, 1383–84 (D.C. Cir.1980) ("[T]he present state of the law does not necessarily preclude class certification after a judgment on the merits in Rule 23(b)(3) class actions; it suggests there may be equitable reasons for allowing post-judgment certification in some cases." Citing some other authority; holding that in instant case equitable considerations justified post-judgment decision on certification); *Cowen v. Bank United of Texas, F.S.B.,* 70 F.3d 937, 941 (7th Cir.1995)(usually certification will be addressed before summary judgment, but facts of particular case may justify different sequence of events).

78. *See, e.g., Lyons v. Georgia-Pacific Corp. Salaried Employees Retirement Plan,* 221 F.3d 1235, 1253 n. 32 (11th Cir.2000), *cert. denied,* 532 U.S. 967, 121 S.Ct. 1504, 149 L.Ed.2d 388 (2001) ("Rule 23(a) is not immutable;" court retains power under Rule 23(c) and (d) to change prior order if subsequent events make that step appropriate); *Forehand v. Florida State Hospital,* 89 F.3d 1562, 1566 (11th Cir.1996) (court may decertify class previously certified even when case was filed ten years earlier and had proceeded through trial).

79. *See* Rule 23(c)(1) advisory committee notes to 2003 amendments.

80. *See* Rule 23(c)(2) advisory committee notes to 2003 amendments. *See also Eubanks v. Billington,* 110 F.3d 87, 96 (D.C. Cir. 1997) (Rule 23(d) authorizes court to permit party to opt out of class certified under Rule 23(b)(1) or (2) "on a selective basis").

81. *See* Rule 23(c)(2) advisory committee notes to 2003 amendments (noting that classes certified under Rule 23(b)(1) or (2) have no right to opt out, reducing need for notice on that point). *See also* 15 U.S.C.A. § 78u–4 (in litigation within scope of Private Securities Litigation Reform Act of 1995, lead plaintiff must, within twenty days of filing complaint, provide publication notice in "widely circulated national business-oriented publication or wire service" of pending action and potential opportunity to serve as lead plaintiff).

Rule 23(c)(2) also establishes special requirements for notifying class members of pending Rule 23(b)(3) actions. The reason for this provision arises from the special nature of Rule 23(b)(3) suits, in which common questions must predominate and the class suit must be superior to alternative methods of adjudication. Such suits tend to involve the least homogeneous classes. Lack of homogeneity increases the risk that informal notice of the class action may not flow freely within the class. To correct this problem, Rule 23(c)(2) provides that individual members must receive the "best notice practicable," which will often be mail service on all class members whose identities and addresses are known.[82]

Finally, amended Rule 23(c)(2) also requires that if a class action requires certification under both Rule 23(b)(2) and (b)(3), the usually more burdensome notice requirements required for a (b)(3) class must be satisfied for the (b)(3) class.[83]

Elements of Notice to Rule 23(b)(3) Classes

Rule 23(c)(2) specifies that notification will include the following pieces of advice: (1) "the nature of the action, (2) the definition of the class certified, (3) the class claims, issues, or defenses," (4) the right of individual members of the class to appear through counsel if they choose, (5) the right to opt out of the class and not be bound by any judgment,[84] and (6) the binding effect of a class judgment on members of the class who do not opt out.[85]

Expense of Notice

The financial burden of notification in Rule 23(b)(3) cases is borne by the class representatives.[86] Thus, in some cases class representatives should be selected with an eye to their financial resources as well as their dedication to the litigation. When the burden of Rule 23(b)(3) notification is onerous, the possibility of certification under another portion of Rule 23(b) should be explored.

Parties Bound by Judgment

Rule 23(c)(3) affords the court substantial discretion to determine the binding effect of a class action. Class actions certified under either

82. *See generally Schwarzschild v. Tse,* 69 F.3d 293, 295 (9th Cir.1995), *cert. denied,* 517 U.S. 1121, 116 S.Ct. 1355, 134 L.Ed.2d 523 (1996) (in general, Rule 23(c)(2) requires notice to class members before merits are adjudicated; in unusual case where summary judgment is granted prior to certification, plaintiff no longer has duty of notification). *Cf., Mirfasihi v. Fleet Mortgage Corp.,* 356 F.3d 781, 786 (7th Cir. 2004) ("When individual notice is infeasible, notice by publication in a newspaper of national circulation ... is an acceptable substitute.").

83. *See* Rule 23(c)(2) advisory committee notes to 2003 amendments.

84. *See, e.g., Abbott Laboratories, Inc. v. CVS Pharmacy, Inc.,* 290 F.3d 854, 859 (7th Cir. 2002) (if party opts out, party is not bound by judgment; moreover, party cannot be "dragged back in under ... supplemental jurisdiction"); *Sperling v. Hoffmann–LaRoche, Inc.,* 24 F.3d 463, 470 (3d Cir. 1994) ("Members of a Rule 23(b)(3) class are automatically included ... unless they make a timely election to opt-out.").

85. *See generally Eisen v. Carlisle and Jacquelin,* 417 U.S. 156, 94 S.Ct. 2140, 40 L.Ed.2d 732 (1974).

86. *Oppenheimer Fund, Inc. v. Sanders,* 437 U.S. 340, 98 S.Ct. 2380, 57 L.Ed.2d 253 (1978).

Rule 23(b)(1) or (b)(2)(described above) have binding effect on whomever the court finds to be within the membership of the class. There is no requirement that the class members receive notice of the action.[87] Rule 23(b)(3) actions bind class members who did not opt out under Rule 23(c)(2) and whom the court defines as members.[88] Thus it is possible that persons in a (b)(3) class might not get actual notice under Rule 23(c)(2) because their names and/or addresses are unknown, yet be bound because the court found them to be members of the class.

Subclasses

Rule 23(c)(4) authorizes the court to create classes only as to particular issues, and/or to create subclasses within an action.[89] If subclasses are certified, each subclass is treated as an independent class for purposes of the action. The circumstances in which the court is most likely to create subclasses occur when the class members share a cause of action against a class opponent, but also experience differing interests among themselves.[90]

Classes for Settlement

Courts have certified classes created for purposes of settlement only. In such a circumstance, the court may notify potential class members of the possibility of class certification at the time the court notifies class members of the proposed settlement.[91]

87. *See, e.g., Payne v. Travenol Laboratories,* 673 F.2d 798, 812 (5th Cir.1982), *cert. denied,* 459 U.S. 1038, 103 S.Ct. 451, 74 L.Ed.2d 605 (1982)(notice required only in Rule 23(b)(3) classes and at time of dismissal or settlement).

88. *Eisen v. Carlisle and Jacquelin,* 417 U.S. 156, 94 S.Ct. 2140, 40 L.Ed.2d 732 (1974)(Rule 23(c)(2) requirement of notice binds all members of Rule 23(b)(3) class who do not opt out).

89. *In re Visa Check/MasterMoney Antitrust Litigation,* 280 F.3d 124, 141 (2d Cir. 2001) (Individualized damages issues may be handled by "(1) bifurcating liability and damage trials with the same or different juries; (2) appointing a magistrate judge or special master to preside over individual damages proceedings; (3) decertifying the class after the liability trial and providing notice to class members concerning how they may proceed to prove damages; (4) creating subclasses; or (5) altering or amending the class.").

90. *Ortiz v. Fibreboard Corp.,* 527 U.S. 815, 119 S.Ct. 2295, 144 L.Ed.2d 715 (1999) (class comprised of holders of both present and future claims "requires subdivision into homogenous subclasses"). *See, e.g., Hawkins v. Comparet–Cassani,* 251 F.3d 1230 (9th Cir.2001) (convict can represent other convicts on Eighth Amendment claim; however, Fourth Amendment claim can be raised only by individuals not already convicted, and convict/class representative therefore lacks standing; suggesting possibility of subclasses with different subclass representatives under Rule 23(c)(4)); *Marisol A. v. Giuliani,* 126 F.3d 372, 379 (2d Cir.1997) (court emphasizes need to locate appropriate representatives for each subclass and to establish that each subclass of instant case meet requirements of Rule 23(b)(2); otherwise, describing value of subclasses as: (1) helping to focus discovery; (2) identifying claims for which there is no adequate representative, so that such claims can be dismissed; and (3) opportunity for notice to defendants of specific charges). *See also Bogosian v. Gulf Oil Corp.,* 561 F.2d 434, 456 (3d Cir.1977) (if liability is common issue, but calculation of damages is peculiar to individual members of class, court should consider limited class certification under Rule 23(c)(4)).

91. *See, e.g., In re General Motors Corp. Pick–Up Truck Fuel Tank Products Liability Litigation,* 55 F.3d 768 (3d Cir.1995), *cert. denied,* 516 U.S. 824, 116 S.Ct. 88, 133 L.Ed.2d 45 (1995)(standard requirements of Rule 23(a) and (b) must be met; class is typically certified formally at same time court approves settlement). *But cf., Ortiz v. Fibreboard Corp.,* 527 U.S. 815, 119 S.Ct. 2295, 144 L.Ed.2d 715 (1999) (trial court is obligated to ensure that requirements of Rule 23(a) and (b) are met; "A fairness hearing under subdivision (e) can no more swallow the preceding protective requirements of Rule 23 in

RULE 23(d). ORDERS IN CONDUCT OF ACTIONS

CORE CONCEPT

Rule 23(d) provides the court explicit authority to craft orders governing class suits. Central to class actions is a need to protect the interests of parties who are less active than persons engaged in more conventional litigation. At the same time, the potential administrative complexity of class actions requires that the court have tools immediately at hand to ensure that the litigation remains manageable.

APPLICATIONS

Undue Repetition of Evidence

Rule 23(d) explicitly vests the court with broad discretion to limit cumulative or repetitive evidence.

Additional Notice to Class Members

Rule 23(d)(2) allows the court to order additional notice to class members to ensure fair treatment of passive members of the class.[92] The court's authority under this provision is very broad, and encompasses discretion to order notice to the class of almost any important event in the litigation.[93] The court may use its power in a variety of circumstances, including: notice to a class of pending litigation; discussion of proposed judgments; identification of class representatives to the whole class; and informing the class of key decision points in the suit so the class can participate in decisions, or evaluate opportunities to seek to participate more actively as class representatives.

Supervision of Class Representatives and Intervenors

Rule 23(d)(3) provides explicit authority for the court to monitor class representatives and intervenors, and thereby supports both fair representation for the class and expeditious processing of the entire case.

Rejecting Class Certification

Rule 23(d)(4) allows the court to enter an order stripping a case of allegations concerning class representation. This provision is typically employed when the court has already refused, under Rule 23(c)(1), to certify the case as a class action. It may also be used if the court originally certified a class, but later altered its decision and refused

a subdivision (b)(1)(B) action than in one under subdivision (b)(3).").

92. *See, e.g., Southern Ute Indian Tribe v. Amoco Production Co.,* 2 F.3d 1023 (10th Cir. 1993)(using Rule 23(d) to order representatives of defendant class—not plaintiff—to notify passive members of defendant class of pending litigation).

93. *See, e.g., Jefferson v. Ingersoll International, Inc.,* 195 F.3d 894, 898 (7th Cir.1999) (suggesting possible certification under Rule 23(b)(2), but with use of Rule 23(d)(2) and (5) to notify members of class seeking both money and equitable relief and to provide opportunity to opt out). *But cf., Cruz v. American Airlines, Inc.,* 356 F.3d 320, 331 (D.C. Cir. 2004) (expressing doubt that Rule 23(d)(2) grants authority to order notice to a class that has not been certified).

certification. In either circumstance, Rule 23(d)(4) contemplates that a suit denied class certification may still proceed as conventional litigation, assuming that the requirements of such litigation are satisfied.

Other Procedural Matters

Rule 23(d)(5) makes explicit that the authority of the court to issue orders to process a class suit expeditiously and fairly is not limited to the other provisions of Rule 23(d).[94] In so doing, Rule 23(d)(5) re-emphasizes the broad discretion a trial court enjoys in class litigation. However, in regulating communications between class lawyers or class representatives to potential class members, the court will explain with particularity the need for such regulation.[95]

Alteration of Prior Rulings

As a practical matter, Rule 23(d)'s declaration that the court may alter prior orders as necessary to the conduct of the suit means the court is not bound by its own interlocutory decisions in class actions. Thus the court enjoys almost complete flexibility to adjust class litigation as events may require. In particular, courts are prepared to change earlier orders appointing class representatives if events show that the representatives are not protecting adequately the interests of the whole class.

RULE 23(e). DISMISSAL OR COMPROMISE

CORE CONCEPT

Rule 23(e) requires court approval of voluntary dismissal or compromise, and requires that proposals to settle the case be submitted to the entire class for approval. This requirement of court supervision recognizes the fact that class actions are especially vulnerable to the possibility that the class representatives or the class attorneys may be placed in circumstances where their personal interests conflict with the interests of passive class members. The risk of inappropriate collaboration between class representatives, or class counsel, and the class opponent is probably greatest when questions of settlement or voluntary dismissal are at issue.[96] Rule 23(e) attempts to suppress the possibility of such conflicts by imposing a series of obligations on both the court and the parties seeking approval of the proposed settlement.

APPLICATIONS

Authority to Settle: Judicial Approval

As amended in 2003, Rule 23(e)(1)(A) expressly authorizes class

94. *See, e.g., Molski v. Gleich,* 318 F.3d 937, 947 (9th Cir.2003) (even with class certified under rule 23(b)(2), "a district court may require notice and the right to opt-out under its discretionary authority provided in Rule 23(d)(2)").

95. *Gulf Oil Co. v. Bernard,* 452 U.S. 89, 101 S.Ct. 2193, 68 L.Ed.2d 693 (1981)(requiring district court to explain the abuse such regulations are intended to address; reversing such regulations in the absence of explanation).

96. *See, e.g., In re Vitamins Antitrust Class Actions,* 215 F.3d 26 (D.C. Cir.2000) (noting that "settlement dynamics" can cause even well-intentioned parties to give insufficient weight to interests of class as a whole).

representatives to settle claims, issues or defenses as appropriate.[97] However, this authority is subject to other provisions in Rule 23(e) that have the effect of giving the power to approve or veto settlement to the district court, which in turn must solicit the views of class members before making its decision.

Comparison With Conventional Litigation

Rule 23(e) is an exception to the standard practice that parties may normally settle their disputes without the approval of the court.[98]

All Class Actions

Rule 23(e) applies to all actions certified under any portion of Rule 23(b).[99] There is also authority that the notice requirement of Rule 23(e) applies even in some situations where the class was decertified or never certified at all.[100]

Effect on Individual Claims

The power of the court to approve or reject settlements of class litigation does not extend to individual claims which members of the class may possess separate from the class claims. By its terms, the approval power of Rule 23(e)(1)(A) is limited to class litigation only.[101]

Notice of Proposed Settlement

As amended, Rule 23(e)(1)(C) expressly requires the district court to hold a hearing and make findings before approving a class settlement or voluntary dismissal. The findings must include a determination that the proposed course of resolution for the class action is "fair, reasonable, and adequate." [102] Within the limits of due process, courts may treat the requirements of Rule 23(e) as satisfied by less notice than, for example, the requirement of first-class mail that may accompany notice obligations under Rule 23(c)(2)(governing notice in Rule 23(b)(3) "predominance of common questions" classes).[103] Moreover, because the

97. *See* Rule 23(e)(1)(A) advisory committee notes to 2003 amendments.

98. *See, e.g., In re Painewebber Limited Partnerships Litigation,* 147 F.3d 132, 137 (2d Cir. 1998) (plaintiff's authority to dismiss an action voluntarily under Rule 41(a)(1) is expressly subject to court's authority under Rule 23(e)). *See also, In the Matter of Cook,* 49 F.3d 263 (7th Cir.1995)(in a class action settlement involving a common fund, Rule 23(e) provides court with authority to monitor closely attorneys' fees).

99. *See, e.g., Grimes v. Vitalink Communications Corp.,* 17 F.3d 1553, 1557 (3d Cir.1994), *cert. denied,* 513 U.S. 986, 115 S.Ct. 480, 130 L.Ed.2d 393 (1994)(duty to monitor fairness of settlement is "particularly acute" in Rule 23(b)(1) and (2) class actions, because members of those classes cannot opt out of the class litigation).

100. *See, e.g., Culver v. City of Milwaukee,* 277 F.3d 908, 914–15 (7th Cir.2002) (acknowledging issue is "not yet definitively settled," but holding that all classes, without regard to status of certification, need notice to enable them to protect against, e.g, statute of limitations problems; but accepting contrary result if violation of Rule 23(e) is harmless).

101. *See* Rule 23(e)(1)(A) advisory committee notes to 2003 amendments.

102. *See also* Rule 23(e)(1)(C) advisory committee notes to 2003 amendments.

103. *See, e.g., Mendoza v. Tucson School District No. 1,* 623 F.2d 1338 (9th Cir.1980), *cert. denied sub nom., Sanchez v. Tucson Unified School District No. 1,* 450 U.S. 912, 101 S.Ct. 1351, 67 L.Ed.2d 336 (1981). *But cf.,* Rule 23(e)(1)(B) advisory committee notes to 2003 amendments (notice of Rule 23(c)(2)(B) may be

litigation has moved toward settlement and the class representatives can now see what the potential outcome of the suit might be, the burdens of notice when Rule 23(e) is relevant are sometimes much less onerous than the burdens established by Rule 23(c)(2).[104]

Disclosure

As amended, Rule 23(e)(2) requires the proponents of a proposed settlement or voluntary dismissal to disclose any agreements that have been made that relate to the proposal.[105]

Settlement

The power to approve settlement of a class action lies within the court's discretion, and such decisions are rarely disturbed on appeal.[106] However, some important considerations may restrict judicial discretion. First, while the court is authorized to determine whether the settlement is fair to passive members of the class,[107] the court must still give substantial deference to a consensus of class members on the wisdom of the settlement.[108] Disregarding such a consensus is not

appropriate if class members must take such individual actions as filing proofs of claim or if individual class members have option of opting out of settlement pursuant to Rule 23(e)(3)).

104. *See, e.g., Gottlieb v. Wiles,* 11 F.3d 1004, 1013 (10th Cir.1993)(suggesting that notice requirements of Rule 23(e) are less rigorous than those of Rule 23(b)(3) and (c)(2)). *See also Crawford v. F. Hoffman–La Roche Ltd.,* 267 F.3d 760, 764 (8th Cir.2001) ("[N]otice is not necessarily required if a class has not been certified."). *But see, White v. Alabama,* 74 F.3d 1058, 1066 n. 27 (11th Cir.1996)(newspaper ads in small type, using "legalese" that attorneys might not fully understand, did not satisfy Rule 23(e) notice requirements). *See also* 15 U.S.C.A. § 78u–4 (in litigation controlled by Private Securities Litigation Reform Act of 1995, notice must include, inter alia, disclosure of recovery to class members; reason for settlement; agreements or disagreements as to damages individual class members would potentially recover if class had achieved victory rather than settlement; and likely payments to lawyers).

105. *See* Rule 23(e)(2) advisory committee notes to 2003 amendments.

106. *See, e.g., Durkin v. Shea & Gould,* 92 F.3d 1510, 1512 n. 6 (9th Cir.1996), *cert. denied,* 520 U.S. 1197, 117 S.Ct. 1553, 137 L.Ed.2d 702 (1997) (standard for approving settlement is whether it is "fundamentally fair, adequate, and reasonable"). *See also, Hanlon v. Chrysler Corp.,* 150 F.3d 1011 (9th Cir.1998) (for settlement approval prior to formal certification, court should make a "more probing inquiry" into terms of proposed settlement). *But see, In re Painewebber Limited Partnerships Litigation,* 147 F.3d 132 (2d Cir.1998) (notwithstanding Rule 23(e), members of potential class that is not yet certified are free to settle individual claims without court supervision; but Rule 23(e) applies once a class is certified). *But cf., Devlin v. Scardelletti,* 536 U.S. 1, 122 S.Ct. 2005, 153 L.Ed.2d 27 (2002) (class member who was not named party and who objects to settlement has right to appeal without first intervening in case; where class member has no choice to opt out of litigation, as when class was certified under, e.g., Rule 23(b)(1), the right of class members to appeal settlement has even greater force).

107. *See, e.g., In the Matter of Mexico Money Transfer Litigation,* 267 F.3d 743, 748 (7th Cir. 2001), *cert. denied,* 535 U.S. 1018, 122 S.Ct. 1607, 152 L.Ed.2d 621 (2002) (fact that "everyone other than the plaintiffs has been paid in cash"–plaintiffs got coupons–does not of itself make settlement unfair; noting, however, "[m]aybe class actions would be prosecuted more vigorously if the class and class counsel had to accept the same coin"); *Hanlon v. Chrysler Corp.,* 150 F.3d 1011, 1026 (9th Cir.1998) (court should consider: "the strengths of the plaintiff's case; the risk, expense, complexity, and likely duration of further litigation; the risk of maintaining a class action status throughout the trial; the amount offered in settlement; the extent of discovery completed and the stage of the proceedings; the experience and views of counsel; . . . and the reaction of the class members to the proposed settlement").

108. *See, e.g., County of Suffolk v. Long Island Lighting Co.,* 266 F.3d 131, 135 (2d Cir. 2001) (notice provided to nearly one million class

automatically abuse of discretion, but is likely to enhance the chances that the trial court's decision will be overturned on appeal. Second, while the court must pass on the fairness of the proposal, it may not rewrite the settlement to make it conform to the court's view of a satisfactory settlement.[109] Third, the court's duty is primarily to the members of the class.[110] If persons have previously opted out of the class, the court has no power or duty to use the settlement process to address their interests.[111] Finally, the court's authority to certify a class created for purposes of settlement and to approve the proposed settlement is subject to a determination that the proposed class meets the requirements of Rule 23(a) and (b).[112]

Legislation Authorizing Judicial Review of Settlements Involving "Coupons"

Congress has authorized district courts, when reviewing proposed settlements of class actions that involve an award of coupons, on motion of a party, to obtain expert testimony on the issue of the actual value to class members of coupons that are redeemed.[113] Moreover, in such cases, the court must hold a hearing and determine, in a written finding, that the settlement is fair, reasonable, and adequate to class members.[114] Finally, the court has discretion to require that a settlement provide for distribution of some portion of the value of unredeemed coupons to charitable or governmental organizations, per an agreement by the parties.[115] However, such a distribution may not be included as part of the basis for calculating attorneys' fees.[116]

members; four hearings held in various places; audience numbered in hundreds; time for briefing was extended; class expert testified that settlement was fair; all expert testimony was subject to cross-examination); *Paradise v. Wells,* 686 F.Supp. 1442, 1444 (M.D.Ala.1988)(first place court should look is to views of class).

109. *Evans v. Jeff D.,* 475 U.S. 717, 726, 106 S.Ct. 1531, 1537, 89 L.Ed.2d 747 (1986)(under rule 23(e), court has authority to approve or reject settlement, but cannot impose a settlement on unwilling parties).

110. *See, e.g., In re Cendant Corp. Litigation,* 264 F.3d 286, 295 (3d Cir.2001) (district court has no duty to assess fairness of settlement to corporate opponent of class; such issues are more properly the subject of separate shareholder derivative litigation); *Tennessee Association of Health Maintenance Organizations, Inc. v. Grier,* 262 F.3d 559, 566 (6th Cir.2001) ("[U]nder Rule 23(e), non-class members have no standing to object to a lack of notice."). *But cf., Local No. 93, International Association of Firefighters,* 478 U.S. 501, 106 S.Ct. 3063, 92 L.Ed.2d 405 (1986) (intervenors are entitled to heard, but they have no right to a "quasi-trial" or to block the settlement by refusing to agree).

111. *See, e.g., In re Vitamins Antitrust Class Actions,* 215 F.3d 26 (D.C. Cir.2000) (non-parties "fall outside the zone of interests protected by Rule 23(e)").

112. *Amchem Products, Inc. v. Windsor,* 521 U.S. 591, 117 S.Ct. 2231, 138 L.Ed.2d 689 (1997). *See also Ortiz v. Fibreboard Corp.,* 527 U.S. 815, 119 S.Ct. 2295, 144 L.Ed.2d 715 (1999) (fairness hearing under Rule 23(e) cannot adequately substitute for failure of class certification movants to demonstrate that certification requirements of Rule 23(a) and (b) are met).

113. 28 U.S.C.A. § 1712(d).

114. 28 U.S.C.A. § 1712(e).

115. Id.

116. Id.

Protection against Loss by Class Members

In 28 U.S.C.A. § 1713, Congress provided the district court with authority to approve a proposed settlement involving a payment by members of the class to class counsel that would be a net loss to the class members. However, that authority is restricted to cases in which the court, by a written finding, concludes that nonmonetary benefits to the class "substantially" outweigh the monetary loss.[117] This provision of § 1713 is not restricted to cases involving "coupon" settlements, and appears to apply to class action settlements generally.

Protection against Geographic Discrimination

Congress has prohibited approval of a proposed settlement in which some members of the class receive greater amounts of value than others based "solely" on their closer geographic ties to the location of the court hearing the case.[118] This provision appears to apply not only to "coupon" settlements but to class action settlements generally.

Additional Opportunity to Opt Out of Class

As amended, Rule 23(e)(3) provides members of classes previously certified under Rule 23(b)(3) with an additional opportunity to opt out of the proposed settlement or voluntary dismissal. The notification obligations attendant on this opportunity will be the same as those required for initial certification of a Rule 23(b)(3) class under Rule 23(c)(2)(B). There are some restrictions on this new opportunity to opt out. First, it applies only to classes certified under Rule 23(b)(3). Second, only individual class members may exercise the option to opt out if they choose. No one has standing to attempt to opt out for other members of the class.[119]

Special Provisions for "Coupon" Settlements

Congress has enacted a number of provisions that are effective in class actions in which some or all members of the class will receive their award in the form of coupons. Section 1712(a) provides that when the attorney will receive a contingency fee based on the value of the coupons, the fee shall be based on the value to class members of the coupons that are actually redeemed.[120] The effect of this provision is to reduce at least somewhat any apparent disparities between the award of contingency fees to class counsel and the nominal value of coupons to class members.

Additionally, if a proposed settlement will provide the class with coupons, but the attorney's fee is not measured solely as a contingency award, § 1712(b) provides that the additional portion of the attorney's fee shall be based on the reasonable amount of time the lawyer expended on the case.[121]

117. 28 U.S.C.A. § 1713.

118. 28 U.S.C.A. § 1714.

119. *See* Rule 23(e)(3) advisory committee notes to 2003 amendments.

120. 28 U.S.C.A. § 1712(a).

121. 28 U.S.C.A. § 1712(b)(1).

The foregoing provisions are subject to review and approval by the court. They include authorization for an appropriate fee in cases involving equitable relief. Moreover, in making calculations as to the appropriate amount to be awarded as an attorney's fees, § 1712 expressly authorizes (but does not require) the use of a lodestar/multiplier method of determining fees.[122] This method of calculation is discussed at greater length on immediately preceding pages.

If the proposed settlement contains both coupons and equitable relief, § 1712(c) provides § 1712(a) shall govern the calculation of that portion of the attorney's fees applicable to the award of coupons and § 1712(b) shall govern the calculation of that portion of the attorney's fee attributable to considerations other than the award of coupons.[123]

Section 1712(d) provides the court with authority, upon motion of one of the parties, to obtain expert testimony on the issue of the actual value to class members of the coupons that are redeemed.[124] This provision appears to be relevant not only to calculation of an attorney's fee, but also to the value and appropriateness of the settlement to the class. Judicial review of the appropriateness of a settlement to the class is discussed elsewhere in the analysis of Rule 23 and related material.

Finally, § 1712(e) authorizes the court to require that a portion of the value of unclaimed coupons be distributed to charitable or governmental organizations, as the parties choose. Such a distribution, however, cannot be used to calculated attorneys' fees under § 1712.[125]

Objections to Settlement

Rule 23(e)(4) affords standing to any member of a class who wants to object to a proposed settlement or voluntary dismissal of a kind that requires judicial approval under Rule 23(e)(1)(A). Once such an objection has been made, it can be withdrawn only with the court's approval.[126]

NOTE: Limitations on the court's discretion notwithstanding, judicial control of settlements in class litigation is still profound.[127] To ensure that the court will approve settlements the parties reach, it is probably wise to invite the court to participate in settlement discussions whenever that is practical.

Legislative Expansion of Notice Requirements for Settlement

Congress has enacted a series of additional notice requirements for proposed settlements of class actions. First, within ten days of the filing of a proposed settlement with the district court, each defendant participating in the proposed settlement must serve notice of the proposed settlement, to include the following documents on both the appropriate

122. 28 U.S.C.A. § 1712(b)(2).

123. 28 U.S.C.A. § 1712(c).

124. 28 U.S.C.A. § 1712(d).

125. 28 U.S.C.A. § 1712(e).

126. *See* Rule 23(e)(4) advisory committee notes to 2003 amendments (also providing examples of circumstances in which approval of withdrawal of objection may be obtained).

127. *See, e.g., Kloster v. McColl,* 350 F.3d 747, 751 (8th Cir. 2003) (Rule 23(e) makes district court "fiduciary" and "guardian" of rights of passive members of class).

federal official and the appropriate state official in each state in which any class member resides: (1) the complaint, amended complaint (if any) and material filed with such pleadings (unless such documents are available electronically, in which case an appropriate explanation of access to the documents will suffice); (2) notice of any scheduled hearing in the case; (3) notice of any proposed or final notification to class members of their right to seek exclusion from the case or a statement that no such right exists, as well as a copy of the proposed settlement; (4) a copy of the final settlement; (5) a copy of any contemporaneous agreement reached between class counsel and defendants' counsel; (6) any final judgment or notice of dismissal; (7) if feasible, names of the class members residing in each state and an estimate of the proportion of the settlement likely to be distributed in each state, or if that information is not reasonable available, a reasonable estimate of such information; and (8) any written judicial opinions relating to items three through six.[128]

For purposes of this provision, the appropriate federal official is the Attorney General of the United States. The appropriate state official is that person with primary regulatory authority over the business in which the defendant engages. If there is no such person, the appropriate state official is the state attorney general. If the defendant is a federal or state depositary institution, a foreign bank, or a subsidiary of any such institution, the appropriate federal official is not the Attorney General, but the person who has primary federal regulatory authority over such an entity. The appropriate state official also becomes the corresponding state officials with similar regulatory authority when a defendant is a state financial institution.[129]

Presumably so that appropriate federal or state officials may participate in the settlement process, § 1715(d) provides that a final order approving a settlement may not issue until at least 90 days after the latest date of notification to federal or state officials required under § 1715(b).[130] If a class member is able to establish that the requirements of § 1715(b) were not met, the class member has the option to refuse to comply with the settlement agreement. No such option exists if the defendants have complied with § 1715(b).[131]

RULE 23(f). APPEALS

CORE CONCEPT

Rule 23(f) creates the possibility that a district court's decision granting or denying class certification could be appealed on an interlocutory basis. That is, the parties might not have to wait until the end of the litigation in the district court to learn whether the decision to certify (or not) would be upheld.

128. 28 U.S.C.A. § 1715(b).

129. 28 U.S.C.A. § 1715(a).

130. 28 U.S.C.A. § 1715(d).

131. 28 U.S.C.A. § 1715(e).

APPLICATIONS

Appellate Discretion

Rule 23(f) vests discretion in appellate courts to permit or deny an appeal granting or denying class certification, and circuit courts have begun to develop standards for determining whether to permit an appeal. Although their discretion is substantially uncurbed,[132] there seems to be general agreement that review under Rule 23(f) should not be a commonplace event.[133] Nevertheless, several situations arise where a circuit court is more likely than not to permit Rule 23(f) interlocutory appellate review of a class certification decision. These situations may sometimes be found together in the same case, but each by itself may justify review. First, if a denial of class certification would probably preclude any realistic chance that individual claims could be prosecuted and the district court's decision was questionable, circuits are inclined to grant review.[134] Second, if a district court's grant of class certification puts substantial pressure on a defendant to settle without regard to the merits of a case and the certification grant was questionable, review is appropriate.[135] Third, circuits generally agree that review is appropriate if it will help develop law regarding class actions.[136] For this last possibility to apply, some circuit courts do not require that there be evidence of some error by the district court,[137] but other courts have imposed additional caveats that the development of law must be both important to the instant litigation and class action law generally, as well as unlikely to be subject to review at the termination of the case in the district court.[138]

Another possibility for obtaining review under Rule 23(f) arises if a party can demonstrate that the district court's certification decision is

132. *See, e.g., Shin v. Cobb County Board of Education,* 248 F.3d 1061, 1063–65 (11th Cir. 2001) (discretion is "unfettered").

133. *See, e.g., In re Lorazepam & Clorazepate Antitrust Litigation,* 289 F.3d 98, 105 (D.C. Cir. 2002) ("As is true for all the circuits, we are of the view that Rule 23(f) review should be granted rarely where a case does not fall within one of these ... categories."); *Waste Management Holdings, Inc. v. Mowbray,* 208 F.3d 288, 294 (1st Cir.2000) (court will "exercise discretion judiciously").

134. *See, e.g., In re Sumitomo Copper Litigation,* 262 F.3d 134, 140 (2d Cir.2001) (review likely if certification denial is death knell for case, and certification decision was questionable); *Waste Management Holdings, Inc. v. Mowbray,* 208 F.3d 288, 293–94 (1st Cir.2000) (same); *Blair v. Equifax Check Services, Inc.,* 181 F.3d 832, 834 (7th Cir.1999) (same). *See also In re Lorazepam & Clorazepate Antitrust Litigation,* 289 F.3d 98, 105 (D.C. Cir.2002) (approving review that is death-knell situation for either plaintiff or defendant where the district court's decision is questionable).

135. *See, e.g., Tardiff v. Knox County,* 365 F.3d 1, 3 (1st Cir. 2004) ("One reason for review is a threat of liability so large as to place on the defendant an 'irresistible pressure to settle.' "); *In re Lorazepam & Clorazepate Antitrust Litigation,* 289 F.3d 98, 106 (D.C. Cir.2002); *In re Sumitomo Copper Litigation,* 262 F.3d 134 (2d Cir.2001); *Blair v. Equifax Check Services, Inc.,* 181 F.3d 832, 834 (7th Cir.1999).

136. *See, e.g., Carnegie v. Household International, Inc.,* 376 F.3d 656 (7th Cir. 2004) ("the more important the resolution of the issue is either to the particular litigation or to the general development of class action law," the greater is the likelihood that appeal will be heard).

137. *See, e.g., Blair v. Equifax Check Services, Inc.,* 181 F.3d 832, 835 (7th Cir. 1999).

138. *In re Lorazepam & Clorazepate Antitrust Litigation,* 289 F.3d 98, 105 (D.C. Cir. 2002); *In re Sumitomo Copper Litigation,* 262 F.3d 134 (2d Cir.2001) (same); *Waste Management Holdings, Inc. v. Mowbray,* 208 F.3d 288, 293–94 (1st Cir.2000) (same).

clear error. In that circumstance some circuits have held that review should normally occur without regard to whether other factors, such as those discussed immediately above, are present.[139]

Circuit courts that emphasize the appropriateness of appellate review in the circumstance of clear error have also adopted a slightly different characterization of the factors that other courts have used. Instead of identifying the three independent circumstances in which appellate review may be appropriate, these circuits have melded the factors together in a way that weighs all of them, plus one or two others. In such circuits Rule 23(f) petitions may be granted if consideration of these factors—taken together, not independently—justify review: (1) the "death knell" consideration, discussed above; (2) potential abuse of discretion by the district court in making its certification decision; (3) whether the appeal presents an unsettled legal question of general importance and importance in the instant litigation that might not be susceptible to review at a later point in the case; (4) the status of the case in the district court, including consideration of progress in discovery, other unresolved motions, and the passage of time since initiation of the case; and (5) the possibility that at some future time it will be clear that prompt review now was appropriate.[140] Courts that follow this approach weigh most heavily the presence of manifest error in the district court's decision. When such error is found it may be unnecessary for the appellate court to find that the other factors favor review before granting a Rule 23(f) petition.[141]

Yet another court has adopted the three independent factors discussed above, plus the additional independent ground for review when a decision is clearly erroneous.[142]

Time

By its terms, Rule 23(f) requires that any application for such an appeal be made to the circuit court within 10 days after the district court has entered its order granting or denying class certification.[143] It

139. *See, e.g., Prado–Steiman ex rel. Prado v. Bush,* 221 F.3d 1266, 1275 (11th Cir.2000) (clear error means review could be appropriate "even if none of the other factors supports granting the Rule 23(f) petition"). *See also Lienhart v. Dryvit Systems, Inc.,* 255 F.3d 138, 145–46 (4th Cir. 2001) (manifest error justifies review even where other factors are not met). *Cf., Carnegie v. Household International, Inc.,* 376 F.3d 656 (7th Cir. 2004) ("the more novel the issue presented by the appeal and so the less likely that the district court's resolution of it will stand . . . the stronger the case for allowing the appeal").

140. *See, e.g., Prado–Steiman v. Bush,* 221 F.3d 1266, 1274–75 n. 10 (11th Cir.2000). *See also Lienhart v. Dryvit Systems, Inc.,* 255 F.3d 138, 146 (4th Cir.2001) (same).

141. *Lienhart v. Dryvit Systems, Inc.,* 255 F.3d 138, 146 (4th Cir.2001); *Prado-Steiman v. Bush,* 221 F.3d 1266, 1275 (11th Cir.2000).

142. *Newton v. Merrill Lynch, Pierce, Fenner & Smith,* 259 F.3d 154, 165 (3d Cir.2001).

143. *Cf., Chevron U.S.A., Inc. v. School Board Vermilion Parish,* 294 F.3d 716 (5th Cir. 2002) (ten day time limit of Rule 23(f) is jurisdictional and may not be waived); *Gary v. Sheahan,* 188 F.3d 891, 892 (7th Cir.1999) (failure to seek appellate review within time limit of rule 23(f) means "appeal must wait until the final judgment"). *But see Shin v. Cobb County Board of Education,* 248 F.3d 1061, 1063–65 (11th Cir. 2001) (motion for reconsideration filed within 10 days of order granting or denying certification stays time for Rule 23(f) appeal until district court decides reconsideration motion; also, when time is calculated it excludes weekends and legal holidays, per Rule 6).

appears settled that the computation of time for Rule 23(f) is governed by Rule 6(a), which is discussed elsewhere in this text.[144]

Raising Other Issues

Rule 23(f) authorizes appeal of class certification only. In general, other issues will not be considered when the basis for appeal is Rule 23(f). One exception to that practice is standing, which appellate courts are willing to consider on an appeal under Rule 23(f).[145]

Relation to 28 U.S.C. § 1292

Section 1292(b) governs some of the circumstances in which a party may seek authorization for an interlocutory appeal from the decision of a district court. Section 1292(b) provides no fixed time limit for seeking such an appeal. However, it appears that when an interlocutory appeal might lie under Rule 23(f), neither district courts nor potential appellants should seek interlocutory relief under § 1292(b).[146]

Stay of District Court Proceedings

If the circuit court allows an appeal under Rule 23(f), the appeal does not automatically stay proceedings in the district court.[147] Instead,

144. *See, e.g., In re Veneman,* 309 F.3d 789, 793 (D.C. Cir.2002) (appellate courts have held unanimously that Rule 6(a) controls).

145. *See, e.g., Rivera v. Wyeth–Ayerst Laboratories,* 283 F.3d 315, 319 (5th Cir.2002) ("[S]tanding may–indeed must–be addressed even under the limits of a Rule 23(f) appeal."); *Bertulli v. Independent Association of Continental Pilots,* 242 F.3d 290, 294 (5th Cir.2001) (enunciating this general rule, but deciding that issues of standing are an exception and may be heard on a Rule 23(f) appeal); *Carter v. West Publishing Co.,* 225 F.3d 1258, 1262 (11th Cir. 2000) (under Rule 23(f) court may also evaluate standing, but not merits of case); *Prado-Steiman v. Bush,* 221 F.3d 1266, 1273 (11th Cir.2000) ("Rule 23(f) should not be a vehicle for courts of appeals to micro-manage complex class action litigation as it unfolds in the district court."). *But see McKowan Lowe & Co. v. Jasmine, Ltd.,* 295 F.3d 380 (3d Cir.2002), *cert. denied,* 537 U.S. 1088, 123 S.Ct. 691, 154 L.Ed.2d 631 (2002) (refusing to review dismissal of plaintiff's underlying claims when hearing Rule 23(f) appeal of denial of class certification; Rule 23(f) does not extend to any other type order, "even where that order has some impact on another portion of Rule 23"); *In re Lorazepam & Clorazepate Antitrust Litigation,* 289 F.3d 98, 107–08 (D.C. Cir 2002) (refusing to consider antitrust standing under Rule 23(f). "The fact that [defendant's] challenge would be dispositive of the class action is not unlike a variety of issues of law on the merits of a class action," but review of such issues "would inappropriately mix the issue of class certification with the merits of a case." However, acknowledging authority for evaluating constitutional standing under Rule 23(f); but distinguishing such cases because such standing goes to court's jurisdiction, while antitrust standing does not). *See also Samuel-Bassett v. Kia Motors America, Inc.,* 357 F.3d 392, 395 (3d Cir. 2004) (circuit court hearing Rule 23(f) issue has obligation to examine subject matter jurisdiction); *Lienhart v. Dryvit Systems, Inc.,* 255 F.3d 138, 143 n. 2 (4th Cir.2001) (acknowledging that "on occasion" merits may be examined when appellate court decides whether to permit early appeal of certification issue pursuant to Rule 23(f)).

146. *Richardson Electronics, Ltd. v. Panache Broadcasting of Pennsylvania, Inc.,* 202 F.3d 957, 959 (7th Cir.2000) (When issue "is an arguable candidate for a rule 23(f) appeal, the appellants may not use § 1292(b) to circumvent the 10–day limitation in Rule 23(f). . . .Should a case arise in which a class-certification order is appealable under [§] 1292(b) but not under [Rule] 23(f), perhaps because it presents an issue that while it satisfies the criteria of the statute does not involve the merits of class certification, the appellant can protect himself by seeking the district judge's permission to take a [§] 1292(b) appeal at the same time that the appellant asks us to entertain his appeal under [Rule] 23(f).").

147. *See, e.g., Prado–Steiman v. Bush,* 221 F.3d 1266, 1273 n. 8 (11th Cir.2000) ("Rule 23(f) contemplates that in most cases discovery (at the very least, merits discovery) will continue not-

a party seeking such a stay must apply to either the district court or the court of appeals.

RULE 23(g). CLASS COUNSEL

CORE CONCEPT

Rule 23(g) is an amendment to Rule 23, effective in late 2003. It governs the manner in which a court will supervise the appointment of counsel to represent the class. Previously there was no precise counterpart to Rule 23(g), but courts had previously used authority derived from Rule 23(a)(4) to develop substantial precedent guiding decisions courts had to make in this area. Additionally, the precepts adopted for class litigation in the area of securities law,[148] themselves heavily borrowed from case law, will also undoubtedly provide guidance to federal courts as they attempt to flesh out the requirements of new Rule 23(g).

APPLICATIONS

Relationship of Rule 23(a)(4) to Rule 23(g)

Until the addition of Rule 23(g), courts had routinely employed Rule 23(a)(4) (governing evaluation of whether class representatives would adequately protect class interests) to examine the adequacy of class counsel.[149] The standards developed by that case law[150] have been incorporated almost in their entirety into new Rule 23(g), giving courts broad discretion to inquire and evaluate the appropriateness of permitting any particular lawyers' representation of the class.

Reverse Auctions

Historically, courts have discouraged reverse auctions–"the practice whereby the defendant in a series of class actions picks the most ineffectual class lawyers to negotiate a settlement with in the hope that the district court will approve a weak settlement that will preclude other claims against the defendant." [151] Rule 23(g)(1)(C)(iii) and

withstanding the pendency of an appeal of the class certification order.").

148. 15 U.S.C.A. § 78u–4(a)(3)(B).

149. *Amchem Products, Inc. v. Windsor,* 521 U.S. 591, 626 n. 20, 117 S.Ct. 2231, 2251 n. 20, 138 L.Ed.2d 689 (1997) ("The adequacy heading also factors in competency and conflicts of class counsel."). *See, e.g., Greisz v. Household Bank, N.A.,* 176 F.3d 1012, 1013 (7th Cir. 1999) (Rule 23(a)(4) requires assessment of competence of counsel for class).

150. *See, e.g., Fymbo v. State Farm Fire and Casualty Co.,* 213 F.3d 1320, 1320–21 (10th Cir. 2000) (rule 23(a)(4) prevents non-attorney from serving as pro se class representative; plaintiff's pleadings were also evidence of lack of competence); *Hanlon v. Chrysler Corp.,* 150 F.3d 1011, 1021 (9th Cir. 1998) (Rule 23(a)(4) requires evaluation of counsel's ability; also, in settlement class, court must also examine "rationale for not pursuing further litigation"); *In re Fine Paper Antitrust Litigation,* 617 F.2d 22, 27 (3d Cir. 1980) (trial judge has "constant duty" to monitor "professional competency and behavior of class counsel").

151. *Reynolds v. Beneficial National Bank,* 288 F.3d 277, 282 (7th Cir. 2002). *See also In re Cendant Corp. Litigation,* 264 F.3d 201 (3d Cir. 2001), *cert. denied,* 535 U.S. 929, 122 S.Ct. 1300, 152 L.Ed.2d 212 (2002) (disapproving choice of lead counsel by reverse auction in case controlled by Private Securities Litigation Reform Act).

(g)(2)(C) now provide the court with express authority to examine and propose appropriate terms for compensation and to include those requirements as part of the order appointing class counsel. The result should be to control attorneys' fees and costs while ensuring that the class opponent is not in a position to choose, unilaterally, the lawyers who will cost the least and who may not do the best work. These portions of Rule 23(g) harmonize closely with Rule 23(h), governing awards of attorney fees. Rule 23(h) is discussed immediately below.

RULE 23(h). ATTORNEY FEES AWARD

CORE CONCEPT

Rule 23(h) governs the award of attorneys' fees in class actions. Heretofore this issue was controlled by case law as well as statutes applicable to particular kinds of class actions, such as the Private Securities Litigation Reform Act of 1995.[152] New Rule 23(h) establishes no substantive standards for determining the appropriateness of a particular fee award. Instead, it establishes a procedure by which a fee application may be made and objections to that application may be heard.

APPLICATIONS

Existing Case Law

Outside of the area of class actions, the general American approach to attorney's fees is to require each party to bear its own burden. However, class actions present a special problem, because the nature of such litigation is that the work of attorneys may enrich an entire group of people. In such a situation it would be unfair to require that the attorneys be compensated, if at all, only by those few individuals who began the litigation.[153] New Rule 23(h) recognizes that principle by permitting attorneys to petition for fees that are taxable, in appropriate cases, against the entire class.

The basis and source of such fees has depended partly on the nature of the cause of action and the judgment or settlement obtained. For example, fees might have been available from the defendant when authorized under an applicable statute.[154] When such a statute was not applicable (and usually even when it was), the district court had substantial authority to determine the method of calculating fees and the amount that would be awarded. Rule 23(h), in essence, codifies that existing practice. Thus, it is likely that for at least the near future courts will rely on precedent developed prior to enactment of Rule 24(h) to determine the appropriateness of a fee award in a particular case.

152. 15 U.S.C.A. § 78u–4(a)(6).

153. *See, e.g, Savoie v. Merchants Bank,* 166 F.3d 456, 460 (2d Cir. 1999) ("A party whose initiative confers a benefit upon a class of people is entitled to recover its costs–including attorneys' fees–from the common fund."). *See also In re Synthroid Marketing Litigation,* 264 F.3d 712, 717 (7th Cir. 2001) ("Unless a class contracts privately over attorneys' fees, lawyers in class-fund cases must petition the court for their compensation.").

154. *See, e.g.,* 42 U.S.C.A. § 1988 (governing attorneys' fees in civil rights litigation).

Methods of Calculation

Measurement of the appropriate amount of a few has usually been determined through one of two methods. If a fund was available, courts have awarded the lawyers a percentage of the money available.[155] In circumstances where the court believed another approach was appropriate or where no fund was available, *e.g.*, where the class sought injunctive relief, courts typically measured the appropriate fee through a "lodestar" approach.[156] In the context of a class action, this calculation begins by determining appropriate hourly rates for individual lawyers, which are then multiplied by the number of hours actually and reasonably expended on the project. Finally, factors such as difficulty of the case, quality of legal work, risk of failure, etc., may be used in some cases to modify the result (up or down) reached by the simple multiplication of hours and rates.[157] It should be noted that while the lodestar method has been available in many class actions, the use of so-called "risk multipliers," *e.g.*, difficulty of the case, etc., has *not* been available in class actions where a fee is imposed based on a fee shifting statute. In such cases it appears that district courts have made their lodestar calculation based only on the reasonable hourly rate multiplied by the reasonable number of hours devoted to the case.[158]

Motion Required

Rule 23(h) requires that an application for attorneys' fees must be made by motion, subject to Rule 54(d) (governing taxation of costs).

155. *Blum v. Stenson,* 465 U.S. 886, 900 n. 16, 104 S.Ct. 1541, 1550 n. 16, 79 L.Ed.2d 891 (1984) (approving calculation based on percentage of fund). *See, e.g., Hanlon v. Chrysler Corp.,* 150 F.3d 1011, 1029 (9th Cir. 1998) (approving approximately 4.5% of very large fund as appropriate compensation).

156. 28 U.S.C.A. § 1712(b)(2) (expressly authorizing, but not mandating, use of lodestar method to calculate attorney's fee). *See, e.g., In re Synthroid Marketing Litigation,* 264 F.3d 712, 718 (7th Cir. 2001) ("We have held repeatedly that, when deciding on appropriate fee levels in common-fund cases, courts must do their best to award counsel the market price for legal services, in light of the risk of nonpayment and the normal rate of compensation in the market at the time."); *In re Cendant Corp. PRIDES Litigation,* 243 F.3d 722, 732 (3d Cir.), *cert. denied,* 534 U.S. 889, 122 S.Ct. 202, 151 L.Ed.2d 143 (2001) (lodestar applicable when anticipated relief is too small to justify use of percentage-of-recovery method but case still has potential social benefit). *Compare, e.g., Savoie v. Merchants Bank,* 166 F.3d 456, 460 (2d Cir. 1999) (suggesting that Second Circuit will use only lodestar method to determine compensation, even in cases involving common fund) *with Goldberger v. Integrated Resources, Inc.,* 209 F.3d 43, 50 (2d Cir. 2000) (acknowledging that lodestar method is approved, but is not "exclusive methodology in common fund cases").

157. *See, e.g., Gunter v. Ridgewood Corp.,* 223 F.3d 190, 195 n. 1 (3d Cir. 2000) (factors to consider "include: (1) the size of the fund created and the number of persons benefited; (2) the presence or absence of substantial objection by members of the class to the settlement terms and/or fees requested by counsel; (3) the skill and efficiency of the attorneys involved; (4) the complexity and duration of the litigation; (5) the risk of nonpayment; (6) the amount of time devoted to the case by plaintiff's counsel; and (7) the awards in similar cases"); *Goldberger v. Integrated Resources, Inc.,* 209 F.3d 43, 53 (2d Cir. 2000) (lodestar case: "[o]f course contingency risk and quality of representation must be considered in settling a reasonable fee").

158. *City of Burlington v. Dague,* 505 U.S. 557, 565–66, 112 S.Ct. 2638, 2642–43, 120 L.Ed.2d 449 (1992) (rejecting use of risk multipliers in cases using lodestar method to calculate attorneys' fees under federal fee-shifting statutes).

Notice

Rule 23(h) requires that the motion for fees must be served on all parties. If the motion is made by class counsel, as it typically will be, it must also "be directed to class members in a reasonable manner."

Objections, Hearing and Findings

Rule 23(h) provides that both class members and the party who may have to pay the fees have standing to object to the motion. The court has discretion–not an obligation–to hold a hearing on the motion. The court must make findings of fact and conclusions of law in a manner consistent with the requirements of Rule 52(a) (governing the court's duty in such matters when issues are tried to the court).

Special Masters and Magistrate Judges

Rule 23(h) permits the district court to refer matters relating to fees to special masters or magistrate judges.

Special Provisions for "Coupon" Settlements

Congress has enacted a number of provisions that are effective in class actions in which some or all members of the class will receive their award in the form of coupons. Section 1712(a) provides that when the attorney will receive a contingency fee based on the value of the coupons, the fee shall be based on the value to class members of the coupons that are actually redeemed.[159] The effect of this provision is to reduce at least somewhat any apparent disparities between the award of contingency fees to class counsel and the nominal value of coupons to class members.

Additionally, if a proposed settlement will provide the class with coupons, but the attorney's fee is not measured solely as a contingency award, § 1712(b) provides that the additional portion of the attorney's fee shall be based on the reasonable amount of time the lawyer expended on the case.[160]

The foregoing provisions are subject to review and approval by the court. They include authorization for an appropriate fee in cases involving equitable relief. Moreover, in making calculations as to the appropriate amount to be awarded as an attorney's fees, § 1712 expressly authorizes (but does not require) the use of a lodestar/multiplier method of determining fees.[161] This method of calculation is discussed at greater length on immediately preceding pages.

If the proposed settlement contains both coupons and equitable relief, § 1712(c) provides § 1712(a) shall govern the calculation of that portion of the attorney's fees applicable to the award of coupons and § 1712(b) shall govern the calculation of that portion of the attorney's fee attributable to considerations other than the award of coupons.[162]

159. 28 U.S.C.A. § 1712(a).

160. 28 U.S.C.A. § 1712(b)(1).

161. 28 U.S.C.A. § 1712(b)(2).

162. 28 U.S.C.A. § 1712(c).

Section 1712(d) provides the court with authority, upon motion of one of the parties, to obtain expert testimony on the issue of the actual value to class members of the coupons that are redeemed.[163] This provision appears to be relevant not only to calculation of an attorney's fee, but also to the value and appropriateness of the settlement to the class. Judicial review of the appropriateness of a settlement to the class is discussed elsewhere in the analysis of Rule 23 and related material.

Finally, § 1712(e) authorizes the court to require that a portion of the value of unclaimed coupons be distributed to charitable or governmental organizations, as the parties choose. Such a distribution, however, cannot be used to calculated attorneys' fees under § 1712.[164]

Protection against Loss by Class Members

In 28 U.S.C.A. § 1713, Congress provided the district court with authority to approve a proposed settlement involving a payment by members of the class to class counsel that would be a net loss to the class members. However, that authority is restricted to cases in which the court, by a written finding, concludes that nonmonetary benefits to the class "substantially" outweigh the monetary loss.[165] This provision of § 1713 is not restricted to cases involving "coupon" settlements, and appears to apply to class action settlements generally.

Reverse Auctions

Historically, courts have discouraged reverse auctions–"the practice whereby the defendant in a series of class actions picks the most ineffectual class lawyers to negotiate a settlement with in the hope that the district court will approve a weak settlement that will preclude other claims against the defendant." [166] Provisions of new Rule 23(g) that permit the court to consider the impact of attorneys' fees even at an early stage of the case when the court is considering appointment of class counsel are likely to further dampen enthusiasm for reverse auctions. In this area the provisions of Rule 23(h), giving the court final approval of attorneys' fees, complement the provisions of Rule 23(g) that authorize the court to restrict fees as a condition of appointment of counsel. Rule 23(g) is discussed in greater detail above.

ADDITIONAL RESEARCH REFERENCES

Wright & Miller, *Federal Practice and Procedure* §§ 1751–1805.

C.J.S. Federal Civil Procedure §§ 63–92, 170.

West's Key No. Digests, Federal Civil Procedure ⚷161–189.

163. 28 U.S.C.A. § 1712(d).

164. 28 U.S.C.A. § 1712(e).

165. 28 U.S.C.A. § 1713.

166. *Reynolds v. Beneficial National Bank,* 288 F.3d 277, 282 (7th Cir. 2002). *See also In re Cendant Corp. Litigation,* 264 F.3d 201 (3d Cir. 2001), *cert. denied,* 535 U.S. 929, 122 S.Ct. 1300, 152 L.Ed.2d 212 (2002) (disapproving choice of lead counsel by reverse auction in case controlled by Private Securities Litigation Reform Act).

RULE 23.1

DERIVATIVE ACTIONS BY SHAREHOLDERS

In a derivative action brought by one or more shareholders or members to enforce a right of a corporation or of an unincorporated association, the corporation or association having failed to enforce a right which may properly be asserted by it, the complaint shall be verified and shall allege (1) that the plaintiff was a shareholder or member at the time of the transaction of which the plaintiff complains or that the plaintiff's share or membership thereafter devolved on the plaintiff by operation of law, and (2) that the action is not a collusive one to confer jurisdiction on a court of the United States which it would not otherwise have. The complaint shall also allege with particularity the efforts, if any, made by the plaintiff to obtain the action the plaintiff desires from the directors or comparable authority and, if necessary, from the shareholders or members, and the reasons for the plaintiff's failure to obtain the action or for not making the effort. The derivative action may not be maintained if it appears that the plaintiff does not fairly and adequately represent the interests of the shareholders or members similarly situated in enforcing the right of the corporation or association. The action shall not be dismissed or compromised without the approval of the court, and notice of the proposed dismissal or compromise shall be given to shareholders or members in such manner as the court directs.

[Added effective July 1, 1966; amended effective August 1, 1987.]

AUTHORS' COMMENTARY ON RULE 23.1

PURPOSE AND SCOPE

In a shareholder derivative suit, a shareholder sues on behalf of a corporation and/or its shareholders by alleging that the officers and directors who control the corporation will not institute the suit. In fact, often the officers and directors are themselves defendants in the derivative suit. The utility of shareholder derivative suits is balanced by the risk that this type of litigation can be used to harass corporate officers and directors into settlements favorable to the plaintiffs, at the expense of degrading corporate assets that are the common property of all shareholders. Through a series of procedural requirements not normally imposed on other kinds of litigation, Rule 23.1 attempts to preserve the social value of derivative suits, while reducing the risk of inappropriate harassment. Some of these requirements bear substantial similarity to elements of Rule 23, governing class actions.

APPLICATIONS

Applicability

For the requirements of Rule 23.1 to apply to a case, a plaintiff must be a "shareholder" or "member" seeking to enforce a right of a corporation or unincorporated association. Other types of derivative claims need not meet the standards of Rule 23.1.[1]

Subject Matter Jurisdiction

If the cause of action is based exclusively on state law, the requirements of diversity jurisdiction must be satisfied. Diversity jurisdiction and other kinds of subject matter jurisdiction are discussed at §§ 2.10–2.13. Because the corporation is normally treated as an indispensable party needed for just adjudication, alignment of the corporate entity as a plaintiff or defendant can have significant consequences for jurisdiction. Although there is no absolute rule governing this issue, it is likely that the court will not align the corporation in a way that defeats diversity jurisdiction. The courts still retain discretion in this area, however, and have on occasion aligned the corporation in a way that defeats diversity.[2]

Personal Jurisdiction

Personal jurisdiction over defendants who are natural persons is obtained in derivative suits in the same manner as in other litigation. For corporations aligned as defendants, however, Congress has enacted a special service of process provision. 28 U.S.C.A. § 1695 allows plaintiffs in shareholder derivative suits to serve process on such corporate defendants "in any district where [they are] organized or licensed to do business or . . . doing business."

Venue

A special statute for derivative suits, 28 U.S.C.A. § 1401, provides that the plaintiff may sue in any judicial district where the corporation might have sued the same defendants. As a practical matter, this means § 1401 should be read in conjunction with § 1391(a) and (b),

1. *Daily Income Fund, Inc. v. Fox,* 464 U.S. 523, 528, 104 S.Ct. 831, 834, 78 L.Ed.2d 645 (1984)(Rule 23.1 applies only when "a shareholder claims a right that could have been, but was not, 'asserted' by the corporation."); *see also, Kayes v. Pacific Lumber Co.,* 51 F.3d 1449, 1462–63 (9th Cir.1995), *cert. denied,* 516 U.S. 914, 116 S.Ct. 301, 133 L.Ed.2d 206 (1995). (Rule 23.1 applies narrowly; it is not applicable to "plan beneficiaries" seeking "to enforce the right of the plan against its fiduciaries").

2. *See, e.g., Liddy v. Urbanek,* 707 F.2d 1222, 1224 (11th Cir.1983)([F]inal alignment of the parties should reflect the actual antagonisms between the plaintiffs, the corporation, and the directors; held, corporation should be joined where appropriate, even when joinder will destroy diversity); *Frank v. Hadesman and Frank, Inc.,* 83 F.3d 158 (7th Cir.1996)(in derivative suit, corporation is aligned as plaintiff if shareholders have suffered harm in common; citing state law; dismissing because corporation is not diverse from defendant).

governing the venue requirements for diversity suits and many claims based on federal questions.

Verification of Complaint

Complaints that initiate shareholders' derivative actions must be sworn to and notarized. This is a departure from the general practice in federal civil procedure, which usually imposes no federal requirement for verification of a complaint. The practical impact of a verification requirement in derivative suits may be limited, however, because it is not applied in a way that prohibits a layperson from relying on competent information in bringing a derivative suit.[3] Thus, any shareholder who has undertaken a reasonable investigation, in person or through the advice of qualified persons, of the allegations in the complaint, should be able to satisfy the verification requirement without undue difficulty.[4]

Standing: Continuous Ownership Requirement

Under Rule 23.1(1), the complaint must state that the derivative suit is initiated on behalf of a person who: (1) was a shareholder at the time the cause of action arose, or who became a shareholder by operation of law from someone who had been a shareholder at that time; and (2) who remained a shareholder at the time the suit was filed.[5] If the plaintiff is divested of ownership while the suit is pending, the suit will usually be dismissed.[6] In diversity suits, these standing requirements of rule 23.1 will apparently apply even if state law might be less strict. The matter is not entirely free from doubt, however, and attorneys should consult the local practice.[7]

Collusive Attempts to Invoke Federal Jurisdiction

Rule 23.1(2) requires that the plaintiff swear that a shareholder derivative suit based on diversity jurisdiction was not brought to

3. *Surowitz v. Hilton Hotels Corp.,* 383 U.S. 363, 86 S.Ct. 845, 15 L.Ed.2d 807 (1966).

4. *See, e.g., Lewis v. Curtis*, 671 F.2d 779, 788 (3d Cir.1982), *cert. denied,* 459 U.S. 880, 103 S.Ct. 176, 74 L.Ed.2d 144 (1982)(reliance on Wall Street Journal article satisfies requirement).

5. *See, e.g., In re Bank of New York Derivative Litigation,* 320 F.3d 291, 298 (2d Cir.2003) (requiring plaintiff to own stock "*throughout* the course of the activities that constitute the *primary basis* of the complaint;" rejecting use of continuing wrong doctrine to expand definition of transaction; holding that plaintiff need not have owned stock during "the entire course of all relevants," but plaintiff must have owned stock "before the case of the allegedly wrongful conduct transpired"); *Rosenbaum v. MacAllister,* 64 F.3d 1439, 1443 n. 2 (10th Cir.1995) (explaining requirements of contemporaneous ownership and continuing ownership; also identifying one exception to those requirements).

6. *See, e.g., Johnson v. United States,* 317 F.3d 1331, 1333–34 (Fed. Cir.2003) (plaintiff who loses shareholder status through bankruptcy proceeding while instant lawsuit was pending loses standing upon cancellation of shares); *Schilling v. Belcher,* 582 F.2d 995, 999 (5th Cir.1978) ("It is generally held that the ownership requirement continues throughout the life of the suit and that the action will abate if the plaintiff ceases to be a shareholder before the litigation ends.").

7. *See, e.g., Kona Enterprises, Inc. v. Estate of Bishop,* 179 F.3d 767, 769 (9th Cir.1999) (holding that standing requirement of Rule 23.1 "is procedural in nature and thus applicable in diversity actions"). *But cf., Batchelder v. Kawamoto,* 147 F.3d 915, 917–18 (9th Cir.1998), *cert. denied,* 525 U.S. 982, 119 S.Ct. 446, 142 L.Ed.2d 400 (1998) (where choice of law clause provided that Japanese law governed rights of interest holders, neither Rule 23.1 nor state law applied).

manufacture federal court jurisdiction on behalf of the corporation. This issue could arise only if the corporation had the same citizenship as the defendants.

Pleading With Particularity

Rule 23.1 requires that certain allegations of the shareholder derivative complaint be pleaded with particularity. This means that the plaintiff must provide additional factual detail that is not normally required under the "notice pleading" policy of the Federal Rules. The requirement of particularity is usually satisfied without difficulty by plaintiffs who simply explain the facts behind their conclusory allegation.[8]

Explanation of Efforts to Encourage Corporation to Protect Its Own Interest

Rule 23.1 requires that a plaintiff allege in the complaint, "with particularity," the following facts: (1) the efforts plaintiff made, if any, to encourage those who control the corporation—shareholders, officers and/or directors—to take action; and (2) the reasons why the efforts were unsuccessful, or reasons why no effort was made.[9]

Demand: Futility

Rule 23.1 requires the plaintiff to make a demand on the corporate officers to pursue the suit. The facts of this demand must be pleaded with particularity.[10]

The requirement that the plaintiff demand that the corporation bring the lawsuit may be waived, however, if it is clear from the facts of a case that such a demand would be clearly futile. Rule 23.1 requires the plaintiff to plead with particularity the facts establishing futility, but the standard by which the facts are evaluated is a matter of state law.[11]

8. *See, e.g., In re Abbott Laboratories Derivative Shareholders Litigation,* 325 F.3d 795, 804 (7th Cir.2003) (holding requirement satisfied when "[a]lthough plaintiffs have a conclusory paragraph in their claim of demand futility, they have also incorporated all of the detailed factual allegations"); *Stepak v. Addison*, 20 F.3d 398, 400 (11th Cir.1994)(mere allegation that law firm was "conflicted" did not satisfy requirement of particularity in Rule 23.1; but allegations that law firm defended corporate officers in criminal matters related to plaintiff's demand, and then gave advice to board about demand, satisfied requirement).

9. *Id.* at 402 (Rule 23.1 imposes "more stringent pleading requirements" than Rules 8 and 12(b)(6)). *See, e.g., Frank v. Hadesman and Frank, Inc.,* 83 F.3d 158 (7th Cir.1996) (noting plaintiff's duty to make demand on corporate board to pursue claim).

10. *See, e.g., In re Abbott Laboratories Derivative Shareholders Litigation,* 325 F.3d 795, 804 (7th Cir.2003) (holding requirement satisfied when "[a]lthough plaintiffs have a conclusory paragraph in their claim of demand futility, they have also incorporated all of the detailed factual allegations"); *Starrels v. First National Bank of Chicago,* 870 F.2d 1168, 1171 (7th Cir. 1989)(conclusory allegations adequate for standard notice pleading may not meet particularity requirements of Rule 23.1).

11. *Kamen v. Kemper Financial Services, Inc.*, 500 U.S. 90, 111 S.Ct. 1711, 114 L.Ed.2d 152 (1991)(Rule 23.1 controls adequacy of pleadings. State law controls substantive standard). *See, e.g., McCall v. Scott,* 239 F.3d 808, 816 (6th Cir.2001) (demand may be excused "because either the directors were incapable of making an impartial decision, or the directors wrongfully refused a demand to sue"). *See also, Boland v.*

Special Litigation Committees

When officers of a business entity are faced with a Rule 23.1 demand to pursue a lawsuit, a typical response has been to appoint a special litigation committee to investigate the matter. In that circumstance courts will usually grant a request to stay proceedings in the derivative action until the committee can make a report recommending a course of action, *e.g.*, terminate the litigation, take it over, or authorize the original plaintiff to continue it. The court has authority to accept or reject the recommendation.[12]

Adequacy of Representation

The plaintiff in a shareholder derivative suit must be a person who will adequately represent the best interests of those—the corporation and other shareholders—on whose behalf the suit is prosecuted.[13] Perhaps because Rule 23.1 derivative suits present fewer of the case management problems associated with Rule 23 class actions, the courts seem less concerned in derivative suits with the quality and experience of the plaintiff's counsel.

Settlement Subject to Court Approval

Derivative suits may not be dismissed or settled without prior judicial approval. The district court enjoys broad, but not totally unfettered, discretion to evaluate a proposed settlement.[14] In determining whether to approve a settlement, the court may consider the reaction of persons, such as other shareholders, who will be affected by the outcome of the case.[15] In theory, the court should not re-write a proposed settlement, but should limit itself to approving or disapproving the proposal.[16] In practice, courts have substantial ability to influence the contents of a settlement by indicating what the court deems a satisfactory compromise.

Engle, 113 F.3d 706 (7th Cir.1997) (state law determines whether demand would be futile, but Rule 23.1 requires plaintiff to provide court with information sufficient to determine whether demand is futile).

12. *See, e.g., Strougo v. Padegs,* 986 F.Supp. 812, 814 (S.D.N.Y.1997) (explaining process and noting courts' awareness of special litigation committee's potential bias toward protecting corporate board and officers).

13. *But see Powers v. Eichen,* 229 F.3d 1249, 1254 (9th Cir.2000) (concluding that Rule 23.1 does not offer as much protection as Rule 23; "Unlike ... Rule 23, in shareholder derivative suits under Rule 23.1, a preliminary affirmative determination that the named plaintiffs will fairly and adequately represent the interests of the other class members is not a prerequisite to the maintenance of the action. Rather, the rule provides only that the derivative suit may not be maintained if it appears that the named shareholder does not fairly and adequately represent the other shareholders. ... In addition, there is no opt-out provision in shareholder derivative suits. Thus, all shareholders are bound by the outcome regardless of their objections."[internal quotation marks omitted]).

14. *See, e.g., McDannold v. Star Bank, N.A.,* 261 F.3d 478, 488 (6th Cir.2001) (district court "enjoys wide discretion in evaluating the settlement of derivative actions").

15. *See, e.g., Bell Atlantic Corp. v. Bolger,* 2 F.3d 1304 (3d Cir.1993)("We also consider the response of other shareholders to the lawsuit.").

16. *See, e.g., United Founders Life Insurance Co. v. Consumers National Life Insurance Co.,* 447 F.2d 647, 655 (7th Cir.1971)("The business judgment of the court is not to be substituted for that of the parties.").

Notice of Settlement

Rule 23.1 requires that the court will order notice of voluntary dismissals or proposed settlements to interested persons. The court has substantial discretion, within the circumstances of the particular case, to determine the manner in which notification will occur.[17]

Bond Requirements

Many states require that plaintiffs in derivative suits post bonds, from which the defendants will be compensated for litigation expenses if the defendants prevail. Rule 23.1 contains no such requirement. In diversity suits, however, it is settled that federal courts will enforce requirements established under state law.[18]

Numerosity Requirements

Rule 23.1 does not require that the plaintiff represent any number of similarly situated persons. Thus it will often be to the advantage of a shareholder who is one among a small group of similarly situated people to file a derivative action, rather than try to file a class action, which requires a greater number of plaintiffs.

ADDITIONAL RESEARCH REFERENCES

Wright & Miller, *Federal Practice and Procedure* §§ 1821–41.

C.J.S. Corporations §§ 397–413; Federal Civil Procedure §§ 84–91, 139, 149, 298.

West's Key No. Digests, Corporations ⚷202–214.

17. *See, e.g., Kyriazi v. Western Electric Co.*, 647 F.2d 388, 395 (3d Cir.1981)(manner of notification within court's discretion, provided notice satisfies dues process).

18. *Cohen v. Beneficial Industrial Loan Corp.*, 337 U.S. 541, 69 S.Ct. 1221, 93 L.Ed. 1528 (1949)(state bond requirement applicable to diversity suit).

RULE 23.2

ACTIONS RELATING TO UNINCORPORATED ASSOCIATIONS

An action brought by or against the members of an unincorporated association as a class by naming certain members as representative parties may be maintained only if it appears that the representative parties will fairly and adequately protect the interests of the association and its members. In the conduct of the action the court may make appropriate orders corresponding with those described in Rule 23(d), and the procedure for dismissal or compromise of the action shall correspond with that provided in Rule 23(e).

[Added effective July 1, 1966.]

AUTHORS' COMMENTARY ON RULE 23.2

PURPOSE AND SCOPE

Rule 23.2 extends some of the procedural protections of class actions under Rule 23 and shareholder derivative suits under Rule 23.1 to members of unincorporated associations who are sued through representatives, or on whose behalf representatives have initiated suit. The three rules all address situations where persons will be affected by the outcome of suits without necessarily having an opportunity to participate fully in litigation. Rule 23.2 is devoted to ensuring that representatives of the unincorporated association's membership adequately represent the interest of the entire membership.

NOTE: Rule 23.2 does not *create* a right for representatives of an unincorporated association to sue or be sued. Rather, it governs such a suit when the applicable state or federal law provides a cause of action by or against the unincorporated association, but does not permit suit by or against the association as an entity.[1]

APPLICATIONS

Fair and Adequate Representation

The court's first concern is to ascertain whether the interests of the unincorporated association's representatives conflict with those of the

1. *See, e.g., Northbrook Excess and Surplus Insurance Co. v. Medical Malpractice Joint Underwriting Ass'n of Massachusetts,* 900 F.2d 476, 477 (1st Cir.1990)("Rule 23.2 provides a mechanism by which an association may sue or be sued through a representative where state law prevents the association from doing so in its own name."). *Cf., Benn v. Seventh–Day Adventist Church,* 304 F.Supp.2d 716, 723 (D. Md. 2004) (most courts hold that where state law permits suit by unincorporated association as an entity, "Rule 23.2 is unavailable.").

association or its membership. However, the case law is divided as to whether an association's representatives in a Rule 23.2 case must meet the standards developed for adequate class representation in Rule 23(a), governing class actions.[2]

Orders Regulating Proceedings

Rule 23.2 explicitly incorporates Rule 23(d), governing the court's power to issue orders in the course of class action litigation. Because the court's authority under Rule 23(d) is broad, the effect of this incorporation is to give the trial court greater discretion to issue orders ensuring both the efficient processing of the case and substantial protection for passive members of the unincorporated association. Elements of Rule 23(d) should therefore also be consulted in the course of applying Rule 23.2.

Approval of Settlement

Rule 23.2 also explicitly incorporates Rule 23(e), which provides a court substantial authority to approve or disapprove settlements in class actions. As a practical matter, the effect is to require not only consultation of Rule 23(e), but also strong consideration of the possibility of inviting the trial judge to participate in settlement discussions whenever the discussions have advanced sufficiently to make participation practicable.

Numerosity

Rule 23.2 contains no requirement that the membership of the unincorporated association rise above some minimum number.[3] Nevertheless, counsel should investigate local precedent before proceeding with a Rule 23.2 action.

Citizenship for Diversity Jurisdiction

Where an unincorporated association may sue or be sued through representatives, the established practice is to determine diversity by examining the citizenship of the representatives.[4] Thus, an unincorporated association often can create diversity jurisdiction by selecting a representative who is a citizen of a different state from the defendants (provided that the amount in controversy exceeds $75,000, exclusive of interest and costs).

2. *Compare Gravenstein v. Campion,* 96 F.R.D. 137, 140 (D.Alaska 1982)(Rule 23 requirements applied to Rule 23.2 lawsuit) *with* [*Curley v. Brignoli, Curley & Roberts Associates,* 915 F.2d 81, 86 (2d Cir.1990), *cert. denied,* 499 U.S. 955, 111 S.Ct. 1430, 113 L.Ed.2d 484 (1991)(requirements of Rule 23(a) do not apply to cases proceeding under Rule 23.2)].

3. *See, e.g., Curley v. Brignoli, Curley & Roberts Associates,* 915 F.2d 81, 86 (2d Cir.1990), *cert. denied,* 499 U.S. 955, 111 S.Ct. 1430, 113 L.Ed.2d 484 (1991)(numerosity and other prerequisites of Rule 23(a) inapplicable in Rule 23.2 case).

4. *See, e.g., Aetna Casualty & Surety Co. v. Iso–Tex, Inc.,* 75 F.3d 216, 218 (5th Cir. 1996)(diversity tested by looking to citizenship of named representatives); *Murray v. Scott,* 176 F.Supp.2d 1249 (M.D.Ala.2001) (same).

Amount in Controversy

The prevailing practice in federal district courts is to determine the amount in controversy by examining the individual claims of the membership of the unincorporated association. This approach creates a substantial hurdle to achieving diversity jurisdiction. Thus, if an unincorporated association has a claim for $1,000,000, the claim would appear to exceed the more–than–$75,000 requirement by a safe margin. If, however, the association has 10,000 members, and each member has an equal share in the aggregate claim of $1,000,000, the value of the suit to each member is only one hundred dollars—well short of the threshold for diversity jurisdiction.

ADDITIONAL RESEARCH REFERENCES

Wright & Miller, *Federal Practice and Procedure* § 1861.

C.J.S. Associations §§ 8, 40–48, 51–53; Federal Civil Procedure §§ 76–93.

West's Key No. Digests, Associations ⚷20(1); Federal Civil Procedure ⚷186.5.

RULE 24

INTERVENTION

(a) Intervention of Right. Upon timely application anyone shall be permitted to intervene in an action: (1) when a statute of the United States confers an unconditional right to intervene; or (2) when the applicant claims an interest relating to the property or transaction which is the subject of the action and the applicant is so situated that the disposition of the action may as a practical matter impair or impede the applicant's ability to protect that interest, unless the applicant's interest is adequately represented by existing parties.

(b) Permissive Intervention. Upon timely application anyone may be permitted to intervene in an action: (1) when a statute of the United States confers a conditional right to intervene; or (2) when an applicant's claim or defense and the main action have a question of law or fact in common. When a party to an action relies for ground of claim or defense upon any statute or executive order administered by a federal or state governmental officer or agency or upon any regulation, order, requirement or agreement issued or made pursuant to the statute or executive order, the officer or agency upon timely application may be permitted to intervene in the action. In exercising its discretion the court shall consider whether the intervention will unduly delay or prejudice the adjudication of the rights of the original parties.

(c) Procedure. A person desiring to intervene shall serve a motion to intervene upon the parties as provided in Rule 5. The motion shall state the grounds therefor and shall be accompanied by a pleading setting forth the claim or defense for which intervention is sought. The same procedure shall be followed when a statute of the United States gives a right to intervene. When the constitutionality of an act of Congress affecting the public interest is drawn in question in any action in which the United States or an officer, agency, or employee thereof is not a party, the court shall notify the Attorney General of the United States as provided in Title 28, U.S.C. § 2403. When the constitutionality of any statute of a State affecting the public interest is drawn in question in any action in which that State or any agency, officer, or employee thereof is not a party, the court shall notify the attorney general of the State as provided in Title 28, U.S.C. § 2403. A party challenging the constitutionality of legislation should call the attention of the court to its consequential duty, but failure to do so is not a waiver of any constitutional right otherwise timely asserted.

[Amended effective March 19, 1948; October 20, 1949; July 1, 1963; July 1, 1966; August 1, 1987; December 1, 1991.]

AUTHORS' COMMENTARY ON RULE 24

PURPOSE AND SCOPE

Rule 24 governs situations in which persons not already parties may intervene in existing litigation. Unlike most Rule 19 situations, where persons who are already parties seek to serve process on non-parties and conscript them into the litigation, in most Rule 24 situations the non-party seeks to join in litigation to which the non-party was not previously invited. Rule 24 attempts to balance the interest of the person seeking intervention with the burdens such intervention may impose on parties to pending suits. The Rule divides intervenors into two basic groups: those seeking intervention as of right under Rule 24(a); and those who seek the court's permission to intervene under Rule 24(b). Notwithstanding the terminology of those two portions of Rule 24, the court enjoys substantial discretion when deciding whether to permit intervention under either Rule 24(a) or Rule 24(b). There remain, however, important distinctions in the factors courts consider in exercising discretion under Rule 24(a) and Rule 24(b). Finally, while cases granting applications to intervene often declare that intervention provisions are to be construed liberally,[1] the application of Rule 24 to particular motions is not always as generous as such general statements might suggest.

NOTE: Rule 24 is another Rule that was changed substantially in 1966, thereby making much of the case law decided prior to that time unreliable. Additionally, the last two sentences of Rule 24(c) were added in December 1991.

RULE 24(a). INTERVENTION OF RIGHT

CORE CONCEPT

Rule 24(a) identifies two distinct circumstances in which a person may be entitled to intervene in pending litigation: where a federal statute confers a right to intervene; and where the intervenor is able to satisfy all elements for intervention as of right.[2]

1. *See, e.g., South Dakota v. United States Department of Interior,* 317 F.3d 783, 785 (8th Cir.2003) ("... Rule 24 should be liberally construed with all doubts resolved in favor of the proposed intervenor.").

2. *See, e.g., United States v. City of New York,* 198 F.3d 360, 364 (2d Cir.1999) (movant must satisfy timeliness plus three elements enumerated in Rule 23(a)(2)). *See also Martin v. Wilks,* 490 U.S. 755, 109 S.Ct. 2180, 104 L.Ed.2d 835 (1989) (Rule 24 does not require intervention; it is permissive in nature, not mandatory; drawing contrast with Rule 19).

APPLICATIONS

Timing

Rule 24(a) explicitly imposes a "timeliness" requirement on motions to intervene.[3] However, unlike timing elements in some other Federal Rules, the actual time limits are not set out in Rule 24(a).[4] Generally speaking, courts weigh four factors in determining timeliness: (1) length of delay in seeking intervention;[5] (2) prejudicial impact of such delay on existing parties;[6] (3) prejudice to intervenor if intervention is denied; and (4) other factors affecting fairness in an individual case.[7] Thus, courts enjoy substantial discretion to make very fact-specific rulings on the timeliness of a Rule 24(a) motion.[8] An initial decision to reject intervention on grounds of lack of timeliness is rarely

3. *See, e.g., Associated Builders & Contractors, Inc. v. Herman,* 166 F.3d 1248, 1257 (D.C.Cir.1999) ("If the motion was not timely, there is no need for the court to address the other factors that enter into an intervention analysis.").

4. *See, e.g., Heaton v. Monogram Credit Card Bank of Georgia,* 297 F.3d 416 (5th Cir.2002) ("There are no absolute measures of timeliness; it is determined from all the circumstances."); *United States v. Washington,* 86 F.3d 1499, 1503 (9th Cir.1996)("[A]ny substantial lapse of time weighs heavily against intervention."); *Atlantic Mutual Insurance Co. v. Northwest Airlines, Inc.,* 24 F.3d 958, 961 (7th Cir.1994)(timeliness means intervenor applicant must "act with dispatch").

5. *See, e.g., League of United Latin American Citizens v. Wilson,* 131 F.3d 1297, 1302 (9th Cir.1997) (27 month delay in moving to intervene makes intervention motion "an uphill battle").

6. *Cf., Effjohn International Cruise Holdings, Inc. v. A&L Sales, Inc.,* 346 F.3d 552, 561 (5th Cir. 2003) (noting prejudice factor, but explaining, "[t]he inquiry for this factor is whether other parties were prejudiced *by the delay,* not whether they would be prejudiced *by the addition of the claim* (obviously, in the sense that they may obtain less, existing parties are always prejudiced by new claims) [emphasis in original]").

7. *See, e.g., Heaton v. Monogram Credit Card Bank of Georgia,* 297 F.3d 416 (5th Cir.2002); *see also, Associated Builders & Contractors, Inc. v. Herman,* 166 F.3d 1248, 1257 (D.C.Cir.1999) (unexplained failure to take clear opportunity to intervene at trial is ground for denying intervention after judgment); *Arrow v. Gambler's Supply, Inc.,* 55 F.3d 407 (8th Cir.1995)(weighing: (1) how far litigation had proceeded; (2) intervenor's prior knowledge of case; (3) reason for any delay in seeking intervention; and (4) risk of prejudice to parties). *See also Roeder v. Islamic Republic of Iran,* 333 F.3d 228, 233 (D.C. Cir.2003), *cert. denied,* ___ U.S. ___, 124 S.Ct. 2836, 159 L.Ed.2d 287 (2004) (timeliness measured from point at which intervenor knew or should have know interest was directly at stake in litigation); *Jordan v. Michigan Conference of Teamsters Welfare Fund,* 207 F.3d 854, 862 (6th Cir.2000) (timeliness evaluated through five factors: "1) the point to which the suit has progressed; 2) the purpose for which the intervention is sought; 3) the length of time preceding the application during which the proposed intervenor knew or reasonably should have known of his interest in the case; 4) the prejudice to the original parties due to the proposed intervenor's failure, after he knew or reasonably should have known of his interest in the case, to apply promptly for intervention; and 5) the existence of unusual circumstances militating against or in favor of intervention;" denying intervention after judgment when intervention should have been sought earlier). *See also Acree v. Republic of Iraq,* 370 F.3d 41, 49 (D.C. Cir. 2004) ("Courts are generally reluctant to permit intervention after a suit has proceeded to final judgment, particularly where the applicant had the opportunity to intervene prior to judgment."). *But cf., Associated Builders and Contractors, Saginaw Valley Area Chapter v. Perry,* 115 F.3d 386 (6th Cir.1997) (original party's decision not to appeal may create grounds for intervention even after trial court's decision).

8. *See, e.g., Edwards v. City of Houston,* 37 F.3d 1097 (5th Cir.1994)(held, intervention in district court was properly denied, but intervention for appeal should be granted). *But see Acree v. Republic of Iraq,* 370 F.3d 41, 49 (D.C. Cir. 2004) ("Courts are generally reluctant to permit intervention after a suit has proceeded to final judgment, particularly where the applicant had the opportunity to intervene prior to judgment.").

disturbed on appeal.[9] This is probably the most important kind of discretion courts possess when considering applications to intervene under Rule 24(a).

"Collateral Purpose" Exception

Some courts modify the timeliness requirement of Rule 24(a) when the purpose of the intervention application is only to modify, e.g., an existing protective order.[10] This view has not been adopted in all circuits,[11] and lawyers must consult the local precedent.

Subject Matter Jurisdiction

If an applicant seeks to intervene as a plaintiff in a case based on diversity jurisdiction, the would-be intervenor should be of diverse citizenship from all defendants. Generally, the courts have held that supplemental jurisdiction does not extend to situations in which the intervenor-plaintiff is not of diverse citizenship from the defendants.[12] However, supplemental jurisdiction is available to persons intervening as defendants.[13] Supplemental jurisdiction is discussed further at greater length elsewhere in this text.

Personal Jurisdiction

When a person attempts to intervene under Rule 24, that person submits to the jurisdiction of the court.[14]

Statutory Right Narrowly Construed

Rule 24(a)(1) explicitly defers to any other federal statute that confers on qualifying persons an unconditional right to intervene in pending litigation. If applicants for statutory intervention demonstrate a right to intervene under Rule 24(a)(1), they "need not show inadequacy of representation or that their interests may be impaired if not allowed to intervene" as is required for intervention under Rule 24(a)(2).[15] However, the case law demonstrates a clear judicial tenden-

9. *See, e.g., Caterino v. Barry,* 922 F.2d 37, 40 (1st Cir.1990)(trial court entitled to "substantive deference" on timeliness).

10. *See, e.g., United Nuclear Corp. v. Cranford Insurance Co.,* 905 F.2d 1424, 1427 (10th Cir.1990), *cert. denied,* 498 U.S. 1073, 111 S.Ct. 799, 112 L.Ed.2d 860 (1991). *See also Pansy v. Borough of Stroudsburg,* 23 F.3d 772, 780 n. 9 (3d Cir.1994).

11. *See, e.g., Empire Blue Cross & Blue Shield of Connecticut, Inc. v. Janet Greeson's A Place for Us, Inc.,* 62 F.3d 1217, 1221 (9th Cir. 1995); *Banco Popular de Puerto Rico v. Greenblatt,* 964 F.2d 1227, 1230–34 (1st Cir.1992) (refusing to modify timeliness requirement for limited purpose motion).

12. *See, e.g., Development Finance Corp. v. Alpha Housing & Health Care, Inc.,* 54 F.3d 156 (3d Cir.1995)(citing to cases generally refusing to find supplemental jurisdiction in such circumstances).

13. *See, e.g., id.* (noting that 28 U.S.C.A. § 1367(b) does not prohibit use of supplemental jurisdiction in such circumstances).

14. *See, e.g., County Security Agency v. Ohio Department of Commerce,* 296 F.3d 477 (6th Cir.2002) (refusing to permit reservation of objections to jurisdiction made by petitioning intervenor; "a motion to intervene is fundamentally incompatible with an objection to personal jurisdiction").

15. *Ruiz v. Estelle,* 161 F.3d 814, 828 (5th Cir.1998), *cert. denied,* 526 U.S. 1158, 119 S.Ct. 2046, 144 L.Ed.2d 213 (1999) ("Under Rule 24(a)(1), intervenors need not even prove a 'sufficient' interest relating to the subject matter of the controversy, since Congress has already declared that interest sufficient by granting the

cy to construe statutory intervention rights narrowly.[16] As a practical result, persons seeking to intervene under Rule 24(a) should routinely consider arguing for intervention under the "interest" test of Rule 24(a)(2)—even in circumstances where they believe they might qualify for intervention as a statutory right under Rule 24(a)(1).[17]

Amicus Curiae Briefs

There may appear to be a superficial similarity between the process of intervention and the opportunity to file an amicus curiae brief. However, courts do not equate amicus status with the rights and responsibilities of a party joined through intervention.[18]

Denying Intervention of Right—Standard of Review

On issues of the timeliness of intervention, as mentioned above, district courts enjoy substantial discretion. However, as to other substantive requirements for intervention under Rule 24(a), there is a split of authority in the courts of appeal as to the proper standard of review. Some appellate courts use a *de novo* standard;[19] others apply an "abuse of discretion" standard;[20] and sometimes a combination of the standards is employed.[21] Where applied, the *de novo* standard is less deferential to the decision of the district court.

Right to Intervene Based on Interest in Litigation

The right to intervene under Rule 24(a)(2) exists only when the court holds that a person seeking intervention has established three

statutory right to intervene." However, statutory intervention is still subject to a determination of timeliness, over which the district court enjoys substantial discretion.). *See also Newdow v. United States Congress,* 313 F.3d 495, 497 (9th Cir.2002) (statute granting right to intervene in instant case also imposes requirement of timely application).

16. *See, e.g., Equal Employment Opportunity Commission v. American Telephone and Telegraph Co.,* 506 F.2d 735 (3d Cir.1974); *see also, Phar-Mor, Inc. v. Coopers & Lybrand,* 22 F.3d 1228, 1232 (3d Cir.1994) ("[C]ourts have construed Rule 24(a)(1) narrowly; these courts have been reluctant to interpret statutes to grant an unconditional right to intervene to private parties.").

17. *Cf., Yorkshire v. United States,* 26 F.3d 942, 944 (9th Cir.1994), *cert. denied,* 513 U.S. 989, 115 S.Ct. 487, 130 L.Ed.2d 399 (1994)(Rule 24(a)(2) "is construed broadly in favor of the applicants").

18. *See, e.g., United States v. City of Los Angeles,* 288 F.3d 391, 400 (9th Cir.2002) ("[A]micus status is insufficient to protect the [petitioner for intervention's] rights because such status does not allow the [petitioner] to raise issues or arguments formally and gives it no right of appeal."); *Coalition of Arizona/New Mexico Counties for Stable Economic Growth v. Department of the Interior,* 100 F.3d 837, 844 (10th Cir.1996) ("[T]he right to file a brief as amicus curiae is no substitute for the right to intervene as a party in the action under Rule 24(a)(2).").

19. *See, e.g., United States v. BDO Seidman,* 337 F.3d 802 (7th Cir.2003), *cert. denied,* 540 U.S. 1178, 124 S.Ct. 1410, 158 L.Ed.2d 78 (2004) (applying de novo standard to all requirements but timeliness requirement); *Alameda Water & Sanitation District v. Browner,* 9 F.3d 88, 89 (10th Cir.1993)(acknowledging split of authority and applying *de novo* standard).

20. *See, e.g., In re Sierra Club,* 945 F.2d 776, 779 (4th Cir.1991)(explicitly adopting "abuse of discretion" standard). *But cf., Public Service Co. of New Hampshire v. Patch,* 136 F.3d 197, 204 (1st Cir.1998) (using abuse of discretion standard, but "discretion is more circumscribed when Rule 24(a) is in play").

21. *See, e.g., Vollmer v. Publishers Clearing House & Campus Subscriptions, Inc.,* 248 F.3d 698, 705 (7th Cir.2001)(timeliness reviewed for abuse of discretion; other factors reviewed *de novo*).

elements: (1) an interest in the subject matter of the pending litigation; (2) a substantial risk that the litigation will impair the interest; and (3) existing parties do not adequately protect that interest. These three elements are *not* weighing factors. *All* must be satisfied before an applicant may exercise a right to intervene under Rule 24(a)(2).[22]

Interest in the Subject Matter

The definition of an "interest" that satisfies Rule 24(a)(2) is unclear.[23] An economic interest in the subject matter of the litigation may satisfy this element of the Rule.[24] Also, if the intervening party will be legally bound by the judgment in the pending litigation, an "interest" exists that satisfies Rule 24(a)(2).[25] Other cases construe the concept of "interest" more broadly, including precedent allowing parents of schoolchildren to intervene in litigation affecting the resources available to certain schools.[26]

22. *See, e.g., Purcell v. BankAtlantic Financial Corp.,* 85 F.3d 1508 (11th Cir.1996), *cert. denied,* 519 U.S. 867, 117 S.Ct. 178, 136 L.Ed.2d 118 (1996)(citing three requirements, plus timeliness); *Americans United for Separation of Church and State v. City of Grand Rapids,* 922 F.2d 303, 305 (6th Cir.1990)(intervenor must satisfy all elements).

23. *See, e.g., Utahns for Better Transportation v. United States Department of Transportation,* 295 F.3d 1111 (10th Cir.2002) ("The sufficiency of an applicant's interest is a highly fact-specific determination." Also noting that "[t]here is some value in having the parties before the court so that they will be bound by the result."); *Daggett v. Commission on Governmental Ethics & Election Practices,* 172 F.3d 104, 110 (1st Cir.1999) (noting that narrow reading of interest is disfavored, "although clear outer boundaries have yet to be developed").

24. *See, e.g., Fund For Animals, Inc. v. Norton,* 322 F.3d 728, 733 (D.C.Cir.2003) (interest of foreign government agency in protecting flow of tourist dollars meets interest requirement of Rule 24(a)); *Utahns for Better Transportation v. United States Department of Transportation,* 295 F.3d 1111 (10th Cir.2002) ("The threat of economic injury from the outcome of the litigation undoubtedly gives a petitioner the requisite interest."); *United States v. Peoples Benefit Life Insurance Co.,* 271 F.3d 411, 416 (2d Cir.2001) (constructive trust may sometimes be sufficient interest to support intervention in forfeiture case, but not when property to be forfeited is not traceable to trust; also noting other facts that distinguish this case from constructive trust cases in which court permitted intervention); *Sierra Club v. Espy,* 18 F.3d 1202, 1207 (5th Cir.1994)(citing economic interest for intervention). *But see, Montana v. Environmental Protection Agency,* 137 F.3d 1135, 1142 (9th Cir. 1998), *cert. denied,* 525 U.S. 921, 119 S.Ct. 275, 142 L.Ed.2d 227 (1998) ("[A] speculative and purely economic interest does not create a protectable interest in litigation concerning a statute that regulates environmental, not economic interests."); *Greene v. United States,* 996 F.2d 973, 976 (9th Cir.1993)(economic interest alone is insufficient); *Mountain Top Condominium Association v. Dave Stabbert Master Builder, Inc.,* 72 F.3d 361, 366 (3d Cir.1995)("mere" economic interest might be insufficient, but interest in specific fund that is at risk will satisfy "interest" requirement of Rule 24(a)(2)); *Gould v. Alleco, Inc.,* 883 F.2d 281, 285 (4th Cir.1989), *cert. denied,* 493 U.S. 1058, 110 S.Ct. 870, 107 L.Ed.2d 953 (1990) ("In a sense, every company's stockholders, bondholders, directors and employees have a stake in the outcome of any litigation involving the company, but this alone is insufficient to imbue them with the degree of 'interest' required for Rule 24(a) intervention.").

25. *See, e.g., Triax Co. v. TRW,* 724 F.2d 1224, 1227 (6th Cir.1984)(collateral estoppel). *See also, Mova Pharmaceutical Corp. v. Shalala,* 140 F.3d 1060, 1074 (D.C.Cir.1998) (to meet "interest" requirement of Rule 24, intervenor need only demonstrate standing to sue).

26. *See, e.g., Smuck v. Hobson,* 408 F.2d 175 (D.C.Cir.1969). *See also, Roeder v. Islamic Republic of Iran,* 333 F.3d 228, 233 (D.C.Cir.2003), *cert. denied,* ___ U.S. ___, 124 S.Ct. 2836, 159 L.Ed.2d 287 (2004) (interest in protecting diplomatic agreement with foreign sovereign that might be affected by litigation gave United States interest that met intervention requirement); *In re Grand Jury Subpoena,* 274 F.3d 563, 570 (1st Cir.2001) (appropriate intervention by attorney and corporate officers to attempt to quash grand jury subpoena; "[c]olorable claims of attorney-client and work product privilege

Impairment of Interest

Rule 24(a)(2) declares that risk of impairment to an applicant's interest may include legal impairment, such as a risk that principles of stare decisis may apply.[27] At the same time, other practical consequences of litigation may also satisfy the "impairment" element. For example, even though a party may not, through res judicata or collateral estoppel, be bound by the judgment, a substantial risk of practical impairments can sometimes constitute sufficient risk of "impairment" to a party seeking to intervene.[28]

Adequate Representation by Existing Parties

Even if the person seeking intervention demonstrates that the elements of "interest" and "impairment" are satisfied, intervention under Rule 24(a)(2) will be denied if the interest at risk is represented adequately by persons already parties to the action.[29] Lack of adequate

qualify as sufficient interests to ground intervention as of right"); *Cotter v. Massachusetts Association of Minority Law Enforcement Officers,* 219 F.3d 31, 34–36 (1st Cir.2000), *cert. denied,* 531 U.S. 1072, 121 S.Ct. 762, 148 L.Ed.2d 663 (2001) (black police officers previously promoted have interest in intervening in suit alleging racial discrimination in promotions harmful to white officers; interest is in protecting promotions of black officers; organization of officers also has interest in intervening to protect interests of black officers who are not parties to suit); *Grutter v. Bollinger,* 188 F.3d 394, 398 (6th Cir.1999) (proposed intervenors' interest in continued use of race as factor in university admissions satisfies interest requirement of rule 24, even if interest is not a specifically protectable legal or equitable interest; " 'close cases should be resolved in favor of recognizing an interest under Rule 24(a)' "); *Loyd v. Alabama Department of Corrections,* 176 F.3d 1336, 1339 (11th Cir.1999), *cert. denied,* 528 U.S. 1061, 120 S.Ct. 613, 145 L.Ed.2d 509 (1999)(state attorney general need not demonstrate standing before intervening in lawsuit over prisoners' rights, provided that existing parties have satisfied requirement of justiciable case or controversy); *Coalition of Arizona/New Mexico Counties for Stable Economic Growth v. Department of the Interior,* 100 F.3d 837, 841 (10th Cir.1996) (granting intervention where there is little economic interest, but intervenor has interest based on involvement with issue and record of advocacy of protection of affected wildlife); *but cf., Kootenai Tribe of Idaho v. Veneman,* 313 F.3d 1094, 1108 (9th Cir. 2002) (where statute creates liability only for government, private party cannot meet rigorous standard of interest that justifies intervention; however, permissive intervention under Rule 24(b) may still be possible, because lower standard of common question of law or fact may still be met); *Standard Heating & Air Conditioning Co. v. City of Minneapolis,* 137 F.3d 567, 571 (8th Cir.1998) (remote interests or interests requiring a sequence of events before becoming colorable do not meet requirements of Rule 24(a)); *City of Cleveland, Ohio v. Nuclear Regulatory Commission,* 17 F.3d 1515 (D.C.Cir. 1994)(per curiam)(interest should be "legally protectable;" otherwise intervenor would lack standing). *See generally, Rio Grande Pipeline Co. v. Federal Energy Regulatory Commission,* 178 F.3d 533 (D.C.Cir.1999) (noting uncertainty as to how great an interest an intervention applicant must demonstrate; making comparison to constitutional requirement of standing and citing cases).

27. *See, e.g., Sierra Club v. Espy,* 18 F.3d 1202, 1207 (5th Cir.1994)(stare decisis effect of decision is sufficient potential impairment to satisfy requirements of Rule 24(a)(2)). *See also United States v. City of Los Angeles,* 288 F.3d 391, 401 (9th Cir.2002) (potential impairment is sufficient; no requirement that outcome will necessarily impair interest).

28. *See, e.g., Utah Association of Counties v. Clinton,* 255 F.3d 1246, 1253 (10th Cir.2001) (question of impairment cannot be separated from question of existence of interest; moreover, " 'the court is not limited to consequences of a strictly legal nature' "); *Grutter v. Bollinger,* 188 F.3d 394, 400 (6th Cir.1999) ("minimal requirements" of impairment satisfied by likely prospect that access of minority students to university will be impaired if university stops using race as criterion in admissions); *Edwards v. City of Houston,* 78 F.3d 983, 1004 (5th Cir. 1996)(practical impairment is sufficient—legal impairment not required).

29. *See, e.g., Daggett v. Commission on Governmental Ethics & Election Practices,* 172 F.3d

representation is most easily demonstrated if the interest is not currently represented at all, or if the persons already parties have positions clearly adverse to those of the intervention applicant.[30] Moreover, a difference in tactics does not of itself necessarily indicate a lack of adequate representation.[31]

Burden of Proof

Most courts require the intervenor to show that its interest is not

104, 111 (1st Cir.1999) (rebuttable presumption that government's defense of validity of statute adequately represents interests of citizens who support statute); *Clark v. Putnam County,* 168 F.3d 458, 461 (11th Cir.1999) ("weak" presumption of adequate representation when "existing party seeks the same objectives as the would-be intervenor").

30. *See, e.g., Twelve John Does v. District of Columbia,* 117 F.3d 571 (D.C.Cir.1997) (existing representation is generally adequate where there is no conflicting interest between representative and would-be intervenor and where representative has ability to litigate the issues with vigor); *but cf., Supreme Beef Processors, Inc. v. United States Department of Agriculture,* 275 F.3d 432, 437–38 (5th Cir.2001) (intervenors need only show that current representation "may be" inadequate; possibility that current party's fate in Chapter 7 bankruptcy proceeding could be liquidation–which would render instant case moot–could mean intervenor might have to litigate issue all over again even though current party won on those issues in district court; held, intervention justified); *Jordan v. Michigan Conference of Teamsters Welfare Fund,* 207 F.3d 854, 863 (6th Cir.2000) (movant's burden is only to show that representation "may be" inadequate, not that representation "will in fact be inadequate"; but burden of demonstrating inadequate representation not met where: "1) no collusion is shown between the existing party and the opposition; 2) the existing party does not have any interests adverse to the intervenor; and 3) the existing party has not failed in the fulfillment of its duty"); *Sierra Club v. Espy,* 18 F.3d 1202 (5th Cir.1994)(burden of demonstrating inadequate existing representation is "minimal.").

31. *See, e.g., United States v. City of Miami,* 278 F.3d 1174, 1179 (11th Cir.2002) (police associations concerned with advancement of blacks and women is adequately represented by government interest in ending discrimination for all minorities); *Massachusetts Food Association v. Massachusetts Alcoholic Beverages Control Commission,* 197 F.3d 560, 566 (1st Cir.1999), *cert. denied,* 529 U.S. 1105, 120 S.Ct. 1846, 146 L.Ed.2d 788 (2000) (courts generally presume that government defendant will adequately represent interest of all private defenders of relevant law "unless there is a showing to the contrary"); *Grutter v. Bollinger,* 188 F.3d 394, 401 (6th Cir.1999) (prospect that university, in defending against challenge to admissions program based partly on race, may not present evidence of its own past discrimination; minority students have therefore demonstrated that existing representation by university is inadequate); *B.H. v. McDonald,* 49 F.3d 294 (7th Cir. 1995)(party's preference to in-chamber conferences as opposed to open court hearings does not constitute inadequate representation). *But see Utahns for Better Transportation v. United States Department of Transportation,* 295 F.3d 1111 (10th Cir.2002) (burden of showing inadequacy of representation is minimal; relying on government creates potential conflict between government's duty to protect public interest and private interests of private intervention petitioners; also, private parties have expertise that government lacks; finally, government's silence on its intent to protect private parties is "deafening"); *United States v. City of Los Angeles,* 288 F.3d 391, 401–02 (9th Cir.2002) (presumption that government will adequately represent interests "arises when the government is acting on behalf of a constituency that it represents. ...The situation is different when the government acts as an employer, as here. ...The presumption has not been applied to parties who are antagonists in the collective bargaining process."); *Turn Key Gaming, Inc. v. Oglala Sioux Tribe,* 164 F.3d 1080, 1082 (8th Cir.1999) (lender/holder of security interest in personalty purchased with proceeds of loan has interest in outcome of lawsuit over, among other issues, whether security interest is valid; current party that was responsible for development of project financed with loan did not adequately represent security interest holder's interest because current party was subject of counterclaim; and it was conceivable that current party would settle counterclaim in way that was detrimental to validity of security interest). *See also, Public Service Co. of New Hampshire v. Patch,* 136 F.3d 197, 207 (1st Cir.1998) (intervenor need make only "minimal showing" of inadequacy of repre-

adequately represented.[32]

Status of Intervenor: Standing

Assuming that an intervenor applicant satisfies the requirements of Rule 24(a)(2), the intervenor may participate as a party. However, left open is whether the intervenor, like a party, must satisfy requirements such as standing. The courts are divided on this issue, and an attorney must consult local precedent.[33]

Class Action Settlements: Standing

It is settled that if a non-named class member objects in a timely manner to a proposed settlement, that member need not intervene in order to appeal the settlement.[34]

Conditional Intervention

It appears that if a court permits intervention as of right, it may impose conditions on such intervention.[35]

RULE 24(b). PERMISSIVE INTERVENTION

CORE CONCEPT

Rule 24(b) contains provisions under which a person may move to intervene, but does not confer a right to intervene. Rule 24(b) applies a substantially more relaxed approach to motions to intervene. A person seeking permission to intervene under Rule 24(b) need not demonstrate the sort of interest required for intervention under Rule 24(a)(2). The court's discretion to reject Rule 24(b)(2) intervention applications, however, is substantially greater than its capacity to reject a Rule 24(a)(2) application.

sentation, but there must still be "some tangible basis" for claim of inadequacy).

32. *See, e.g., Maine v. Director, United States Fish & Wildlife Service,* 262 F.3d 13, 18 (1st Cir.2001) ("Some burden of showing inadequacy is placed on the proposed intervenor."). *Gottlieb v. Wiles,* 11 F.3d 1004, 1008 (10th Cir. 1993)(would-be intervenors bear burden of showing inadequacy of representation). *Buf cf., Southwest Center for Biological Diversity v. Berg,* 268 F.3d 810, 819–20 (9th Cir.2001) (Circuits hold "that a district court is required to accept as true the non-conclusory allegations made in support of an intervention motion."). *See also Brennan v. New York City Board of Education,* 260 F.3d 123, 129 (2d Cir.2001) (court cannot go to merits of case to conclude that movant's claim of interest is factually or legally weak).

33. *Compare, e.g., Building and Construction Trades Department, AFL–CIO v. Reich,* 40 F.3d 1275, 1282 (D.C.Cir.1994)(intervenor is on "equal footing" with parties, and must satisfy standing requirements of Article III of the Constitution) *with, e.g., Jones v. Prince George's County,* 348 F.3d 1014, 1018 (D.C. Cir. 2003) ("As the Rule's plain text indicates, intervenors of right need only an 'interest' in the litigation–not a 'cause of action' or 'permission to sue.' "). *See also, Mausolf v. Babbitt,* 85 F.3d 1295 (8th Cir.1996)(collecting cases).

34. *Devlin v. Scardelletti,* 536 U.S. 1, 122 S.Ct. 2005, 153 L.Ed.2d 27 (2002) (held, such a party easily satisfies standing requirement, and right to appeal is not restricted to named parties).

35. *See, e.g., Walsh v. Walsh,* 221 F.3d 204, 213 (1st Cir.2000), *cert. denied,* 531 U.S. 1159, 121 S.Ct. 1113, 148 L.Ed.2d 982 (2001) ("[I]t was well within the district court's discretion to limit [a person's] intervention, which took place long after trial and judgment, to a distinct legal issue that required no additional factfinding."); *Beauregard, Inc. v. Sword Services, L.L.C.,* 107 F.3d 351, 352 (5th Cir.1997) (permitting intervention provided, *inter alia,* that intervenor

APPLICATIONS

Common Question of Law or Fact

The bedrock requirement for Rule 24(b)(2) permissive intervention is a demonstration by the person seeking intervention that there exists a common question of law or fact between that person's claim or defense and the pending litigation.[36]

Discretion

A district court's decision to deny permissive intervention is almost never overturned on appeal.[37]

Subject Matter Jurisdiction

Persons attempting to intervene under Rule 24(b)(2) must establish an independent basis for subject matter jurisdiction. Supplemental jurisdiction is not available to would-be permissive intervenors.[38]

Timing

Applications to intervene under Rule 24(b) must be "timely". The determination of what constitutes a timely application rests within the court's discretion in the context of the facts in a particular case.[39] Because Rule 24(b) intervention questions do not typically affect the interests of non-parties as importantly as Rule 24(a) cases, courts tend to hold motions for permissive intervention to a more rigorous standard of timeliness than would be applied to motions for intervention of right.[40]

Delay or Prejudice

Rule 24(b) expressly authorizes the court to deny permissive intervention if intervention will unduly delay or prejudice the pending litigation. The provision permits denial of intervention if undue delay to existing parties will result even from an arguably timely application. That might occur if the complexity added by an intervenor would

agreed to seize asset and help pay cost of maintaining asset; noting contrary scholarly authority).

36. *See, e.g., Kootenai Tribe of Idaho v. Veneman,* 313 F.3d 1094, 1108 (9th Cir.2002) (standard for permissive intervention under rule 24(b) is common question of law or fact, not more rigorous standard of interest that may be impaired); *Griffith v. University Hospital, L.L.C.,* 249 F.3d 658, 661 (7th Cir.2001) (Rule 24(b) is appropriate way for third party to challenge protective order); *E.E.O.C. v. National Children's Center, Inc.,* 146 F.3d 1042, 1045 (D.C. Cir.1998) (same; collecting circuit decisions). *Cf., Trans Chemical, Ltd. v. China National Machinery Import & Export Corp.,* 332 F.3d 815, 824 (5th Cir.2003) (lack of common question of law or fact means permissive intervention is inappropriate).

37. *See, e.g., Purcell v. BankAtlantic Financial Corp.,* 85 F.3d 1508, 1513 (11th Cir.), *cert. denied,* 519 U.S. 867, 117 S.Ct. 178, 136 L.Ed.2d 118 (1996)(Rule 24(b) intervention is "wholly discretionary" even where the requirements of Rule 24(b) are satisfied); *Shea v. Angulo,* 19 F.3d 343, 346 (7th Cir.1994)(reversal of district court's decision denying permissive intervention " 'is a very rare bird indeed, so seldom seen as to be unique.' ").

38. *See, e.g., E.E.O.C. v. National Children's Center, Inc.,* 146 F.3d 1042, 1046 (D.C.Cir.1998) ("Permissive intervention ... has always required an independent basis for jurisdiction.").

39. *See, e.g., Caterino v. Barry,* 922 F.2d 37, 40 (1st Cir.1990)(trial court entitled to "substantial deference").

40. *See, e.g., Banco Popular de Puerto Rico v. Greenblatt,* 964 F.2d 1227, 1230 (1st Cir.

prolong the litigation excessively.[41] Similarly, inappropriate prejudice to existing parties might occur if the presence of the intervenor might shift the focus of the litigation from the pending issues to those introduced by the intervenor.[42]

There is authority for the position that the "prejudice" evaluation of Rule 24(b)(2) should include an evaluation of the merits of the proposed party's claim. To the extent that the claim is duplicative or weak on its merits, the court will be inclined to give greater weight to concerns about delay or prejudice.[43]

Permissive Statutory Intervention

Fewer cases deal with permissive statutory intervention. Such statutes as exist, and which clearly contemplate permissive statutory intervention, generally accord the court authority to allow intervention by some public official such as the United States Attorney General.[44] In other circumstances it is less clear whether the statute is intended to allow intervention as of right or permissive intervention. Although the paucity of case law makes conclusions difficult, the inclination of courts to construe narrowly statutes that clearly contemplate intervention as of right may suggest that courts will be inclined to construe the uncertain statutes as authorizing permissive statutory intervention under Rule 24(b)(1) rather than statutory intervention as of right under Rule 24(a)(1). As a practical matter, that inclination provides the courts with greater opportunities to use discretion to reject an application for permissive intervention.

Standing for Non-statutory Permissive Intervention

Although a person seeking intervention under Rule 24(b)(2) need not demonstrate an "interest" within the kinds contemplated by Rule 24(a)(2), the person seeking permissive intervention must nonetheless have a sufficient stake in the litigation to satisfy ordinary requirements for standing.[45]

Permissive Intervention for Public Officials

Rule 24(b) authorizes intervention by officers or agencies if the pending litigation raises questions of law administered by the officer or

1992)(timeliness standard more strict for Rule 24(a) than Rule 24(b)).

41. *See, e.g., Massachusetts v. Microsoft Corp.,* 373 F.3d 1199 (D.C. Cir. 2004) (prejudice evaluation "captures all the possible drawbacks of piling on parties," including extra cost and increased risk of error). *See also Farmland Dairies v. Commissioner of New York State Department of Agriculture and Markets,* 847 F.2d 1038, 1044 (2d Cir.1988)(post-judgment intervention is disfavored).

42. *See, e.g., Alaniz v. Tillie Lewis Foods,* 572 F.2d 657, 659 (9th Cir.1978), (per curiam) *cert. denied sub nom., Beaver v. Alaniz,* 439 U.S. 837, 99 S.Ct. 123, 58 L.Ed.2d 134 (1978)(post-resolution intervention often unfairly hard on existing parties).

43. *See, e.g., Massachusetts v. Microsoft Corp.,* 373 F.3d 1199 (D.C. Cir. 2004) (but in instant case intervention is appropriate because concerns about delay or prejudice are minimal).

44. *See, e.g.,* 42 U.S.C.A. § 2000a–3(a).

45. *See, e.g., United States v. Napper,* 887 F.2d 1528, 1532 (11th Cir.1989) (standing is required for both intervenors of right and permissive intervenors). *But cf., In re Vitamins Antitrust Class Actions,* 215 F.3d 26 (D.C. Cir.2000) (expressing uncertainty as to whether standing is required).

agency, or questions of regulations issued by the officer or agency.[46]

Conditional Permissive Intervention

If intervention is permitted under Rule 24(b), the court has substantial authority to impose conditions on the intervention.[47]

RULE 24(c). PROCEDURE

CORE CONCEPT

Rule 24(c) contains the provisions for notice and service of process of the motion to intervene. It also contains special notice provisions when the constitutionality of public acts of the United States or of any state will be at issue in the litigation, so that a federal or state attorney general may have an opportunity to intervene.

APPLICATIONS

Service of Process

The motion to intervene should be filed with the court and served on all persons already parties to the pending litigation, as provided in Rule 5.

Service of Proposed Pleading

In addition to the motion to intervene, Rule 24(c) also requires that the applicant for intervention file and serve a proposed pleading explaining the claim or defense that is the purpose of the intervention.[48] This proposed pleading should also be served consistent with the requirements of Rule 5, governing service on persons already parties.

Constitutionality of Federal Acts

In cases where the pending litigation raises questions as to the constitutionality of a federal law "affecting the public interest," Rule 24(c) imposes on the court a requirement to notify the United States Attorney General of the pendency of the case, so that the Attorney General has an opportunity to seek intervention.[49]

Constitutionality of State Acts

In cases where the pending litigation raises questions as to the constitutionality of a state law "affecting the public interest," Rule

46. *See, e.g., Harris v. Amoco Production Co.,* 768 F.2d 669, 680 (5th Cir.1985), *cert. denied,* 475 U.S. 1011, 106 S.Ct. 1186, 89 L.Ed.2d 302 (1986)(citing federal law authorizing permissive intervention for federal agency).

47. *See, e.g., Beauregard, Inc. v. Sword Services, L.L.C.,* 107 F.3d 351, 352 n. 2 (5th Cir. 1997) ("It is undisputed that virtually any condition may be attached to a grant of permissive intervention.").

48. *See, e.g., Retired Chicago Police Association v. City of Chicago,* 7 F.3d 584, 595 (7th Cir.1993), *cert. denied,* 519 U.S. 932, 117 S.Ct. 305, 136 L.Ed.2d 222 (1996) (for purposes of Rule 24(c), intervenor should provide an original pleading, not merely an adoption by reference of prior pleadings; Rule 10(c), permitting adoption by reference in other situations, does not apply to pleadings required under Rule 24(c)).

49. *Caprio v. Bell Atlantic Sickness & Accident Plan,* 374 F.3d 217 (3d Cir. 2004) (Rule 24(c) imposes duty on district court to notify Attorney General of the United States).

24(c) imposes on the court a requirement to notify the attorney general of the affected state, so that the state attorney general has an opportunity to seek intervention.[50]

Parties' Duty to Notify Court of Constitutional Challenge

Rule 24(c) requires the parties to bring to the court's attention its duty to notify the federal or state attorney general when the constitutionality of a statute is at issue.[51] However, Rule 24(c) also makes clear that there is no sanction if the parties fail to do so.

Consequences if Court Fails to Notify an Attorney General

It appears settled that no consequence to the pending litigation follows if the court should neglect to notify an attorney general pursuant to Rule 24(c).[52]

Procedure

The appropriate means of seeking to intervene in a case is through application to intervene. A motion to join, when made by a non-party, is inappropriate.[53]

ADDITIONAL RESEARCH REFERENCES

Wright & Miller, *Federal Practice and Procedure* §§ 1900–23.

C.J.S. Federal Civil Procedure §§ 128–155.

West's Key No. Digests, Federal Civil Procedure ⚷311–345.

50. *Caprio v. Bell Atlantic Sickness & Accident Plan,* 374 F.3d 217 (3d Cir. 2004) (Rule 24(c) imposes duty on district court to notify state attorney general).

51. *Caprio v. Bell Atlantic Sickness & Accident Plan,* 374 F.3d 217 (3d Cir. 2004) (party challenging constitutionality of statute has duty to point out court's notification obligation).

52. *See, e.g., Tonya K. v. Board of Education of the City of Chicago,* 847 F.2d 1243, 1247 (7th Cir.1988)("Failure to notify the Attorney General is not a jurisdictional defect.").

53. *See, e.g, Thompson v. Boggs,* 33 F.3d 847, 858 n. 10 (7th Cir.1994), *cert. denied,* 514 U.S. 1063, 115 S.Ct. 1692, 131 L.Ed.2d 556 (1995). (Rule 24 motion to intervene is "proper course;" courts do not grant motions to join when motion is made by a non-party).

RULE 25

SUBSTITUTION OF PARTIES

(a) Death.

(1) If a party dies and the claim is not thereby extinguished, the court may order substitution of the proper parties. The motion for substitution may be made by any party or by the successors or representatives of the deceased party and, together with the notice of hearing, shall be served on the parties as provided in Rule 5 and upon persons not parties in the manner provided in Rule 4 for the service of a summons, and may be served in any judicial district. Unless the motion for substitution is made not later than 90 days after the death is suggested upon the record by service of a statement of the fact of the death as provided herein for the service of the motion, the action shall be dismissed as to the deceased party.

(2) In the event of the death of one or more of the plaintiffs or of one or more of the defendants in an action in which the right sought to be enforced survives only to the surviving plaintiffs or only against the surviving defendants, the action does not abate. The death shall be suggested upon the record and the action shall proceed in favor of or against the surviving parties.

(b) Incompetency. If a party becomes incompetent, the court upon motion served as provided in subdivision (a) of this rule may allow the action to be continued by or against the party's representative.

(c) Transfer of Interest. In case of any transfer of interest, the action may be continued by or against the original party, unless the court upon motion directs the person to whom the interest is transferred to be substituted in the action or joined with the original party. Service of the motion shall be made as provided in subdivision (a) of this rule.

(d) Public Officers; Death or Separation From Office.

(1) When a public officer is a party to an action in an official capacity and during its pendency dies, resigns, or otherwise ceases to hold office, the action does not abate and the officer's successor is automatically substituted as a party. Proceedings following the substitution shall be in the name of the substituted party, but any misnomer not affecting the substantial rights of the parties shall be disregarded. An order of substitution may be entered at any time,

but the omission to enter such an order shall not affect the substitution.

(2) A public officer who sues or is sued in an official capacity may be described as a party by the officer's official title rather than by name; but the court may require the officer's name to be added.

[Amended effective October 20, 1949; July 19, 1961; July 1, 1963; August 1, 1987.]

AUTHORS' COMMENTARY ON RULE 25

PURPOSE AND SCOPE

Rule 25 prescribes the steps to employ when, in any of four distinct circumstances described in the Rule, it becomes necessary to substitute a party in a case. Rule 25 applies only to cases already pending when the substitution becomes necessary. It does not apply to substitutions in circumstances where suit has not already commenced. Such circumstances are more likely to be controlled by Rule 17, governing a person's capacity to initiate a suit.

RULE 25(a). DEATH

CORE CONCEPT

Rule 25(a) prescribes the procedure to follow for substituting a party when a plaintiff or defendant in pending litigation dies during the course of the proceedings. The Rule expressly defers to state or federal substantive law to determine whether the cause of action survives the death of the party, and is only applicable if the suit is not extinguished by the death.

APPLICATIONS

Motion for Substitution

Rule 25(a)(1) provides that any party, or the persons affiliated with the deceased party, may make a motion for substitution.[1] It is important to note that until a motion for substitution has been made and granted, the court has no authority to proceed with the deceased party's case.[2]

Service

The motion should be filed and served on all parties consistent with the requirements of Rule 5. If the circumstances are such that service

1. *See, e.g., Unicorn Tales, Inc. v. Banerjee*, 138 F.3d 467 (2d Cir.1998) (so holding; suggestion can be made by widow who is not a party, and need not be made by formally appointed representative of estate).

2. *See, e.g., Younts v. Fremont County*, 370 F.3d 748, 752 (8th Cir. 2004) ("Because the deceased . . . is not a proper party on appeal and no proper party has been substituted for her, we cannot address the merits of the appeal raised on [her] behalf.").

on non-parties is also appropriate, the non-parties shall be served consistent with the requirements for service of a summons under Rule 4, which controls service at the beginning of a suit. Rule 25(a)(1) authorizes service of such process in any federal judicial district.

Hearing

If there is a dispute as to the appropriateness of the proposed substituted party, the court has a duty to resolve the issue and may hold a hearing before ruling on the motion.[3] The notice of hearing should be filed and served on all parties in the manner provided by Rule 5.

Time

The time in which the motion for substitution must be made is 90 days from when the death of the party is "suggested" on the record of the case. Thus, a party may have been deceased for a substantial period before a suggestion of death is made, and that fact will have no consequence for the 90–day limitation.[4]

Suggestion of Death

Death of a party is suggested by written notice on the record, which should be filed and served on all parties pursuant to Rule 5.[5] Non-party representatives of the deceased should be served pursuant to Rule 4.[6]

Failure to Move for Substitution Within 90 Days

If more than 90 days elapses following the suggestion of death without a motion for substitution, Rule 25(a)(1) provides that the suit will be dismissed as to the deceased party. However, notwithstanding the apparently mandatory language of the Rule, the cases generally hold that the courts have discretion to extend the time in which a party may move for substitution.[7]

Status of Successor

A party who replaces a deceased party receives the status the deceased party possessed at the time of death. For example, if the

3. *See, e.g., Escareno v. Noltina Crucible and Refractory Corp.*, 139 F.3d 1456 (11th Cir.1998) (court has duty to determine whether substitute party–here an administrator of estate–was properly appointed; issue in instant case was whether probate court had jurisdiction to appoint administrator).

4. *See, e.g., Grandbouche v. Lovell*, 913 F.2d 835 (10th Cir.1990). *But see, Miles, Inc. v. Scripps Clinic & Research Foundation*, 810 F.Supp. 1091, 1102 (S.D.Cal.1993)(party who delays unreasonably in filing suggestion of death may be denied permission to substitute a party).

5. *See, e.g., Barlow v. Ground*, 39 F.3d 231, 233–34 (9th Cir.1994) (90 days does not start to run until representative of estate is properly served).

6. See, e.g., id. at 233 (requiring service on non-party representatives under Rule 4).

7. *See, e.g., Continental Bank, N.A. v. Meyer*, 10 F.3d 1293, 1297 (7th Cir.1993)(extensions of 90–day time period may be granted liberally). *But see, Russell v. City of Milwaukee*, 338 F.3d 662, 668 (7th Cir. 2003) (affirming dismissal where counsel failed to demonstrate excusable neglect).

deceased party had already consented to trial by a magistrate judge, the successor is bound by that consent.[8]

Death of a Party for Whom Substitution Cannot Be Made

Before Rule 25(a) can be employed to substitute a new party for a deceased party, the substantive law controlling the suit must allow survival of the cause of action. If the cause of action does not survive the death of a party, there can be no substitution for that party under Rule 25(a).[9] In multi-party litigation, however, it is possible that substantive law would extinguish the cause of action as to a deceased party, but that sufficient parties would remain to continue the action. In that circumstance, Rule 25(a)(2) directs that the action may continue as to surviving parties, with appropriate record made of the death.

RULE 25(b). INCOMPETENCY

CORE CONCEPT

Rule 25(b) addresses the possibility of substitution for parties who become incompetent in the course of litigation. It requires a motion to substitute a representative for the incompetent party, and it expressly adopts the same service provisions applicable to substitution for deceased parties found in Rule 25(a).

APPLICATIONS

Survival of the Action

Incompetency will not extinguish a cause of action.

Timing

Rule 25(b) contains no reference to time limitations for motions to substitute parties. There is little or no case law on the point.

RULE 25(c). TRANSFER OF INTEREST

CORE CONCEPT

Rule 25(c) addresses substitution in circumstances in which, during the course of the litigation, an interest is transferred from a party to another entity. It also controls the procedure for substitution when one corporate entity loses its identity through dissolution or merger with another corporate entity.

APPLICATIONS

Option to Substitute Parties

Rule 25(c) does not require that the person now holding the

8. *See, e.g., Brook, Weiner, Sered, Kreger & Weinberg v. Coreq, Inc.*, 53 F.3d 851, 852 (7th Cir.1995)("A successor takes over without any other change in the status of the case," and therefore decedent's consent to trial by magistrate judge binds successor.).

9. *See, e.g., Asklar v. Honeywell, Inc.*, 95 F.R.D. 419, 422 (D.Conn.1982)(substantive law, not Rule 25(a), determines whether case may proceed after death of party).

interest transferred be substituted for the transferor-party.[10] Instead, the Rule allows the action to continue in the name of the transferor unless the court chooses to order substitution, or joinder, of the transferee.[11] Thus the case may go to judgment without any substitution of parties having occurred, and the absence of a formal substitution will have no consequence.[12] If it is appropriate in the circumstances of the particular case, both the transferor and transferee will be bound by the court's judgment.[13]

Personal Jurisdiction

Courts generally hold that when successors in interest are joined under Rule 25(c), they are subject to the personal jurisdiction of the court simply because they are successors in interest, "without regard to whether they had any other minimum contacts." [14]

Timing

Rule 25(c) contains no time limit in which substitution must take place.

Subject Matter Jurisdiction: Relation to Rule 19

Joinder of a nondiverse party under rule 25(c) does not usually destroy diversity jurisdiction.[15] However, if the joined party was someone who would have been indispensable under Rule 19 at the time the case was filed, joinder of a nondiverse party destroys diversity jurisdiction.[16]

Extinguishing Corporate Causes of Action

Rule 25(c) is subordinate to substantive law on the issue of survival of a cause of action after corporate reorganizations. Thus if substantive law directs that dissolution of a corporation also extinguishes the corporation's causes of action, Rule 25(c) will not save the cause of action.[17]

10. *See, e.g., Educational Credit Management Corp. v. Bernal,* 207 F.3d 595, 598 (9th Cir.2000) (Rule 25(c) requires no action by anyone after a transfer of interest; judgment binds successor in interest even if successor is not named).

11. *See, e.g., Burka v. Aetna Life Insurance Co.,* 87 F.3d 478 (D.C.Cir.1996)(noting that Rule 25(c) affords option of replacing one party with another, or joining a person with original party).

12. *See, e.g., Arnold Graphics Industries, Inc. v. Independent Agent Center, Inc.,* 775 F.2d 38, 40 (2d Cir.1985)(enforcing judgment against successor corporation where substitution was made only after judgment).

13. *See, e.g., Luxliner P.L. Export Co. v. RDI/Luxliner, Inc.,* 13 F.3d 69, 71 (3d Cir. 1993)(even if no substitution is sought, judgment against original defendant can bind successor).

14. *LiButti v. United States,* 178 F.3d 114 (2d Cir.1999) (collecting other case authority).

15. *Freeport-McMoRan, Inc. v. K N Energy, Inc.,* 498 U.S. 426, 428, 111 S.Ct. 858, 859, 112 L.Ed.2d 951 (1991) (per curiam) (any other result would impede "normal business transactions during the pendency of what might be lengthy litigation").

16. *Freeport–McMoRan, Inc. v. K N Energy, Inc.,* 498 U.S. 426, 111 S.Ct. 858, 112 L.Ed.2d 951 (1991)(per curiam).

17. *See, e.g., ELCA Enterprises, Inc. v. Sisco Equipment Rental & Sales Inc.,* 53 F.3d 186, 190 n. 4 (8th Cir.1995)("Rule 25 does not substantively determine what actions survive the transfer of an interest; rather, it provides substitution procedures for an action that does survive."). *See also Organic Cow, L.L.C. v. Center for New England Dairy Compact Research,* 335

Status of Successor

A party who enters a case as the legal successor of a corporation receives the status which the predecessor corporation possessed at the time the successor entered the case. For example, if the predecessor corporation had already consented to trial by a magistrate judge, the successor is bound by that consent.[18]

Service of Process

If a motion to substitute parties is made under Rule 25(c), service should meet the requirements established in Rule 25(a) for motions to make substitutions for deceased parties.

Relation to Rule 17

Rule 25(c) governs transfers of interest during the pendency of a case. Rule 17(a), by contrast, governs situations in which an interest is transferred before the suit is filed.[19]

RULE 25(d). PUBLIC OFFICERS; DEATH OR SEPARATION FROM OFFICE

CORE CONCEPT

Rule 25(d) governs substitution in which public officers are named parties to actions in their official capacities. It does not control substitution in suits where parties, who also happen to be public officers, are suing or being sued personally.[20] Rule 25(d) provides that if substitution of a successor to a public officer is necessary in a pending suit, the substitution shall be automatic. Rule 25(d) applies to circumstances involving death of a public officer or departure from public office for any reason.

APPLICATIONS

Motions

Because the substitution under Rule 25(d) occurs automatically,

F.3d 66 (2d Cir.2003) (when mandate of commission created by Congress to administer dairy compact expired without renewal, private entity could not be substituted under Rule 25(c) because private entity had no authority to perform role of commission).

18. *See, e.g., Andrews v. Lakeshore Rehabilitation Hospital,* 140 F.3d 1405, 1408 (11th Cir. 1998) (where transfer of interest occurs prior to trial, Rule 25(c) is not applicable and therefore "does not save plaintiff's amendments from the statute of limitations"). *Brook, Weiner, Sered, Kreger & Weinberg v. Coreq, Inc.,* 53 F.3d 851, 852 (7th Cir.1995)("A successor takes over without any other change in the status of the case," and therefore a successor to a corporation is bound by the corporation's previous consent to trial by a magistrate judge.).

19. *See, e.g., FDIC v. Deglau,* 207 F.3d 153, 159 (3d Cir.2000) (Rule 17 governs transfers prior to filing of lawsuit; after lawsuit begins, Rule 25 governs).

20. *See, e.g., Bunn v. Conley,* 309 F.3d 1002, 1009 (7th Cir.2002) (*Bivens* claim is suit against government officer in individual (not official) capacity; thus newly appointed officer cannot be substituted for officer originally sued in individual capacity); *Ellison v. Chilton County Board of Education,* 894 F.Supp. 415, 417 n. 3 (M.D.Ala. 1995)(substitution available for school board members whose terms have expired, to the extent they were sued officially; but claims for individual liability of former board members continue unaffected by official substitution).

there is no need to file or serve a motion seeking the substitution.[21]

Timing

For the same reason that no motion is necessary under Rule 25(d), Rule 25(d) imposes no time requirements.

Survival of the Action

Rule 25(d) provides expressly that a suit by or against a public officer does not abate when a substitution occurs.[22]

Events Prior to Substitution: Stipulations, Admissions, Etc.

It appears settled that substitution of an official for a predecessor in office binds the successor to the results of previous events in the case as surely as if no substitution had been made.[23]

Substitutions in the Style of the Case

Rule 25(d) directs that proceedings subsequent to the substitution shall be in the name of the substituted party. However, this provision is usually no more than a formality, for no consequence attaches to erroneous use of the name of the original party—unless such error somehow has an adverse effect on the case.[24]

Order of Substitution

The court has discretion to order that a new public officer be substituted for a predecessor, but need not do so. Whatever the court decides, Rule 25(d) provides that the presence or absence of such an order does not alter the fact that the automatic substitution has already occurred.[25]

Suit by Title Rather than Individual Name

Rule 25(d) allows suit by or against a public officer under either that person's official title or personal name. The court, however, may

21. *Cheney v. United States District Court,* 541 U.S. 913, ___, 124 S.Ct. 1391, 1395, 158 L.Ed.2d 225 (2004) (substitution is automatic). *See, e.g., Negron Gaztambide v. Hernandez Torres,* 145 F.3d 410 (1st Cir.1998), *cert. denied,* 525 U.S. 1149, 119 S.Ct. 1049, 143 L.Ed.2d 55 (1999) (per curiam) (new officeholders are substituted automatically for their predecessors and automatically have same standing to litigate case).

22. *See, e.g., Saldana–Sanchez v. Lopez–Gerena,* 256 F.3d 1, 10, n. 16 (1st Cir.2001) ("As Fed. R. Civ. P. 25(d)(1) makes clear, the substitution of a public official by his or her successor in an official capacity suit does not affect the underlying action.").

23. *See, e.g., Feliciano v. Rullan,* 303 F.3d 1, 7–8 (1st Cir.2002) (holding that substituted party cannot repudiate stipulations to which predecessor agreed).

24. *See, e.g., Cable v. Ivy Tech State College,* 200 F.3d 467, 475 (7th Cir.1999) (Rule 17(d) "expressly directs that any misnomer of the parties that does not affect their substantive rights shall be disregarded even without a motion or order for substitution"); *Presbytery of New Jersey of Orthodox Presbyterian Church v. Florio,* 40 F.3d 1454, 1458 n. 4 (3d Cir.1994), *cert. denied,* 520 U.S. 1155, 117 S.Ct. 1334, 137 L.Ed.2d 494 (1997)(failure to amend caption to reflect election of new governor/defendant does not affect case).

25. *See, e.g., Shakman v. Democratic Organization of Cook County,* 919 F.2d 455, 456 (7th Cir.1990)(challenger who wins election against official defendant "automatically became a party to . . . consent decree").

add the individual's name in cases where the official title alone has been used. The primary advantage of suing a public officer by title, rather than individual name, is that departure of the person from office thereby does not require consideration of a substitution of names under Rule 25(d).

ADDITIONAL RESEARCH REFERENCES

Wright & Miller, *Federal Practice and Procedure* §§ 1951–62.

C.J.S. Federal Civil Procedure §§ 156–168 et seq.

West's Key No. Digests, Federal Civil Procedure ⚿351–366, 391.

V. DEPOSITIONS AND DISCOVERY

RULE 26

GENERAL PROVISIONS GOVERNING DISCOVERY; DUTY OF DISCLOSURE

(a) Required Disclosures; Methods to Discover Additional Matter.

(1) *Initial Disclosures.* Except in categories of proceedings specified in Rule 26(a)(1)(E), or to the extent otherwise stipulated or directed by order, a party must, without awaiting a discovery request, provide to other parties:

(A) the name and, if known, the address and telephone number of each individual likely to have discoverable information that the disclosing party may use to support its claims or defenses, unless solely for impeachment, identifying the subjects of the information;

(B) a copy of, or a description by category and location of, all documents, data compilations, and tangible things that are in the possession, custody, or control of the party and that the disclosing party may use to support its claims or defenses, unless solely for impeachment;

(C) a computation of any category of damages claimed by the disclosing party, making available for inspection and copying as under Rule 34 the documents or other evidentiary material, not privileged or protected from disclosure, on which such computation is based, including materials bearing on the nature and extent of injuries suffered; and

(D) for inspection and copying as under Rule 34 any insurance agreement under which any person carrying on an insurance business may be liable to satisfy part or all of a judgment which may be entered in the action or to indemnify or reimburse for payments made to satisfy the judgment.

(E) The following categories of proceedings are exempt from initial disclosure under Rule 26(a)(1):

(i) an action for review on an administrative record;

(ii) a petition for habeas corpus or other proceeding to challenge a criminal conviction or sentence;

(iii) an action brought without counsel by a person in custody of the United States, a state, or a state subdivision;

(iv) an action to enforce or quash an administrative summons or subpoena;

(v) an action by the United States to recover benefit payments;

(vi) an action by the United States to collect on a student loan guaranteed by the United States;

(vii) a proceeding ancillary to proceedings in other courts; and

(viii) an action to enforce an arbitration award.

These disclosures must be made at or within 14 days after the Rule 26(f) conference unless a different time is set by stipulation or court order, or unless a party objects during the conference that initial disclosures are not appropriate in the circumstances of the action and states the objection in the Rule 26(f) discovery plan. In ruling on the objection, the court must determine what disclosures—if any—are to be made, and set the time for disclosure. Any party first served or otherwise joined after the Rule 26(f) conference must make these disclosures within 30 days after being served or joined unless a different time is set by stipulation or court order. A party must make its initial disclosures based on the information then reasonably available to it and is not excused from making its disclosures because it has not fully completed its investigation of the case or because it challenges the sufficiency of another party's disclosures or because another party has not made its disclosures.

(2) *Disclosure of Expert Testimony.*

(A) In addition to the disclosures required by paragraph (1), a party shall disclose to other parties the identity of any person who may be used at trial to present evidence under Rules 702, 703, or 705 of the Federal Rules of Evidence.

(B) Except as otherwise stipulated or directed by the court, this disclosure shall, with respect to a witness who is retained or specially employed to provide expert testimony in the case or whose duties as an employee of the party regularly involve giving expert testimony, be accompanied by a written report prepared and signed by the witness. The report shall contain a complete statement of all opinions to be expressed and the basis and reasons therefor; the data or other information considered by the witness in forming the opinions; any exhibits to be used as a summary of or support for the opinions; the qualifications of the witness, including a list of all publications authored by the witness within the preceding ten years; the compensation to be paid for the study and testimony; and a listing of any other cases in which the witness has testified as an expert at trial or by deposition within the preceding four years.

(C) These disclosures shall be made at the times and in the sequence directed by the court. In the absence of other directions from the court or stipulation by the parties, the disclosures shall be made at least 90 days before the trial date or the date the case is to be ready for trial or, if the evidence is intended solely to contradict or rebut evidence on the same subject matter identified by another party under paragraph (2)(B), within 30 days after the disclosure made by the other party. The parties shall supplement these disclosures when required under subdivision (e)(1).

(3) *Pretrial Disclosures.* In addition to the disclosures required by Rule 26(a)(1) and (2), a party must provide to other parties and promptly file with the court the following information regarding the evidence that it may present at trial other than solely for impeachment:

(A) the name and, if not previously provided, the address and telephone number of each witness, separately identifying those whom the party expects to present and those whom the party may call if the need arises;

(B) the designation of those witnesses whose testimony is expected to be presented by means of a deposition and, if not taken stenographically, a transcript of the pertinent portions of the deposition testimony; and

(C) an appropriate identification of each document or other exhibit, including summaries of other evidence, separately identifying those which the party expects to offer and those which the party may offer if the need arises.

Unless otherwise directed by the court, these disclosures must be made at least 30 days before trial. Within 14 days thereafter, unless a different time is specified by the court, a party may serve and promptly file a list disclosing (i) any objections to the use under Rule 32(a) of a deposition designated by another party under Rule 26(a)(3)(B), and (ii) any objection, together with the grounds therefor, that may be made to the admissibility of materials identified under Rule 26(a)(3)(C). Objections not so disclosed, other than objections under Rules 402 and 403 of the Federal Rules of Evidence, are waived unless excused by the court for good cause.

(4) *Form of Disclosures.* Unless the court orders otherwise, all disclosures under Rules 26(a)(1) through (3) must be made in writing, signed, and served.

(5) *Methods to Discover Additional Matter.* Parties may obtain discovery by one or more of the following methods: depositions upon oral examination or written questions; written interrogatories; production of documents or things or permission to enter upon land or other property under Rule 34 or 45(a)(1)(C), for inspection and other purposes; physical and mental examinations; and requests for admission.

(b) Discovery Scope and Limits. Unless otherwise limited by order of the court in accordance with these rules, the scope of discovery is as follows:

(1) *In General.* Parties may obtain discovery regarding any matter, not privileged, that is relevant to the claim or defense of any party, including the existence, description, nature, custody, condition, and location of any books, documents, or other tangible things and the identity and location of persons having knowledge of any discoverable matter. For good cause, the court may order discovery of any matter relevant to the subject matter involved in the action. Relevant information need not be admissible at the trial if the discovery appears reasonably calculated to lead to the discovery of admissible evidence. All discovery is subject to the limitations imposed by Rule 26(b)(2)(i), (ii), and (iii).

(2) *Limitations.* By order, the court may alter the limits in these rules on the number of depositions and interrogatories or the length of depositions under Rule 30. By order or local rule, the court may also limit the number of requests under Rule 36. The frequency or extent of use of the discovery methods otherwise permitted under these rules and by any local rule shall be limited by the court if it determines that: (i) the discovery sought is unreasonably cumulative or duplicative, or is obtainable from some other source that is more convenient, less burdensome, or less expensive; (ii) the party seeking discovery has had ample opportunity by discovery in the action to obtain the information sought; or (iii) the burden or expense of the proposed discovery outweighs its likely benefit, taking into account the needs of the case, the

amount in controversy, the parties' resources, the importance of the issues at stake in the litigation, and the importance of the proposed discovery in resolving the issues. The court may act upon its own initiative after reasonable notice or pursuant to a motion under Rule 26(c).

(3) *Trial Preparation: Materials.* Subject to the provisions of subdivision (b)(4) of this rule, a party may obtain discovery of documents and tangible things otherwise discoverable under subdivision (b)(1) of this rule and prepared in anticipation of litigation or for trial by or for another party or by or for that other party's representative (including the other party's attorney, consultant, surety, indemnitor, insurer, or agent) only upon a showing that the party seeking discovery has substantial need of the materials in the preparation of the party's case and that the party is unable without undue hardship to obtain the substantial equivalent of the materials by other means. In ordering discovery of such materials when the required showing has been made, the court shall protect against disclosure of the mental impressions, conclusions, opinions, or legal theories of an attorney or other representative of a party concerning the litigation.

A party may obtain without the required showing a statement concerning the action or its subject matter previously made by that party. Upon request, a person not a party may obtain without the required showing a statement concerning the action or its subject matter previously made by that person. If the request is refused, the person may move for a court order. The provisions of Rule 37(a)(4) apply to the award of expenses incurred in relation to the motion. For purposes of this paragraph, a statement previously made is (A) a written statement signed or otherwise adopted or approved by the person making it, or (B) a stenographic, mechanical, electrical, or other recording, or a transcription thereof, which is a substantially verbatim recital of an oral statement by the person making it and contemporaneously recorded.

(4) *Trial Preparation: Experts.*

(A) A party may depose any person who has been identified as an expert whose opinions may be presented at trial. If a report from the expert is required under subdivision (a)(2)(B), the deposition shall not be conducted until after the report is provided.

(B) A party may, through interrogatories or by deposition, discover facts known or opinions held by an expert who has been retained or specially employed by another party in anticipation of litigation or preparation for trial and who is not expected to be called as a witness at trial only as provided in Rule 35(b) or upon a showing of exceptional circumstances under which it is impracticable for the party seeking discovery to obtain facts or opinions on the same subject by other means.

(C) Unless manifest injustice would result, (i) the court shall require that the party seeking discovery pay the expert a reasonable fee for time spent in responding to discovery under this subdivision; and (ii) with respect to discovery obtained under subdivision (b)(4)(B) of this rule the court shall require the party seeking discovery to pay the other party a fair portion of the fees and expenses reasonably incurred by the latter party in obtaining facts and opinions from the expert.

(5) *Claims of Privilege or Protection of Trial Preparation Materials.* When a party withholds information otherwise discoverable under these rules by claiming that it is privileged or subject to protection as trial preparation material, the party shall make the claim expressly and shall describe the nature of the documents, communications, or things not produced or disclosed in a manner that, without revealing information itself privileged or protected, will enable other parties to assess the applicability of the privilege or protection.

(c) Protective Orders. Upon motion by a party or by the person from whom discovery is sought, accompanied by a certification that the movant has in good faith conferred or attempted to confer with other affected parties in an effort to resolve the dispute without court action, and for good cause shown, the court in which the action is pending or alternatively, on matters relating to a deposition, the court in the district where the deposition is to be taken may make any order which justice requires to protect a party or person from annoyance, embarrassment, oppression, or undue burden or expense, including one or more of the following:

(1) that the disclosure or discovery not be had;

(2) that the disclosure or discovery may be had only on specified terms and conditions, including a designation of the time or place;

(3) that the discovery may be had only by a method of discovery other than that selected by the party seeking discovery;

(4) that certain matters not be inquired into, or that the scope of the disclosure or discovery be limited to certain matters;

(5) that discovery be conducted with no one present except persons designated by the court;

(6) that a deposition, after being sealed, be opened only by order of the court;

(7) that a trade secret or other confidential research, development, or commercial information not be revealed or be revealed only in a designated way; and

(8) that the parties simultaneously file specified documents or information enclosed in sealed envelopes to be opened as directed by the court.

If the motion for a protective order is denied in whole or in part, the court may, on such terms and conditions as are just, order that any party or other person provide or permit discovery. The provisions of Rule 37(a)(4) apply to the award of expenses incurred in relation to the motion.

(d) *Timing and Sequence of Discovery.* Except in categories of proceedings exempted from initial disclosure under Rule 26(a)(1)(E), or when authorized under these rules or by order or agreement of the parties, a party may not seek discovery from any source before the parties have conferred as required by Rule 26(f). Unless the court upon motion, for the convenience of parties and witnesses and in the interests of justice, orders otherwise, methods of discovery may be used in any sequence, and the fact that a party is conducting discovery, whether by deposition or otherwise, does not operate to delay any other party's discovery.

(e) Supplementation of Disclosures and Responses. A party who has made a disclosure under subdivision (a) or responded to a request for discovery with a disclosure or response is under a duty to supplement or correct the disclosure or response to include information thereafter acquired if ordered by the court or in the following circumstances:

(1) A party is under a duty to supplement at appropriate intervals its disclosures under subdivision (a) if the party learns that in some material respect the information disclosed is incomplete or incorrect and if the additional or corrective information has not otherwise been made known to the other parties during the discovery process or in writing. With respect to testimony of an expert from whom a report is required under subdivision (a)(2)(B)

the duty extends both to information contained in the report and to information provided through a deposition of the expert, and any additions or other changes to this information shall be disclosed by the time the party's disclosures under Rule 26(a)(3) are due.

(2) A party is under a duty seasonably to amend a prior response to an interrogatory, request for production, or request for admission if the party learns that the response is in some material respect incomplete or incorrect and if the additional or corrective information has not otherwise been made known to the other parties during the discovery process or in writing.

(f) Conference of Parties; Planning for Discovery. Except in categories of proceedings exempted from initial disclosure under Rule 26(a)(1)(E) or when otherwise ordered, the parties must, as soon as practicable and in any event at least 21 days before a scheduling conference is held or a scheduling order is due under Rule 16(b), confer to consider the nature and basis of their claims and defenses and the possibilities for a prompt settlement or resolution of the case, to make or arrange for the disclosures required by Rule 26(a)(1), and to develop a proposed discovery plan that indicates the parties' views and proposals concerning:

(1) what changes should be made in the timing, form, or requirement for disclosures under Rule 26(a), including a statement as to when disclosures under Rule 26(a)(1) were made or will be made:

(2) the subjects on which discovery may be needed, when discovery should be completed, and whether discovery should be conducted in phases or be limited to or focused upon particular issues;

(3) what changes should be made in the limitations on discovery imposed under these rules or by local rule, and what other limitations should be imposed; and

(4) any other orders that should be entered by the court under Rule 26(c) or under Rule 16(b) and (c).

The attorneys of record and all unrepresented parties that have appeared in the case are jointly responsible for arranging the conference, for attempting in good faith to agree on the proposed discovery plan, and for submitting to the court within 14 days after the conference a written report outlining the plan. A court may order that the parties or attorneys attend the conference in person.

If necessary to comply with its expedited schedule for Rule 16(b) conferences, a court may by local rule (i) require that the conference between the parties occur fewer than 21 days before the scheduling conference is held or a scheduling order is due under Rule 16(b), and (ii) require that the written report outlining the discovery plan be filed fewer than 14 days after the conference between the parties, or excuse the parties from submitting a written report and permit them to report orally on their discovery plan at the Rule 16(b) conference.

(g) Signing of Disclosures, Discovery Requests, Responses, and Objections.

(1) Every disclosure made pursuant to subdivision (a)(1) or subdivision (a)(3) shall be signed by at least one attorney of record in the attorney's individual name, whose address shall be stated. An unrepresented party shall sign the disclosure and state the party's address. The signature of the attorney or party constitutes a certification that to the best of the signer's knowledge, information, and belief, formed after a reasonable inquiry, the disclosure is complete and correct as of the time it is made.

(2) Every discovery request, response, or objection made by a party represented by an attorney shall be signed by at least one attorney of record in the attorney's individual name, whose address shall be stated. An unrepresented party shall sign the request, response, or objection and state the party's address. The signature of the attorney or party constitutes a certification that to the best of the signer's knowledge, information, and belief, formed after a reasonable inquiry, the request, response, or objection is:

(A) consistent with these rules and warranted by existing law or a good faith argument for the extension, modification, or reversal of existing law;

(B) not interposed for any improper purpose, such as to harass or to cause unnecessary delay or needless increase in the cost of litigation; and

(C) not unreasonable or unduly burdensome or expensive, given the needs of the case, the discovery already had in the case, the amount in controversy, and the importance of the issues at stake in the litigation.

If a request, response, or objection is not signed, it shall be stricken unless it is signed promptly after the omission is called to the attention of the party making the request, response, or objection, and a party shall not be obligated to take any action with respect to it until it is signed.

(3) If without substantial justification a certification is made in violation of the rule, the court, upon motion or upon its own initiative, shall impose upon the person who made the certification, the party on whose behalf the disclosure, request, response, or objection is made, or both, an appropriate sanction, which may include an order to pay the amount of the reasonable expenses incurred because of the violation, including a reasonable attorney's fee.

[Amended December 27, 1946, effective March 19, 1948; January 21, 1963, effective July 1, 1963; February 28, 1966, effective July 1, 1966; March 30, 1970, effective July 1, 1970; April 29, 1980, effective August 1, 1980; April 28, 1983, effective August 1, 1983; March 2, 1987, effective August 1, 1987; April 22, 1993, effective December 1, 1993; April 17, 2000, effective December 1, 2000.]

AUTHORS' COMMENTARY ON RULE 26

PURPOSE AND SCOPE

Rule 26 contains the general provisions governing discovery. It sets forth the general discovery procedures, controls the scope of inquiry allowed, provides for protective orders, and imposes a duty to supplement discovery responses. The general provisions in Rule 26 apply to the specific discovery devices in Rules 27 through 37.

NOTE: Rule 26 and the other discovery rules were substantially revised in 1970, 1993, and 2000. Therefore, great care should be exercised when citing or relying on decisions pertaining to Rule 26.

RULE 26(a). REQUIRED DISCLOSURES; METHODS TO DISCOVER ADDITIONAL MATTER

CORE CONCEPT

Rule 26(a) requires that parties disclose certain information automatically, without the need for discovery requests, at three points during the litigation. First, all parties must make broad initial disclosures at or shortly after they conduct the discovery meeting under Rule 26(f). Second, Rule 26(a) requires disclosures about expert testimony 90 days before trial. Third, Rule 26(a) specifies the pretrial disclosures to be made 30 days before trial. Rule 26(a) also establishes the exclusive list of available discovery methods to supplement the automatic disclosures. In general, the only discovery devices that parties may use are: depositions upon oral examination (Rules 30, 27, 28, and 32); depositions upon written questions (Rules 31, 27, 28, and 32); written interrogatories (Rule 33); production of documents and things and entry onto land for inspection (Rule 34); physical and mental inspections (Rule 35); and requests for admission (Rule 36).

RULE 26(a)(1). INITIAL DISCLOSURES

CORE CONCEPT

At the commencement of discovery, each party must disclose the identity of witnesses, a description of documents by category and location, a computation of each category of damages, and insurance information.

APPLICATIONS

Time for Initial Disclosure

Parties must make their initial disclosures at or within 14 days after the discovery meeting required by Rule 26(f), unless a different time is set by court order or stipulation. Thus, Rule 26 establishes the following typical sequence for the early discovery events: first, the court schedules an initial scheduling conference; second, the parties conduct a discovery meeting at least 21 days before the court's initial scheduling conference; third, the parties make their voluntary disclosures; and fourth, the parties meet with the judge for the scheduling conference, where the timetable for the balance of the discovery events will be established. Parties joined or served after the Rule 26(f) conference must make the initial disclosures within 30 days after being joined or served, unless a different time is set by stipulation or court order.

Content of Initial Disclosure

Rule 26(a)(1) requires automatic initial disclosure of four categories of information:

(A) *Witnesses*: Parties must disclose the name, and if known the address and telephone number,[1] of each individual likely to have discoverable information that the disclosing party may use to support its claims or defenses.[2] Parties must also identify the subjects of such information.

(B) *Documents*: Parties must provide a copy of, or a description by category and location of, all documents, data compilations, and tangible things that the disclosing party may use to support its claims or defenses.[3] Computerized data and other electronically-

1. *Scaife v. Boenne*, 191 F.R.D. 590, 594 (N.D.In.2000) (Rule 26(a)(1)(A) contemplates disclosure of address and telephone number so the other party can contact the witnesses, if appropriate).

2. *Cummings v. General Motors Corp.*, 365 F.3d 944, 954 (10th Cir. 2004) (a party is not obligated to disclose witnesses or documents, whether favorable or unfavorable, that it does not intend to use); *Intel Corp. v. VIA Technologies, Inc.*, 204 F.R.D. 450, 451–52 (N.D.Cal.2001) (witness identity must be disclosed if the witness may be used to support claims or defenses in the context of a motion or at trial, but an affidavit or declaration is work product and need not be disclosed).

3. *Lovato v. Burlington Northern and Santa Fe Ry. Co.*, 200 F.R.D. 448 (D.Colo. 2001), *rev'd on other grounds*, 201 F.R.D. 509 (D. Colo.2001) (medical records must be disclosed).

recorded information are deemed documents for purposes of the initial disclosure.[4] Except in cases with very few documents, most parties will disclose categories and locations rather than producing all the documents. Parties must provide or describe all disclosable documents in their possession, control, or custody.[5]

(C) *Damages Computations*: Each party must provide a computation of any category of damages claimed by that party.[6] Each party must also produce the non-privileged documents supporting the computation, including documents bearing on the nature and extent of injuries suffered.

(D) *Insurance*: Each party must provide all insurance policies that may provide coverage for part or all of any judgment that might be entered in the action.[7]

Additional disclosures may be required by directive.

Information to Support Claims or Defenses

Rule 26(a)(1) requires disclosure only of information and documents that the disclosing party may use to support its claims or defenses. This provision dovetails with the exclusionary sanction of Rule 37(c)(1), so that a party may not use information or documents not disclosed initially or by supplement.[8]

Impeachment

Information and documents that a party may use solely for impeachment need not be disclosed.[9]

Excluded Proceedings

Rule 26(a)(1)(E) excludes 8 categories of proceedings from the initial disclosures:

(1) appeals from administrative proceedings;

(2) petitions for habeaus corpus or like challenges to criminal convictions or sentences;

(3) pro se prisoner actions;

4. *Super Film of America, Inc. v. UCB Films, Inc.*, 219 F.R.D. 649, 657 (D.Kan. 2004); *In re Bristol–Myers Squibb Securities Litigation*, 205 F.R.D. 437, 440–41 (D.N.J.2002) (the Rule applies to electronic documents in existence at the time of the disclosure, but not to documents scanned for purposes of trial preparation); The Advisory Committee Note to the 1993 Amendments to Rule 26(a)(1).

5. See Rule 34(a) for an explanation of the scope of documents within a party's possession, custody, or control.

6. *Williams v. Trader Pub. Co.*, 218 F.3d 481, 487 (5th Cir.2000) (damages for emotional distress are not susceptible to the type of calculation contemplated by Rule 26(a)(1)); *Morrison Knudsen Corp. v. Fireman's Fund Ins. Co.*, 175 F.3d 1221 (10th Cir.1999).

7. *Gluck v. Ansett Australia Ltd.*, 204 F.R.D. 217, 222 (D.D.C.2001). *Flores v. Southern Peru Copper Corp.*, 203 F.R.D. 92 (S.D.N.Y.2001).

8. The 2000 Amendment to the Advisory Committee Note to Rule 26(a)(1).

9. *Searles v. Van Bebber*, 251 F.3d 869 (10th Cir.2001), *cert. denied,* 536 U.S. 904, 122 S.Ct. 2356, 153 L.Ed.2d 179 (2002); *Lomascolo v. Otto Oldsmobile–Cadillac, Inc.*, 253 F.Supp.2d 354, 359 (N.D.N.Y. 2003) (documents must be used ***solely*** for impeachment).

(4) actions to enforce or quash an administrative summons or subpoena;

(5) actions by the United States to recover benefit payments;

(6) actions by the United States to collect on student loans guaranteed by the United States;

(7) proceedings ancillary to proceedings in other courts; and

(8) actions to enforce arbitration awards.

Investigation for Initial Disclosure

The parties must make their initial disclosures based on the information then "reasonably available." Rule 26(a)(1) expressly provides that a party may not avoid the initial disclosure requirements by claiming that its investigation is not yet complete.

Failure to Disclose

Failure to make the initial disclosures required by Rule 26(a)(1) can result in the exclusion of the undisclosed witness or information,[10] unless the failure was harmless or there was substantial justification.[11]

Other Party's Failure to Disclose

A party may not refuse to make the Rule 26(a) disclosures because another party has also failed to do so.[12] Likewise, a party believing that another party's disclosure was not sufficient must nonetheless make its own disclosures.

Disclosures Automatic

The initial disclosures are automatically required, without any need for a request or demand.

Stipulations Not to Disclose

The parties may stipulate to the elimination or modification of the initial disclosures, unless precluded from doing so by local rule or court order.

Form of Disclosures

The initial disclosures should be in writing, signed, and served on other parties unless otherwise directed by local rule or court order.[13]

10. *Wilson v. AM General Corp.*, 167 F.3d 1114 (7th Cir.1999) (rejecting claim that the witnesses were impeachment witnesses and excluding their testimony). *But see Hernandez–Torres v. Intercontinental Trading, Inc.*, 158 F.3d 43, 49 (1st Cir.1998) (witnesses need not be listed until 30 days before trial, as required by Rule 20(a)(3)(C)).

11. *Pfingston v. Ronan Engineering Co.*, 284 F.3d 999, 1005 (9th Cir.2002) (examining prejudice to the other party caused by delayed disclosure); *Trost v. Trek Bicycle Corp.*, 162 F.3d 1004 (8th Cir.1998).

12. *See Jacobsen v. Deseret Book Co.*, 287 F.3d 936, 954 (10th Cir.2002), *cert. denied,* 537 U.S. 1066, 123 S.Ct. 623, 154 L.Ed.2d 555 (2002) .

13. *See S.E.C. v. TheStreet.Com*, 273 F.3d 222, 233 (2d Cir.2001) (initial disclosures under Rule 26(a)(1) are not filed unless ordered by the court or used in a subsequent stage of the proceedings).

The signature constitutes a certification that the disclosure is complete and accurate under Rule 26(g)(1).

Objections

A party believing that Rule 26(a)(1) initial disclosures are "not appropriate in the circumstances of the action" may object during the Rule 26(f) discovery conference. The objection should then be stated in the Rule 26(f) discovery plan filed with the court. Disclosures are not required thereafter except as ordered by the court.[14] In ruling on the objection, the court must determine what disclosures, if any, will be made and set the time for such disclosures.

New or Late Served Parties

Parties that have not been joined or served at the time of the initial disclosures or the Rule 26(f) discovery conference must still make initial disclosures. The time for their disclosures will be 30 days from when they are served or joined, unless modified by stipulation or order. The scope of such parties' disclosures will be similar to the original parties with respect to any stipulations or court orders.[15]

RULE 26(a)(2). DISCLOSURE OF EXPERT TESTIMONY

CORE CONCEPT

Each party must disclose the identity of its expert witnesses and produce an expert report for each expert witness.

APPLICATIONS

Time for Expert Disclosure

The time for expert disclosures can be set by the court or stipulated by the parties.[16] In the absence of a court order or stipulation, the expert disclosures must be made 90 days before the trial date.[17] If the expert testimony is purely to contradict or rebut testimony disclosed by another party, then the disclosure must be made within 30 days after the disclosure by the other party.[18]

Content of Expert Disclosure

Rule 26(a)(2) requires automatic disclosure of the identity of persons who "may" testify as expert witnesses and production of a report for each such witness.

14. The 2000 Amendment to the Advisory Committee Note to Rule 26(a)(1).

15. The Advisory Committee Note to the 2000 Amendment to Rule 26(a)(1).

16. *See Southern Union Company v. Southwest Gas Corp.*, 180 F.Supp.2d 1021, 1059–60 (D.Ariz.2002) (the disclosures should be sufficiently in advance of trial that opposing parties have a reasonable opportunity to prepare for effective cross examination and perhaps arrange for expert testimony from other witnesses).

17. *School Bd. of Collier County, Fla. v. K.C.*, 285 F.3d 977, 981 (11th Cir.2002).

18. *Callahan v. A.E.V., Inc.*, 182 F.3d 237, 259 (3d Cir.1999) (expert witness designated as "rebuttal expert" allowed to testify during case-in-chief).

Expert Report

Each expert report must be in writing and signed by the expert,[19] and must contain: a complete statement of all the expert's opinions and the basis and reasons therefore;[20] the data and information considered by the expert, including documents provided by counsel;[21] any exhibits to be used as support for or a summary of the opinions; the qualifications of the expert and all publications authored by the expert in the past 10 years; the expert's compensation for his review and testimony; and a list of all other cases in which the expert has testified at trial or at deposition in the past 4 years.[22] The report itself should contain all the required information with considerable detail,[23] and may not satisfy Rule 26(a)(2)(B) by incorporating interrogatory answers.[24]

Failure to Disclose Report

The failure to disclose a report meeting the requirements of Rule 26(a)(2)(B) may preclude that witness from testifying, either altogether[25] or as to specific opinions not disclosed in the report.[26] Such sanctions are "automatic and mandatory" unless the party failing to disclose can show the failure was justified or harmless.[27] Disclosure of

19. *Gust v. Jones,* 162 F.3d 587 (10th Cir. 1998); *Trigon Ins. Co. v. United States*, 204 F.R.D. 277, 292–93 (E.D.Va.2001) (the report must be prepared by the expert, but the attorney may assist).

20. *King v. Ford Motor Co.*, 209 F.3d 886, 900 (6th Cir.2000), *cert. denied*, 531 U.S. 960, 121 S.Ct. 386, 148 L.Ed.2d 298 (2000).

21. *Herman v. Marine Midland Bank*, 207 F.R.D. 26 (W.D.N.Y.2002) (the rule require the disclosure of all information provided to the expert, including work product); *Southern Union Company v. Southwest Gas Corp.*, 180 F.Supp.2d 1021, 1059–60 (D.Ariz.2002) (documents provided to the expert must be disclosed even if not relied upon by the expert in forming his or her opinions).

22. *Doblar v. Unverferth Manuf. Co., Inc.*, 185 F.R.D. 258 (D.S.D.1999) (awarding sanctions against the expert because many instances of prior testimony were not disclosed); *Coleman v. Dydula*, 190 F.R.D. 316, 318 (W.D.N.Y.1999) (the list of cases should, at a minimum, include the name of the court where the testimony occurred, the names of the parties, the case number, and whether the testimony was given at a deposition or trial); *Zic v. Italian Government Travel Office*, 130 F.Supp.2d 991, 1001 (N.D.Ill. 2001) (names of the parties in other cases in which the expert has testified is sufficient, although not ideal). *Cf. Trunk v. Midwest Rubber & Supply Co.*, 175 F.R.D. 664, 665 (D.Colo.1997) (Rule 26(a)(2)(B) report does not require a party to produce reports offered by its expert witness in unrelated litigation).

23. *Hilt v. SFC, Inc.*, 170 F.R.D. 182, 184–85 (D.Kan.1997) (report must provide the substantive rationale in detail with respect to the basis and reasons for the proffered opinions).

24. *Smith v. State Farm Fire and Casualty Co.*, 164 F.R.D. 49 (S.D.W.Va.1995).

25. *Ortiz-Lopez v. Sociedad Espanola de Auxilio Mutuo Y Beneficiencia de Puerto Rico,* 248 F.3d 29 (1st Cir.2001).

26. *Brandt Distributing Co., Inc. v. Federal Ins. Co.*, 247 F.3d 822 (8th Cir.2001); *Salgado v. General Motors Corp.*, 150 F.3d 735, 742 (7th Cir.1998) (expert report must contain a detailed description of expert opinions and bases therefore); *Lamarca v. United States*, 31 F.Supp.2d 110, 122–23 (E.D.N.Y.1998) (expert opinion not in report excluded even though disclosed during deposition); *Coastal Fuels of Puerto Rico v. Caribbean Petroleum Corp.*, 79 F.3d 182 (1st Cir. 1996), *cert. denied*, 519 U.S. 927, 117 S.Ct. 294, 136 L.Ed.2d 214 (1996).

27. *Jacobsen v. Deseret Book Co.*, 287 F.3d 936, 952–53 (10th Cir.2002), *cert. denied,* 537 U.S. 1066, 123 S.Ct. 623, 154 L.Ed.2d 555 (2002) (listing factors to be considered in determining the existence of substantial justification or harmlessness); *NutraSweet Co. v. X–L Engineering Co.*, 227 F.3d 776, 785–86 (7th Cir.2000).

the expert opinions or required information in deposition has been held not to be a substitute for inclusion in the expert disclosure.[28]

Stipulations Not to Disclose Expert Reports

The parties may stipulate to the elimination or modification of the expert report disclosures, unless precluded from doing so by local rule or court order.

Testimony is Measure, Not Witness Qualification

The expert disclosures are required if the testimony is expert in nature, not factual; expert disclosures are not required if an expert is being called to give percipient factual testimony.[29]

Experts Employed by a Party

A party must produce an expert report for any employee whose duties regularly involve giving expert testimony or who was specially employed to provide expert testimony.[30] This requirement will only apply, however, if the employee is giving expert testimony.[31]

Treating Physicians

An expert report is generally not required for a treating physician to testify regarding the treatment,[32] although a minority of courts require an expert report when the treating physician will offer testimony as to causation.[33]

Always Disclose Experts Identities

In circumstances where no expert report is required, such as by stipulation, for employees whose duties do not include regularly testifying, or for treating physicians, the party must still disclose the identity of the expert witness or the witness will not be permitted to testify.[34]

Rebuttal Experts

Leave may be obtained to disclose an expert report for a rebuttal expert witness after the time for expert disclosures under Rule 26(a)(2).[35]

28. *Commercial Data Servers, Inc. v. International Business Machines Corp.*, 262 F.Supp.2d 50 (S.D.N.Y. 2003).

29. *Gomez v. Rivera Rodriguez*, 344 F.3d 103, 113 (1st Cir. 2003) (Rule 26(a)(2) does not encompass a percipient witness who happens to be an expert).

30. *Prieto v. Malgor*, 361 F.3d 1313, 1318 (11th Cir. 2004); *Rollins ex rel Rollins v. Barlow*, 188 F.Supp.2d 660, 661–62 (S.D.W.Va.2002) (report not required for police officer expert witness neither retained nor employed by the plaintiff); *Brown v. Best Foods*, 169 F.R.D. 385, 387 (N.D.Ala.1996) (treating physician may give expert opinion testimony without filing an expert report because the physician was not "retained or specifically employed" to render expert testimony).

31. *Long v. Cottrell, Inc.*, 265 F.3d 663, 668 (8th Cir.2001), *cert. denied*, 535 U.S. 931, 122 S.Ct. 1304, 152 L.Ed.2d 215 (2002) (expert report not required even though employee regularly testified for the party as an expert witness because the testimony at issue was fact testimony, not expert testimony).

32. *See Brandon v. Village of Maywood*, 179 F.Supp.2d 847 (N.D.Ill. 2001) (discussing when a report is required for a treating physician); *Brundidge v. City of Buffalo*, 79 F.Supp.2d 219, 224 (W.D.N.Y.1999).

33. *See Musser v. Gentiva Health Services*, 356 F.3d 751, 757 (7th Cir. 2004); *Martin v. CSX Transp., Inc.*, 215 F.R.D. 554 (S.D.Ind. 2003).

34. *Hamburger v. State Farm Mut. Auto. Ins. Co.*, 361 F.3d 875, 883, n.4 (5th Cir. 2004).

35. *See Nyama v. Ashcroft*, 357 F.3d 812, 816 (8th Cir. 2004); *Eckelkamp v. Beste*, 315 F.3d 863, 872 (8th Cir.2002).

Disclosures Automatic

The expert disclosures are automatically required, without any need for a request or demand.

Form of Disclosures

The expert disclosures should be in writing, signed, and served on other parties, unless otherwise directed by local rule or court order.[36] The signature constitutes a certification that the disclosure is complete and accurate under Rule 26(g)(1).

Objections

The court's case management order may designate a period for filing objections to the sufficiency of expert disclosures, in which case such objections are waived if not timely raised.[37] Otherwise, sanctions for an insufficient disclosure are governed by the sanctions provisions in Rule 37(c)(1).

Standard on Appeal

In reviewing a trial court's order for exclusion of expert testimony for failure to disclose, the appellate court will apply an abuse of discretion standard.[38]

RULE 26(a)(3). PRETRIAL DISCLOSURES

CORE CONCEPT

Prior to trial, each party must disclose the witnesses that may testify at trial, the deposition testimony that may be offered at trial, and the exhibits that may be offered at trial.

APPLICATIONS

Time for Pretrial Disclosure

The time for pretrial disclosures is often set by the court. In the absence of a court order, the expert disclosures must be made 30 days before the trial date. Parties will not be required to respond to discovery requests seeking the information covered by Rule 26(a)(3) at an earlier stage in the litigation.[39]

Content of Pretrial Disclosure

Rule 26(a)(3) requires a pretrial disclosure of the following information:

36. *See S.E.C. v. TheStreet.Com*, 273 F.3d 222, 233 (2d Cir.2001) (initial disclosures under Rule 26(a)(2) are not filed unless ordered by the court or used in a subsequent stage of the proceedings).

37. *McCoy v. Whirlpool Corp.*, 214 F.R.D. 646, 648–49 (D.Kan. 2003).

38. *Tompkin v. Philip Morris USA, Inc.*, 362 F.3d 882, 894–95 (6th Cir. 2004).

39. *Banks v. Office of Senate Sergeant–At–Arms*, 222 F.R.D. 7, 15 (D.D.C. 2004).

(A) *Witnesses*: Each party must disclose the name and, unless already disclosed, the address and phone number of each witness that may testify at trial. The disclosure should indicate those witnesses who are expected to testify and those who may be called if needed.

(B) *Depositions*: Each party must designate the testimony that the party intends to introduce in the form of a deposition. If the deposition was recorded other than stenographically, then the party must provide a transcript of the pertinent parts of the testimony.[40]

(C) *Exhibits*: Each party must identify all exhibits, including demonstrative or summary exhibits. The disclosure should indicate those exhibits that the party expects to introduce and those that the party may introduce if needed.

Impeachment

The pretrial disclosure is not required to include documents or testimony to be introduced solely for impeachment.[41]

Failure to Disclose

Any witnesses, depositions, or exhibits not properly disclosed under Rule 26(a)(3) may be excluded from use at trial.[42]

Objections to Deposition Testimony or Exhibits

Any objections to the use of a deposition or exhibit must be served and filed within 14 days of the disclosure of the intent to use the deposition or exhibit. The statement of the objections should state the grounds for the objections. Failure to disclose such an objection is a waiver of the objection, except for objections to relevancy under Rules 402 and 403 of the Federal Rules of Evidence. Note that the disclosure of the objection is not the same as making the objection; a party must still object when the deposition or exhibit is offered at trial.[43]

Disclosures Automatic

The pretrial disclosures are automatically required, without any need for a request or demand.

Form of Disclosures

The pretrial disclosures should be in writing, signed, served on other parties, and filed with the court, unless otherwise directed by local rule or court order. The signature constitutes a certification that the disclosure is complete and accurate under Rule 26(g)(1).

40. *Tilton v. Capital Cities/ABC, Inc.*, 115 F.3d 1471, 1478 (10th Cir.1997).

41. *Halbasch v. Med–Data, Inc.*, 192 F.R.D. 641 (D.Or.2000) (discussing the various interpretations of "solely for impeachment"); *DeBiasio v. Illinois Central Railroad*, 52 F.3d 678 (7th Cir.1995), *cert. denied*, 516 U.S. 1157, 116 S.Ct. 1040, 134 L.Ed.2d 188 (1996).

42. The Advisory Committee Note to the 1993 Amendment to Rule 26.

43. The Advisory Committee Note to the 1993 Amendment to Rule 26.

RULE 26(a)(4). FORM OF DISCLOSURES; FILING

CORE CONCEPT

The automatic disclosures under Rule 26(a) should be in writing, signed, served on other parties, unless otherwise directed by local rule or court order. Only the pretrial disclosure under Rule 26(a)(3) must be filed. The signature constitutes a certification that the disclosure is complete and accurate under Rule 26(g)(1).

RULE 26(a)(5). METHODS TO DISCOVER ADDITIONAL MATTER

CORE CONCEPT

There are a few situations in which discovery methods other than those listed in Rules 26–37 are available. Informal methods of discovery, such as interviews of witnesses, are permissible discovery tools.[44] Rule 34 governing production of documents and things allows a party to initiate an independent action in the nature of a bill of discovery to obtain the right to inspect documents or things in the possession of a non-party (but note that such an action may be unnecessary under the subpoena power presently available under Rule 45). Rule 69 provides that a party may conduct discovery in aid of execution under the Federal Rules or under state rules or practices. Discovery of evidence located in a foreign country is controlled by the Hague Convention and the laws of the foreign country, and may be achieved in various manners (see Rule 28 for a more detailed description of deposing a witness in a foreign country).

RULE 26(b)(1). DISCOVERY SCOPE AND LIMITS—IN GENERAL

CORE CONCEPT

In general, discovery is allowed of any matter that is relevant to the claim or defense of any party in the pending action and is not privileged.[45] Discovery is more limited with respect to trial preparation materials, non-testifying expert witnesses, and physical or mental examinations.

APPLICATIONS

Covered Actions

The discovery rules apply to all civil actions in federal court, except for the narrow exceptions listed in Rule 81 (such as certain admiralty matters and matters in arbitration pursuant to federal statute). The

44. *Lovato v. Burlington Northern and Santa Fe Ry. Co.*, 200 F.R.D. 448 (D.Colo. 2001), *rev'd on other grounds*, 201 F.R.D. 509 (D.Colo.2001) ("informal interviews may often be the most efficient and effective discovery method").

45. *Schoffstall v. Henderson*, 223 F.3d 818, 823 (8th Cir.2000).

Rules apply in bankruptcy proceedings, patent actions, and civil contempt proceedings. They apply in habeas corpus actions if the court grants leave to conduct discovery.

"Relevant" Defined

The term "relevant" is not defined by the Rules, but was extremely broad prior to the 2000 Amendments.[46] Courts have defined "relevant" to encompass "any matter that bears on, or that reasonably could lead to other matters that could bear on, any issue that is or may be in the case." [47] Courts also have defined "relevant" as "germane." [48] However, although Rule 26(b)(1) continues to use the word "relevant" after the 2000 Amendments, the scope of discovery has been narrowed and we may see the courts construing "relevant" less broadly in the future.[49]

Claim or Defense vs. Subject Matter

The 2000 Amendments changed the scope of discovery from matters "relevant to the subject matter involved in the pending action" to matters "relevant to the claim or defense of any party."[50] The Advisory Committee did not define the distinction, but indicated that it wants the focus of discovery to be the actual claims and defenses in the action, and does not want discovery to be used to develop new claims or defenses not already pleaded.[51] However, information such as other incidents of the same type or involving the same product or information about a party's organizational structure may be relevant to the claims in the action.[52]

Motion to Expand the Scope

For "good cause," the court may expand discovery to include matters relevant to the subject matter involved in the action.[53] This determination might be made in the context of a motion to compel a more broad response to particular discovery requests, or possibly could be raised in the Rule 26(f) discovery report and addressed during the initial status conference with the court.[54] The "good cause" standard is

46. *Behnia v. Shapiro*, 176 F.R.D. 277, 280 (N.D.Ill.1997); *but see Food Lion, Inc. v. United Food and Commercial Workers Int'l Union*, 103 F.3d 1007, 1012–14 (D.C.Cir.1997) (finding that "relevant" did not extend to third and fourth party documents).

47. *Oil, Chemical & Atomic Workers Local Union v. N.L.R.B.*, 711 F.2d 348, 360 (D.C.Cir. 1983) ; *Kidwiler v. Progressive Paloverde Ins. Co.*, 192 F.R.D. 193, 199 (N.D.W.Va.2000).

48. *Oppenheimer Fund, Inc. v. Sanders*, 437 U.S. 340, 351, 98 S.Ct. 2380, 2389–90, 57 L.Ed.2d 253 (1978).

49. *See In re PE Corp. Securities Litigation*, 221 F.R.D. 20, 24 (D.Conn. 2003); *Behler v. Hanlon*, 199 F.R.D. 553, 555 (D.Md. 2001) (amended Rule 26 is more narrow).

50. *See Sanyo Laser Products Inc. v. Arista Records, Inc.*, 214 F.R.D. 496 (S.D.Ind.2003) (discussing the effects of the 2000 Amendments).

51. The Advisory Committee Note to the 2000 Amendment to Rule 26(b)(1).

52. The Advisory Committee Note to the 2000 Amendment to Rule 26(b)(1).

53. *Castillo v. Norton*, 219 F.R.D. 155, 160, n.2 (D.Ariz. 2003); *In re Maxim Group, Inc. Securities Litigation*, 2002 WL 987660 (N.D.Ga. 2002).

54. The Advisory Committee Note to the 2000 Amendment to Rule 26(b)(1).

meant to be flexible, giving broad discretion to the court.[55]

Relevant to Potential Claims

A party may discover any matter that is relevant to any claim, issue, or defense that is pleaded in the case, regardless of which party raises the claim, issue, or defense. Discovery is not permitted as to potential additional claims or defenses, absent a court order expanding the scope of discovery.[56] Thus, discovery is permitted with respect to claims that have been challenged by a motion to dismiss or motion for summary judgment. However, if a claim has been dismissed, further discovery that is relevant to that claim only will not be allowed.[57]

Relevant vs. Admissible

Evidence need not be admissible to be relevant, and thus discoverable.[58] Rule 26(b)(1) states that relevant inadmissible evidence is discoverable if it is "reasonably calculated to lead to the discovery of admissible evidence."[59] Conversely, admissible evidence is almost always discoverable.[60]

Limitations on Discovery

The broad scope of discovery under Rule 26(b)(1) must be read in conjunction with the three limitations in Rule 26(b)(2) relating to discovery that is cumulative or unduly burdensome. Although this has been the case for years, the 2000 amendments added a specific reference in Rule 26(b)(1) to these limitations to prompt the courts to apply the limitations more vigorously.[61]

Jurisdictional Issues

Discovery is allowed with respect to jurisdictional issues.[62] Thus, parties may conduct discovery pertaining to other parties' citizenship, the amount in controversy, a party's contacts with the forum state, and other jurisdictional issues.

Location of Evidence

Rule 26(b)(1) explicitly authorizes discovery about the location and existence of documents and other evidence and about the identity and

55. The Advisory Committee Note to the 2000 Amendment to Rule 26(b)(1).

56. The Advisory Committee Note to the 2000 Amendment to Rule 26(b)(1).

57. *Oppenheimer Fund, Inc. v. Sanders,* 437 U.S. 340, 351, 98 S.Ct. 2380, 2389–90, 57 L.Ed.2d 253 (1978).

58. *Seattle Times Co. v. Rhinehart,* 467 U.S. 20, 104 S.Ct. 2199, 81 L.Ed.2d 17 (1984), *cert. denied,* 467 U.S. 1230, 104 S.Ct. 2690, 81 L.Ed.2d 884 (1984); *Bruggeman ex rel. Bruggeman v. Blagojevich*, 219 F.R.D. 430, 432 (N.D.Ill. 2004).

59. *Glover v. South Carolina Law Enforcement Division*, 170 F.3d 411 (4th Cir.1999), *cert. dism'd*, 528 U.S. 1146, 120 S.Ct. 1005, 145 L.Ed.2d 1065 (2000).

60. *Terwilliger v. York Int'l. Corp.*, 176 F.R.D. 214, 218 (W.D.Va.1997).

61. The Advisory Committee Note to the 2000 Amendment to Rule 26(b)(1).

62. *Oppenheimer Fund, Inc. v. Sanders,* 437 U.S. 340, 351 n. 13, 98 S.Ct. 2380, 2389–90 n. 13, 57 L.Ed.2d 253 (1978).

location of persons having knowledge of discoverable matters. The latter provision includes the identity of investigators hired by a party.

Matters Known to Others

A party must provide information and documents it possesses, regardless of who else possesses that information. Thus, it generally is not proper to object on the basis that the party already has the information it is requesting or that information is in the public record [63] or is otherwise available to the party[64] (although the court might curtail such requests as unduly burdensome in some circumstances).

Impeachment

Discovery is generally allowed of matters that would be used to impeach other parties' witnesses.[65] Thus, one normally may ask whether the responding party has any criminal convictions and may inquire as to prior statements.[66] It is less clear whether one may inquire as to what other parties will use for impeachment. The courts are divided as to whether a party may ask whether opponents are aware of any prior injuries of the party or whether opponents have surveillance movies of the party.

Discovery of Attorneys

Attorneys with discoverable facts not covered by attorney-client privilege or work product protection are subject to discovery despite being retained by one of the parties to represent it in the litigation.[67]

Privileges

Privileged matters are protected from discovery.[68] Privileges in federal court depend upon whether the action involves a state law issue before the court under diversity or supplemental jurisdiction, or whether the action involves a federal cause of action. If a state's substantive laws are being applied, that state's laws of privilege also apply,[69] except as to the attorney work product protection, which is governed by federal common law.[70] If the action is governed by federal law, then Rule 501 of the Federal Rules of Evidence applies. Essentially, Rule 501 instructs the federal courts to develop a body of federal common law

63. *Mid-Atlantic Recycling Technologies, Inc. v. City of Vineland*, 222 F.R.D. 81 (D.N.J. 2004); *Petruska v. Johns–Manville,* 83 F.R.D. 32, 35 (E.D.Pa.1979).

64. *Abrahamsen v. Trans-State Express*, Inc., 92 F.3d 425, 428 (6th Cir.1996).

65. *Hickman v. Taylor,* 329 U.S. 495, 511, 67 S.Ct. 385, 394, 91 L.Ed. 451 (1947); *Varga v. Rockwell International Corp.*, 242 F.3d 693, 697 (6th Cir.2001), *cert. denied,* 534 U.S. 821, 122 S.Ct. 53, 151 L.Ed.2d 23 (2001) (a party may not hold back materials responsive to a proper discovery request because it prefers to use the evidence as surprise impeachment evidence at trial).

66. *See Curro v. Watson*, 884 F.Supp. 708 (E.D.N.Y.1995)(limiting impeachment discovery to areas related to expected testimony).

67. *United Phosphorus, Ltd. v. Midland Fumigant, Inc.*, 164 F.R.D. 245 (D.Kan.1995).

68. *Goodyear Tire & Rubber Co. v. Chiles Power Supply, Inc.*, 332 F.3d 976 (6th Cir.2003).

69. *Brown v. Waco Fire & Cas. Co.,* 73 F.R.D. 297 (S.D.Miss.1976).

70. *Tompkins v. R.J. Reynolds Tobacco Co.*, 92 F.Supp.2d 70 (N.D.N.Y.2000).

privileges. When a deposition is taken in a state other than the state in which the action is pending, the analysis becomes very complicated, and depends upon each state's choice of law provisions.

Raising Claim of Privilege

The normal manner for raising a privilege is by objecting to a particular request or inquiry. For example, at a deposition, a party may orally raise an objection to an individual question, then refuse to provide the privileged information (by counsel instructing the witness not to answer). In response to interrogatories, document requests, or requests for admission, a party may make a written objection to individual questions or requests and withhold the privileged information. The objection must include sufficient information so that the court and opposing counsel can assess the applicability of the privilege.[71]

Burden of Proof

The party raising a privilege has the burden of establishing the existence of the privilege.[72] Likewise, a party claiming that requested discovery is not relevant has the burden to show that the discovery is outside the scope of the rules.[73]

Who May Assert

Usually, a privilege may only be asserted by the person holding the privilege. Certainly, one party may not assert a privilege of a non-party witness or another party. When an attorney or doctor is deposed it is unclear who may assert the privilege—the privilege technically belongs to the client, but some courts allow the attorney to assert the privilege if asked about the attorney-client communication.

Waiver of Privilege

Privileges generally are waived by voluntary disclosure,[74] either during discovery or elsewhere. Thus, caution should be exercised in discussing or responding to discovery requests pertaining to privileged matters.

Documents Containing Privileged and Non-privileged Matters

If part of a document contains privileged matters and part does not, a party must provide the non-privileged matter, but may redact the privileged matter.

71. Rule 26(b)(5); *Burns v. Imagine Films Entertainment, Inc.*, 164 F.R.D. 589 (W.D.N.Y. 1996).

72. *McCoo v. Denny's Inc.*, 192 F.R.D. 675 (D.Kan.2000); *Heathman v. United States District Court,* 503 F.2d 1032, 1033 (9th Cir.1974).

73. *Simpson v. University of Colorado*, 220 F.R.D. 354, 359 (D.Colo. 2004) (when the discovery sought appears relevant, the party resisting the discovery has the burden to establish the lack of relevance by demonstrating that the requested discovery (1) does not come within the scope of relevance, or (2) is of such marginal relevance that the potential harm occasioned by discovery would outweigh the ordinary presumption in favor of broad disclosure); *General Elec. Capital Corp. v. Lear Corp.*, 215 F.R.D. 637(D.Kan.2003).

74. *In re Grand Jury Proceedings Subpoena to Testify to: Wine,* 841 F.2d 230, 234 (8th Cir.1988).

Privileged Matters to be Introduced at Trial

A majority of courts hold that a party cannot assert a privilege at the discovery stage, then introduce the privileged matter at trial.[75] Consequently, any matter intended to be introduced at trial should be produced during discovery if requested. This principle does not apply to the attorney work product protections.

Particular Privileges

A detailed analysis of every potential privilege is beyond the scope of this book. The following is an overview of the most commonly asserted privileges:

- *Attorney–Client:* The attorney-client privilege applies to all confidential communications between a client and the client's attorney that occur in connection with legal representation or in the process of obtaining legal representation.[76] It applies to communications to an in-house attorney if the attorney is providing legal services. The privilege does not protect communications between one party and the attorney for another party. It does not protect documents or other physical evidence provided to the attorney (other than written communications to the attorney), nor does it protect information or evidence gathered by the attorney from other sources or notes and memoranda prepared by the attorney (but see the discussion of attorney-work product under Rule 26(b)(3)).
- *Self–Incrimination:* The Fifth Amendment to the United States Constitution provides all persons (whether or not parties to a litigation) with a privilege against testifying in a manner that would tend to incriminate them.[77] The privilege applies at depositions,[78] interrogatories, requests for admission, and production of documents,[79] as well as at trial. Corporations may not assert the privilege, but corporate representatives may assert it if their testimony would incriminate them personally, regardless of whether they are testifying in their individual or representative capacities.[80] There can be no penalties or sanctions for properly exercising the Fifth Amendment privilege. However, in a civil proceeding it appears that opposing parties may comment on a party's exercise of the Fifth Amendment (in contrast to the prohibition on such comments in a criminal proceeding).[81]
- *Governmental Privileges:* The United States and the individual States must produce all relevant, non-privileged matter, just as

75. *Doe v. Eli Lilly & Co., Inc.*, 99 F.R.D. 126, 127 (D.D.C.1983).

76. *Diversified Industries, Inc. v. Meredith*, 572 F.2d 596, 612 (8th Cir.1977).

77. *De Vita v. Sills*, 422 F.2d 1172 (3d Cir. 1970).

78. *In re Folding Carton Antitrust Litigation*, 609 F.2d 867 (7th Cir.1979).

79. *Gordon v. Federal Deposit Ins. Corp.*, 427 F.2d 578, 580 (D.C.Cir.1970).

80. *United States v. Kordel*, 397 U.S. 1, 8, 90 S.Ct. 763, 767, 25 L.Ed.2d 1 (1970), *cert. denied*, 400 U.S. 821, 91 S.Ct. 41, 27 L.Ed.2d 49 (1970).

81. *Baxter v. Palmigiano*, 425 U.S. 308, 96 S.Ct. 1551, 47 L.Ed.2d 810 (1976).

any other party.[82] However, the United States has some extra privileges:

- *Governmental Informer Privilege:* The United States has a qualified privilege to refuse to reveal the identity of an informer.[83] When the privilege is asserted, the court will balance the litigant's need for the information against the government's interest in protecting its informer's identity. The privilege belongs to the government, and protects only the identity of the informer, not the information provided by the informer. The government may not assert the privilege if it intends for the informer to testify at trial.
- *Government's Privilege for Military or State Secrets:* The United States has a qualified privilege for matters that involve military or state secrets. In order to assert the privilege, the head of the department that has control over the matter must lodge a formal claim of privilege. The court will then rule on the privilege by balancing the litigant's need against the government's interest in keeping the matter secret.[84]
- *Government's Statutory Privilege:* Some statutes require governmental agencies and other entities to file certain documents or reports, and designate the submissions as confidential. Under these statutes, the privilege is generally absolute. A common example is income tax returns. Under the regulation,[85] the United States receives and keeps tax returns, but is not required to produce them to private litigants. Note that the privilege belongs to the United States only—the individual filing the return may be required to produce it (although other objections, such as relevance, might apply).
- *Executive Privilege:* The Executive branch of the United States government has a general qualified privilege, grounded in the need for the executive branch to gather information. The privilege generally must be asserted by the head of the relevant department. The court will then balance the litigant's need against the governmental interest asserted.[86]

- *Other Privileges:* In some states, communications with spouses, physicians, clergy, journalists,[87] accountants, and social workers are privileged.

82. *United States v. Procter & Gamble Co.,* 356 U.S. 677, 681, 78 S.Ct. 983, 986, 2 L.Ed.2d 1077 (1958).

83. *Roviaro v. United States,* 353 U.S. 53, 59, 77 S.Ct. 623, 627, 1 L.Ed.2d 639 (1957).

84. *United States v. Reynolds,* 345 U.S. 1, 73 S.Ct. 528, 97 L.Ed. 727 (1953).

85. 26 C.F.R. § 301.6103(a–1(c)).

86. *United States v. Nixon,* 418 U.S. 683, 94 S.Ct. 3090, 41 L.Ed.2d 1039 (1974).

87. *In re: Madden,* 151 F.3d 125, 128 (3d Cir.1998) (recognizing qualified journalists' privilege); *Gonzales v. National Broadcasting Co., Inc.,* 155 F.3d 618, 626–27 (2d Cir.1998) (journalists' privilege applies only to confidential information).

RULE 26(b)(2). LIMITATIONS

CORE CONCEPT

Rule 26(b)(2) provides the court with authority to limit discovery that is unreasonably cumulative or duplicative,[88] is obtainable from another source more conveniently, or is unduly burdensome[89] or expensive given the nature and circumstances of the case.[90] The court may also limit discovery if the party seeking the discovery has had "ample opportunity" to obtain the information during prior discovery.

APPLICATIONS

Objections to Specific Requests

One method of asserting the limitations in Rule 26(b)(2) is by making an objection to a discovery request, such as objecting to an interrogatory or request for production as cumulative or overly burdensome.

Motion for Protective Order

A party seeking to have the use of certain discovery procedures limited should make a motion for a protective order under Rule 26(c). The motion must be accompanied by a certification that the parties met prior to the filing of the motion and attempted to resolve their dispute without intervention by the court.

Limits Established by Rules

Other Rules place limits on the duration of depositions and on the number of interrogatories and depositions, which may be altered by court order.[91] These limits may also be altered by stipulation under Rule 29. The Rules do not contain any limit on the number of requests for admission, but such limits can be set by local rule, court order, or stipulation.

RULE 26(b)(3). TRIAL PREPARATION: MATERIALS

CORE CONCEPT

Rule 26(b)(3) provides limited protection to otherwise discoverable trial preparation and work product materials.[92] Such materials must be produced in discovery *only* when the information contained there is not

88. *Bayer AG v. Betachem, Inc.*, 173 F.3d 188 (3d Cir.1999).

89. *In re Microcrystalline Cellulose Antitrust Litigation*, 221 F.R.D. 428 (E.D.Pa. 2004).

90. *See Patterson v. Avery Dennison Corp.*, 281 F.3d 676, 681–82 (7th Cir.2002) (before restricting discovery, the court should consider the totality of the circumstances, weighing the value of the material sought against the burden of providing it, and taking into account society's interest in furthering the truthseeking function); *Koch v. Koch Industries, Inc.*, 203 F.3d 1202, 1238 (10th Cir.2000) (parties are not entitled to conduct a "fishing expedition"), *cert. denied*, 531 U.S. 926, 121 S.Ct. 302, 148 L.Ed.2d 242 (2000).

91. *Andamiro U.S.A. v. Konami Amusement of America, Inc.*, 2001 WL 535667 (C.D.Cal. 2001) (setting forth the factors for a motion to take more than 10 depositions).

92. *See In re Perrigo Co.*, 128 F.3d 430, 437 (6th Cir.1997) (noting that the work product

reasonably available from any other source.[93] Note that the work product protection is broader than the attorney-client privilege, but is less absolute.[94]

APPLICATIONS

Documents Only

The work product protection applies only to documents[95] prepared in anticipation of litigation.[96] It does not apply to facts known or gathered relating to the litigation, which generally are discoverable.[97] It is unsettled whether the work product protection applies to compilations of documents, such as documents selected for deposition preparation.[98] The protection has been held not to apply to electronic images of documents created for use in the litigation.[99]

Prepared in Anticipation of Litigation

The work product protection applies only to documents prepared in anticipation of litigation.[100] Most courts apply the protection to documents prepared when litigation is expected but has not yet been commenced;[101] rather, to be protected, the documents must be primarily concerned with legal assistance.[102] Conversely, the protection does not apply to documents prepared in the regular course of business while

doctrine creates a qualified immunity rather than a privilege).

93. Rule 26(b)(3) is essentially a codification of the principles announced by the Supreme Court in *Hickman v. Taylor,* 329 U.S. 495, 67 S.Ct. 385, 91 L.Ed. 451 (1947), which contains an excellent discussion of the work product protection. *See also In re Ford Motor Co.*, 110 F.3d 954 (3d Cir.1997).

94. *In re Sealed Case,* 107 F.3d 46, 51 (D.C.Cir.1997).

95. *In re Perrigo Co.*, 128 F.3d 430, 437 (6th Cir.1997); *Sadowski v. Gudmundsson,* 206 F.R.D. 25, 27 (D.D.C. 2002).

96. *In re Ford Motor Company*, 110 F.3d 954 (3d Cir.1997) (work product doctrine extends to materials prepared by an agent of an attorney provided that material was prepared in anticipation of litigation).

97. *See In re Cendant Corp. Securities Litigation*, 343 F.3d 658, 662 (3rd Cir.2003); *Vardon Golf Co., Inc. v. Karsten Mfg. Corp.*, 213 F.R.D. 528, 534 (N.D.Ill. 2003); *but see In re: Grand Jury Subpoena Dated Oct. 22, 2001*, 282 F.3d 156, 161 (2d Cir.2002) (we see no reason why work product cannot encompass facts as well as opinions and strategy).

98. *In re Grand Jury Subpoenas Dated March 19, 2002 and August 2*, 2002, 318 F.3d 379, 385 (2nd Cir.2003); *Nutramax Laboratories, Inc. v. Twin Laboratories, Inc.*, 183 F.R.D. 458 (D.Md.1998) (containing a detailed analysis of this issue).

99. *Hines v. Widnall,* 183 F.R.D. 596 (N.D.Fla.1998).

100. *Heath v. F/V ZOLOTOI*, 221 F.R.D. 545 (W.D.Wash. 2004) (more than the mere possibility of litigation must be evident for materials to be considered immune from discovery under the work-product doctrine); *In re Sealed Case,* 146 F.3d 881, 884 (D.C.Cir.1998); *Southern Union Co. v. Southwest Gas Corp.*, 205 F.R.D. 542, 549 (D.Ariz.2002) ("litigation" includes administrative proceedings provided there is an opportunity for cross examination).

101. *Equal Employment Opportunity Commission v. Lutheran Social Services,* 186 F.3d 959 (D.C.Cir.1999); *Binks Mfg. Co. v. National Presto Industries, Inc.,* 709 F.2d 1109, 1119 (7th Cir.1983); *Navigant Consulting, Inc. v. Wilkinson,* 220 F.R.D. 467, 476–77 (N.D.Tex. 2004) .

102. *In re Lernout & Hauspie Securities Litigation*,222 F.R.D. 29 (D.Mass. 2004) (litigation need not be imminent, as long as the primary motivating purpose behind the creation of the document was to aid in possible future litigation); *North Shore Gas Co. v. Elgin, Joliet & Eastern Ry. Co.*, 164 F.R.D. 59, 61 (N.D.Ill.1995); but see *In re Ford Motor Co.*, 110 F.3d 954 (3d Cir.1997) (materials deemed to be prepared in anticipation of litigation for purposes of work product protection did not necessarily include legal advice).

litigation is pending.[103] The trend seems to be to apply the protection to documents prepared in anticipation of any litigation, not just the pending action.[104]

Investigators' Reports

The work product protection applies to reports prepared by investigators or others on behalf of a party.[105]

Parties Only

The work product protection only applies to parties and their agents.[106] Thus, if a witness prepares a document for the witness's own purposes, it is generally not work product. However, when an insurance company is defending a party, the protection may extend to documents prepared by or on behalf of the insurance company.[107]

Obtaining Work Product

Work product is discoverable if the attorney makes a sufficient showing that there is no reasonable alternative source for the same or substantially equivalent information,[108] and that the attorney has a *substantial* need for the information.[109] For example, a party may obtain a written statement in opposing counsel's files if the witness is no longer available.[110] Similarly, there may be no substitute for photographs or statements taken shortly after an incident. Work product is also discoverable in an action where the work product is directly at issue, such as in an action for legal malpractice.[111]

103. *JumpSport, Inc. v. Jumpking, Inc.*, 213 F.R.D. 329, 344 (N.D.Cal. 2003); *Simon v. G.D. Searle & Co.*, 816 F.2d 397, 401 (8th Cir.1987), *cert. denied,* 484 U.S. 917, 108 S.Ct. 268, 98 L.Ed.2d 225 (1987).

104. *In re Ford Motor Co.*, 110 F.3d 954 (3d Cir.1997) (looking to literal language of the Rule); *but see In re Grand Jury Subpoena*, 220 F.R.D. 130, 148 (D.Mass. 2004) (containing a detailed discussion of this issue); *Burton v. R.J. Reynolds Tobacco Co.*, 177 F.R.D. 491 (D.Kan. 1997) (documents must pertain to a specific claim or potential litigation, particularly for an insurance company whose entire business involves claims).

105. *See, In re: In re Grand Jury Subpoena* (Mark Torf/Torf Environmental Management), 357 F.3d 900, 907 (9th Cir. 2004) (the work product doctrine applies to documents created by investigators working for attorneys, provided the documents were created in anticipation of litigation); *Grand Jury Subpoena Dated Oct. 22, 2001*, 282 F.3d 156, 161 (2d Cir.2002).

106. *In re Grand Jury Subpoena*, 220 F.R.D. 130, 144 (D.Mass. 2004) (courts typically do not extend work product protection to documents prepared by non-parties or their agents); *Duck v. Warren*, 160 F.R.D. 80 (E.D.Va.1995)(police internal affairs investigation documents were not prepared by the party police officer being sued, and thus were not work product).

107. *See Tayler v. Travelers Ins. Co.*, 183 F.R.D. 67, 69 (N.D.N.Y.1998).

108. *United Kingdom v. United States*, 238 F.3d 1312, 1322 (11th Cir.2001), *cert. denied,* 534 U.S. 891, 122 S.Ct. 206, 151 L.Ed.2d 146 (2001); *Hendrick v. Avis Rent A Car System, Inc.*, 916 F.Supp. 256, 261 (W.D.N.Y. 1996)(expense in obtaining the information independently is a factor which may be considered by a court in determining whether to order disclosure of work product).

109. *Corley v. Rosewood Care Ctr., Inc.*, 142 F.3d 1041, 1052 (7th Cir.1998); *Melhelm v. Meijer, Inc.*, 206 F.R.D. 609 (S.D.Ohio 2002).

110. *McCoo v. Denny's Inc.*, 192 F.R.D. 675 (D.Kan.2000) (statements from witnesses who failed to appear for their depositions must be produced).

111. *Rutgard v. Haynes*, 61 F.Supp.2d 1082 (S.D.Cal.1999).

Mental and Legal Impressions

The mental impressions and legal evaluations of an attorney, investigator, or claims agent (sometimes referred to as "core" or "opinion" work product) enjoy an almost absolute privilege from disclosure.[112] Thus, an attorney may redact statements reflecting mental and legal impressions from work product that must be disclosed under Rule 26(b)(3). Note, however, that the protections in Rule 26(b)(3) do not apply to interrogatories, which may require the respondent to make legal conclusions requiring the application of law to facts (in other words, the responding attorney may not interpose an objection on the basis that such a legal conclusion is the attorney's work product).

Statement of a Party

A party may always obtain a copy of the party's own statement, whether a signed written statement or a recording of an oral statement.[113] A party may similarly obtain a copy of a statement by the party's agent or representative.[114] The method for obtaining such a statement is by document request under Rule 34.

Statement of a Witness

A non-party witness has a right to a copy of the witness' own statement, whether a signed written statement or a recording of an oral statement. If a party refuses to provide a witness with a copy of the witness' statement, the witness may move to compel and for sanctions under Rule 37(a)(4). Parties, in contrast, do not have an absolute right to a copy of a non-party witness' statement.[115] A party can attempt to get a copy of a witness' statement directly from the witness or by making the showing of necessity required to obtain attorney-work product.[116]

Controlling Law

Unlike most privileges, the work product doctrine is controlled by federal common law, even in diversity cases.[117]

Burden of Proof

The party asserting the work product doctrine has the burden of

112. *In re Cendant Corp. Securities Litigation*, 343 F.3d 658, 663 (3rd Cir. 2003); *Baker v. General Motors Corp.*, 209 F.3d 1051, 1054 (8th Cir.2000); *In re Allen*, 106 F.3d 582, 607 (4th Cir.1997), *cert. denied, McGraw v. Better Gov't Bureau, Inc.*, 522 U.S. 1047, 118 S.Ct. 689, 139 L.Ed.2d 635 (1998); *but see Conoco Inc. v. Boh Brothers Construction Co.*, 191 F.R.D. 107 (W.D.La.1998); *Hager v. Bluefield Regional Medical Center*, 170 F.R.D. 70, 78 (D.D.C.1997) ("near absolute protection given by courts to opinion work product must give way" when attorney is designated as an expert witness).

113. *Corley v. Rosewood Care Center, Inc. of Peoria*, 142 F.3d 1041, 1052 (7th Cir.1998); *Crenshaw v. R & B Falcon Drilling, USA, Inc.*, 2003 WL 21010746 (E.D.La. 2003).

114. *Woodard v. Nabors Offshore Corp.*, 2001 WL 13339 (E.D.La. 2001).

115. *Garcia v. City of El Centro*, 214 F.R.D. 587, 594–95 (S.D.Cal. 2003).

116. *Garcia v. City of El Centro*, 214 F.R.D. 587, 594–95 (S.D.Cal. 2003) (there is a split as to whether the mere passage of time creates a substantial need for a witness statement).

117. *Meoli v. American Medical Service of San Diego*, 287 B.R. 808, 813 (S.D.Cal. 2003).

demonstrating that the subject documents are work product.[118] The party seeking the opponent's work product then has the burden of showing the necessity of obtaining the work product.[119]

Waiver

Disclosure of documents to an adverse party, or in a manner such that an adverse party may see the documents,[120] constitutes a waiver of the work product protection with respect to those documents.[121] Disclosure of documents to a non-adverse party, such as a co-defendant, will not constitute a waiver of the work product protection if the documents fall within the scope of a proper joint defense agreement.[122] Disclosure of fact work product to a testifying expert may also constitute waiver.[123] Disclosure to a third-party who does not share a common interest in developing legal theories and analyses of documents may also constitute a waiver.[124] Note that this differs from most privileges, which are waived by disclosure to anyone, not just parties.[125] The courts are divided as to which party has the burden of proving non-waiver.[126]

Discovery Stage Only

Work product may be withheld as privileged during discovery, then used at trial. Note the contrast with most other privileges, which cannot be asserted during discovery then waived at trial.

RULE 26(b)(4). TRIAL PREPARATION: EXPERTS

CORE CONCEPT

Parties may depose expert witnesses who may testify at trial. Rule 26(b)(4) allows only very limited discovery with respect to non-testifying experts.[127]

118. *Gulf Islands Leasing, Inc. v. Bombardier Capital, Inc.*, 215 F.R.D. 466 (S.D.N.Y. 2003).

119. *Ferko v. National Ass'n For Stock Car Auto Racing, Inc.*, 219 F.R.D. 396, 400 (E.D.Tex. 2003); *Pippenger v. Gruppe*, 883 F.Supp. 1201 (S.D.Ind.1994).

120. *United States ex rel. Bagley v. TRW, Inc.*, 212 F.R.D. 554, 560 (C.D.Cal.2003) (required disclosure of a document to the United States does not waive the attorney work product doctrine).

121. *United States v. M.I.T.*, 129 F.3d 681, 687 (1st Cir.1997) (disclosure of a contractor's documents to a Defense Contract Audit Agency constitutes disclosure to a potential adversary which forfeits work product protection for disclosed documents); *Oxyn Telecommunications, Inc. v. Onse Telecom*, 2003 WL 660848 (S.D.N.Y. 2003).

122. *U.S. v. Duke Energy Corp.*, 214 F.R.D. 383, 389 (M.D.N.C.2003).

123. *Johnson v. Gmeinder*, 191 F.R.D. 638, 644 (D.Kan.2000).

124. *Judicial Watch, Inc. v. U.S. Postal Service*, 297 F.Supp.2d 252, 268 (D.D.C. 2004).

125. *See In re Columbia/HCA Healthcare Corp. Billing Practices Litigation*, 293 F.3d 289, 314 (6th Cir.2002) (disclosure to third parties does not waive the work product protection).

126. *See Granite Partners, L.P. v. Bear, Stearns & Co. Inc.*, 184 F.R.D. 49, 54 (S.D.N.Y. 1999) (party making work product claim has the burden of proving non-waiver); *Johnson v. Gmeinder*, 191 F.R.D. 638, 643 (D.Kan.2000) (party claiming waiver must prove waiver).

127. *Employer's Reinsurance Corp. v. Clarendon Nat. Ins. Co.*, 213 F.R.D. 422 (D.Kan. 2003); *Agron v. Trustees of Columbia Univ.*, 176 F.R.D. 445, 449 (S.D.N.Y.1997) (limitation on discovery is virtually inapplicable where adverse party has not objected to discovery of its expert).

APPLICATIONS

Depositions of Experts

Parties may take the deposition of any expert witness that may testify at trial.[128]

Time for Expert Depositions

If an expert report is to be disclosed for the witness, then the deposition may not occur before the report is disclosed.

Experts Specially Retained but Not Expected to Testify

A party may obtain discovery pertaining to experts not expected to testify only upon a showing of exceptional circumstances rendering it impracticable to obtain facts or opinions on the same subject by other means.[129] Such further discovery might be allowed when the particular consulting expert was the only expert to examine evidence that is no longer available (such as a blood sample).[130]

Discovery of Examining Physician

Discovery pertaining to treating or examining health professionals is available under Rule 35(b).[131] There is a split of authority as to whether a treating physician is a fact witness or an expert witness for purposes of the provisions of Rule 26(b)(4).[132]

Experts Informally Consulted

No discovery is permitted of experts informally consulted but not retained.[133]

Experts Generally Retained

Full discovery is permitted regarding an expert who is a full-time employee of a party, or who was retained generally, rather than in connection with pending or anticipated litigation.[134] No expert fees are awarded in connection with such discovery.

128. *Lovato v. Burlington Northern and Santa Fe Ry. Co.*, 200 F.R.D. 448 (D.Colo. 2001), *rev'd on other grounds*, 201 F.R.D. 509 (D.Colo. 2001).

129. *Lowery v. Circuit City Stores, Inc.*, 158 F.3d 742, 765 (4th Cir.1998), *cert. granted, judgment vacated on other grounds*, 527 U.S. 1031, 119 S.Ct. 2388, 144 L.Ed.2d 790 (1999). *But see American Crop Protection Ass'n v. U.S. E.P.A.*, 182 F.Supp.2d 89, 93 (D.D.C.2002) (non-testifying experts are shielded from discovery only in the action with respect to which they are consulted; full discovery is permitted of their writings and opinions in subsequent matters).

130. *See, e.g., Spearman Industries, Inc. v. St. Paul Fire and Marine Ins. Co.*, 128 F.Supp.2d 1148 (N.D.Ill.2001) (describing circumstances where a party might obtain discovery from a non-testifying expert).

131. *But see Coleman v. Dydula*, 190 F.R.D. 320, 321–24 (W.D.N.Y.1999) (awarding deposition attendance fees to treating physicians under Rule 26(b)(4)).

132. *See, e.g., Demar v. United States*, 199 F.R.D. 617 (N.D.Ill.2001) (treating physician not entitled to expert fees from the party noticing the physician's deposition); *Grant v. Otis Elevator Co.*, 199 F.R.D. 673, 675–76 (N.D.Okla.2001) (treating physician entitled to expert fee compensation for deposition testimony).

133. *West Tennessee Chapter of Associated Builders and Contractors, Inc. v. City of Memphis*, 219 F.R.D. 587, 591 (W.D.Tenn. 2004).

134. *Dunn v. Sears, Roebuck & Co.*, 639 F.2d 1171, 1174 (5th Cir.1981).

Experts Who Witnessed or Participated in Events

Discovery pertaining to an expert who acquired his knowledge and facts through witnessing or participating in the events that form the basis for the complaint is not covered by Rule 26(b)(4), which is limited to information acquired or developed in anticipation of litigation.[135] Thus, full fact discovery is allowed regarding such experts, and no expert fees are awarded.[136]

Party Who Is an Expert

A party cannot avoid discovery or obtain expert fees by claiming to be an expert witness.

Ex Parte Communications with Experts

All communications with an opposing party's expert should be through the procedures set forth in Rule 26, such as a Rule 26(b)(4) deposition; a party should not have *ex parte* communications with an expert for another party.[137]

Testifying Expert Fees

The court must impose on the party seeking expert discovery of a testifying expert the reasonable expert fees incurred in responding to the discovery[138] unless manifest injustice would result.[139] For a deposition, the fee normally includes compensation for time testifying but not preparation time.[140] However, if the expert charges more than a "reasonable" fee, the party retaining that expert must pay over and above the "reasonable" rate for that witness' deposition by an adversary.[141]

Non-testifying Expert Fees

If discovery is sought of non-testifying experts, the court must also require the party to pay a fair share of the expenses already expended

135. *Battle ex rel. Battle v. Memorial Hosp. at Gulfport*, 228 F.3d 544, 551 (5th Cir.2000).

136. The Advisory Committee Note to Rule 26(b)(4); *Paquin v. Federal Nat'l. Mortgage Assn.*, 119 F.3d 23, 33 (D.C.Cir.1997) (denying payment of fees for alleged experts with personal knowledge).

137. *Sewell v. Maryland Dept. of Transp.*, 206 F.R.D. 545 (D.Md.2002).

138. *Trepel v. Roadway Express, Inc.*, 266 F.3d 418, 426–27 (6th Cir.2001); *Haarhuis v. Kunnan Enterprises, Ltd.*, 177 F.3d 1007 (D.C.Cir.1999) ($300 per hour for deposition, including time traveling to and from deposition, was reasonable). *See also, Hansen v. Sea Ray Boats, Inc.*, 160 F.R.D. 166 (D.Utah 1995)(limiting the recovery of expert fees to the statutory $40.00 witness fee).

139. *Research Systems Corp. v. IPSOS Publicite*, 276 F.3d 914, 920 (7th Cir.2002), *cert. denied*, 537 U.S. 878, 123 S.Ct. 78, 154 L.Ed.2d 133 (2002); *Royal Maccabees Life Ins. Co. v. Malachinski*, 2001 WL 290308 (N.D.Ill. 2001) ("The "manifest injustice" requirement, however, is a "stringent standard," and only applies in special circumstances.").

140. *Frydman v. Department of Justice*, 852 F.Supp. 1497 (D.Kan.1994)(holding that a large lapse of time can warrant compensation for preparation time). *But see McNerney v. Archer Daniels Midland Co.*, 164 F.R.D. 584, 587 (W.D.N.Y.1995)(Holding plaintiff's expert was entitled to charge defendant up to 4 hours time in preparing for the deposition and reviewing and signing the transcript).

141. *Frederick v. Columbia University*, 212 F.R.D. 176, 177 (S.D.N.Y.2003) (setting forth a test for reasonableness of expert fees).

for the experts to form their opinions, in addition to the experts' fees for the time testifying or responding to the discovery.

RULE 26(b)(5). CLAIMS OF PRIVILEGE OR PROTECTION OF TRIAL PREPARATION MATERIALS

CORE CONCEPT

A party who withholds information based on a claim of privilege or attorney work product protection must state the claim expressly and describe the nature of the documents or information so withheld in a manner that will enable other parties to assess the claim of privilege or protection.[142]

APPLICATIONS

Failure to State Claim of Privilege

If a party withholds information without properly disclosing the basis, the party may be subject to sanctions under Rule 37(b)(2), and may have waived the privilege.[143]

Privilege Log

Many courts read Rule 26(b)(5) to require a party asserting a privilege to produce a privilege log describing the documents withheld.[144] The respondent may wait until the court rules upon pending objections before generating the privilege log if the objections pertain to the allegedly privileged documents.[145] Privileges may be waived broadly for failure to produce a privilege log[146] or specifically for any documents omitted from the privilege log.[147]

RULE 26(c). PROTECTIVE ORDERS

CORE CONCEPT

The court may enter orders designed to protect the parties and witnesses during the discovery process.

142. *U.S. v. Philip Morris Inc.*, 347 F.3d 951, 954 (D.C.Cir. 2003); *In re Santa Fe Intern. Corp.*, 272 F.3d 705, 710 (5th Cir.2001) (party asserting the privilege has the burden of demonstrating its applicability).

143. *Anderson v. Marion County Sheriff's Dept.*, 220 F.R.D. 555, 563 (S.D.Ind. 2004) ("the time to make the showing that certain information is privileged is at the time the privilege is asserted, not months later when the matter is before the Court on a motion to compel"); *Ritacca v. Abbott Laboratories*, 203 F.R.D. 332, (N.D.Ill.2001) ("Minor procedural violations, good faith attempts at compliance, and other such mitigating circumstances militate against finding waiver."); The Advisory Committee Note to the 1993 Amendment to Rule 26.

144. *Horton v. United States*, 204 F.R.D. 670, 673 (D.Colo.2002) ("The information provided in the privilege log must be sufficient to enable the court to determine whether each element of the asserted privilege is satisfied."); *Avery Dennison Corp. v. Four Pillars*, 190 F.R.D. 1, 1–2 (D.D.C. 1999) (a privilege log has become "the universally accepted means of asserting privileges in discovery in the federal courts").

145. *United States v. Philip Morris Inc.*, 314 F.3d 612, 621 (D.C.Cir.2003).

146. *Banks v. Office of Senate Sergeant–At–Arms*, 222 F.R.D. 7, 15 (D.D.C. 2004).

147. *Robinson v. Texas Auto. Dealers Ass'n*, 214 F.R.D. 432, 456 (E.D.Tex.2003), *vac'd in part*, 2003 WL 21911333 (5th Cir.2003).

APPLICATIONS

Motion

Protective orders are obtained by motion filed in the district where the action is pending.[148] In the case of a deposition that is to occur in a different district, a motion may also be filed where the deposition is to occur.[149]

Certificate of Conference

A motion for protective order must include a certification that the movant has in good faith conferred or attempted to confer with the other party in an effort to resolve the dispute without court action.[150]

Timing

Normally, the motion must be filed before the discovery is to occur, unless there is no opportunity to do so.[151]

Who May File

A motion may be made by a party or by a witness from whom discovery is sought.[152] The motion must be brought by the individual whose interests are affected. Thus, a party may not move for a protective order to protect the interests of another, but may move to protect the party's own interests when discovery is sought from another.

Good Cause

Protective orders are entered for "good cause." [153] The court has almost complete discretion in determining what constitutes good cause,[154] and such determinations are rarely disturbed on appeal.[155] Rule 26(c) specifically instructs the court to limit the frequency or extent of discovery if justice so requires to protect a party or witness

148. *Kirshner v. Uniden Corp. of America*, 842 F.2d 1074 (9th Cir.1988).

149. *In re: Sealed Case*, 141 F.3d 337 (D.C.Cir.1998) (non-party witness has a right to have a motion for protective order heard in the district where the deposition is to occur). The Advisory Committee Note to Rule 26(c).

150. *Lockwood v. City of Philadelphia*, 205 F.R.D. 448, 450 (E.D.Pa.2002).

151. *Mims v. Central Mfrs. Mut. Ins. Co.*, 178 F.2d 56 (5th Cir.1949); *Drexel Heritage Furnishings, Inc. v. Furniture USA, Inc.*, 200 F.R.D. 255 (M.D.N.C.2001).

152. *Silkwood v. Kerr–McGee Corp.*, 563 F.2d 433 (10th Cir.1977).

153. *Foltz v. State Farm Mut. Auto. Ins. Co.*, 331 F.3d 1122 (9th Cir.2003) (a party seeking a protective order must show, for each particular document it seeks to protect, that specific prejudice or harm will result if no protective order is granted); *Chicago Tribune Co. v. Bridgestone/Firestone, Inc.*, 263 F.3d 1304, 1310 (11th Cir.2001) (applying the good cause standard, and rejecting the press' argument that a compelling interest was required to keep documents from the press).

154. *Flatow v. Islamic Republic of Iran*, 308 F.3d 1065, 1074 (9th Cir.2002), *cert. denied*, 538 U.S. 944, 123 S.Ct. 1632, 155 L.Ed.2d 485 (2003); *Wiggins v. Burge*, 173 F.R.D. 226, 229 (N.D.Ill.1997) ("In deciding whether good cause exists, the district court must balance interests involved: the harm to the party seeking the protective order and the importance of disclosure to the public.").

155. *But see Citizens First National Bank of Princeton v. Cincinnati Ins. Co.*, 178 F.3d 943, 944 (7th Cir.1999) (court must make an actual determination of good cause, and may not allow the parties to seal whatever portions of the record they choose).

from annoyance, embarrassment,[156] oppression, or undue burden or expense.[157] Rule 26(b)(1) instructs the court to limit the frequency or extent of discovery if: (i) the discovery sought is unreasonably cumulative or is obtainable from a more convenient or less burdensome or expensive source; (ii) the party seeking the discovery has had ample opportunity to obtain the information; or (iii) the discovery is unduly burdensome[158] or expensive taking into account the circumstances of the particular case. A court may grant a protective order prohibiting the taking of a deposition when it believes the information sought is wholly irrelevant to the issues or to prospective relief.[159] In general, the court will balance the need of the party seeking the discovery against the burden on the party responding.[160]

Burden of Proof

The party seeking the protective order has the burden of showing that good cause exists by stating particular and specific facts.[161]

Depositions

Motions for protective orders are most common in connection with depositions, because such motions are the only mechanism for challenging a deposition in advance of its occurrence. With interrogatories, document requests, and requests for admission, a party can make objections to individual requests without providing a substantive response. The onus then shifts to the party seeking the discovery to move to compel an answer under Rule 37(a). The scheduling of a second deposition of the same person without good cause will generally support finding of annoyance and undue burden, and thus allow the entrance of a protective order.[162]

Types of Protective Order

Rule 26(c) lists eight kinds of protective orders, which are discussed immediately below. The list is not exclusive, however, and the court may make any type of protective order required by justice. The specifically enumerated categories are:

(1) *Order that Disclosure or Discovery Not be Had:* Rule 26(c)(1) allows the court to order that the automatic disclosure or

156. *Miscellaneous Docket Matter #1 v. Miscellaneous Docket Matter #2*, 197 F.3d 922, 925 (8th Cir.1999).

157. *Stagman v. Ryan*, 176 F.3d 986 (7th Cir.1999), *cert. denied,* 528 U.S. 986, 120 S.Ct. 446, 145 L.Ed.2d 363 (1999).

158. *Cummings v. General Motors Corp.*, 365 F.3d 944, 954 (10th Cir. 2004) (it is not enough that the discovery be burdensome, that burden must be "undue").

159. *Leighr v. Beverly Enterprises–Kansas Inc.*, 164 F.R.D. 550, 551 (D.Kan.1996).

160. *In re Wilson*, 149 F.3d 249, 252 (4th Cir.1998); A *Helping Hand, LLC v. Baltimore County, Md.*, 295 F.Supp.2d 585, 592 (D.Md. 2003).

161. *Gulf Oil Co. v. Bernard,* 452 U.S. 89, 102, 101 S.Ct. 2193, 2201, 68 L.Ed.2d 693 (1981); *Rivera v. Nibco, Inc.*, 364 F.3d 1057, 1063 (9th Cir. 2004); *Phillips ex rel. Estates of Byrd v. General Motors Corp.*, 307 F.3d 1206,-1211, n.1 (9th Cir.2002); *In re PE Corp. Securities Litigation*, 221 F.R.D. 20, 26 (D.Conn. 2003) (courts require a particular and specific demonstration of fact, as distinguished from stereotyped and conclusory statements).

162. *Sentry Insurance v. Shivers*, 164 F.R.D. 255, 256 (D.Kan.1996).

requested discovery not occur. Such orders are occasionally entered with respect to interrogatories or document requests, since the court can examine the requests. Such orders are rarely granted with respect to depositions.[163]

(2) *Specified Terms and Conditions:* The court can impose terms and conditions on the automatic disclosure or the taking of discovery under Rule 26(c)(2). The court may designate the time and location of a deposition,[164] or the time to respond to interrogatories, document requests, or requests for admission. The court may order the party seeking discovery to pay the responding party's resulting expenses.[165] The court may set deadlines for the completion of various phases of discovery or order that discovery be conducted in a particular sequence.[166] The court may also modify any of the terms and conditions in subsequent orders.[167]

(3) *Method of Discovery:* The court may restrict discovery to a particular method (such as no depositions or depositions only upon written questions) under Rule 26(c)(3). The general principle is that the parties may select their own discovery methods without unnecessary interference from the court.[168] Thus, most motions to restrict the discovery methods are denied unless the moving party shows special circumstances.[169]

(4) *Limit of Scope or Time:* The court may limit the scope of the automatic disclosures or discovery to specific areas of inquiry or to a specific time period.[170] The court may also stay discovery, either while a dispositive motion is pending,[171] or except with respect to a critical or threshold issue.[172] For example, if a jurisdictional dispute exists, the court may restrict discovery to the jurisdictional issues, then permit broad discovery if jurisdiction is found to exist.[173] Similarly, if liability and damages are

163. *Simmons Foods, Inc. v. Willis*, 191 F.R.D. 625, 630 (D.Kan.2000) (although courts rarely grant a protective order which totally prohibits a deposition, a request to take the deposition of the opposing party's counsel may justify such an order).

164. *Philadelphia Indemnity Insurance Co. v. Federal Insurance Co*, 215 F.R.D. 492 (E.D.Pa. 2003).

165. *Medtronic Sofamor Danek, Inc. v. Michelson*, 2003 WL 21468573 (W.D.Tenn.2003).

166. *Builders Ass'n of Greater Chicago v. City of Chicago*, 170 F.R.D. 435, 437 (N.D.Ill. 1996) (order setting the sequence of discovery appropriate when a potentially dispositive threshold issue has been raised).

167. *Martin v. Reynolds Metals Corp.*, 297 F.2d 49 (9th Cir.1961).

168. *National Life Ins. Co. v. Hartford Acc. & Indem. Co.*, 615 F.2d 595 (3d Cir.1980).

169. *Nguyen v. Excel Corp.*, 197 F.3d 200, 208–09 (5th Cir.1999) (for "good cause shown," court may order discovery taken by a method other than that selected by the party seeking the discovery).

170. *See* Rule 26(c)(4).

171. *Johnson v. New York Univ. School of Educ.*, 205 F.R.D. 433, 434 (S.D.N.Y. 2002); *GTE Wireless v. Qualcomm, Inc.*, 192 F.R.D. 284, 285–86 (S.D.Cal.2000) (before staying discovery, the court should "take a preliminary peek" at the merits to see if there is an "immediate and clear possibility" that the dispositive motion will be granted).

172. *Vivid Technologies, Inc. v. American Science & Engineering, Inc.*, 200 F.3d 795, 804 (staying discovery on all other issues until critical issue is resolved).

173. *Orchid Biosciences, Inc. v. St. Louis University*, 198 F.R.D. 670 (S.D.Cal. 2001).

to be tried separately, the court may restrict discovery to liability issues until the first phase of the case is complete.

(5) *Persons Present:* The court may exclude the public, the press, other witnesses, or other non-parties from a deposition or access to documents produced in discovery under Rule 26(c)(5).[174] The court generally will not exclude the parties or their attorneys.

(6) *Sealed Transcript:* The court may order a deposition transcript sealed, and thus not part of the public record, under Rule 26(c)(6).[175] Similar orders have been entered with respect to interrogatory answers or documents to be produced,[176] although such orders are not expressly authorized by 26(c)(6).[177] Once a sealing order has been entered, parties are prohibited from disclosing to third persons information obtained pursuant to the court order. The prohibition does not apply, however, to information already in a party's possession when the order is entered.[178]

(7) *Confidential Information:* The court may enter an order restricting disclosure of trade secrets and confidential research, development, or commercial information[179] obtained during discovery.[180] Sealing a document is sometimes viewed as extraordinary relief, and there is a presumptive right to access to discovery in civil cases.[181] There is no absolute privilege or protection with respect to such matters.[182] The normal procedure is for the responding party to claim that certain information is confidential. Then, if the parties cannot agree to a

174. *Phillips v. General Motors Corp.*, 307 F.3d 1206. 1210 (9th Cir.2002) (the public generally, and the press in particular, are presumptively entitled to access to documents produced in discovery, and good cause must be demonstrated to shield document from such access); *Jones v. Circle K Stores, Inc.*, 185 F.R.D. 223 (M.D.N.C.1999).

175. *In re Estate of Martin Luther King, Jr., Inc. v. CBS, Inc.*, 184 F.Supp.2d 1353, 1362 (N.D.Ga. 2002) (only the court may seal documents; the parties cannot do so by stipulation).

176. *United States v. Nine Million Forty One Thousand Five Hundred Ninety Eight Dollars and Sixty Eight Cents,* 163 F.3d 238, 250 (5th Cir.1998) (even after the record is sealed, the court may still deny a request for an unredacted copy of sealed documents), *cert. denied*, 527 U.S. 1023, 119 S.Ct. 2369, 144 L.Ed.2d 773 (1999).

177. *Morgan v. United States Dept. of Justice,* 923 F.2d 195 (D.C.Cir.1991).

178. *See Rodgers v. United States Steel Corp.*, 536 F.2d 1001 (3d Cir.1976); *International Prods. Corp. v. Koons,* 325 F.2d 403, 408–09 (2d Cir.1963).

179. *Phillips v. General Motors Corp.*, 289 F.3d 1117 (9th Cir.2002), *opinion amended and superseded*, 307 F.3d 1206 (9th Cir.2002) (the enumerated categories of confidential information are not exclusive, and settlement information can be protected); *Drexel Heritage Furnishings, Inc. v. Furniture USA, Inc.*, 200 F.R.D. 255 (M.D.N.C.2001) (making a distinction between trade secrets and other confidential research and commercial information).

180. *Seattle Times v. Rhinehart,* 467 U.S. 20, 104 S.Ct. 2199, 81 L.Ed.2d 17 (1984), *cert. denied*, 467 U.S. 1230, 104 S.Ct. 2690, 81 L.Ed.2d 884 (1984); *Pearson v. Miller* 211 F.3d 57 (3d Cir.2000).

181. *Loussier v. Universal Music Group, Inc.*, 214 F.R.D. 174, 176–77 (S.D.N.Y.2003).

182. *Federal Open Market Committee v. Merrill,* 443 U.S. 340, 99 S.Ct. 2800, 61 L.Ed.2d 587 (1979); *Sprinturf, Inc. v. Southwest Recreational Industries, Inc.*, 216 F.R.D. 320 (E.D.Pa.2003) (the party seeking the order must show that the information sought is a trade secret or other confidential information protected by Rule 26(c)(7), and that good cause exists to prevent the disclosure of this information).

confidentiality stipulation, the responding party can move for a protective order or the party seeking the discovery can move to compel under Rule 37(a). The party seeking the discovery will have the burden of showing that the information is relevant and needed.[183] In most cases, the discovery will be allowed, but under restricted conditions regarding further disclosure. The court can fashion any order it sees fit, limiting how the information may be used, who may see it, etc. The court may also order disclosure of limited portions of confidential information, such as ordering disclosure of the ingredients of a product, but not the formula. The court can also designate an impartial third person to examine the confidential information.

(8) *Simultaneous Exchange:* The court may order the parties to simultaneously file designated documents or information in sealed envelopes, to be opened as directed by the court. This procedure is most common in patent cases, where it can be an advantage to know an opponent's claims.

Order Compelling Discovery

If the court denies a motion for a protective order, it may at the same time issue an order compelling the discovery. Such an order can facilitate obtaining sanctions under Rule 37.

Discovery While Motion for Protective Order Pending

Technically, a motion for protective order does not automatically stay the discovery that is the subject of the motion.[184] Thus, for example, a motion for protective order to prevent a deposition should not be filed on the day of the deposition, unless it was not practical to file it sooner. However, some local rules provide for an automatic stay of the subject discovery.[185]

Expenses and Attorney Fees

The court has discretion to require the party losing a motion for protective order to pay the expenses the opposing party incurred in connection with the motion, including reasonable attorney fees, under Rule 26(c) and Rule 37(a)(4).

Appeal of Discovery Order by Party

Discovery orders are normally interlocutory, not final, and thus not appealable until the end of the lawsuit.[186] A discovery order will be final if the underlying motion was the entire proceeding, such as with an order granting or denying a deposition to perpetuate testimony under Rule 27, an order denying discovery in aid of execution, an order

183. *Bruno & Stillman, Inc. v. Globe Newspaper Co.*, 633 F.2d 583 (1st Cir.1980).

184. *Creative Solutions Group, Inc. v. Pentzer Corp.*, 199 F.R.D. 443, 444 (D.Mass.2001) (motion to stay discovery does not stay discovery).

185. *Ecrix Corp. v. Exabyte Corp.*, 191 F.R.D. 611, 617 (D.Col.2000).

186. *Cipollone v. Liggett Group, Inc.*, 785 F.2d 1108, 1116 (3d Cir.1986).

granting or denying letters rogatory under Rule 28, or an order denying the deposition of a non-party that was entered in another district.[187]

Appeal of Discovery Order by Non-party

In general, non-parties cannot appeal discovery orders.[188] If the discovery is denied, they have no need to appeal. If the order is granted, their only recourse is to disobey, then appeal any contempt judgment.

Discretion of the Trial Court

The trial court enjoys considerable discretion in deciding discovery matters and may be reversed only for abuse of discretion. [189]

Appeal as Interlocutory Order

Interlocutory orders may be appealed under the Interlocutory Appeals Act of 1958, 28 U.S.C. § 1292(b), if the issues meet the criteria of the Act (such as issues that present a controlling question of law justifying immediate review).[190] Normally, discovery orders will not qualify for interlocutory review.

Appeal at Conclusion

Interlocutory discovery orders may be appealed at the conclusion of the case, and will be reviewed for abuse of discretion.[191] In general, however, it will be difficult to have a verdict overturned based upon a discovery order.

RULE 26(d). TIMING AND SEQUENCE OF DISCOVERY

CORE CONCEPT

Parties may not conduct discovery prior to their discovery conference meeting under Rule 26(f). Thereafter, each party may conduct whatever discovery that party chooses, in any sequence, regardless of the discovery undertaken by other parties. The various discovery devices may be used in any order or simultaneously.

APPLICATIONS

Commencement of Discovery

Parties may not conduct discovery prior to their discovery confer-

187. *United States v. Sciarra,* 851 F.2d 621, 628 (3d Cir.1988), *cert. denied,* 489 U.S. 1068, 109 S.Ct. 1345, 103 L.Ed.2d 814 (1989).

188. *National Super Spuds, Inc. v. New York Mercantile Exchange,* 591 F.2d 174 (2d Cir. 1979). *See also In re Ford Motor Co.*, 110 F.3d 954 (3d Cir.1997).

189. *See Cummings v. General Motors Corp.*, 365 F.3d 944, 953 (10th Cir. 2004); *Food Lion, Inc. v. United Food and Commercial Workers Int'l Union*, 103 F.3d 1007, 1012 (D.C.Cir.1997).

190. *See S.E.C. v. TheStreet.Com*, 273 F.3d 222, 228 (2d Cir.2001) (Rule 26(c) order immediately appealable if such order (1) conclusively determined the disputed question; (2) "resolved an important issue completely separate from the merits of the action; and (3) was effectively unreviewable on appeal from a final judgment").

191. *Thomas v. International Business Machines*, 48 F.3d 478 (10th Cir.1995).

ence under Rule 26(f).[192] This limitation may be altered by court order or stipulation.[193]

Court Orders

The court may order discovery in a specified sequence or according to a schedule "for the convenience of the parties and witnesses and in the interests of justice." Such orders are authorized under Rule 26(c)(2), and are within the broad discretion of the court.[194]

Simultaneous Discovery

The parties may conduct discovery simultaneously. There is no obligation for any party to wait until others have completed their discovery.[195]

Failure to Answer by One Party

A party is not excused from answering discovery because another party has failed to answer discovery. The proper remedy if another party fails to answer discovery is a motion to compel under Rule 37, not a refusal to comply with valid discovery requests.

No Mutuality

There is no requirement that a party conduct discovery in a manner like that used by other parties. Each party is free to conduct any authorized discovery in any sequence regardless of the discovery conducted by other parties.[196]

Excluded Proceedings

The moratorium on early discovery established by Rule 26(d) does not apply to the proceedings exempted from the initial disclosures and discovery conference process by Rule 26(a)(1)(E).

RULE 26(e). SUPPLEMENTATION OF DISCLOSURES AND RESPONSES

CORE CONCEPT

Parties have a duty to supplement automatic disclosures and discovery responses under certain limited conditions set forth in Rule 26(e).[197] Otherwise, there is no general duty to supplement.

192. *Alston v. Parker*, 363 F.3d 229, 236, n.11 (3rd Cir. 2004).

193. *See Semitool, Inc. v. Tokyo Electron America, Inc.*, 208 F.R.D. 273 (N.D.Cal.2002) (applying the good cause standard to a motion to conduct discovery prior to a Rule 26(f) conference); The Advisory Committee Note to the 2000 Amendment to Rule 26(d) (the 2000 Amendment removed the option to eliminate the Rule 26(d) discovery moratorium by local rule).

194. *Doebele v. Sprint Corp.*, 2001 WL 392513 (D.Kan.2001). *But see Ortiz–Rivera v. Municipal Government of Toa Alta*, 214 F.R.D. 51, 54 (D.Puerto Rico 2003) (only the most obviously compelling reasons are sufficient to justify a departure from the rule).

195. *George C. Frey Ready–Mixed Concrete, Inc. v. Pine Hill Concrete Mix Corp.*, 554 F.2d 551 (2d Cir.1977).

196. *Keller v. Edwards*, 206 F.R.D. 412 (D.Md.2002).

197. *See, e.g., Rodowicz v. Massachusetts Mut. Life Ins. Co.*, 279 F.3d 36, 45, n.10 (1st Cir.2002).

APPLICATIONS

Conditions Requiring Supplemental Responses

The following three conditions require supplemental answers:

(1) *Automatic Disclosures:* A party must at reasonable intervals supplement its initial, expert,[198] and pretrial disclosures under Rule 26(a) if the party learns that the information disclosed was incomplete or incorrect;[199]

(2) *Incorrect Response:* A party must supplement a response to an interrogatory, request for production, or request for admission that the party learns was incorrect or incomplete when made;[200] and

(3) *Court Order:* The duty to supplement may also arise by court order.

Timing of Supplemental Responses

No specific time periods are established for the duty to supplement. Any supplements to the disclosures under Rule 26(a) should be made "at appropriate intervals."[201] Any supplements to interrogatories, document requests, or requests for admission should be made "seasonably."[202]

Supplementing Expert Discovery

The obligations to supplement described above apply to both expert reports disclosed under Rule 26(a)(2)(B)[203] and depositions of such experts. Supplemental expert information should be disclosed by the time the pretrial disclosures are made under Rule 26(a)(3), 30 days before trial unless otherwise set by the court.[204]

Information Already Provided

A party need not supplement a disclosure or discovery response if the other parties have already received the additional or corrective information in writing.[205]

198. *Miller v. Pfizer, Inc.*, 356 F.3d 1326, 1332 (10th Cir. 2004).

199. *Klonoski v. Mahlab*, 156 F.3d 255, 268 (1st Cir.1998) (duty to supplement is broad), *cert. denied*, 526 U.S. 1039, 119 S.Ct. 1334, 143 L.Ed.2d 498 (1999).

200. *Rodriguez v. Ibp, Inc.*, 243 F.3d 1221, 1229 (10th Cir.2001), *cert. denied,* 534 U.S. 1055, 122 S.Ct. 645, 151 L.Ed.2d 563 (2001).

201. *Chimie v. PPG Industries, Inc.*, 303 F.Supp.2d 502, 507, n.11 (D.Del. 2004).

202. *United States v. Boyce*, 148 F.Supp.2d 1069 (S.D.Cal.2001) (party cannot wait until the eve of trial to supplement discovery responses).

203. *See Macaulay v. Anas*, 321 F.3d 45, 50 (1st Cir.2003); *Jacobsen v. Deseret Book Co.*, 287 F.3d 936, 951 (10th Cir.2002), *cert. denied,* 537 U.S. 1066, 123 S.Ct. 623, 154 L.Ed.2d 555 (2002).

204. *Reid v. Lockheed Martin Aeronautics Co.*, 205 F.R.D. 655, 662 (N.D.Ga.2001) (Rule 26(e) is not to be used to delay disclosures until 30 days before trial by calling them supplements).

205. *See Williams v. Morton*, 343 F.3d 212, 222 (3rd Cir. 2003); *Troknya v. Cleveland Chiropractic Clinic*, 280 F.3d 1200, 1205 (8th Cir. 2002).

No Other Duty

The duties described in Rule 26(e) are the only duties to supplement. Thus, an instruction in a set of interrogatories that the interrogatories are continuing or purporting to impose a duty to supplement is ineffective.

Sanctions

Failure to supplement a disclosure or discovery response is the equivalent of providing incorrect information in the initial disclosure or response. The court may exclude certain evidence[206] or claims,[207] may order a continuance and further discovery, or take any other action it deems appropriate[208] (*see* Rule 37 for a more detailed analysis of the available sanctions).

RULE 26(f). MEETING OF PARTIES; PLANNING FOR DISCOVERY

CORE CONCEPT

The parties must confer and develop a proposed discovery plan, to be submitted to the court in writing, addressing the discovery schedule and any modifications to the limits or scope of discovery.

APPLICATIONS

Time for Conference

Rule 26(f) directs that the parties confer "as soon as practicable and in any event at least 21 days before a scheduling conference is held or a scheduling order is due under Rule 16(b)."[209] The timing of the discovery conference may be modified by local rule or court order, and specified actions may be exempted from the discovery conference requirement.

In Person Attendance

The rules do not require that the Rule 26(f) conference be conducted in person, and the parties may participate by telephone.[210] However, the court can order the parties to participate in person.

Agenda for Discovery Conference

At the discovery conference, the parties must discuss the nature and basis of their claims and defenses and the possibilities of prompt

206. *W.G. Pettigrew Distributing Co. v. Borden, Inc.*, 976 F.Supp. 1043, 1050 (S.D.Tx.1996).

207. *U.S. v. Philip Morris USA, Inc.*, 219 F.R.D. 198, 200–01 (D.D.C. 2004); *Loral Fairchild Corp. v. Victor Company of Japan, Ltd.*, 911 F.Supp. 76, 80 (E.D.N.Y.1996).

208. *Townsend v. Daniel, Mann, Johnson & Mendenhall*, 196 F.3d 1140, 1151 (10th Cir.1999) (no sanction warranted where conduct not culpable and no harm to defendant).

209. *Coleman v. Sears, Roebuck & Co.*, 221 F.R.D. 433 (W.D.Pa. 2003).

210. The Advisory Committee Note to the 2000 Amendment to Rule 26(f) expresses a preference for in person meetings, but recognizes that the distances some counsel would have to travel and the resulting expenses may outweigh the benefits of an in person meeting.

settlement or resolution of the case. They must also make or arrange for the initial automatic disclosures required by Rule 26(a)(1), discuss orders that the court should enter,[211] and develop a proposed discovery plan, as described below. The parties may also attempt to reach a consensus as to the disputed facts alleged in the pleadings with particularity for purpose of the disclosures under Rule 26(a).

Content of Discovery Plan

The discovery plan should indicate the parties' positions or proposals concerning:

(1) *Automatic Disclosures*: Any changes to the timing, form, or requirement for disclosures under Rule 26(a).[212] The plan must explicitly state when the initial disclosures were or are to be made;

(2) *Discovery Scope and Schedule*: The likely subjects of discovery, the completion date for discovery, and any discovery that should be conducted in phases or limited to or focused on particular issues;

(3) *Discovery Limits*: Any changes to the discovery limits established by the Rules or by local rule, plus any additional limits; and

(4) *Other Orders*: Any other case management or protective orders proposed to the court for consideration at the court's scheduling conference.

Submission of Plan

The parties should submit to the court a written report outlining the plan within 14 days of the discovery meeting. The court may order that the discovery plan be submitted at a different time or that the plan be submitted orally at the Rule 16 conference with the court. Form 35 of the Appendix of Forms to the Rules (printed in Part IV) contains a sample report.

Good Faith Participation

Rule 26(f) places a joint obligation on the attorneys (and on unrepresented parties) to schedule the discovery conference and to attempt in good faith to agree on a proposed discovery plan and a report outlining the plan.

Excluded Proceedings

A discovery conference and discovery plan are not required in proceedings listed in Rule 26(a)(1)(E) as exempted from initial disclosures.[213] Additionally, the parties may be excused from the discovery conference and plan requirements by court order.

211. *Mallinckrodt, Inc. v. Masimo Corp.*, 254 F.Supp.2d 1140, 1157 (C.D.Cal.2003).

212. *In re Bristol–Myers Squibb Securities Litigation*, 205 F.R.D. 437, 440–41 (D.N.J.2002) (the discovery conference should include a discussion of what documents are available in electronic format, and the format to be used for disclosures and production of such documents).

213. *See, e.g., Orbe v. True*, 201 F.Supp.2d 671 (E.D.Va.2002) (habeas corpus proceedings exempt from Rule 26(f)).

RULE 26(g). SIGNING OF DISCLOSURES, DISCOVERY REQUESTS, RESPONSES, AND OBJECTIONS

CORE CONCEPT

Every disclosure, request for discovery, and response or objection must be signed by at least one attorney of record. The signature constitutes a certification that to the best of the signer's knowledge, information, and belief, the document is complete and correct, and is being served for proper purposes within the Rules.

APPLICATIONS

Signature and Certification

Every discovery request, response, or objection must be signed by at least one attorney of record.[214] The document must also state the address of the attorney. The signature constitutes a certification to the best of the signer's knowledge, information, and belief formed after "reasonable inquiry"[215] that:

(A) The document is consistent with the Rules and existing law, or with a good faith argument for extension, modification, or reversal of existing law;

(B) The document is not imposed for any improper purpose, such as to harass, delay, or cause needless expense for an opponent;[216] and

(C) The discovery is not unreasonably or unduly burdensome or expensive, given the nature of the case, the discovery already conducted, the amount in controversy, and the importance of the issues at stake in the litigation.[217]

Duty of Inquiry

The signer of a discovery document is under an obligation to make a reasonable inquiry into the issues covered by his certification before signing the document.[218]

Unsigned Discovery Documents

If without substantial justification a discovery disclosure, request, response, or objection is unsigned, other parties should advise the party

214. *Dugan v. Smerwick Sewerage Co.*, 142 F.3d 398, 407 (7th Cir.1998).

215. *Allender v. Raytheon Aircraft Co.*, 220 F.R.D. 661, 666 (D.Kan. 2004) ("counsel's unrepentant failure to consider, follow, and cite the Tenth Circuit's holding in *Biocore* also amounts to a violation of the 'reasonable inquiry' requirement of Rule 26(g)").

216. *United States v. Kouri–Perez*, 187 F.3d 1, 6 (1st Cir.1999).

217. *See Legault v. Zambarano*, 105 F.3d 24, 27 (1st Cir.1997).

218. *Green Leaf Nursery v. E.I. DuPont De Nemours and Co.*, 341 F.3d 1292, 1305 (11th Cir. 2003) (the signature certifies that the lawyer has made a reasonable effort to assure that the client has provided all the information and documents available to him that are responsive to the discovery demand); *Legault v. Zambarano*, 105 F.3d 24, 28 (1st Cir.1997) (certifying attorney must make a reasonable effort to ensure that the client has provided all responsive information and documents to a discovery request).

making the disclosure, request, response, or objection. If counsel for that party fails to sign the document promptly, the unsigned document will be stricken, and no party is obligated to respond to the unsigned document.

Unrepresented Parties

An unrepresented party should sign disclosures, discovery requests, responses, and objections and should list the party's address.

Automatic Disclosures

The initial disclosure (Rule 26(a)(1)) and the pretrial disclosure (Rule 26(a)(3)) must be signed by at least one attorney of record. The disclosure must also state the address of the attorney. The signature constitutes a certification to the best of the signer's knowledge, information, and belief formed after "reasonable inquiry" that the disclosure is complete and correct.[219]

Sanctions

If without a substantial justification a certification is made in violation of Rule 26(g), the court will impose an appropriate sanction[220] on the party, the attorney, or both.[221] The sanction may include expenses incurred because of the violation, including attorney fees.[222] Generally, a discovery sanction is not a final appealable order.[223]

ADDITIONAL RESEARCH REFERENCES

Wright & Miller, *Federal Practice and Procedure* §§ 2001–2052.

C.J.S. Federal Civil Procedure §§ 526–535.

West's Key No. Digests, Federal Civil Procedure ⚷1261–1278.

219. *Metropolitan Opera Ass'n, Inc. v. Local 100, Hotel Employees and Restaurant Employees Intern. Union*, 212 F.R.D. 178, 222, n.28 (S.D.N.Y.2003).

220. *PLX, Inc. v. Prosystems, Inc.*, 220 F.R.D. 291, 296 (N.D.W.Va. 2004) (court has broad discretion in determining the appropriate sanction).

221. *Maynard v. Nygren*, 332 F.3d 462 (7th Cir.2003) (attorney may not be sanctioned absent a knowing improper certification or violation of the discovery Rules); *McCoo v. Denny's Inc.*, 192 F.R.D. 675 (D.Kan.2000) (sanctions should be assessed against counsel absent evidence that the party was aware of the wrongdoing).

222. *Starlight International, Inc. v. Herlihy*, 190 F.R.D. 587 (D.Kan.1999) (containing a detailed discussion of the criteria for awarding attorney fees as a sanction); *Deese v. Springfield Thoracic and Cardiovascular Surgeons, S.C.*, 183 F.R.D. 534 (C.D.Ill.1998) (awarding fees for attempted introduction of audio tape not properly disclosed during discovery).

223. *United States v. Kouri–Perez*, 187 F.3d 1, 6 (1st Cir.1999).

RULE 27

DEPOSITIONS BEFORE ACTION OR PENDING APPEAL

(a) Before Action.

(1) *Petition.* A person who desires to perpetuate testimony regarding any matter that may be cognizable in any court of the United States may file a verified petition in the United States district court in the district of the residence of any expected adverse party. The petition shall be entitled in the name of the petitioner and shall show: 1, that the petitioner expects to be a party to an action cognizable in a court of the United States but is presently unable to bring it or cause it to be brought, 2, the subject matter of the expected action and the petitioner's interest therein, 3, the facts which the petitioner desires to establish by the proposed testimony and the reasons for desiring to perpetuate it, 4, the names or a description of the persons the petitioner expects will be adverse parties and their addresses so far as known, and 5, the names and addresses of the persons to be examined and the substance of the testimony which the petitioner expects to elicit from each, and shall ask for an order authorizing the petitioner to take the depositions of the persons to be examined named in the petition, for the purpose of perpetuating their testimony.

(2) *Notice and Service.* The petitioner shall thereafter serve a notice upon each person named in the petition as an expected adverse party, together with a copy of the petition, stating that the petitioner will apply to the court, at a time and place named therein, for the order described in the petition. At least 20 days before the date of hearing the notice shall be served either within or without the district or state in the manner provided in Rule 4(d) for service of summons; but if such service cannot with due diligence be made upon any expected adverse party named in the petition, the court may make such order as is just for service by publication or otherwise, and shall appoint, for persons not served in the manner provided in Rule 4(d), an attorney who shall represent them, and, in case they are not otherwise represented, shall cross-examine the deponent. If any expected adverse party is a minor or incompetent the provisions of Rule 17(c) apply.

(3) *Order and Examination.* If the court is satisfied that the perpetuation of the testimony may prevent a failure or delay of

justice, it shall make an order designating or describing the persons whose depositions may be taken and specifying the subject matter of the examination and whether the depositions shall be taken upon oral examination or written interrogatories. The depositions may then be taken in accordance with these rules; and the court may make orders of the character provided for by Rules 34 and 35. For the purpose of applying these rules to depositions for perpetuating testimony, each reference therein to the court in which the action is pending shall be deemed to refer to the court in which the petition for such deposition was filed.

(4) *Use of Deposition.* If a deposition to perpetuate testimony is taken under these rules or if, although not so taken, it would be admissible in evidence in the courts of the state in which it is taken, it may be used in any action involving the same subject matter subsequently brought in a United States district court, in accordance with the provisions of Rule 32(a).

(b) Pending Appeal. If an appeal has been taken from a judgment of a district court or before the taking of an appeal if the time therefor has not expired, the district court in which the judgment was rendered may allow the taking of the depositions of witnesses to perpetuate their testimony for use in the event of further proceedings in the district court. In such case the party who desires to perpetuate the testimony may make a motion in the district court for leave to take the depositions, upon the same notice and service thereof as if the action was pending in the district court. The motion shall show (1) the names and addresses of persons to be examined and the substance of the testimony which the party expects to elicit from each; (2) the reasons for perpetuating their testimony. If the court finds that the perpetuation of the testimony is proper to avoid a failure or delay of justice, it may make an order allowing the depositions to be taken and may make orders of the character provided for by Rules 34 and 35, and thereupon the depositions may be taken and used in the same manner and under the same conditions as are prescribed in these rules for depositions taken in actions pending in the district court.

(c) Perpetuation by Action. This rule does not limit the power of a court to entertain an action to perpetuate testimony.

[Amended effective March 19, 1948; October 20, 1949; July 1, 1971; August 1, 1987.]

AUTHORS' COMMENTARY ON RULE 27

PURPOSE AND SCOPE

Sometimes it will be important to preserve or perpetuate testimony before an action is commenced or during the appeal of an action. Rule 27 provides one mechanism for perpetuating such testimony by taking a deposition.

RULE 27(a). BEFORE ACTION

CORE CONCEPT

Rule 27 is most commonly used to perpetuate testimony when there is a danger that important testimony will be lost, but for one reason or another a civil action cannot yet be commenced.

APPLICATIONS

Verified Petition

A request for a deposition under Rule 27 must be by *verified* petition (*i.e.,* a petition accompanied by a statement signed by the petitioner that the factual averments are accurate).[1]

Contents of Petition

A Rule 27 petition must contain the following:

(1) A statement that the petitioner expects to be a party to an action in federal court, but is presently unable to bring the action;

(2) A description of the subject matter of the anticipated action and the petitioner's relationship to the action;

(3) The facts that the petitioner intends to establish by the testimony, and the petitioner's need for perpetuating it;

(4) The identities and addresses of the persons expected to be adverse parties in the action; and

(5) The identity of the deponent(s) and a detailed description of the substance of their testimony.[2]

The petition must also include a proposed order describing the procedure and scope of the deposition.

Testimony Only

The general rule appears to be that one may not obtain documents or interrogatory responses under Rule 27, only deposition testimony.[3]

1. *In re Chester County Elec., Inc.,* 208 F.R.D. 545, 546–47 (E.D.Pa. 2002).

2. *Penn Mutual Life Insurance Co. v. United States,* 68 F.3d 1371, 1374, 1376 (D.C.Cir. 1995)(Instructing the district court on remand of a Rule 27 ruling to require a "narrowly tailored showing of the substance" of the testimony).

3. *United States v. Van Rossem,* 180 F.R.D. 245, 247 (W.D.N.Y.1998). *But see Application of Deiulemar Compagnia Di Navigazione S.p.A,* 198 F.3d 473, 478, n. 5 (4th Cir.1999), *cert.*

Certainty of Litigation Unnecessary

A party need not demonstrate that litigation is absolutely certain in order to file a motion to perpetuate; instead, the party must be found to be acting in anticipation of litigation.[4]

Need to Perpetuate

It is not necessary to show that the deponents are on their death beds. Rather, one must show that there is a danger of the testimony or evidence being lost,[5] such as when circumstances indicate that memories may fade.[6] In making this determination, however, the deponent's age alone can present a sufficient risk the deponent will be unable to testify.[7]

Pre-Litigation Only

Once litigation has been commenced, Rule 27(a) may no longer be used to perpetuate testimony, and Rules 26 and 30 take over.[8]

Inability to Bring Suit

One requirement for petitions to perpetuate testimony under Rule 27(a) is that the movant not be able to bring a law suit.[9] One basis for such inability is a lack of sufficient information to draft the complaint under the constraints of Rule 11.[10] However, Rule 27 may not be used to uncover or discover testimony necessary to file suit,[11] and applies only where known testimony is to be preserved.[12]

Place of Filing

The petition may be filed in the district in which any of the adverse parties reside. If *all* adverse parties are both not American citizens and not residing in the United States, the petition may be filed in any district.

denied, 529 U.S. 1109, 120 S.Ct. 1962, 146 L.Ed.2d 794 (2000); *Ashafa v. City of Chicago*, 146 F.3d 459, 461 (7th Cir.1998) (Rule 27 petition for names of officers involved in an incident). *But see Pacific Technology Corp. v. Ehrenwald*, 2000 WL 1634393 (S.D.N.Y.2000) (recognizing that Rule 27 does not allow for the obtaining of documents, but allowing it nonetheless because of the importance of the documents).

4. *Calderon v. U.S. Dist. Court*, 144 F.3d 618 (9th Cir.1998).

5. *Calderon v. U.S. Dist. Court*, 144 F.3d 618 (9th Cir.1998); *Lucas v. Riddle*, 2004 WL 1084719 (D.Conn. 2004); *Tennison v. Henry*, 203 F.R.D. 435, 440 (N.D.Cal.2001) (the movant must show a substantial risk of the evidence being lost).

6. *Arizona v. California*, 292 U.S. 341, 54 S.Ct. 735, 78 L.Ed. 1298 (1934).

7. *Penn Mutual Life Insurance Co. v. United States*, 68 F.3d 1371, 1375 (D.C.Cir.1995).

8. *19th Street Baptist Church v. St. Peters Episcopal Church*, 190 F.R.D. 345, 348 (E.D.Pa. 2000).

9. *In re Town of Amenia, NY*, 200 F.R.D. 200 (S.D.N.Y.2001) (party can take a Rule 27 deposition when a declaratory judgment is technically possible but the parties are still negotiating).

10. *In the Matter of Petition of Alpha Industries, Inc.*, 159 F.R.D. 456 (S.D.N.Y.1995).

11. *Application of Deiulemar Compagnia Di Navigazione S.p.A*, 198 F.3d 473, 485 (4th Cir. 1999), *cert. denied*, 529 U.S. 1109, 120 S.Ct. 1962, 146 L.Ed.2d 794 (2000); *In re Yancey L.L.C.*, 2000 WL 1515179 (E.D.La. 2000) ("Rule 27(a) was not designed as an aid to help counsel frame a complaint.").

12. *In re Petition of Sheila Roberts Ford*, 170 F.R.D. 504, 507 (M.D.Ala.1997).

Notice and Service

At least 20 days prior to the hearing, the petitioner must send notice and a copy of the petition to all expected adverse parties.[13] The notice may be served in the manner provided for service of a summons under Rule 4(d). If personal service cannot be made, the court can order service by publication or otherwise. In such cases, the court must appoint an attorney to represent those not personally served. If an expected party is a minor or incompetent, then the provisions of Rule 17(c) apply.

Ruling by the Court

The court will order the deposition if it is satisfied that the perpetuation of the testimony may prevent a future failure or delay of justice.[14] The court may also make orders of the type allowable under Rules 34 (production of documents) and 35 (mental examinations).[15]

Conduct of the Deposition

The court must designate the deponent(s), the subject matter of the examination, and whether the deposition will be oral or written.[16] The deposition is then taken in accordance with the court order and Rules pertaining to depositions (*see* Rule 30 and Rule 31).

Scope of Deposition

An inquiry under Rule 27 may include inspection of documents and mental and physical examinations. However, the scope of a deposition under Rule 27 is often more narrow than a typical discovery deposition, and generally will be governed by the court's order.[17] In general, courts have required that the evidence to be preserved be material and competent, not merely discoverable under general discovery provisions.[18]

Use of the Transcript

A deposition taken pursuant to Rule 27 may be used in any subsequent action in federal court involving the subject matter identified in the petition, under the general terms and conditions governing use of depositions in Rule 32(a).

Subject Matter Jurisdiction

A proceeding to perpetuate testimony is not a separate civil action, and does not require its own basis for jurisdiction. However, the

13. *In re Chester County Elec., Inc.*, 208 F.R.D. 545, 546–47 (E.D.Pa.2002); *In re Solorio*, 192 F.R.D. 709 (D.Utah 2000) (notice is a "condition precedent" to discovery under Rule 27).

14. *19th Street Baptist Church v. St. Peters Episcopal Church*, 190 F.R.D. 345 (E.D.Pa.2000).

15. *Lucas v. Riddle*, 2004 WL 1084719 (D.Conn. 2004).

16. *Martin v. Reynolds Metals Corp.*, 297 F.2d 49, 55 (9th Cir.1961).

17. *Nevada v. O'Leary*, 63 F.3d 932, 936 (9th Cir.1995).

18. *In re Hopson Marine Transportation, Inc.*, 168 F.R.D. 560, 565 (E.D.La.1996).

petition must demonstrate that the anticipated legal action will proceed in federal court.[19]

Bankruptcy Proceedings

Rule 27 does not apply in contested matters before a bankruptcy court.[20]

Appeals

A grant or denial of a Rule 27 petition is appealable as a final order.[21] It is reviewed under the abuse of discretion standard.[22]

RULE 27(b). PENDING APPEAL

CORE CONCEPT

Rule 27 may be used while a case is on appeal, or while the period to appeal is running, to preserve testimony in the event that further proceedings are needed.[23] A request for a deposition pending an appeal is made by motion (not petition) to the district court where the action proceeded.[24] The motion must include the names and addresses of the deponents, the substance of their testimony, and the reasons for perpetuating their testimony.[25] Otherwise, a motion pursuant to Rule 27(b) is subject to the notice, service, and other requirements and conditions for a petition under Rule 27(a) described immediately above.

RULE 27(c). PERPETUATION BY ACTION

CORE CONCEPT

Rule 27 is not the exclusive method of perpetuating testimony.[26] Thus, for example, a deposition that would be admissible in a subsequent proceeding in state court will also be admissible in federal court, even though the offering party may not have complied with Rule 27.

19. *Dresser Industries, Inc. v. United States,* 596 F.2d 1231 (5th Cir.1979); *In re Complaint of Financial Indemnity Co.*, 173 F.R.D. 435, 437 (W.D.La.1997) (implicit in showing that legal action will proceed in federal court is requirement that in diversity cases, petitioner must prove by a preponderance of the evidence that the amount in controversy exceeds the jurisdictional amount). *But see Application of Deiulemar Compagnia Di Navigazione S.p.A,* 198 F.3d 473, 479 (4th Cir.1999), *cert. denied,* 529 U.S. 1109, 120 S.Ct. 1962, 146 L.Ed.2d 794 (2000) (allowing Rule 27 discovery to preserve evidence for an arbitration).

20. *See Sweetland v. Szadkowski,* 198 B.R. 140, 141 n. 1 (Bkrtcy.D.Md.1996). *See also* Fed. Rules Bankr.Proc.Rule 9014.

21. *Martin v. Reynolds Metals Corp.,* 297 F.2d 49 (9th Cir.1961).

22. *Application of Deiulemar Compagnia Di Navigazione S.p.A,* 198 F.3d 473, 479 (4th Cir. 1999), *cert. denied,* 529 U.S. 1109, 120 S.Ct. 1962, 146 L.Ed.2d 794 (2000); *Shore v. Acands, Inc.,* 644 F.2d 386 (5th Cir.1981).

23. *See Schreier v. Weight Watchers Northeast Region, Inc.,* 872 F.Supp. 1 (E.D.N.Y.1994).

24. *United States v. Van Rossem,* 180 F.R.D. 245, 247 (W.D.N.Y.1998) (motion to compel Rule 27 discovery denied because need to perpetuate testimony was not demonstrated).

25. *Foy v. Dicks,* 1996 WL 745501 (E.D.Pa. 1996) (petitioners' Rule 27 motion denied for failure to assert reasons why perpetuation of evidence was necessary).

26. *See Nissei Sangyo America, Ltd. v. United States,* 31 F.3d 435 (7th Cir.1994)(action to perpetuate foreign bank records).

Likewise, a party may preserve testimony under a method authorized by statute.

ADDITIONAL RESEARCH REFERENCES

Wright & Miller, *Federal Practice and Procedure* §§ 2071–2076. Lisnek & Kaufman, *Depositions: Procedure, Strategy and Technique.*

C.J.S. Federal Civil Procedure §§ 544–547.

West's Key No. Digests, Federal Civil Procedure ⚷1291–1299.

RULE 28

PERSONS BEFORE WHOM DEPOSITIONS MAY BE TAKEN

(a) Within the United States. Within the United States or within a territory or insular possession subject to the jurisdiction of the United States, depositions shall be taken before an officer authorized to administer oaths by the laws of the United States or of the place where the examination is held, or before a person appointed by the court in which the action is pending. A person so appointed has power to administer oaths and take testimony. The term officer as used in Rules 30, 31 and 32 includes a person appointed by the court or designated by the parties under Rule 29.

(b) In Foreign Countries. Depositions may be taken in a foreign country (1) pursuant to any applicable treaty or convention, or (2) pursuant to a letter of request (whether or not captioned a letter rogatory), or (3) on notice before a person authorized to administer oaths in the place where the examination is held, either by the law thereof or by the law of the United States, or (4) before a person commissioned by the court, and a person so commissioned shall have the power by virtue of the commission to administer any necessary oath and take testimony. A commission or a letter of request shall be issued on application and notice and on terms that are just and appropriate. It is not requisite to the issuance of a commission or a letter of request that the taking of the deposition in any other manner is impracticable or inconvenient; and both a commission and a letter of request may be issued in proper cases. A notice or commission may designate the person before whom the deposition is to be taken either by name or descriptive title. A letter of request may be addressed "To the Appropriate Authority in [here name the country]." When a letter of request or any other device is used pursuant to any applicable treaty or convention, it shall be captioned in the form prescribed by that treaty or convention. Evidence obtained in response to a letter of request need not be excluded merely because it is not a verbatim transcript, because the testimony was not taken under oath, or because of any similar departure from the requirements for depositions taken within the United States under these rules.

(c) Disqualification for Interest. No deposition shall be taken before a person who is a relative or employee or attorney or counsel of any of the parties, or is a relative or employee of such attorney or counsel, or is financially interested in the action.

[Amended December 27, 1946, effective March 19, 1948; January 21, 1963, effective July 1, 1963; April 29, 1980, effective August 1, 1980; March 2, 1987, effective August 1, 1987; April 22, 1993, effective December 1, 1993.]

AUTHORS' COMMENTARY ON RULE 28

PURPOSE AND SCOPE

Rule 28 specifies the type of person who must be present at a deposition to administer the oath and to record the testimony.

RULE 28(a). WITHIN THE UNITED STATES

CORE CONCEPT

In the United States, or a territory or insular possession, depositions may be taken before an officer authorized to administer oaths under federal or state law.[1] Typically, a stenographer is such an officer. A deposition may also be taken before someone appointed by the court, or before a person designated by the parties pursuant to Rule 29.[2]

RULE 28(b). IN FOREIGN COUNTRIES

CORE CONCEPT

The procedures for taking depositions in a foreign country depend upon the particular country. Some countries have treaties with the United States that facilitate such depositions. Other countries strictly prohibit such depositions altogether.

NOTE: In some countries, the taking of evidence under unauthorized procedures may subject the interrogator to severe—even criminal—sanctions. Before taking such evidence, a practitioner should consult the Hague Convention and all treaty supplements thereto.[3]

APPLICATIONS

Alternatives

Depending upon the laws of the foreign country, a deposition in a foreign country may be taken:

1. *Hudson v. Spellman High Voltage*, 178 F.R.D. 29, 32 (E.D.N.Y.1998).

2. *Popular Imports, Inc. v. Wong's Int'l Inc.*, 166 F.R.D. 276, 279–80 (E.D.N.Y.1996).

3. The Hague Convention on the Taking of Evidence Abroad in Civil or Commercial Matters is reproduced as a note to 28 U.S.C.A. § 1781, and may also be found on WESTLAW in the IEL database, **ci(vii-b & text)**. *Also see* Lowenfeld, International Litigation and Arbitration: Selected Treaties, Statutes and Rules, page 262 (1993). *See Societe Nationale Industrielle Aerospatiale v. United States District Court for the Southern District of Iowa,* 482 U.S. 522, 107 S.Ct. 2542, 96 L.Ed.2d 461 (1987).

(1) Pursuant to any applicable treaty or convention (such as the Hague Convention described above); *International Ins. Co. v. Caja Nacional De Ahoroo Y Seguro*, 2004 WL 555618 (N.D.Ill. 2004).

(2) Pursuant to a letter request (or letter rogatory), which is a formal communication between the court in which an action is proceeding and another court requesting that the testimony of a foreign witness be taken under the direction of the foreign court;

(3) Upon a notice of deposition by any person authorized to administer oaths either by the laws of the foreign country or the United States; and

(4) Before persons commissioned by the court, who will have power to administer an oath and hear testimony by virtue of their oaths.

Method Optional

A party seeking to depose a witness in a foreign country may use any of the methods listed in Rule 28(b) allowed by the foreign country's laws, and may even combine two or more methods.

Issuance of Letter Requests

All courts of the United States are authorized to issue letter requests or letters rogatory,[4] which are typically channeled through the United States Department of State.

Testimony Pursuant to a Letter Request

The evidence taken pursuant to a letter request varies according to the foreign country's laws. Sometimes the foreign judge examines the witness, then makes a written summary of the testimony, which is acknowledged as correct by the witness. The United States court will then decide on the weight to be given to the evidence depending upon the method of recording.

Compelling Attendance of Witness

If the witness is a party, then the witness is subject to the United States court's sanctions if the witness fails to appear as noticed. If the witness is a United States citizen, then the witness still may be subject to the United States court's subpoena power. However, if the witness is an alien, then the party will have to rely on a letter request.

RULE 28(c). DISQUALIFICATION FOR INTEREST

CORE CONCEPT

The officer at a deposition may not be a relative, employee, attor-

4. *See United States v. Reagan,* 453 F.2d 165 (6th Cir.1971), *cert. denied,* 406 U.S. 946, 92 S.Ct. 2049, 32 L.Ed.2d 334 (1972).

ney, or counsel of any of the parties,[5] or an employee or relative of an attorney for a party, or anyone with a financial interest in the action.[6]

APPLICATIONS

Objections

Objections to the officer must be raised before the deposition starts, or as soon thereafter as the interest of the officer becomes known or should have become known, with due diligence. Otherwise, the objection is waived.[7]

ADDITIONAL RESEARCH REFERENCES

Wright & Miller, *Federal Practice and Procedure* §§ 2081–2084.

C.J.S. Federal Civil Procedure § 593.

West's Key No. Digests, Federal Civil Procedure ⚷1371.

5. *See United States v. Washington,* 46 M.J. 477, 482 (C.A.A.F.1997), *cert. denied,* 522 U.S. 1051, 118 S.Ct. 698, 139 L.Ed.2d 642 (1998) (defendant objected to the appointment of a prosecutor on the basis that he had prior prosecutorial involvement in the case).

6. *Ott v. Stipe Law Firm,* 169 F.R.D. 380, 381 (E.D.Okla.1996) (plaintiff is not permitted to administer oath).

7. See Rule 32(d)(2).

RULE 29

STIPULATIONS REGARDING DISCOVERY PROCEDURE

Unless otherwise directed by the court, the parties may by written stipulation (1) provide that depositions may be taken before any person, at any time or place, upon any notice, and in any manner and when so taken may be used like other depositions, and (2) modify other procedures governing or limitations placed upon discovery, except that stipulations extending the time provided in Rules 33, 34, and 36 for responses to discovery may, if they would interfere with any time set for completion of discovery, for hearing of a motion, or for trial, be made only with the approval of the court.

[Amended March 30, 1970, effective July 1, 1970; April 22, 1993, effective December 1, 1993.]

AUTHORS' COMMENTARY ON RULE 29

PURPOSE AND SCOPE

For their convenience, the parties may stipulate to modified procedures for taking depositions and for other discovery methods as long as the stipulation does not interfere with a hearing or trial date or the discovery deadline.

NOTE: Rule 29 was revised in 1993, and care should be exercised when citing decisions pertaining to Rule 29.

APPLICATIONS

Writings

Rule 29 states that stipulations must be in writing.[1] Although not expressly required by Rule 29, the stipulation should be signed by the parties.[2]

Depositions

The parties may designate the person before whom a deposition will occur, and the time, location, notice requirements, and method of taking

1. *In re Carney*, 258 F.3d 415, 419 (5th Cir. 2001) (stipulation not effective if not in writing); *Venture Funding, Ltd. v. United States*, 190 F.R.D. 209, 212 (E.D.Mich.1999) (oral agreement that only certain documents need to be produced is unenforceable); *Pescia v. Auburn Ford–Lincoln Mercury, Inc.*, 177 F.R.D. 509, 510 (M.D.Ala.1997) (oral agreement, even though confirmed in writing, did not satisfy the requirement of Rule 29 that stipulations must be in writing).

2. *Land Ocean Logistics, Inc. v. Aqua Gulf Corp.*, 181 F.R.D. 229, 243 (W.D.N.Y.1998) (competing unsigned stipulations are unenforceable).

the deposition.[3] Thereafter, a deposition taken in accordance with the stipulation may be used as if taken in accordance with the provisions governing depositions in Rules 30 and 31.

Other Discovery Methods

The parties may also stipulate to any other discovery method, except that the parties need court approval to modify the time to respond to interrogatories, document requests, and requests for admission set forth in Rules 33, 34, and 36 if the extension would interfere with the court's discovery deadline or with a hearing or trial date.[4]

Court Override

The court can order that parties perform under the Rules as written, vitiating any stipulations.[5]

ADDITIONAL RESEARCH REFERENCES

Wright & Miller, *Federal Practice and Procedure* §§ 2091–2092.

C.J.S. Federal Civil Procedure § 566.

West's Key No. Digests, Federal Civil Procedure ⚷1326.

3. *Hudson v. Spellman High Voltage*, 178 F.R.D. 29, 32 (E.D.N.Y.1998).

4. *See Laborers' Pension Fund v. Blackmore Sewer Const., Inc.*, 298 F.3d 600, 605–06 (7th Cir.2002); *Jayne H. Lee, Inc. v. Flagstaff Indus. Corp.*, 173 F.R.D. 651, 654 n. 8 (D.Md.1997).

5. The Advisory Note to the 1970 amendment of Rule 29.

RULE 30

DEPOSITIONS UPON ORAL EXAMINATION

(a) When Depositions May Be Taken; When Leave Required.

(1) A party may take the testimony of any person, including a party, by deposition upon oral examination without leave of court except as provided in paragraph (2). The attendance of witnesses may be compelled by subpoena as provided in Rule 45.

(2) A party must obtain leave of court, which shall be granted to the extent consistent with the principles stated in Rule 26(b)(2), if the person to be examined is confined in prison or if, without the written stipulation of the parties,

(A) a proposed deposition would result in more than ten depositions being taken under this rule or Rule 31 by the plaintiffs, or by the defendants, or by third-party defendants;

(B) the person to be examined already has been deposed in the case; or

(C) a party seeks to take a deposition before the time specified in Rule 26(d) unless the notice contains a certification, with supporting facts, that the person to be examined is expected to leave the United States and be unavailable for examination in this country unless deposed before that time.

(b) Notice of Examination: General Requirements; Method of Recording; Production of Documents and Things; Deposition of Organization; Deposition by Telephone.

(1) A party desiring to take the deposition of any person upon oral examination shall give reasonable notice in writing to every other party to the action. The notice shall state the time and place for taking the deposition and the name and address of each person to be examined, if known, and, if the name is not known, a general description sufficient to identify the person or the particular class or group to which the person belongs. If a subpoena duces tecum is to be served on the person to be examined, the designation of the materials to be produced as set forth in the subpoena shall be attached to, or included in, the notice.

(2) The party taking the deposition shall state in the notice the method by which the testimony shall be recorded. Unless the court orders otherwise, it may be recorded by sound, sound-and-

visual, or stenographic means, and the party taking the deposition shall bear the cost of the recording. Any party may arrange for a transcription to be made from the recording of a deposition taken by nonstenographic means.

(3) With prior notice to the deponent and other parties, any party may designate another method to record the deponent's testimony in addition to the method specified by the person taking the deposition. The additional record or transcript shall be made at that party's expense unless the court otherwise orders.

(4) Unless otherwise agreed by the parties, a deposition shall be conducted before an officer appointed or designated under Rule 28 and shall begin with a statement on the record by the officer that includes (A) the officer's name and business address; (B) the date, time, and place of the deposition; (C) the name of the deponent; (D) the administration of the oath or affirmation to the deponent; and (E) an identification of all persons present. If the deposition is recorded other than stenographically, the officer shall repeat items (A) through (C) at the beginning of each unit of recorded tape or other recording medium. The appearance or demeanor of deponents or attorneys shall not be distorted through camera or sound-recording techniques. At the end of the deposition, the officer shall state on the record that the deposition is complete and shall set forth any stipulations made by counsel concerning the custody of the transcript or recording and the exhibits, or concerning other pertinent matters.

(5) The notice to a party deponent may be accompanied by a request made in compliance with Rule 34 for the production of documents and tangible things at the taking of the deposition. The procedure of Rule 34 shall apply to the request.

(6) A party may in the party's notice and in a subpoena name as the deponent a public or private corporation or a partnership or association or governmental agency and describe with reasonable particularity the matters on which examination is requested. In that event, the organization so named shall designate one or more officers, directors, or managing agents, or other persons who consent to testify on its behalf, and may set forth, for each person designated, the matters on which the person will testify. A subpoena shall advise a non-party organization of its duty to make such a designation. The persons so designated shall testify as to matters known or reasonably available to the organization. This subdivision (b)(6) does not preclude taking a deposition by any other procedure authorized in these rules.

(7) The parties may stipulate in writing or the court may upon motion order that a deposition be taken by telephone or other remote electronic means. For the purposes of this rule and Rules 28(a), 37(a)(1), and 37(b)(1), a deposition taken by such means is taken in the district and at the place where the deponent is to answer questions.

(c) Examination and Cross–Examination; Record of Examination; Oath; Objections. Examination and cross-examination of witnesses may proceed as permitted at the trial under the provisions of the Federal Rules of Evidence except Rules 103 and 615. The officer before whom the deposition is to be taken shall put the witness on oath or affirmation and shall personally, or by someone acting under the officer's direction and in the officer's presence, record the testimony of the witness. The testimony shall be taken stenographically or recorded by any other method authorized by subdivision (b)(2) of this rule. All objections made at the time of the examination to the qualifications of the officer taking the deposition, to the manner of taking it, to the evidence presented, to the conduct of any party, or to any other aspect of the proceedings shall be noted by the officer upon the record of the deposition; but the examination shall proceed, with the testimony being taken subject to the objections. In lieu of participating in the oral examination, parties may serve written questions in a sealed envelope on the party taking the deposition and the party taking the deposition shall transmit them to the officer, who shall propound them to the witness and record the answers verbatim.

(d) Schedule and Duration; Motion to Terminate or Limit Examination.

(1) Any objection during a deposition must be stated concisely and in a non-argumentative and non-suggestive manner. A person may instruct a deponent not to answer only when necessary to preserve a privilege, to enforce a limitation directed by the court, or to present a motion under Rule 30(d) (4).

(2) Unless otherwise authorized by the court or stipulated by the parties, a deposition is limited to one day of seven hours. The court must allow additional time consistent with Rule 26(b)(2) if needed for a fair examination of the deponent or if the deponent or another person, or other circumstance, impedes or delays the examination.

(3) If the court finds that any impediment, delay, or other conduct has frustrated the fair examination of the deponent, it may

impose upon the persons responsible an appropriate sanction, including the reasonable costs and attorney's fees incurred by any parties as a result thereof.

(4) At any time during a deposition, on motion of a party or of the deponent and upon a showing that the examination is being conducted in bad faith or in such manner as unreasonably to annoy, embarrass, or oppress the deponent or party, the court in which the action is pending or the court in the district where the deposition is being taken may order the officer conducting the examination to cease forthwith from taking the deposition, or may limit the scope and manner of the taking of the deposition as provided in Rule 26(c). If the order made terminates the examination, it may be resumed thereafter only upon the order of the court in which the action is pending. Upon demand of the objecting party or deponent, the taking of the deposition must be suspended for the time necessary to make a motion for an order. The provisions of Rule 37(a)(4) apply to the award of expenses incurred in relation to the motion.

(e) Review by Witness; Changes; Signing. If requested by the deponent or a party before completion of the deposition, the deponent shall have 30 days after being notified by the officer that the transcript or recording is available in which to review the transcript or recording and, if there are changes in form or substance, to sign a statement reciting such changes and the reasons given by the deponent for making them. The officer shall indicate in the certificate prescribed by subdivision (f)(1) whether any review was requested and, if so, shall append any changes made by the deponent during the period allowed.

(f) Certification and Filing by Officer; Exhibits; Copies.

(1) The officer must certify that the witness was duly sworn by the officer and that the deposition is a true record of the testimony given by the witness. This certificate must be in writing and accompany the record of the deposition. Unless otherwise ordered by the court, the officer must securely seal the deposition in an envelope or package indorsed with the title of the action and marked "Deposition of [here insert name of witness]" and must promptly send it to the attorney who arranged for the transcript or recording, who must store it under conditions that will protect it against loss, destruction, tampering, or deterioration. Documents and things produced for inspection during the examination of the witness must, upon the request of a party, be marked for identifica-

tion and annexed to the deposition and may be inspected and copied by any party, except that if the person producing the materials desires to retain them the person may (A) offer copies to be marked for identification and annexed to the deposition and to serve thereafter as originals if the person affords to all parties fair opportunity to verify the copies by comparison with the originals, or (B) offer the originals to be marked for identification, after giving to each party an opportunity to inspect and copy them, in which event the materials may then be used in the same manner as if annexed to the deposition. Any party may move for an order that the original be annexed to and returned with the deposition to the court, pending final disposition of the case.

(2) Unless otherwise ordered by the court or agreed by the parties, the officer shall retain stenographic notes of any deposition taken stenographically or a copy of the recording of any deposition taken by another method. Upon payment of reasonable charges therefor, the officer shall furnish a copy of the transcript or other recording of the deposition to any party or to the deponent.

(3) The party taking the deposition shall give prompt notice of its filing to all other parties.

(g) Failure to Attend or to Serve Subpoena; Expenses.

(1) If the party giving the notice of the taking of a deposition fails to attend and proceed therewith and another party attends in person or by attorney pursuant to the notice, the court may order the party giving the notice to pay to such other party the reasonable expenses incurred by that party and that party's attorney in attending, including reasonable attorney's fees.

(2) If the party giving the notice of the taking of a deposition of a witness fails to serve a subpoena upon the witness and the witness because of such failure does not attend, and if another party attends in person or by attorney because that party expects the deposition of that witness to be taken, the court may order the party giving the notice to pay to such other party the reasonable expenses incurred by that party and that party's attorney in attending, including reasonable attorney's fees.

[Amended January 21, 1963, effective July 1, 1963; March 30, 1970, effective July 1, 1970; March 1, 1971, effective July 1, 1971; November 20, 1972, effective July 1, 1975; April 29, 1980, effective August 1, 1980; March 2, 1987, effective August 1, 1987; April 22, 1993, effective December 1, 1993; April 17, 2000, effective December 1, 2000.]

AUTHORS' COMMENTARY ON RULE 30

PURPOSE AND SCOPE

Rule 30 sets forth the procedures for the taking of depositions by oral examination. Rule 30 must be considered in conjunction with the other discovery rules, and in particular Rule 26 governing the scope of discovery.

NOTE: Rule 30 was substantially revised in 1993 and 2000, and great care should be exercised when citing decisions pertaining to Rule 30.

RULE 30(a). WHEN DEPOSITIONS MAY BE TAKEN; WHEN LEAVE REQUIRED

CORE CONCEPT

In general, a party may take the deposition of up to 10 witnesses, party or otherwise, at any time after the parties have conducted the discovery conference under Rule 26(d).

APPLICATIONS

Persons Subject to Deposition

Rule 30 applies to parties and nonparties alike.[1] A party may even take the party's own deposition if, for example, the party will be unable to attend trial. One may also take the deposition of attorneys, including the attorneys for parties,[2] although the attorney-client privilege may protect most of an attorney's testimony. Depositions are also permitted of public officials, the United States, individual states, and other governmental subdivisions.[3]

Number of Depositions

The plaintiffs as a group are limited to 10 depositions total, by written and/or oral examination, as are the defendants and third-party defendants.[4] Subpoenas to produce documents do not count towards the 10 deposition limit.[5] It is not clear whether expert depositions count toward the limit.[6] This number may be increased by stipulation or by order of court.[7]

1. *CSC Holdings, Inc. v. Redisi*, 309 F.3d 988, 993 (7th Cir.2002) (a party has a general right to compel any person to appear at a deposition).

2. *Shelton v. American Motors Corp.*, 805 F.2d 1323 (8th Cir.1986); *Prevue Pet Products, Inc. v. Avian Adventures, Inc.*, 200 F.R.D. 4135 (N.D.Ill.2001) (describing the criteria for taking the deposition of opposing counsel).

3. *United States v. Procter & Gamble Co.*, 356 U.S. 677, 78 S.Ct. 983, 2 L.Ed.2d 1077 (1958).

4. *Finova Capital Corp. v. Lawrence*, 2000 WL 1808276 (N.D.Tex. 2000) (depositions of parties and nonparties alike both count towards the 10 deposition limit).

5. *Andamiro U.S.A. v. Konami Amusement of America, Inc.*, 2001 WL 535667 (C.D.Cal. 2001).

6. *Express One Intern., Inc. v. Sochata*, 2001 WL 363073 (N.D.Tex. 2001).

7. *Raniola v. Bratton*, 243 F.3d 610, 628 (2d Cir.2001); *Barrow v. Greenville Independent School Dist.*, 202 F.R.D. 480, 482 (N.D.Tex.

Repeat Depositions

Leave of court is required to depose someone a second time (although leave of court is not required to reconvene and continue a deposition that was suspended or not completed the first day).[8] This restriction arguably applies to depositions of a corporate representative under Rule 30(b)(6).[9] Leave shall be granted subject to the principles in Rule 26(b)(2), such as when the sought-after information could not have been obtained in the first deposition.[10]

When Depositions May be Conducted

Depositions generally may be taken at any time after the Rule 26(d) discovery conference and before the cut-off date for discovery established by the court. Leave of court is generally required to depose someone prior to the time when the parties conduct the discovery conference under Rule 26(d). An exception occurs when the deponent is expected to leave the United States. In such instances, the notice of deposition must contain a certification with the facts supporting the need for the early deposition.[11] Additionally, in proceedings listed in Rule 26(a)(1)(E) as exempt from initial disclosures, there is no preliminary waiting period for depositions.

Postjudgment Depositions

A judgment creditor is entitled to take depositions of the judgment debtor to inquire into the assets necessary to satisfy the judgment.[12]

Deponent in Prison

Leave of court must be obtained in order to take the deposition of a person confined in prison.[13]

RULE 30(b)(1). NOTICE OF EXAMINATION: GENERAL REQUIREMENTS

CORE CONCEPT

A party desiring to take a deposition must serve a written notice upon all other parties identifying the deponent and time and location of the deposition. Depositions are only binding on parties properly noticed or actually represented at the deposition.

2001) (magistrate judge's ruling denying leave to take more than 10 depositions reviewed on an abuse of discretion standard).

8. *In re Tutu Water Wells Contamination CERCLA Litigation*, 189 F.R.D. 153, 155 (D.Vi. 1999) (balancing need for testimony against burden of second deposition); *Melhorn v. New Jersey Transit Rail Operations, Inc.*, 203 F.R.D. 176 (E.D.Pa.2001) ("Absent some showing of need or good reason for doing so, a deponent should not be required to appear for a second deposition.").

9. *See Ameristar Jet Charter, Inc. v. Signal Composites, Inc.*, 244 F.3d 189 (1st Cir.2001).

10. *Collins v. International Dairy Queen*, 189 F.R.D. 496, 498 (M.D.Ga.1999).

11. *19th Street Baptist Church v. St. Peters Episcopal Church*, 190 F.R.D. 345, 348 n. 5 (E.D.Pa.2000).

12. *Credit Lyonnais v. SGC International, Inc.*, 160 F.3d 428, 430 (8th Cir.1998).

13. *See Ashby v. McKenna*, 331 F.3d 1148(10th Cir.2003) (prisoner plaintiff sanctioned for refusing to participate in deposition without court order); *Davis v. Artuz*, 2001 WL 50887 (S.D.N.Y.2001).

APPLICATIONS

Content of Notice

The notice must state the time and place of the deposition. It must also state the name and address of the deponent, if known, or a general description sufficient to identify the deponent. If a subpoena duces tecum (seeking documents) is to be served under Rule 45, then the notice must include a description of the documents sought.[14] There is no need to state the subject of the inquiry.

Filing of Notice

The notice need not be filed.

Notice to Party

Parties must comply with a notice of deposition or they are potentially subject to sanctions from the court. A corporate party is required to produce directors, officers, and managing agents pursuant to a notice of deposition; a subpoena is required for other employees.[15] Parties that believe that they should not be required to attend can file motions for protective orders.

Failure to Notify

If a party does not receive a notice of a deposition and does not appear, or is not represented at the deposition, the testimony cannot be used against that party, even if the party had actual knowledge.[16]

Notice to Non-party

A notice of deposition is not binding on a non-party. Instead, a subpoena must be issued pursuant to Rule 45 to force a non-party to attend a deposition.

Reasonable Notice

Rule 30(b)(1) states that a party must give reasonable notice.[17] There is no bright line as to what is reasonable notice, and the determination is extremely fact-specific.[18] If the parties cannot agree on a mutually acceptable date, then unreasonable notice may be challenged by a motion to enlarge or shorten the time for taking the deposition pursuant to Rule 30(b)(3) or by a motion for a protective order under Rule 26(c). An order vacating a deposition notice based upon unreasonable notice does not preclude further discovery with proper notice.

14. *Orleman v. Jumpking, Inc.*, 2000 WL 1114849 (D.Kan.2000) (description of documents to be produced must be attached to or included in the notice).

15. *U.S. Fidelity & Guar. Co. v. Braspetro Oil Services Co.*, 2001 WL 43607 (S.D.N.Y.2001).

16. *Lauson v. Stop–N–Go Foods, Inc.*, 133 F.R.D. 92 (W.D.N.Y.1990).

17. *Howard v. Everex Systems, Inc.*, 228 F.3d 1057, 1067 (9th Cir.2000); *United States v. Philip Morris Inc.*, 312 F.Supp.2d 27 (D.D.C. 2004) (3 days notice for busy professionals is not reasonable).

18. *In re Stratosphere Corp. Securities Litigation*, 183 F.R.D. 684, 687 (D.Nev.1999) (six days notice not reasonable).

Sanctions

The sanctions for failure to appear at a deposition depend upon whether the witness is a party. Non-party witnesses may be held in contempt of court for failure to obey a subpoena. Party witnesses are subject to the sanctions described in Rule 37(d).

Place of Examination

For a party deponent, one may select any location for the deposition, subject to the party's right to move for a protective order (but see the general rules below). For a non-party witness, the witness must travel up to 100 miles from the place where the witness resides, is employed, or regularly transacts business.

General Rules for Deposition Location

The court has discretion to control the location of a deposition.[19] In general, however, plaintiffs will be required to travel to the district where the suit is pending for their depositions,[20] whereas defendants can have their depositions taken where they work or live.[21] Also, in general, the deposition of a corporation occurs at its principal place of business.[22] These general principles are, of course, subject to extenuating circumstances, such as a plaintiff who is too sick to travel.

Motion for Protective Order

If a notice of deposition is facially valid, then the witness must attend or file a motion for a protective order pursuant to Rule 26(c).[23] The motion must be made before the time scheduled for the deposition, and must show good reason for the requested protection. The motion must be accompanied by a certification that the parties met prior to the filing of the motion and attempted to resolve their dispute without intervention by the court.

RULE 30(b)(2). NOTICE OF EXAMINATION: GENERAL REQUIREMENTS

CORE CONCEPT

The notice of deposition must specify the method for recording the deposition testimony.

19. *In re Standard Metals Corp.*, 817 F.2d 625, 628 (10th Cir.1987); *Starlight International Inc. v. Herlihy*, 186 F.R.D. 626, 644 (D.Kan. 1999) (court will consider each case on its own facts and the equities of the particular situation).

20. *United States v. Rock Springs Vista Development*, 185 F.R.D. 603 (D.Nev.1999) (wheelchair-bound out-of-state plaintiffs must travel to the forum of the suit for their depositions); *Dollar Systems, Inc. v. Tomlin*, 102 F.R.D. 93 (D.Tenn.1984).

21. *Rapoca Energy Comapny, L.P. v. Amci Export Corp.*, 199 F.R.D. 191, 193 (W.D.Va. 2001).

22. *Custom Form Mfg., Inc. v. Omron Corp.*, 196 F.R.D. 333, 336 (N.D.Ind.2000); *Chris-Craft Industrial Products, Inc. v. Kuraray Co., Ltd.*, 184 F.R.D. 605 (N.D.Ill.1999).

23. *Collins v. Wayland,* 139 F.2d 677 (9th Cir.1944), *cert. denied,* 322 U.S. 744, 64 S.Ct. 1151, 88 L.Ed. 1576 (1944).

APPLICATIONS

Methods Available

The party taking the deposition may have it recorded by audio, audio visual, or stenographic means, unless the court orders otherwise.[24] Other parties may arrange for additional methods of recording under Rule 30(b)(3).

Cost of Recording

The party taking the deposition bears the cost of the party's chosen method(s) of recording.[25]

Transcript

Any party may, at its own expense, arrange for a transcript to be made of a deposition recorded by nonstenographic means.[26]

Use of Nonstenographic Depositions

In order to use a nonstenographically recorded deposition at trial or in connection with a dispositive motion, a party must submit a transcript of the portions to be introduced for the court's use.[27]

Objections

Objections to the nonstenographic recording of a deposition should be raised prior to the commencement of the deposition via a motion for protective order under Rule 26(c) or at the commencement of the deposition under Rule 30(c).[28]

RULE 30(b)(3). NOTICE OF EXAMINATION: METHOD OF RECORDING

CORE CONCEPT

Any party may arrange for a method of recording a deposition in addition to that specified in the notice of deposition. The party desiring such additional method of recording must send prior notice to all other parties and to the deponent,[29] and will bear the expense of the additional recording unless otherwise ordered by the court.

24. *Planned Parenthood of Columbia/Willamette, Inc. v. American Coalition of Life Activists*, 290 F.3d 1058 (9th Cir.2002) ("nonstenographic" means audio or visual); *Wilson v. Olathe Bank*, 184 F.R.D. 395, 397 (D.Kan.1999) (availability of witnesses to tetify at trial does not affect the noticing party's right to select the manner of recording).

25. *Morrison v. Reichhold Chemicals, Inc.*, 97 F.3d 460, 464 (11th Cir.1996); *Hudson v. Spellman High Voltage*, 178 F.R.D. 29 (E.D.N.Y. 1998). *See also Cherry v. Champion International Corp.*, 186 F.3d 442, 448–49 (4th Cir.1999) (discussing the recovery of alternative means of recording as costs under 28 U.S.C. § 1920).

26. *Hudson v. Spellman High Voltage*, 178 F.R.D. 29 (E.D.N.Y.1998).

27. Rule 26(a)(3)(B) and Rule 32(c); *But see Hudson v. Spellman High Voltage*, 178 F.R.D. 29 (E.D.N.Y.1998) ("there is no requirement that a party taking a deposition by non-stenographic means provide a written transcript of the entire deposition to other parties.").

28. *Fanelli v. Centenary College*, 211 F.R.D. 268 (D.N.J.2002) (anxiety over videotaping not good cause sufficient to warrant a protective order).

29. *Ogden v. Keystone Residence*, 226 F.Supp.2d 588, 605 (M.D.Pa.2002).

RULE 30(b)(4). NOTICE OF DEPOSITION: GENERAL REQUIREMENTS

CORE CONCEPT

At the beginning of a deposition, the officer shall place on the record administrative details identifying and describing the deposition. During the deposition, the demeanor of the witnesses shall not be distorted in the recording.

APPLICATIONS

Statement at Deposition Beginning

The officer recording the deposition shall begin the record with a statement that includes:

A) the officer's name and business address;

B) the date, time, and place of deposition;

C) the name of the deponent;

D) the administration of the oath or affirmation to the deponent; and

E) an identification of all persons present.

If the deposition is recorded other than stenographically, then each separate tape or unit of recording must begin with the officer's name and business address, the date, time and place of the deposition, and the deponent's name.

Statement at Deposition End

The officer recording the deposition shall close the record by stating that the deposition is complete and setting forth any administrative stipulations regarding the deposition.

Witness Demeanor

The recording device should accurately and neutrally depict the witness' demeanor and appearance.

RULE 30(b)(5). NOTICE OF DEPOSITION: PRODUCTION OF DOCUMENTS AND THINGS

CORE CONCEPT

A witness may be compelled to bring documents to a deposition by including a description of the documents in the notice of deposition (for a party witness) or by issuing a subpoena duces tecum under Rule 45(a)(1)(C) and including a description in the notice (for a non-party witness).[30] However, if the witness is a party, then the witness must be accorded 30 days to interpose objections to the document request[31] (the rationale being that one should not be able to circumvent the 30–day

30. *Lee v. U.S. Dept. of Justice*, 287 F.Supp.2d 15, 22 (D.D.C. 2003).

31. *Howell v. Standard Motor Products, Inc.*, 2001 WL 456241 (N.D.Tex.2001).

period in the document request rules by issuing a notice of deposition).[32]

RULE 30(b)(6). NOTICE OF EXAMINATION: DEPOSITION OF ORGANIZATION

CORE CONCEPT

Rule 30(b)(6) allows a party to notice the deposition of a corporation, partnership,[33] association, or governmental agency[34] and to specify the areas of inquiry. The named organization must then designate one or more representatives to testify as to the areas of inquiry.

APPLICATIONS

Subpoena

If the corporation or organization is not a party, then one must issue a subpoena to compel attendance.[35] If the corporation or organization is a party, a notice of deposition is sufficient.

Content of Notice

The notice (and the subpoena, if necessary) must state that the corporation has the duty to designate a representative, and must specify the areas of inquiry with reasonable particularity.[36]

Designation of Agent

Corporations may be compelled to name an officer, director, or managing agent.[37] Statements by the designated representative are then treated as statement of the party.[38] The term "managing agent" is not defined. Courts look to whether the individual has general powers to exercise discretion with respect to corporate matters, whether the individual's interests coincide with those of the corporation, and whether the individual can be depended on to give testimony at the corporation's direction.[39]

Selection of Representatives

The representative does not have to be an officer or director of the organization, and in fact does not even need to be employed by the

32. *See Canal Barge Co. v. Commonwealth Edison Co.*, 2001 WL 817853 (N.D.Ill.2001) (discussing the relationship between document requests under Rule 34 and requests to bring documents to depositions).

33. *Starlight International Inc. v. Herlihy*, 186 F.R.D. 626, 638 (D.Kan.1999) (Rule 30(b)(6) applies to partnerships and joint ventures).

34. *McKesson v. Islamic Republic of Iran*, 185 F.R.D. 70 (D.D.C.1999) (allowing a Rule 30(b)(6) deposition of Iran).

35. *See Mattel, Inc. v. Walking Mountain Productions*, 353 F.3d 792, 797 (9th Cir. 2003); *Cates v. LTV Aerospace Corp.*, 480 F.2d 620 (5th Cir.1973).

36. *Steil v. Humana Kansas City, Inc.*, 197 F.R.D. 442 (D.Kan.2000); *Starlight International Inc. v. Herlihy*, 186 F.R.D. 626, 638 (D.Kan. 1999).

37. *Atlantic Cape Fisheries v. Hartford Fire Ins. Co.*, 509 F.2d 577, 579 (1st Cir.1975); *Travelers Indemnity Co. v. Hash Management, Inc.*, 173 F.R.D. 150, 155 (M.D.N.C.1997).

38. *Stone v. Morton Int'l Inc.*, 170 F.R.D. 498, 500 (D.Utah 1997).

39. *Terry v. Modern Woodmen of America*, 57 F.R.D. 141 (W.D.Mo.1972).

organization. Regardless of the status of the representative, however, the organization will be bound by the representative's testimony and must prepare the representative to testify as to the organization's collective knowledge and information. If no single individual can provide the corporation's testimony as to all the designated topics, the corporation can name more than one representative.[40] Sometimes, corporate counsel are selected as the corporate representative.[41]

Particular Officer

To depose a specific officer, director, or managing agent, there is no need to use Rule 30(b)(6); a notice of deposition may be sent indicating that the individual's testimony is sought in the individual's official capacity.[42] The corporation is then subject to sanctions if the named representative fails to appear.[43] The party moving for such sanctions has the burden of proving that the individual was an officer, director, or managing agent.

Officer vs. Employee

One cannot compel the attendance at a deposition of an employee who is not an officer, director, or managing agent of the organization merely by sending a notice.[44] Such an employee may be served with a subpoena,[45] and the employee is then subject to sanctions if the employee fails to appear. The corporation is not bound by the statements of such employees.[46]

Status of Individual

The court determines whether a particular individual is a corporate representative and "speaks for the corporation" when the testimony is offered into evidence or when sanctions are sought for failure to appear. The individual's status is measured as of the time of the deposition, not the time of the trial or hearing.[47]

Sanctions Against Organization

If the designated officer, director, or managing agent fails to appear for a deposition, the corporation or organization is subject to sanctions. Likewise, if a corporation provides witnesses who cannot answer ques-

40. *Ferko v. National Ass'n for Stock Car Auto Racing, Inc.*, 218 F.R.D. 125, 142 (E.D.Tex. 2003).

41. *See In re Pioneer Hi–Bred Intern., Inc.*, 238 F.3d 1370, 1376 (Fed.Cir.2001) (addressing the attorney client privilege issues when counsel is designated as the corporate representative).

42. *Cummings v. General Motors Corp.*, 365 F.3d 944, 953 (10th Cir. 2004); *Folwell v. Hernandez*, 210 F.R.D. 169, 172 (M.D.N.C.2002) (Rule 30(b)(6) does not eliminate the prior Rule 30(a)(1) method of examination which permits the opposing party to select an officer, director, or managing agent for deposition).

43. *Bon Air Hotel, Inc. v. Time, Inc.*, 376 F.2d 118 (5th Cir.1967), *cert. denied,* 393 U.S. 859, 89 S.Ct. 131, 21 L.Ed.2d 127 (1968).

44. *See Folwell v. Hernandez*, 210 F.R.D. 169, 173 (M.D.N.C.2002) (the definition of a managing agent is made on a case-by-case factual determination).

45. *Phildelphia Indem. Ins. Co. v. Federal Ins. Co.*, 215 F.R.D. 492 (E.D.Pa.2003).

46. *Burns Bros. v. The B & O No. 177,* 21 F.R.D. 142 (E.D.N.Y.1957).

47. *Bon Air Hotel, Inc. v. Time, Inc.*, 376 F.2d 118 (5th Cir.1967), *cert. denied,* 393 U.S. 859, 89 S.Ct. 131, 21 L.Ed.2d 127 (1968).

tions listed in notice of deposition, then corporation has failed to comply with its obligations under the rule and may be subject to sanctions.[48]

Scope of Testimony

The corporation or organization must select an individual or individuals who can testify to the areas specified in the notice.[49] The individual(s) must testify to all matters known or reasonably available to the corporation,[50] which may necessitate some gathering of documents and information and having the individual(s) review and become familiar with the documents and information.[51] The courts are divided as to whether the examination of the representative is limited to the areas of inquiry identified in the notice of deposition.[52]

Legal Matters

Many courts are reluctant to allow depositions of opposing counsel, and will closely examine notices under Rule 30(b)(6) that are "back door" attempts to depose opposing counsel.[53]

Duty to Prepare

If the representative(s) cannot testify as to the corporation's collective information on the matters requested, then the corporation has a duty to gather the information and prepare the representative(s) so that the representatives can give complete, knowledgeable, and binding testimony.[54] Failure to adequately prepare the representative can result in sanctions.[55]

Effect of Testimony

Testimony by a Rule 30(b)(6) representative has the effect of an evidentiary admission, not a judicial admission, and thus may be controverted or explained by the party.[56] The organization may then be prohibited from using theories or information not disclosed during the

48. *Reilly v. NatWest Markets Group Inc.*, 181 F.3d 253 (2d Cir.1999), *cert. denied*, 528 U.S. 1119, 120 S.Ct. 940, 145 L.Ed.2d 818 (2000) (corporation precluded from offering testimony from witnesses not designated in response to Rule 30(b)(6) notice); *King v. Pratt & Whitney*, 161 F.R.D. 475 (S.D.Fla.1995).

49. *Poole v. Textron, Inc.*, 192 F.R.D. 494 (D.Md.2000) (a corporation should make a "diligent inquiry" to determine the individual(s) best suited to testify).

50. *Media Services Group, Inc. v. Lesso, Inc.*, 45 F.Supp.2d 1237 (D.Kan.1999).

51. *Poole v. Textron, Inc.*, 192 F.R.D. 494 (D.Md.2000); *Alexander v. Federal Bureau of Investigation*, 186 F.R.D. 148 (D.D.C.1999) (listing 5 obligations of recipient of a Rule 30(b)(6) notice).

52. *See Paparelli v. Prudential Insurance Co. of America*, 108 F.R.D. 727 (D.Mass.1985); *Starlight International Inc. v. Herlihy*, 186 F.R.D. 626, 639 (D.Kan.1999) (for questions outside the areas in the notice, the general deposition principles apply, and no sanctions attach if the witness does not know the answer); *King v. Pratt & Whitney*, 161 F.R.D. 475 (S.D.Fla.1995)(the notice limits the corporation's duty to prepare, but not the examining attorney's inquiry).

53. *See S.E.C. v. Buntrock*, 217 F.R.D. 441, 445 (N.D.Ill. 2003) (3 factor test for obtaining the deposition of opposing counsel).

54. *In re Vitamins Antitrust Litigation*, 216 F.R.D. 168 (D.D.C. 2003); *Paul Revere Life Ins. Co. v. Jafari*, 206 F.R.D. 126, 127 (D.Md.2002).

55. *Black Horse Lane Assoc., L.P. v. Dow Chemical Corp.*, 228 F.3d 275, 301–05 (3d Cir. 2000).

56. *Interstate Narrow Fabrics, Inc. v. Century USA, Inc.*, 218 F.R.D. 455, 462 (M.D.N.C. 2003); *Media Services Group, Inc. v. Lesso, Inc.*, 45 F.Supp.2d 1237 (D.Kan.1999).

Rule 30(b)(6) deposition unless the information was unavailable at the time of the deposition.[57]

RULE 30(b)(7). NOTICE OF EXAMINATION: DEPOSITION BY TELEPHONE

CORE CONCEPT

The parties may stipulate to a deposition by telephone or may move the court for an order that a deposition be taken by telephone.[58] Such depositions are deemed to occur in the district where the deponent is located when answering the questions,[59] and the court reporter should be in the presence of the witness, not the attorneys.[60]

RULE 30(c). EXAMINATION AND CROSS–EXAMINATION; RECORD OF EXAMINATION; OATH; OBJECTIONS

CORE CONCEPT

In general, the examination of witnesses at a deposition proceeds much like at trial, except that most objections are reserved until the testimony is offered into evidence.

APPLICATIONS

Oath or Affirmation

The officer before whom the deposition is to be taken (usually the stenographer) will put the witness on oath or affirmation at the beginning of the deposition.

Recording

The officer will also arrange to have the testimony recorded, either stenographically or otherwise (as discussed above under Rule 30(b)(2)).

Expense of Recording

The party noticing the deposition arranges for and pays the cost of recording but the other parties pay for their copies of the recording. If the party taking the deposition does not order a transcript, then any other party can order one, and the court then has discretion as to who bears the expense.[61]

Examination

Examination proceeds as at trial, with direct examination and

57. *Rainey v. American Forest and Paper Assoc., Inc.*, 26 F.Supp.2d 82, 94 (D.D.C.1998).

58. *Nagele v. Electronic Data Systems Corp.*, 193 F.R.D. 94 (W.D.N.Y. 2000); *Advani Enterprises, Inc. v. Underwriters at Lloyds*, 2000 WL 1568255 (S.D.N.Y. 2000) ("permission should be granted unless an objecting party will likely be prejudiced or the method employed 'would not reasonably ensure accuracy and trustworthiness' ").

59. *Hudson v. Spellman High Voltage*, 178 F.R.D. 29, 32 (E.D.N.Y.1998).

60. *Aquino v. Automotive Service Industry Assoc.*, 93 F.Supp.2d 922 (N.D.Ill.2000).

61. The Advisory Committee Note to the 1970 amendment of Rule 30(c).

cross-examination.[62] Unlike trial, cross-examination is not limited to matters raised on direct, although the admission at trial of the deposition transcript may be limited on that basis.

Witness's Rights

At a deposition, the witness has the same rights as at trial, and may refresh his recollection with former testimony.[63] The extent to which a witness has the right to confer with counsel during a deposition is unsettled.[64]

Refusal to Answer Question

If a witness refuses to answer a question, the examining party may suspend the proceedings to seek an order under Rule 37(a)(2) compelling an answer or may reserve the right to move for an order to compel and proceed to other areas. The losing party to such a motion to compel may then be subject to sanctions under Rule 37(a)(4).

Objections to Questions

Objections must be stated in a non-suggestive manner.[65] Some objections to questions must be raised at the time of the deposition or they are waived, others are reserved until trial. The way to determine whether an objection must be made is to determine whether the examiner could rephrase the question to cure the objection. Thus, parties must object to leading questions in order to give the examiner an opportunity to ask the question in a non-leading fashion. Conversely, parties do not need to raise objections such as relevancy or competency that cannot be cured.

Objections to Officer or Procedures

All objections to the qualifications of the officer, to the manner of recording, or to any other procedure must be raised at the deposition and noted by the officer or they are waived.

Objections to Exhibits

Exhibits that have been objected to are taken and appended to the transcript subject to a subsequent ruling on the objection.

Procedure after Objections

After an objection to the officer recording the deposition, the manner of taking the deposition, the evidence, the conduct of a party, or any other aspect of the deposition, the deposition should continue

62. *Sperling v. City of Kennesaw Dept.*, 202 F.R.D. 325, 329 (N.D.Ga.2001) (adverse party entitled to review and use writing used by witness to refresh recollection).

63. *See Magee v. The Paul Revere Life Ins. Co.*, 172 F.R.D. 627, 637 (E.D.N.Y.1997) (deponent repeatedly consulted his notes to refresh his memory at the deposition).

64. *See, e.g., In re Stratosphere Corp. Securities Litigation,* 182 F.R.D. 614, 620 (D.Nev.1998) (witness not permitted to confer while a question is pending); *Hall v. Clifton Precision*, 150 F.R.D. 525, 526 (E.D.Pa.1993).

65. See the commentary to Rule 30(d), below.

subject to such objections.[66] Exceptions to this principle are matters like questions seeking attorney-client information, as discussed under Rule 30(d).

Attendance by Other Witnesses

Other witnesses are not excluded from observing deposition absent a court order under Rule 26(c)(5).[67]

Written Questions

Instead of attending a deposition in person, a party can send written questions to the party taking the deposition, who will then ask the questions to the deponent on the record. This procedure is rarely used.

RULE 30(d). SCHEDULE AND DURATION; MOTION TO TERMINATE OR LIMIT EXAMINATION

CORE CONCEPT

Objections to questions must be stated in a non-suggestive and non-argumentative manner. The Rules provide for a 7 hour time limit on depositions, which may be extended by court order. Rule 30(d) also provides protection from unreasonable or vexatious examination during a deposition.

APPLICATIONS

Stating Objections

Objections must be stated in a non-suggestive manner.[68] Attorneys should not use an objection to instruct the witnesses how to answer (or not answer) a question.[69] However, the specific nature of the objection should be stated so that the court later can rule on the objection (*i.e.* "objection, leading" or "objection, lack of foundation").[70]

Instruction Not to Answer

Directions to a witness not to answer a question are only allowed in three narrow circumstances: to claim a privilege (*i.e.*, attorney client communication);[71] to enforce a court directive limiting the scope or length of the deposition;[72] or to suspend the deposition for purposes of

66. *Morales v. Zondo, Inc.*, 204 F.R.D. 50 (S.D.N.Y.2001).

67. The Advisory Committee Note to the 1993 Amendment to Rule 30; *In re Terra Int'l., Inc.*, 134 F.3d 302, 305–06 (5th Cir.1998)(party moving to exclude other witnesses must show good cause why such witnesses should not attend).

68. *Methode Electronics, Inc. v. Finisar Corp.*, 205 F.R.D. 552, 553 (N.D.Cal. 2001).

69. *Calzaturficio S.C.A.R.P.A. s.p.a. v. Fabiano Shoe Co., Inc.*, 201 F.R.D. 33 (D.Mass. 2001); *Quantachrome Corp. v. Micromeritics Instrument Corp.*, 189 F.R.D. 697, 700 (S.D.Fla.1999).

70. *Moloney v. United States*, 204 F.R.D. 16, 20–21 (D.Mass.2001) (certain privileges were waived because the objection did not identify those privileges).

71. *Moloney v. United States*, 204 F.R.D. 16, 20–21 (D.Mass.2001); *United States v. Philip Morris Inc.*, 209 F.R.D. 13, 19 (D.D.C. 2002).

72. *S.E.C. v. Oakford Corp.*, 141 F.Supp.2d 435 (S.D.N.Y. 2001).

a motion under Rule 30(d)(3) relating to improper harassing conduct.[73] Thus, it is inappropriate for counsel to instruct a witness not to answer a question on the basis of relevance,[74] on the basis that the question has been asked and answered,[75] or on the basis that the question is outside the areas of inquiry identified in the notice of deposition for a Rule 30(b)(6) deposition of a party representative.[76]

Duration of Depositions

Rule 30(d)(2) sets a time limit for depositions of 1 day of 7 hours. The time period includes only time spent examining the witness; lunch and other breaks are not counted.[77] The parties can extend or eliminate the time limitation by stipulation, or can file a motion to extend the time limit for specified depositions or for the case in general (discussed below).

Motion to Extend Time

A party may file a motion to extend the 1 day 7 hour limitation.[78] The court must allow additional time if needed for a "fair examination" of the witness or if the examination has been impeded or delayed by another person or by circumstances. Examples of situations in which an extended deposition would be warranted include: witnesses who need interpreters; examinations covering long periods of time or numerous and/or lengthy documents (although the Advisory Committee suggests that a prerequisite might be sending the documents to the witness to review prior to the deposition); instances where documents were requested but not produced prior to the deposition; multi-party cases (if the parties have taken measures to avoid duplicative questioning); depositions in which the lawyer for the witness also wants to ask questions; depositions of expert witnesses; depositions interrupted by power outage, health emergency, or other like event; and depositions in which improper objections or other conduct by other attorneys or the witness has impeded the examination.[79] The court need not order an extended deposition if the extended deposition would be cumulative or unreasonably burdensome, as provided by Rule 26(b)(2). The burden will be on the party moving for an extension to show good cause why the extension is warranted.

73. *See Cobell v. Norton*, 213 F.R.D. 16, 27 (D.D.C.2003) (counsel may not instruct the witness not to answer because the question is harassing, but only to suspend the deposition to seek a court order protecting the witness from harassment); *Mathias v. Jacobs*, 167 F.Supp.2d 606, 626 (S.D.N.Y.2001) (Rule 30(d) is the only mechanism for redressing harassing conduct at a deposition).

74. *Resolution Trust Corp. v. Dabney*, 73 F.3d 262, 266 (10th Cir.1995); *Banks v. Office of Senate Sergeant–At–Arms*, 222 F.Supp.2d 1, 6 (D.D.C. 2004); *Gober v. City of Leesburg*, 197 F.R.D. 519, 520 (M.D.Fla.2000).

75. *Athridge v. Aetna Casualty and Surety Co.*, 184 F.R.D. 200, 208 (D.D.C.1998).

76. *Paparelli v. Prudential Insurance Co. of America*, 108 F.R.D. 727, 730–31 (D.Mass.1985).

77. The Advisory Committee Note to the 2000 Amendment to Rule 30(d).

78. *See Dunkin' Donuts Incorporated v. Mary's Donuts, Inc.*, 206 F.R.D. 518, 522 (S.D.Fla.2002).

79. The Advisory Committee Note to the 2000 Amendment to Rule 30(d). *See also United States v. Kattar*, 191 F.R.D. 33, 38 (D.N.H.1999) (pre–2000 Amendment case in which additional time was allowed to cure improper objections and instructions not to answer).

Designated Representatives

If a corporation or entity designates more than 1 representative in response to a deposition notice under Rule 30(b)(6), the 1 day 7 hour limitation will apply separately to each representative.[80]

Sanctions for Impediment or Delay

Parties or witnesses should not engage in conduct that unreasonably impedes, delays, or otherwise frustrates a deposition.[81] When such conduct occurs, the court may impose the costs of such conduct, including attorney fees, on the party engaging in the obstructional behavior.[82] Non-party witnesses are also subject to such sanctions.

Motion to Terminate or Limit Deposition

In order to prevail on a motion to terminate or limit an examination, the moving party must demonstrate that the examination was being conducted in bad faith or in an unreasonably annoying, embarrassing, or oppressive manner.[83] The court can then order the deposition concluded or can limit the time and/or scope of the deposition,[84] and may impose upon the persons responsible an appropriate sanction, including the reasonable costs and attorney's fees incurred by any parties as a result.[85]

Which Court for Motion to Terminate

A motion under Rule 30(d)(3) may be filed either in the court where the case is pending or in the district where the deposition is occurring.

Suspension of Deposition

A party desiring to make a Rule 30(d)(3) motion may suspend the deposition for the period of time necessary to make the motion.

Expenses of Motion to Terminate

In ruling on a Rule 30(d)(3) motion, the court must consider awarding expenses to the prevailing party, in accordance with Rule 37(a)(4).

Resuming Terminated Deposition

Once a deposition has been terminated by the court upon a Rule 30(d)(3) motion, it cannot be resumed or re-noticed without leave of court.

80. The Advisory Committee Note to the 2000 Amendment to Rule 30(d)(2).

81. *Royal Maccabees Life Ins. Co. v. Malachinski*, 2001 WL 290308 (N.D.Ill.2001).

82. *See Higginbotham v. KCS Intern., Inc.*, 202 F.R.D. 444, 458–59 (D.Md.2001) (advising the witness to leave the deposition before it was completed frustrated the fair examination of the witness, warranting sanctions); *Oleson v. Kmart Corp.*, 175 F.R.D. 570, 573 (D.Kan.1997) (extension of the length of time of the deposition caused by attorney's interference was a factor in court's decision to order sanction).

83. *Garland v. Torre,* 259 F.2d 545 (2d Cir. 1958), *cert. denied,* 358 U.S. 910, 79 S.Ct. 237, 3 L.Ed.2d 231 (1958).

84. *S.E.C. v. Oakford Corp.*, 141 F.Supp.2d 435 (S.D.N.Y.2001).

85. *Hague v. Celebrity Cruises, Inc.*, 2001 WL 546519 (S.D.N.Y.2001).

Parallel to Protective Order

A party may seek the same types of protection for a deposition under Rule 30(d) that are available under a protective order under Rule 26(c).[86] A motion for a protective order under Rule 26(c) provides similar protection before a deposition begins, at which point Rule 30(d) takes over.

RULE 30(e). REVIEW BY WITNESS; CHANGES; SIGNING

CORE CONCEPT

The opportunity to review and correct the transcript is available upon timely request.

APPLICATIONS

Request to Review

To obtain an opportunity to review and correct the transcript, the deponent or a party must make a request prior to the completion of the deposition.

Submission of Changes

If a review is requested, the witness must submit a signed statement describing any changes within 30 days of submission by the officer.[87] The statement should state the reasons for the changes[88] and be signed by the witness. The time for submission of changes may be extended by the court upon motion.[89] Any changes that are submitted are attached to the transcript.

Changes in Form

Changes in form, such as typographic errors, are entered into the transcript with an explanation as to the reason for the change.

Changes in Substance

The courts vary as to whether and when they will allow a witness to make changes in the substance of the testimony,[90] which are also entered into the transcript with an explanation as to the reason for the change.[91] With changes in substance, the deposition can be recon-

86. *In re CFS–Related Securities Fraud Litigation*, 256 F.Supp.2d 1227, 1240 (N.D.Okla. 2003) (a deposition transcript may be placed under seal under Rule 30(d)).

87. *Margo v. Weiss*, 213 F.3d 55 (2d Cir. 2000); *World Impressions, Inc. v. McDonald's Corp.*, 235 F.Supp.2d 831, 840 (N.D.Ill.2002).

88. *DeLoach v. Philip Morris Companies, Inc.*, 206 F.R.D. 568 (M.D.N.C.2002).

89. *Statzer v. Town of Lebanaon, VA*, 2001 WL 604160 (W.D.Va.2001).

90. *See Banks v. Office of Senate Sergeant–At–Arms*, 222 F.R.D. 7, 9 (D.D.C. 2004) (if a motion for summary judgment has been filed, allowing the witness to modify what she said can so disrupt the movant's legal arguments that a court may hesitate to permit the change); *Burn v. Board of County Com'rs of Jackson County*, 330 F.3d 1275, 1281–82 (10th Cir.2003) (setting forth a test for when a witness may contradict his or her deposition testimony); *Thorn v. Sundstrand Aerospace Corp.*, 207 F.3d 383, 388–89 (7th Cir.2000) (witness may not directly contradict testimony).

91. *Podell v. Citicorp Diners Club, Inc.*, 112 F.3d 98, 103 (2d Cir.1997); *Wigg v. Sioux Falls School Dist.* 49–5, 274 F.Supp.2d 1084, 1090

vened.[92] A deponent who changes the answers may be impeached with the former answers.[93]

Failure to Submit Changes

A witness who fails to submit any changes or return the signed errata sheet within the time period allowed waives the right to make corrections to the transcript.[94]

RULE 30(f). CERTIFICATION AND DELIVERY BY OFFICER; EXHIBITS; COPIES

CORE CONCEPT

The officer must certify that the witness was duly sworn and that the deposition transcript was a true record of the testimony given by the deponent.

APPLICATIONS

Certificate

The officer shall prepare a written certificate to accompany the record of the deposition.[95] The certificate should indicate that the witness was sworn, that the deposition is a true and accurate record of the testimony, and whether review of the record was requested.

Filing of Transcript

Ordinarily, deposition transcripts should not be filed. However, under Rule 5(d), once a deposition is used in a proceeding, the attorney must file it.

Copies of the Transcript

Any party or the deponent can obtain a copy of the recording of the deposition for a reasonable charge.[96] If the deposition was recorded stenographically and has not been transcribed, then the party seeking the transcript will normally have to pay the transcription costs, unless the court orders otherwise.

Exhibits

Upon the request of a party, a document produced at a deposition (or any other document) may be marked for identification and annexed

(D.S.D. 2003), affirmed in part, reversed in part, 382 F.3d 807 (8th Cir.2004); *Holland v. Cedar Creek Min., Inc.*, 198 F.R.D. 651, 653 (S.D.W.Va. 2001) (without an explanation for the changes, the changes are not allowed).

92. *Tingley Sys., Inc. v. CSC Consulting, Inc.*, 152 F.Supp.2d 95, 120 (D.Mass.2001).

93. *Thorn v. Sundstrand Aerospace Corp.*, 207 F.3d 383, 388–89 (7th Cir.2000); *Podell v. Citicorp Diners Club, Inc.*, 112 F.3d 98 (2d Cir. 1997) (the changes made do not replace the deponent's original answers; the original information remains part of the record and may be introduced at trial).

94. *Green v. Louisiana*, 2001 WL 474280 (E.D.La.2001).

95. *Orr v. Bank of America, NT & SA*, 285 F.3d 764, 774 (9th Cir.2002); *Fenje v. Feld*, 301 F.Supp.2d 781, 817 (N.D.Ill. 2003).

96. *Rivera v. DiSabato*, 962 F.Supp. 38, 39–40 (D.N.J.1997).

to the deposition transcript. A copy of a document may be substituted for the original. If documents are produced at a deposition, any party has a right to inspect and copy them.

Retaining Recording

The officer should retain a copy of the transcript or recording of the deposition.

RULE 30(g). FAILURE TO ATTEND OR SERVE SUBPOENA

CORE CONCEPT

The court may award expenses, including attorney fees, to a party that appears for a deposition that does not occur because either: (1) the party noticing the deposition does not attend; or (2) the party fails to subpoena a witness and that witness does not appear. In both cases, the party noticing the deposition may be ordered to pay the expenses of other parties incurred as a result of appearing for the deposition.

ADDITIONAL RESEARCH REFERENCES

Wright & Miller, *Federal Practice and Procedure* §§ 2101–2120.

C.J.S. Federal Civil Procedure §§ 548–583 et seq., 600–644 et seq.

West's Key No. Digests, Federal Civil Procedure ⚷1311–1456.

RULE 31

DEPOSITIONS UPON WRITTEN QUESTIONS

(a) Serving Questions; Notice.

(1) A party may take the testimony of any person, including a party, by deposition upon written questions without leave of court except as provided in paragraph (2). The attendance of witnesses may be compelled by the use of subpoena as provided in Rule 45.

(2) A party must obtain leave of court, which shall be granted to the extent consistent with the principles stated in Rule 26(b)(2), if the person to be examined is confined in prison or if, without the written stipulation of the parties,

(A) a proposed deposition would result in more than ten depositions being taken under this rule or Rule 30 by the plaintiffs, or by the defendants, or by third-party defendants;

(B) the person to be examined has already been deposed in the case; or

(C) a party seeks to take a deposition before the time specified in Rule 26(d).

(3) A party desiring to take a deposition upon written questions shall serve them upon every other party with a notice stating (1) the name and address of the person who is to answer them, if known, and if the name is not known, a general description sufficient to identify the person or the particular class or group to which the person belongs, and (2) the name or descriptive title and address of the officer before whom the deposition is to be taken. A deposition upon written questions may be taken of a public or private corporation or a partnership or association or governmental agency in accordance with the provisions of Rule 30(b)(6).

(4) Within 14 days after the notice and written questions are served, a party may serve cross questions upon all other parties. Within 7 days after being served with cross questions, a party may serve redirect questions upon all other parties. Within 7 days after being served with redirect questions, a party may serve recross questions upon all other parties. The court may for cause shown enlarge or shorten the time.

(b) Officer to Take Responses and Prepare Record. A copy of the notice and copies of all questions served shall be delivered by the party taking the deposition to the officer designated in the notice, who shall proceed promptly, in the manner provided by Rule 30(c), (e), and (f), to take the testimony of the witness in response to the questions and to prepare, certify, and file or mail the deposition, attaching thereto the copy of the notice and the questions received by the officer.

(c) Notice of Filing. When the deposition is filed the party taking it shall promptly give notice thereof to all other parties.

[Amended March 30, 1970, effective July 1, 1970; March 2, 1987, effective August 1, 1987; April 22, 1993, effective December 1, 1993.]

AUTHORS' COMMENTARY ON RULE 31

PURPOSE AND SCOPE

Rule 31 contains the procedures for taking depositions through written questions.

RULE 31(a). SERVING QUESTIONS; NOTICE

CORE CONCEPT

Any party may take depositions by serving written questions, which are asked by the deposition officer (stenographer) and answered orally by the witness. Depositions by written question are rarely used, and their only advantage seems to be that they may be less expensive than depositions by oral question.

APPLICATIONS

Notice

A notice of deposition by written question must state the name and address of the deponent, if known, or a general description sufficient to identify the deponent.

Timing of Notice

The notice of written deposition may be served at any time after the parties have conducted the discovery conference under Rule 26(d), or earlier with leave of court. In proceedings listed in Rule 26(a)(1)(E) as exempt from initial disclosures, there is no preliminary waiting period for written depositions.

Subpoenas

Subpoenas must be used to compel the attendance of non-party witnesses. Party witnesses and representatives of corporations are compelled to attend by virtue of the notice alone.

Service of Direct–Examination

The written deposition questions for direct examination are served upon all parties with the notice.[1]

Cross, Redirect, and Recross

Within 14 days of service of the notice and direct examination questions, any other party may serve cross-examination questions. The noticing party may then serve redirect examination questions within 7 days, and the other party may serve re-cross examination questions within 7 more days. The court may shorten or lengthen these time periods upon motion and for cause shown. All questions should be served on all parties.

Number of Depositions

The plaintiffs as a group are limited to 10 depositions total, by written and/or oral examination, as are the defendants and the third-party defendants. This number may be increased by stipulation or by leave of court.

Scope of Questions

The scope of the written deposition questions is the same as oral questions, and is controlled by Rule 26.

Persons Subject

Both parties and non-parties are subject to written depositions.

Corporate Representative

A party may require a corporation or organization to designate a representative to respond to the questions, as described in detail under Rule 30(b)(6).

Repeat Depositions

Leave of court is required to depose someone a second time.

Deponent in Prison

If the deponent is in prison, leave of court is required to take a written deposition.

Objections

Objections to the form of a written question (*i.e.,* because it is leading) must be served in writing upon the party propounding the question within the time for serving succeeding questions and within 5 days of the last questions authorized.[2]

RULE 31(b). OFFICER TO TAKE RESPONSES AND PREPARE RECORD

1. *Lenders Mortgage Services, Inc.*, 224 B.R. 707, 710 (Bkrtcy.E.D.Mo.1997).

2. *See* Rule 32(d)(3)(C).

CORE CONCEPT

Once all the questions have been served, the party initiating the deposition provides all the questions to the deposition officer. The officer then promptly takes the deposition by reading the questions and recording the answers. A transcript is then prepared and submitted to the witness as provided in Rule 30 governing oral depositions.

RULE 31(c). NOTICE OF FILING

CORE CONCEPT

Local rules usually determine whether the officer files a sealed transcript with the court. If so, the party noticing the deposition must promptly give notice of the filing of the transcript to all other parties.

ADDITIONAL RESEARCH REFERENCES

Wright & Miller, *Federal Practice and Procedure* §§ 2131–2133.

C.J.S. Federal Civil Procedure §§ 591–592.

West's Key No. Digests, Federal Civil Procedure ⚷1369–1370.

RULE 32

USE OF DEPOSITIONS IN COURT PROCEEDINGS

(a) Use of Depositions. At the trial or upon the hearing of a motion or an interlocutory proceeding, any part or all of a deposition, so far as admissible under the rules of evidence applied as though the witness were then present and testifying, may be used against any party who was present or represented at the taking of the deposition or who had reasonable notice thereof, in accordance with any of the following provisions:

(1) Any deposition may be used by any party for the purpose of contradicting or impeaching the testimony of deponent as a witness, or for any other purpose permitted by the Federal Rules of Evidence.

(2) The deposition of a party or of anyone who at the time of taking the deposition was an officer, director, or managing agent, or a person designated under Rule 30(b)(6) or 31(a) to testify on behalf of a public or private corporation, partnership or association or governmental agency which is a party may be used by an adverse party for any purpose.

(3) The deposition of a witness, whether or not a party, may be used by any party for any purpose if the court finds:

(A) that the witness is dead; or

(B) that the witness is at a greater distance than 100 miles from the place of trial or hearing, or is out of the United States, unless it appears that the absence of the witness was procured by the party offering the deposition; or

(C) that the witness is unable to attend or testify because of age, illness, infirmity, or imprisonment; or

(D) that the party offering the deposition has been unable to procure the attendance of the witness by subpoena; or

(E) upon application and notice, that such exceptional circumstances exist as to make it desirable, in the interest of justice and with due regard to the importance of presenting the testimony of witnesses orally in open court, to allow the deposition to be used.

A deposition taken without leave of court pursuant to a notice under Rule 30(a)(2)(C) shall not be used against a party who demonstrates that, when served with the notice, it was unable through the exercise of diligence to obtain counsel to represent it at the taking of the deposition; nor shall a deposition be used against a party who, having received less than 11 days notice of a deposition, has promptly upon receiving such notice filed a motion for a protective order under Rule 26(c)(2) requesting that the deposition not be held or be held at a different time or place and such motion is pending at the time the deposition is held.

(4) If only part of a deposition is offered in evidence by a party, an adverse party may require the offeror to introduce any other part which ought in fairness to be considered with the part introduced, and any party may introduce any other parts.

Substitution of parties pursuant to Rule 25 does not affect the right to use depositions previously taken; and, when an action has been brought in any court of the United States or of any State and another action involving the same subject matter is afterward brought between the same parties or their representatives or successors in interest, all depositions lawfully taken and duly filed in the former action may be used in the latter as if originally taken therefor. A deposition previously taken may also be used as permitted by the Federal Rules of Evidence.

(b) Objections to Admissibility. Subject to the provisions of Rule 28(b) and subdivision (d)(3) of this rule, objection may be made at the trial or hearing to receiving in evidence any deposition or part thereof for any reason which would require the exclusion of the evidence if the witness were then present and testifying.

(c) Form of Presentation. Except as otherwise directed by the court, a party offering deposition testimony pursuant to this rule may offer it in stenographic or nonstenographic form, but, if in nonstenographic form, the party shall also provide the court with a transcript of the portions so offered. On request of any party in a case tried before a jury, deposition testimony offered other than for impeachment purposes shall be presented in nonstenographic form, if available, unless the court for good cause orders otherwise.

(d) Effect of Errors and Irregularities in Depositions.

(1) *As to Notice.* All errors and irregularities in the notice for taking a deposition are waived unless written objection is promptly served upon the party giving the notice.

(2) *As to Disqualification of Officer.* Objection to taking a deposition because of disqualification of the officer before whom it

is to be taken is waived unless made before the taking of the deposition begins or as soon thereafter as the disqualification becomes known or could be discovered with reasonable diligence.

(3) *As to Taking of Deposition.*

(A) Objections to the competency of a witness or to the competency, relevancy, or materiality of testimony are not waived by failure to make them before or during the taking of the deposition, unless the ground of the objection is one which might have been obviated or removed if presented at that time.

(B) Errors and irregularities occurring at the oral examination in the manner of taking the deposition, in the form of the questions or answers, in the oath or affirmation, or in the conduct of parties, and errors of any kind which might be obviated, removed, or cured if promptly presented, are waived unless seasonable objection thereto is made at the taking of the deposition.

(C) Objections to the form of written questions submitted under Rule 31 are waived unless served in writing upon the party propounding them within the time allowed for serving the succeeding cross or other questions and within 5 days after service of the last questions authorized.

(4) *As to Completion and Return of Deposition.* Errors and irregularities in the manner in which the testimony is transcribed or the deposition is prepared, signed, certified, sealed, indorsed, transmitted, filed, or otherwise dealt with by the officer under Rules 30 and 31 are waived unless a motion to suppress the deposition or some part thereof is made with reasonable promptness after such defect is, or with due diligence might have been, ascertained.

[Amended March 30, 1970, effective July 1, 1970; November 20, 1972, effective July 1, 1975; April 29, 1980, effective August 1, 1980; March 2, 1987, effective August 1, 1987; April 22, 1993, effective December 1, 1993.]

AUTHORS' COMMENTARY ON RULE 32

PURPOSE AND SCOPE

Rule 32 specifies the circumstances in which a deposition is admissible at trial. Any analysis, however, must always include reference to the applicable rules of evidence.

RULE 32(a). USE OF DEPOSITIONS

CORE CONCEPT

A deposition may be used to impeach the witness if it is admissible under Rule 32 and under the Federal Rules of Evidence. Deposition testimony may also be used for any purpose if the witness is unavailable.

APPLICATIONS

Impeachment

Rule 32(a)(1) allows the use of a deposition to impeach or contradict a witness. A party may use a deposition to impeach the party's own witness, if permitted by the applicable rules of evidence. The Federal Rules of Evidence allow the use of a prior inconsistent statement made at the deposition as substantive evidence (as opposed to for impeachment purposes only).[1]

Deposition of Adverse Party

Rule 32(a)(2) allows the deposition of an adverse party to be used for any purpose (*i.e.,* as substantive evidence or for impeachment).[2] Rule 32(a)(2) applies to the deposition of an officer, director, or managing agent of a party organization,[3] and to a representative of a party designated pursuant to a Rule 30(b)(6) deposition notice.[4]

Deposition of Non-party Witness

Under Rule 32(a)(3), the deposition of a witness may be used as substantive, non-impeachment evidence only under certain circumstances (but see Rules 801(d) and 801(d)(2) of the Federal Rules of Evidence relating to hearsay). The general requirement is that the witness be unavailable. Rule 32(a)(3) enumerates five situations in which the deposition may be used for non-impeachment purposes:

(A) The witness is dead.[5] However, if the witness dies during the taking of the deposition, so that one party does not have a full opportunity to examine the witness, then the Court has discretion as to whether to admit the testimony;

(B) The witness is more than 100 miles from the courthouse (measured "as the crow flies")[6] or outside the United States,

1. Fed.R.Evid. 801(d).

2. *C.R. Bard, Inc. v. M3 Systems Inc.*, 866 F.Supp. 362 (N.D.Ill.1994).

3. *Shanklin v. Norfolk Southern Ry. Co.*, 369 F.3d 978 (6th Cir. 2004); *Palmer Coal & Rock Co. v. Gulf Oil Co. U.S.*, 524 F.2d 884 (10th Cir.1975), *cert. denied,* 424 U.S. 969, 96 S.Ct. 1466, 47 L.Ed.2d 736 (1976); *Wilstein v. San Tropai Condominium Master Assoc.*, 189 F.R.D. 371, 382 (N.D.Ill.1999).

4. The Advisory Note to the 1970 amendment to Rule 32(a)(2).

5. *See Dellwood Farms, Inc. v. Cargill*, 128 F.3d 1122, 1128 (7th Cir.1997).

6. *Chrysler Intern. Corp. v. Chemaly*, 280 F.3d 1358, 1359 (11th Cir.2002); *Ueland v. U.S.*, 291 F.3d 993, 996 (7th Cir.2002); *Young & Associates Public Relations, L.L.C. v. Delta Air Lines, Inc.*, 216 F.R.D. 521, 524 (D.Utah 2003) (distance from the courthouse should be evaluated at all times during trial).

unless it appears that the party offering the testimony procured the absence of the witness;[7]

(C) The deponent is unable to attend trial because of age, sickness,[8] infirmity, or imprisonment;

(D) The party offering the deposition was unable to procure the deponent's attendance at trial by subpoena;[9] or

(E) Exceptional other circumstances.[10] Note, however, that the general policy favoring live testimony leads to a restrictive reading of this "catch-all" clause.[11]

Rules of Evidence

Once the criteria in Rule 32 for use of a deposition have been satisfied, the deposition must still be admissible under the rules of evidence.[12] The rules of evidence are applied as though the deponent were present and testifying. Thus, the effect of Rule 32 is to negate the hearsay objection.[13] Furthermore, as with any evidence, the admission of deposition testimony is subject to the Court's discretion.[14]

Use of Part of a Deposition

If a party introduces only part of a deposition, any adverse party may require the offering party to introduce additional parts necessary to clarify the offered text.[15] Such adverse parties have the right to have the additional text introduced immediately following the admission of the offered testimony.[16] The admission of the additional parts is still subject to evidentiary objections.[17]

7. *Wilson v. Philadelphia Detention Ctr.*, 986 F.Supp. 282, 291 n. 13 (E.D.Pa.1997).

8. *Cognitronics Imaging Systems, Inc. v. Recognition Research Inc.*, 83 F.Supp.2d 689, 699, n. 14 (E.D.Va.2000).

9. *Griman v. Makousky*, 76 F.3d 151, 154 (7th Cir.1996)(Counsel must have used reasonable diligence to secure witness' attendance); *Hangarter v. Paul Revere Life Ins. Co.*, 236 F.Supp.2d 1069, 1091 (N.D.Cal.2002).

10. *See Battle ex rel. Battle v. Memorial Hosp. at Gulfport*, 228 F.3d 544, 554 (5th Cir. 2000) (videotaped deposition of physician allowed); *Hague v. Celebrity Cruises, Inc.*, 2001 WL 546519 (S.D.N.Y. 2001) (courts are divided as to whether a physician's busy schedule constitutes exceptional circumstances).

11. *Griman v. Makousky*, 76 F.3d 151, 153 (7th Cir.1996); *Young & Associates Public Relations, L.L.C. v. Delta Air Lines, Inc.*, 216 F.R.D. 521, 522–23 (D.Utah 2003).

12. *Reeg v. Shaughnessy*, 570 F.2d 309 (10th Cir.1978); *Haseotes and CM Acquisitions, Inc. v. Cumberland Farms*, 216 B.R. 690, 694 (D.Mass. 1997) (applying Rule 32 in bankruptcy adversary proceeding).

13. *Ueland v. United States*, 291 F.3d 993 (7th Cir.2002).

14. *Coletti v. Cudd Pressure Control*, 165 F.3d 767, 773 (10th Cir.1999) (upholding trial court's refusal to admit deposition testimony as substantive evidence).

15. *Lentomyynti Oy v. Medivac, Inc.*, 997 F.2d 364 (7th Cir.1993); *Heary Bros. Lightning Protection Co., Inc. v. Lightning Protection Institute*, 287 F.Supp.2d 1038, 1065, n.10 (D.Ariz. 2003) (other parts of the deposition transcript should be admitted "in fairness"); *Blue Cross and Blue Shield of New Jersey, Inc. v. Philip Morris, Inc.*, 199 F.R.D. 487, 489–90 (E.D.N.Y. 2001).

16. *Westinghouse Electric Corp. v. Wray Equip. Corp.*, 286 F.2d 491, 494 (1st Cir.1961), *cert. denied*, 366 U.S. 929, 81 S.Ct. 1650, 6 L.Ed.2d 388 (1961); *Trepel v. Roadway Express, Inc.*, 194 F.3d 708, 710 (6th Cir.1999).

17. *See Heary Bros. Lightning Protection Co., Inc. v. Lightning Protection Institute*, 287 F.Supp.2d 1038, 1065, n.10 (D.Ariz. 2003).

Deposition Taken in Another Matter

A deposition from another matter may be used if the witness is unavailable and if the party against whom the testimony is offered (or the party's predecessor in interest) had an opportunity and similar motive to examine the witness at the deposition.[18]

Documents Attached to Transcript

A document attached to a deposition transcript may be used under the same circumstances as the transcript itself.[19]

Who May Use

Deposition transcripts may be used by any party, regardless of who noticed the deposition.[20]

Use of One's Own Deposition

Parties may notice their own deposition for use at trial if they know they will be "unavailable" under the provisions of Rule 32(a)(3).[21] The court will evaluate whether the party truly was "unavailable." [22]

Against Whom

The deposition may be used against any party who had reasonable notice of the deposition. A deposition cannot be used against a party who demonstrates that it was unable to obtain counsel to represent it at the deposition despite the exercise of diligence. Likewise, the deposition cannot be used against a party who received less than 11 days notice and who has filed a motion for a protective order that was pending at the time of the deposition.

Discovery Depositions

Rule 32 does not draw any distinctions between depositions taken for discovery purposes and those taken "for use at trial."[23]

Substitution of Parties

Substitution of parties pursuant to Rule 25 (such as upon the death of a party) does not affect the use of a deposition transcript unless the substitution significantly alters the nature of the claim.

Motion for Summary Judgment

Deposition transcripts may be used in support of or in opposition to

18. *See* Fed.R.Evid. 804(b)(1), Part X, infra; *Nippon Credit Bank, Ltd. v. Matthews*, 291 F.3d 738 (11th Cir.2002); *Clay v. Buzas*, 208 F.R.D. 636 (D.Utah 2002).

19. *Gore v. Maritime Overseas Corp.*, 256 F.Supp. 104, 119 (E.D.Pa.1966), *reversed on other grounds*, 378 F.2d 584 (3d Cir.1967).

20. *Savoie v. Lafourche Boat Rentals, Inc.*, 627 F.2d 722 (5th Cir.1980).

21. *Richmond v. Brooks*, 227 F.2d 490 (2d Cir.1955).

22. *Vevelstad v. Flynn*, 230 F.2d 695 (9th Cir.1956), *cert. denied*, 352 U.S. 827, 77 S.Ct. 40, 1 L.Ed.2d 49 (1956).

23. *Manley v. Ambase Corp.*, 337 F.3d 237, 247 (2nd Cir. 2003).

motions for summary judgment.[24] The use of depositions in connection with summary judgment is governed by Rule 56(c).

RULE 32(b). OBJECTIONS TO ADMISSIBILITY

CORE CONCEPT

Objections to the admissibility of a deposition under Rule 32 must be made at the time the testimony is offered at trial or the objections are waived.

APPLICATIONS

Rules of Evidence

A deposition admissible under Rule 32 must also be admissible under the rules of evidence.[25] Evidentiary rulings are made as though the deponent were present and testifying.

Compare to Objections at Deposition

Objections that can be cured by rephrasing the question, such as leading questions, must be raised at the deposition or they are waived. These objections are covered by Rule 32(d)(3). All other objections, such as relevance,[26] capacity, etc., are reserved until the testimony is offered at trial.[27]

Non-jury Trial

In a non-jury trial, the court can admit a deposition transcript subject to future rulings on objections.

RULE 32(c). FORM OF PRESENTATION

CORE CONCEPT

Deposition testimony may be offered in stenographic or nonstenographic form. In jury trials, any party may require that the nonstenographic form be used if available.

APPLICATIONS

Nonstenographic Forms

A party expecting to use a nonstenographic form of deposition at trial must provide other parties with a transcript in advance of trial under Rule 26(a)(3)(B). When nonstenographic forms of testimony are

24. *Carmen v. San Francisco Unified School Dist.*, 237 F.3d 1026, 1028 (9th Cir.2001); *Beiswenger Enterprises, Corp. v. Carletta*, 46 F.Supp.2d 1297 (M.D.Fla.1999) (allowing the use of a deposition from another action to support a motion for summary judgment); *In re KZK Livestock, Inc.*, 221 B.R. 471, 475 (Bkrtcy.C.D.Ill. 1998) (allowing the use of a deposition transcript that did not meet the requirements for use at trial, but did meet the requirements for an affidavit).

25. *Marshall v. Planz*, 145 F.Supp.2d 1258 (M.D.Ala. 2001).

26. *In re Stratosphere Corp. Securities Litigation*, 182 F.R.D. 614, 618 (D.Nev.1998).

27. *Cronkrite v. Fahrbach*, 853 F.Supp. 257 (W.D.Mich.1994).

offered, the offering party shall also provide the court a transcript.[28] Rule 32 does not authorize the submission of deposition summaries in lieu of the transcript.[29]

Jury Trials

In a jury trial, any party may require that depositions be offered in nonstenographic form if available unless the deposition is being used for impeachment or unless the court orders otherwise for good cause shown.

RULE 32(d). EFFECT OF ERRORS AND IRREGULARITIES IN DEPOSITIONS

CORE CONCEPT

Objections to the procedures at a deposition must be asserted as soon as practicable or they are waived.

APPLICATIONS

Defects in Notice

Objections to the notice must be made in writing to the party issuing the notice,[30] unless there was no opportunity to object.[31]

Disqualification of Officer

Objections to the qualifications of the officer (*e.g.*, stenographer), which are set forth in Rule 28, must be made before the start of the deposition or they are waived.

Objections to Testimony

Objections that can be cured by rephrasing the question, such as leading questions, must be raised at the deposition.[32] These objections are covered by Rule 32(d)(3). All other objections, such as relevance,[33] capacity, etc., are reserved until the testimony is offered at trial.[34]

Objections to Written Deposition Questions

Objections to the form of a written question (*e.g.*, because it is leading) must be served in writing upon the party propounding the

28. *Tilton v. Capital Cities,* 115 F.3d 1471, 1479 (10th Cir.1997) (a party intending to use a videotape deposition must provide a transcript).

29. *Planned Parenthood of Columbia/Willamette, Inc. v. American Coalition of Life Activists*, 290 F.3d 1058, 1117 (9th Cir.2002).

30. *Bobrosky v. Vickers,* 170 F.R.D. 411, 415 (W.D.Va.1997) (only objections to the form of the notice are waived by failure to promptly to serve written objection).

31. *Oates v. S.J. Groves & Sons Co.,* 248 F.2d 388 (6th Cir.1957).

32. *Daubach v. Wnek*, 2001 WL 290181 (N.D.Ill. 2001); *Boyd v. University of Maryland Med. System,* 173 F.R.D. 143, 147 n. 8 (D.Md. 1997) (containing a list of the ten most common objections to the form of the question).

33. *Quantachrome Corp. v. Micromeritics Instrument Corp.*, 189 F.R.D. 697, 700 (S.D.Fla. 1999); *In re Stratosphere Corp. Securities Litigation*, 182 F.R.D. 614, 618 (D.Nev.1998).

34. *Cronkrite v. Fahrbach*, 853 F.Supp. 257 (W.D.Mich.1994).

question within the time for serving succeeding questions and within 5 days of the last questions authorized.

Objections as to Manner of Transcription

Objections as to the manner of transcription or as to the procedures used in correcting and signing the transcript must be made in the form of a motion to suppress, which must be made with "reasonable promptness" after the defect is discovered or should have been discovered with due diligence.[35]

ADDITIONAL RESEARCH REFERENCES

Wright & Miller, *Federal Practice and Procedure* §§ 2142–2157.

C.J.S. Federal Civil Procedure §§ 544–568, 633–638 et seq.

West's Key No. Digests, Federal Civil Procedure ⚷1297, 1298, 1334, 1432–1440.

35. *Trade Development Bank v. Continental Ins. Co.*, 469 F.2d 35 (2d Cir.1972).

RULE 33

INTERROGATORIES TO PARTIES

(a) Availability. Without leave of court or written stipulation, any party may serve upon any other party written interrogatories, not exceeding 25 in number including all discrete subparts, to be answered by the party served or, if the party served is a public or private corporation or a partnership or association or governmental agency, by any officer or agent, who shall furnish such information as is available to the party. Leave to serve additional interrogatories shall be granted to the extent consistent with the principles of Rule 26(b)(2). Without leave of court or written stipulation, interrogatories may not be served before the time specified in Rule 26(d).

(b) Answers and Objections.

(1) Each interrogatory shall be answered separately and fully in writing under oath, unless it is objected to, in which event the objecting party shall state the reasons for objection and shall answer to the extent the interrogatory is not objectionable.

(2) The answers are to be signed by the person making them, and the objections signed by the attorney making them.

(3) The party upon whom the interrogatories have been served shall serve a copy of the answers, and objections if any, within 30 days after the service of the interrogatories. A shorter or longer time may be directed by the court or, in the absence of such an order, agreed to in writing by the parties subject to Rule 29.

(4) All grounds for an objection to an interrogatory shall be stated with specificity. Any ground not stated in a timely objection is waived unless the party's failure to object is excused by the court for good cause shown.

(5) The party submitting the interrogatories may move for an order under Rule 37(a) with respect to any objection to or other failure to answer an interrogatory.

(c) Scope; Use at Trial. Interrogatories may relate to any matters which can be inquired into under Rule 26(b)(1), and the answers may be used to the extent permitted by the rules of evidence.

An interrogatory otherwise proper is not necessarily objectionable merely because an answer to the interrogatory involves an opinion or contention that relates to fact or the application of law to fact, but the court may order that such an interrogatory need not be answered until after designated discovery has been completed or until a pre-trial conference or other later time.

(d) Option to Produce Business Records. Where the answer to an interrogatory may be derived or ascertained from the business records of the party upon whom the interrogatory has been served or from an examination, audit or inspection of such business records, including a compilation, abstract or summary thereof, and the burden of deriving or ascertaining the answer is substantially the same for the party serving the interrogatory as for the party served, it is a sufficient answer to such interrogatory to specify the records from which the answer may be derived or ascertained and to afford to the party serving the interrogatory reasonable opportunity to examine, audit or inspect such records and to make copies, compilations, abstracts or summaries. A specification shall be in sufficient detail to permit the interrogating party to locate and to identify, as readily as can the party served, the records from which the answer may be ascertained.

[Amended December 27, 1946, effective March 19, 1948; March 30, 1970, effective July 1, 1970; April 29, 1980, effective August 1, 1980; April 22, 1993, effective December 1, 1993.]

AUTHORS' COMMENTARY ON RULE 33

PURPOSE AND SCOPE

Rule 33 sets forth the procedures for using interrogatories. It must be read in conjunction with Rule 26, which establishes the scope of all the discovery rules.

NOTE: Rule 33 was substantially revised in 1970 and 1993, and great care should be exercised when citing decisions pertaining to Rule 33.

RULE 33(a). AVAILABILITY

CORE CONCEPT

Any party may serve written interrogatories or questions on any other party, who must respond in writing within 30 days.

APPLICATIONS

Who May Serve

Any party may serve interrogatories.

Who May Be Served

Interrogatories are limited to parties to the action,[1] although the party need not be an adverse party. The interrogatories must be addressed to the party. Thus, if the party is a corporation, interrogatories should be addressed to the corporation, not to a corporate officer or the attorney.[2] In a class action, the courts are split as to whether only the named representatives can be served.[3]

Time for Service

Interrogatories can be served after the parties have conducted the discovery conference under Rule 26(f), or earlier with leave of court. In proceedings listed in Rule 26(a)(1)(E) as exempt from initial disclosures, there is no preliminary waiting period for interrogatories. The Rules do not set an outer limit on how late in the case interrogatories may be served, but many local rules or case management orders will set such a limit. Usually, when such a limit exists, interrogatories must be served so that the answers are due before the close of discovery.[4]

Number

Each party may serve up to 25 interrogatories,[5] including subparts,[6] on each other party.[7] Additional interrogatories may be served pursuant to a court order or stipulation.[8]

Form

Parties have a great deal of latitude in framing interrogatories, as long as the responding party can reasonably determine the information to include in the answer. Only rarely will a question be so ambiguous that it does not require an answer, although the responding party can limit the scope of its answer.

Proceedings Where Interrogatories Available

Rule 33 applies to all civil actions in district court, including post-judgment proceedings (*i.e.*, interrogatories in aid-of-execution). Rule 33

1. *United States v. Lot 41, Berryhill Farm Estates*, 128 F.3d 1386, 1397 (10th Cir.1997); *Alcon Laboratories, Inc. v. Pharmacia Corp.*, 225 F.Supp.2d 340, 344 (S.D.N.Y.2002).

2. *Holland v. Minneapolis–Honeywell Regulator Co.*, 28 F.R.D. 595 (D.D.C.1961).

3. *Brennan v. Midwestern United Life Ins. Co.*, 450 F.2d 999 (7th Cir.1971), *cert. denied*, 405 U.S. 921, 92 S.Ct. 957, 30 L.Ed.2d 792 (1972)(unnamed members of class required to respond); *Wainwright v. Kraftco Corp.*, 54 F.R.D. 532 (N.D.Ga.1972)(unnamed members of class not required to respond).

4. *Thomas v. Pacificorp*, 324 F.3d 1176, (10th Cir.2003).

5. *Walker v. Lakewood Condominium Owners Assoc.*, 186 F.R.D. 584, 586–89 (C.D.Cal. 1999) (interrogatories count toward the limit of 25 even though the respondent objects instead of answering, and such interrogatories may not be withdrawn to allow for additional interrogatories).

6. *Banks v. Office of Senate Sergeant–At–Arms*, 222 F.R.D. 7, 10 (D.D.C. 2004) (discussing the counting of subparts); *Nyfield v. Virgin Islands Telephone Corp.*, 200 F.R.D. 246 (D.V.I. 2001) (discussing the counting of subparts).

7. The Advisory Committee Note to the 1993 Amendment to Rule 33; *Chudasama v. Mazda Motor Corp.*, 123 F.3d 1353, 1357 (11th Cir. 1997); *Nagele v. Electronic Data Systems Corp.*, 193 F.R.D. 94 (W.D.N.Y.2000) (allowing more than 25 interrogatories where the recipient failed to object).

8. *Duncan v. Paragon Pub., Inc.*, 204 F.R.D. 127, 128 (S.D.Ind.2001); *Berry v. Rite Aid Corp.*, 2001 WL 527815 (E.D.Pa.2001).

does not apply to habeas proceedings.[9]

RULE 33(b). ANSWERS AND OBJECTIONS

Answers

Each interrogatory must be answered separately and fully[10] in writing,[11] unless an objection is interposed in lieu of an answer. The answer must include all information within the party's control or known by the party's agents.[12] This includes *facts* in an attorney's possession and information supplied to the party by others.[13] If no such information is available, the answer may so state.[14] If only some information is available, that information must be provided, and may be prefaced with a statement placing the answer in context.

Time to Answer

Answers and objections are due within 30 days of service.[15] Failure to serve a response in a timely manner (i.e. within 30 days of service) may constitute a waiver of all objections.[16] The time to answer may be extended by written agreement under Rule 29.[17]

Who Answers

The party must answer the interrogatories, not the party's attorney (although it is common practice for the attorney to draft the answers). The attorney interposes the objections. If the party is a corporation or organization, an officer or agent will answer for the corporation.[18] In this case, the attorney may answer the interrogatories as agent for the corporation.[19] The answering officer or agent need not have first-hand knowledge of the information being provided.[20] However, the responding agent's answers must provide the composite knowledge available to the party.[21] If the party is an infant, the infant's attorney or next

9. *Harris v. Nelson*, 394 U.S. 286, 293–94, 89 S.Ct. 1082, 1087, 22 L.Ed.2d 281 (1969); Sloan v. Pugh, 351 F.3d 1319, 1322 (10th Cir. 2003).

10. *Somerset Marine, Inc. v. Briese Schiffahrts GMBH & Co.*, 2002 WL 1933723 (E.D.La. 2002).

11. *Wsol v. Fiduciary Management Associates, Inc.*, 2000 WL 748143 (N.D.Ill.2000) (oral answers are not permitted).

12. *Cage v. New York Cent. R. Co.*, 276 F.Supp. 778, 786–87 (W.D.Pa.1967), *affirmed*, 386 F.2d 998 (3d Cir.1967); *Hansel v. Shell Oil Corp.*, 169 F.R.D. 303, 305 (E.D.Pa.1996) ("Parties must provide true, explicit, responsive, complete, and candid answers to interrogatories.").

13. *Hickman v. Taylor*, 329 U.S. 495, 504, 67 S.Ct. 385, 390, 91 L.Ed. 451 (1947).

14. *Hansel v. Shell Oil Corp.*, 169 F.R.D. 303, 305 (E.D.Pa.1996) (answer should set forth the efforts used to attempt to obtain the requested information).

15. *See Verkuilen v. South Shore Building & Mortgage Co.*, 122 F.3d 410, 411 (7th Cir.1997).

16. *Banks v. Office of Senate Sergeant–At–Arms*, 222 F.R.D. 7, 21 (D.D.C. 2004); *Jayne H. Lee, Inc. v. Flagstaff Indus. Corp.*, 173 F.R.D. 651, 653 (D.Md.1997).

17. *Jayne H. Lee, Inc. v. Flagstaff Indus. Corp.*, 173 F.R.D. 651, 654 (D.Md.1997).

18. *General Dynamics Corp. v. Selb Mfg. Co.*, 481 F.2d 1204 (8th Cir.1973), *cert. denied*, 414 U.S. 1162, 94 S.Ct. 926, 39 L.Ed.2d 116 (1974).

19. *Wilson v. Volkswagen of America, Inc.*, 561 F.2d 494, 508 (4th Cir.1977), *cert. denied*, 434 U.S. 1020, 98 S.Ct. 744, 54 L.Ed.2d 768 (1978).

20. *See Duff v. Lobdell–Emery Mfg. Co.*, 926 F.Supp. 799, 802 (N.D.Ind.1996).

21. *Law v. NCAA*, 167 F.R.D. 464, 476 (D.Kan.1996), *vacated on other grounds, Univ. of Texas at Austin v. Vratil*, 96 F.3d 1337 (10th Cir.1996).

friend may answer.[22]

Verification

When the party is an individual, the party, not the attorney,[23] must sign a verification or affidavit as to the accuracy of the answers.[24] This is one of the few exceptions to the general principle under the Federal Rules of Civil Procedure that the attorney may sign all pleadings and papers. A representative, including counsel,[25] of a corporate party may verify interrogatory answers without personal knowledge of every response by furnishing the information available to the corporation.[26]

Objections

If the responding party determines that a particular interrogatory is outside the scope of discovery, the party may object to the question in lieu of answering it. The objection must be made in writing, must state the grounds of the objection with specificity,[27] and must be signed by the attorney for the responding party.[28] Some common objections are:

- *Overly broad, unduly vague, and ambiguous:* When a question is written broadly so that it extends to information not relevant to the complaint (such as a question not limited in time to the events relevant to the complaint), the question may be overly broad.[29] When a question is susceptible to numerous meanings, it may be unduly vague and ambiguous. In general, these objections are probably not justification for refusing to answer a question altogether, but the responding party can raise the objection, then expressly limit the scope of the response.
- *Burdensome and oppressive:* In general, the responding party must produce the information available without undue effort or expense. Thus, questions that require extensive research, compilation of data, or evaluation of data may be objectionable.[30] The

22. *Hall v. Hague,* 34 F.R.D. 449 (D.Md. 1964).

23. *Overton v. City of Harvey,* 29 F.Supp.2d 894, 901 (N.D.Ill.1998).

24. *Davidson v. Goord,* 215 F.R.D. 73, 77 (W.D.N.Y. 2003); *Buffalo Carpenters Pension Fund v. CKG Ceiling and Partition Co., Inc.*, 192 F.R.D. 95 (W.D.N.Y.2000) (defendant must redraft and reserve interrogatory answers because the first response was not under oath).

25. *Rea v. Wichita Mortg. Corp.*, 747 F.2d 567 (10th Cir.1984); *Wilson v. Volkswagen of America, Inc.*, 561 F.2d 494, 508 (4th Cir.1977), *cert. denied*, 434 U.S. 1020, 98 S.Ct. 744, 54 L.Ed.2d 768 (1978); *Gluck v. Ansett Australia Ltd.*, 204 F.R.D. 217, 221 (D.D.C.2001).

26. *Shepherd v. American Broadcasting Companies, Inc.*, 62 F.3d 1469, 1482 (D.C.Cir. 1995).

27. *PLX, Inc. v. Prosystems, Inc.*, 220 F.R.D. 291, 293 (N.D.W.Va. 2004) (mere recitation of the familiar litany that an interrogatory is overly broad, burdensome, oppressive, and irrelevant will not suffice); *Drexel Heritage Furnishings, Inc. v. Furniture USA, Inc.*, 200 F.R.D. 255 (M.D.N.C.2001); *Pulsecard, Inc. v. Discover Card Services, Inc.*, 168 F.R.D. 295, 303 (D.Kan.1996) ("Use of general, reserved objections is disfavored.").

28. *Sonnino v. University Kansas Hosp. Authority*, 220 F.R.D. 633, 655 (D.Kan. 2004); *Momah v. Albert Einstein Medical Center*, 164 F.R.D. 412, 417 (E.D.Pa.1996).

29. *Jewish Hospital Ass'n of Louisville v. Struck Const. Co.*, 77 F.R.D. 59 (W.D.Ky.1978).

30. *IBP, Inc. v. Mercantile Bank of Topeka*, 179 F.R.D. 316, 321 (D.Kan.1998) (interrogatory asking for every fact and application of law to fact supporting claim held burdensome).

responding party is not required to prepare the adverse party's case. The reasonableness of an interrogatory is within the court's discretion.

- *Privileged information:* Questions that seek information protected by the attorney-client privilege or by another privilege are objectionable. When privileged information is withheld, the responding party must explicitly state the objection and describe the nature of the information not provided sufficiently to enable other parties to assess the applicability of the privilege. Care should be exercised in responding to such interrogatories, because the privilege may be waived by revealing part or all of the privileged communication.
- *Attorney work product:* Rule 26(b)(3) provides that trial preparation materials may be discovered only upon a showing that the party is unable to obtain the equivalent information through other means without undue hardship.[31]
- *Non-discoverable expert information:* Rule 26(b)(4) limits the scope of discovery directed towards experts. It generally requires the responding party to provide an expert for each expert it may call as a witness, and thereafter allows other parties to depose such experts. Further discovery with respect to such witnesses is available only upon motion. Rule 26(b)(4)(B) does not allow any discovery with respect to experts not intended to be called as witnesses, absent "exceptional circumstances." [32]
- *Not calculated to lead to the discovery of admissible evidence:* Rule 26 takes a very broad approach with respect to what information is discoverable. The requested information need not be admissible, only relevant.[33]

Failure to Object Is Waiver

All grounds for objection must be specifically stated in a timely response[34] or they are waived,[35] unless excused by the court for good cause shown.[36]

Objection to Part of Interrogatory

If only part of an interrogatory is objectionable, the responding party must answer the interrogatory to the extent that it is not

31. *See* Rule 26(b)(3)(in-depth discussion of discovery of work product).

32. *See* Rule 26(b)(4)(in-depth discussion of discovery directed toward experts).

33. *See* Rule 26(b)(1)(in-depth discussion of the scope of discovery).

34. *Maloney v. Universalcom, Inc.*, 2001 WL 8589 (E.D.La.2001); *Starlight International, Inc. v. Herlihy*, 181 F.R.D. 494, 496 (D.Kan.1998) (objections in response served 4 days late deemed waived).

35. *Davidson v. Goord*, 215 F.R.D. 73, 77 (W.D.N.Y.2003); *Nagele v. Electronic Data Systems Corp.*, 193 F.R.D. 94 (W.D.N.Y. 2000) (failure to object to interrogatories in excess of 25 results in waiver).

36. *Banks v. Office of Senate Sergeant–At–Arms*, 222 F.R.D. 7, 21 (D.D.C. 2004); *Puricelli v. Borough of Morrisville*, 136 F.R.D. 393, 396 (E.D.Pa.1991)(failure to raise an objection with sufficient specificity within the time period prescribed by Rule 33, without an extension, may be deemed waiver).

objectionable.[37] Thus, if an interrogatory is overly broad, it must be answered to the extent it is not overly broad.[38]

Motion for a Protective Order

As an alternative to making objections to individual questions, the responding party may make a motion for a protective order under Rule 26(c). A motion for a protective order is appropriate when most or all of a set of interrogatories is too burdensome or cumulative. The burden is on the moving party to show hardship or injustice.[39] The motion must be accompanied by a certification that the parties met prior to the filing of the motion and attempted to resolve their dispute without intervention by the court.

Motion to Compel

If the responding party fails to answer or objects to a question, the propounding party may file a motion to compel under Rule 37(a). The court will award the prevailing party its reasonable expenses, including attorney fees, incurred in connection with the motion to compel, unless the conduct of the losing party was justified (*i.e.*, not frivolous). The motion must be accompanied by a certification that good faith attempts were made to resolve discovery disputes before relief was sought from the court.

Burden of Persuasion

In a motion to compel, the burden is on the responding party (the non-moving party) to convince the court that an interrogatory is objectionable.

Discretion of Court

The district court has extremely broad discretion in ruling on objections to interrogatories.[40] The court will balance the need and the burden, but will generally require an answer unless the administration of justice would be impeded.

Appeals

The court's rulings on objections to interrogatories are reviewed on an abuse of discretion standard.[41] Usually, such rulings are not final orders, and cannot be appealed until the conclusion of the case.

Sanctions for Failure to Answer

If a party files no response to an interrogatory, the court may impose certain sanctions specified in Rule 37(b)(2), such as deeming certain facts established or refusing to allow the party to oppose or

37. *Omega Engineering, Inc. v. Omega, S.A.*, 2001 WL 173765 (D.Conn.2001); the Advisory Committee Note to the 1993 Amendment to Rule 33.

38. *See Walls v. International Paper Co.*, 192 F.R.D. 294 (D.Kan.2000).

39. *Roesberg v. Johns–Manville Corp.*, 85 F.R.D. 292 (E.D.Pa.1980).

40. *Mack v. Great Atlantic and Pacific Tea Co.*, 871 F.2d 179, 186 (1st Cir.1989).

41. *Mack v. Great Atlantic and Pacific Tea Co.*, 871 F.2d 179, 186 (1st Cir.1989).

support certain claims.[42] Furthermore, the court must award reasonable expenses, including attorney fees, caused by the responding party's failure to answer, unless the court finds that the failure to answer was justified.

Sanctions for Incomplete Answers or Improper Objections

If the responding party makes an incomplete answer or makes an improper objection, the propounding party can make a motion to compel under Rule 37(a). The court will award the prevailing party its reasonable expenses, including attorney fees, incurred in connection with the motion to compel, unless the conduct of the losing party was justified. If the motion is granted in part and denied in part, then the court will award expenses as it sees fit.

Sanctions for Failure to Obey Order to Answer

If, in response to a motion to compel, the court orders an answer or a more complete answer, and if the responding party fails to comply, then the court can impose the sanctions specified in Rule 37(b)(2), such as deeming certain facts established or refusing to allow the party to oppose or support certain claims. Furthermore, the court must award reasonable expenses, including attorney fees, caused by the responding party's failure to answer, unless the court finds that the failure to answer was justified.

Sanctions for Untrue Answers

If an answer is untrue, either at the time it was made or subsequently, and is not supplemented, the court may exclude certain testimony or make whatever order justice requires.

Duty to Supplement

Rule 26(e)(2) provides that a party must supplement their response to an interrogatory. If the party learns that the response is in some material respect incomplete or incorrect and if the additional or corrective information has not been provided to the other parties in writing or at a deposition.[43]

RULE 33(c). SCOPE; USE AT TRIAL

CORE CONCEPT

The scope of interrogatories is the broad discovery available under Rule 26. If an interrogatory is too burdensome or exceeds the allowable areas of inquiry, then a party may object. Interrogatory answers are not admissions, but generally may be used as though made in court by the party.

APPLICATIONS

Scope of Questions

The scope of interrogatories, and all other discovery forms, is

42. *See* Rule 37(d).

43. *See* Rule 26(e)(2).

controlled by Rule 26(b).[44] The information sought must be relevant to the issues in the case, but need not be admissible evidence. Privileged information is not discoverable, and discovery is limited with respect to expert witnesses and trial preparation materials.

Requests for Documents

Interrogatories may not be used to obtain documents.[45] Rather, a document request must be made under Rule 34. However, interrogatories may inquire about the existence of documents and the facts contained therein. Furthermore, documents may, under certain circumstances, be produced in lieu of answering an interrogatory, as discussed below under Rule 33(d).

Opinions or Contentions

Rule 33(c) explicitly states that an interrogatory is not objectionable because it seeks an opinion or contention that relates to fact or the application of law to fact.[46] However, the court may order that a contention interrogatory not be answered until discovery is complete or until after the pre-trial conference is held.[47] Rule 33(c) does not authorize a question that asks for a pure legal conclusion, without application to the facts.[48]

Use of Interrogatory Answers at Trial

Answers to interrogatories are treated like any other evidence, and may be offered[49] and admitted into evidence as allowed by the Federal Rules of Evidence.[50] They may be objected to as irrelevant, prejudicial, confusing, cumulative, or for any other applicable reason. Interrogatory answers are generally not hearsay with respect to the party making the answer because they are party admissions. However, they may be hearsay if offered against another party. If only part of an answer is read, the responding party may require that other parts of the answer be admitted at the same time in order to clarify the portion offered.[51]

Answers Not Binding

Answers to interrogatories are not admissions, and a party is not bound by its answers. Thus, a party can supplement or amend its

44. *Pulsecard, Inc. v. Discover Card Services, Inc.,* 168 F.R.D. 295, 310 (D.Kan.1996).

45. *Alltmont v. United States,* 177 F.2d 971 (3d Cir.1949), *cert. denied,* 339 U.S. 967, 70 S.Ct. 999, 94 L.Ed. 1375 (1950).

46. *Banks v. Office of Senate Sergeant–At–Arms,* 222 F.R.D. 7, 13 (D.D.C. 2004) (a party's opinions and contentions are discoverable by interrogatory); *E.E.O.C. v. Carrols Corp.,* 215 F.R.D. 46, 54 (N.D.N.Y.2003) (contention interrogatories are most useful to narrow and sharpen issues, a major purpose of discovery).

47. *McCarthy v. Paine Webber Group, Inc.,* 168 F.R.D. 448, 450 (D.Conn.1996).

48. *United States v. Boyce,* 148 F.Supp.2d 1069 (S.D.Cal.2001) (party must respond to interrogatories because they do not go to issues of "pure law"); *Coles v. Jenkins,* 179 F.R.D. 179, 181 (W.D.Va.1998).

49. *Cimino v. Raymark Industries, Inc.,* 151 F.3d 297, 309 (5th Cir.1998) (interrogatory answers are not part of the record unless formally offered into evidence).

50. *Melius v. National Indian Gaming Com'n,* 2000 WL 1174994 (D.D.C.2000) (the purpose of interrogatories is not merely to gather information but also to obtain statements that can be admitted at trial).

51. *Grace & Co. v. City of Los Angeles,* 278 F.2d 771 (9th Cir.1960).

answers, and is obligated to do so under certain circumstances discussed above. Even absent an amendment, a party may take a different position at trial unless it would prejudice another party.[52] Opposing parties may then impeach by questioning the reason for the changed answer.

Use of Interrogatory Answers in a Summary Judgment Motion

Interrogatory answers may be used in support of or in opposition to a motion for summary judgment, as provided in Rule 56(c).[53]

RULE 33(d). OPTION TO PRODUCE BUSINESS RECORDS

CORE CONCEPT

A party may produce business records in lieu of answering an interrogatory when the burden of extracting the requested information would be substantially equal for either party.

APPLICATIONS

Business Records Only

Only business records may be used in lieu of interrogatory answers. Thus, one cannot produce pleadings[54] or deposition transcripts[55] instead of answering an interrogatory.

Documents Must Contain Information

In order to respond to an interrogatory by producing business records, a party must state that the documents contain the requested information.[56] It is not sufficient to state that the documents *may* contain the information.[57]

Identify Specific Documents

A party responding to an interrogatory by producing business records must provide sufficient detail so that the propounding party can identify which individual documents contain the information requested.[58]

52. The Advisory Committee Note to Rule 33(b).

53. *Kirkpatrick v. Merit Behavioral Care Corp.*, 128 F.Supp.2d 186, 191 (D.Vt.2000).

54. *Melius v. National Indian Gaming Com'n*, 2000 WL 1174994 (D.D.C.2000).

55. *Starlight International, Inc. v. Herlihy*, 190 F.R.D. 587 (D.Kan.1999).

56. *Bujnicki v. American Paving and Excavating, Inc.*, 2004 WL 1071736 (W.D.N.Y. 2004) (to the extent that the information sought in the interrogatory is not contained in the documents produced, defendants must respond to the interrogatory); *United States S.E.C. v. Elfindepan, S.A.*, 206 F.R.D. 574, 576 (M.D.N.C.2002); *Mackey v. IBP, Inc.*, 167 F.R.D. 186, 198 (D.Kan.1996) (a party electing to produce documents must affirmatively state so under oath).

57. *Daiflon, Inc. v. Allied Chemical Corp.*, 534 F.2d 221 (10th Cir.1976), *cert. denied,* 429 U.S. 886, 97 S.Ct. 239, 50 L.Ed.2d 168 (1976).

58. *Rainbow Pioneer No. 44–18–04A v. Hawaii–Nevada Inv. Corp.*, 711 F.2d 902 (9th Cir. 1983); *In re G–I Holdings Inc.*, 218 F.R.D. 428, 438 (D.N.J. 2003) (the responding party has a duty to specify, by category and location, the records from which it knows the answers to the interrogatories can be found); *United States S.E.C. v. Elfindepan, S.A.*, 206 F.R.D. 574, 576 (M.D.N.C.2002) (the response must specify for each interrogatory the actual documents where the information may be found; document dumps

Equal Burden

In order to respond to interrogatories by producing business records, the burden of deriving or ascertaining the answer must be substantially equal for the requesting party and the producing party.[59] If the sufficiency of the response is challenged, the producing party will bear the burden of making this showing.[60]

Privileged Documents

A party cannot elect to produce business records and then withhold the documents as privileged in order to prevent a party from deriving an answer.[61]

Copies or Originals

The responding party may allow the propounding party to inspect and copy the originals or may make copies.[62]

Expense of Compiling Records

Under proper circumstances, the court will, upon motion for a protective order, require the propounding party to pay the cost of compiling the records.[63]

Motion to Compel

If the propounding party believes that its burden to find the answers from the records is substantially greater than that of the responding party, the propounding party can file a motion to compel an answer.[64] Note that the court may find the burden not substantially the same, yet nonetheless deny the motion to compel, if the court finds that the burden on the responding party to answer fully would be excessive or unreasonable.[65] The motion to compel must be accompanied by a certification that the parties met prior to the filing of the motion and attempted to resolve their dispute without intervention by the court.

ADDITIONAL RESEARCH REFERENCES

Wright & Miller, *Federal Practice and Procedure* §§ 2161–2182.

C.J.S. Federal Civil Procedure §§ 645–695 et seq.

West's Key No. Digests, Federal Civil Procedure ⚿1471–1542.

do not suffice); *O'Connor v. Boeing North American, Inc.*, 185 F.R.D. 272 (C.D.Cal.1999) (the burden is not equal unless the producing party provides detailed references to the location of the responsive information).

59. *United States v. Rachel*, 289 F.Supp.2d 688, 693 (D.Md. 2003); *United States S.E.C. v. Elfindepan, S.A.*, 206 F.R.D. 574, 577 (M.D.N.C. 2002).

60. *United States S.E.C. v. Elfindepan, S.A.*, 206 F.R.D. 574, 577 (M.D.N.C.2002).

61. *Ampex v. Mitsubishi Elec. Corp.*, 937 F.Supp. 352, 355 (D.Del.1996).

62. *Neal v. Siegel–Robert, Inc.*, 171 F.R.D. 264, 267 (E.D.Mo.1996).

63. *See* Rule 26(c)(2)(detail on costs).

64. *See Matthews v. USAir, Inc.*, 882 F.Supp. 274 (N.D.N.Y.1995)(may not respond by producing documents that are unintelligible).

65. The Advisory Committee Note to the 1970 amendment of Rule 33(c).

RULE 34

PRODUCTION OF DOCUMENTS AND THINGS AND ENTRY UPON LAND FOR INSPECTION AND OTHER PURPOSES

(a) Scope. Any party may serve on any other party a request (1) to produce and permit the party making the request, or someone acting on the requestor's behalf, to inspect and copy, any designated documents (including writings, drawings, graphs, charts, photographs, phonorecords, and other data compilations from which information can be obtained, translated, if necessary, by the respondent through detection devices into reasonably usable form), or to inspect and copy, test, or sample any tangible things which constitute or contain matters within the scope of Rule 26(b) and which are in the possession, custody or control of the party upon whom the request is served; or (2) to permit entry upon designated land or other property in the possession or control of the party upon whom the request is served for the purpose of inspection and measuring, surveying, photographing, testing, or sampling the property or any designated object or operation thereon, within the scope of Rule 26(b).

(b) Procedure. The request shall set forth, either by individual item or by category, the items to be inspected, and describe each with reasonable particularity. The request shall specify a reasonable time, place, and manner of making the inspection and performing the related acts. Without leave of court or written stipulation, a request may not be served before the time specified in Rule 26(d).

The party upon whom the request is served shall serve a written response within 30 days after the service of the request. A shorter or longer time may be directed by the court or, in the absence of such an order, agreed to in writing by the parties, subject to Rule 29. The response shall state, with respect to each item or category, that inspection and related activities will be permitted as requested, unless the request is objected to, in which event the reasons for the objection shall be stated. If objection is made to part of an item or category, the part shall be specified and inspection permitted of the remaining parts. The party submitting the request may move for an order under Rule 37(a) with respect to any objection to or other failure to respond to the request or any part thereof, or any failure to permit inspection as requested.

A party who produces documents for inspection shall produce them as they are kept in the usual course of business or shall organize and label them to correspond with the categories in the request.

(c) Persons Not Parties. A person not a party to the action may be compelled to produce documents and things or to submit to an inspection as provided in Rule 45.

[Amended December 27, 1946, effective March 19, 1948; March 30, 1970, effective July 1, 1970; April 29, 1980, effective August 1, 1980; March 2, 1987, effective August 1, 1987; April 30, 1991, effective December 1, 1991; April 22, 1993, effective December 1, 1993.]

AUTHORS' COMMENTARY ON RULE 34

PURPOSE AND SCOPE

Rule 34 sets forth the procedures for obtaining access to documents and things within the control of other parties, and for gaining entry upon other parties' land for inspection. It must be read in conjunction with Rule 26, which establishes the scope of all discovery rules.

NOTE: Rule 34 was substantially revised in 1970, 1991, and 1993, and great care should be exercised when citing decisions pertaining to Rule 34.

RULE 34(a). SCOPE

CORE CONCEPT

The scope of document requests and other discovery under Rule 34 is the broad discovery available under Rule 26. Generally, any relevant, non-privileged document is discoverable unless it was prepared in anticipation of litigation, pertains to expert witnesses, or would be unreasonably burdensome to produce.

APPLICATIONS

Documents

"Documents" is broadly defined to include all forms of recorded information. Rule 34(a) specifically lists writings, drawings, graphs, charts, photographs, phonorecords, and other data compilations. Generally, a party is not required to create documents meeting the document requests, only to produce documents already in existence.[1] A party is entitled to inspect and copy discoverable documents.

1. *Alexander v. F.B.I.*, 194 F.R.D. 305, 310 (D.D.C.2000); *but see Harris v. Athol–Royalston Regional School District Committee*, 200 F.R.D. 18 (D.Mass.2001) (party required to create a handwriting exemplar for examination by the opposing party's expert).

Electronic Data

Rule 34 is deliberately flexible so as to include new forms of technology such as the various methods of data storage used by computers.[2]

Tangible Things

Rule 34 allows a party to inspect and copy, test, or sample tangible things relevant to the action.[3]

Property

A party has the right to enter onto another party's land and inspect, measure, survey, photograph, test, or sample property or a designated object or operation thereon if relevant to the pending action.[4]

Parties Only

Only parties are obligated to respond to document requests.[5] "Party" is sometimes liberally construed, such as to include experts,[6] insurance companies,[7] and garnishees.[8] Note, however, that documents may be obtained from non-parties by a subpoena under Rule 45.[9]

Documents Within Party's Control

A party must produce all discoverable documents or things responsive to a request that are in the party's possession, custody, or control.[10] Documents are deemed to be within the possession, custody, or control of a party if the party has actual possession, custody, control, or the legal right to obtain the documents on demand.[11] Documents held by

2. *In re Ford Motor Co.*, 345 F.3d 1315, 1316–17 (11th Cir. 2003); *Simon Property Group L.P. v. mySimon, Inc.*, 194 F.R.D. 639, 640 (S.D. Ind. 2000) (computer records, including records that have been deleted, are documents discoverable under Rule 34); the Advisory Committee Note to the 1970 amendment to Rule 34(a).

3. *Macort v. Goodwill Industries–Manasota, Inc.*, 220 F.R.D. 377, 379 (M.D.Fla. 2003) (inspection of property); *Harris v. Athol–Royalston Regional School Dist. Committee*, 206 F.R.D. 30, 32–33 (D.Mass.2002) (fingerprint samples may be obtained under either Rule 34 or Rule 35).

4. *Albany Bank & Trust Co. v. Exxon Mobil Corp.*, 310 F.3d 969, 974 (7th Cir.2002); *Micro Chemical, Inc. v. Lextron, Inc.*, 193 F.R.D. 667, 669–70 (D.Colo.2000) (allowing the president of the opposing party to attend the inspection of the plant, but not allowing the discovering party to alter the machine of the responding party to allow better observation of its operation).

5. *In re Greenwood Air Crash*, 161 F.R.D. 387 (S.D.Ind.1995)(discussion of who constitutes a "party" under Rule 34).

6. *Alper v. United States*, 190 F.R.D. 281, 283 (D.Mass.2000)(document request to the party's expert is deemed a document request to the party).

7. *See, e.g., Parrett v. Ford Motor Co.*, 47 F.R.D. 22, 24 (W.D.Mo.1968).

8. *See, e.g., Conversion Chem. Corp. v. Dr.–Ing. Max Schloetter Fabrik Fur Galvanotechnik*, 49 F.R.D. 126 (D.Conn.1969).

9. *Price Waterhouse LLP v. First American Corp.*, 182 F.R.D. 56, 61 (S.D.N.Y.1998).

10. *Kissinger v. Reporters Com. for Freedom of the Press*, 445 U.S. 136, 166, 100 S.Ct. 960, 976, 63 L.Ed.2d 267 (1980).

11. *In Re Bankers Trust Co.*, 61 F.3d 465, 469 (6th Cir.1995); *Rosie D. v. Romney*, 256 F.Supp.2d 115, 119 (D.Mass.2003) (control may be established by the existence of a principal-agent relationship or a legal right pursuant to a contractual provision). *But see United States v. Skeddle*, 176 F.R.D. 258, 261 (N.D.Ohio 1997) ("in practice the courts have sometimes interpreted Rule 34 to require production if the party has practical ability to obtain the documents

the party's attorney,[12] expert,[13] insurance company,[14] accountant,[15] spouse,[16] or agent[17] are deemed to be within the party's control. Likewise, documents held by a subsidiary, affiliated corporation, or branch office in another state may be within a party's control.[18] Moreover, documents owned by a third person but possessed by a party are within the party's control.[19] A party may also be deemed to have possession, custody or control of documents which the party may release by authorization, such as medical records.[20]

Documents Available From Another Source

The fact that documents are available from another source, such as public records, is not, by itself, a valid basis for objecting or refusing to produce such documents if they are within the possession, custody, or control of the responding party.[21] Depending on the circumstances, however, the availability of alternative sources for the requested documents may support an objection on the basis of undue burden.

Proceedings Where Requests Available

Document requests are available in all civil actions in federal court, subject to certain narrow exceptions listed in Rule 81. Document requests are available in bankruptcy proceedings.

from another, irrespective of his legal entitlement to the documents").

12. *In re Ruppert,* 309 F.2d 97 (6th Cir. 1962); *Johnson v. Askin Capital Management, L.P.,* 202 F.R.D. 112, 114 (S.D.N.Y.2001) (documents held by the party's attorney or former attorney are within the party's control and must be produced).

13. *Alper v. United States,* 190 F.R.D. 281, 283 (D.Mass.2000) (documents held by the party's expert are within the party's control).

14. *Henderson v. Zurn Industries, Inc.,* 131 F.R.D. 560, 567 (S.D.Ind.1990). *But see Japan Halon Co., Ltd. v. Great Lakes Chemical Corp.,* 155 F.R.D. 626 (N.D.Ind.1993) (subsidiary not required to obtain documents from parent in another country).

15. *Wardrip v. Hart,* 934 F.Supp. 1282, 1286 (D.Kan.1996) (financial records of defendant in possession of defendant's accountant are in defendant's control).

16. *Monroe's Estate v. Bottle Rock Power Corp.,* 2004 WL 737463 (E.D.La. 2004).

17. *United States ex rel. Stewart v. Louisiana Clinic,* 2003 WL 21283944 (E.D.La.2003).

18. *Novartis Pharmaceuticals Corp. v. Eon Labs Mfg., Inc.,* 206 F.R.D. 392, 395 (D.Del.2002) (documents held by a subsidiary in the control of the parent); *Uniden America Corp. v. Ericsson Inc.,* 181 F.R.D. 302, 306 (M.D.N.C.1998) (party required to produce documents from sister corporation); *but see Kestrel Coal Pty. Ltd. v. Joy Global, Inc.,* 362 F.3d 401, 405 (7th Cir. 2004) (One uses Rule 34 to get documents from firms that possess them, not from their corporate affiliates).

19. *Societe Internationale Pour Participations Industrielles Et Commerciales, S.A. v. Rogers,* 357 U.S. 197, 78 S.Ct. 1087, 2 L.Ed.2d 1255 (1958); *Commerce and Industry Ins. Co. v. Grinnell Corp.,* 2001 WL 96377 (E.D.La.2001).

20. *Preservation Products, LLC v. Nutraceutical Clinical Laboratories Intern., Inc.,* 214 F.R.D. 494, 495 (N.D.Ill. 2003) (plaintiff must supply authorization for SEC testimony sought by defendant); *J.J.C. v. Fridell,* 165 F.R.D. 513, 517 (D.Minn.1995) (in considering authorization for release of medical records, the court must balance the patient's right to privacy with the need for such records in obtaining a fair trial); *but see Clark v. Vega Wholesale Inc.,* 181 F.R.D. 470, 472 (D.Nev.1998) (medical records not deemed in the plaintiff's control).

21. *Sabouri v. Ohio Bureau of Employment Services,* 2000 WL 1620915 (S.D.Ohio 2000) (party required to produce a pleading that could also be obtained from the courthouse). *But see Bleecker v. Standard Fire Ins. Co.,* 130 F.Supp.2d 726 (E.D.N.C. 2000) (discovery is not required when documents are readily obtainable by the party seeking a motion to compel).

Procedure to Perpetuate Testimony

A party may file a motion to obtain documents in connection with an action to perpetuate testimony under Rule 27.

Procedures in Aid of Execution

Document requests may be served following the entry of judgment, as part of procedures in aid of execution.

Motion for a Protective Order

As an alternative to making objections to individual document requests, the responding party may make a motion for a protective order under Rule 26(c).[22] A motion for a protective order is appropriate when most or all of a set of document requests is too burdensome or cumulative. The burden is on the moving party to show hardship or injustice. The motion must be accompanied by a certification that the parties met prior to the filing of the motion and attempted to resolve their dispute without intervention by the court.

Contractual Agreements

Parties sometimes have previously entered into agreements defining a right to inspect designated documents (such as an agreement restricting one party's right to inspect another party's financial records for one year). Such agreements may be upheld by the court, if reasonable.

RULE 34(b). PROCEDURE

CORE CONCEPT

Any party may serve document requests on any other party,[23] who must respond in writing within 30 days.

APPLICATIONS

Who May Serve

Any party may serve document requests.

Who May Be Served

Document requests are limited to parties to the action, although the party need not be an adverse party (documents are obtained from non-parties by a subpoena under Rule 45). The document requests must be addressed to the party. Thus, if the party is a corporation, document requests should be addressed to the corporation, not to a corporate officer or the attorney. In a class action, the courts are split as to whether only the named representatives can be served.[24] Copies of the document requests should be served upon all parties.

22. *Minnesota Mining & Mfg. Co., Inc. v. Nippon Carbide Indus. Co., Inc.*, 171 F.R.D. 246 (D.Minn.1997).

23. *McKesson v. Islamic Republic of Iran*, 185 F.R.D. 70 (D.D.C.1999) (compelling a foreign nation defendant to allow the plaintiff's expert to enter the country and conduct an inspection).

24. *Brennan v. Midwestern United Life Ins. Co.*, 450 F.2d 999 (7th Cir.1971), *cert. denied*, 405 U.S. 921, 92 S.Ct. 957, 30 L.Ed.2d 792

Time for Service

Document requests can be served after the parties have conducted the discovery conference under Rule 26(f), or earlier with leave of court. In proceedings listed in Rule 26(a)(1)(E) as exempt from initial disclosures, there is no preliminary waiting period for document requests. The Rules do not set an outer limit on how late in the case document requests may be served, but many local rules or case management orders will set such a limit. Usually, when such a limit exists, document requests must be served so that the response is due before the close of discovery.[25]

Number

The Rule contains no limitation on the number of document requests.[26] Some districts have local rules limiting the number of document requests.

Designation of Documents

Documents to be produced must be designated with "reasonable particularity."[27] Rule 34(b) permits requests for categories of documents as long as the category is described with reasonable particularity.[28] Essentially, the test is whether the responding party can determine what documents to produce.

Form of Requests

A request for inspection should be a formal document[29] setting forth the items to be inspected with "reasonable particularity."[30] What constitutes "reasonable particularity" depends on the circumstances. The request should also specify a reasonable time, place, and manner for the inspection.[31] The time designated should be after the time to respond has elapsed (30 days). As an alternative, the serving party may designate "a time and manner convenient to the parties," then reach an agreement with opposing counsel.

Response

A party served with a document request must serve a written response[32] or move for a protective order under Rule 26(c). Otherwise,

(1972)(unnamed members of class required to respond); *Wainwright v. Kraftco Corp.*, 54 F.R.D. 532 (N.D.Ga.1972)(unnamed members of class not required to respond).

25. *Thomas v. Pacificorp*, 324 F.3d 1176, 1179 (10th Cir.2003).

26. *Bourguignon v. Spielvogel*, 2004 WL 743668 (D.Conn. 2004).

27. *Bruggeman ex rel. Bruggeman v. Blagojevich*, 219 F.R.D. 430, 436 (N.D.Ill. 2004); *St. Paul Reinsurance Co., Ltd. v. Commercial Financial Corp.*, 198 F.R.D. 508, 514 (N.D.Iowa 2000).

28. *Goosman v. A. Duie Pyle, Inc.*, 320 F.2d 45 (4th Cir.1963).

29. *Suid v. Cigna Corp.*, 203 F.R.D. 227, 229–29 (D.Virgin Islands 2001) (letters between counsel are not document requests under Rule 34).

30. *Roebling v. Anderson*, 257 F.2d 615, 620 (D.C.Cir.1958).

31. *Southern Estate Services, Inc. v. Puritan Financial Services, Inc.*, 2000 WL 1725086 (E.D.La. 2000).

32. *Starcher v. Correctional Medical Systems, Inc.*, 144 F.3d 418, 420–21 (6th Cir.1998), *cert.*

the party will be subject to the sanctions in Rule 37(d). The response may state that the request will be complied with in the manner requested. It may also state that the request will be complied with, but at some other time or place, or in some other manner. The response may also raise objections to some or all of the requests. Finally, the response may advise that the party has no such documents in its possession, custody, or control.[33]

Time to Answer

A written response is due within 30 days of service.[34] The time to answer may be extended by written agreement under Rule 29.[35] If the responding party intends to object to some of the document requests, the stipulation should specify that the time is extended to answer and file objections.[36] The period for responding may also be shortened or lengthened by the court, typically upon motion by one of the parties.[37]

Service of Response

The response must be served upon all parties.

Objections

If the responding party determines that a particular document request is outside the scope of discovery, the party may object to the request in lieu of producing the documents. The objection must be made in writing, must state the grounds of the objection with specificity,[38] and must be signed by the attorney for the responding party. Some common objections are:

- *Overly broad, unduly vague, and/or ambiguous:* When a document request is written broadly so that it extends to documents not relevant to the complaint (such as a request not limited in time to the events relevant to the complaint), the request may be overly broad.[39] When a request is susceptible to numerous meanings, it may be unduly vague and ambiguous. In general, these objections are probably not justification for refusing to provide documents altogether, but the responding party can raise the objection, then expressly limit the scope of the response.
- *Burdensome and oppressive:* In general, the responding party must produce the documents available without undue effort or

granted, 525 U.S. 1098, 119 S.Ct. 864, 142 L.Ed.2d 716 (1999).

33. *See Fishel v. BASF*, 175 F.R.D. 525, 531 (S.D.Iowa 1997) ("Even if there are no such documents, plaintiff is entitled to a response as required by Fed.R.Civ.P. 34(b) and the Court will so order.").

34. *Jayne H. Lee, Inc. v. Flagstaff Indus. Corp.*, 173 F.R.D. 651, 654 (D.Md.1997).

35. *Tropix, Inc. v. Lyon & Lyon*, 169 F.R.D. 3, *3–4 (D.Mass.1996).

36. *Coregis Ins. Co. v. Baratta & Fenerty, Ltd.*, 187 F.R.D. 528, 530 (E.D.Pa.1999).

37. *Ellsworth Associates v. United States*, 917 F.Supp. 841, 844 (D.D.C.1996)(motion for expedited discovery is particularly appropriate with a claim for injunctive relief).

38. *United States v. Philip Morris Inc.*, 347 F.3d 951, 954 (D.C.Cir. 2003); *Athridge v. Aetna Casualty and Surety Co.*, 184 F.R.D. 181, 190–91 (D.D.C.1998) (general boilerplate objections are ineffective).

39. *Westhemeco Ltd. v. New Hampshire Ins. Co.*, 82 F.R.D. 702 (S.D.N.Y.1979).

expense. Thus, requests that require extensive research, compilation, or evaluation of documents may be objectionable.[40] The responding party is not required to prepare the adverse party's case. The reasonableness of a request is within the court's discretion.

- *Privileged information:* Requests that seek documents protected by the attorney-client privilege or by another privilege are objectionable.[41] When privileged documents are withheld, the responding party must explicitly state the objection and describe the nature of the documents not produced sufficiently to enable other parties to assess the applicability of the privilege.[42] A log of the documents withheld on the basis of privilege should be provided to the requesting party, either at the time of the responses or at a mutually agreeable time.[43] Care should be exercised in responding to such requests, because the privilege may be waived by revealing part or all of the privileged documents.
- *Attorney work product:* Rule 26(b)(3) provides that trial preparation materials may be discovered only upon a showing that the party is unable to obtain the equivalent information through other means without undue hardship.[44]
- *Non-discoverable expert information:* Rule 26(b)(4) limits the scope of discovery directed towards experts. It generally requires the responding party to provide an expert report for each expert the party may call as a witness, and thereafter allows other parties to depose such experts. Further discovery with respect to such witnesses is available only upon motion. Rule 26(b)(4)(B) does not allow any discovery with respect to experts not intended to be called as witnesses, absent "exceptional circumstances."[45]
- *Not calculated to lead to the discovery of admissible evidence:* Rule 26 takes a very broad approach with respect to what information is discoverable. The requested information need not be admissible, only relevant. Information that is neither admissible nor reasonably calculated to lead to the discovery of admissible evidence, however, is not discoverable.[46]

Failure to Object Is Waiver

All grounds for objection must be specifically stated in a timely[47] response or they are waived,[48] unless excused by the court for good

40. *Chambers v. Capital Cities/ABC*, 154 F.R.D. 63 (S.D.N.Y.1994).

41. *Nat. Union Fire Ins. Co. of Pittsburgh, Pa. v. Midland Bancor, Inc.*, 159 F.R.D. 562 (D.Kan.1994).

42. *United States v. Philip Morris Inc.*, 347 F.3d 951, 954 (D.C.Cir. 2003).

43. *Strougo v. Bea Associates*, 199 F.R.D. 515, 521 (S.D.N.Y. 2001).

44. *See* Rule 26(b)(3)(discovery of work product).

45. *See* Rule 26(b)(4)(in-depth discussion of discovery directed toward experts).

46. *See* Rule 26(b)(1)(in-depth discussion of the scope of discovery).

47. *Land Ocean Logistics, Inc. v. Aqua Gulf Corp.*, 181 F.R.D. 229, 236–37 (W.D.N.Y.1998).

48. *Drexel Heritage Furnishings, Inc. v. Furniture USA, Inc.*, 200 F.R.D. 255 (M.D.N.C.2001)

cause shown.[49]

Objection to Part of Request

If any part of a request is objectionable, the responding party must specify the objectionable part and respond to the remaining parts.[50]

Production of Documents

The responding party has the option of allowing the serving party to inspect and copy the documents as they are normally kept (*i.e.*, "There is our file room.").[51] The responding party may also produce selected responsive documents, in which case the party must organize and label them to correspond to the categories requested.[52] The responding party may make copies for the requesting party, but is not obligated to do so.

Use of Documents at Trial

Documents produced in response to document requests are treated like any other evidence, and are admissible as allowed by the rules of evidence. They may be objected to as irrelevant, prejudicial, confusing, cumulative, or any other applicable objection.

Cost of Copying

The requesting party is responsible for the cost of copying the requested documents,[53] although parties sometimes agree (formally or informally) that the responding party pays copying costs. The requesting party may inspect the produced documents before copying in order to avoid duplicative copying of documents already in the requesting party's possession.[54]

Production of Computer Data

It is settled that computer data is discoverable under Rule 34.[55] A party is normally required to convert computer data into an intelligible

(waiver is implicit in Rule 34's requirement that objections be explicitly stated); *Rivera v. Kmart Corp.*, 190 F.R.D. 298, 300–01 (D.Puerto Rico 2000).

49. *Starlight International, Inc. v. Herlihy*, 181 F.R.D. 494 (D.Kan.1998) (attorney inadvertence not good cause).

50. *Cotracom Commodity Trading Co. v. Seaboard Corp.*, 189 F.R.D. 655, 666 (D.Kan. 1999).

51. *In re G–I Holdings Inc.*, 218 F.R.D. 428, 439–40 (D.N.J. 2003) (producing party does not have to organize and label documents that are produced as they are kept); *Rowlin v. Alabama Dept. of Public Safety*, 200 F.R.D. 459 (M.D.Ala. 2001); *but see Bonilla v. Trebol Motors Corp.*, 1997 WL 178844, *68 (D.Puerto Rico), *reversed in part, vacated in part*, 150 F.3d 88 (1st Cir. 1998) (responding party may not utilize a system of record-keeping which conceals rather than discloses relevant records or which makes production of the documents excessively burdensome and costly).

52. *Ferrito v. IKON Office Solutions, Inc.*, 2000 WL 1477188 (D.Kan. 2000) (production of 2,000 pages of documents that were neither Bates stamped nor otherwise organized did not satisfy Rule 34); *Stiller v. Arnold*, 167 F.R.D. 68, 71 (N.D.Ind.1996) (discovery sanctions were warranted where producing party failed to organize and label the 7,000 documents it produced).

53. *Obiajulu v. City of Rochester, Dept. of Law*, 166 F.R.D. 293, 297 (W.D.N.Y.1996) (plaintiff may copy documents by bringing in his own portable copying machine or by paying the defendant a reasonable copying cost.)

54. *Stiller v. Arnold*, 167 F.R.D. 68, 70 (N.D.Ind.1996).

55. *Illinois Tool Works, Inc. v. Metro Mark Products, Ltd.*, 43 F.Supp.2d 951 (N.D.Ill.1999).

format (*i.e.,* make a printed copy). Normally, the cost of the conversion is born by the responding party, unless the burden would be unreasonable enough to warrant a protective order under Rule 26(c). If the computer or software is the subject of the lawsuit, the court can fashion a suitable method of inspection balancing both parties' rights.

Limitations on Inspection

The responding party can set reasonable limitations on the time, place, and manner of an inspection.

Motion to Compel

If the responding party fails to respond to a document request or to allow an inspection, or objects to a document request, the propounding party may file a motion to compel under Rule 37(a).[56] The court will award the prevailing party its reasonable expenses, including attorney fees, incurred in connection with the motion to compel, unless the conduct of the losing party was justified (*i.e.,* not frivolous).

NOTE: Rule 37 requires the moving party to certify in writing that good faith attempts were made to resolve discovery disputes before relief was sought from the court.

Burden of Persuasion

In a motion to compel, the burden is on the responding party (the non-moving party) to convince the court that a document request is objectionable.

Discretion of Court

The district court has extremely broad discretion in ruling on objections to document requests. The court will balance the need for the documents and the burden of producing them, but will generally require production unless the administration of justice would be impeded. The court may allow inspection under limited conditions, and may restrict further disclosure of sensitive documents. The court may also privately inspect the documents before ruling.

Appeals

The court's rulings on objections to document requests are reviewed on an abuse of discretion standard.[57] Usually, such rulings are not final orders, and cannot be appealed until the conclusion of the case.

Sanctions for Failure to Respond

If a party files no response to a document request, the court may impose certain sanctions under Rule 37(b)(2), such as deeming certain facts established or refusing to allow the party to oppose or support certain claims.[58] The court may also deem objections to the document

56. *United States v. Kattar,* 191 F.R.D. 33, 35–36 (D.N.H.1999) (such a motion must comply with the requirements of Rule 37(a)).

57. *Swanner v. United States,* 406 F.2d 716, 719 (5th Cir.1969).

58. *See* Rule 37(d); *Land Ocean Logistics, Inc. v. Aqua Gulf Corp.,* 181 F.R.D. 229, 235

request waived by the failure to file a timely response.[59] Furthermore, the court must award reasonable expenses, including attorney fees, caused by the responding party's failure to answer, unless the court finds that the failure to answer was justified.

Sanctions for Failure to Obey Order to Produce Documents

If, in response to a motion to compel, the court orders a party to produce certain documents, and if the responding party fails to comply, then the court can impose the sanctions specified in Rule 37(b)(2), such as deeming certain facts established or refusing to allow the party to oppose or support certain claims. Furthermore, the court must award reasonable expenses, including attorney fees, caused by the responding party's failure to produce the documents, unless the court finds that the failure was justified.

RULE 34(c). PERSONS NOT PARTIES

CORE CONCEPT

Although document requests or requests for inspection cannot be served on a non-party, documents or inspections can be obtained from a non-party by a subpoena under Rule 45.[60] Furthermore, Rule 34 does not preclude an independent action for production of documents or things or for permission to enter onto land (but such actions may be unnecessary under the expanded subpoena powers in Rule 45).[61]

ADDITIONAL RESEARCH REFERENCES

Wright & Miller, *Federal Practice and Procedure* §§ 2201–2218.

C.J.S. Federal Civil Procedure §§ 696–740 et seq.

West's Key No. Digests, Federal Civil Procedure ⚷1551–1640.

(W.D.N.Y.1998) (preclusion of evidence is a harsh sanction reserved for exceptional cases).

59. *Scaturro v. Warren and Sweat Manufacturing Co., Inc.*, 160 F.R.D. 44 (M.D.Pa.1995).

60. *In re Greenwood Air Crash*, 161 F.R.D. 387 (S.D.Ind.1995)(discussion of who constitutes a "party" under Rule 34).

61. The Advisory Committee Note to the 1970 amendment to Rule 34(c).

RULE 35

PHYSICAL AND MENTAL EXAMINATIONS OF PERSONS

(a) Order for Examination. When the mental or physical condition (including the blood group) of a party or of a person in the custody or under the legal control of a party, is in controversy, the court in which the action is pending may order the party to submit to a physical or mental examination by a suitably licensed or certified examiner or to produce for examination the person in the party's custody or legal control. The order may be made only on motion for good cause shown and upon notice to the person to be examined and to all parties and shall specify the time, place, manner, conditions, and scope of the examination and the person or persons by whom it is to be made.

(b) Report of Examiner.

(1) If requested by the party against whom an order is made under Rule 35(a) or the person examined, the party causing the examination to be made shall deliver to the requesting party a copy of the detailed written report of the examiner setting out the examiner's findings, including results of all tests made, diagnoses and conclusions, together with like reports of all earlier examinations of the same condition. After delivery the party causing the examination shall be entitled upon request to receive from the party against whom the order is made a like report of any examination, previously or thereafter made, of the same condition, unless, in the case of a report of examination of a person not a party, the party shows that the party is unable to obtain it. The court on motion may make an order against a party requiring delivery of a report on such terms as are just, and if an examiner fails or refuses to make a report the court may exclude the examiner's testimony if offered at trial.

(2) By requesting and obtaining a report of the examination so ordered or by taking the deposition of the examiner, the party examined waives any privilege the party may have in that action or any other involving the same controversy, regarding the testimony of every other person who has examined or may thereafter examine the party in respect of the same mental or physical condition.

(3) This subdivision applies to examinations made by agreement of the parties, unless the agreement expressly provides otherwise. This subdivision does not preclude discovery of a report of

an examiner or the taking of a deposition of the examiner in accordance with the provisions of any other rule.

[Amended effective July 1, 1970; August 1, 1987; November 18, 1988; December 1, 1991.]

AUTHORS' COMMENTARY ON RULE 35

PURPOSE AND SCOPE

Rule 35 requires a party to submit to a mental or physical examination when the party's mental or physical condition is at issue in the action. In contrast to most other discovery procedures, mental or physical examinations are available only for "good cause."

RULE 35(a). ORDER FOR EXAMINATION

CORE CONCEPT

Examination is compulsory only if ordered by the court. Examination will be ordered for good cause shown, which will generally exist in every case in which the plaintiff is claiming personal injuries.

APPLICATIONS

Motion

Technically, a request for examination must be made by motion, with a proposed order attached, served upon the person to be examined and all parties,[1] meeting the requirements described below.[2] Typically, however, examination is arranged by consent.

Order

If the court grants a motion for a Rule 35 examination, it must issue an order that specifies the time, place, manner, conditions, and scope of the examination and the examiner.[3] These topics are discussed individually below. The order may also include protective measures deemed appropriate by the court.[4]

Condition at Issue

Examinations for a particular condition are allowed only when that

1. *Smith v. Koplan*, 215 F.R.D. 11, 12 (D.D.C.2003).

2. *See Cabana v. Forcier*, 200 F.R.D. 9 (D.Mass. 2001) (the movant complied with Rule 35 by providing a time and place for the exam as well as the name of the examiner and a general idea of the exam's intended scope).

3. *Ziemba v. Armstrong*, 2004 WL 834685 (D.Conn. 2004); *Hertenstein v. Kimberly Home Health Care, Inc.*, 189 F.R.D. 620, 623 (D.Kan. 1999).

4. *Hertenstein v. Kimberly Home Health Care, Inc.*, 189 F.R.D. 620, 624 (D.Kan.1999).

condition is in controversy.[5]

Good Cause

The court will order an examination "for good cause shown." [6] The burden of demonstrating good cause rests with the moving party.[7] The requirement of good cause is not a formality; the court must genuinely balance the need for the information with the right to privacy and safety of the party.[8] In a tort action where the plaintiff seeks to recover for personal injuries, good cause will almost always be found to exist.[9] It becomes less clear when the party has not put the party's own mental or physical condition at issue.[10]

Time for Filing Motion

There is no time limit on the filing of a motion for an examination.

Who Conducts Exam

Rule 35 states that the examination may be conducted by any suitably licensed or certified examiner or examiners.[11] It does not address the selection of a particular examiner. In general, the court will allow the movant to select the examiner unless the person to be examined raises a valid objection.[12] The court may reject a particular examiner upon a showing of bias[13] or, arguably, if a person requests a doctor of the same gender. Some local rules have provisions regarding

5. *Green v. Branson*, 108 F.3d 1296, 1304 (10th Cir.1997) (denying motion by the plaintiff to have himself examined where purpose was for the plaintiff, a prisoner, to obtain treatment); *Cauley v. Ingram Micro, Inc.*, 216 F.R.D. 241(W.D.N.Y.2003) (claim of severe emotional harm justifies mental examination); *Gattegno v. Pricewaterhousecoopers, LLP*, 204 F.R.D. 228, 231–33 (D.Conn.2001) (describing a good cause test when emotional distress claims are brought); *Bowen v. Parking Authority of City of Camden*, 214 F.R.D. 188, 193 (D.N.J. 2003) ("garden variety" emotional distress claim does not put the plaintiff's mental condition at issue).

6. *Schlagenhauf v. Holder,* 379 U.S. 104, 85 S.Ct. 234, 13 L.Ed.2d 152 (1964) (describing "good cause" as a determination that must be made on a case-by-case basis); *Johnson v. City of Ecorse*, 137 F.Supp.2d 886, 894 (E.D.Mich. 2001) ("A demonstration of good cause requires, initially, that the desired information cannot be obtained by other means.").

7. *Cauley v. Ingram Micro, Inc.*, 216 F.R.D. 241 (W.D.N.Y.2003).

8. *Schlagenhauf v. Holder*, 379 U.S. 104, 118, 85 S.Ct. 234, 242, 13 L.Ed.2d 152 (1964); *Houghton v. M & F Fishing, Inc.*, 198 F.R.D. 666 (S.D.Cal. 2001); *but see Simpson v. University of Colorado*, 220 F.R.D. 354, 362 (D.Colo. 2004) (the rule is to be construed liberally in favor of granting the examination).

9. *See Chaney v. Venture Transport, Inc.*, 2004 WL 445134 (E.D.La. 2004); *Nyfield v. Virgin Islands Telephone Corp.*, 2001 WL 378858 (D.Virgin Islands 2001).

10. *See Ali v. Wang Labs., Inc.*, 162 F.R.D. 165 (M.D.Fla.1995).

11. *Merritt v. Stolt Offshore, Inc.*, 2004 WL 224578 (E.D.La. 2004) (holding that the court may order more than one examiner, but noting that some states hold differently); *Fischer v. Coastal Towing, Inc.*, 168 F.R.D. 199, 201 (E.D.Tex.1996) (vocational-rehabilitation expert deemed a "suitably licensed and/or certified examiner").

12. *Douponce v. Drake*, 183 F.R.D. 565, 566 (D.Colo.1998) (allowing the defendant's selected examiner despite allegations of bias); *Lahr v. Fulbright & Jaworski, L.L.P.*, 164 F.R.D. 196, 202–03 (N.D.Tex.1995).

13. *See Nyfield v. Virgin Islands Telephone Corp.*, 2001 WL 378858 (D.Virgin Islands 2001) ("There is no requirement that a Rule 35 examination be conducted by a physician wholly unconnected with either party and absent evidence of bias, Defendants should be allowed their chosen examiner.").

the selection of a neutral examiner.[14] The court order must designate the examiner, and may be invalid if it fails to do so.

Testimony of Examiner

The party conducting the examination may call the examiner to testify as an expert witness (assuming the criteria for expert testimony are satisfied). The courts are split as to whether the party who was examined may call the examiner as an expert.[15]

Type of Exams

The type of exams allowable depends on the circumstances of the case. Exams can include blood tests, x-rays, electrocardiograms, fingerprint analysis,[16] and other safe, medically accepted tests indicated by the condition at issue.[17] Vocational exams are also permissible under Rule 35.[18] The burden on the movant to show good cause will be greater if the tests are more invasive, painful, or burdensome, or if repeated examinations are sought. However, a party that objects to a particular test as too painful or invasive may be precluded from offering evidence of the type that would result from the test. A court may also limit testing to only those tests that have been specifically identified.[19]

Mental Examinations

Psychiatric examinations are allowable if a person's mental condition is at issue.[20] The examination may be conducted by a psychiatrist or psychologist. Courts are divided as to whether a claim for emotional distress places the plaintiff's mental condition at issue.[21]

Safety of Tests

In order to oppose a mental or physical exam on the grounds that the exam is unsafe, a party must demonstrate that the proposed test is

14. *But see Hunt v. R & B Falcon Drilling USA, Inc.*, 2000 WL 1838327 (E.D.La.2000) (a motion for a court appointed examiner is more properly brought under Federal Rule of Evidence 706).

15. *Lehan v. Ambassador Programs, Inc.*, 190 F.R.D. 670 (E.D.Wash.2000) (discussing the various positions taken by the courts on this issue).

16. *Harris v. Athol–Royalston Regional School Dist. Committee*, 206 F.R.D. 30, 32–33 (D.Mass.2002) (fingerprint samples may be obtained under either Rule 34 or Rule 35).

17. *See Jefferys v. LRP Publications, Inc.*, 184 F.R.D. 262, 263 (E.D.Pa.1999) (allowing interview by vocational expert).

18. *See Storms v. Lowe's Home Centers, Inc.*, 211 F.R.D. 296, 297 (W.D.Va.2002); *Douris v. County of Bucks*, 2000 WL 1358481 (E.D.Pa. 2000).

19. *Hirschheimer v. Associated Metals & Minerals Corp.*, 1995 WL 736901, at *4 (S.D.N.Y. 1995); *contra Ragge v. MCA/Universal Studios*, 165 F.R.D. 605, 609 (C.D.Cal.1995).

20. *Sarko v. Penn–Del Directory Co.*, 170 F.R.D. 127, 131 (E.D.Pa.1997). *See also Smith v. J.I. Case Corp.*, 163 F.R.D. 229, 230 (E.D.Pa. 1995)(discussing four possible situations in which a party's mental condition is in controversy).

21. *See E.E.O.C. v. Grief Bros. Corp.*, 218 F.R.D. 59, 61 (W.D.N.Y. 2003) (mental examinations may be obtained where a plaintiff's allegations of emotional distress amount to more than a claim for garden variety emotional distress damages); *Ford v. Contra Costa County*, 179 F.R.D. 579, 579–80 (N.D.Cal.1998) (mere claim for emotional distress damages does not place mental condition at issue); *E.E.O.C. v. Old Western Furniture Corp.*, 173 F.R.D. 444, 445–46 (W.D.Tex.1996); *Neal v. Siegel–Robert, Inc.*, 171 F.R.D. 264 (E.D.Mo.1996).

potentially dangerous. Thereafter, the burden shifts to the party requesting the examination to show that it is both necessary and safe.[22]

Second Examinations

When permanent injuries are claimed or under other appropriate circumstances, the court may allow a second examination just before trial.[23] A stronger showing of necessity is usually required for a second examination.[24]

Time and Location

The court will designate the time and location of the examination in the order. Usually, the plaintiff will be required to travel to the district where the action is pending to be examined.[25]

Cost of Examination

The moving party must pay the medical or professional expenses of the examination. The person to be examined is not compensated, however, for transportation costs[26] and lost time.

Who Is Present at Examination

The court has discretion to determine who may be present at the examination.[27] Some courts allow the person being examined by a doctor to bring his own physician, others do not.[28] It is also unsettled as to whether attorneys have a right to be present.[29]

Persons Subject to Examination

Any party is subject to examination upon motion by any other party, provided that the physical or mental condition of the party to be examined is at issue.[30] Additionally, a person who is within the control of a party is subject to examination. Thus, a parent suing on behalf of an injured child may have to produce the child for examination.[31] This principle has also been extended to a spouse when one spouse is suing

22. *Pena v. Troup*, 163 F.R.D. 352, 353–54 (D.Colo.1995).

23. See *Galieti v. State Farm Mutual Automobile Ins. Co.*, 154 F.R.D. 262 (D.Colo.1994).

24. *Furlong v. Circle Line Statue of Liberty Ferry, Inc.*, 902 F.Supp. 65 (S.D.N.Y.1995).

25. *Landry v. Green Bay & Western R. Co.*, 121 F.R.D. 400 (E.D.Wis.1988).

26. *McCloskey v. UPS*, 171 F.R.D. 268, 270 (D.Or.1997).

27. *See Bethel v. Dixie Homecrafters, Inc.*, 192 F.R.D. 320 (N.D. Ga. 2000); *Ali v. Wang Labs., Inc.*, 162 F.R.D. 165, 168 (M.D.Fla.1995).

28. *Shirsat v. Mutual Pharmaceutical Co., Inc.*, 169 F.R.D. 68, 71 (E.D.Pa.1996).

29. *Marsch v. Rensselaer County*, 218 F.R.D. 367, 371 (N.D.N.Y. 2003) (although attorneys are generally not permitted to be present during the examination, Fifth Amendment concerns dictated allowing counsel to be present); *Cabana v. Forcier*, 200 F.R.D. 9 (D.Mass. 2001) (the clear majority of federal courts have refused to permit third party observers at Rule 35 examinations); *Gensbauer v. May Department Stores Co.*, 184 F.R.D. 552 (E.D.Pa.1999).

30. *Schlagenhauf v. Holder*, 379 U.S. 104, 85 S.Ct. 234, 13 L.Ed.2d 152 (1964).

31. The Advisory Committee Note to the 1970 amendment of Rule 35(a); *but see Caban v. 600 E. 21st Street Co.*, 200 F.R.D. 176 (E.D.N.Y. 2001) (a guardian suing on behalf of a child is not the party or within the control of the party, and thus is not subject to examination under Rule 35).

for injuries to the other.[32] In such case, the party has a duty to make a good faith effort to obtain the person's presence.[33]

Sanctions

If a party fails to comply with the order, most of the sanctions in Rule 37(b)(2) are available, such as deeming certain facts established or refusing to allow the violator to oppose or support certain claims. However, contempt sanctions are not available for failure to submit to the examination.[34] If a person within the control of a party is to be examined, no sanctions apply to that person because he is not a party. The party's duty is to make a good faith effort to obtain the person's presence, and the party will be subject to the sanctions if the party fails to make the requisite good faith effort.[35]

Actions Applicable

Examinations are available in all civil actions in federal court,[36] subject to certain narrow exceptions in Rule 81. The court may also order an examination in connection with a deposition to perpetuate testimony under Rule 27.[37]

Appeal

An order directing or refusing an examination is interlocutory, and thus generally not appealable until the end of the action.[38] It is reviewed under the abuse of discretion standard.[39]

RULE 35(b). REPORT OF EXAMINER

CORE CONCEPT

Upon request by the party or person examined, the party moving for the examination must provide a copy of a detailed written report by the examiner, together with any reports of earlier examinations for the same condition.[40] Following the delivery of such a copy, the examined party must provide copies of reports of the results of any other examinations for the same condition, whether conducted before or after the Rule 35 examination.

32. *In re Certain Asbestos Cases,* 112 F.R.D. 427, 434 (N.D.Tex.1986).

33. The Advisory Committee Note to the 1970 amendment of Rule 35(a).

34. *Sibbach v. Wilson & Co.,* 312 U.S. 1, 61 S.Ct. 422, 85 L.Ed. 479 (1941).

35. The Advisory Committee Note to the 1970 amendment of Rule 35(a).

36. *Caban v. 600 E. 21st Street Co.,* 200 F.R.D. 176 (E.D.N.Y.2001) (Rule 35 governs in diversity cases even in the face of conflicting state rules regarding examinations of parties).

37. *See* Rules 27(a)(3) and 27(b).

38. *O'Malley v. Chrysler Corp.,* 160 F.2d 35 (7th Cir.1947).

39. *Green v. Branson,* 108 F.3d 1296, 1304 (10th Cir.1997).

40. *See Grajales–Romero v. American Airlines, Inc.,* 194 F.3d 288, 298 (1st Cir.1999) (duty to exchange applies to an examination voluntarily submitted to by the plaintiff).

APPLICATIONS

Examination by Agreement

The report exchanging provisions apply to examinations by agreement unless the agreement expressly provides otherwise.

Effect of Report

Testimony by the examiner will be limited to the opinions disclosed in the report.[41]

Waiver of Privilege

A request for a report under Rule 35 acts as a waiver of the doctor-patient or psychologist-patient privilege for other examinations for the same condition.[42] Thus, the examined party may not refuse to produce other reports on the basis of privilege once the party has requested a copy of the report of the Rule 35 examination. Note that the Rule 35 waiver may be avoided by attempting to obtain the reports via another discovery rule or another procedural device.

Other Discovery Procedures

The parties may use other discovery procedures in lieu of or in addition to the report exchange procedures in Rule 35, such as document requests or depositions of the examiner.

Failure to Exchange

If either party fails to provide covered reports, the court can order production.

Failure to Draft Report

If the examiner fails to prepare or provide a report, the court may exclude the examiner's testimony.

Extraneous Material

If the report contains extraneous or unreasonably prejudicial material, the court can order certain portions excised.

Reports for Persons Under Control of Party

If a person is examined under Rule 35 because that person is in the control of a party, the party is entitled to the same reporting rights and obligations as the person would be.

ADDITIONAL RESEARCH REFERENCES

Wright & Miller, *Federal Practice and Procedure* §§ 2231–2239.

C.J.S. Federal Civil Procedure §§ 752–755.

West's Key No. Digests, Federal Civil Procedure ⚷1651–1664.

41. *Licciardi v. TIG Insurance Group*, 140 F.3d 357 (1st Cir.1998) (testimony beyond the scope of the report excluded).

42. *Cunningham v. Connecticut Mutual Life Insurance*, 845 F.Supp. 1403 (S.D.Cal.1994).

RULE 36

REQUESTS FOR ADMISSION

(a) Request for Admission. A party may serve upon any other party a written request for the admission, for purposes of the pending action only, of the truth of any matters within the scope of Rule 26(b)(1) set forth in the request that relate to statements or opinions of fact or of the application of law to fact, including the genuineness of any documents described in the request. Copies of documents shall be served with the request unless they have been or are otherwise furnished or made available for inspection and copying. Without leave of court or written stipulation, requests for admission may not be served before the time specified in Rule 26(d).

Each matter of which an admission is requested shall be separately set forth. The matter is admitted unless, within 30 days after service of the request, or within such shorter or longer time as the court may allow or as the parties may agree to in writing, subject to Rule 29, the party to whom the request is directed serves upon the party requesting the admission a written answer or objection addressed to the matter, signed by the party or by the party's attorney. If objection is made, the reasons therefor shall be stated. The answer shall specifically deny the matter or set forth in detail the reasons why the answering party cannot truthfully admit or deny the matter. A denial shall fairly meet the substance of the requested admission, and when good faith requires that a party qualify an answer or deny only a part of the matter of which an admission is requested, the party shall specify so much of it as is true and qualify or deny the remainder. An answering party may not give lack of information or knowledge as a reason for failure to admit or deny unless the party states that the party has made reasonable inquiry and that the information known or readily obtainable by the party is insufficient to enable the party to admit or deny. A party who considers that a matter of which an admission has been requested presents a genuine issue for trial may not, on that ground alone, object to the request; the party may, subject to the provisions of Rule 37(c), deny the matter or set forth reasons why the party cannot admit or deny it.

The party who has requested the admissions may move to determine the sufficiency of the answers or objections. Unless the court determines that an objection is justified, it shall order that an answer be served. If the court determines that an answer does not comply with the requirements of this rule, it may order either that the matter is admitted or that an amended answer be served. The court may, in lieu of these orders, determine that final disposition of the request be made at a pre-trial conference or at a designated time prior to trial. The provisions of Rule 37(a)(4) apply to the award of expenses incurred in relation to the motion.

(b) Effect of Admission. Any matter admitted under this rule is conclusively established unless the court on motion permits withdrawal or amendment of the admission. Subject to the provision of Rule 16 governing amendment of a pre-trial order, the court may permit withdrawal or amendment when the presentation of the merits of the action will be subserved thereby and the party who obtained the admission fails to satisfy the court that withdrawal or amendment will prejudice that party in maintaining the action or defense on the merits. Any admission made by a party under this rule is for the purpose of the pending action only and is not an admission for any other purpose nor may it be used against the party in any other proceeding.

[Amended December 27, 1946, effective March 19, 1948; March 30, 1970, effective July 1, 1970; March 2, 1987, effective August 1, 1987; April 22, 1993, effective December 1, 1993.]

AUTHORS' COMMENTARY ON RULE 36

PURPOSE AND SCOPE

Rule 36 allows each party to require other parties to admit each relevant fact not in controversy, thereby eliminating the need to produce witnesses and evidence in support of these facts. It must be read in conjunction with Rule 26, which establishes the scope of all discovery rules.

RULE 36(a). REQUESTS FOR ADMISSION

CORE CONCEPT

Rule 36 establishes a procedure whereby one party serves requests for admission on another party, who must investigate and either admit, deny with specificity, or object to each requested admission.

APPLICATIONS

Who May Serve

Any party may serve requests for admission.

Who May Be Served

Requests for admission are limited to parties to the action, although the party need not be an adverse party.

Time for Service

Requests for admission can be served after the parties have conducted the discovery conference under Rule 26(f).[1] In proceedings listed in Rule 26(a)(1)(E) as exempt from initial disclosures, there is no preliminary waiting period for requests for admission. The Rules do not set an outer limit on how late in the case requests for admission may be served, and courts are split as to whether requests for admission are discovery devices subject to a general discovery cutoff.[2] However, many local rules or case management orders will set a limit for requests for admission. Usually, when such a time limit exists, requests for admission must be served so that the response is due before the specified deadline.[3]

Contents of Request

Each fact[4] or matter for which admission is requested should be set forth in a separate paragraph. All facts that are part of the request should be set forth in the request—it is improper to incorporate facts by reference to other text.

Scope

The scope of requests for admission is the broad discovery available under Rule 26.[5] Generally, any relevant, non-privileged matter is covered unless it was prepared in anticipation of litigation or pertains to expert witnesses. The requests may pertain to any issue that is or may be in the case, including the ultimate facts at issue,[6] the application of law to fact,[7] jurisdiction, or the statute of limitations.

Number

Rule 36 contains no limitation on the number of requests for admission. Some districts have local rules limiting the number of requests.

1. *DIRECTV, Inc. v. DeVries*, 302 F.Supp.2d 837, 838 (W.D.Mich. 2004).

2. *Banks v. Office of Senate Sergeant–At–Arms*, 222 F.R.D. 7 (D.D.C. 2004). *Gluck v. Ansett Australia Ltd.*, 204 F.R.D. 217, 218–19 (D.D.C.2001) (discussing the split and citing cases on both sides).

3. *Laborers' Pension Fund v. Blackmore Sewer Const., Inc.*, 298 F.3d 600, 605 (7th Cir. 2002).

4. *United States v. Block 44, Lots 3, 6*, 177 F.R.D. 695 (M.D.Fla.1997) (requests for admission apply to facts only, not to conclusions of law).

5. *Johnson v. Royal Coal Co.*, 326 F.3d 421, 424, n.2 (4th Cir.2003); *City of Rome v. United States*, 450 F.Supp. 378 (D.D.C.1978), *affirmed*, 446 U.S. 156, 100 S.Ct. 1548, 64 L.Ed.2d 119 (1980).

6. *In re Carney*, 258 F.3d 415, 419 (5th Cir. 2001). *But see North Louisiana Rehabilitation Center, Inc. v. United States*, 179 F.Supp.2d 658, 663 (W.D.La.2001) (allowing withdrawal of an admission because the ultimate issues are better decided on the merits).

7. *In re Carney*, 258 F.3d 415, 419 (5th Cir. 2001).

Authenticity of Documents

A request may ask that the genuineness or authenticity of a document be admitted.[8] If so, a copy of the document should be attached, unless already provided.

Who Must Receive Copies

All parties must be served with a copy of the requests for admissions.

Time to Answer

A written response is due within 30 days of service. The time to answer may be extended by written agreement under Rule 29.[9] Additionally, the court has discretion to lengthen or shorten the time in which a party must respond.[10]

Service of Response

Copies of the response should be served on the propounding party and all other parties, unless the court has ordered otherwise. The original should be filed with the court, except where local rule provides otherwise (in which case it should be retained by the responding party).

Form of Response

The response should be in writing and signed by the party or the attorney.[11] It should be a single document organized in numbered paragraphs to correspond to the requests.

Responses

The responding party essentially has four possible responses to a request for admission. The party can admit the request (in part or in full), deny the request (in part or in full), set forth reasons why the party cannot admit or deny the request, or object to the request (by a specific objection or by a motion for a protective order).

Duty to Supplement

Rule 26(e) imposes a duty to supplement a denial or statement of inability to admit or deny if the party learns that the original response is in some material respect incomplete or incorrect, and if the additional or corrective information has not been provided to the other parties in writing or at a deposition.

Denials

A denial must specifically address the substance of the requested

8. *Booth Oil Site Administrative Group v. Safety–Kleen Corporation*, 194 F.R.D. 76, 80 (W.D.N.Y. 2000).

9. *Simien v. Chemical Waste Management, Inc.*, 30 F.Supp.2d 939, 941, n. 1 (W.D.La.1998).

10. *Manatt v. Union Pacific R.R. Co.*, 122 F.3d 514, 517 (8th Cir.1997), *cert. denied*, 522 U.S. 1050, 118 S.Ct. 697, 139 L.Ed.2d 641 (1998); *Equal Employment Opportunity Commission v. TruGreen Limited Partnership*, 185 F.R.D. 552, 554 (W.D.Wis.1998).

11. The Advisory Committee Note to Rule 36(a).

admission.[12] The denial may be as simple as the single word "denied,"[13] or may be a longer sentence, but may not sidestep the request or be evasive.[14] If the propounding party feels that the denial is not sufficiently specific, the party can move the court to determine the sufficiency of the denial. If the court deems the denial not sufficiently specific, it can deem the denial an admission or order a more specific answer.

Partial Denial

If the responding party believes that part of a requested admission is accurate and part is not, the proper response is to admit the accurate portion and deny the balance.[15]

Inability to Admit or Deny

If the responding party is genuinely unable to admit or deny the requested admission, the party can so state, but must describe in detail why after reasonable inquiry the party cannot admit or deny.[16] A general statement that the responding party has insufficient information to respond will be treated as an insufficient answer, and upon motion the court will treat the answer as an admission or will order a further answer.[17]

Objections

Objections must be made in writing within the time allowed for answering. If answering some requests and objecting to others, the objections should be included in the document containing the answers. Typical grounds for objections to requests for admission are:

- *Privilege:* If a response requires the disclosure of privileged matters, it is objectionable.[18] *See* Rule 26 (discussion of commonly asserted privileges).
- *Vague or Ambiguous:* A request may be objectionable if it is so vague or ambiguous that the responding party cannot answer it.
- *Outside the Scope of Discovery:* Rule 36 is limited to relevant matters, as defined by Rule 26. Thus, if a requested admission is

12. The Advisory Committee Note to Rule 36(a); *ATD Corp. v. Lydall, Inc.*, 159 F.3d 534, 548 (Fed.Cir.1998).

13. *Caruso v. Coleman Co.*, 1995 WL 347003 (E.D.Pa.1995); *Wanke v. Lynn's Transp. Co.*, 836 F.Supp. 587 (N.D.Ind.1993).

14. *Asea, Inc. v. Southern Pac. Transp. Co.*, 669 F.2d 1242, 1245 (9th Cir.1981) (evasive denial may be deemed an admission); *Caruso v. Coleman Co.*, 1995 WL 347003 (E.D.Pa.1995) (an evasive answer does not specifically deny).

15. *ATD Corp. v. Lydall, Inc.*, 159 F.3d 534, 549 (Fed.Cir.1998); *Henry v. Champlain Enterprises, Inc.*, 212 F.R.D. 73, 78 (N.D.N.Y. 2003).

16. *Taborn v. Unknown Officers*, 2001 WL 138908 (N.D.Ill. 2001) (reasonable inquiry includes investigation and inquiry of any of defendant's officers, administrators, agents, employees, servants, enlisted or other personnel who may have information which may lead to or furnish the necessary and appropriate response); *Uniden America Corp. v. Ericsson Inc.*, 181 F.R.D. 302, 303 (M.D.N.C.1998) (respondent may even have a duty to make an inquiry of third parties).

17. *City of Rome v. United States,* 450 F.Supp. 378 (D.D.C.1978), *affirmed,* 446 U.S. 156, 100 S.Ct. 1548, 64 L.Ed.2d 119 (1980).

18. *United States v. One Tract of Real Property Together With all Buildings, Improvements, Appurtenances, and Fixtures*, 95 F.3d 422, 428 (6th Cir.1996).

irrelevant to the issues that are or may be in the case, it is objectionable.[19]

Improper Objections

An improper objection is not the same as an admission, and the proper response to an improper objection is to file a motion to compel a further response.[20] It is irrelevant who has the burden of proof with respect to the matter for which admission is requested. Likewise, a party cannot refuse to answer a request on the basis that the serving party already knows the answer. Similarly, a party cannot refuse to answer a request on the basis that it pertains to ultimate facts in the case or facts for proof at trial.[21]

Opinions and Conclusions

Rule 36 explicitly states that a request for admission is not objectionable because it involves an opinion or contention that relates to fact or the application of law to fact.[22] Rule 36 does not authorize a request that requires a pure legal conclusion, without application to the facts.[23]

Motion for a Protective Order

As an alternative to making objections to individual requests for admission, the responding party may make a motion for a protective order under Rule 26(c). A motion for a protective order is appropriate when most or all of a set of requests is objectionable. The motion must be accompanied by a certification that the parties met prior to the filing of the motion and attempted to resolve their dispute without intervention of the court.

Failure to Respond

Failure to respond in a timely fashion is deemed an admission.[24] The court has discretion to allow a party to submit responses after the allowed time for a response.[25]

Motion to Determine Sufficiency

If a party believes that a response is insufficient or that an objection is improper, the party can move the court to determine the

19. *But see Bell v. Domino's Pizza, Inc.*, 2000 WL 1780266 (D.D.C.2000) (relevance concerns are diminished with requests for admission because they cannot be used in any other proceeding).

20. *Butler v. Oak Creek–Franklin School Dist.*, 172 F.Supp.2d 1102, 1122, n.9 (E.D.Wis. 2001).

21. *Taborn v. Unknown Officers*, 2001 WL 138908 (N.D.Ill. 2001); the Advisory Committee Note to Rule 36(a).

22. *Marchand v. Mercy Medical Center*, 22 F.3d 933 (9th Cir.1994); *Sepatis v. City and County of San Francisco*, 217 F.Supp.2d 992, 1006 (N.D.Cal.2002).

23. *Tulip Computers Intern., B.V. v. Dell Computer Corp.*, 210 F.R.D. 100, 108 (D.Del. 2002); *United States v. Estate of Dickerson ex rel. Tate*, 189 F.Supp.2d 622, 625–26 (W.D.Tex. 2001).

24. *Walsh v. McCain Foods, Ltd.*, 81 F.3d 722, 726 (7th Cir.1996); *Kansas City Cable Partners ex rel. Time Warner Entertainment Co., L.P. v. Espy*, 250 F.Supp.2d 1296, 1297 (D.Kan.2003).

25. *In re Heritage Bond Litigation*, 220 F.R.D. 624, 626 (C.D.Cal. 2004).

sufficiency of the answer.[26] Note that "insufficient" refers to the specificity of the response, not whether the response is correct or in good faith.[27] The burden will be on the party raising an objection to show that the objection was proper. If the court determines that the answer was insufficient, it can deem the answer an admission or can order a more complete answer.[28] The court may also defer ruling until later in the pretrial proceedings.[29]

Expenses of Motion to Determine Sufficiency

The party losing a motion to determine the sufficiency of a response pays the other party's expenses, including a reasonable attorney fee, incurred in connection with the motion, pursuant to Rule 37(a)(4).[30]

Sanctions

The sanctions available depend upon the conduct of the responding party. The sanction for failure to respond is that the requests are deemed admitted.[31] The sanction for improperly denying a request is that the responding party will be required to pay the costs of the other party incurred in proving the matter, including attorney fees, under Rule 37(c).[32] The sanction for an insufficient answer or improper objection is that the response may be deemed an admission, plus the responding party will be liable for the other party's expenses in bringing the motion, including a reasonable attorney fee. The sanctions for failing to obey a court order to make a further response are the sanctions set forth in Rule 37(b)(2), such as deeming certain facts established or refusing to allow the party to oppose or support certain claims. Furthermore, the court must award reasonable expenses, including attorney fees, caused by the responding party's failure to comply with the order, unless the court finds that the failure was justified. Sanctions can be awarded against the party under Rule 37(c) and/or against the attorney under Rule 26(g).[33]

Appeals

The court's rulings on the sufficiency of and objections to requests for admissions are reviewed under an abuse of discretion standard. Usually, such rulings are not final orders, and cannot be appealed until the conclusion of the case.

26. *In re Heritage Bond Litigation*, 220 F.R.D. 624, 626 (C.D.Cal. 2004).

27. *Foretich v. Chung*, 151 F.R.D. 3 (D.D.C. 1993).

28. *See Medtronic Sofamor Danek, Inc. v. Michelson*, 2003 WL 23200031 (W.D.Tenn. 2003); *Security Ins. Co. of Hartford v. DHL Worldwide Exp. NV*, 2001 WL 55460 (N.D.Ill. 2001).

29. The Advisory Committee Note to Rule 36(a).

30. *Epling v. UCB Films, Inc.*, 2000 WL 1466216 (D.Kan.2000).

31. *See In the Matter of the Complaint of Fisherman's Wharf Fillet, Inc.*, 83 F.Supp.2d 651, 660–61 (E.D.Va.1999).

32. *National Semiconductor Corp. v. Ramtron International Corp.*, 265 F.Supp.2d 71 (D.D.C.2003); *Johnson International Co. v. Jackson National Life Ins. Co.*, 812 F.Supp. 966 (D.Neb.1993), *affirmed*, 19 F.3d 431 (8th Cir. 1994).

33. *Johnson International Co. v. Jackson National Life Ins. Co.*, 19 F.3d 431 (8th Cir.1994).

RULE 36(b). EFFECT OF ADMISSION

CORE CONCEPT

An admission is deemed conclusively established unless the court permits withdrawal or amendment of the admission.[34]

APPLICATIONS

Proceedings Covered

An admission is only binding within the action in which the request was served.[35] An admission may be introduced at trial or in the context of a motion, such as a motion for summary judgment.[36]

Evidentiary Objections

Admissions are still subject to evidentiary objections at trial, such as hearsay.[37] However, adverse parties can use the exception to the hearsay rule for admissions of party opponents.[38]

Party Making Admission

The party making the admission may not introduce it at trial.[39]

Coparties Not Bound

An admission will only be binding on the admitting party and will not be binding on any coparties.[40]

Withdrawal

A party may move to withdraw or amend an admission.[41] The court may allow withdrawal or amendment when it will aid in the resolution of the matter on the merits and when the party who obtained the admission will not be prejudiced by the amendment or withdrawal.[42]

34. *Tate v. Farmland Industries, Inc.*, 268 F.3d 989, 998–99 (10th Cir.2001); *T. Rowe Price Small-Cap Fund, Inc. v. Oppenheimer & Co., Inc.*, 174 F.R.D. 38, 44 (S.D.N.Y.1997) ("Rule 36 responses become, in effect, sworn evidence that is binding upon the respondent at trial.").

35. *American Civil Liberties Union v. The Florida Bar*, 999 F.2d 1486 (11th Cir.1993); *Bell v. Domino's Pizza, Inc.*, 2000 WL 1780266 (D.D.C.2000).

36. *Essex Ins. Co. v. McManus*, 299 F.Supp.2d 939, 942 (E.D.Mo. 2003); *Eber v. Harris County Hosp. Dist.*, 130 F.Supp.2d 847, 853 (S.D.Tex.2001).

37. *Walsh v. McCain Foods Ltd.*, 81 F.3d 722, 726 (7th Cir.1996).

38. *Id.*

39. *In re Air Crash*, 982 F.Supp. 1060, 1067 (D.S.C.1996), *aff'd*, 105 F.3d 1042 (5th Cir.1997), *cert. denied*, 522 U.S. 824, 118 S.Ct. 82, 139 L.Ed.2d 40 (1997).

40. *Becerra v. Asher*, 921 F.Supp. 1538, 1544 (S.D.Tex.1996), *cert. denied*, 522 U.S. 824, 118 S.Ct. 82, 139 L.Ed.2d 40 (1997).

41. *In re Carney*, 258 F.3d 415, 419 (5th Cir.2001) (discussing the standards for a motion to withdraw an admission). *Kalis v. Colgate–Palmolive Co.*, 231 F.3d 1049, 1059 (7th Cir. 2000) (the proper procedural vehicle to withdraw admissions is a motion under Rule 36(b)).

42. *Gallegos v. City of Los Angeles*, 308 F.3d 987, 993 (9th Cir.2002) (The prejudice relates to the difficulty a party may face in proving its case, such as problems caused by the unavailability of key witnesses, or the sudden need to obtain evidence with respect to the questions previously deemed admitted); *Perez v. Miami–Dade County*, 297 F.3d 1255, 1265 (11th Cir. 2002), *cert. denied*, 537 U.S. 1193, 123 S.Ct.

Normally, changed circumstances or honest error will be valid grounds.[43] Amendment or withdrawal will not be allowed where prejudice will result to the opponent from reliance on the admission.[44] The court has broad discretion in ruling on motions to withdraw or amend admissions.[45]

Binding Nature of Formal Admissions

A matter formally admitted under Rule 36 is conclusively established.[46] In contrast, an informal, extrajudicial admission is evidence, but not conclusive.[47]

Proof of Admission by Failure to Answer

In order to use the failure to answer as an admission, the offering party must prove service of the requests and the failure to answer.[48]

ADDITIONAL RESEARCH REFERENCES

Wright & Miller, *Federal Practice and Procedure* §§ 2251–2265.

C.J.S. Federal Civil Procedure §§ 756–774 et seq.

West's Key No. Digests, Federal Civil Procedure ⚷1671–1686.

1291, 154 L.Ed.2d 1028 (2003) (a district court abuses its discretion in denying a motion to withdraw or amend admissions when it applies some other criterion beyond the two-part test—or grossly misapplies the two-part test—in making its ruling).

43. *See ADM Agri–Industries, Ltd. v. Harvey*, 200 F.R.D. 467 (M.D.Ala.2001) (courts should be reluctant to deny motions to withdraw or amend when final disposition of the case may result from mere discovery noncompliance rather than the merits).

44. *Sonoda v. Cabrera*, 255 F.3d 1035, 1039 (9th Cir.2001) (prejudice refers to the difficulty the non-moving party will have in proving its case, such as by the unavailability of witnesses related to the delay); *In re: Durability Inc.*, 212 F.3d 551 (10th Cir.2000) (the court's focus in a motion to withdraw an admission is the prejudice on the opposing party, not on the excuse of the moving party).

45. *Kress v. Food Employers Labor Relations Ass'n*, 285 F.Supp.2d 678, (D.Md. 2003); *Nguyen v. CNA Corp.,* 44 F.3d 234 (4th Cir.1995); *Rohman v. Chemical Leaman Tank Lines, Inc.*, 923 F.Supp. 42, 46 (S.D.N.Y.1996)(holding that although party failed to respond and failed to provide an explanation for not responding to a request for admission, the subject of the request was too important to the merits of the case not to be presented).

46. *In re Carney*, 258 F.3d 415, 420 (5th Cir.2001); *ADM Agri–Industries, Ltd. v. Harvey*, 200 F.R.D. 467 (M.D.Ala. 2001).

47. *Murrey v. United States*, 73 F.3d 1448, 1455 (7th Cir.1996).

48. *Gilbert v. General Motors Corp.,* 133 F.2d 997 (2d Cir.1943), *cert. denied,* 319 U.S. 743, 63 S.Ct. 1031, 87 L.Ed. 1700 (1943).

RULE 37

FAILURE TO MAKE DISCLOSURE OR COOPERATE IN DISCOVERY: SANCTIONS

(a) Motion for Order Compelling Disclosure or Discovery. A party, upon reasonable notice to other parties and all persons affected thereby, may apply for an order compelling disclosure or discovery as follows:

(1) *Appropriate Court.* An application for an order to a party shall be made to the court in which the action is pending. An application for an order to a person who is not a party shall be made to the court in the district where the discovery is being, or is to be, taken.

(2) *Motion.*

(A) If a party fails to make a disclosure required by Rule 26(a), any other party may move to compel disclosure and for appropriate sanctions. The motion must include a certification that the movant has in good faith conferred or attempted to confer with the party not making the disclosure in an effort to secure the disclosure without court action.

(B) If a deponent fails to answer a question propounded or submitted under Rules 30 or 31, or a corporation or other entity fails to make a designation under Rule 30(b)(6) or 31(a), or a party fails to answer an interrogatory submitted under Rule 33, or if a party, in response to a request for inspection submitted under Rule 34, fails to respond that inspection will be permitted as requested or fails to permit inspection as requested, the discovering party may move for an order compelling an answer, or a designation, or an order compelling inspection in accordance with the request. The motion must include a certification that the movant has in good faith conferred or attempted to confer with the person or party failing to make the discovery in an effort to secure the information or material without court action. When taking a deposition on oral examination, the proponent of the question may complete or adjourn the examination before applying for an order.

(3) *Evasive or Incomplete Disclosure, Answer, or Response.* For purposes of this subdivision an evasive or incomplete disclo-

sure, answer, or response is to be treated as a failure to disclose, answer, or respond.

(4) *Expenses and Sanctions.*

(A) If the motion is granted or if the disclosure or requested discovery is provided after the motion was filed, the court shall, after affording an opportunity to be heard, require the party or deponent whose conduct necessitated the motion or the party or attorney advising such conduct or both of them to pay to the moving party the reasonable expenses incurred in making the motion, including attorney's fees, unless the court finds that the motion was filed without the movant's first making a good faith effort to obtain the disclosure or discovery without court action, or that the opposing party's nondisclosure, response, or objection was substantially justified, or that other circumstances make an award of expenses unjust.

(B) If the motion is denied, the court may enter any protective order authorized under Rule 26(c) and shall, after affording an opportunity to be heard, require the moving party or the attorney filing the motion or both of them to pay to the party or deponent who opposed the motion the reasonable expenses incurred in opposing the motion, including attorney's fees, unless the court finds that the making of the motion was substantially justified or that other circumstances make an award of expenses unjust.

(C) If the motion is granted in part and denied in part, the court may enter any protective order authorized under Rule 26(c) and may, after affording an opportunity to be heard, apportion the reasonable expenses incurred in relation to the motion among the parties and persons in a just manner.

(b) Failure to Comply With Order.

(1) *Sanctions by Court in District Where Deposition Is Taken.* If a deponent fails to be sworn or to answer a question after being directed to do so by the court in the district in which the deposition is being taken, the failure may be considered a contempt of that court.

(2) *Sanctions by Court in Which Action Is Pending.* If a party or an officer, director, or managing agent of a party or a person designated under Rule 30(b)(6) or 31(a) to testify on behalf of a party fails to obey an order to provide or permit discovery, including an order made under subdivision (a) of this rule or Rule 35, or

if a party fails to obey an order entered under Rule 26(f), the court in which the action is pending may make such orders in regard to the failure as are just, and among others the following:

(A) An order that the matters regarding which the order was made or any other designated facts shall be taken to be established for the purposes of the action in accordance with the claim of the party obtaining the order;

(B) An order refusing to allow the disobedient party to support or oppose designated claims or defenses, or prohibiting that party from introducing designated matters in evidence;

(C) An order striking out pleadings or parts thereof, or staying further proceedings until the order is obeyed, or dismissing the action or proceeding or any part thereof, or rendering a judgment by default against the disobedient party;

(D) In lieu of any of the foregoing orders or in addition thereto, an order treating as a contempt of court the failure to obey any orders except an order to submit to a physical or mental examination;

(E) Where a party has failed to comply with an order under Rule 35(a) requiring that party to produce another for examination, such orders as are listed in paragraphs (A), (B), and (C) of this subdivision, unless the party failing to comply shows that that party is unable to produce such person for examination.

In lieu of any of the foregoing orders or in addition thereto, the court shall require the party failing to obey the order or the attorney advising that party or both to pay the reasonable expenses, including attorney's fees, caused by the failure, unless the court finds that the failure was substantially justified or that other circumstances make an award of expenses unjust.

(c) Failure to Disclose; False or Misleading Disclosure; Refusal to Admit.

(1) A party that without substantial justification fails to disclose information required by Rule 26(a) or 26(e)(1), or to amend a prior response to discovery as required by Rule 26(e)(2), is not, unless such failure is harmless, permitted to use as evidence at a trial, at a hearing, or on a motion any witness or information not so disclosed. In addition to or in lieu of this sanction, the court, on motion and after affording an opportunity to be heard, may impose

other appropriate sanctions. In addition to requiring payment of reasonable expenses, including attorney's fees, caused by the failure, these sanctions may include any of the actions authorized under Rule 37(b)(2)(A), (B), and (C) and may include informing the jury of the failure to make the disclosure.

(2) If a party fails to admit the genuineness of any document or the truth of any matter as requested under Rule 36, and if the party requesting the admissions thereafter proves the genuineness of the document or the truth of the matter, the requesting party may apply to the court for an order requiring the other party to pay the reasonable expenses incurred in making that proof, including reasonable attorney's fees. The court shall make the order unless it finds that (A) the request was held objectionable pursuant to Rule 36(a), or (B) the admission sought was of no substantial importance, or (C) the party failing to admit had reasonable ground to believe that the party might prevail on the matter, or (D) there was other good reason for the failure to admit.

(d) Failure of Party to Attend at Own Deposition or Serve Answers to Interrogatories or Respond to Request for Inspection. If a party or an officer, director, or managing agent of a party or a person designated under Rule 30(b)(6) or 31(a) to testify on behalf of a party fails (1) to appear before the officer who is to take the deposition, after being served with a proper notice, or (2) to serve answers or objections to interrogatories submitted under Rule 33, after proper service of the interrogatories, or (3) to serve a written response to a request for inspection submitted under Rule 34, after proper service of the request, the court in which the action is pending on motion may make such orders in regard to the failure as are just, and among others it may take any action authorized under subparagraphs (A), (B), and (C) of subdivision (b)(2) of this rule. Any motion specifying a failure under clause (2) or (3) of this subdivision shall include a certification that the movant has in good faith conferred or attempted to confer with the party failing to answer or respond in an effort to obtain such answer or response without court action. In lieu of any order or in addition thereto, the court shall require the party failing to act or the attorney advising that party or both to pay the reasonable expenses, including attorney's fees, caused by the failure unless the court finds that the failure was substantially justified or that other circumstances make an award of expenses unjust.

The failure to act described in this subdivision may not be excused on the ground that the discovery sought is objectionable unless the party failing to act has a pending motion for a protective order as provided by Rule 26(c).

(e) Subpoena of Person in Foreign Country [Abrogated].

(f) Expenses Against United States [Repealed].

(g) Failure to Participate in the Framing of a Discovery Plan. If a party or a party's attorney fails to participate in good faith in the development and submission of a proposed discovery plan as required by Rule 26(f), the court may, after opportunity for hearing, require such party or attorney to pay to any other party the reasonable expenses, including attorney's fees, caused by the failure.

[Amended December 29, 1948, effective October 20, 1949; March 30, 1970, effective July 1, 1970; April 29, 1980, effective August 1, 1980; amended by Pub.L. 96–481, Title II, § 205(a), October 21, 1980, 94 Stat. 2330, effective October 1, 1981; amended March 2, 1987, effective August 1, 1987; April 22, 1993, effective December 1, 1993; April 17, 2000, effective December 1, 2000.]

AUTHORS' COMMENTARY ON RULE 37

PURPOSE AND SCOPE

Rule 37 contains the mechanisms for enforcing the provisions of the other discovery rules by imposing sanctions on parties who violate the Rules. In general, obtaining sanctions is a two-step process in which a party must first obtain an order compelling discovery under Rule 37(a), then move for sanctions under Rule 37(b) for failure to comply with the order. If, however, the responding party totally fails to respond to an entire discovery request, the sanctions may be available immediately.

NOTE: Rule 37 was revised in 1993 and 2000, and care should be exercised when citing case law pertaining to Rule 37.

RULE 37(a). MOTION FOR ORDER COMPELLING DISCLOSURE OR DISCOVERY

CORE CONCEPT

The first step in obtaining sanctions is to make a motion for an order compelling the discovery sought.[1] A motion to compel is filed after the opponent fails to make the automatic disclosures required by Rule 26(a), fails to respond to discovery served pursuant to the discov-

1. *Helfand v. Gerson*, 105 F.3d 530, 536 (9th Cir.1997) (failure to bring a motion to compel is a waiver of any future objections).

ery rules, or makes an improper or incomplete disclosure or discovery response.

APPLICATIONS

Procedures

Motions to compel are served on all parties and filed with the court.

Certification of Conference

The motion to compel must be accompanied by a certification that the movant has in good faith conferred or attempted to confer with the other party or person in an effort to resolve the dispute without court action.[2]

Which Court

The proper court in which to file a motion to compel depends on the location and status of the person that is the subject of the motion. If the individual or entity is a party, then a motion to compel must be filed in the court where the action is pending. If the motion to compel pertains to a non-party witness, pursuant to a subpoena for deposition or to produce documents, then only the court issuing the subpoena can enforce it through the court's contempt powers.[3]

Expenses

In general, the victorious party in a motion to compel is entitled to recover its expenses, including a reasonable attorney fee,[4] from the losing party.[5] The movant is also entitled to expenses if the respondent provides a disclosure or discovery response after the motion was filed.[6] The award of expenses by the court is mandatory unless the movant failed to confer with the respondent in good faith prior to filing the motion or the losing party demonstrates that its conduct was "substantially justified,"[7] or if other circumstances render an award of expenses

2. *Naviant Marketing Solutions, Inc. v. Larry Tucker, Inc.*, 339 F.3d 180 (3rd Cir. 2003); *LaFleur v. Teen Help*, 342 F.3d 1145, 1152 (10th Cir. 2003); *Kalis v. Colgate–Palmolive Co.*, 231 F.3d 1049, 1059 (7th Cir.2000); *Williams v. Board of County Com'rs of Unified Government of Wyandotte County and Kansas City, Kan.*, 192 F.R.D. 698, 699 (D.Kan.2000) (a single letter between counsel addressing a discovery dispute does not satisfy the duty to confer); *but see Oleson v. Kmart Corp.*, 175 F.R.D. 570, 571 (D.Kan.1997) (entertaining a motion for sanctions where the correspondence between the parties indicated that the dispute would not have been resolved by additional efforts to confer).

3. See Rule 45 (discussing subpoenas). *But see Platypus Wear, Inc. v. K.D. Co.*, 905 F.Supp. 808, 810 (S.D.Cal.1995)(holding that a disputed claim of privilege should be presented to the court where the action is pending regardless of the location of the deposition).

4. *Cobell v. Norton*, 231 F.Supp.2d 295 (D.D.C.2002) (discussing the calculation of a reasonable attorney fee).

5. *See Interactive Products Corp. v. a2z Mobile Office Solutions, Inc.*, 326 F.3d 687, 700 (6th Cir.2003) (motion for leave to take depositions deemed motion to compel, and expenses awarded against unsuccessful movant); *Stein v. Foamex Intern., Inc.*, 204 F.R.D. 270, 271 (E.D.Pa. 2001) (court may not reduce the amount of attorney fees awarded if the amount claimed is demonstrated to be reasonable).

6. *Tuszkiewicz v. Allen–Bradley Co., Inc.*, 172 F.R.D. 396, 398 (E.D.Wis.1997).

7. *Dolquist v. Heartland Presbytery*, 221 F.R.D. 564 (D.Kan. 2004).

"unjust."[8]

- *Substantially Justified:* The precise meaning of "substantially justified" is not well-defined. Good faith is generally not enough; the losing party must demonstrate some unsettled issue of law or like circumstance.[9] The burden is on the losing party to show that the party's behavior was "substantially justified."
- *Opportunity to be Heard*: The court must provide the non-moving party with an opportunity to be heard, either orally or in writing.[10]
- *Who Pays Expenses:* The court may impose the expenses on the party, the attorney, or both.[11]
- *Motion Granted in Part:* If a motion to compel is granted in part and denied in part, the court may apportion the expenses as it sees fit.[12]
- *Non-parties:* The expense provisions apply only to certain motions involving non-parties.[13] Fees will be awarded in connection with a non-party making a motion to obtain a copy of the non-party's statement. A non-party may be required to pay expenses incurred because of the non-party's failure to attend a deposition if a court order had already been entered compelling the non-party's attendance.
- *Applicable Discovery Motions:* The expense provisions apply to all but a small group of discovery motions. The expense provisions do *not* apply to: Rule 27—(petition to perpetuate testimony); Rule 28(b)—(application for a commission or letter rogatory to take a deposition in a foreign country); Rule 30(a)—(motion for leave of court to take a deposition); Rule 30(b)(3)—(motion to enlarge or shorten the time for taking a deposition); Rule 30(b)(4)—(motion that testimony at a deposition be recorded by other than stenographic means); Rule 33(a)—(motion that a shorter or longer time be allowed to answer interrogatories); Rule 34(b)—(motion that a shorter or longer time be allowed to serve a response to a request for inspection); Rule 35(a)—(motion to compel a physical or mental examination); Rule

8. *Rickels v. City of South Bend, Ind.*, 33 F.3d 785 (7th Cir.1994); *PLX, Inc. v. Prosystems, Inc.*, 220 F.R.D. 291, 298 (N.D.W.Va. 2004) (the losing party has the burden of showing that fees should not be awarded).

9. *Pierce v. Underwood,* 487 U.S. 552, 565, 108 S.Ct. 2541, 2550, 101 L.Ed.2d 490 (1988); *Neumont v. Monroe County, Fla.*, 220 F.R.D. 380, 382 (S.D.Fla. 2004) (a party's objection is substantially justified if reasonable people could differ as to the appropriateness of the contested action).

10. *McCoo v. Denny's Inc.*, 192 F.R.D. 675 (D.Kan.2000) (written submissions provide an adequate opportunity to be heard).

11. *Hoffman v. United Parcel Service, Inc.*, 206 F.R.D. 506, 507 (D.Kan.2002) (fees should be imposed on the person or entity responsible for the sanctionable conduct).

12. *Sonnino v. University Kansas Hosp. Authority*, 220 F.R.D. 633, 656 (D.Kan. 2004); *Alexander v. Federal Bureau of Investigation*, 192 F.R.D. 23 (D.D.C.2000).

13. *Athridge v. Aetna Casualty and Surety Co.*, 184 F.R.D. 200, 208 (D.D.C.1998); *Cuthbertson v. Excel Industries, Inc.*, 179 F.R.D. 599, 602 (D.Kan.1998) (non-party who appeared voluntarily at a deposition without subpoena was not subject to the court's jurisdiction or to sanctions).

35(b)(1)—(motion to compel delivery of report of a physical or mental examination); Rule 37(c)—(motion to assess expenses for failure to make requested admission); and Rule 45(d)(1)—(motion to compel deponent to permit inspection and copying of documents and things subpoenaed for deposition).

- *Fees From United States:* Attorney fees can be awarded against the United States.[14]
- *Appeal of Fee Award:* An award of attorney fees under Rule 37(a)(4) is not a final, applicable order.[15]

Basis for Motion to Compel

Generally, a motion to compel may only be filed after a discovery request has been properly served and the opposing party has failed to respond. A motion to compel may be filed after a witness improperly refuses to answer a deposition question.[16] A party cannot bring a motion to compel where the subject is not a discovery request to which the other party has not adequately responded.[17]

Evasive or Incomplete Answer

Rule 37(a)(3) states that an evasive or incomplete answer or disclosure is treated as a failure to answer or disclose.[18]

Motion Denied

If a motion to compel is denied, the court can at the same time enter a protective order under Rule 26(c).

RULE 37(b). FAILURE TO COMPLY WITH ORDER

CORE CONCEPT

The sanctions listed in Rule 37(b) become available if a party or deponent fails to obey a court order regarding discovery. The court has broad discretion to impose one or more[19] of the listed sanctions or any other sanction it deems appropriate.[20]

14. *United States v. Horn,* 29 F.3d 754 (1st Cir.1994)(fees may be assessed against the United States as a sanction); *Cook v. Watt,* 597 F.Supp. 552 (D.Alaska 1984).

15. *Cunningham v. Hamilton County, Ohio,* 527 U.S. 198, 200, 119 S.Ct. 1915, 1917, 144 L.Ed.2d 184 (1999) (fee award against attorney is not immediately appealable even if attorney has withdrawn).

16. *Cabana v. Forcier,* 200 F.R.D. 9 (D.Mass. 2001).

17. *Mitchell v. National R.R. Passenger Corp.,* 217 F.R.D. 53, 57–58 (D.D.C. 2003) (prevailing party not entitled to expenses under Rule 37(a) where motion was to take additional depositions).

18. *Dotson v. Bravo,* 321 F.3d 663, 667 (7th Cir.2003) (incomplete or evasive responses to interrogatories can support dismissal of the entire action).

19. *Young v. Office of U.S. Senate Sergeant at Arms,* 217 F.R.D. 61, 65, n.2 (D.D.C. 2003) (the sanctions are not mutually exclusive)

20. *Anderson v. Foundation for Advancement, Education and Employment of American Indians,* 155 F.3d 500, 504 (4th Cir.1998).

APPLICATIONS

Order Prerequisite

The court may not impose sanctions under Rule 37(b) unless it has already issued a discovery order with which a party or deponent has failed to comply.[21] The order may be pursuant to a motion to compel under Rule 37(a) or may be issued in a discovery conference under Rule 26(f).[22] Note, however, that the court may impose certain sanctions under Rules 37(c) and 37(d) without having first issued a discovery order, under the circumstances discussed below.

Sanctions by Court Where Deposition to Occur

If a non-party witness fails to comply with an order to appear and be sworn in for a deposition or an order to answer a question at a deposition, the court in the district where the deposition was to occur may treat the failure as a contempt of court under Rule 37(b)(1).[23]

Sanctions by Court Where Action Pending

Rule 37(b)(2) lists specific categories of sanctions that may be imposed by the court where the action is pending on a party who fails to obey an order to permit or provide discovery:

- *Deem Facts Established:* The court may deem as established the facts that the moving party was seeking to establish.[24] Thus, where an individual claiming to be totally disabled refused to submit to a physical examination, the court deemed it established that he was not totally disabled.[25]
- *Prohibit Evidence:* The court may refuse to allow the disobedient party to introduce certain matters into evidence, or to support or oppose certain claims.[26] Thus, where a party failed to comply

21. *In re: Williams*, 156 F.3d 86, 89 n. 1 (1st Cir.1998), *cert. denied*, 525 U.S. 1123, 119 S.Ct. 905, 142 L.Ed.2d 904 (1999); *Nike Inc. v. Wolverine World Wide, Inc.*, 43 F.3d 644 (Fed.Cir. 1994)(oral order sufficient to support sanctions); *United States v. Matusoff Rental Co.*, 204 F.R.D. 396, 398 (S.D.Ohio 2001). *But see Dotson v. Bravo*, 202 F.R.D. 559, 570 (N.D.Ill. 2001) (a prior order is not required when extreme discovery abuses have occurred).

22. *Lipscher v. LRP Publications, Inc.*, 266 F.3d 1305, 1322–23 (11th Cir.2001) (Rule 37(b) sanctions not available for violation of a protective order under Rule 26(c)), *but see Paul Revere Life Ins. Co. v. Jafari*, 206 F.R.D. 126, 127 (D.Md.2002) (allowing sanctions for violation of a protective order). *Buffalo Carpenters Pension Fund v. CKG Ceiling and Partition Co., Inc.*, 192 F.R.D. 95 (W.D.N.Y.2000) (sanctions may be imposed for failure to comply with any discovery order, not just an order under Rule 37(a)).

23. *In re: Sealed Case*, 141 F.3d 337 (D.C.Cir.1998).

24. Rule 37(b)(2)(A); *Insurance Corp. of Ireland, Ltd. v. Compagnie des Bauxites de Guinee*, 456 U.S. 694, 102 S.Ct. 2099, 72 L.Ed.2d 492 (1982)(deeming personal jurisdiction established as a discovery sanction); *Navellier v. Sletten*, 262 F.3d 923, 947–48 (9th Cir.2001), *cert. denied* 536 U.S. 941, 122 S.Ct. 2623, 153 L.Ed.2d 806 (2002) (deeming breach of duty established when witness failed to answer questions at a deposition after being ordered to do so); *Knowlton v. Teltrust Phones, Inc.*, 189 F.3d 1177, 1182 (10th Cir.1999) (deeming certain facts established can be tantamount to summary judgment, triggering a higher level of scrutiny).

25. *McMullen v. Travelers Ins. Co.*, 278 F.2d 834 (9th Cir.1960), *cert. denied*, 364 U.S. 867, 81 S.Ct. 110, 5 L.Ed.2d 89 (1960).

26. *In re TMI Litigation*, 193 F.3d 613, 721 (3d Cir.1999), *cert. denied*, 530 U.S. 1225, 120 S.Ct. 2238, 147 L.Ed.2d 266 (2000) (listing the factors for the exclusion of evidence); *Trilogy Communications, Inc. v. Times Fiber Communications, Inc.*, 109 F.3d 739, 745 (Fed.Cir.1997)

with discovery orders regarding damages, the party was precluded from offering evidence as to its damages.[27]

- *Strike Pleadings:* The court may strike any pleading or portion of a pleading.[28]
- *Issue Stay:* The court may stay further proceedings until the order is obeyed.[29]
- *Dispositive Ruling:* In extreme situations, the court may dismiss an action or portions of the action.[30] The court may also enter judgment against the disobedient party.[31]
- *Contempt:* The court may treat the failure to obey its order as a contempt of court,[32] with the exception of a failure to submit to a mental or physical examination (which is punishable by other sanctions, but not as contempt).[33]

List Not Exclusive

The court is not limited to the sanctions listed in Rule 37(b)(2), and may make any order that is "just." [34] In practice, however, courts generally have imposed only those sanctions listed.

Failure to Produce Another for Examination

If a party fails to comply with an order to produce another for a mental or physical examination, the party is subject to the same

(barring expert testimony submitted after due date for expert reports had passed); *Melendez v. Illinois Bell Tel. Co.*, 79 F.3d 661, 671–72 (7th Cir.1996)(barring expert's testimony concerning the validity of a standardized cognitive ability test when the party failed to disclose that there was an ongoing project to revise the test).

27. *Ware v. Rodale Press, Inc.*, 322 F.3d 218 (3rd Cir.2003).

28. *See Creative Gifts, Inc. v. UFO*, 235 F.3d 540, 544 (10th Cir.2000).

29. Rule 37(b)(2)(C).

30. *Young v. Gordon*, 330 F.3d 76, 81 (1st Cir.2003) (disobedience of court orders is inimical to the orderly administration of justice and, in and of itself, can constitute extreme misconduct); *Rio Properties, Inc. v. Rio Intern. Interlink*, 284 F.3d 1007, 1022 (9th Cir. 2002)(describing 5 factors for evaluating dismissal as a sanction), *cert. denied*, 526 U.S. 1064, 119 S.Ct. 1455, 143 L.Ed.2d 542 (1999); *Simmons v. Chatham Nursing Home, Inc.*, 93 F.Supp.2d 1265 (S.D.Ga.2000) (dismissal pursuant to Rule 37 deemed on the merits and with prejudice). *See also Atchison, Topeka and Santa Fe Railway Co. v. Hercules Inc.*, 146 F.3d 1071, 1074 (9th Cir.1998) (court may not dismiss a separate but related action).

31. Rule 37(b)(2)(C); *Computer Task Group, Inc. v. Brotby*, 364 F.3d 1112, 1115 (9th Cir. 2004) (listing 5 factors for imposing sanction of default); *Fair Housing of Marin v. Combs*, 285 F.3d 899, 905 (9th Cir.2002), *cert. denied*, 537 U.S. 1018, 123 S.Ct. 536, 154 L.Ed.2d 425 (2002) (judgment as a sanction is appropriate only in extreme circumstances); *Chrysler Corp. v. Carey*, 186 F.3d 1016, 1022 (8th Cir.1999).

32. *General Ins. Co. v. Eastern Consol. Util., Inc.*, 126 F.3d 215, 220 (3d Cir.1997) (a nonparty may be held in contempt of court for violating an order requiring the nonparty to produce documents and attend a deposition); *Maynard v. Nygren*, 332 F.3d 462, 470 (7th Cir.2003) (fines are permissible sanctions).

33. Rule 37(b)(2)(D).

34. *Valley Engineers Inc. v. Electric Engineering Co.*, 158 F.3d 1051, 1056 (9th Cir.1998) (justice is the central factor in a sanctions order under rule 37(b)), *cert. denied*, 526 U.S. 1064, 119 S.Ct. 1455, 143 L.Ed.2d 542 (1999); *Harris v. City of Philadelphia*, 47 F.3d 1311 (3d Cir. 1995); *Thompson v. U.S. Dept. of Housing and*

sanctions that would apply if the party failed to appear, unless the party can show that the party was unable to produce the individual.[35]

Multiple Sanctions

The court may impose any combination of sanctions it deems appropriate.[36]

Expenses

The court will also require the party not complying with the court order and/or the party's attorney[37] to pay all expenses, including a reasonable attorney fee, incurred by the moving party as a result of the failure to comply.[38] This includes expenses incurred in the motion for sanctions, but not expenses incurred in obtaining the order compelling the discovery (although these expenses may be recoverable under Rule 37(a) as discussed above). The court must award such expenses unless it finds that the failure was "substantially justified" or that other circumstances exist that would make the award "unjust."[39] The amount of monetary damages must be related to the expenses incurred as a result of the violations.[40]

Corporate Representative

The court may also impose sanctions on a party that is a corporation or organization if its officer, director, managing agent, or designated representative fails to obey an order.[41] The party noticing the deposition will have the burden of showing that the person had the necessary relationship to the corporation.

Waiver of Sanctions

A party might be deemed to have waived its rights to sanctions by not strictly enforcing the order, such as by failing to make attempts to schedule a physical examination[42] or by failing to bring a motion for sanctions in a reasonable period of time.[43]

Conflicts with Regulations

Where compliance with a discovery order would force a party to violate a federal agency regulation, compliance with the discovery order

Urban Development, 219 F.R.D. 93, 101 (D.Md. 2003) (list of sanctions is non-exclusive).

35. *Societe Internationale v. Rogers*, 357 U.S. 197, 78 S.Ct. 1087, 2 L.Ed.2d 1255 (1958).

36. *See O'Neill v. AGWI Lines*, 74 F.3d 93 (5th Cir.1996)(dismissing the action and imposing attorney's fees).

37. *Stuart I. Levin & Associates, P.A. v. Rogers*, 156 F.3d 1135, 1140 (11th Cir.1998); *Heath v. F/V ZOLOTOI*, 221 F.R.D. 545 (W.D.Wash. 2004).

38. *Watkins & Son Pet Supplies v. Iams Co.*, 197 F.Supp.2d 1030, 1032 (S.D.Ohio 2002) (attorney fees must be reasonable); *Cobell v. Babbitt*, 188 F.R.D. 122, 125 (D.D.C.1999) (discussing the calculation of the attorney fees award).

39. *Koehler v. Bank of Bermuda, Ltd.*, 2003 WL 289640 (S.D.N.Y.2003).

40. *Tollett v. City of Kemah*, 285 F.3d 357 (5th Cir.2002), *cert. denied*, 537 U.S. 883, 123 S.Ct. 105, 154 L.Ed.2d 141 (2002) (discussing the method of proving attorney fees); *Martin v. Brown*, 63 F.3d 1252, 1263–64 (3d Cir.1995).

41. *Bon Air Hotel, Inc. v. Time, Inc.*, 376 F.2d 118 (5th Cir.1967), *cert. denied*, 393 U.S. 859, 89 S.Ct. 131, 21 L.Ed.2d 127 (1968).

42. *Hinson v. Michigan Mut. Liability Co.*, 275 F.2d 537 (5th Cir.1960).

43. *United States Fidelity & Guar. Co. v. Baker Material Handling, Corp.*, 62 F.3d 24, 29 (1st Cir.1995); *Tolliver v. Federal Republic of Nigeria*, 265 F.Supp.2d 873 (W.D.Mich.2003).

will be excused.[44]

Appeals

The entry of sanctions under Rule 37 is reviewed under the abuse of discretion standard.[45]

RULE 37(c). FAILURE TO DISCLOSE; FALSE OR MISLEADING DISCLOSURE; REFUSAL TO ADMIT

CORE CONCEPT

If a party improperly fails to make the automatic disclosures under Rule 26(a) or makes false or misleading disclosures, or if a party fails to supplement a prior discovery response as required by Rule 26(e)(2), the party is subject to a variety of sanctions. If a party improperly fails to admit a matter, Rule 37(c) imposes on that party the cost to the other party in proving the matter.

APPLICATIONS

Failure to Disclose

If a party fails to make the automatic disclosures under Rule 26(a) in a timely manner[46] or makes false or misleading disclosures, the party will not be permitted to use at trial or in a motion[47] the documents or witnesses[48] not properly disclosed, unless the party had "substantial justification"[49] or the failure was harmless.[50]

Failure to Supplement

If a party fails to supplement a prior discovery response as required under Rule 26(e)(2), the party will not be permitted to use at trial the documents, information, opinions,[51] or witnesses not properly disclosed,

44. *In re Bankers Trust Co.*, 61 F.3d 465, 469–70 (6th Cir.1995) *cert. dismissed,* 517 U.S. 1205, 116 S.Ct. 1711, 134 L.Ed.2d 808 (1996).

45. *Computer Task Group, Inc. v. Brotby*, 364 F.3d 1112, 1115 (9th Cir. 2004) (sanctions reversed only if appellate court has a definite and firm conviction that the trial court committed a clear error of judgment); *In re Golant*, 239 F.3d 931, 37 Bankr.Ct.Dec. 106 (7th Cir.2001).

46. *Trost v. Trek Bicycle Corp.*, 162 F.3d 1004, 1008 (8th Cir.1998) (failure to disclose in a timely manner is equivalent to failure to disclose); *Transclean Corp. v. Bridgewood Services, Inc.*, 77 F.Supp.2d 1045, 1063 (D.Minn.1999), *affirmed in part, vacated in part on other grounds*, 290 F.3d 1364 (Fed.Cir.2002).

47. *Shepard v. Frontier Communications Services, Inc.*, 92 F.Supp.2d 279 (S.D.N.Y.2000).

48. *Musser v. Gentiva Health Services*, 356 F.3d 751, 758 (7th Cir. 2004).

49. *McCarthy v. Option One Mortg. Corp.*, 362 F.3d 1008, 1012 (7th Cir. 2004).

50. *Sommer v. Davis*, 317 F.3d 686, 692 (6th Cir.2003) (harmless involves an honest mistake on the part of a party coupled with sufficient knowledge on the part of the other party); *Wilson v. Bradlees of New England, Inc.*, 250 F.3d 10 (1st Cir.2001) (mandatory preclusion is the required sanction in the ordinary case); Saudi *v.* *Valmet–Appleton, Inc.*, 219 F.R.D. 128, 132, n.5 (E.D.Wis. 2003) (the 2000 Amendment that replaced "shall" with "is" was stylistic, and did not lessen the mandatory nature of the sanctions).

51. *Southern States Rack And Fixture, Inc. v. Sherwin–Williams Co.*, 318 F.3d 592, 595–96 (4th Cir.2003)

unless the party had "substantial justification" or the failure was harmless.[52]

Additional Sanctions

In addition to or in lieu of[53] precluding the evidence, upon motion and after an opportunity to be heard,[54] the court may impose additional sanctions, including:

- payment of reasonable expenses, including attorney and/or expert fees, caused by the failure;[55]
- informing the jury of the failure to make the disclosure;[56]
- deeming certain matters established;
- precluding the non-disclosing party from supporting or opposing designated claims or defenses;[57]
- striking pleadings or portions thereof;[58]
- staying the action pending proper disclosure; or
- dismissing or entering judgment as to part or all of the action.[59]

Failure to Admit

If a party fails to admit a matter that another party subsequently proves at trial,[60] the other party can move after trial for its reasonable expenses, including a reasonable attorney fee, incurred in proving the matter.[61] The court must then award expenses unless one of the following four conditions exists:

(1) The request was objectionable;[62]

52. *Wilson v. Bradlees of New England, Inc.*, 250 F.3d 10 (1st Cir.2001) (party seeking to avoid the sanction has the burden of demonstrating that the failure to supplement was substantially justified or harmless); *Fenje v. Feld*, 301 F.Supp.2d 781, 814–15 (N.D.Ill. 2003) (since the plaintiff was aware of the witnesses' roles, the failure to supplement was harmless); the Advisory Committee Note to the 2000 Amendment to Rule 37(c)(1).

53. *Dura Automotive Systems of Indiana, Inc. v. CTS Corp.*, 285 F.3d 609, 615–16 (7th Cir.2002) (additional sanctions may be imposed in lieu of evidence exclusion only if the failure to disclose was substantially justified).

54. *Paladin Associates, Inc. v. Montana Power Co.*, 328 F.3d 1145, 1164–65 (9th Cir. 2003)(the opportunity to submit briefs was an opportunity to be heard).

55. *Speedplay, Inc. v. Bebop, Inc.*, 211 F.3d 1245, 1260 (Fed.Cir.2000).

56. *Central States Indus. Supply, Inc. v. McCullough*, 279 F.Supp.2d 1005, 1025 (N.D.Iowa 2003); *Tarlton v. Cumberland County Correctional Facility*, 192 F.R.D. 165 (D.N.J. 2000).

57. *Patterson v. State Auto. Mut. Ins. Co.*, 105 F.3d 1251, 1252 (8th Cir.1997) (expert's testimony about his unannounced second visit to site was precluded due to prejudice on opposing party).

58. *Second Chance Body Armor, Inc. v. American Body Armor, Inc.*, 177 F.R.D. 633, 637 (N.D.Ill.1998).

59. *Maynard v. Nygren*, 332 F.3d 462, 467–68 (7th Cir.2003) (dismissal is a draconian sanction, and the circuit court will be vigilant in reviewing a dismissal sanction).

60. *Joseph v. Fratar*, 197 F.R.D. 20 (D.Mass. 2000) (motion for expenses for improper failure to admit may not be made until after trial).

61. *Bradshaw v. Thompson*, 454 F.2d 75 (6th Cir.1972), *cert. denied*, 409 U.S. 878, 93 S.Ct. 130, 34 L.Ed.2d 131 (1972); *National Semiconductor Corp. v. Ramtron International Corp.*, 265 F.Supp.2d 71 (D.D.C.2003).

62. *Russo v. Baxter Healthcare Corp.*, 51 F.Supp.2d 70, 78 (D.R.I.1999).

(2) The admission sought was of no substantial importance, such as when the proof of the matter was trivial;[63]

(3) The party refusing to admit had reasonable grounds to believe that it would be successful on the matter;[64] or

(4) Other good reasons exist for the failure to admit, such as a genuine inability to determine the truth of the matter.[65]

Party Only

Expenses and fees under Rule 37(c) may be awarded against the party only, not against the attorney, in contrast to other provisions of Rule 37.[66]

Improper Statement of Inability to Admit

The sanctions in Rule 37(c) apply to an improper statement of inability to admit or deny, as well as to an improper denial.

Failure to Respond to Requests for Admissions

The sanctions in Rule 37(c) do not apply to a failure to respond to a request for admissions because such a failure is deemed an admission.[67]

Explanation of Sanctions

The court order must state the basis for its decision to impose sanctions so that the appellate court can conduct a meaningful review.[68]

RULE 37(d). FAILURE OF A PARTY TO ATTEND AT OWN DEPOSITION OR SERVE ANSWERS TO INTERROGATORIES OR RESPOND TO REQUEST FOR INSPECTION

CORE CONCEPT

Rule 37(d) provides that upon motion sanctions are immediately available against a party who completely fails to participate in the discovery process.

APPLICATIONS

When Available

Sanctions under Rule 37(d) are available when the party fails to

63. *Read-Rite Corp. v. Burlington Air Express, Inc.*, 183 F.R.D. 545, 547 (N.D.Cal.1998).

64. *Mutual Service Ins. Co. v. Frit Industries, Inc.*, 358 F.3d 1312, 1326 (11th Cir. 2004) (the true test is not whether a party prevailed at trial, but whether it acted reasonably in believing that it might prevail); *Washington State Dep't of Transp. v. Washington Natural Gas Co.*, 59 F.3d 793, 805–06 (9th Cir.1995); *Caruthers v. Proctor & Gamble Manufacturing Co.*, 177 F.R.D. 667, 669 (D.Kan.1998).

65. *Maynard v. Nygren*, 332 F.3d 462, 470 (7th Cir.2003) (attorneys can be sanctioned for failure-to-disclose violations under Rule 26(g)(3)).

66. *Apex Oil Co. v. Belcher Co. of New York, Inc.*, 855 F.2d 1009, 1013–14 (2d Cir.1988).

67. *West Ky. Coal Co. v. Walling*, 153 F.2d 582, 587 (6th Cir.1946).

68. *Mutual Service Ins. Co. v. Frit Industries, Inc.*, 358 F.3d 1312, 1326 (11th Cir. 2004) ("[I]n cases invoking the sanction power of Rule 37 the district court must 'clearly state its reasons so that meaningful review may be had on appeal.' ").

appear for the party's deposition after being served with proper notice,[69] fails to answer or object to properly-served interrogatories,[70] or fails to serve a written response to a properly-served request to inspect documents or things. Thus, a court order is not a prerequisite to sanctions under Rule 37(d).[71] Rule 37(d) does not specify when the motion for sanctions must be filed, but some courts have held that the motion must be filed without "unreasonable delay,"[72] or before the entry of judgment.[73]

Certification of Conference

A motion for sanctions under Rule 37(d) for failure to respond to interrogatories or requests for inspection must include a certification that the movant has in good faith conferred or attempted to confer with the other party or person in an effort to obtain a response without court action.[74] Note that this requirement does not apply to the failure to appear for a deposition.[75]

Sanctions

Rule 37(d) states that the court may impose whatever sanctions as are "just,"[76] including those listed in Rules 37(b)(2)(A), (B), and (C), which are essentially the sanctions discussed above except for contempt of court sanctions.[77] The court has broad discretion in deciding what sanction to impose, and an award of sanctions is reviewed for abuse of discretion.[78] The court can consider all the circumstances, such as whether the failure was accidental or in bad faith in determining the sanctions to impose.[79]

Expenses

The court must require that the party failing to participate in discovery and/or the party's attorney pay the resulting expenses of the other party, including a reasonable attorney fee.[80] The court must award such expenses unless it finds that the failure was "substantially

69. *Haraway v. National Ass'n For Stock Car Auto Racing, Inc.*, 213 F.R.D. 161, 165 (D.Del. 2003).

70. *Jayne H. Lee, Inc. v. Flagstaff Indus. Corp.*, 173 F.R.D. 651, 653 (D.Md.1997).

71. *Guidry v. Continental Oil Co.*, 640 F.2d 523, 533 (5th Cir.1981), *cert. denied,* 454 U.S. 818, 102 S.Ct. 96, 70 L.Ed.2d 87 (1981); *Inmuno Vital, Inc. v. Telemundo Group, Inc.*, 203 F.R.D. 561, 566 (S.D.Fla.2001).

72. *See Lancaster v. Independent School District No. 5*, 149 F.3d 1228, 1237 (10th Cir.1998).

73. *See Mercy v. County of Suffolk*, 748 F.2d 52, 55–56 (2d Cir.1984).

74. *Black Horse Lane Assoc., L.P. v. Dow Chemical Corp.*, 228 F.3d 275, 301 (3d Cir.2000).

75. *Grand Oaks, Inc. v. A.W. Anderson*, 175 F.R.D. 247, 250 (N.D.Miss.1997).

76. *Coan v. Hutter*, 207 B.R. 981, 986 (Bkrtcy.D.Conn.1997).

77. *See Bishop v. First Mississippi Financial Group, Inc.*, 221 F.R.D. 461 (S.D.Miss. 2004) (dismissal for failure to appear at depositions and respond to motions); *Viswanathan v. Scotland County Bd. of Educ.*, 165 F.R.D. 50 (M.D.N.C.1995)(dismissing action after claimant failed to appear at a scheduled deposition three times), *affirmed,* 76 F.3d 377 (4th Cir.1996).

78. *Black Horse Lane Assoc., L.P. v. Dow Chemical Corp.*, 228 F.3d 275, 301 (3d Cir.2000); *Webb v. District of Columbia*, 146 F.3d 964 (D.C.Cir.1998).

79. *In re Sumitomo Copper Litigation*, 204 F.R.D. 58, 60–61 (S.D.N.Y.2001) (case dismissed based on willful failure to appear at deposition).

80. *Hyde & Drath v. Baker*, 24 F.3d 1162 (9th Cir.1994).

justified"[81] or that other circumstances exist that would make the award "unjust."[82] The award of expenses can be in addition to or instead of other sanctions.

Objections to Discovery/Protective Order

It is not a defense to a motion for sanctions under Rule 37(d) to argue that the discovery request was objectionable.[83] The proper response to an objectionable discovery request is to file a motion for a protective order under Rule 26(c), not to ignore the discovery request.[84]

Court Order

Although a court order is not a prerequisite to a motion for sanctions under Rule 37(d), the motion may still be brought if the party failing to participate in discovery had been ordered to participate.[85]

Procedure

A motion for sanctions under Rule 37(d) is filed in the court in which the action is pending.

Corporate Representative

A corporation or organization that is a party is subject to the sanctions in Rule 37(d) if its officer, director, managing agent, or person designated to testify under Rule 30(b)(6) fails to appear for a deposition after being properly noticed.[86] Likewise, if a party refuses to designate a representative, the party will be subject to sanctions under Rule 37(d).[87] In extreme cases, a party who produces an unprepared or inappropriate representative may also be subject to sanctions under Rule 37(d).[88]

Party Who Refuses to Be Sworn In

A party appearing at the designated time but who refuses to be sworn in generally is not subject to Rule 37(d) sanctions.[89]

81. *Telluride Management Solutions, Inc. v. Telluride Investment Group*, 55 F.3d 463 (9th Cir.1995)(good faith but incorrect belief that the action had been dismissed was not sufficient to excuse absence from a deposition); *Lee v. Walters*, 172 F.R.D. 421, 429 (D.Or.1997).

82. *Miller v. International Paper Co.*, 408 F.2d 283, 292–94 (5th Cir.1969).

83. *Magee v. Paul Revere Life Ins.Co.*, 178 F.R.D. 33, 38 (E.D.N.Y.1998).

84. *Ferko v. National Ass'n for Stock Car Auto Racing, Inc.*, 218 F.R.D. 125, 143–44 (E.D.Tex. 2003).

85. *Independent Productions Corp. v. Loew's Inc.*, 283 F.2d 730 (2d Cir.1960).

86. *Atlantic Cape Fisheries v. Hartford Fire Ins. Co.*, 509 F.2d 577 (1st Cir.1975); *Precisionflow Technologies, Inc. v. CVD Equipment Corp.*, 140 F.Supp.2d 195, (N.D.N.Y.2001) (corporation that agrees to produce employees sanctioned when employees do not appear for their depositions); *Starlight International Inc. v. Herlihy*, 186 F.R.D. 626, 639 (D.Kan.1999) (producing an unprepared witness is tantamount to not producing any witness at all); *but see Stone v. Morton Int'l, Inc.*, 170 F.R.D. 498, 503 (D.Utah 1997) (questioning the ability to sanction a corporation for failure of its officer to appear).

87. *Ferko v. National Ass'n for Stock Car Auto Racing, Inc.*, 218 F.R.D. 125, 133 (E.D.Tex. 2003).

88. *Ferko v. National Ass'n for Stock Car Auto Racing, Inc.*, 218 F.R.D. 125, 142–43 (E.D.Tex. 2003) (if the representative is not knowledgeable about the designated subject matter, the appearance is, for all practical purposes, no appearance at all).

89. *Aziz v. Wright*, 34 F.3d 587 (8th Cir. 1994), *cert. denied*, 513 U.S. 1090, 115 S.Ct. 752, 130 L.Ed.2d 652 (1995).

Refusal to Answer Specific Questions

A party who appears and is sworn in, but who then refuses to answer a specific question or questions is not subject to sanctions under Rule 37(d). The proper procedure is for the party taking the deposition to move to compel answers under Rule 37(a), then move for sanctions under Rule 37(b) if the party still refuses to answer.[90] The same result is reached with respect to evasive or incomplete answers. However, if the party refuses to answer all or substantially all of the questions, Rule 37(d) will apply.[91]

Continuation of Deposition

Sanctions under Rule 37(d) do not apply to a party who fails to appear for the continuation of a deposition if the date of the continuation was not specified in a notice.[92]

Incomplete Response to Interrogatories or Document Requests

Rule 37(d) only applies if the party fails altogether to serve a response to interrogatories or document requests. If the party serves an incomplete or evasive response, the proper procedure is a motion to compel under Rule 37(a), then a motion for sanctions under Rule 37(b) if the party does not comply with the court order.[93]

Failure to Preserve Evidence

Dismissal may be imposed as a sanction against parties who bring actions with knowledge that their own actions, or actions of a third party, have caused the spoliation or loss of key pieces of evidence which render defense of the action difficult.[94]

Compliance After Motion

Once a motion for sanctions has been filed, the non-participating party cannot avoid sanctions by responding to the discovery request. However, the court can consider that conduct in deciding what sanctions to impose.[95]

RULE 37(g). FAILURE TO PARTICIPATE IN THE FRAMING OF A DISCOVERY PLAN

CORE CONCEPT

90. *Independent Productions Corp. v. Loew's Inc.*, 283 F.2d 730 (2d Cir.1960).

91. *Black Horse Lane Assoc., L.P. v. Dow Chemical Corp.*, 228 F.3d 275, 301 (3d Cir.2000) (producing an unprepared Rule 30(b)(6) corporate representative is tantamount to not producing a witness at all); *Starlight International Inc. v. Herlihy*, 186 F.R.D. 626, 639 (D.Kan.1999) (producing an unprepared witness is tantamount to not producing any witness at all). *But see Garcia v. Senkowski*, 919 F.Supp. 609, 613–14 (N.D.N.Y.1996)(denying sanction of dismissal where deponent appeared, refused to answer questions orally, but submitted written answers).

92. *Miller v. International Paper Co.*, 408 F.2d 283, 292–294 (5th Cir.1969).

93. *Fjelstad v. American Honda Motor Co., Inc.*, 762 F.2d 1334 (9th Cir.1985).

94. *Thiele v. Oddy's Auto and Marine, Inc.*, 906 F.Supp. 158, 161–62 (W.D.N.Y.1995).

95. *Antico v. Honda of Camden,* 85 F.R.D. 34, 36 (E.D.Pa.1979).

If a party fails to participate in developing a proposed discovery plan as required by Rule 26(f), the court may, after opportunity for a hearing, require the party failing to participate to pay the expenses of the other party, including a reasonable attorney fee, caused by the failure.

ADDITIONAL RESEARCH REFERENCES

Wright & Miller, *Federal Practice and Procedure* §§ 2281–2293.

C.J.S. Federal Civil Procedure §§ 535–547, 640–644, 694, 695, 748–774.

West's Key No. Digests, Federal Civil Procedure ⚷1278, 1299, 1451–1456, 1537–1542, 1636–1640, 1663–1664, 1685.

VI. TRIALS

RULE 38

JURY TRIAL OF RIGHT

(a) Right Preserved. The right of trial by jury as declared by the Seventh Amendment to the Constitution or as given by a statute of the United States shall be preserved to the parties inviolate.

(b) Demand. Any party may demand a trial by jury of any issue triable of right by a jury by (1) serving upon the other parties a demand therefor in writing at any time after the commencement of the action and not later than 10 days after the service of the last pleading directed to such issue, and (2) filing the demand as required by Rule 5(d). Such demand may be indorsed upon a pleading of the party.

(c) Same: Specification of Issues. In the demand a party may specify the issues which the party wishes so tried; otherwise the party shall be deemed to have demanded trial by jury for all the issues so triable. If the party has demanded trial by jury for only some of the issues, any other party within 10 days after service of the demand or such lesser time as the court may order, may serve a demand for trial by jury of any other or all of the issues of fact in the action.

(d) Waiver. The failure of a party to serve and file a demand as required by this rule constitutes a waiver by the party of trial by jury. A demand for trial by jury made as herein provided may not be withdrawn without the consent of the parties.

(e) Admiralty and Maritime Claims. These rules shall not be construed to create a right to trial by jury of the issues in an admiralty or maritime claim within the meaning of Rule 9(h).

[Amended February 28, 1966, effective July 1, 1966; March 2, 1987, effective August 1, 1987; April 22, 1993, effective December 1, 1993.]

AUTHORS' COMMENTARY ON RULE 38

PURPOSE AND SCOPE

Rule 38 governs the parties' right to a trial by jury and how the parties exercise their right to such a trial. Rule 38 essentially serves two functions: (1) Rules 38(a) and 38(e) describe the issues for which the parties have a right to a jury trial; and (2) Rules 38(b), 38(c), and 38(d) control the procedural aspects of making a jury trial demand and the consequences of failing to do so.

NOTE: The right to a jury trial is waived unless a jury trial demand is served within 10 days of the answer or last pleading.

RULE 38(a). RIGHT PRESERVED

CORE CONCEPT

Rule 38 essentially codifies the Constitution's Seventh Amendment, which provides that the parties have a right to trial by jury for all suits at law with more than $20.00 in controversy.[1]

APPLICATIONS

Law vs. Equity

Under Rule 38, one has a right to a jury in all actions that historically would have been tried at law, such as actions for damages, but no right to a jury in actions that historically would have been tried in the courts of equity, such as actions for specific performance[2] or injunctive relief.[3]

Declaratory Judgment Actions

The right to a jury trial is preserved in declaratory judgment actions. If the issues would have been triable by a jury had something other than declaratory relief been sought, a right to a jury trial exists in a declaratory judgment action.[4]

Individual Issues

The right to a jury trial is evaluated claim by claim, not for the entire case.[5] If one claim triable at law is present in the case, then the parties have a right to a jury trial on that claim; whether the primary or principal claim is legal or equitable is immaterial.[6]

Policy Favors Jury Trials

There is a strong policy in favor of jury trials, so courts will tend to allow jury trials if it is unclear whether an issue historically would have

1. *International Financial Services Corp. v. Chromas Technologies Canada, Inc.*, 356 F.3d 731, 735 (7th Cir. 2004) (there is a right to a jury trial where either the Seventh Amendment or an ordinary statute of the United States so requires); *GTFM, LLC v. TKN Sales, Inc.*, 257 F.3d 235, 239–40 (2d Cir.2001).

2. *See Tull v. United States*, 481 U.S. 412, 417, 107 S.Ct. 1831, 1835, 95 L.Ed.2d 365 (1987); *Parklane Hosiery Co. v. Shore,* 439 U.S. 322, 99 S.Ct. 645, 58 L.Ed.2d 552 (1979).

3. *National Ass'n For Advancement of Colored People v. Acusport Corp.*, 226 F.Supp.2d 391, 397 (E.D.N.Y.2002).

4. *See Simler v. Conner*, 372 U.S. 221, 83 S.Ct. 609, 9 L.Ed.2d 691 (1963); *Beacon Theatres, Inc. v. Westover*, 359 U.S. 500, 79 S.Ct. 948, 3 L.Ed.2d 988 (1959).

5. *Bleecker v. Standard Fire Ins. Co.*, 130 F.Supp.2d 726, 737 (E.D.N.C.2000).

6. *Beacon Theatres, Inc. v. Westover,* 359 U.S. 500, 79 S.Ct. 948, 3 L.Ed.2d 988 (1959).

been triable at law.[7]

Governing Law

Federal law generally governs whether an issue is legal or equitable, not state law.[8] The determination of whether a party has a right to a jury trial is a legal determination subject to de novo review.[9]

Right Depends on Facts

The court bases its rulings on the issues raised by the *facts* alleged in the pleadings, not on the labels used by the parties or the relief claimed in the WHEREFORE clause.[10]

Jury Issues First

When there are jury and non-jury issues or claims present, the jury first determines the jury trial issues, then the court resolves any remaining issues. Any factual findings made by the jury are then binding on the court when trying the non-jury issues. The court may also conduct completely separate trials of jury and non-jury issues.[11]

Procedural Posture

The procedural device by which the parties arrive at court is irrelevant; legal issues are tried by jury even if the claims are brought under the historically equitable joinder provisions such as class actions, derivative actions, and intervention.[12]

RULE 38(b). DEMAND

CORE CONCEPT

Any party may make a jury trial demand. The demand then applies to all parties for the duration of the case.[13]

APPLICATIONS

Form of Demand

The jury trial demand should be in writing,[14] and can be part of another pleading[15] or a separate signed document. To avoid timing

7. *Beacon Theatres, Inc. v. Westover,* 359 U.S. 500, 79 S.Ct. 948, 3 L.Ed.2d 988 (1959).

8. *Simler v. Conner,* 372 U.S. 221, 83 S.Ct. 609, 9 L.Ed.2d 691 (1963); *International Financial Services Corp. v. Chromas Technologies Canada, Inc.*, 356 F.3d 731, 735 (7th Cir. 2004) (even where a district court is applying the substantive law of a state, federal procedural law controls the question of whether there is a right to a jury trial).

9. *Indiana Lumbermens Mutual Ins. Co. v. Timberland Pallet and Lumber Co., Inc.*, 195 F.3d 368, 374 (8th Cir.1999).

10. *Dairy Queen, Inc. v. Wood,* 369 U.S. 469, 82 S.Ct. 894, 8 L.Ed.2d 44 (1962).

11. *Beacon Theatres, Inc. v. Westover,* 359 U.S. 500, 79 S.Ct. 948, 3 L.Ed.2d 988 (1959).

12. *Ross v. Bernhard,* 396 U.S. 531, 90 S.Ct. 733, 24 L.Ed.2d 729 (1970).

13. *Kramer v. Banc of America Securities,* LLC, 355 F.3d 961, 967 (7th Cir. 2004).

14. *U.S. Leather, Inc. v. Mitchell Mfg. Group, Inc.*, 276 F.3d 782, 790 (6th Cir.2002) (oral jury demand during proceedings before a magistrate judge deemed insufficient).

15. *Metzger v. City of Leawood,* 144 F.Supp.2d 1225 (D.Kan.2001) ("While it is not desirable to bury the demand in the text of the

problems, it is advisable to include the jury demand on the complaint or answer. Note that it is probably not sufficient to indicate a jury trial on the civil coversheet or legal backer.[16] Likewise, a jury trial demand in a motion is probably not effective.[17]

Timing

A party wishing a jury trial for an issue must *serve* a jury trial demand within 10 days after service of the last pleading raising or responding to that issue.[18] Normally, the last pleading is the answer to the pleading raising the issue.[19] The party must then *file* the jury trial demand within a reasonable time, as provided in Rule 5(d). If a jury trial demand is served after the 10th day, the court has discretion to consider the demand.[20]

Service

To be effective, the jury demand must be served on other parties within the 10 day time limit of Rule 38(b).[21] If the last pleading was served by mail, the date of service is the mailing date plus 3 days.[22]

Other Parties

Once one party has made a jury demand, the other parties are entitled to rely on that demand and do not need to file jury demands of their own.[23]

Amendments

An amended or supplemental pleading does not restart the jury

pleading, plaintiff is correct in stating that demand may be incorporated in a pleading.").

16. *Johnson v. Dalton*, 57 F.Supp.2d 958, 959 (C.D.Cal.1999). *But see Wright v. Lewis*, 76 F.3d 57, 59 (2d Cir.1996)(a jury trial demand on a civil cover sheet can satisfy Rule 38(b) if the cover sheet is served).

17. *Bogosian v. Woloohojian Realty Corp.*, 323 F.3d 55, 62 (1st Cir.2003); *Hunt v. HEB Fed. Credit Union,* 215 B.R. 505, 509 (Bkrtcy. W.D.Tex.1997) (jury trial demand contained in a motion to withdraw reference to bankruptcy court is not effective).

18. *Burns v. Lawther,* 44 F.3d 960 (11th Cir.1995) (look to Rule 7 for definition of pleading); *Triad Elec. & Controls, Inc. v. Power Sys. Eng'g, Inc.*, 117 F.3d 180, 195 (5th Cir.1997); *In re Apponline.Com., Inc.*, 303 B.R. 723 (E.D.N.Y. 2004) (an amended complaint revives the right to a jury demand only if it adds new issues for which there is a right to a jury trial).

19. *See Shelton v. Consumer Products Safety Com'n*, 277 F.3d 998, 1011 (8th Cir.2002) (amended complaint does not trigger a new period to file a jury demand for issues raised in the original complaint); *United States v. California Mobile Home Park Management Co.*, 107 F.3d 1374, 1378 (9th Cir.1997) ("last pleading" is the answer to the intervenor's complaint, rather than the answer to the original complaint filed); *Tropez v. Veneman*, 2004 WL 574733 (E.D.La. 2004).

20. *Zivkovic v. Southern California Edison Co.*, 302 F.3d 1080, (9th Cir.2002) (the district court's discretion is narrow and does not permit a court to grant relief when the failure to make a timely demand results from an oversight or inadvertence, such as a good faith mistake with respect to the deadline for demanding a jury trial); *Members v. Paige,* 140 F.3d 699 (7th Cir. 1998) (district judge may require a litigant who requests an untimely jury trial to offer a reason for not meeting the deadline); *Miller v. Merrill Lynch Credit Corp.*, 2004 WL 813029 (D.Conn. 2004) (a court's discretion to permit a late jury demand is somewhat broader in removed cases than original actions).

21. *Ruiz v. Rodriguez*, 206 F.R.D. 501, 503–04 (E.D.Cal.2002).

22. *See* Rule 6(e).

23. *I & M Rail Link, LLC v. Northstar Nav., Inc.*, 2001 WL 460028 (N.D.Ill.2001).

trial demand clock for issues raised in the original pleading.[24] The focus is the issue, not the remedy.[25] Therefore, if the original complaint seeks specific performance of a breached contract and the amended complaint adds a damages claim arising out of the same breach, under the majority approach, the parties do not have the right to demand a jury trial 10 days after service of the amended complaint, unless the court directs the party to make such a demand.[26]

Removal

The removing party may make a jury trial demand within 10 days of filing the petition.[27] Others may make demands within 10 days of service of the petition. If a pleading is filed after the petition, then all parties have 10 days from service of the pleading.[28] If, prior to removal, a party has made a jury demand in accordance with state procedures or has made a jury demand that would satisfy federal requirements,[29] or if state procedures do not require an express demand, then no jury demand is necessary following removal.[30]

Objections to Jury Trial Demand

A party objecting to a jury trial demand may challenge it by filing a motion to strike. The Rules do not specify a time limit for moving to strike a jury trial demand.[31]

Appeals

A party that believes that the court has incorrectly denied its right to a jury trial may either seek a Writ of Mandamus or take an appeal after final judgment.[32]

RULE 38(c). SPECIFICATION OF ISSUES

CORE CONCEPT

A party may limit a jury trial demand to specific issues.[33] Other parties then have 10 days to make a jury trial demand for remaining issues.

24. *Huff v. Dobbins, Fraker, Tennant, Joy & Perlstein*, 243 F.3d 1086 (7th Cir.2001).

25. *See National Union Fire Ins., Co. of Pittsburgh, Pa. v. L.E. Myers Co. Group*, 928 F.Supp. 394, 396 (S.D.N.Y.1996).

26. *See, e.g., Hostrop v. Board of Jr. College Dist. No. 515,* 523 F.2d 569 (7th Cir.1975), *cert. denied,* 425 U.S. 963, 96 S.Ct. 1748, 48 L.Ed.2d 208 (1976).

27. *Polywell Intern., Inc. v. Hauppauge Computer Works, Inc.*, 2003 WL 22176616 (N.D.Tex. 2003); *Avne Systems, Ltd. v. Marketsource Corp.*, 191 F.R.D. 56, 57 (S.D.N.Y.2000) (greater leniency is appropriate in cases originally filed in state court); *Williams v. J.F.K. Int'l Carting Co.*, 164 F.R.D. 340, 341–42 (S.D.N.Y.1996).

28. *See* Rule 81(c).

29. *Wyatt v. Hunt Plywood Co., Inc.*, 297 F.3d 405, 415, n.26 (5th Cir.2002), *cert. denied*, 537 U.S. 1188, 123 S.Ct. 1254, 154 L.Ed.2d 1020 (2003).

30. Rule 81(c); *Williams v. J.F.K. Int'l Carting Co.*, 164 F.R.D. 340, 341–42 (S.D.N.Y. 1996)(failure to make a demand by the deadline set by the court constitutes waiver).

31. *Jones-Hailey v. Corp. of TVA*, 660 F.Supp. 551, 553 (E.D.Tenn.1987) (motion to strike jury trial demand allowed one month before trial because Rule 38 contains no time limit).

32. *Dairy Queen, Inc. v. Wood,* 369 U.S. 469, 82 S.Ct. 894, 8 L.Ed.2d 44 (1962).

33. *Athridge v. Iglesias*, 2003 WL 23100036 (D.D.C. 2003).

NOTE: A demand that does not specify individual issues is deemed a demand for a jury trial on all issues that are properly triable to a jury.[34]

RULE 38(d). WAIVER

CORE CONCEPT

Failure to serve and file a timely jury trial demand is a waiver of the right, even if the failure was inadvertent.[35]

APPLICATIONS

Waiver Following Demand

A party making timely jury trial demand waives that right if the party participates in a non-jury trial without objecting.[36]

Withdrawal of Demand

Once a jury trial demand has been made, it cannot be withdrawn except with the consent of all parties.[37] Note, however, that if the case develops such that the right to a jury trial no longer exists, the court can designate the case as non-jury without the consent of the party initially making the jury demand.[38]

RULE 38(e). ADMIRALTY AND MARITIME LAW

CORE CONCEPT

Rule 38 does not create a right to a jury trial for admiralty or maritime claims.[39] However, jury trials in an admiralty claim are not forbidden.[40]

34. *See Allison v. Citgo Petroleum*, 151 F.3d 402 (5th Cir.1998).

35. *Bogosian v. Woloohojian Realty Corp.*, 323 F.3d 55, 62 (1st Cir.2003) (cursory objection to bench trial cannot resurrect a waived jury trial right); *Garcia-Ayala v. Lederle Parenterals, Inc.*, 212 F.3d 638, 645 (1st Cir.2000) (the right to a jury trial is constitutionally protected and casual waivers are not to be presumed).

36. *Thompson v. Mahre,* 110 F.3d 716, 721 (9th Cir.1997), *cert. denied*, 522 U.S. 967, 118 S.Ct. 414, 139 L.Ed.2d 317 (1997); *but see United States v. California Mobile Home Park Management Co.*, 107 F.3d 1374, 1379–80 (9th Cir.1997) (plaintiff's filing a continuing demand for a jury trial and objecting several times prior to trial was sufficient to preserve her right to a jury trial even though she went to bench trial and did not object at trial); *Jennings v. McCormick*, 154 F.3d 542, 545 (5th Cir.1998) (participation in bench trial by a *pro se* party is not a waiver).

37. *Middle Tennessee News Co., Inc. v. Charnel of Cincinnati, Inc.*, 250 F.3d 1077 (7th Cir. 2001); *Allison v. Citgo Petroleum*, 151 F.3d 402 (5th Cir.1998).

38. *Kramer v. Banc of America Securities,* LLC, 355 F.3d 961, 968 (7th Cir. 2004), *cert. denied*, ___ U.S. ___, 124 S.Ct. 2876, 159 L.Ed.2d 798 (2004).

39. *See Foulk v. Donjon Marine Co., Inc.*, 144 F.3d 252 (3d Cir.1998); *Windsor Mount Joy Mut. Ins. Co. v. Johnson*, 264 F.Supp.2d 158 (D.N.J. 2003); *Group Therapy, Inc. v. White,* 280 F.Supp.2d 21, 32 (W.D.N.Y. 2003).

40. *See American River Transp. Co., Inc. v. Paragon Marine Services, Inc.*, 329 F.3d 946, 947 (8th Cir.2003).

ADDITIONAL RESEARCH REFERENCES

Wright & Miller, *Federal Practice and Procedure* §§ 2301–2322.

C.J.S. Admiralty §§ 216–218; Federal Civil Procedure §§ 943–950; Juries §§ 9, 11, 84–113 et seq.

West's Key No. Digests, Admiralty ⚷80; Jury ⚷9–37.

RULE 39

TRIAL BY JURY OR BY THE COURT

(a) By Jury. When trial by jury has been demanded as provided in Rule 38, the action shall be designated upon the docket as a jury action. The trial of all issues so demanded shall be by jury, unless (1) the parties or their attorneys of record, by written stipulation filed with the court or by an oral stipulation made in open court and entered in the record, consent to trial by the court sitting without a jury or (2) the court upon motion or of its own initiative finds that a right of trial by jury of some or of all those issues does not exist under the Constitution or statutes of the United States.

(b) By the Court. Issues not demanded for trial by jury as provided in Rule 38 shall be tried by the court; but, notwithstanding the failure of a party to demand a jury in an action in which such a demand might have been made of right, the court in its discretion upon motion may order a trial by a jury of any or all issues.

(c) Advisory Jury and Trial by Consent. In all actions not triable of right by a jury the court upon motion or of its own initiative may try any issue with an advisory jury or, except in actions against the United States when a statute of the United States provides for trial without a jury, the court, with the consent of both parties, may order a trial with a jury whose verdict has the same effect as if trial by jury had been a matter of right.

AUTHORS' COMMENTARY ON RULE 39

PURPOSE AND SCOPE

Rule 39 describes the mechanisms for allocating issues for trial by jury or non-jury (other than by filing a jury trial demand pursuant to Rule 38). Rule 39 also covers advisory juries.

RULE 39(a). BY JURY

CORE CONCEPT

Once a jury trial has been demanded, the docket will be so designated and the claim will be tried to a jury unless the parties stipulate otherwise or the court determines that no right to a jury trial exists under the Constitution or federal statute.[1]

APPLICATIONS

Stipulations

The parties may stipulate to a non-jury trial, even if a timely jury trial demand has been filed.[2] The parties may also stipulate to trial by the court of specific issues.[3] Such a stipulation should be clear and unambiguous,[4] and must be made either:

- in writing and filed with the court;[5] or
- orally in open court and entered in the record.[6]

Striking Improper Jury Demand

When a party has filed a jury trial demand for an equity claim, the court should order a non-jury trial, either *sua sponte*[7] or upon motion.[8]

Jury Verdict Binding

If a trial occurs before a jury following a jury trial demand, the verdict is binding and may not be treated as advisory.

Waiver

Participating in a bench trial without objection may constitute a waiver of the right to a jury trial, even if a timely demand has been filed.[9]

RULE 39(b). BY THE COURT

CORE CONCEPT

Claims for which no party has filed a jury trial demand are tried by the court.

1. *South Port Marine, LLC v. Gulf Oil Ltd. Partnership*, 234 F.3d 58, 62 (1st Cir.2000).

2. *Clark v. Runyon*, 218 F.3d 915, 917–18 (8th Cir.2000).

3. *Gaworski v. ITT Commercial Finance Corp.*, 17 F.3d 1104 (8th Cir.1994).

4. *Hupp v. Siroflex of America*, 159 F.R.D. 29 (S.D.Tex.1994)(failure to object is not a stipulation).

5. *Garcia-Ayala v. Lederle Parenterals, Inc.*, 212 F.3d 638, 645 (1st Cir.2000).

6. *Fuller v. City of Oakland, Cal.*, 47 F.3d 1522 (9th Cir.1995).

7. *Tegal Corp. v. Tokyo Electron America, Inc.*, 257 F.3d 1331, 1341 (Fed.Cir.2001), *cert. denied*, 535 U.S. 927, 122 S.Ct. 1297, 152 L.Ed.2d 209 (2002); *Kennedy v. Alabama State Board of Education*, 78 F.Supp.2d 1246, 1259 (M.D.Ala.2000).

8. *Kramer v. Banc of America Securities*, LLC, 355 F.3d 961, 967–68 (7th Cir. 2004), *cert. denied*, ___ U.S. ___, 124 S.Ct. 2876, 159 L.Ed.2d 798 (2004); *Hobleman v. Kentucky Fried Chicken*, 260 F.Supp.2d 801, 804–05 (D.Neb. 2003); *General Instrument Corp. of Del. v. Nu-Tek Elecs. & Mfg., Inc.*, 1996 WL 184794 (E.D.Pa. 1996) (holding that a party may unilaterally revoke a demand for a jury trial where a jury trial is not a matter of right).

9. *United States v. Rangel de Aguilar*, 308 F.3d 1134, 1138 (10th Cir.2002), *cert. denied*, 537 U.S. 1241, 123 S.Ct. 1372, 155 L.Ed.2d 211 (2003) (allowing waiver of jury trial right by oral stipulation entered in the record); *Wilcher v. City of Wilmington*, 139 F.3d 366 (3d Cir.1998).

APPLICATIONS

No Jury Without Demand or Motion

The court may not impanel a jury without a demand or motion,[10] except in an advisory capacity.[11]

Rules Governing Trial by Court

Other Rules govern the procedures for trial by the court. *See* Rule 41(b)(pertaining to involuntary dismissal), Rule 43(c)(pertaining to offers of proof), Rule 52 (pertaining to findings of fact), Rules 53(b) and (e)(2)(pertaining to reference to a master), Rule 58 (pertaining to entry of judgments), and Rule 59(c)(pertaining to grounds for a new trial).

Motion for Jury Trial

When a jury demand is omitted or filed out-of-time, the court, upon motion[12] and in its discretion, may order a jury trial of claims for which a jury trial could properly have been made.[13] Courts are split on the standard for granting such motions.[14] On appeal, rulings on motions for jury trials are reviewed under the abuse of discretion standard.[15]

RULE 39(c). ADVISORY JURY

CORE CONCEPT

The judge may impanel an advisory jury if the case will not be tried to a binding jury.

10. *Sartin v. Cliff's Drilling Co.*, 2004 WL 551209 (E.D.La. 2004) (Rule 39(b) requires a motion by a party; the court may not employ Rule 39(b) of its own initiative).

11. *Swofford v. B & W, Inc.*, 336 F.2d 406, 409 (5th Cir.1964), *cert. denied,* 379 U.S. 962, 85 S.Ct. 653, 13 L.Ed.2d 557 (1965).

12. *Sartin v. Cliff's Drilling Co.*, 2004 WL 551209 (E.D.La. 2004) (Rule 39(b) requires a motion by a party; the court may not employ Rule 39(b) of its own initiative).

13. *United States Securities and Exchange Commission v. The Infinity Group Co.*, 212 F.3d 180 (3d Cir.2000), *cert. denied*, 532 U.S. 905, 121 S.Ct. 1228, 149 L.Ed.2d 138 (2001); *Pyramid Co. of Holyoke v. Homeplace Stores Two, Inc.*, 175 F.R.D. 415, 421 (D.Mass.1997) (motion must be done formally, be well supported, and be addressed to the trial judge in whose discretion the decision resides).

14. *See Ruiz v. Rodriguez*, 206 F.R.D. 501 (E.D.Cal.2002) (discussing the different standards applied by various courts); *Green Construction Co. v. Kansas Power & Light Co.*, 1 F.3d 1005 (10th Cir.1993)(jury trial should be granted in the absence of strong and compelling reasons to the contrary); *Pacific Fisheries Corp. v. HIH Cas. & General Ins., Ltd.*, 239 F.3d 1000, 1002 (9th Cir.2001), *cert. denied*, 534 U.S. 944, 122 S.Ct. 324, 151 L.Ed.2d 242 (2001) (discretion to grant an untimely jury trial is narrow, and does not permit a court to grant relief when the failure to make a timely demand results from an oversight or inadvertence); *Members v. Paige*, 140 F.3d 699, 703 (7th Cir.1998) (court may request a reason the deadline has not been met and then approach the "application under Rule 39(b) with an open mind and an eye to the factual situation of that particular case, rather than with a fixed policy").

15. *Mile High Industries v. Cohen*, 222 F.3d 845, 855 (10th Cir.2000).

APPLICATIONS

Verdict Non-binding

The judge is the ultimate trier of fact as to equitable claims,[16] and has complete discretion to adopt or reject the verdict of an advisory jury.[17]

Findings of Fact and Conclusions of Law

The court must make its own findings of fact and conclusions of law in cases tried with an advisory jury.[18]

Broad Discretion

The court has broad discretion as to whether to impanel an advisory jury.[19]

Binding Jury With Consent

If no claims at law are present, the judge still may impanel a normal, binding jury with the consent (either express or by failure to object) of *all* parties.[20] Consent of the parties does not require the judge to empanel a jury, it merely gives the court the discretion to do so.[21] The exception to this rule is that certain statutes prohibit jury trials in specified actions against the United States.[22]

Advisory Jury With Legal Claims

Rule 39(c) states that a judge may impanel an advisory jury "[i]n all actions not triable of right by a jury. . . ."[23] Some courts construe this language broadly to include any action for which the right has not been exercised.

16. *N.A.A.C.P. v. AcuSport, Inc.*, 271 F.Supp.2d 435, 469 (E.D.N.Y. 2003) (the judge in an equitable action is the ultimate trier of fact even when the judge has invoked the discretionary right to empanel an advisory jury).

17. *Hyde Properties v. McCoy*, 507 F.2d 301 (6th Cir.1974); *Hine v. Mineta*, 238 F.Supp.2d 497, 499 (E.D.N.Y.2003) (it is wholly within the discretion of the trial court whether to accept or reject in whole or in part the verdict of the advisory jury).

18. Rule 52(a); *Kolstad v. American Dental Assoc.*, 108 F.3d 1431, 1440 (D.C.Cir.1997), *cert. denied*, 525 U.S. 964, 119 S.Ct. 408, 142 L.Ed.2d 331 (1998).

19. *Kramer v. Banc of America Securities*, LLC, 355 F.3d 961, 968, n.2 (7th Cir. 2004), *cert. denied*, ___ U.S. ___, 124 S.Ct. 2876, 159 L.Ed.2d 798 (2004); *Indiana Lumbermens Mutual Ins. Co. v. Timberland Pallet and Lumber Co., Inc.*, 195 F.3d 368, 374 (8th Cir.1999) (district court's discretion is not unlimited); *Hamm v. Nasatka Barriers, Inc.*, 166 F.R.D. 1, 2 (D.D.C.1996) (permitting the use of an advisory jury in a case where the United States was the defendant).

20. *See Pals v. Schepel Buick & GMC Truck, Inc.*, 220 F.3d 495, 501 (7th Cir.2000) (failure to object to a trial before a jury is the equivalent of consenting); *Crane v. Green & Freedman Baking Co., Inc.*, 134 F.3d 17, 22 (1st Cir.1998).

21. *Ed Peters Jewelry Co., Inc. v. C & J Jewelry Co., Inc.*, 215 F.3d 182 (1st Cir.2000).

22. *See Palischak v. Allied Signal Aerospace Co.*, 893 F.Supp. 341, 342 (D.N.J.1995).

23. *Mota v. University of Texas Houston Health Science Center*, 261 F.3d 512, 526, n. 45 (5th Cir.2001) (although front pay was equitable remedy to be decided by the court, an advisory jury could be empaneled); *Epstein v. Kalvin–Miller Intern., Inc.*, 2000 WL 1761052 (S.D.N.Y. 2000) (court of its own initiative has the right to try issue with advisory jury where the claim was not triable of right by a jury, even when parties not given notice of the advisory jury in advance of trial).

ADDITIONAL RESEARCH REFERENCES

Wright & Miller, *Federal Practice and Procedure* §§ 2323–2350.

C.J.S. Federal Civil Procedure §§ 933, 946, 1028–1030; Juries §§ 11, 91–98.

West's Key No. Digests, Federal Civil Procedure ⚷1991, 2251, 2252; Jury ⚷25(1), 28(6).

RULE 40

ASSIGNMENT OF CASES FOR TRIAL

The district courts shall provide by rule for the placing of actions upon the trial calendar (1) without request of the parties or (2) upon request of a party and notice to the other parties or (3) in such other manner as the courts deem expedient. Precedence shall be given to actions entitled thereto by any statute of the United States.

AUTHORS' COMMENTARY ON RULE 40

PURPOSE AND SCOPE

Rule 40 allows individual district courts to formulate their own rules for placing cases on the trial calendar.

APPLICATIONS

Broad Discretion

Individual judges have broad discretion in enforcing the district court's rules regarding assignment of cases. They may give precedence to cases of public importance or cases in which delay will cause hardship.[1]

Precedence by Statute

Some statutes provide for precedence for actions brought thereunder.

Motion for Continuance

The trial judge has great discretion in ruling on motions for continuance.[2]

ADDITIONAL RESEARCH REFERENCES

Wright & Miller, *Federal Practice and Procedure* §§ 2351–2352.

C.J.S. Federal Civil Procedure § 934.

West's Key No. Digests, Federal Civil Procedure ⚷1993–1994.

1. *Clinton v. Jones*, 520 U.S. 681, 707–708, 117 S.Ct. 1636, 1650–51, 137 L.Ed.2d 945 (1997) (the court abused its discretion in deferring trial until after president left office).

2. *Clinton v. Jones*, 520 U.S. 681, 706–707, 117 S.Ct. 1636, 1650–51, 137 L.Ed.2d 945 (1997).

RULE 41

DISMISSAL OF ACTIONS

(a) Voluntary Dismissal: Effect Thereof.

(1) *By Plaintiff; By Stipulation.* Subject to the provisions of Rule 23(e), of Rule 66, and of any statute of the United States, an action may be dismissed by the plaintiff without order of court (i) by filing a notice of dismissal at any time before service by the adverse party of an answer or of a motion for summary judgment, whichever first occurs, or (ii) by filing a stipulation of dismissal signed by all parties who have appeared in the action. Unless otherwise stated in the notice of dismissal or stipulation, the dismissal is without prejudice, except that a notice of dismissal operates as an adjudication upon the merits when filed by a plaintiff who has once dismissed in any court of the United States or of any state an action based on or including the same claim.

(2) *By Order of Court.* Except as provided in paragraph (1) of this subdivision of this rule, an action shall not be dismissed at the plaintiff's instance save upon order of the court and upon such terms and conditions as the court deems proper. If a counterclaim has been pleaded by a defendant prior to the service upon the defendant of the plaintiff's motion to dismiss, the action shall not be dismissed against the defendant's objection unless the counterclaim can remain pending for independent adjudication by the court. Unless otherwise specified in the order, a dismissal under this paragraph is without prejudice.

(b) Involuntary Dismissal: Effect Thereof. For failure of the plaintiff to prosecute or to comply with these rules or any order of court, a defendant may move for dismissal of an action or of any claim against the defendant. Unless the court in its order for dismissal otherwise specifies, a dismissal under this subdivision and any dismissal not provided for in this rule, other than a dismissal for lack of jurisdiction, for improper venue, or for failure to join a party under Rule 19, operates as an adjudication upon the merits.

(c) Dismissal of Counterclaim, Cross–Claim, or Third–Party Claim. The provisions of this rule apply to the dismissal of any counterclaim, cross-claim, or third-party claim. A voluntary dismissal by the claimant alone pursuant to paragraph (1) of subdivision (a) of this rule shall be made before a responsive pleading is served or, if there is none, before the introduction of evidence at the trial or hearing.

(d) Costs of Previously Dismissed Action. If a plaintiff who has once dismissed an action in any court commences an action based upon or including the same claim against the same defendant, the court may make such order for the payment of costs of the action previously dismissed as it may deem proper and may stay the proceedings in the action until the plaintiff has complied with the order.

[Amended effective March 19, 1948; July 1, 1963; July 1, 1966; July 1, 1968; August 1, 1987; December 1, 1991.]

AUTHORS' COMMENTARY ON RULE 41

PURPOSE AND SCOPE

Rule 41 controls the procedural aspects and effects of dismissals. It addresses both voluntary and involuntary dismissals, as well as the plaintiff's ability to initiate another action based on the same cause of action.

NOTE: The second voluntary dismissal by the plaintiff acts as an adjudication on the merits and will bar subsequent actions based on the same claims.

RULE 41(a)(1). VOLUNTARY DISMISSAL BY THE PLAINTIFF OR BY STIPULATION

CORE CONCEPT

The plaintiff may dismiss an action without consent of the court either by stipulation of all parties or unilaterally if the defendant has not yet filed an answer or motion for summary judgment.[1]

APPLICATIONS

Notice of Dismissal

Dismissal under Rule 41(a)(1) is achieved by filing a *notice* of dismissal, not by motion, and no court order is required.[2] The notice is effective when filed,[3] but must be served on all parties pursuant to Rule 5(a).

1. *Wilson v. City of San Jose*, 111 F.3d 688, 692 (9th Cir.1997); *SmithKline Beecham Corp. v. Pentech Pharmaceuticals, Inc.*, 261 F.Supp.2d 1002, 1004 (N.D.Ill.2003).

2. *Torres v. Walker*, 356 F.3d 238, 243 (2nd Cir. 2004); *Finley Lines Joint Protective Bd. Unit 200 v. Norfolk S. Corp.* 109 F.3d 993, 995 (4th Cir.1997).

3. *Marques v. Federal Reserve Bank of Chicago*, 286 F.3d 1014, 1018 (7th Cir.2002) (a judgment entered after a proper voluntary dismissal is void); *Commercial Space Management Co.,*

Notice Unconditional

A notice of dismissal must be unconditional[4] and unequivocal[5] in both dismissals by the plaintiff and by stipulation, although the parties may privately impose conditions (such as the payment of a sum of money) on their participation in a stipulation for dismissal.

Effect of Dismissal

A voluntary dismissal leaves the situation as if the lawsuit had never been filed,[6] unless the dismissal is specified as with prejudice. A voluntary dismissal that is specified as with prejudice is given the same res judicata effect as any other judgment.[7]

Absolute Right

Generally, the right to voluntarily dismiss an action is considered absolute, not requiring assent by the court or opposing parties.[8] Likewise, the court cannot impose conditions in connection with a voluntary dismissal[9] (although it can do so under Rule 41(a)(2)).[10]

Stipulation

A stipulation for dismissal must be signed by all parties who have appeared in the action or it is not effective.[11]

Dismissal Without Prejudice (Two Dismissal Rule)

Dismissals by stipulation are presumed without prejudice unless they specify otherwise.[12] Dismissals unilaterally by the plaintiff are governed by the Two Dismissal Rule: the first voluntary dismissal of a given claim is without prejudice; the second dismissal acts as a final

Inc. v. The Boeing Co., Inc., 193 F.3d 1074, 1076 (9th Cir.1999) (once the notice of dismissal is filed, the court loses jurisdiction over the action). *But see University of South Alabama v. American Tobacco Co.*, 168 F.3d 405, 409 (11th Cir. 1999) (dismissal not effective where court did not have subject matter jurisdiction and motion to remand was pending).

4. *Hyde Constr. Co. v. Koehring Co.*, 388 F.2d 501, 507 (10th Cir.1968), *cert. denied*, 391 U.S. 905, 88 S.Ct. 1654, 20 L.Ed.2d 419 (1968); *Scam Instrument Corp. v. Control Data Corp.*, 458 F.2d 885 (7th Cir.1972).

5. *Carter v. Beverly Hills Sav. and Loan Ass'n*, 884 F.2d 1186 (9th Cir.1989), *cert. denied*, 497 U.S. 1024, 110 S.Ct. 3270, 111 L.Ed.2d 780 (1990).

6. *City of South Pasadena v. Mineta*, 284 F.3d 1154, 1157 (9th Cir.2002).

7. *Norfolk Southern Corp. v. Chevron, U.S.A., Inc.*, 371 F.3d 1285 (11th Cir. 2004).

8. *Marques v. Federal Reserve Bank of Chicago*, 286 F.3d 1014, 1017 (7th Cir.2002) (a party does not need a good reason, or even a sane reason, for a voluntary dismissal); *American Soccer Co., Inc. v. Score First Enterprises*, 187 F.3d 1108, 1111 (9th Cir.1999) (the amount of time and effort expended does not affect the plaintiff's right to a voluntary dismissal).

9. *Commercial Space Management Co., Inc. v. The Boeing Co., Inc.*, 193 F.3d 1074, 1076 (9th Cir.1999); *Hester Industries, Inc. v. Tyson Foods, Inc.*, 160 F.3d 911, 916 (2d Cir.1998), *cert. denied*, 526 U.S. 1131, 119 S.Ct. 1805, 143 L.Ed.2d 1009 (1999).

10. *Commercial Space Management Co., Inc. v. The Boeing Co., Inc.*, 193 F.3d 1074, 1078 (9th Cir.1999).

11. *Mutual Assignment and Indemnification Co. v. Lind–Waldock & Co., LLC*, 364 F.3d 858, 860 (7th Cir. 2004); *Camacho v. Mancuso*, 53 F.3d 48 (4th Cir.1995)(Stipulation of dismissal signed by the plaintiff only is not effective even though all parties admit that they consented).

12. *Bowers v. National Collegiate Athletic Ass'n*, 346 F.3d 402, 413 (3rd Cir. 2003); *West v. Macht*, 197 F.3d 1185, 1188 (7th Cir.1999).

adjudication on the merits and will preclude a third action based on the same claim.[13]

Dismissal With Prejudice

A dismissal stipulation may specifically provide that dismissal is with prejudice.[14]

Actions in State Court

The Two Dismissal Rule applies to actions filed in state court on the first occasion. However, if the second action is filed and dismissed in state court, it will not trigger the Two Dismissal Rule [15] unless the state has a similar rule.[16] Once an action is barred in federal court by the Two Dismissal Rule, it will also be barred in state court.

Statute of Limitations

An action dismissed without prejudice does not toll the statute of limitations.[17]

Class Actions, Receivers, etc.

Rule 41 is expressly subject to the provisions of Rule 23(e)(requiring court approval for the dismissal of a class action)[18] and Rule 66 (governing cases in which a receiver has been appointed). Rule 41 also may not apply in other statutorily controlled areas, such as stockholders' derivative actions.[19] Rule 41 does apply to appeals of certain proceedings to a federal court, such as an appeal of a decision by the Board of Veterans' Appeals.[20]

Removal

Rule 41 applies with equal force to cases removed from state court.[21]

Rule 12 Motions

In general, a motion to dismiss pursuant to Rule 12(b) for failure to state a claim or for lack of jurisdiction or venue does not terminate the

13. *Commercial Space Management Co., Inc. v. The Boeing Co., Inc.*, 193 F.3d 1074, 1076 (9th Cir.1999); *ASX Investment Corp. v. Newton*, 183 F.3d 1265, 1267–68 (11th Cir.1999) (Two Dismissal Rule does not count a dismissal by court order under Rule 41(a)(2)); *Pacheco de Perez v. AT & T Co.*, 139 F.3d 1368 (11th Cir.1998); *Tate v. Riverboat Services, Inc.*, 305 F.Supp.2d 916, 924–25 (N.D.Ind. 2004).

14. *Norfolk Southern Corp. v. Chevron, U.S.A., Inc.*, 371 F.3d 1285 (11th Cir. 2004) (a stipulation of dismissal with prejudice is given the same res judicata effect as any other judgment).

15. *Rader v. Baltimore & O.R. Co.*, 108 F.2d 980 (7th Cir.1940), *cert. denied*, 309 U.S. 682, 60 S.Ct. 722, 84 L.Ed. 1026 (1940).

16. *Manning v. South Carolina Dept. of Highway and Public Transp.*, 914 F.2d 44 (4th Cir.1990).

17. *Beck v. Caterpillar Inc.*, 50 F.3d 405 (7th Cir.1995).

18. *Crawford v. F. Hoffman–La Roche Ltd.*, 267 F.3d 760, 764 (8th Cir.2001); *In re Painewebber Limited Partnerships Litigation*, 147 F.3d 132, 137 (2d Cir.1998).

19. *Baker v. America's Mortgage Servicing, Inc.*, 58 F.3d 321 (7th Cir.1995).

20. *Graves v. Principi*, 294 F.3d 1350 (Fed. Cir.2002).

21. *Grivas v. Parmelee Transp. Co.*, 207 F.2d 334 (7th Cir.1953), *cert. denied*, 347 U.S. 913, 74 S.Ct. 477, 98 L.Ed. 1069 (1954).

plaintiff's unilateral right to dismiss.[22] An exception may arise if the court has held extensive hearings on the motion,[23] or converted the motion to dismiss into a motion for summary judgment.[24]

Dismissal of Part of Action

Courts differ as to the proper procedural mechanism for voluntarily dismissing part of an action. The majority allow voluntary dismissal of part of an action by notice pursuant to Rule 41.[25] Some courts require a motion to amend pursuant to Rule 15(a).[26] A third party plaintiff may voluntarily dismiss the third party complaint under Rule 41(a)(1).[27]

Costs

Following a voluntary dismissal under Rule 41, the district court retains jurisdiction over the matter such that the court may award costs to the defendant.[28]

Enforcement of Settlement Agreement

Normally, a federal court does not have jurisdiction over an action to enforce the terms of a settlement agreement. In order to vest the court with such jurisdiction, the parties can include language in their Rule 41(a)(1)(ii) stipulation for dismissal providing that the court will retain jurisdiction for purposes of enforcing the settlement agreement.[29]

Appeals

The first voluntary dismissal under Rule 41(a)(1) is normally not considered a final order and thus not appealable.[30] The second dismissal, however, is a final, appealable order.[31]

RULE 41(a)(2). DISMISSAL BY ORDER OF COURT

22. *Manze v. State Farm Ins. Co.,* 817 F.2d 1062, 1066 (3d Cir.1987).

23. *Harvey Aluminum, Inc. v. American Cyanamid Co.,* 203 F.2d 105 (2d Cir.1953), *cert. denied,* 345 U.S. 964, 73 S.Ct. 949, 97 L.Ed. 1383 (1953).

24. *Swedberg v. Marotzke*, 339 F.3d 1139 (9th Cir.2003); *Hamm v. Rhone–Poulenc Rorer Pharmaceuticals, Inc.*, 187 F.3d 941, 950 (8th Cir.1999), *cert. denied*, 528 U.S. 1117, 120 S.Ct. 937, 145 L.Ed.2d 815 (2000); *Finley Lines Joint Protective Bd. Unit 200 v. Norfolk So. Corp.*, 109 F.3d 993 (4th Cir.1997).

25. *See Bowers v. National Collegiate Athletic Ass'n*, 346 F.3d 402, 413 (3rd Cir. 2003) (allowing dismissal of part of a third party complaint); *Commercial Space Management Co., Inc. v. The Boeing Co., Inc.*, 193 F.3d 1074, 1079 (9th Cir.1999) (stipulation of dismissal as to some defendants); *Public Interest Research Group of New Jersey, Inc. v. Windall*, 51 F.3d 1179 (3d Cir.1995).

26. *Gobbo Farms & Orchards v. Poole Chem. Co.*, 81 F.3d 122, 123 (10th Cir.1996)(holding that a voluntary dismissal must be for all claims within an action); *Bragg v. Robertson*, 54 F.Supp.2d 653, 659 (S.D.W.Va.1999).

27. *Century Mfg. Co., Inc. v. Central Transport Intern., Inc.*, 209 F.R.D. 647 (D.Mass.2002).

28. *Sequa Corp. v. Cooper*, 245 F.3d 1036, 1037 (8th Cir.2001).

29. *Kokkonen v. Guardian Life Ins. Co. of Am.*, 511 U.S. 375, 378–81, 114 S.Ct. 1673, 1675-1677, 128 L.Ed.2d 391 (1994); *Municipality of San Juan v. Rullan*, 318 F.3d 26, 30 (1st Cir. 2003).

30. *State Treasurer of the State of Michigan v. Barry*, 168 F.3d 8, 11 (11th Cir.1999).

31. *Muzikowski v. Paramount Pictures Corp.*, 322 F.3d 918, 923–24 (7th Cir.2003).

CORE CONCEPT

Except as provided in Rule 41(a)(1) above (dismissal by stipulation or before an answer or motion for summary judgment has been filed), dismissal of an action must be by court order.[32]

APPLICATIONS

Prejudice

A dismissal by order of court can be with or without prejudice.[33] A court order granting voluntary dismissal is presumed to be without prejudice unless it explicitly specifies otherwise.[34]

Discretion of Court

The decision whether to grant or deny the plaintiff's motion for voluntary dismissal is within the sound discretion of the court,[35] although some courts hold that the court had no discretion to deny a motion to dismiss *with prejudice* (reasoning that it is unfair to force an unwilling plaintiff to go to trial).[36] A court should grant a Rule 41(a)(2) motion for voluntary dismissal unless a defendant can show that it will suffer some plain legal prejudice as a result.[37] In general, courts are more likely to grant motions for voluntary dismissal at earlier stages of the litigation.[38]

Conditions

The court may include terms and conditions in its order granting voluntary dismissal in order to prevent prejudice to the defendant.[39] These conditions may be proposed by the parties or *sua sponte* by the court. Examples of such conditions include the payment of costs[40]

32. *Wilson v. City of San Jose,* 111 F.3d 688, 692 (9th Cir.1997); *Home American Credit, Inc. v. Investors Title Ins. Co.*, 199 F.R.D. 563, 564–65 (E.D.N.C.2001) (leave of court is required for a dismissal once the defendant has answered or filed a motion for summary judgment).

33. *See, e.g., Minnesota Mining And Mfg. Co. v. Barr Laboratories, Inc.*, 289 F.3d 775, 779 (Fed.Cir.2002).

34. *LeBlang Motors, Ltd. v. Subaru of America, Inc.*, 148 F.3d 680, 687 (7th Cir.1998) (dismissal deemed with prejudice even though the defendant's motion only asked for dismissal without prejudice); *Palmieri v. Defaria,* 88 F.3d 136, 140 (2d Cir.1996).

35. *Minnesota Mining And Mfg. Co. v. Barr Laboratories, Inc.*, 289 F.3d 775, 779 (Fed.Cir. 2002) (describing considerations for the court in exercising its discretion); *Pontenberg v. Boston Scientific Corp.*, 252 F.3d 1253 (11th Cir.2001) (a voluntary dismissal should be granted unless the defendant will suffer clear legal prejudice, other then the mere prospect of a subsequent lawsuit).

36. *Smoot v. Fox,* 340 F.2d 301 (6th Cir. 1964).

37. *County of Santa Fe, N.M. v. Public Service Co. of New Mexico*, 311 F.3d 1031, 1047 (10th Cir.2002) (the important aspect is whether the opposing party will suffer prejudice).

38. *Jones v. Simek*, 193 F.3d 485, 491 (7th Cir.1999); *Berry v. General Star National Ins. Co.*, 190 F.R.D. 697, 698 (M.D.Ala.2000).

39. *Elbaor v. Tripath Imaging, Inc.*, 279 F.3d 314, 316, n.1 (5th Cir.2002) ("Rule 41(a)(2), which is designed to protect non-movants from prejudice occasioned by unconditional dismissals, is not a proper mechanism to punish non-compliance with court orders."); *D'Alto v. Dahon Cal., Inc.*, 100 F.3d 281, 283–4 (2d Cir.1996) (court outlines five factors to determine if dismissing would prejudice defendant).

40. *Chavez v. Illinois State Police*, 251 F.3d 612 (7th Cir.2001); *ACEquip, Ltd. v. Am. Eng'g Corp.*, 219 F.R.D. 44, 46 (D.Conn. 2003) (deciding not to award costs, but requiring that any future action be filed in the same court).

and/or attorney fees,[41] the production of specified documents,[42] making the dismissal with prejudice,[43] and an agreement not to assert specified claims in another action. If the plaintiff is unhappy with the conditions imposed by the court, the plaintiff may decline the dismissal.[44]

Counterclaims

If the defendant has filed a counterclaim, then the plaintiff cannot dismiss the action against the defendant's objections unless the counterclaim can remain pending for adjudication.[45] The defendant may dismiss its own counterclaim in the same manner that Rule 41 provides for dismissal of the plaintiff's claims.[46]

Dismissal of Part of Action

The plaintiff may dismiss some, but not all, of the defendants.[47] Courts differ as to the proper procedural mechanism for voluntarily dismissing part of an action after an answer or summary judgment motion has been filed.[48] Some courts allow voluntary dismissal by court order pursuant to Rule 41(a)(2). Some courts require a motion to amend pursuant to Rule 15(a).[49]

Enforcement of Settlement Agreement

Normally, a federal court does not have jurisdiction over an action to enforce the terms of a settlement and stipulated dismissal.[50] In order to vest the district court with such jurisdiction, the court may, at its discretion, make the parties' compliance with a settlement agreement part of its dismissal order.[51]

41. *Brown v. Local 58, Int'l Bhd. of Elec. Workers*, 76 F.3d 762, 766–67 (6th Cir.1996); *Hinfin Realty Corp. v. The Pittston Co.*, 212 F.R.D. 461, 462 (E.D.N.Y.2002) (courts often grant fee awards when a plaintiff dismisses a suit without prejudice under Rule 41(a)(2)); *BD v. Debuono*, 193 F.R.D. 117 (S.D.N.Y.2000) (attorney fees awarded only where conduct of the plaintiff was in bad faith or vexatious).

42. *In re Vitamins Antitrust Litigation*, 198 F.R.D. 296 (D.D.C.2000) (dismissal conditioned on the plaintiff responding to outstanding document requests and interrogatories).

43. *Elbaor v. Tripath Imaging, Inc.*, 279 F.3d 314, 316, n.1 (5th Cir.2002) (the court may require the dismissal to be with prejudice to protect the defendant, but not to punish the plaintiff); *Woodzicka v. Artifex Limited*, 25 F.Supp.2d 930, 934 (E.D.Wis.1998).

44. *Elbaor v. Tripath Imaging, Inc.*, 279 F.3d 314, 320 (5th Cir.2002); *Babcock v. McDaniel*, 148 F.3d 797, 799 (7th Cir.1998) (if the plaintiff moves for dismissal without prejudice, the court may not dismiss with prejudice without offering the plaintiff an opportunity withdraw the motion).

45. *See Underwriters at Interest on Cover Note JHB92M10582079 v. Nautronix, Ltd.*, 79 F.3d 480, 483–85 (5th Cir.1996); *Wyandotte Nation v. City of Kansas City, Kansas*, 200 F.Supp.2d 1279, 1283 (D.Kan.2002).

46. *eCash Technologies, Inc. v. Guagliardo*, 127 F.Supp.2d 1069, 1081–82 (C.D.Cal.2000).

47. *Protocomm Corp. v. Novell, Inc.*, 171 F.Supp.2d 459, 471 (E.D.Pa.2001)(dismissal of some defendants is permissible even in the presence of cross-claims).

48. *See Jet, Inc. v. Sewage Aeration Systems*, 223 F.3d 1360, 1364 (Fed.Cir.2000) (Rule 41(a)(2) and Rule 15(a) are functionally interchangeable); *State Treasurer of State of Michigan v. Barry*, 168 F.3d 8, 18 (11th Cir.1999).

49. *See Boyce v. Augusta–Richmond County*, 111 F.Supp.2d 1363, 1374 (S.D.Ga.2000).

50. *Solv-Ex Corp. v. Quillen*, 186 F.R.D. 313, 315 (S.D.N.Y.1999); *Lee v. Runyon*, 18 F.Supp.2d 649, 653 (E.D.Tex.1998).

51. *Kokkonen v. Guardian Life Ins. Co. of America*, 511 U.S. 375, 114 S.Ct. 1673, 128 L.Ed.2d 391 (1994); *Bragg v. Robertson*, 54 F.Supp.2d 653, 662–63 (S.D.W.Va.1999).

Circumvention of Rule 39(b)

A district court may not use Rule 41(a)(2) to allow an untimely jury demand (by dismissal, then refiling a new complaint with a jury demand) if it would be prohibited from doing so under Rule 39(b), as that would introduce an unnecessary conflict between the two federal rules.[52]

Appeal

The granting or denial of a motion for voluntary dismissal is normally not appealable.[53] However, mandamus will lie if the motion was to dismiss with prejudice.[54] The defendant may appeal a notice of voluntary dismissal[55] or an order granting a motion for voluntary dismissal.[56] The plaintiff may be able to appeal the granting of its own motion to dismiss if the court imposes conditions on the dismissal that prejudice the plaintiff and to which the plaintiff has not acquiesced.[57] The plaintiff may not appeal prior rulings in an action if the action is dismissed without prejudice.[58]

RULE 41(b). INVOLUNTARY DISMISSAL

CORE CONCEPT

Rule 41(b) governs two types of involuntary dismissals: dismissal for failure to prosecute; and dismissal for failure to comply with other Rules or with a court order.

NOTE: Rule 41(b) was amended in 1991, and care should be exercised when citing decisions pertaining to Rule 41(b).

APPLICATIONS

Disfavored

Involuntary dismissal is within the discretion of the court,[59] but is disfavored and is granted sparingly.[60]

52. *Russ v. Standard Ins. Co.*, 120 F.3d 988, 990 (9th Cir.1997); *but see Hoffmann v. Alside, Inc.*, 596 F.2d 822, 823 (8th Cir.1979).

53. *See Briseno v. Ashcroft*, 291 F.3d 377 (5th Cir.2002).

54. *In re International Business Machines Corp.*, 687 F.2d 591 (2d Cir.1982).

55. *Harvey Aluminum, Inc. v. American Cyanamid Co.*, 203 F.2d 105 (2d Cir.1953).

56. *Pontenberg v. Boston Scientific Corp.*, 252 F.3d 1253 (11th Cir.2001) (order granting dismissal is reviewed under the abuse of discretion standard).

57. *See Chavez v. Illinois State Police*, 251 F.3d 612 (7th Cir.2001); *Belle-Midwest, Inc. v. Missouri Property & Casualty Ins. Guarantee Ass'n*, 56 F.3d 977 (8th Cir.1995).

58. *Martens v. Thomann*, 273 F.3d 159, 183 (2d Cir.2001) ("interlocutory orders should not ordinarily merge with a final judgment dismissing an action for failure to prosecute"); *Chappelle v. Beacon Communications Corp.*, 84 F.3d 652, 654 (2d Cir.1996).

59. *Bishop v. Lewis*, 155 F.3d 1094, 1096 (9th Cir.1998).

60. *LeSane v. Hall's Sec. Analyst, Inc.*, 239 F.3d 206, 209 (2d Cir.2001) (involuntary dismissal is a harsh remedy to be utilized only in extreme situations, particularly when *pro se* plaintiffs are involved); *Hunt v. City of Minneapolis, Minnesota*, 203 F.3d 524, 527 (8th Cir. 2000) (involuntary dismissal should be used when lesser sanctions prove futile).

Failure to Prosecute

The court may dismiss for failure to prosecute *sua sponte* or upon motion.[61] Local Rules frequently specify the conditions for dismissal based on inactivity (typically, lack of activity for a period of one year).[62]

Failure to Comply With Rules or With Order

The court may grant a motion for involuntary dismissal or dismiss an action *sua sponte* based on the plaintiff's failure to comply with the Rules or with a court order.[63] For example, the plaintiff may risk involuntary dismissal by persistently refusing to file a pretrial statement. To determine whether dismissal is an appropriate sanction for violation of a particular Rule, the practitioner should also review the author commentary and case law discussing that Rule.[64]

With Prejudice

Involuntary dismissals are presumed to be with prejudice unless the court specifies otherwise.[65] Additionally, involuntary dismissal under Rule 41(b) and dismissals not under Rule 41 (other than dismissals for lack of jurisdiction,[66] lack of venue,[67] or failure to join a party under Rule 19) operate as adjudications on the merits for purposes of res judicata or collateral estoppel.[68]

61. *Pomales v. Celulares Telefonica, Inc.*, 342 F.3d 44, 50, n.5 (1st Cir. 2003) (warning is not strictly required before dismissal, but without a warning, the circumstances must show knowledge of the potential consequences of the party's conduct); *Aura Lamp & Lighting Inc. v. International Trading Corp.*, 325 F.3d 903, 908 (7th Cir.2003) (setting forth the factors for involuntary dismissal for failure to prosecute); *O'Rourke Bros., Inc. v. Nesbitt Burns, Inc.*, 201 F.3d 948, 953 (7th Cir.2000) (involuntary dismissal based on failure to serve the complaint).

62. *See Wagner v. Ashcroft*, 214 F.R.D. 78 (N.D.N.Y.2003).

63. *Slack v. McDaniel*, 529 U.S. 473, 120 S.Ct. 1595, 146 L.Ed.2d 542 (2000); *Wynder v. McMahon*, 360 F.3d 73, 78 (2nd Cir. 2004) (court may not dismiss based on failure to comply with an order that imposes requirements greater than those authorized by the Rules); *Olsen v. Mapes*, 333 F.3d 1199 (10th Cir.2003) (setting forth criteria for involuntary dismissal for violation of a court order).

64. *See, e.g., Jackson v. City of New York*, 22 F.3d 71 (2d Cir.1994).

65. *Styskal v. Weld County Bd. of County Com'rs*, 365 F.3d 855, 858–59 (10th Cir. 2004); *Owens v. Kaiser Foundation Health Plan, Inc.*, 244 F.3d 708, 714 (9th Cir.2001) (dismissal for failure to prosecute acts as an adjudication on the merits); *Proctor v. Millar Elevator Service Co.*, 8 F.3d 824 (D.C.Cir.1993). *Cf. Criales v. American Airlines, Inc.*, 105 F.3d 93, 95 (2d Cir.1997), *cert. denied*, 522 U.S. 906, 118 S.Ct. 264, 139 L.Ed.2d 190 (1997) (dismissal for failure to exhaust state or administrative remedies is usually without prejudice).

66. *County of Mille Lacs v. Benjamin*, 361 F.3d 460, 464–65 (8th Cir. 2004); *Matosantos Commercial Corp. v. Applebee's Intern., Inc.*, 245 F.3d 1203, 1209 (10th Cir.2001) (noting that the first adjudication will have estoppel effect as to the jurisdictional issues actually determined by the court).

67. *See Vasquez v. Bridgestone/Firestone, Inc.*, 325 F.3d 665, 678 (5th Cir.2003) (dismissal for forum non conveniens is not dismissal for lack of venue, and this is a dismissal with prejudice).

68. *See Semtek Intern. Inc. v. Lockheed Martin Corp.*, 531 U.S. 497, 121 S.Ct. 1021, 149 L.Ed.2d 32 (2001) (Rule 41 determines that the dismissal is on the merits, but in diversity cases, state law then determines the preclusive effect of the dismissal on another action); *Orca Yachts, L.L.C. v. Mollicam, Inc.*, 287 F.3d 316, 319 (4th Cir.2002).

Motion Formalities

If the defendant makes the motion for involuntary dismissal at the close of plaintiff's case, it may be oral and without notice. Otherwise, the defendant must comply with the normal procedural formalities.

Dismissal Under Other Rules

Rule 41(b) governs only the two specified types of involuntary dismissal. Other types of dismissal are addressed elsewhere, such as in Rule 12(b), governing dismissal for reasons such as failure to state a claim and lack of jurisdiction.[69]

Appeal

The plaintiff may appeal an involuntary dismissal as a final order.[70] The order will be reviewed under the abuse of discretion standard.[71]

RULE 41(c). DISMISSAL OF COUNTERCLAIMS, ETC.

CORE CONCEPT

The provisions of Rule 41 apply to counterclaims, crossclaims, and third-party claims with equal force.[72] For example, the right to unilateral voluntary dismissal ends with the filing of a responsive pleading or motion for summary judgment directed toward the counterclaim, crossclaim, or third-party claim.

RULE 41(d). COSTS OF PREVIOUSLY DISMISSED ACTION

CORE CONCEPT

If a plaintiff who has already *voluntarily* dismissed an action commences another action on the same claim, the court, in its discretion, can stay the second action until the plaintiff[73] pays such costs of the first action as the court deems appropriate.[74] The courts are split as to whether an award of costs under Rule 41(d) may include attorneys

69. *See Blue Cross and Blue Shield of Ala. v. Fondren*, 966 F.Supp. 1093, 1097 (M.D.Ala.1997) (case due to be dismissed for lack of subject matter jurisdiction is due to be dismissed without prejudice).

70. *Wynder v. McMahon*, 360 F.3d 73, 76 (2nd Cir. 2004) (a dismissal without prejudice that does not give leave to amend and closes the case is a final, appealable order); *Rodgers v. Curators of the Univ. of Missouri*, 135 F.3d 1216, 1219 (8th Cir.1998) (applying an abuse of discretion standard).

71. *Cintron-Lorenzo v. Departamento de Asuntos del Consumidor*, 312 F.3d 522, 526 (1st Cir.2002).

72. *Orca Yachts, L.L.C. v. Mollicam, Inc.*, 287 F.3d 316, 319 (4th Cir.2002).

73. *Duffy v. Ford Motor Co.*, 218 F.3d 623, 636 (6th Cir.2000) (Rule 41(d) discusses the imposition of costs upon the plaintiffs, not counsel).

74. *Pontenberg v. Boston Scientific Corp.*, 252 F.3d 1253 (11th Cir.2001) (Rule 41(d) authorizes the district court to require the plaintiff to pay the defendant's costs of the dismissed action upon refiling the action); *Rogers v. Wal–Mart Stores, Inc.*, 230 F.3d 868, 874 (6th Cir. 2000), *cert. denied*, 532 U.S. 953, 121 S.Ct. 1428, 149 L.Ed.2d 367 (2001) (part of the purpose of Rule 41(d) is to avoid forum shopping; it is not necessary to show bad faith or vexatious conduct).

fees.[75]

ADDITIONAL RESEARCH REFERENCES

Wright & Miller, *Federal Practice and Procedure* §§ 2361–2376.

C.J.S. Federal Civil Procedure §§ 486, 775–819 et seq., 839–869 et seq.

West's Key No. Digests, Federal Civil Procedure ⚷1691–1715, 1721–1729, 1741, 1758–1765, 1821–1842.

75. *See Rogers v. Wal–Mart Stores, Inc.*, 230 F.3d 868, 875 (6th Cir.2000), *cert. denied*, 532 U.S. 953, 121 S.Ct. 1428, 149 L.Ed.2d 367 (2001) (noting the split and determining that fees are not available in the 6th Circuit); *Esposito v. Piatrowski*, 223 F.3d 497 (7th Cir.2000) (attorneys fees may be recovered only when an underlying statute defines costs as including attorneys fees).

RULE 42

A CONSOLIDATION; SEPARATE TRIALS

(a) Consolidation. When actions involving a common question of law or fact are pending before the court, it may order a joint hearing or trial of any or all the matters in issue in the actions; it may order all the actions consolidated; and it may make such orders concerning proceedings therein as may tend to avoid unnecessary costs or delay.

(b) Separate Trials. The court, in furtherance of convenience or to avoid prejudice, or when separate trials will be conducive to expedition and economy, may order a separate trial of any claim, cross-claim, counterclaim, or third-party claim, or of any separate issue or of any number of claims, cross-claims, counterclaims, third-party claims, or issues, always preserving inviolate the right of trial by jury as declared by the Seventh Amendment to the Constitution or as given by a statute of the United States.

[Amended effective July 1, 1966.]

AUTHORS' COMMENTARY ON RULE 42

PURPOSE AND SCOPE

Rule 42 allows the court to control the manner in which the cases on its docket are tried; the court may consolidate several actions into a single proceeding or may conduct separate trials of various issues within a single action.

RULE 42(a). CONSOLIDATION

CORE CONCEPT

When actions pending[1] before the court share common issues of law or fact, the court can consolidate the actions, either completely or for limited proceedings or stages.[2]

1. *Mourik Intern. B.V. v. Reactor Services Intern., Inc.*, 182 F.Supp.2d 599, 602 (S.D.Tex. 2002) (the case must be properly pending before the court to be consolidated; an improperly removed case could not be consolidated).

2. *Lewis v. ACB Bus. Services Inc.*, 135 F.3d 389, 412 (6th Cir.1998).

APPLICATIONS

Court's Discretion

In deciding whether to consolidate actions, the court should balance the savings to the judicial system against the possible inconvenience, delay, or prejudice to the parties.[3] The court has broad discretion in this balancing process,[4] and does not need the parties' consent.[5]

Common Issues Necessary

Although the court has broad discretion, it may not consolidate actions that do not share common issues of law or fact.[6]

Limited Consolidation

The court may consolidate actions for all purposes, for pretrial proceedings only, or for specified hearings or issues.

Actions in Different Districts

Actions in different districts may not be consolidated. However, if actions are pending in different districts that ought to be consolidated, the actions may be transferred to a single district, then consolidated, as provided in 28 U.S.C.A. § 1407.

Actions Remain Separate

In general, consolidated actions retain their separate identity.[7] Thus, the pleadings will remain separate and the court will enter separate judgments in each action. However, the court can order that briefs and rulings apply to all consolidated cases.[8]

Conflicts of Interest

Consolidation may be improper if it aligns parties who have conflicting interests.[9]

3. *Arnold v. Eastern Air Lines, Inc.*, 681 F.2d 186, 193 (4th Cir.1982), *cert. denied,* 460 U.S. 1102, 103 S.Ct. 1801, 76 L.Ed.2d 366 (1983); *Kos Pharmaceuticals, Inc. v. Barr Laboratories, Inc.*, 218 F.R.D. 387 (S.D.N.Y. 2003) (balancing competing factors in evaluating consolidation); *Nieto v. Kapoor*, 210 F.R.D. 244, 248 (D.N.M.2002).

4. *Young v. Augusta, Ga. Through DeVaney*, 59 F.3d 1160, 1168 (11th Cir.1995); *Saudi Basic Industries Corp. v. Exxonmobil Corp.*, 194 F.Supp.2d 378, 416 (D.N.J. 2002).

5. *Connecticut General Life Ins. Co. v. Sun Life Assurance Co. Of Canada*, 210 F.3d 771 (7th Cir.2000).

6. *Malcolm v. National Gypsum Co.*, 995 F.2d 346 (2d Cir.1993); *Philips Electronics North America Corp. v. Contec Corp.*, 220 F.R.D. 415, 418 (D.Del. 2004); *Saudi Basic Industries Corp. v. Exxonmobil Corp.*, 194 F.Supp.2d 378, 416 (D.N.J.2002), *order vac'd in part,* 364 F.3d 102 (3d Cir.2004) (Rule 42(a) does not require that the cases be identical, merely that there be a common question of law or fact).

7. *Boardman Petroleum, Inc. v. Federated Mut. Ins. Co.*, 135 F.3d 750, 752 (11th Cir.1998); *Lewis v. ACB Bus. Services, Inc.*, 135 F.3d 389, 412 (6th Cir.1998); *Narragansett Indian Tribe of Rhode Island v. Rhode Island*, 296 F.Supp.2d 153, 159 (D.R.I. 2003) (each action must have an independent basis of federal jurisdiction); *State v. Microsoft Corp.*, 209 F.Supp.2d 132 (D.D.C. 2002) (consolidation does not make the parties to one action parties to the other).

8. *Specht v. Netscape Communications Corp.*, 150 F.Supp.2d 585, 586, n.1 (S.D.N.Y.2001).

9. *Dupont v. Southern Pac. Co.*, 366 F.2d 193 (5th Cir.1966); *Atkinson v. Roth,* 297 F.2d 570 (3d Cir.1961).

Arbitration

Many courts do not permit consolidation of arbitrations unless there is an express provision in the arbitration agreements providing for consolidation.[10]

Procedures

Consolidation is achieved by motion of any party or by the court *sua sponte*.[11] Local rules may determine to which judge a motion to consolidate should be presented if the matters are pending before different judges.[12] Once actions have been consolidated, the court manages the proceedings. In unusual circumstances, the court may appoint one counsel as lead or liaison counsel.

Appeals

An order granting or denying a motion for consolidation is not appealable as a final judgment,[13] although mandamus may be available under extreme circumstances.[14]

RULE 42(b). SEPARATE TRIALS

CORE CONCEPT

The court may conduct separate trials of any claim or issue.[15]

APPLICATIONS

Court's Discretion

In deciding whether to order separate trials, the court should balance the savings to the judicial system against the possible inconvenience, delay, or prejudice to the parties.[16] The court has broad discretion in this balancing process.[17]

10. *Champ v. Siegel Trading Co.*, 55 F.3d 269, 274 (7th Cir.1995); *but see Office & Professional Employees Intern. Union, AFL–CIO v. Sea–Land Service, Inc.*, 210 F.3d 117, 123 (2d Cir.2000), *cert. denied*, 531 U.S. 1076, 121 S.Ct. 771, 148 L.Ed.2d 670 (2001) (developing common law of labor contracts empowered district court to consolidate two arbitration proceedings without consideration of whether such consolidation was authorized by Fed.R.Civ.P. 42(a)).

11. *Tucker v. Kenney,* 994 F.Supp. 412 (E.D.N.Y.1998) (court may order consolidation upon its own motion, and the consent of the parties is not required).

12. *Stewart v. O'Neill*, 225 F.Supp.2d 16, 21 (D.D.C.2002) (local rule providing that the motion to consolidate should be presented in the matter first filed).

13. *NAACP of Louisiana v. Michot,* 480 F.2d 547, 548 (5th Cir.1973).

14. *In re Repetitive Stress Injury Litigation*, 11 F.3d 368 (2d Cir.1993).

15. *Simon v. Philip Morris Inc.*, 200 F.R.D. 21, 27 (E.D.N.Y.2001) (the court may order a separate trial of any claim, cross-claim, counterclaim, or third-party claim, or of any separate issue or of any number of claims, cross-claims, counterclaims, third-party claims, or issues).

16. *Lindsey v. Prive Corp.*, 161 F.3d 886, 892 (5th Cir.1998); *Quintanilla v. City of Downey*, 84 F.3d 353, 356 (9th Cir.1996), *cert. denied*, 519 U.S. 1122, 117 S.Ct. 972, 136 L.Ed.2d 856 (1997); *William Reber, LLC v. Samsung Electronics America, Inc.*, 220 F.R.D. 533, 536 (N.D.Ill. 2004) (prejudice is the most important factor, and bifurcation should be the exception, not the rule).

17. *Houseman v. United States Aviation Underwriters*, 171 F.3d 1117 (7th Cir.1999); *TVT Records v. Island Def Jam Music Group*, 257 F.Supp.2d 737, 747 (S.D.N.Y.2003).

Burden of Proof

The burden is on the moving party to demonstrate that bifurcation is justified even in cases where bifurcation is not uncommon.[18]

Single Action

A separation under Rule 42 separates aspects of the action for trial, but the aspects remain part of a single action, and result in a single judgment.[19] This contrasts with claims that are severed pursuant to Rule 21.[20]

Liability and Damages

The most common instance of separate trials is when the court first conducts a trial as to liability, then as to damages if necessary.[21]

Separate Trials for Each Defendant

The court may order separate trials for each defendant, particularly if one is in bankruptcy, as long as the defendants are not indispensable parties.[22]

Procedure

The court may order separate trials *sua sponte* or by motion of any party.

Federal Law Controls

Bifurcated trials are permissible under Rule 42 even when the state law would prohibit bifurcation.[23]

Jury Trials

The procedures for separate trials do not affect the parties' rights to a jury trial.[24] Separate trials may be conducted before one jury or different juries. If there are jury and non-jury claims present, the jury claims may have to be tried first, so that the court does not make factual findings that should properly have been made by the jury.

18. *Thorndike ex rel. Thorndike v. Daimler-chrysler Corp.*, 220 F.R.D. 6, 8 (D.Me. 2004); *Real v. Bunn–O–Matic Corp.*, 195 F.R.D. 618, 620 (N.D.Ill.2000) (the party seeking bifurcation has the burden of demonstrating that judicial economy would be served and that no party would be prejudiced by separate trials); *Industrias Metalicas Marva, Inc. v. Lausell,* 172 F.R.D. 1, 2 (D.P.R.1997) (bifurcation is not and should not be routine, but should be encouraged where experienced has demonstrated its worth).

19. *White v. ABCO Engineering Corp.*, 199 F.3d 140, 145 (3d Cir.1999); *Hecht v. City of New York*, 217 F.R.D. 148, 149–50 (S.D.N.Y. 2003); *In re Brand–Name Prescription Drugs Antitrust Litigation*, 264 F.Supp.2d 1372 (Jud.Pan. Mult.Lit. 2003).

20. *Rice v. Sunrise Express, Inc.*, 209 F.3d 1008, 1014–16 (7th Cir.2000), *cert. denied*, 531 U.S. 1012, 121 S.Ct. 567, 148 L.Ed.2d 486 (2000).

21. *See Gafford v. General Electric Co.*, 997 F.2d 150 (6th Cir.1993); *Colon ex rel. Molina v. Bic USA, Inc.*, 199 F.Supp.2d 53, 97–98 (S.D.N.Y.2001).

22. *Hecht v. City of New York*, 217 F.R.D. 148, 150 (S.D.N.Y. 2003).

23. *Oulds v. Principal Mutual Life Ins. Co.*, 6 F.3d 1431 (10th Cir.1993).

24. *Danjaq LLC v. Sony Corp.*, 263 F.3d 942, 961–62 (9th Cir.2001) (in ordering separate trials, the court must "always preserv[e] inviolate the right of trial by jury as declared by the Seventh Amendment to the Constitution").

State Law Claims

The court may conduct a separate trial of an issue over which it could not exercise independent jurisdiction. Thus, if a court exercised supplemental jurisdiction over a state law claim that otherwise could not have been brought as a separate action, the court may at the trial stage conduct a separate trial for that state law claim.[25]

Appeals

An order granting or denying a motion for bifurcation is not appealable as a final judgment, although mandamus may be available under extreme circumstances.[26] The decision ultimately may be reviewed under the "abuse of discretion" standard.[27]

ADDITIONAL RESEARCH REFERENCES

Wright & Miller, *Federal Practice and Procedure* §§ 2381–2392.

C.J.S. Federal Civil Procedure §§ 611, 916–918.

West's Key No. Digests, Federal Civil Procedure ⚷8–9, 1953–1965.

25. *Travelers Indem. Co. v. Miller Mfg. Co.*, 276 F.2d 955 (6th Cir.1960).

26. *See In re Repetitive Stress Injury Litigation*, 11 F.3d 368 (2d Cir.1993).

27. *Palace Exploration Co. v. Petroleum Development Co.*, 316 F.3d 1110, 1118–19 (10th Cir.2003); *Athey v. Farmers Ins. Exchange*, 234 F.3d 357, 362 (8th Cir.2000).

RULE 43

TAKING OF TESTIMONY

(a) Form. In every trial, the testimony of witnesses shall be taken in open court, unless a federal law, these rules, the Federal Rules of Evidence, or other rules adopted by the Supreme Court provide otherwise. The court may, for good cause shown in compelling circumstances and upon appropriate safeguards, permit presentation of testimony in open court by contemporaneous transmission from a different location.

(b) [Abrogated].

(c) [Abrogated].

(d) Affirmation in Lieu of Oath. Whenever under these rules an oath is required to be taken, a solemn affirmation may be accepted in lieu thereof.

(e) Evidence on Motions. When a motion is based on facts not appearing of record the court may hear the matter on affidavits presented by the respective parties, but the court may direct that the matter be heard wholly or partly on oral testimony or deposition.

(f) Interpreters. The court may appoint an interpreter of its own selection and may fix the interpreter's reasonable compensation. The compensation shall be paid out of funds provided by law or by one or more of the parties as the court may direct, and may be taxed ultimately as costs, in the discretion of the court.

[Amended effective July 1, 1966; July 1, 1975; August 1, 1987, December 1, 1996.]

AUTHORS' COMMENTARY ON RULE 43

PURPOSE AND SCOPE

Rule 43, formerly entitled "Evidence" was largely supplanted by the Federal Rules of Evidence. The remaining provisions govern the manner in which testimony is taken, the manner in which evidence is presented in support of motions, and the use of interpreters. A discussion of the Federal Rules of Evidence is beyond the scope of this book.

RULE 43(a). FORM

CORE CONCEPT

There is a preference in federal court for testimony taken in open court.[1] All testimony shall be in such form unless otherwise authorized by the Federal Rules of Evidence,[2] federal statute, or Supreme Court rule, or if stipulated by the parties.[3]

APPLICATIONS

Live Testimony

The Rules place a strong emphasis on live testimony taken in open court.[4] Rule 43(a) reflects the permissible use of other forms of communication, such as writing or sign language, if the witness cannot speak.[5]

Remote Testimony

Rule 43(a) allows the transmitting of testimony from a different location.[6] However, the Rules continue to emphasize live testimony in court, and transmitted testimony is permitted only for good cause shown in compelling circumstances.[7] In cases where remote testimony is to be used, the court must employ appropriate safeguards to protect the procedure and the parties' interests.[8] Transmitted testimony might be allowed when unexpected circumstances, such as an accident or illness, render a witness unable to appear in court.[9]

RULES 43(b)–(c). ABROGATED

RULE 43(d). AFFIRMATION IN LIEU OF OATH

CORE CONCEPT

A party who, for religious reasons or otherwise, chooses not to take

1. *In re Stevinson*, 194 B.R. 509, 511 (D.Colo. 1996) (approving use of written direct testimony and live cross-examination).

2. *Kuntz v. Sea Eagle Diving Adventures Corp.*, 199 F.R.D. 665, 667 (D.Hawai'i 2001) (Federal Rules of Evidence authorize the submission of testimony by affidavit).

3. *Charlton Mem. Hosp. v. Sullivan*, 816 F.Supp. 50 (D.Mass.1993); *Saverson v. Levitt*, 162 F.R.D. 407, 408 (D.D.C.1995).

4. *Rusu v. U.S. I.N.S.*, 296 F.3d 316 (4th Cir.2002).

5. The Advisory Committee Note to the 1996 Amendment to Rule 43.

6. *Beltran–Tirado v. I.N.S.*, 213 F.3d 1179, 1185–86 (9th Cir.2000) (rejecting a due process challenge to telephonic testimony).

7. *See F.T.C. v. Swedish Match North America, Inc.*, 197 F.R.D. 1, 2 (D.D.C.2000) (serious inconvenience to the witness constitutes good cause); *United States v. Gigante,* 971 F.Supp. 755 (E.D.N.Y.1997), *aff'd*, 166 F.3d 75 (2d Cir. 1999) (recognizing the use of televised presentation of evidence under Rule 43).

8. *F.T.C. v. Swedish Match North America, Inc.*, 197 F.R.D. 1 (D.D.C.2000) (in assessing the safeguards of remote testimony, the courts focus on whether the testimony was made in open court, under oath, and whether the opportunity for cross examination was available).

9. The Advisory Committee Note to the 1996 Amendment to Rule 43.

an oath, may make a "solemn affirmation" instead.[10]

RULE 43(e). EVIDENCE ON MOTIONS

CORE CONCEPT

A party may submit affidavits in support of or in opposition to a motion in order to demonstrate facts not found in the record.[11] The court, in its discretion, may order oral evidence taken[12] or may request deposition transcripts. The court may also consider preliminary injunction applications under Rule 43(e).[13]

RULE 43(f). INTERPRETERS

CORE CONCEPT

The court may, in its discretion, appoint an interpreter,[14] who then should take an oath or affirmation that the translation will be accurate. If an interpreter is appointed, the court may determine the interpreter's fees. The court may order that one party pay the fees, and may award the fees as costs after the conclusion of the trial.

ADDITIONAL RESEARCH REFERENCES

Wright & Miller, *Federal Practice and Procedure* §§ 2401–2417.

C.J.S. Courts § 1–110; Federal Civil Procedure §§ 368, 373, 935; Witnesses §§ 320–326.

West's Key No. Digests, Courts ⚷56; Federal Civil Procedure ⚷921, 2011; Witnesses ⚷227, 228, 230.

10. *Doe v. Phillips*, 81 F.3d 1204 (2d Cir. 1996), *cert. denied*, 520 U.S. 1115, 117 S.Ct. 1244, 137 L.Ed.2d 326 (1997).

11. *Valentin v. Hospital Bella Vista*, 254 F.3d 358, 364 (1st Cir.2001); *Spurlock v. Lawson*, 881 F.Supp. 436, 438 (E.D.Ark.1995)(evidence not in the record considered in ruling on a motion for new trial); *Tiberi v. CIGNA Ins. Co.*, 40 F.3d 110 (5th Cir.1994)(holding that faxed affidavits are admissible).

12. *March v. Levine*, 249 F.3d 462 (6th Cir. 2001), *cert. denied*, 534 U.S. 1080, 122 S.Ct. 810, 151 L.Ed.2d 695 (2002) (oral testimony is not favored in summary judgment proceedings due to the well founded reluctance to turn a summary judgment hearing into a trial); *Thompson v. Mahre,* 110 F.3d 716, 719 (9th Cir.1997), *cert. denied*, 522 U.S. 967, 118 S.Ct. 414, 139 L.Ed.2d 317 (1997) (district courts may in their discretion "sparingly and with great care" take oral testimony under Rule 43(e) on a summary judgment motion); *PAR Microsystems, Inc. v. Pinnacle Dev. Corp.*, 995 F.Supp. 655 (N.D.Tex.1997) (oral testimony permitted only when a controlling credibility question is presented).

13. *Jones v. Bush*, 122 F.Supp.2d 713, 715 (N.D.Tex.2000).

14. *Pedraza v. Phoenix*, 1994 WL 177285 (S.D.N.Y.1994)(no right to a court-ordered translation of pre-trial motions).

RULE 44

PROOF OF OFFICIAL RECORD

(a) Authentication.

(1) *Domestic.* An official record kept within the United States, or any state, district, or commonwealth, or within a territory subject to the administrative or judicial jurisdiction of the United States, or an entry therein, when admissible for any purpose, may be evidenced by an official publication thereof or by a copy attested by the officer having the legal custody of the record, or by the officer's deputy, and accompanied by a certificate that such officer has the custody. The certificate may be made by a judge of a court of record of the district or political subdivision in which the record is kept, authenticated by the seal of the court, or may be made by any public officer having a seal of office and having official duties in the district or political subdivision in which the record is kept, authenticated by the seal of the officer's office.

(2) *Foreign.* A foreign official record, or an entry therein, when admissible for any purpose, may be evidenced by an official publication thereof; or a copy thereof, attested by a person authorized to make the attestation, and accompanied by a final certification as to the genuineness of the signature and official position (i) of the attesting person, or (ii) of any foreign official whose certificate of genuineness of signature and official position relates to the attestation or is in a chain of certificates of genuineness of signature and official position relating to the attestation. A final certification may be made by a secretary of embassy or legation, consul general, vice consul, or consular agent of the United States, or a diplomatic or consular official of the foreign country assigned or accredited to the United States. If reasonable opportunity has been given to all parties to investigate the authenticity and accuracy of the documents, the court may, for good cause shown, (i) admit an attested copy without final certification or (ii) permit the foreign official record to be evidenced by an attested summary with or without a final certification. The final certification is unnecessary if the record and the attestation are certified as provided in a treaty or convention to which the United States and the foreign country in which the official record is located are parties.

(b) Lack of Record. A written statement that after diligent search no record or entry of a specified tenor is found to exist in the records designated by the statement, authenticated as provided in subdivision (a)(1) of this rule in the case of a domestic record, or complying with the requirements of subdivision (a)(2) of this rule for a summary in the case of a foreign record, is admissible as evidence that the records contain no such record or entry.

(c) Other Proof. This rule does not prevent the proof of official records or of entry or lack of entry therein by any other method authorized by law.

[Amended effective July 1, 1966; August 1, 1987; December 1, 1991.]

AUTHORS' COMMENTARY ON RULE 44

PURPOSE AND SCOPE

Rule 44 describes certain methods for authenticating official records of the United States or foreign governments. It also provides methods to demonstrate the absence of a particular official document or record.

RULE 44(a)(1). DOMESTIC

CORE CONCEPT

An official record kept within the United States is authenticated if it is an official publication or if it is a copy of an official record which is attested to by the legal custodian and accompanied by a certificate made by a judge or public officer with a seal of office.

APPLICATIONS

Official Record

"Official record" is not a defined term, but includes such documents as weather bureau records, records of conviction, tax returns, marriage and birth certificates, and selective service files. "Official" does not mean "public"; the public need not have access to "official records."

No Summaries

The Rule applies only to the record itself, not to summaries of the contents of the record.

Authentication Only

Rule 44 only *authenticates* records. It does not render the records immune from other objections, such as hearsay (but see the exception to the hearsay rule for official records), nor does it govern the import of those records.[1]

1. *Moreno v. Macaluso*, 844 F.Supp. 736 (M.D.Fla.1994).

Entries in Record

The Rule applies equally to entire records or individual entries.

Official Publication

When a document has been printed by government authority, its authenticity is established.

Documents Kept in the United States

Rule 44 applies to all official federal, state, or local records physically maintained within the United States or within territories subject to United States jurisdiction, not just to United States official records. Thus, it includes foreign government records maintained in the United States.

Attested Copy

A copy of an official record may be attested to by the officer having legal custody of the record or by the officer's deputy.

Certificate

The attested copy must be accompanied by a certificate that the attesting individual has custody of the record. The certificate must be made by a judge in the district or political subdivision in which the document is kept, or by a public official with duties in the district or political subdivision in which the document is kept, provided that the official has a seal of office and authenticates the certificate with that seal.[2]

RULE 44(a)(2). FOREIGN

CORE CONCEPT

A foreign official record may be authenticated in essentially the same manner as a domestic record (described immediately above), with some minor variations.

APPLICATIONS

Official Publication

As with a domestic official record, official publications of foreign official records are self-authenticating.[3]

Attested Copy With Certificate

A foreign official record may be attested to by any person authorized by the laws of that country to attest records if the signature is certified by a secretary of embassy or legation, consul general, consul, vice consul or consular agent of the United States, or a diplomatic or consular official of the foreign country assigned or accredited to the

2. *Espinoza v. Immigration & Naturalization Service*, 45 F.3d 308 (9th Cir.1995).

3. *Construction Drilling, Inc. v. Chusid*, 63 F.Supp.2d 509 514 (D.N.J.1999).

United States.[4] The certification will not be necessary if the United States and the foreign country are signatories to a treaty providing for proof of foreign records without a certification and the foreign record is submitted in accordance with the treaty.[5] In particular, see the Hague Public Documents Convention,[6] and the Convention Abolishing the Requirement of Legalization for Foreign Public Documents.[7]

Chain of Certificate

An attestation may also be certified via a chain of certifications, as long as the chain leads to one of the officials listed above.[8]

Attested Copy Without Certificate

The court has discretion to admit an attested copy of a foreign official record without a certificate if all parties have had a reasonable opportunity to investigate the authenticity and accuracy of the record, or for good cause.[9]

RULE 44(b). LACK OF RECORD

CORE CONCEPT

One may prove the absence of a particular record with a written statement that after diligent search, no record or entry of the specified nature exists. The statement must be authenticated in the same manner as for an official record.

RULE 44(c). OTHER PROOF

CORE CONCEPT

The methods in Rule 44 are not exclusive. Quite often, an official will testify as to the authenticity of an official record. Similarly, certain documents are self-authenticating under Rule 902 of the Federal Rules of Evidence.

ADDITIONAL RESEARCH REFERENCES

Wright & Miller, *Federal Practice and Procedure* §§ 2431–2437.

C.J.S. Evidence § 634 et seq.

West's Key No. Digests, Evidence ⚷366.

4. *United States v. Squillacote*, 221 F.3d 542 (4th Cir.2000), *cert. denied*, 532 U.S. 971, 121 S.Ct. 1601, 149 L.Ed.2d 468 (2001) (the certification may be a separate document—the Rule does not require that the document itself be signed).

5. *Ocean Rig ASA v. Safra National Bank of New York*, 72 F.Supp.2d 193, 204–05 (S.D.N.Y. 1999).

6. Reprinted in *Martindale Hubbell,* International Law Digests.

7. The Convention Abolishing the Requirement of Legalization for Foreign Public Documents may be found on WESTLAW in the IEL database, **ci(vii-c & text)**.

8. *See United States v. Squillacote*, 221 F.3d 542 (4th Cir.2000), *cert. denied*, 532 U.S. 971, 121 S.Ct. 1601, 149 L.Ed.2d 468 (2001) (second official certified identity of first official and that first official was authorized to attest to the authenticity of the documents).

9. *Batista v. Ashcroft*, 270 F.3d 8, 17, n.8 (1st Cir.2001).

RULE 44.1

DETERMINATION OF FOREIGN LAW

A party who intends to raise an issue concerning the law of a foreign country shall give notice by pleadings or other reasonable written notice. The court, in determining foreign law, may consider any relevant material or source, including testimony, whether or not submitted by a party or admissible under the Federal Rules of Evidence. The court's determination shall be treated as a ruling on a question of law.

[Added effective July 1, 1966; amended effective July 1, 1975; August 1, 1987.]

AUTHORS' COMMENTARY ON RULE 44.1

PURPOSE AND SCOPE

Rule 44.1 contains the provisions for raising and determining issues concerning the law of a foreign country. A party must give notice of its intent to raise an issue of foreign law. Thereafter, the judge will determine the applicable law of the foreign country.

NOTE: Rule 44.1 (which became effective in 1966) presents a significant diversion from past law, so be wary of citing any authority before 1966.

APPLICATIONS

Notice of Foreign Law Issue

A party must give written notice to the court and all other parties of its intent to raise an issue concerning foreign law.[1] The notice should specify the issues or claims purportedly governed by foreign law, but need not state the specific provisions of the foreign law. Failure to provide the required notice of intent to raise an issue concerning foreign law can result in a waiver of the right to raise the issue.[2]

Form of Notice

The notice may be included in a pleading or may be a separate document.[3]

1. *DP Aviation v. Smiths Industries Aerospace and Defense Systems Ltd.*, 268 F.3d 829, 846 (9th Cir.2001) (presenting a detailed analysis of what constitutes sufficient notice).

2. *In re Magnetic Audiotape Antitrust Litigation*, 334 F.3d 204(2d Cir.2003).

3. *Local 875 I.B.T. Pension Fund v. Pollack,* 992 F.Supp. 545 (E.D.N.Y.1998) (raising issue of foreign law in reply papers is not sufficient notice under Rule 44.1); *see also Canadian Imperial Bank of Commerce v. Saxony Carpet Co.*, 899 F.Supp. 1248, 1253 (S.D.N.Y.1995)(raising issues of foreign law in motion papers was adequate notice).

Timing for Notice

Rule 44.1 does not set a specific time for filing the notice. If the notice is a separate document, it should be served as soon as possible to give a reasonable opportunity to all parties to prepare.[4] If not already raised, issues of foreign law are sometimes raised at the pretrial conference.[5]

Party Giving Notice

Notice is normally given by the party whose claim or defense is based on foreign law, but may be raised by any party. If parties believe that a different foreign law applies from the law raised by another party, they should issue separate notices.

Court Determines Foreign Law

The determination of foreign law is now considered a matter of law,[6] not a matter of fact, and is therefore made by the court.[7]

Materials Used by the Court

The court may consider any relevant material or source to determine foreign law,[8] regardless of whether it is admissible.[9] A common method of proving foreign law is through expert testimony[10] and treatises.[11] The court may also do its own research[12] or seek the aid of an

4. *See Club Car, Inc. v. Club Car (Quebec) Import, Inc.*, 362 F.3d 775, 782 (11th Cir. 2004) (notice 2 weeks before trial held reasonable); *Mutual Service Ins. Co. v. Frit Industries, Inc.*, 358 F.3d 1312, 1321 (11th Cir. 2004) (notice at pretrial conference held reasonable); *Thyssen Steel Co. v. M/V Kavo Yerakas*, 911 F.Supp. 263, 266 (S.D.Tex.1996)(holding that notice of intent to rely on foreign law served after the case was remanded was sufficient).

5. *But see Whirlpool Fin. Corp. v. Sevaux*, 96 F.3d 216, 221 (7th Cir.1996) (choice-of-law issue is waived if party brings it up after summary judgment is rendered).

6. *Pazcoguin v. Radcliffe*, 292 F.3d 1209 (9th Cir.2002).

7. *U.S. Fidelity and Guar. Co. v. Braspetro Oil Services Co.*, 369 F.3d 34 (2nd Cir. 2004); *S.E.C. v. Dunlap*, 253 F.3d 768 (4th Cir.2001); *Sidali v. Immigration and Naturalization Serv.*, 107 F.3d 191, 197 (3d Cir.1997).

8. *Prewitt Enterprises, Inc. v. Organization of Petroleum Exporting Countries*, 353 F.3d 916, 924, n.11 (11th Cir. 2003); *Pazcoguin v. Radcliffe*, 292 F.3d 1209 (9th Cir.2002); *Johnson v. Ventra Group, Inc.*, 191 F.3d 732, 738 (6th Cir. 1999).

9. *General Star Nat. Ins. Co. v. Administratia Asigurarilor de Stat*, 289 F.3d 434, 439 (6th Cir.2002); *Society of Lloyd's v. Ashenden*, 233 F.3d 473 (7th Cir.2000) (in answering questions about foreign law, a court is not limited to the consideration of evidence that would be admissible under the Federal Rules of Evidence; any relevant material or source may be consulted).

10. *Primavera Familienstifung v. Askin*, 130 F.Supp.2d 450, 520, n.73 (S.D.N.Y.2001) (courts may consider the statements of foreign attorneys on issues affected by foreign law); *Consorcio Rive, S.A. de C.V. v. Briggs of Cancun, Inc.*, 2001 WL 46875 (E.D.La.2001) (testimony of foreign attorney admitted to prove foreign law).

11. *See Access Telecom, Inc. v. MCI Telecommunications Corp.*, 197 F.3d 694, 713 (5th Cir. 1999), *cert. denied*, 531 U.S. 917, 121 S.Ct. 275, 148 L.Ed.2d 200 (2000).

12. *Brockmeyer v. May*, 361 F.3d 1222, 1241 (9th Cir. 2004) (courts may reject even the uncontradicted conclusions of an expert witness and reach their own decisions on the basis of independent examination of foreign legal authorities); *Universe Sales Co., Ltd. v. Silver Castle, Ltd.*, 182 F.3d 1036, 1038 (9th Cir.1999), *cert. denied*, 530 U.S. 1275, 120 S.Ct. 2742, 147 L.Ed.2d 1006 (2000); *Medline Industries Inc. v. Maersk Medical Ltd.*, 230 F.Supp.2d 857, 862 (N.D.Ill.2002) (both trial and appellate courts are urged to research and analyze foreign law independently).

expert witness to help in the interpretation of foreign law.[13]

Summary Judgment

As an issue of law, a determination of foreign law is appropriate for summary judgment.[14]

Applies in All Cases

Rule 44.1 applies in diversity cases and federal question cases. Note, however, that the state conflict of law rules will determine *which* laws apply in diversity cases. Rule 44.1 is implicated only after the court has determined that a foreign country's laws apply.

Appellate Review

Determinations of foreign law are legal determinations fully reviewable by the Courts of Appeals.[15] However, a ruling as to foreign law is interlocutory, and cannot be immediately appealed.

ADDITIONAL RESEARCH REFERENCES

Wright & Miller, *Federal Practice and Procedure* §§ 2441–2447.

C.J.S. Evidence §§ 12–26.

West's Key No. Digests, Evidence ⚿37, 51.

13. *ID Sec. Systems Canada, Inc. v. Checkpoint Systems, Inc.*, 198 F.Supp.2d 598, 623 (E.D.Pa.2002); *Thomson Consumer Elec., Inc. v. Innovatron, S.A.*, 3 F.Supp.2d 49 (D.D.C.1998) (no express hierarchy of sources exists for questions of foreign law).

14. *McKesson HBOC, Inc. v. Islamic Republic of Iran*, 271 F.3d 1101, 1108 (D.C.Cir.2001), *cert. denied*, 537 U.S. 941, 123 S.Ct. 341, 154 L.Ed.2d 248 (2002); *Korea Life Ins. Co., Ltd. v. Morgan Guar. Trust Co. of New York*, 269 F.Supp.2d 424 (S.D.N.Y.2003) (a disagreement of the experts as to an issue of foreign law does not foreclose the granting of a motion for summary judgment).

15. *Karaha Bodas Co., L.L.C. v. Perusahaan Pertambangan Minyak Dan Gas Bumi Negara ("Pertamina")*, 313 F.3d 70, 80 (2d Cir.2002), *cert. denied*, 539 U.S. 904, 123 S.Ct. 2256, 156 L.Ed.2d 113 (2003).

RULE 45

SUBPOENA

(a) Form; Issuance.

(1) Every subpoena shall

(A) state the name of the court from which it is issued; and

(B) state the title of the action, the name of the court in which it is pending, and its civil action number; and

(C) command each person to whom it is directed to attend and give testimony or to produce and permit inspection and copying of designated books, documents or tangible things in the possession, custody or control of that person, or to permit inspection of premises, at a time and place therein specified; and

(D) set forth the text of subdivisions (c) and (d) of this rule.

A command to produce evidence or to permit inspection may be joined with a command to appear at trial or hearing or at deposition, or may be issued separately.

(2) A subpoena commanding attendance at a trial or hearing shall issue from the court for the district in which the hearing or trial is to be held. A subpoena for attendance at a deposition shall issue from the court for the district designated by the notice of deposition as the district in which the deposition is to be taken. If separate from a subpoena commanding the attendance of a person, a subpoena for production or inspection shall issue from the court for the district in which the production or inspection is to be made.

(3) The clerk shall issue a subpoena, signed but otherwise in blank, to a party requesting it, who shall complete it before service. An attorney as officer of the court may also issue and sign a subpoena on behalf of

(A) a court in which the attorney is authorized to practice; or

(B) a court for a district in which a deposition or production is compelled by the subpoena, if the deposition or production pertains to an action pending in a court in which the attorney is authorized to practice.

(b) Service.

(1) A subpoena may be served by any person who is not a party and is not less than 18 years of age. Service of a subpoena upon a person named therein shall be made by delivering a copy thereof to such person and, if the person's attendance is commanded, by tendering to that person the fees for one day's attendance and the mileage allowed by law. When the subpoena is issued on behalf of the United States or an officer or agency thereof, fees and mileage need not be tendered. Prior notice of any commanded production of documents and things or inspection of premises before trial shall be served on each party in the manner prescribed by Rule 5(b).

(2) Subject to the provisions of clause (ii) of subparagraph (c)(3)(A) of this rule, a subpoena may be served at any place within the district of the court by which it is issued, or at any place without the district that is within 100 miles of the place of the deposition, hearing, trial, production, or inspection specified in the subpoena or at any place within the state where a state statute or rule of court permits service of a subpoena issued by a state court of general jurisdiction sitting in the place of the deposition, hearing, trial, production, or inspection specified in the subpoena. When a statute of the United States provides therefor, the court upon proper application and cause shown may authorize the service of a subpoena at any other place. A subpoena directed to a witness in a foreign country who is a national or resident of the United States shall issue under the circumstances and in the manner and be served as provided in Title 28, U.S.C. § 1783.

(3) Proof of service when necessary shall be made by filing with the clerk of the court by which the subpoena is issued a statement of the date and manner of service and of the names of the persons served, certified by the person who made the service.

(c) Protection of Persons Subject to Subpoenas.

(1) A party or an attorney responsible for the issuance and service of a subpoena shall take reasonable steps to avoid imposing undue burden or expense on a person subject to that subpoena. The court on behalf of which the subpoena was issued shall enforce this duty and impose upon the party or attorney in breach of this duty an appropriate sanction, which may include, but is not limited to, lost earnings and a reasonable attorney's fee.

(2)(A) A person commanded to produce and permit inspection and copying of designated books, papers, documents or tangible things, or inspection of premises need not appear in person at the place of production or inspection unless commanded to appear for deposition, hearing or trial.

(B) Subject to paragraph (d)(2) of this rule, a person commanded to produce and permit inspection and copying may, within 14 days after service of the subpoena or before the time specified for compliance if such time is less than 14 days after service, serve upon the party or attorney designated in the subpoena written objection to inspection or copying of any or all of the designated materials or of the premises. If objection is made, the party serving the subpoena shall not be entitled to inspect and copy the materials or inspect the premises except pursuant to an order of the court by which the subpoena was issued. If objection has been made, the party serving the subpoena may, upon notice to the person commanded to produce, move at any time for an order to compel the production. Such an order to compel production shall protect any person who is not a party or an officer of a party from significant expense resulting from the inspection and copying commanded.

(3)(A) On timely motion, the court by which a subpoena was issued shall quash or modify the subpoena if it

(i) fails to allow reasonable time for compliance;

(ii) requires a person who is not a party or an officer of a party to travel to a place more than 100 miles from the place where that person resides, is employed or regularly transacts business in person, except that, subject to the provisions of clause (c)(3)(B)(iii) of this rule, such a person may in order to attend trial be commanded to travel from any such place within the state in which the trial is held, or

(iii) requires disclosure of privileged or other protected matter and no exception or waiver applies, or

(iv) subjects a person to undue burden.

(B) If a subpoena

(i) requires disclosure of a trade secret or other confidential research, development, or commercial information, or

(ii) requires disclosure of an unretained expert's opinion or information not describing specific events or occurrences in dispute and resulting from the expert's study made not at the request of any party, or

(iii) requires a person who is not a party or an officer of a party to incur substantial expense to travel more than 100 miles to attend trial, the court may, to protect a person subject to or affected by the subpoena, quash or modify the subpoena or, if the party in whose behalf the subpoena is issued shows a substantial need for the testimony or material that cannot be otherwise met without undue hardship and assures that the person to whom the subpoena is addressed will be reasonably compensated, the court may order appearance or production only upon specified conditions.

(d) Duties in Responding to Subpoena.

(1) A person responding to a subpoena to produce documents shall produce them as they are kept in the usual course of business or shall organize and label them to correspond with the categories in the demand.

(2) When information subject to a subpoena is withheld on a claim that it is privileged or subject to protection as trial preparation materials, the claim shall be made expressly and shall be supported by a description of the nature of the documents, communications, or things not produced that is sufficient to enable the demanding party to contest the claim.

(e) Contempt. Failure by any person without adequate excuse to obey a subpoena served upon that person may be deemed a contempt of the court from which the subpoena issued. An adequate cause for failure to obey exists when a subpoena purports to require a non-party to attend or produce at a place not within the limits provided by clause (ii) of subparagraph (c)(3)(A).

[Amended effective March 19, 1948; October 20, 1949; July 1, 1970; August 1, 1980; August 1, 1985; August 1, 1987; December 1, 1991.]

AUTHORS' COMMENTARY ON RULE 45

PURPOSE AND SCOPE

Rule 45 governs subpoenas, both for discovery purposes and for hearings or trial. It addresses subpoenas *ad testificandum,* pertaining to testimony, and subpoenas *duces tecum,* pertaining to documents.

NOTE: Rule 45 was substantially revised in 1991, and many of the procedures for subpoenas were changed.

RULE 45(a). FORM; ISSUANCE

CORE CONCEPT

Parties to legal proceedings have the power to obtain a subpoena compelling a witness to appear and testify at a designated time and location.[1]

APPLICATIONS

Issued by Clerk

A subpoena may be issued by the clerk of court. The clerk will issue subpoenas with the name of the recipient left blank, to be filled in by the party.

Issued by Attorney

A subpoena may also be issued by an attorney, acting as an officer of the court.[2] To be effective, the subpoena must be signed by the issuing attorney.[3] An attorney may issue a subpoena on behalf of any court before which the attorney is authorized to practice. An attorney may also issue a subpoena on behalf of a court where a deposition is to occur, provided that the deposition pertains to a matter pending in a court where the attorney is authorized to practice. This applies equally to attorneys admitted *pro hac vice* (for one matter only).

Which Court

A subpoena commanding attendance at a trial or hearing shall be issued from the court in which the trial is to occur. A subpoena for attendance at a deposition shall be issued from the court for the district in which the deposition is to occur, bearing the same case name and number as the case in the court where trial is to occur.[4] If a separate subpoena is issued commanding the production of documents or an inspection of premises, the subpoena shall issue from the court for the district in which the production or inspection is to occur.[5]

Subject Matter Jurisdiction

In order to issue a valid, enforceable subpoena in a lawsuit, the lawsuit must properly be before a federal court with subject matter

1. *Gomez v. Gates*, 25 F.3d 761 (9th Cir. 1994), *cert. denied*, 513 U.S. 1109, 115 S.Ct. 898, 130 L.Ed.2d 783 (1995)("when the subpoena is ad testificandum, there can be no pinch hitters.").

2. *United States v. Santiago–Lugo*, 904 F.Supp. 43, 46 (D.P.R.1995).

3. *Atlantic Inv. Management, LLC v. Millennium Fund I, Ltd.*, 212 F.R.D. 395, 397 (N.D.Ill. 2002) (lack of signature waived by conduct of recipient).

4. *Amgen Inc. v. Kidney Center of Delaware County, Ltd.*, 879 F.Supp. 878 (N.D.Ill.1995).

5. *Mabe v. San Bernardino County, Dept. of Public Social Services*, 237 F.3d 1101, 1112 (9th Cir.2001); *Cusumano v. Microsoft Corp.*, 162 F.3d 708, 711 (1st Cir.1998) (motion to compel docketed as an independent matter in court where documents were to be produced); *Crafton v. U.S. Specialty Ins. Co.*, 218 F.R.D. 175, 177 (E.D.Ark. 2003) (quashing document subpoena served on a corporate agent in one state where documents and corporate headquarters were in a different state more than 100 miles from service).

jurisdiction.[6]

Contents

Every subpoena should:

(1) state the name of the court issuing the subpoena;

(2) state the name of the court where the action is pending;

(3) contain the caption and civil action number of the case;[7]

(4) command the recipient to appear and give testimony, to produce for inspection the documents or things described in the subpoena or in an attachment thereto,[8] or to permit inspection of premises, at a designated time and location; and

(5) recite the language in subsections (c) and (d) of Rule 45.[9]

NOTE: Blank subpoenas generally are available at the clerk's office and will include the requisite language.

Scope

The scope of documents or information that can be obtained by subpoena is the same as the scope of discovery generally under Rule 26.[10]

Multiple Commands

A subpoena to produce documents or to inspect premises may be issued separately or joined with a command to appear to testify.

Number

There is no limit on the number of subpoenas in a civil action.

Time

Courts are split as to whether subpoenas are subject to the discovery deadline established by the court, with the majority not allowing subpoenas after the deadline.[11]

Documents

Witnesses may be compelled to produce all documents which they possess, have custody of, *or control.*[12] Thus, a corporation must produce

6. *Olcott v. Delaware Flood Co.*, 76 F.3d 1538, 1552 (10th Cir.1996).

7. *U.S. v. Patiwana*, 267 F.Supp.2d 301 (E.D.N.Y.2003) (enforcing subpoena despite failure to include a civil action number).

8. *Orleman v. Jumpking, Inc.*, 2000 WL 1114849 (D.Kan.2000); *Insituform Technologies, Inc. v. Cat Contracting, Inc.*, 168 F.R.D. 630, 633 (N.D.Ill.1996).

9. *Elam v. Ryder Automotive Operations, Inc.*, 179 F.R.D. 413, 415 (W.D.N.Y.1998) (subpoena enforced despite omission of language from Rule 45(c) and (d) based on absence of real prejudice); *Anderson v. Government of the Virgin Islands*, 180 F.R.D. 284 (D.Vi.1998).

10. *Graham v. Casey's General Stores*, 206 F.R.D. 251, 253–54 (S.D.Ind.2002).

11. *Dreyer v. GACS Inc.*, 204 F.R.D. 120, 122–23 (N.D.Ind.2001).

12. *Hay Group, Inc. v. E.B.S. Acquisition Corp.*, 360 F.3d 404, 408 (3rd Cir. 2004) (there is no need to bring a witness in to testify when only documents are sought); *In re: Citric Acid Litigation*, 191 F.3d 1090, 1106–07 (9th Cir. 1999), *cert. denied*, 529 U.S. 1037, 120 S.Ct. 1531, 146 L.Ed.2d 346 (2000) ("control" is de-

documents in the possession of its agent, attorney, or subsidiary, even if these documents are located outside the district.[13]

Inspection

A subpoena may be used to obtain inspection of the property of a non-party.[14]

Privileges

The recipient of a subpoena *duces tecum* may refuse to produce privileged documents. If the issuing party contests the asserted privilege, that party can request that the court conduct an *in camera* inspection of such documents.

Challenge

The proper method for challenging a subpoena is by motion to quash. The court can modify or quash the subpoena if it is unreasonable or oppressive.[15] Expense is not a reason to quash, but the court may condition compliance on the advancement of the expenses of complying by the issuing party.[16] A motion to quash may only be brought by the witness; the parties do not have standing to bring the motion on behalf of the witness.[17] If the subpoena is issued in one district for an action pending in another district, a motion to quash should be brought in the court issuing the subpoena.[18] In addition, if the subpoena is for a deposition, the witness may move for a protective order under the discovery provisions in Rule 26(c). If the subpoena is for the production of documents, the recipient may serve written objections on the issuer within 14 days of receipt of the subpoena, or before the date for production if sooner than 14 days from receipt of the subpoena.[19]

Parties

A subpoena is not necessary to take the deposition of a party or an officer, director, or managing agent of a party, or to compel a party to produce documents;[20] a notice of deposition pursuant to Rules 30(b) and 31(a) is sufficient.[21]

fined as the legal right to obtain documents upon demand); *Insituform Technologies, Inc. v. Cat Contracting, Inc.*, 168 F.R.D. 630, 633 (N.D.Ill.1996) (subpoena recipient must produce all existing documents within its control, but is not required to create documents).

13. *See Crafton v. U.S. Specialty Ins. Co.*, 218 F.R.D. 175, 177 (E.D.Ark. 2003) (quashing document subpoena served on a corporate agent in one state where documents and corporate headquarters were in a different state more than 100 miles from service).

14. *Fitzpatrick v. Arco Marine, Inc.*, 199 F.R.D. 663, 664 (C.D.Cal.2001) (allowing inspection of a non-party's ship).

15. *Ariel v. Jones,* 693 F.2d 1058 (11th Cir. 1982).

16. *SEC v. Arthur Young & Co.*, 584 F.2d 1018 (D.C.Cir.1978), *cert. denied,* 439 U.S. 1071, 99 S.Ct. 841, 59 L.Ed.2d 37 (1979).

17. *Brown v. Braddick,* 595 F.2d 961, 967 (5th Cir.1979).

18. *In re: Sealed Case*, 141 F.3d 337, 340 (D.C.Cir.1998).

19. *See* Rule 45(c) below.

20. *Dixon v. Ford Motor Credit Co.*, 2000 WL 1182274 (E.D.La.2000) (Rule 34, not Rule 45, provides the proper way for a party to obtain documents from another party).

21. *COMSAT Corp. v. National Science Foundation*, 190 F.3d 269, 278 (4th Cir.1999); but see *First City, Texas–Houston, N.A. v. Rafidain Bank*, 197 F.R.D. 250, 254 (S.D.N.Y.2000)

Corporations

In deposing a corporation, one may describe the information sought in the subpoena (or notice) and require the corporation to designate a representative qualified to testify about the designated issues.[22]

United States

As a general rule, representatives of the United States must comply with subpoenas.[23]

RULE 45(b). SERVICE

CORE CONCEPT

Subpoenas may be served by any non-party not under the age of 18.

APPLICATIONS

Personal Service

Service must be personal;[24] the subpoena may not be left at the witness's dwelling or work place.[25]

Proof of Service

If necessary, service can be proved by filing a statement of the date and manner of service, certified by the person making service, with the clerk of the court issuing the subpoena.

Time for Service

Rule 45 does not establish any cutoff or deadline for serving subpoenas. However, a subpoena for a deposition or for the production of documents may be governed by the discovery deadline.[26]

Not on Lawyer

Service upon the witness's lawyer is not sufficient.

Corporations

Service on the agent of a corporation is sufficient.[27]

(nothing in the Rules prevents issuing a subpoena to a party).

22. *Price Waterhouse LLP v. First American Corp.*, 182 F.R.D. 56, 61 (S.D.N.Y.1998).

23. *Linder v. Calero–Portocarrero*, 251 F.3d 178 (D.C.Cir.2001).

24. *See Catskill Development, L.L.C. v. Park Place Entertainment Corp.*, 206 F.R.D. 78, 84, n.5 (S.D.N.Y. 2002); *King v. Crown Plastering Corp.*, 170 F.R.D. 355, 356 (E.D.N.Y.1997) ("personal service" does not necessarily mean in hand delivery).

25. *United States v. Philip Morris Inc.*, 312 F.Supp.2d 27 (D.D.C. 2004). *But see Doe v. Hersemann*, 155 F.R.D. 630 (N.D.Ind.1994) (certified mail satisfies Rule 45(b)(1) as delivery by a non-party adult).

26. *See Alper v. United States*, 190 F.R.D. 281, 283 (D.Mass.2000).

27. *Sabatier v. Barnes*, 2001 WL 175234 (E.D.La.2001) (service on a secretary or receptionist is technically sufficient, but not advisable); *In re: Motorsports Merchandise Antitrust Litigation*, 186 F.R.D. 344 (W.D.Va.1999) (look to Rule 4 to determine proper service on a corporation).

Expenses

If the recipient's attendance is commanded, service must be accompanied by the tender of the fees and expenses for a 1–day appearance, unless the issuing party is the United States or officer or agency thereof.[28] There is no requirement to tender witness fees and expenses when the subpoena is only for the production of documents, and no witness is commanded to appear.[29] The amount of fees and expenses is controlled by 28 U.S.C.A. § 1821.[30]

Place of Service

A subpoena may be served at any place within the district, at any place within 100 miles of the hearing, deposition, production, or trial, or at any place within the state where a subpoena could be served under state law.[31] The 100–mile limit is extended by statute under some circumstances, such as in some bankruptcy proceedings.

Service in Multiparty, Multiforum Actions

When jurisdiction of the district court is based in whole or in part on the multiparty, multiforum statute,[32] a subpoena for attendance at a hearing or trial may, if authorized by the court upon motion for good cause shown, be served at any place within the United States, or anywhere outside the United States if otherwise permitted by law.[33] The court may impose terms and conditions on service under this provision.[34]

Foreign Countries

Under certain circumstances, a witness subject to the jurisdiction of the court may be in a foreign country. The procedure for issuing a subpoena to such a witness is governed by 28 U.S.C.A. § 1783 (The Walsh Act), which provides for the issuance of such a subpoena if the court finds that the witness's testimony or documents are "necessary in the interest of justice," and it is not possible to obtain the testimony or documents by other means. The person serving such a subpoena must advance the recipient estimated travel expenses.

NOTE: The Walsh Act, 28 U.S.C.A. § 1783, only governs issuing a subpoena to a witness. Rule 30 discusses when foreign witnesses may be deposed.

28. *In re Dennis*, 330 F.3d 696, 704–05 (5th Cir.2003) (Rule 45(b)(1) requires simultaneous tendering of witness fees and the reasonably estimated mileage allowed by law with service of a subpoena; mileage need not be precise, only a reasonable estimate); *In re Hunt*, 238 F.3d 1098, 1100 (9th Cir.2001) (subpoena quashed because service not accompanied by witness fee and mileage).

29. *United States E.E.O.C. v. Laidlaw Waste, Inc.*, 934 F.Supp. 286, 290 n.6 (N.D.Ill.1996).

30. 28 U.S.C.A. § 1821 is reprinted in Part VIII of this book. *See also Fisher v. Ford Motor Co.*, 178 F.R.D. 195 (N.D.Ohio 1998).

31. *Vass v. Volvo Trucks North America, Inc.*, 304 F.Supp.2d 851, 857 (S.D.W.Va. 2004); *In re Security Life Ins. Co. of America*, 228 F.3d 865, 871 (8th Cir.2000) (100 mile limitation does not apply to a subpoena for documents); *Robertson v. Kiamichi Railroad Co., L.L.C.*, 42 F.Supp.2d 651 (E.D.Tex.1999).

32. 28 U.S.C. § 1369.

33. 28 U.S.C. § 1783.

34. 28 U.S.C. § 1783.

Service on Other Parties

If the subpoena is for a deposition, a notice of deposition must be served on all parties pursuant to Rule 30 or 31. If the subpoena requires the production of documents or inspection of premises, notice must be served upon all parties prior to service on the recipient so that they may assert any privileges or objections and may obtain the same or additional documents.[35]

RULE 45(c). PROTECTION OF PERSONS SUBJECT TO SUBPOENA

CORE CONCEPT

An attorney has a duty not to issue a subpoena for improper purposes or to impose undue burden on the recipient of the subpoena. Rule 45(c) also provides mechanisms for recipients of subpoenas to challenge the subpoenas.

NOTE: The cautionary language in Rule 45(c) *must* be reprinted on every subpoena.

APPLICATIONS

Duty to Avoid Undue Burden

An attorney issuing a subpoena has a duty to avoid causing undue burden or expense on the recipient.[36]

Remedy for Undue Burden

If compliance with a subpoena would cause undue burden[37] or expense, the court issuing the subpoena will shift some or all of the costs to the party issuing the subpoena,[38] or otherwise impose an "appropriate" sanction.[39] The sanction may include wages lost because of the improperly issued subpoena, and may also include attorney fees.[40]

35. *Butler v. Biocore Medical Technologies, Inc.*, 348 F.3d 1163, 1173 (10th Cir. 2003); *Murphy v. Board of Educ. of Rochester City School Dist.*, 196 F.R.D. 220, 222–23 (W.D.N.Y.2000) (attorney sanctioned for repeatedly failing to serve copies of subpoenas on other parties in order to prevent their objections); *Schweizer v. Mulvehill*, 93 F.Supp.2d 376 (S.D.N.Y.2000) (subpoenas must be served on other parties prior to service on respondent).

36. *Northwestern Memorial Hosp. v. Ashcroft*, 362 F.3d 923, 938 (7th Cir. 2004); *Federal Deposit Ins. Corp. v. Garner*, 126 F.3d 1138, 1145–46 (9th Cir.1997); *Liberty Mut. Ins. Co. v. Diamante*, 194 F.R.D. 20, 23 (D.Mass.2000) (good faith is not sufficient, but rather the issue is whether the issuing party took reasonable steps to avoid imposing undue burden or expense on the person subject to the subpoena).

37. *Flatow v. Islamic Republic of Iran*, 201 F.R.D. 5, 8 (D.D.C.2001) (describing test for evaluating undue burden).

38. *Heidelberg Americas, Inc. v. Tokyo Kikai Seisakusho, Ltd.*, 333 F.3d 38 (1st Cir.2003) (a court "shall" quash or modify a subpoena if the subpoena subjects a person to undue burden); *In re Law Firms of McCourts and McGrigor Donald*, 2001 WL 345233 (S.D.N.Y. 2001) (the court is required to protect the non-party from undue burden or expense, but that does not mean that the non-party cannot absorb some of the cost of compliance).

39. *Dravo Corp. v. Liberty Mut. Ins. Co.*, 160 F.R.D. 123 (D.Neb.1995).

40. *Mattel, Inc. v. Walking Mountain Productions*, 353 F.3d 792, 814 (9th Cir. 2003).

Attendance by Person Producing Documents

A person subpoenaed to produce documents or things or to permit an inspection need not actually appear at the designated time, as long as the person complies with the subpoena.

Objection to Subpoena to Produce Documents

A person subpoenaed to produce documents or things or to permit an inspection may serve an objection to all or part of the subpoena within fourteen days after service of the subpoena (or before the time designated in the subpoena, if sooner).[41] Objections to subpoenas are customarily made by letter.[42] All grounds for objection should be asserted or they may be waived.[43] Once an objection has been served on the party issuing the subpoena, the subpoena recipient is not obligated to comply with the subpoena.[44] Failure to serve timely objections may constitute a waiver of objections to the subpoena other than objections relating to service.[45]

Motion to Compel

If a subpoena recipient serves an objection to the subpoena, the serving party may file a motion to compel in the court from which the subpoena was issued.[46] The motion must be served on the subpoena recipient. In ruling on such a motion, the court will protect non-parties from "significant" expense.[47] Respondents to motions to compel should raise the issue of expenses or risk waiver.[48] Some courts and local rules require counsel for the moving party to make a reasonable effort to confer with opposing counsel prior to filing a motion to compel.[49]

Motion to Quash or Modify

A subpoena recipient[50] may move to quash a subpoena in the court

41. *McCabe v. Ernst & Young, LLP*, 221 F.R.D. 423 (D.N.J. 2004); *McCoy v. Southwest Airlines Co., Inc.*, 211 F.R.D. 381, 384 (C.D.Cal. 2002) (only the nonparty can prevent disclosure by objection; the party to whom the subpoenaed records pertain cannot simply object).

42. *See Tuite v. Henry*, 98 F.3d 1411, 1416 (D.C.Cir.1996).

43. *DG Acquisition Corp. v. Dabah*, 151 F.3d 75, 81 (2d Cir.1998); *McCoy v. Southwest Airlines Co., Inc.*, 211 F.R.D. 381, 385 (C.D.Cal. 2002).

44. *Pamida, Inc. v. E.S. Originals, Inc.*, 281 F.3d 726, 732 (8th Cir.2002).

45. *Judicial Watch, Inc. v. U.S. Dept. of Commerce*, 196 F.R.D. 1, 2 (D.D.C.2000).

46. *McCabe v. Ernst & Young, LLP*, 221 F.R.D. 423 (D.N.J. 2004); *Dravo Corp. v. Liberty Mut. Ins. Co.*, 160 F.R.D. 123 (D.Neb.1995).

47. *McCabe v. Ernst & Young, LLP*, 221 F.R.D. 423 (D.N.J. 2004); *First American Corp. v. Price Waterhouse LLP*, 184 F.R.D. 234, 238 (S.D.N.Y.1998) (respondent awarded expenses plus a portion of attorney's fees).

48. *First American Corp. v. Price Waterhouse LLP*, 184 F.R.D. 234, 238–39 (S.D.N.Y.1998).

49. *See Medical Components, Inc. v. Classic Medical, Inc.*, 210 F.R.D. 175, 178 (M.D.N.C. 2002).

50. *Nova Products, Inc. v. Kisma Video, Inc.*, 220 F.R.D. 238, 241 (S.D.N.Y. 2004) (a party ordinarily lacks standing to quash a subpoena directed at a nonparty unless the party is seeking to protect a personal privilege or right); *Transcor, Inc. v. Furney Charters, Inc.*, 212 F.R.D. 588, 590 (D.Kan.2003) (a motion to quash or modify a subpoena duces tecum may only be made by the party to whom the subpoena is directed except where the party seeking to challenge the subpoena has a personal right or privilege with respect to the subject matter requested in the subpoena).

from which the subpoena was issued.[51] If the court finds the subpoena objectionable, it may either quash it altogether or modify it to cure the objection.[52] The motion must be "timely" filed, and should certainly be filed before the subpoena's return date.[53] Failure to file a motion to quash may constitute a waiver of objections to the subpoena.[54] A motion to quash is normally filed in the district where the subpoena was issued, but the court where the matter is pending also has the authority to issue protective orders and generally control the scope of discovery.[55] Some courts and local rules require counsel for the moving party to make a reasonable effort to confer with opposing counsel prior to filing a motion to quash.[56] Rule 45(c)(3) lists situations in which a subpoena will be quashed or modified:

(1) *Time to Comply:* Rule 45(c)(3)(A)(i) requires that the subpoena recipient be provided reasonable time to comply.[57]

(2) *Distance to Travel:* Rule 45(c)(3)(A)(ii) provides for the quashing of a subpoena requiring a person not a party or officer of a party to travel too far. Generally, such a person must travel up to 100 miles.[58] When the subpoena is for trial, such a person must travel anywhere within the state.[59] These distances are measured from any place that the person resides, is employed, or regularly transacts business.[60] Thus, a non-party witness

51. *Pamida, Inc. v. E.S. Originals, Inc.*, 281 F.3d 726, 729, n.3 (8th Cir.2002).

52. *CSC Holdings, Inc. v. Redisi*, 309 F.3d 988, 993 (7th Cir.2002); *Flatow v. Islamic Republic of Iran*, 196 F.R.D. 203, 209 (D.D.C.2000) (court should, when appropriate, consider modifying the subpoena rather than quashing it).

53. *See United States ex rel. Pogue v. Diabetes Treatment Centers of America, Inc.*, 238 F.Supp.2d 270, 278 (D.D.C.2002) ("Timely" is not defined in the rule nor elaborated upon in the advisory committee's notes); *First City, Texas–Houston, N.A. v. Rafidain Bank*, 197 F.R.D. 250, 254 (S.D.N.Y.2000) (objections raised more than one year after respondent held in contempt were waived).

54. *In re Flat Glass Antitrust Litigation*, 288 F.3d 83, 90 (3d Cir.2002) (failure to file motion to quash constitutes waiver of objections to manner of service of subpoena).

55. *GFL Advantage Fund, LTD v. Colkitt*, 216 F.R.D. 189 (D.D.C.2003); *Static Control Components, Inc. v. Darkprint Imaging*, 201 F.R.D. 431, 437 (M.D.N.C.2001); *Goodyear Tire & Rubber Co. v. Kirk's Tire & Auto Servicenter of Haverstraw, Inc.*, 211 F.R.D. 658, 660 (D.Kan. 2003) (it is within the discretion of the court that issued the subpoena to transfer motions involving the subpoena to the district in which the action is pending); *but see In re Subpoenas Served on Wilmer, Cutler & Pickering and Goodwin Proctor LLP*, 255 F.Supp.2d 1, 2 (D.D.C. 2003) (a district court has no authority to transfer a Rule 45(c) motion to the district in which the underlying litigation is pending).

56. *See In re Bennett Funding Group, Inc.*, 259 B.R. 243, 250 (N.D.N.Y.2001) (if a subpoena is served on a non-party and it forces the non-party to travel more than 100 miles from where it resides, the court must quash or modify the subpoena); *Smith v. Midland Brake, Inc.*, 162 F.R.D. 683, 685 (D.Kan.1995).

57. *Paul v. Stewart Enterprises, Inc.*, 2000 WL 1171120 (E.D.La.2000) (one business day's notice is clearly unreasonable in light of the requirement in Rule 45(c)(2)(B) that a subpoenaed person be permitted 14 days to object); *United States v. Woods*, 931 F.Supp. 433, 442 n. 3 (E.D.Va.1996) (obtaining subpoenas 7 days before the hearing was not a reasonable enough time to comply).

58. *In re Edelman*, 295 F.3d 171, 174 (2nd Cir.2002).

59. *Chung v. Chrysler Corp.*, 903 F.Supp. 160, 165 (D.D.C.1995).

60. *See Idlewild Creek Ltd. Partnership v. Travelers Property Cas.*, 2000 WL 1717566 (D.Me.2000); *Price Waterhouse LLP v. First American Corp.*, 182 F.R.D. 56, 62 (S.D.N.Y. 1998) (when the subpoena seeks a corporate representative, travel distance is measured for the representative, not the corporation).

must attend a deposition if his residence or place of employment is within 100 miles of the deposition location.

(3) *Privileged Matters:* Rule 45(c)(3)(A)(iii) provides that a subpoena may be quashed if it requires the disclosure of privileged or other protected matters.[61]

(4) *Undue Burden:* Rule 45(c)(3)(A)(iv) provides that a subpoena may be quashed if it subjects the recipient to undue burden.[62] This provision is sometimes used as justification for imposing the non-party's expenses on the party issuing the subpoena to cure the undue burden on the non-party.[63]

Substantial Need of Serving Party

Rule 45(c)(3)(B) lists circumstances in which a subpoena will be quashed unless the serving party shows a "substantial need" for the testimony, documents, or inspection. In such cases, the court will condition compliance on the serving party compensating the recipient. These circumstances are:

(1) *Trade Secrets:* Rule 45(c)(3)(B)(i) provides limited protection for trade secrets and other confidential research, development, and commercial information.[64]

(2) *Unretained Experts:* Rule 45(c)(3)(B)(ii) provides limited protection for experts who have not been retained, so that parties cannot obtain their testimony without paying their fees.[65]

(3) *Undue Travel:* Rule 45(c)(3)(B)(iii) provides limited protection to persons who are not parties or officers of parties who would

61. *Ferko v. National Ass'n For Stock Car Auto Racing, Inc.*, 219 F.R.D. 396, 402 (E.D.Tex. 2003) (asserting Rule 45(c)(3)(A)(iii) as to attorney work product); *Cmedia, LLC v. Lifekey Heathcare, LLC*, 216 F.R.D. 387 (N.D.Tex.2003); *Royal Surplus Lines Ins. Co. v. Sofamor Danek Group, Inc.*, 190 F.R.D. 463, 474 (W.D.Tenn. 1999) (whoever asserts the privilege has the burden of proving that the information sought by the subpoena is privileged).

62. *Northwestern Memorial Hosp. v. Ashcroft*, 362 F.3d 923, 927 (7th Cir. 2004) (balancing the burden and the need for the information); *Jones v. Hirschfeld*, 219 F.R.D. 71 (S.D.N.Y. 2003) (court is particularly sensitive to burden when subpoena served on high ranking government official); *Linder v. Department of Defense*, 133 F.3d 17, 24 (D.C.Cir.1998); *Flatow v. The Islamic Republic of Iran*, 196 F.R.D. 203, 206–07 (D.D.C.2000) (undue burden can be identified through looking at factors such as relevance, the need of the party for the documents, the breadth of the document request, the time period covered by it, the particularity with which the documents are described and the burden imposed); *Rimsat, Ltd. v. Hilliard*, 207 B.R. 964, 969 (D.D.C.1997) (mere assertions that compliance would be burdensome are insufficient to establish an undue burden).

63. *See Medical Components, Inc. v. Classic Medical, Inc.*, 210 F.R.D. 175, 179 (M.D.N.C. 2002).

64. *Mattel, Inc. v. Walking Mountain Productions*, 353 F.3d 792, 814 (9th Cir. 2003); *In re Vitamins Antitrust Litigation*, 267 F.Supp.2d 738 (S.D.Ohio 2003); *Mycogen Plant Science, Inc. v. Monsanto Co.*, 164 F.R.D. 623, 625 (E.D.Pa. 1996)(Court should balance the need for the confidential information against the privacy interests).

65. *Statutory Committee of Unsecured Creditors v. Motorola, Inc.*, 218 F.R.D. 325, 326–27 (D.D.C. 2003); *Express One Intern., Inc. v. Sochata*, 2001 WL 363073 (N.D.Tex.2001) (witness was an employee who has not consented to serve as an expert and cannot be forced to testify as an expert); *Sprague v. Liberty Mut. Ins. Co.*, 177 F.R.D. 78 (D.N.H.1998).

incur substantial expenses to travel more than 100 miles to attend trial.[66]

RULE 45(d). DUTIES IN RESPONDING TO SUBPOENA

CORE CONCEPT

Documents may be produced as they are normally kept or may be separated and organized. When privileges are asserted, the privilege must be expressly described.

NOTE: The cautionary language in Rule 45(d) *must* be reprinted on every subpoena.

APPLICATIONS

Production of Documents

The scope of production under a subpoena is the same as the scope for discovery generally under Rule 26.[67] The responding party has the option of allowing the serving party to inspect and copy the documents where they are normally kept (*e.g.*, "There is our file room.")[68] The responding party may also collect the responsive documents and organize and label them to correspond to the categories requests. The responding party may make copies for the requesting party, but is not obligated to do so.

Asserting a Privilege

When the subpoena recipient seeks to withhold information that is privileged, the recipient must expressly claim the privilege and describe the nature of the documents, communications, or things not produced in sufficient detail that the court and parties can assess the privilege.[69]

RULE 45(e). CONTEMPT

CORE CONCEPT

Failure to obey a valid subpoena without adequate excuse is a contempt of the court issuing the subpoena.[70] However, sanctions may not be available without a court order compelling compliance.[71]

66. *Kisser v. Coalition for Religious Freedom*, 1995 WL 590169 (E.D.Pa.1995)(ordering party to reimburse non-party for reasonable attorney's fees and travel expenses).

67. *Transcor, Inc. v. Furney Charters, Inc.*, 212 F.R.D. 588, 591, n.4 (D.Kan.2003).

68. *In re Copper Market Antitrust Litigation*, 200 F.R.D. 213 (S.D.N.Y.2001).

69. *In re Grand Jury Subpeona*, 274 F.3d 563, 575–76 (1st Cir.2001); *Goodyear Tire & Rubber Co. v. Kirk's Tire & Auto Servicenter of Haverstraw, Inc.*, 211 F.R.D. 658, 660 (D.Kan. 2003).

70. *In re Sealed Case*, 141 F.3d 337, 341 (D.C.Cir.1998); *Blackmer v. United States*, 284 U.S. 421, 52 S.Ct. 252, 76 L.Ed. 375 (1932); *Public Service Co. of NH v. Portland Natural Gas*, 218 F.R.D. 361, 362, n.2 (D.N.H. 2003).

71. *Cruz v. Meachum*, 159 F.R.D. 366 (D.Conn.1994).

APPLICATIONS

Challenge to Subpoena

If a party believes that a subpoena is not valid, the proper response is a motion to quash or a motion for a protective order. *See* Rule 26(c). If the motion is unsuccessful and the party disobeys the subpoena nonetheless, the party can also raise validity grounds again at the contempt proceedings.[72] However, if the lawsuit is not before a federal court with subject matter jurisdiction, the subpoena will not be enforceable and a disobedient recipient is not subject to contempt sanctions.[73]

Adequate Excuse

Inability to comply is an adequate excuse.[74] The fact that the subpoena would require the recipient to travel greater distances than those listed in Rule 45(c)(3)(A)(iii) is also an adequate excuse.[75] Likewise, a timely objection to the subpoena is an adequate excuse.[76] Preferring to work instead of comply with the subpoena is not an adequate excuse.[77]

Appeal

Orders pertaining to subpoenas are ordinarily interlocutory, and thus not appealable. An exception exists when one district clerk issues a discovery subpoena for an action proceeding in another district, and that subpoena is quashed. Such an order is immediately appealable as a final order.[78] To be reversed, an order pertaining to a subpoena must be plainly arbitrary.

ADDITIONAL RESEARCH REFERENCES

Wright & Miller, *Federal Practice and Procedure* §§ 2451–2463.

C.J.S. Federal Civil Procedure §§ 582–583 et seq., 644; Witnesses §§ 13–27 et seq.

West's Key No. Digests, Federal Civil Procedure ⚷1353–1354, 1456; Witnesses ⚷7–16, 21.

72. *United States v. Ryan,* 402 U.S. 530, 533, 91 S.Ct. 1580, 1582, 29 L.Ed.2d 85 (1971).

73. *Olcott v. Delaware Flood Co.*, 76 F.3d 1538, 1552 (10th Cir.1996).

74. *Fisher v. Marubeni Cotton Corp.,* 526 F.2d 1338, 1342 (8th Cir.1975); *Tranchant v. Environmental Monitoring Service, Inc.*, 2001 WL 617426 (E.D.La.2001) ("For a person to be held in contempt for failing to produce documents, it must be proven that the documents actually exist.").

75. *See Hillard v. Guidant Corp.*, 76 F.Supp.2d 566, 570 (M.D.Pa.1999); *National Property Investors VIII v. Shell Oil Co.*, 917 F.Supp. 324, 328 (D.N.J.1995).

76. *Flatow v. Islamic Republic of Iran*, 196 F.R.D. 203, 208 (D.D.C.2000).

77. *Higginbotham v. KCS Intern., Inc.*, 202 F.R.D. 444, 455 (D.Md.2001).

78. *CF & I Steel Corp. v. Mitsui & Co. (U.S.A.), Inc.*, 713 F.2d 494 (9th Cir.1983); *Horizons Titanium Corp. v. Norton,* 290 F.2d 421 (1st Cir.1961).

RULE 46

EXCEPTIONS UNNECESSARY

Formal exceptions to rulings or orders of the court are unnecessary; but for all purposes for which an exception has heretofore been necessary it is sufficient that a party, at the time the ruling or order of the court is made or sought, makes known to the court the action which the party desires the court to take or the party's objection to the action of the court and the grounds therefor; and, if a party has no opportunity to object to a ruling or order at the time it is made, the absence of an objection does not thereafter prejudice the party.

[Amended effective August 1, 1987.]

AUTHORS' COMMENTARY ON RULE 46

PURPOSE AND SCOPE

Rule 46 abolishes the formality of noting "exceptions" when the court overrules an objection or takes some action contrary to a request.[1]

NOTE: An attorney still needs to voice an objection to a court's ruling in the first instance; Rule 46 only relieves the need to note exceptions to the court's ruling.

APPLICATIONS

Applies to All Stages

Rule 46 applies to all stages of a trial, from voir dire through jury instructions. The attorney must object even to questions asked by the judge, although the appeals court may be more lenient about the form and timing of such objections.

Form of Objection

In order to preserve an issue for appeal, an attorney must state the particular grounds upon which the objection rests.[2] It is not sufficient to state simply, "objection," or to make a general objection. The primary purpose of the specificity requirement is to apprise the court of the litigant's position so that the court can correct its ruling if appropri-

1. *Kasper v. Saint Mary of Nazareth Hospital,* 135 F.3d 1170, 1175 (7th Cir.1998).

2. *Kasper v. Saint Mary of Nazareth Hospital,* 135 F.3d 1170, 1176 (7th Cir.1998); *Rice v. Community Health Assoc.*, 40 F.Supp.2d 788 (S.D.W.Va.1999), *aff'd in part, vac'd in part,* 203 F.3d 283 (4th Cir.2000) .

ate.[3] Consequently, if the grounds are obvious to the trial judge, an appellate court may overlook a lack of specificity.[4] If the judge's ruling is ambiguous, a party cannot challenge it on appeal without first attempting to have the judge clarify the ruling.[5]

Exceptions

It is not necessary to note an exception or take any other action to preserve a properly raised but overruled objection.[6]

Failure to Object

In general, failure to object to a ruling or issue constitutes a waiver of the ruling or issue.[7] Rule 46 provides that an attorney need not object if there is no opportunity to do so.[8] Additionally, the appeals court may consider on appeal an issue to which no objection was asserted when the basis was so clear that no objection was necessary, such as when the attorney has already objected to the same evidence.[9] Also, the appellate court may overlook the lack of an objection if the error was so fundamental that it caused a miscarriage of justice.[10]

Unsuccessful Motion in Limine

If a party files an unsuccessful motion in limine where the exclusion of certain evidence is sought, that party does not have to formally object at trial when the evidence in question is introduced as long as two conditions are met: (1) the party filed a written pre-trial motion setting forth reasons and case citations in support of the request that the evidence be excluded; and (2) the district court made a "definitive" ruling with no suggestion that it would reconsider the matter at trial.[11]

ADDITIONAL RESEARCH REFERENCES

Wright & Miller, *Federal Practice and Procedure* §§ 2471–2473.

C.J.S. Federal Civil Procedure §§ 370 et seq., 941–942.

West's Key No. Digests, Federal Civil Procedure ⚷928, 2017–2019.

3. *Kasper v. Saint Mary of Nazareth Hospital*, 135 F.3d 1170, 1176 (7th Cir.1998); *In re Wedtech Corp.*, 196 B.R. 274, 277 (Bankr. S.D.N.Y.1996).

4. *New England Newspaper Pub. Co. v. Bonner*, 68 F.2d 880 (1st Cir.1934), *cert. denied*, 292 U.S. 625, 54 S.Ct. 630, 78 L.Ed. 1480 (1934).

5. *Kasper v. Saint Mary of Nazareth Hospital*, 135 F.3d 1170, 1176 (7th Cir.1998).

6. *Fogarty v. Near North Insurance Brokerage, Inc.*, 162 F.3d 74, 81 (2d Cir.1998).

7. *See Krieger v. Fadely*, 211 F.3d 134 (D.C.Cir.2000).

8. *Boeing Co. v. Cascade Corp.*, 207 F.3d 1177, 1191 n. 46 (9th Cir.2000).*Angelo v. Armstrong World Industries, Inc.*, 11 F.3d 957 (10th Cir.1993).

9. *Beech Aircraft Corp. v. Rainey,* 488 U.S. 153, 109 S.Ct. 439, 102 L.Ed.2d 445 (1988).

10. *Sibbach v. Wilson & Co.*, 312 U.S. 1, 16, 61 S.Ct. 422, 427, 85 L.Ed. 479 (1941).

11. *Walden v. Georgia–Pacific Corp.*, 126 F.3d 506, 518 (3d Cir.1997), *cert. denied*, 523 U.S. 1074, 118 S.Ct. 1516, 140 L.Ed.2d 669 (1998). *See also Inter Medical Supplies, Ltd. v. EBI Medical Systems, Inc.*, 181 F.3d 446, 455 (3d Cir.1999) (objection unnecessary following motion in limine where the court has made a definitive ruling on the issue and is unlikely to reconsider).

RULE 47

SELECTION OF JURORS

(a) Examination of Jurors. The court may permit the parties or their attorneys to conduct the examination of prospective jurors or may itself conduct the examination. In the latter event, the court shall permit the parties or their attorneys to supplement the examination by such further inquiry as it deems proper or shall itself submit to the prospective jurors such additional questions of the parties or their attorneys as it deems proper.

(b) Peremptory Challenges. The court shall allow the number of peremptory challenges provided by 28 U.S.C. § 1870.

(c) Excuse. The court may for good cause excuse a juror from service during trial or deliberation.

[Amended effective July 1, 1966; December 1, 1991.]

AUTHORS' COMMENTARY ON RULE 47

PURPOSE AND SCOPE

Rule 47 addresses the examination of prospective jurors (voir dire) and contains provisions for alternate jurors.

RULE 47(a). EXAMINATION OF JURORS

CORE CONCEPT

The court and/or the parties may ask prospective jurors questions in order to determine bias and to enable the parties to exercise their peremptory challenges in a meaningful manner.

APPLICATIONS

Scope of Examinations

The court has broad discretion with respect to the scope of voir dire.[1] It may conduct the examination itself or allow the parties to do so. If the court conducts the examination, the parties may submit proposed questions, which the court may ask if it deems them proper.[2] In exercising its discretion, the court must allow sufficient questioning so that the selection process is meaningful.

1. *Smith v. Vicorp, Inc.*, 107 F.3d 816, 817 (10th Cir.1997).

2. *Butler v. City of Camden, City Hall*, 352 F.3d 811, 815 (3rd Cir. 2003).

Challenges for Cause

Challenges for cause are ruled on by the court. The party making the challenge has the burden of persuading the court. Partiality is the main grounds for such challenges. Parties can challenge the entire panel or the selection process. Such challenges should be made at the time of jury selection, not in a motion for new trial.[3]

Qualifications for Jurors

The qualifications for jurors is governed by the Jury Selection and Service Act of 1968, 28 U.S.C. § 1861 *et seq*. Essentially, jurors must be United States citizens, have resided in the district for at least one year, must meet minimum literacy requirements and be fluent in English, must be mentally and physically capable of service, and must be free from pending charges or past convictions of crimes punishable by imprisonment for more than 2 years.

Excluded Groups

The Jury Selection and Service Act of 1968 also provides for the establishment of certain groups who are precluded or excused from serving. Generally, these include: persons providing vital services (such as members of the armed services and policemen); persons for whom service would be a particular hardship (such as sole proprietors, mothers with young children, persons with gravely ill family members); and those excluded by the court for partiality or because they are likely to be disruptive.

Conduct of Jurors

The court has great latitude with respect to such issues as note taking by jurors, sequestration, questions by the jury, etc.

Alternate Jurors

Alternate jurors are no longer used in federal court.

RULE 47(b). PEREMPTORY CHALLENGES

CORE CONCEPT

Rule 47(b) provides that peremptory challenges are governed by 28 U.S.C.A. § 1870, which provides that each party has 3 peremptory challenges, and generally need not give any explanation for using those challenges. Peremptory challenges are not constitutionally protected fundamental rights, but are merely one means to the constitutional end of an impartial jury and a fair trial.[4] When there are multiple plaintiffs or defendants, the court may require them to exercise the challenges collectively or may allow additional challenges.[5]

3. *Atlas Roofing Mfg. Co. v. Parnell*, 409 F.2d 1191 (5th Cir.1969).

4. *United States v. Allen–Brown*, 243 F.3d 1293, 1299 (11th Cir.2001), *cert. denied*, 534 U.S. 1010, 122 S.Ct. 496, 151 L.Ed.2d 407 (2001).

5. *Polec v. Northwest Airlines, Inc.*, 86 F.3d 498, 518–519 (6th Cir.1996).

APPLICATIONS

Improper Grounds

It is improper to use a peremptory challenge to exclude a juror on the basis of race[6] or gender.[7]

RULE 47(c). EXCUSE

CORE CONCEPT

The court may excuse a juror for reasons of sickness, family emergency, juror misconduct, or for other "good cause shown."[8] A juror's refusal to join the majority is not grounds for excuse.[9]

APPLICATIONS

Considerations for Excuse

Characteristics of a juror to be scrutinized pursuant to Rule 47(c) include not only spoken words, but gestures and attitudes in order to ensure the jury's impartiality and competence.[10]

ADDITIONAL RESEARCH REFERENCES

Wright & Miller, *Federal Practice and Procedure* §§ 2481–2485. Bennett & Hirschhorn, Bennett's *Guide to Jury Selection and Trial Dynamics in Civil and Criminal Litigation.*

C.J.S. Juries §§ 208–250 et seq., 251–285 et seq.

West's Key No. Digests, Jury ⚷83–142.

6. *Edmonson v. Leesville Concrete Co.*, 500 U.S. 614, 111 S.Ct. 2077, 114 L.Ed.2d 660 (1991).

7. *Montanez v. Puerto Rico Police Department*, 33 F.Supp.2d 106, 108 (D.Puerto Rico 1999).

8. *See Harris v. Folk Construction Co.*, 138 F.3d 365, 371 (8th Cir.1998); *Interpool Limited v. Patterson*, 874 F.Supp. 616 (S.D.N.Y. 1995)(juror excused because of important business trip).

9. *See also Murray v. Laborers Union Local No. 324*, 55 F.3d 1445, 1450–51 (9th Cir.1995), *cert. denied*, 517 U.S. 1219, 116 S.Ct. 1847, 134 L.Ed.2d 948 (1996).

10. *Harris v. Folk Construction Co.*, 138 F.3d 365, 371 (8th Cir.1998).

RULE 48

NUMBER OF JURORS—PARTICIPATION IN VERDICT

The court shall seat a jury of not fewer than six and not more than twelve members and all jurors shall participate in the verdict unless excused from service by the court pursuant to Rule 47(c). Unless the parties otherwise stipulate, (1) the verdict shall be unanimous and (2) no verdict shall be taken from a jury reduced in size to fewer than six members.

[Amended effective December 1, 1991.]

AUTHORS' COMMENTARY ON RULE 48

PURPOSE AND SCOPE

The court may select any number of jurors from 6 to 12, inclusive. Unless the parties stipulate otherwise, the verdict must be unanimous.

APPLICATIONS

Verdicts Normally Unanimous

Absent a stipulation, verdicts must be unanimous.[1] However, verdicts are considered unanimous even if 1 or more jurors reluctantly joins just to reach a verdict.[2] If a jury reports being unable to reach a unanimous verdict, the majority of the courts allow an instruction to the jury to deliberate further to attempt to break the deadlock.[3]

Polling the Jury

A party may demand that the jury be polled to verify that the verdict is unanimous. If 1 or more jurors dissents, the court may require the jury to deliberate further or may declare a mistrial. Polling must occur before the verdict is recorded and the jury is discharged.

Excused Jurors

If a juror is excused for illness or other reason under Rule 47(c), a unanimous verdict among the remaining jurors will be valid if at least 6

1. *Jazzabi v. Allstate Ins. Co.*, 278 F.3d 979, 985 (9th Cir.2002) (jury must be unanimous as to affirmative defense as well as ultimate verdict); *Robinson v. Cattaraugus County*, 147 F.3d 153, 161 (2d Cir.1998).

2. *See Cary v. Allegheny Technologies Inc.*, 267 F.Supp.2d 43 (W.D.Pa.2003) (allowing a charge to the jury about the benefits of reaching a verdict).

3. *Cary v. Allegheny Technologies Inc.*, 267 F.Supp.2d 442, 446 (W.D.Pa. 2003) (the "vast majority" of the courts allow supplemental "Allen" instructions to civil juries).

jurors remain. If fewer than 6 remain, the parties may consent to allow the trial or deliberations to continue and to then be bound by the verdict.[4]

Stipulations

By stipulation, the parties can agree that a unanimous decision is not necessary, and that the decision of a specified majority will be taken as the decision of the jury.[5] The parties may also stipulate to fewer than 6 jurors.[6]

Alternate Jurors

Alternate jurors are not used in federal court.[7]

Advisory Jury

It does not appear that the provisions of Rule 48 regarding unanimity pertain to advisory juries.[8]

ADDITIONAL RESEARCH REFERENCES

Wright & Miller, *Federal Practice and Procedure* §§ 2491–2492. Bennett & Hirschhorn, Bennett's *Guide to Jury Selection and Trial Dynamics in Civil and Criminal Litigation.*

C.J.S. Federal Civil Procedure §§ 995 et seq.; Juries § 4.

West's Key No. Digests, Federal Civil Procedure ⚷2191; Jury ⚷4.

4. *Meyers v. Wal–Mart Stores, East, Inc.*, 257 F.3d 625, 633 (6th Cir.2001) (approving a trial with 4 jurors based on the parties' stipulation, and noting that a bench trial is essentially a stipulation to trial before zero jurors); *N.A.A.C.P v. Acusport, Inc.*, 253 F.Supp.2d 459 (E.D.N.Y. 2003).

5. *Baxter Healthcare Corp. v. Spectramed, Inc.*, 49 F.3d 1575 (Fed.Cir.1995), *cert. denied*, 516 U.S. 906, 116 S.Ct. 272, 133 L.Ed.2d 194 (1995); *NAACP v. AcuSport, Inc.*, 271 F.Supp.2d 435 (E.D.N.Y.2003).

6. *Meyers v. Wal–Mart Stores, East, Inc.*, 77 F.Supp.2d, 826, 827 (E.D.Mich.1999) (both parties stipulated to 4 jurors).

7. *Delaney v. Detella*, 2004 WL 525007 (N.D.Ill. 2004) (no legal or procedural error resulted from the selection of a jury without alternates).

8. *N.A.A.C.P v. Acusport, Inc.*, 253 F.Supp.2d 459 (E.D.N.Y.2003).

RULE 49

SPECIAL VERDICTS AND INTERROGATORIES

(a) Special Verdicts. The court may require a jury to return only a special verdict in the form of a special written finding upon each issue of fact. In that event the court may submit to the jury written questions susceptible of categorical or other brief answer or may submit written forms of the several special findings which might properly be made under the pleadings and evidence; or it may use such other method of submitting the issues and requiring the written findings thereon as it deems most appropriate. The court shall give to the jury such explanation and instruction concerning the matter thus submitted as may be necessary to enable the jury to make its findings upon each issue. If in so doing the court omits any issue of fact raised by the pleadings or by the evidence, each party waives the right to a trial by jury of the issue so omitted unless before the jury retires the party demands its submission to the jury. As to an issue omitted without such demand the court may make a finding; or, if it fails to do so, it shall be deemed to have made a finding in accord with the judgment on the special verdict.

(b) General Verdict Accompanied by Answer to Interrogatories. The court may submit to the jury, together with appropriate forms for a general verdict, written interrogatories upon one or more issues of fact the decision of which is necessary to a verdict. The court shall give such explanation or instruction as may be necessary to enable the jury both to make answers to the interrogatories and to render a general verdict, and the court shall direct the jury both to make written answers and to render a general verdict. When the general verdict and the answers are harmonious, the appropriate judgment upon the verdict and answers shall be entered pursuant to Rule 58. When the answers are consistent with each other but one or more is inconsistent with the general verdict, judgment may be entered pursuant to Rule 58 in accordance with the answers, notwithstanding the general verdict, or the court may return the jury for further consideration of its answers and verdict or may order a new trial. When the answers are inconsistent with each other and one or more is likewise inconsistent with the general verdict, judgment shall not be entered, but the court shall return the jury for further consideration of its answers and verdict or shall order a new trial.

[Amended effective July 1, 1963; August 1, 1987.]

AUTHORS' COMMENTARY ON RULE 49

PURPOSE AND SCOPE

Rule 49 provides mechanisms for directing specific questions to the jury. There are 2 alternative methods: special verdicts, which allow the jury to make findings as to each issue of fact; and written interrogatories which, together with a general verdict, allow the parties to verify that the jury is applying the law to the facts in the manner instructed by the court.

RULE 49(a). SPECIAL VERDICTS

CORE CONCEPT

The court may require the jury to return special verdicts as to each factual issue, instead of a general verdict in favor of one party.[1]

APPLICATIONS

Comparison With General Verdict

A general verdict is a single statement disposing of the entire case ("We find in favor of the defendant.").[2] Special verdicts ask the jury to decide specific factual questions ("At the time of the accident, the vehicle was proceeding at an excessive rate of speed.").[3]

Court's Discretion

The court has virtually absolute discretion as to the use of special verdicts.[4] This discretion extends to determining the content and layout of the verdict form, and any interrogatories submitted to the jury, provided the questions asked are reasonably capable of an interpretation that would allow the jury to address all factual issues essential to judgment.[5] Generally, special verdicts are more appropriate in complex cases.[6] Special verdicts are also valuable when the status of the law is uncertain because if the trial court is reversed on the law, sufficient special verdicts may render a new trial unnecessary.

1. *Lee v. Coss*, 39 F.Supp.2d 170 (D.Conn. 1999).

2. *Mason v. Ford Motor Co., Inc.*, 307 F.3d 1271, 1274 (11th Cir.2002).

3. *Zhang v. American Gem Seafoods, Inc.*, 339 F.3d 1020, 1031 (9th Cir. 2003) (comparing special and general verdicts); *Lavin v. Emery Air Freight Corp.*, 980 F.Supp. 93, 98 (D.Conn.1997), *aff'd*, 141 F.3d 1151 (2d Cir.1998) (court looks to two factors when determining whether a verdict is general or special, its own intent and the substantive charge given).

4. *Broadcast Satellite Intern., Inc. v. National Digital Television Center, Inc.*, 323 F.3d 339, 342 (5th Cir.2003).

5. *United States v. Real Property Located at 20832 Big Rock Drive, Malibu, CA 90265*, 51 F.3d 1402, 1408 (9th Cir.1995).

6. *Dinco v. Dylex Ltd.*, 111 F.3d 964, 969 (1st Cir.1997).

Scope of Questions

The special verdicts should fairly present the case, and should cover all factual issues.[7] Although special verdicts should not ask purely legal questions, they sometimes will contain a mixture of law and fact.

Form of Questions

Special verdicts may take different forms. Sometimes the questions will require the jury to write a brief answer (such as "yes" or "no"). Sometimes alternative special verdicts will be written out, and the jury need only choose one alternative.

Instructions to Jury

Rule 49(a) requires the court to give the jury sufficient instructions so that they can determine each issue before them.[8] When an issue before the jury involves mixed questions of fact and law, the court must give instructions as to the applicable law.[9]

Omission of Issues

If the court submits special verdicts to the jury and omits a question of fact raised by the pleadings or evidence, each party must object to the omission before the jury retires or that party waives the right to a jury trial on that issue (note that one party cannot rely on the objection of another party).[10] As to issues not submitted to the jury and not objected to, the court may make a finding.[11] If the court merely issues a general verdict, the court will be deemed to have ruled in a consistent fashion on issues not submitted to the jury.[12]

Return of Verdict

The jury's verdicts must be certain, unequivocal, and consistent. If there is a construction of the verdicts that renders them consistent, it will be adopted.[13] Otherwise, the court may require the jury to deliber-

7. *Broadcast Satellite Intern., Inc. v. National Digital Television Center, Inc.*, 323 F.3d 339, 342 (5th Cir.2003).

8. *Romano v. Howarth*, 998 F.2d 101 (2d Cir.1993). *But see Aerotech Resources, Inc. v. Dodson Aviation, Inc.*, 191 F.Supp.2d 1209, 1220 (D.Kan.2002) (with special interrogatories, the jury makes findings of fact as to each contested fact, then the court applies the law to those facts, so instructions of the law to the jury are unnecessary).

9. *Manufacturers Hanover Trust Co. v. Drysdale Sec. Corp.*, 801 F.2d 13, 26 (2d Cir.1986), *cert. denied*, 479 U.S. 1066, 107 S.Ct. 952, 93 L.Ed.2d 1001 (1987); *Tights, Inc. v. Acme–McCrary Corp.*, 541 F.2d 1047, 1061 (4th Cir. 1976), *cert. denied*, 429 U.S. 980, 97 S.Ct. 493, 50 L.Ed.2d 589 (1976).

10. *Becker v. Poling Transp. Corp.*, 356 F.3d 381, 390 (2nd Cir. 2004); *Reynolds v. City of Chicago*, 296 F.3d 524 (7th Cir.2002); *Lynch v. City of Boston*, 180 F.3d 1, 11 (1st Cir.1999).

11. *Roberts v. Karimi*, 251 F.3d 404, 407–08 (2d Cir.2001); *Ramos v. Davis & Geck, Inc.*, 224 F.3d 30, 32 (1st Cir.2000) (issue must be raised by the pleadings); *Parrish v. Sollecito*, 280 F.Supp.2d 145, 158 (S.D.N.Y. 2003).

12. *Ansin v. River Oaks Furniture, Inc.*, 105 F.3d 745, 756 (1st Cir.1997), *cert. denied*, 522 U.S. 818, 118 S.Ct. 70, 139 L.Ed.2d 31 (1997).

13. *Technical Resource Services, Inc. v. Dornier Medical Sys.*, 134 F.3d 1458, 1464 (11th Cir.1998) (test to be applied in reconciling potential conflicts between the jury's answers is whether the answers may fairly be said to represent a logical and probable decision on the relevant issues as submitted).

ate further[14] or may declare a mistrial. The court may not, however, make findings contrary to the jury verdict.[15]

Failure to Find

If the jury fails to unanimously agree on some of the answers to special interrogatories, the judge has several available procedures prior to dismissing the jury. The judge can: resubmit the interrogatories to the jury for further deliberations; ask the parties if they would be willing to accept the majority responses; enter judgment on the basis of the unanimous interrogatory answers if they are dispositive; declare the entire case a mistrial; or order a partial retrial of the issues not unanimously agreed upon.[16]

Objections

Objections to the instructions to the jury should be made before the jury retires.[17] Objections to the jury's responses or to the verdict to be entered based on the jury's responses should be made, if possible, before the jury is discharged. Failure to do so may result in a waiver of the objections.[18]

Law Governing

The use of special verdicts or interrogatories is a procedural issue governed by federal law, not by state law.[19]

Appellate Review

The trial court's use of special verdicts is reviewed under the "abuse of discretion" standard.[20]

RULE 49(b). GENERAL VERDICT ACCOMPANIED BY ANSWER TO INTERROGATORIES

CORE CONCEPT

The court may submit to the jury a general verdict[21] and written interrogatories about specific factual issues.

14. *Selgas v. American Airlines, Inc.*, 858 F.Supp. 316 (D.P.R.1994), *aff'd in part, vac'd in part*, 69 F.3d 1205 (1st Cir.1995).

15. *Ramos v. Davis & Geck, Inc.*, 224 F.3d 30, 32 (1st Cir.2000).

16. *Baxter Healthcare Corp. v. Spectramed, Inc.*, 49 F.3d 1575 (Fed.Cir.1995), *cert. denied*, 516 U.S. 906, 116 S.Ct. 272, 133 L.Ed.2d 194 (1995).

17. *Austin v. Paramount Parks, Inc.*, 195 F.3d 715, 725 (4th Cir.1999); *Wilson v. Maritime Overseas Corp.*, 150 F.3d 1, 6 (1st Cir.1998).

18. *Marcano-Rivera v. Pueblo International, Inc.*, 232 F.3d 245, 253 n.4 (1st Cir.2000); *Denny v. Ford Motor Co.*, 42 F.3d 106 (2d Cir.1994). *But see Heno v. Sprint/United Management Co.*, 208 F.3d 847, 851 (10th Cir.2000) (a party is not required to object to inconsistent special verdicts before the jury retires in order to preserve the issue for a subsequent motion to the court).

19. *Affiliated FM Ins. Co. v. Neosho Construction Co., Inc.*, 192 F.R.D. 662, 673 (D. Kan. 2000); *Dewitt v. Smith*, 152 F.R.D. 162 (W.D.Ark.1993).

20. *Bills v. Aseltine*, 52 F.3d 596 (6th Cir. 1995); *Davis v. Ford Motor Co.*, 128 F.3d 631, 633 (8th Cir.1997).

21. *Zhang v. American Gem Seafoods, Inc.*, 339 F.3d 1020 (9th Cir.2003) (the Rules do not define general verdicts, but they imply that general verdicts do not involve factual findings but rather ultimate legal conclusions).

APPLICATIONS

Purpose

Written interrogatories can serve 2 functions. First they focus the jury's attention on important factual issues and insure that the general verdict is consistent with the factual findings. Second, if the court is subsequently reversed on a legal issue, a new trial may be avoided if the interrogatories contain sufficient findings.

Court's Discretion

As with special verdicts, the court has virtually absolute discretion with respect to the use of written interrogatories to the jury and with respect to the format of the questions.[22] The court also has broad discretion in evaluating the consistency of the interrogatories and the general verdict, and in selecting the remedy for any inconsistencies as described below.[23]

Content of Interrogatories

Because there is a general verdict, the content of the interrogatories is not as critical as with special verdicts—every issue need not be covered.

Interrogatory Answers and Verdict Consistent

If the general verdict is consistent with the interrogatory answers, then the court will enter judgment accordingly. Any ambiguity will be resolved in favor of consistency.[24]

Interrogatory Answers and Verdict Not Consistent

If the interrogatory answers are internally consistent but not consistent with the general verdict, the court has 3 options: it can order the jury to deliberate further;[25] it can enter judgment based on the interrogatories if they are sufficient;[26] or it can declare a mistrial.[27] If the interrogatory answers are internally inconsistent and inconsistent with the general verdict, the court can order further deliberations or declare a mistrial, but cannot enter judgment.[28] However, an inconsistency or failure to answer an interrogatory will not prevent entry of judgment if the interrogatory is not necessary to the judgment.

22. *JGR, Inc. v. Thomasville Furniture Indust., Inc.*, 370 F.3d 519 (6th Cir. 2004); *Cruz v. Town of Cicero, Ill.*, 275 F.3d 579, 591 (7th Cir.2001); *Hostetler v. Consol. Rail Corp.*, 123 F.3d 387, 393 (6th Cir.1997).

23. *Beard v. Flying J. Inc.*, 116 F.Supp.2d 1077, 1088 (S.D.Iowa 2000).

24. *Turyna v. Martam Construction Co., Inc.*, 83 F.3d 178, 181 (7th Cir.1996).

25. *Kerman v. City of New York*, 261 F.3d 229, 244 (2d Cir.2001).

26. *Zhang v. American Gem Seafoods, Inc.*, 339 F.3d 1020, 1038 (9th Cir. 2003).

27. *See Intermatic Inc. v. Lamson & Sessions Co.*, 273 F.3d 1355, 1369 (Fed.Cir.2001).

28. *King v. Ford Motor Co.*, 209 F.3d 886 (6th Cir.2000), *cert. denied*, 531 U.S. 960, 121 S.Ct. 386, 148 L.Ed.2d 298 (2000) (court has broad discretion as to whether to send the jury out for further deliberations or order a new trial), *cert. denied,* 531 U.S. 960, 121 S.Ct. 386, 148 L.Ed.2d 298 (2000); *Loughman v. Consol–Pennsylvania Coal Company*, 6 F.3d 88 (3d Cir. 1993).

Inconsistent Interrogatories

When the interrogatory answers are internally inconsistent, the court may order the jury to deliberate further or may order a new trial.[29]

Inconsistent General Verdicts

When general verdicts on different claims are inconsistent, a court may not simply mold one of the two verdicts to be consistent with the other. Faced with inconsistent general verdicts, the court may take one of four approaches: (1) "in certain circumstances, ... allow the verdict to stand;" (2) "attempt to read the verdict in a manner that will resolve the inconsistencies;" (3) "resubmit the question to the jury;" or (4) "order an entirely new trial."[30]

Objections to Interrogatories

The courts are divided as to whether objections to interrogatories are waived unless raised before the jury retires.[31]

ADDITIONAL RESEARCH REFERENCES

Wright & Miller, *Federal Practice and Procedure* §§ 2501–2513. Bennett & Hirschhorn, Bennett's *Guide to Jury Selection and Trial Dynamics in Civil and Criminal Litigation.*

C.J.S. Federal Civil Procedure §§ 1009–1027 et seq.

West's Key No. Digests, Federal Civil Procedure ⚷2211–2220, 2231–2242.

29. *Zhang v. American Gem Seafoods, Inc.*, 339 F.3d 1020, 1038 (9th Cir. 2003); *King v. Ford Motor Co.*, 209 F.3d 886, 895 (6th Cir. 2000), *cert. denied*, 531 U.S. 960, 121 S.Ct. 386, 148 L.Ed.2d 298 (2000)(the court has wide discretion as to which option to employ).

30. *Mosley v. Wilson*, 102 F.3d 85, 90–91 (3d Cir.1996) (quoting *Los Angeles v. Heller*, 475 U.S. 796, 106 S.Ct. 1571, 89 L.Ed.2d 806 (1986)) (internal quotes omitted).

31. *Correia v. Fitzgerald*, 354 F.3d 47, 57 (1st Cir. 2003) (failure to object to an alleged inconsistency while the jury is still in the box forfeits a party's objection, subject only to the possibility of relief for plain error); *Mason v. Ford Motor Co., Inc.*, 307 F.3d 1271, 1274 (11th Cir.2002) (if the jury rendered inconsistent general verdicts, failure to object timely waives that inconsistency as a basis for seeking retrial); *Fleet National Bank v. Anchor Media Television, Inc., KOVR*, 831 F.Supp. 16 (D.R.I.1993).

RULE 50

JUDGMENT AS A MATTER OF LAW IN JURY TRIALS; ALTERNATIVE MOTION FOR NEW TRIAL; CONDITIONAL RULINGS

(a) Judgment as a Matter of Law.

(1) If during a trial by jury a party has been fully heard on an issue and there is no legally sufficient evidentiary basis for a reasonable jury to find for that party on that issue, the court may determine the issue against that party and may grant a motion for judgment as a matter of law against that party with respect to a claim or defense that cannot under the controlling law be maintained or defeated without a favorable finding on that issue.

(2) Motions for judgment as a matter of law may be made at any time before submission of the case to the jury. Such a motion shall specify the judgment sought and the law and the facts on which the moving party is entitled to the judgment.

(b) Renewing Motion for Judgment After Trial; Alternative Motion for New Trial. If, for any reason, the court does not grant a motion for judgment as a matter of law made at the close of all the evidence, the court is considered to have submitted the action to the jury subject to the court's later deciding the legal questions raised by the motion. The movant may renew its request for judgment as a matter of law by filing a motion no later than 10 days after entry of judgment—and may alternatively request a new trial or join a motion for a new trial under Rule 59. In ruling on a renewed motion, the court may:

(1) if a verdict was returned:

(A) allow the judgment to stand,

(B) order a new trial, or

(C) direct entry of judgment as a matter of law; or

(2) if no verdict was returned:

(A) order a new trial, or

(B) direct entry of judgment as a matter of law.

(c) Granting Renewed Motion for Judgment as a Matter of Law; Conditional Rulings; New Trial Motion.

(1) If the renewed motion for judgment as a matter of law is granted, the court shall also rule on the motion for a new trial, if

any, by determining whether it should be granted if the judgment is thereafter vacated or reversed, and shall specify the grounds for granting or denying the motion for the new trial. If the motion for a new trial is thus conditionally granted, the order thereon does not affect the finality of the judgment. In case the motion for a new trial has been conditionally granted and the judgment is reversed on appeal, the new trial shall proceed unless the appellate court has otherwise ordered. In case the motion for a new trial has been conditionally denied, the appellee on appeal may assert error in that denial; and if the judgment is reversed on appeal, subsequent proceedings shall be in accordance with the order of the appellate court.

(2) Any motion for a new trial under Rule 59 by a party against whom judgment as a matter of law is rendered shall be filed no later than 10 days after entry of the judgment.

(d) Same: Denial of Motion for Judgment as a Matter of Law. If the motion for judgment as a matter of law is denied, the party who prevailed on that motion may, as appellee, assert grounds entitling the party to a new trial in the event the appellate court concludes that the trial court erred in denying the motion for judgment. If the appellate court reverses the judgment, nothing in this rule precludes it from determining that the appellee is entitled to a new trial, or from directing the trial court to determine whether a new trial shall be granted.

[Amended January 21, 1963, effective July 1, 1963; March 2, 1987, effective August 1, 1987; April 30, 1991, effective December 1, 1991; April 22, 1993, effective December 1, 1993; April 27, 1995, effective December 1, 1995.]

AUTHORS' COMMENTARY ON RULE 50

PURPOSE AND SCOPE

Rule 50 contains the provisions governing motions for judgment as a matter of law during and following jury trials. These remedies are generally available when the evidence in the record could not reasonably support a particular verdict.

NOTE: A motion for judgment after trial can be filed only if a motion for judgment as a matter of law was filed at the close of the record, and must be filed within 10 days of entry of the verdict.

NOTE: Rule 50 was substantially revised in 1991. The new terminology, "judgment as a matter of law," replaces the former "directed verdict" and "judgment notwithstanding the verdict."[1]

RULE 50(a). JUDGMENT AS A MATTER OF LAW

CORE CONCEPT

Rule 50(a) allows the court to take a case away from the jury by entering a judgment if there is not sufficient evidence to raise a genuine factual controversy.[2]

APPLICATIONS

Content of Motion

A motion for judgment as a matter of law must state the judgment sought (*i.e.,* the counts or issues upon which judgment is sought) and the law and facts supporting the judgment.[3]

Form and Timing of Motion

A motion for judgment as a matter of law may be made orally or in writing, but must be made on the record.[4] The motion may be made after the opposing party has been fully heard on an issue, at any time before submission of the case to the jury.[5] Such motions are typically made at the close of the plaintiff's case (by the defendant), at the close of the record, or both. Regardless of when the motion is first made, it must be made or renewed at the close of the record in order to preserve future rights for appeal.[6]

Subject of Motion

A motion for judgment as a matter of law may seek judgment on entire claims or defenses or on specific issues that are not wholly dispositive of a claim or defense.[7]

1. *Young Dental Mfg. Co., Inc. v. Q3 Special Products, Inc.*, 112 F.3d 1137, 1142, n. 1 (Fed. Cir.1997).

2. *Wimmer v. Suffolk County Police Dept.*, 176 F.3d 125, 134 (2d Cir.1999), *cert. denied*, 522 U.S. 1109, 118 S.Ct. 1039, 140 L.Ed.2d 105 (1998); *CVI/Beta Ventures, Inc. v. Tura LP*, 112 F.3d 1146, 1152 (Fed.Cir.1997), *cert. denied*, 522 U.S. 1109, 118 S.Ct. 1039, 140 L.Ed.2d 105 (1998).

3. *Smith v. Northwest Fin. Acceptance, Inc.*, 129 F.3d 1408, 1415 (10th Cir.1997); *Zeigler v. Fisher–Price, Inc.*, 302 F.Supp.2d 999, 1007 (N.D.Iowa 2004) (although the grounds do not have to be stated with technical precision, the movant must give fair notice to the court of the grounds for the motion); Frazier v. Boyle, 206 F.R.D. 480, 490–91 (E.D.Wis.2002).

4. *Ross v. Rhodes Furniture, Inc.*, 146 F.3d 1286, 1289 (11th Cir.1998).

5. *Bristol v. Board of County Com'rs of County of Clear Creek*, 281 F.3d 1148, 1163 (10th Cir.2002), *vac'd in part on reh'g en banc*, 312 F.3d 1213 (10th Cir.2002); *Wolfgang v. Mid–America Motorsports, Inc.*, 111 F.3d 1515, 1521 (10th Cir.1997).

6. *MacArthur v. University of Texas Health Center at Tyler*, 45 F.3d 890 (5th Cir.1995).

7. *Ross v. Rhodes Furniture, Inc.*, 146 F.3d 1286, 1289–90 (11th Cir.1998) (grounds for motion must be clear from the record so that the appeals court can ensure that setting aside the verdict would not be a surprise to the non-movant); *Chesapeake Paper Products Co. v. Stone & Webster Engineering Corp.*, 51 F.3d 1229, 1236 (4th Cir.1995).

Opportunity to Cure

A major purpose of the motion is to call a deficiency in the evidence to the attention of the court so the opposing counsel may cure the defect.[8] The court then has a duty to apprise the non-moving party of the materiality of the dispositive fact and provide that party with an opportunity to present any available evidence.[9]

Sufficiency of Evidence

The sufficiency of the evidence is an issue of law to be determined by the judge.[10] The primary consideration is whether the evidence in the record could properly support a particular verdict.[11] The court must view all evidence in the light most favorable to the party opposing the motion; [12] it may not make credibility determinations or weigh the evidence.[13] However, the court may disregard testimony that is opposed to undisputed physical facts.[14] Moreover, a "mere scintilla" of evidence is not sufficient.[15]

Inferences

The court must draw all reasonable inferences from the evidence that favor the party opposing the motion.[16] Thus, even if all the facts are undisputed, a motion for judgment as a matter of law will still be denied if the evidence is susceptible of conflicting inferences.[17] However, inferences created by statute or doctrine, such as *res ipsa loquitur,* may raise different issues requiring specific research.

8. *Laborers' Pension Fund v. A & C Environmental, Inc.*, 301 F.3d 768, 775 (7th Cir.2002).

9. *Waters v. Young*, 100 F.3d 1437, 1441 (9th Cir.1996) (adding that the court's duty is especially important when confronted with pro se litigants).

10. *Lange v. Penn Mut. Life Ins. Co.*, 843 F.2d 1175, 1181 (9th Cir.1988).

11. *Anderson v. Liberty Lobby, Inc.*, 477 U.S. 242, 106 S.Ct. 2505, 91 L.Ed.2d 202 (1986); *Acevedo-Garcia v. Monroig*, 351 F.3d 547, 565 (1st Cir. 2003); *Murray v. Chicago Transit Authority*, 252 F.3d 880 (7th Cir.2001) (the test for a Rule 50 motion is whether there is no legally sufficient evidentiary basis for a reasonable jury to find for the non-moving party on the issues that are the subject of the motion).

12. *Galloway v. United States,* 319 U.S. 372, 63 S.Ct. 1077, 87 L.Ed. 1458 (1943); *Perez v. Volvo Car Corp.*, 247 F.3d 303 (1st Cir.2001); *Cobb v. Pozzi*, 363 F.3d 89, 101 (2nd Cir. 2004) (essentially, the standard for a Rule 50 motion is the same as the standard for a summary judgment motion under Rule 56).

13. *This Is Me, Inc. v. Taylor,* 157 F.3d 139, 142 (2d Cir.1998); *Andrade v. Jamestown Housing Authority*, 82 F.3d 1179, 1186 (1st Cir.1996); *Rand-Whitney Containerboard Ltd. Partnership v. Town of Montville*, 289 F.Supp.2d 62, 66 (D.Conn. 2003).

14. *See, e.g., O'Connor v. Pennsylvania R.R. Co.,* 308 F.2d 911 (2d Cir.1962) (testimony about snowfall disregarded when contrary to the records of the Weather Bureau); *Grant v. Cia Anonima Venezolana de Navegacion,* 228 F.Supp. 232 (E.D.La.1964), *affirmed*, 343 F.2d 757 (5th Cir.1965) (testimony that a winch was operated electrically disregarded when a physical inspection showed that the winch was operated hydraulically).

15. *A.B. Small Co. v. Lamborn & Co.,* 267 U.S. 248, 254, 45 S.Ct. 300, 303, 69 L.Ed. 597 (1925); *DP Solutions, Inc. v. Rollins, Inc.*, 353 F.3d 421, 427 (5th Cir. 2003).

16. *Laxton v. Gap Inc.*, 333 F.3d 572, 577 (5th Cir.2003). *Green v. Administrators of Tulane Educational Fund*, 284 F.3d 642, 652 (5th Cir.2002).

17. *Daniels v. Twin Oaks Nursing Home,* 692 F.2d 1321, 1325 (11th Cir.1982).

Jury Trials Only

Rule 50 applies only to binding jury cases.[18] The appropriate motion in non-jury trials and trials with an advisory jury is a motion for judgment on partial findings under Rule 52(c).[19]

Motions Held Under Consideration

The court is under no obligation to grant a motion for judgment as a matter of law even if the record supports the motion. Courts often allow the jury to reach a verdict in order to minimize the likelihood of needing a new trial, then if necessary enter judgment contrary to the verdict.[20]

Motion Granted

If the court grants a motion for judgment as a matter of law, it will enter the appropriate verdict without involvement of the jury.

Motion Denied

If the motion for judgment as a matter of law is denied, the defendant may put on evidence. However, if the plaintiff's case lacked a certain element and that element is brought out during the defendant's case, the deficiency will be cured.[21]

Who May Make Motion

Both defendants and plaintiffs may make motions for judgment as a matter of law. Thus, if the plaintiff enters evidence sufficient to support each element of the plaintiff's case and that evidence is not contradicted during the defendant's case, the plaintiff will be entitled to a judgment as a matter of law.[22] In addition, the judge may grant a judgment as a matter of law *sua sponte*.[23]

Prerequisite to Appeal

A motion for judgment as a matter of law at the close of the record is a prerequisite to challenging the sufficiency of the evidence on appeal.[24] Note, however, that appellate issues other than those relating to the sufficiency of the evidence are not affected.[25] An exception to this principle occurs if the verdict constitutes plain error on the face of

18. *Nieto v. Kapoor*, 268 F.3d 1208, 1217 (10th Cir.2001).

19. *Northeast Drilling, Inc. v. Inner Space Services, Inc.*, 243 F.3d 25, 37 (1st Cir.2001).

20. *Colonial Lincoln–Mercury, Inc. v. Musgrave*, 749 F.2d 1092, 1098 (4th Cir.1984); *United States v. Singleton*, 702 F.2d 1159, 1172 (D.C.Cir.1983).

21. *Trustees of University of Pa. v. Lexington Ins. Co.*, 815 F.2d 890, 903 (3d Cir.1987); *Peterson v. Hager*, 724 F.2d 851, 854 (10th Cir.1984).

22. *Hurd v. American Hoist & Derrick Co.*, 734 F.2d 495, 499 (10th Cir.1984); *Walter E. Heller & Co. v. Video Innovations, Inc.*, 730 F.2d 50, 54 (2d Cir.1984).

23. *American & Foreign Ins. Co. v. Bolt*, 106 F.3d 155, 160 (6th Cir.1997).

24. *Chemetall GMBH v. ZR Energy, Inc.*, 320 F.3d 714, 719 (7th Cir.2003).

25. *Ruyle v. Continental Oil Co.*, 44 F.3d 837 (10th Cir.1994), *cert. denied*, 516 U.S. 906, 116 S.Ct. 272, 133 L.Ed.2d 193 (1995).

the record, and a miscarriage of justice would result if the verdict remained in effect.[26]

Standard of Review

On appeal, the appellate court applies the same standard as the district court, without deference to the ruling of the trial judge.[27]

RULE 50(b). RENEWAL OF MOTION FOR JUDGMENT AFTER TRIAL; ALTERNATIVE MOTION FOR NEW TRIAL

CORE CONCEPT

The court can enter a judgment that is inconsistent with the jury's verdict if it determines that the verdict was not supported by the evidence. However, a prerequisite to a motion for judgment after trial is a motion for a judgment as a matter of law at the close of the record.[28]

APPLICATIONS

Content of Motion

A motion for judgment after trial must state the grounds for relief,[29] and may include only those grounds raised in the motion for judgment as a matter of law.[30]

Timing

The motion must be filed not later than 10 days after the *entry* of the judgment[31] (not the notice of entry of the judgment). If the jury does not return a verdict, such as with a mistrial, the parties have 10 days from the discharge of the jury.[32] This strict time limit cannot be enlarged.[33]

26. *Stephenson v. Doe*, 332 F.3d 68, 75–76 (2nd Cir.2003).

27. *Cobb v. Pozzi*, 363 F.3d 89, 101 (2nd Cir. 2004).

28. *Graves v. City of Coeur D'Alene*, 339 F.3d 828 (9th Cir.2003) (failure to raise lack of a Rule 50(a) motion was a waiver of the defect); *Nichols v. Ashland Hosp. Corp.*, 251 F.3d 496, 502, n.1 (4th Cir.2001).

29. *Andreas v. Volkswagen of America, Inc.*, 336 F.3d 789 (8th Cir.2003) (Rule 50(b) motion must put the court and the parties on notice of the issues being raised).

30. *Ross v. Rhodes Furniture, Inc.*, 146 F.3d 1286, 1289–90 (11th Cir.1998) (grounds for motion must be clear from the record so that the appeals court can ensure that setting aside the verdict would not be a surprise to the nonmovant); *Staley v. Bridgestone/Firestone, Inc.*, 106 F.3d 1504, 1508 (10th Cir.1997).

31. *Green v. Administrators of Tulane Educational Fund*, 284 F.3d 642, 652 (5th Cir.2002) (Rule 50(b) motion timely when delivered to the clerk's office within 10 days even though the clerks did not file the motion until after 10 days); *Fruit of the Loom, Inc. v. American Marketing Enterprises, Inc.*, 192 F.3d 73, 75–76 (2d Cir.1999).

32. Rule 50(b) is silent about the deadline for filing a post-trial motion if a judgment is not entered. However, the best interpretation is that the 10 day limit also applies when judgment is not entered, such as with a mistrial. *See Wiehoff v. GTE Directories Corp.*, 851 F.Supp. 1322 (D. Minn. 1993), *affirmed in part, reversed in part*, 61 F.3d 588 (8th Cir.1995) (stating without discussion that a rule 50(b) motion may be filed 10 days after the jury has been discharged following a mistrial).

33. *Andreas v. Volkswagen of America, Inc.*, 336 F.3d 789 (8th Cir.2003); *Hodge ex rel. Skiff v. Hodge*, 269 F.3d 155, 157 (2d Cir.2001).

Rule 59 Motion for New Trial

A Rule 50(b) motion is often combined with a motion for new trial under Rule 59(a).[34]

Motion for Judgment as a Matter of Law After Trial

A party cannot make a motion for judgment after trial unless it has filed a motion for judgment as a matter of law at the close of the evidence.[35] Moreover, the post trial motion is limited to the issues raised in the pre-verdict motion.[36] However, there are two recognized exceptions to this rule: (1) if a court indicates renewal is not necessary to preserve the challenge;[37] (2) if not allowing the claim would result in a manifest miscarriage of justice.[38] In addition, if the moving party fails to file a motion at the close of evidence, but the non-moving party fails to raise the waiver issue, the non-moving party is precluded from raising the waiver issue on appeal.[39] If there was no motion for judgment as a matter of law but the evidence does not support the verdict, the court can order a new trial.[40]

Motion for a New Trial

A party may join a motion for a new trial with a motion for judgment after trial, or request a new trial in the alternative.[41] The standard is the same as with a motion for new trial under Rule 59; the motion will be granted if the verdict is contrary to the clear weight of the evidence. A new trial is favored over a judgment contrary to the verdict when it appears that the party could present sufficient evidence to support the verdict at a future date.

Rulings

If the jury returned a verdict, the court may allow the verdict to stand, order a new trial, or direct entry of judgment as a matter of law. If no verdict was returned, the court may order a new trial or direct the entry of judgment as a matter of law. When a motion for new trial is

34. *See, e.g., Frazier v. Boyle*, 206 F.R.D. 480 (E.D.Wis.2002); *Pickett v. Detella*, 163 F.Supp.2d 999 (N.D.Ill.2001).

35. *Rinehimer v. Cemcolift, Inc.*, 292 F.3d 375 (3d Cir.2002); *American & Foreign Ins. Co. v. Bolt*, 106 F.3d 155, 160 (6th Cir.1997) (holding a judge may not *sua sponte* raise a new issue in a Rule 50(b) motion); *Hoechst Celanese Corp. v. BP Chemicals Limited*, 78 F.3d 1575, 1581–82 (Fed.Cir.1996), *cert. denied*, 519 U.S. 911, 117 S.Ct. 275, 136 L.Ed.2d 198 (1996).

36. *Freund v. Nycomed Amersham*, 347 F.3d 752, 761 (9th Cir. 2003).

37. *Pahuta v. Massey–Ferguson, Inc.*, 170 F.3d 125, 129 (2d Cir.1999).

38. *C.K. Greenwood v. Societe Francaise De*, 111 F.3d 1239, 1244 (5th Cir.1997), *cert. denied*, 522 U.S. 995, 118 S.Ct. 558, 139 L.Ed.2d 400 (1997) (holding that a motion made at the close of the plaintiff's case, coupled with an objection to jury charge, can be sufficient to preserve appeal); *BE & K Const. v. United Brotherhood of Carpenters & Joiners of America*, 90 F.3d 1318, 1325 (8th Cir.1996).

39. *Desrosiers v. Flight International of Florida Inc.*, 156 F.3d 952, 956 (9th Cir.1998); *Thompson & Wallace of Memphis, Inc. v. Falconwood Corp.*, 100 F.3d 429, 435 (5th Cir.1996).

40. *Johnson v. New York, N.H. & H.R. Co.*, 344 U.S. 48, 54, 73 S.Ct. 125, 128, 97 L.Ed. 77 (1952).

41. *Willis v. State Farm Fire and Cas. Co.*, 219 F.3d 715 (8th Cir.2000) (moved for judgment as a matter of law and, in the alternative, for a new trial).

joined with a motion for judgment after trial, Rule 50 specifically requires that the court rule on both motions.

Appeals

Rulings on motions for judgment after trial are final, appealable orders. In contrast, an order granting a new trial may not be a final, appealable order.[42] On appeal, legal determinations are reviewed de novo.[43] In diversity cases, questions of evidence sufficiency are reviewed under the standard used by the forum state. When there is a federal question, evidence sufficiency is reviewed in a light most favorable to the non-moving party and motions are granted only when reasonable minds could not come to a conclusion other than the one favoring the movant.[44]

RULE 50(c). GRANTING RENEWED MOTION FOR JUDGMENT AS A MATTER OF LAW; CONDITIONAL RULINGS; NEW TRIAL MOTION

CORE CONCEPT

If the court grants a motion for judgment as a matter of law after trial and a motion for a new trial was also filed, the court will make a conditional ruling on the motion for a new trial.[45]

APPLICATIONS

Rulings Conditional on Reversal

The trial court's rulings on the motion for a new trial are applicable if the appeals court reverses the granting of the judgment after trial.[46] In that case, the appeals court will generally enter the original verdict or order a new trial, depending on the trial court's conditional ruling. However, the appeals court also may review the trial court's conditional ruling on the motion for a new trial.

Granting of Both Motions

If the trial court grants both a motion for judgment notwithstanding the verdict and a motion for a new trial, the ruling on the motion for a new trial is automatically deemed conditional.

Motion for New Trial

If the court grants a motion for judgment after trial, the party against whom judgment was entered may file a motion for a new trial no later than 10 days after the entry of judgment, pursuant to Rule 59.

42. *Binder v. Long Island Lighting Co.*, 57 F.3d 193 (2d Cir.1995).

43. *Graves v. City of Coeur D'Alene*, 339 F.3d 828 (9th Cir.2003).

44. *K & T Enterprises, Inc. v. Zurich Ins. Co.*, 97 F.3d 171, 175–176 (6th Cir.1996).

45. *Rhone Poulenc Rorer Pharmaceuticals, Inc. v. Newman Glass Works*, 112 F.3d 695, 698 (3d Cir.1997); *Computer Access Technology Corp. v. Catalyst Enterprises, Inc.*, 273 F.Supp.2d 1063 (N.D.Cal.2003).

46. *Fioto v. Manhattan Woods Golf Enterprises, LLC.*, 304 F.Supp.2d 541 (S.D.N.Y. 2004).

Failure to Issue a Conditional Ruling

If a court fails to issue a conditional ruling, the appellate court has the authority to either remand to the trial court to decide the new trial motion or decide the new trial motion itself.[47]

RULE 50(d). SAME: DENIAL OF MOTION FOR JUDGMENT AS A MATTER OF LAW

CORE CONCEPT

If the losing party appeals the denial of a motion for judgment after trial, the prevailing party may on appeal assert grounds for a new trial in the event that the court reverses the denial of the motion for judgment after trial. If the appellate court does reverse, it may order the entry of judgment, order a new trial, or remand to the trial court to determine whether a new trial is warranted.

ADDITIONAL RESEARCH REFERENCES

Wright & Miller, *Federal Practice and Procedure* §§ 2521–2540.

C.J.S. Federal Civil Procedure §§ 958–977 et seq., 1034, 1089, 1093, 1219–1226 et seq.

West's Key No. Digests, Federal Civil Procedure ⚷2111–2156, 2601–2610.

47. *Acosta v. San Francisco*, 83 F.3d 1143, 1149 (9th Cir.1996), *cert. denied*, 519 U.S. 1009, 117 S.Ct. 514, 136 L.Ed.2d 403 (1996).

RULE 51

INSTRUCTIONS TO JURY; OBJECTIONS; PRESERVING A CLAIM OF ERROR

(a) Requests.

(1) A party may, at the close of the evidence or at an earlier reasonable time that the court directs, file and furnish to every other party written requests that the court instruct the jury on the law as set forth in the requests.

(2) After the close of the evidence, a party may:

(A) file requests for instructions on issues that could not reasonably have been anticipated at an earlier time for requests set under Rule 51(a)(1), and

(B) with the court's permission file untimely requests for instructions on any issue.

(b) Instructions. The court:

(1) must inform the parties of its proposed instructions and proposed action on the requests before instructing the jury and before final jury arguments;

(2) must give the parties an opportunity to object on the record and out of the jury's hearing to the proposed instructions and actions on requests before the instructions and arguments are delivered; and

(3) may instruct the jury at any time after trial begins and before the jury is discharged.

(c) Objections.

(1) A party who objects to an instruction or the failure to give an instruction must do so on the record, stating distinctly the matter objected to and the grounds of the objection.

(2) An objection is timely if:

(A) a party that has been informed of an instruction or action on a request before the jury is instructed and before final jury arguments, as provided by Rule 51(b)(1), objects at the opportunity for objection required by Rule 51(b)(2); or

(B) a party that has not been informed of an instruction or action on a request before the time for objection provided under Rule 51(b)(2) objects promptly after learning that the instruction or request will be, or has been, given or refused.

(d) Assigning Error; Plain Error.

(1) A party may assign as error:

(A) an error in an instruction actually given if that party made a proper objection under Rule 51(c), or

(B) a failure to give an instruction if that party made a proper request under Rule 51(a), and—unless the court made a definitive ruling on the record rejecting the request—also made a proper objection under Rule 51(c).

(2) A court may consider a plain error in the instructions affecting substantial rights that has not been preserved as required by Rule 51(d)(1)(A) or (B).

[Amended effective August 1, 1987; March 27, 2003, effective December 1, 2003.]

AUTHORS' COMMENTARY ON RULE 51

PURPOSE AND SCOPE

Before the jury retires to deliberate, the judge must instruct the jury as to the law that they are to apply. The parties have an opportunity to request that certain instructions be given, and to object to the instructions given and to the instructions not given.

NOTE: Rule 51 was substantially revised in 2003. The amendments reorganized Rule 51 into 4 subparts, and codified much of the case law that had evolved under Rule 51.

RULE 51(a). REQUESTS

CORE CONCEPT

The parties may submit proposed jury instructions to the court. Proposed instructions are submitted at the close of the evidence, or at such earlier time as directed by the court.

APPLICATIONS

Timing of Requests

Requests for jury instructions are normally made at the close of the evidence, or earlier if the court so directs. If the court has set a time before the close of evidence for submission of requests for instructions, a party may submit additional requests for instructions after the close of evidence on issues that could not have been anticipated when the requests were submitted.[1] Note, however, that local rules may set the time for making requests for jury instructions. The court, in its discretion, may consider untimely requests.[2]

Form and Content of Requests

Requests normally should be reasonably neutral statements of the law governing the case, and not overly argumentative. Requests are usually written, although they can be oral.

Service

Requests for instruction must be furnished to every other party.[3]

RULE 51(b). INSTRUCTIONS

CORE CONCEPT

The court must inform the parties of its proposed instructions before instructing the jury and before the parties' final arguments to the jury, and must give the parties an opportunity to object on the record and out of the jury's hearing.

APPLICATIONS

Rulings on Requests

The court is required to inform the parties of its rulings on the jury instruction requests before the closing arguments, so that the counsel may adjust their closings accordingly. Failure to do so, however, will not be grounds for a new trial unless it is prejudicial.[4]

Form and Procedure for Instructions

Instructions are given to the jury in open court at any time after trial begins and before the jury is discharged.[5] The judge may repeat portions of the charge or give a supplemental charge at the jury's request, but must afford the parties notice and an opportunity to be present for such additional instruction. The judge may submit a written charge to the jury, although it is not commonly done.

Content of Instructions

The court should give an instruction on every material issue in the case. The instruction should clearly and understandably convey the status of the applicable law. There is no particular wording or order mandated, and the judge need not use the language requested by the parties. Narrowly-tailored instructions are favored over broad statements of the law.

1. Rule 51(a)(2)(A).
2. Rule 51(a)(2)(B).
3. Rule 51(a)(1).
4. *Delano v. Kitch,* 542 F.2d 550 (10th Cir. 1976), *opinion clarified,* 554 F.2d 1004 (10th Cir.1977), *cert. denied,* 456 U.S. 946, 102 S.Ct. 2012, 72 L.Ed.2d 468 (1982).
5. Rule 51(b)(3).

Deadlocked Jury

In the civil context, the judge may instruct a jury claiming to be deadlocked to make further attempts to reach a verdict. The judge may not, however, coerce reluctant jurors to join the majority.

Comments on Evidence

The court, in its discretion, may comment on the evidence and even focus the jury's attention on certain portions of the evidence. If the judge does so, the judge must make it clear to the jury that they, not the judge, are the ultimate fact finders.

Opportunity to Object

The court must give the parties an opportunity to raise objections to the instructions out of the hearing of the jury before the instructions and closing arguments are delivered.[6] If the court fails to give an opportunity to raise the objections, parties with objections should request such an opportunity. However, if instructions are reread or the jury is given additional instructions, an objection may be raised at that time.[7]

RULE 51(c). OBJECTIONS

CORE CONCEPT

Objections to the instructions must be made on the record with a statement of the grounds when the court provides and opportunity for such objections.[8]

APPLICATIONS

Content of Objection

The objection must be stated with sufficient clarity and specificity that the judge can understand the nature of the objection and remedy the problem if the judge agrees.[9] Any appeal must be based upon issues so raised in an objection.[10]

Time of Objections

A party must object to the content of the instructions at the opportunity provided by the court before the instructions and closing

6. *Club Car, Inc. v. Club Car (Quebec) Import, Inc.*, 362 F.3d 775, 782 (11th Cir. 2004).

7. *Barrett v. Orange County Human Rights Commission*, 194 F.3d 341, 349 (2d Cir.1999).

8. *Sherman v. Kasotakis*, 314 F.Supp.2d 843 (N.D.Iowa 2004).

9. *Beaudry v. Corrections Corp. of America*, 331 F.3d 1164, 1168 (10th Cir.2003), *cert. denied*, 540 U.S. 1118, 124 S.Ct. 1059, 157 L.Ed.2d 913 (2004) (merely tendering proposed instructions to a court is insufficient); *Housing 21, L.L.C. v. Atlantic Home Builders Co.*, 289 F.3d 1050, 1054 (8th Cir.2002) (Rule 51 does not require a party to employ the utmost formality in making an objection to avoid waiver); *Medlock v. Ortho Biotech, Inc.*, 164 F.3d 545, 553 (10th Cir.1999), *cert. denied*, 528 U.S. 813, 120 S.Ct. 48, 145 L.Ed.2d 42 (1999) (Rule 51 requires a litigant to state distinctly the specific objections; a general objection does not preserve the objections).

10. *Schobert v. Illinois Dept. of Transp.*, 304 F.3d 725, 729 (7th Cir.2002); *FHS Properties Limited Partnership v. BC Associates*, 175 F.3d 81, 87 (1st Cir.1999).

arguments are delivered[11], even if the party has previously raised and attempted to preserve the same objection.[12] If a party was not informed of an instruction or action on a request for an instruction prior to the opportunity to object provided by the court, the party may object promptly upon learning that the instruction was or would be given or refused.[13]

Failure to Object

If a party fails to object to an instruction before the jury begins deliberations, the party loses the right to challenge the instruction on appeal.[14] Some courts will undertake appellate review in the absence of a timely objection if the alleged error constitutes plain error[15] or is fundamental,[16] but other courts strictly require a timely objection.[17] Similarly, some courts will undertake appellate review in the absence of a timely objection if an objection would have been a pointless formality.[18]

RULE 51(d). ASSIGNING ERROR; PLAIN ERROR

11. Rule 51(c)(2)(A). *See also Moba, B.V. v. Diamond Automation, Inc.*, 325 F.3d 1306, 1314 (Fed.Cir.2003), *cert. denied*, 540 U.S. 982, 124 S.Ct. 464, 157 L.Ed.2d 371 (2003); *Greene v. Safeway Stores, Inc.*, 210 F.3d 1237 (10th Cir. 2000).

12. *Gray v. Genlyte Group, Inc.*, 289 F.3d 128, 134 (1st Cir.2002), *cert. denied*, 537 U.S. 1001, 123 S.Ct. 485, 154 L.Ed.2d 397 (2002) (it is not enough to refer back to previously raised objections); *Jones Truck Lines, Inc. v. Full Service Leasing Corp.*, 83 F.3d 253, 256 (8th Cir. 1996) (a "concern that the trial judge would prefer no objection or that the objection would be futile does not relieve parties from making an objection to preserve errors for review"); *Libbey–Owens–Ford Company v. Insurance Company of North America*, 9 F.3d 422 (6th Cir. 1993)(objections were waived even though the trial court told the parties that previously raised objections were preserved); *but see Lighting & Power Services, Inc. v. Roberts*, 354 F.3d 817, 820 (8th Cir. 2004) (finding that plaintiff's counsel's fully explained in-chambers objections satisfied Rule 51); *Smith v. Borough of Wilkinsburg*, 147 F.3d 272, 276 (3d Cir.1998) (a definitive ruling rejecting a proposed instruction preserves the issue for appeal).

13. Rule 51(c)(2)(B).

14. *Kanida v. Gulf Coast Medical Personnel LP*, 363 F.3d 568, 580 (5th Cir. 2004); *Walsh v. National Computer Systems, Inc.*, 332 F.3d 1150, (8th Cir.2003); *Medforms, Inc. v. Healthcare Management Solutions, Inc.*, 290 F.3d 98, 111–12 (2d Cir.2002).

15. *Muniz v. Rovira*, 373 F.3d 1 (1st Cir. 2004) (appellant must show that the alleged error seriously affected the fairness or integrity of the trial); *Oden v. Oktibbeha County, Miss.*, 246 F.3d 458, 466 (5th Cir.2001), *cert. denied*, 534 U.S. 948, 122 S.Ct. 341, 151 L.Ed.2d 258 (2001) (to appeal based on the plain error exception, there must be (1) error, (2) that is plain, and (3) that affects substantial rights).

16. *SCS Communications, Inc. v. Herrick Co., Inc.*, 360 F.3d 329, 343 (2nd Cir. 2004); *Ford ex rel. Estate of Ford v. Garcia*, 289 F.3d 1283, 1288 (11th Cir.2002), *cert. denied*, 537 U.S. 1147, 123 S.Ct. 868, 154 L.Ed.2d 849 (2003) (setting forth a 4 part test for fundamental or plain error); *Fashion Boutique of Short Hills, Inc. v. Fendi USA, Inc.*, 314 F.3d 48, 60 (2nd Cir.2002) (to qualify as a fundamental error there must be an error so serious and flagrant that it goes to the very integrity of the trial).

17. *See Monroe v. City of Phoenix, Ariz.*, 248 F.3d 851, 858 (9th Cir.2001).

18. *See Riverwood Intern. Corp. v. R.A. Jones & Co., Inc.*, 324 F.3d 1346, 1353 (Fed.Cir. 2003) (no need to object when issue had already been briefed and objection would have been futile); *Monroe v. City of Phoenix, Ariz.*, 248 F.3d 851, 858 (9th Cir.2001) (an objection may be a pointless formality when: (1) throughout the trial the party argued the disputed matter with the court; (2) it is clear from the record that the court knew the party's grounds for disagreement with the instruction; and (3) the party offered an alternative instruction).

CORE CONCEPT

A party may base an appeal on an instruction if the party made a proper objection pursuant to Rule 51(c) or upon plain error.

APPLICATIONS

Issues On Appeal

In general, a party may only raise on appeal issues regarding the instructions given that the party properly raised as objections pursuant to Rule 51(c).[19] A party may only raise on appeal an issue regarding an instruction not given if the party made a proper request for the instruction and either the court made a definitive ruling on the record rejecting the request or the party made a proper objection regarding the omitted instruction.[20]

Plain Error

The appeals court generally will review only issues to which there was a timely objection, but may, under extreme circumstances when justice demands, reverse even if no objections were made when an instruction contains plain error.[21] Additionally, the appeals court may consider an issue not preserved by objection where there has been a supervening change in the law.[22]

Appellate Review

Whether a jury instruction is legally erroneous is a question of law.[23] On appeal, the court reads the instructions as a whole and considers them in light of the entire charge to the jury.[24] There is a presumption that the jury followed the instructions[25] and that an erroneous instruction was prejudicial.[26]

ADDITIONAL RESEARCH REFERENCES

Wright & Miller, *Federal Practice and Procedure* §§ 2551–2558. Devitt, Blackmar, Wolff & O'Malley, *Federal Jury Practice and Instructions.*

C.J.S. Federal Civil Procedure §§ 983–994 et seq.

West's Key No. Digests, Federal Civil Procedure ⚷2171–2185.

19. *Connelly v. Hyundai Motor Co.*, 351 F.3d 535, 544 (1st Cir. 2003) (an objection on one ground does not preserve appellate review of a different ground).

20. Rule 51(d)(1)(B).

21. *Tompkins v. Cyr*, 202 F.3d 770, 783–84 (5th Cir.2000); *Beatty v. Michael Business Machines Corp.*, 172 F.3d 117 (1st Cir.1999).

22. *See Cadena v. Pacesetter Corp.*, 224 F.3d 1203, 1212 (10th Cir.2000); *Anixter v. Home–Stake Production Company*, 77 F.3d 1215, 1230–31 (10th Cir.1996).

23. *Advanced Display Systems, Inc. v. Kent State University*, 212 F.3d 1272, 1282 (Fed.Cir. 2000), *cert. denied*, 532 U.S. 904, 121 S.Ct. 1226, 149 L.Ed.2d 136 (2001).

24. *Advanced Display Systems, Inc. v. Kent State University*, 212 F.3d 1272, 1282 (Fed.Cir. 2000), *cert. denied*, 532 U.S. 904, 121 S.Ct. 1226, 149 L.Ed.2d 136 (2001).

25. Rule 51(d)(2). *See also Pittman v. Littlefield,* 438 F.2d 659, 662 (1st Cir.1971).

26. *United States v. River Rouge Improvement Co.,* 269 U.S. 411, 421, 46 S.Ct. 144, 148, 70 L.Ed. 339 (1926).

RULE 52

FINDINGS BY THE COURT; JUDGMENT ON PARTIAL FINDINGS

(a) Effect. In all actions tried upon the facts without a jury or with an advisory jury, the court shall find the facts specially and state separately its conclusions of law thereon, and judgment shall be entered pursuant to Rule 58; and in granting or refusing interlocutory injunctions the court shall similarly set forth the findings of fact and conclusions of law which constitute the grounds of its action. Requests for findings are not necessary for purposes of review. Findings of fact, whether based on oral or documentary evidence, shall not be set aside unless clearly erroneous, and due regard shall be given to the opportunity of the trial court to judge of the credibility of the witnesses. The findings of a master, to the extent that the court adopts them, shall be considered as the findings of the court. It will be sufficient if the findings of fact and conclusions of law are stated orally and recorded in open court following the close of the evidence or appear in an opinion or memorandum of decision filed by the court. Findings of fact and conclusions of law are unnecessary on decisions of motions under Rule 12 or 56 or any other motion except as provided in subdivision (c) of this rule.

(b) Amendment. On a party's motion filed no later than 10 days after entry of judgment, the court may amend its findings—or make additional findings—and may amend the judgment accordingly. The motion may accompany a motion for a new trial under Rule 59. When findings of fact are made in actions tried without a jury, the sufficiency of the evidence supporting the findings may be later questioned whether or not in the district court the party raising the question objected to the findings, moved to amend them, or moved for partial findings.

(c) Judgment on Partial Findings. If during a trial without a jury a party has been fully heard on an issue and the court finds against the party on that issue, the court may enter judgment as a matter of law against that party with respect to a claim or defense that cannot under the controlling law be maintained or defeated without a favorable finding on that issue, or the court may decline to render any judgment until the close of all the evidence. Such a judgment shall be supported by findings of fact and conclusions of law as required by subdivision (a) of this rule.

[Amended December 27, 1946, effective March 19, 1948; January 21, 1963, effective July 1, 1963; April 28, 1983, effective August 1, 1983; April 29, 1985, effective August 1, 1985; April 30, 1991, effective December 1, 1991; April 22, 1993, effective December 1, 1993; April 27, 1995, effective December 1, 1995.]

AUTHORS' COMMENTARY ON RULE 52

PURPOSE AND SCOPE

Following a non-jury trial, Rule 52 requires that the trial judge make findings of fact and conclusions of law. Rule 52 also sets forth the standard of review for such findings, and allows the judge to enter judgment during the trial if a party fails to carry its burden of proof.

RULE 52(a). EFFECT

CORE CONCEPT

The trial judge shall explicitly state findings of fact and conclusions of law upon which the judge bases the verdict. Findings of fact will not be disturbed on appeal unless clearly erroneous. Conclusions of law are fully reviewable on appeal.

APPLICATIONS

Findings Mandatory

The requirement that the judge make findings of fact and conclusions of law is mandatory, and cannot be waived.[1] The parties do not need to request findings.

Content of Findings

The findings must be sufficient to indicate the factual basis for the ultimate conclusion,[2] and permit meaningful appellate review,[3] but need not address all the evidence presented at trial.[4] The court need not make findings on uncontested or stipulated facts.[5]

1. *See Golden Blount, Inc. v. Robert H. Peterson Co.*, 365 F.3d 1054, 1060–61 (Fed.Cir. 2004); *Francis v. Goodman*, 81 F.3d 5, 8 (1st Cir.1996).

2. *American Canoe Ass'n v. Murphy Farms, Inc.*, 326 F.3d 505, 522 (4th Cir.2003); *Liddell v. Board of Education of the City of St. Louis*, 20 F.3d 326 (8th Cir.1994) (holding that a reference to "the totality of the circumstances" was not sufficient).

3. *Folger Coffee Co. v. Olivebank*, 201 F.3d 632, 635 (5th Cir.2000); *Duffie v. Deere & Co.*, 111 F.3d 70, 73 (8th Cir.1997) (without findings of fact, a trial court's conclusions are considered suspect).

4. *Zack v. C.I.R.*, 291 F.3d 407 (6th Cir. 2002). *But see Kidd v. Illinois State Police*, 167 F.3d 1084, 1101 (7th Cir.1999) (court should address conflicting testimony in its findings); *League of United Latin American Citizens, Council No. 4434 v. Clements*, 986 F.2d 728 (5th Cir.1993), *cert. denied*, 510 U.S. 1071, 114 S.Ct. 878, 127 L.Ed.2d 74 (1994)(the court should address all substantial evidence contrary to its opinion).

5. *Simeonoff v. Hiner*, 249 F.3d 883, 891 (9th Cir.2001) ("We will affirm the district court if . . . there can be no genuine dispute about omitted findings").

Proposed Findings and Conclusions

The court may require the parties to submit proposed findings of fact and conclusions of law,[6] although the court's wholesale adoption of the prevailing party's submission is discouraged.[7]

Proceedings Covered by Rule 52

Rule 52 requires findings of fact and conclusions of law in non-jury trials, trials with advisory juries,[8] proceedings for preliminary or permanent injunctions,[9] and when the court grants a motion for dismissal after the plaintiff has presented evidence pursuant to Rule 52(c).[10] Rule 52 does not apply to motions for summary judgment under Rule 56,[11] motions under Rule 12(b)[12] (such as motions to dismiss), motions for attorney fees,[13] or any other motion other than a motion for judgment on partial findings under Rule 52(c).[14] Likewise, findings are not required for actions before administrative agencies that submit reports and recommendations to the district court,[15] or in proceedings where the district court reviews rulings made by the bankruptcy court.

Findings in Jury Trials

In jury trials, Rule 52 applies to any issues decided by the court instead of the jury. The court must also make findings of fact and conclusions of law in a case tried before an advisory jury.[16]

6. *American River Trans. Co. v. Kavo Kaliakra SS*, 148 F.3d 446, 449 (5th Cir. 1998)(proposed findings adopted by the court are entitled to the same deference as findings crafted by the court).

7. *McLennan v. American Eurocopter Corp., Inc.*, 245 F.3d 403, 409 (5th Cir.2001) ("the district court's decision to adopt one party's proposed findings and conclusions without change may cause us to approach such findings with greater caution, and as a consequence to apply the standard of review more rigorously"); *Counihan v. Allstate Ins. Co.*, 194 F.3d 357, 365 (2d Cir.1999).

8. *Transmatic, Inc. v. Gulton Industries, Inc.*, 53 F.3d 1270 (Fed.Cir.1995).

9. *See Prairie Band of Potawatomi Indians v. Pierce*, 253 F.3d 1234, 1245 (10th Cir.2001); *Ciena Corp. v. Jarrard*, 203 F.3d 312 (4th Cir. 2000); *but see Dresser–Rand Co. v. Virtual Automation Inc.*, 361 F.3d 831, 847 (5th Cir. 2004) (findings not required at when addressing a request for a permanent injunction at the conclusion of a jury trial).

10. *Nieto v. Kapoor*, 268 F.3d 1208, 1217 (10th Cir.2001).

11. *Grossman v. Berman*, 241 F.3d 65, 68 (1st Cir.2001) (on a motion for summary judgment, a trial court has no obligation either to make specific findings of fact or to elaborate upon its view of the controlling legal principles); *but see Holly D. v. California Institute of Technology*, 339 F.3d 1158, 1180 (9th Cir. 2003) (Rule 52(a) does not relieve a court of the burden of stating its reasons somewhere in the record when its underlying holdings would otherwise be ambiguous).

12. *Souza v. Pina*, 53 F.3d 423 (1st Cir. 1995)(noting that, although not required, findings would be helpful).

13. *W.G. v. Senatore*, 18 F.3d 60 (2d Cir. 1994)(suggesting that findings regarding attorney fees would have been helpful, even though not required); *but see Kelly v. Golden*, 352 F.3d 344, 352 (8th Cir. 2003) (when awarding attorney fees, the court must make findings).

14. *Enzo Biochem, Inc. v. Calgene, Inc.*, 188 F.3d 1362, 1379 (Fed.Cir.1999).

15. *But see Muller v. First Unum Life Ins. Co.*, 341 F.3d 119, 124 (2nd Cir. 2003) (findings are required in ruling on a motion for judgment on the administrative record).

16. *Kolstad v. American Dental Ass'n*, 108 F.3d 1431, 1440 (D.C.Cir.1997), *cert. denied*, 525 U.S. 964, 119 S.Ct. 408, 142 L.Ed.2d 331 (1998). *See also*, Rule 39(c) and the author commentary discussing advisory juries.

Injunctions

The court must make findings of fact and conclusions of law when ruling on a motion for a preliminary injunction.[17] If a temporary restraining order is to be extended beyond the period allowed by Rule 65, it becomes a preliminary injunction and findings are required.[18] In ruling on a permanent injunction, the court must make findings if the ruling hinges on factual issues,[19] but the court will not be bound by findings made at the preliminary injunction stage.[20] Findings are not required in ruling on a motion to dissolve an injunction.[21]

Failure to Make Sufficient Findings

The appellate court may vacate and remand if the trial court's findings of fact are insufficient.[22] The appellate court may also direct the trial judge to order a new trial [23] or hearing to supplement the record.[24] The appellate court may also decide the appeal on the record, if possible.[25]

Form

The findings of fact may be a separate document or may be included in an opinion.[26] The court may also make its findings orally on the record.[27] If the court makes separate findings, then on appeal those findings control over any contradictory factual statements in an opinion.[28]

Objections

Rule 52 explicitly states that there is no need to request findings of fact and that no objection is necessary on the basis that the evidence does not support the findings.

17. *Bonnell v. Lorenzo*, 241 F.3d 800 (6th Cir.2001), *cert. denied*, 534 U.S. 951, 122 S.Ct. 347, 151 L.Ed.2d 262 (2001); *Hoechst Diafoil Co. v. Nan Ya Plastics Corp.*, 174 F.3d 411 (4th Cir.1999) (findings help the parties understand the grounds for the court's ruling and permits the appellate court to conduct a meaningful review).

18. *Hoechst Diafoil Co. v. Nan Ya Plastics Corp.*, 174 F.3d 411 (4th Cir.1999).

19. *Alberti v. Cruise*, 383 F.2d 268 (4th Cir. 1967); *but see Dresser–Rand Co. v. Virtual Automation Inc.*, 361 F.3d 831, 847 (5th Cir. 2004) (findings not required at when addressing a request for a permanent injunction at the conclusion of a jury trial).

20. *TEC Engineering Corp. v. Budget Molders Supply, Inc.*, 82 F.3d 542, 545 (1st Cir.1996).

21. *Baltimore & O. R. Co. v. Chicago River & I.R. Co.*, 170 F.2d 654 (7th Cir.1948), *cert. denied*, 336 U.S. 944, 69 S.Ct. 811, 93 L.Ed. 1101 (1949).

22. *Hatahley v. United States*, 351 U.S. 173, 76 S.Ct. 745, 100 L.Ed. 1065 (1956); *Federal Trade Com'n. v. Enforma Natural Products, Inc.*, 362 F.3d 1204, 1212 (9th Cir. 2004).

23. *Andre v. Bendix Corp.*, 774 F.2d 786, 801 (7th Cir.1985).

24. *Cordova v. Cox*, 351 F.2d 269 (10th Cir. 1965).

25. *E.E.O.C. v. Severn Trent Services, Inc.*, 358 F.3d 438, 442 (7th Cir. 2004) (the absence of explanation can be forgiven when the justification for the injunction is clear from the record); *TEC Engineering Corp. v. Budget Molders Supply, Inc.*, 82 F.3d 542, 545 (1st Cir.1996) (failure to comply with Rule 52 is harmless error when the "record substantially eliminates all reasonable doubt as to the basis of the district court's decision").

26. *See In re Hongisto*, 293 B.R. 45 (N.D.Cal. 2003).

27. *Federal Trade Com'n. v. Enforma Natural Products, Inc.*, 362 F.3d 1204, 1212 (9th Cir. 2004); *Ciena Corp. v. Jarrard*, 203 F.3d 312, 321 (4th Cir.2000).

28. *Snow Machines, Inc. v. Hedco, Inc.*, 838 F.2d 718, 727 (3d Cir.1988).

Record on Appeal

On appeal, the record includes the court's findings. Courts are divided as to whether the record includes proposed but not adopted findings.

Standard of Review

Findings of fact are presumed correct, and are only disturbed if clearly erroneous.[29] "Clearly erroneous" has been defined by the Supreme Court as when, after reviewing all of the evidence, the appeals court is "left with the definite and firm conviction that a mistake has been committed." [30] The appellate court's deference for findings is not quite as strong as for jury verdicts, but findings are not set aside merely because the appellate court would have decided differently.[31] Conclusions of law are reviewed de novo.[32] Courts are split as to whether mixed questions of law and fact are reviewed under the clearly erroneous standard or de novo.[33]

Review of Credibility Determinations

Appellate courts are particularly hesitant to set aside findings based on evaluations of witness credibility.[34] The same applies to expert testimony,[35] except for evidentiary rulings such as foundation and methodology. On the other hand, findings based solely on documents in the record may not be accorded such high deference.[36]

Review of Inferences

Inferences from the evidence are reviewed under the same standard as any factual finding.[37]

29. *See Hurley v. Irish–American Gay, Lesbian and Bisexual Group of Boston*, 515 U.S. 557, 115 S.Ct. 2338, 132 L.Ed.2d 487 (1995); *Shire US Inc. v. Barr Laboratories, Inc.*, 329 F.3d 348, 352 (3rd Cir.2003).

30. *United States v. U.S. Gypsum Co.*, 333 U.S. 364, 395, 68 S.Ct. 525, 541, 92 L.Ed. 746 (1948); *Beaver v. Clingman*, 363 F.3d 1048, 1053 (10th Cir. 2004), *cert. granted*, ___ U.S. ___, 125 S.Ct. 27, 159 L.Ed.2d 857 (2004); *Presley v. U.S. Postal Service*, 317 F.3d 167, 174 (2nd Cir.2003).

31. *See Nelson-Salabes, Inc. v. Morningside Development, LLC*, 284 F.3d 505, 512 (4th Cir. 2002); *Damon v. Sun Co., Inc.*, 87 F.3d 1467, 1472 (1st Cir.1996) (but, findings of fact based on errors of law receive diminished respect).

32. *Coady Corp. v. Toyota Motor Distributors, Inc.*, 361 F.3d 50, 54 (1st Cir. 2004); *Koam Produce, Inc. v. DiMare Homestead, Inc.*, 329 F.3d 123, 126 (2nd Cir.2003); *Cerros v. Steel Technologies, Inc.*, 288 F.3d 1040, 1044 (7th Cir.2002).

33. *See Phansalkar v. Andersen Weinroth & Co., L.P.*, 344 F.3d 184, 199 (2nd Cir. 2003) (de novo); *Ringling Bros.-Barnum & Bailey Combined Shows, Inc. v. Utah Division of Travel Development*, 170 F.3d 449, 461 (4th Cir.1999), *cert. denied*, 528 U.S. 923, 120 S.Ct. 286, 145 L.Ed.2d 239 (1999)(clearly erroneous).

34. *Adzick v. UNUM Life Ins. Co. of America*, 351 F.3d 883, 889 (8th Cir. 2003) (findings based on credibility can virtually never be clear error); *McCrary v. Runyon*, 515 F.2d 1082 (4th Cir.1975), *affirmed*, 427 U.S. 160, 96 S.Ct. 2586, 49 L.Ed.2d 415 (1976); *Trustees of Nat. Elevator Industry Pension, Health Benefit and Educational Funds v. Lutyk*, 332 F.3d 188, 194 (3rd Cir. 2003).

35. *Graver Tank & Mfg. Co. v. Linde Air Prods. Co.*, 336 U.S. 271, 274, 69 S.Ct. 535, 537, 93 L.Ed. 672 (1949).

36. *Hall v. Nat'l Gypsum Co.*, 105 F.3d 225, 228 (5th Cir.1997); *but see Shire US Inc. v. Barr Laboratories, Inc.*, 329 F.3d 348, 352 (3d Cir. 2003) (the clearly erroneous standard applies to the district court's factual findings whether based on oral or documentary evidence).

37. *United States v. U.S. Gypsum Co.*, 333 U.S. 364, 68 S.Ct. 525, 92 L.Ed. 746 (1948).

Review of Mixed Fact and Law

Often findings or conclusions by the trial court are actually mixtures of fact and law. Such mixed holdings are generally fully reviewable, and not subject to the "clearly erroneous" standard.[38] However, the line between issues of fact and law is often blurry. The appellate court will not rely on the trial court's label, but will determine on its own whether a holding is factual or legal.

Review of Findings of Master

If the report and recommendation of a master is adopted, those findings are subject to the same standard as the court's findings.[39] The standard of review is less clear when the trial court rejects or modifies the master's findings.

RULE 52(b). AMENDMENT

CORE CONCEPT

Upon motion, the court may amend its findings and/or judgment.

APPLICATIONS

Timing

Motions to amend the findings must be filed no later than 10 days after entry of judgment.[40] This time period is absolute, and cannot be enlarged by the court.[41] The motion may be filed before entry of judgment.

Grounds

Proper grounds for a Rule 52(b) motion to amend include newly discovered evidence, a change in the law, or a manifest error of fact or law by the trial court.[42] A Rule 52(b) motion to amend should not merely relitigate old issues or rehear the merits of the case.[43]

Prerequisites for Appeal

Challenges to the sufficiency of the evidence supporting the findings in a non-jury trial may be made on appeal, even absent an

38. *Muller v. Committee on Special Education of East Islip Union Free School District*, 145 F.3d 95, 102 (2d Cir.1998); *Hirschfeld v. Spanakos*, 104 F.3d 16, 19 (2d Cir.1997).

39. *AccuSoft Corp. v. Palo*, 237 F.3d 31, 39 (1st Cir.2001); *Berger v. Iron Workers Reinforced Rodmen, Local 201*, 170 F.3d 1111, 1119 (D.C.Cir.1999).

40. *Cayuga Indian Nation of New York v. Pataki*, 188 F.Supp.2d 223, 229–30 (N.D.N.Y. 2002).

41. *Martin v. Monumental Life Ins. Co.*, 240 F.3d 223, 237–38 (3d Cir.2001).

42. *Sherman v. Kasotakis*, 314 F.Supp.2d 843 (N.D.Iowa 2004); *Padilla v. Miller*, 143 F.Supp.2d 479, 487 (M.D.Pa.2001); *Hollis v. City of Buffalo*, 189 F.R.D. 260, 262 (W.D.N.Y.1999).

43. *Gutierrez v. Ashcroft*, 289 F.Supp.2d 555, 561 (D.N.J. 2003); *Diebitz v. Arreola*, 834 F.Supp. 298 (E.D.Wis.1993).

objection to the findings, motion to amend the findings, or motion for partial findings before the district court.[44] However, challenges other than to the sufficiency of the evidence may need to be raised at the trial level to be raised on appeal. For example, a motion under Rule 52(b) to request additional findings may be a prerequisite to basing an appeal on the lack of such findings.[45] Likewise, a party may not be permitted to first raise objections to the form of the finding on appeal.[46]

Tolls Appeal Period

The filing of a motion to amend the findings tolls the running of the time to file an appeal.[47] The appeal clock starts over when the court enters an order granting or denying the motion to amend.

RULE 52(c). JUDGMENT ON PARTIAL FINDINGS

CORE CONCEPT

At any time in a non-jury trial after a party has presented all its evidence with respect to a particular issue, the court may enter judgment against that party if the evidence failed to persuade the judge.[48]

APPLICATIONS

Proceedings Applicable

Rule 52(c) applies only in non-jury trials.[49] The parallel for jury trials is a judgment as a matter of law under Rule 50(a).

Timing of Motion

A Rule 52(c) motion may be made at any time after all the evidence has been presented on a particular topic;[50] the movant need not wait until the opposing party has rested.[51]

Standard for Granting

The trial judge rules on motions for judgment on partial findings as a final factfinder, reviewing all evidence presented thus far without presumptions in favor of either party.[52] The judge grants the motion if,

44. *Glaverbel Societe Anonyme v. Northlake Marketing & Supply, Inc.*, 45 F.3d 1550 (Fed.Cir. 1995).

45. *See Northeast Drilling, Inc. v. Inner Space Services, Inc.*, 243 F.3d 25, 35 (1st Cir. 2001).

46. *Miller v. Bittner*, 985 F.2d 935 (8th Cir. 1993).

47. *Weyant v. Okst*, 198 F.3d 311, 314–15 (2d Cir.1999).

48. *Lamarca v. United States*, 31 F.Supp.2d 110, 123 (E.D.N.Y.1998) (judgment on partial findings may be rendered in favor of plaintiffs or defendants).

49. *Fillmore v. Page*, 358 F.3d 496, 502–03 (7th Cir. 2004); *Northeast Drilling, Inc. v. Inner Space Services, Inc.*, 243 F.3d 25, 35 (1st Cir. 2001).

50. *First Virginia Banks, Inc. v. BP Exploration & Oil, Inc.*, 206 F.3d 404, 407 (4th Cir.2000) (Rule 52 does not create a right to introduce all the evidence on a topic that the party wishes; the court may exclude evidence if cumulative or not probative).

51. *Cajun Electric Power Cooperative, Inc. v. Gulf States Utilities Company*, 848 F.Supp. 71 (M.D.La.1994).

52. *Ortloff v. U.S.*, 335 F.3d 652, 660 (7th Cir.2003), *cert. denied,* 540 U.S. 1225, 124 S.Ct. 1520, 158 L.Ed.2d 164 (2004) (contrasting the standard under Rule 52(c) to the standard under

upon the evidence already presented, the judge would find against the party that has already presented evidence and in favor of the moving party.

Scope of Judgment

The judge will enter judgment on the claim or issue that is the subject of the motion and on any other claim, issue, counterclaim, crossclaim, or third-party claim that is determined by the outcome of the issue that is the subject of the motion.

Findings of Fact

If the judge grants a motion for judgment on partial findings, the judge must make findings of fact pursuant to Rule 52(a).[53]

Deferred Ruling

The judge, in an exercise of discretion, may defer ruling until all evidence has been presented.[54]

Appeals

The appeals court will review judgments on partial findings under the "clearly erroneous" standard because such findings represent the judge's factual determinations.[55] Conclusions of law are reviewed *de novo*.[56] The appeals court will probably review all the evidence in the record. Thus, if the motion is denied and the defendant elects to offer evidence, the plaintiff may be able to cure the purported deficiency in its case.

ADDITIONAL RESEARCH REFERENCES

Wright & Miller, *Federal Practice and Procedure* §§ 2571–2591.

C.J.S. Federal Civil Procedure §§ 1036–1056 et seq.

West's Key No. Digests, Federal Civil Procedure ⚷2261–2293.

Rule 52(a)); *Geddes v. Northwest Missouri State University*, 49 F.3d 426 (8th Cir.1995).

53. *Burger v. New York Inst. of Technology*, 94 F.3d 830, 835 (2d Cir.1996) (explaining that a "one-sentence statement in no way constitutes the requisite findings under Rule 52"); *Quantachrome Corp. v. Micromeritics Instrument Corp.*, 97 F.Supp.2d 1181 (S.D. Fla.2000).

54. *United States v. Davis*, 20 F.Supp.2d 326, 331 (D.R.I.1998), *aff'd in part, remanded in part*, 261 F.3d 1 (1st Cir.2001).

55. *Samson v. Apollo Resources, Inc.*, 242 F.3d 629, 633 (5th Cir.2001), *cert. denied*, 534 U.S. 825, 122 S.Ct. 63, 151 L.Ed.2d 31 (2001).

56. *Mullin v. Town of Fairhaven*, 284 F.3d 31, 36 (1st Cir.2002).

RULE 53

MASTERS

(a) Appointment.

(1) Unless a statute provides otherwise, a court may appoint a master only to:

(A) perform duties consented to by the parties;

(B) hold trial proceedings and make or recommend findings of fact on issues to be decided by the court without a jury if appointment is warranted by

(i) some exceptional condition, or

(ii) the need to perform an accounting or resolve a difficult computation of damages; or

(C) address pretrial and post-trial matters that cannot be addressed effectively and timely by an available district judge or magistrate judge of the district.

(2) A master must not have a relationship to the parties, counsel, action, or court that would require disqualification of a judge under 28 U.S.C. § 455 unless the parties consent with the court's approval to appointment of a particular person after disclosure of any potential grounds for disqualification.

(3) In appointing a master, the court must consider the fairness of imposing the likely expenses on the parties and must protect against unreasonable expense or delay.

(b) Order Appointing Master.

(1) *Notice.* The court must give the parties notice and an opportunity to be heard before appointing a master. A party may suggest candidates for appointment.

(2) *Contents.* The order appointing a master must direct the master to proceed with all reasonable diligence and must state:

(A) the master's duties, including any investigation or enforcement duties, and any limits on the master's authority under Rule 53(c);

(B) the circumstances—if any—in which the master may communicate ex parte with the court or a party;

(C) the nature of the materials to be preserved and filed as the record of the master's activities;

(D) the time limits, method of filing the record, other procedures, and standards for reviewing the master's orders, findings, and recommendations; and

(E) the basis, terms, and procedure for fixing the master's compensation under Rule 53(h).

(3) *Entry of Order.* The court may enter the order appointing a master only after the master has filed an affidavit disclosing whether there is any ground for disqualification under 28 U.S.C. § 455 and, if a ground for disqualification is disclosed, after the parties have consented with the court's approval to waive the disqualification.

(4) *Amendment.* The order appointing a master may be amended at any time after notice to the parties, and an opportunity to be heard.

(c) Master's Authority. Unless the appointing order expressly directs otherwise, a master has authority to regulate all proceedings and take all appropriate measures to perform fairly and efficiently the assigned duties. The master may by order impose upon a party any noncontempt sanction provided by Rule 37 or 45, and may recommend a contempt sanction against a party and sanctions against a nonparty.

(d) Evidentiary Hearings. Unless the appointing order expressly directs otherwise, a master conducting an evidentiary hearing may exercise the power of the appointing court to compel, take, and record evidence.

(e) Master's Orders. A master who makes an order must file the order and promptly serve a copy on each party. The clerk must enter the order on the docket.

(f) Master's Reports. A master must report to the court as required by the order of appointment. The master must file the report and promptly serve a copy of the report on each party unless the court directs otherwise.

(g) Action on Master's Order, Report, or Recommendations.

(1) *Action.* In acting on a master's order, report, or recommendations, the court must afford an opportunity to be heard and may receive evidence, and may: adopt or affirm; modify; wholly or partly reject or reverse; or resubmit to the master with instructions.

(2) *Time To Object or Move.* A party may file objections to—or a motion to adopt or modify—the master's order, report, or recommendations no later than 20 days from the time the master's order, report, or recommendations are served, unless the court sets a different time.

(3) *Fact Findings.* The court must decide de novo all objections to findings of fact made or recommended by a master unless the parties stipulate with the court's consent that:

(A) the master's findings will be reviewed for clear error, or

(B) the findings of a master appointed under Rule 53(a)(1)(A) or (C) will be final.

(4) *Legal Conclusions.* The court must decide de novo all objections to conclusions of law made or recommended by a master.

(5) *Procedural Matters.* Unless the order of appointment establishes a different standard of review, the court may set aside a master's ruling on a procedural matter only for an abuse of discretion.

(h) Compensation.

(1) *Fixing Compensation.* The court must fix the master's compensation before or after judgment on the basis and terms stated in the order of appointment, but the court may set a new basis and terms after notice and an opportunity to be heard.

(2) *Payment.* The compensation fixed under Rule 53(h)(1) must be paid either:

(A) by a party or parties; or

(B) from a fund or subject matter of the action within the court's control.

(3) *Allocation.* The court must allocate payment of the master's compensation among the parties after considering the nature and amount of the controversy, the means of the parties, and the extent to which any party is more responsible than other parties for the reference to a master. An interim allocation may be amended to reflect a decision on the merits.

(i) Appointment of Magistrate Judge. A magistrate judge is subject to this rule only when the order referring a matter to the magistrate judge expressly provides that the reference is made under this rule.

[Amended February 28, 1966, effective July 1, 1966; April 28, 1983, effective August 1, 1983; March 2, 1987, effective August 1, 1987; April 30, 1991, effective December 1, 1991; April 22, 1993, effective December 1, 1993; March 27, 2003, effective December 1, 2003.]

AUTHORS' COMMENTARY ON RULE 53

PURPOSE AND SCOPE

Rule 53 provides the procedures governing the reference of designated aspects of an action to a master.

> **NOTE:** Rule 53 was substantially revised in 2003 to reflect changing practices in using masters. The amendment recognizes that special masters are used for a variety of pretrial and post-trial functions as well as to conduct trials. The amendment also changes the standard of review for findings of fact by a master.

RULE 53(a). APPOINTMENT

CORE CONCEPT

The court in which an action is pending may appoint a special master to conduct trials in limited circumstances and to conduct certain pretrial and post-trial functions.

APPLICATIONS

Functions Performed by Master

Rule 53 defines three categories of functions that a master may perform:

Duties consented to by the parties;[1]

Hold trial proceedings and make recommended findings of fact on non-jury issues if the appointment is warranted by an exceptional condition or by the need to perform an accounting or resolve a difficult computation of damages;[2] or

Address pretrial[3] or post-trial matters[4] if they cannot be addressed effectively and timely by the court.

Jury Trials

The 2003 Amendments eliminated the use of masters in matters to

1. Rule 53(a)(1)(A).

2. Rule 53(a)(1)(B).

3. Rule 53(a)(1)(C). *See also* The Advisory Committee Note to the 2003 Amendment to Rule 53 ("A pretrial master should be appointed only when the need is clear.").

4. Rule 53(a)(1)(C). *See also* The Advisory Committee Note to the 2003 Amendment to Rule 53 (reliance on a master is appropriate when a complex decree requires ongoing policing).

be tried to a jury unless the parties consent.[5]

Ineligible Persons

One cannot be master if related to the parties, the action, or the court under the same standards that govern disqualification of a judge set forth in 28 U.S.C. § 455.[6] The clerk of court and the clerk's deputies are also ineligible. The parties can waive this restriction with the court's approval.[7]

Court's Discretion—Fairness

In determining whether to appoint a master, the court must consider the fairness of imposing the cost of the master's compensation on the parties and the effects of delay.[8] The court has discretion as to whether to refer a matter to a master,[9] but reference should be the exception, not the rule.[10] The court also has discretion to refuse to appoint a master even if the parties have consented.[11]

Magistrate Judges

The court may appoint a United States Magistrate Judge to serve as a special master.[12] The provisions regarding compensation do not apply when a United States Magistrate Judge is designated to serve as a special master.

Common References

References are most common in patent, trademark, and copyright actions. They are also used occasionally to supervise discovery, following summary judgment on liability when the damages are difficult to calculate, and to oversee compliance.[13]

RULE 53(b). ORDER APPOINTING MASTER

CORE CONCEPT

A master is appointed by an order setting forth the duties and parameters of the reference.

5. The Advisory Committee Note to the 2003 Amendments to Rule 53.

6. *In re Kensington Intern. Ltd.*, 353 F.3d 211, 222 (3rd Cir. 2003).

7. Rule 53(a)(2).

8. Rule 53(a)(3).

9. *Middle Tennessee News Co., Inc. v. Charnel of Cincinnati, Inc.*, 250 F.3d 1077 (7th Cir. 2001) ("The district court did not need the consent of the parties to refer "complicated" issues to an independent accountant under Rule 53."); *United States v. State of Washington*, 157 F.3d 630, 660 (9th Cir.1998), *cert. denied*, 526 U.S. 1060, 119 S.Ct. 1376, 143 L.Ed.2d 535 (1999).

10. *United States v. State of Wash.*, 135 F.3d 618, 646 (9th Cir.1998), *amended and superseded on denial of rehearing*, 157 F.3d 630 (9th Cir.1998), *cert. denied*, 526 U.S. 1060, 119 S.Ct. 1376, 143 L.Ed.2d 535 (1999).

11. The Advisory Committee Note to the 2003 Amendments to Rule 53.

12. *Securities and Exchange Commission v. AMX, International, Inc.*, 872 F.Supp. 1541 (N.D.Tex.1994).

13. *See United States v. Microsoft Corp.*, 147 F.3d 935, (D.C.Cir.1998) (discussing the "well established tradition allowing use of special masters to oversee compliance.").

APPLICATIONS

Notice and Opportunity to Be Heard

The court must give notice of the proposed appointment of a master to the parties and provide an opportunity to be heard before appointing the master.[14] Written submissions will provide an "opportunity to be heard" unless the circumstances require live testimony.[15]

Candidates for Appointment

A party may suggest candidates for appointment as master.[16]

Contents of Order

The order appointing a master must:

- Direct the master to proceed with all reasonable diligence;[17]
- State the master's duties and any limits on the master's authority;[18]
- State the circumstances, if any, in which the master may communicate *ex parte* with the court or a party;[19]
- State the nature of the materials to be preserved and filed as the record of the master's activities;[20]
- State the time limits, methods of filing the record, other procedures, and standards for reviewing the master's orders, findings, and recommendations;[21] and
- State the basis, terms, and procedures for determining the master's compensation under Rule 53(h).[22]

Affidavit re Disqualification

Before the court can enter the order appointing the master, the master must file an affidavit disclosing whether there is any ground for disqualification under 28 U.S.C. § 455.[23] If a ground for disqualification is disclosed, the court may not enter the order unless the parties have consented with the court's approval to waive the disqualification.[24]

Amendment of Order

The order appointing the master may be amended at any time after notice to the parties and an opportunity to be heard.[25]

14. Rule 53(b)(1).

15. The Advisory Committee Note to the 2003 Amendment to Rule 53.

16. Rule 53(b)(1).

17. Rule 53(b)(2).

18. Rule 53(b)(2)(A).

19. Rule 53(b)(2)(B). *See also* The Advisory Committee Note to the 2003 Amendment to Rule 53 (ordinarily, the order should prohibit *ex parte* communications).

20. Rule 53(b)(2)(C). *See also* The Advisory Committee Note to the 2003 Amendment to Rule 53 (a basic requirement is that the master must make and file a complete record of the evidence considered in making or recommending findings of fact).

21. Rule 53(b)(2)(D).

22. Rule 53(b)(2)(E).

23. Rule 53(b)(3).

24. Rule 53(b)(3).

25. Rule 53(b)(4).

Challenging Reference

The proper method for contesting a reference is a motion to amend, vacate or revoke the reference.[26] Failure to make such a motion may be deemed a consent or waiver.[27] If the motion to vacate is denied, the disgruntled party may attempt to compel the court to vacate by a writ of mandamus.[28] Orders of reference are interlocutory, and may not be appealed directly, but may be appealed at the conclusion of the district court proceedings.[29]

RULE 53(c). MASTER'S AUTHORITY

CORE CONCEPT

Absent specific limitations in the order appointing the master, the master has all powers necessary to perform the referred matters, including the powers necessary to regulate the proceedings, rule on evidentiary issues, place witnesses under oath, and examine witnesses.[30] The master has discretion as to what procedures to employ, with the only requirement being that when the master determines that a hearing is necessary, the master shall make a record of the evidence offered and excluded in the same manner and subject to the same limitations as provided in the Federal Rules of Evidence for a non-jury trial.[31] The court has the duty to oversee the special master's performance of his duties to ensure that they are appropriately discharged.[32]

APPLICATIONS

Sanctions

The master may impose on a party any non-contempt sanction provided by Rule 37 or 45. The master may also recommend contempt sanctions against a party and sanctions against a non-party.

RULE 53(d). EVIDENTIARY HEARINGS

CORE CONCEPT

Unless otherwise limited by the order appointing the master, the master may exercise the powers of the court to compel (by subpoena under Rule 45), take, and record evidence.

26. *Fajardo Shopping Center, S.E. v. Sun Alliance Ins. Co. of Puerto Rico, Inc.*, 167 F.3d 1, 6 (1st Cir.1999).

27. *Fajardo Shopping Center, S.E. v. Sun Alliance Ins. Co. of Puerto Rico, Inc.*, 167 F.3d 1, 6 (1st Cir.1999); *Spaulding v. University of Washington,* 740 F.2d 686, 693 (9th Cir.1984), *cert. denied,* 469 U.S. 1036, 105 S.Ct. 511, 83 L.Ed.2d 401 (1984).

28. *La Buy v. Howes Leather Co.,* 352 U.S. 249, 77 S.Ct. 309, 1 L.Ed.2d 290 (1957); *United States v. Microsoft Corp.,* 147 F.3d 935 (D.C.Cir. 1998).

29. *Sierra Club v. Clifford*, 257 F.3d 444 (5th Cir.2001).

30. *United States v. Clifford Matley Family Trust,* 354 F.3d 1154, 1159 (9th Cir. 2004) (the order referring the case is the source and the limit of the master's duties and powers).

31. *United States v. Clifford Matley Family Trust,* 354 F.3d 1154, 1159 (9th Cir. 2004).

32. *Cordoza v. Pacific States Steel Corp.*, 320 F.3d 989, 999 (9th Cir.2003) (court has the duty to reduce special master's compensation if appropriate).

RULE 53(e). MASTER'S ORDERS

CORE CONCEPT

A master who makes an order must file the order with the clerk and promptly serve a copy on each party. The clerk must enter the order on the docket.

RULE 53(f). MASTER'S REPORTS

CORE CONCEPT

A master must prepare reports as directed by the order of appointment. The master must file such reports with the clerk and promptly serve a copy upon each party unless the court directs otherwise.[33]

APPLICATIONS

Supporting Materials

The master should provide all portions of the record that the master deems relevant to the report. The parties may seek to designate additional materials from the record, and may seek to supplement the record. The court may provide that additional materials from the record be filed.[34]

Sealed Report

Sealing of the report from public access may be appropriate, particularly with respect to pre-trial and post-trial masters. A report detailing a continuing or failed settlement effort is one example of a report that might be sealed.[35]

RULE 53(g). ACTION ON MASTER'S ORDER, REPORT, OR RECOMMENDATIONS

CORE CONCEPT

Rule 53(g) sets forth the procedures for the court to act on the masters report and the standards by which the court should review the report.

APPLICATIONS

Actions by the Court

When considering an order, report, or recommendation from a master, the court may adopt or affirm, modify, reject or reverse in whole or in part, or resubmit to the master with instructions.[36]

33. *See Schaefer Fan Co., Inc. v. J & D Mfg.*, 265 F.3d 1282, 1289 (Fed.Cir.2001); *In re Latex Glove Products Liability Litigation*, 2004 WL 1118691 (E.D.Pa. 2004).

34. The Advisory Committee Note to the 2003 Amendment to Rule 53.

35. The Advisory Committee Note to the 2003 Amendment to Rule 53.

36. Rule 53(g)(1).

Opportunity to be Heard

Before taking action on an order, report, or recommendation from a master, the court must provide the parties with an opportunity to be heard. Written submissions will provide an "opportunity to be heard" unless the circumstances require live testimony.[37]

Time for Objections

A party may file objections to the master's order, report, or recommendations no later than 20 days from the time the order, report, or recommendations are served, unless the court sets a different time. The parties may also file a motion to adopt or modify the order, report, or recommendations in the same time frame.[38] This time period is not jurisdictional, and the court has the authority to consider a late objection or motion.[39]

Findings of Fact

Absent a stipulation otherwise,[40] the court must decide *de novo* all objections to findings of fact made or recommended by a master.[41] The court may also review *de novo* findings of fact made or recommended by a master in the absence of an objection.[42] The parties may stipulate, with the court's consent, that the master's findings of fact will only be reviewed for clear error.[43] The parties may also stipulate, with the court's consent, that the master's findings of fact will be final if the master was appointed by consent or was appointed to address pretrial or post-trial matters.[44] The court may withdraw its consent to a stipulation for clear error review or finality, may reopen the opportunity for the parties to object.[45]

Conclusions of Law

The court must decide *de novo* all objections to conclusions of law made or recommended by a master.[46] The court may also review *de novo* findings of fact made or recommended by a master in the absence of an objection.[47]

37. The Advisory Committee Note to the 2003 Amendment to Rule 53.

38. Rule 53(g)(2).

39. *See Wallace v. Skadden, Arps, Slate, Meagher & Flom, LLP*, 362 F.3d 810, 816 (D.C.Cir. 2004); The Advisory Committee Note to the 2003 Amendment to Rule 53.

40. *AgGrow Oils, L.L.C. v. National Union Fire Ins. Co. of Pittsburgh*, PA, 276 F.Supp.2d 999, 1005 (D.N.D. 2003) (when the parties stipulate that a master's findings of fact shall be final, the district court shall only consider questions of law).

41. *United States v. KPMG LLP*, 316 F.Supp.2d 30 (D.D.C. 2004); Rule 53(g)(3).

42. The Advisory Committee Note to the 2003 Amendment to Rule 53.

43. Rule 53(g)(3)(A). *See also* The Advisory Committee Note to the 2003 Amendment to Rule 53 (suggesting that clear error review is more likely to be appropriate with respect to findings that do not go to the merits of the claims or defenses, such as findings of fact going to a privilege issue).

44. Rule 53(g)(3)(B).

45. The Advisory Committee Note to the 2003 Amendment to Rule 53.

46. *United States v. KPMG LLP*, 316 F.Supp.2d 30 (D.D.C. 2004); Rule 53(g)(4).

47. The Advisory Committee Note to the 2003 Amendment to Rule 53.

Procedural Matters

In the absence of a different standard set by the order of appointment, the court reviews a master's ruling on a procedural matter for abuse of discretion.[48]

Appeals

The report of the master is not appealable until adopted by the court. Thereafter, the report of the master becomes the findings of the court and is appealable under the same "clearly erroneous" standard used for all findings of fact by the court, as set forth in Rule 52.[49]

RULE 53(h). COMPENSATION

CORE CONCEPT

The court sets the compensation for a master. The master's compensation will be allocated among the parties or taken from the subject matter of the litigation.

APPLICATIONS

Amount of Compensation

The court fixes the compensation for a master,[50] and the amount will not be disturbed on appeal absent an abuse of discretion.[51] The court may also require the posting of a bond to secure payment of the fee or require the payment of the fee into escrow.[52] The amount of compensation will be controlled by the order of appointment, but the court may set a new basis and terms after notice to the parties and an opportunity to be heard.[53]

Source of Compensation

The court may impose the master's fee upon either party or may apportion it among the parties.[54] The court may also direct that the fee be paid from any fund[55] or subject matter of the action in the custody of the court.

48. Rule 53(g)(5). *See also* The Advisory Committee Note to the 2003 Amendment to Rule 53 (suggesting that the abuse of discretion standard may be more searching for a master's rulings than an appellate court exercises over a district court).

49. *See Charter Oak Fire Ins. Co. v. Hedeen & Companies*, 280 F.3d 730, 738 (7th Cir.2002); *Bogosian v. Woloohojian*, 831 F.Supp. 47 (D.R.I. 1993)

50. *Cordoza v. Pacific States Steel Corp.*, 320 F.3d 989, 999 (9th Cir.2003) (court has the duty to reduce special master's compensation if appropriate).

51. *Roy v. County of Lexington, South Carolina*, 141 F.3d 533 (4th Cir.1998).

52. *Allapattah Services, Inc. v. Exxon Corp.*, 157 F.Supp.2d 1291, 1325 (S.D.Fla.2001).

53. Rule 53(h)(1).

54. *See Roy v. County of Lexington, S.C.*, 141 F.3d 533, 549 (4th Cir.1998); *Hook v. State of Arizona*, 907 F.Supp. 1326, 1336–37 (D.Ariz. 1995)(charging special master fees against Arizona despite a state statute purporting to insulate the state from such fees).

55. *See Six L's Packing Co., Inc. v. Post & Taback, Inc.*, 132 F.Supp.2d 306, 309 (S.D.N.Y. 2001).

Allocation Among Parties

If the compensation is to be paid by the parties, the court must allocate the compensation among the parties. The court should consider the nature and amount of the controversy, the parties' financial means, and the extent to which any party is more responsible for the reference to the master.[56] The court may make interim allocations and may adjust the interim allocation later to reflect the decision on the merits.[57]

Collection of Compensation

The master may obtain a writ of execution against a party not paying his share of the master's fee. The master may not withhold the report to obtain payment.

RULE 53(i). APPOINTMENT OF MAGISTRATE JUDGE

CORE CONCEPT

The provisions of Rule 53 do not pertain to matters referred to magistrate judges unless the order of reference specifically states that it is made pursuant to Rule 53.[58]

ADDITIONAL RESEARCH REFERENCES

Wright & Miller, *Federal Practice and Procedure* §§ 2601–2615.

C.J.S. Federal Civil Procedure §§ 890–904; United States Commissioners § 3.

West's Key No. Digests, Federal Civil Procedure ⚷1871–1908; United States Magistrates ⚷14.

56. Rule 53(h)(3).

57. Rule 53(h)(3).

58. *See Wallace v. Skadden, Arps, Slate, Meagher & Flom, LLP*, 362 F.3d 810, 814–16 (D.C.Cir. 2004); *Gonzalez v. Rakkas*, 846 F.Supp. 229 (E.D.N.Y.1994).

VII. JUDGMENT

RULE 54

JUDGMENTS; COSTS

(a) Definition; Form. "Judgment" as used in these rules includes a decree and any order from which an appeal lies. A judgment shall not contain a recital of pleadings, the report of a master, or the record of prior proceedings.

(b) Judgment Upon Multiple Claims or Involving Multiple Parties. When more than one claim for relief is presented in an action, whether as a claim, counterclaim, cross-claim, or third-party claim, or when multiple parties are involved, the court may direct the entry of a final judgment as to one or more but fewer than all of the claims or parties only upon an express determination that there is no just reason for delay and upon an express direction for the entry of judgment. In the absence of such determination and direction, any order or other form of decision, however designated, which adjudicates fewer than all the claims or the rights and liabilities of fewer than all the parties shall not terminate the action as to any of the claims or parties, and the order or other form of decision is subject to revision at any time before the entry of judgment adjudicating all the claims and the rights and liabilities of all the parties.

(c) Demand for Judgment. A judgment by default shall not be different in kind from or exceed in amount that prayed for in the demand for judgment. Except as to a party against whom a judgment is entered by default, every final judgment shall grant the relief to which the party in whose favor it is rendered is entitled, even if the party has not demanded such relief in the party's pleadings.

(d) Costs; Attorneys' Fees.

(1) *Costs Other Than Attorneys' Fees.* Except when express provision therefor is made either in a statute of the United States or in these rules, costs other than attorneys' fees shall be allowed as of course to the prevailing party unless the court otherwise directs; but costs against the United States, its officers, and agencies shall be imposed only to the extent permitted by law. Such costs may be taxed by the clerk on one day's notice. On motion served within 5 days thereafter, the action of the clerk may be reviewed by the court.

(2) *Attorneys' Fees.*

(A) Claims for attorneys' fees and related nontaxable expenses shall be made by motion unless the substantive law governing the action provides for the recovery of such fees as an element of damages to be proved at trial.

(B) Unless otherwise provided by statute or order of the court, the motion must be filed no later than 14 days after entry of judgment; must specify the judgment and the statute, rule, or other grounds entitling the moving party to the award; and must state the amount or provide a fair estimate of the amount sought. If directed by the court, the motion shall also disclose the terms of any agreement with respect to fees to be paid for the services for which claim is made.

(C) On request of a party or class member, the court shall afford an opportunity for adversary submissions with respect to the motion in accordance with Rule 43(e) or Rule 78. The court may determine issues of liability for fees before receiving submissions bearing on issues of evaluation of services for which liability is imposed by the court. The court shall find the facts and state its conclusions of law as provided in Rule 52(a).

(D) By local rule the court may establish special procedures by which issues relating to such fees may be resolved without extensive evidentiary hearings. In addition, the court may refer issues relating to the value of services to a special master under Rule 53 without regard to the provisions of Rule 53(a)(1) and may refer a motion for attorneys' fees to a magistrate judge under Rule 72(b) as if it were a dispositive pretrial matter.

(E) The provisions of subparagraphs (A) through (D) do not apply to claims for fees and expenses as sanctions for violations of these rules or under 28 U.S.C. § 1927.

[Amended December 27, 1946, effective March 19, 1948; April 17, 1961, effective July 19, 1961; March 2, 1987, effective August 1, 1987; April 22, 1993, effective December 1, 1993; amended April 29, 2002, effective December 1, 2002; March 27, 2003, effective December 1, 2003.]

AUTHORS' COMMENTARY ON RULE 54

PURPOSE AND SCOPE

Rule 54 defines the term "judgment", discusses the limits of recovery on a judgment, and allows the taxation of costs. The Rule also permits the federal court to enter judgment as to one adjudicated claim or the adjudicated rights of one party, and thus permit an immediate appeal from that judgment.

RULE 54(a). DEFINITION OF "JUDGMENT"

CORE CONCEPT

A judgment is any appealable decree or order. A judgment must be in writing and must be set forth in a separate document, free of extraneous materials.[1]

APPLICATIONS

To be a "judgment" within the meaning of Rule 54(a), the decree or order must be a ruling from which an appeal can be taken.[2] A ruling that results in a partial judgment or other non-final order is generally not a Rule 54(b) judgment.[3]

RULE 54(b). JUDGMENTS UPON MULTIPLE CLAIMS OR INVOLVING MULTIPLE PARTIES

CORE CONCEPT

A judgment entered as to less than all claims in a lawsuit, or as to less than all parties in a lawsuit, is not immediately appealable. Instead, the appeal must generally await the entry of judgment as to all remaining claims and parties. However, the district court can make a judgment as to less than all claims or parties "final", and thus immediately appealable, by expressly determining that no just cause exists to delay the appeal and by directing the entry of judgment.

1. *See Cooper v. Town of East Hampton*, 83 F.3d 31, 35 (2d Cir.1996) ("separate document" requirement applies to all judgments, including orders certified under Rule 54(b)). *But see Dinunzio v. Apfel*, 101 F.Supp.2d 1028, 1031 (N.D.Ill.2000) (noting that consent judgments, draft orders, and minute orders can constitute valid judgments if the language indicates an end to the litigation).

2. *See Brown v. Local 58, Int'l Bhd. of Elec. Workers, AFL–CIO*, 76 F.3d 762, 767 (6th Cir. 1996)(whether order is a "judgment" is determined by whether an appeal could be taken from the order); *Maristuen v. National States Ins. Co.*, 57 F.3d 673, 679 (8th Cir.1995) (judgment defined to include any decree or order from which an appeal lies); *National Basketball Ass'n v. Minnesota Professional Basketball, Ltd. Partnership*, 56 F.3d 866, 872 (8th Cir. 1995)(definition of judgment encompasses interlocutory orders appealable as of right, such as preliminary injunction rulings); *Balla v. Idaho State Bd. of Corrections*, 869 F.2d 461, 466 (9th Cir.1989)(noting that Rule 54 encompasses final judgments and appealable interlocutory orders). *See also United States v. Haynes*, 158 F.3d 1327, 1329 (D.C.Cir.1998) (holding that order denying Rule 60(b) motion is a "judgment" under Rule 54(a)).

3. *See Dishman v. UNUM Life Ins. Co. of America*, 269 F.3d 974, 990–91 (9th Cir.2001) (holding that post-judgment interest does not begin to accrue when district court enters a partial or non-final judgment because the ruling doesn't qualify under Rule 54(a)); *Resolution Trust Corp. v. O'Bear, Overholser, Smith & Huffer*, 886 F.Supp. 658, 671 n. 11 (N.D. Ind. 1995) (summary judgment granted as to less than entire claim is not a "judgment" but merely a partial, pretrial adjudication of certain issues).

APPLICATIONS

Purpose

Separate, piecemeal appeals during a single litigation are often inefficient and uneconomical, and thus are contrary to the historic federal policy favoring one appeal on all issues at the conclusion of the lawsuit.[4] Rule 54(b) determinations allowing immediate appeal permit exceptions from this general policy for those infrequent instances where awaiting a final judgment would be unduly harsh or unjust.[5]

"Certification" Nomenclature

Often in the case law, the Rule 54(b) determination procedure is described as a "certification". One court of appeals has counseled against this nomenclature as a "misnomer born of confusion".[6] The term "certification" is also used to describe the procedure for seeking immediate appellate review of interlocutory orders under 28 U.S.C. § 1292(b). Under this permissive relief of interlocutory orders, a Rule 54(b) determination, if granted, effectively severs what becomes a *final* judgment (albeit as to one or more but fewer than all claims or parties) from the remaining claims and parties in the case.[7]

Prerequisites to Rule 54(b) Judgments

In evaluating whether to grant a Rule 54(b) determination, the district courts function somewhat like a "dispatcher".[8] The district courts must decide whether three prerequisites for an immediately appealable partial judgment exist:

- ***1: Multiple Claims or Parties Fully Resolved:*** To be eligible for immediate appeal under Rule 54(b), a partial adjudication must *either* (a) finally resolve at least one claim or (b) finally resolve the rights and liabilities of at least one party. A claim or a party's interest *must* be adjudicated to finality, such that there is nothing more to do on that claim or for that party but await the conclusion of the remaining portions of the litigation.[9] This

4. *See Reiter v. Cooper*, 507 U.S. 258, 263, 113 S.Ct. 1213, 1217, 122 L.Ed.2d 604 (1993); *Curtiss-Wright Corp. v. General Elec. Co.*, 446 U.S. 1, 8, 100 S.Ct. 1460, 1464–65, 64 L.Ed.2d 1 (1980); *O'Bert ex rel. Estate of O'Bert v. Vargo*, 331 F.3d 29, 40 (2d Cir.2003). *Cf. Williams v. County of Westchester*, 171 F.3d 98, 102 (2d Cir.1999) (holding that interlocutory orders are, by their nature, subject to modification or adjustment by the trial court prior to the entry of a final judgment adjudicating the claims to which they pertain).

5. *See O'Bert ex rel. Estate of O'Bert v. Vargo*, 331 F.3d 29, 40–41 (2d Cir.2003). *Oklahoma Turnpike Authority v. Bruner*, 259 F.3d 1236, 1241–42 (10th Cir.2001); *In re Southeast Banking Corp.*, 69 F.3d 1539, 1547 (11th Cir.1995); *PYCA Indus. v. Harrison County Waste Water Management Dist.*, 81 F.3d 1412, 1421 (5th Cir. 1996).

6. *See James v. Price Stern Sloan, Inc.*, 283 F.3d 1064, 1067–68 n. 6 (9th Cir.2002).

7. *See James v. Price Stern Sloan, Inc.*, 283 F.3d 1064, 1067–68 n. 6 (9th Cir.2002) ("Referring to a Rule 54(b) severance order as a 'certification' misleadingly brings to mind the kind of rigorous judgment embodied in the section 1292(b) certification process. In reality, issuance of a Rule 54(b) order is a fairly routine act that is reversed only in the rarest instances").

8. *See Ultra–Precision Mfg. Ltd. v. Ford Motor Co.*, 338 F.3d 1353, 1357 (Fed.Cir.2003).

9. *See Curtiss-Wright Corp. v. General Elec. Co.*, 446 U.S. 1, 7, 100 S.Ct. 1460, 1464, 64 L.Ed.2d 1 (1980); *State Street Bank & Trust Co.*

limitation is a pivotal one. Rule 54(b) does not alter the normal rules of appellate finality for individual claims, and no appeal may be taken from district court rulings on any particular claim until the court finally resolves that claim.[10] Thus, for example, if an affirmative defense to a claim otherwise completely adjudicated would still remain for trial, the claim has not been finally resolved and immediate appeal is improper.[11]

- *"Claim Defined":* A "claim" has been defined to include all legal grounds based on closely related facts.[12] Multiple claims exist where each claim is factually separate and independent,[13] where each claim could be enforced separately,[14] where there is more than one potential recovery, or where different types of relief are requested.[15] If, however, only one recovery is possible (even though several legal theories are offered to support that recovery) or if alternative recoveries either substantially overlap or are mutually exclusive, the claims cannot be immediately appealed under Rule 54(b).[16]

- ***2: No Just Cause for Delay:*** The district court must state, in clear and unmistakable language, that there is no just cause to delay the appeal of the adjudicated claim or the adjudicated

v. Brockrim, Inc., 87 F.3d 1487, 1489 (1st Cir. 1996); *In re Southeast Banking Corp.*, 69 F.3d 1539, 1547 (11th Cir.1995); *National Union Fire Ins. Co. v. City Savings, F.S.B.*, 28 F.3d 376 (3d Cir.1994); *Williams v. Kentucky*, 24 F.3d 1526 (6th Cir.1994). *See Compagnie De Reassurance D'Ile de France v. New England Reinsurance Corp.*, 57 F.3d 56, 69 n. 11 (1st Cir. 1995)(although the "better practice" requires that counterclaims be denied explicitly, court held that where district court's intention to do so was apparent from other rulings, all claims were deemed to be fully adjudicated for Rule 54(b) purposes), *cert. denied*, 516 U.S. 1009, 116 S.Ct. 564, 133 L.Ed.2d 490 (1995).

10. *See Ultra-Precision Mfg. Ltd. v. Ford Motor Co.*, 338 F.3d 1353, 1357 (Fed.Cir.2003); *In re Lull Corp.*, 52 F.3d 787, 788 (8th Cir.1995). *See also N.W. Enters. Inc. v. City of Houston*, 352 F.3d 162, 179 (5th Cir. 2003) (Rule 54(b) judgment improper where district court only authorized appeal of elements of claims, and not entire claims), *modified in part on reh'g on other grounds*, 372 F.3d 333 (5th Cir. 2004); *Information Resources, Inc. v. Dun & Bradstreet Corp.*, 294 F.3d 447, 451–52 (2d Cir.2002) (Rule 54(b) judgment is improper if court enters judgment on something less than a final disposition of an entire claim).

11. *See Waldorf v. Shuta*, 142 F.3d 601, 611 (3d Cir.1998).

12. *See Greenwell v. Aztar Indiana Gaming Corp.*, 268 F.3d 486, 490 (7th Cir.2001), *cert. denied*, 535 U.S. 1034, 122 S.Ct. 1790, 152 L.Ed.2d 649 (2002).

13. *See Seatrain Shipbuilding Corp. v. Shell Oil Co.*, 444 U.S. 572, 100 S.Ct. 800, 63 L.Ed.2d 36 (1980); *Advanced Magnetics, Inc. v. Bayfront Partners, Inc.*, 106 F.3d 11, 16 n. 21 (2d Cir. 1997). *See Lawyers Title Ins. Corp. v. Dearborn Title Corp.*, 118 F.3d 1157 (7th Cir.1997) (noting that test for "separate claims" is whether the claim at issue so overlaps the claims remaining that any appeal at the end of the case on the remaining claims would require the appellate court to cover the same ground addressed on the Rule 54(b) appeal).

14. *See Advanced Magnetics, Inc. v. Bayfront Partners, Inc.*, 106 F.3d 11, 16 n. 21 (2d Cir. 1997); *Rieser v. Baltimore & Ohio R.R.*, 224 F.2d 198 (2d Cir.1955). *Cf. General Acquisition, Inc. v. GenCorp., Inc.*, 23 F.3d 1022, 1028 (6th Cir. 1994)(if the action seeks to vindicate only one legal right, but merely alleges several elements of damage, only one claim is presented and Rule 54(b) does not apply).

15. *See Advanced Magnetics, Inc. v. Bayfront Partners, Inc.*, 106 F.3d 11, 16 n. 21 (2d Cir. 1997); *In re Southeast Banking Corp.*, 69 F.3d 1539, 1547 (11th Cir.1995) (if more than one possible recovery exists or if different sorts of recoveries are sought, the claims are "separately enforceable" under Rule 54(b), even though the claims may arise from a single transaction or occurrence).

16. *See In re Southeast Banking Corp.*, 69 F.3d 1539, 1547 (11th Cir.1995).

rights and liabilities of a party. This determination ordinarily can be made only where delay in appealing presents some risk of hardship or injustice that would be avoided by an immediate appellate review, where a plaintiff could be prejudiced by a delay in recovering a monetary judgment, or where an expensive, duplicative trial could be avoided by reviewing a dismissed claim promptly before the remaining claims reach trial.[17] Whether "just cause" exists is a determination made on a case-by-case basis.[18] Certain criteria guide the court's consideration:

- The relationship between adjudicated and unadjudicated claims;
- The possibility that the need for appellate review might be mooted by future developments in the district court;
- The possibility that the district court might be obligated to consider the same issue on a later occasion;
- The presence (or absence) of a claim or counterclaim that could result in a set-off against the judgment now sought to be made final and appealed; and
- Other factors, including delay, economic and solvency concerns, shortening of trial time, frivolity of competing claims, and expense.[19]

- ***3: Entry of Judgment:*** In clear and unmistakable language, the district court must also direct that judgment is entered as to that one claim or one party.[20]

Use of "Magic Language"

There is some authority for the proposition that the district court need not expressly incant the phrase "no just cause for delay" in order to permit a Rule 54(b) appeal, so long as the trial judge's intent to certify is unmistakably clear from the order and/or the record.[21]

17. *See Advanced Magnetics, Inc. v. Bayfront Partners, Inc.*, 106 F.3d 11, 16 (2d Cir.1997).

18. *See Sears, Roebuck & Co. v. Mackey,* 351 U.S. 427, 76 S.Ct. 895, 100 L.Ed. 1297 (1956). *See also Doe v. City of Chicago*, 360 F.3d 667, 673 (7th Cir. 2004) (ruling that there was "just reason for delay" and, thus, Rule 54(b) relief was not available, where factual development of certain claim was necessary).

19. *See Akers v. Alvey*, 338 F.3d 491, 495 (6th Cir.2003) (same); *Waldorf v. Shuta*, 142 F.3d 601, 609 (3d Cir.1998) (same); *Braswell Shipyards, Inc. v. Beazer East, Inc.*, 2 F.3d 1331, 1335–36 (4th Cir.1993)(same). *Cf. Credit Francais Int'l, S.A. v. Bio–Vita, Ltd.*, 78 F.3d 698, 707 (1st Cir.1996) (certification is particularly suspect when the appellants remain litigants before the trial court).

20. *See Kelley v. Michaels*, 59 F.3d 1055, 1057 (10th Cir.1995)(noting that premature appeal, taken before entry of Rule 54(b) judgment, matures upon entry of order).

21. *See Carringer v. Tessmer*, 253 F.3d 1322, 1324 n.1 (11th Cir.2001); *Briargrove Shopping Ctr. Joint Venture v. Pilgrim Enters., Inc.*, 170 F.3d 536, 539 (5th Cir.1999). *But cf. Berckeley Inv. Group, Ltd. v. Colkitt*, 259 F.3d 135, 141–42 (3d Cir.2001) *See also Downie v. City of Middleburg Heights*, 301 F.3d 688, 693 (6th Cir.2002) (district court need not enter partial final judgment in its certification, but it must recognize that such a partial final judgment has been entered).

Explanation by the District Court

In its order entering a Rule 54(b) judgment, the district court must clearly and cogently explain why it has concluded that an immediate appellate review of the order is advisable,[22] or those reasons must be readily apparent from the record.[23] The district court should not simply reprint, in boilerplate, the formula of the Rule.[24] The court of appeals may, in the absence of such a written explanation, dismiss the appeal as inappropriately allowed under Rule 54(b).[25] Although dismissal of the appeal is permitted (and perhaps even likely) without a corresponding explanation from the trial court, dismissal is not compulsory; the failure to offer a written explanation is *not* a jurisdictional defect that *compels* the appeal's dismissal.[26]

Duty of Counsel in Explanation Requirement

In moving for a Rule 54(b) determination, the courts expect counsel, as officers of the court and advocates for an immediate appeal, to

22. *See O'Bert ex rel. Estate of O'Bert v. Vargo*, 331 F.3d 29, 42 (2d Cir.2003) (court ordinarily must offer reasoned, yet brief, explanation); *Federal Home Loan Mortgage Corp. v. Scottsdale Ins. Co.*, 316 F.3d 431, 440 (3d Cir. 2003) (court should clearly articulate reasons and factors underlying decision to permit Rule 54(b) appeal); *Ebrahimi v. City of Huntsville Bd. of Educ.*, 114 F.3d 162, 166 (11th Cir.1997) (certifying court must support its conclusion by clearly, cogently explaining its reasoning, together with supporting factual and legal determinations); *Nichols v. Cadle Co.*, 101 F.3d 1448, 1449 (1st Cir.1996) (district judge must explain its reasoning, at least where explanation is not obvious from the record); *HBE Leasing Corp. v. Frank*, 48 F.3d 623, 631 (2d Cir.1995)(noting that court abused its discretion where judgment was accompanied by a mere incantation of the language "there is no just reason for delay," without any explanation for such a conclusion); *Justice v. Pendleton Place Apts.*, 40 F.3d 139, 141 (6th Cir.1994)(noting that Rule 54(b) requires that district court articulate its reasons for entering the final order); *Braswell Shipyards, Inc. v. Beazer East, Inc.*, 2 F.3d 1331, 1336 (4th Cir.1993). *But cf. Building Industry Ass'n of Superior Cal. v. Babbitt*, 161 F.3d 740 (D.C.Cir.1998) (in cases where it is not self-evident that Rule 54(b) certification is appropriate, further explanation by district court may be necessary).

23. *See O'Bert ex rel. Estate of O'Bert v. Vargo*, 331 F.3d 29, 41 (2d Cir.2003) (noting that courts, on "rare occasions", have excused full explanations where reasons for Rule 54(b) entry were obvious and remand would only unnecessarily delay appeal process); *Cooper Power Sys., Inc. v. Union Carbide Chemicals & Plastics Co.*, 123 F.3d 675, 679 n. 1 (7th Cir.1997) (commenting that court failed to set forth explicitly its reasons for certification, but those reasons were apparent from record which incorporated rationale of litigant's motion for Rule 54(b) order).

24. *See Akers v. Alvey*, 338 F.3d 491, 495 (6th Cir.2003); *O'Bert ex rel. Estate of O'Bert v. Vargo*, 331 F.3d 29, 41 (2d Cir.2003); *Federal Home Loan Mortgage Corp. v. Scottsdale Ins. Co.*, 316 F.3d 431, 440 (3d Cir.2003).

25. *See Smith ex rel. Smith v. Half Hollow Hills Cent. Sch. Dist.*, 298 F.3d 168, 171 (2d Cir.2002) (dismissing appeal, ruling that district courts must not "merely repeat the formulaic language" of Rule 54(b), but must offer "a brief, reasoned explanation" for the decision to allow an immediate appeal); *Advanced Magnetics, Inc. v. Bayfront Partners, Inc.*, 106 F.3d 11, 16 n. 21 (2d Cir.1997) (holding that trial court's failure to offer appropriate explanation is basis for dismissal).

26. *See Carter v. City of Philadelphia*, 181 F.3d 339 (3d Cir.1999) (not jurisdictional). *See also Smith ex rel. Smith v. Half Hollow Hills Cent. Sch. Dist.*, 298 F.3d 168, 171 (2d Cir.2002) (noting that, under rare certain circumstances, the reason for certification may be sufficiently obvious that no explanation is required and the court of appeals is able to provide meaningful review without an explanation from the trial judge of why certification was deemed appropriate).

assist the district court by making appropriate submissions that express the reasons for and basis of a Rule 54(b) determination.[27]

Burden of Proof

The moving party bears the burden of establishing that a partial judgment should be entered under Rule 54(b).[28]

Discretion of District Judge

The court is not *required* to enter a final judgment in an action involving multiple parties where the court resolves claims involving less than all parties or less than all claims.[29] To the contrary, whether to enter a judgment under Rule 54(b) is reserved for the sound discretion of the district judge.[30] Indeed, such judgments are contrary to the historic federal policy against piecemeal appeals, particularly during a period when the courts of appeals' caseload has grown faster than any other segment of the federal bench.[31] For this reason, Rule 54(b) orders are not granted routinely,[32] or merely with the hope of avoiding a trial,[33] or as an accommodation to counsel.[34] Instead, the district court must carefully balance the needs of the parties for an immediate appeal against the interest of efficient management of the litigation.[35]

27. *See Federal Home Loan Mortgage Corp. v. Scottsdale Ins. Co.*, 316 F.3d 431, 441–42 (3d Cir.2003)

28. *See Braswell Shipyards, Inc. v. Beazer East, Inc.*, 2 F.3d 1331, 1335 (4th Cir.1993); *Anthuis v. Colt Indus. Operating Corp.*, 971 F.2d 999, 1003 (3d Cir.1992).

29. *See generally Ruiz v. Blentech Corp.*, 89 F.3d 320, 323 (7th Cir.1996), *cert. denied*, 519 U.S. 1077, 117 S.Ct. 737, 136 L.Ed.2d 677 (1997)(court has two options in placing into final form individual orders in multi-party cases: Rule 54(b) finality order or final order disposing of all claims respecting all parties).

30. *See Curtiss–Wright Corp. v. General Elec. Co.*, 446 U.S. 1, 100 S.Ct. 1460, 64 L.Ed.2d 1 (1980). *See also Sears, Roebuck & Co. v. Mackey*, 351 U.S. 427, 437, 76 S.Ct. 895, 900, 100 L.Ed. 1297 (1956)(noting that discretion lies primarily with the district court "as the one most likely to be familiar with the case and with any justifiable reasons for delay"); *Bingham v. City of Manhattan Beach*, 341 F.3d 939, 942 n.1 (9th Cir. 2003); *Akers v. Alvey*, 338 F.3d 491, 495 (6th Cir.2003); *Federal Home Loan Mortgage Corp. v. Scottsdale Ins. Co.*, 316 F.3d 431, 440 (3d Cir. 2003); *Harris v. Secretary, United States Dep't of Army*, 119 F.3d 1313 (8th Cir.1997).

31. *See In re Southeast Banking Corp.*, 69 F.3d 1539, 1548 (11th Cir.1995). *See also Reiter v. Cooper*, 507 U.S. 258, 263, 113 S.Ct. 1213, 1218, 122 L.Ed.2d 604 (1993); *Curtiss-Wright Corp. v. General Elec. Co.*, 446 U.S. 1, 8, 100 S.Ct. 1460, 1465, 64 L.Ed.2d 1 (1980); *Soliday v. Miami County*, 55 F.3d 1158, 1163 (6th Cir. 1995) (reiterating that Rule 54(b) does not permit the piecemeal review of claims, nor should it be used indiscriminately).

32. *See O'Bert ex rel. Estate of O'Bert v. Vargo*, 331 F.3d 29, 40–41 (2d Cir.2003); *Smith ex rel. Smith v. Half Hollow Hills Cent. Sch. Dist.*, 298 F.3d 168, 171 (2d Cir.2002); *Oklahoma Turnpike Authority v. Bruner*, 259 F.3d 1236, 1242 (10th Cir.2001); *L.B. Foster Co. v. America Piles, Inc.*, 138 F.3d 81, 86 (2d Cir.1998); *Ebrahimi v. City of Huntsville Bd. of Educ.*, 114 F.3d 162, 166 (11th Cir.1997); *Advanced Magnetics, Inc. v. Bayfront Partners, Inc.*, 106 F.3d 11, 16 (2d Cir.1997); *Nichols v. Cadle Co.*, 101 F.3d 1448, 1449 (1st Cir.1996).

33. *See Credit Francais Int'l, S.A. v. Bio–Vita, Ltd.*, 78 F.3d 698, 706 (1st Cir.1996)(possibility of avoiding a trial is "rarely, if ever, a self-sufficient basis for a Rule 54(b) certification").

34. *See Braswell Shipyards, Inc. v. Beazer East, Inc.*, 2 F.3d 1331, 1335 (4th Cir.1993). *See Curtiss–Wright Corp. v. General Elec. Co.,* 446 U.S. 1, 10, 100 S.Ct. 1460, 1466, 64 L.Ed.2d 1 (1980)(writing that sound judicial administration does not require that Rule 54(b) requests be granted routinely); *PYCA Indus. v. Harrison County Waste Water Management Dist.*, 81 F.3d 1412, 1421 (5th Cir.1996)(not entered routinely as courtesies to counsel).

35. *See L.B. Foster Co. v. America Piles, Inc.*, 138 F.3d 81, 86 (2d Cir.1998) (certification should be reserved for "the infrequent harsh case" where danger exists for hardship or injustice through delay, which could be alleviated by immediate appeal); *PYCA Indus. v. Harrison County Waste Water Management Dist.*, 81 F.3d 1412, 1421 (5th Cir.1996)(certification should be granted only where some danger of hardship or injustice through delay exists); *General Acquisi-*

Determination by Trial Judge Is *Not* Conclusive on Court of Appeals

That the district judge allowed a ruling for an immediate appeal under Rule 54(b) is not wholly dispositive. The courts of appeals will still review the matter to ensure that the trial judge allowed a ruling that was eligible for immediate review under the Rule.[36]

Procedure for Obtaining Rule 54(b) Determination

The Rule sets no defined procedure for obtaining a determination under Rule 54(b). The district court may grant such a determination *sua sponte* to accompany the order at issue. Alternatively, the parties may separately move the district court under Rule 54(b) to grant a determination. The time for making such a motion is not specified in the Rule. Prudent practitioners will seek Rule 54(b) determination promptly, and within the familiar 10–day period allotted for alterations or amendments to "judgments". Although Rule 54(b) motions are technically not motions seeking Rule 59 or Rule 60 relief (and, thus, might not technically fall within the ambit of the 10–day limit), this type of prompt action is consistent with the moving party's claim that the order qualifies as a "judgment" under the Rule and comports with the Rule 54(b) objective of permitting some piecemeal appeals where delay would be unduly harsh or unjust.[37] If an appeal is taken prior to the district court's determination under Rule 54(b), most Circuits have ruled that the belated determination will "ripen" an otherwise improper appeal, so long as the determination issues prior to the date the court of appeals considers the appeal.[38]

Effect of Rule 54(b) Judgments

Once a Rule 54(b) judgment is entered, the time for appeal on the judgment begins to run,[39] as does post-judgment interest.[40] Note, however, that some courts have ruled that the time for appeal following a Rule 54(b) determination can begin to run even earlier, before entry on the docket–on the date the order granting Rule 54(b) relief was signed and mailed to the parties.[41] Accordingly, prudent counsel should file their appeal promptly after the Rule 54(b) order is served.

tion, Inc. v. GenCorp., Inc., 23 F.3d 1022, 1027 (6th Cir.1994).

36. *See Schudel v. General Elec. Co.*, 120 F.3d 991, 994 (9th Cir.1997), *cert. denied*, 523 U.S. 1094, 118 S.Ct. 1560, 140 L. Ed. 2d 792 (1998); *Ebrahimi v. City of Huntsville Bd. of Educ.*, 114 F.3d 162, 166 (11th Cir.1997).

37. There does not appear to be published case law resolving this issue, a factor that all the more urgently counsels in favor of prompt action by the moving party.

38. *See, e.g., United States v. Brown*, 348 F.3d 1200, 1206 (10th Cir. 2003); *Lewis v. B.F. Goodrich Co.*, 850 F.2d 641 (10th Cir.1988); *Tidler v. Eli Lilly & Co.*, 824 F.2d 84, 85–87 (D.C. Cir.1987) (per curiam); *Coalition for Equitable Minority Participation in Architectural Contracts in Tenn. (COMPACT) v. Metropolitan Gov't of Nashville & Davidson County*, 786 F.2d 227, 228 & n. 1 (6th Cir.1986); *Lac Courte Oreilles Band of Lake Superior Chippewa Indians v. Wisconsin*, 760 F.2d 177, 180–81 (7th Cir.1985); *Metallurgical Indus., Inc. v. Fourtek, Inc.*, 771 F.2d 915, 916 (5th Cir.1985) (per curiam); *Freeman v. Hittle*, 747 F.2d 1299, 1301–02 (9th Cir.1984); *Hayden v. McDonald*, 719 F.2d 266, 268 (8th Cir. 1983) (per curiam); *Tilden Fin. Corp. v. Palo Tire Serv., Inc.*, 596 F.2d 604, 606–07 (3d Cir. 1979).

39. *See FDIC v. Tripati*, 769 F.2d 507 (8th Cir.1985).

40. *See* 28 U.S.C.A. § 1961; *Hooks v. Washington Sheraton Corp.*, 642 F.2d 614 (D.C.Cir. 1980).

41. *See Silivanch v. Celebrity Cruises, Inc.*, 333 F.3d 355, 364–65 (2d Cir.2003), *cert. denied*, 540 U.S. 1105, 124 S.Ct. 1047, 157 L.Ed.2d 890

Effect of Dismissals Without Rule 54(b) Judgment

Unless the court enters a separate judgment under Rule 54(b), litigants in a multi-party case who are dismissed may technically remain in the case until the final resolution of all claims as to all parties. Dismissed litigants are, however, entitled to rely on the dismissal until notified that they have been rejoined as parties. Thus, until notified otherwise, dismissed litigants need not participate in discovery, in pretrial proceedings, or in the trial itself.[42]

Scope of "Determination"

On appeal following a Rule 54(b) determination, the court of appeals will confine its review only to those specific rulings for which determination was granted. All other rulings by the district court will not be examined during the interlocutory appeal.[43]

No "Tag–Along" Partial Appeals

A decision to permit an immediate appeal of one part of a litigation is not, by itself, sufficient justification to grant Rule 54(b) relief for another part.[44]

Appealability of Denials of Rule 54(b) Requests

Allowing immediate appellate review of "partial" final judgments is a practice that departs from the federal courts' traditional opposition to piecemeal appeals. Rule 54(b), thus, represents an unusual exception to this settled policy. Predictably, the courts reject attempts to immediately challenge denials of Rule 54(b) judgments as premature and unappealable until a final ruling is entered on the merits.[45]

Adversary Proceedings in Bankruptcy Require Determination

The majority view holds that litigants who lose and then seek to immediately appeal from an adversary proceeding ruling in bankruptcy are required to obtain a Rule 54(b) determination from the trial court in order to press the appeal.[46]

Rule 54(b) and Tax Court Rulings

Although there is some division of authority on the point, recent case law supports the application of Rule 54(b) procedures to partial

(2004) (commenting that "[t]here is no requirement that such a certification be docketed in order for it to become effective", and thus the order became effective, and the appeal period began to run, when the order "was signed and mailed to the parties"). *But cf. Brown v. Mississippi Valley State Univ.,* 311 F.3d 328, 331–32 (5th Cir.2002) (noting that, for purposes of Rule 4 of the Federal Rules of Appellate Procedure 4, judgment becomes final on the date Rule 54(b) determination is entered).

42. *See Bennett v. Pippin*, 74 F.3d 578, 587 (5th Cir.1996), *cert. denied*, 519 U.S. 817, 117 S.Ct. 68, 136 L.Ed.2d 29 (1996).

43. *See Monsanto Co. v. McFarling*, 363 F.3d 1336, 1343 n.1 (Fed.Cir. 2004), *petition for cert. filed*, Nos. 03–1177 & 03–1228 (U.S. July 6, 2004); *New Castle County v. Hartford Accident & Indemnity Co.*, 933 F.2d 1162, 1178 n. 33 (3d Cir.1991); *McCall v. Deeds*, 849 F.2d 1259, 1259 (9th Cir.1988); *Makuc v. American Honda Motor Co.*, 692 F.2d 172 (1st Cir.1982).

44. *See O'Bert ex rel. Estate of O'Bert v. Vargo*, 331 F.3d 29, 43 (2d Cir.2003).

45. *See United Indus. v. Eimco Process Equip. Co.*, 61 F.3d 445, 448 (5th Cir.1995).

46. *See In re Boca Arena, Inc.*, 184 F.3d 1285 (11th Cir.1999).

rulings by the United States Tax Court.[47]

RULE 54(c). DEMAND FOR JUDGMENT

CORE CONCEPT

The district court generally must grant all the relief to which the prevailing party is entitled, whether or not such relief was requested in the pleadings. Pleadings serve as "guides" to the nature of the case, but the lawsuit is ultimately measured by what is pleaded and proven, not merely by what was demanded.[48] In default judgments, however, the district court may not award relief beyond that sought in the complaint.

APPLICATIONS

Default Judgments

Because a non-appearing defendant may be relying on the demand (or WHEREFORE) clause contained in the complaint, a plaintiff may not receive a default judgment for more than the amount sought in the complaint.[49]

Non-default Judgments

Where the defendant has answered or otherwise appeared to defend the lawsuit, a plaintiff may receive a judgment for an amount greater or less than that sought in the complaint,[50] and containing types of relief not mentioned in the complaint's demand clause.[51] It is the court's duty to grant all appropriate relief.[52]

47. *See New York Football Giants, Inc. v. C.I.R.*, 349 F.3d 102, 106–07 (3d Cir. 2003) (so holding, and surveying division among Circuits).

48. *See Minyard Enters. v. Southeastern Chem. & Solvent Co.*, 184 F.3d 373 (4th Cir. 1999); *Baker v. John Morrell & Co.*, 266 F.Supp.2d 909, 929 (N.D.Iowa 2003).

49. *See Scala v. Moore McCormack Lines, Inc.*, 985 F.2d 680, 683 (2d Cir.1993); *Appleton Elec. Co. v. Graves Truck Line,* 635 F.2d 603 (7th Cir.1980), *cert. denied,* 451 U.S. 976, 101 S.Ct. 2058, 68 L.Ed.2d 357 (1981).

50. *See Avitia v. Metropolitan Club of Chicago, Inc.*, 49 F.3d 1219, 1229 (7th Cir. 1995)(holding that, except for "special damages" under Rule 9(g), plaintiffs are not obligated to itemize their damages in their complaints); *Stineman v. Fontbonne College,* 664 F.2d 1082 (8th Cir.1981).

51. *See Holt Civic Club v. Tuscaloosa*, 439 U.S. 60, 65–66, 99 S.Ct. 383, 387–388, 58 L.Ed.2d 292 (1978) (writing that federal courts should not dismiss meritorious constitutional claims because the pleadings specify one remedy, rather than another, appropriate one). *See also In re Bennett*, 298 F.3d 1059, 1069–70 (9th Cir. 2002) (counterclaim not required to seek attorney's fee award, since trial court must grant such relief despite absence of formal demand in pleadings); *North Alamo Water Supply Corp. v. City of San Juan*, 90 F.3d 910, 918–19 (5th Cir.1996), *cert. denied*, 519 U.S. 1029, 117 S.Ct. 586, 136 L.Ed.2d 515 (1996)(courts enjoy broad discretion to fashion a remedy, even where remedy is not specifically requested in prayer); *Commercial Union Ins. Co. v. Walbrook Ins. Co.*, 41 F.3d 764, 773 n. 15 (1st Cir.1994)(court may grant the victors any relief to which they are entitled, even if such relief was not included in original pleadings); *Felce v. Fiedler*, 974 F.2d 1484, 1501 (7th Cir.1992)(court will grant all relief to which party is entitled, including injunctive relief not requested in pleadings, so long as defendant is not prejudiced by decision).

52. *See Felce v. Fiedler*, 974 F.2d 1484, 1501 (7th Cir.1992)(noting that Rule 54(c) is to be liberally construed so that there is no doubt but that the court must grant whatever relief is appropriate). *See Feldman v. Philadelphia Housing Auth.*, 43 F.3d 823, 832 (3d Cir. 1994)(commenting that nature of relief is "determined by the merits of the case, not by the pleadings").

Limitations on Awarding Relief Beyond What Was Demanded

Although the court is entitled to award all relief to which a party is entitled, even if not demanded in the pleadings, this entitlement is not unbounded. A party may not recover on issues not presented to and not actually litigated before the factfinder, nor may the party recover relief which has been lost due to failures in the pleadings or failure in proof.[53] Nor may a litigant obtain relief from a particular defendant unless relief of some kind has first been sought from that defendant,[54] or where the award would otherwise be unfairly prejudicial or unjust.[55] A remedy that none of the parties desire, however, will not be forced upon them.[56] Moreover, a party will generally be held bound by representations made during a pretrial conference or in a pretrial order that had outlined the claims in the case and the relief requested.[57]

Prejudgment Interest

If prejudgment interest is authorized under the applicable substantive law, the court will award it even if it has not been expressly demanded in the pleadings.[58]

RULE 54(d). TAXATION OF COSTS

CORE CONCEPT

The district court may, in its discretion, award costs to the prevailing party in a lawsuit, unless an express provision regarding costs is made by federal statute or court rule.

53. *See Old Republic Ins. Co. v. Employers Reinsurance Corp.*, 144 F.3d 1077, 1080 (7th Cir.1998) (trial court may not award relief upon theory not properly raised at trial); *Gilbane Bldg. Co. v. Federal Reserve Bank*, 80 F.3d 895, 904 (4th Cir.1996)(alternative relief only permitted where the factfinder has found all factual conclusions necessary to support that relief); *Rodriguez v. Doral Mortgage Corp.*, 57 F.3d 1168, 1173 (1st Cir.1995)(commenting that the thesis of Rule 54(c) is "hollow at its core", because the Rule creates no entitlement to any relief based on issues not presented to and tried before the factfinder).

54. *See Powell v. National Bd. of Med. Examiners*, 364 F.3d 79, 86 (2d Cir. 2004); *NAACP v. United States Sugar Corp.*, 84 F.3d 1432, 1438 (D.C.Cir.1996).

55. *See Powell v. National Bd. of Med. Examiners*, 364 F.3d 79, 86 (2d Cir. 2004); *Pinkley, Inc. v. City of Frederick*, 191 F.3d 394, 400 (4th Cir.1999), *cert. denied*, 528 U.S. 1155, 120 S.Ct. 1161, 145 L.Ed.2d 1072 (2000); *Minyard Enters. v. Southeastern Chem. & Solvent Co.*, 184 F.3d 373 (4th Cir.1999). *See also United Phosphorus, Ltd. v. Midland Fumigant, Inc.*, 205 F.3d 1219, 1235 (10th Cir.2000) (although jury award exceeding relief requested does not invalidate jury's award, remittitur may be necessary to avoid a double recovery).

56. *See Minyard Enters. v. Southeastern Chem. & Solvent Co.*, 184 F.3d 373, 386 n. 14 (4th Cir.1999).

57. *See Walker v. Anderson Elec. Connectors*, 944 F.2d 841, 844 (11th Cir.1991)(limiting plaintiff to the relief demanded at the pretrial conference, and finding no conflict between Rule 54(c) and requirement that plaintiff set forth, at the pretrial conference, all relief sought), *cert. denied*, 506 U.S. 1078, 113 S.Ct. 1043, 122 L.Ed.2d 352 (1993). *See also Seven Words LLC v. Network Solutions*, 260 F.3d 1089, 1098 (9th Cir. 2001) (where damages claim was made years into litigation, after various representations that only declaratory and injunctive relief was sought, after a motion to dismiss, and only days before oral argument on appeal, court joins other courts of appeals in declining to read damages claim into complaint).

58. *See, e.g., Baker v. John Morrell & Co.*, 266 F.Supp.2d 909, 931 n.4 (N.D.Iowa 2003); *J.A. McDonald, Inc. v. Waste Sys. Int'l Moretown Landfill, Inc.*, 247 F.Supp.2d 542, 546 (D.Vt. 2002); *Stanford Square, L.L.C. v. Nomura Asset Capital Corp.*, 232 F.Supp.2d 289, 290–91 (S.D.N.Y.2002).

APPLICATIONS

"Prevailing Party" Defined

A prevailing plaintiff is generally one who succeeds on some significant issue in the litigation and thereby achieves some of the benefit sought in filing the lawsuit.[59] Thus, a prevailing plaintiff is one who obtains relief that materially alters the parties' legal relationship by modifying the behavior of the defendant in a way that directly benefits the plaintiff.[60] A judgment for *any* amount of damages necessarily modifies the defendant's behavior to the plaintiff's benefit, thus a plaintiff who obtains only nominal damages may still become a prevailing party.[61] Thus, a litigant need not succeed on all issues to qualify as a prevailing party.[62]

A prevailing defendant is one who defeats the litigation and obtains a denial of relief. Thus, a dismissal, with prejudice and on the merits, of all claims against a defendant will generally make that defendant a prevailing party.[63]

There are no prevailing parties if the case is dismissed for lack of jurisdiction.[64]

Against Whom May Costs Be Taxed

Under Rule 54(d), costs may be taxed only against the non-prevailing party; costs may not be taxed under this Rule against counsel for a litigant.[65]

Types of Taxable Costs

The types of costs that are generally taxed in favor of the prevailing party in a federal litigation are set by statute.[66] These costs include:

1. Clerk and U.S. Marshal fees;

59. *Cf. Texas State Teachers Ass'n v. Garland Independent Sch. Dist.*, 489 U.S. 782, 791–92, 109 S.Ct. 1486, 1493–94, 103 L.Ed.2d 866 (1989)(applying definition in civil rights litigation under 42 U.S.C.A. § 1988); *Hensley v. Eckerhart*, 461 U.S. 424, 433, 103 S.Ct. 1933, 1939, 76 L.Ed.2d 40 (1983)(same); *Testa v. Village of Mundelein*, 89 F.3d 443, 447 (7th Cir.1996).

60. *See Farrar v. Hobby*, 506 U.S. 103, 111–13, 113 S.Ct. 566, 573, 121 L.Ed.2d 494 (1992).

61. *See Farrar v. Hobby*, 506 U.S. 103, 111–13, 113 S.Ct. 566, 573, 121 L.Ed.2d 494 (1992); *Barber v. T.D. Williamson, Inc.*, 254 F.3d 1223, 1234 (10th Cir.2001).

62. *See Fireman's Fund Ins. Co. v. Tropical Shipping & Const. Co.*, 254 F.3d 987, 1012–13 (11th Cir.2001) (noting precedent supporting an award of costs where the prevailing party obtains a judgment "on even a fraction of the claims advanced").

63. *See Power Mosfet Techs, L.L.C. v. Siemens AG*, 378 F.3d 1396 (Fed.Cir. 2004) (prevailing party is one who "wins completely on every claim at issue", and thus party who "had all claims against it dismissed with prejudice" so qualifies); *Weaver v. Toombs*, 948 F.2d 1004 (6th Cir.1991)(a dismissal, whether on the merits or not, defines the defendant as the prevailing party).

64. *See Miles v. California*, 320 F.3d 986, 988 (9th Cir.2003).

65. *See Wilder v. GL Bus Lines*, 258 F.3d 126, 127–31 (2d Cir.2001).

66. *See* 28 U.S.C.A. § 1920. *See also* 28 U.S.C.A. §§ 1911–31 (defining costs provisions generally). In addition, the Rules allow costs to be taxed in other instances: when an attorney violates Rule 11, conducts discovery improperly in violation of Rule 37, or rejects unwisely an offer of settlement under Rule 68.

2. Deposition expenses, when the transcript is received in evidence or was otherwise reasonably necessary for the trial;[67] these expenses may include costs for videotape depositions;[68]
3. Printing fees;
4. Witness fees and witnesses' travel and subsistence expenses, where the witnesses' testimony was material, relevant, and reasonably necessary to the case;[69]
5. Fees to "exemplify" documents (which may include reimbursement for many methods of illustration, including models, charts, graphs, and even computerized presentation systems[70]), and fees to print copies of papers necessary for use in the case;[71]
6. Certain docket fees; and
7. Fees for court-appointed experts and interpreters.[72]

67. *See Mitchell v. City of Moore, Oklahoma*, 218 F.3d 1190 (10th Cir.2000) (recovery permitted for costs of all depositions reasonably necessary to litigation); *Corder v. Lucent Techs. Inc.*, 162 F.3d 924, 928–29 (7th Cir.1998) (affirming taxation of costs for expedited delivery transcripts, given district court's conclusion that such transcripts were necessary given the discovery and motion schedule set for the case); *Cengr v. Fusibond Piping Sys., Inc.*, 135 F.3d 445, 455 (7th Cir.1998) (inquiry is whether deposition was reasonably necessary as of the time it was taken, not whether the deposition was used in a motion or at a court proceeding); *Zotos v. Lindbergh Sch. Dist.*, 121 F.3d 356, 363 (8th Cir. 1997) (same); *Manildra Mill. Corp. v. Ogilvie Mills, Inc.*, 76 F.3d 1178, 1184 (Fed.Cir. 1996)(includes both trial transcripts and deposition transcripts); *Jones v. Unisys Corp.*, 54 F.3d 624, 633 (10th Cir.1995)(court reporter fees for transcripts); *Barber v. Ruth*, 7 F.3d 636, 645 (7th Cir.1993)(noting that transcript need not be "absolutely indispensable"; instead, it need only be "reasonably necessary"). *See also Virginia Panel Corp. v. Mac Panel Co.*, 887 F.Supp. 880, 886 (W.D.Va.1995)(cost of daily copies of trial transcripts is recoverable if daily copy is "indispensable", and not a convenience for counsel).

68. *See Tilton v. Capital Cities/ABC, Inc.*, 115 F.3d 1471, 1477–79 (10th Cir.1997); *Barber v. Ruth*, 7 F.3d 636, 645 (7th Cir.1993); *Garonzik v. Whitman Diner*, 910 F.Supp. 167, 170–71 (D.N.J.1995)(allowing recovery of recording and playback costs for videotape depositions). *But cf. Cherry v. Champion Int'l Corp.*, 186 F.3d 442 (4th Cir.1999) (although costs of video depositions may be taxed, prevailing party must make a showing why *both* the transcript and the video deposition were "necessary").

69. *See Rank v. Balshy*, 590 F.Supp. 787 (M.D.Pa.1984). *Cf. Jones v. Unisys Corp.*, 54 F.3d 624, 633 (10th Cir.1995)(fees for expert witnesses not allowable if witnesses do not appear in court).

70. *See Cefalu v. Village of Elk Grove*, 211 F.3d 416, 427–28 (7th Cir.2000) (affirming reimbursement for cost of computerized, multi-media system used to present exhibits to jury). *But cf. Kohus v. Toys R US, Inc.*, 282 F.3d 1355, 1357–61 (Fed.Cir.2002) (reversing award of $12,950 for video model/animation as unauthorized under federal law), *cert. denied*, 537 U.S. 1044, 123 S.Ct. 659, 154 L.Ed.2d 515 (2002); *Arcadian Fertilizer, L.P. v. MPW Indus. Services, Inc.*, 249 F.3d 1293, 1297 (11th Cir.2001) (refusing reimbursement for videotape exhibits and computer animation, since they are not "copies of paper" or "exemplifications").

71. *See Concord Boat Corp. v. Brunswick Corp.*, 309 F.3d 494, 497–98 (8th Cir.2002), *mandate amended*, 318 F.3d 1156 (8th Cir.2003) (allowing costs for photocopies "necessarily obtained for use in the case"); *Cengr v. Fusibond Piping Sys., Inc.*, 135 F.3d 445, 455 (7th Cir. 1998) (rejecting party's objection to $12.60 copying as "border[ing] on dopiness"); *Jones v. Unisys Corp.*, 54 F.3d 624, 633 (10th Cir.1995)(fees for copies of papers "necessarily obtained for use in the case").

72. Guardians ad litem may be taxed as costs. *See Gaddis v. United States*, 381 F.3d 444 (5th Cir. 2004) (court may award guardian ad litem fees as court costs, even against government); *Kollsman, a Div. of Sequa Corp. v. Cohen*, 996 F.2d 702 (4th Cir.1993)(noting that such costs may be taxed); *Hull v. United States*, 971 F.2d 1499 (10th Cir.1992)(noting that taxing guardian ad litem expenses depends on role of guardian), *cert. denied*, 507 U.S. 1030, 113 S.Ct. 1844, 123 L.Ed.2d 469 (1993). Fees and ex-

The district court may not award costs under Rule 54(d) that are not authorized by statute or court rule.[73]

Attorney's Fees as Costs

In the absence of a federal statute to the contrary, the Supreme Court has ruled that attorney's fees may not be taxed as costs beyond the modest provisions set forth in 28 U.S.C.A. § 1923.[74]

Exception: Attorney's fees, however, may be taxed against a common fund generated in a class action or shareholders' derivative action.[75] Attorney's fees may also be taxed where a party instituted, defended, or conducted litigation in bad faith.[76]

Diversity Jurisdiction Cases

Federal law governs the taxation of costs in the district courts, even where the district court's jurisdiction is premised on diversity of citizenship.[77]

Discretion of District Court

Rule 54(d) provides that costs shall be taxed "as of course".[78] The courts have interpreted this mandate to create a presumption in favor of the award of costs in favor of the prevailing party,[79] but reserving for

penses to a Special Master are also recoverable costs. *See also Hook v. Arizona*, 907 F.Supp. 1326, 1339 (D.Ariz.1995), *aff'd*, 73 F.3d 369 (9th Cir.1995)(Table).

73. *See United States v. Merritt Meridian Const. Corp.*, 95 F.3d 153, 171 (2d Cir. 1996)(noting that district judge lacks discretion to award costs not authorized by statute or contractual provision). *Cf. Brisco-Wade v. Carnahan*, 297 F.3d 781, 782 (8th Cir.2002) (reversing as improper taxation of costs of mediation against defendants); *Jones v. Unisys Corp.*, 54 F.3d 624, 633 (10th Cir.1995)(costs for computer-assisted legal research not statutorily authorized); *O'Bryhim v. Reliance Standard Life Ins. Co.*, 997 F.Supp. 728, 737–38 (E.D.Va.1998), *aff'd*, 188 F.3d 502 (4th Cir.1999) (denying costs for postage, long distance telephone calls, Federal Express service, Messenger Service, facsimile transmissions, transportation, and parking); *Garshman Co. v. General Elec. Co.*, 993 F.Supp. 25, 29 (D.Mass.1998), *aff'd*, 176 F.3d 1 (1st Cir. 1999) (denying costs for travel, postage, telecopier, and computer research expenses); *Mary M. v. North Lawrence Community Sch. Corp.*, 951 F.Supp. 820, 833 (S.D.Ind.1997), *rev'd on other grounds*, 131 F.3d 1220 (7th Cir.1997), *cert. denied*, 524 U.S. 952, 118 S.Ct. 2369, 141 L.Ed.2d 737 (1998) (acknowledging it as well established that computer research costs are not recoverable); *Ortega v. IBP, Inc.*, 883 F.Supp. 558, 562–63 (D.Kan.1995)(costs for legal research, long distance telephone calls, postage, fax transmissions, mileage, travel, lodging, and meals are not recoverable); *Thomas v. Treasury Management Ass'n, Inc.*, 158 F.R.D. 364, 372 (D.Md. 1994)(paralegal costs to serve subpoena, in-house photocopying, costs of computer research, couriers, postage, telecopier, overnight deliveries, and local transportation expenses not awarded). *But see Snell v. Reno Hilton Resort*, 930 F.Supp. 1428, 1434 (D.Nev.1996)(in its discretion, court may allow as costs reasonable photocopying, paralegal, telephone, facsimile, LEXIS, and other client charges normally charged to a fee-paying).

74. *See Alyeska Pipeline Serv. Co. v. Wilderness Soc'y*, 421 U.S. 240, 95 S.Ct. 1612, 44 L.Ed.2d 141 (1975).

75. *See Mills v. Electric Auto–Lite Co.*, 396 U.S. 375, 90 S.Ct. 616, 24 L.Ed.2d 593 (1970).

76. *See Chambers v. NASCO, Inc.*, 501 U.S. 32, 111 S.Ct. 2123, 115 L.Ed.2d 27 (1991).

77. *See Gobbo Farms & Orchards v. Poole Chem. Co.*, 81 F.3d 122, 123 (10th Cir.1996).

78. *See Miles v. California*, 320 F.3d 986, 988 (9th Cir.2003); *Concord Boat Corp. v. Brunswick Corp.*, 309 F.3d 494, 497–98 (8th Cir.2002), *mandate amended*, 318 F.3d 1156 (8th Cir.2003). *See also In re Paoli R.R. Yard PCB Litig.*, 221 F.3d 449 (3d Cir.2000) (tracing history of award of costs from English inception).

79. *See Delta Air Lines, Inc. v. August*, 450 U.S. 346, 352, 101 S.Ct. 1146, 1150, 67 L.Ed.2d 287 (1981); *Rodriguez v. Whiting Farms, Inc.*,

the district judge the discretion to deny costs in appropriate circumstances.[80] If the court chooses not to award costs to a prevailing party, the court must explain its good reasons for not doing so.[81]

Reasons for Denying Costs

The proper exercise of a trial court's discretion to deny costs will hinge on whether the costs are of a type authorized by law and whether the costs pay for materials necessarily obtained for use in the case.[82] Costs may be denied, for example, where both parties partially prevail in the litigation,[83] where a prevailing plaintiff fails to prove that federal jurisdiction was proper (either because plaintiff fails to recover the $75,000 jurisdictional minimum in a diversity case or because plaintiff fails to win on the federal question counts),[84] where the prevailing party needlessly prolongs the litigation or otherwise acts in bad faith,[85] or,

360 F.3d 1180, 1190–91 (10th Cir. 2004); *Champion Produce, Inc. v. Ruby Robinson Co.*, 342 F.3d 1016, 1022 (9th Cir. 2003); *Park v. City of Chicago*, 297 F.3d 606, 617 (7th Cir.2002); *In re Paoli R.R. Yard PCB Litig.*, 221 F.3d 449 (3d Cir.2000); *Cherry v. Champion Int'l Corp.*, 186 F.3d 442 (4th Cir.1999); *Greaser v. State Dep't of Corrections*, 145 F.3d 979, 985 (8th Cir.1998), *cert. denied*, 525 U.S. 1056, 119 S.Ct. 620, 142 L.Ed.2d 559 (1998); *Neal & Co. v. United States*, 121 F.3d 683, 686 (Fed.Cir.1997).

80. *See Crawford Fitting Co. v. J. T. Gibbons, Inc.*, 482 U.S. 437, 107 S.Ct. 2494, 96 L.Ed.2d 385 (1987); *Farmer v. Arabian American Oil Co.*, 379 U.S. 227, 85 S.Ct. 411, 13 L.Ed.2d 248 (1964); *Rodriguez v. Whiting Farms, Inc.*, 360 F.3d 1180, 1190–91 (10th Cir. 2004); *Champion Produce, Inc. v. Ruby Robinson Co.*, 342 F.3d 1016, 1022 (9th Cir. 2003); *Perlman v. Zell*, 185 F.3d 850 (7th Cir.1999); *Cherry v. Champion Int'l Corp.*, 186 F.3d 442 (4th Cir. 1999); *Greaser v. State Dep't of Corrections*, 145 F.3d 979, 985 (8th Cir.1998), *cert. denied*, 525 U.S. 1056, 119 S.Ct. 620, 142 L.Ed.2d 559 (1998); *United States v. Merritt Meridian Const. Corp.*, 95 F.3d 153, 171 (2d Cir.1996); *Mathews v. Lancaster General Hosp.*, 87 F.3d 624, 642 (3d Cir.1996).

81. *See Rodriguez v. Whiting Farms, Inc.*, 360 F.3d 1180, 1190–91 (10th Cir. 2004); *Champion Produce, Inc. v. Ruby Robinson Co.*, 342 F.3d 1016, 1022 (9th Cir. 2003); *Chapman v. AI Transport*, 229 F.3d 1012, 1039 (11th Cir.2000); *In re Paoli R.R. Yard PCB Litig.*, 221 F.3d 449 (3d Cir.2000); *Krocka v. City of Chicago*, 203 F.3d 507, 518 (7th Cir.2000); *Cherry v. Champion Int'l Corp.*, 186 F.3d 442 (4th Cir.1999); *Neal & Co. v. United States*, 121 F.3d 683, 686 (Fed. Cir.1997). *See also Allison v. Bank One–Denver*, 289 F.3d 1223, 1248–49 (10th Cir.2002) (trial court abuses its discretion when it rests its ruling on an erroneous legal conclusion or where no rational basis supports the ruling).

82. *See Allison v. Bank One–Denver*, 289 F.3d 1223, 1248 (10th Cir.2002).

83. *See Barber v. T.D. Williamson, Inc.*, 254 F.3d 1223, 1234–35 (10th Cir.2001) (noting that in cases where prevailing party has been only partially successful, some courts have chosen to apportion costs among parties or to reduce size of prevailing party's award); *Perlman v. Zell*, 185 F.3d 850 (7th Cir.1999) (noting that plaintiff's modest recovery (in relation to original demand) implies that defendants won more of the dispute than they lost, and therefore award of costs could be refused); *Cherry v. Champion Int'l Corp.*, 186 F.3d 442 (4th Cir.1999) (limited value of prevailing party's victory could justify denying award of costs); *AeroTech, Inc. v. Estes*, 110 F.3d 1523, 1526 (10th Cir.1997) (costs may be denied when the prevailing party only partially succeeds); *Amarel v. Connell*, 102 F.3d 1494, 1523 (9th Cir.1996) (district court may require each party to bear their own costs in the event of a mixed judgment), *cert. denied*, 539 U.S. 903, 123 S.Ct. 2248, 156 L.Ed.2d 111 (2003); *Testa v. Village of Mundelein*, 89 F.3d 443, 447 (7th Cir.1996)(in viewed of mixed outcome, district court did not abuse its discretion in requiring each party to bear its own costs).

84. *See Miles v. California*, 320 F.3d 986, 988 (9th Cir.2003); *Perlman v. Zell*, 185 F.3d 850 (7th Cir.1999).

85. *See Farrar v. Hobby*, 506 U.S. 103, 115–16, 113 S.Ct. 566, 575, 121 L.Ed.2d 494 (1992)(commenting that, having considered the amount and nature of the plaintiff's success on the merits, district courts may award modest fees or no fees at all); *Champion Produce, Inc. v. Ruby Robinson Co.*, 342 F.3d 1016, 1022 (9th Cir. 2003); *Mother & Father v. Cassidy*, 338 F.3d 704, 708 (7th Cir.2003) (costs can be denied for

perhaps, where the losing party is unable to pay or would be rendered indigent by paying,[86] or is incarcerated,[87] or where the prevailing party's recovery was nominal or "substantially less" than what was sought,[88] where the or where there would be some other "injustice" in approving an award of costs.[89] Generally, a district court may not deny costs simply upon a finding that the case was brought and litigated in "good faith" and without a vexatious motive,[90] because a significant disparity exists between the parties' financial resources,[91] because the case was "complex" or a "close call",[92] because the prevailing party had rejected

party's misconduct); *In re Paoli R.R. Yard PCB Litig.*, 221 F.3d 449 (3d Cir.2000) (prevailing party's "unclean hands" is relevant factor for consideration); *Cherry v. Champion Int'l Corp.*, 186 F.3d 442 (4th Cir.1999) ("misconduct by the prevailing party worthy of a penalty" may justify denial of costs); *Greaser v. State Dep't of Corrections*, 145 F.3d 979, 985 (8th Cir.1998) (costs should be denied only if there is some misconduct or other action worthy of penalty on the part of the prevailing party), *cert. denied*, 525 U.S. 1056, 119 S.Ct. 620, 142 L.Ed.2d 559 (1998); *AeroTech, Inc. v. Estes*, 110 F.3d 1523, 1526–27 (10th Cir.1997) (noting that denying costs is a severe penalty, justified only if "some apparent reason to penalize" exists); *National Information Servs., Inc. v. TRW, Inc.*, 51 F.3d 1470, 1472 (9th Cir.1995)(presumption can be overcome by demonstrating some impropriety on the part of the prevailing part, and citing case law examples such as where prevailing party called unnecessary witnesses, pressed unnecessary issues, or encumbered the record).

86. *See Champion Produce, Inc. v. Ruby Robinson Co.*, 342 F.3d 1016, 1022 (9th Cir. 2003) (losing party's "limited financial resources" may be considered); *Lampkins v. Thompson*, 337 F.3d 1009, 1017 (8th Cir. 2003) (party's indigency properly considered); *Mother & Father v. Cassidy*, 338 F.3d 704, 708 (7th Cir.2003) (noting proper "pragmatic exercise of discretion" to deny or limit award of costs if losing party is indigent); *Chapman v. AI Transport*, 229 F.3d 1012, 1039 (11th Cir.2000) (noting that non-prevailing party's financial status is factor to be considered, but court must first require substantial documentation of true inability to pay costs); *In re Paoli R.R. Yard PCB Litig.*, 221 F.3d 449 (3d Cir.2000) (commenting that "most important" factor is defeated party's indigency or inability to pay which may, but need not automatically, excuse taxation of costs); *Cherry v. Champion Int'l Corp.*, 186 F.3d 442 (4th Cir.1999) (costs may possibly be denied if litigant is of sufficiently modest means). *But see Rodriguez v. Whiting Farms, Inc.*, 360 F.3d 1180, 1190–91 (10th Cir. 2004) (finding no error in district court's rejection of party's indigency as possible justification to deny costs).

87. *See Lampkins v. Thompson*, 337 F.3d 1009, 1017 (8th Cir. 2003).

88. *See Champion Produce, Inc. v. Ruby Robinson Co.*, 342 F.3d 1016, 1022–23 (9th Cir. 2003).

89. *See Cherry v. Champion Int'l Corp.*, 186 F.3d 442 (4th Cir.1999). *See also Barber v. T.D. Williamson, Inc.*, 254 F.3d 1223, 1234–35 (10th Cir.2001) (noting that courts have refused to award costs where neither side entirely prevailed, both sides prevailed, or litigation resulted from fault on both parties).

90. *See In re Paoli R.R. Yard PCB Litig.*, 221 F.3d 449 (3d Cir.2000) (agreeing that "good faith" is not relevant factor); *Cherry v. Champion Int'l Corp.*, 186 F.3d 442 (4th Cir.1999) (rejecting district court's decision to deny costs on basis of plaintiff's good faith in filing, since to hold otherwise would frustrate the Rule's operations because most cases are filed in good faith); *National Information Servs., Inc. v. TRW, Inc.*, 51 F.3d 1470, 1471–72 (9th Cir.1995)(specifically rejecting position that prosecuting lawsuit in "good faith" is sufficient to defeat presumption in favor of an award of costs). *But see Champion Produce, Inc. v. Ruby Robinson Co.*, 342 F.3d 1016, 1022 (9th Cir. 2003) (whether losing party litigated in good faith could be considered).

91. *See In re Paoli R.R. Yard PCB Litig.*, 221 F.3d 449 (3d Cir.2000) (rejecting relative wealth of parties as relevant factor); *Cherry v. Champion Int'l Corp.*, 186 F.3d 442 (4th Cir. 1999) (rejecting "comparative economic power" argument, noting that it would frequently favor defendant, thus ignoring plain language of Rule and undermining foundation of legal system that justice is administered to all equally, regardless of wealth or status).

92. *See In re Paoli R.R. Yard PCB Litig.*, 221 F.3d 449 (3d Cir.2000) (complexity or closeness of issues not appropriate factors for consideration); *National Information Servs., Inc. v. TRW, Inc.*, 51 F.3d 1470, 1473 (9th Cir.1995)(rejecting view that costs may be denied in cases presenting "close and difficult" legal issues); *Klein v. Grynberg*, 44 F.3d 1497, 1506 (10th Cir.

the defendant's Rule 68 offer of judgment,[93] or because the case involved significant matters in the public interest.[94] In many cases, the district court will also be precluded from denying costs merely because the prevailing party failed to pray for them in a pleading.[95]

Note, however, that the Circuits are not always uniform in their approaches to these various factors. Indeed, one court of appeals has explained that denying costs is "in the nature of a severe penalty" and, as such, the party opposing the taxing of costs will be obligated to offer a reason why the prevailing party ought to be "penalized" by a refusal of costs.[96]

Burden of Proof

The burden of proving the amount of compensable costs and expenses lies with the party seeking costs.[97] Once the prevailing party demonstrates the amount of its costs and that they fall within an allowable category of taxable costs, the prevailing party enjoys the "strong presumption" that its costs will be awarded "in full measure".[98] The party opposing the award of costs bears the burden of demonstrating that the award would be improper.[99]

1995)(rejecting premise that costs may be denied because litigation was complex or lengthy), *cert. denied*, 516 U.S. 810, 116 S.Ct. 58, 133 L.Ed.2d 22 (1995). *See also Rodriguez v. Whiting Farms, Inc.*, 360 F.3d 1180, 1190–91 (10th Cir. 2004) (finding no error in district court's rejection of claim that case involved "close and difficult call" as possible justification to deny costs). Note, however, that the case law in this area is not developing uniformly. *See Champion Produce, Inc. v. Ruby Robinson Co.*, 342 F.3d 1016, 1022 (9th Cir. 2003) ("close and difficult" issues in case may be considered); *Cherry v. Champion Int'l Corp.*, 186 F.3d 442 (4th Cir.1999) (commenting that factors that could justify denying award of costs include the closeness and difficulty of the issues decided); *Luckey v. Baxter Healthcare Corp.*, 183 F.3d 730 (7th Cir.1999) (observing that district judge might require each side to bear its own costs when the case is close, or when the side with the better position loses on a technicality), *cert. denied*, 528 U.S. 1038, 120 S.Ct. 562, 145 L.Ed.2d 439 (1999).

93. *See Champion Produce, Inc. v. Ruby Robinson Co.*, 342 F.3d 1016, 1022–24 (9th Cir. 2003).

94. *See Mitchell v. City of Moore, Oklahoma*, 218 F.3d 1190 (10th Cir.2000) (presumption in favor of awarding costs applies even where prevailing party is defendant in civil rights case); *Cherry v. Champion Int'l Corp.*, 186 F.3d 442 (4th Cir.1999) (holding that presumptive award of costs cannot be defeated on the basis of the nature of the underlying litigation). *But see Champion Produce, Inc. v. Ruby Robinson Co.*, 342 F.3d 1016, 1022 (9th Cir. 2003) ("the chilling effect of imposing ... high costs on future civil rights litigants" may be considered, as well as whether the case involved "a landmark issue of national importance"). *Stanley v. University of So. Cal.*, 178 F.3d 1069, 1079 (9th Cir.1999) (directing courts, in civil rights cases, to consider plaintiff's financial resources and amount of cost so as to avoid unnecessarily chilling civil rights litigation; "Without civil rights litigants who are willing to test the boundaries of our laws, we would not have made much of the progress that has occurred in this nation since Brown v. Board of Educ."), *cert. denied*, 528 U.S. 1022, 120 S.Ct. 533, 145 L.Ed.2d 413 (1999).

95. *See Flynn v. AK Peters, Ltd.*, 377 F.3d 13, 26 (1st Cir. 2004) (right to attorney's fees not waived where prayer for fees not listed as "special damages" in complaint); *Port of Stockton v. Western Bulk Carrier KS*, 371 F.3d 1119, 1121–22 (9th Cir. 2004) (same effect).

96. *See Rodriguez v. Whiting Farms, Inc.*, 360 F.3d 1180, 1190–91 (10th Cir. 2004).

97. *See Allison v. Bank One–Denver*, 289 F.3d 1223, 1248–49 (10th Cir.2002).

98. *See Concord Boat Corp. v. Brunswick Corp.*, 309 F.3d 494, 497–98 (8th Cir.2002), *mandate amended*, 318 F.3d 1156 (8th Cir.2003).

99. *See Rodriguez v. Whiting Farms, Inc.*, 360 F.3d 1180, 1190–91 (10th Cir. 2004); *Save Our Valley v. Sound Transit*, 335 F.3d 932, 944–45 (9th Cir.2003); *Concord Boat Corp. v. Brunswick Corp.*, 309 F.3d 494, 497–98 (8th Cir.2002), *mandate amended*, 318 F.3d 1156 (8th Cir.2003); *In re Paoli R.R. Yard PCB Litig.*, 221 F.3d 449 (3d Cir.2000).

Taxing Costs For or Against the United States

The United States may be awarded costs in the same manner as any prevailing party.[100] Costs may be taxed against the United States in accordance with the list set forth in 28 U.S.C.A. § 1920,[101] except that in non-tort actions, the district court may refuse to tax costs upon a finding that the United States' position was substantially justified or where special circumstances make an award of costs unjust.[102]

Taxing Costs Against States

Some courts have construed the Eleventh Amendment to the United States Constitution as prohibiting a district court's right to tax costs against a State.[103] To ensure that costs may be so taxed against a State, the court will consult the source of the substantive law under which the suit is brought to determine whether provision is made for such an award of costs against a State.

Costs in Pauper Actions

The district court may, in its discretion, permit a civil litigant, criminal defendant, or appellant to proceed without the prepayment of costs upon receiving an affidavit showing an inability to pay costs.[104]

Procedure for Obtaining Award of Non–Attorney's Fee Costs

To obtain an award of costs, the prevailing party must file a "Bill of Costs" with the clerk (the district court may have a preprinted form for this purpose). The Bill of Costs must be verified by affidavit. The clerk may tax costs on one-day notice. Within 5 days thereafter, a disappointed party may seek court review of the clerk's assessment. Some courts have ruled that a failure to seek review within this 5–day period waives the losing party's right to challenge the award.[105] Other courts have noted that the time period is not jurisdictional and untimely objections may, in the trial court's discretion, be considered.[106] The district court is authorized to conduct a *de novo* review of the clerk's assessments.[107] Costs may be taxed against multiple losing parties either in allocated amounts or jointly and severally.[108] The time for filing a Bill of Costs is typically regulated by local court rule, but usually is set after the court has rendered its decision in the case.[109]

100. *See E.E.O.C. v. W & O, Inc.*, 213 F.3d 600, 620 (11th Cir.2000); *United States v. Lynd,* 349 F.2d 785 (5th Cir.1965).

101. *See* 28 U.S.C.A. § 1920.

102. *See* 28 U.S.C.A. § 2412.

103. *See Alyeska Pipeline Serv. Co. v. Wilderness Soc'y,* 421 U.S. 240, 269 n. 44, 95 S.Ct. 1612, 1627 n. 44, 44 L.Ed.2d 141 (1975).

104. *See* 28 U.S.C.A. § 1915.

105. *See Bloomer v. United Parcel Serv., Inc.*, 337 F.3d 1220, 1221 (10th Cir.2003); *Cooper v. Eagle River Mem'l Hosp., Inc.*, 270 F.3d 456, 464 (7th Cir.2001); *Walker v. California*, 200 F.3d 624, 626 (9th Cir.1999).

106. *See In re Paoli R.R. Yard PCB Litig.*, 221 F.3d 449 (3d Cir.2000).

107. *See In re Paoli R.R. Yard PCB Litig.*, 221 F.3d 449 (3d Cir.2000).

108. *In re Paoli R.R. Yard PCB Litig.*, 221 F.3d 449 (3d Cir.2000).

109. *See S.A. Healy Co. v. Milwaukee Metropolitan Sewerage Dist.*, 60 F.3d 305 (7th Cir. 1995)(commenting that because Rule 54(d) specifies no uniform national deadline for filing Bills of Costs, such timing is typically governed by local court rules), *cert. denied*, 516 U.S. 1010, 116 S.Ct. 566, 133 L.Ed.2d 491 (1995).

Procedure for Obtaining Award of Attorney's Fees

Where an award of attorney's fees is appropriate, Rule 54(d)(2) fixes the procedure for obtaining an award of such fees and related non-taxable expenses. This procedure does *not* apply to attorney's fees recoverable as an element of damages (*e.g.*, under terms of a contract) or to fees and expenses awarded as sanctions.[110] The procedure follows:

1. *Motion Required:* The prevailing party must apply for such an award by motion. The motion must: (a) specify the judgment; (b) identify the legal source authorizing such an award of fees or expenses; and (c) state the amount, or a fair estimate of the amount, of the requested award.[111]

   Court-Implemented Settlements: In cases where a settlement must be implemented by the court, the district court may also require that the motion disclose any fee agreement affecting the litigation.

2. *Time for Service:* Ordinarily, the motion must be served within 14 days after entry of judgment. This deadline helps both to ensure that the opponent receives proper notice of the fees claim and to promote a prompt fees ruling from the district court, thus permitting simultaneous appellate review of both the merits and the fees award.[112] Failure to serve within this allotted time constitutes a waiver of a party's right to recover such fees or expenses.[113] Nevertheless, because the 14–day time period is not jurisdictional, some courts have held that the district judge may exercise discretion to extend the time period.[114]

   Local Rules & Standing Orders: Practitioners must *carefully* consult the applicable local rules on Rule 54(d) attorneys fee motions. This 14–day period may be modified "by statute or order of the court".[115] Several courts have ruled that local rules

110. *See* Rule 54(d)(2)(E). *See also United Indus. v. Simon–Hartley, Ltd.*, 91 F.3d 762, 766 (5th Cir.1996). *Cf. Capital Asset Research Corp. v. Finnegan*, 216 F.3d 1268 (11th Cir.2000) (holding that failure to make explicit request for attorney's fees in pleadings is not defect depriving district court of subject matter jurisdiction).

111. *See* Rule 54(d)(2)(A)-(2)(B). *See also United Indus. v. Simon–Hartley, Ltd.*, 91 F.3d 762, 766–67 (5th Cir.1996).

112. *See United Indus. v. Simon–Hartley, Ltd.*, 91 F.3d 762, 766 (5th Cir.1996).

113. *See Committee for Idaho's High Desert, Inc. v. Yost*, 92 F.3d 814 (9th Cir.1996)(affirming district court's refusal to extend 14–day period); *United Indus. v. Simon–Hartley, Ltd.*, 91 F.3d 762, 767 (5th Cir.1996)(noting waiver rule); *Mathews v. Lancaster General Hosp.*, 87 F.3d 624, 642 n. 12 (3d Cir.1996)(holding that district court did not abuse its discretion in refusing fees where petition was not timely filed); *Sol Salins, Inc. v. W.M. Ercanbrack Co.*, 155 F.R.D. 4 (D.D.C.1994). *But cf. Johnson v. Lafayette Fire Fighters Ass'n Local 472*, 51 F.3d 726, 729 (7th Cir.1995)(holding that local court rule, as a uniform "order of court", modified the 14–day period set forth in Rule 54(d)(2)(B)).

114. *See Green v. Administrators of Tulane Educ. Fund*, 284 F.3d 642, 664 (5th Cir.2002); *Amarel v. Connell*, 102 F.3d 1494 (9th Cir.1996). *See also Tancredi v. Metropolitan Life Ins.*, 378 F.3d 220, 227–28 (2d Cir. 2004) (before extension to 14–day deadline may be granted, trial court must find "excusable neglect").

115. *See* Rule 54(d)(2)(B).

which adopt longer periods for making attorney's fee motions qualify as "standing orders" and, thus, are authorized modifications of the 14–day period.[116]

3. *Time for Service*: Originally, Rule 54(d) required that a motion for attorney's fees must be *both* served and filed within 14 days. This requirement was changed in the 2002 amendments to the Rule. Now, filing must be made, as with any other document under Rule 5(d), "within a reasonable time after service".[117]
4. *Opponent's Response:* Upon request, the court must provide the opponent with the opportunity to present evidence in opposition to the requested award.
5. *Court's Delegation:* The court may enlist the help of a Special Master for setting the proper value to be awarded for the attorney services provided. The court may also refer the entire motion to a magistrate judge for a Report & Recommendation (akin to dispositive pretrial matters).
6. *Court's Ruling:* In ruling on a Rule 54(d)(2) motion, the court must issue findings of fact and conclusions of law as required under Rule 52(a), and must issue a separate judgment as required under Rule 58. The court may, at its option, bifurcate its consideration of the motion to resolve liability issues first, before considering the amount of an appropriate award.
7. *Additional Procedures By Local Rule:* Rule 54(d)(2) permits the district courts to promulgate local rules to govern procedures for claims without the need for extensive evidentiary hearings.[118]

Effect of an Attorney's Fees Motion on Judgment's "Finality"

The filing of a Rule 54(d)(2) motion for an award of attorney's fees does not ordinarily affect the finality of the underlying judgment.[119] However, when a *timely* motion for fees is made and so long as no notice of appeal has yet been filed (or become effective), the district court may enter an order directing that the fees motion be deemed to have the same effect as a timely Rule 59 motion and, thereby, toll the time for taking an appeal until after the motion is resolved.[120] This

116. *See Planned Parenthood of Cent. New Jersey v. Attorney General of New Jersey*, 297 F.3d 253, 259–61 (3d Cir.2002) (ruling that 14–day period was properly extended by local rule, which qualifies as a standing court order); *Green v. Administrators of Tulane Educ. Fund*, 284 F.3d 642, 664 (5th Cir.2002) (same).

117. *See* Rule 5(d). *See also* Rule 54(d)(2)(B) advisory committee note to 2002 amendments (noting deletion of 14–day filing requirement "to establish a parallel with Rules 50, 52, and 59. Service continues to be required under Rule 5(a)").

118. Local rules *must* be consulted on this point. The advisory committee notes suggest that, by local rule, the district courts may even adopt schedules listing customary attorney's fees or factors that affect attorney's fees within a particular legal community. *See* Rule 54(d)(2)(D) advisory committee note.

119. *See* Rule 58(c)(1). *See also Moody Nat'l Bank of Galveston v. GE Life & Annuity Assur. Co.*, 383 F.3d 249, 250, at *1 (5th Cir. 2004).

120. *See* Rule 58(c)(2). *See also Moody Nat'l Bank of Galveston v. GE Life & Annuity Assur. Co.*, 383 F.3d 249, 253 (5th Cir. 2004).

extension option applies only to fees motions, not to the taxation of costs.[121]

ADDITIONAL RESEARCH REFERENCES

Wright & Miller, *Federal Practice and Procedure* §§ 2651–79.

C.J.S. Federal Civil Procedure §§ 1105–1120 et seq., 1236; Federal Courts § 293(17).

West's Key No. Digests, Federal Civil Procedure ⚷2391–2399, 2571–2587, 2721–2742.5; Federal Courts ⚷660.

121. *See Moody Nat'l Bank of Galveston v. GE Life & Annuity Assur. Co.*, 383 F.3d 249, 253 (5th Cir. 2004)

RULE 55

DEFAULT

(a) Entry. When a party against whom a judgment for affirmative relief is sought has failed to plead or otherwise defend as provided by these rules and that fact is made to appear by affidavit or otherwise, the clerk shall enter the party's default.

(b) Judgment. Judgment by default may be entered as follows:

(1) *By the Clerk.* When the plaintiff's claim against a defendant is for a sum certain or for a sum which can by computation be made certain, the clerk upon request of the plaintiff and upon affidavit of the amount due shall enter judgment for that amount and costs against the defendant, if the defendant has been defaulted for failure to appear and is not an infant or incompetent person.

(2) *By the Court.* In all other cases the party entitled to a judgment by default shall apply to the court therefor; but no judgment by default shall be entered against an infant or incompetent person unless represented in the action by a general guardian, committee, conservator, or other such representative who has appeared therein. If the party against whom judgment by default is sought has appeared in the action, the party (or, if appearing by representative, the party's representative) shall be served with written notice of the application for judgment at least 3 days prior to the hearing on such application. If, in order to enable the court to enter judgment or to carry it into effect, it is necessary to take an account or to determine the amount of damages or to establish the truth of any averment by evidence or to make an investigation of any other matter, the court may conduct such hearings or order such references as it deems necessary and proper and shall accord a right of trial by jury to the parties when and as required by any statute of the United States.

(c) Setting Aside Default. For good cause shown the court may set aside an entry of default and, if a judgment by default has been entered, may likewise set it aside in accordance with Rule 60(b).

(d) Plaintiffs, Counterclaimants, Cross–Claimants. The provisions of this rule apply whether the party entitled to the judgment by default is a plaintiff, a third-party plaintiff, or a party who has pleaded a cross-claim or counterclaim. In all cases a judgment by default is subject to the limitations of Rule 54(c).

(e) Judgment Against the United States. No judgment by default shall be entered against the United States or an officer or agency thereof unless the claimant establishes a claim or right to relief by evidence satisfactory to the court.

[Amended effective August 1, 1987.]

AUTHORS' COMMENTARY ON RULE 55

PURPOSE AND SCOPE

Rule 55 sets the procedure for defaults and default judgments in the federal courts. Because default judgments are not favored by the courts, Rule 55 also defines the procedure for setting aside defaults and default judgments.

RULE 55(a). ENTRY OF DEFAULT

CORE CONCEPT

Upon motion of a party, the clerk of court may enter a default against a party who has failed to plead or otherwise defend.

APPLICATIONS

Distinguished From Default Judgment

The clerk's entry of a party's default is merely the official recognition that the party is in default.[1] The entry of default is a prerequisite for the entry of judgment upon that default.[2] It is, in effect, akin to a finding of liability with the entry of final judgment yet to come.[3] Thus, there are two stages in a default proceeding–the establishment of the default itself, followed by the entry of a default judgment.[4]

Prerequisites

The party against whom the default is entered must have been properly served with process, and the district court must enjoy subject

1. *See New York Life Ins. Co. v. Brown*, 84 F.3d 137, 141 (5th Cir.1996)(entry of default is made by clerk, once default established by affidavit or otherwise, after which application can be made for judgment upon that default); *Pinaud v. County of Suffolk*, 52 F.3d 1139, 1152 n. 11 (2d Cir.1995)(noting crucial distinction between entry of default and entry of default judgment; entry of default is essentially a formal matter, and is not a judgment); *Dahl v. Kanawha Investment Holding Co.*, 161 F.R.D. 673 (N.D.Iowa 1995)(commenting the entry of default is first of two steps prior to entry of default judgment).

2. *See Johnson v. Dayton Elec. Mfg. Co.*, 140 F.3d 781, 783 (8th Cir.1998); *Inman v. American Home Furniture Placement, Inc.*, 120 F.3d 117 (8th Cir.1997); *Lee v. Brotherhood of Maintenance of Way Employees*, 139 F.R.D. 376 (D.Minn.1991).

3. *See Alameda v. Secretary of Health, Educ. & Welfare*, 622 F.2d 1044, 1048 n. 3 (1st Cir. 1980).

4. *See In re Catt*, 368 F.3d 789, 793 (7th Cir. 2004).

matter jurisdiction and either personal or quasi-in-rem/in-rem jurisdiction over the defaulting party.[5] The clerk must also be satisfied, by the moving party's affidavit or otherwise, that the defaulting party has failed to plead or otherwise defend.[6]

Contested Motions for Entry of Default

Where a motion for entry of default is opposed by a party who has entered an appearance, the courts may, in considering the contested motion, apply the criteria guiding motions to set aside a default.[7]

Effect of Entry of Default

A defaulting party is deemed to have admitted all well-pleaded allegations of the complaint.[8]

Appealability

Entry of default is an interlocutory order, from which an immediate appeal ordinarily cannot be taken.[9]

RULE 55(b). ENTRY OF DEFAULT JUDGMENTS

CORE CONCEPT

Where the defendant has defaulted for failing to appear and the moving party has submitted evidence by affidavit establishing damages in a sum certain or in a sum that can be made certain by computation, the clerk of court may enter a default judgment upon motion. In all other cases, the *court* (and *not* the clerk of court) may enter a default judgment.

APPLICATIONS

Defendant's "Appearance"

A defendant "appears" in the action by making some presentation or submission to the court (*e.g.*, serving a responsive pleading, filing an entry of appearance, serving a Rule 12 motion to dismiss, or having

5. *See Maryland State Firemen's Ass'n v. Chaves*, 166 F.R.D. 353 (D.Md.1996)(noting that it is "axiomatic" that process must be properly served before a default or a default judgment may be entered); *Dahl v. Kanawha Investment Holding Co.*, 161 F.R.D. 673 (N.D.Iowa 1995)(as precondition for entry of default or default judgment, movant must show that proper service was made on defendants).

6. *See New York Life Ins. Co. v. Brown*, 84 F.3d 137, 141 (5th Cir.1996)(entry of default is made by clerk, once default established by affidavit or otherwise); *Martin v. Coughlin*, 895 F.Supp. 39 (N.D.N.Y.1995).

7. *See* Rule 55(c). *See also Schmir v. Prudential Ins. Co.*, 220 F.R.D. 4, 5 (D.Me. 2004) (applying Rule 55(c) factors, namely (1) whether default was willful, (2) prejudice to adversary, (3) whether meritorious defense is presented, (4) nature of explanation for default, (5) good faith of parties, (6) amount of money involved, (7) timing of motion, and (8) general philosophy favoring decisions on merits).

8. *See In re The Home Restaurants, Inc.*, 285 F.3d 111, 114 (1st Cir.2002); *Adkins v. Teseo*, 180 F.Supp.2d 15, 17 (D.D.C. 2001); *Taylor Made Golf Co. v. Carsten Sports, Ltd.*, 175 F.R.D. 658, 661 (S.D.Cal.1997); *Wing v. East River Chinese Restaurant*, 884 F.Supp. 663, 669 (E.D.N.Y.1995).

9. *See In re Lam*, 192 F.3d 1309, 1311 (9th Cir.1999); *Ackra Direct Mktg. Corp. v. Fingerhut Corp.*, 86 F.3d 852, 855 (8th Cir.1996).

counsel attend a conference on the client's behalf).[10] Some courts have taken an even wider view, ruling that "appearing" within the meaning of Rule 55(b) is defined broadly and is not necessarily limited to a formal filing in court.[11] In those courts, informal acts such as correspondence or telephone calls between counsel can constitute the requisite appearance,[12] as can engaging in settlement negotiations under certain circumstances.[13] Given the judicial philosophy disfavoring default judgments, the courts may search to find that an appearance has occurred.[14] Nevertheless, merely accepting or waiving service of process will not qualify as "appearing" within the meaning of this Rule.[15]

The Appearance 3–Day Rule

If a default judgment is being sought against a party who has "appeared" (as that term is used in Rule 55(b)), that party must be served with *written* notice of the application for a default judgment at least 3 days before the hearing.[16]

Default Judgment by Clerk of Court

The clerk of court may only enter a default judgment where the following three prerequisites are met:

1. The defendant was defaulted because of a failure to appear; and
2. The defendant is not an infant or incompetent person; and
3. The moving party submits an affidavit establishing that the amount due is either a sum certain or a sum that can be made certain by computation.

- *"Sum Certain" Defined:* A claim is not a "sum certain" under Rule 55 unless there is no doubt as to the amount that must be awarded.[17] The definition contemplates a context in

10. *See Sun Bank of Ocala v. Pelican Homestead & Savings Ass'n*, 874 F.2d 274, 276 (5th Cir.1989) (filing motion to dismiss constitutes "appearing"); *Hudson v. North Carolina*, 158 F.R.D. 78, 80 (E.D.N.C. 1994) (same); *ABI Investment Group v. FDIC*, 860 F.Supp. 911, 915 (D.N.H.1994) (same). *See also Lutwin v. City of New York*, 106 F.R.D. 502, 504 n.1 (S.D.N.Y. 1985) (attendance at conference sufficient to "appear"), *aff'd*, 795 F.2d 1004 (2d Cir.1986) (Table).

11. *See Silverman v. RTV Communications Group, Inc.*, 2002 WL 483421, at *3 (S.D.N.Y. 2002) (holding that appearance "is broadly defined and is not limited to a formal court filing"). *See also Rogers v. Hartford Life & Accident Ins. Co.*, 167 F.3d 933, 936–37 (5th Cir. 1999) (noting that Fifth Circuit does not construe "appeared" as requiring the filing of responsive papers or actual in-court actions by the defendant). *But see Town & Country Kids, Inc. v. Protected Venture Investment Trust #1, Inc.*, 178 F.R.D. 453, 455 (E.D.Va.1998) (holding that, for purposes of Rule 55(b), parties "appear" in action only where they make a presentation or submission to the court).

12. *See Sun Bank of Ocala v. Pelican Homestead & Savings Ass'n*, 874 F.2d 274, 276–77 (5th Cir.1989).

13. *See S.E.C. v. Getanswers, Inc.*, 219 F.R.D. 698, 700 (S.D.Fla. 2004).

14. *See Franchise Holding II, LLC. v. Huntington Restaurants Group, Inc.*, 375 F.3d 922, 927 (9th Cir. 2004).

15. *See Rogers v. Hartford Life & Accident Ins. Co.*, 167 F.3d 933, 936–37 (5th Cir.1999).

16. *See* Rule 55(b)(2).

17. *See Franchise Holding II, LLC. v. Huntington Restaurants Group, Inc.*, 375 F.3d 922, 928–29 (9th Cir. 2004); *KPS & Assocs., Inc. v. Designs By FMC, Inc.*, 318 F.3d 1, 19–20 (1st Cir.2003).

which, once liability is established, the amount due is beyond question (such as actions on money judgments or negotiable instruments).[18] This standard is not met where some portion of damages, such as "reasonable" attorney's fees or punitive damages, still needs to be fixed.[19]

Default Judgment by Court

In all other circumstances, the court may enter the default judgment:

1. Where the defendant has "appeared", in which case the appearing defendant must be served with written notice of the application for default judgment at least 3 days before any hearing on the application;[20]
2. Where the defendant is an infant or incompetent person, in which case a default judgment may be entered only if the infant or incompetent is represented;
3. Where the amount due is not certain, in which case the court may conduct a hearing, bench trial, or jury trial to assess damages; [21]

 Note: The court may either conduct an evidentiary hearing,[22] or may choose to rely simply on affidavits or other documentary evidence.[23] Whether to convene a hearing is a decision committed to the trial judge's discretion.[24] So long as there is a proper basis for awarding the damages specified in the default judgment, a hearing is not necessarily required.[25] If an evidentiary hearing is convened, the party seeking default bears the burden of proof[26], and the plead-

18. *See KPS & Assocs., Inc. v. Designs By FMC, Inc.*, 318 F.3d 1, 19–20 (1st Cir.2003)

19. *See Dailey v. R & J Commercial Contracting*, 2002 WL 484988, at *3 (S.D.Ohio 2002) (error for clerk to enter requested judgment involving punitive damages); *Combs v. Coal & Mineral Management Servs., Inc.*, 105 F.R.D. 472 (D.D.C.1984).

20. *See Canal Ins. Co. v. Dale Ashmore*, 61 F.3d 15 (8th Cir.1995)(abuse of discretion to fail to set aside default judgment where defendant never received notice); *D.B. v. Bloom*, 896 F.Supp. 166 (D.N.J.1995)(court must be satisfied that party received notice of motion).

21. *See Chudasama v. Mazda Motor Corp.*, 123 F.3d 1353, 1364 n. 27 (11th Cir.1997) (commenting that where amount of damages is disputed, only court—after determining the amount of damages—may enter default judgment); *Wing v. East River Chinese Restaurant*, 884 F.Supp. 663, 669 (E.D.N.Y.1995)(unless amount of damages is certain, court required to make independent determination of sum to be awarded; factors for court's consideration include amount potentially involved, whether material factual issues exist, whether default is "largely technical", prejudice to the movant, harshness of judgment, likelihood that default would be set aside).

22. *See Cablevision Sys. New York City Corp. v. Lokshin*, 980 F.Supp. 107, 111–12 (E.D.N.Y. 1997); *In re Crazy Eddie Secs. Litig.*, 948 F.Supp. 1154, 1160 (E.D.N.Y.1996).

23. *See Time Warner Cable of New York City v. Foote*, 2002 WL 1267993, at *4 (E.D.N.Y. 2002); *Cablevision Sys. New York City Corp. v. Lokshin*, 980 F.Supp. 107, 111–12 (E.D.N.Y. 1997); *In re Crazy Eddie Secs. Litig.*, 948 F.Supp. 1154, 1160 (E.D.N.Y.1996).

24. *See DIRECTV, Inc. v. Huynh*, 318 F.Supp.2d 1122, 1129 (M.D.Ala. 2004); *In re Crazy Eddie Secs. Litig.*, 948 F.Supp. 1154, 1160 (E.D.N.Y.1996).

25. *See Directv, Inc. v. Griffin*, 290 F.Supp.2d 1340, 1343–44 (M.D.Fla. 2003).

26. *See In re Catt*, 368 F.3d 789, 793 (7th Cir. 2004); *Oberstar v. F.D.I.C.*, 987 F.2d 494, 505 n. 9 (8th Cir.1993); *In re Crazy Eddie Secs. Litig.*, 948 F.Supp. 1154, 1160 (E.D.N.Y.1996).

ing's allegations regarding the amount of damages are not presumed true.[27] All reasonable inferences from the evidence offered, however, are drawn in the moving party's favor.[28]

4. Where the defendant has been defaulted for a reason other than a failure to appear (*e.g.,* failure to plead or otherwise defend).

Note: The entry of a default deprives a defendant of the right to contest the factual allegations of the complaint (unless the default is set aside),[29] but does not prevent the defendant from appearing to challenge the amount of damages.

Default in Multiple Defendant Cases

Where the plaintiff alleges joint liability against multiple defendants or the defendants have closely related defenses, the default of one defendant usually will not result in a judgment against that defendant. Instead, the court will allow the lawsuit to proceed as to the other, non-defaulting defendants. The result in the litigation (*e.g.*, judgment for plaintiff or judgment for defendants) will then simply be entered as to the defaulting defendant as well.[30]

Defaulting Defendants in the Military

The federal Soldiers' and Sailors' Civil Relief Act of 1940[31] prohibits the entry of any federal or State judgment by default against absent military defendants, unless the court first appoints counsel to represent the absent defendants' interests. Often, the court may simply stay a lawsuit against the absent military defendants until their return.

Note: In seeking a default judgment, a plaintiff must either set forth facts showing that the defaulting defendant is not in the military or provide an affidavit attesting to that fact.

Limitation on Default Judgments

No judgment by default can be greater in amount or different in kind from the demand contained in the complaint.[32]

27. *See In re Catt*, 368 F.3d 789, 793 (7th Cir. 2004).

28. *See Time Warner Cable of New York City v. Foote*, 2002 WL 1267993, at *4 (E.D.N.Y. 2002); *In re Crazy Eddie Secs. Litig.*, 948 F.Supp. 1154, 1160 (E.D.N.Y.1996).

29. *See Ramos–Falcon v. Autoridad de Energia Electrica*, 301 F.3d 1, 2 (1st Cir.2002) (if court examines complaint, it may take all well-pleaded factual allegations as true).

30. *See Frow v. De La Vega,* 82 U.S. (15 Wall.) 552, 21 L.Ed. 60 (1872). *But see Whelan v. Abell*, 953 F.2d 663 (D.C.Cir.1992), *cert. denied,* 506 U.S. 906, 113 S.Ct. 300, 121 L.Ed.2d 223 (1992)(construing *Frow* narrowly to hold that a default order that is inconsistent with a judgment on the merits must be set aside only where the liability is actually "joint" (i.e., where the theory of recovery would render all defendants (even the defaulting defendant) liable if any one of the defendants is liable)); *In re Uranium Antitrust Litig.*, 617 F.2d 1248, 1257–58 (7th Cir.1980) (same); *Douglas v. Metro Rental Servs., Inc.*, 827 F.2d 252 (7th Cir.1987)(same); *Martin v. Coughlin*, 895 F.Supp. 39 (N.D.N.Y. 1995)(same, and noting Second Circuit view that it is "most unlikely" that *Frow* principle survived promulgation of Rule 54(b)).

31. 50 U.S.C.A.App. § 501.

32. *See* Rule 55(d) and Rule 54(c).

Discretion of District Court

Judgments by default are disfavored and are never granted as a matter of right.[33] Whether to enter a judgment by default is a decision entrusted to the sound discretion of the district court.[34] Thus, a defendant's default does not necessarily entitle the plaintiff to an automatic default judgment.[35] Before exercising their discretion and entering a default judgment, some courts will examine the standards for setting aside a default.[36]

Appealability

The entry of a judgment by default is a final order, and is subject to immediate appeal.[37]

RULE 55(c). SETTING ASIDE DEFAULT

CORE CONCEPT

The court may set aside the entry of default for good cause shown, and may vacate a judgment by default in accordance with Rule 60(b)(which governs some of the grounds upon which a party may seek relief from the judgment).

APPLICATIONS

Setting Aside a Default

Rule 55(c) authorizes the district courts, "for good cause shown", to set aside the entry of a default.[38] Not susceptible to a precise definition, "good cause" has been labeled a liberal and "mutable" standard, one that varies from situation to situation.[39] In many jurisdictions, however, mere "good cause" alone is not sufficient. Instead, the courts examine many equitable criteria in determining whether to set aside a default. These criteria include: (1) proof that the default was not willful or culpable;[40] (2) prompt action by the defaulting party

33. *See Kauffman v. Cal Spas*, 37 F.Supp.2d 402, 404 (E.D.Pa.1999); *Patray v. Northwest Publ'g, Inc.*, 931 F.Supp. 865, 868 (S.D.Ga.1996).

34. *See Bender Shipbuilding & Repair Co., Inc. v. Vessel DRIVE OCEAN V*, 123 F.Supp. 2d 1201, 1208 (S.D.Cal.1998); *Patray v. Northwest Publ'g, Inc.*, 931 F.Supp. 865, 868 (S.D.Ga.1996); *D.B. v. Bloom*, 896 F.Supp. 166 (D.N.J.1995).

35. *See Philip Morris USA, Inc. v. Castworld Prods., Inc.*, 219 F.R.D. 494, 498 (C.D.Cal. 2003).

36. *See Philip Morris USA, Inc. v. Castworld Prods., Inc.*, 219 F.R.D. 494, 498 (C.D.Cal. 2003).

37. *See Ackra Direct Mktg. Corp. v. Fingerhut Corp.*, 86 F.3d 852, 855 n. 3 (8th Cir.1996).

38. *See African Methodist Episcopal Church, Inc. v. Ward*, 185 F.3d 1201, 1202 (11th Cir. 1999) (noting that district court may set aside entry of default only if good reason is provided).

39. *See Compania Interamericana Export–Import, S.A. v. Compania Dominicana de Aviacion*, 88 F.3d 948, 951 (11th Cir.1996).

40. *See SEC v. McNulty*, 137 F.3d 732, 738 (2d Cir.1998), *cert. denied*, 525 U.S. 931, 119 S.Ct. 340, 142 L.Ed.2d 281 (1998) (explaining that "willfulness" refers to more than merely negligent or careless conduct, but may be found where conduct was egregious and not adequately explained). *See also Franchise Holding II, LLC. v. Huntington Restaurants Group, Inc.*, 375 F.3d 922, 925–26 (9th Cir. 2004); *Effjohn Int'l Cruise Holdings, Inc. v. A & L Sales, Inc.*, 346 F.3d 552, 563 (5th Cir. 2003); *O.J. Distrib., Inc. v. Hornell Brewing Co.*, 340 F.3d 345, 353 (6th Cir.2003); *KPS & Assocs., Inc. v. Designs By FMC, Inc.*, 318 F.3d 1, 12 (1st Cir.2003) (same); *Pecarsky v. Galaxiworld.com Ltd.*, 249 F.3d 167, 170 (2d Cir.2001).

to correct the default;[41] (3) the existence of a meritorious defense;[42] (4) an absence of prejudice to the opponent;[43] (5) whether the default resulted from a good faith mistake in following a rule of procedure;[44] (6) the nature of the defendant's explanation for defaulting;[45] (7) the amount in controversy;[46] (8) the availability of effective alternative sanctions;[47] and (9) whether entry of a default would produce a harsh or unfair result.[48] Each particular consideration need not necessarily be satisfied,[49] and the list is generally seen as non-exhaustive, intended instead to serve only as a series of indicators of circumstances that could warrant setting aside a default.[50] Such determinations are neces-

41. *See Effjohn Int'l Cruise Holdings, Inc. v. A&L Sales, Inc.*, 346 F.3d 552, 563 (5th Cir. 2003); *KPS & Assocs., Inc. v. Designs By FMC, Inc.*, 318 F.3d 1, 12 (1st Cir.2003); *Lacy v. Sitel Corp.*, 227 F.3d 290, 291 (5th Cir.2000); *Compania Interamericana Export–Import, S.A. v. Compania Dominicana de Aviacion*, 88 F.3d 948, 951 (11th Cir.1996); *Jones v. Phipps*, 39 F.3d 158, 162 (7th Cir.1994).

42. *See also Franchise Holding II, LLC. v. Huntington Restaurants Group, Inc.*, 375 F.3d 922, 925–26 (9th Cir. 2004); *Effjohn Int'l Cruise Holdings, Inc. v. A & L Sales, Inc.*, 346 F.3d 552, 563 (5th Cir. 2003); *O.J. Distrib., Inc. v. Hornell Brewing Co.*, 340 F.3d 345, 353 (6th Cir.2003); *KPS & Assocs., Inc. v. Designs By FMC, Inc.*, 318 F.3d 1, 12 (1st Cir.2003); *Pecarsky v. Galaxiworld.com Ltd.*, 249 F.3d 167, 170 (2d Cir.2001).

43. *See SEC v. McNulty*, 137 F.3d 732, 740 (2d Cir.1998) (noting prejudice element, but clarifying that mere absence of prejudice would not automatically entitle defaulting party to relief), *cert. denied*, 525 U.S. 931, 119 S.Ct. 340, 142 L.Ed.2d 281 (1998); *East Coast Express, Inc. v. Ruby, Inc.*, 162 F.R.D. 37 (E.D.Pa.1995)(prejudice means a loss of evidence or the impairment of plaintiff's ability to press claim; prejudice not established merely by showing that litigation will continue absent default); *Momah v. Albert Einstein Medical Ctr.*, 161 F.R.D. 304, 307 (E.D.Pa.1995)(same); *Mathon v. Marine Midland Bank, N.A.*, 875 F.Supp. 986, 992 (E.D.N.Y. 1995)(noting that real prejudice is indicated by loss of evidence, unavailability of witnesses, or roadblocks to discovery). *See also Franchise Holding II, LLC. v. Huntington Restaurants Group, Inc.*, 375 F.3d 922, 925–26 (9th Cir. 2004); *Effjohn Int'l Cruise Holdings, Inc. v. A & L Sales, Inc.*, 346 F.3d 552, 563 (5th Cir. 2003); *O.J. Distrib., Inc. v. Hornell Brewing Co.*, 340 F.3d 345, 353 (6th Cir.2003); *KPS & Assocs., Inc. v. Designs By FMC, Inc.*, 318 F.3d 1, 12 (1st Cir.2003); *Pecarsky v. Galaxiworld.com Ltd.*, 249 F.3d 167, 170 (2d Cir.2001). Note that the practical reality that, absent default, the moving party would be required to litigate on the merits ordinarily does *not* qualify as "prejudice" within the meaning of Rule 55(c). *See Thiemann v. Electrical Insulation Suppliers, Inc.*, 180 F.R.D. 200, 201 (D.P.R.1998).

44. *See KPS & Assocs., Inc. v. Designs By FMC, Inc.*, 318 F.3d 1, 12 (1st Cir.2003); *Conetta v. National Hair Care Ctrs., Inc.*, 186 F.R.D. 262, 268–69 (D.R.I.1999); *Richardson v. Nassau County*, 184 F.R.D. 497, 501 (E.D.N.Y.1999); *Momah v. Albert Einstein Med. Ctr.*, 161 F.R.D. 304, 308 (E.D.Pa.1995).

45. *See KPS & Assocs., Inc. v. Designs By FMC, Inc.*, 318 F.3d 1, 12 (1st Cir.2003).

46. *See KPS & Assocs., Inc. v. Designs By FMC, Inc.*, 318 F.3d 1, 12 (1st Cir.2003); *Compania Interamericana Export–Import, S.A. v. Compania Dominicana de Aviacion*, 88 F.3d 948, 951 (11th Cir.1996).

47. *See Kauffman v. Cal Spas*, 37 F.Supp.2d 402, 404 (E.D.Pa.1999).

48. *See Richardson v. Nassau County*, 184 F.R.D. 497, 501 (E.D.N.Y.1999); *Canfield v. VSH Restaurant Corp.*, 162 F.R.D. 431 (N.D.N.Y. 1995).

49. *See Franchise Holding II, LLC. v. Huntington Restaurants Group, Inc.*, 375 F.3d 922, 926 (9th Cir. 2004) (commenting that factors are disjunctive, and motion for relief could be denied if any factor was true); *Conetta v. National Hair Care Ctrs., Inc.*, 186 F.R.D. 262, 268–69 (D.R.I. 1999) (commenting that no precise formula is required, and each case will turn on its own particular facts). *But see Messick v. Toyota Motor Mfg., Ky., Inc.*, 45 F.Supp.2d 578, 582 (E.D.Ky. 1999) (holding that movant *must* independently satisfy each of three factors—absence of culpability, absence of prejudice to the adversary, and existence of meritorious defense).

50. *See Effjohn Int'l Cruise Holdings, Inc. v. A&L Sales, Inc.*, 346 F.3d 552, 563 (5th Cir. 2003) (noting factors are non-exclusive, and "are to be regarded simply as a means to identify good cause"); *KPS & Assocs., Inc. v. Designs By FMC, Inc.*, 318 F.3d 1, 12 (1st Cir.2003) (noting court will consider "panoply of relevant equita-

sarily case-specific, and are made in a "practical, commonsense manner, without rigid adherence to, or undue reliance upon, a mechanical formula".[51] Note, however, that some courts conclude that the first criterion (willfulness) can, by itself, justify ending the inquiry and preserving the default.[52]

Note: In practice, any of the grounds that justify vacating a default judgment will likely also constitute adequate "good cause" to warrant setting aside the entry of a default. This "good cause" test is more lenient than the Rule 60(b) standard,[53] however, and some circumstances that might not justify relief from judgment under Rule 60(b) could still permit the setting aside of the entry of default under Rule 55(c)(*e.g.,* illness of counsel, mistake of counsel).

Vacating a Judgment by Default

Once a judgment is entered upon a party's default, the task of vacating it becomes more difficult. The court may vacate a default judgment if (1) the defaulting party meets the "good cause" test noted above, *and also* (2) satisfies one of the Rule 60(b) reasons for vacating a judgment (*i.e.*, mistake, inadvertence, surprise, excusable neglect, newly discovered evidence, misconduct by an adverse party, void judgment, or satisfied or discharged judgment).[54] The time for filing such motions is set forth in Rule 60(b).

Discretion of District Court

Defaults and default judgments are disfavored, as such remedies are inconsistent with the federal courts' preference for resolving disputes on their merits.[55] Thus, defaults are extreme sanctions[56] re-

ble factors"); *Fink v. Swisshelm*, 185 F.R.D. 353 (D.Kan.1999) (commenting that factors are not talismanic, and others may be considered); *Richardson v. Nassau County*, 184 F.R.D. 497, 501 (E.D.N.Y.1999) (same effect). *But cf. Conetta v. National Hair Care Ctrs., Inc.*, 186 F.R.D. 262, 269 (D.R.I.1999) (court may deny vacation where party claims to have simply "misplaced" the legal papers, to have negligently ignored deadlines, or to have avoided the case in the hope it "would all go away").

51. *See KPS & Assocs., Inc. v. Designs By FMC, Inc.*, 318 F.3d 1, 12 (1st Cir.2003).

52. *See Lacy v. Sitel Corp.*, 227 F.3d 290, 291 (5th Cir.2000) (commenting that a finding of intentional failure of responsive pleadings ends the need for further findings).

53. *See Dennis Garberg & Assocs., Inc. v. Pack–Tech Int'l Corp.*, 115 F.3d 767, 775 n. 6 (10th Cir.1997); *American Alliance Ins. Co. v. Eagle Ins. Co.*, 92 F.3d 57 (2d Cir.1996).

54. *See Brien v. Kullman Indus.*, 71 F.3d 1073, 1077 (2d Cir.1995) (noting factors including willfulness, the existence of a meritorious defense, and the level of prejudice to the non-defaulting party); *Enron Oil Corp. v. Diakuhara*, 10 F.3d 90, 96 (2d Cir.1993)(noting that factors for vacating a default judgment are largely the same as those for setting aside a default, except that the courts apply the factors more rigorously in cases of default judgments); *O'Brien v. R.J. O'Brien & Assocs., Inc.*, 998 F.2d 1394 (7th Cir.1993)(same); *East Coast Express, Inc. v. Ruby, Inc.*, 162 F.R.D. 37 (E.D.Pa. 1995)(court must consider defendant's meritorious defense, prejudice to plaintiff, culpability of defendant's conduct, and effectiveness of other sanctions).

55. *See Enron Oil Corp. v. Diakuhara*, 10 F.3d 90, 95–96 (2d Cir.1993); *United States on Behalf of and for Use of Time Equip. Rental & Sales, Inc. v. Harre*, 983 F.2d 128, 130 (8th Cir.1993);. *Richardson v. Nassau County*, 184 F.R.D. 497, 501 (E.D.N.Y.1999) (in deciding Rule 55(c) motion, court must be mindful of longstanding preference in the federal courts that litigation disputes be resolved on their merits).

56. *See D.B. v. Bloom*, 896 F.Supp. 166 (D.N.J.1995); *Martin v. Coughlin*, 895 F.Supp. 39 (N.D.N.Y.1995)(default judgment is extreme

served for rare occasions, the "good faith" criteria are applied generously,[57] and doubts are resolved in favor of lifting the default.[58] Whether to set aside the entry of default or vacate a default judgment is left to the discretion of the district judge.[59]

RULE 55(d). RULE 55 APPLIES TO PLAINTIFFS, AS WELL AS COUNTERCLAIMANTS, CROSS–CLAIMANTS, AND THIRD–PARTY PLAINTIFFS

CORE CONCEPT

The default provisions of Rule 55 apply equally to plaintiffs, third-party plaintiffs, counterclaimants, and cross-claimants.[60]

APPLICATIONS

Same Rule 55 Standards Apply

Third-party plaintiffs, counterclaimants, and cross-claimants may also invoke the default provisions of Rule 55.[61] In ruling on default applications by these claimants, the same standards apply as would for a plaintiff.[62]

RULE 55(e). DEFAULT JUDGMENT AGAINST THE UNITED STATES

CORE CONCEPT

No default judgment may be entered against the United States or any federal agency or officer, unless the plaintiff establishes for the court, by satisfactory evidence, a claim or right to relief.

APPLICATIONS

Policy

The entry of default judgments against the United States is not favored. The courts reason that federal taxpayers (on whom the

sanction, and "a weapon of last, and not first, resort").

57. *See Martin v. Coughlin*, 895 F.Supp. 39 (N.D.N.Y.1995).

58. *See Powerserve Int'l, Inc. v. Lavi*, 239 F.3d 508, 514 (2d Cir.2001); *Lacy v. Sitel Corp.*, 227 F.3d 290, 291 (5th Cir.2000); *Enron Oil Corp. v. Diakuhara*, 10 F.3d 90, 96 (2d Cir.1993); *Choice Hotels Int'l, Inc. v. Pennave Assocs., Inc.*, 192 F.R.D. 171, 173–74 (E.D.Pa.2000); *Conetta v. National Hair Care Ctrs., Inc.*, 186 F.R.D. 262, 268 (D.R.I.1999); *Richardson v. Nassau County*, 184 F.R.D. 497, 501 (E.D.N.Y.1999); *Canfield v. VSH Restaurant Corp.*, 162 F.R.D. 431 (N.D.N.Y. 1995).

59. *See O.J. Distrib., Inc. v. Hornell Brewing Co.*, 340 F.3d 345, 353 (6th Cir.2003); *Bailey v. United Airlines*, 279 F.3d 194, 204 (3d Cir.2002); *Powerserve Int'l, Inc. v. Lavi*, 239 F.3d 508, 514 (2d Cir.2001); *Lacy v. Sitel Corp.*, 227 F.3d 290, 291 (5th Cir.2000).

60. *See Viveros v. Nationwide Janitorial Ass'n, Inc.*, 200 F.R.D. 681, 684 (N.D.Ga.2000) (granting default for defendant where plaintiff failed to answer counterclaim).

61. *See Iraola & CIA, S.A. v. Kimberly–Clark Corp.*, 31 F.Supp.2d 1378, 1380 (N.D.Ga.1998) (entering default on counterclaim).

62. *See, e.g., Continental Casualty Co. v. Diversified Indus.*, 884 F.Supp. 937, 963 (E.D.Pa. 1995)(noting same judicial discretion whether to enter default judgment).

burden of the default judgment would ultimately rest) should not be called upon to pay a penalty imposed as the consequence of the neglect of some government official, if to do so would cause a windfall to the litigant.[63]

Applies Only to Judgments, Not Defaults

Although default judgments may not be entered against the United States, the default itself may be entered.[64]

Claim-or-Right-to-Relief Inquiry

The court's inquiry to determine whether the plaintiff has a claim or a right-to-relief against the United States (and, thus, should be entitled to seek a default judgment) does not necessarily require a hearing, or either more or different evidence than would otherwise be received.[65] (Although at least one court has ruled that the burden for default against the United States is "higher", and requires a demonstration of an evidentiary basis that is legally sufficient for a reasonable jury to find for the plaintiff.[66]) Instead, the courts assume a flexible approach in determining the procedures necessary to conduct this inquiry.[67]

ADDITIONAL RESEARCH REFERENCES

Wright & Miller, *Federal Practice and Procedure* §§ 2681–2702.

C.J.S. Federal Civil Procedure §§ 1122–1134 et seq.

West's Key No. Digests, Federal Civil Procedure ⚷2411–2455.

63. *See Compania Interamericana Export–Import, S.A. v. Compania Dominicana de Aviacion*, 88 F.3d 948, 951 (11th Cir.1996); *ABI Investment Group v. FDIC*, 860 F.Supp. 911, 914 (D.N.H.1994). The Foreign Sovereign Immunities Act, 28 U.S.C.A. § 1608(e), provides foreign sovereigns with this same protection against default judgments in federal courts. *See Commercial Bank of Kuwait v. Rafidain Bank*, 15 F.3d 238, 242 (2d Cir.1994); *Nationsbank of Florida v. Banco Exterior de Espana*, 867 F.Supp. 167, 174 (S.D.N.Y.1994)(commenting that court's preference for denying motion for default judgment is particularly strong where the defendant is a foreign sovereign; when foreign sovereign defaults, movant bears the burden to show sufficient evidence that default judgment is appropriate).

64. *See Alameda v. Secretary of Health, Educ. & Welfare*, 622 F.2d 1044, 1048 (1st Cir. 1980)(noting that default may be entered, and commenting that the exemption from default judgments "heightens" the United States' obligation to cooperate with the court).

65. *See Commercial Bank of Kuwait v. Rafidain Bank*, 15 F.3d 238, 242 (2d Cir.1994).

66. *See Smith ex rel. Smith v. Islamic Emirate of Afghanistan*, 262 F.Supp.2d 217, 223–24 (S.D.N.Y.2003).

67. *See Gadoury v. United States*, 187 B.R. 816, 822 (D.R.I.1995).

RULE 56

SUMMARY JUDGMENT

(a) For Claimant. A party seeking to recover upon a claim, counterclaim, or cross-claim or to obtain a declaratory judgment may, at any time after the expiration of 20 days from the commencement of the action or after service of a motion for summary judgment by the adverse party, move with or without supporting affidavits for a summary judgment in the party's favor upon all or any part thereof.

(b) For Defending Party. A party against whom a claim, counterclaim, or cross-claim is asserted or a declaratory judgment is sought may, at any time, move with or without supporting affidavits for a summary judgment in the party's favor as to all or any part thereof.

(c) Motion and Proceedings Thereon. The motion shall be served at least 10 days before the time fixing for the hearing. The adverse party prior to the day of hearing may serve opposing affidavits. The judgment sought shall be rendered forthwith if the pleadings, depositions, answers to interrogatories, and admissions on file, together with the affidavits, if any, show that there is no genuine issue as to any material fact and that the moving party is entitled to a judgment as a matter of law. A summary judgment, interlocutory in character, may be rendered on the issue of liability alone although there is a genuine issue as to the amount of damages.

(d) Case Not Fully Adjudicated on Motion. If on motion under this rule judgment is not rendered upon the whole case or for all the relief asked and a trial is necessary, the court at the hearing of the motion, by examining the pleadings and the evidence before it and by interrogating counsel, shall if practicable ascertain what material facts exist without substantial controversy and what material facts are actually and in good faith controverted. It shall thereupon make an order specifying the facts that appear without substantial controversy, including the extent to which the amount of damages or other relief is not in controversy, and directing such further proceedings in the action as are just. Upon the trial of the action the facts so specified shall be deemed established, and the trial shall be conducted accordingly.

(e) Form of Affidavits; Further Testimony; Defense Required. Supporting and opposing affidavits shall be made on personal knowledge, shall set forth such facts as would be admissible in evidence, and shall show affirmatively that the affiant is competent to testify to the matters stated therein. Sworn or certified copies of all papers or parts thereof referred to in an affidavit shall be attached thereto or served therewith. The court may permit affidavits to be supplemented or opposed by depositions, answers to interrogatories, or further affidavits. When a motion for summary judgment is made and supported as provided in this rule, an adverse party may not rest upon the mere allegations or denials of the adverse party's pleading, but the adverse party's response, by affidavits or as otherwise provided in this rule, must set forth specific facts showing that there is a genuine issue for trial. If the adverse party does not so respond, summary judgment if appropriate, shall be entered against the adverse party.

(f) When Affidavits Are Unavailable. Should it appear from the affidavits of a party opposing the motion that the party cannot for reasons stated present by affidavit facts essential to justify the party's opposition, the court may refuse the application for judgment or may order a continuance to permit affidavits to be obtained or depositions to be taken or discovery to be had or may make such other order as is just.

(g) Affidavits Made in Bad Faith. Should it appear to the satisfaction of the court at any time that any of the affidavits presented pursuant to this rule are presented in bad faith or solely for the purpose of delay, the court shall forthwith order the party employing them to pay to the other party the amount of the reasonable expenses which the filing of the affidavits caused the other party to incur, including reasonable attorney's fees, and any offending party or attorney may be adjudged guilty of contempt.

[Amended effective March 19, 1948; July 1, 1963; August 1, 1987.]

AUTHORS' COMMENTARY ON RULE 56

PURPOSE AND SCOPE

Rule 56 sets the procedure by which a party may request or oppose summary judgment, and the standards the federal courts consider when ruling on motions for summary judgment.

COMPARISONS WITH OTHER RULES OF ADJUDICATION

Dismissals and Judgments on the Pleadings: When granting a dismissal under Rule 12(b)(6) or a judgment on the pleadings under Rule 12(c), the district judge generally examines only the allegations contained in the non-moving party's pleadings to determine whether the averments of law and fact, if true, are legally sufficient. In contrast, a motion for summary judgment under Rule 56 permits the district judge to consult not only the pleadings, but also any affidavits, depositions, interrogatory answers, admissions, and other evidence to determine whether any factual dispute exists between the parties.

Note: A motion to dismiss under Rule 12(b)(6) for failing to state a claim upon which relief can be granted, or a motion for judgment on the pleadings under Rule 12(c), will be converted into a Rule 56 motion for summary judgment if the court considers matters outside the pleadings in ruling on the motion.[1]

Judgments as a Matter of Law: The prerequisites for and effect of summary judgments is much the same as judgments as a matter of law, entered under Rule 50 (the federal equivalent of a "directed verdict").[2] Both motions test for whether, on the evidence then before the court, a reasonable jury could return a verdict in the nonmoving party's favor. Both motions, if granted, will result in a "judgment" in the movant's favor. The difference between the motions is largely one of timing. Summary judgment motions are filed before trial begins and are supported by pleadings, discovery responses, affidavits, deposition excerpts, documents, and other "cold" evidence. Conversely, motions for judgment as a matter of law are made during trial, after the close of the plaintiff's case (and, possibly, the defendant's case), with the trial judge having listened to a full, live evidentiary presentation. Thus, Rule 50 motions challenge whether there is any need for the trial—then underway—to reach the jury deliberation stage; Rule 56 motions challenge whether there is any need to convene a trial at all.

RULE 56(a)–(b). PARTIES WHO MAY MAKE MOTION

CORE CONCEPT

Motions for summary judgment may be filed in any federal court action—whether at law or equity—by any party, plaintiff or defendant, and against any party, including the United States, its agencies and officers.

APPLICATIONS

Motions by Claimants

Summary judgment is not only a defensive tool; claimants can move

1. *See* Rule 12(b) & Rule 12(c). *See also* **Authors' Commentary** to Rule 12(b) & Rule 12(c).

2. *See Anderson v. Liberty Lobby, Inc.*, 477 U.S. 242, 250–51, 106 S.Ct. 2505, 2511, 91 L.Ed.2d 202 (1986) (noting that summary judgment standard "mirrors the standard for a directed verdict under Federal Rule of Civil Procedure 50(a), which is that the trial judge must direct a verdict if, under the governing law, there can be but one reasonable conclusion as to the verdict").

for summary judgment on their own claims as well.[3] There is a timing restriction on motions by claimants, however. Claimants must wait to file such motions until 20 days after the lawsuit was commenced or immediately after the defendant files her motion for summary judgment, whichever is earlier.[4]

Motions by Defending Parties

Defending parties may move for summary judgment at any time.[5] Note, however, that the case law is unclear whether moving for summary judgment tolls the time for filing an answer to the complaint.[6] The filing of an answer is clearly not, however, a prerequisite for filing a summary judgment motion.[7]

"Premature" Motions

Recent appellate courts seem to have rejected the notion that a summary judgment motion (which otherwise comports with Rule 56(a) or Rule 56(b)) can be "premature" simply because it was filed before discovery is completed or even begun.[8] Such a conclusion is somewhat at odds with the Supreme Court's admonition in 1986 that summary judgment may be granted only after the nonmoving party has had an "adequate time for discovery".[9] It would seem, therefore, that prediscovery summary judgments should more appropriately be the exception, rather than the rule.[10]

3. *See Bouchat v. Baltimore Ravens Football Club, Inc.*, 346 F.3d 514, 521 (4th Cir. 2003), *cert. denied*, ___ U.S. ___, 124 S.Ct. 2171, 158 L.Ed.2d 732 (2004).

4. *See G & G Fire Sprinklers, Inc. v. Bradshaw*, 136 F.3d 587 (9th Cir.1998), *amended and superseded on other grounds*, 156 F.3d 893 (9th Cir.1998), *vacated on other grounds*, 526 U.S. 1061, 119 S.Ct. 1450, 143 L.Ed.2d 538 (1999)(rejecting argument that plaintiff's motion for summary judgment was "premature" when it was filed more than 20 days after lawsuit was commenced and no motion under Rule 56(f) was pending); *United States v. Cannabis Cultivators Club*, 5 F.Supp.2d 1086 (N.D.Cal.1998) (ruling that plaintiff's motion for summary judgment was premature where it was filed at the same time as the lawsuit itself).

5. *See Jefferson v. Chattanooga Pub. Co.*, 375 F.3d 461, 463 (6th Cir. 2004); *Alexander v. Pathfinder, Inc.*, 189 F.3d 735, 744 (8th Cir.1999); *Mattei v. Mattei*, 126 F.3d 794, 807 (6th Cir. 1997), *cert. denied*, 523 U.S. 1120, 118 S.Ct. 1799, 140 L.Ed.2d 939 (1998); *Brill v. Lante Corp.*, 119 F.3d 1266 (7th Cir.1997); *Cupit v. United States*, 964 F.Supp. 1104, 1106 (W.D.La. 1997).

6. *Compare Poe v. Cristina Copper Mines, Inc.*, 15 F.R.D. 85 (D.Del.1953)(holding that summary judgment motion does not automatically toll the period for answering) *with Rashidi v. Albright*, 818 F.Supp. 1354 (D.Nev. 1993)(holding that summary judgment motion will toll the period for answering), *aff'd*, 39 F.3d 1188 (9th Cir.1994)(table).

7. *See HS Resources, Inc. v. Wingate*, 327 F.3d 432, 440 (5th Cir.2003).

8. *See, e.g., Alholm v. American Steamship Co.*, 144 F.3d 1172, 1177 (8th Cir.1998) (noting that Rule 56 does not require that discovery be closed before motion can be heard); *G & G Fire Sprinklers, Inc. v. Bradshaw*, 136 F.3d 587 (9th Cir.1998), *amended and superseded on other grounds*, 156 F.3d 893 (9th Cir.1998), *vacated on other grounds*, 526 U.S. 1061, 119 S.Ct. 1450, 143 L.Ed.2d 538 (1999) (rejecting argument that plaintiff's motion for summary judgment was "premature" when it was filed more than 20 days after lawsuit was commenced and no motion under Rule 56(f) was pending); *Brill v. Lante Corp.*, 119 F.3d 1266, 1275 (7th Cir.1997) (commenting that plaintiff's argument that summary judgment should not have been granted while discovery remained open is an argument that "hardly concerns us because a party can file a motion for summary judgment at any time, indeed, even before discovery has begun").

9. *Celotex Corp. v. Catrett*, 477 U.S. 317, 322, 106 S.Ct. 2548, 2552, 91 L.Ed.2d 265 (1986). *Accord Jefferson v. Chattanooga Pub. Co.*, 375 F.3d 461, 463 (6th Cir. 2004).

10. *See Patton v. General Signal Corp.*, 984 F.Supp. 666, 670 (W.D.N.Y.1997) (commenting

Cross–Motions

Both parties may file for summary judgment in the same action, with "cross-motions" under Rule 56.

RULE 56(c). MOTION AND PROCEEDINGS FOR SUMMARY JUDGMENT

Core Concept

The district court may enter summary judgment when the motion papers, affidavits, and other evidence submitted to the court show that no genuine issue exists as to any material fact, and that the moving party is entitled to judgment as a matter of law.

APPLICATIONS

Purpose of Summary Judgment

The purpose of summary judgment is to isolate, and then terminate, claims and defenses that are factually unsupported.[11] The Supreme Court has emphasized that summary judgment is to be viewed not as a disfavored technical shortcut, but rather as an integral component of the Federal Rules.[12] Summary judgment motions must be resolved not only with an appropriate regard for the rights of those asserting claims and defenses to have their positions heard by a factfinder, but also with due regard for the rights of persons opposing such claims and defenses to demonstrate, under this Rule and *before* trial, that the claims and defenses have no factual basis.[13] Thus, a party moving for summary judgment forces the opponent to come forward with at least one sworn averment of specific fact essential to that opponent's claims or defenses, before the time-consuming process of litigation will continue.[14]

Seventh Amendment Jury Rights: A proper entry of summary judgment does not violate the nonmoving party's constitutional

that "pre-discovery summary judgment remains the exception rather than the rule, and will be 'granted only in the clearest of cases' "). *See also Information Handling Servs., Inc. v. Defense Automated Printing Servs.*, 338 F.3d 1024, 1032 (D.C.Cir.2003) (commenting that summary judgment is ordinarily proper only when plaintiff has had adequate time for discovery); *Miller v. Wolpoff & Abramson, L.L.P.*, 321 F.3d 292, 303–04 (2d Cir.2003), *cert.denied,* 540 U.S. 823, 124 S.Ct. 153, 157 L.Ed.2d 44 (2003) (pre-discovery summary judgment granted in only rarest cases), *petition for cert. filed*, 71 U.S.L.W. 3791 (U.S. June 17, 2003) (No. 02–1820); *Vaughn v. United States Small Bus. Admin.*, 65 F.3d 1322, 1325 n. 1 (6th Cir.1995) (defendant's summary judgment motion cannot ordinarily be considered until the plaintiff has had the opportunity to conduct discovery).

11. *See Celotex Corp. v. Catrett*, 477 U.S. 317, 323–24, 106 S.Ct. 2548, 2552–53, 91 L.Ed.2d 265 (1986).

12. *See Celotex Corp. v. Catrett*, 477 U.S. 317, 327, 106 S.Ct. 2548, 2554, 91 L.Ed.2d 265 (1986).

13. *See Celotex Corp. v. Catrett*, 477 U.S. 317, 327, 106 S.Ct. 2548, 2554, 91 L.Ed.2d 265 (1986).

14. *See Lujan v. National Wildlife Fed'n*, 497 U.S. 871, 888–89, 110 S.Ct. 3177, 3188–89, 111 L.Ed.2d 695 (1990).

right under the Seventh Amendment to a trial by jury; a properly entered Rule 56 judgment means that no triable issue exists to be submitted to a jury.[15]

Standards for Granting or Denying Summary Judgment

Summary judgment is to be rendered "forthwith" when, after an adequate period for discovery,[16] one party is unable to show a genuine issue as to a material fact on which that party will bear the burden of proof at trial, so long as judgment against that party is appropriate as a matter of law.[17]

Genuine Issue: A "genuine issue" exists where the evidence before the court is of such a nature that a reasonable jury could return a verdict in favor of the non-moving party. This standard parallels the test for judgment as a matter of law under Rule 50(a): a mere "scintilla" of evidence, or evidence that is only "colorable" or is not sufficiently probative, is not enough to defeat summary judgment. Instead, there must be evidence upon which a jury could reasonably find in the non-moving party's favor.[18] Conversely, where the evidence presented in support of the motion fails to demonstrate the absence of a genuine issue, summary judgment will be denied even though no opposing evidentiary matter is submitted.[19]

Controlling Legal Standard: The court will test for a "genuine issue" through the prism of the applicable controlling legal standard—the quantum and quality of proof necessary to support liability under the claims raised. Thus, if the plaintiff must prove its case by clear and convincing evidence, the court will assess whether the evidence in the summary judgment record would allow a rational factfinder to find for the plaintiff by that standard of clear and convincing evidence.[20]

Material Fact: Whether a fact is "material" hinges on the substantive law at issue. A fact is "material" if it might affect the

15. *See Shannon v. Graves*, 257 F.3d 1164, 1167 (10th Cir.2001) (citing *Fidelity & Deposit Co. v. United States*, 187 U.S. 315, 319–20, 23 S.Ct. 120, 121-122, 47 L.Ed. 194 (1902)).

16. *See Celotex Corp. v. Catrett*, 477 U.S. 317, 322, 106 S.Ct. 2548, 2552, 91 L.Ed.2d 265 (1986). *See* **Authors' Commentary** to Rule 56(a)–(b), *supra*, "Premature" Motions, (discussion of pre-discovery motions for summary judgment).

17. *See Department of Commerce v. U.S. House of Representatives*, 525 U.S. 316, 327, 119 S.Ct. 765, 772, 142 L.Ed.2d 797 (1999); *Nebraska v. Wyoming*, 507 U.S. 584, 589, 113 S.Ct. 1689, 1694, 123 L.Ed.2d 317 (1993); *Celotex Corp. v. Catrett*, 477 U.S. 317, 322, 106 S.Ct. 2548, 2552, 91 L.Ed.2d 265 (1986). *See also United States Fidelity & Guaranty Co. v. Planters Bank & Trust Co.*, 77 F.3d 863, 866 (5th Cir.1996)(noting that court of appeals recognizes a "hint of a distinction" between the standard applied in jury cases and an arguably more lenient standard in certain non-jury cases).

18. *See Anderson v. Liberty Lobby, Inc.*, 477 U.S. 242, 248–52, 106 S.Ct. 2505, 2510–12, 91 L.Ed.2d 202 (1986). *Cf. Matsushita Elec. Indus. Co. v. Zenith Radio Corp.*, 475 U.S. 574, 587, 106 S.Ct. 1348, 1356, 89 L.Ed.2d 538 (1986)(commenting that where factual context of claim or defense is implausible, the non-moving party must come forward with more persuasive evidence than would otherwise be necessary).

19. *See Torres–Rosado v. Rotger–Sabat*, 335 F.3d 1, 9 (1st Cir.2003).

20. *See Anderson v. Liberty Lobby, Inc.*, 477 U.S. 242, 254, 106 S.Ct. 2505, 2513, 91 L.Ed.2d 202 (1986).

outcome of the case.[21] Disputes over irrelevant or unnecessary facts are insufficient to defeat a motion for summary judgment.[22]

Appropriate As A Matter Of Law: Judgment is appropriate "as a matter of law" when the nonmoving party has failed to make an adequate showing on an essential element of her case, as to which she has the burden of proof.[23]

Predominantly Legal Disputes

Summary judgment is often especially appropriate in cases where the remaining unresolved disputes are primarily legal, rather than factual in nature.[24]

Discretion of District Court

The court *must* deny summary judgment when a genuine issue of material fact remains to be tried, or where the moving party is not entitled to a judgment as a matter of law. In all other cases, the court enjoys some discretion to deny summary judgment where the court concludes that a fuller factual development is necessary[25] or where there is some particular reason to believe that the wiser course would be to proceed to trial.[26]

Warning to Unrepresented Parties

Before summary judgment may be entered against unrepresented litigants, some courts require that the unrepresented party first be expressly informed of the consequences that may follow from failing to come forward with contradicting evidence (*e.g.*, the party must be told he or she cannot rely merely on the allegations of the pleadings, and risks dismissal in doing so).[27] Other courts recognize this special warning duty, but only in the context of incarcerated unrepresented parties.[28] As to nonprisoner unrepresented parties, those courts would

21. *See Anderson v. Liberty Lobby, Inc.*, 477 U.S. 242, 248, 106 S.Ct. 2505, 2510, 91 L.Ed.2d 202 (1986). *See also Wright ex rel. Trust Co. of Kansas v. Abbott Laboratories, Inc.*, 259 F.3d 1226, 1231–32 (10th Cir.2001) ("material" if, under substantive law, fact is "essential to the proper disposition of the claim"); *Hoffman-Dombrowski v. Arlington Int'l Racecourse, Inc.*, 254 F.3d 644, 650 (7th Cir.2001) ("material" if fact "might affect the outcome of the suit under the governing law").

22. *See Anderson v. Liberty Lobby, Inc.*, 477 U.S. 242, 248, 106 S.Ct. 2505, 2510, 91 L.Ed.2d 202 (1986). *See also State Auto. Ins. Co. v. Lawrence*, 358 F.3d 982, 985 (8th Cir. 2004) ("dispute must be outcome determinative under prevailing law".)

23. *See Cleveland v. Policy Management Sys. Corp.*, 526 U.S. 795, 804, 119 S.Ct. 1597, 1603, 143 L.Ed.2d 966 (1999); *Celotex Corp. v. Catrett*, 477 U.S. 317, 323, 106 S.Ct. 2548, 2552, 91 L.Ed.2d 265 (1986); *Waterhouse v. District of Columbia*, 298 F.3d 989, 922 (D.C.Cir.2002). *See also Young Dental Mfg. Co., Inc. v. Q3 Special Prods., Inc.*, 112 F.3d 1137, 1141 (Fed.Cir.1997) (even if material facts remain disputed, summary judgment may be proper if, after all inferences are drawn in the nonmoving party's favor, the moving party is entitled to judgment as a matter of law).

24. *See Koehn v. Indian Hills Cmty. Coll.*, 371 F.3d 394, 396 (8th Cir. 2004).

25. *See Kennedy v. Silas Mason Co.*, 334 U.S. 249, 68 S.Ct. 1031, 92 L.Ed. 1347 (1948).

26. *See Anderson v. Liberty Lobby, Inc.*, 477 U.S. 242, 255, 106 S.Ct. 2505, 2513, 91 L.Ed.2d 202 (1986).

27. *See United States v. Ninety Three Firearms*, 330 F.3d 414, 427 (6th Cir.2003) (collecting cases); *Bryant v. Madigan*, 84 F.3d 246, 248 (7th Cir.1996) (Posner, J.).

28. *See United States v. Ninety Three Firearms*, 330 F.3d 414, 427–28 (6th Cir.2003).

require no special warning.[29]

Burden of Proof

The party moving for summary judgment always has the burden of persuasion on such a motion. The burden of going forward, however, shifts during the motion process.

The moving party must first make a prima facie showing that summary judgment is appropriate under Rule 56. This does not require the moving party to disprove the opponent's claims or defenses. Instead, this prima facie burden is discharged simply by pointing out for the court an absence of evidence in support of the non-moving party's claims or defenses. The burden of going forward then shifts to the non-moving party to show, by affidavit or otherwise, that a genuine issue of material fact remains for the factfinder to resolve.[30] The non-moving party must carry this burden as to each essential element on which she bears the burden of proof.[31] A party does *not* meet this burden simply by theorizing a "plausible scenario" in support of the party's claims, when that proffered scenario conflicts with direct, contrary evidence.[32]

The burden of showing the existence or absence of a disputed issue of material fact will rarely shift to the trial judge. Most courts that have considered the issue have ruled that the trial judge is not generally obligated to conduct an independent review of the record, sifting through the often voluminous record, unguided, searching for a genuine issue of fact sufficient to defeat summary judgment.[33] Not all courts agree, however. Some courts seem to hold that the district judge has such an independent obligation generally,[34] or must conduct such an independent search in certain cases, such as those involving the First Amendment.[35]

Doubts and Inferences

In ruling on a motion for summary judgment, the court will never weigh the evidence or find the facts. Instead, the court's role under

29. *See United States v. Ninety Three Firearms*, 330 F.3d 414, 428 (6th Cir.2003) (citing other precedent in concluding that this distinction "was only fair because parties choosing to have counsel 'must bear the risk of their attorney's mistakes,' and thus, 'a litigant who chooses himself as a legal representative should be treated no differently' ").

30. *See Celotex Corp. v. Catrett,* 477 U.S. 317, 106 S.Ct. 2548, 91 L.Ed.2d 265 (1986).

31. *See Wheeler v. Aventis Pharms.*, 360 F.3d 853, 857 (8th Cir. 2004).

32. *See Swanson v. Leggett & Platt, Inc.*, 154 F.3d 730, 733 (7th Cir.1998).

33. *See Amnesty America v. Town of West Hartford*, 288 F.3d 467, 470 (2d Cir.2002); *Carmen v. San Francisco Unified Sch. Dist.*, 237 F.3d 1026, 1030–31 (9th Cir.2001); *Jackson v. Finnegan, Henderson, Farabow, Garrett & Dunner*, 101 F.3d 145, 154 (D.C.Cir.1996); *L.S. Heath & Son, Inc. v. AT & T Information Sys., Inc.*, 9 F.3d 561, 567 (7th Cir.1993); *Guarino v. Brookfield Township Trustees*, 980 F.2d 399, 405–06 (6th Cir.1992); *Skotak v. Tenneco Resins, Inc.*, 953 F.2d 909, 915 n. 7 & 916 n. 8 (5th Cir.1992), *cert. denied*, 506 U.S. 832, 113 S.Ct. 98, 121 L.Ed.2d 59 (1992).

34. *See Stepanischen v. Merchants Despatch Trans. Corp.*, 722 F.2d 922, 931 (1st Cir.1983) (holding that Rule 56(c) imposes on trial courts the duty to examine all evidence "on file").

35. *See Anderson v. McCotter*, 100 F.3d 723, 725 (10th Cir.1996) (noting that when First Amendment values are implicated, the court must independently examine whole record to ensure that its judgment does not improperly intrude on the field of free expression).

Rule 56 is narrowly limited to assessing the threshold issue of whether a genuine issue exists as to material facts requiring a trial.[36] Thus, the evidence of the non-moving party will be believed as true, all doubts will be resolved against the moving party, all evidence will be construed in the light most favorable to the non-moving party, and all reasonable inferences will be drawn in the non-moving party's favor.[37]

"Reasonable" inferences are inferences reasonably drawn from all the facts then before the court, after sifting through the universe of all possible inferences the facts could support. "Reasonable" inferences are not necessarily more probable or likely than other inferences that might tilt in the moving party's favor. Instead, so long as more than one reasonable inference can be drawn, and that inference creates a genuine issue of material fact, the trier of fact is entitled to decide which inference to believe and summary judgment is not appropriate.[38]

Ordinarily, an appropriately supported summary judgment motion cannot be defeated by inferences that are improbable, allegations that are conclusory, or rank speculation.[39]

Credibility Questions

The court will not weigh the credibility of witnesses or other evidence in ruling on a motion for summary judgment. Evaluating credibility, weighing evidence, and drawing factual inferences are all functions reserved for the jury.[40]

State of Mind Questions

Summary judgment is never automatically foreclosed merely because a person's state of mind (such as motive, knowledge, intent, good faith or bad faith, malice, fraud, conspiracy, or consent) is at issue.[41] But such cases will seldom lend themselves to a summary disposition

36. *See Anderson v. Liberty Lobby, Inc.*, 477 U.S. 242, 249, 106 S.Ct. 2505, 2510, 91 L.Ed.2d 202 (1986).

37. *See Hunt v. Cromartie*, 526 U.S. 541, 550–55, 119 S.Ct. 1545, 1551–52, 143 L.Ed.2d 731 (1999); *Eastman Kodak Co. v. Image Technical Servs., Inc.*, 504 U.S. 451, 456, 112 S.Ct. 2072, 2076, 119 L.Ed.2d 265 (1992); *Anderson v. Liberty Lobby, Inc.*, 477 U.S. 242, 255, 106 S.Ct. 2505, 2513, 91 L.Ed.2d 202 (1986); *Adickes v. S.H. Kress & Co.*, 398 U.S. 144, 157–59, 90 S.Ct. 1598, 1608–09, 26 L.Ed.2d 142 (1970).

38. *See Hunt v. Cromartie*, 526 U.S. 541, 552, 119 S.Ct. 1545, 1552, 143 L.Ed.2d 731 (1999); *Patterson & Wilder Const. Co., Inc. v. United States*, 226 F.3d 1269, 1273 (11th Cir. 2000).

39. *See Rathbun v. Autozone, Inc.*, 361 F.3d 62, 66 (1st Cir. 2004).

40. *See Anderson v. Liberty Lobby, Inc.*, 477 U.S. 242, 255, 106 S.Ct. 2505, 2513, 91 L.Ed.2d 202 (1986).

41. *See Ward v. Bechtel Corp.*, 102 F.3d 199, 202 (5th Cir.1997) (holding that summary judgment is not precluded simply because questions of intent are at issue); *Fennell v. First Step Designs, Ltd.*, 83 F.3d 526, 535 (1st Cir. 1996)(summary judgment may be proper in cases involving "elusive concepts" like intent or motive); *Ennis v. National Ass'n of Business & Educational Radio, Inc.*, 53 F.3d 55, 62 (4th Cir.1995)(although courts must consider summary judgment carefully when "intent" is at issue, an otherwise valid motion is not defeated by "the mere incantation of intent or state of mind")(citation omitted); *In re Varrasso*, 37 F.3d 760, 764 (1st Cir.1994)(holding that issues involving a litigant's state of mind can be resolved at summary judgment stage, although courts must be "exceptionally cautious" in this regard).

because questions of credibility will ordinarily abound.[42] Thus, summary judgment is used "sparingly" and "seldom granted" in cases involving peculiarly intensive state of mind questions such as employment actions, discrimination claims, and antitrust cases.[43]

Form of Motion

Motions for summary judgment generally must be in writing.[44] Local rules may prescribe the briefing requirements for summary judgment motions, and these rules should always be consulted before briefing. In some judicial districts, the local rules may also require the moving parties to compile a list of all material facts they believe are not in dispute, and require non-moving parties to submit a counterstatement listing material facts they believe to be disputed.[45] Such requirements have been enforced strictly, and practitioners should take care to notice these district-specific obligations when consulting the local rules.[46]

42. *See Hutchinson v. Proxmire,* 443 U.S. 111, 99 S.Ct. 2675, 61 L.Ed.2d 411 (1979); *Graham v. Long Island R.R.*, 230 F.3d 34, 38 (2d Cir.2000) (commenting that summary judgment is used "sparingly" where intent and state of mind are implicated); *EMI Catalogue Partnership v. Hill, Holliday, Connors, Cosmopulos Inc.*, 228 F.3d 56, 61 (2d Cir.2000) ("caution" must be observed with issues involving defendant's intent); *Seamons v. Snow*, 206 F.3d 1021, 1027–28 (10th Cir.2000) (noting that grant of summary judgment is "especially questionable" in cases delving into party's state of mind); *United States ex rel. Cantekin v. University of Pittsburgh*, 192 F.3d 402, 411 (3d Cir.1999) (noting "basic rule" that state of mind issues typically should not be decided on summary judgment), *cert. denied*, 531 U.S. 880, 121 S.Ct. 192, 148 L.Ed.2d 133 (2000); *Mendocino Envt'l Ctr. v. Mendocino County*, 192 F.3d 1283, 1302 (9th Cir.1999) (observing that state of mind questions are factual issues inappropriate for summary judgment); *Geier v. Medtronic, Inc.*, 99 F.3d 238, 240 (7th Cir.1996) (applying summary judgment standards with "especial scrutiny" where cases turn on issues of intent or credibility); *Hossaini v. Western Missouri Med. Ctr.*, 97 F.3d 1085, 1088 (8th Cir.1996) (recognizing difficulty of disposing of intent issues at the summary judgment stage).

43. *See, e.g., Duncan v. Delta Consol. Indus., Inc.*, 371 F.3d 1020, 1024 (8th Cir. 2004) ("seldom" granted in discrimination cases); *Feingold v. New York*, 366 F.3d 138, 148–49 (2d Cir. 2004) (summary judgments affirmed "sparingly" in discrimination cases); *Ashley Creek Phosphate Co. v. Chevron USA, Inc.*, 315 F.3d 1245, 1253 (10th Cir.2003) ("sparingly" in antitrust cases), *cert. denied*, 540 U.S. 820, 124 S.Ct. 103, 157 L.Ed.2d 38 (2003). *But cf. PepsiCo, Inc. v. Coca–Cola Co.*, 315 F.3d 101, 104–05 (2d Cir.2002) (noting that summary judgment is "particularly favored" in antitrust cases due to the risk that protracted litigation will chill pro-competitive market forces).

44. *See National Fire Ins. v. Bartolazo*, 27 F.3d 518, 520 (11th Cir.1994); *Hanson v. Polk County Land, Inc.*, 608 F.2d 129, 131 (5th Cir. 1979).

45. *See, e.g.,* M.D. Pa. Loc. R. 56.1 ("Upon any motion for summary judgment pursuant to Fed.R.Civ.P. 56, there shall be filed with the motion a separate, short and concise statement of the material facts, in numbered paragraphs, as to which the moving party contends there is no genuine issue to be tried. The papers opposing a motion for summary judgment shall include a separate, short and concise statement of the material facts, responding to the numbered paragraphs set forth in the statement required in the foregoing paragraph, as to which it is contended that there exists a genuine issue to be tried.").

46. *See, e.g., A.M. Capen's Co. v. American Trading & Production Corp.*, 202 F.3d 469, 472 (1st Cir.2000) (finding that trial court properly admitted uncontested facts when non-moving party failed to comply with local rules in opposing motion with proper format), *cert. denied*, 531 U.S. 823, 121 S.Ct. 68, 148 L.Ed.2d 32 (2000); *Jackson v. Finnegan, Henderson, Farabow, Garrett & Dunner*, 101 F.3d 145, 154 (D.C.Cir.1996) (citing local rule, deeming "admitted" all facts which the nonmoving party did not dispute when filing its counterstatement); *Buchanan v. Sherrill*, 51 F.3d 227, 228–29 (10th Cir. 1995)(citing local court practice requiring con-

Materials Accompanying the Motion

A moving party may choose to submit the motion papers alone, or may supplement the motion with affidavits, pleadings, deposition transcripts, interrogatory answers, admissions, stipulations, transcripts from another proceeding, oral testimony, authenticated exhibits, other proper exhibits, and anything of which the court may properly take judicial notice. To be considered, the facts contained in these materials must be admissible or usable at trial, although for purposes of summary judgment, the facts need not be presented to the court in a form admissible at trial.[47]

Documents and Other Exhibits: Many courts require that documents submitted with summary judgment motions be attached to a Rule 56(e) affidavit that, upon personal knowledge, both identifies and authenticates each document.[48] Documents that fail to satisfy this affidavit authentication requirement may be properly disregarded by those courts when analyzing the pending motion.[49]

Party Admissions: Admissions by a party–whether express (intentional acknowledgement) or through default (*e.g.*, where a party fails to deny Rule 36 requests for admission)–are considered conclusive as to the matters admitted, cannot be contradicted by affidavit or otherwise, and can support a grant of summary judgment.[50]

Transcribed Oral Testimony: Deposition testimony may be used to support a motion for summary judgment, so long as the testimony meets the competence and admissibility requirements of Rule 56(e).[51]

Live Oral Testimony: Entertaining live oral testimony in conjunction with a summary judgment motion is rare and problematic. Because the summary judgment procedure is intended to offer a speedy resolution when the material facts are undisputed, and because the trial court may not, under Rule 56, resolve any facts

cise statements regarding disputed and undisputed facts); *Johnson v. Gudmundsson*, 35 F.3d 1104, 1108 (7th Cir.1994)(noting court's strict enforcement of local rule requiring statement); *Professional Programs Group v. Department of Commerce*, 29 F.3d 1349, 1353 (9th Cir. 1994)(noting local rule requiring non-moving party to file genuine issue statement).

47. *See Stinnett v. Iron Works Gym/Executive Health SPA, Inc.*, 301 F.3d 610, 613 (7th Cir. 2002). *See also Celotex Corp. v. Catrett*, 477 U.S. 317, 324, 106 S.Ct. 2548, 2553, 91 L.Ed.2d 265 (1986)(commenting that party need not depose its own witnesses in order to defeat a summary judgment motion). Indeed, the most frequently submitted support on a summary judgment motion—affidavits—generally are only admissible at trial when the affiant is legally unavailable.

48. *See Woods v. City of Chicago*, 234 F.3d 979, 988 (7th Cir.2000), *cert. denied*, 534 U.S. 955, 122 S.Ct. 354, 151 L.Ed.2d 268 (2001); *Carmona v. Toledo*, 215 F.3d 124, 131 (1st Cir. 2000); *Stuart v. General Motors Corp.*, 217 F.3d 621, 635 n. 20 (8th Cir.2000); *Carmona v. Toledo*, 215 F.3d 124, 131 (1st Cir.2000); *In re Citric Acid Litig.*, 191 F.3d 1090, 1101 (9th Cir.1999), *cert. denied*, 529 U.S. 1037, 120 S.Ct. 1531, 146 L.Ed.2d 346 (2000); *Berk v. Ascott Inv. Corp.*, 759 F.Supp. 245, 249 (E.D.Pa.1991).

49. *See Stuart v. General Motors Corp.*, 217 F.3d 621, 635 n.20 (8th Cir.2000); *Stuart v. General Motors Corp.*, 217 F.3d 621, 635 n. 20 (8th Cir.2000); *Carmona v. Toledo*, 215 F.3d 124, 131 (1st Cir.2000).

50. *See In re Carney*, 258 F.3d 415, 420 (5th Cir.2001).

51. *See Carmen v. San Francisco Unified School Dist.*, 237 F.3d 1026, 1028 n.4 (9th Cir. 2001).

that remain disputed, oral testimony in summary judgment proceedings will only be granted "sparingly" and "with great care".[52]

Briefs: The court may consider concessions in a party's brief or during oral argument in gauging whether a genuine issue of material fact exists; otherwise, however, the parties' briefs are not evidence.[53]

Responding to the Motion

When the moving party supplements the motion by affidavit or other material, the non-moving party cannot respond with mere allegations or denials.[54] Instead, the non-moving party must show, by affidavit, deposition testimony, or otherwise, that a genuine issue of material fact remains for trial.[55]

Time for Service and Response

The non-moving party must be served with the motion papers at least 10 days before any hearing or disposition on the motion.[56] The purpose of this 10–day notice rule is to allow non-moving parties a specific period of time in which to marshal their resources and offer into the summary judgment record additional materials and arguments.[57] The 10–day period is an essential and mandatory component of the Rule, and not a mere technicality.[58] However, if the non-moving party has had ample opportunity to oppose the motion, or if the 10–day period would not have developed additional materials that could have defeated summary judgment, a failure to provide the 10–day notice may be deemed harmless error and excused.[59]

52. *See Seamons v. Snow*, 206 F.3d 1021, 1025–26 (10th Cir.2000).

53. *See Orson, Inc. v. Miramax Film Corp.*, 79 F.3d 1358, 1372 (3d Cir.1996)(legal memoranda and oral argument are not evidence and cannot create a factual dispute that prevents summary judgment); *American Title Ins. Co. v. Lacelaw Corp.*, 861 F.2d 224, 226–27 (9th Cir. 1988)(noting that district court, in its discretion, may consider statements of fact contained in summary judgment briefing as party admissions for Rule 56 purposes); *Stallard v. United States*, 12 F.3d 489, 496 n. 27 (5th Cir.1994)(noting same practice).

54. *See First Nat'l Bank v. Cities Serv. Co.*, 391 U.S. 253, 289, 88 S.Ct. 1575, 1592, 20 L.Ed.2d 569 (1968).

55. *See Millar v. Houghton*, 115 F.3d 348, 350 (5th Cir.1997). *See also* Rule 56(e); *Anderson v. Liberty Lobby, Inc.*, 477 U.S. 242, 257, 106 S.Ct. 2505, 2514, 91 L.Ed.2d 202 (1986).

56. *See Ross v. University of Texas at San Antonio*, 139 F.3d 521, 527 (5th Cir.1998); *Employers Ins. of Wausau v. Petroleum Specialties, Inc.*, 69 F.3d 98, 105 (6th Cir.1995); *Whiting v. Maiolini*, 921 F.2d 5 (1st Cir.1990).

57. *See Restigouche, Inc. v. Town of Jupiter*, 59 F.3d 1208, 1213 (11th Cir.1995); *United States v. Houston Pipeline Co.*, 37 F.3d 224, 228 (5th Cir.1994)(purpose is to allow nonmoving party time "to put its best foot forward").

58. *See Celestine v. Petroleos de Venezuella SA*, 266 F.3d 343, 350 (5th Cir.2001) (commenting that "strict enforcement of the ten day notice requirement of Rule 56(c) is necessary because summary judgment is a final adjudication on the merits"); *Beaird v. Seagate Tech., Inc.*, 145 F.3d 1159, 1165 (10th Cir.1998), *cert. denied*, 525 U.S. 1054, 119 S.Ct. 617, 142 L.Ed.2d 556 (1998) (holding that court "lacks authority" to enter a summary judgment prior to 10 days from motion filing); *Massey v. Congress Life Ins. Co.*, 116 F.3d 1414, (11th Cir.1997) (requirement of notice and opportunity to respond has been strictly enforced); *Employers Ins. of Wausau v. Petroleum Specialties, Inc.*, 69 F.3d 98, 105 (6th Cir.1995)(commenting that failure to comply with Rule 56's time provision deprives the trial court of its authority to grant summary judgment).

59. *See Celestine v. Petroleos de Venezuella SA*, 266 F.3d 343, 350 (5th Cir.2001) (failure to give 10–days notice may be harmless if non-

Uncontested Summary Judgment Motions

Summary judgment will not be entered automatically if the non-moving party fails to file an opposition to the motion.[60] Summary judgment may be entered only if it is appropriate to do so.[61] Consequently, although it is assuredly a dangerous practice to fail to oppose a summary judgment motion, even uncontested motions must be examined carefully by the district court to determine whether no genuine issue of material fact remains and whether judgment is appropriate as a matter of law.[62] The trial court may not accept as true the moving party's itemization of undisputed facts; instead, the court must satisfy itself that the evidence in the summary judgment record supports this relief.[63] This does not necessarily require the court to review all evidentiary materials on file, but it must at least review those materials supporting the motion itself.[64] Moreover, the district court's order should recount that it addressed the underlying motion on its merits.[65]

New Evidence in Reply

If the moving party introduces new evidence in a reply brief or memoranda, the trial court should not accept and consider the new evidence without first affording the non-moving party an opportunity to respond.[66]

moving party admits that no additional evidence would be offered or if appellate court evaluates all additional evidence and finds no genuine issue of material fact); *Restigouche, Inc. v. Town of Jupiter*, 59 F.3d 1208, 1213 (11th Cir. 1995)(violation of notice period deemed harmless where supplemental materials would not have prevented entry of summary judgment); *In re Harris Pine Mills*, 44 F.3d 1431, 1439–40 (9th Cir.1995)(commenting that although court may not ordinarily enter relief under Rule 56 without 10 days notice and an opportunity to oppose, judgment may be entered without notice if losing party has had a full and fair opportunity to address the issues implicated in the motion), *cert. denied*, 515 U.S. 1131, 115 S.Ct. 2555, 132 L.Ed.2d 809 (1995);

60. *See De La Vega v. San Juan Star, Inc.*, 377 F.3d 111, 115–16 (1st Cir. 2004); *Vermont Teddy Bear Co. v. 1–800 Beargram Co.*, 373 F.3d 241, 244–46 (2d Cir. 2004); *United States v. One Piece of Real Prop. Located at 5800 SW 74th Ave., Miami, Fla.*, 363 F.3d 1099, 1101–02 (11th Cir. 2004).

61. *See* Rule 56(c) (summary judgment entered forthwith, but only if no genuine issue of material facts exists *and* movant is entitled to judgment); Rule 56(e) ("If the adverse party does not so respond, summary judgment *if appropriate*, shall be entered against the adverse party") (emphasis added). *See also United States v. One Piece of Real Prop. Located at 5800 SW 74th Ave., Miami, Fla.*, 363 F.3d 1099, 1101 (11th Cir. 2004) (noting that summary judgment, even when unopposed, may be entered only when appropriate).

62. *See* Rule 56(e) ("If the adverse party does not so respond, summary judgment *if appropriate*, shall be entered against the adverse party") (emphasis added). *Accord De La Vega v. San Juan Star, Inc.*, 377 F.3d 111, 115–16 (1st Cir. 2004); *Vermont Teddy Bear Co. v. 1–800 Beargram Co.*, 373 F.3d 241, 244–46 (2d Cir. 2004); *Custer v. Pan American Life Ins. Co.*, 12 F.3d 410, 416 (4th Cir. 1993).

63. *See Vermont Teddy Bear Co. v. 1–800 Beargram Co.*, 373 F.3d 241, 244 (2d Cir. 2004).

64. *See United States v. One Piece of Real Prop. Located at 5800 SW 74th Ave., Miami, Fla.*, 363 F.3d 1099, 1101–02 (11th Cir. 2004).

65. *See United States v. One Piece of Real Prop. Located at 5800 SW 74th Ave., Miami, Fla.*, 363 F.3d 1099, 1101–02 (11th Cir. 2004).

66. *See Seay v. Tennessee Valley Auth.*, 339 F.3d 454, 481–82 (6th Cir.2003); *Beaird v. Seagate Tech., Inc.*, 145 F.3d 1159, 1163–65 (10th Cir.1998), *cert. denied*, 525 U.S. 1054, 119 S.Ct. 617, 142 L.Ed.2d 556 (1998).

Hearings and Oral Argument

Although the district court may, in its discretion, entertain a hearing or oral argument on the Rule 56 motion, hearings and oral argument are not obligatory.[67]

Multiple Summary Judgment Motions

The district court may permit a second motion for summary judgment, especially where there has been an intervening change in the controlling law, where new evidence has become available or the factual record has otherwise expanded through discovery, or where a clear need arises to correct a manifest injustice.[68]

Stipulated Facts and Cross Motions

If the parties stipulate to the facts, obviously no genuine dispute as to material facts then exists for a factfinder to resolve.[69] Nevertheless, the summary judgment standard remains the same. The court must draw inferences from the stipulated facts, and resolve those inferences in favor of the non-moving party.[70] Similarly, cross-motions for sum-

67. *See* Rule 78 (authorizing determination of motions without oral argument). *See Cruz v. Melecio*, 204 F.3d 14, 19 (1st Cir.2000) (refusing to vacate summary judgment in absence of oral argument, holding that summary judgment upon written submissions only is neither "fundamentally unfair" nor a denial of due process); *AD/SAT, Div. of Skylight, Inc. v. Associated Press*, 181 F.3d 216, 226 (2d Cir.1999) (decision to permit oral argument lies within trial court's discretion); *McCormack v. Citibank, N.A.*, 100 F.3d 532, 541 (8th Cir.1996); *Deutsch v. Burlington Northern R.R.*, 983 F.2d 741, 744 n. 2 (7th Cir.1992), *cert. denied*, 507 U.S. 1030, 113 S.Ct. 1845, 123 L.Ed.2d 470 (1993); *L.S.T., Inc. v. Crow*, 49 F.3d 679, 684 n. 9 (11th Cir.1995); *Cray Communications, Inc. v. Novatel Computer Sys., Inc.*, 33 F.3d 390, 396 (4th Cir.1994), *cert. denied,* 513 U.S. 1191, 115 S.Ct. 1254, 131 L.Ed.2d 135 (1995); *Kennedy v. Meacham*, 540 F.2d 1057, 1061 n. 3 (10th Cir.1976).

68. *See Garvin v. Wheeler*, 304 F.3d 628, 632 (7th Cir.2002); *Whitford v. Boglino*, 63 F.3d 527, 530 (7th Cir.1995), *cert. denied*, 529 U.S. 1075, 120 S.Ct. 1691, 146 L.Ed.2d 497 (2000). *See also Kovacevich v. Kent State Univ.*, 224 F.3d 806, 835 (6th Cir.2000) (permitting renewed or successive motions where factual record has expanded); *Enlow v. Tishomingo County*, 962 F.2d 501, 506 (5th Cir.1992) (successive summary judgment motion allowed when new facts were presented by amended pleading); *Williamsburg Wax Museum, Inc. v. Historic Figures, Inc.*, 810 F.2d 243, 251 (D.C.Cir.1987)(noting that subsequent motion for summary judgment premised upon expanded record is always permitted); *Shearer v. Homestake Mining Co.*, 727 F.2d 707, 709 (8th Cir.1984)(finding no error in permitting second or renewed motion based upon substantial discovery of facts not previously before the court). *Gulezian v. Drexel Univ.*, 1999 WL 200675, at *2 (E.D.Pa.1999) (noting that courts may entertain successive summary judgment motions, particularly when parties have expanded factual record on which summary judgment is sought); *Holloman v. Neily*, 1998 WL 828413, at *1 (E.D.Pa.1998) (same); *Bank One, Texas, N.A. v. FDIC*, 16 F.Supp.2d 698, 715 (N.D.Tex.1998) (noting possibility of summary judgment on subsequent motion). *See also Gann v. Fruehauf Corp.*, 52 F.3d 1320, 1324 (5th Cir. 1995)(reversing district court's sanctioning of counsel for filing a second motion for summary judgment where arguments presented in both motions differed).

69. *See Centennial Ins. Co. v. Ryder Truck Rental, Inc.*, 149 F.3d 378 (5th Cir.1998) (noting that factual stipulations can be the basis for summary judgment); *Miyazawa v. City of Cincinnati*, 45 F.3d 126, 127 (6th Cir.1995); *Luden's Inc. v. Local Union No. 6 of Bakery, Confectionery & Tobacco Workers' Int'l Union of America*, 28 F.3d 347, 353 (3d Cir.1994).

70. *See Leebaert v. Harrington*, 332 F.3d 134, 138–39 (2d Cir.2003); *Luden's Inc. v. Local Union No. 6 of Bakery, Confectionery & Tobacco Workers' Int'l Union of America*, 28 F.3d 347, 353 (3d Cir.1994). *But see United Paperworkers Int'l Union Local 14, AFL–CIO–CLC v. International Paper Co.*, 64 F.3d 28, 31 (1st Cir. 1995)(noting that summary judgment standard may be modified where dispute arrives as a "case stated"; in that instance, trial judge is

mary judgment are examined under the same standards.[71] Each cross-motion must be evaluated on its own merits, with the court viewing all facts and reasonable inferences in the light most favorable to the nonmoving party.[72] Thus, the mere fact that cross motions have been filed does not, by itself, necessarily justify the entry of a summary judgment,[73] nor will the denial of one cross motion compel the grant of the other cross motion.[74]

Entry of Summary Judgment in Favor of *Non-Moving Party*

In unusual circumstances, the trial court may not only deny the moving party's motion for summary judgment, but may enter summary judgment in favor of the non-moving party (even though that party has not sought such relief). Such judgments are generally only entered if the court is convinced that the factual record is fully developed, that the non-moving party is "clearly" entitled to judgment, and that entry of the judgment would not result in procedural prejudice to the moving party.[75] Because such motions are, in effect, *sua sponte* motions for summary judgment, the trial court should generally abide by the standards for entry of *sua sponte* relief.[76]

Sua Sponte Motions

The court may enter summary judgment *sua sponte*.[77] The case law, however, cautions great care in the grant of *sua sponte* summary

free to engage in certain factfinding, including the drawing of inferences). *But see also United States Fidelity & Guaranty Co. v. Planters Bank & Trust Co.*, 77 F.3d 863, 866 (5th Cir. 1996)(noting that court of appeals recognizes a "hint of a distinction" between the standard applied in jury cases and an arguably more lenient standard in certain non-jury cases).

71. *See Westfield Ins. Co. v. Tech Dry, Inc.*, 336 F.3d 503, 506 (6th Cir.2003); *Cochran v. Quest Software, Inc.*, 328 F.3d 1, 6 (1st Cir. 2003); *Mellen v. Bunting*, 327 F.3d 355, 363 (4th Cir.2003).

72. *See Westfield Ins. Co. v. Tech Dry, Inc.*, 336 F.3d 503, 506 (6th Cir.2003); *Mellen v. Bunting*, 327 F.3d 355, 363 (4th Cir.2003); *Metropolitan Life Ins. Co. v. Johnson*, 297 F.3d 558, 561–62 (7th Cir.2002); *Chandler v. City of Arvada*, 292 F.3d 1236, 1240 (10th Cir.2002); *Murphy Exploration & Prod. Co. v. Oryx Energy Co.*, 101 F.3d 670, 673 (Fed.Cir.1996).

73. *See Atlantic Richfield Co. v. Farm Credit Bank of Wichita*, 226 F.3d 1138, 1148 (10th Cir.2000); *Wightman v. Springfield Terminal Ry. Co.*, 100 F.3d 228, 230 (1st Cir.1996).

74. *See Atlantic Richfield Co. v. Farm Credit Bank of Wichita*, 226 F.3d 1138, 1148 (10th Cir.2000).

75. *See Armijo v. Atchison, Topeka & Santa Fe Ry.*, 27 F.3d 481, 482–83 (10th Cir.1994); *Dickeson v. Quarberg*, 844 F.2d 1435, 1444 n. 8 (10th Cir.1988); *E.C. Ernst, Inc. v. General Motors Corp.*, 537 F.2d 105, 109 (5th Cir.1976).

76. *See Madewell v. Downs*, 68 F.3d 1030, 1049 (8th Cir.1995) (commenting that liability of the nonmoving party was "derivative" of the motion, such that when motion leaves no genuine issue of material fact as to the *nonmoving* party's right to summary judgment, *sua sponte* summary judgment is proper). *See also* **Authors' Commentary** on *Sua Sponte* Motions, *infra*.

77. *See Celotex Corp. v. Catrett*, 477 U.S. 317, 326, 106 S.Ct. 2548, 2554, 91 L.Ed.2d 265 (1986)(noting district court's right to enter *sua sponte* motions under Rule 56); *United States v. Hoyts Cinemas Corp.*, 380 F.3d 558 (1st Cir. 2004); *Gibson v. Mayor of Wilmington*, 355 F.3d 215, 222 (3d Cir. 2004); *Athridge v. Rivas*, 141 F.3d 357, 361 (D.C.Cir.1998) ; *Ross v. University of Texas at San Antonio*, 139 F.3d 521, 527 (5th Cir.1998); *GBJ Corp. v. Eastern Ohio Paving Co.*, 139 F.3d 1080, 1090 (6th Cir.1998); *National Presto Indus. v. West Bend Co.*, 76 F.3d 1185, 1188 (Fed.Cir.1996) *But cf. Baker v. Metropolitan Life Ins. Co.*, 364 F.3d 624, 632 (5th Cir. 2004) (commenting that *sua sponte* summary judgment may not be granted "on grounds not requested by the moving party").

judgments.[78] In practice, *sua sponte* summary judgments should be unnecessary because the trial court may always invite a party to file a summary judgment motion.[79] Where the court considers entering a *sua sponte* judgment, it must first ensure that proper advance notice of this intention (at least 10 days) has been made.[80] The court must also confirm that the litigants have a full and fair duty to respond.[81] Discovery must either be completed or clearly be of no further benefit.[82] These notice-and-opportunity requirements apply even when the *sua sponte* summary judgment is entered against a party who, herself, has moved for summary judgment.[83] An order granting summary judgment *sua sponte* without notice will generally be reversed unless the nonmoving party has waived this right or unless it is clear that the non-moving party suffered no prejudice (*e.g.*, because there was no additional evidence for the record or because none of the evidence would create a genuine issue of material fact).[84] Other courts have excused this notice and response requirement where three criteria are met: the summary judgment record is fully developed, there is no prejudice to the non-

78. *See Ramsey v. Coughlin*, 94 F.3d 71, 74 (2d Cir.1996)("great care"); *Goldstein v. Fidelity & Guaranty Ins. Underwriters, Inc.*, 86 F.3d 749, 751 (7th Cir.1996)("special caution" warranted with this "just a bit risky" practice, which the court of appeals does not want to encourage); *Employers Ins. of Wausau v. Petroleum Specialties, Inc.*, 69 F.3d 98, 105 (6th Cir. 1995)(although no per se prohibition against *sua sponte* summary judgments, it is a practice the court discourages).

79. *See Goldstein v. Fidelity & Guaranty Ins. Underwriters, Inc.*, 86 F.3d 749, 751 (7th Cir. 1996).

80. *See United States v. Hoyts Cinemas Corp.*, 380 F.3d 558 (1st Cir. 2004); *Verizon Del., Inc. v. Covad Communications Co.*, 377 F.3d 1081, 1092 (9th Cir. 2004); *Gibson v. Mayor of Wilmington*, 355 F.3d 215, 223 (3d Cir. 2004); *American Road Serv. Co. v. Consolidated Rail Corp.*, 348 F.3d 565, 567 (6th Cir. 2003); *HS Resources, Inc. v. Wingate*, 327 F.3d 432, 441 (5th Cir.2003); *Lindsey v. Jewels by Park Lane, Inc.*, 205 F.3d 1087, 1094 (8th Cir.2000); *Bridgeway Corp. v. Citibank*, 201 F.3d 134, 139–40 (2d Cir.2000); *Athridge v. Rivas*, 141 F.3d 357, 361 (D.C.Cir.1998); *Oluwa v. Gomez*, 133 F.3d 1237, 1239 (9th Cir.1998); *Sports Racing Servs., Inc. v. Sports Car Club of America, Inc.*, 131 F.3d 874, 892 (10th Cir.1997); *National Presto Indus. v. West Bend Co.*, 76 F.3d 1185, 1188 (Fed.Cir. 1996). *But cf. Enowmbitang v. Seagate Tech., Inc.*, 148 F.3d 970 (8th Cir.1998) (holding that trial court may grant *sua sponte* summary judgment without prior notice for failure to state claim upon which relief may be granted).

81. *See American Road Serv. Co. v. Consolidated Rail Corp.*, 348 F.3d 565, 567 (6th Cir. 2003); *HS Resources, Inc. v. Wingate*, 327 F.3d 432, 441 (5th Cir.2003); *North Texas Production Credit Ass'n v. McCurtain County Nat'l Bank*, 222 F.3d 800 (10th Cir.2000); *Lindsey v. Jewels by Park Lane, Inc.*, 205 F.3d 1087, 1094 (8th Cir.2000); *Shelby County Health Care Corp. v. Southern Council of Indus.*, 203 F.3d 926, 931 (6th Cir.2000); *Bank v. International Bus. Machs. Corp.*, 145 F.3d 420, 431 (1st Cir.1998); *Ramsey v. Coughlin*, 94 F.3d 71, 73–74 (2d Cir. 1996); *Berkovitz v. Home Box Office, Inc.*, 89 F.3d 24, 29 (1st Cir.1996)(holding that targeted party must have an adequate opportunity "to dodge the bullet"); *Chambers Dev't Co. v. Passaic County Utilities Auth.*, 62 F.3d 582, 584 n. 5 (3d Cir.1995). *See also Massey v. Del Labs., Inc.*, 118 F.3d 1568 (Fed.Cir.1997) (holding that court may grant *sua sponte* summary judgment without notice only if the losing party has had a "full and fair opportunity to ventilate the issues involved in the motion").

82. *See Bank v. International Bus. Machs. Corp.*, 145 F.3d 420, 431 (1st Cir.1998) (ruling that litigation should be sufficiently advanced that parties have had reasonable opportunity to present material evidence in their favor); *Ramsey v. Coughlin*, 94 F.3d 71, 74 (2d Cir.1996); *Berkovitz v. Home Box Office, Inc.*, 89 F.3d 24, 29 (1st Cir.1996).

83. *See Bridgeway Corp. v. Citibank*, 201 F.3d 134, 139–40 (2d Cir.2000).

84. *See American Road Serv. Co. v. Consolidated Rail Corp.*, 348 F.3d 565, 567 (6th Cir. 2003); *Love v. National Med. Enters.*, 230 F.3d 765, 770–71 (5th Cir.2000); *Bridgeway Corp. v. Citibank*, 201 F.3d 134, 139–40 (2d Cir.2000).

moving party, and the decision rests on a purely legal issue.[85]

Any objection to this procedural error must be appropriately preserved for appeal, however. Thus, filing a motion for reconsideration that contests a *sua sponte* grant of summary judgment, but that omits from that motion a challenge to the procedural propriety of the order, will be reviewed narrowly for "plain error" only.[86]

Effect of Summary Judgment Rulings—"Law Of The Case"

The "law of the case" doctrine holds that when a court decides upon a rule of law, that decision should generally control the same issues throughout the subsequent stages in the same case.[87] It is based on the sound, salutary policy of judicial finality—that all litigation should come to an end.[88] This is a prudential doctrine; it guides and influences the court's exercise of discretion, but it does not limit the court's jurisdiction or power.[89] Because *denials* of summary judgment generally do nothing more than acknowledge that a genuine issue of material fact remains for trial, such denials are typically not accorded any preclusive effect nor do they become "law of the case".[90]

Appealability

Ordinarily, an order denying a party's motion for summary judgment is interlocutory and, therefore, not immediately appealable.[91] Conversely, an order granting summary judgment is appealable only when it constitutes the "final order" in the case.[92]

Exceptions: Practitioners must be wary. Exceptions to these general rules are numerous. For example, if the motion asserts questions of

85. *See Gibson v. Mayor of Wilmington*, 355 F.3d 215, 222 (3d Cir. 2004).

86. *See Love v. National Med. Enters.*, 230 F.3d 765, 771 (5th Cir.2000).

87. *See Arizona v. California*, 460 U.S. 605, 618, 103 S.Ct. 1382, 1391, 75 L.Ed.2d 318 (1983).

88. *See Lyons v. Fisher*, 888 F.2d 1071 (5th Cir.1989), *cert. denied*, 495 U.S. 948, 110 S.Ct. 2209, 109 L.Ed.2d 535 (1990). *See also Gindes v. United States*, 740 F.2d 947, 949 (Fed.Cir.1984) (commenting that doctrine rests upon important public policy litigants do not enjoy the right to cover the same ground twice, hoping that passage of time or changes in court's composition will alter outcome), *cert. denied*, 469 U.S. 1074, 105 S.Ct. 569, 83 L.Ed.2d 509 (1984).

89. *See Arizona v. California*, 460 U.S. 605, 618, 103 S.Ct. 1382, 1391, 75 L.Ed.2d 318 (1983); *Sejman v. Warner–Lambert Co.*, 845 F.2d 66, 68–69 (4th Cir.1988).

90. *See Murphy v. Missouri Dep't of Corrections*, 372 F.3d 979, 986 (8th Cir. 2004); *Kovacevich v. Kent State Univ.*, 224 F.3d 806 (6th Cir.2000); *United States v. Palmer*, 122 F.3d 215, 220–21 (5th Cir.1997); *Trustees of Indiana Univ. v. Aetna Cas. & Sur. Co.*, 920 F.2d 429, 435 (7th Cir.1990). *But see Federal Ins. Co. v. Scarsella Bros.*, 931 F.2d 599, 601 n. 4 (9th Cir.1991) (holding that doctrine is not amenable to such broad generalizations, and may apply to summary judgment denials when trial court intends to resolve definitively the legal questions in issue).

91. *See Padfield v. AIG Life Ins. Co.*, 290 F.3d 1121, 1124 (9th Cir.2002), *cert. denied*, 537 U.S. 1067, 123 S.Ct. 602, 154 L.Ed.2d 556 (2002); *Ahrenholz v. Board of Trustees of Univ. of Illinois*, 219 F.3d 674 (7th Cir.2000); *Hermes Int'l v. Lederer de Paris Fifth Ave., Inc.*, 219 F.3d 104, 109 (2d Cir.2000); *Helm Fin. Corp. v. MNVA R.R., Inc.*, 212 F.3d 1076, 1079 (8th Cir.2000); *Acevedo-Garcia v. Vera–Monroig*, 204 F.3d 1, 7 (1st Cir.2000); *Roberts v. Roadway Express, Inc.*, 149 F.3d 1098 (10th Cir.1998).

92. *See Santaella v. Metropolitan Life Ins. Co.*, 123 F.3d 456, 461 (7th Cir.1997). *See also* 28 U.S.C.A. § 1291. *But see* 28 U.S.C.A. § 1292 (permitting certification by district court of interlocutory orders); Rule 54(b)(permitting entry of partial judgment that resolves one claim or all rights of one party).

immunity from suit, a denial of summary judgment may be immediately appealable.[93] Similarly, a denial of a cross-motion for summary judgment may be immediately appealable along with a challenge to that portion of the cross-motion that was granted.[94]

Effect of Non–Appealable Summary Judgment Denials: Because such rulings only determine that a genuine issue of material fact remains for trial, denials of summary judgment motions ordinarily do not merge into the final judgment and, therefore, are typically not independently appealable even where the case proceeds to trial and a later appeal.[95]

RULE 56(d). PARTIAL SUMMARY ADJUDICATION

CORE CONCEPT

The court may enter a summary ruling on the issue of liability alone, even though a genuine issue of material fact exists as to damages. The court may also summarily resolve other individual issues as to which there remain no genuine issue of material fact.

APPLICATIONS

Purpose of Partial Summary Adjudications

Where a summary judgment is not possible (or not requested) and the dispute will have to go to trial, the district court is nevertheless permitted to declare certain facts—those which it determines appear without substantial controversy—as established for purposes of the case.[96] Partial summary adjudications allow the trial court to salvage some constructive result from its efforts in ruling upon an otherwise denied summary judgment motion.[97] Partial summary adjudications accelerate litigations by narrowing the triable issues and eliminating—pretrial—those matters involving no genuine issues of material fact.[98]

93. *See Swint v. Chambers County Comm'n*, 514 U.S. 35, 115 S.Ct. 1203, 131 L.Ed.2d 60 (1995)(district court orders denying summary judgment not immediately appealable unless appellant raised qualified immunity defense); *Mitchell v. Forsyth*, 472 U.S. 511, 530, 105 S.Ct. 2806, 2817, 86 L.Ed.2d 411 (1985)(same); *Christy v. Pennsylvania Turnpike Comm'n*, 54 F.3d 1140 (3d Cir.1995)(permitting immediate appeal from denials of summary judgment on Eleventh Amendment grounds), *cert. denied*, 516 U.S. 932, 116 S.Ct. 340, 133 L.Ed.2d 238 (1995). *But cf. Jones v. City of Jackson*, 203 F.3d 875, 878 (5th Cir.2000) (even with immunity motions, summary judgment denials are not immediately appealable if disputed and material factual issues are present).

94. *See Padfield v. AIG Life Ins. Co.*, 290 F.3d 1121, 1124 (9th Cir.2002), *cert. denied*, 537 U.S. 1067, 123 S.Ct. 602, 154 L.Ed.2d 556 (2002); *National Coalition For Students With Disabilities Educ. v. Allen*, 152 F.3d 283 (4th Cir.1998); *McIntosh v. Scottsdale Ins. Co.*, 992 F.2d 251, 253 (10th Cir.1993).

95. *See Iacobucci v. Boulter*, 193 F.3d 14, 22 (1st Cir.1999).

96. *See Algie v. RCA Global Communications, Inc.*, 891 F.Supp. 875, 882–83 (S.D.N.Y. 1994), *aff'd*, 60 F.3d 956 (2d Cir.1995); *FDIC v. Massingill*, 24 F.3d 768 (5th Cir.1994), *opinion supplemented*, 30 F.3d 601 (5th Cir.1994).

97. *See Access Solutions Int'l, Inc. v. Data/Ware Dev't, Inc.*, 70 F.Supp.2d 92, 95–96 (D.R.I. 1999); *National Union Fire Ins. Co. of Pittsburgh v. L.E. Myers Co. Group*, 937 F.Supp. 276, 285 (S.D.N.Y.1996); *URI Cogeneration Partners, L.P. v. Board of Governors for Higher Educ.*, 915 F.Supp. 1267, 1279 (D.R.I.1996).

98. *See National Union Fire Ins. Co. of Pittsburgh v. L.E. Myers Co. Group*, 937 F.Supp. 276, 285 (S.D.N.Y.1996).

Liability Alone

Under Rule 56(c), the court may summarily enter an interlocutory judgment on liability questions, where the issue of damages must await trial.

Standards for Granting or Denying Partial Summary Adjudication

In resolving a motion for partial summary adjudication, the court will apply the same standards and criteria used for evaluating full motions for summary judgment.[99]

District Court's Discretion

Similar to motions for "full" summary judgment, the district judge has the discretion (subject to the familiar summary judgment standards generally) to defer a partial adjudication ruling until the proper time arrives for making a complete adjudication on all issues in the case.[100]

Effect of Partial Summary Adjudications—"Law Of The Case"

Partial summary adjudications are not "judgments" and do not become "final orders" until the district court enters a judgment disposing of the entire case.[101] Nevertheless, such adjudications are still rulings on a "dispositive motion",[102] and will be accorded treatment as "law of the case".[103] Thus, the parties are entitled to rely on the conclusiveness of the partial summary adjudication[104] and, absent good reason for doing so, the district court will not generally revisit or alter the issues adjudicated under Rule 56(d).[105] Nevertheless, such partial adjudications are not immutable and have no *res judicata* effect; they may, under appropriate circumstances, be revisited.[106] If the court later decides that good reasons exist to alter a partial summary adjudication, the court must so inform the parties and permit them an opportunity to present evidence concerning any of the revisited issues.[107]

99. *See Russell v. Enterprise Rent–A–Car Co. of Rhode Island*, 160 F.Supp.2d 239, 249 (D.R.I. 2001); *Melvin v. Patterson*, 965 F.Supp. 1212, 1214 (S.D.Ind.1997); *Pettengill v. United States*, 867 F.Supp. 380, 381 (E.D.Va.1994).

100. *See Colasanto v. Life Ins. Co. of North America*, 100 F.3d 203, 210 (1st Cir.1996); *Department of Toxic Substances Control v. Interstate Non–Ferrous Corp.*, 99 F.Supp.2d 1123, 1125 (E.D.Cal.2000).

101. *See Alberty-Velez v. Corporacion de Puerto Rico Para La Difusion Publica*, 361 F.3d 1, 6 n.5 (1st Cir. 2004); *Burkhart v. Washington Metro. Area Transit Auth.*, 112 F.3d 1207, 1215–16 (D.C.Cir.1997); *Palmer v. Fox Software, Inc.*, 107 F.3d 415, 419 (6th Cir.1997), *cert. denied*, 522 U.S. 860, 118 S.Ct. 162, 139 L.Ed.2d 106 (1997).

102. *See Burkhart v. Washington Metro. Area Transit Auth.*, 112 F.3d 1207, 1215–16 (D.C.Cir.1997).

103. *See Burge v. Parish of St. Tammany*, 187 F.3d 452, 467 (5th Cir.1999); *Carr v. O'Leary*, 167 F.3d 1124, 1126 (7th Cir.1999); *Palmer v. Fox Software, Inc.*, 107 F.3d 415, 419 (6th Cir.1997), *cert. denied*, 522 U.S. 860, 118 S.Ct. 162, 139 L.Ed.2d 106 (1997).

104. *See Huss v. King Co.*, 338 F.3d 647, 650–51 (6th Cir.2003), *cert. denied*, 541 U.S. 1015, 124 S.Ct. 2080, 158 L.Ed.2d 629 (2004); *Leddy v. Standard Drywall, Inc.*, 875 F.2d 383, 386 (2d Cir.1989).

105. *See Carr v. O'Leary*, 167 F.3d 1124, 1126 (7th Cir.1999).

106. *See Alberty-Velez v. Corporacion de Puerto Rico Para La Difusion Publica*, 361 F.3d 1, 6 n.5 (1st Cir. 2004); *Burge v. Parish of St. Tammany*, 187 F.3d 452, 467 (5th Cir.1999).

107. *See Alberty-Velez v. Corporacion de Puerto Rico Para La Difusion Publica*, 361 F.3d 1, 6 n.5 (1st Cir. 2004); *Huss v. King Co.*, 338 F.3d 647, 650–51 (6th Cir.2003); *Leddy v. Standard Drywall, Inc.*, 875 F.2d 383, 386 (2d Cir. 1989). *See also Joseph P. Caulfield & Assocs., Inc. v. Litho Prods., Inc.*, 155 F.3d 883, 888 (7th

Appealability

Ordinarily, rulings that grant[108] or deny[109] partial summary adjudications are considered interlocutory, subject to revision by the district court, and thus not immediately appealable. This rule is, however, subject to exceptions.[110]

RULE 56(e). USE OF AFFIDAVITS IN SUMMARY JUDGMENT PRACTICE

CORE CONCEPT

When submitted to support or oppose a summary judgment motion, an affidavit must be based on personal knowledge, must set forth facts that would be admissible at time of trial, and must establish the affiant's competence to testify.

APPLICATIONS

When Affidavits or Other Materials Are Required

When a summary judgment motion is supported with affidavits or other material, the non-moving party cannot rely on mere allegations or denials found in the pleadings. Rather, the non-moving party must demonstrate, by affidavit, deposition testimony, or otherwise, that a genuine issue of material fact remains for trial.[111]

Affidavit Prerequisites

To be considered on a motion for summary judgment, an affidavit must satisfy three prerequisites: it must be sworn upon personal knowledge; it must state specific facts admissible in evidence at time of trial; and it must be offered by a competent affiant. In ruling upon a motion for summary judgment, the court generally will not consider affidavits that fail to satisfy these prerequisites.[112]

Cir.1998) (holding that proper procedure to seek a revisitation of the adjudicated issues is to file a motion to vacate the ruling and request either that the issues be added to the trial or that they be resolved as a matter of law in favor of the moving party).

108. *See Lovejoy-Wilson v. NOCO Motor Fuel, Inc.*, 263 F.3d 208, 219 n.6 (2d Cir.2001); *CAE Screenplates Inc. v. Heinrich Fiedler GmbH & Co.*, 224 F.3d 1308 (Fed.Cir.2000); *Williamson v. UNUM Life Ins. Co. of America*, 160 F.3d 1247, 1250 (9th Cir.1998); *Construction Aggregates, Ltd. v. Forest Commodities Corp.*, 147 F.3d 1334 (11th Cir.1998), *cert. denied*, 526 U.S. 1039, 119 S.Ct. 1335, 143 L.Ed.2d 500 (1999); *E.E.O.C. v. Sears, Roebuck & Co.*, 839 F.2d 302, 352 n.53 (7th Cir.1988).

109. *See American Airlines, Inc. v. Herman*, 176 F.3d 283, 288 (5th Cir.1999); *Burns-Vidlak ex rel. Burns v. Chandler*, 165 F.3d 1257 (9th Cir.1999).

110. *See* **Authors' Commentary** to Rule 56(c), *supra*, "Appealability".

111. *See* Rule 56(e).

112. *See Patterson v. County of Oneida*, 375 F.3d 206, 219 (2d Cir. 2004); *Lantec, Inc. v. Novell, Inc.*, 306 F.3d 1003, 1019 (10th Cir. 2002); *Markel v. Board of Regents of Univ. of Wisc. Sys.*, 276 F.3d 906, 912 (7th Cir.2002); *Lopez-Carrasquillo v. Rubianes*, 230 F.3d 409, 414 (1st Cir.2000); *Aucutt v. Six Flags Over Mid-America, Inc.*, 85 F.3d 1311, 1317 (8th Cir. 1996). *But see* **Authors' Commentary** to Rule 56(e), *infra*, "Striking Affidavits" (discussing waiver of objections to defective affidavits); *Ruby v. Springfield R-12 Pub. Sch. Dist.*, 76 F.3d 909, 912 n. 8 (8th Cir.1996)(absent motion to strike or other timely objection, district judge may consider a document which fails to conform to Rule 56(e)'s formal requirements).

Sworn: A summary judgment affidavit must be "sworn" or verified.[113]

Personal Knowledge: A summary judgment affidavit must be made on personal knowledge.[114] Affidavits based on "information and belief"—facts that the affiant *believes* are true, but does not *know* are true—are not proper.[115] Likewise, inferences and opinions must be premised on first-hand observations or personal experience.[116] Although "self-serving", an affidavit of the party herself can suffice under Rule 56(e) provided the affidavit contains specific factual information, is made upon personal knowledge, and otherwise satisfies the Rule's requirements.[117]

Specific Admissible Facts: A summary judgment affidavit must also contain specific facts[118] which, in turn, must be admissible in

113. *See Markel v. Board of Regents of Univ. of Wisc. Sys.*, 276 F.3d 906, 912 (7th Cir.2002) (affidavit improper where not sworn or certified); *Watts v. Kroger Co.*, 170 F.3d 505, 508 (5th Cir.1999) (handwritten statements from co-workers that were signed but not sworn, notarized, or in affidavit form, were not competent summary judgment evidence under Rule 56(e)); *Chaiken v. VV Publ'g Corp. d/b/a Village Voice*, 119 F.3d 1018 (2d Cir.1997), *cert. denied*, 522 U.S. 1149, 118 S.Ct. 1169, 140 L.Ed.2d 179 (1998) (unsworn letters do not meet prerequisites for summary judgment affidavits); *Berwick Grain Co. v. Illinois Dep't of Agric.*, 116 F.3d 231, 234 (7th Cir.1997) (transcript of witness interview insufficient); *Neal v. Kelly*, 963 F.2d 453, 457 (D.C.Cir.1992) (verified statement under 28 U.S.C.A. § 1746 will qualify as summary judgment "affidavit").

114. *See Patterson v. County of Oneida*, 375 F.3d 206, 219 (2d Cir. 2004); *Murphy v. Missouri Dep't of Corrections*, 372 F.3d 979, 982 (8th Cir. 2004); *Bolen v. Dengel*, 340 F.3d 300, 313 (5th Cir.2003), *cert. denied* 541 U.S. 959, 124 S.Ct. 1714, 158 L.Ed.2d 399 (2004); *Payne v. Pauley*, 337 F.3d 767, 772 (7th Cir.2003); *Norita v. Northern Mariana Islands*, 331 F.3d 690, 697 (9th Cir.2003); *Lantec, Inc. v. Novell, Inc.*, 306 F.3d 1003, 1019 (10th Cir.2002); *Sperle v. Michigan Dep't of Corrections*, 297 F.3d 483, 495 (6th Cir.2002); *Pace v. Capobianco*, 283 F.3d 1275, 1278–79 (11th Cir.2002); *Perez v. Volvo Car Corp.*, 247 F.3d 303, 315–16 (1st Cir.2001); *Evans v. Technologies Applications & Serv. Co.*, 80 F.3d 954, 962 (4th Cir.1996). *Cf. Leary v. Dalton*, 58 F.3d 748, 754 (1st Cir.1995)(ruling that "cursory submissions" do not satisfy the "specific facts" showing necessary to defeat a motion for summary judgment).

115. *See Automatic Radio Mfg. Co. v. Hazeltine Research Inc.*, 339 U.S. 827, 831, 70 S.Ct. 894, 896, 94 L.Ed. 1312 (1950); *Murphy v. Missouri Dep't of Corrections*, 372 F.3d 979, 986 (8th Cir. 2004); *Bolen v. Dengel*, 340 F.3d 300, 313 (5th Cir.2003),*cert. denied* 541 U.S. 959, 124 S.Ct. 1714, 158 L.Ed.2d 399 (2004); *Pace v. Capobianco*, 283 F.3d 1275, 1278–79 (11th Cir. 2002); *Cadle Co. v. Hayes*, 116 F.3d 957 (1st Cir.1997).

116. *See Payne v. Pauley*, 337 F.3d 767, 772 (7th Cir.2003) (personal knowledge may include reasonable inferences grounded in observation or other first-hand experience; they may not be "flights of fancy, speculations, hunches, intuitions, or rumors about matters remote from that experience"); *Buchanan v. City of Bolivar*, 99 F.3d 1352, 1355 n. 2 (6th Cir.1996) (plaintiff's sworn statement of facts surrounding her son's detainment were disregarded because plaintiff was not present and, thus, could have no personal knowledge of the events described); *Visser v. Packer Eng'g Assocs., Inc.*, 924 F.2d 655, 659 (7th Cir.1991)(inferences and opinions may not be based on "flights of fancy, speculations, hunches, intuitions, or rumors about matters remote from" personal experience).

117. *See Santiago–Ramos v. Centennial P.R. Wireless Corp.*, 217 F.3d 46, 53 (1st Cir.2000) (explaining when party's own affidavit will suffice). *See also In re Kaypro*, 218 F.3d 1070, 1075 (9th Cir.2000) ("self-serving" affidavit is not necessarily disqualified, so long as foundation was adequate).

118. *See Moore v. J.B. Hunt Transport, Inc.*, 221 F.3d 944 (7th Cir.2000) (affidavit cannot defeat summary judgment motion where it lacks specific facts and offers only conclusory statements); *Santiago-Ramos v. Centennial P.R. Wireless Corp.*, 217 F.3d 46, 53 (1st Cir.2000) (affidavit is insufficient if it merely reiterates allegations from complaint, without providing specific factual information made on the basis of personal knowledge); *Doren v. Battle Creek Health Sys.*, 187 F.3d 595, 598–99 (6th Cir.1999) (requiring specific facts).

evidence at time of trial.[119] Thus, hearsay statements,[120] conclusory averments,[121] unfounded self-serving declarations, [122] speculation or conjecture,[123] and inadmissible expert opinions[124] are generally improper in Rule 56(e) affidavits. A party's promise that he or she has certain unidentified "additional evidence", which will be produced at trial, is insufficient to avoid summary judgment.[125]

Competence: The summary judgment affidavit must demonstrate that the affiant is competent to testify as to the facts contained in the affidavit.[126] Competence to testify may be inferred from the affidavits themselves.[127] Ordinarily, statements of counsel in a memorandum of law are not competent to support or oppose a motion for summary judgment.[128]

119. *See Santos v. Murdock*, 243 F.3d 681, 682 (2d Cir.2001); *Perez v. Volvo Car Corp.*, 247 F.3d 303, 315–16 (1st Cir.2001); *Porter v. Whitehall Labs., Inc.*, 9 F.3d 607, 612 (7th Cir.1993); *Salas v. Carpenter*, 980 F.2d 299, 305 (5th Cir. 1992).

120. *See Patterson v. County of Oneida*, 375 F.3d 206, 219 (2d Cir. 2004); *Murphy v. Missouri Dep't of Corrections*, 372 F.3d 979, 982 (8th Cir. 2004); *Sperle v. Michigan Dep't of Corrections*, 297 F.3d 483, 495 (6th Cir.2002); *Vazquez v. Lopez–Rosario*, 134 F.3d 28, 33 (1st Cir.1998); *U.S. Structures, Inc. v. J.P. Structures, Inc.*, 130 F.3d 1185, 1189 (6th Cir.1997); *Scosche Indus., Inc. v. Visor Gear Inc.*, 121 F.3d 675, 680–81 (Fed.Cir.1997); *Thomas v. International Bus. Machs.*, 48 F.3d 478, 485 (10th Cir.1995). *But see J.F. Feeser, Inc. v. Serv–A–Portion, Inc.*, 909 F.2d 1524, 1542 (3d Cir.1990)(noting Third Circuit rule that hearsay evidence produced in an affidavit opposing summary judgment may be considered if the out-of-court declarant could later present the evidence through direct testimony at trial), *cert. denied*, 499 U.S. 921, 111 S.Ct. 1313, 113 L.Ed.2d 246 (1991).

121. *See Patterson v. County of Oneida*, 375 F.3d 206, 219 (2d Cir. 2004); *Lantec, Inc. v. Novell, Inc.*, 306 F.3d 1003, 1019 (10th Cir. 2002); *Moore v. J.B. Hunt Transport, Inc.*, 221 F.3d 944 (7th Cir.2000); *Doren v. Battle Creek Health Sys.*, 187 F.3d 595, 598–99 (6th Cir. 1999); *Delange v. Dutra Const. Co.*, 183 F.3d 916 (9th Cir.1999). *See Lujan v. National Wildlife Fed'n*, 497 U.S. 871, 888, 110 S.Ct. 3177, 3188, 111 L.Ed.2d 695 (1990)(noting that object of Rule 56 is not to replace conclusory averments in a pleading with conclusory allegations in an affidavit).

122. *See Evans v. Technologies Applications & Serv. Co.*, 80 F.3d 954, 962 (4th Cir.1996); *Hall v. Bellmon*, 935 F.2d 1106, 1111 (10th Cir.1991). *See also In re Kaypro*, 218 F.3d 1070, 1075 (9th Cir.2000) ("self-serving" affidavit is not necessarily disqualified, so long as foundation was adequate); *Delange v. Dutra Const. Co.*, 183 F.3d 916 (9th Cir.1999) (when nonmoving party relies only on his own affidavit to oppose summary judgment, his affidavit may not be conclusory or unsupported by factual data).

123. *See Stagman v. Ryan*, 176 F.3d 986, 995 (7th Cir.1999), *cert. denied*, 528 U.S. 986, 120 S.Ct. 446, 145 L.Ed.2d 363 (1999).

124. *See Ruffin v. Shaw Indus., Inc.*, 149 F.3d 294 (4th Cir.1998) (because expert's opinions are inadmissible under Supreme Court's *Daubert* test, expert's affidavits and deposition testimony cannot be considered on summary judgment motion). *But cf. Morganroth & Morganroth v. DeLorean*, 213 F.3d 1301, 1311 (10th Cir.2000) (expert opinion evidence in affidavit form may be considered on motion for summary judgment).

125. *See Geske & Sons, Inc. v. NLRB*, 103 F.3d 1366, 1376 (7th Cir.1997), *cert. denied*, 522 U.S. 808, 118 S.Ct. 46, 139 L.Ed.2d 13 (1997); *Roche v. John Hancock Mut. Life Ins. Co.*, 81 F.3d 249, 253 (1st Cir.1996).

126. *See Patterson v. County of Oneida*, 375 F.3d 206, 219 (2d Cir. 2004); *Lantec, Inc. v. Novell, Inc.*, 306 F.3d 1003, 1019 (10th Cir. 2002); *Markel v. Board of Regents of Univ. of Wisc. Sys.*, 276 F.3d 906, 912 (7th Cir.2002); *Perez v. Volvo Car Corp.*, 247 F.3d 303, 315–16 (1st Cir.2001); *El Deeb v. University of Minnesota*, 60 F.3d 423, 428–29 (8th Cir.1995); *Davis v. Portline Transportes Maritime Internacional*, 16 F.3d 532, 537 n. 6 (3d Cir.1994). *Cf. Garside v. Osco Drug, Inc.*, 895 F.2d 46, 50 (1st Cir.1990) (expert's affidavit not competent if expert lacks pertinent scientific knowledge).

127. *See Barthelemy v. Air Lines Pilots Ass'n*, 897 F.2d 999, 1018 (9th Cir.1990)(noting that affiant's competence could be inferred from position with the company).

128. *See Orson, Inc. v. Miramax Film Corp.*, 79 F.3d 1358, 1372 (3d Cir.1996)(noting that

Verifications

For purposes of Rule 56(e), the federal courts will accept verified statements made under the penalties of perjury in lieu of an affidavit.[129] Thus, verified complaints (ordinarily not required under the Rules) may be treated as summary judgment "affidavits",[130] so long as they otherwise satisfy the Rule 56(e) prerequisites.[131]

Affidavits to Authenticate Summary Judgment Documents and Exhibits

Parties may submit documents and other exhibits to support or oppose motions for summary judgment. Most courts require that those documents be attached to a Rule 56(e) affidavit that, upon personal knowledge, both identifies and authenticates each document.[132] Documents that fail to satisfy this affidavit authentication requirement may be properly disregarded by those courts when analyzing the pending motion.[133]

"Vouching" Risk with Summary Judgment Affidavits

At least one court has ruled that a party offering a Rule 56(e) affidavit effectively concedes that the affidavit qualifies for consideration under the Rule (that is, that the statements made are sworn, made upon personal knowledge, factually specific, admissible, and competent). The court may properly deny a party's later, pretrial *in limine* motion to strike testimony that the same moving party had earlier itself offered in support of a summary judgment brief, especially where the *in limine* motion purports to challenge an aspect of the testimony that the proffering party had earlier implicitly conceded.[134]

legal memoranda and oral argument are not evidence and cannot independently create a genuine issue of disputed fact sufficient to preclude summary judgment); *Lopez v. Corporacion Azucarera de Puerto Rico*, 938 F.2d 1510, 1516 n. 11 (1st Cir.1991).

129. *See* 28 U.S.C.A. § 1746; *Neal v. Kelly*, 963 F.2d 453, 457 (D.C.Cir.1992).

130. *See Monahan v. New York City Dep't of Corrections*, 214 F.3d 275, 292 (2d Cir.2000); *Ford v. Wilson*, 90 F.3d 245, 247 (7th Cir.1996) (though not "condon[ing] the practice," court holds that verifying the complaint converts the pleading into an affidavit, and it is immaterial that the verification was not captioned "affidavit"), *cert. denied*, 520 U.S. 1105, 117 S.Ct. 1110, 137 L.Ed.2d 311 (1997); *Hayes v. Marriott*, 70 F.3d 1144, 1148 (10th Cir.1995)(same).

131. *See Schroeder v. McDonald*, 55 F.3d 454, 460 (9th Cir.1995) (verified complaint may be considered as opposing affidavit if based on personal knowledge and if it sets forth specific, admissible facts). *But see Lantec, Inc. v. Novell, Inc.*, 306 F.3d 1003, 1019 (10th Cir.2002) (district court properly refused to consider verified complaint as summary judgment affidavit where its allegations were merely conclusory).

132. *See Scott v. Edinburg*, 346 F.3d 752, 759–60 & 760 n.7 (7th Cir. 2003); *Orr v. Bank of America, NT & SA*, 285 F.3d 764, 773–74 (9th Cir.2002); *Woods v. City of Chicago*, 234 F.3d 979, 988 (7th Cir.2000), *cert. denied*, 534 U.S. 955, 122 S.Ct. 354, 151 L.Ed.2d 268 (2001); *Carmona v. Toledo*, 215 F.3d 124, 131 (1st Cir. 2000); *Stuart v. General Motors Corp.*, 217 F.3d 621, 635 n. 20 (8th Cir.2000); *Berk v. Ascott Inv. Corp.*, 759 F.Supp. 245, 249 (E.D.Pa.1991).

133. *See Scott v. Edinburg*, 346 F.3d 752, 759–60 & 760 n.7 (7th Cir. 2003); *Citizens for Better Forestry v. United Stated Dep't of Agric.*, 341 F.3d 961, 972 n.7 (9th Cir.2003); *Stuart v. General Motors Corp.*, 217 F.3d 621, 635 n.20 (8th Cir.2000); *Carmona v. Toledo*, 215 F.3d 124, 131 (1st Cir.2000).

134. *See Williams v. Trader Pub'g Co.*, 218 F.3d 481, 485 (5th Cir.2000) (in an employment case, party offered affidavits of certain male employees to support its summary judgment position, then later attempted to argue that the testimony of these same male employees was inadmissible because the male employees were not in situations "nearly identical" to the plaintiff; court ruled that the testimony was properly admitted because defendant, by introducing this

Contradictory Sworn Evidence from Same Party

A party ordinarily cannot defeat summary judgment by simply denying, in an affidavit, a statement that the party had earlier admitted in a sworn statement. To create a genuine issue for trial sufficient to defeat summary judgment, the party must, in addition to the denial itself, offer an explanation for the inconsistency that the district court finds adequate to allow a reasonable juror to *both* accept the current denial and yet still assume either the truth of, or the party's good faith belief in, the earlier sworn statement.[135] Where, however, the original statement was truly ambiguous, and the later affidavit serves to clarify the testimony, the subsequent statement may be accepted.[136]

Striking Affidavits

A party may move to strike a Rule 56 affidavit. In resolving such motions, the courts use "a scalpel, not a butcher knife".[137] Only those improper portions of an affidavit are disallowed; all properly stated facts are allowed.[138] Moreover, if a party fails to move to strike an improper affidavit or improper portions thereof, the objection is waived.[139]

RULE 56(f). WHEN AFFIDAVITS ARE UNAVAILABLE

CORE CONCEPT

Once a motion for summary judgment is filed, the non-moving party must prove to the court that a genuine and material factual dispute exists to defeat summary judgment. If the non-moving party is still engaged in valuable discovery or for some other reason is not yet ready or able to making that showing, he or she may file an affidavit explaining why a ruling on summary judgment should be postponed.

same evidence at the summary judgment stage, contended that the evidence would be relevant and admissible at trial).

135. *See Cleveland v. Policy Management Sys. Corp.*, 526 U.S. 795, 804, 119 S.Ct. 1597, 1603, 143 L.Ed.2d 966 (1999). *See also Bausman v. Interstate Brands Corp.*, 50 F.Supp.2d 1028 (D.Kan.1999) (conflicting affidavit can only be disregarded if court determines it was merely an attempt to create "sham fact issue"), *aff'd in part, rev'd in part*, 252 F.3d 1111 (10th Cir. 2001).

136. *See Selenke v. Medical Imaging of Colorado*, 248 F.3d 1249, 1258 (10th Cir.2001).

137. *See Perez v. Volvo Car Corp.*, 247 F.3d 303, 315–16 (1st Cir.2001).

138. *See Perez v. Volvo Car Corp.*, 247 F.3d 303, 315–16 (1st Cir.2001); *Hollander v. American Cyanamid Co.*, 172 F.3d 192, 198 (2d Cir. 1999); *Evans v. Technologies Applications & Serv. Co.*, 80 F.3d 954, 962 (4th Cir.1996); *Lee v. National Life Assurance Co. of Canada*, 632 F.2d 524 (5th Cir.1980).

139. *See Ruby v. Springfield R–12 Pub. Sch. Dist.*, 76 F.3d 909, 912 n. 8 (8th Cir.1996)(absent motion to strike or other timely objection, district judge may consider a document which fails to conform to Rule 56(e)'s formal requirements); *In re Unisys Sav. Plan Litig.*, 74 F.3d 420, 437 n. 12 (3d Cir.1996), (party waived objection to form of affidavit by failing to move to strike or otherwise object), *cert. denied*, 519 U.S. 810, 117 S.Ct. 56, 136 L.Ed.2d 19 (1996); *Humane Soc'y of United States v. Babbitt*, 46 F.3d 93, 96 n. 5 (D.C.Cir.1995)(agreeing with sister circuits that Rule 56(e) defects are deemed waived if motion to strike not filed in the district court); *Casas Office Machs., Inc. v. Mita Copystar America, Inc.*, 42 F.3d 668, 682 (1st Cir.1994)(commenting that, absent motion to strike (which specifies objectionable portions of affidavit and grounds for challenge), objections to Rule 56(e) affidavit are deemed waived).

The court, in its discretion, may then grant a temporary reprieve if the affidavit of reasons is persuasive.

APPLICATIONS

Affidavit Required

Some courts will not consider a Rule 56(f) request unless it is accompanied by a sworn affidavit.[140] In any event, every request under Rule 56(f) must specifically seek that the court defer ruling on the then-pending summary judgment motion until further discovery is completed.[141]

When Affidavit May Not Be Required

There is some tension between an absolute requirement that a Rule 56(f) affidavit be filed and the established principle that summary judgment is only properly entered after an adequate time for discovery.[142] To reconcile this tension, some courts have held that a postponement in entering summary judgment may still be appropriate, even in the absence of a Rule 56(f) affidavit, where the nonmoving party adequately notifies the trial court that summary judgment is premature and that additional discovery is necessary, and where the nonmoving party–through no fault of her own–has had little or no opportunity for discovery.[143] Practitioners should be cautioned against relying on this case-specific liberalizing approach, however; even in those cases where this approach is followed, the court has "hasten[ed] to add that parties who ignore Rule 56(f)'s affidavit requirement do so at their peril".[144]

140. *See Ball v. Union Carbide Corp.*, 376 F.3d 554, 561 (6th Cir. 2004); *American Chiropractic Ass'n v. Trigon Healthcare, Inc.*, 367 F.3d 212, 237 (4th Cir. 2004); *Di Benedetto v. Pan Am World Serv., Inc.*, 359 F.3d 627, 630 (2d Cir. 2004); *United States v. Kitsap Physicians Serv.*, 314 F.3d 995, 1000 (9th Cir.2002); *Bradley v. United States*, 299 F.3d 197, 208 (3d Cir.2002); *Woods v. City of Chicago*, 234 F.3d 979, 990 (7th Cir.2000), *cert. denied*, 534 U.S. 955, 122 S.Ct. 354, 151 L.Ed.2d 268 (2001); *Price ex rel. Price v. Western Resources, Inc.*, 232 F.3d 779, 783–84 (10th Cir.2000); *Stanback v. Best Diversified Prods., Inc.*, 180 F.3d 903, 911 (8th Cir.1999); *Byrd v. United States EPA*, 174 F.3d 239, 248 n. 8 (D.C.Cir.1999), *cert. denied*, 529 U.S. 1018, 120 S.Ct. 1418, 146 L.Ed.2d 311 (2000); *Harbert Int'l, Inc. v. James*, 157 F.3d 1271, 1280 (11th Cir.1998). *See also Pastore v. Bell Tel. Co. of Pa.*, 24 F.3d 508 (3d Cir.1994)(noting that affidavit requirement ensures that Rule 56(f) protection is being invoked in good faith and provides trial court with the showing necessary to assess the merits of the party's opposition to the motion). *But cf. Cacevic v. City of Hazel Park*, 226 F.3d 483, 488–89 (6th Cir.2000) (noting how some courts suggest that request for Rule 56(f) can take form other than affidavit); *Stults v. Conoco, Inc.*, 76 F.3d 651, 657–58 (5th Cir.1996)(affidavit form not required).

141. *See Velez v. Awning Windows, Inc.*, 375 F.3d 35, 40 (1st Cir. 2004); *Vargas-Ruiz v. Golden Arch Dev't, Inc.*, 368 F.3d 1, 3–4 (1st Cir. 2004).

142. *See Celotex Corp. v. Catrett*, 477 U.S. 317, 322, 106 S.Ct. 2548, 2552, 91 L.Ed.2d 265 (1986) (setting forth principle).

143. *See Harrods Ltd. v. Sixty Internet Domain Names*, 302 F.3d 214, 244 (4th Cir.2002).

144. *See Harrods Ltd. v. Sixty Internet Domain Names*, 302 F.3d 214, 246 n. 19 (4th Cir. 2002) (making comment, and "reiterat[ing] that our court expects full compliance with Rule 56(f)"). *See also Bradley v. United States*, 299 F.3d 197, 207 (3d Cir.2002) (noting "strong presumption against a finding of constructive compliance with Rule 56(f)").

Prerequisites for Postponing Summary Judgment

Relief under this Rule does not come automatically.[145] Before the courts will postpone a summary judgment ruling pending further discovery, the courts will generally require a Rule 56(f) movant to make three showings: (1) a description of the particular discovery the movant intends to seek; (2) an explanation showing how that discovery would preclude the entry of summary judgment; and (3) a statement justifying why this discovery had not been or could not have been obtained earlier.[146] Although the affidavit (or, where permitted, a non-affidavit submission) need not contain evidentiary facts,[147] the showing made in the affidavit must be specific—vague or baldly conclusory statements will not suffice.[148] Moreover, the affidavit containing these showings must be authoritative (that is, it must be taken by someone with first-hand knowledge of the statements made).[149] The Rule 56(f) request must also be made in a timely fashion, which generally means before any summary judgment response is filed or, in any event, prior to oral argument on the motion.[150] The court is unlikely to grant such a request where the moving party has not been diligent in beginning discovery; the request must verify that the moving party has been diligent in pursuing discovery.[151] A party may not, for example, directly attempt to defeat the summary judgment motion on its merits and then, when an adverse ruling is entered, seek a Rule 56(f) extension of

145. *See Allen v. CSX Transp., Inc.*, 325 F.3d 768, 775 (6th Cir.2003) (movant "has no absolute right to additional time for discovery"); *Price ex rel. Price v. Western Resources, Inc.*, 232 F.3d 779, 783–84 (10th Cir.2000).

146. *See Ball v. Union Carbide Corp.*, 376 F.3d 554, 561 (6th Cir. 2004); *Velez v. Awning Windows, Inc.*, 375 F.3d 35, 40 (1st Cir. 2004); *Price ex rel. Price v. Western Resources, Inc.*, 232 F.3d 779, 783–84 (10th Cir.2000); *In re Silicon Graphics Inc. Secs. Litig.*, 183 F.3d 970 (9th Cir.1999); *Harbert Int'l, Inc. v. James*, 157 F.3d 1271, 1280 (11th Cir.1998); *Duffy v. Wolle*, 123 F.3d 1026, 1040 (8th Cir.1997), *cert. denied*, 523 U.S. 1137, 118 S.Ct. 1839, 140 L.Ed.2d 1090 (1998); *United States v. Bloom*, 112 F.3d 200, 205 n. 17 (5th Cir.1997); *Simmons Oil Corp. v. Tesoro Petroleum Corp.*, 86 F.3d 1138, 1144 (Fed.Cir.1996); *Evans v. Technologies Applications & Serv. Co.*, 80 F.3d 954, 961 (4th Cir. 1996); *St. Surin v. Virgin Islands Daily News, Inc.*, 21 F.3d 1309 (3d Cir.1994) (same).

147. *See Price ex rel. Price v. Western Resources, Inc.*, 232 F.3d 779, 783–84 (10th Cir. 2000).

148. *See Ball v. Union Carbide Corp.*, 376 F.3d 554, 561 (6th Cir. 2004); *Byrd v. United States EPA*, 174 F.3d 239, 248 n. 8 (D.C.Cir. 1999), *cert. denied*, 529 U.S. 1018, 120 S.Ct. 1418, 146 L.Ed.2d 311 (2000); *Grundstad v. Ritt*, 166 F.3d 867, 873 (7th Cir.1999).

149. *See C.B. Trucking, Inc. v. Waste Management, Inc.*, 137 F.3d 41, 44 n. 2 (1st Cir. 1998). *But cf. Simas v. First Citizens' Fed. Credit Union*, 170 F.3d 37, 46 n. 4 (1st Cir.1999) (although movant must attest to personal knowledge of recited grounds, statement need not be presented in form admissible at trial, so long as it rises sufficiently above mere speculation; thus, reliance on hearsay is not necessarily a dispositive defect under Rule 56(f)).

150. *See Simas v. First Citizens' Fed. Credit Union*, 170 F.3d 37, 46 n. 4 (1st Cir.1999) (must be made within reasonable time after summary judgment motion is filed); *Massachusetts Sch. of Law at Andover, Inc. v. American Bar Ass'n*, 142 F.3d 26, 44 (1st Cir.1998).

151. *See Velez v. Awning Windows, Inc.*, 375 F.3d 35, 40 (1st Cir. 2004); *Chance v. Pac–Tel Teletrac Inc.*, 242 F.3d 1151, 1161 n.6 (9th Cir. 2001); *Beattie v. Madison County Sch. Dist.*, 254 F.3d 595, 606 (5th Cir.2001); *Grundstad v. Ritt*, 166 F.3d 867, 873 (7th Cir.1999); *Berkeley v. Home Ins. Co.*, 68 F.3d 1409 (D.C.Cir.1995), *cert. denied*, 517 U.S. 1208, 116 S.Ct. 1825, 134 L.Ed.2d 930 (1996); *Druid Hills Civic Ass'n v. Federal Highway Admin.*, 833 F.2d 1545 (11th Cir.1987), *cert. denied*, 488 U.S. 819, 109 S.Ct. 60, 102 L.Ed.2d 38 (1988).

discovery.[152] If the moving party fails to adequately make any of these showings, the court may deny the requested postponement and rule upon the pending summary judgment motion.[153]

Postponing Very Early Filed Motions for Summary Judgment

When a summary judgment motion is filed very early in the litigation, before a realistic opportunity for discovery, courts generally grant Rule 56(f) postponements freely.[154] Summary judgment is granted in only rare cases where the plaintiff has not had the opportunity for discovery.[155] With such early filed motions, the courts recognize that the Rule 56(f) affiant may not be capable of framing its postponement request with great specificity.[156]

Burden on the Movant

The party moving to postpone the summary judgment ruling bears the burden of demonstrating the requisite basis for relief under Rule 56(f).[157]

District Court's Discretion and Options

Whether to grant or deny a Rule 56(f) postponement is committed to the district court's discretion.[158] In ruling, the district court must balance the moving party's need for the requested discovery against the burden the discovery and delay will place on the opposing party.[159] Ordinarily, such requests are construed generally and are granted

152. *See Rodriguez–Cuervos v. Wal–Mart Stores, Inc.*, 181 F.3d 15, 23 (1st Cir.1999).

153. *See Cervantes v. Jones*, 188 F.3d 805 (7th Cir.1999) (affirming denial of Rule 56(f) motion where excuse for failing to conduct the deposition earlier was a desire to refrain from beginning discovery in order to "foster an atmosphere conducive to settlement"), *cert. denied*, 528 U.S. 1154, 120 S.Ct. 1159, 145 L.Ed.2d 1071 (2000); *Kelly v. Marcantonio*, 187 F.3d 192 (1st Cir.1999) (affirming denial of motion where party failed to specify any material evidence that they would likely uncover if given additional discovery); *In re Silicon Graphics Inc. Secs. Litig.*, 183 F.3d 970 (9th Cir.1999) (noting that failure to comply with Rule 56(f) requirements is proper ground for denying discovery and proceeding to summary judgment); *Stanback v. Best Diversified Prods., Inc.*, 180 F.3d 903, 911 (8th Cir.1999) (noting that where "party fails to carry burden under Rule 56(f), postponement of summary judgment ruling is not justified"); *Byrd v. United States EPA*, 174 F.3d 239, 248 n. 8 (D.C.Cir.1999) (affirming denial where movant, without more, alleged merely that "there may well be" evidence helpful to the claim), *cert. denied*, 529 U.S. 1018, 120 S.Ct. 1418, 146 L.Ed.2d 311 (2000).

154. *See Burlington No. Santa Fe R. Co. v. Assiniboine & Sioux Tribes of Fort Peck Reservation*, 323 F.3d 767, 773–74 (9th Cir.2003)

155. *See Miller v. Wolpoff & Abramson, L.L.P.*, 321 F.3d 292, 303–04 (2d Cir.2003), *cert. denied*, 540 U.S. 823, 124 S.Ct. 153, 157 L.Ed.2d 44 (2003) (No. 02–1820).

156. *See Burlington No. Santa Fe R. Co. v. Assiniboine & Sioux Tribes of Fort Peck Reservation*, 323 F.3d 767, 773–74 (9th Cir.2003) (noting that affiant cannot be expected to frame motion with great specificity as to nature of discovery likely to develop useful information because ground for such specificity has not yet been laid).

157. *See Summers v. Leis*, 368 F.3d 881, 887 (6th Cir. 2004); *Chance v. Pac–Tel Teletrac Inc.*, 242 F.3d 1151, 1161 n.6 (9th Cir.2001); *Stanback v. Best Diversified Prods., Inc.*, 180 F.3d 903, 911 (8th Cir.1999).

158. *See Ball v. Union Carbide Corp.*, 376 F.3d 554, 561 (6th Cir. 2004); *Chance v. Pac–Tel Teletrac Inc.*, 242 F.3d 1151, 1161 n.6 (9th Cir. 2001); *Beattie v. Madison County Sch. Dist.*, 254 F.3d 595, 606 (5th Cir.2001); *Massachusetts Sch. of Law at Andover, Inc. v. American Bar Ass'n*, 142 F.3d 26, 44 (1st Cir.1998).

159. *See Harbert Int'l, Inc. v. James*, 157 F.3d 1271, 1280 (11th Cir.1998).

liberally.[160] On the basis of the party's meritorious Rule 56(f) showings, the district court may: (1) deny the motion for summary judgment; (2) grant a continuance to allow affidavits to be prepared and submitted; (3) permit discovery; or (4) make any other order as is just.

RULE 56(g). AFFIDAVITS MADE IN BAD FAITH

CORE CONCEPT

If the district court concludes that an affidavit submitted under Rule 56(c) or Rule 56(f) was presented in bad faith or solely for purposes of delay, the court will order the offending party to pay reasonable expenses incurred by the party's adversary (including attorney's fees) as a result of the improper affidavits.

APPLICATIONS

Prerequisites of Bad Faith or Delay

Rarely invoked or granted,[161] this Rule requires the court to compensate an adversary who confronted affidavits submitted either in bad faith or for purposes of delay.[162] Merely because one party disbelieves the other party is not a basis for invoking this Rule,[163] nor is the Rule properly invoked merely because the affidavit conflicts with the affiant's prior sworn testimony.[164] Instead, the Rule has been granted in "particularly egregious" circumstances[165] where the district court finds that the affidavit was, in fact, submitted in bad faith or with the purpose of delay.[166] Very little case law exists to guide the court's assessment of

160. *See Beattie v. Madison County Sch. Dist.*, 254 F.3d 595, 606 (5th Cir.2001). *See also Simas v. First Citizens' Fed. Credit Union*, 170 F.3d 37, 46 n. 4 (1st Cir.1999) (when all Rule 56(f) preconditions are met, a "strong presumption arises in favor of relief").

161. *See Fort Hill Builders, Inc. v. National Grange Mut. Ins. Co.*, 866 F.2d 11, 16 (1st Cir. 1989).

162. *See In re Gioioso*, 979 F.2d 956 (3d Cir.1992)(noting that once bad faith is found, court is obligated to assess costs and fees).

163. *See Moorer v. Grumman Aerospace Corp.*, 964 F.Supp. 665, 676 (E.D.N.Y.1997), *aff'd*, 162 F.3d 1148 (2d Cir.1998).

164. *See Bausman v. Interstate Brands Corp.*, 50 F.Supp.2d 1028 (D.Kan.1999), *aff'd in part, rev'd in part*, 252 F.3d 1111 (10th Cir.2001) (conflicting affidavit can only be disregarded if court determines it was merely an attempt to create "sham fact issue"). *See also Cleveland v. Policy Management Sys. Corp.*, 526 U.S. 795, 804, 119 S.Ct. 1597, 1603, 143 L.Ed.2d 966 (1999) (party ordinarily cannot defeat summary judgment by simply denying, in an affidavit, a statement that the party had earlier admitted in a sworn statement unless an adequate explanation for the inconsistency is offered).

165. *See Fort Hill Builders, Inc. v. National Grange Mut. Ins. Co.*, 866 F.2d 11, 16 (1st Cir. 1989).

166. *See Klein v. Stahl GMBH & Co. Maschinefabrik*, 185 F.3d 98, 110 (3d Cir.1999) (bad faith required); *Murray v. Board of Educ. of New York*, 111 F.Supp.2d 349 (S.D.N.Y.2000) (same); *Rogers v. AC Humko Corp.*, 56 F.Supp.2d 972 (W.D.Tenn.1999) (granting sanctions where affiant made a representation upon personal knowledge, relating to a crucial issue, in a manner favorable to his employer, which later proved to be false, and where representation was not a simple mistake but either a highly reckless representation of an important fact or a deliberate and calculated misrepresentation abetted by counsel and designed to thwart justice); *Hunt v. Tektronix, Inc.*, 952 F.Supp. 998, 1010 (W.D.N.Y. 1997) (denying sanctions where affiant's actions, though "unfortunate", were not deliberately taken in bad faith); *Feltner v. Partyka*, 945 F.Supp. 1188, 1192 (N.D.Ind.1996) (denying sanctions where affiant, although technically deficient, was not "willful[ly]" deficient).

"bad faith" under the Rule, and the courts possess wide discretion in making this analysis.[167] Courts have found "bad faith" to be egregious conduct (*e.g.*, averring perjurious or blatantly false allegations or facts) related and necessary to issues central to the disposition of the case.[168] If, however, the improper affidavit is not considered in resolving the summary judgment motion, sanctions under Rule 56(g) may be deemed inappropriate.[169]

Prescribed Remedies For Bad Faith Affidavits

When a court determines that an affidavit has been presented in bad faith, the court will order the presenting party to reimburse its adversaries for all expenses—including attorney's fees—attributable to the additional litigation generated by the bad faith affidavit.[170] At least one court has ruled that relief is mandatory–once the court finds that the affidavit was presented in bad faith or solely for purpose of delay, compensation to the responding party is not discretionary and must be awarded.[171]

Improper Affidavits May Be Stricken

In addition to sanctioning the submitting party, the court also has discretion to strike sham summary judgment affidavits.[172]

Other Penalties

In addition to the sanctions permitted under Rule 56(g), the court may also hold the attorney and the offending party in contempt of court,[173] and false swearing to the court could also give rise to criminal penalties.[174]

Affidavits from *Pro Se* Litigants

Some courts apply the affidavit sanction rule more gently in cases involving affidavits submitted by *pro se* litigants.[175]

167. *See Cobell v. Norton,* 214 F.R.D. 13, 20 (D.D.C.2003).

168. *See Fort Hill Builders, Inc. v. National Grange Mut. Ins. Co.,* 866 F.2d 11, 16 (1st Cir. 1989); *Boggs v. Die Fliedermaus, LLP,* 286 F.Supp.2d 291, 302 (S.D.N.Y. 2003); *Jaisan, Inc. v. Sullivan,* 178 F.R.D. 412, 415–16 (S.D.N.Y. 1998).

169. *See Laney v. American Equity Inv. Life Ins. Co.,* 243 F.Supp.2d 1347, 1358 (M.D.Fla. 2003).

170. *See Klein v. Stahl GMBH & Co. Maschinefabrik,* 185 F.3d 98, 110 (3d Cir.1999).

171. *See Cobell v. Norton,* 214 F.R.D. 13, 20 (D.D.C.2003).

172. *See Bausman v. Interstate Brands Corp.,* 50 F.Supp.2d 1028 (D.Kan.1999), *aff'd in part, rev'd in part,* 252 F.3d 1111 (10th Cir. 2001).

173. *See Klein v. Stahl GMBH & Co. Maschinefabrik,* 185 F.3d 98, 110 (3d Cir.1999).

174. *See* 18 U.S.C.A. § 1623 (prescribing that person who makes a knowingly false material declaration to a court is subject to a $10,000 fine, five years in prison, or both).

175. *See Boggs v. Die Fliedermaus, LLP,* 286 F.Supp.2d 291, 302 (S.D.N.Y. 2003) (finding sanctions inappropriate where litigant appeared *pro se*, no bad faith evidence existed, there had not been repeated unmeritorious filings, and no prior warnings to litigant had been given by the court).

ADDITIONAL RESEARCH REFERENCES

Wright & Miller, *Federal Practice and Procedure* §§ 2711–2742.

C.J.S. Federal Civil Procedure §§ 1135–1187 et seq., 1189–1216 et seq.

West's Key No. Digests, Federal Civil Procedure ⚷2461–2559.

RULE 57

DECLARATORY JUDGMENTS

The procedure for obtaining a declaratory judgment pursuant to Title 28 U.S.C. § 2201, shall be in accordance with these rules, and the right to trial by jury may be demanded under the circumstances and in the manner provided in Rules 38 and 39. The existence of another adequate remedy does not preclude a judgment for declaratory relief in cases where it is appropriate. The court may order a speedy hearing of an action for a declaratory judgment and may advance it on the calendar.

[Amended effective October 20, 1949.]

AUTHORS' COMMENTARY ON RULE 57

PURPOSE AND SCOPE

Rule 57 permits parties to obtain a declaratory judgment to determine their rights and obligations in cases involving actual controversies. The Rule operates in conjunction with the federal Declaratory Judgment Act, 28 U.S.C.A. §§ 2201–02.

APPLICATIONS

Purpose

A declaratory judgment declares the rights and obligations of litigants. Its purpose is to afford litigants an early opportunity to resolve their federal disputes so as to avoid the threat of impending litigation.[1] This procedure is particularly useful for defendants confronting numerous lawsuits, who may seek declaratory relief to avoid a multiplicity of actions and achieve an adequate, expedient, and comparably inexpensive declaration of rights.[2]

Relationship between Rule 57 and Declaratory Judgment Act

Courts have held that the federal Declaratory Judgment Act, 28 U.S.C.A. §§ 2201–02, is "mirrored by" and "functionally equivalent to" Rule 57.[3]

1. *See Biodiversity Legal Found. v. Badgley*, 309 F.3d 1166, 1172 (9th Cir.2002).

2. *See Biodiversity Legal Found. v. Badgley*, 309 F.3d 1166, 1172 (9th Cir.2002).

3. *See Ernst & Young v. Depositors Econ. Prot. Corp.*, 45 F.3d 530, 534 n.8 (1st Cir. 1995).

The Constitutional Requirements: Subject Matter Jurisdiction, Actual Controversy, and Ripeness

Subject Matter Jurisdiction. A plaintiff seeking declaratory relief must establish an independent basis for the district court's subject matter jurisdiction (*e.g.,* diversity of citizenship or federal question).[4] Neither Rule 57 nor the Declaratory Judgment Act expands the court's jurisdiction; these provisions only provide a declaratory remedy in cases properly brought in federal court.[5]

Note: In federal question cases, the district courts will apply the "well-pleaded complaint" rule to assess whether the plaintiff's action involves a federal question. Thus, where the federal nature of plaintiff's claim comes only from plaintiff's anticipation that the defendant will assert a federal defense, the court is likely to find that the plaintiff's claim lacks subject matter jurisdiction.[6]

Actual Controversy. The district court may only enter a declaratory judgment where the dispute between the parties is definite and concrete, affecting the parties' adverse legal interests with sufficient immediacy as to justify relief.[7] No declaratory judgment may be entered where the parties' dispute is hypothetical, abstract, or academic.

Ripeness. The actual controversy requirement obligates the court to determine that the case is "ripe" for adjudication.[8] This "ripeness" must remain throughout the lawsuit. Thus, the district court must decide at the time it is about to enter judgment whether an actual controversy still exists between the parties. Thus, even if an actual controversy existed at the time the lawsuit was filed, the court will not enter a declaratory judgment if later events ended the controversy and

4. For further discussion on this point, see Part II of this text §§ 2.10–2.13 on subject matter jurisdiction.

5. *See Schilling v. Rogers*, 363 U.S. 666, 677, 80 S.Ct. 1288, 1295, 4 L.Ed.2d 1478 (1960)(commenting that the Act is not an independent source of federal jurisdiction); *Aetna Life Ins. Co. v. Haworth*, 300 U.S. 227, 240, 57 S.Ct. 461, 463, 81 L.Ed. 617 (1937)(writing that Act is only procedural). *See also TIG Ins. Co. v. Reliable Research Co.*, 334 F.3d 630, 634 (7th Cir.2003); *Heydon v. MediaOne of Southeast Mich., Inc.*, 327 F.3d 466, 470 (6th Cir.2003); *Commercial Union Ins. Co. v. Walbrook Ins. Co.*, 41 F.3d 764, 775 (1st Cir.1994)(commenting that declaratory judgment is a type of relief, not a theory of recovery).

6. *See Public Serv. Comm'n v. Wycoff Co.*, 344 U.S. 237, 73 S.Ct. 236, 97 L.Ed. 291 (1952). *See also Skelly Oil Co. v. Phillips Petroleum Co.*, 339 U.S. 667, 673, 70 S.Ct. 876, 880, 94 L.Ed. 1194 (1950)("It would turn into the federal courts a vast amount of litigation indubitably arising under State law, in the sense that the right to be vindicated was State-created, if a suit for a declaration of rights could be brought into the federal courts merely because an anticipated defense derived from federal law").

7. *See Maryland Cas. Co. v. Pacific Coal & Oil Co.*, 312 U.S. 270, 61 S.Ct. 510, 85 L.Ed. 826 (1941); *Aetna Life Ins. Co. v. Haworth,* 300 U.S. 227, 57 S.Ct. 461, 81 L.Ed. 617 (1937). *Cf. Calderon v. Ashmus*, 523 U.S. 740, 118 S.Ct. 1694, 140 L.Ed.2d 970 (1998) (holding that declaratory judgments cannot be sought merely for the purpose of testing the validity of a defense that a State may possibly raise in some future, as yet unfiled habeas proceeding).

8. *See Pic-A-State Pa., Inc. v. Reno*, 76 F.3d 1294, 1298 (3d Cir.1996)(in pre-enforcement challenge to statute, court tests for ripeness by examining the adversity of the parties' interests, the conclusiveness of the judicial judgment sought, and the usefulness of the judgment requested), *cert. denied*, 517 U.S. 1246, 116 S.Ct. 2504, 135 L.Ed.2d 194 (1996).

the dispute has become moot.[9]

Note: The courts recognize an exception to this mootness limitation where the plaintiff is able to show a substantial likelihood that the dispute will re-occur in the future.[10]

The Prudential Concerns: Exercise of the District Court's Discretion

Declaratory relief is never automatic. Whether to grant or deny declaratory relief is vested in the sound discretion of the district court.[11] If the court decides not to entertain the declaratory proceeding, it may either stay or dismiss the federal action, and may enter such an order before trial or after all arguments come to a close.[12]

Factors for Court's Consideration

To decide whether to entertain a declaratory judgment action, courts may consider various factors, including whether the declaratory judgment proceeding will resolve the controversy, whether such a proceeding would serve a useful purpose in clarifying the legal relations in dispute, whether the proceeding is being initiated for the purpose of forum shopping, "racing to res judicata", or to procedurally "fence" with the opponent, whether the declaratory judgment action would be inequitable to the allegedly injured party, whether a State court action is already pending in which the controversy could be fully litigated, whether the district court would increase friction between federal and State court systems by hearing the case or would otherwise encroach upon State jurisdiction, whether some alternate relief might be better or more effective, and whether the federal court is a convenient forum

9. *See Preiser v. Newkirk,* 422 U.S. 395, 95 S.Ct. 2330, 45 L.Ed.2d 272 (1975); *Golden v. Zwickler,* 394 U.S. 103, 89 S.Ct. 956, 22 L.Ed.2d 113 (1969). *See also Bauer v. Texas,* 341 F.3d 352, 358 (5th Cir.2003) (substantial and continuing controversy between adverse parties required); *United States v. Braren,* 338 F.3d 971, 975 (9th Cir.2003) (discussing elements for constitutional and prudential ripeness); *Skysign Int'l, Inc. v. City & County of Honolulu,* 276 F.3d 1109, 1114 (9th Cir.2002) (declaratory judgment action is "live", not moot, if facts alleged, under the circumstances, show substantial controversy between parties having adverse legal interests of sufficient immediacy and reality to warrant issuance of declaratory relief).

10. *See Super Tire Eng'g Co. v. McCorkle,* 416 U.S. 115, 94 S.Ct. 1694, 40 L.Ed.2d 1 (1974); *Malowney v. Federal Collection Deposit Group,* 193 F.3d 1342, 1347 (11th Cir.1999) (holding that declaratory judgment remedy is only proper where plaintiffs assert a reasonable expectation that injury will continue or will be repeated in the future), *cert. denied,* 529 U.S. 1055, 120 S.Ct. 1558, 146 L.Ed.2d 463 (2000).

11. *See Provident Tradesmens Bank & Trust Co. v. Patterson,* 390 U.S. 102, 88 S.Ct. 733, 19 L.Ed.2d 936 (1968). *See also Wilton v. Seven Falls Co.,* 515 U.S. 277, 281, 115 S.Ct. 2137, 2140, 132 L.Ed.2d 214 (1995)(noting that, even when subject matter jurisdiction prerequisites are otherwise satisfied, district courts enjoy discretion to determine whether, in what circumstances, to entertain declaratory judgment action); *Hewitt v. Helms,* 482 U.S. 755, 762, 107 S.Ct. 2672, 2676, 96 L.Ed.2d 654 (1987) ("The fact that a court can enter a declaratory judgment does not mean that it should"); *Public Serv. Comm'n v. Wycoff Co.,* 344 U.S. 237, 241, 73 S.Ct. 236, 239, 97 L.Ed. 291 (1952)(noting that the declaratory judgment statute "is an enabling act, which confers a discretion on the courts rather than an absolute right upon the litigant"); *Brillhart v. Excess Ins. Co.,* 316 U.S. 491, 494, 62 S.Ct. 1173, 1175, 86 L.Ed. 1620 (1942) (vesting discretion). *But see Public Affairs Assocs., Inc. v. Rickover,* 369 U.S. 111, 112, 82 S.Ct. 580, 581, 7 L.Ed.2d 604 (1962)(writing that court may not decline to exercise its discretion "as a matter of whim of personal disinclination").

12. *See Wilton v. Seven Falls Co.,* 515 U.S. 277, 287, 115 S.Ct. 2137, 2143, 132 L.Ed.2d 214 (1995).

for parties and witnesses and would otherwise serve the interests of judicial economy.[13]

Note: When another lawsuit involving the same dispute is pending in state court, the district judge may defer to the State forum, particularly where the State case was filed first.[14]

Statement of Circumstances Supporting Declaratory Judgment

If a party contests the prudence of the district court's exercise of discretion to hear a declaratory judgment claim, the court must articulate the factual circumstances supporting the award of declaratory relief.[15]

Realignment of the Parties

In determining whether to grant a declaratory judgment, the courts may realign the parties in order to reflect the nature of the actual, underlying controversy.[16]

Burden of Proof

A party seeking a declaratory judgment bears the burden of proving the existence of an actual case or controversy.[17] But the courts are divided on the question of the merits burden of proof in declaratory judgment actions. Because a declaratory judgment plaintiff often seeks a determination that the defendant lacks some type of right that, had defendant filed suit first, the defendant would bear the burden of proving, some courts permit a shift in the burden of proof.[18] Practition-

13. *See, e.g., Bituminous Cas. Corp. v. J & L Lumber Co.*, 373 F.3d 807, 813 (6th Cir. 2004) (listing several factors for consideration); *St. Paul Fire & Marine Ins. Co. v. Runyon*, 53 F.3d 1167, 1169 (10th Cir.1995)(same); *Commercial Union Ins. Co. v. Walbrook Ins. Co.*, 41 F.3d 764, 775 (1st Cir.1994)(same); *St. Paul Ins. Co. v. Trejo*, 39 F.3d 585, 590–91 (5th Cir.1994)(same). *See International Ass'n of Entrepreneurs of America v. Angoff*, 58 F.3d 1266, 1270 (8th Cir. 1995)(noting reluctance to grant such relief where the action is filed to obtain a "tactical advantage" over an opponent or to open an otherwise closed avenue into federal court by asserting what is essentially a defensive action, reactive to State court litigations), *cert. denied*, 516 U.S. 1072, 116 S.Ct. 774, 133 L.Ed.2d 726 (1996); *BASF Corp. v. Symington*, 50 F.3d 555, 558–59 (8th Cir.1995)(emphasizing that declaratory judgment actions may merit closer inspection to ensure that the plaintiff is not simply forum shopping, and such proceedings may be refused where the plaintiff asserts principally an affirmative defense in a declaratory judgment action brought to deny an injured party its otherwise proper choice of forum and time for suit).

14. *See Geni-Chlor Int'l, Inc. v. Multisonics Dev't Corp.*, 580 F.2d 981 (9th Cir.1978).

15. *See Government Employees Ins. Co. v. Dizol*, 133 F.3d 1220, 1225 (9th Cir.1998).

16. *See BASF Corp. v. Symington*, 50 F.3d 555, 557 (8th Cir.1995).

17. *See Cardinal Chem. Co. v. Morton Int'l, Inc.*, 508 U.S. 83, 94, 113 S.Ct. 1967, 1974, 124 L.Ed.2d 1 (1993); *E.R. Squibb & Sons, Inc. v. Lloyd's & Cos.*, 241 F.3d 154, 177 (2d Cir.2001); *Indium Corp. of America v. Semi–Alloys, Inc.*, 781 F.2d 879 (Fed.Cir.1985), *cert. denied,* 479 U.S. 820, 107 S.Ct. 84, 93 L.Ed.2d 37 (1986).

18. *See Reliance Life Ins. Co. v. Burgess*, 112 F.2d 234 (8th Cir.1940), *cert. denied,* 311 U.S. 699, 61 S.Ct. 137, 85 L.Ed. 453 (1940). *See also American Eagle Ins. Co. v. Thompson*, 85 F.3d 327, 331 (8th Cir.1996)(burden remains on the party asserting the affirmative on an issue); *Utah Farm Bureau Ins. Co. v. Dairyland Ins. Co.*, 634 F.2d 1326 (10th Cir.1980)(noting divergent views on burden of proof in declaratory judgment actions); *Fireman's Fund Ins. Co. v. Videfreeze Corp.*, 540 F.2d 1171 (3d Cir.1976), *cert. denied,* 429 U.S. 1053, 97 S.Ct. 767, 50 L.Ed.2d 770 (1977)(same); *Allstate Ins. Co. v. Sprout*, 782 F.Supp. 999 (M.D.Pa.1991)(same).

ers should consult their local rules and substantive case law on this issue.

Type of Relief Available

The court may grant a successful plaintiff whatever relief is warranted by the evidence, regardless of the demand in the plaintiff's complaint. The Declaratory Judgment Act provides that further relief can be awarded after reasonable notice and hearing. The courts, for example, possess "broad power" to make damages awards in declaratory judgment actions where appropriate.[19]

Note: The Eleventh Amendment ordinarily does not preclude declaratory judgment proceedings instituted against State officials.[20]

Cumulative, Auxiliary Remedy

Declaratory relief cannot be defeated merely by showing that an adequate remedy other than a declaratory judgment exists.[21] A declaratory judgment may be entered whether or not further relief is sought or could have been awarded.[22] Nevertheless, the existence of another, adequate remedy may counsel the district court to exercise its discretion to deny declaratory relief in favor of some better or more effective remedy.[23]

Partial Remedy

If it exercises its discretion to hear a declaratory judgment case, the trial court is not obligated to rule on every issue presented. The court may, instead, properly choose to decide some of the issues raised and decline to decide others.[24]

Any Party May Seek Declaratory Judgment

Any party who has an interest in an actual controversy has standing to seek a declaratory judgment.

Who Declaratory Judgments Benefit

Ordinarily, a declaratory judgment is effective only as to the plaintiffs who obtained it.[25] Often, however, such relief has far broader ramifications (such as in cases declaring the invalidity of a statute or patent).

19. *See BancInsure, Inc. v. BNC Nat'l Bank, N.A.*, 263 F.3d 766, 772 (8th Cir.2001).

20. *See Native Village of Noatak v. Blatchford*, 38 F.3d 1505, 1513–14 (9th Cir.1994).

21. *See Exxon Shipping Co. v. Airport Depot Diner, Inc.*, 120 F.3d 166 (9th Cir.1997). *But see National Private Truck Council, Inc. v. Oklahoma Tax Com'n*, 515 U.S. 582, 589, 115 S.Ct. 2351, 2356, 132 L.Ed.2d 509 (1995)(commenting that the availability of an adequate remedy at law makes declaratory relief unwarranted).

22. *See Powell v. McCormack*, 395 U.S. 486, 89 S.Ct. 1944, 23 L.Ed.2d 491 (1969); *Nautilus Ins. Co. v. Winchester Homes, Inc.*, 15 F.3d 371, 379 (4th Cir.1994).

23. *See Universal Underwriters Serv. Corp. v. Melson*, 953 F.Supp. 385, 388 (M.D.Ala.1996).

24. *See Henglein v. Colt Indus. Operating Corp.*, 260 F.3d 201, 210–11 (3d Cir.2001), *cert. denied*, 535 U.S. 955, 122 S.Ct. 1358, 152 L.Ed.2d 354 (2002).

25. *See Tesmer v. Granholm*, 333 F.3d 683, 701 (6th Cir.2003), *cert. granted*, 540 U.S. 1148, 124 S.Ct. 1144, 157 L.Ed.2d 1041 (2004).

Rules of Procedure

All rules of procedure applicable generally to civil lawsuits apply in a declaratory judgment action.[26]

Expedited Treatment

The district court may order a speedy hearing in declaratory judgment cases, and may move such cases to the top of the court's calendar.

Jury Trial

The right to a jury trial is preserved in declaratory judgment actions. If the issues would have been triable by a jury had something other than declaratory relief been sought, a right to a jury trial exists.[27]

Common Uses

Declaratory judgments are often used in insurance disputes to determine the validity of a policy, the extent of coverage, the insurance company's duty to defend, or a waiver of conditions.[28] Declaratory judgments are also commonly used in patent, copyright, and trademark cases to determine such questions as patent validity and patent infringement.[29] Declaratory judgments can be also be sought to determine a party's immunity status.[30]

Cautious Uses

The district court frequently will refrain from declaratory relief in cases involving important public issues, where the concreteness of a monetary or injunctive dispute is more advisable.[31] The district judge will also often deny declaratory relief that would act to interfere with a State criminal prosecution.[32]

Declaratory Relief Unavailable in Many Tax Cases

Declaratory relief is often not available in federal and State tax cases, particularly where State law provides for efficient tax challenges

26. *See Cloverland–Green Spring Dairies, Inc. v. Pennsylvania Milk Mktg. Bd.*, 298 F.3d 201, 210 n. 12 (3d Cir.2002) (noting that standards for granting summary judgment in declaratory judgment case is same as for all other types of relief).

27. *See Simler v. Conner,* 372 U.S. 221, 83 S.Ct. 609, 9 L.Ed.2d 691 (1963); *Beacon Theatres, Inc. v. Westover*, 359 U.S. 500, 79 S.Ct. 948, 3 L.Ed.2d 988 (1959). *See also Marseilles Hydro Power, LLC v. Marseilles Land & Water Co.*, 299 F.3d 643, 649 (7th Cir.2002) (if declaratory judgment action fits into none of existing equitable patterns, but is instead an "inverted law suit") (a claim by a litigant who, at common law, would have been a defendant, then a jury right exists; if, however, the action is the counterpart of an equity suit, no jury right exists); *Owens-Illinois, Inc. v. Lake Shore Land Co.*, 610 F.2d 1185, 1189 (3d Cir.1979) (same).

28. *See, e.g., Aetna Life Ins. Co. v. Haworth,* 300 U.S. 227, 57 S.Ct. 461, 81 L.Ed. 617 (1937).

29. *See Verizon Communications, Inc. v. Inverizon Int'l, Inc.*, 295 F.3d 870, 873 (8th Cir. 2002); *Phillips Plastics Corp. v. Kato Hatsujou Kabushiki Kaisha,* 57 F.3d 1051, 1053–54 (Fed. Cir.1995).

30. *See In re B–727 Aircraft Serial No. 21010*, 272 F.3d 264, 270 (5th Cir.2001).

31. *See Public Affairs Assocs., Inc. v. Rickover,* 369 U.S. 111, 82 S.Ct. 580, 7 L.Ed.2d 604 (1962).

32. *See Samuels v. Mackell,* 401 U.S. 66, 91 S.Ct. 764, 27 L.Ed.2d 688 (1971).

and remedies, and where the action contests the constitutionality of a State tax provision.

Exception: Congress allows declaratory judgment remedies in cases brought under Section 7428 of the Internal Revenue Code (relating to the status and classification of certain organizations for tax purposes) and Sections 505 and 1146 of the Bankruptcy Code (relating to determinations of tax liability in bankruptcy cases).

Declaratory Relief Unavailable Where Specific Relief Otherwise Provided

A declaratory judgment may not be sought where a statute provides a specific alternate type of proceeding, or where the parties have agreed privately on some other type of proceeding (*e.g.*, a contractual arbitration clause).

Appealability

Whether a declaratory judgment order is immediately appealable depends upon the nature of the court's ruling. Once the court disposes of all the issues presented in the declaratory judgment action (either by ruling upon them or by declining to rule upon them), the resulting declaratory judgment becomes complete, final, and appealable.[33] Conversely, if the court enters an order resolving certain of the issues presented, but expressly leaves open for later resolution other issues in the case, the order is merely interlocutory and, therefore, not immediately appealable under the final order doctrine.[34]

ADDITIONAL RESEARCH REFERENCES:

Wright & Miller, *Federal Practice and Procedure* §§ 2751–2771.

C.J.S. Declaratory Judgments §§ 1–24 et seq., 25–75, 76–126, 127–142 et seq., 143–165.

West's Key No. Digests, Declaratory Judgment ⚷1–395.

33. *See Henglein v. Colt Indus. Operating Corp.*, 260 F.3d 201, 211 (3d Cir.2001), *cert. denied*, 535 U.S. 955, 122 S.Ct. 1358, 152 L.Ed.2d 354 (2002).

34. *See Henglein v. Colt Indus. Operating Corp.*, 260 F.3d 201, 211 (3d Cir.2001), *cert. denied*, 535 U.S. 955, 122 S.Ct. 1358, 152 L.Ed.2d 354 (2002).

RULE 58

ENTRY OF JUDGMENT

(a) Separate Document.

(1) Every judgment and amended judgment must be set forth on a separate document, but a separate document is not required for an order disposing of a motion:

(A) for judgment under Rule 50(b);

(B) to amend or make additional findings of fact under Rule 52(b);

(C) for attorney fees under Rule 54;

(D) for a new trial, or to alter or amend the judgment, under Rule 59; or

(E) for relief under Rule 60.

(2) Subject to Rule 54(b):

(A) unless the court orders otherwise, the clerk must, without awaiting the court's direction, promptly prepare, sign, and enter the judgment when:

(i) the jury returns a general verdict,

(ii) the court awards only costs or a sum certain, or

(iii) the court denies all relief;

(B) the court must promptly approve the form of the judgment, which the clerk must promptly enter, when:

(i) the jury returns a special verdict or a general verdict accompanied by interrogatories, or

(ii) the court grants other relief not described in Rule 58(a)(2).

(b) Time of Entry. Judgment is entered for purposes of these rules:

(1) if Rule 58(a)(1) does not require a separate document, when it is entered in the civil docket under Rule 79(a), and

(2) if Rule 58(a)(1) requires a separate document, when it is entered in the civil docket under Rule 79(a) and when the earlier of these events occurs:

(A) when it is set forth on a separate document, or

(B) when 150 days have run from entry in the civil docket under Rule 79(a).

(c) Cost or Fee Awards.

(1) Entry of judgment may not be delayed, nor the time for appeal extended, in order to tax costs or award fees, except as provided in Rule 58(c)(2).

(2) When a timely motion for attorney fees is made under Rule 54(d)(2), the court may act before a notice of appeal has been filed and has become effective to order that the motion have the same effect under Federal Rule of Appellate Procedure 4(a)(4) as a timely motion under Rule 59.

(d) Request for Entry. A party may request that judgment be set forth on a separate document as required by Rule 58(a)(1).

[Amended December 27, 1946, effective March 19, 1948; January 21, 1963, effective July 1, 1963; April 22, 1993, effective December 1, 1993; April 29, 2002, effective December 1, 2002.]

AUTHORS' COMMENTARY ON RULE 58

PURPOSE AND SCOPE

Rule 58 sets the procedure by which the district court enters judgments on its docket records. The date a judgment is "entered" on the district court docket triggers the time for making post-trial motions, for taking an appeal, and for executing on the relief awarded.

APPLICATIONS

2002 Amendments–*Citation Warning*

Rule 58 was substantially rewritten in 2002 to address the "separate document" requirement for the entry of a federal judgment. The Rule revision took effect December 1, 2002. Practitioners should cite pre-amendment case law construing and applying Rule 58 (particularly case law discussing the "separate document" requirement) with great care.

Contents of Judgment

The judgment document must clearly state which parties are entitled to what relief.[1]

1. *See Citizens Elec. Corp. v. Bituminous Fire & Marine Ins. Co.*, 68 F.3d 1016, 1021(7th Cir. 1995)(proper judgments say who is liable for how much, then stop).

Entry of Judgment

Unless it is a "partial" final judgment under Rule 54(b),[2] all federal judgments are entered either by the clerk or by the court:

By The Clerk: Unless the court otherwise orders, the clerk of court must, without awaiting any further direction from the court, promptly prepare, sign, and enter judgment when (i) the jury returns a general verdict, (ii) the court awards only costs or a sum certain, or (iii) the court denies all relief.[3]

By The Court: The court must review and promptly approve the form of judgment (which the clerk then must promptly enter) when (i) the jury returns a special verdict or a general verdict accompanied by interrogatories, or (ii) the court grants other relief not described above.[4]

The "Old" Separate Document Rule

Prior to the December 2002 amendments to Rule 58, a judgment was required to be (1) set forth in writing, (2) in a "separate document", and (3) entered on the docket. These requirements were intended to create a "bright line" for litigants and the courts in determining when finality attached and, thus, when the period for seeking an appeal began.[5] To abate any uncertainty as to when the appeal "clock" would start ticking, the courts generally applied these requirements mechanically.[6] Until each requirement was met, the judgment was not deemed to have been entered[7] and the time for filing an appeal would not begin to run.[8]

What resulted was a significant body of interpretative case law construing the "separate document" requirement, and deciding what, if any, effect it would have on the appeal period. Some cases explained how rulings orally announced from the bench[9] or included within the text of a minute-order, a memorandum, or a written opinion[10] could not qualify as "judgments" under Rule 58. Other cases explained how a little, but not much, collateral discussion by the trial court might be

2. *See* Rule 54(b) (permitting court to direct the entry of final judgment "as to one or more but fewer than all of the claims or parties only upon an express determination that there is no just reason for delay and upon an express direction for the entry of judgment").

3. *See* Rule 58(a)(2)(A). *See also Otis v. City of Chicago*, 29 F.3d 1159, 1163 (7th Cir.1994) (observing that Rule 58 places on clerk of court the onus of preparing the judgment).

4. *See* Rule 58(a)(2)(B).

5. *See Fogade v. ENB Revocable Trust*, 263 F.3d 1274, 1285–86 (11th Cir.2001); *United States v. Haynes*, 158 F.3d 1327, 1329 (D.C.Cir. 1998).

6. *See Trotter v. Regents of Univ. of New Mexico*, 219 F.3d 1179 (10th Cir.2000).

7. *See United States v. Indrelunas*, 411 U.S. 216, 93 S.Ct. 1562, 36 L.Ed.2d 202 (1973); *Miller v. Marriott Int'l, Inc.*, 300 F.3d 1061, 1064–65 (9th Cir.2002); *Constitution Bank v. Tubbs*, 68 F.3d 685, 692 n. 7 (3d Cir.1995).

8. *See Fogade v. ENB Revocable Trust*, 263 F.3d 1274, 1286 (11th Cir.2001); *Trotter v. Regents of Univ. of New Mexico*, 219 F.3d 1179 (10th Cir.2000).

9. *Atlantic Richfield Co. v. Monarch Leasing Co.*, 84 F.3d 204 (6th Cir.1996).

10. *See United States v. Johnson*, 254 F.3d 279, 285 (D.C.Cir.2001); *Transit Management of S.E. La., Inc. v. Group Ins. Admin., Inc.*, 226 F.3d 376, 382 (5th Cir.2000); *Radio Television Espanola S.A. v. New World Entertainment, Ltd.*, 183 F.3d 922 (9th Cir.1999).

overlooked when included on the "judgment" document.[11] Still other cases explained that the "separate document" requirement could be waived because it was not jurisdictional.[12] Thus, the courts determined that waiver could occur by express agreement of the parties[13] or by failing to timely object.[14] In still other instances, the courts would simply excuse a "separate document" failure entirely where the circumstances made it plain that the court's decision was final.[15]

Ultimately, a split developed among the circuits over how to address the nagging spectre of an appeal period being postponed indefinitely by the failure to meet the requirements of a "separate document" judgment.[16]

The Current Separate Document Rule

The amended Rule 58 changes the "separate document" requirement in order to "ensure that appeal time does not linger on indefinitely".[17] The amendment, however, was expressly not intended to sort through the confusion in the case law with the contents of a separate document, and the drafters directed the courts and litigants to the Appendix of Forms for guidance.[18] Under the new Rule, the separate document requirement will *not apply at all* in certain circumstances:

> *Separate Document Required:* Every judgment and amended judgment must be labeled "judgment" and must be set forth on a separate document.[19] Neither a judicial memorandum or opinion[20]

11. *See Kidd v. District of Columbia*, 206 F.3d 35, 39 (D.C.Cir.2000); *Pacific Employers Ins. Co. v. Domino's Pizza, Inc.*, 144 F.3d 1270, 1278 (9th Cir.1998).

12. *See Bankers Trust Co. v. Mallis*, 435 U.S. 381, 98 S.Ct. 1117, 55 L.Ed.2d 357 (1978); *Henglein v. Colt Indus. Operating Corp.*, 260 F.3d 201, 209 n.5 (3d Cir.2001), *cert. denied*, 535 U.S. 955, 122 S.Ct. 1358, 152 L.Ed.2d 354 (2002); *Missouri ex rel. Nixon v. Prudential Health Care Plan, Inc.*, 259 F.3d 949, 952 (8th Cir.2001).

13. *See Pohl v. United Airlines, Inc.*, 213 F.3d 336, 338 (7th Cir.2000).

14. *See American Disability Ass'n, Inc. v. Chmielarz*, 289 F.3d 1315, 1318 n. 1 (11th Cir. 2002); *Puerto Rico Aqueduct & Sewer Auth. v. Constructora Lluch, Inc.*, 169 F.3d 68, 76 (1st Cir.1999), *cert. denied*, 528 U.S. 872, 120 S.Ct. 175, 145 L.Ed.2d 147 (1999).

15. *See Allison v. Bank One–Denver*, 289 F.3d 1223, 1232–33 (10th Cir.2002); *First Ins. Funding Corp. v. Federal Ins. Co.*, 284 F.3d 799, 804 n. 3 (7th Cir.2002). *See also Quinn v. Haynes*, 234 F.3d 837, 843 (4th Cir.2000) (separate-document requirement may be excused where (1) trial court evidenced its intent that order constituted final decision in the case, (2) judgment was docketed by the clerk, and (3) no objection was made to the procedural violation), *cert. denied*, 532 U.S. 1024, 121 S.Ct. 1968, 149 L.Ed.2d 762 (2001); *Reynolds v. Golden Corral Corp.*, 213 F.3d 1344, 1347 n. 2 (11th Cir.2000) (same).

16. *Compare White v. Fair*, 289 F.3d 1, 6 (1st Cir.2002) (noting court rule that waiver will be inferred where a party fails to act within 3 months to resolve a separate document failure) *with Hammack v. Baroid Corp.*, 142 F.3d 266, 270 (5th Cir.1998) (rejecting First Circuit's 3–month inferred waiver rule); *United States v. Haynes*, 158 F.3d 1327, 1330–31 (D.C.Cir.1998) (same); *Rubin v. Schottenstein, Zox & Dunn*, 143 F.3d 263, 270 (6th Cir.1998) (en banc) (same).

17. *See* Rule 58 advisory committee notes to 2002 amendment.

18. *See* Rule 58 advisory committee notes to 2002 amendment (noting that Forms 31 and 32 "provide examples" of a proper separate document judgment). The Appendix of Forms is reprinted in Part IV of this text.

19. *See* Rule 58(a)(1). *See also Silivanch v. Celebrity Cruises, Inc.*, 333 F.3d 355, 363 (2d Cir.2003), *cert. denied,* 540 U.S. 1105, 124 S.Ct. 1047, 157 L.Ed.2d 890 (2004) (must be labeled a "judgment").

20. *See Silivanch v. Celebrity Cruises, Inc.*, 333 F.3d 355, 363 (2d Cir.2003).

nor marginal entry orders[21] satisfy this requirement. Thus, to qualify as a "separate document", the judgment must (1) be a self-contained, separate document, (2) state the relief granted, and (3) omit the reasoning used by the district court to dispose of pending motions (which should, instead, be contained in the court's opinion).[22] There remains, however, a division among the Circuits as to whether a document marked "order" can ever qualify as a separate document "judgment" under this Rule.[23]

Separate Document Not Required: A separate document is not required for an order disposing of a Rule 50(b) renewed motion for judgment after trial, a Rule 52(b) motion to amend or make additional findings of fact, a Rule 54(d) motion for attorney's fees, a Rule 59 motion for new trial or to alter or amend a judgment, or a Rule 60 motion for relief from a judgment or order.[24]

Time of Entry of Judgment

A judgment must always be entered on the docket.[25] To avoid the uncertainty created by the old "separate document" requirement (which could, theoretically, have allowed for months or years to pass before the appeals clock might begin to run), the revised Rule now imposes an outside time limit for triggering the appeal period:

When Separate Document Required: If a separate document is required, the judgment is deemed to be entered when (1) it is entered on the docket *and* (2) it is actually set forth on a qualifying separate document *or* 150 days passes after the entry on the docket, whichever occurs earlier.[26]

When Separate Document Not Required: If a separate document is not required (*i.e.*, involving a qualifying Rule 50(b), 52(b), 54(d), 59, or 60 motion), the judgment is deemed to be entered when it is entered on the docket.[27]

The 150–day outside time limit should be disregarded, however, where it serves no purpose.[28] Thus, for example, assessing the propriety of an

21. *See Inland Bulk Transfer Co. v. Cummins Engine Co.*, 332 F.3d 1007, 1015 n.7 (6th Cir.2003).

22. *See Selkridge v. United of Omaha Life Ins. Co.*, 360 F.3d 155, 160 n.2 (3d Cir. 2004). *See also Local Union No. 1992 of Int'l Bhd. of Elec. Workers v. Okonite Co.*, 358 F.3d 278, 284–85 (3d Cir. 2004) (separate document requirement satisfied where order was self-contained and separate from opinion, had separate caption, was separately (not consecutively) paginated, was separately signed, was separately file-stamped, and was separately docketed).

23. *See Local Union No. 1992 of Int'l Bhd. of Elec. Workers v. Okonite Co.*, 358 F.3d 278, 285–86 (3d Cir. 2004) (finding "order" may qualify, and discussing case law); *United States v. Johnson*, 254 F.3d 279, 285–86 & 286 n.7 (D.C. Cir. 2001) (same); *Mirpuri v. ACT Mfg., Inc.*, 212 F.3d 624, 628–29 (1st Cir.2000) (same). *See also* Rule 54(a) (defining "judgment" to include "a decree and any order from which an appeal lies"). *But see Kanematsu–Gosho Ltd. v. M/T Messiniaki Aigli*, 805 F.2d 47, 48–49 (2d Cir. 1986) (per curiam) ("order" does not qualify as judgment).

24. *See* Rule 58(a)(1).

25. *See* Rule 79 (providing for entries on the official court docket).

26. *See* Rule 58(b)(2). *See Funk v. LFLM Defendants*, 382 F.3d 1058, 1064 (10th Cir. 2004); *Freudensprung v. Offshore Tech. Servs., Inc.*, 379 F.3d 327 (5th Cir. 2004).

27. *See* Rule 58(b)(1).

28. *See* Rule 58 advisory committee notes to 2002 amendments.

appeal from a collateral order should *not* be complicated by the separate document requirement.[29] To the contrary, appeal periods for collateral orders should start to run when the collateral order is entered, and should not await either the creation of a separate document or the passing of 150 days.[30]

Attorney Initiatives to Satisfy Separate Document Requirement

Before the 2002 amendments, Rule 58 prohibited attorneys from drafting and submitting proposed forms of judgment, unless directed to do so by the court.[31] This prohibition was designed to avoid delays encountered by such drafting and submission and to avoid occasionally inept drafting results.[32] The former prohibition was "replaced" by the drafters with a new provision that expressly permits a party to request the entry of a separate document judgment.[33]

Taxation of Costs / Award of Attorney's Fees

The entry of judgment ordinarily may not be delayed or extended pending the taxation of costs.[34] However, the court may, in its discretion, enter an order deeming a motion for an award of attorney's fees to be the equivalent of a Rule 59 request.[35] The court may only enter such an order if: (1) the motion for fees is timely made (within 14 days after entry of judgment)[36], (2) no effective notice of appeal is in place, but (3) a timely notice of appeal is still possible.[37] If the court enters such an order, the 30–day period for filing an appeal will not begin to run until the court enters its order resolving the fees claim.[38] That

29. *See* Rule 58 advisory committee notes to 2002 amendments.

30. *See* Rule 58 advisory committee notes to 2002 amendments.

31. *See* Rule 58 (former language: "Attorneys shall not submit forms of judgment except upon direction of the court, and these directions shall not be given as a matter of course").

32. *See* Rule 58 advisory committee notes to 2002 amendment. *See also Matteson v. United States*, 240 F.2d 517, 519 (2d Cir.1956) (commenting that earlier practice of having lawyers prepare form of judgment caused delay in the entry of judgment and forced the court to sift through "the normal excess of detail supplied by zealous advocates in their natural desire to press home all conceivable ad hoc advantages from the judgment").

33. *See* Rule 58(d). *See also id.* advisory committee notes to 2002 amendment ("The new provision allowing any party to move for entry of judgment on a separate document will protect all needs for prompt commencement of the periods for motions, appeals, and execution or other enforcement").

34. *See* Rule 58(c)(1). *See also Richards v. Government of the Virgin Islands,* 579 F.2d 830 (3d Cir.1978). *But see Maristuen v. National States Ins. Co.*, 57 F.3d 673, 678 (8th Cir. 1995)(award of specific sum in attorney's fees required for final order where such award was integral part of claim—in this instance, bad faith claim).

35. *See* Rule 58(c)(2). *See also Gilda Marx, Inc. v. Wildwood Exercise, Inc.*, 85 F.3d 675, 680 n. 5 (D.C.Cir.1996)(from the perspective of the appellate courts, it is obviously desirable to have merits appeals and fees order appeals decided together).

36. *See Cooper v. Pentecost*, 77 F.3d 829 (5th Cir.1996)(noting that 14–day period for petitioning for fee award does not begin to run until judgment is entered in a separate document).

37. *See Mendes Junior Int'l Co. v. Banco do Brasil, S.A.*, 215 F.3d 306 (2d Cir.2000) (the filing of a fees-and-costs motion cannot rescue an otherwise out-of-time appeal; if the 30–day appeal clock has run, a ruling on the fees-and-costs motion will not revive the time to appeal).

38. *See Wikol ex rel. Wikol v. Birmingham Pub. Schs. Bd. of Educ.*, 360 F.3d 604, 607–08 (6th Cir. 2004); *Deboard v. Sunshine Mining & Refining Co.*, 208 F.3d 1228, 1236 (10th Cir. 2000).

order granting or denying fees must likewise include an order satisfying the separateness requirement.[39] Note, however, that this appeal time postponement provision applies only to attorneys' fees awards, and not to costs.[40]

Warning: Unless the district court grants–and *properly* grants–a request under Rule 58(c)(2) to postpone the running of the appeal clock, that clock will continue to run throughout the time that the attorneys' fees motion remains pending. Consequently, a mistaken reliance that the open fees motion is automatically tolling the time for taking an appeal can lead to a complete loss of all appellate rights on the underlying merits.[41]

Implications for Appeal

Ripeness: The clerk's entry of a judgment is evidence of, but not a requirement for, finality and ripeness for appeal.[42] Thus, an order can become final, and thus appealable, even without qualifying as a separate document.[43] The significance is this: absent a waiver of the Rule 58 requirements, an appeal *may* be taken from a final, appealable order that fails the separate document test, but the "clock" for a timely appeal will not begin running until the order is entered on the docket and, if a separate document is required, actually set forth on a separate document *or* 150 days have passed following entry (whichever is earlier).[44] In the meanwhile, the district court never loses its jurisdiction over the case.[45] Where the court enters an order of dismissal that grants plaintiff leave, within a prescribed period of time, to amend or otherwise cure the basis for the dismissal, the finality of the dismissal order may be deemed suspended until the prescribed period has closed.[46]

Waiver By Appellant: By not starting the appeal clock until either a qualifying separate document judgment has been entered or 150 days has passed, the 150–day clock benefits the appellant. The appellant

39. *See Deboard v. Sunshine Mining & Refining Co.*, 208 F.3d 1228, 1237 (10th Cir.2000).

40. *See Moody Nat'l Bank of Galveston v. GE Life & Annuity Assur. Co.*, 383 F.3d 249, 252-53 (5th Cir. 2004).

41. *See Wikol ex rel. Wikol v. Birmingham Public Schs. Bd. of Educ.*, 360 F.3d 604, 609–10 (6th Cir. 2004). The ambiguity of the current wording of Rule 58(c)(2) prompted harsh comments from this Court of Appeals. *See id.* at 610 ("As a final comment on this issue, we cannot help but express dismay over the complexity of the rules regarding the timeliness of an appeal under the present circumstances. There should be no need to have to parse the language of four different rules of procedure in order to find an answer to whether an appeal is timely filed. . . . Perhaps this is a topic that should be considered by the Advisory Committee to the Federal Rules of Appellate Procedure").

42. *See* Rule 54(b). *See also American Int'l Specialty Lines Ins. Co. v. Electronic Data Sys. Corp.*, 347 F.3d 665, 669 (7th Cir. 2003); *Franklin v. District of Columbia*, 163 F.3d 625, 630 (D.C.Cir.1998).

43. *See American Int'l Specialty Lines Ins. Co. v. Elec. Data Sys. Corp.*, 347 F.3d 665, 669 (7th Cir. 2003).

44. *See* Rule 58(b). *See also Shalala v. Schaefer*, 509 U.S. 292, 113 S.Ct. 2625, 125 L.Ed.2d 239 (1993) (decided under pre–2002 amendment, but noting that trial court's failure to enter judgment on a separate document kept the time for appeal open); *American Int'l Specialty Lines Ins. Co. v. Electronic Data Sys. Corp.*, 347 F.3d 665, 669 (7th Cir. 2003).

45. *See Fogade v. ENB Revocable Trust*, 263 F.3d 1274, 1286 (11th Cir.2001).

46. *See Otis v. City of Chicago*, 29 F.3d 1159 (7th Cir.1994).

may, however, waive this benefit and file an appeal at any point within the 150–day period without affecting the validity of the appeal.[47] (Other conduct, like filing a Rule 60 motion for relief from judgment, can also qualify as a waiver of the separate document rule.)[48] Conversely, the appellee cannot object to this waiver and compel the appellant to return to the district court to insist upon compliance with the separate document rule.[49]

Triggering the Appeal Clock: To ensure prompt appeals, the prevailing parties should quickly confirm with the clerk's office that both Rule 58 requirements (separate writing and entry) have been satisfied.

Transferring Judgments to Another Judicial District

A judgment for money or property entered by one federal district court may be transferred to, and executed upon in, another district court. Such transfers are accomplished by filing a certified copy of the judgment in the new district court *after* the judgment has become final after appeal, by the expiration of time for appeal, or when, still pending appeal, the court so orders for good cause.[50] The transferred judgment will have the same effect as any other judgment entered in the new district.[51]

ADDITIONAL RESEARCH REFERENCES

Wright & Miller, *Federal Practice and Procedure* §§ 2781–2787.

C.J.S. Federal Civil Procedure §§ 1227–1231 et seq.

West's Key No. Digests, Federal Civil Procedure ⚷2621–2628.

47. *See de Jesus–Mangual v. Rodriguez*, 383 F.3d 1, 5 (1st Cir. 2004); *Peng v. Penghu*, 335 F.3d 970, 975 n.4 (9th Cir.2003), *cert. denied,* 540 U.S. 1218, 124 S.Ct. 1506, 158 L.Ed.2d 153 (2004).

48. *See Casey v. Albertson's Inc.*, 362 F.3d 1254, 1256–59 (9th Cir. 2004), *petition for cert. filed*, No. 02–57198 (U.S. July 6, 2004).

49. *See Peng v. Penghu*, 335 F.3d 970, 975 n.4 (9th Cir.2003), *cert. denied,* 540 U.S. 1218, 124 S.Ct. 1506, 158 L.Ed.2d 153 (2004).

50. *See Stanford v. Utley,* 341 F.2d 265 (8th Cir.1965).

51. *See* 28 U.S.C.A. § 1963.

RULE 59

NEW TRIALS; AMENDMENT OF JUDGMENTS

(a) Grounds. A new trial may be granted to all or any of the parties and on all or part of the issues (1) in an action in which there has been a trial by jury, for any of the reasons for which new trials have heretofore been granted in actions at law in the courts of the United States; and (2) in an action tried without a jury, for any of the reasons for which rehearings have heretofore been granted in suits in equity in the courts of the United States. On a motion for a new trial in an action tried without a jury, the court may open the judgment if one has been entered, take additional testimony, amend findings of fact and conclusions of law or make new findings and conclusions, and direct the entry of a new judgment.

(b) Time for Motion. Any motion for a new trial shall be filed no later than 10 days after entry of the judgment.

(c) Time for Serving Affidavits. When a motion for new trial is based on affidavits, they shall be filed with the motion. The opposing party has 10 days after service to file opposing affidavits, but the period may be extended for up to 20 days, either by the court for good cause or by the parties' written stipulation. The court may permit reply affidavits.

(d) On Court's Initiative; Notice; Specifying Grounds. No later than 10 days after entry of judgment the court, on its own, may order a new trial for any reason that would justify granting one on a party's motion. After giving the parties notice and an opportunity to be heard, the court may grant a timely motion for a new trial for a reason not stated in the motion. When granting a new trial on its own initiative or for a reason not stated in a motion, the court shall specify the grounds in its order.

(e) Motion to Alter or Amend Judgment. Any motion to alter or amend a judgment shall be filed no later than 10 days after entry of the judgment.

[Amended effective March 19, 1948; July 1, 1966; April 27, 1995, effective December 1, 1995.]

AUTHORS' COMMENTARY ON RULE 59

PURPOSE AND SCOPE

When appropriate to prevent a miscarriage of justice, the district court may set aside a verdict and order a new trial or, alternatively, alter or amend a judgment.

NOTE: A party moving for either a new trial or an order altering or amending a judgment must file such a motion no later than 10 days after the judgment is entered. The district court may *not* extend this 10 day period.

RULE 59(a). GROUNDS FOR GRANTING NEW TRIAL

CORE CONCEPT

In both jury and bench trials, the court may grant a new trial for any reason for which new trials (jury trials) or rehearings (bench trials) were formerly granted, such as where the verdict is against the weight of the evidence or is either excessive or inadequate, where probative evidence is newly discovered, or where conduct by the court, counsel, or the jury improperly influenced the deliberative process.

APPLICATIONS

Procedure

Motions for new trial are usually made in writing and must state with particularity the grounds for relief.

Discretion of District Court

Whether the circumstances justify the granting of a new trial is a decision left to the sound discretion of the trial judge.[1] So broad is this discretion in certain contexts, that one court has described it as "virtually unassailable on appeal".[2] In exercising this discretion, the trial judge may reopen a judgment, hear additional testimony, and amend (or make new) findings of fact and conclusions of law.[3]

Grounds for New Trials

The district courts may grant new trials for several reasons. New trials may be granted, for example, where:

1. *See Allied Chem. Corp. v. Daiflon, Inc.*, 449 U.S. 33, 101 S.Ct. 188, 66 L.Ed.2d 193 (1980)(noting that the authority to grant a new trial "is confided almost entirely to the exercise of discretion on the part of the trial court"). *See also Rivera Castillo v. Autokirey, Inc.*, 379 F.3d 4 (1st Cir. 2004); *Manley v. Ambase Corp.*, 337 F.3d 237, 244–45 (2d Cir.2003); *Peyton v. DiMario*, 287 F.3d 1121, 1125–28 (D.C.Cir.2002); *Ecolab, Inc. v. Paraclipse, Inc.*, 285 F.3d 1362, 1369 (Fed. Cir.2002); *Defenders of Wildlife v. Bernal*, 204 F.3d 920, 928–29 (9th Cir.2000); *Neal v. Honeywell, Inc.*, 191 F.3d 827, 831 (7th Cir. 1999); *Sibley v. Lemaire*, 184 F.3d 481 (5th Cir. 1999), *cert. denied*, 529 U.S. 1019, 120 S.Ct. 1420, 146 L.Ed.2d 312 (2000).

2. *See Children's Broad. Corp. v. Walt Disney Co.*, 357 F.3d 860, 867 (8th Cir. 2004) (in context of denial of new trials on against the weight of the evidence claims).

3. *See Defenders of Wildlife v. Bernal*, 204 F.3d 920, 928–29 (9th Cir.2000).

- *Verdict Against the Weight of Evidence:* when the district court concludes that the factfinder's verdict is against the "clear" or "great" weight of the evidence, and a new trial is therefore necessary to prevent a miscarriage of justice;[4]
- *Verdict is Excessive or Inadequate:* when the district court determines that the amount of the verdict is so unreasonable that it shocks the conscience;[5]

  "Remittitur": If the court decides that the verdict is excessive, the court may offer the verdict winner a reduction—called a "remittitur"—in exchange for the court's denial of a motion for a new trial.[6] If the verdict winner accepts the court's offer, the verdict winner waives the right of appeal.[7] If remitted, the jury's verdict will usually be reduced to the maximum amount the jury could have awarded without being excessive.[8]

  "Additur": If the court finds that the verdict is inadequate, the court may *not* offer the verdict winner an increase in verdict size—called an "additur"—in exchange for the court's denial of a motion for new trial.

4. *See Byrd v. Blue Ridge Rural Elec. Cooperative, Inc.*, 356 U.S. 525, 540, 78 S.Ct. 893, 902, 2 L.Ed.2d 953 (1958); *Rivera Castillo v. Autokirey, Inc.*, 379 F.3d 4 (1st Cir. 2004); *Manley v. Ambase Corp.*, 337 F.3d 237, 244–45 (2d Cir.2003); *Susan Wakeen Doll Co. v. Ashton Drake Galleries*, 272 F.3d 441, 449–50 (7th Cir. 2001). *See also Latino v. Kaizer*, 58 F.3d 310, 314 (7th Cir.1995)(ruling that jury's verdict should be accorded greater deference under Rule 59 in cases involving simple issues with highly disputed facts, than in cases involving complex issues with facts that are not as disputed).

5. *See Rivera Castillo v. Autokirey, Inc.*, 379 F.3d 4 (1st Cir. 2004) (must exceed "any rational appraisal or estimate of the damage that could be based on the evidence before the jury"); *Eiland v. Westinghouse Elec. Corp.*, 58 F.3d 176, 183 (5th Cir.1995)(jury's award may be disturbed only upon a "clear showing of excessiveness" such that the verdict is "contrary to right reason" or "entirely disproportionate to the injury sustained"); *Starceski v. Westinghouse Elec. Corp.*, 54 F.3d 1089, 1100 (3d Cir. 1995)(remittitur allowed only where court concludes that evidence clearly does not support verdict and exceeds amount needed to make plaintiff whole). *But see Gasperini v. Center for Humanities, Inc.*, 518 U.S. 415, 116 S.Ct. 2211, 135 L.Ed.2d 659 (1996) (citing the *Erie* doctrine in applying New York's state law standard for judging "excessiveness", where state standard differed from federal "shocks the conscience" benchmark).

6. *See Linn v. United Plant Guard Workers of America, Local 114*, 383 U.S. 53, 65–66, 86 S.Ct. 657, 664–65, 15 L.Ed.2d 582 (1966) (holding that if damages award is excessive, trial judge has the "duty" to require a remittitur or grant a new trial); *Cline v. Wal-Mart Stores, Inc.*, 144 F.3d 294, 305 n. 2 (4th Cir.1998) (describing remittitur procedure and Seventh Amendment concerns); *Atlas Food Sys. & Servs., Inc. v. Crane Nat'l Vendors, Inc.*, 99 F.3d 587, 593 (4th Cir.1996) (noting remittitur's history, dating back to 1822); *Tingley Sys., Inc. v. Norse Sys., Inc.*, 49 F.3d 93, 96 (2d Cir. 1995)(instructing that district courts, upon finding jury verdict to be excessive, may order a new trial, may order a partial new trial limited to damages, or may offer to deny the new trial motion on the condition that plaintiff accepts damages in reduced amount). Note, however, that the court ordinarily may not reduce plaintiff's damages award without first offering plaintiff a new trial. *See In re Joint Eastern & Southern Dist. Asbestos Litig.*, 52 F.3d 1124, 1139 (2d Cir.1995).

7. *See Donovan v. Penn Shipping Co.*, 429 U.S. 648, 97 S.Ct. 835, 51 L.Ed.2d 112 (1977)(per curiam).

8. *See Eiland v. Westinghouse Elec. Corp.*, 58 F.3d 176, 183 (5th Cir.1995). *See Earl v. Bouchard Transp. Co.*, 917 F.2d 1320, 1328–30 (2d Cir.1990)(adopting same rule, but discussing the three views on remittitur and scholarly commentary's preferences).

Where the verdict is inadequate, the court's only option is ordering a new trial.[9]

- *Newly Discovered Evidence:* when the district court learns of a party's newly discovered evidence. To entitle the moving party to a new trial, the "newly discovered evidence" generally: (1) must have existed as of the time of trial; (2) must have been excusably overlooked by the moving party, notwithstanding the moving party's due diligence in attempting to discover it; (3) must be admissible; and (4) must be likely to alter the trial's outcome.[10] In addition to a new trial under Rule 59, newly discovered evidence may also entitle the moving party to relief from judgment under Rule 60(b)(2);
- *Improper Conduct by Counsel or the Court:* when improper conduct by either an attorney or the court unfairly influenced the verdict;[11]
- *Improper Conduct Affecting the Jury:* when the jury verdict was not unanimous or was facially inconsistent, or when the jury was improperly influenced,[12] or when an erroneous jury instruction likely misled or confused the jury.[13] Note, however, that after the verdict is returned, jurors may not impeach or alter their verdict except to testify as to improper, extrinsic influences.[14]

Prejudice

Trial errors may only give rise to a new trial if they affect the substantive rights of the parties and are not cured by the trial judge's cautionary instructions to the jury.[15]

9. *See Dimick v. Schiedt,* 293 U.S. 474, 55 S.Ct. 296, 79 L.Ed. 603 (1935)(finding that additur violates Constitution's Seventh Amendment right to a jury verdict).

10. *See Peacock v. Board of Sch. Comm'rs,* 721 F.2d 210 (7th Cir.1983). *See also Advanced Display Sys., Inc. v. Kent State Univ.*, 212 F.3d 1272, 1284 (Fed.Cir.2000) (stating three-prong test: probability of affecting outcome, reasonably discoverable earlier, and more than merely cumulative or impeaching), *cert. denied*, 532 U.S. 904, 121 S.Ct. 1226, 149 L.Ed.2d 136 (2001); *Defenders of Wildlife v. Bernal*, 204 F.3d 920, 928–29 (9th Cir.2000) (criteria include: evidence discovered after trial, not fairly discoverable earlier, and likelihood of changing outcome); *Joseph v. Terminix Int'l Co.*, 17 F.3d 1282, 1285 (10th Cir.1994) (listing newly discovered evidence criteria).

11. *See Wharf v. Burlington Northern R. Co.*, 60 F.3d 631 (9th Cir.1995)(granting new trial where counsel permitted district court to read to the jury an untruthful stipulated fact concerning plaintiff); *Aggarwal v. Ponce Sch. of Med.*, 837 F.2d 17 (1st Cir.1988)(before conduct of judge will warrant a new trial, the moving party must be "so seriously prejudiced as to be deprived of a fair trial"); *City of Cleveland v. Peter Kiewit Sons' Co.*, 624 F.2d 749 (6th Cir.1980)(moving for new trial where counsel injected into trial notion that insurance company would pay any award).

12. *Cf. Parker v. Gladden,* 385 U.S. 363, 87 S.Ct. 468, 17 L.Ed.2d 420 (1966)(per curiam)(statement by bailiff that defendant was a "wicked fellow" who was guilty, and that the higher courts would correct a guilty verdict if it was wrong).

13. *See Susan Wakeen Doll Co. v. Ashton Drake Galleries*, 272 F.3d 441, 452 (7th Cir. 2001).

14. *See Carson v. Polley,* 689 F.2d 562 (5th Cir.1982); *Smallwood v. Pearl Brewing Co.,* 489 F.2d 579 (5th Cir.1974), *cert. denied,* 419 U.S. 873, 95 S.Ct. 134, 42 L.Ed.2d 113 (1974).

15. *See* Rule 61 (directing that harmless errors are to be disregarded).

Waiver

A party may not seek a new trial on grounds not brought contemporaneously to the trial judge's attention.[16] The courts recognize a narrow exception to this waiver rule where a trial error is so fundamental that gross injustice would result were it not corrected.

Bench Trials

Following a bench trial, the court may open a judgment already entered, hear additional testimony, revise or add findings of fact and conclusions of law, and direct the entry of a new judgment.

Partial New Trials

The court may grant a partial new trial limited only to certain issues, provided the error justifying the new trial did not affect the determination of the remaining issues[17], and provided that the singular issue for retrial is so clearly distinct and separate from all other issues that a retrial of it alone will not be unjust.[18] If, however, the trial court concludes that passion influenced the jury, a partial new trial on the issue of damages alone is ordinarily improper; the court must instead order a new trial on all issues.[19] When a partial new trial is granted, those portions of the original judgment that were not set aside by the court become part of the single, ultimate judgment following the new trial. Most commonly, courts have granted partial new trials on damages, following an error-free trial on liability issues, but partial new trials can be granted as to any "separable matter".[20]

Appealability

An order granting a new trial is generally interlocutory and not immediately appealable, absent a showing that the court lacked authority to enter the order.[21] An order denying a new trial is also usually not immediately appealable because the party's proper appeal is often an appeal from the final judgment, not from the denial of a new trial.[22]

16. *See United States v. Walton,* 909 F.2d 915 (6th Cir.1990). *But cf. Pulla v. Amoco Oil Co.,* 72 F.3d 648, 656 (8th Cir.1995)(party may move for new trial under Rule 59 "based on the overwhelming evidence contrary to the verdict without ever previously raising such an objection").

17. *See Anderson v. Siemens Corp.*, 335 F.3d 466, 475–76 (5th Cir.2003); *Eximco, Inc. v. Trane Co.*, 737 F.2d 505 (5th Cir.1984).

18. *See Gasoline Prods. v. Champlin Refining Co.*, 283 U.S. 494, 500, 51 S.Ct. 513, 515, 75 L.Ed. 1188 (1931); *Anderson v. Siemens Corp.*, 335 F.3d 466, 475–76 (5th Cir.2003); *Rice v. Community Health Ass'n*, 203 F.3d 283, 290 (4th Cir.2000).

19. *See Sanford v. Crittenden Mem'l Hosp.*, 141 F.3d 882, 885 (8th Cir.1998).

20. *See Rice v. Community Health Ass'n*, 203 F.3d 283, 290 (4th Cir.2000).

21. *See Allied Chem. Corp. v. Daiflon, Inc.*, 449 U.S. 33, 101 S.Ct. 188, 66 L.Ed.2d 193 (1980); *Schudel v. General Elec. Co.*, 120 F.3d 991, 994–95 (9th Cir.1997), *cert. denied*, 523 U.S. 1094, 118 S.Ct. 1560, 140 L.Ed.2d 792 (1998).

22. *See, e.g., Clark v. Heidrick*, 150 F.3d 912 (8th Cir.1998) (in absence of exceptional circumstances, orders denying motion for new trial are not immediately appealable); *Bethel v. McAllister Bros., Inc.,* 81 F.3d 376, 382 (3d Cir.1996)(order granting new trial is interlocutory and therefore nonappealable; but once new trial is complete, appellate court may review Rule 59 order).

Note that even ultimate appellate review of denials of new trials may be further limited by Seventh Amendment constitutional concerns.[23]

RULE 59(b). TIME FOR MAKING MOTION FOR NEW TRIAL

CORE CONCEPT

A party must file a motion for new trial within 10 days after the entry of judgment.

APPLICATIONS

10 Days to File Motion for New Trial

A party seeking a new trial must *file* the Rule 59 motion within 10 days after the district court enters its judgment on the docket.[24]

Amended Judgments

Where an amended judgment is filed and alters the legal rights or obligations of the parties, the court may find that a new 10–day period for filing Rule 59 motions is triggered.[25]

Early Motions

A party may move for a new trial before the formal entry of judgment and at any time during the 10 days following the entry of judgment.

No Extensions or Waiver

This 10–day period is jurisdictional, and may not be extended by court order or waived by the parties.[26] Nor will the fact that one party moves for relief under Rule 59 excuse all other parties seeking such relief from timely filing separately.[27] Although the 10–day limitation is mandatory, courts may consider untimely Rule 59 motions as requests for relief under Rule 60.[28]

3–Day Service–By–Mail Extension Does Not Apply

Rule 6(e) extends a party's time for acting by 3 days if the relevant time period is to begin upon service by mail. Because Rule 59(b)

23. *See Jocks v. Tavernier*, 316 F.3d 128, 137 (2d Cir.2003) (commenting that district court's determination that jury's verdict was not against weight of evidence is not reviewable on appeal due to limitations imposed by Seventh Amendment).

24. *See Schudel v. General Elec. Co.*, 120 F.3d 991 (9th Cir.1997), *cert. denied*, 523 U.S. 1094, 118 S.Ct. 1560, 140 L.Ed.2d 792 (1998) (noting that Rule 59, as amended in 1995, requires that such motions be filed, not served, within 10 days following entry of judgment).

25. *See Walker v. Bain*, 257 F.3d 660, 670 (6th Cir.2001), *cert. denied*, 535 U.S. 1095, 122 S.Ct. 2291, 152 L.Ed.2d 1050 (2002).

26. Rule 6(b). *See Schneider ex rel. Estate of Schneider v. Fried*, 320 F.3d 396, 402–03 (3d Cir.2003); *Lichtenberg v. Besicorp Group Inc.*, 204 F.3d 397, 401 (2d Cir.2000); *U.S. Leather, Inc. v. H & W Partnership*, 60 F.3d 222 (5th Cir.1995).

27. *See Hertz Corp. v. Alamo Rent–A–Car, Inc.*, 16 F.3d 1126 (11th Cir.1994).

28. *See Feathers v. Chevron U.S.A., Inc.*, 141 F.3d 264, 268 (6th Cir.1998) (where party failed to file timely Rule 59 motion, court appropriately could consider motion under Rule 60).

requires *filing* (not service) no later than 10 days after entry of judgment, this 3–day service-by-mail extension does not apply.[29]

Motion Tolls Appeal Period

A timely-filed motion for a new trial delays the finality of the underlying judgment and tolls the time for appeal. Originally, a notice of appeal, filed prematurely before the trial court had ruled upon a pending motion for a new trial, would have been deemed a "nullity".[30] Under recent amendments to Federal Rule of Appellate Procedure 4(a)(4), a prematurely filed appeal is now treated as filed as of the date the trial court ultimately disposes of the pending Rule 59 motion.[31]

Motion Filed After Notice of Appeal

The filing of a notice of appeal is jurisdictional; once filed, the district court is divested of jurisdiction over those aspects of the case implicated in the appeal, and jurisdiction is conferred upon the court of appeals.[32] Consequently, a party seeking to move the district court for a new trial after a notice of appeal has been filed must file a motion with the district judge, and the judge may then request a remand of the case from the court of appeals.[33]

RULE 59(c). TIME FOR SERVING AFFIDAVITS

CORE CONCEPT

A party may support a motion for new trial with affidavits. Supporting affidavits must be filed with the motion. Opposing affidavits may be filed 10 days thereafter, unless an additional period not to exceed 20 days is permitted by the court for good cause shown or by stipulated agreement of the parties.

APPLICATIONS

10 Days to File Affidavits

Parties intending to oppose new trial affidavits by submitting affidavits of their own must *file* those opposing affidavits within 10 days after service of the moving party's affidavits.

RULE 59(d). ORDER OF NEW TRIAL ON COURT'S INITIATIVE

29. *See Cavaliere v. Allstate Ins. Co.*, 996 F.2d 1111, 1112–14 (11th Cir.1993). *See also Adams v. Trustees of N.J. Brewery Employees' Pension Trust Fund*, 29 F.3d 863, 870–71 (3d Cir.1994)(applying same reasoning in construing Rule 59(e)); *Derrington–Bey v. District of Columbia Dep't of Corrections*, 39 F.3d 1224, 1225 (D.C.Cir.1994) (same).

30. *See Griggs v. Provident Consumer Discount Co.*, 459 U.S. 56, 61, 103 S.Ct. 400, 403, 74 L.Ed.2d 225 (1982)(per curiam). *Accord Acosta v. Louisiana Dep't of Health & Human Resources*, 478 U.S. 251, 254, 106 S.Ct. 2876, 2877, 92 L.Ed.2d 192 (1986).

31. *See* Fed. R. App. P. 4(a)(4). *See also Leader Nat'l Ins. Co. v. Industrial Indemn. Ins. Co.*, 19 F.3d 444 (9th Cir.1994)(noting that, after 1993 amendment, appeal is no longer a nullity but is merely held in abeyance).

32. *See Griggs v. Provident Consumer Discount Co.*, 459 U.S. 56, 58, 103 S.Ct. 400, 402, 74 L.Ed.2d 225 (1982)(per curiam).

33. *See Hattersley v. Bollt,* 512 F.2d 209 (3d Cir.1975).

CORE CONCEPT

The court may grant a new trial entirely on its own initiative, or, upon reviewing a party's motion, may grant a new trial for a reason not stated in the moving papers.

APPLICATIONS

Grounds

The court may grant a new trial for any reason that a party could have permissibly requested by motion.[34]

Time

A court that intends to grant a new trial on its own initiative must do so within 10 days after the entry of judgment. When a court receives a motion, but decides to grant a new trial for reasons not specified in the motion, the timing is less clear. One court has held that this 10–day requirement does not apply to such rulings.[35]

Granting on Different Grounds

When a court decides to grant a new trial for reasons different from those set forth in the moving party's papers, the court must give the parties notice of this intention and an opportunity to be heard.

Nature of Order

When the court grants a motion for a new trial on its own initiative or on grounds different from those stated in a party's motion papers, the order must specify the grounds for the court's decision.

RULE 59(e). MOTION TO ALTER OR AMEND A JUDGMENT

CORE CONCEPT

The court may alter or amend its judgment upon motion by a party.

APPLICATIONS

Grounds

Rule 59(e) preserves the district court's right to alter or amend a judgment after the judgment is entered. Motions to alter or amend a judgment are appropriate where they involve reconsideration of matters properly encompassed in the decision on the merits.[36] The case law acknowledges four grounds that justify altering or amending a judgment: to incorporate an intervening change in the law,[37] to reflect new

34. *See Pryer v. C.O. 3 Slavic*, 251 F.3d 448, 453 (3d Cir.2001) (noting principle, and ruling that new trial may be granted where verdict is against the great weight of the evidence).

35. *See Kelly v. Moore*, 376 F.3d 481, 484 (5th Cir. 2004).

36. *See White v. New Hampshire Dep't of Employment Sec.*, 455 U.S. 445, 451, 102 S.Ct. 1162, 1166, 71 L.Ed.2d 325 (1982).

37. *See In re Benjamin Moore & Co.*, 318 F.3d 626, 629 (5th Cir.2002); *United States ex rel. Becker v. Westinghouse Savannah River Co.*, 305 F.3d 284, 290 (4th Cir.2002), *cert. denied*, 538 U.S. 1012, 123 S.Ct. 1929, 155 L.Ed.2d 848 (2003); *Zimmerman v. City of Oakland*, 255 F.3d 734, 740 (9th Cir.2001); *Servants of Paraclete v. Does*, 204 F.3d 1005, 1012 (10th Cir.2000).

evidence not available at the time of trial,[38] to correct a clear legal error,[39] and to prevent a manifest injustice.[40] Thus, for example, a Rule 59(e) motion is appropriate where the court misunderstood the facts, a party's arguments, or the controlling law,[41] where the original judgment failed to provide that relief which the court found a party entitled to receive,[42] or where the party seeks a post-judgment award of prejudgment interest.[43]

District Court's Discretion

The decision whether to alter or amend a judgment is generally committed to the discretion of the trial judge.[44] Exercising this discretion calls upon the court to balance two competing interests–the need to bring litigation to a close and the need to render just rulings based on

38. *See Infusion Res., Inc. v. Minimed, Inc.*, 351 F.3d 688, 696–97 (5th Cir. 2003) (new facts must (1) probably change outcome, (2) be actually newly discovered and could not have been discovered earlier by proper diligence, and (3) not merely be cumulative or impeaching), *cert. denied*, ___ U.S. ___, 124 S.Ct. 2881, 159 L.Ed.2d 778(2004). *See also United States ex rel. Becker v. Westinghouse Savannah River Co.*, 305 F.3d 284, 290 (4th Cir.2002), *cert. denied*, 538 U.S. 1012, 123 S.Ct. 1929, 155 L.Ed.2d 848 (2003); *Zimmerman v. City of Oakland*, 255 F.3d 734, 740 (9th Cir.2001); *Landrau-Romero v. Banco Popular De Puerto Rico*, 212 F.3d 607, 612 (1st Cir.2000); *Servants of Paraclete v. Does*, 204 F.3d 1005, 1012 (10th Cir.2000). *Cf. Certain Underwriters at Lloyd's, London & Other Cos. v. St. Joe Minerals Corp.*, 90 F.3d 671 (2d Cir.1996)(affirming refusal to hear additional evidence after dismissal; party could have proffered such evidence earlier).

39. *See Munafo v. Metropolitan Transp. Auth.*, 381 F.3d 99, 105 (2d Cir. 2004); *Templet v. HydroChem Inc.*, 367 F.3d 473, 478–79 (5th Cir. 2004); *United States ex rel. Becker v. Westinghouse Savannah River Co.*, 305 F.3d 284, 290 (4th Cir.2002), *cert. denied*, 538 U.S. 1012, 123 S.Ct. 1929, 155 L.Ed.2d 848 (2003).

40. *See Munafo v. Metropolitan Transp. Auth.*, 381 F.3d 99, 105 (2d Cir. 2004); *Templet v. HydroChem Inc.*, 367 F.3d 473, 478–79 (5th Cir. 2004); *United States ex rel. Becker v. Westinghouse Savannah River Co.*, 305 F.3d 284, 290 (4th Cir.2002), *cert. denied*, 538 U.S. 1012, 123 S.Ct. 1929, 155 L.Ed.2d 848 (2003); *Zimmerman v. City of Oakland*, 255 F.3d 734, 740 (9th Cir. 2001); *Landrau-Romero v. Banco Popular De Puerto Rico*, 212 F.3d 607, 612 (1st Cir.2000); *Servants of Paraclete v. Does*, 204 F.3d 1005, 1012 (10th Cir.2000); *Divane v. Krull Elec. Co.*, 194 F.3d 845, 850 (7th Cir.1999). *See also Ford Motor Credit Co. v. Bright*, 34 F.3d 322, 324 (5th Cir.1994)(in considering Rule 59(e) motion, court may take into account attorney's conduct). *But cf. Frietsch v. Refco, Inc.*, 56 F.3d 825, 828 (7th Cir.1995)(affirming refusal to consider affidavit filed after dismissal; Rule 59(e) does not "enable a party to complete presenting his case after the court has ruled against him").

41. *See Servants of Paraclete v. Does*, 204 F.3d 1005, 1012 (10th Cir.2000).

42. *See Continental Cas. Co. v. Howard*, 775 F.2d 876 (7th Cir.1985), *cert. denied*, 475 U.S. 1122, 106 S.Ct. 1641, 90 L.Ed.2d 186 (1986).

43. *See Osterneck v. Ernst & Whinney*, 489 U.S. 169, 109 S.Ct. 987, 103 L.Ed.2d 146 (1989). *But see Buchanan v. Stanships, Inc.*, 485 U.S. 265, 108 S.Ct. 1130, 99 L.Ed.2d 289 (1988)(seeking an allowance of costs under Rule 54(d) is not appropriate for a Rule 59(e) motion, because such costs are collateral to the merits of the action); *White v. New Hampshire Dep't of Employment Sec.*, 455 U.S. 445, 102 S.Ct. 1162, 71 L.Ed.2d 325 (1982)(seeking an award of attorney's fees is not appropriate for a Rule 59(e) motion).

44. *See Minton v. National Ass'n of Secs. Dealers, Inc.*, 336 F.3d 1373, 1379 (5th Cir. 2003); *Zivitz v. Greenberg*, 279 F.3d 536, 539 (7th Cir.2002); *Callantine v. Staff Builders, Inc.*, 271 F.3d 1124, 1134 (8th Cir.2001); *Vaughn v. Lawrenceburg Power Sys.*, 269 F.3d 703, 710 (6th Cir.2001); *Pacific Ins. Co. v. American Nat'l Fire Ins. Co.*, 148 F.3d 396 (4th Cir.1998), *cert. denied*, 525 U.S. 1104, 119 S.Ct. 869, 142 L.Ed.2d 771 (1999); *Phelps v. Hamilton*, 122 F.3d 1309, 1324 (10th Cir.1997).

all the facts.[45] However, this liberal discretion standard does not apply to Rule 59(e) motions seeking review of a grant of summary judgment; as to those motions, a *de novo* standard applies.[46] This sort of reconsideration of a judgment is an extraordinary remedy and is used only sparingly.[47]

10 Days to File Motion to Alter or Amend a Judgment

A party seeking to alter or amend a judgment must *file* the motion within 10 days after the district court enters its judgment on the docket.[48]

No Extensions

The court may not grant a party any extensions to this 10 day rule.[49]

3–Day Service–By–Mail Extension Does Not Apply

Rule 6(e) extends a party's time for acting by 3 days if the relevant time period is to begin upon service by mail. Because Rule 59(e) requires *filing* (not service) no later than 10 days after entry of judgment, this 3–day service-by-mail extension does not apply.[50]

Prisoner Plaintiffs

The prisoner "mailbox rule" has been adopted by some courts for Rule 59(e) motions. Consequently, a *pro se* prisoner's papers will be deemed filed when deposited with the post office.[51]

Motion Tolls Appeal Period

Like Rule 59(b) motions for new trial, a timely-filed Rule 59(e) motion to alter or amend the judgment tolls the time for appeal.[52] As

45. *See Templet v. HydroChem Inc.*, 367 F.3d 473, 478–79 (5th Cir. 2004).

46. *See Cockrel v. Shelby County Sch. Dist.*, 270 F.3d 1036, 1047 (6th Cir.2001), *petition for cert. filed*, 537 U.S. 813, 123 S.Ct. 73, 154 L.Ed.2d 15 (2002).

47. *See Templet v. HydroChem Inc.*, 367 F.3d 473, 479 (5th Cir. 2004).

48. *See Schudel v. General Elec. Co.*, 120 F.3d 991 (9th Cir.1997) (noting that Rule 59, as amended in 1995, requires that such motions be filed, not served, within 10 days following entry of judgment), *cert. denied*, 523 U.S. 1094, 118 S.Ct. 1560, 140 L.Ed.2d 792 (1998). *See also Life Ins. Co. of North America v. Von Valtier*, 116 F.3d 279, 282–83 (7th Cir.1997) (considering motion to be timely filed where it was delivered to district court, as required by standing chambers order, but trial judge delayed in transmitting motion to clerk's office for formal filing).

49. *See* Rule 6(b). *See also Weitz v. Lovelace Health Sys., Inc.*, 214 F.3d 1175, 1179 (10th Cir.2000); *Wight v. Bankamerica Corp.*, 219 F.3d 79, 84 (2d Cir.2000).

50. *See Albright v. Virtue*, 273 F.3d 564, 567 (3d Cir.2001); *FHC Equities, L.L.C. v. MBL Life Assur. Corp.*, 188 F.3d 678 (6th Cir.1999); *Halicki v. Louisiana Casino Cruises, Inc.*, 151 F.3d 465, 466–67 (5th Cir.1998), *cert. denied*, 526 U.S. 1005, 119 S.Ct. 1143, 143 L.Ed.2d 210 (1999); *Derrington-Bey v. District of Columbia Dep't of Corrections*, 39 F.3d 1224, 1225 (D.C.Cir.1994). *See also Cavaliere v. Allstate Ins. Co.*, 996 F.2d 1111, 1112–14 (11th Cir.1993)(applying same reasoning in construing Rule 59(b)).

51. *See Edwards v. United States*, 266 F.3d 756, 758 (7th Cir.2001).

52. *See, e.g., Bass v. United States Dep't of Agriculture*, 211 F.3d 959, 962 (5th Cir.2000); *Innovative Home Health Care, Inc. v. P.T.-O.T. Assocs. of Black Hills*, 141 F.3d 1284, 1286 (8th Cir.1998).

in the case of Rule 59(b) motions, a prematurely filed appeal during the pendency of a Rule 59(e) motion is held in abeyance until the date the district court resolves the pending motion.[53] An untimely Rule 59(e) motion will not toll the time for appeal,[54] nor will a second or later Rule 59(e) motion when multiple such motions are filed.[55]

To qualify for this tolling effect, the Rule 59(e) motion must satisfy the "particularity" requirement of Rule 7(b)(1). Accordingly, a "skeleton" motion that fails to alert the court or the other litigants of the grounds for which an alteration or amendment is sought may be deemed improper and, thus, ineffective in tolling the appeal period.[56]

Appeal Must Name Correct Order: The filing of a timely, proper Rule 59(e) motion can toll the time for filing an appeal from the original underlying *merits* ruling, and not just from the court's disposition of the Rule 59(e) motion itself.[57] However, to benefit from that *merits* tolling effect, the litigant must list the *merits* ruling on the Notice of Appeal (in addition to any other orders from which the appeal is taken).[58] Although the appellate courts will liberally construe the Notice of Appeal to give effect to the parties' intentions if clearly obvious (and in the absence of prejudice to the adversary),[59] litigants have been cautioned by the courts "that such rescue missions are not automatic, and litigants will do well to draft notices of appeal with care".[60]

Motions for "Reconsideration"

The Rules do not expressly recognize motions for "reconsideration".[61] Instead, such motions are treated typically as motions to alter or amend a judgment under Rule 59(e) or motions for relief from judgments or orders under Rule 60(b). Often, whether a "reconsideration" motion is governed by Rule 59(e) or Rule 60(b) will depend on the date it is filed. If filed within the 10–day period set for Rule 59(e)

53. *See* Fed. R. App. P. 4(a)(4)(as amended Dec. 1, 1993); *Schroeder v. McDonald*, 55 F.3d 454, 458 (9th Cir.1995)(applying Fed.R.App.P. 4(a)(4) to Rule 59(e) motion).

54. *See Garcia-Velazquez v. Frito Lay Snacks Caribbean*, 358 F.3d 6, 9 (1st Cir. 2004); *Panhorst v. United States*, 241 F.3d 367, 370 (4th Cir.2001); *Wight v. Bankamerica Corp.*, 219 F.3d 79, 84 (2d Cir.2000).

55. *See Acevedo–Villalobos v. Hernandez*, 22 F.3d 384 (1st Cir.1994).

56. *See Talano v. Northwestern Med. Faculty Found., Inc.*, 273 F.3d 757, 760–61 (7th Cir. 2001) ("if a party could file a skeleton motion and later fill it in, the purpose of the time limitation would be defeated").

57. *See Chamorro v. Puerto Rican Cars, Inc.*, 304 F.3d 1, 3 (1st Cir.2002).

58. *See Chamorro v. Puerto Rican Cars, Inc.*, 304 F.3d 1, 3 (1st Cir.2002) (an appeal taken only from the order denying the Rule 59(e) motion will generally not be considered an appeal from the underlying merits judgment); *Correa v. Cruisers, a Div. of KCS Int'l, Inc.*, 298 F.3d 13, 21 n. 3 (1st Cir.2002) (same).

59. *See Chamorro v. Puerto Rican Cars, Inc.*, 304 F.3d 1, 3 (1st Cir.2002) (commenting that "formalism is not obligatory", and Notice will be construed liberally and examined in the context of the record as a whole, "with a recognition that the core purpose of a notice of appeal is to 'facilitate a proper decision on the merits' "); *Correa v. Cruisers, a Div. of KCS Int'l, Inc.*, 298 F.3d 13, 21 n. 3 (1st Cir.2002) (same effect).

60. *See Chamorro v. Puerto Rican Cars, Inc.*, 304 F.3d 1, 3 (1st Cir.2002).

61. *See Computerized Thermal Imaging, Inc. v. Bloomberg, L.P.*, 312 F.3d 1292, 1296 n.3 (10th Cir.2002); *Bass v. United States Dep't of Agriculture*, 211 F.3d 959, 962 (5th Cir.2000).

motions, the "reconsideration" will be evaluated under Rule 59(e).[62] Otherwise, the courts will examine the motion under Rule 60(b).[63] Motions for "reconsideration" will not be granted absent "highly unusual circumstances"[64]—they do not provide litigants with an opportunity for a "second bite at the apple"[65] or allow them, like Emperor Nero, to "fiddle as Rome burns",[66] or license a litigation "game of hopscotch", allowing parties to switch from one legal theory to a new one "like a bee in search of honey".[67] Such motions are not vehicles for relitigating old issues.[68] Courts properly decline to consider new arguments or new evidence on reconsideration where those arguments or evidence were available earlier.[69]

Motions to Include Prejudgment Interest

Generally, motions to amend to include an award of either mandatory or discretionary prejudgment interest are treated under this Rule and, thus, must be sought within 10 days of entry of the judgment or be deemed waived.[70]

62. *See United States v. $23,000 in U.S. Currency*, 356 F.3d 157, 165 n.9 (1st Cir. 2004); *Texas A&M Research Found. v. Magna Transp., Inc.*, 338 F.3d 394, 400 (5th Cir.2003); *Dudley ex rel. Estate of Patton v. Penn–America Ins. Co.*, 313 F.3d 662, 675 (2d Cir.2002); *Computerized Thermal Imaging, Inc. v. Bloomberg, L.P.*, 312 F.3d 1292, 1296 n.3 (10th Cir.2002); *Inge v. Rock Fin. Corp.* 281 F.3d 613, 617 (6th Cir.2002); *American Ironworks & Erectors, Inc. v. North American Const. Corp.*, 248 F.3d 892, 898–99 (9th Cir.2001).

63. *See Texas A&M Research Found. v. Magna Transp., Inc.*, 338 F.3d 394, 400 (5th Cir. 2003); *Dudley ex rel. Estate of Patton v. Penn–America Ins. Co.*, 313 F.3d 662, 675 (2d Cir. 2002); *Computerized Thermal Imaging, Inc. v. Bloomberg, L.P.*, 312 F.3d 1292, 1296 n.3 (10th Cir.2002); *American Ironworks & Erectors, Inc. v. North American Const. Corp.*, 248 F.3d 892, 898–99 (9th Cir.2001); *Small v. Hunt*, 98 F.3d 789, 797 (4th Cir.1996); *Helm v. Resolution Trust Corp.*, 43 F.3d 1163, 1166 (7th Cir.1995).

64. *See McDowell v. Calderon*, 197 F.3d 1253, 1255 (9th Cir.1999), *cert. denied*, 529 U.S. 1082, 120 S.Ct. 1708, 146 L.Ed.2d 511 (2000). *See also United States ex rel. Becker v. Westinghouse Savannah River Co.*, 305 F.3d 284, 290 (4th Cir.2002) (simple disagreement with the court's ruling will not support Rule 59(e) relief), *cert. denied*, 538 U.S. 1012, 123 S.Ct. 1929, 155 L.Ed.2d 848 (2003).

65. *See Sequa Corp. v. GBJ Corp.*, 156 F.3d 136 (2d Cir.1998); *Bhatnagar v. Surrendra Overseas Ltd.*, 52 F.3d 1220, 1231 (3d Cir.1995); *Senza–Gel Corp. v. Seiffhart*, 803 F.2d 661, 664 (Fed.Cir.1986).

66. *Vasapolli v. Rostoff*, 39 F.3d 27, 36 (1st Cir.1994)(Selya, J.)("Unlike the Emperor Nero, litigants cannot fiddle as Rome burns. A party who sits in silence, withholds potentially relevant information, allows his opponent to configure the summary judgment record, and acquiesces in a particular choice of law does so at his peril").

67. *See Cochran v. Quest Software, Inc.*, 328 F.3d 1, 11 (1st Cir.2003) (noting that litigants "frame the issues in a case before the trial court rules" and, once framed, should not be permitted to switch from theory to theory thereafter).

68. *See Templet v. HydroChem Inc.*, 367 F.3d 473, 478–79 (5th Cir. 2004); *Servants of Paraclete v. Does*, 204 F.3d 1005, 1012 (10th Cir. 2000); *Sequa Corp. v. GBJ Corp.*, 156 F.3d 136 (2d Cir.1998); *Sault Ste. Marie Tribe of Chippewa Indians v. Engler*, 146 F.3d 367, 374 (6th Cir.1998).

69. *See Templet v. HydroChem Inc.*, 367 F.3d 473, 478–79 (5th Cir. 2004); *Rivera v. Puerto Rico Aqueduct & Sewers Auth.*, 331 F.3d 183, 193 (1st Cir.2003); *Moysis v. DTG Datanet*, 278 F.3d 819, 829 n. 3 (8th Cir.2002); *Divane v. Krull Elec. Co.*, 194 F.3d 845, 850 (7th Cir.1999); *Sequa Corp. v. GBJ Corp.*, 156 F.3d 136 (2d Cir.1998); *Pacific Ins. Co. v. American Nat'l Fire Ins. Co.*, 148 F.3d 396 (4th Cir.1998) *cert. denied*, 525 U.S. 1104, 119 S.Ct. 869, 142 L.Ed.2d 771 (1999).

70. *See Osterneck v. Ernst & Whinney*, 489 U.S. 169, 173–78, 109 S.Ct. 987, 989–82, 103 L.Ed.2d 146 (1989) (mandatory prejudgment interest); *McCalla v. Royal MacCabees Life Ins. Co.*, 369 F.3d 1128, 1130–34 (9th Cir. 2004) (mandatory prejudgment interest); *Crowe v. Bol-*

ADDITIONAL RESEARCH REFERENCES

Wright & Miller, *Federal Practice and Procedure* §§ 2801–21.

C.J.S. Federal Civil Procedure §§ 1061–1103 et seq., 1233–1251 et seq.

West's Key No. Digests, Federal Civil Procedure ⚷2311–2377, 2641–2662.

duc, 365 F.3d 86, 92–93 (1st Cir. 2004) (mandatory or discretionary prejudgment interest).

RULE 60

RELIEF FROM JUDGMENT OR ORDER

(a) Clerical Mistakes. Clerical mistakes in judgments, orders or other parts of the record and errors therein arising from oversight or omission may be corrected by the court at any time of its own initiative or on the motion of any party and after such notice, if any, as the court orders. During the pendency of an appeal, such mistakes may be so corrected before the appeal is docketed in the appellate court, and thereafter while the appeal is pending may be so corrected with leave of the appellate court.

(b) Mistakes; Inadvertence; Excusable Neglect; Newly Discovered Evidence; Fraud, etc. On motion and upon such terms as are just, the court may relieve a party or a party's legal representative from a final judgment, order, or proceeding for the following reasons: (1) mistake, inadvertence, surprise, or excusable neglect; (2) newly discovered evidence which by due diligence could not have been discovered in time to move for a new trial under Rule 59(b); (3) fraud (whether heretofore denominated intrinsic or extrinsic), misrepresentation, or other misconduct of an adverse party; (4) the judgment is void; (5) the judgment has been satisfied, released, or discharged, or a prior judgment upon which it is based has been reversed or otherwise vacated, or it is no longer equitable that the judgment should have prospective application; or (6) any other reason justifying relief from the operation of the judgment. The motion shall be made within a reasonable time, and for reasons (1), (2), and (3) not more than one year after the judgment, order, or proceeding was entered or taken. A motion under this subdivision (b) does not affect the finality of a judgment or suspend its operation. This rule does not limit the power of a court to entertain an independent action to relieve a party from a judgment, order, or proceeding, or to grant relief to a defendant not actually personally notified as provided in Title 28, U.S.C., § 1655, or to set aside a judgment for fraud upon the court. Writs of coram nobis, coram vobis, audita querela, and bills of review and bills in the nature of a bill of review, are abolished, and the procedure for obtaining any relief from a judgment shall be by motion as prescribed in these rules or by an independent action.

[Amended effective March 19, 1948; October 20, 1949; August 1, 1987.]

AUTHORS' COMMENTARY ON RULE 60

PURPOSE AND SCOPE

The district judge may grant relief from a judgment or order to correct clerical errors or in circumstances justifying an alteration of the judgment or order.

Motions to correct clerical errors may be made at any time. Motions for relief from judgment founded on other reasons must be made within a "reasonable" time after the judgment is entered and, in some cases, no later than 1 year after the judgment is entered. Motions for relief on the basis that the judgment is void may be made at any time.

RULE 60(a). CLERICAL MISTAKES

CORE CONCEPT

The district court, on its own initiative or on motion of a party, may correct clerical errors in judgments, orders, or other parts of the record, and errors arising from oversight or omission.

APPLICATIONS

Procedure

Motions to correct clerical errors are made to the district court that rendered the judgment sought to be corrected, rather than to any court where such a judgment may have been transferred.

Sua Sponte Corrections

Upon notice to the parties, the court *sua sponte* may raise clerical errors for correction.[1]

Types of Errors

Clerical mistakes are minor, ministerial errors arising from simple oversight or omission, rather than substantive factual or legal errors.[2]

1. *See In re West Texas Mktg. Corp.*, 12 F.3d 497, 503 n. 4 (5th Cir.1994).

2. *See In re West Texas Mktg. Corp.*, 12 F.3d 497, 504–05 (5th Cir.1994)("As long as the intentions of the parties are clearly defined and all the court need do is employ a judicial eraser to obliterate a mechanical or mathematical mistake, the modification will be allowed" under Rule 60(a)). *See, e.g. United States v. Mosbrucker*, 340 F.3d 664, 665–67 (8th Cir.2003) (permitting correction to note that easement tract was not partially released, only that government's mortgage was subordinated to utility easement); *Big Bear Lodging Ass'n v. Snow Summit, Inc.*, 182 F.3d 1096 (9th Cir.1999) (finding that Rule 60(a) motion was proper vehicle to clarify whether district court had ruled on pending state law claims, and, if so, whether they were dismissed on merits or for lack of jurisdiction); *Rezzonico v. H & R Block, Inc.*, 182 F.3d 144 (2d Cir.1999) (Rule 60(a) could be used to correct district court's omission of word "not" from judgment, where accompanying opinion clearly indicated court's intention and, thus, insertion of word "not" would not change court's intended result), *cert. denied*, 528 U.S. 1189, 120 S.Ct. 1243, 146 L.Ed.2d 101 (2000); *Hale Container Line, Inc. v. Houston Sea Packing Co.*, 137 F.3d 1455, 1474 (11th Cir.1998) (Rule 60(a) may correct damages award containing erroneous mathematical computation); *McNamara v. City of Chicago*, 138 F.3d 1219, 1221 (7th Cir.1998) (under Rule 60(a), district court could replace "Chicago Po-

This distinction between clerical mistakes ("blunders in execution") and substantive errors ("where the court changes its mind") is significant.[3] Where the error lies in accurately reducing the court's original intentions to paper, a Rule 60(a) motion is appropriate; however, where the written order accurately captures the court's intentions, but that ruling is allegedly in error, a Rule 60(a) motion is not proper.[4]

Whose Errors

Relief under Rule 60(a) is not limited to clerical mistakes committed only by the clerk; the Rule applies to mistakes by the court, the parties, and the jury as well.[5]

Time for Correction

The district court may correct clerical errors even after an appeal is taken;[6] once the case is docketed in the appellate court, however, the district court may correct clerical errors only upon leave of the court of appeals.

Implications for Appeal

Historically, whether a party's post-entry motion was a motion to alter or amend under Rule 59(e) or a motion for relief under Rule 60 had great appellate significance—Rule 59(e) motions tolled the time for appeal, but Rule 60 motions did not.[7] This effect was changed in a recent amendment to the Federal Rules of Appellate Procedure. Now, Rule 60 motions (like Rule 59(e) motions) will toll the appeal period, but only so long as those motions are filed within 10 days after judgment is entered.[8] Conversely, Rule 60 motions filed beyond the 10–day period

lice Department" with "Chicago Fire Department" in one sentence of opinion), *cert. denied*, 525 U.S. 981, 119 S.Ct. 444, 142 L.Ed.2d 398 (1998); *Paddington Partners v. Bouchard*, 34 F.3d 1132, 1139 (2d Cir.1994)(Rule 60(a) may be invoked in the context of an award of pre-judgment interest so long as correction simply gives effect to the actual intention of the court's earlier judgment); *Kosnoski v. Howley*, 33 F.3d 376, 379 (4th Cir.1994)(Rule 60(a) properly invoked by court in performing a calculation, based upon its earlier determined formula, in order to fix the total amount of judgment).

3. *See Harman v. Harper*, 7 F.3d 1455, 1457 (9th Cir.1993), *cert. denied*, 513 U.S. 814, 115 S.Ct. 68, 130 L.Ed.2d 24 (1994). *See also In re Walter*, 282 F.3d 434, 440–41 (6th Cir.2002) (citing quotation with approval), *cert. denied*, 537 U.S. 885, 123 S.Ct. 118, 154 L.Ed.2d 144 (2002).

4. *See Lowe v. McGraw–Hill Cos.*, 361 F.3d 335, 341 (7th Cir. 2004) ("defining element" is that litigants knew error "was by pure inadvertence, rather than a mistaken exercise of judgment"); *United States v. Mosbrucker*, 340 F.3d 664, 666 (8th Cir.2003) (Rule 60(a) permits correction to reflect "what was understood, intended, and agreed upon by parties and court"); *In re Craddock*, 149 F.3d 1249, 1254 n. 4, (10th Cir. 1998) (holding that Rule 60(a) can be invoked where "the thing spoken, written or recorded is not what the person intended to speak, write or record"; Rule may not be used "to correct something that was deliberately done but later discovered to be wrong"). *See also In re Transtexas Gas Corp.*, 303 F.3d 571, 581 (5th Cir.2002); *In re Walter*, 282 F.3d 434, 440–41 (6th Cir.2002), *cert. denied*, 537 U.S.885, 123 S.Ct. 118, 154 L.Ed.2d 144 (2002).

5. *See In re Walter*, 282 F.3d 434, 440–41 (6th Cir.2002), *cert. denied*, 537 U.S. 885, 123 S.Ct. 118, 154 L.Ed.2d 144 (2002); *In re West Texas Mktg. Corp.*, 12 F.3d 497, 503–04 (5th Cir.1994); *Pattiz v. Schwartz*, 386 F.2d 300 (8th Cir.1968).

6. *See In re U.S. Healthcare, Inc.*, 193 F.3d 151, 158 n. 2 (3d Cir.1999), *cert. denied*, 530 U.S. 1242, 120 S.Ct. 2687, 147 L.Ed.2d 960 (2000).

7. *See* Fed. R. App. P. 4(a)(4)(A)(vi) advisory committee notes to 1993 amendment.

8. *See* Fed. R. App. P. 4(a)(4)(A)(vi). *But see Hodge ex rel. Skiff v. Hodge*, 269 F.3d 155, 158 (2d Cir.2001) (citing authorities, and holding

will not toll the time for appeal.[9]

Nature of Appellate Review

An appeal from a district court order denying relief under Rule 60(a) implicates only the propriety of that denial, and not the underlying merits of the contested judgment itself.[10]

RULE 60(b). RELIEF FOR OTHER REASONS

CORE CONCEPT

In its discretion, the district court may grant a motion for relief from a final judgment, order, or proceeding for various enumerated reasons.

APPLICATIONS

Purpose

The essential purpose of permitting substantive relief from a judgment or order is to allow the federal courts to strike the proper balance between two often conflicting principles–that litigation must be brought to a final close and that justice must be done.[11]

Reasons for Granting Relief

The Rule provides five specified reasons for which relief may be granted, and adds a sixth catch-all category for reasons not specifically listed.

Reason 1—Mistake, Inadvertence, Surprise, or Excusable Neglect

Relief from a judgment or order may be granted for mistakes by any person, not just a party.[12] This category permits relief where the order or judgment results from such circumstances as an inability to consult with counsel,[13] a misunderstanding regarding the duty to appear,[14] a failure to receive service,[15] or, in some circumstances, an attorney's negligent failure to meet a deadline.[16] The standard, howev-

that Rule 60(a) motion does not extend time for filing postjudgment motions).

9. *See American Fed'n of Grain Millers, Local 24 v. Cargill, Inc.*, 15 F.3d 726, 728 (7th Cir.1994); *Harman v. Harper*, 7 F.3d 1455, 1457 (9th Cir.1993), *cert. denied*, 513 U.S. 814, 115 S.Ct. 68, 130 L.Ed.2d 24 (1994).

10. *See Paddington Partners v. Bouchard*, 34 F.3d 1132, 1147 (2d Cir.1994).

11. *See Coltec Indus., Inc. v. Hobgood*, 280 F.3d 262, 271 (3d Cir.2002), *cert. denied*, 537 U.S. 885, 123 S.Ct. 411, 154 L.Ed.2d 291 (2002).

12. *See Associates Discount Corp. v. Goldman*, 524 F.2d 1051 (3d Cir.1975).

13. *See Falk v. Allen*, 739 F.2d 461 (9th Cir.1984).

14. *See Ellingsworth v. Chrysler*, 665 F.2d 180 (7th Cir.1981).

15. *See Blois v. Friday*, 612 F.2d 938 (5th Cir.1980).

16. *See Robb v. Norfolk & Western Ry. Co.*, 122 F.3d 354 (7th Cir.1997) (noting that circuit discontinues its "hard-and-fast" rule barring trial judges from, in their discretion, finding that attorney negligence in missing a deadline constitutes "excusable neglect", but sternly cautioning counsel against expecting such relief to be granted automatically). *See also United States v. $23,000 in U.S. Currency*, 356 F.3d 157, 164 (1st Cir. 2004).

er, is a demanding one.[17] Whether relief is appropriate is assessed on a case-by-case analysis; not every error or omission in the course of litigation will qualify as "excusable neglect",[18] nor will routine carelessness[19], a confusion concerning the Rules,[20] or a party's misunderstanding of the consequences of her actions (even after advice of counsel) qualify for relief.[21] Moreover, otherwise careful clients can be penalized for omissions of their careless attorneys.[22] As a threshold showing, the moving party must demonstrate that the error made did not result from his or her own culpable conduct.[23] To qualify as "excusable neglect", the conduct is tested against an equitable standard, considering: (1) prejudice to the opponent; (2) length of delay and impact on the proceedings; (3) reason for the delay; and (4) the moving party's good faith.[24]

Note: This provision has been applied for seeking relief under Rule 60(b) from default judgments, and, so applied, generally obligates the moving party to show good cause for defaulting, quick action in correcting the default, and the existence of a meritorious defense.[25]

Reason 2—Newly Discovered Evidence

Relief from an order or judgment may also be granted where (1) the evidence has been newly discovered since trial, (2) the moving party was diligent in discovering the new evidence, (3) the new evidence is not merely cumulative or impeaching, (4) the new evidence is material, and (5) in view of the new evidence, a new trial would probably produce a different result.[26] Implicit in these elements is the recognition that the

17. *See United States v. $23,000 in U.S. Currency*, 356 F.3d 157, 164 (1st Cir. 2004).

18. *See Rodgers v. Wyoming Attorney Gen.*, 205 F.3d 1201, 1206 (10th Cir.2000) (party who simply misunderstands the legal consequences of his deliberate acts might not be deemed excusably neglectful); *United States for Use & Benefit of Familian Northwest, Inc. v. RG & B Contractors, Inc.*, 21 F.3d 952, 956 (9th Cir.1994). *See also Robinson v. Armontrout*, 8 F.3d 6, 7 (8th Cir.1993)(party's and attorney's failure to object does not justify relief).

19. *See Easley v. Kirmsee*, 382 F.3d 693, 698 (7th Cir. 2004); *Negron v. Celebrity Cruises, Inc.*, 316 F.3d 60, 62 (1st Cir.2003).

20. *See United States v. $23,000 in U.S. Currency*, 356 F.3d 157, 164 (1st Cir. 2004).

21. *See Cashner v. Freedom Stores, Inc.*, 98 F.3d 572, 577–78 (10th Cir.1996).

22. *See United States v. Reyes*, 307 F.3d 451, 456 (6th Cir.2002).

23. *See Weiss v. St. Paul Fire & Marine Ins. Co.*, 283 F.3d 790, 794 (6th Cir.2002), *cert. denied*, 537 U.S. 885, 123 S.Ct. 105, 154 L.Ed.2d 141 (2002).

24. *See Laurino v. Syringa General Hosp.*, 279 F.3d 750, 753 (9th Cir.2002)(listing considerations from Supreme Court's decision in *Pioneer*, noting that they were not exclusive listing).

25. *See Rogers v. Hartford Life & Acc. Ins. Co.*, 167 F.3d 933, 938–39 (5th Cir.1999); *United We Stand America, Inc. v. United We Stand, America New York, Inc.*, 128 F.3d 86, 89 (2d Cir.1997), *cert. denied*, 523 U.S. 1076, 118 S.Ct. 1521, 140 L.Ed.2d 673 (1998); *Jones v. Phipps*, 39 F.3d 158, 162 (7th Cir.1994).

26. *See General Universal Sys., Inc. v. Lee*, 379 F.3d 131 (5th Cir. 2004); *Feature Realty, Inc. v. City of Spokane*, 331 F.3d 1082, 1093 (9th Cir.2003); *Waddell v. Hendry County Sheriff's Office*, 329 F.3d 1300, 1309 (11th Cir.2003); *Boule v. Hutton*, 328 F.3d 84, 95 (2d Cir.2003); *Karak v. Bursaw Oil Corp.*, 288 F.3d 15, 20 (1st Cir.2002); *Coregis Ins. Co. v. Baratta & Fenerty, Ltd.*, 264 F.3d 302, 309–10 (3d Cir.2001); *Schwieger v. Farm Bureau Ins. Co.*, 207 F.3d 480, 487 (8th Cir.2000); *Jones v. Lincoln Elec. Co.*, 188 F.3d 709 (7th Cir.1999), *cert. denied*, 529 U.S. 1067, 120 S.Ct. 1673, 146 L.Ed.2d 482 (2000). *See also Casella v. Equifax Credit Information Servs.*, 56 F.3d 469, 476 (2d Cir.1995)(no abuse of discretion in denying Rule 60(b)(2) motion where evidence, even if newly discovered,

newly-discovered evidence must be evidence of facts that were in existence at the time of trial.[27] Moreover (and implicitly), the newly discovered evidence must be both admissible and credible.[28] These requirements are strictly enforced.[29] If the movant fails to meet *any* of these prerequisites, the Rule 60(b)(2) motion may be denied.[30] Relief under this Rule is considered an "extraordinary remedy" to be granted only in exceptional circumstances.[31]

Note: The same principles apply whether relief is sought for this reason under Rule 59 or Rule 60(b).[32]

Reason 3—Fraud, Misrepresentation, Other Adversary Misconduct

Relief from a judgment or order may be permitted where (1) the moving party possessed a meritorious claim at trial, (2) the adverse party engaged in fraud, misrepresentation, or other misconduct, and (3) the adverse party's conduct prevented the moving party from fully and fairly presenting its case during trial.[33] This Rule is reserved for judgments that were unfairly obtained, not at those that are claimed to be just factually in error.[34] In appropriate cases, relief under this Rule may be granted to remedy belatedly uncovered misconduct during discovery, but only where the challenged behavior substantially interfered with the moving party's ability to fully and fairly try the case.[35] A party's entitlement to relief must be proven by clear and convincing evidence.[36]

would not have altered result in case); *Atkinson v. Prudential Property Co.*, 43 F.3d 367, 371 n. 3 (8th Cir.1994)(suggesting that where moving party has "newly discovered" evidence entire time, the party's belated "discovery" of the evidence may be insufficient for Rule 60(b)(2) purposes).

27. *See General Universal Sys., Inc. v. Lee*, 379 F.3d 131 (5th Cir. 2004); *Betterbox Communications Ltd. v. BB Tech., Inc.*, 300 F.3d 325 (3d Cir.2002).

28. *See Goldstein v. MCI WorldCom*, 340 F.3d 238, 257 (5th Cir.2003).

29. *See Waddell v. Hendry County Sheriff's Office*, 329 F.3d 1300, 1309 (11th Cir.2003).

30. *See Jones v. Lincoln Elec. Co.*, 188 F.3d 709 (7th Cir.1999) (commenting that if any of these prerequisites is not satisfied, Rule 60(b)(2) motion must fail), *cert. denied*, 529 U.S. 1067, 120 S.Ct. 1673, 146 L.Ed.2d 482 (2000); *McCormack v. Citibank, N.A.*, 100 F.3d 532, 542 (8th Cir.1996) (commenting that even if movant could meet many prerequisites, he would fail to meet at least one).

31. *See Jones v. Lincoln Elec. Co.*, 188 F.3d 709 (7th Cir.1999), *cert. denied*, 529 U.S. 1067, 120 S.Ct. 1673, 146 L.Ed.2d 482 (2000).

32. *See Jones v. Aero/Chem Corp.*, 921 F.2d 875 (9th Cir.1990).

33. *See General Universal Sys., Inc. v. Lee*, 379 F.3d 131 (5th Cir. 2004); *State Street Bank & Trust Co. v. Inversiones Errazuriz Limitada*, 374 F.3d 158, 176 (2d Cir. 2004); *Tiller v. Baghdady*, 294 F.3d 277, 280–83 (1st Cir.2002); *De Saracho v. Custom Food Mach., Inc.*, 206 F.3d 874, 880 (9th Cir.2000), *cert. denied*, 531 U.S. 876, 121 S.Ct. 183, 148 L.Ed.2d 126 (2000); *Frederick v. Kirby Tankships, Inc.*, 205 F.3d 1277, 1287 (11th Cir.2000), *cert. denied*, 531 U.S. 813, 121 S.Ct. 46, 148 L.Ed.2d 16 (2000); *Cowan v. Strafford R–VI Sch. Dist.*, 140 F.3d 1153, 1159 (8th Cir.1998); *Tobel v. City of Hammond*, 94 F.3d 360, 362 (7th Cir.1996). *See also Assmann v. Fleming*, 159 F.2d 332 (8th Cir.1947) (noting possibility of relief, irrespective of whether the fraud is considered "extrisic" or "intrinsic").

34. *See General Universal Sys., Inc. v. Lee*, 379 F.3d 131, 156 (5th Cir. 2004).

35. *See General Universal Sys., Inc. v. Lee*, 379 F.3d 131 (5th Cir. 2004); *Summers v. Howard Univ.*, 374 F.3d 1188, 1193 (D.C.Cir. 2004); *Cummings v. General Motors Corp.*, 365 F.3d 944, 955 (10th Cir. 2004); *Klonoski v. Mahlab*, 156 F.3d 255, 275 (1st Cir.1998), *cert. denied*, 526 U.S. 1039, 119 S.Ct. 1334, 143 L.Ed.2d 498 (1999).

36. *See Cummings v. General Motors Corp.*, 365 F.3d 944, 955 (10th Cir. 2004); *Waddell v. Hendry County Sheriff's Office*, 329 F.3d 1300,

Reason 4—Void Judgment

Relief may also be granted where the judgment or order is void, whether because the court lacked jurisdiction over the subject matter, lacked personal jurisdiction over the parties, acted in some manner inconsistent with constitutional due process, or otherwise acted beyond the powers granted to it under the law.[37] When a motion challenges a judgment as void, the district court lacks discretion: either the judgment is void (in which case relief must be granted) or it is not.[38] However, some courts require that this jurisdictional error be "egregious" ("a clear usurpation of judicial power") before relief will be granted.[39]

Note: A wrong judgment is not void; only those judgments entered beyond the court's authority to act are "void".[40]

Reason 5—Changed Circumstances

Relief from a judgment or order may also be granted where the circumstances justifying the ruling have changed, such as (1) when the judgment is satisfied, released, or discharged, (2) where a prior judgment on which the present judgment is based has been reversed or otherwise vacated, or (3) in any other circumstance where the continued enforcement of the judgment would be inequitable (*e.g.,* a change in legislative or decisional law, or a change in critical facts).[41] This encom-

1309 (11th Cir.2003); *U.S. Steel v. M. DeMatteo Const. Co.*, 315 F.3d 43, 52–53 (1st Cir.2002).

37. *See Callon Petroleum Co. v. Frontier Ins. Co.*, 351 F.3d 204, 208 (5th Cir. 2003); *Burke v. Smith*, 252 F.3d 1260, 1263 (11th Cir.2001); *Robinson Eng'g Co. Pension Plan & Trust v. George*, 223 F.3d 445 (7th Cir.2000); *United States v. Berke*, 170 F.3d 882, 883 (9th Cir.1999); *Eberhardt v. Integrated Design & Const., Inc.*, 167 F.3d 861, 871 (4th Cir.1999); *Grun v. Pneumo Abex Corp.*, 163 F.3d 411, 422 (7th Cir.1998), *cert. denied*, 526 U.S. 1087, 119 S.Ct. 1496, 143 L.Ed.2d 651 (1999).

38. *See Central Vermont Pub. Serv. Corp. v. Herbert*, 341 F.3d 186, 189 (2d Cir.2003); *Carter v. Fenner*, 136 F.3d 1000, 1005 (5th Cir.1998), *cert. denied*, 525 U.S. 1041, 119 S.Ct. 591, 142 L.Ed.2d 534 (1998).

39. *See Central Vermont Pub. Serv. Corp. v. Herbert*, 341 F.3d 186, 190 (2d Cir.2003) (must be "total want of jurisdiction and no arguable basis" to support jurisdiction); *In re G.A.D., Inc.*, 340 F.3d 331, 336 (6th Cir.2003) (must be "so glaring as to constitute 'a total want of jurisdiction' "); *United States v. Tittjung*, 235 F.3d 330, 334 (7th Cir.2000), *cert. denied*, 533 U.S. 931, 121 S.Ct. 2554, 150 L.Ed.2d 721 (2001).

40. *See United States v. Buck*, 281 F.3d 1336, 1344 (10th Cir.2002); *United States v. Berke*, 170 F.3d 882, 883 (9th Cir.1999); *Eberhardt v. Integrated Design & Const., Inc.*, 167 F.3d 861, 871 (4th Cir.1999); *In re Crivello*, 134 F.3d 831, 838 (7th Cir.1998). *Chambers v. Armontrout*, 16 F.3d 257, 260 (8th Cir.1994).

41. *See Agostini v. Felton*, 521 U.S. 203, 117 S.Ct. 1997, 138 L.Ed.2d 391 (1997) (allowing relief under Rule 60(b)(5) to alter permanent injunction in light of Supreme Court's decision to overrule earlier constitutional precedent on which injunction was based); *Rufo v. Inmates of Suffolk County Jail*, 502 U.S. 367, 112 S.Ct. 748, 116 L.Ed.2d 867 (1992)(parties seeking a modification of an order entered by consent bear the burden of demonstrating a "significant change" in circumstances to warrant relief from the decree). *See also Reynolds v. McInnes*, 338 F.3d 1221, 1227 (11th Cir.2003) (modification may be warranted where significant time has passed since order was entered and, despite defendants' efforts, objectives of original agreement have not been met); *Maraziti v. Thorpe*, 52 F.3d 252, 254 (9th Cir.1995)(noting that nearly every court order causes some reverberations into the future, and mere "continuing consequences" do not equate with the "prospective application" required under Rule 60(b)(5); instead, standard for Rule 60(b)(5) is whether judgment is "executory" or implicates "supervision of changing conduct or conditions"); *Valentine Sugars, Inc. v. Sudan*, 34 F.3d 320, 321–22 (5th Cir. 1994)(modification under Rule 60(b)(5) is granted cautiously and only when dangers have al-

passes the traditional power invested in a court of equity to modify its decree when appropriate in view of changed circumstances.[42] In evaluating such motions, the courts consider whether a substantial change in circumstances or law has occurred since the contested order was entered, whether complying with the contested order would cause extreme and unexpected hardship, and whether a good reason for modification exists.[43] The proposed modification must be "suitably tailored" to meet the new legal or factual circumstances.[44] Relief under the "changed circumstances" category is only available where there is a prospective effect to the challenged judgment; the mere fact that a ruling will have future collateral estoppel effect (something obviously common to many rulings)[45] or otherwise causes "some reverberations into the future"[46] does not provide the requisite "prospective" effect necessary for relief under this provision. Ordinarily, money judgments will not possess the required "prospective" effect because the set nature of the monetary outlay provides the finality.[47]

Note: The Supreme Court has confirmed that the lower courts should not apply Rule 60(b)(5) in *anticipation* of the Supreme Court's overruling of an earlier precedent. To the contrary, the Supreme Court instructs that where one of its precedents applies directly to the circumstances at hand, even though the precedent's reasoning has been undermined by other opinions, the lower courts should nevertheless follow the precedent and leave to the Supreme Court the prerogative of overruling its own decisions.[48]

Reason 6—In the Interests of Justice

Finally, relief from a judgment or order may be permitted to further the interests of justice if such relief will not affect the substantial rights of the parties. This "catch-all" category is reserved for extraordinary circumstances.[49] Used sparingly, relief under this catch-

most disappeared, moving party is experiencing significantly extreme and unexpected hardship and oppression, and movant's case is unanswerable).

42. *See Frew ex rel. Frew v. Hawkins*, 540 U.S. 431, 441, 124 S.Ct. 899, 905–06, 157 L.Ed.2d 855 (2004).

43. *See United States v. Kayser–Roth Corp.*, 272 F.3d 89, 95 (1st Cir.2001); *Parton v. White*, 203 F.3d 552, 555 (8th Cir.2000), *cert. denied*, 531 U.S. 963, 121 S.Ct. 392, 148 L.Ed.2d 302 (2000); *Bellevue Manor Assocs. v. United States*, 165 F.3d 1249, 1254 (9th Cir.1999).

44. *See Reynolds v. McInnes*, 338 F.3d 1221 (11th Cir.2003).

45. *See Coltec Indus., Inc. v. Hobgood*, 280 F.3d 262, 271–72 (3d Cir.2002), *cert. denied*, 537 U.S. 947, 123 S.Ct. 411, 154 L.Ed.2d 291, (2002) ("If this [collateral estoppel argument] were enough to satisfy Rule 60(b)(5)'s threshold requirement, then the Rule's requirement of 'prospective application' would be meaningless").

46. *See Kalamazoo River Study Group v. Rockwell Int'l Corp.*, 355 F.3d 574, 587–88 (6th Cir. 2004).

47. *See Kalamazoo River Study Group v. Rockwell Int'l Corp.*, 355 F.3d 574, 587–88 (6th Cir. 2004).

48. *See Agostini v. Felton*, 521 U.S. 203, 117 S.Ct. 1997, 138 L.Ed.2d 391 (1997).

49. *See, e.g., Old Republic Ins. Co. v. Pacific Fin. Servs. of America, Inc.*, 301 F.3d 54, 59 (2d Cir.2002) (noting that moving party must show "extraordinary circumstances" to warrant relief); *Coltec Indus., Inc. v. Hobgood*, 280 F.3d 262, 273 (3d Cir.2002) (same), *cert. denied*, 537 U.S. 947, 123 S.Ct. 411, 154 L.Ed.2d 291 (2002); *Reform Party of Allegheny County v. Allegheny County Dep't of Elections*, 174 F.3d 305, 311 (3d Cir.1999) (available only in extraordinary circumstances, and commenting that intervening developments in the law will, by themselves, rarely constitute basis for relief under Rule 60(b)(6)); *Lehman v. United States*, 154 F.3d

all provision also generally requires a showing of actual injury and the presence of circumstances beyond the movant's control that prevented timely action to protect her interests.[50] Several courts have ruled that relief under this category is appropriate where a client seeking relief from a default judgment demonstrates gross negligence on the part of counsel.[51]

Note: The "catch-all" category and the preceding five specific categories are generally viewed as mutually exclusive. If the reason for which relief is sought fits within one of the five specific categories but fails to meet the prerequisites for relief (*e.g.*, the neglect is not truly excusable, the time period for seeking relief under that Rule provision has passed, etc.), the catch-all category will not permit relief.[52]

Burden of Proof

The party seeking relief from a judgment or order bears the burden of demonstrating that the prerequisites for such relief are satisfied.[53]

Discretion of District Judge

Whether to grant relief under Rule 60(b) is left to the discretion of the trial court, and will not be disturbed on appeal unless that discretion has been abused.[54] In the case of "void" judgments attacked under Rule 60(b)(4), however, the district court's discretion is almost illusory,

1010, 1017 (9th Cir.1998), *cert. denied*, 526 U.S. 1040, 119 S.Ct. 1336, 143 L.Ed.2d 500 (1999) (used "sparingly"); *Computer Professionals for Social Responsibility v. United States Secret Service,* 72 F.3d 897, 903 (D.C.Cir.1996)(Rule 60(b)(6) applies only to "extraordinary circumstances;" however, relief is appropriate where previously undisclosed evidence indicated that government source had reasonable expectation of confidentiality; order directing disclosure of source's identity should therefore be modified under Rule 60(b)(6)).

50. *See Lehman v. United States*, 154 F.3d 1010, 1017 (9th Cir.1998), *cert. denied*, 526 U.S. 1040, 119 S.Ct. 1336, 143 L.Ed.2d 500 (1999).

51. *See Community Dental Servs. v. Tani*, 282 F.3d 1164, 1169 (9th Cir.2002) (neglect must be "so gross that it is inexcusable"); *Shepard Claims Serv., Inc. v. William Darrah & Assocs.*, 796 F.2d 190, 195 (6th Cir.1986); *Boughner v. Secretary of Health, Educ. & Welfare*, 572 F.2d 976, 978 (3d Cir.1978); *L.P. Steuart, Inc. v. Matthews*, 329 F.2d 234, 235 (D.C.Cir.1964), *cert. denied*, 379 U.S. 824, 85 S.Ct. 50, 13 L.Ed.2d 35 (1964).

52. *See Liljeberg v. Health Servs. Acquisition Corp.,* 486 U.S. 847, 108 S.Ct. 2194, 100 L.Ed.2d 855 (1988). *See also McCurry ex rel. Turner v. Adventist Health Sys./Sunbelt, Inc.*, 298 F.3d 586, 592–96 (6th Cir.2002); *Fiskars, Inc. v. Hunt Mfg. Co.*, 279 F.3d 1378, 1383 (Fed. Cir.2002); *Lyon v. Agusta S.P.A.*, 252 F.3d 1078, 1088–89 (9th Cir.2001), *cert. denied,* 534 U.S. 1079, 122 S.Ct. 809, 151 L.Ed.2d 694 (2002); *Warren v. Garvin*, 219 F.3d 111, 114 (2d Cir.2000), *cert. denied*, 531 U.S. 968, 121 S.Ct. 404, 148 L.Ed.2d 312 (2000); *Baltia Air Lines, Inc. v. Transaction Management, Inc.*, 98 F.3d 640, 642 (D.C.Cir. 1996); *Williams v. United States Drug Enforcement Admin.*, 51 F.3d 732, 736 n. 1 (7th Cir. 1995); *Schultz v. Commerce First Financial*, 24 F.3d 1023 (8th Cir.1994); *de la Torre v. Continental Ins. Co.*, 15 F.3d 12 (1st Cir.1994).

53. *See McCurry ex rel. Turner v. Adventist Health Sys./Sunbelt, Inc.*, 298 F.3d 586, 592 (6th Cir.2002).

54. *See McCurry ex rel. Turner v. Adventist Health Sys./Sunbelt, Inc.*, 298 F.3d 586, 592 (6th Cir.2002); *Provident Life & Acc. Ins. Co. v. Goel*, 274 F.3d 984, 997 (5th Cir.2001); *Davila-Alvarez v. Escuela de Medicina Universidad Central Del Caribe*, 257 F.3d 58, 63–64 (1st Cir.2001); *Liberty Mut. Ins. Co. v. FAG Bearings Corp.*, 153 F.3d 919, 924 (8th Cir.1998); *Robb v. Norfolk & Western Ry. Co.*, 122 F.3d 354 (7th Cir.1997); *Twelve John Does v. District of Columbia,* 841 F.2d 1133 (D.C.Cir.1988).

if it exists at all. Void judgments are "legal nullities", and the court's refusal to vacate such judgments is a *per se* abuse of discretion.[55]

Procedure

Motions under this Rule should be made to the court that rendered the judgment.[56] Absent a local rule dictating otherwise, the court is not required to convene a hearing on Rule 60(b) motions, but may choose to do so in its discretion.[57] The court generally does not need to enter findings of fact and conclusions of law to grant Rule 60(b) relief.[58]

Who May Seek Relief

Relief under this Rule may be requested by a party, the party's legal representative,[59] or one in privity with a party.[60]

Sua Sponte Motions

The Circuits are divided on whether a district court may, on its own initiative, grant relief from a judgment under Rule 60(b).[61]

Time for Motion

All motions under Rule 60(b) must be made within a "reasonable" time, except:

- *Void Judgments:* Motions can be made at any time; [62] Laches and similar finality principles generally have no effect on void judgments; the courts have held that the mere passage of time will not convert a void judgment into a proper one.[63] However, if a party attacks the court's jurisdiction and loses on that issue, the question of jurisdiction becomes *res judicata* and, accordingly,

55. *See, e.g., Central Vermont Pub. Serv. Corp. v. Herbert*, 341 F.3d 186, 189 (2d Cir. 2003); *Jackson v. FIE Corp.*, 302 F.3d 515, 522 (5th Cir.2002); *Robinson Eng'g Co. Pension Plan & Trust v. George*, 223 F.3d 445 (7th Cir.2000).

56. *See Board of Trustees, Sheet Metal Workers' Nat'l Pension Fund v. Elite Erectors, Inc.*, 212 F.3d 1031, 1034 (7th Cir.2000).

57. *See Atkinson v. Prudential Property Co.*, 43 F.3d 367, 374 (8th Cir.1994).

58. *See Atkinson v. Prudential Property Co.*, 43 F.3d 367, 374 (8th Cir.1994).

59. *See In re El Paso Refinery, LP*, 37 F.3d 230, 234 (5th Cir.1994) (defining phrase "party's legal representative" as person standing in the place, and in the stead, of another (such as an heir at law), who either holds position tantamount to that of the party, or whose legal rights were so tied to the party that his or her rights were directly affected by final judgment).

60. *See Eyak Native Village v. Exxon Corp.*, 25 F.3d 773 (9th Cir.1994), *cert. denied*, 513 U.S. 1102, 115 S.Ct. 779, 130 L.Ed.2d 673 (1995).

61. *See United States v. Pauley*, 321 F.3d 578, 581 & 581 n.1 (6th Cir.2003) (describing Circuit split). *Compare United States v. Pauley*, 321 F.3d 578, 581 & 581 n.1 (6th Cir.2003) (no *sua sponte* relief) *and Dow v. Baird*, 389 F.2d 882, 884–85 (10th Cir.1968) (same) *with Fort Knox Music Inc. v. Baptiste*, 257 F.3d 108, 111 (2d Cir.2001) (*sua sponte* relief not prohibited) *and Kingvision Pay–Per–View Ltd. v. Lake Alice Bar*, 168 F.3d 347, 351 (9th Cir.1999) (same) *and McDowell v. Celebrezze*, 310 F.2d 43, 44 (5th Cir.1962) (same) *and United States v. Jacobs*, 298 F.2d 469, 472 (4th Cir.1961) (same).

62. *See Central Vermont Pub. Serv. Corp. v. Herbert*, 341 F.3d 186, 189 (2d Cir.2003); *Jackson v. FIE Corp.*, 302 F.3d 515, 523–24 (5th Cir.2002); *Hertz Corp. v. Alamo Rent–A–Car, Inc.*, 16 F.3d 1126, 1130 (11th Cir.1994).

63. *See Jackson v. FIE Corp.*, 302 F.3d 515, 523–24 (5th Cir.2002); *United States v. One Toshiba Color Television*, 213 F.3d 147, 157–58 (3d Cir.2000).

the judgment is not void; the party's only recourse in such a case is a proper, timely merits appeal, not relief under this Rule.[64]

- *Mistake, Inadvertence, Surprise, or Excusable Neglect:* One–Year time limit: motions must be made within 1 year after judgment, order, or proceeding was entered or taken;[65]
- *Newly Discovered Evidence:* One–Year time limit: motions must be made within 1 year after judgment, order, or proceeding was entered or taken;[66]
- *Fraud, Misrepresentation, or Other Misconduct By An Adverse Party:* One–Year time limit: motions must be made within 1 year after judgment, order, or proceeding was entered or taken.[67] This time limit on the fraud category is "absolute", and is not tolled during the pendency of an appeal from the same judgment.[68]

In all other instances, the courts determine whether the time of filing is "reasonable" on a case-by-case basis, by examining the prejudice to the party opposing the motion and whether the moving party had good reason for not acting sooner.[69]

No Extensions

Where a time limit is specified in Rule 60(b), the district court lacks the authority to extend the time for bringing a motion.[70]

Enforceability of Judgment

Rule 60(b) specifically provides that a judgment challenged under that Rule remains valid and enforceable unless and until the Rule 60(b) motion is granted.[71]

Effect of Appeals

Taking an appeal does not extend the Rule 60(b) 1–year or "reasonable" time limits.[72] However, a Rule 60 motion filed within 10 days after entry of the judgment will toll the time for taking an appeal.[73] Otherwise, a Rule 60(b) motion filed more than 10 days following entry

64. *See Durfee v. Duke,* 375 U.S. 106, 84 S.Ct. 242, 11 L.Ed.2d 186 (1963); *American Surety Co. v. Baldwin,* 287 U.S. 156, 53 S.Ct. 98, 77 L.Ed. 231 (1932).

65. *See In re G.A.D., Inc.*, 340 F.3d 331, 334 (6th Cir.2003).

66. *See In re G.A.D., Inc.*, 340 F.3d 331, 334 (6th Cir.2003).

67. *See In re G.A.D., Inc.*, 340 F.3d 331, 334 (6th Cir.2003).

68. *See King v. First American Investigations, Inc.*, 287 F.3d 91, 94 (2d Cir.2002), *cert. denied*, 537 U.S. 960, 123 S.Ct. 393, 154 L.Ed.2d 314 (2002).

69. *See In re G.A.D., Inc.*, 340 F.3d 331, 334–35 (6th Cir.2003); *Old Republic Ins. Co. v. Pacific Fin. Servs. of America, Inc.*, 301 F.3d 54, 59 (2d Cir.2002); *Watkins v. Lundell*, 169 F.3d 540, 544 (8th Cir.1999), *cert. denied*, 528 U.S. 928, 120 S.Ct. 324, 145 L.Ed.2d 253 (1999); *Travelers Ins. Co. v. Liljeberg Enters.*, 38 F.3d 1404, 1410 (5th Cir.1994).

70. *See* Rule 6(b).

71. *See, e.g., Balark v. City of Chicago,* 81 F.3d 658, 663 (7th Cir.1996), *cert. denied*, 519 U.S. 1006, 117 S.Ct. 507, 136 L.Ed.2d 398 (1996)(Rule 60(b) order "operates prospectively only").

72. *See Cashner v. Freedom Stores, Inc.*, 98 F.3d 572, 579 n. 4 (10th Cir.1996).

73. *See* Fed. R. App. P. 4(a)(4)(A)(vi).

of judgment will generally not postpone the finality of the judgment and the appeal period begins to run.[74] In such cases, a pending Rule 60(b) motion does not prevent an otherwise proper notice of appeal from conferring jurisdiction on the appellate court.[75] Once an appeal is taken, the district court's ability to act on Rule 60(b) motions is limited. Although the district court may *deny* such motions, it may not *grant* them without a remand from the court of appeals.[76] If the district court is inclined to grant a Rule 60(b) motion during the pendency of an appeal, the court should issue a brief memorandum so notifying the movant, and the movant, thereafter, should seek a limited remand of the appeal for that purpose.[77]

Nature of Appellate Review

An appeal from a district court order denying relief under Rule 60(b) implicates only the propriety of that denial, and not the underlying merits of the contested judgment itself.[78]

Other Methods for Seeking Relief From Judgments

Rule 60(b) does not prevent the use of any of the following three other methods for seeking relief from a judgment or order:

- *Independent Action:* Litigants may also seek relief from judgment by filing an "independent action", a proceeding that sounds in equity.[79] Although Rule 60(b) expressly preserves this procedure, independent actions are permitted in only exceptional cases to prevent grave miscarriages of justice.[80] An independent action may be maintained where:

  (1) the judgment should not, in good conscience, be enforced;

  (2) a good defense exists to the plaintiff's lawsuit;

  (3) fraud, accident, or mistake prevented the defendant from obtaining the benefit of the good defense;

  (4) the defendant is free of fault and negligence; *and*

74. *See Carpenter v. Williams,* 86 F.3d 1015 (10th Cir.1996)(Rule 60(b) motion filed more than ten days after district court dismissed case does not toll time for filing notice of appeal).

75. *See Hatfield v. Board of County Comm'rs*, 52 F.3d 858, 861 (10th Cir.1995).

76. *See Fobian v. Storage Tech. Corp.*, 164 F.3d 887, 890–91 (4th Cir.1999); *Cashner v. Freedom Stores, Inc.*, 98 F.3d 572, 579 n. 4 (10th Cir.1996); *Travelers Ins. Co. v. Liljeberg Enters.*, 38 F.3d 1404, 1407 n. 3 (5th Cir.1994). *See also Brooks v. Celeste*, 16 F.3d 104, 108 (6th Cir.1994) (noting that once notice of appeal is filed, district court will generally lack jurisdiction to consider Rule 60(b) motions), *vacated on other grounds on reconsideration*, 39 F.3d 125 (6th Cir.1994).

77. *See Mahone v. Ray*, 326 F.3d 1176, 1180 (11th Cir.2003); *Morse v. McWhorter*, 290 F.3d 795, 799 (6th Cir.2002); *Fobian v. Storage Tech. Corp.*, 164 F.3d 887, 890–91 (4th Cir.1999); *Cashner v. Freedom Stores, Inc.*, 98 F.3d 572, 579 n. 4 (10th Cir.1996); *Travelers Ins. Co. v. Liljeberg Enters.*, 38 F.3d 1404, 1407 n. 3 (5th Cir.1994).

78. *See Browder v. Director*, 434 U.S. 257, 263 n. 7, 98 S.Ct. 556, 560 n. 7, 54 L.Ed.2d 521 (1978).

79. *See United States v. Beggerly*, 524 U.S. 38, 118 S.Ct. 1862, 141 L.Ed.2d 32 (1998).

80. *See United States v. Beggerly*, 524 U.S. 38, 118 S.Ct. 1862, 141 L.Ed.2d 32 (1998); *Appling v. State Farm Mut. Auto. Ins. Co.*, 340 F.3d 769, 780 (9th Cir.2003).

(5) there is no adequate remedy at law.[81]

The Rule 60(b) time limits do not apply to independent actions in equity.[82] If the independent action is filed in the same court that granted the judgment, supplemental jurisdiction exists—regardless of diversity or federal question jurisdiction.[83]

- *Statutory Relief:* Relief from judgments is available where provided by statute.
- *Fraud on the Court:* The district court enjoys the inherent power to grant relief where the judgment or order is obtained through a fraud on the court.[84] No time limits apply.[85] The court may grant the relief on its own initiative or on motion. Such fraud must be proven by clear and convincing evidence.[86]

  Note: To constitute as a fraud on the court, the alleged misconduct must be something more than fraud among the litigants. Instead, the misconduct must be an assault on the integrity of the judicial process, which defiles the court itself or is perpetrated by officers of the court in such a manner that the impartial system of justice fails to function.[87] Fraud in the discovery process, to the extent it meets this standard, can support an independent action.[88]

Old Writs Abolished

The old common law writs of coram nobis, coram vobis, audita querela, and bills of review are abolished in civil proceedings.[89] Filings

81. *See In re West Texas Mktg. Corp.*, 12 F.3d 497, 503 n. 3 (5th Cir.1994)(listing criteria); *Great Coastal Express, Inc. v. International Bhd. of Teamsters, Chauffeurs, Warehousemen & Helpers of America*, 675 F.2d 1349, 1358 (4th Cir.1982)(same), *cert. denied,* 459 U.S. 1128, 103 S.Ct. 764, 74 L.Ed.2d 978 (1983) .

82. *See Robinson v. Volkswagenwerk AG*, 56 F.3d 1268, 1274 (10th Cir.1995), *cert. denied,* 516 U.S. 1045, 116 S.Ct. 705, 133 L.Ed.2d 661 (1996); *In re West Texas Mktg. Corp.*, 12 F.3d 497, 503 n. 3 (5th Cir.1994).

83. *See United States v. Beggerly*, 524 U.S. 38, 118 S.Ct. 1862, 141 L.Ed.2d 32 (1998); *Cresswell v. Sullivan & Cromwell*, 922 F.2d 60, 70 (2d Cir.1990).

84. *Universal Oil Prods. Co. v. Root Refining Co.,* 328 U.S. 575, 66 S.Ct. 1176, 90 L.Ed. 1447 (1946); *Hazel–Atlas Glass Co. v. Hartford–Empire Co.,* 322 U.S. 238, 64 S.Ct. 997, 88 L.Ed. 1250 (1944).

85. *See King v. First American Investigations, Inc.*, 287 F.3d 91, 95 (2d Cir.2002), *cert. denied*, 537 U.S. 960, 123 S.Ct. 393, 154 L.Ed.2d 314 (2002).

86. *See King v. First American Investigations, Inc.*, 287 F.3d 91, 95 (2d Cir.2002), *cert. denied*, 537 U.S. 960, 123 S.Ct. 393, 154 L.Ed.2d 314 (2002).

87. *See Appling v. State Farm Mut. Auto. Ins. Co.*, 340 F.3d 769, 780 (9th Cir.2003). *King v. First American Investigations, Inc.*, 287 F.3d 91, 95 (2d Cir.2002), *cert. denied*, 537 U.S. 960, 123 S.Ct. 393, 154 L.Ed.2d 314 (2002). *See also Baltia Air Lines, Inc. v. Transaction Management, Inc.*, 98 F.3d 640, 642 (D.C.Cir.1996) (citing bribery of a judge or an attorney's knowing participation in the presentation of perjured testimony).

88. *See Appling v. State Farm Mut. Auto. Ins. Co.*, 340 F.3d 769, 780 (9th Cir.2003).

89. At the old common law, a writ of coram nobis (if sought at the King's Bench) or writ of coram vobis (if sought in the Courts of Common Pleas) were the procedural tools to correct errors of fact by petitioning to bring before the court certain facts which, if known earlier, would have prevented the entry of judgment. *See* 18 Am. Jur. 2d *Coram Nobis & Allied Statutory Remedies* §§ 1–2 (1985). A person against whom execution has issued or was about to issue could seek a writ of audita querela to prevent execution where the execution would be contrary to

under these ancient writs may be treated by the courts as motions for relief under Rule 60(b).[90]

ADDITIONAL RESEARCH REFERENCES

Wright & Miller, *Federal Practice and Procedure* §§ 2851–73.

C.J.S. Federal Civil Procedure §§ 368, 373, 1233–1251 et seq.

West's Key No. Digests, Federal Civil Procedure ⚷921, 2641–2662.

justice. *See* 7 Am. Jur. 2d *Audita Querela* § 1 (1997). Finally, a bill of review was a new action, filed in equity, that sought the correction, reversal, alteration, or explanation of a decree issued in an earlier proceeding. *See* 27A Am. Jur. 2d *Equity* § 256 (1996). Each of these ancient writs—in civil actions only—have been abolished by the Federal Rules.

90. *See Green v. White*, 319 F.3d 560, 563 n.1 (3d Cir.2003) (treating request for writ in the nature of a writ of coram nobis as motion under Rule 60(b)).

RULE 61

HARMLESS ERROR

No error in either the admission or the exclusion of evidence and no error or defect in any ruling or order or in anything done or omitted by the court or by any of the parties is ground for granting a new trial or for setting aside a verdict or for vacating, modifying or otherwise disturbing a judgment or order, unless refusal to take such action appears to the court inconsistent with substantial justice. The court at every stage of the proceeding must disregard any error or defect in the proceeding which does not affect the substantial rights of the parties.

AUTHORS' COMMENTARY ON RULE 61

PURPOSE AND SCOPE

Rule 61 codifies the principle that "harmless" errors by the district court—those errors that do not affect the parties' substantial rights—will not justify a new trial, setting aside a verdict, or vacating, modifying, or otherwise disturbing the court's order.

APPLICATIONS

Standard for "Harmlessness"

Rule 61 defines a harmless error as one that does not affect the substantial rights of the parties or does not defeat substantial justice.[1] Generally, an error will not be discounted as harmless if the court is left with a grave doubt as to whether the error had a substantial influence in the ultimate verdict.[2] In making this evaluation, the court considers the entire record and applies the harmlessness standard on a case-by-case basis.[3] Every reasonable possibility of prejudice need not be dis-

1. Rule 61. *See Brandt v. Vulcan, Inc.*, 30 F.3d 752 (7th Cir.1994)(harmless error calls into question the fundamental fairness of the trial).

2. *See Krulewitch v. United States*, 336 U.S. 440, 444–45, 69 S.Ct. 716, 718–19, 93 L.Ed. 790 (1949)(defining harmlessness in criminal context); *General Motors Corp. v. New A.C. Chevrolet, Inc.*, 263 F.3d 296, 329 (3d Cir.2001) (non-constitutional legal errors are harmless if it is "highly probable that the error did not affect the judgment"); *Nieves-Villanueva v. Soto–Rivera*, 133 F.3d 92, 102 (1st Cir.1997) (court assumes error affected the verdict if court is in "grave doubt" about its effect on verdict); *Malek v. Federal Ins. Co.*, 994 F.2d 49, 55 (2d Cir. 1993)(error is not harmless where it would have affected the outcome of the case). *See also Barber v. Ruth*, 7 F.3d 636, 641 (7th Cir.1993)(in bench trial, trial error is harmless if the record indicates that trial court would have reached the same judgment regardless of the error).

3. *See Nieves-Villanueva v. Soto–Rivera*, 133 F.3d 92, 102 (1st Cir.1997); *Brewer v. Jeep Corp.*, 724 F.2d 653 (8th Cir.1983).

proved.[4] In describing when something will rise to the level of "harmless error", it is nearly impossible to avoid the subjectivity inherent in the inquiry itself.[5] At its core, the harmless error inquiry examines whether the trial error "affected the outcome of a case to the substantial disadvantage of the losing party".[6]

Burden of Proof

The party moving for a mistrial or for post-trial relief bears the burden of establishing that a trial error affected that party's substantial rights and, thus, was not harmless.[7]

Applies to All Errors

The harmless error rule applies to all types of errors, including most constitutional errors. The courts of appeals review rulings of the district courts under this standard as well.[8]

Federal Law Controls

Under *Erie* principles,[9] the federal (not State) construction of the harmless error rule usually controls where the federal and State standards are inconsistent.[10]

Errors in Rulings on Pleadings

Technical errors in pleadings will generally be discounted as harmless.[11]

4. *See General Motors Corp. v. New A.C. Chevrolet, Inc.*, 263 F.3d 296, 329 (3d Cir.2001).

5. *See United States v. O'Keefe*, 169 F.3d 281, 287 n. 5 (5th Cir.1999) (citing formulations by Judge Traynor and Justice Rutledge as among the clearest formulations) (citing 11 Charles Alan Wright, Arthur R. Miller, & Mary Kay Kane, *Federal Practice & Procedure* § 2883, at 445–47 (2d ed. 1995)). *Cf.* Roger Traynor, *The Riddle of Harmless Error* 35 (1970) ("[U]nless the appellate court believes it highly probable that the error did not affect the judgment, it should reverse"); *Kotteakos v. United States*, 328 U.S. 750, 760, 66 S.Ct. 1239, 1245, 90 L.Ed. 1557 (1946) (Rutledge, J.) ("Do not be technical, where technicality does not really hurt the party whose rights in the trial and in its outcome the technicality affects").

6. *See United States v. O'Keefe*, 169 F.3d 281, 287 n. 5 (5th Cir.1999).

7. *See Palmer v. Hoffman*, 318 U.S. 109, 116, 63 S.Ct. 477, 481–82, 87 L.Ed. 645 (1943)(moving party bears the burden of showing resulting prejudice); *Tesser v. Board of Educ. of City Sch. Dist. of New York*, 370 F.3d 314, 319–20 (2d Cir. 2004) (same); *Dresser-Rand Co. v. Virtual Automation Inc.*, 361 F.3d 831, 842 (5th Cir. 2004) (same); *Nieves-Villanueva v. Soto-Rivera*, 133 F.3d 92, 102 (1st Cir.1997) (same); *Burkhart v. Washington Metro. Area Transit Auth.*, 112 F.3d 1207, 1214 (D.C.Cir. 1997) (same); *Phoenix Eng'g & Supply Inc. v. Universal Elec. Co.*, 104 F.3d 1137, 1142 (9th Cir.1997) (same).

8. *See* 28 U.S.C.A. § 2111 (fixing harmlessness standard for appeals). *See also McDonough Power Equip., Inc. v. Greenwood*, 464 U.S. 548, 554, 104 S.Ct. 845, 849, 78 L.Ed.2d 663 (1984)(noting that appellate courts must act in accordance with the salutary policy embodied in Rule 61); *General Motors Corp. v. New A.C. Chevrolet, Inc.*, 263 F.3d 296, 329 n.18 (3d Cir. 2001) (same).

9. *See Erie R.R. v. Tompkins*, 304 U.S. 64, 58 S.Ct. 817, 82 L.Ed. 1188 (1938)(in diversity cases, the federal courts will apply federal rules of procedure but State substantive law). *See* discussion of the *Erie* Doctrine in Part II of this text.

10. *See Sokol Crystal Prods., Inc. v. DSC Communications Corp.*, 15 F.3d 1427 (7th Cir. 1994); *Smith v. Chesapeake & Ohio Ry.*, 778 F.2d 384 (7th Cir.1985).

11. *See Toth v. Corning Glass Works*, 411 F.2d 912 (6th Cir.1969)(refusal to strike a pleading's claim deemed harmless).

Errors in Admitting or Excluding Evidence

The district court enjoys broad discretion to admit or exclude evidence.[12] Errors in such rulings are harmless if the party raises no objection,[13] if the evidence wrongfully admitted or excluded was cumulative,[14] if adequate curative instructions are given[15], or if the rulings are otherwise determined not to have caused substantial prejudice or to have substantially influenced the jury.[16] However, evidentiary rulings that affected the substantial rights of a party are *not* harmless, and the rulings must be reversed.[17] Thus, if the trial evidence is not sufficient to support the verdict without the wrongfully admitted evidence, the ruling is prejudicial.[18] In making this "harmlessness" evaluation, the court considers the centrality of the evidence and the prejudicial effect of the inclusion or exclusion of the evidence.[19] If the court can say "with fair assurance" that the judgment was not substantially affected by the wrongfully admitted or excluded evidence, the error will be considered harmless.[20]

12. *See United States v. Kim*, 111 F.3d 1351, 1363 (7th Cir.1997); *Abrams v. Lightolier Inc.*, 50 F.3d 1204, 1213 (3d Cir.1995); *Norton v. Caremark, Inc.*, 20 F.3d 330, 338 (8th Cir.1994).

13. *See Abrams v. Lightolier Inc.*, 50 F.3d 1204, 1213 (3d Cir.1995); *Sokol Crystal Prods., Inc. v. DSC Communications Corp.*, 15 F.3d 1427, 1435 (7th Cir.1994).

14. *See In re Air Crash Disaster*, 86 F.3d 498, 531 (6th Cir.1996); *La Crosse County v. Gershman, Brickner & Bratton, Inc.*, 982 F.2d 1171, 1175 (7th Cir.1993).

15. *See Grizzle v. Travelers Health Network, Inc.*, 14 F.3d 261, 269 (5th Cir.1994)(court must consider curative instructions when assessing harmlessness). In ruling on the effect of the curative instructions, a court will assume that the jury obeyed the court and followed its instructions. *Trademark Research Corp. v. Maxwell Online, Inc.*, 995 F.2d 326, 340 (2d Cir. 1993). *Compare Davidson v. Smith*, 9 F.3d 4 (2d Cir.1993)(improper testimony not cured by trial instructions) *with Trademark Research Corp. v. Maxwell Online, Inc.*, 995 F.2d 326 (2d Cir.1993) (trial error deemed cured by court's instructions).

16. *Fort v. C.W. Keller Trucking, Inc.*, 330 F.3d 1006 1013 (7th Cir.2003); *Blake v. Pellegrino*, 329 F.3d 43, 49 (1st Cir.2003); *Anderson v. WBMG–42*, 253 F.3d 561, 563 (11th Cir.2001); *Romano v. U–Haul Int'l*, 233 F.3d 655, 667 (1st Cir.2000), *petition for cert. filed*, 534 U.S. 815, 122 S.Ct. 41, 151 L.Ed.2d 14 (2001); *Odetics, Inc. v. Storage Tech. Corp.*, 185 F.3d 1259, 1276 (Fed.Cir.1999); *Innes v. Howell Corp.*, 76 F.3d 702, 711 (6th Cir.1996)(expert's testimony); *Ricketts v. City of Hartford*, 74 F.3d 1397, 1412 (2d Cir.1996), *cert. denied*, 519 U.S. 815, 117 S.Ct. 65, 136 L.Ed.2d 26 (1996); *Phillips v. U.S. IRS*, 73 F.3d 939, 945 (9th Cir.1996); *In re CLDC Management Corp.*, 72 F.3d 1347, 1353 (7th Cir.1996), *cert. denied*, 519 U.S. 861, 117 S.Ct. 166, 136 L.Ed.2d 108 (1996). *See also Hynes v. Coughlin*, 79 F.3d 285, 291 (2d Cir. 1996)(tests for whether improperly admitted evidence substantially influenced the jury include: examining whether evidence was unimportant in relation to all other issues jury considered, whether evidence bore on an issue that was plainly critical to the jury's deliberations, and whether the evidence was emphasized during jury argument).

17. *See Concord Boat Corp. v. Brunswick Corp.*, 207 F.3d 1039, 1057 (8th Cir.2000), *cert. denied*, 531 U.S. 979, 121 S.Ct. 428, 148 L.Ed.2d 436 (2000); *Becker v. ARCO Chem. Co.*, 207 F.3d 176, 180 (3d Cir.2000); *Costantino v. David M. Herzog, M.D., P.C.*, 203 F.3d 164, 174 (2d Cir. 2000).

18. *See Havrum v. United States*, 204 F.3d 815, 818 (8th Cir.2000) (wrongly admitted evidence is harmless error if factfinder would have reached the same conclusion without the challenged evidence); *Sokol Crystal Prods., Inc. v. DSC Communications Corp.*, 15 F.3d 1427, 1435 (7th Cir.1994).

19. *See Nieves–Villanueva v. Soto–Rivera*, 133 F.3d 92, 102 (1st Cir.1997).

20. *See Tesser v. Board of Educ. of City Sch. Dist. of New York*, 370 F.3d 314, 319–20 (2d Cir. 2004); *Blake v. Pellegrino*, 329 F.3d 43, 49 (1st Cir.2003). *See also Mihailovich v. Laatsch*, 359 F.3d 892, 913–14 (7th Cir. 2004) (errors in evidence satisfy standard only if significant chance exists that errors affected trial's outcome), *petition for cert. filed* (U.S. Aug. 3, 2004); *Goodman v. Pennsylvania Turnpike Com'n*, 293 F.3d 655,

Expert Testimony: This same harmless error standard applies to challenges to expert testimony as well.[21]

Effect of Multiple Errors: Although each individual evidentiary error might not, standing alone, have affected a party's substantial rights, the court may find that the collective effect of multiple evidentiary errors deprived the moving party of a fair trial.[22]

Errors in Jury Instructions

Jury instructions must be considered in their entirety.[23] If the charging errors would not have changed the trial result,[24] or if the parties waived the errors by failing to timely object,[25] challenges to jury instructions will be rejected as harmless.[26] Conversely, if the jury may have based their verdict on an erroneous instruction, a new trial is warranted.[27]

Errors in Ruling on Counsel's Conduct During Trial

Misconduct by counsel during trial will be deemed harmless unless the court determines that the misconduct affected the verdict.[28]

667 (3d Cir.2002) (evidentiary admission error is harmless, and not grounds for reversal, if it is "highly probable" that jury would have reached same result otherwise).

21. *See Dresser–Rand Co. v. Virtual Automation Inc.*, 361 F.3d 831, 842 (5th Cir. 2004).

22. *See Gomez v. Rivera Rodriguez*, 344 F.3d 103, 118 (1st Cir. 2003); *Phoenix Assocs. III v. Stone*, 60 F.3d 95, 105 (2d Cir.1995); *Kopf v. Skyrm*, 993 F.2d 374, 381 (4th Cir.1993).

23. *See Elwell v. University Hosps. Home Care Servs.*, 276 F.3d 832, 844 (6th Cir.2002); *Dadian v. Village of Wilmette*, 269 F.3d 831, 839 (7th Cir.2001).

24. *See Richards v. Relentless, Inc.*, 341 F.3d 35, 48 (1st Cir.2003) (new trial necessary only if instruction error could have affected jury's deliberation); *Elwell v. University Hosps. Home Care Servs.*, 276 F.3d 832, 844 (6th Cir.2002) (assessing ruling in context of instructions as a whole, ruling "harmless because risk of jury confusion was minimal"); *Dadian v. Village of Wilmette*, 269 F.3d 831, 839 (7th Cir.2001) (testing whether instructions, as a whole, sufficiently informed jury correctly as to applicable law and thus did not affect substantial rights of parties).

25. *See Foley v. Commonwealth Elec. Co.*, 312 F.3d 517, 520 (1st Cir.2002) (if party properly objects to jury instruction, harmless error Rule 61 applies; if proper objection not made, plain error rule applies which requires proof of: (1) error, (2) that error was plain, (3) that error likely altered outcome, and (4) that error was sufficiently fundamental to threaten fairness, integrity, or public reputation of judicial proceedings).

26. *See Terminate Control Corp., Nu-Life Const. Corp. v. Horowitz*, 28 F.3d 1335 (2d Cir. 1994)(jury instructions warrant a new trial only if the court is persuaded, based on the record as a whole, that the error was prejudicial or the charge was highly confusing).

27. *See S.E.C. v. Yun*, 327 F.3d 1263, 1282 (11th Cir.2003) (granting new trial due to court's erroneous jury instruction, reinforced in counsel's closing argument); *Jannotta v. Subway Sandwich Shops, Inc.*, 125 F.3d 503, 515 (7th Cir.1997) (holding that instructional error was not harmless if it provided jury with inadequate understanding of the law and caused prejudice to the complaining party); *Coleman v. B–G Maintenance Mgmt. of Colo., Inc.*, 108 F.3d 1199, 1204–05 (10th Cir.1997)(because the jury, in all probability, based its verdict on erroneous instruction, jury's verdict must be reversed)..

28. *Cf.* Rule 39(c)(relating to advisory juries). *See Peterson v. Willie*, 81 F.3d 1033, 1036 (11th Cir.1996)(noting that statements made during oral arguments will not constitute reversible error unless they are plainly unwarranted and clearly injurious); *Westfarm Assocs. Ltd. Partnership v. Washington Suburban Sanitary Com'n*, 66 F.3d 669, 685 n. 10 (4th Cir. 1995)(inappropriate allusion made during closing argument, followed by proper instructions from the court, is not basis for reversal), *cert. denied,* 517 U.S. 1103, 116 S.Ct. 1318, 134 L.Ed.2d 471 (1996).

Error in Granting or Denying Jury Trial

The court's mistaken decision to grant a jury trial is generally harmless error,[29] but an improper denial of a jury trial is usually grounds for reversal.[30]

ADDITIONAL RESEARCH REFERENCES

Wright & Miller, *Federal Practice and Procedure* §§ 2881–88.

C.J.S. Federal Civil Procedure §§ 1062–1100 et seq., 1241–1247 et seq.

West's Key No. Digests, Federal Civil Procedure ⚷2333–2353, 2651–2656.

29. *See Mateyko v. Felix,* 924 F.2d 824, 828 (9th Cir.1990), *cert. denied,* 502 U.S. 814, 112 S.Ct. 65, 116 L.Ed.2d 40 (1991). *See also Venture Properties, Inc. v. First Southern Bank,* 79 F.3d 90, 92 (8th Cir.1996)(movant demonstrated no prejudice from court's decision to conduct a jury trial rather than a bench trial).

30. *See Burns v. Lawther,* 53 F.3d 1237, 1241–42 (11th Cir.1995) (harmless error rule may be applied to improper denials of trial by jury, but only if the issues could have been resolved by summary judgment or judgment as a matter of law); *King v. United Benefit Fire Ins. Co.,* 377 F.2d 728, 731 (10th Cir.1967)(denial will be deemed harmless where only a question of law is involved or where a verdict for the movant would have been set aside), *cert. denied,* 389 U.S. 857, 88 S.Ct. 99, 19 L.Ed.2d 124 (1967). *See also Sailor v. Hubbell, Inc.*, 4 F.3d 323 (4th Cir.1993)(denial of jury trial harmless if it did not affect party's rights, such as where no reasonable jury could have found in that party's favor).

RULE 62

STAY OF PROCEEDINGS TO ENFORCE A JUDGMENT

(a) Automatic Stay; Exceptions—Injunctions, Receiverships, and Patent Accountings. Except as stated herein, no execution shall issue upon a judgment nor shall proceedings be taken for its enforcement until the expiration of 10 days after its entry. Unless otherwise ordered by the court, an interlocutory or final judgment in an action for an injunction or in a receivership action, or a judgment or order directing an accounting in an action for infringement of letters patent, shall not be stayed during the period after its entry and until an appeal is taken or during the pendency of an appeal. The provisions of subdivision (c) of this rule govern the suspending, modifying, restoring, or granting of an injunction during the pendency of an appeal.

(b) Stay on Motion for New Trial or for Judgment. In its discretion and on such conditions for the security of the adverse party as are proper, the court may stay the execution of or any proceedings to enforce a judgment pending the disposition of a motion for a new trial or to alter or amend a judgment made pursuant to Rule 59, or of a motion for relief from a judgment or order made pursuant to Rule 60, or of a motion for judgment in accordance with a motion for a directed verdict made pursuant to Rule 50, or of a motion for amendment to the findings or for additional findings made pursuant to Rule 52(b).

(c) Injunction Pending Appeal. When an appeal is taken from an interlocutory or final judgment granting, dissolving, or denying an injunction, the court in its discretion may suspend, modify, restore, or grant an injunction during the pendency of the appeal upon such terms as to bond or otherwise as it considers proper for the security of the rights of the adverse party. If the judgment appealed from is rendered by a district court of three judges specially constituted pursuant to a statute of the United States, no such order shall be made except (1) by such court sitting in open court or (2) by the assent of all the judges of such court evidenced by their signatures to the order.

(d) Stay Upon Appeal. When an appeal is taken the appellant by giving a supersedeas bond may obtain a stay subject to the exceptions contained in subdivision (a) of this rule. The bond may be given at or after the time of filing the notice of appeal or of procuring the order allowing the appeal, as the case may be. The stay is effective when the supersedeas bond is approved by the court.

(e) Stay in Favor of the United States or Agency Thereof. When an appeal is taken by the United States or an officer or agency thereof or by direction of any department of the Government of the United States and the operation or enforcement of the judgment is stayed, no bond, obligation, or other security shall be required from the appellant.

(f) Stay According to State Law. In any state in which a judgment is a lien upon the property of the judgment debtor and in which the judgment debtor is entitled to a stay of execution, a judgment debtor is entitled, in the district court held therein, to such stay as would be accorded the judgment debtor had the action been maintained in the courts of that state.

(g) Power of Appellate Court Not Limited. The provisions in this rule do not limit any power of an appellate court or of a judge or justice thereof to stay proceedings during the pendency of an appeal or to suspend, modify, restore, or grant an injunction during the pendency of an appeal or to make any order appropriate to preserve the status quo or the effectiveness of the judgment subsequently to be entered.

(h) Stay of Judgment as to Multiple Claims or Multiple Parties. When a court has ordered a final judgment under the conditions stated in Rule 54(b), the court may stay enforcement of that judgment until the entering of a subsequent judgment or judgments and may prescribe such conditions as are necessary to secure the benefit thereof to the party in whose favor the judgment is entered.

[Amended effective March 19, 1948; October 20, 1949; July 19, 1961; August 1, 1987.]

AUTHORS' COMMENTARY ON RULE 62

PURPOSE AND SCOPE

Rule 62 provides for stays to prevent the enforcement of judgments pending post-trial motions and appeals.

NOTE: Except for a ten-day stay immediately following entry of judgment as provided by Rule 62(a), post-trial motions and appeals do not automatically stay enforcement of judgments.

RULE 62(a). AUTOMATIC STAY; EXCEPTIONS— INJUNCTIONS, RECEIVERSHIPS, AND PATENT ACCOUNTINGS

CORE CONCEPT

The automatic stay postpones enforcement of a judgment for ten days from the date of entry of the judgment. However, Rule 62(a) provides no automatic stay in three circumstances: (1) an interlocutory or final judgment in an action for an injunction; (2) an interlocutory or final judgment in a receivership action; and (3) a judgment or order directing an accounting in an action for infringement of letters patent.

APPLICATIONS

Effect

An automatic stay will prevent the enforcement of the judgment, but the stay will not affect the appealability of the judgment or the running of the appeal time.[1] Additionally, the judgment has *res judicata* effect during the pendency of the appeal.[2]

Judgments Covered

The automatic stay applies to any judgment defined in Rule 54(a).[3]

Expiration of Stay Period

Once the automatic stay period expires, a party may seek enforcement of the judgment.[4]

Armed Services Personnel

The Soldiers and Sailors Civil Relief Act of 1940, 50 U.S.C.A. §§ 203–04, Appendix §§ 523–24, provides that a court may stay the execution of any judgment entered against a person in the military service, or vacate or stay an attachment or garnishment.

Relation to Rule 6(a)

Although there is little authority on point, it appears that for purposes of 10–day stays under Rule 62(a), time shall be computed under the standards of Rule 6(a).[5]

RULE 62(b). STAY ON MOTION FOR NEW TRIAL OR FOR JUDGMENT

1. FED.R.APP.P. 4(a).

2. *See, e.g., Fish Market Nominee Corp. v. Pelofsky*, 72 F.3d 4, 7 (1st Cir.1995)(noting distinction between bar to enforcing judgment and absence of bar to *res judicata*).

3. *But cf., Arnold v. Garlock, Inc.*, 278 F.3d 426, 437 (5th Cir.2001) (remand of pending case to state court is not final judgment and therefore Rule 62 has no applicability to remands).

4. *See, e.g., Acevedo–Garcia v. Vera–Monroig*, 368 F.3d 49, 58 (1st Cir. 2004) ("The federal rules contemplate that, absent a stay, a victorious plaintiff may execute on the judgment even while an appeal of that judgment is pending.").

5. *See, e.g., KRW Sales, Inc. v. Kristel Corp.*, 154 F.R.D. 186, 188 (N.D.Ill.1994)(computing 10 days for purposes of Rule 62(a) under standards of Rule 6(a)).

CORE CONCEPT

After judgment, a court has discretion to order a stay while it considers post-trial motions. The court also has discretion to establish conditions for the security of the adverse party during the pendency of the stay.

APPLICATIONS

Security

The court has discretion not only to order a stay pending post-trial motions, but may order the movant to post security, including the amount of the judgment and interest, during the period of the stay. The court may also require the bond to include costs and damages for delay or any other loss that may result during the period of the stay. Additionally, the court may order the movant to provide written notice to the opposing parties of any material disposition of the movant's assets.

Effect of Denial

When the court denies a stay pending disposition of a post trial motion, judgment is binding (and may be enforced) until vacated by the court or reversed on appeal.

Procedure

The filing of post-trial motions does not stay execution of the judgment or the proceeding in execution. Hence, a party should assert the motion for stay before the end of the 10–day automatic stay period, provided under Rule 62(a). Once the motion for stay is made, the court has discretion to stay execution or enforcement of the judgment pending disposition of the post-trial motions.

RULE 62(c). INJUNCTION PENDING APPEAL

CORE CONCEPT

Rule 62(c) authorizes the district judge or a district court of three judges having granted, dissolved, or denied a preliminary or final injunction to stay its decision or grant other interim relief pending appeal.[6]

NOTE: There are no automatic stays in injunction actions. Injunction actions may be stayed only by court order. The district court has discretion to determine whether to grant a stay.[7]

6. *See also A & M Records, Inc. v. Napster, Inc.*, 284 F.3d 1091, 1099 (9th Cir.2002) (Rule 62(c) "authorizes a district court to continue supervising compliance with the injunction." Affirming district court's decision to continue to supervise defendant's compliance with injunction.).

7. *See, e.g., LiButti v. United States*, 178 F.3d 114, 121 (2d Cir.1999) ("It has been long-established law that simply filing an appeal from the grant or denial of an injunction–absent a stay of further proceedings–does not enjoin the operative effect of the trial court's ruling from which the appeal is taken.").

APPLICATIONS

Scope

Rule 62(c) expressly covers interlocutory as well as final judgments in injunction cases and applies to cases where the court has denied an injunction as well as granted an injunction. However, the district court may not dissolve an injunction that has been appealed. Instead, the court may only modify the injunction while it is being appealed, with the purpose of maintaining the status quo.[8]

Time for Motion

A party should make a motion to stay an injunction immediately after the notice of appeal has been filed and may make this motion at any time while the appeal is pending.[9]

Which Court

The movant should first assert the motion in the district court. If the district court denies relief or the district court provides inadequate relief, the movant may assert the motion in the court of appeals.[10] Where submission to a panel would prejudice the movant, the motion can be made to a single judge of the court of appeals.[11] In extraordinary circumstances, pending disposition of an application for writ of certiorari and during the pendency of an appeal to the court of appeals [12] or from a final judgment of the court of appeals,[13] a single justice of the Supreme Court, sitting as a single Circuit Justice, may take any action provided in Rule 62(g).[14] In addition, a judge of the court rendering the judgment may grant a stay on application for writ of certiorari to the Supreme Court.[15]

Requirements

Rule 62(c) authorizes the court to issue a stay to maintain the status quo or the effectiveness of the final judgment during the pendency of an appeal. When a party makes a motion under Rule 62(c),

8. *See, e.g., Mayweathers v. Newland,* 258 F.3d 930, 935 (9th Cir.2001) (filing of notice of appeal generally strips district court of jurisdiction over case, but Rule 62(c) is exception; under Rule 62(c) district court may issue second injunction while first injunction is under appeal–provided that new injunction does not change status quo); *Natural Resources Defense Council v. Southwest Marine, Inc.,* 242 F.3d 1163, 1166 (9th Cir.2001) (Rule 62(c) gives district court authority only to take steps to maintain status quo while case is pending on appeal; district court has no authority to re-visit the merits of case on appeal).

9. *See, e.g., Minnesota Humane Society v. Clark,* 184 F.3d 795, 797 (8th Cir.1999) (denial of preliminary injunction that was sought to bar removal and killing of geese should have caused plaintiff to seek prompt appeal under 28 U.S.C. § 1292 and request for injunction pending appeal).

10. FED.R.APP. 8(a). *See Rakovich v. Wade,* 834 F.2d 673, 675 (7th Cir.1987)(movant should first seek relief in district court; if district court denies relief, movant may then seek stay in court of appeals).

11. FED.R.APP. 8(a).

12. *Atiyeh v. Capps,* 449 U.S. 1312, 101 S.Ct. 829, 66 L.Ed.2d 785 (1981)(per Justice Rehnquist).

13. *Graddick v. Newman,* 453 U.S. 928, 102 S.Ct. 4, 69 L.Ed.2d 1025 (1981); *Holtzman v. Schlesinger,* 414 U.S. 1304, 94 S.Ct. 1, 38 L.Ed.2d 18 (1973)(per Justice Marshall).

14. 28 U.S.C.A. § 1651(a); U.S.Sup.Ct.R. 23.

15. 28 U.S.C.A. 2101(f).

the courts will require the movant to show the following elements:[16] (a) a strong likelihood of success on the merits of the appeal; (b) that unless the motion is granted the movant will suffer irreparable injury; (c) no substantial harm will come to other interested parties; and (d) a grant of the motion will not harm the public interest. The courts have often balanced the irreparable injury to the movant if the court did not issue the stay against the harm the stay would cause to the other parties and to the public. The governing considerations are the same whether the party applies to the district court or to the appellate courts under Rule 62(g).

Requirements of Order

An injunctive order issued pursuant to Rule 62(c) must set forth the reasons for its issuance and be specific in its terms in compliance with the requirements of Rule 65(d).

Security for Stay

The court may order the movant to post security during the period of the stay or the injunction.

Three Judge District Court

When a district court of three judges, sitting by statute, renders judgment in an injunction case, a motion to that judgment should be addressed to all three judges. Such a court may only issue a stay pending an appeal in open court or by signature of all three judges.

RULE 62(d). STAY UPON APPEAL

CORE CONCEPT

The act of appealing a judgment does not automatically create a stay of the judgment pending appeal.[17] However, a party may obtain a stay by filing a supersedeas bond with the court (*i.e.,* a bond posted as security against an appeal) that is approved by the court. Unless state law provides otherwise (as described in Rule 62(f)), Rule 62(d) governs the only circumstances in which a party may obtain a stay of enforcement of a money judgment pending appeal,[18] beyond the automatic 10–day period provided by Rule 62(a).

APPLICATIONS

Stay as of Right

By posting a supersedeas bond with the court and approval of the bond by the court, a party may obtain a stay upon appeal as a matter of course.[19]

16. *See, e.g., Michigan Coalition of Radioactive Material Users, Inc. v. Griepentrog,* 945 F.2d 150, 153 (6th Cir.1991).

17. *See, e.g., Correa v. Cruisers,* 298 F.3d 13, 29 (1st Cir.2002) ("[T]here is no requirement that the judgment become final before it can be enforced.").

18. *See, e.g., Cleveland Hair Clinic, Inc. v. Puig,* 104 F.3d 123, 125 (7th Cir.1997)(Rule 62(d) stay may also prevent enforcement of final decision to sanction parties and attorney for misconduct in case; applicability of Rule 62(d) not limited to circumstances involving only judgments).

19. *See, e.g., Hoban v. Washington Metropolitan Area Transit Authority,* 841 F.2d 1157, 1159 (D.C.Cir.1988) (per curiam)(posting bond under

Amount of Bond

The amount of the bond will usually be an amount sufficient to satisfy the judgment plus interest. The court may also require the bond to include costs,[20] plus any damages for delay. The court has the discretion to provide a lesser amount or other types of security.[21] Local rule may provide the amount required.

Alternatives to Bond

Although Rule 62(d) speaks only of bonds, courts may permit "other forms of judgment guarantee." [22]

Deadline for Posting Bond

Rule 62(d) permits the bond to be posted at the time a party files a notice of appeal (or receives permission to appeal), or later. However, because the stay does not become effective until the court approves the bond, it is wise to post the bond within the 10–day period of the automatic stay provided by Rule 62(a).[23]

Actions Not Stayed

Rule 62(d), by its own terms, does not apply to the three circumstances enunciated in Rule 62(a). Those circumstances are: judgments in injunction actions; judgments in receivership actions; and judgments requiring an accounting in patent infringement cases. In such cases an

Rule 62(d) creates stay). *But see, National Labor Relations Board v. Westphal,* 859 F.2d 818, 819 (9th Cir.1988)(Rule 62(d) stay as of right limited to money judgments; no right to stay order enforcing subpoenas).

20. F.R.A.P. 7.

21. *See, e.g., Olcott v. Delaware Flood Co.,* 76 F.3d 1538, 1559 (10th Cir.1996)(bond normally equals amount of judgment; trial court, however, has discretion to require lesser amount; but no discretion, apparently to require bond in amount greater than judgment). *Dillon v. City of Chicago,* 866 F.2d 902 (7th Cir.1988) (identifying circumstances when other guarantees are appropriate).

22. *See, e.g., Arban v. West Publishing Corp.,* 345 F.3d 390, 409 (6th Cir. 2003) (bond that meets requirements of Rule 62(d) entitles party to stay as of right; however, even in absence of bond, court has discretion to issue stay); *Dale M. v. Board of Education,* 237 F.3d 813, 815 (7th Cir.2001) (judgment debtor who pays judgment and does not choose to post bond under Rule 62(d) has not rendered appeal moot and is entitled to repayment of judgment if reversed); *In the Matter of Carlson,* 224 F.3d 716, 719 (7th Cir.2000) (waiver of bond requirement "is appropriate only if the appellant has a clearly demonstrated ability to satisfy the judgment if the appeal is unsuccessful and there is no other concern that the appellee's rights will be compromised by a failure adequately to secure the judgment"); *FDIC v. Ann–High Associates,* 129 F.3d 113 (2d Cir.1997) (per curiam) (court has discretion to waive bond requirement "if the appellant provides an acceptable alternative means of securing the judgment"); *Olympia Equipment Leasing Corp. v. Western Union Telegraph Co.,* 786 F.2d 794, 796 (7th Cir.1986) ("[A]n inflexible requirement of a bond would be inappropriate in two sorts of case: where the defendant's ability to pay the judgment is so plain that the cost of the bond would be a waste of money; and–the opposite case, one of increasing importance in an age of titanic damage judgments–where the requirement would put the defendant's other creditors in undue jeopardy.").

23. *But see, Equal Employment Opportunity Commission v. Clear Lake Dodge,* 25 F.3d 265, 273 (5th Cir.1994)(Rule 62(d) permits posting of bond at or after filing notice of appeal; thus, to post bond prior to appealing is inappropriate).

appealing party may not post a bond and obtain a stay of judgment under Rule 62(d).

Judgments for Damages and Injunctions

If a party seeks to use Rule 62(d) to stay a judgment by which the court ordered both money damages and equitable relief, the stay under Rule 62(d) is effective only to stop enforcement of the damage award.[24] Unless the appealing party can persuade the court to stay the injunction under Rule 62(c), the injunction portion of the judgment may be enforced pending appeal.

Failure to Post Bond

Failure to post bond under Rule 62(d) does not affect a party's right to appeal.[25] However, in the absence of a stay ordered pursuant to Rule 62(d), an adverse party may enforce a judgment while the appeal is pending,[26] which sometimes may render the appeal moot.

Impact of Appeal by Prevailing Party

If the prevailing party also appeals some facet of a district court's judgment, there is some conflict in the cases as to whether the judgment debtor must post a bond to stay execution of judgment pending the judgment debtor's appeal.[27] Attorneys are urged to consult local precedent.

Relation to Rule 11

Inappropriate use of Rule 62(d) bonds may be grounds for sanctions under Rule 11.

RULE 62(e). STAY IN FAVOR OF THE UNITED STATES OR AGENCY THEREOF

24. *N.L.R.B. v. Westphal*, 859 F.2d 818 (9th Cir.1988) (Rule 62(d) cannot stay injunctions). *But cf., Venus Lines Agency v. CVG Industria Venezolana De Aluminio, C.A.*, 210 F.3d 1309, 1313 (11th Cir.2000) (per curiam) (seizure of property to secure enforcement of any award issued in pending arbitration proceeding; held, determination that stay is justified in circumstances of a non-money judgment depends on following factors: "(1) whether the stay applicant has made a strong showing that [it] is likely to succeed on the merits; (2) whether the applicant will be irreparably injured absent a stay; (3) whether the issuance of a stay will substantially injure the other parties interested in the proceeding; and (4) where the public interest lies"; brackets in original).

25. *See, e.g., In re American President Lines, Inc.*, 779 F.2d 714, 718 (D.C.Cir.1985)(per curiam)(failure to post bond leaves appellant vulnerable to enforcement of judgment, but does not forfeit right of appeal).

26. *See, e.g., id.*

27. *Compare Tennessee Valley Authority v. Atlas Machine and Iron Works, Inc.*, 803 F.2d 794, 797 (4th Cir.1986) (appeal by prevailing party suspends judgment; thus losing party need not post supersedeas bond to prevent execution on judgment while losing party's appeal is pending), *with Trustmark Insurance Co. v. Gallucci*, 193 F.3d 558–59 (1st Cir.1999) (noting split of authority; concluding that appeal by prevailing party eliminates obligation of judgment debtor to post bond under Rule 62(d) to stay execution of money judgment only when basis of prevailing party's appeal is inconsistent with enforcement of judgment; requiring bond when prevailing party's appeal was only for denial of pre-judgment interest, which is not inconsistent with immediate enforcement of judgment).

CORE CONCEPT

The United States is not required to post a bond to obtain a stay of the enforcement of a judgment pending appeal. This exemption also extends to officers and agents of the United States government, and any party acting under the direction of any department or agency of the government, as provided by 28 U.S.C.A. § 2408.

RULE 62(f). STAY ACCORDING TO STATE LAW

CORE CONCEPT

When the judgment creates a lien upon the debtor's property and the judgment debtor is entitled to a stay under applicable state law, the district court shall stay the enforcement of the judgment to the same extent that state law directs a state court to enter a stay.[28] The court has no discretion to deny such a stay.[29] Moreover, while the normal practice anticipates that the judgment debtor will file a motion for a stay, there appears to be no requirement for such a motion and the stay can become effective even in the absence of a motion.[30]

RULE 62(g). POWER OF APPELLATE COURT NOT LIMITED

CORE CONCEPT

The provisions of Rule 62 apply only to district courts, and do not limit appellate courts.

RULE 62(h). STAY OF JUDGMENT AS TO MULTIPLE CLAIMS OR MULTIPLE PARTIES

CORE CONCEPT

When a court issues a partial judgment under Rule 54(b), it may allow immediate enforcement of the partial judgment or it may stay enforcement of the partial judgment pending a further adjudication.

APPLICATIONS

Time for Filing

A party must make a motion for stay upon partial judgment after the entry of the partial judgment and during the ten-day automatic stay period.

28. *See, e.g., Hoban v. Washington Metropolitan Area Transit Authority*, 841 F.2d 1157, 1159 (D.C.Cir.1988)(per curiam)(if state law authorizes stay without requiring a supersedeas bond, stay imposed under rule 62(f) must also be unencumbered by bond).

29. *Cf., Rodriguez–Vazquez v. Lopez–Martinez*, 345 F.3d 13, 14 (1st Cir. 2003) ("Our own inclination is to think that where a lien can be procured [under state law] by minor ministerial acts, this minor burden on the judgment-creditor should not preclude a stay under Rule 62(f)." Citing division of authority in district courts).

30. *See, e.g., Whitehead v. Food Max of Mississippi, Inc.*, 332 F.3d 796, 804–05 (5th Cir. 2003) (en banc) (no requirement for a formal motion to grant a Rule 62(f) stay; if sanctions under Rule 11 are appropriate because prevailing party violated stay, the absence of a Rule 62(f) motion does not prevent imposition).

Standards for Granting a Stay

The court has discretion to decide a motion for stay, balancing the equities of the parties and considering the administration of the case.[31]

Independent Actions

When a court consolidates several independent actions and renders judgment on one of the independent actions, this is not considered a partial judgment under Rule 54(b), and a stay will not be granted under Rule 62(h).[32]

Posting of Security

When issuing a stay of a particular judgment, the court may require security to be posted to secure that part of the judgment.

ADDITIONAL RESEARCH REFERENCES

Wright & Miller, *Federal Practice and Procedure: Civil 2d* §§ 2901–20.

C.J.S. Federal Civil Procedure § 1263; Federal Courts § 294(1–5) et seq.

West's Key No. Digests, Federal Civil Procedure ⚷2700; Federal Courts ⚷684–687.

31. *See, e.g., North Penn Transfer, Inc. v. Maple Press Co.,* 176 B.R. 372, 375–77 (M.D.Pa. 1995)(judgment for plaintiff on unpaid shipping charges stayed under Rule 62(h) so that defendant can challenge reasonableness of shipping rates before regulatory agency; citing possibility that immediate enforcement of judgment would make defendant insolvent).

32. *In re Massachusetts Helicopter Airlines, Inc.,* 469 F.2d 439, 442 (1st Cir.1972)(Rule 62(h) applicable only to circumstances governed by Rule 54(b); independent actions cannot be stayed under Rule 62(h)).

RULE 63

INABILITY OF A JUDGE TO PROCEED

If a trial or hearing has been commenced and the judge is unable to proceed, any other judge may proceed with it upon certifying familiarity with the record and determining that the proceedings in the case may be completed without prejudice to the parties. In a hearing or trial without a jury, the successor judge shall at the request of a party recall any witness whose testimony is material and disputed and who is available to testify again without undue burden. The successor judge may also recall any other witness.

[Amended effective August 1, 1987; December 1, 1991.]

AUTHORS' COMMENTARY ON RULE 63

PURPOSE AND SCOPE

When a judge withdraws after the commencement of a trial or hearing, any other judge of the court may proceed with the case. The successor judge will read the pertinent portions of the record, certify familiarity with that record, and then decide whether he or she may proceed with the case without causing prejudice to the parties. In a non-jury hearing or trial format, if the successor judge proceeds with the case, he or she must recall any witnesses requested by the parties, if their testimony is material and disputed and where the witnesses are available to testify again without undue burden. In addition, the successor judge may recall any witnesses in order to become more familiar with the record.

CAUTION: Rule 63 was substantially amended in 1991 to expand the Rule's scope and to alter certain constructions given to the Rule by the courts. Decisions that predate the 1991 amendment, thus, should be cited with exceptional care.[1]

APPLICATIONS

Conditions for Inability to Proceed

A judge's withdrawal must rest on compelling reasons, such as sickness, death, or other disability, including recusal and disqualification.[2] A judge may not withdraw for personal convenience.[3]

1. *But see Zand v. Commissioner*, 143 F.3d 1393, 1400 (11th Cir.1998) (court may look to pre–1991 decisions for guidance given facts of particular case).

2. *See* Rule 63 advisory committee notes to 1991 amendment. *See also* 28 U.S.C. §§ 144 & 455 (providing for disqualification of judges).

3. *See* Rule 63 advisory committee notes to 1991 amendment.

Statement of Grounds for Withdrawal

The withdrawing judge must state on the record the reasons for his or her withdrawal.[4]

Timing of Substitution

The original text of Rule 63 implied that, once a trial or hearing had begun, district judges could not be substituted unless the departing judge had already filed findings of fact and conclusions of law. The courts embraced this implication and, unless the parties stipulated otherwise, required new trials where the departing judge had not filed the findings and conclusions.[5]

This "negative inference" mandate ascribed to Rule 63 was abolished in 1991. Citing the increasing length of trials in federal court and the expected concomitant increase in the number of trials interrupted by a judge's disability,[6] the drafters provided that a substitution may be made after trial commences and even in the absence of filed findings and conclusions, if the replacement judge (1) can certify his or her familiarity with the proceedings in the case to date, and (2) can continue the proceedings without prejudicing the parties.

Certifying Familiarity With the Record

Once a trial or hearing has begun, no substitute judge can replace a departing judge without first "certifying familiarity with the record". It is this certification procedure that ensures that Due Process is not violated when the case resumes.[7] Although an express "certification" is plainly preferred,[8] the court of appeals will likely not reverse in the absence of an express certification so long as the successor judge's statements confirm compliance with the record familiarity requirement.[9] This certification requirement obligates the substitute judge to read and consider all relevant portions of the record.[10] What portions of the record the successor judge is required to learn depends upon the nature of the successor judge's role in the case. For example, if the

4. *See* Rule 63 advisory committee notes to 1991 amendment.

5. *See, e.g., In re Higginbotham*, 917 F.2d 1130, 1132 (8th Cir.1990); *Olle v. Henry & Wright Corp.*, 910 F.2d 357, 361 (6th Cir.1990); *Home Placement Serv., Inc. v. Providence Journal Co.*, 819 F.2d 1199, 1202 (1st Cir.1987); *Whalen v. Ford Motor Credit Co.*, 684 F.2d 272, 274 n. 5 (4th Cir.1982), *cert. denied*, 459 U.S. 910, 103 S.Ct. 216, 74 L.Ed.2d 172 (1982); *Thompson v. Sawyer*, 678 F.2d 257, 268–69 (D.C.Cir.1982); *Arrow-Hart, Inc. v. Philip Carey Co.*, 552 F.2d 711, 713 (6th Cir.1977).

6. *See* Rule 63 advisory committee notes to 1991 amendment. *See also Mergentime Corp. v. Washington Metro. Area Transit Auth.*, 166 F.3d 1257, 1262 (D.C.Cir.1999) (noting motivation for Rule change, and commenting that successor judges may now take over at any point after the trial begins, subject to certain additional responsibilities imposed upon the successor judges).

7. *See Patelco Credit Union v. Sahni*, 262 F.3d 897, 905 (9th Cir.2001).

8. *See, e.g., Vescio v. Merchants Bank*, 272 B.R. 413, 420 (D.Vt.2001) ("The Court hereby certifies pursuant to Fed.R.Civ.P. 63 that it has reviewed the transcript of the trial, together with the exhibits, and that the proceedings in this case may be completed without prejudice to the parties").

9. *See Mergentime Corp. v. Washington Metro. Area Transit Auth.*, 166 F.3d 1257, 1265 (D.C.Cir.1999).

10. *See Mergentime Corp. v. Washington Metro. Area Transit Auth.*, 166 F.3d 1257, 1265 (D.C.Cir.1999); *Canseco v. United States*, 97 F.3d 1224, 1226 (9th Cir.1996) (as amended Dec. 18, 1996).

successor judge inherits a jury trial before the evidence has closed, she must become familiar with the entire record so as to properly rule upon relevance-based evidentiary objections; but if the successor judge inherits the case after the entry of verdict or judgment, she need only review those portions of the record relevant to the particular issues challenged by post-trial motions.[11]

Prerequisite for Substitution

In order for a judge to be substituted, there must be an available transcript or a videotape to permit the replacement judge to become familiar with the proceedings that occurred prior to the substitution. The Committee Notes encourage the prompt preparation of the trial or videotape transcript, so as to prevent delaying the jury longer than necessary.[12]

Bench Trials

In a non-jury trial, the successor judge may make new factual findings based on the testimony heard by the withdrawing judge in limited circumstances:

(1) *Testimony of Available Witness:* When a witness is available, the successor judge may decide to hear the witness' testimony if the testimony is material or disputed. It may be error for the court to decline to hear the testimony of a witness whose credibility is material to a finding of fact, particularly if a party so requests.[13]

(2) *Testimony of Unavailable Witness:* If a witness has become unavailable, such that a subpoena to compel testimony at trial is unavailable, the successor judge can consider the testimony recorded at trial or, if the testimony was not material or not disputed, may choose not to hear the testimony at all.[14]

Previously Litigated Issues

Unless the controlling law has changed, the successor judge will not ordinarily revisit rulings made by the withdrawing judge. However, the successor judge is required to consider and rule upon allegations of trial error properly raised in post-trial motions.[15]

11. *See Mergentime Corp. v. Washington Metro. Area Transit Auth.*, 166 F.3d 1257, 1265 (D.C.Cir.1999).

12. *See* Rule 63 advisory committee notes to 1991 amendment.

13. *See* Rule 63 advisory committee notes to 1991 amendment. *See also Mergentime Corp. v. Washington Metro. Area Transit Auth.*, 166 F.3d 1257, 1266 (D.C.Cir.1999) (holding that, upon request of party, district court must recall any witness whose testimony is material and disputed and who, without undue burden, is available to testify again); *Canseco v. United States*, 97 F.3d 1224, 1227 (9th Cir.1996) (as amended Dec. 18, 1996) (where credibility of witness is questioned, and where sufficiency of the evidence hinges on that witness's testimony and credibility cannot be determined from the record, substitute judge must recall the witness, if available without undue burden, and make own credibility determination); *Chemoil Holding Co. v. Delta Commodities, Inc.*, 1998 WL 474216, at *2 (E.D.La.1998) (recalling witnesses where litigation involved factual disputes necessitating credibility determinations).

14. *See* Rule 63 advisory committee notes to 1991 amendment.

15. *See Mergentime Corp. v. Washington Metro. Area Transit Auth.*, 166 F.3d 1257, 1263 (D.C.Cir.1999) (holding that successor judge may not refuse to consider post-trial motions out of deference to the original judge).

Option To Enter Summary Judgment

If, after reviewing the trial transcript, the court decides that no credibility determinations are required and that one party is entitled to a judgment as a matter of law, summary judgment can be entered as an alternative to the successor judge "stepping into the shoes" of the unavailable trial judge.[16]

Removed Cases

Where the parties or issues permit a belated removal of a State court proceeding, the federal court may enter judgment upon the State court jury's verdict.[17]

Waiver of Right to Object to New Judge

Following the departure of the original judge, the litigants may be deemed to have waived any objection to the case's reassignment to a new judge if the litigants fail either to timely seek a new trial or timely object to a reassignment.[18]

ADDITIONAL RESEARCH REFERENCES

Wright & Miller, *Federal Practice and Procedure: Civil 2d* §§ 2921–30.

C.J.S. Judges §§ 35–68.

West's Key No. Digests, Judges ⚷21, 32.

16. *See Patelco Credit Union v. Sahni*, 262 F.3d 897, 906 (9th Cir.2001).

17. *See Sweeney v. Resolution Trust Corp.*, 16 F.3d 1, 5–6 (1st Cir.1994), *cert. denied*, 513 U.S. 914, 115 S.Ct. 291, 130 L.Ed.2d 206 (1994).

18. *See Zand v. Commissioner*, 143 F.3d 1393, 1400 (11th Cir.1998) (ruling that parties had "cleverly tiptoe[d]" across a "procedural tightrope", refusing to consent to a reassignment while, simultaneously, failing to seek the added expense of a retrial; therefore, an unfavorable verdict by the successor judge could not be challenged under Rule 63).

VIII. PROVISIONAL AND FINAL REMEDIES

RULE 64

SEIZURE OF PERSON OR PROPERTY

At the commencement of and during the course of an action, all remedies providing for seizure of person or property for the purpose of securing satisfaction of the judgment ultimately to be entered in the action are available under the circumstances and in the manner provided by the law of the state in which the district court is held, existing at the time the remedy is sought, subject to the following qualifications: (1) any existing statute of the United States governs to the extent to which it is applicable; (2) the action in which any of the foregoing remedies is used shall be commenced and prosecuted or, if removed from a state court, shall be prosecuted after removal, pursuant to these rules. The remedies thus available include arrest, attachment, garnishment, replevin, sequestration, and other corresponding or equivalent remedies, however designated and regardless of whether by state procedure the remedy is ancillary to an action or must be obtained by an independent action.

AUTHORS' COMMENTARY ON RULE 64

PURPOSE AND SCOPE

After the commencement of an action and until the time of judgment, Rule 64 provides means by which a claimant may seek an order of court to seize a person or property in order to secure satisfaction of the eventual judgment. Relief under Rule 64 is infrequently granted and should be infrequently sought.

APPLICATIONS

Time to Seek an Order

At any time after the commencement of an action and until the time of judgment,[1] a party may assert an ancillary claim in the pending action or file an independent action to seize property under Rule 64.

1. *See, e.g., Rosen v. Cascade International, Inc.*, 21 F.3d 1520, 1530 (11th Cir.1994)(Rule 64 authorizes prejudgment attachment in some situations); *But see, Credit Managers Association of Southern California v. Kennesaw Life and Accident Insurance Co.*, 25 F.3d 743, 750 (9th Cir.1994)(permitting use of Rule 64 to satisfy existing judgment; but Rule 64 deferred to state law, which prohibited satisfaction on instant facts).

Sources of Remedies

The claimant must seek the applicable federal remedy, if a specific federal remedy exists.[2] The Advisory Committee Notes to Rule 64 list some of the federal remedies. Otherwise, the movant may choose any provisional remedy under applicable state law.[3]

Method for Obtaining Relief

Where a federal remedy exists, the procedure for obtaining relief will be provided by the relevant statute and the Rules. When relief is sought under a state remedy, state law generally supplies the procedures, except to the extent that the Rules apply. The method for obtaining relief will vary from state to state and district to district. However, in all cases a U.S. Marshal rather than a state officer would seize the goods or property.

Jurisdiction

Procedures under Rule 64 whether asserted in a pending action or in an independent action do not require a separate basis of subject matter jurisdiction.

Constitutional Limitations

The seizure of a person or property without notice or a prior hearing may often be a violation of constitutional due process.[4]

Relation to Rule 65

It now appears settled that in cases involving only money damages on an unsecured claim, a party may not use Rule 65 (governing preliminary injunctions and temporary restraining orders) to obtain a prejudgment injunction aimed at preventing dissipation of assets. Instead, such relief must be sought under other provisions, such as Rule 64's authorization to use state law prejudgment attachment provisions.[5] However, if the lawsuit also seeks equitable relief, the district court is not restricted by Rule 64 and may still grant a prejudgment injunction that freezes specific assets that are the subject of a restitution or

2. *See, e.g., Hoult v. Hoult*, 373 F.3d 47, 54 (1st Cir. 2004) ("federal statute governs to the extent applicable").

3. *See, e.g., Goya Foods, Inc. v. Wallack Management Co.*, 290 F.3d 63, 70 (1st Cir.2002), *cert. denied*, 537 U.S. 974, 123 S.Ct. 434, 154 L.Ed.2d 330 (2002) ("By its terms [Rule 64] allows a federal court to borrow provisional remedies created by state law."); *Stephens v. National Distillers and Chemical Corp.*, 69 F.3d 1226, 1228 n. 2 (2d Cir.1995) (noting that Rule 64 incorporates state remedies).

4. *North Georgia Finishing, Inc. v. Di-Chem, Inc.*, 419 U.S. 601, 95 S.Ct. 719, 42 L.Ed.2d 751 (1975) (*Fuentes v. Shevin* is weakened); *Mitchell v. W.T. Grant Co.*, 416 U.S. 600, 94 S.Ct. 1895, 40 L.Ed.2d 406 (1974); *Fuentes v. Shevin*, 407 U.S. 67, 92 S.Ct. 1983, 32 L.Ed.2d 556 (1972).

5. *Grupo Mexicano de Desarrollo, S.A. v. Alliance Bond Fund, Inc.*, 527 U.S. 308, 330–31, 119 S.Ct. 1961, 1968–75, 144 L.Ed.2d 319 (1999) (in case involving only general creditor seeking damages at law and with no lien in specific property of defendant, Rule 65 may not be used to obtain prejudgment injunction because, *inter alia*, such use of Rule 65 would render Rule 64 "a virtual irrelevance. Why go through the trouble of complying with local attachment and garnishment standards when this all-purpose prejudgment injunction is available?").

recission claim or that preserves the power of the court to grant final injunctive relief.[6]

Armed Services Personnel

Provisional relief under Rule 64 is subject to the Soldiers' and Sailors' Civil Relief Act of 1940, 50 U.S.C.A. §§ 203, 204, Appendix §§ 523, 524, which prohibits seizure of the assets of absent military personnel in many circumstances.

Execution

A plaintiff who recovers judgment is entitled to an execution sale of the previously seized property in satisfaction of the judgment.

ADDITIONAL RESEARCH REFERENCES

Wright & Miller, *Federal Practice and Procedure: Civil 2d* §§ 2931–40.

C.J.S. Federal Civil Procedure §§ 233–241, 1271.

West's Key No. Digests, Federal Civil Procedure ⚷581–590, 601–610.

6. *See, e.g., United States ex rel. Rahman v. Oncology Associates,* 198 F.3d 489, 495–97 (4th Cir.1999) (explaining relationship of *Grupo Mexicano* to earlier Supreme Court precedent authorizing use of prejudgment injunction in equity cases; also noting that equity court "has enhanced authority when the public interest is involved"). *See also De Beers Consolidated Mines, Ltd. v. United States,* 325 U.S. 212, 219, 65 S.Ct. 1130, 1133–34, 89 L.Ed. 1566 (1945) ("A preliminary injunction is always appropriate to grant intermediate relief of the same character as that which may be granted finally"; however, in instant case property affected by injunction lies outside issues of case; also noting, *inter alia,* that relief government requested was not available under Rule 64); *Deckert v. Independence Shares Corp.,* 311 U.S. 282, 289, 61 S.Ct. 229, 233, 85 L.Ed. 189 (1940) (in case where equitable remedy of recission is sought, district court has authority to issue prejudgment injunction freezing assets as means of preserving status quo pending final outcome of case).

RULE 65

INJUNCTIONS

(a) Preliminary Injunction.

(1) *Notice.* No preliminary injunction shall be issued without notice to the adverse party.

(2) *Consolidation of Hearing With Trial on Merits.* Before or after the commencement of the hearing of an application for a preliminary injunction, the court may order the trial of the action on the merits to be advanced and consolidated with the hearing of the application. Even when this consolidation is not ordered, any evidence received upon an application for a preliminary injunction which would be admissible upon the trial on the merits becomes part of the record on the trial and need not be repeated upon the trial. This subdivision (a)(2) shall be so construed and applied as to save to the parties any rights they may have to trial by jury.

(b) Temporary Restraining Order; Notice; Hearing; Duration. A temporary restraining order may be granted without written or oral notice to the adverse party or that party's attorney only if (1) it clearly appears from specific facts shown by affidavit or by the verified complaint that immediate and irreparable injury, loss, or damage will result to the applicant before the adverse party or that party's attorney can be heard in opposition, and (2) the applicant's attorney certifies to the court in writing the efforts, if any, which have been made to give the notice and the reasons supporting the claim that notice should not be required. Every temporary restraining order granted without notice shall be indorsed with the date and hour of issuance; shall be filed forthwith in the clerk's office and entered of record; shall define the injury and state why it is irreparable and why the order was granted without notice; and shall expire by its terms within such time after entry, not to exceed 10 days, as the court fixes, unless within the time so fixed the order, for good cause shown, is extended for a like period or unless the party against whom the order is directed consents that it may be extended for a longer period. The reasons for the extension shall be entered of record. In case a temporary restraining order is granted without notice, the motion for a preliminary injunction shall be set down for hearing at the earliest possible time and takes precedence of all matters except older matters of the same character; and when the motion comes on for hearing the party who obtained the temporary restraining order shall proceed with the application for a preliminary injunction and, if the party does not do so, the court shall dissolve the temporary restraining order. On 2 days' notice to the party who obtained the temporary restraining order without notice or on such shorter notice to that party as the court may prescribe, the adverse party may appear and move its dissolution or modification and in that event the court shall proceed to hear and determine such motion as expeditiously as the ends of justice require.

(c) Security. No restraining order or preliminary injunction shall issue except upon the giving of security by the applicant, in such sum as the court deems proper, for the payment of such costs and damages as may be incurred or suffered by any party who is found to have been wrongfully enjoined or restrained. No such security shall be required of the United States or of an officer or agency thereof.

The provisions of Rule 65.1 apply to a surety upon a bond or undertaking under this rule.

(d) Form and Scope of Injunction or Restraining Order. Every order granting an injunction and every restraining order shall set forth the reasons for its issuance; shall be specific in terms; shall describe in reasonable detail, and not by reference to the complaint or other document, the act or acts sought to be restrained; and is binding only upon the parties to the action, their officers, agents, servants, employees, and attorneys, and upon those persons in active concert or participation with them who receive actual notice of the order by personal service or otherwise.

(e) Employer and Employee; Interpleader; Constitutional Cases. These rules do not modify any statute of the United States relating to temporary restraining orders and preliminary injunctions in actions affecting employer and employee; or the provisions of Title 28, U.S.C., § 2361, relating to preliminary injunctions in actions of interpleader or in the nature of interpleader; or Title 28, U.S.C., § 2284, relating to actions required by Act of Congress to be heard and determined by a district court of three judges.

(f) Copyright Impoundment. This rule applies to copyright impoundment proceedings.

[Amended effective March 19, 1948; October 20, 1949; July 1, 1966; August 1, 1987; April 23, 2001, effective December 1, 2001.]

AUTHORS' COMMENTARY ON RULE 65

PURPOSE AND SCOPE

Rule 65 establishes the procedural requirements for obtaining a temporary restraining order or a preliminary injunction. It is important to note that although a party must satisfy the procedures of Rule 65 before a court will grant such injunctive relief, the substantive requirements for an injunction are separate from and additional to Rule 65, and they must also be satisfied.[1]

The substantive requirements for injunctions are found predominantly in federal case law, as well as federal statutes authorizing injunctions in certain circumstances and limiting their applicability in others. Although there can be substantial variations in the requirements from one circuit to another, courts deciding whether to grant an injunction generally weigh some or all of the following factors: (1) whether the potential harm to the person seeking injunctive relief is irreparable,[2] *i.e.,* whether such harm could be cured through an award of money damages instead of an injunction;[3] (2) whether the person against whom an injunction would be entered would be harmed excessively by the injunction; (3) whether, and to what extent, the grant or denial of an injunction would affect interests of third persons, including public interests; and (4) when a motion for a temporary restraining order or a preliminary injunction is before the court, whether the person seeking such relief is likely to prevail on the merits when the case comes to trial.[4]

NOTE: It is important to keep in mind that most of Rule 65 applies only to requests for preliminary relief. With the exception of Rule 65(d), discussed

1. *See, e.g. United States v. Cohen,* 152 F.3d 321, 324 (4th Cir.1998) ("[Rule] 65 is not a source of power for a district court to enter an injunction. Rather, it regulates the issuance of injunctions otherwise authorized.").

2. *See, e.g., Rodriguez v. DeBuono,* 175 F.3d 227, 235 (2d Cir.1999) (per curiam) (noting that both preliminary and permanent injunction require a showing of irreparable harm; however, standard for obtaining preliminary injunction is nevertheless more stringent, because moving party must also demonstrate "imminence" of harm, which is not required for grant of permanent injunction). *But cf., Prayze FM v. Federal Communications Commission,* 214 F.3d 245, 250 (2d Cir.2000) (where government seeks preliminary injunction for violation of statute irreparable nature of injury is rebuttably presumed; distinguishing private injunction claims).

3. *Cf., Grupo Mexicano de Desarrollo, S.A. v. Alliance Bond Fund, Inc.,* 527 U.S. 308, 119 S.Ct. 1961, 144 L.Ed.2d 319 (1999) (in action for money damages on contract claim district court lacks jurisdiction to issue preliminary injunction preventing defendants' transfer of assets prior to judgment).

4. *See, e.g., Prairie Band of Potawatomi Indians v. Pierce,* 253 F.3d 1234 (10th Cir.2001) (citing all four factors, but observing that if party seeking preliminary relief can establish last three factors, application of first factor is "less strict"); *United States v. Power Engineering Co.,* 191 F.3d 1224, 1230 (10th Cir.1999), *cert. denied,* 529 U.S. 1086, 120 S.Ct. 1718, 146 L.Ed.2d 640 (2000) (citing use of all four factors; also noting that "[a] mandatory preliminary injunction (*i.e.,* one that directs a party to act) imposes an even heavier burden on [the movant] of showing that the four factors . . . weigh heavily and compellingly in movant's favor"). *But cf., Heideman v. South Salt Lake City,* 348 F.3d 1182, 1189 (10th Cir. 2003) (if movant can show that latter three "harm" factors tip "*decidedly*" in its favor, it is entitled to a "somewhat relaxed" burden on probability of success standard; however, no such leniency applies to application for injunction against government action undertaken in public interest); *New Comm Wireless Services, Inc. v. SprintCom, Inc.,* 287 F.3d 1, 9 (1st Cir.2002) ("The sine qua non of this four-part inquiry is likelihood of success on the merits: if the moving party cannot demonstrate that he is likely to succeed in his quest, the remaining factors become matters of idle curiosity.").

below, Rule 65 has no application to grants or denials of permanent injunctions.[5]

RULE 65(a). PRELIMINARY INJUNCTION

CORE CONCEPT

Rule 65(a) contains two distinct concepts. The first portion of the Rule ensures that courts will not grant applications for preliminary injunctions until affected parties receive notice and an opportunity to oppose the proposed preliminary injunction. The second part of Rule 65(a) provides that the court may consolidate an application for a preliminary injunction with a trial on the merits, to the extent that consolidation is feasible under the facts of the particular case.

APPLICATIONS

Purpose

The purpose of a preliminary injunction is usually to maintain the status quo until the merits of a case can be decided.[6] Courts grant preliminary injunctions ordering an alteration of the status quo only in unusual circumstances where the merits clearly favor one party over another.[7] A preliminary injunction can only apply during the pendency of the case, at the end of which the court may consider whether to enter a permanent injunction.

Relation to Rule 64

It now appears settled that in cases involving only money damages on an unsecured claim, a party may not use Rule 65 (governing preliminary injunctions and temporary restraining orders) to obtain a prejudgment injunction aimed at preventing dissipation of assets. Instead, such relief must be sought under other provisions, such as Rule 64's authorization to use state law prejudgment attachment provisions.[8] However, if the lawsuit also seeks equitable relief, the district court is

5. *See, e.g., United States v. Criminal Sheriff, Parish of Orleans,* 19 F.3d 238 (5th Cir. 1994)(Rule 65 does not apply to permanent injunctions).

6. *See, e.g., Resolution Trust Corp. v. Cruce,* 972 F.2d 1195, 1198 (10th Cir.1992)(primary purpose of preliminary injunction is to preserve status quo).

7. *See, e.g., Dominion Video Satellite, Inc. v. EchoStar Satellite Corp.,* 269 F.3d 1149, 1154–55 (10th Cir.2001) (movant has "heightened burden of showing that the traditional four factors weigh heavily and compellingly in its favor before obtaining a preliminary injunction. . . . The heightened burden applies to preliminary injunctions that (1) disturb the status quo, (2) mandatory rather than prohibitory, or (3) provide the movant substantially all the relief it could feasibly attain after a full trial on the merits. . . . This court disfavors such injunctions."); *Aoude v. Mobil Oil Corp.,* 862 F.2d 890, 893 (1st Cir. 1988)("[On] the peculiar facts of this case, the preliminary injunction is not vulnerable to attack even if it is seen as changing the status quo.").

8. *Grupo Mexicano de Desarrollo, S.A. v. Alliance Bond Fund, Inc.,* 527 U.S. 308, 330–31, 119 S.Ct. 1961, 1968–75, 144 L.Ed.2d 319 (1999) (in case involving only general creditor seeking damages at law and with no lien in specific property of defendant, Rule 65 may not be used to obtain prejudgment injunction because, *inter alia,* such use of Rule 65 would render Rule 64 "a virtual irrelevance. Why go through the trouble of complying with local attachment and garnishment standards when this all-purpose prejudgment injunction is available?").

not restricted by Rule 64 and may still grant a prejudgment injunction that freezes specific assets that are the subject of a restitution or recission claim or that preserves the power of the court to grant final injunctive relief.[9]

Comparison With Temporary Restraining Order

A temporary restraining order is also directed at freezing circumstances in place until further action can be taken. However, in certain circumstances discussed below, Rule 65(b) permits a temporary restraining order to issue without notice to the opposing party. Temporary restraining orders issued without notice are effective for no more than ten days, and may be extended without the consent of the opposing party only once, for a maximum of ten additional days. Courts often use temporary restraining orders to maintain the status quo until there is an opportunity for a fuller hearing on a motion for a preliminary injunction.[10]

Appeal

A court's decision to grant, deny, dissolve, continue, or modify a preliminary injunction is immediately appealable of right pursuant to 28 U.S.C.A. § 1292(a)(1).[11]

(1). NOTICE

Contents of Notice

Rule 65(a)(1) prohibits issuance of a preliminary injunction without notice to the opposing party.[12] However, the Rule contains no provisions governing what constitutes adequate notice. Generally, courts require at a minimum that opposing parties be served with copies of the motion for a preliminary injunction and any supporting documents, along with notification of the date of a proposed hearing.[13]

9. *See, e.g., United States ex rel. Rahman v. Oncology Associates,* 198 F.3d 489, 495–97 (4th Cir.1999) (explaining relationship of *Grupo Mexicano* to earlier Supreme Court precedent authorizing use of prejudgment injunction in equity cases; also noting that equity court "has enhanced authority when public interest is involved"). *See also De Beers Consolidated Mines, Ltd. v. United States,* 325 U.S. 212, 219, 65 S.Ct. 1130, 1133–34, 89 L.Ed. 1566 (1945) ("A preliminary injunction is always appropriate to grant intermediate relief of the same character as that which may be granted finally"; however, in instant case property affected by injunction lies outside issues of case; also noting, *inter alia,* that relief government requested was not available under Rule 64); *Deckert v. Independence Shares Corp.,* 311 U.S. 282, 289, 61 S.Ct. 229, 233, 85 L.Ed. 189 (1940) (in case where equitable remedy of recission is sought, district court has authority to issue prejudgment injunction freezing assets as means of preserving status quo pending final outcome of case).

10. *See, e.g., Hospital Resource Personnel, Inc. v. United States,* 860 F.Supp. 1554, 1556 (S.D.Ga.1994)(granting restraining order so that court can "conduct a thorough inquiry" on injunction).

11. *See, e.g., Nutrasweet Co. v. Vit–Mar Enterprises, Inc.,* 112 F.3d 689 (3d Cir.1997) (so noting).

12. *Cf., Western Water Management, Inc. v. Brown,* 40 F.3d 105, 109 (5th Cir.1994) (prohibiting modification of injunction in absence of notice).

13. *Granny Goose Foods, Inc. v. Brotherhood of Teamsters & Auto Truck Drivers Local No. 70,* 415 U.S. 423, 433 n. 7, 94 S.Ct. 1113, 1122, 39 L.Ed.2d 435 (1974) (same day notice is inadequate; distinguishing between less formal notice requirements of restraining order versus requirement of Rule 65(a) that "implies a hearing

Scope of Hearing

Rule 65 requires that the court hold a hearing before granting or refusing a preliminary injunction. However, the scope of such a hearing is subject to the discretion of the trial court.[14]

Timing of Service

A motion for a preliminary injunction should meet the timeliness requirements of Rule 6(d), which generally provides that motions should be served no less than five days before the date of a proposed hearing on the motion.[15]

(2). CONSOLIDATION OF HEARING WITH TRIAL ON MERITS

Standard for Consolidation

The court has discretion to consolidate the preliminary injunction hearing with the trial on the merits.[16] Parties seeking a quick decision in the case may consent to consolidation, because Rule 65(a)(2) provides that the schedule for the trial will be advanced to the date of the preliminary injunction hearing. However, the tactical consequences that can follow from such an approach should not be overlooked.[17] If the

in which the defendant is given a fair opportunity to oppose the application and to prepare for such opposition"). *See, e.g., United States v. Microsoft Corp.,* 147 F.3d 935 (D.C.Cir.1998) (held, preliminary injunction entered without adequate notice; plaintiff's request for contempt citation, arising from previous consent decree, did not constitute adequate notice because standards for contempt and for preliminary injunction are different); *Parker v. Ryan,* 960 F.2d 543, 544 (5th Cir.1992) (notice should provide opponent with at least a fair opportunity to prepare opposition); generally such notice "should comply with Rule 6(d), which requires five days notice before a hearing on a motion". *But cf., Dominion Video Satellite, Inc. v. EchoStar Satellite Corp.,* 269 F.3d 1149, 1154 (10th Cir.2001) (noting that most circuits have not incorporated Rule 6(d)'s five day notice requirement into Rule 65(a)(1)); holding that three days was sufficient in circumstances of instant case; *Harris County, Texas v. CarMax Auto Superstores, Inc.,* 177 F.3d 306 (5th Cir.1999) (notice under Rule 65(a)(1) should normally comply with Rule 6(d), which normally requires notice of at least five days; in apparent dicta, however, court observed that while defendant received only three days formal notice, defendant had "ample" informal notice; court also observed that at hearing, defendant called witnesses, presented exhibits, engaged in vigorous cross-examination, and never sought postponement of hearing).

14. *See, e.g., McDonald's Corp. v. Robertson,* 147 F.3d 1301, 1311–13 (11th Cir.1998) ("Rule 65 does not [always] require an evidentiary hearing;" undisputed material facts require no hearing, but "bitterly disputed" facts do; in cases where facts are clear but dispute exists as to which important inferences to draw, trial court has substantial discretion as to whether to hold evidentiary hearing); *Campbell Soup Co. v. Giles,* 47 F.3d 467 (1st Cir.1995) (sometimes it is acceptable to consider documentary evidence only; evidentiary hearing may be curtailed or eliminated when speedy decision is required); *Schulz v. Williams,* 38 F.3d 657, 658 (2d Cir. 1994) (per curiam)(parties entitled only to "reasonable opportunity" to contest evidence).

15. *Cf., e.g., Gomperts v. Chase,* 404 U.S. 1237, 92 S.Ct. 16, 30 L.Ed.2d 30 (1971)(Douglas, J., in chambers)(three days insufficient to prepare for or implement preliminary injunction).

16. *See, e.g., American Train Dispatchers Department of the Brotherhood of Locomotive Engineers v. Fort Smith Railroad Co.,* 121 F.3d 267, 270 (7th Cir.1997), *cert. denied,* 522 U.S. 1016, 118 S.Ct. 602, 139 L.Ed.2d 490 (1997) (so holding; noting also that district court must provide parties with "clear and unambiguous notice" of intent to do so).

17. *See, e.g., Rodriguez v. DeBuono,* 175 F.3d 227, 235 (2d Cir.1999) (per curiam) (standard for permanent injunction is less stringent than standard for preliminary injunction because, *e.g.,* motion for permanent injunction does not have to demonstrate potential for "imminent" irreparable harm, while motion for preliminary injunction must make such a showing).

case on the merits is not yet ripe for trial, as when discovery is not yet completed, courts will not consolidate the trial with the preliminary injunction hearing.[18]

Timing of Order to Consolidate

Rule 65(a)(2) permits the court to order consolidation before or after commencement of the hearing on the preliminary injunction. This authorization is construed to mean that courts will not order consolidation unless all parties had adequate warning of the possibility of consolidation and a reasonable opportunity to prepare their positions on the merits.[19]

Preliminary Injunction Evidence

If the court decides not to consolidate the preliminary injunction hearing with trial on the merits, evidence presented at the hearing is nonetheless preserved as part of the record. Significantly, Rule 65(a)(2) provides that the evidence need not be repeated for trial and may be used as it was inserted in the record of the hearing, consistent with the rules of evidence.

Trial by Jury

Rule 65(a)(2) directs that it be construed so that consolidation and/or preservation of evidence for trial does not interfere with a party's right to a jury trial. Thus, if the court decides a motion for a preliminary injunction by ruling on some issues of fact, evidence presented on those issues of fact is preserved for trial. However, the trier of fact at trial is not bound by the previous findings of fact made by the court in the preliminary injunction hearing.[20]

Modifying or Dissolving a Preliminary Injunction

Although Rule 65(a) is silent on the matter, a preliminary injunction can be modified or dissolved on motion of party who demonstrates

18. *Pughsley v. 3750 Lake Shore Drive Cooperative Building*, 463 F.2d 1055, 1057 (7th Cir. 1972)("A litigant applying for a preliminary injunction should seldom be required either to forego discovery in order to seek emergency relief, or to forego a prompt application for an injunction in order to prepare adequately for trial.").

19. *University of Texas v. Camenisch*, 451 U.S. 390, 101 S.Ct. 1830, 68 L.Ed.2d 175 (1981)(parties entitled to clear notice of intent to consolidate so that parties can prepare). *See also, American Train Dispatchers of International Brotherhood of Locomotive Engineers v. Fort Smith Railroad Co.,* 121 F.3d 267 (7th Cir.1997), *cert. denied,* 522 U.S. 1016, 118 S.Ct. 602, 139 L.Ed.2d 490 (1997) ("Because different standards of proof may apply in the hearing than in the trial, parties must be given a clear chance to object or to propose special procedures for the consolidation."). *But cf., Aponte v. Calderon,* 284 F.3d 184, 190 (1st Cir.2002), *cert. denied,* 537 U.S. 886, 123 S.Ct. 128, 154 L.Ed.2d 145 (2002) (although notice must be early enough "to allow the parties time to assemble and present their evidence," an objection to lack of timely notice is lost if a "party does not object contemporaneously with the court's notice of consolidation"); *Campaign for Family Farms v. Glickman,* 200 F.3d 1180, 1186 (8th Cir.2000) (When dealing "with a purely legal issue on a fixed administrative standard ... a district court may properly reach the merits in such a case without expressly ordering consolidation under Rule 65 and without giving the parties adequate notice.").

20. *University of Texas v. Camenisch,* 451 U.S. 390, 395, 101 S.Ct. 1830, 1834, 68 L.Ed.2d 175 (1981) ("[F]indings of fact and conclusions of law made by a court granting a preliminary injunction are not binding at trial on the merits.").

that the purpose of the injunction has been fulfilled.[21] Thus, a preliminary injunction not to interfere with the destruction of a derelict building is fulfilled when the building is destroyed.

RULE 65(b). TEMPORARY RESTRAINING ORDER; NOTICE; HEARING; DURATION

CORE CONCEPT

Rule 65(b) provides the procedure for obtaining a temporary restraining order. Although the Rule permits a party to obtain a temporary restraining order without first providing notice to opposing parties, it restricts such relief to circumstances where it is clear that notice was not feasible, and limits the duration of such restraining orders to a maximum of twenty days.

APPLICATIONS

Purpose

The purpose of a temporary restraining order is generally to hold the status quo in place until the court has an opportunity to hear a request for fuller relief, such as a preliminary injunction.[22]

Comparison With Preliminary Injunction

A preliminary injunction is also usually directed at freezing circumstances in place until there is greater opportunity to hear the merits of a case.[23] However, a preliminary injunction cannot be issued unless all parties are provided with notice of the motion for such relief, whereas it is possible in some circumstances to obtain a temporary restraining order without first providing notice to opposing parties. Preliminary injunctions may be effective for the pendency of the case, whereas temporary restraining orders issued without notice are effective, with a single renewal, for a maximum of twenty days.[24] When courts grant temporary restraining orders, it is often with an eye to holding a prompt hearing on a motion for a preliminary injunction.[25] In one respect, temporary restraining orders are identical to preliminary injunctions, i.e., the substantive requirements for both (discussed above)

21. *United States v. United Shoe Machinery Corp.,* 391 U.S. 244, 88 S.Ct. 1496, 20 L.Ed.2d 562 (1968). See also, *Favia v. Indiana University of Pennsylvania,* 7 F.3d 332, 337 (3d Cir.1993) (modification proper only when change of circumstances makes continuation of original order inequitable).

22. *See, e.g., Hospital Resource Personnel, Inc. v. United States,* 860 F.Supp. 1554, 1556 (S.D.Ga.1994)(granting temporary restraining order to preserve status quo until hearing on preliminary or permanent injunction).

23. *See, e.g., CMM Cable Rep., Inc. v. Ocean Coast Properties, Inc.,* 48 F.3d 618, 620 (1st Cir.1995)("The purpose of a preliminary injunction is to preserve the status quo," pending full adjudication later.).

24. *Cf., Bennett v. Medtronic, Inc.,* 285 F.3d 801, 804 (9th Cir.2002) (if district court's order exceeds time limits of temporary restraining order, order should be reviewed under standards of preliminary injunction).

25. *Granny Goose Foods, Inc. v. Brotherhood of Teamsters and Auto Truck Drivers Local No. 70 of Alameda County,* 415 U.S. 423, 94 S.Ct. 1113, 39 L.Ed.2d 435 (1974).

are identical.[26]

Order Without Notice to Opposing Party

Although much of Rule 65(b) is devoted to the circumstances in which a party may obtain a temporary restraining order without first notifying opponents of the motion, it is important to note that such ex parte temporary restraining orders are disfavored.[27] Before granting one, the court will search the facts carefully to ascertain the need for ex parte relief, and will require that the party seeking relief satisfy *all* the requirements in Rule 65 for a temporary restraining order, as well as substantive prerequisites in case law governing such equitable remedies as restraining orders and injunctions.[28]

Oral Notice

The preferred method of notice for a temporary restraining order is formal service of written documents upon the opposing party. However, the court has substantial discretion to approve lesser notice.[29] Additionally, Rule 65(b) provides that if written notice is impractical, a party seeking relief under the Rule should attempt to notify the adversary orally.

Orders Issuing Without Prior Notice

Rule 65(b) permits issuance of a temporary restraining order without prior notice to the opposing party, but imposes two additional requirements before such an order is granted: proof of irreparable injury and a statement of the efforts made to notify the opposing party.

Irreparable Injury

Rule 65(b)(1) requires a party to show by affidavit or verified complaint the irreparable injury that will occur if the order is not granted until the opposing parties are notified and have an opportunity to appear.[30]

(1) *Affidavit or Complaint:* The quality and detail required in an affidavit or complaint vary substantially, but the explanation should be sufficient for the court to understand the risk of irreparable injury, along with other relevant facts that will help the court understand the need for prompt action.[31]

26. *See, e.g., Bieros v. Nicola,* 857 F.Supp. 445, 446 (E.D.Pa.1994)("The standards for a temporary restraining order are the same as those for a preliminary injunction.").

27. *See, e.g., Redken Laboratories v. Levin,* 843 F.2d 226, 228 (6th Cir.1988), *cert. denied* 488 U.S. 852, 109 S.Ct. 137, 102 L.Ed.2d 110 (1988)(Ex parte temporary restraining orders "often [exact] manifest injustices.").

28. *See, e.g., Phillips v. Chas. Schreiner Bank,* 894 F.2d 127, 131 (5th Cir.1990)(noting "stringent restrictions" of Rule 65(b) on ex parte temporary restraining orders).

29. *Cf., People of Illinois ex rel. Hartigan v. Peters,* 871 F.2d 1336, 1340 (7th Cir.1989)("[w]e leave the question of what constitutes sufficient notice primarily to the district court's discretion.").

30. *See, e.g., American Can Co. v. Mansukhani,* 742 F.2d 314, 321–24 (7th Cir.1984)(failure to comply with Rule 65(b)(1) is abuse of discretion).

31. *See, e.g., Id.*

(2) *Irreparable Injury:* The concept of what constitutes irreparable injury is so flexible as to be elusive. However, it seems clear that a party can demonstrate that the loss likely to occur if an ex parte temporary restraining order is not issued is an irreparable loss when the damages will be of a nature as are difficult to calculate.[32] Thus, substantial risk of lost future profits or business reputation might constitute irreparable injury. Alternatively, if the loss will be of a nature that the courts normally consider beyond compensation by money, however calculated, the injury is likely to be irreparable. Thus, risk of damage to unique property, such as land, might also meet the standard of irreparable injury.

Efforts to Notify Adversary

Rule 65(b)(2) requires that an applicant for a temporary restraining order explain, in writing, whatever efforts have been made to notify the opposing party, and the reasons why no further efforts at notification before issuance of the order are justified. Although the Rule does not literally require that an applicant make efforts to notify an adversary, the court may treat failure to make efforts that would have been reasonable as a ground for denying the motion for a temporary restraining order.[33]

Date and Time of Issuance

If a party is able to obtain a temporary restraining order without first providing notice to opposing parties, Rule 65(b) requires that the order be indorsed with the date and time it was issued. This indorsement is significant because it begins the running of the ten-day period, discussed below, for which the order is effective.

Filing With Clerk

Once an order is issued without prior notice, it must be filed "forthwith" with the clerk of court and entered as part of the record of the case.

Explanation of Injury and Lack of Notice

The court's temporary restraining order will explain the apprehended irreparable injury in detail sufficient to inform an appellate court,[34] and will also explain the reasons why the court found it necessary to issue the order without first hearing from opposing parties.

Duration of Temporary Restraining Order

If an order issues under Rule 65(b) without prior notice to opposing parties, the order will expire no later than ten days after issuance.[35]

32. *Cf., In re Arthur Treacher's Franchisee Litigation*, 689 F.2d 1137, 1145 (3d Cir. 1982)("we have never upheld an injunction where the claimed injury constituted a loss of money, a loss capable of recoupment in a proper action at law.").

33. *See, e.g., American Can Co. v. Mansukhani,* 742 F.2d 314, 321–24 (7th Cir.1984)(failure to make reasonable efforts make grant of order an abuse of discretion).

34. *See, e.g., Ben David v. Travisono,* 495 F.2d 562, 564–65 (1st Cir.1974)("Expansive" injunction against "brutalization" of prisoners must be based on "express findings that the prohibited conduct is likely").

35. *Cf., CVI/Beta Ventures, Inc. v. Custom Optical Frames, Inc.*, 859 F.Supp. 945, 948 (D.Md.1994)(but if order issues only after notice to opponent, order may extend for longer period;

The court may provide for expiration of the order in a lesser period. Additionally, even temporary restraining orders issued with notice cannot continue indefinitely unless they meet the standards required for preliminary injunctions.[36]

Consent to Extension

If the opposing party consents to an extension of the temporary restraining order, the order may be extended for any length of time to which the parties agree.[37]

Judicial Extension of Time

Temporary restraining orders issued without prior notice may be extended by judicial order for an additional period not greater than the length of time in the original order, and in no event for more than ten additional days.

Obtaining an Extension

A party seeking judicial extension of an order must move for the extension within the time limitation of the original order, and must show good cause for the extension. Good cause might be a continuation of the circumstances of irreparable injury that justified the original order, or such new circumstances as the temporary restraining order produced. For example, if the court is considering issuance of a preliminary injunction, extension of a temporary restraining order might be appropriate to allow the court more time to decide the preliminary injunction question.

Recording of Reasons for Extension

If a temporary restraining order is extended, Rule 65(b) provides that the court must record its reasons for granting the extension.[38]

Timing of Hearing on Preliminary Injunction

If the court grants a temporary restraining order without prior notice to opposing parties, Rule 65(b) directs that a hearing on a motion for a preliminary injunction will be held "at the earliest possible time." The preliminary injunction hearing must move to the head of the

order is then analogous to preliminary injunction).

36. *See, e.g., United States v. Crawford,* 329 F.3d 131, 137 (2d Cir.2003), *cert. denied*, 540 U.S. 881, 124 S.Ct. 329, 157 L.Ed.2d 147 (2003) (where temporary restraining order was unambiguous as to its continuing nature and was originally granted only upon notice and hearing, it properly continued beyond time limit as a preliminary injunction).

37. *See, e.g., In re Arthur Treacher's Franchise Litigation,* 689 F.2d 1150 (3d Cir.1982); *Cf., Hudson v. Barr,* 3 F.3d 970, 973 (6th Cir. 1993)(noting that temporary restraining order can be extended beyond 20 days only with consent of parties).

38. *But cf., Reliance Insurance Co. v. Mast Construction Co.,* 159 F.3d 1311, 1316 (10th Cir.1998) (extension of expiration date of order does not require that operative language of order must be restated; it is sufficient that extension incorporated by reference such language as was previously laid out when order was originally granted).

court's docket, second only to preliminary injunction matters that are already pending.

Failure to Seek a Preliminary Injunction

If a party obtained a temporary restraining order without prior notice, and then fails to pursue an application for a preliminary injunction at the scheduled hearing, the court will terminate the temporary restraining order.

Motion to Modify or Dissolve Order

Like preliminary injunctions, temporary restraining orders may be modified or dissolved on motion of a party. Grounds for dissolution include a demonstration that the purpose of the order has been fulfilled. An order may also be modified or dissolved if the court is persuaded that the circumstances requiring the order have changed.

Notice

A party subject to a temporary restraining order issued without prior notice may move to dissolve or modify the order. Rule 65(b) requires that the moving party provide other parties at least two days notice of a hearing on the motion to dissolve, unless the court permits less notice.

Timing of Hearing

Rule 65(b) establishes no time limit within which the court must hear a motion to dissolve or modify a temporary restraining order, but the Rule clearly encourages a prompt hearing, "as expeditiously as the ends of justice require."

Appeal

Generally, a court's decision to grant, deny, modify, continue, or dissolve a temporary restraining order is not appealable.[39]

RULE 65(c). SECURITY

CORE CONCEPT

Rule 65(c) requires that, as a condition of granting a preliminary injunction or temporary restraining order, the court must impose a bond or other security.[40] The party bound by the injunction or order is entitled to recover damages from the posted security if the injunction or order is subsequently found to have been erroneously granted. The

39. *See, e.g., In re Lorillard Tobacco Co.,* 370 F.3d 982, 986 (9th Cir. 2004) (temporary restraining orders "are generally not appealable as of right"); *Robinson v. Lehman,* 771 F.2d 772, 782 (3d Cir.1985)(temporary restraining order not appealable unless denial of order effectively decides the case).

40. *Cf., Mead Johnson & Co. v. Abbott Laboratories,* 209 F.3d 1032, 1033 (7th Cir.2000) (per curiam), *cert. denied,* 531 U.S. 917, 121 S.Ct. 276, 148 L.Ed.2d 200 (2000) (posting bond may be required to obtain preliminary injunction, but "posting a bond is [still] voluntary"; if party chooses to do so, party can decline to pay bond and drop the suit).

court retains substantial discretion to determine the amount of the security.

APPLICATIONS

Mandatory Security

Although the language of Rule 65(c) seems to direct a court to impose a bond, many cases treat the decision to impose a bond as a matter of discretion for the court.[41]

Timing

If a bond is required, it must be posted when the court grants a preliminary injunction or temporary restraining order.[42] There is no requirement to post security when a party initially seeks such relief.

Amount of Security

The maximum amount of security that may be required is the court's estimate of the potential loss to a party proximately caused by erroneous issuance of the injunction or order.[43] The court has discretion to require posting of lesser amounts than the bound party's estimated potential loss.[44] In practice, that means in some cases the

41. *See, e.g., Doctor's Associates, Inc. v. Stuart,* 85 F.3d 975 (2d Cir.1996)(affirming district court's decision not to require bond); *Moltan Co. v. Eagle-Picher Industries, Inc.,* 55 F.3d 1171, 1176 (6th Cir.1995)("While we recognize that the language of Rule 65(c) appears to be mandatory, and that many circuits have so interpreted it, the rule in our circuit has long been that the district court possesses discretion over whether to require the posting of security"); *Temple University v. White,* 941 F.2d 201, 219 (3d Cir.1991), *cert. denied sub nom., Snider v. Temple University,* 502 U.S. 1032, 112 S.Ct. 873, 116 L.Ed.2d 778 (1992)(sometimes a strict reading of bond requirements may be "inappropriate"); *Sprint Communications Co. v. CAT Communications International, Inc.,* 335 F.3d 235 n.4 (3d Cir.2003) (suggesting that exceptions to bond requirement are rare). *See also Ty, Inc. v. Publications International, Inc.,* 292 F.3d 512, 516 (7th Cir.2002), *cert. denied,* 537 U.S. 1110, 123 S.Ct. 892, 154 L.Ed.2d 783 (2003) (bond requirement of Rule 65(c) applies only to temporary restraining order or preliminary injunction, ... "not for a permanent injunction").

42. *See, e.g., Massachusetts Mutual Life Insurance Co. v. Associated Dry Goods Corp.,* 786 F.Supp. 1403, 1419 (N.D.Ind.1992)(bond covering loss is "precondition" to injunction, imposed upon grant of order). *But Compare Kos Pharmaceuticals, Inc. v. Andrix Corp.,* 369 F.3d 700, 728 (3d Cir. 2004) (court should determine amount of bond by evaluation of potential financial damages; however, decision to grant injunction should be separate from determination of bond amount), *with Corning, Inc. v. PicVue Electronics, Ltd.,* 365 F.3d 156, 158 (2d Cir. 2004) ("While it might have been within the discretion of the district court to decide that, under the circumstances, no security was required, ... the district court was required to make this determination before it entered the preliminary injunction.").

43. *See, e.g., Hoechst Diafoil Co. v. Nan Ya Plastics Corp.,* 174 F.3d 411, 421 (4th Cir.1999) (court must impose bond of an amount that considers magnitude of both defendant's potential loss and plaintiff's potential enrichment, as well as likelihood that harm will actually occur; citing authority for bond amount of zero if no evidence supported likelihood of harm). *But cf., Connecticut General Life Insurance Co. v. New Images of Beverly Hills,* 321 F.3d 878, 883 (9th Cir.2003) (party affected by injunction has obligation to present evidence that bond in a particular amount is needed).

44. *See, e.g., GoTo.com, Inc. v. Walt Disney Co.,* 202 F.3d 1199, 1211 (9th Cir.2000) (refusing to raise bond from $25,000 to $20,000,000; noting discretion of district court and practical result); *International Association of Machinists and Aerospace Workers v. Eastern Airlines, Inc.,* 925 F.2d 6 (1st Cir.1991)(district court has "substantial discretion" to set terms of bond).

court may limit security to a nominal amount, if such a small sum is in the interest of justice.[45]

Requests for Increase in Bond

If a party believes the amount designated for the bond is insufficient to cover damages, the party may seek an increase in the bond during the time when the preliminary relief is in effect–or when the preliminary remedy has been lifted, but might still be re-imposed. However, once an injunction or restraining order has been reversed and will not be replaced, the amount of the bond cannot be increased.[46]

Standard for "Wrongfully Enjoined"

A party has been wrongfully enjoined "if it is ultimately found that the enjoined party had at all times the right to do the enjoined act." [47]

Damages Recoverable

An injured party's maximum recovery is generally limited to the amount of the bond.[48] However, a party may pursue an independent action for malicious prosecution in the unusual cases where the elements of that tort are satisfied.[49]

Actions Involving the United States

Rule 65(c) exempts the United States, its officers, and agencies from the obligation to post security.

Relation to Rule 65.1

Rule 65.1 governs the procedure by which a party may seek recovery against security posted pursuant to Rule 65(c).

45. *See, e.g., Davis v. Mineta,* 302 F.3d 1104 (10th Cir.2002) ("Ordinarly, where a party is seeking to vindicate the public interest served by [federal environmental law], a minimal bond amount should be considered."); *Cronin v. United States Department of Agriculture,* 919 F.2d 439, 445 (7th Cir.1990)(citing circuits that require only nominal bonds in environmental cases). *But see, Mead Johnson & Co. v. Abbott Laboratories,* 201 F.3d 883, 888 (7th Cir.2000), *cert. denied,* 531 U.S. 917, 121 S.Ct. 276, 148 L.Ed.2d 200 (2000) ("When setting the amount of security, district courts should err on the high side"; partly because bond acts to limit damages recoverable); *MacDonald v. Chicago Park District,* 132 F.3d 355, 358 (7th Cir.1997) (per curiam) (finding error in imposition of $100 bond on plaintiff of modest means; loss to defendant is potentially much larger).

46. *See, e.g., Mead Johnson & Co. v. Abbott Laboratories,* 209 F.3d 1032, 1033 (7th Cir.2000) (per curiam), *cert. denied,* 531 U.S. 917, 121 S.Ct. 276, 148 L.Ed.2d 200 (2000) ("To permit changes in the bond after an injunction's reversal would be to overturn the rule [that recoverable damages are limited to amount of the bond] in fact, if not in name.").

47. *Blumenthal v. Merrill Lynch, Pierce, Fenner & Smith, Inc.,* 910 F.2d 1049, 1054 (2d Cir.1990). *See also Milan Express, Inc. v. Averitt Express, Inc.,* 254 F.3d 966 (11th Cir.2001) (elements are: (1) wrongfully enjoined; and (2) proximately caused damage).

48. *W.R. Grace & Co. v. Local Union 759, International Union of United Rubber, Cork, Linoleum & Plastic Workers of America,* 461 U.S. 757, 770, 103 S.Ct. 2177, 2185, 76 L.Ed.2d 298 (1983) ("A party injured by the issuance of an injunction later determined to be erroneous has no action for damages in the absence of a bond."). *See, e.g., Coyne–Delany Co. v. Capital Development Board,* 717 F.2d 385, 393–94 (7th Cir.1983)(bond is a ceiling on damages, except where plaintiff acted in bad faith).

49. *Meyers v. Block,* 120 U.S. 206, 211, 7 S.Ct. 525, 528, 30 L.Ed. 642 (1887)(bond sets limit of recovery, in absence of suit for malicious prosecution).

RULE 65(d). FORM AND SCOPE OF INJUNCTION OR RESTRAINING ORDER

CORE CONCEPT

Rule 65(d) governs the information that must be contained in injunctions and temporary restraining orders. The Rule also describes categories of persons who are bound by an injunction or order.

APPLICATIONS

Reasons for Issuance

The injunction or order must contain an explanation of the reasons for its issuance. A sufficient explanation will state specifically the facts found by the court as well as the conclusions of law upon which the court's decision is based.[50] An explanation of the reason for the court's action is usually direct, without excessive detail.

Relation to Rule 52

Alongside the Rule 65(d) requirement of reasons for issuance of an injunction or restraining order, Rule 52(a) provides that district courts must make findings of fact and conclusions of law when granting or denying a request for an interlocutory injunction.[51] This issue is discussed in greater detail under Rule 52.

Description of Acts Proscribed: Requirement of Writing

Rule 65(d) ordinarily requires that the injunction or order describe the prohibited acts with sufficient detail and clarity so that a layperson who was bound by the order could distinguish between acts that were permitted and acts the injunction or order prohibited.[52] Thus, a court

50. *Schmidt v. Lessard,* 414 U.S. 473, 476, 94 S.Ct. 713, 715, 38 L.Ed.2d 661 (1974) ("The specificity provisions of Rule 65(d) are no mere technical requirements. The Rule was designed to prevent uncertainty and confusion on the part of those faced with injunction orders, and to avoid the possible founding of a contempt citation on a decree too vague to be understood."). *But cf., EEOC v. Severn Trent Services, Inc.,* 358 F.3d 438, 442 (7th Cir. 2004) ("The explanation can be oral rather than written ... and the absence of explanation can be forgiven when the justification for the injunction is clear from the record.").

51. *See, e.g., Prairie Band of Potawatomi Indians v. Pierce,* 253 F.3d 1234 (10th Cir.2001) ("[W]ithout adequate findings of fact and conclusions of law, appellate review is in general not possible."). *But cf., Knapp Shoes, Inc. v. Sylvania Shoe Manufacturing Corp.,* 15 F.3d 1222, 1228 (1st Cir.1994), *cert. denied,* 517 U.S. 1245, 116 S.Ct. 2500, 135 L.Ed.2d 191 (1996) ("conclusory findings are not enough, [but court may make] brief, definite, pertinent findings and conclusions upon the contested matters; there is no necessity for over-elaboration of detail or particularization of facts" [internal quotation marks omitted]).

52. *See, e.g., Fortyune v. American Multi–Cinema, Inc.,* 364 F.3d 1075, 1087 (9th Cir. 2004) (district court has no duty to explain *how* to enforce injunction, only to explain what must or must not be done); *A & M Records, Inc. v. Napster, Inc.,* 284 F.3d 1091, 1097 (9th Cir.2002) ("We do not set aside injunctions under [Rule 65(d)] 'unless they are so vague that they have no reasonably specific meaning.' "); *Prairie Band of Potawatomi Indians v. Pierce,* 253 F.3d 1234 (10th Cir.2001) (finding sufficient specificity in order barring state from enforcing state motor vehicle registration and titling laws against vehicles registered and titled under tribal motor vehicle code; use of words "applying" and "enforcing" in instant context are clear; "Rule 65(d) does not require the impossible.");

will ordinarily not use highly technical language unless there is no other way to describe the acts and the parties affected are likely to be uniquely capable of understanding such language.

Part of the requirement of describing with reasonable precision the prohibited conduct is a companion requirement that the court's order must be reduced to writing.[53]

Incorporation by Reference

The Rule specifically provides that prohibited acts *may not* be described only by reference to the complaint or other documents in the action.[54] However, Rule 65(d) is satisfied if a document specifically describing the prohibited acts is "physically appended" to the injunction order.[55]

Persons Bound

Rule 65(d) describes the categories of persons subject to an injunction or order: (1) parties;[56] (2) their officers, agents, servants, employees, and attorneys;[57] and (3) other persons "in active concert or participation with [parties]." [58]

Power v. Summers, 226 F.3d 815, 819 (7th Cir. 2000) (prohibition on "retaliation" against plaintiffs who are suing for alleged violation of free speech rights is not unduly vague); *CPC International, Inc. v. Skippy, Inc.,* 214 F.3d 456, 459 (4th Cir.2000) (order that tells defendant with specificity what to remove from website but provides no clear reason for the redaction violates Rule 65(d)); *Burton v. City of Belle Glade,* 178 F.3d 1175 (11th Cir.1999) (enjoining city to abstain from racial discrimination in annexation policies does "no more than instruct the City to 'obey the law' " and therefore does not meet specificity requirement of Rule 65(d)); *Reliance Insurance Co. v. Mast Construction Co.,* 159 F.3d 1311, 1316 (10th Cir.1998) (temporary restraining order blocking transfer of assets of bank account in which "defendants have or maintain an interest" is sufficiently specific under Rule 65(d); "interest" is not ambiguous "when used to describe rights in a bank account"); *PMC, Inc. v. Sherwin–Williams Co.,* 151 F.3d 610, 619 (7th Cir.1998), *cert. denied,* 525 U.S. 1104, 119 S.Ct. 871, 142 L.Ed.2d 772 (1999) (injunction requiring defendant to take "full responsibility" for cleanup of toxic waste site is "hopelessly vague;" defendant should bear no risk of responsibility for past or future pollution caused by others; remanded for redrafting); *IDS Life Insurance Co. v. SunAmerica Life Insurance Co.,* 136 F.3d 537, 543 (7th Cir.1998) (injunction prohibiting encouragement of "unlawful insurance practices" is vacated; but district court may try to reformulate injunction more precisely); *Peregrine Myanmar, Ltd. v. Segal,* 89 F.3d 41 (2d Cir.1996)(prohibition against "spurious" lawsuits is overbroad, unless district court on remand can define that term more precisely).

53. *See, e.g., Lau v. Meddaugh,* 229 F.3d 121, 123 (2d Cir.2000), *cert. denied,* 534 U.S. 833, 122 S.Ct. 81, 151 L.Ed.2d 44 (2001) (failure to memorialize order is reversible error).

54. *See, e.g., Advent Electronics, Inc. v. Buckman,* 112 F.3d 267 (7th Cir.1997) (order must state reasons for issuance and specific terms "without reference to another document"); *Dunn v. New York State Department of Labor,* 47 F.3d 485 (2d Cir.1995)(unacceptable to incorporate consent decree from related case; because consent decree can be modified, incorporation of such decree risks confusion in instant case).

55. *LeBlanc-Sternberg v. Fletcher,* 143 F.3d 748 (2d Cir.1998). *But cf., California v. Campbell,* 138 F.3d 772 (9th Cir.1998), *cert. denied,* 525 U.S. 822, 119 S.Ct. 64, 142 L.Ed.2d 51 (1998) (purpose of prohibition on incorporation by reference is to ensure notice; however, where notice is otherwise adequate, incorporation of state administrative order into injunction is not fatal when order is physically attached to injunction).

56. *See, e.g., United States v. Vitek Supply Corp.,* 151 F.3d 580 (7th Cir.1998) (Rule 65(d) extends scope of injunction to bind alter egos); *Hernandez v. O'Malley,* 98 F.3d 293, 294 (7th Cir.1996) (injunction against public official also applies to successor in office).

57. *See, e.g., Planned Parenthood of Columbia/Willamette, Inc. v. American Coalition of Life Activists,* 290 F.3d 1058, 1088 n. 19 (9th Cir. 2002) (en banc) (individual employee/agent of

58. See note 58 on page 919.

Notice to Persons Bound

No one is bound by an injunction or order until that person receives fair notice of the judicial act. However, formal notice, in the form of service of documents, is not necessarily required to bind a party or those in privity with a party. A party or a person in a close relationship with a party may be bound if they simply have actual knowledge of the injunction or order.[59]

Personal Jurisdiction

Persons outside the jurisdiction of the court are not subject to its orders.[60] For a further discussion of jurisdiction over persons and things, see §§ 2.2–2.10.

Persons in Active Concert

This broad category of persons who may be subject to an injunction or order is necessarily fact-specific in application.[61] Generally, however, assignees who take an interest from a party with actual or constructive notice of an injunction or order prohibiting that party from performing a certain act relating to the interest may also be barred from performing the act.[62]

party is appropriately within scope of injunction); *American Civil Liberties Union v. Johnson,* 194 F.3d 1149 (10th Cir.1999) (preliminary injunction against enforcement by governor and attorney general of criminal statute also binds state's district attorneys). *But cf., Doctor's Associates, Inc. v. Reinert & Duree,* 191 F.3d 297, 302–303 (2d Cir.1999) (violation of Rule 65(d) to enjoin preliminarily franchisees of defendant who are not parties to current litigation in federal court from pursuing their separate claims in state court).

58. *Regal Knitwear Co. v. National Labor Relations Board,* 324 U.S. 9, 65 S.Ct. 478, 89 L.Ed. 661 (1945). *But cf., R.M.S. Titanic, Inc. v. Haver,* 171 F.3d 943, 957–58 (4th Cir.1999), *cert. denied,* 528 U.S. 825, 120 S.Ct. 74, 145 L.Ed.2d 63 (1999) (shipping company that agreed to transport enjoined party to site of sunken vessel is not in privity with party prohibited from approaching or photographing wreckage); *Additive Controls & Measurement Systems, Inc. v. Flowdata, Inc.,* 96 F.3d 1390, 1395 (Fed.Cir.1996) ("Having a relationship to an enjoined party of the sort set forth in Rule 65(d) exposes a nonparty to contempt for assisting the party to violate the injunction, but does not justify granting injunctive relief against the non-party in its separate capacity.").

59. *Spallone v. United States,* 493 U.S. 265, 110 S.Ct. 625, 107 L.Ed.2d 644 (1990).

60. *See, e.g., R.M.S. Titanic, Inc. v. Haver,* 171 F.3d 943, 957–58 (4th Cir.1999), *cert. denied,* 528 U.S. 825, 120 S.Ct. 74, 145 L.Ed.2d 63 (1999) ("[A] party cannot obtain injunctive relief against another without first obtaining in personam jurisdiction over that person or someone in legal privity with that person."); *Parker v. Ryan,* 960 F.2d 543, 546 (5th Cir.1992)(nonparty acting independently of defendant is not subject to court's jurisdiction under Rule 65(d)). *But see, Waffenschmidt v. MacKay,* 763 F.2d 711, 714 (5th Cir.1985), cert. denied, 474 U.S. 1056, 106 S.Ct. 794, 88 L.Ed.2d 771 (1986)(nonparties residing outside territorial jurisdiction are nevertheless subject to court's jurisdiction if they intentionally and knowingly aid and abet violation of court's order).

61. *See, e.g., Reliance Insurance Co. v. Mast Construction Co.,* 84 F.3d 372 (10th Cir.1996) (nonparties bound include alter egos, and also those "with actual notice" who assist defendant or privy in violation of order); *United States v. International Brotherhood of Teamsters, Chauffeurs, Warehousemen and Helpers of America, AFL-CIO,* 964 F.2d 180, 184 (2d Cir.1992) (whether a person is bound "always depends on the precise relationship of that person to the underlying litigation").

62. *Regal Knitwear Co. v. National Labor Relations Board,* 324 U.S. 9, 65 S.Ct. 478, 89 L.Ed. 661 (1945). *See, e.g., Chicago Truck Drivers v. Brotherhood Labor Leasing,* 207 F.3d 500, 507–08 (8th Cir.2000) (non-party who is sole shareholder, corporate officer and agent of cor-

Permanent Injunctions

Unlike other provisions of Rule 65, Rule 65(d) does not refer only to preliminary injunctions or temporary restraining orders. Thus, Rule 65(d)'s provisions for a satisfactory explanation of the court's decision, an adequate description of prohibited acts, and the categories of persons bound by an injunction or order apply equally to permanent injunctions.[63]

Standing to Enforce Permanent Injunction

As is described above, there are many circumstances in which persons who are not parties may nonetheless be bound by an injunction. However, only those who are parties to a lawsuit have standing to seek enforcement of a final injunction.[64]

Failure to Comply with Injunction or Order

Persons within the categories of Rule 65(d) who have notice of an injunction or order and who do not comply are subject to the court's power of contempt.[65]

RULE 65(e). EMPLOYER AND EMPLOYEE; INTERPLEADER; CONSTITUTIONAL CASES

CORE CONCEPT

Rule 65(e) provides that nothing in Rule 65 shall be construed to modify statutes relating to labor relations, interpleader actions, or actions subject to the jurisdiction of a three-judge court.

APPLICATION

Alterations to Courts' Injunctive Power

In each of the three areas of law addressed by Rule 65(e)—labor law, statutory interpleader, and three-judge courts—federal statutes alter the typical power of courts to issue injunctions and restraining orders. Rule 65(e) makes clear that when those statutes are applicable to a case and conflict with a provision of Rule 65, the statute governs.

RULE 65(f). COPYRIGHT IMPOUNDMENT

CORE CONCEPT

porations easily falls within scope of Rule 65(d) for purposes of contempt; however, such non-party has no personal liability for payment obligations of corporations when non-party has not been sued in underlying litigation).

63. *See, e.g., Reich v. ABC/York–Estes Corp.,* 64 F.3d 316, 320 (7th Cir.1995)(holding that failure to comply with Rule 65(d) meant no permanent injunction existed).

64. *See, e.g., Planned Parenthood of Idaho, Inc. v. Wasden,* 376 F.3d 908 (9th Cir. 2004) ("Only a proper party to an action can enforce an injunction that results from a final judgment.").

65. *Gunn v. University Committee to End the War in Viet Nam,* 399 U.S. 383, 90 S.Ct. 2013, 26 L.Ed.2d 684 (1970). *See also, Reliance Insurance Co. v. Mast Construction Co.,* 84 F.3d 372, 376 (10th Cir.1996)("Generally speaking, a person who violates an injunction or temporary restraining order during its pendency is subject to a compensatory civil contempt judgment.").

Rule 65(f), scheduled to become effective on December 1, 2001 unless Congress acts prior to that date, provides that other provisions of Rule 65 apply to copyright impoundment proceedings.

ADDITIONAL RESEARCH REFERENCES

Wright & Miller, *Federal Practice and Procedure* §§ 2941–62.

C.J.S. Injunctions §§ 4–54, 60–110, 111–158, 160–206, 213–263, 264–314, 320–341.

West's Key No. Digests, Injunction ⚷132–188.

RULE 65.1

SECURITY: PROCEEDINGS AGAINST SURETIES

Whenever these rules, including the Supplemental Rules for Certain Admiralty and Maritime Claims, require or permit the giving of security by a party, and security is given in the form of a bond or stipulation or other undertaking with one or more sureties, each surety submits to the jurisdiction of the court and irrevocably appoints the clerk of the court as the surety's agent upon whom any papers affecting the surety's liability on the bond or undertaking may be served. The surety's liability may be enforced on motion without the necessity of an independent action. The motion and such notice of the motion as the court prescribes may be served on the clerk of the court, who shall forthwith mail copies to the sureties if their addresses are known.

[Added effective July 1, 1966; amended effective August 1, 1987.]

AUTHORS' COMMENTARY ON RULE 65.1

PURPOSE AND SCOPE

Rule 65.1 provides a summary procedure by which parties can enforce their rights against a surety who has posted security.

APPLICATIONS

Scope

Rule 65.1 applies to proceedings to enforce a surety's liability on an appeal bond, a supersedeas bond, or an injunction bond posted pursuant to Rule 65(c). The Rule also applies when the Supplemental Rules for Certain Admiralty and Maritime Claims require the posting of bond. Finally, Rule 65.1 applies to the satisfaction of provisional remedies under Rule 64, when state law requires a bond.

Injunction Bonds: Rebuttable Presumption

The majority of courts hold that a party wrongfully enjoined under Rule 65 enjoys a rebuttable presumption in favor of recovering provable damages up to the limit of any bond required under Rule 65(c). Only in "rare cases" will the wrongfully enjoined party not be entitled to recovery on the bond.[1]

1. *Nintendo of America, Inc. v. Lewis Galoob Toys, Inc.*, 16 F.3d 1032, 1039 (9th Cir.1994), *cert. denied*, 513 U.S. 822, 115 S.Ct. 85, 130 L.Ed.2d 37 (1994)(presumption in favor of recov-

Alternative Procedures

Rule 65.1 is not the only means by which a party can seek to collect on a bond. Instead of employing the Rule, a party may bring an independent action against the surety in a state or federal court.[2]

Motion for Judgment

The appropriate method for seeking to collect from a surety under Rule 65.1 is a motion for judgment on the bond.

Timing

Generally, a party may seek recovery under Rule 65.1 once the court has terminated or altered the relief that the bond secured. Thus, if a court determines that a preliminary injunction was improvidently granted, or was of excessive scope, the party previously enjoined may then move against the bond for damages.[3]

Consent to Personal Jurisdiction

Rule 65.1 provides that when a surety posts a bond or other security, the surety submits to the personal jurisdiction of the court for purposes of any litigation relating to liability on the bond.[4] Personal jurisdiction is discussed further at §§ 2.3–2.7.

Service of Process

Upon posting bond, a surety also irrevocably appoints the clerk of court as the surety's agent to receive service of process in matters relating to liability on the bond.

Notice

A party seeking to collect on a bond should serve the motion on the clerk of court, along with such other notice as the court may require. Rule 65.1 requires that the clerk shall "forthwith" mail copies of the documents to all affected sureties whose addresses are known.

Injunction Staying Enforcement

Although Rule 65.1 is intended to provide an expeditious means of recovering damages from a bond, there are situations in which Rule 65.1 proceedings will be stayed. In particular, if a court enjoins

ery of proven damages). *But cf., Bass v. First Pacific Networks, Inc.*, 219 F.3d 1052, 1053 (9th Cir.2000) (attorney's fees allegedly incurred in collecting on bond under Rule 65.1 cannot be recovered under that Rule; contrary state law is irrelevant to bond enforcement under Rule 65.1).

2. *See, e.g., Alabama ex rel. Siegelman v. United States Environmental Protection Agency*, 925 F.2d 385, 388 (11th Cir.1991)(permitting independent action when bond is unavailable). *See also De Boer Structures (U.S.A.), Inc. v. Shaffer Tent & Awning Co.*, 187 F.Supp.2d 910, 925 (S.D.Ohio 2001) (noting that appointment of receiver is extraordinary remedy justified only in extreme situations).

3. *See, e.g., American Bible Society v. Blount*, 446 F.2d 588, 595 n. 12 (3d Cir.1971)(liability on bond arises after defendant prevails on merits).

4. *See, e.g., Instant Air Freight Co. v. C.F. Air Freight, Inc.*, 882 F.2d 797, 804 (3d Cir. 1989)(noting that Rule 65.1 requires that surety submit to jurisdiction of court).

proceedings against the bond, the injunction must be obeyed until it is modified or dissolved.[5]

Collecting From Principals

Although Rule 65.1 addresses the means by which a party may seek damages on a surety's bond or other undertaking, courts also permit the use of Rule 65.1 for similar relief against a surety's principal.[6]

Subject Matter Jurisdiction

If a party seeks in the original action to collect against a bond under Rule 65.1, the court will have supplemental jurisdiction over the claim.[7] If a party seeks to enforce a bond in an independent action, the court has subject matter jurisdiction under 28 U.S.C.A. § 1352, governing independent actions on bonds posted pursuant to federal law.[8] Subject matter jurisdiction is discussed further at §§ 2.10–2.13.

ADDITIONAL RESEARCH REFERENCES

Wright & Miller, *Federal Practice and Procedure* §§ 2971–74.

C.J.S. Federal Civil Procedure §§ 1273–1295.

West's Key No. Digests, Federal Civil Procedure ⚿2732–2733.

5. *Celotex Corp. v. Edwards,* 514 U.S. 300, 115 S.Ct. 1493, 131 L.Ed.2d 403 (1995) (notwithstanding Rule 65.1, a bankruptcy court's injunction may stay collection from a debtor's surety until injunction is modified or dissolved).

6. *See, e.g., Willis v. Celotex Corp.,* 970 F.2d 1292 (4th Cir.1992)(Rule 65.1 permits recovery against both surety and principal).

7. *See, e.g., Buddy Systems, Inc. v. Exer–Genie, Inc.,* 545 F.2d 1164, 1166 (9th Cir.1976), *cert. denied,* 431 U.S. 903, 97 S.Ct. 1694, 52 L.Ed.2d 387 (1977)(jurisdiction over collection against bond exists until bond is discharged).

8. *See, e.g., Milan Express, Inc. v. Averitt Express, Inc.,* 208 F.3d 975, 980 (11th Cir.2000) (28 U.S.C. § 1352 provides jurisdiction over claims against injunction bond issued under Rule 65; further, claim for damages in excess of bond, based on allegation of bad faith, could be heard under supplemental jurisdiction of court, 28 U.S.C. § 1367).

RULE 66

RECEIVERS APPOINTED BY FEDERAL COURTS

An action wherein a receiver has been appointed shall not be dismissed except by order of the court. The practice in the administration of estates by receivers or by other similar officers appointed by the court shall be in accordance with the practice heretofore followed in the courts of the United States or as provided in rules promulgated by the district courts. In all other respects the action in which the appointment of a receiver is sought or which is brought by or against a receiver is governed by these rules.

[Amended effective March 19, 1948; October 20, 1949.]

AUTHORS' COMMENTARY ON RULE 66

PURPOSE AND SCOPE

Rule 66 provides that, when appointed by district courts, federal equity receivers shall administer estates in accordance with prior federal practice and local court rules. Once an equity receiver is appointed in a particular lawsuit, the action may not thereafter be dismissed without the court's prior approval.

APPLICATIONS

Role of Federal Equity Receiver

Receivership is an extraordinary equitable remedy, justified only in extreme circumstances.[1] Federal courts appoint equity receivers to assume custody, control, and management of property that either is presently involved or is likely to become involved in litigation.[2] The receiver is charged to preserve the property, and any rents or profits the property earns, until a final disposition by the court. Although typically appointed only to care for property, a federal equity receiver may be appointed where other, extraordinary circumstances compel intimate judicial supervision.[3]

1. *See Hollywood Healthcare Corp. v. Deltec, Inc.*, 2004 WL 1118610, at *10 (D.Minn. May 17, 2004); *Sumpter v. United States*, 314 F.Supp.2d 684, 690 (E.D.Mich. 2004).

2. *See Gilchrist v. General Elec. Capital Corp.*, 262 F.3d 295, 302 (4th Cir.2001) (noting that federal courts have equity power to appoint receivers and administer receiverships).

3. *See Morgan v. McDonough*, 540 F.2d 527 (1st Cir.1976)(affirming appointment of federal receiver for public high school, to implement desegregation orders), *cert. denied,* 429 U.S. 1042, 97 S.Ct. 743, 50 L.Ed.2d 755 (1977). *See also De Boer Structures (U.S.A.), Inc. v. Shaffer Tent & Awning Co.*, 187 F.Supp.2d 910, 925 (S.D.Ohio 2001) (noting that appointment of re-

- *Officer of the Court:* An equity receiver is not an agent of any of the parties to the litigation. Instead, the receiver is deemed to be an officer of the court.[4]
- *Auxiliary Remedy Only:* The appointment of a receiver is not permitted as an end in itself; receivers are only appointed as an auxiliary remedy necessary to some other, primary requested relief.[5]

Administration of Estates By Receivers

Traditional federal practice and, where promulgated, local court rules guide a federal equity receiver in administering the receivership property.

- *State Law:* The substantive law of the State in which the receivership property is located dictates the manner in which the receiver must manage and operate the receivership property.[6]

Federal Rules Control Litigations Involving Receivers

The Rules govern all actions in which a party seeks the appointment of a federal equity receiver, as well as all actions brought by or against the receiver once appointed.[7]

Appointment of Receivers

Rule 66 does not create a substantive right to the appointment of a receiver; a statute or general principle of equity must first justify the appointment. Federal law controls whether an equity receiver should be appointed, even in a diversity case.[8]

- *Who May Seek An Appointment:* The appointment of a receiver may be requested by any person having a legally recognized right to the property—a mere interest or claim to the property will not be sufficient to justify the appointment of a receiver.[9] Receivers

ceiver is extraordinary remedy justified only in extreme situations).

4. *See Hollywood Healthcare Corp. v. Deltec, Inc.*, 2004 WL 1118610, at *9 (D.Minn. May 17, 2004); *Federal Home Loan Mortgage Corp. v. Spark Tarrytown, Inc.*, 829 F.Supp. 82, 85 n. 6 (S.D.N.Y.1993).

5. *See Gordon v. Washington*, 295 U.S. 30, 37 n. 4, 55 S.Ct. 584, 588 n. 4, 79 L.Ed. 1282 (1935)("A receivership is only a means to reach some legitimate end sought through the exercise of the power of a court of equity. It is not an end in itself"); *See also Sumpter v. United States*, 314 F.Supp.2d 684, 690 (E.D.Mich. 2004); *New York Life Ins. Co. v. Watt West Investment Corp.*, 755 F.Supp. 287, 291 n. 6 (E.D.Cal. 1991)(commenting that appointment of receiver is ancillary remedy).

6. *See* 28 U.S.C.A. § 959(b). *See also Gilchrist v. General Elec. Capital Corp.*, 262 F.3d 295, 302 (4th Cir.2001); *Federal Home Loan Mortgage Corp. v. Spark Tarrytown, Inc.*, 829 F.Supp. 82, 85 (S.D.N.Y.1993).

7. *See Phelan v. Middle States Oil Corp.*, 210 F.2d 360 (2d Cir.1954), *aff'd,* 220 F.2d 593 (2d Cir.1955), *cert. denied,* 349 U.S. 929, 75 S.Ct. 772, 99 L.Ed. 1260 (1955); *World Fuel Servs. Corp. v. Moorehead*, 229 F.Supp.2d 584, 596 (N.D.Tex.2002); *Varsames v. Palazzolo*, 96 F.Supp.2d 361, 365 (S.D.N.Y.2000).

8. *See National Partnership Inv. Corp. v. National Housing Dev't Corp.*, 153 F.3d 1289, 1291–92 (11th Cir.1998); *Aviation Supply Corp. v. R.S.B.I. Aerospace, Inc.*, 999 F.2d 314, 317 (8th Cir.1993); *Hollywood Healthcare Corp. v. Deltec, Inc.*, 2004 WL 1118610, at *9 (D.Minn. May 17, 2004); *Sumpter v. United States*, 314 F.Supp.2d 684, 690 (E.D.Mich. 2004).

9. *See Santibanez v. Wier McMahon & Co.*, 105 F.3d 234, 241 (5th Cir.1997)(appointments sought by judgment creditors); *Piambino v. Bailey*, 757 F.2d 1112 (11th Cir.1985), *cert. denied,*

are appointed frequently at the request of secured creditors, mortgagees, judgment creditors, and plaintiffs in shareholder derivative actions.[10]

- *Prerequisites for Appointment:* The appointment of a receiver is an extraordinary remedy, available only upon a clear showing that a receivership is essential to protect the property from some threatened loss or injury pending a final disposition by the court.[11] Thus, the court may consider the following factors in deciding whether an appointment is necessary:

    - the existence of a valid claim by the party seeking the appointment;
    - the imminent nature of any danger to the property, to its concealment or removal, or to its value;
    - the adequacy of other legal remedies;
    - the lack of a less drastic equitable remedy;
    - the plaintiff's probable success in the lawsuit and the risk of irreparable injury to the property;
    - whether the defendant has engaged, or may engage, in any fraudulent actions with respect to the property;
    - the likelihood that appointing the receiver will do more good than harm; *and*
    - whether the potential harm to the plaintiff outweighs the injury to others.[12]

Each factor need not be satisfied, so long as the court determines that its review favors the receiver's appointment.[13] Courts have held that the existence of an express contractual right to the appointment of a receiver, along with adequate *prima facie* evidence of default, can suffice to justify appointment.[14]

476 U.S. 1169, 106 S.Ct. 2889, 90 L.Ed.2d 976 (1986); *Mintzer v. Arthur L. Wright & Co.*, 263 F.2d 823 (3d Cir.1959).

10. *See Santibanez v. Wier McMahon & Co.*, 105 F.3d 234, 241 (5th Cir.1997) (appointments sought by judgment creditors).

11. *See Gordon v. Washington*, 295 U.S. 30, 55 S.Ct. 584, 79 L.Ed. 1282 (1935); *Aviation Supply Corp. v. R.S.B.I. Aerospace, Inc.*, 999 F.2d 314, 317 (8th Cir.1993); *Hollywood Healthcare Corp. v. Deltec, Inc.*, 2004 WL 1118610, at *10 (D.Minn. May 17, 2004); *Sumpter v. United States*, 314 F.Supp.2d 684, 690 (E.D.Mich. 2004); *World Fuel Servs. Corp. v. Moorehead*, 229 F.Supp.2d 584, 596 (N.D.Tex.2002); *Varsames v. Palazzolo*, 96 F.Supp.2d 361, 365 (S.D.N.Y.2000).

12. *See Santibanez v. Wier McMahon & Co.*, 105 F.3d 234, 241–42 (5th Cir.1997); *Aviation Supply Corp. v. R.S.B.I. Aerospace, Inc.*, 999 F.2d 314, 317 (8th Cir.1993); *Hollywood Healthcare Corp. v. Deltec, Inc.*, 2004 WL 1118610, at *9—*10 (D.Minn. May 17, 2004); *Fleet Business Credit, L.L.C. v. Wings Rests., Inc.*, 291 B.R. 550, 556 (N.D.Okla.2003); *Pioneer Capital Corp. v. Environamics Corp.*, 2003 WL 345349, at *9 (D.Me.2003) (decision of Magistrate Judge), *aff'd*, 2003 WL 1923765 (D.Me.2003); *World Fuel Servs. Corp. v. Moorehead*, 229 F.Supp.2d 584, 596 (N.D.Tex. 2002); *De Boer Structures (U.S.A.), Inc. v. Shaffer Tent & Awning Co.*, 187 F.Supp.2d 910, 925 (S.D.Ohio 2001); *Varsames v. Palazzolo*, 96 F.Supp.2d 361, 365 (S.D.N.Y.2000); *Select Creations, Inc. v. Paliafito America, Inc.*, 828 F.Supp. 1301, 1367 (E.D.Wis.1992); *RTC v. Fountain Circle Assocs. Ltd. Partnership*, 799 F.Supp. 48, 50–51 (N.D.Ohio 1992).

13. *See Fleet Bus. Credit, L.L.C. v. Wings Rests., Inc.*, 291 B.R. 550, 556 (N.D.Okla.2003) (appointing receiver where "several of the factors weigh in favor of the propriety of appointing a receiver").

14. *See Pioneer Capital Corp. v. Environamics Corp.*, 2003 WL 345349, at *9 (D.Me.2003) (decision of Magistrate Judge), *aff'd*, 2003 WL 1923765 (D.Me.2003).

Consent to Appointment

The court may appoint a receiver where the defendant both admits liability for the claim asserted in the litigation and consents to the appointment of a receiver—provided that there has been no improper attempt by the parties to collusively manufacture federal jurisdiction.[15]

Discretion of the District Court

Whether to appoint a receiver lies within the district judge's sound discretion.[16]

Who May Be Appointed

The court may appoint as the receiver any person deemed capable of serving in that capacity. However, federal statutes prevent the judge from appointing as a receiver any person related to the judge by consanguinity within the fourth degree,[17] a clerk or deputy of the court (absent special circumstances),[18] or a federal employee or person employed by the appointing judge.[19]

Place of Appointment

Because the appointment of a receiver is a type of *in rem* proceeding, the appointing court must enjoy a strong relationship to the contemplated receivership: a substantial portion of the defendant's business must be conducted in the host district, or a substantial portion of the anticipated receivership property must be located within the host district.

- *Conflicting Claims to Jurisdiction:* If two courts of concurrent and coordinate jurisdiction (*e.g.,* two federal courts) attempt to assert a claim to the same property, the court where the legal papers are first filed assumes exclusive jurisdiction, irrespective of whether its receiver is the first to obtain physical possession of the property. If the two courts are not of the same or concurrent jurisdiction (*e.g.,* one State and one federal court), and where the subject matter in the one litigation is not the same as in the other litigation, or where no constructive possession of the property is obtained through the filing, the court whose receiver first obtains actual possession of the property assumes exclusive jurisdiction.[20]

Notice of Appointment

Generally, the court gives notice to all parties before appointing an equity receiver. But where notice is impractical or self-defeating, or

15. *See In re Reisenberg,* 208 U.S. 90, 28 S.Ct. 219, 52 L.Ed. 403 (1908).

16. *See Santibanez v. Wier McMahon & Co.,* 105 F.3d 234, 241 (5th Cir.1997); *De Boer Structures (U.S.A.), Inc. v. Shaffer Tent & Awning Co.,* 187 F.Supp.2d 910, 925 (S.D.Ohio 2001); *Varsames v. Palazzolo,* 96 F.Supp.2d 361, 365 (S.D.N.Y.2000); *Insussary v. Adminstaff Cos., Inc.,* 1999 WL 305102, at *1–*2 (S.D.N.Y.1999).

17. 28 U.S.C.A. § 458; 18 U.S.C.A. § 1910.

18. 28 U.S.C.A. § 957.

19. 28 U.S.C.A. § 958.

20. *See Harkin v. Brundage,* 276 U.S. 36, 48 S.Ct. 268, 72 L.Ed. 457 (1928).

where the appointment must be made immediately, the court enjoys the power to appoint a receiver *ex parte*.[21]

Effect of Appointment

Once a receiver is appointed and gives the bond required by the court, the court and the receiver obtain exclusive jurisdiction of all of the defendant's property, no matter where it is kept. To obtain such jurisdiction over property outside the appointing district, the receiver must first file a copy of the complaint and appointment order in that foreign district.[22]

Actions by Receivers

A federal equity receiver is authorized to commence and prosecute any action necessary to accomplish the objectives of the receivership.[23] The receiver may be directed to bring suit on specific instructions from the court, or the receiver may independently institute lawsuits pursuant to the receiver's general duties of receiving, controlling, and managing the receivership property.

- *May Sue In Any Jurisdiction:* The receiver may bring suit in any federal district, including those districts outside the court in which the receiver was formally appointed.[24]
- *Equitable Defenses*: Receivers are deemed to have stepped into the shoes of the persons or entities for whom they act. Thus, absent statutory provisions dictating otherwise, defenses that could be asserted against the original plaintiff are equally available against the plaintiff's equity receiver. However, equitable defenses (such as unclean hands) that could be asserted against the original plaintiff might not be effective against the receiver.[25]

Actions Against Receivers

A person may sue an equity receiver, without leave of court, for any of the receiver's actions taken after the receiver was appointed and during the receiver's management and operation of the receivership property.[26]

- *Leave of Court Needed:* Leave of court is required before the receiver may be sued for claims that arise from the property owner's actions or for claims that do not challenge the receiver's actions since appointment.

21. *See Arkansas Louisiana Gas Co. v. Kroeger*, 303 F.2d 129 (5th Cir.1962), *cert. denied*, 371 U.S. 887, 83 S.Ct. 183, 9 L.Ed.2d 121 (1962).

22. 28 U.S.C.A. § 754.

23. *See Gilchrist v. General Elec. Capital Corp.*, 262 F.3d 295, 302 (4th Cir.2001) (noting that, when appointed, federal equity receivers may sue and be sued as provided by federal law).

24. 28 U.S.C.A. § 754.

25. *See FDIC v. O'Melveny & Myers*, 61 F.3d 17 (9th Cir.1995)(commenting that while party may be denied right or defense due to its misdeeds, the same punishment should not be imposed upon innocent receiver who assumes control pursuant to court order or by operation of law).

26. 28 U.S.C.A. § 959(a). *See Gilchrist v. General Elec. Capital Corp.*, 262 F.3d 295, 301 (4th Cir.2001) (noting that, when appointed, federal equity receivers may sue and be sued as provided by federal law).

- *Subject to Court's General Equity Power:* Suits against receivers remain subject to the court's general equity powers, which the court may exercise to achieve the ends of justice.

Jurisdiction in Actions Involving Receivers

Receivers may only sue or be sued when the district court would enjoy subject matter jurisdiction over the dispute.

- *Diversity Cases:* In diversity jurisdiction cases, the citizenship of the appointed receiver is examined to determine whether complete diversity exists.[27]
- *Federal Question Cases:* The district court's act of appointing a federal receiver probably will suffice to vest that district court with subject matter jurisdiction over actions brought by or against the receiver in that district.[28] Thus, when instituted in the appointing district, suits by the receiver intended to accomplish the objectives of the receivership are deemed ancillary to the appointing court's subject matter jurisdiction.[29] Likewise, suits may be maintained against the receiver in the receiver's appointing district even though no independent basis for subject matter jurisdiction is present.[30]
- *Outside Appointing District:* Suits by or against receivers instituted outside the appointing district will generally require an independent basis for federal subject matter jurisdiction.[31]

Dismissal of Actions Involving Receivers

After the court appoints a receiver in a litigation, the parties may not thereafter dismiss the litigation without first obtaining the court's approval. This requirement protects against a waste of the court's time in unnecessarily establishing a receivership.

Vacating or Terminating the Receivership

The district court may vacate the order appointing the receiver or terminate the receivership when the objectives of the receivership have been obtained or the need for the receiver has abated.

Appeals

The district court's decision to appoint a receiver may be immediately appealed.[32] The court of appeals will review the appointment under the lenient abuse of discretion standard. If the appointment is

27. *See Barber v. Powell,* 135 F.2d 728 (4th Cir.1943), *cert. denied,* 320 U.S. 752, 64 S.Ct. 56, 88 L.Ed. 447 (1943).

28. *See Gay v. Ruff,* 292 U.S. 25, 54 S.Ct. 608, 78 L.Ed. 1099 (1934).

29. *See Pope v. Louisville, N.A. & C. Ry. Co.,* 173 U.S. 573, 19 S.Ct. 500, 43 L.Ed. 814 (1899); *Haile v. Henderson Nat'l Bank,* 657 F.2d 816 (6th Cir.1981), *cert. denied,* 455 U.S. 949, 102 S.Ct. 1450, 71 L.Ed.2d 663 (1982).

30. *See Rouse v. Hornsby,* 161 U.S. 588, 16 S.Ct. 610, 40 L.Ed. 817 (1896); *Robinson v. Michigan Consolidated Gas Co.,* 918 F.2d 579 (6th Cir.1990).

31. *See United States v. Franklin Nat'l Bank,* 512 F.2d 245 (2d Cir.1975).

32. 28 U.S.C.A. § 1292(a)(2).

found to have been improvident, the court of appeals may reverse and tax the costs and expenses incurred in the receivership on the persons who procured the receivership.[33]

Orders refusing to wind up the receivership or that otherwise have the effect of either ousting persons from their property or injuring the property may also be immediately appealed.[34]

All other orders involving receivers may only be appealed after entry of a final order.

ADDITIONAL RESEARCH REFERENCES

Wright & Miller, *Federal Practice and Procedure* §§ 2981–86.

C.J.S. Mechanics Liens § 214; Receivers §§ 1–30 et seq., 52–103 et seq., 105–150 et seq., 163–208 et seq., 227–256 et seq., 283–325 et seq., 365–411 et seq., 418–431 et seq.

West's Key No. Digests, Receivers ⚷1–220.

33. *See Tucker v. Baker,* 214 F.2d 627 (5th Cir.1954).

34. 28 U.S.C.A. § 1292(a)(2).

RULE 67

DEPOSIT IN COURT

In an action in which any part of the relief sought is a judgment for a sum of money or the disposition of a sum of money or the disposition of any other thing capable of delivery, a party, upon notice to every other party, and by leave of court, may deposit with the court all or any part of such sum or thing, whether or not that party claims all or any part of the sum or thing. The party making the deposit shall serve the order permitting deposit on the clerk of the court. Money paid into court under this rule shall be deposited and withdrawn in accordance with the provisions of Title 28, U.S.C., §§ 2041 and 2042; the Act of June 26, 1934, c. 756, § 23, as amended (48 Stat. 1236, 58 Stat. 845), U.S.C., Title 31, § 725v; or any like statute. The fund shall be deposited in an interest-bearing account or invested in an interest-bearing instrument approved by the court.

[Amended effective October 20, 1949; August 1, 1983.]

AUTHORS' COMMENTARY ON RULE 67

PURPOSE AND SCOPE

Rule 67 governs the circumstances in which a court may accept deposits of money and other personal assets pending the outcome of a case.

APPLICATIONS

Common Uses

Parties have used Rule 67 in cases concerning Rule 22 and statutory interpleader[1] and when Rule 62 provides for security as a condition of a stay pending appeal.[2] Rule 67 has no applicability to payments permitted or ordered in criminal cases.[3]

Time for Deposit

A party may move pursuant to Rule 67 at any time during an action.

1. *See, e.g., Southtrust Bank of Florida, N.A. v. Wilson,* 971 F.Supp. 539, 542 (M.D.Fla.1997) (using Rule 67 to accept deposit in interpleader case).

2. *Cf., e.g., Kotsopoulos v. Asturia Shipping Co.,* 467 F.2d 91, 94 (2d Cir.1972) (by paying amount of judgment into court, party can stop running of interest against that party during pendency of appeal).

3. *See, e.g., United States v. Sun Growers of California,* 212 F.3d 603, 606 (D.C.Cir.2000) (Rule 67 applies "only to civil actions.").

Stakeholder's Decision

Rule 67 provides the holder of a disputed asset with an opportunity to seek relief from the burden of safeguarding the asset. However, it provides no authority for another party to demand surrender of the asset.[4]

Leave of Court

Deposits may only be made with leave of court, on motion and with notice to all other parties.[5] If funds are actually deposited with the court, one effect may be to stop the accrual of interest on claims until the case is decided.[6]

Content of Motion

In the motion, the movant should state that opposing parties dispute the ownership of the property or money as well as the particular reasons for making the deposit, such as to avoid responsibility for the property or money.

Method of Deposit

When the court grants leave to make the deposit, the party must serve the order on the clerk of court at the time of making the deposit.

Administration of Deposit

The clerk of court must invest any money paid into the court in an interest-bearing account or in an interest-bearing instrument approved by the court in the name and to the credit of the court.

Withdrawal of Deposit

A person seeking the money deposited in court must make a motion asserting a judgment or any other document establishing that person's judicially defined interest in the deposit. The court may not disburse any deposit until it establishes ownership by court order, unless the parties have stipulated to the ownership of the property under the direction of the court.

The Merits

Rule 67 provides a potential safe haven for an asset until a court determines rights in the asset. However, Rule 67 does not of itself offer a forum for adjudicating such rights. The question of the merits is reserved for some separate proceeding.[7]

4. *See, e.g., Cajun Electric Power Cooperative, Inc. v. Riley Stoker Corp.,* 901 F.2d 441, 444–45 (5th Cir.1990) ("The ... purpose [of Rule 67] is to relieve the depositor of responsibility for the fund in dispute while the parties hash out their differences with respect to it.").

5. *See, e.g., Garrick v. Weaver,* 888 F.2d 687, 694 (10th Cir.1989) (court has discretion to decide whether to accept payment).

6. *See, e.g., Cajun Electric Power Cooperative, Inc. v. Riley Stoker Corp.,* 901 F.2d 441, 445 (5th Cir.1990) (so noting).

7. *See, e.g., LTV Corp. v. Gulf States Steel, Inc. of Alabama,* 969 F.2d 1050, 1063 (D.C.Cir. 1992), *cert. denied,* 506 U.S. 1022, 113 S.Ct. 661, 121 L.Ed.2d 586 (1992) (Rule 67 " 'provides a place of safekeeping for disputed funds pending the resolution of a legal dispute, but it cannot be used as a means of altering the contractual relationships and legal duties of the parties.' ").

Deposit Not Claimed

If the deposit is not claimed by the person entitled to the deposit for five years from the date of adjudication or from the date of deposit when the asset deposited is not in dispute, the asset will be transferred to the U.S. Treasury in the name of and to the credit of the United States.[8]

ADDITIONAL RESEARCH REFERENCES

Wright & Miller, *Federal Practice and Procedure* §§ 2991–3000.

C.J.S. Deposits in Court §§ 1–9.

West's Key No. Digests, Deposits in Court ⚷1–12.

8. 28 U.S.C.A. § 2042.

RULE 68

OFFER OF JUDGMENT

At any time more than 10 days before the trial begins, a party defending against a claim may serve upon the adverse party an offer to allow judgment to be taken against the defending party for the money or property or to the effect specified in the offer, with costs then accrued. If within 10 days after the service of the offer the adverse party serves written notice that the offer is accepted, either party may then file the offer and notice of acceptance together with proof of service thereof and thereupon the clerk shall enter judgment. An offer not accepted shall be deemed withdrawn and evidence thereof is not admissible except in a proceeding to determine costs. If the judgment finally obtained by the offeree is not more favorable than the offer, the offeree must pay the costs incurred after the making of the offer. The fact that an offer is made but not accepted does not preclude a subsequent offer. When the liability of one party to another has been determined by verdict or order or judgment, but the amount or extent of the liability remains to be determined by further proceedings, the party adjudged liable may make an offer of judgment, which shall have the same effect as an offer made before trial if it is served within a reasonable time not less than 10 days prior to the commencement of hearings to determine the amount or extent of liability.

[Amended effective March 19, 1948; July 1, 1966; August 1, 1987.]

AUTHORS' COMMENTARY ON RULE 68

PURPOSE AND SCOPE

Rule 68 governs the circumstances in which a party defending against a claim for money damages or property may seek to resolve the claim by offering to allow judgment against that party for a specified amount of money or property. The Rule also establishes the consequences when a party does not accept an offer of judgment.

APPLICATIONS

Contents of Offer

An offer of judgment must be for a specified dollar amount or specified property.[1] Rule 68 provides that the offer must include an offer to pay costs accrued by the claiming party prior to receipt of the offer of judgment.[2] In practice, however, if the offer provides a specified amount for costs or provides that costs are included, the offer satisfies the requirements of the Rule. The court may add an amount for costs only when the offer does not provide for costs.[3]

Relation to Rule 54

Rule 54(d) provides that the party who prevails in a lawsuit is entitled to costs "as of course" unless some other provision of federal law or the federal rules intervenes.[4] When Rule 68 is applicable, it is a provision of the federal rules that overrides Rule 54(d) and can create a situation where a non-prevailing party may recover costs.[5]

Offering Judgment

The appropriate method of offering judgment is to serve a written offer upon the party whose claim is at issue.[6] Although the Rule does not strictly require it, standard practice is to serve copies of the offer upon all other parties to the case. However, until an offer is accepted by the claiming party, it is inappropriate to file a copy of the offer with the clerk's office.[7]

Ambiguities

In accordance with ordinary rules of contract law, ambiguities in Rule 68 offers are construed against the offeror.[8]

1. *See, e.g., Basha v. Mitsubishi Motor Credit of America, Inc.,* 336 F.3d 451 (5th Cir.2003) (offer that proposed to settle all claims but did not quantify damages could not meet Rule 68 requirements); *Marryshow v. Flynn,* 986 F.2d 689, 691 (4th Cir.1993) (offer must be for "specified amount").

2. *See, e.g., McCain v. Detroit II Auto Finance Center,* 378 F.3d 561 (6th Cir. 2004) (defendant's silence on costs means they are recoverable by plaintiff).

3. *Marek v. Chesny,* 473 U.S. 1, 105 S.Ct. 3012, 87 L.Ed.2d 1 (1985). *But compare, Stewart v. Professional Computer Centers, Inc.,* 148 F.3d 937 (8th Cir.1998) (defendant made offer to cover "any and all counts;" plaintiff had sought attorneys' fees and costs in complaint; held, facts were open to more than one interpretation, and therefore no valid offer and acceptance had occurred; judgment based on Rule 68 must therefore be vacated), *with Webb v. James,* 147 F.3d 617 (7th Cir.1998) (defendants' offer did not mention costs; held, plaintiff entitled to attorneys' fees and costs under applicable law; principles of contract recission should not apply to situations involving Rule 68). *See also Hennessy v. Daniels Law Office,* 270 F.3d 551, 553–54 (8th Cir.2001) (where accepted offer is silent as to attorney's fees and no parol evidence exists to resolve ambiguity, defendant is liable for attorney's fees; using contract principle to construe ambiguity against offeror).

4. Fed.R.Civ.P. 54(d).

5. *See, e.g., Payne v. Milwaukee County,* 288 F.3d 1021, 1027 (7th Cir. 2002).

6. *See, e.g., Driver Music Co. v. Commercial Union Insurance Cos.,* 94 F.3d 1428, 1432 (10th Cir.1996) (Rule 68 contemplates that offer will be in writing); *Magnuson v. Video Yesteryear,* 85 F.3d 1424, 1429 (9th Cir.1996)(absent demonstrated special need or consent of opposing party, service by fax or federal express is ineffective service).

7. *See, e.g., Kason v. Amphenol Corp.,* 132 F.R.D. 197 (N.D.Ill.1990). ("[N]o filing is permitted at the time of tender.").

8. *See, e.g., Arbor Hill Concerned Citizens Neighborhood Association v. County of Albany,* 369 F.3d 91, 95 (2d Cir. 2004) (mere promise that is dependent on will or inclination of promisor is not an offer of a mutually binding contract and therefore cannot be an offer of judgment); *Hennessy v. Daniels Law Office,* 270 F.3d 551, 553–54 (8th Cir.2001) (where accepted offer is silent as to attorney's fees and no parol evidence

Timing of Offer

To be effective under Rule 68, an offer of judgment must be served on the party prosecuting a claim at least 11 days before the beginning of a trial. However, if the trial is a bifurcated proceeding, in which liability only is established in a first hearing, a timely offer of judgment may be served after a determination of liability but not less than 10 days before a damages hearing begins.[9]

Method of Accepting an Offer

The appropriate method for accepting an offer of judgment is by written notice of acceptance to the party who made the offer. It is standard practice to serve copies of such notice on all other parties to the case.

Terms of Acceptance

The offer must be accepted in its entirety, or it is deemed rejected.[10]

Timing of Acceptance

A party has 10 days after receipt of service of the written offer to accept the offer of judgment.[11] If the offer is not accepted within the 10–day period, Rule 68 treats the offer as withdrawn, and it cannot thereafter be accepted. However, it is possible for the party that made the offer to renew the offer, or make a different offer, in which event the 10–day period for acceptance begins to run again.

Offers by Plaintiff

Unless a plaintiff is defending against a counterclaim or a cross-claim, as described in Rules 13 and 14, a plaintiff cannot make an offer of judgment.[12] Only parties defending against claims may use Rule 68

exists to resolve ambiguity, defendant is liable for attorney's fees; using contract principle to construe ambiguity against offeror). *Gavoni v. Dobbs House, Inc.,* 164 F.3d 1071, 1077 (7th Cir.1999) (unapportioned offer of $10,000 to three defendants is ineffective to trigger Rule 68; burden is on defendant to make offer with precision); *Herrington v. County of Sonoma,* 12 F.3d 901 (9th Cir.1993)(additionally, extrinsic evidence is admissible to clarify ambiguities). *See also Nordby v. Anchor Hocking Packaging Co.,* 199 F.3d 390, 392 (7th Cir.1999) (additional reasons for construing ambiguities against offeror are that "plaintiff is being asked to give up his right to a trial" and that ambiguities mean plaintiff "can't make an intelligent choice whether to accept [the offer]–and [unlike ordinary contracts] there are consequences either way").

9. *Delta Air Lines v. August,* 450 U.S. 346, 101 S.Ct. 1146, 67 L.Ed.2d 287 (1981).

10. *See, e.g., Whitcher v. Town of Matthews,* 136 F.R.D. 582, 585 (W.D.N.C.1991). (Plaintiffs cannot both accept offer as to money damages and continue action as to equitable relief). *But cf., Gordon v. Gouline,* 81 F.3d 235 (D.C.Cir. 1996) (acceptance is effective even when conditioned upon approval of bankruptcy court).

11. *See, e.g., Perkins v. U.S. West Communications, Inc.,* 138 F.3d 336 (8th Cir.1998) (defendant filed motion for summary judgment; while motion was pending, defendant made offer of judgment under Rule 68; two days after offer of judgment was made, court granted defendant's summary judgment motion; plaintiff, upon notice of grant of summary judgment, accepted Rule 68 offer; held, acceptance bound defendant, notwithstanding grant of summary judgment; possible different result if defendant had conditioned offer of judgment on court's denial of summary judgment motion).

12. *Delta Air Lines v. August,* 450 U.S. 346, 101 S.Ct. 1146, 67 L.Ed.2d 287 (1981).

to make offers of judgment.[13]

Entering Final Judgment

If the party prosecuting a claim accepts the offer of judgment, Rule 68 permits either party to file the offer and notice of acceptance, along with proof of service, with the clerk of court. Rule 68 then directs that the clerk shall enter judgment consistent with the offer and acceptance.

Equitable Claims

Rule 68 generally applies to offers of specific sums or specific property. Typically the Rule is not used to resolve claims in equity where a party seeks an injunction, but Rule 68 itself does not expressly prohibit such an application.[14]

Revocation

It appears settled that except in exceptional circumstances a Rule 68 offer cannot be revoked during the 10 days provided by the Rule.[15] This conclusion is an exception to the general rule that principles of contract law apply to construe a Rule 68 offer and acceptance.[16]

Consequences of Nonacceptance

The consequences of nonacceptance of an offer under Rule 68 depend on the outcome of the litigation. Once final judgment is entered, if the party that did not accept the offer has won a judgment greater than the amount in the offer of judgment, the refusal of the offer has no consequence whatever.[17] If, however, the nonaccepting party receives a favorable final judgment, but for less than the amount in the offer of judgment—Rule 68 requires the nonaccepting party to pay the offering party's costs incurred after the offer was made.[18] Rule

13. *See, e.g., Garcia v. Wal-Mart Stores, Inc.*, 209 F.3d 1170, 1176 (10th Cir.2000) ("Rule 68 governs only defendants' costs."). *Cf., Amati v. City of Woodstock,* 176 F.3d 952, 958 (7th Cir. 1999), *cert. denied* 528 U.S. 985, 120 S.Ct. 445, 145 L.Ed.2d 362 (1999) ("A plaintiff has no right to demand a Rule 68 offer."). *But cf., S.A. Healy Co. v. Milwaukee Metropolitan Sewerage District,* 60 F.3d 305, 310–12 (7th Cir.1995), *cert. denied,* 516 U.S. 1010, 116 S.Ct. 566, 133 L.Ed.2d 491 (1995)(Rule 68 permits offers only by parties defending claims, but in diversity case, state law permitting plaintiff's offer of settlement may be applied).

14. *See, e.g., Chathas v. Local 134 IBEW,* 233 F.3d 508, 511 (7th Cir.2000), *cert. denied*, 533 U.S. 949, 121 S.Ct. 2590, 150 L.Ed.2d 750 (2001) ("Rule 68 offers are much more common in money cases than in equity cases, but nothing in the rule forbids its use in the latter type of case.").

15. *See, e.g., Richardson v. National Railroad Passenger Corp.*, 49 F.3d 760, 764 (D.C.Cir. 1995) (noting that courts treat offers as irrevocable for 10 days). *Cf., Perkins v. U.S. West Communications, Inc.,* 138 F.3d 336 (8th Cir.1998) (revocation permitted only for "good cause").

16. *See, e.g., Herrington v. County of Sonoma,* 12 F.3d 901, 907 (9th Cir.1993) (Rule 68 is subject to standard rules of contract construction.).

17. *See, e.g., Brown v. Lester E. Cox, Medical Centers,* 286 F.3d 1040, 1047 (8th Cir.2002) (plaintiff refused offer of judgment and then won judgment greater than offer; held, plaintiff's right to attorney's fees established by applicable federal civil rights law was therefore unaffected by refusal).

18. *See, e.g., Payne v. Milwaukee County,* 288 F.3d 1021, 1025 (7th Cir.2002) (civil rights case; prevailing plaintiff who won less than offer of judgment is not entitled to recovery attorney's fees that would otherwise have been available under federal civil rights law); *Haworth v. Nevada,* 56 F.3d 1048 (9th Cir.1995) (plaintiff recovering less than offer of judgment cannot recover costs incurred after offer, and must pay defen-

68 may thus permit a party that has made an offer of judgment, and then loses the case, to recover some costs from the prevailing party. To that extent, Rule 68 provides a possible exception to Rule 54(d), which provides that the prevailing party ordinarily will collect costs from the losing party.

When Defendant Prevails

If an opponent of a claim makes an offer of judgment that is not accepted, and if the offeror then wins the case, Rule 68 has *no* effect. Rule 68 is applied, if at all, only when an offer is not accepted, and then the offeree obtains judgment—but for less than the amount of the offer.[19]

Offer to Multiple Plaintiffs

If a defendant makes an offer of judgment to more than one plaintiff in the same case, the offer must itemize the proposed payment to each plaintiff. If the offer does not identify the proposed allocation of money among the plaintiffs, the defendant will not collect costs even if the plaintiffs' final judgment is for less than the offer.[20]

Joint Offer from Multiple Defendants

When more than one defendant makes an offer of judgment to a plaintiff, the defendants should be careful to make clear the proportion of the offer being made by each defendant. Failure to provide more than an unapportioned joint offer creates a significant possibility that, if one of the defendants is somehow excused but another is found liable, the offeror/defendants will not meet their burden of demonstrating that the offer was more favorable than the judgment the plaintiff later obtained.[21]

dant's post-offer costs). *See also Pouillon v. Little,* 326 F.3d 713, 715 (6th Cir.2003) (Rule 68 offer that was not accepted retains cost-shifting effect after plaintiff got reversal on appeal of original loss and won nominal amount upon remand). *Cf., Berkla v. Corel Corp.*, 302 F.3d 909, 922 (9th Cir.2002) (prevailing party won less than rejected offer, but offer did not satisfy elements of Rule 68; held, prevailing party could not be denied costs that would otherwise have been awarded if no offer had been made); *Ortiz v. Regan,* 980 F.2d 138, 141 (2d Cir.1992) (defendant made settlement offer which did not satisfy Rule 68; held, plaintiff's rejection could not be used to reduce fee award that would otherwise have been made).

19. *Delta Air Lines v. August,* 450 U.S. 346, 352, 101 S.Ct. 1146, 1150, 67 L.Ed.2d 287 (1981). *See also, Payne v. Milwaukee County,* 288 F.3d 1021, 1025 (7th Cir.2002) ("Had [plaintiff] not prevailed in some significant sense, [defendant] would be confined to Rule 54(d), and rule 68 would simply have no application."). *MRO Communications, Inc. v. AT&T Corp.*, 197 F.3d 1276, 1280 (9th Cir.1999), *cert. denied*, 529 U.S. 1124, 120 S.Ct. 1995, 146 L.Ed.2d 820 (2000) (under *Delta Air Lines* "Rule 68 is inapplicable in a case in which the defendant obtains judgment"); *Amati v. City of Woodstock,* 176 F.3d 952, 957 (7th Cir.1999), *cert. denied*, 528 U.S. 985, 120 S.Ct. 445, 145 L.Ed.2d 362 (1999) ("Rule 68 bites only when the plaintiff wins but wins less than the defendant's offer of judgment."); *Louisiana Power & Light Co. v. Kellstrom,* 50 F.3d 319, 333 (5th Cir.1995), *cert. denied,* 516 U.S. 862, 116 S.Ct. 173, 133 L.Ed.2d 113 (1995)("If a plaintiff takes nothing . . . Rule 68 does not apply." (citing *Delta Air Lines*)).

20. *See, e.g., Gavoni v. Dobbs House, Inc.,* 164 F.3d 1071, 1075–77 (7th Cir.1999) (defendant has burden of showing that offer was more favorable than final judgment; defendant also has burden of making offer clear, and plaintiffs are entitled to "a clear baseline from which [they] may evaluate the merits of their case relative to the value of the offer").

21. *See, e.g., Harbor Motor Co. v. Arnell Chevrolet–Geo, Inc.,* 265 F.3d 638, 647–49 (7th

Settled Cases

The literal language of Rule 68 bars its use to award costs in cases that settle without going to judgment. Less certain is the result when the parties settle, and the court enters judgment on the settlement.[22] Attorneys are advised to consult local practice.

Offer of Judgment as Evidence

Rule 68 provides that if an offer of judgment is not accepted, the offer may not be used as evidence at trial. The only use to which a nonaccepted offer of judgment may be put is to establish the consequences, if any, to the nonaccepting party when final judgment is entered in the case.

Attorney Fees

Rule 68 is silent as to whether a nonaccepting party may be required to pay another party's attorney fees as part of the other party's "costs". However, it is settled that Rule 68 does not itself create a right to recover attorney fees.[23] Instead, Rule 68 authorizes recovery of attorney fees from a nonaccepting party—who subsequently received a final judgment less favorable than the offer of judgment—if some other provision of federal law permits recovery of attorney fees.[24] Thus, if a defendant who was sued on a federal civil rights claim made an offer of judgment that was not accepted, and the defendant then lost on the merits (but for less than the offer of judgment), the defendant might be entitled to recover costs that included attorney fees if federal civil rights law included attorney fees within the range of recoverable

Cir.2001) (one defendant won at trial, but other lost; held, plaintiff could not have estimated with any confidence what portion of offer was attributable to losing defendant, so offer was ineffective; acknowledging possibility that on different facts court might be able to calculate the share of an unapportioned offer to ascribe to each of several defendants; "We need not go so far as to conclude ... that Rule 68 always requires an exact delineation of the manner in which damages are to be apportioned among multiple parties."); *Johnston v. Penrod Drilling Co.,* 803 F.2d 867, 870 (5th Cir.1986) (plaintiff settled with one defendant, won judgment against another; held, offer of judgment and judgment actually obtained could not be compared because "settlement may have ... had an effect on the damage award;" noting different result if plaintiff's judgment had been won against both defendants). *Cf., Tai Van Le v. University of Pennsylvania,* 321 F.3d 403, 408 (3d Cir.2003) (distinguishing results in other cases where it was not as clear as in instant case that all payments, whether pursuant to Rule 68 or judgment on merits, would be made by one defendant who had duty of indemnification to other defendant).

22. *Compare, e.g., Equal Employment Opportunity Commission v. Hamilton Standard Division, United Technologies Corp.,* 637 F.Supp. 1155, 1158 (D.Conn.1986)(refusing to apply Rule 68 to case ending in settlement and stipulated dismissal), *with Lang v. Gates,* 36 F.3d 73, 77 (9th Cir.1994), *cert. denied,* 513 U.S. 1017, 115 S.Ct. 579, 130 L.Ed.2d 494 (1994)(approving application of Rule 68 to order enforcing settlement).

23. *See, e.g., McCain v. Detroit II Auto Finance Center,* 378 F.3d 561 (6th Cir. 2004) ("[T]he only way in which Rule 68 directly implicates awards of attorney's fees is in situations where such fees are made an element of 'costs'–whether by statute ... or as a matter of contract."); *Poteete v. Capital Engineering, Inc.,* 185 F.3d 804, 807 (7th Cir.1999) ("Rule 68 does not entitle a defendant to recover his attorneys' fees." (citing extensive authority)).

24. *See, e.g., Wilson v. Nomura Securities International, Inc.,* 361 F.3d 86, 89 (2d Cir. 2004) ("Where the underlying statute defines 'costs' to include attorney's fees ... such fees are 'costs' for purposes of Rule 68.").

costs.[25] Moreover, if the statute normally awarded fees to a prevailing plaintiff (who recovered less than the offer), the court has authority to reduce the attorney fees award to the plaintiff.[26]

Multiple Offers

Rule 68 explicitly permits a party whose previous offer of judgment was not accepted to continue making offers, provided that the offers are served more than 10 days before the beginning of a trial.

ADDITIONAL RESEARCH REFERENCES

Wright & Miller, *Federal Practice and Procedure* §§ 3001–10. Lisnek, *Effective Negotiation and Mediation, A Lawyer's Guide.*

C.J.S. Federal Civil Procedure § 1276.

West's Key No. Digests, Federal Civil Procedure ⚷2725.

25. *Marek v. Chesny,* 473 U.S. 1, 105 S.Ct. 3012, 87 L.Ed.2d 1 (1985). *Harbor Motor Co. v. Arnell Chevrolet–Geo, Inc.,* 265 F.3d 638, 646 (7th Cir.2001) (agreeing with *Crossman,* infra, that in cases controlled by fee provision of copyright law "only prevailing parties can receive attorney's fees pursuant to rule 68;" defendant who lost case for less than offer of judgment therefore cannot recover attorney's fees; acknowledging different result in *Jordan v. Time, Inc.,* infra); *Crossman v. Marcoccio,* 806 F.2d 329, 333–34 (1st Cir.1986), *cert. denied,* 481 U.S. 1029, 107 S.Ct. 1955, 95 L.Ed.2d 527 (1987) (where underlying copyright statute awards attorney's fees only to prevailing party, defendant who lost case–but for amount less than offer of judgment–cannot recover attorney's fee because defendant did not prevail in case). *Cf., Haworth v. Nevada,* 56 F.3d 1048 (9th Cir.1995)(because relevant federal statute did not include attorney fees in costs, attorney fees could not be shifted by Rule 68). *But see Jordan v. Time, Inc.,* 111 F.3d 102, 105 (11th Cir.1997) (requiring plaintiff in copyright case who obtained judgment for less than offer of judgment to pay defendant's costs and fees incurred after offer was made).

26. *See, e.g., Dalal v. Alliant Techsystems, Inc.,* 182 F.3d 757 (10th Cir.1999) (affirming reduced award of attorney fees for legal work done between date of offer of judgment and date of judgment; acknowledging lack of precise formula for making calculation); *Haworth v. Nevada,* 56 F.3d 1048 (9th Cir.1995)(reducing plaintiff's recovery of attorney fees because judgment was for less than the offer of judgment).

RULE 69

EXECUTION

(a) In General. Process to enforce a judgment for the payment of money shall be a writ of execution, unless the court directs otherwise. The procedure on execution, in proceedings supplementary to and in aid of a judgment, and in proceedings on and in aid of execution shall be in accordance with the practice and procedure of the state in which the district court is held, existing at the time the remedy is sought, except that any statute of the United States governs to the extent that it is applicable. In aid of the judgment or execution, the judgment creditor or a successor in interest when that interest appears of record, may obtain discovery from any person, including the judgment debtor, in the manner provided in these rules or in the manner provided by the practice of the state in which the district court is held.

(b) Against Certain Public Officers. When a judgment has been entered against a collector or other officer of revenue under the circumstances stated in Title 28, U.S.C., § 2006, or against an officer of Congress in an action mentioned in the Act of March 3, 1875, c. 130, § 8 (18 Stat. 401), U.S.C., Title 2, § 118, and when the court has given the certificate of probable cause for the officer's act as provided in those statutes, execution shall not issue against the officer or the officer's property but the final judgment shall be satisfied as provided in such statutes.

[Amended effective October 20, 1949; July 1, 1970; August 1, 1987.]

AUTHORS' COMMENTARY ON RULE 69

PURPOSE AND SCOPE

Rule 69 provides a mechanism for executing money judgments entered by a federal court. Rule 69 also provides for the execution of judgments entered against district directors of the Internal Revenue Service and officers of Congress.

RULE 69(a). IN GENERAL

CORE CONCEPT

Rule 69(a) provides for the enforcement of money judgments generally through a writ of execution. If enforcement of a money judgment requires ancillary litigation, state law will usually control such litigation unless a federal statute otherwise provides.[1] However, discovery to enforce a money judgment may be conducted pursuant to either the federal discovery rules or the discovery rules of the forum state.

APPLICATIONS

Scope

Rule 69 only applies to an execution of a money judgment entered by a federal court[2] and has no application to state court judgments or other types of judgments.

Subject Matter Jurisdiction

Efforts to collect judgments under Rule 69 fall within the supplemental jurisdiction of district courts.[3]

Supplementing or Supplanting State Procedure

Although Rule 69(a) directs a district court to use state procedure,[4] it also provides that the court may "direct otherwise." At the same time, federal courts apparently have authority to supplement such procedure with federal practice when necessary.[5] Indeed, if state law is an obstacle to enforcement, federal courts may even be able to disregard

1. *See, e.g., United States v. Little,* 52 F.3d 495 (4th Cir.1995)(holding that Rule 69(a) requires application of state law governing enforcement of judgments). *But cf., Apparel Art International, Inc. v. Amertex Enterprises, Ltd.,* 48 F.3d 576 (1st Cir.1995)(Rule 69 requires application of state procedure on execution; however, Rule 69 does not require use of "general state procedural law," such as state doctrine on res judicata).

2. *See, e.g., United States v. Timilty,* 148 F.3d 1, 4 (1st Cir.1998) (enforcement of judgment imposing criminal fine in favor of United States is also controlled by, *inter alia,* Rule 69(a)).

3. *See, e.g., Kokkonen v. Guardian Life Insurance Co.,* 511 U.S. 375, 379, 114 S.Ct. 1673, 1676, 128 L.Ed.2d 391 (1994) (ancillary jurisdiction permits district court, *inter alia,* to "vindicate its authority, and effectuate its decrees"); *Yang v. City of Chicago,* 137 F.3d 522, 525 (7th Cir.1998), *cert. denied,* 525 U.S. 1140, 119 S.Ct. 1031, 143 L.Ed.2d 40 (1999) (citing to extensive authority). *But cf., Sandlin v. Corporate Interiors, Inc.,* 972 F.2d 1212, 1217 (10th Cir.1992) (if enforcement proceeding is an attempt to collect judgment from nonparty on theory distinct from theory underlying judgment, "an independent basis for federal jurisdiction must exist").

4. *Peacock v. Thomas,* 516 U.S. 349, 359 n. 7, 116 S.Ct. 862, 869 n. 7, 133 L.Ed.2d 817 (1996)("Rule 69(a) ... permits judgment creditors to use any execution method consistent with [state] practice and procedure."). *See, e.g., In re Levander,* 180 F.3d 1114, 1120 (9th Cir.1999) (if state law allows amendment of judgment to add additional judgment debtor, federal court may do so under Rule 69(a)). *Cf., United International Holdings, Inc. v. Wharf Holdings, Ltd.,* 210 F.3d 1207, 1235 (10th Cir.2000), *affirmed,* 532 U.S. 588, 121 S.Ct. 1776, 149 L.Ed.2d 845 (2001) (no requirement to make findings of fact before applying Rule 69 unless federal statute or state rules on execution of judgments provides otherwise).

5. *See, e.g., United States v. Harkins Builders, Inc.,* 45 F.3d 830, 833 (4th Cir.1995)(Rule 69(a) permits use of federal procedure to further "the federal policy of affording judgment creditors the right to a writ of execution to enforce money judgments in federal courts."). *But see, Credit Suisse v. United States District Court for the Central District of California,* 130 F.3d 1342, 1344 (9th Cir.1997) (Rule 69(a) authorizes only a writ of execution; it provides no authority for court to order payment into court); *Aetna Casualty & Surety Co. v. Markarian,* 114 F.3d 346, 349 (1st Cir.1997) ("The 'otherwise' clause is narrowly construed. ...It does not authorize enforcement of a civil money judgment by methods other than a writ of execution, except [in unusual circumstances];" vacating writ that required judgment debtor to surrender passport).

state practice.[6] Finally, Rule 69(a) explicitly provides that any applicable federal statute supplants state law.

Stay of Enforcement

Rule 62(a) directs that a federal money judgment may not be executed upon until 10 days after entry of judgment. The court may further stay execution of the final judgment when an appeal is properly taken or when the court reviews post-trial motions, as provided by Rule 62.[7]

Time for Enforcement

State law will determine the time limitation of the writ of execution and how the time limitation may be extended.

Source of Remedies

A party seeking execution of a money judgment may use any applicable federal statute. Federal remedies for executions in aid of judgments are listed at 28 U.S.C.A. §§ 2001 *et seq.* See also the Advisory Committee Notes to Rule 69. Additionally, a party may use any of the provisional remedies of the forum state at the time the remedy is sought, such as garnishment, arrest, mandamus, contempt, or the appointment of a receiver. When a state remedy is utilized, a party need only comply substantially with the provisions of the state remedy.[8]

Registering a Judgment in District Outside Forum State

A judgment for money or property entered by any district court may be registered in any other district court by filing a certified copy of such judgment in the other district after the judgment has become final.[9] A judgment that has been registered has the same effect as the original judgment and may be enforced as would any other judgment. However, a potentially important result of registering a judgment in federal court that was previously awarded in a different federal court in a different state is that the law of the enforcing state–not the judgment state–will normally control.[10]

6. *See, e.g., Hankins v. Finnel,* 964 F.2d 853, 860 (8th Cir.1992), *cert. denied,* 506 U.S. 1013, 113 S.Ct. 635, 121 L.Ed.2d 566 (1992)("Where state law fails to supply the necessary procedure, or actually stands in the way of enforcement, the district court may take the necessary steps to ensure compliance with its judgment."). *But see, Credit Suisse v. United States District Court for the Central District of California,* 130 F.3d 1342, 1344 (9th Cir.1997) (where state law requires service of a notice of levy on the branch office where defendant holds account–and that branch is not within state–service is ineffective).

7. *Cf., Acevedo–Garcia v. Vera–Monroig,* 296 F.3d 13 (1st Cir.2002) ("Absent a stay on some ground, plaintiffs are free to seek execution of the jdugment pursuant to Fed. R. Civ. P. 69.").

8. *Duchek v. Jacobi,* 646 F.2d 415, 417 (9th Cir.1981); (state law requiring that enforcement proceedings be held in state court may properly be disregarded).

9. 28 U.S.C.A. § 1963.

10. *See, e.g., Condaire, Inc. v. Allied Piping, Inc.,* 286 F.3d 353, 357–58 (6th Cir.2002) (collecting other cases on point). *Cf., Gagan v. Monroe,* 269 F.3d 871, 873 (7th Cir.2001) (judgment in Indiana federal district court; when defendant did not pay, plaintiff sought Rule 69 enforcement in Indiana district court; held, because property to be executed upon was in Arizona, Indiana state law required use of Arizona law to determine whether property was subject to execution).

Writ of Execution

A writ of execution is a writ to enforce a judgment by the seizure and sale of property of the debtor in satisfaction of the judgment.

Enforcement of Judgment

Upon obtaining the writ of execution, the judgment creditor may serve the writ on the U.S. Marshal or state officer, who will then execute, by attachment or otherwise, the property of the judgment debtor in the possession of third parties, and may have the judgment debtor's property sold at an execution sale. The specific procedures for obtaining a writ of execution and executing on the property of the judgment debtor will depend upon the remedy sought and will vary from state to state and district to district.

Discovery

A party seeking to enforce a judgment may use either the federal or the state discovery rules [11] to uncover information concerning assets of the debtor and to aid in execution of the judgment. Rule 69(a) expressly provides that such discovery may be directed toward "any person," including persons not parties to the lawsuit.[12]

Property Subject to Levy

State law will designate the property of the judgment debtor which may be levied upon in satisfaction of the judgment.

Fees and Costs

Fees for writs, subpoenas, keeping attached property, seizing or levying on property, and for the sale of property may be taxed as costs.[13]

RULE 69(b). AGAINST CERTAIN PUBLIC OFFICERS

CORE CONCEPT

If a district director of the Internal Revenue Service—a "collector" of revenue—or an officer of Congress has obtained a certificate of probable cause, a judgment entered against such district director [14] or officer [15] for damages resulting from any of the individual's official acts, or for the recovery of any money exacted by or paid to the individual and subsequently paid into the Treasury may only be executed against the United States Treasury, and not against the individual's property.

11. *See, e.g., Natural Gas Pipeline Co. of America v. Energy Gathering, Inc.,* 2 F.3d 1397, 1403 (5th Cir.1993) *cert. denied,* 510 U.S. 1073, 114 S.Ct. 882, 127 L.Ed.2d 77 (1994)(post-judgment discovery may follow federal pre-trial discovery or applicable state discovery law).

12. *See, e.g., Credit Lyonnais, S.A. v. SGC International, Inc.,* 160 F.3d 428, 430 (8th Cir. 1998) (Under Rule 69(a) and applicable state procedure, "[a] party may depose almost anyone, including corporations, who may provide relevant information.").

13. 28 U.S.C.A. § 1921.

14. 28 U.S.C.A. § 2006 (Internal Revenue Officer).

15. 2 U.S.C.A. § 118 (18 Stat. 401)(Officer of Congress).

APPLICATIONS

District Director

"District director" is defined as any district director of the Internal Revenue Service, former district director, or personal representative of a deceased district director.

Obtaining Certificate of Probable Cause

When a judgment creditor seeks to enforce a judgment, the district director or the officer of Congress may apply to the court for a certificate of probable cause. Upon such application, the court will determine whether the director or officer acted with probable and reasonable cause in performing their proper governmental duties. If the court so finds, the court will issue a certificate of probable cause.

Effect of Certificate

The certificate of probable cause converts the action to one against the United States, extinguishing the personal liability of the individual. Subsequently, the judgment creditor may serve the certificate of probable cause, along with the judgment, on the United States Treasury. The Treasury will pay the amount of the judgment.

ADDITIONAL RESEARCH REFERENCES

Wright & Miller, *Federal Practice and Procedure* §§ 3011–3020.

C.J.S. Federal Civil Procedure §§ 1254–1272 et seq.

West's Key No. Digests, Federal Civil Procedure ⚷2691–2714.

RULE 70

JUDGMENT FOR SPECIFIC ACTS; VESTING TITLE

If a judgment directs a party to execute a conveyance of land or to deliver deeds or other documents or to perform any other specific act and the party fails to comply within the time specified, the court may direct the act to be done at the cost of the disobedient party by some other person appointed by the court and the act when so done has like effect as if done by the party. On application of the party entitled to performance, the clerk shall issue a writ of attachment or sequestration against the property of the disobedient party to compel obedience to the judgment. The court may also in proper cases adjudge the party in contempt. If real or personal property is within the district, the court in lieu of directing a conveyance thereof may enter a judgment divesting the title of any party and vesting it in others and such judgment has the effect of a conveyance executed in due form of law. When any order or judgment is for the delivery of possession, the party in whose favor it is entered is entitled to a writ of execution or assistance upon application to the clerk.

AUTHORS' COMMENTARY ON RULE 70

PURPOSE AND SCOPE

Rule 70 provides that the court may convey property or perform any other specific act, when a party ordered to convey property or perform a specific act fails to comply.

APPLICATIONS

Scope

Rule 70 "applies only to parties who have failed to perform specific acts pursuant to a judgment."[1]

1. *See, e.g., Westlake North Property Owners Association v. City of Thousand Oaks,* 915 F.2d 1301, 1304 (9th Cir.1990) (party's attorneys cannot be sanctioned under Rule 70). *Cf., McAlpin v. Lexington 76 Auto Truck Stop, Inc.,* 229 F.3d 491, 504 (6th Cir.2000), *cert. denied,* 532 U.S. 905, 121 S.Ct. 1229, 149 L.Ed.2d 139 (2001) (where judgment contained only one term of twenty-page settlement and otherwise dismissed case, court had no authority under Rule 70 to enforce terms of settlement not incorporated in judgment). *But see Peterson v. Highland Music, Inc.,* 140 F.3d 1313, 1323 (9th Cir.1998), *cert. denied,* 525 U.S. 983, 119 S.Ct. 446, 142 L.Ed.2d 401 (1998) (non-parties who aid parties in defy-

Property Within the District

If a party has failed to obey a court order pertaining to real or personal property physically located within the district in which the court sits, the court may order title transferred directly from the disobedient party to the prevailing party.

Property Outside the District

If the real or personal property is not physically located within the district in which the court sits, the court must appoint a person to convey the property. The act performed by the appointed party has the full effect as it if it were executed by the disobedient party.

Timing

Rule 70 applies to the enforcement of court orders after the entry of judgment and after the time for performing the ordered action has elapsed.[2]

Content of Motion

In a written motion, the movant should allege with specificity the disobedient party's noncompliance, as well as the relief sought to remedy noncompliance.

Alternative Enforcement Remedies

The court may enforce a judgment by requiring a party to convey property or perform a specific act through the following remedies.

(1) *Writ of Attachment or Sequestration:* Upon proper motion to the clerk of court, a prevailing party may obtain a writ of attachment or sequestration authorizing seizure of the disobedient party's property or money until that party complies with a judgment.

(2) *Contempt of Court:* In addition to other remedies under Rule 70, the court retains the authority to enforce a judgment directing the performance of a specific act by finding the disobedient party in contempt of court.[3]

(3) *Writs of Assistance:* Upon a proper motion to the clerk of court, a party may obtain a writ of assistance to enforce the delivery of property to the person entitled to the property under a judgment against a party who refuses to surrender possession.

Costs Against Disobedient Party

A court may tax against the disobedient party the costs of transferring the property or performing the specific act.

ing judgment are also subject to Rule 70; upholding contempt citation).

2. *See, e.g., Barmat, Inc. v. United States*, 159 F.R.D. 578, 582 (N.D.Ga.1994)(Rule 70 "is operative only after entry of judgment").

3. *See, e.g., McMahan & Co. v. Po Folks, Inc.*, 206 F.3d 627, 634 (6th Cir.2000) ("[U]nder Fed.R.Civ.P. 70, a party may be held in civil contempt for violating a garnishment order.").

ADDITIONAL RESEARCH REFERENCES

Wright & Miller, *Federal Practice and Procedure* §§ 3021–3030.

C.J.S. Assistance, Writ of §§ 3, 4; Contempt § 12; Federal Civil Procedure §§ 1254–1260 et seq.

West's Key No. Digests, Assistance, Writ of ⚷2; Contempt ⚷20; Federal Civil Procedure ⚷2691, 2695.

RULE 71

PROCESS IN BEHALF OF AND AGAINST PERSONS NOT PARTIES

When an order is made in favor of a person who is not a party to the action, that person may enforce obedience to the order by the same process as if a party; and, when obedience to an order may be lawfully enforced against a person who is not a party, that person is liable to the same process for enforcing obedience to the order as if a party.

[Amended effective August 1, 1987.]

AUTHORS' COMMENTARY ON RULE 71

PURPOSE AND SCOPE

Rule 71 provides for the enforcement of a court order by any person (including a non-party) in whose favor an order has been entered. Additionally, Rule 71 provides for the enforcement of a court order against a non-party when such enforcement is otherwise lawful.

APPLICATIONS

In Favor of a Non-party

A court order may be enforced by a non-party when that person shares an identity of interest with a prevailing party or is an intended beneficiary of the court order with the right to enforce it.[1] Thus, an assignee of a party who prevailed in a dispute concerning the title of property is entitled under Rule 71 to enforce a judgment in the same manner as the assignor.[2]

1. *See, e.g., Brennan v. Nassau County,* 352 F.3d 60, 65 (2d Cir. 2003) (suggesting that motion to compel may be suitable means of employing Rule 71; but also noting that non-parties must be able to meet requirements of standing); *Beckett v. Air Line Pilots Association*, 995 F.2d 280, 287–88 (D.C.Cir.1993)(Rule 71 permits intended beneficiaries of consent decree to sue to enforce decree; incidental third-party beneficiaries do not have such standing). *See also, Washington Hospital v. White,* 889 F.2d 1294, 1299 (3d Cir.1989)(third-party beneficiary has standing under Rule 71 to enforce court-ordered stipulation of dismissal); *SEC v. Prudential Securities, Inc.*, 136 F.3d 153, 159 (D.C.Cir.1998) ("The test is not . . . only whether the contracting parties intended to confer a benefit directly on the third parties, but also whether the parties intended the third party to be able to sue to protect that benefit.").

2. *See, e.g., Peterson v. Highland Music, Inc.,* 140 F.3d 1313 (9th Cir.1998), *cert. denied*, 525 U.S. 983, 119 S.Ct. 446, 142 L.Ed.2d 401 (1998) (citing rule 71 as authority to hold non-parties in contempt).

Against a Non-party

A court order may be enforced against a non-party when that person's interests are so closely related to a losing party's interests that enforcement against that non-party is not unfair.[3] When enforcing a judgment against non-parties, Rule 71 is explicitly restricted to circumstances where enforcement does not violate due process and is otherwise lawful.[4]

ADDITIONAL RESEARCH REFERENCES

Wright & Miller, *Federal Practice and Procedure* §§ 3031–3040.

C.J.S. Federal Civil Procedure § 1107.

West's Key No. Digests, Federal Civil Procedure ⚷2394.

3. *See, e.g., Irwin v. Mascott,* 370 F.3d 924, 931–32 (9th Cir. 2004) (Rule 71 permits use of contempt power of court to enforce order against non-party who has notice of injunction).

4. *See, e.g., LiButti v. United States,* 178 F.3d 114 (2d Cir.1999) (enforcement of a judgment against a person who is a successor in interest to a party requires that the court first obtain personal jurisdiction over the successor in interest).

IX. SPECIAL PROCEEDINGS

RULE 71A

CONDEMNATION OF PROPERTY

(a) Applicability of Other Rules. The Rules of Civil Procedure for the United States District Courts govern the procedure for the condemnation of real and personal property under the power of eminent domain, except as otherwise provided in this rule.

(b) Joinder of Properties. The plaintiff may join in the same action one or more separate pieces of property, whether in the same or different ownership and whether or not sought for the same use.

(c) Complaint.

(1) *Caption.* The complaint shall contain a caption as provided in Rule 10(a), except that the plaintiff shall name as defendants the property, designated generally by kind, quantity, and location, and at least one of the owners of some part of or interest in the property.

(2) *Contents.* The complaint shall contain a short and plain statement of the authority for the taking, the use for which the property is to be taken, a description of the property sufficient for its identification, the interests to be acquired, and as to each separate piece of property a designation of the defendants who have been joined as owners thereof or of some interest therein. Upon the commencement of the action, the plaintiff need join as defendants only the persons having or claiming an interest in the property whose names are then known, but prior to any hearing involving the compensation to be paid for a piece of property, the plaintiff shall add as defendants all persons having or claiming an interest in that property whose names can be ascertained by a reasonably diligent search of the records, considering the character and value of the property involved and the interests to be acquired, and also those whose names have otherwise been learned. All others may be made defendants under the designation "Unknown Owners." Process shall be served as provided in subdivision (d) of this rule upon all defendants, whether named as defendants at the time of the commencement of the action or subsequently added, and a defendant may answer as provided in subdivision (e) of this rule. The court meanwhile may order such distribution of a deposit as the facts warrant.

(3) *Filing.* In addition to filing the complaint with the court, the plaintiff shall furnish to the clerk at least one copy thereof for the use of the defendants and additional copies at the request of the clerk or of a defendant.

(d) Process.

(1) *Notice; Delivery.* Upon the filing of the complaint the plaintiff shall forthwith deliver to the clerk joint or several notices directed to the defendants named or designated in the complaint. Additional notices directed to defendants subsequently added shall be so delivered. The delivery of the notice and its service have the same effect as the delivery and service of the summons under Rule 4.

(2) *Same; Form.* Each notice shall state the court, the title of the action, the name of the defendant to whom it is directed, that the action is to condemn property, a description of the defendant's property sufficient for its identification, the interest to be taken, the authority for the taking, the uses for which the property is to be taken, that the defendant may serve upon the plaintiff's attorney an answer within 20 days after service of the notice, and that the failure so to serve an answer constitutes a consent to the taking and to the authority of the court to proceed to hear the action and to fix the compensation. The notice shall conclude with the name of the plaintiff's attorney and an address within the district in which action is brought where the attorney may be served. The notice need contain a description of no other property than that to be taken from the defendants to whom it is directed.

(3) *Service of Notice.*

(A) Personal Service. Personal service of the notice (but without copies of the complaint) shall be made in accordance with Rule 4 upon a defendant whose residence is known and who resides within the United States or a territory subject to the administrative or judicial jurisdiction of the United States.

(B) Service by Publication. Upon the filing of a certificate of the plaintiff's attorney stating that the attorney believes a defendant cannot be personally served, because after diligent inquiry within the state in which the complaint is filed the defendant's place of residence cannot be ascertained by the plaintiff or, if ascertained, that it is beyond the territorial limits of personal service as provided in this rule, service of the notice shall be made on this defendant by publication in a newspaper published in the county where the property is located, or if there is no such newspaper, then in a newspaper having a general circulation where the property is located, once a week for not less than three successive weeks. Prior to the last publication, a copy of the notice shall also be mailed to a defendant who cannot be personally served as provided in this rule but whose place of residence is then known. Unknown owners may be served by publication in like manner by a notice addressed to "Unknown Owners."

Service by publication is complete upon the date of the last publication. Proof of publication and mailing shall be made by certificate of the plaintiff's attorney, to which shall be attached a printed copy of the published notice with the name and dates of the newspaper marked thereon.

(4) *Return; Amendment.* Proof of service of the notice shall be made and amendment of the notice or proof of its service allowed in the manner provided for the return and amendment of the summons under Rule 4.

(e) Appearance or Answer. If a defendant has no objection or defense to the taking of the defendant's property, the defendant may serve a notice of appearance designating the property in which the defendant claims to be interested. Thereafter, the defendant shall receive notice of all proceedings affecting it. If a defendant has any objection or defense to the taking of the property, the defendant shall serve an answer within 20 days after the service of notice upon the defendant. The answer shall identify the property in which the defendant claims to have an interest, state the nature and extent of the interest claimed, and state all the defendant's objections and defenses to the taking of the property. A defendant waives all defenses and objections not so presented, but at the trial of the issue of just compensation, whether or not the defendant has previously appeared or answered, the defendant may present evidence as to the amount of the compensation to be paid for the property, and the defendant may share in the distribution of the award. No other pleading or motion asserting any additional defense or objection shall be allowed.

(f) Amendment of Pleadings. Without leave of court, the plaintiff may amend the complaint at any time before the trial of the issue of compensation and as many times as desired, but no amendment shall be made which will result in a dismissal forbidden by subdivision (i) of this rule. The plaintiff need not serve a copy of an amendment, but shall serve notice of the filing, as provided in Rule 5(b), upon any party affected thereby who has appeared and, in the manner provided in subdivision (d) of this rule, upon any party affected thereby who has not appeared. The plaintiff shall furnish to the clerk of the court for the use of the defendants at least one copy of each amendment and shall furnish additional copies on the request of the clerk or of a defendant. Within the time allowed by subdivision (e) of this rule a defendant may serve an answer to the amended pleading, in the form and manner and with the same effect as there provided.

(g) Substitution of Parties. If a defendant dies or becomes incompetent or transfers an interest after the defendant's joinder, the court may order substitution of the proper party upon motion and notice of hearing. If the motion and notice of hearing are to be served upon a person not already a party, service shall be made as provided in subdivision (d)(3) of this rule.

(h) Trial. If the action involves the exercise of the power of eminent domain under the law of the United States, any tribunal specially constituted by an Act of Congress governing the case for the trial of the issue of just compensation shall be the tribunal for the determination of that issue; but if there is no such specially constituted tribunal any party may have a trial by jury of the issue of just compensation by filing a demand therefor within the time allowed for answer or within such further time as the court may fix, unless the court in its discretion orders that, because of the character, location, or quantity of the property to be condemned, or for other reasons in the interest of justice, the issue of compensation shall be determined by a commission of three persons appointed by it.

In the event that a commission is appointed the court may direct that not more than two additional persons serve as alternate commissioners to hear the case and replace commissioners who, prior to the time when a decision is filed, are found by the court to be unable or disqualified to perform their duties. An alternate who does not replace a regular commissioner shall be discharged after the commission renders its final decision. Before appointing the members of the commission and alternates the court shall advise the parties of the identity and qualifications of each prospective commissioner and alternate and may permit the parties to examine each such designee. The parties shall not be permitted or required by the court to suggest nominees. Each party shall have the right to object for valid cause to the appointment of any person as a commissioner or alternate. If a commission is appointed it shall have the authority of a master provided in Rule 53(c) and proceedings before it shall be governed by the provisions of Rule 53(d). Its action and report shall be determined by a majority and its findings and report shall have the effect, and be dealt with by the court in accordance with the practice, prescribed in Rule 53(e), (f), and (g). Trial of all issues shall otherwise be by the court.

(i) Dismissal of Action.

(1) *As of Right.* If no hearing has begun to determine the compensation to be paid for a piece of property and the plaintiff has not acquired the title or a lesser interest in or taken possession, the plaintiff may dismiss the action as to that property, without an order of the court, by filing a notice of dismissal setting forth a brief description of the property as to which the action is dismissed.

(2) *By Stipulation.* Before the entry of any judgment vesting the plaintiff with title or a lesser interest in or possession of property, the action may be dismissed in whole or in part, without an order of the court, as to any property by filing a stipulation of dismissal by the plaintiff and the defendant affected thereby; and, if the parties so stipulate, the court may vacate any judgment that has been entered.

(3) *By Order of the Court.* At any time before compensation for a piece of property has been determined and paid and after motion and hearing, the court may dismiss the action as to that property, except that it shall not dismiss the action as to any part of the property of which the plaintiff has taken possession or in which the plaintiff has taken title or a lesser interest, but shall award just compensation for the possession, title or lesser interest so taken. The court at any time may drop a defendant unnecessarily or improperly joined.

(4) *Effect.* Except as otherwise provided in the notice, or stipulation of dismissal, or order of the court, any dismissal is without prejudice.

(j) Deposit and Its Distribution. The plaintiff shall deposit with the court any money required by law as a condition to the exercise of the power of eminent domain; and, although not so required, may make a deposit when permitted by statute. In such cases the court and attorneys shall expedite the proceedings for the distribution of the money so deposited and for the ascertainment and payment of just compensation. If the compensation finally awarded to any defendant exceeds the amount which has been paid to that defendant on distribution of the deposit, the court shall enter judgment against the plaintiff and in favor of that defendant for the deficiency. If the compensation finally awarded to any defendant is less than the amount which has been paid to that defendant, the court shall enter judgment against that defendant and in favor of the plaintiff for the overpayment.

(k) Condemnation Under a State's Power of Eminent Domain. The practice as herein prescribed governs in actions involving the exercise of the power of eminent domain under the law of a state, provided that if the state law makes provision for trial of any issue by jury, or for trial of the issue of compensation by jury or commission or both, that provision shall be followed.

(*l*) Costs. Costs are not subject to Rule 54(d).

[Adopted April 30, 1951, effective August 1, 1951; amended January 21, 1963, effective July 1, 1963; April 29, 1985, effective August 1, 1985; March 2, 1987, effective August 1, 1987; April 25, 1988, effective August 1, 1988; amended by Pub.L. 100–690, Title VII, § 7050, November 18, 1988, 102 Stat. 4401 (although amendment by Pub.L. 100–690 could not be executed due to prior amendment by Court order which made the same change effective August 1, 1988); amended April 22, 1993, effective December 1, 1993; March 27, 2003, effective December 1, 2003.]

AUTHORS' COMMENTARY ON RULE 71A

PURPOSE AND SCOPE

Rule 71A provides a uniform set of rules for the condemnation of real and personal property under the federal and state powers of eminent domain.

NOTE: Rule 71A(d)(3) and (d)(4) were significantly amended as of December 1, 1991.

RULE 71A(a). APPLICABILITY OF OTHER RULES

CORE CONCEPT

Rule 71A(a) directs that, unless specifically otherwise provided in Rule 71A, the General Civil Rules govern the procedure for the condemnation of real and personal property under the power of eminent domain.

APPLICATIONS

Condemnation of Personal Property

Rule 71A applies to the condemnation of personal property as an appurtenance to real property or as the sole object of the proceeding.[1]

1. *See,* 42 U.S.C.A. §§ 1805, 1811, 1813 (Atomic Energy Act); 50 U.S.C.A. § 79 (nitrates); 50 U.S.C.A. §§ 161–166 (helium gas).

Inverse Condemnation Proceedings

Rule 71A does not apply to inverse condemnation proceedings. An inverse condemnation "is a cause of action by which a landowner recovers just compensation from the government for a taking of his or her property when condemnation proceedings have not been instituted."[2]

Supplementary Condemnation Statutes

Rule 71A does not affect supplementary condemnation statutes, such as the Declaration of Taking Act[3], which permit the Federal Government to take private property for public use under the power of eminent domain.

Uniformity of Procedure

Rule 71A makes the procedure for condemnation of property under all statutes uniform.

Choice of Law

Federal condemnation is strictly governed by federal law and precedent. State law only defines the nature of the real or personal property interest, such as the meaning of property, defining what is taken, or determining the ownership of land.

Condemnation Under State Law

A district court may entertain condemnation proceedings under state law, as provided by Rule 71A(k).

Jurisdiction and Venue

The district courts have original jurisdiction over proceedings to condemn real property for the use of the United States, its agencies, or departments.[4] Venue will be in the district court of the district in which the real property is located or, if located in different districts in the same state, in any such districts.[5]

Rule 71A and the Other Rules

In cases where Rule 71A does not provide a procedure concerning litigation, the court will apply other applicable Rules, such as the discovery Rules.[6]

RULE 71A(b). JOINDER OF PROPERTIES

CORE CONCEPT

Rule 71A(b) permits condemnation of separate properties, including properties belonging to different owners, or properties for different

2. *KLK, Inc. v. United States Department of the Interior,* 35 F.3d 454, 455 n. 1 (9th Cir. 1994)(Rule 71A applicable only to "traditional" condemnation, not inverse condemnation).

3. 40 U.S.C.A. §§ 248a–258e.

4. 28 U.S.C.A. § 1358.

5. 28 U.S.C.A. § 1403.

6. *See also East Tennessee Natural Gas Co. v. Sage,* 361 F.3d 808, 828–29 (4th Cir. 2004) (approving use of Rule 65 to obtain preliminary injunction enabling early occupation of land).

public uses in the same court action.[7] Only in exceptional circumstances is the court required to conduct separate trials. To eliminate jury confusion over the relative value of properties, the court may separate the evidence concerning the damages sustained by each owner.

RULE 71A(c). COMPLAINT

CORE CONCEPT

The requirements for a complaint under Rule 71A(c) are different from those in an ordinary civil action. In the complaint's caption, Rule 71A(c) requires the plaintiff to name as defendants both the property and at least one of the owners. Rule 71A(c) does not require the plaintiff to serve a summons and a complaint on the defendants; rather the clerk of court arranges for notice to all defendants as provided in Rule 71A(d). However, prior to a hearing on compensation, the plaintiff must join all defendants who can be ascertained from a reasonably diligent search of the records.

APPLICATIONS

Caption

The complaint's caption must include the name of the court, the title of the action, the docket number, and the name of the type of pleading being presented.[8] The caption must name as defendants both the property and at least one of the owners. The plaintiff will name the property as the defendant by stating the kind, quantity, and location of the property.

Contents of Complaint

The complaint must contain a short and plain statement of:

(1) the authority for the taking;

(2) the use for which the property is to be taken;[9]

(3) a description of the property sufficient for identification;[10]

(4) the interests to be acquired; and

(5) for each separate piece of property, the owners who have been joined as defendants or who have some interest.

Filing of Complaint and Notice

The plaintiff must file the complaint with the clerk and provide the clerk with at least one copy for the defendants. Upon the request of

7. *See, e.g., McLaughlin v. Mississippi Power Co.*, 376 F.3d 344 (5th Cir. 2004) (also noting that joinder of properties under Rule 71A is "much broader" than joinder of parties under Rules 19 and 20 and joinder of claims under Rule 18).

8. *See,* Official Form 29.

9. *See, e.g., City of Arlington v. Golddust Twins Realty Corp.*, 41 F.3d 960, 964 (5th Cir. 1994)(Rule 71A(c)(2) requires condemning authority to state purpose for which condemnation is sought).

10. *See, e.g., Southern Natural Gas Co. v. Land, Cullman County,* 197 F.3d 1368, 1375 (11th Cir.1999) (a legal description and plat map showing location of pipeline and related easements "easily" satisfies Rule 71A(c)(2)).

the clerk or the defendants, the plaintiff must furnish additional copies. This practice differs from the normal practice under Rule 4, which requires the plaintiff to serve a summons and a copy of the complaint on the defendants.

Joining Parties at Commencement

At the commencement of an action, the condemnor must join as defendants all persons or entities of title record having or claiming an interest in the property whose names are then known. All other persons unascertained or unknown shall be made parties as defendants by description if their names are unknown.

Joining of Interested Parties Prior to Hearing

Prior to a hearing involving compensation, the condemnor must add as defendants all persons who have an interest whose identities can be ascertained by a reasonably diligent search of the records,[11] and also those whose names have been learned. "Reasonably diligent" search means the type of search a title searcher would undertake, but the extent of the search required will depend upon the character and value of the property involved and the interests to be acquired. Property owners joined after the commencement of the action must be served with notice by the clerk and allowed to answer.

Failure to Join a Party

There are no indispensable parties in a condemnation action. Therefore, the failure to join a party will not defeat the condemnor's title to the land because a condemnation action is an action *in rem.*[12] If the condemnor fails to join a party, the omitted party may have the right to sue for compensation in the Claims Court after the condemnation is completed.[13]

RULE 71A(d). PROCESS

CORE CONCEPT

Rule 71A(d) directs that the clerk will deliver a notice of the complaint to a marshal or specially appointed person who will make personal service on the defendants.

11. *See, e.g., Cadorette v. United States,* 988 F.2d 215, 224 (1st Cir.1993)(Rule 71A(c) requires government to make an affirmative search for "lost" heirs).

12. *Fulcher v. United States,* 632 F.2d 278, 282 (4th Cir.1980); ("Persons not identified . . . can be impleaded as unknown.").

13. *See, e.g., United States v. 194.08 Acres of Land,* 135 F.3d 1025, 1035 n. 8 (5th Cir.1998) (failure to join party or give required notice does not invalidate taking; such failure only preserves right of unjoined interested party to challenge taking). *Cadorette v. United States,* 988 F.2d 215, 225 (1st Cir.1993)(person not joined may seek compensation in Claims Court through the device of a takings claim).

APPLICATIONS

Content of Notice

Each notice must state: [14]

(1) the court;

(2) the title of the action;

(3) the name of the defendant to whom it is directed;

(4) the nature of the action (condemning property);

(5) a description of the property sufficient for its identification;

(6) the interest to be taken;

(7) the authority for the taking;

(8) the uses for which the property is being taken;

(9) the time for answering the complaint (the defendant may serve an answer upon the plaintiff's attorney within twenty days after the service of the notice); and

(10) the penalty for failing to answer (a consent to the taking, permitting the court to proceed to hear the action and fix compensation).

Preparation of Notice

The plaintiff may prepare joint or separate notices. However, one notice must be delivered to each named defendant and need contain a description of only that property taken from the particular defendant to whom it is directed.

Filing of Notice

The plaintiff's attorney will prepare a notice and deliver it to the clerk with the complaint. Subsequently, the clerk will file and enter the complaint in the record and deliver a notice of the complaint (but not a copy of the complaint itself) to the marshal or specially-appointed person for service.

Persons Requiring Notice

At the commencement of the case, the clerk need only provide notice to persons whose names are in the complaint. Property owners joined after the filing of the complaint must be served with notice and allowed to answer.

Service

Personal service of the notice (but without copies of the complaint) shall be made in accordance with Rule 4 upon each defendant who resides within the United States or its territories or insular possessions and whose residence is known.

14. *See,* Official Form 28.

Service By Publication

(1) *Persons Served by Publication:* A plaintiff may make service by publication on three types of defendants:[15]

(a) owners who do not reside in the United States, its territories, or insular possessions, and who, therefore, are beyond the territorial limits of personal service;

(b) owners within the state in which the complaint is filed whose place of residence is unknown after a diligent search of the records; and

(c) unknown owners.

(2) *Publication:* The plaintiff must publish the notice in a newspaper in the county where the land is located. When no newspaper exists in the county where the land is located, the plaintiff must publish the notice in a newspaper having a circulation in the area where the land is located. The plaintiff must publish the notice once a week for at least three successive weeks.

(3) *Proof of Publication:* When a plaintiff wishes to make proof of service by publication, the plaintiff's attorney must file with the court a certificate stating that the defendant cannot be served personally because the defendant's residence is beyond the personal service limits or after diligent inquiry defendant's residence is unknown. The plaintiff's attorney must attach to the certificate a printed copy of the published notice marked with the name of the newspaper and the dates of publication.

(4) *Defendants Who Cannot Be Served But Residence Known:* A defendant who cannot be personally served but whose place of residence is known must be mailed a copy of the notice prior to the date of the last publication. Service is complete on the date of the last publication.

RULE 71A(e). APPEARANCE OR ANSWER

CORE CONCEPT

A defendant may respond to a condemnation complaint in two ways. If the defendant intends to either contest the taking or make objections to the complaint, the defendant must file an answer. Alternatively, if the defendant has no defenses or objections to the taking, the defendant simply serves a notice of appearance designating the property in which the defendant has an interest. However, regardless of whether the defendant files an answer or an appearance, a defendant may present evidence at the hearing on compensation and share in the award.[16]

15. *See, e.g., United States v. 499.472 Acres of Land More or Less, in Brazoria County, Texas,* 701 F.2d 545, 551 (5th Cir.1983)(publication service permissible only in the explicit circumstances described in Rule 71A(d)).

16. *See, e.g., Bank One Texas, N.A. v. United States,* 157 F.3d 397 (5th Cir.1998), *cert. denied,* 526 U.S. 1115, 119 S.Ct. 1761, 143 L.Ed.2d 792 (1999).

APPLICATIONS

Answer

The answer is the only document in which defenses or objections may be asserted.[17] Unlike most answers to complaints in ordinary civil actions, the defendant must make specific allegations. In the answer the defendant must identify the property, the defendant's interest in the property, and the defenses to the taking. After filing an answer, the defendant is entitled to receive notice of all of the proceedings affecting the defendant.

Counterclaims and Crossclaims

An answer may not contain a counterclaim or crossclaim.[18] A counterclaim must be brought in a separate action in the district court or the Court of Claims.

Timing of Answer

Within 20 days of service of the notice, the defendant must answer the complaint. This response period may be enlarged by motion, as provided by Rule 6(b).

Appearance

When the defendant has no defenses or objections to the taking or to the complaint, the defendant may serve a notice of appearance. The notice of appearance should designate the property in which the defendant claims an interest. When a defendant has filed an appearance, the defendant is entitled to receive notice of all of the proceedings affecting the defendant.

RULE 71A(f). AMENDMENT OF THE PLEADINGS

CORE CONCEPT

Before the trial on the issue of just compensation, a plaintiff may amend the complaint multiple times without leave of court. However, except as provided by Rule 71A(i), the plaintiff may not amend the complaint to remove the names of defendants or claims. Within 20 days of the notice of each amended complaint, the defendant is entitled to file one amended answer as of right.

APPLICATIONS

Procedure for Amending Complaint

The plaintiff may amend the complaint by filing with the clerk the amended pleading and by serving notice of the amended pleading on

17. *See, e.g., Washington Metropolitan Area Transit Authority v. Precision Small Engines,* 227 F.3d 224, 228 n. 2 (4th Cir.2000) (except for amount of compensation, defenses or objections not raised in answer are waived; "Simply put, no other pleading besides the answer is contemplated.").

18. *See, e.g., United States v. Certain Land Situated in the City of Detroit,* 361 F.3d 305, 308 (6th Cir. 2004) ("A district court lacks jurisdiction to hear counterclaims against the United States in condemnation cases.").

each defendant. The plaintiff need not serve a copy of the amended pleading itself on defendants, a practice that differs from normal civil actions. Instead, if a defendant or the clerk requests additional copies of the amended complaint, the plaintiff must provide the clerk with additional copies.

Service to Persons Who Have Not Entered an Appearance

The plaintiff should serve notice of an amended complaint on persons who have not entered an appearance.[19]

RULE 71A(g). SUBSTITUTION OF PARTIES

CORE CONCEPT

Upon proper motion and notice of hearing, the court may order the substitution of parties when a defendant dies or becomes incompetent, or transfers an interest after the defendant's joinder. If a new party is substituted, the plaintiff must serve a copy of the motion and notice of hearing on the new party, as provided by Rule 71A(d). Rule 25, governing substitution of parties in most civil actions, does not apply to condemnation actions.

RULE 71A(h). TRIAL

CORE CONCEPT

All issues other than the issue of compensation will be decided by the court. The issue of compensation will be decided by either a special tribunal, a commission, a jury, or the court, in condemnation actions instituted by the federal or state government under powers of eminent domain. Federal law may require the issue of compensation to be decided by a tribunal specially constituted by Congress. When any party demands a trial by jury, the court will decide whether to conduct a jury trial or to appoint a commission to decide the issue of compensation.

NOTE: If a commission is appointed to decide the issue of compensation, the commission must issue a report. Within 10 days after service of the commission report, parties must make and serve on the other parties and the court their objections to the report.

APPLICATIONS

Trial by Jury

When any party demands a trial by jury, the court may conduct a jury trial or may appoint a commission to decide the issue of compensation. However, there is no constitutional right to a trial by jury in condemnation cases,[20] and the jury in such cases may decide only the issue of compensation.

19. *See,* Rule 71A(d).

20. *United States v. Reynolds,* 397 U.S. 14, 18, 90 S.Ct. 803, 806, 25 L.Ed.2d 12 (1970).

(1) *Time for Demand:* Within the time allowed for the answer to the condemnation complaint (20 days of service of the notice of the complaint, unless an enlargement of time has extended the period) or a further time fixed by the court, any party may demand a trial by jury.

(2) *Procedure for Trial by Jury:* The trial of a condemnation action is similar to any other civil proceeding involving a trial by jury. However, the judge will determine all issues other than the amount of compensation.[21]

Trial by Commission

(1) *Appointment of Commission:* When a party demands a trial by jury, the court has discretion to appoint a commission to decide the issue of compensation rather than conducting a trial by jury.[22] Although the court is not required to make findings of fact to support its determination to appoint a commission, for purposes of appellate review the court will often state in writing its reasons for appointing a commission.

(a) *Conditions for Reference to Commission:* Courts have appointed commissions for such reasons as: local preference or habit, the preference of the Justice Department, the distance of the property from the courthouse, the complexity of the issues, the character of the land, the nature of the interest or the number of tracts taken, the need for numerous jury trials, the desirability of uniform awards, or to prevent discrimination.

(2) *Number of Commissioners:* A commission is generally composed of three persons. The court may appoint two alternate commissioners to sit at the hearing with the other commissioners.

(3) *Appointment of Commissioners:* The parties may suggest nominees as potential commissioners. Usually, the court will appoint commissioners and alternate commissioners. Often, the court will appoint a lawyer or ex-judge as chair of the commission and one real estate person as a member. After appointing the commissioners, the court will advise the parties of the identity and qualifications of each prospective commissioner and alternate commissioner. The parties may exam-

("[I]t has long been settled that there is no constitutional right to a jury in eminent domain cases."). *See also Southern Natural Gas Co. v. Land, Cullman County,* 197 F.3d 1368, 1373 (11th Cir.1999) (condemnation action pursuant to Natural Gas Act, 15 U.S.C. § 717 *et seq.*; notwithstanding provision in Natural Gas Act providing that condemnation procedure shall conform as closely as possible to state law, Rule 71A(h) permits district court to appoint commission in place of jury; held, Rule 71A(h) supercedes applicable provisions of Natural Gas Act).

21. *See, e.g., United States v. 4.0 Acres of Land,* 175 F.3d 1133 (9th Cir.1999), *cert. denied* 528 U.S. 1047, 120 S.Ct. 582, 145 L.Ed.2d 484 (1999) (jury's sole function is to determine amount of compensation).

22. *But cf., United States v. 320.0 Acres of Land,* 605 F.2d 762, 828 (5th Cir.1979) (acknowledging some contrary authority but holding that "a commission is to be used only for exceptional cases" such as large tracts of land held by many small landowners or tracts too distant for jury to view); *Questar Southern Trails Pipeline Co. v. 4.26 Acres of Land,* 194 F.Supp.2d 1192, 1193 (D.N.M.2002) (in 10th Circuit "jury trial is . . . still the standard").

ine the commissioners and may, for valid cause, object to the appointment of any commissioner.

(4) *Reformation and Revocation of Commission:* When the court believes the judgment of the commission has been affected by bias, the court may reform the commission by replacing some or all of the commissioners.[23] When justice so requires, such as instances of undue delay, the court may vacate the reference to the commission.

(5) *Procedure for Trial by Commission:*

(a) *Powers:* The commission will only try the issue of compensation; all other issues will be decided by the court. The commission has the same powers as a master in a non-jury trial. Proceedings before the commission are governed by Rule 53(c). The commission may regulate its proceedings, require the production of all documents, rule on the admissibility of evidence, call and examine witnesses, and permit the witnesses to be examined by the parties. These powers will be regulated indirectly by the court through its instructions to the commission in the order of reference.

(b) *Instructions:* In its order of reference, the trial judge will instruct the commissioners as to such issues as: the qualifications of expert witnesses, the weight to be given to other opinions of evidence, competent evidence of value, the best evidence of value, the manner of the hearing and the method of conducting it, the right to view the property, the limited purpose of viewing, and the kind of evidence which is inadmissible and the manner of ruling on the admissibility of evidence.

(c) *Admission of Evidence:* Although the court will control the kind of evidence which is admissible, the commission will apply the Federal Rules of Evidence when ruling on the admissibility of the evidence.

(1) *View of Property:* When necessary or conducive to a proper determination of compensation and when not inconvenient or the cause of undue delay or expense, the commission may view the property.

(6) *Findings and Report of Commission:* A majority of the commissioners will decide the amount of compensation to award, and the commission will submit a report. The findings and the report of the commission will follow the provisions of Rule 53(e)(2). In its report, the commission must clearly show a factual basis for its finding, but need not make detailed findings. A suitable commission report will state what evidence and what measure of damages the commission accepted and why the commission reached its award.[24]

23. *But cf., City of Stilwell, Oklahoma v. Ozarks Rural Electric Cooperative Corp.,* 166 F.3d 1064, 1069 (10th Cir.1999) (commissioners need not have "complete and absolute impartiality;" no error in appointment of either customer of cooperative's competitor (owned by city) or owner-members of cooperative, especially when virtually every resident in area used utility services of one or another of the parties).

24. *See, United States v. Merz,* 376 U.S. 192, 198, 84 S.Ct. 639, 643, 11 L.Ed.2d 629 (1964) (conclusory findings are unacceptable; commissioners should explain reasoning, what evidence was used, etc.).

(7) *Objection to Commission Report:* Within 10 days after service of the commission's report, a party must make and file with the court and serve on all other parties objections to the report.[25] The party objecting to the report retains the burden of demonstrating that the report is erroneous.

(8) *Trial Court Review of Commission Report:* The trial court must adopt the report of the commission unless it finds the report to be clearly erroneous.[26] A trial court may find the report clearly erroneous when there was a substantial error in the proceedings, when the report is unsupported by substantial evidence, against the clear weight of the evidence,[27] or involves a misapplication of law. Courts have also found commission reports clearly erroneous when the award was grossly inadequate. When the trial court finds the report clearly erroneous, the court may examine the testimony and make its own judgment or it may recommit the matter to the commission with instructions.[28]

(9) *Commissioners' Compensation:* Commissioners will be compensated in reasonable relation to the services rendered (i.e., the bar association's minimum fee schedule). The commissioners' compensation will be charged to the condemnor and may be included in the damage award, not taxed as costs against the award.

(10) *Appellate Court Review of Commission or Court Decision:* An appellate court reviews the judgment of a trial court under a clearly erroneous standard.[29]

RULE 71A(i). DISMISSAL OF ACTION

CORE CONCEPT

The procedures for dismissal depend on the posture of the proceedings. Prior to a hearing or declaration of taking, the action may be dismissed as of right. Where the government files a declaration of taking, acquires an interest, acquires title, or takes possession of the property before the entry of judgment, neither the plaintiff nor the court may dismiss an action, except by stipulation of the parties.[30] After the entry of judgment the court has discretion to vacate the judgment upon the stipulation of the parties.

25. *See,* Rule 53(e)(2).

26. *United States v. Merz,* 376 U.S. 192, 198, 84 S.Ct. 639, 643, 11 L.Ed.2d 629 (1964)(adopting "clearly erroneous" standard).

27. *Georgia Power Co. v. 138.30 Acres of Land,* 596 F.2d 644 (5th Cir.1979), *rehearing ordered,* 602 F.2d 1243 (5th Cir.1979), *vacated on other grounds,* 617 F.2d 1112 (5th Cir.1980), *cert. denied,* 450 U.S. 936, 101 S.Ct. 1403, 67 L.Ed.2d 372 (1981)(commissioners behaved inconsistently without adequate explanation).

28. *See, e.g., Southern Natural Gas Co. v. Land, Cullman County,* 197 F.3d 1368, 1375 (11th Cir.1999) (district court has discretion to recommit matter to commission or to hear additional evidence itself).

29. *See, e.g., United States v. 179.26 Acres of Land in Douglas County, Kansas,* 644 F.2d 367, 373 (10th Cir.1981)(applying clearly erroneous standard).

30. *Kirby Forest Industries, Inc. v. United States,* 467 U.S. 1, 12 n. 18, 104 S.Ct. 2187, 2195 n. 18, 81 L.Ed.2d 1(1984) (Rule 71A(i)(3) bars dismissal by court if government has acquired interest in property—court must first hold compensation hearing).

APPLICATIONS

Dismissal

(1) *As of Right:* Before a hearing on compensation has begun and before the plaintiff has filed a declaration of taking as provided by statute, acquired title, acquired an interest, or taken possession of the property, the plaintiff may dismiss the action by filing a notice of dismissal stating a brief description of the property.

(2) *By Stipulation:* Before the entry of a judgment vesting plaintiff with title, an interest, or possession of the property, the parties may stipulate to a dismissal in whole or in part without an order of the court. After judgment, the parties may stipulate to a dismissal and the court may vacate the judgment and revest title in the defendant.

(3) *By Court Order:* When the hearing on compensation has begun, but the plaintiff has not filed a declaration of taking, acquired title, acquired an interest, or taken possession, the court will decide whether to grant a voluntary dismissal.[31] However, when the hearing has begun and the plaintiff has filed a declaration of taking, acquired title, acquired an interest, or taken possession, the court must award just compensation for the possession, title, or the interest taken, unless stipulated otherwise by the parties.[32]

Dismissal of Improperly and Unnecessarily Joined Parties

At any time, upon a motion or *sua sponte,* the court may dismiss a defendant who has no interest but has been unnecessarily or improperly joined.

Dismissal Without Prejudice

Unless stated in the order or the stipulation, a dismissal of a condemnation proceeding is without prejudice.

RULE 71A(j). DEPOSIT AND ITS DISTRIBUTION

CORE CONCEPT

Rule 71A(j) describes the procedure for the deposit of money with the court when required or permitted by statute. State substantive law will determine the amount to be deposited in state eminent domain actions, while federal substantive law will determine the amount to be deposited in federal eminent domain actions.

APPLICATIONS

The Declaration of Taking Act

The Declaration of Taking Act supplements the procedure under Rule 71A(j), relating to the deposit and distribution in eminent domain

31. *See, e.g., United States v. 4,970 Acres of Land,* 130 F.3d 712, 714–15 (5th Cir.1997) (if jury has returned verdict but government has not yet engaged in specified acts, government may buy property by tendering the amount of the verdict or may move to dismiss condemnation action; if government sought dismissal of action, court then would have discretion to dismiss; "Condemnation is a means by which the sovereign may find out what any piece of property will cost.").

32. *See, e.g., Id. at* 715 (so noting).

cases. Under the Act, upon the filing of a declaration of taking and a deposit of the estimated compensation with the court, title immediately vests in the federal government.

(1) *Time for Filing:* A declaration of taking may be brought at the commencement of the condemnation action and at any time before a judgment.

(2) *Certification:* The chief of the government department or bureau acquiring the land will certify that the land is within the value prescribed by Congress.

(3) *Surrender of Possession; Encumbrances:* Upon the filing of a declaration of taking, the court will fix the time and the terms upon which the parties in possession will surrender possession of the property to the plaintiff. The court may also make orders concerning encumbrances, liens, rents, taxes, assessments, insurance, etc.

(4) *Amount of Award:* The judgment will include 6 percent interest from the date of the taking to the date of the award. However, no interest will be ordered on money paid into the court. When the court or the jury awards an amount greater than the deposit, the court will enter judgment against the plaintiff and in favor of the defendant for the difference plus 6 percent interest.[33] When the court or the jury awards an amount less than the deposit, the court will enter judgment against the defendant and in favor of the plaintiff for the amount of overpayment. When the deposit exceeds the award the plaintiff will obtain the excess deposit from the clerk.[34]

(5) *Deposit and Distribution:* At the time of the taking and the deposit into the court, the court may order distribution of the deposit to the known defendants.[35]

(6) *Appellate Review:* A transfer of title is not a final appealable judgment until a final judgment on compensation has been entered.[36]

RULE 71A(k). CONDEMNATION UNDER A STATE'S POWER OF EMINENT DOMAIN

CORE CONCEPT

Although most federal court eminent domain cases will involve the federal power of eminent domain, a state may institute an eminent

33. *United States v. 9.20 Acres of Land, More or Less, Situate in Polk County, State of Iowa,* 638 F.2d 1123 (8th Cir.1981) (deposit insufficient); *See also,* 40 U.S.C.A. § 258a.

34. *United States v. Featherston,* 325 F.2d 539, 541 (10th Cir.1963)(if deposit exceeds award, government can get excess from the clerk or sue landowner if landowner received excess).

35. *See,* Rule 71A(c)(2). *See also,* 40 U.S.C.A. § 258a. *Cf., United States v. 8.0 Acres of Land,* 197 F.3d 24, 29 n. 1 (1st Cir.1999) (when United States has taken title to condemned land, it has no standing to participate in proceedings relating to distribution of compensation award once amount of award has been determined; however, when other parties initiate appeal, United States may properly seek to have district court judgment affirmed and to offer government's advice on distribution; citing Rule 71A(j) provision dealing with expediting distribution of money deposited).

36. *Catlin v. United States,* 324 U.S. 229, 65 S.Ct. 631, 89 L.Ed. 911 (1945)(appeal must await final judgment).

domain action in a federal district court when diversity of citizenship exists between the plaintiff (condemnor) and the defendant (landowner) and the amount in controversy exceeds $75,000, exclusive of interest and costs. Similarly, a defendant (landowner) may remove a state eminent domain action to federal district court when the condemnor initiates the suit and the defendant (landowner) is not a citizen of the state in which the action is brought, and the amount in controversy exceeds $75,000, exclusive of interest and costs.[37] These state eminent domain actions must be brought in the federal district court for the district in which the land is situated.

APPLICATIONS

Choice of Law

The federal court will apply the procedure described in Rule 71A. The court will apply state substantive condemnation law.

Trial by Jury

In state eminent domain cases, the court will follow state law provisions for trial by jury or a commission.[38]

Collateral Attack of State Court Judgment

A party may not bring a federal court action challenging a state court judgment in a state eminent domain action.

RULE 71A(*l*). COSTS

CORE CONCEPT

Rule 71A(*l*) governs the assessment of costs in condemnation proceedings decided pursuant to Rule 71A. The normal expenses of the proceeding will be charged to the condemnor. Expenses incurred in the distribution of the award are charged to the condemnee.

APPLICATIONS

Costs Paid by Condemnor

The condemnor shall pay the normal expenses such as the bills for publication of notice, commissioners' fees, the cost of transporting commissioners and jurors for a view, fees for attorneys representing defendants who have failed to answer, and witness' fees. These expenses shall be charged to the government and, when required, be included as damages in the award but will not be taxed against the award, except to the extent permitted by law.[39] In addition, the condemnor shall pay for the expenses of a commissioner who records the deed and executes the conveyance.

37. 28 U.S.C.A. § 1441(a), (b).

38. *West, Inc. v. United States,* 374 F.2d 218, 224 n. 3 (5th Cir.1967)(Rule 71A(k) applies when state has condemned property and diversity jurisdiction causes case to be in federal court).

39. *See,* Advisory Committee Note to Rule 71A(*l*).

Expenses of Distribution

Expenses incurred in the distribution of the award, such as ascertaining the identity of the distributees and deciding between conflicting claimants, are chargeable against the award.[40]

ADDITIONAL RESEARCH REFERENCES

Wright & Miller, *Federal Practice and Procedure* §§ 3041–3056.

C.J.S. Eminent Domain §§ 209–251 et seq., 267–315 et seq., 319–366 et seq., 373–386 et seq.

West's Key No. Digests, Eminent Domain ⚷166–265(5).

40. *See,* Advisory Committee Note to Rule 71A(*l*).

RULE 72

MAGISTRATE JUDGES; PRETRIAL ORDERS

(a) Nondispositive Matters. A magistrate judge to whom a pretrial matter not dispositive of a claim or defense of a party is referred to hear and determine shall promptly conduct such proceedings as are required and when appropriate enter into the record a written order setting forth the disposition of the matter. Within 10 days after being served with a copy of the magistrate judge's order, a party may serve and file objections to the order; a party may not thereafter assign as error a defect in the magistrate judge's order to which objection was not timely made. The district judge to whom the case is assigned shall consider such objections and shall modify or set aside any portion of the magistrate judge's order found to be clearly erroneous or contrary to law.

(b) Dispositive Motions and Prisoner Petitions. A magistrate judge assigned without consent of the parties to hear a pretrial matter dispositive of a claim or defense of a party or a prisoner petition challenging the conditions of confinement shall promptly conduct such proceedings as are required. A record shall be made of all evidentiary proceedings before the magistrate judge, and a record may be made of such other proceedings as the magistrate judge deems necessary. The magistrate judge shall enter into the record a recommendation for disposition of the matter, including proposed findings of fact when appropriate. The clerk shall forthwith mail copies to all parties.

A party objecting to the recommended disposition of the matter shall promptly arrange for the transcription of the record, or portions of it as all parties may agree upon or the magistrate judge deems sufficient, unless the district judge otherwise directs. Within 10 days after being served with a copy of the recommended disposition, a party may serve and file specific, written objections to the proposed findings and recommendations. A party may respond to another party's objections within 10 days after being served with a copy thereof. The district judge to whom the case is assigned shall make a de novo determination upon the record, or after additional evidence, of any portion of the magistrate judge's disposition to which specific written objection has been made in accordance with this rule. The district judge may accept, reject, or modify the recommended decision, receive further evidence, or recommit the matter to the magistrate judge with instructions.

[Former Rule 72 abrogated December 4, 1967, effective July 1, 1968; new Rule 72 adopted April 28, 1983, effective August 1, 1983; amended April 30, 1991, effective December 1, 1991; April 22, 1993, effective December 1, 1993.]

AUTHORS' COMMENTARY ON RULE 72

PURPOSE AND SCOPE

Rule 72 provides that a district judge may refer pretrial, trial, and post-trial matters to a magistrate judge without the consent of the parties under the court's additional duties jurisdiction, as provided by 28 U.S.C.A. § 636(b)(3). A district judge may also refer prisoner petitions challenging conditions of confinement for consideration by a magistrate judge.

NOTE: Rule 72(a) was significantly amended as of December 31, 1991.

RULE 72(a). NONDISPOSITIVE MATTERS

CORE CONCEPT

A district judge may refer, without the consent of the parties, pretrial matters nondispositive of a claim or a defense to a magistrate judge. Such decisions of the magistrate judge may be appealed to the district court for review on a standard of clear error or contrary to law.

NOTE: A party must file written objections to the magistrate judge's order within 10 days after being served with a copy of the order. Failure to make a timely objection may constitute a waiver of appellate review of the magistrate judge's order.[1]

APPLICATIONS

Nondispositive Pretrial Matters

A nondispositive pretrial matter is a matter which is collateral and nonessential to a full disposition of the petitioner's claim and the defendant's liability, such as: (1) motions relating to discovery matters; (2) a motion for sanctions for noncompliance with a discovery order;[2]

1. *See, e.g., Phinney v. Wentworth Douglas Hospital,* 199 F.3d 1, 4 (1st Cir.1999) (Rule 72(a) objection to magistrate judge's order must contain all claims of error; claims of error not raised before district judge cannot be raised in circuit court); *Simpson v. Lear Astronics Corp.,* 77 F.3d 1170, 1174 (9th Cir.1996) ("[A] party who fails to file timely objections to a magistrate judge's nondispositive order . . . forfeits its right to appellate review."); *International Surplus Lines Insurance Co. v. Wyoming Coal Refining Systems, Inc.*, 52 F.3d 901, 904 (10th Cir. 1995)(failure to make timely objection constitutes waiver). *But see Kruger v. Apfel,* 214 F.3d 784, 786–87 (7th Cir.2000) (10 day time limit is not jurisdictional; where appeal is only a few days late and opposing party experienced no unfair prejudice, district court should consider objections to magistrate judge's recommendation de novo; moreover, separate from party's objection, district court should examine recommendation of magistrate judge for clear error).

2. *See, e.g., Hutchinson v. Pfeil,* 105 F.3d 562, 566 (10th Cir.1997), *cert. denied,* 522 U.S. 914, 118 S.Ct. 298, 139 L.Ed.2d 230 (1997) (magistrate judge may impose sanctions in discovery as nondispositive matter).

(3) motions to add claims; and (4) a motion to join a counterclaim. It is unclear whether a magistrate judge may impose sanctions under Rule 72(a) for violations of Rule 11 (governing sanctions for inappropriate pleadings, motions and other papers) or may only recommend such sanctions to the district court pursuant to Rule 72(b).[3]

Dispositive Sanction Not Imposed

If a motion seeks a sanction that would be dispositive, but the magistrate judge denies the motion, the matter is not considered dispositive. Instead, the standard of review is provided by Rule 72(a) (clearly erroneous or contrary to law), rather than Rule 72(b)(de novo review upon the record).[4]

Magistrate Judge's Authority

When appropriate, and to aid further proceedings, Rule 72 authorizes a magistrate judge to enter a written order on the record that constitutes a final adjudication regarding nondispositive pretrial matters, subject to review on appeal by the district court.

Magistrate Judge's Ruling

A magistrate judge's ruling on a pretrial matter on referral from a district judge will follow the Rules. When a magistrate judge decides a nondispositive pretrial matter, the order becomes effective when made, and requires no further action by the district judge.

Review of Nondispositive Pretrial Matter

The district judge who assigned the case retains ultimate authority over the case and shall modify or set aside any portion of the magistrate judge's order found to be clearly erroneous or contrary to law. Even if no objections are presented, the district judge may rehear or reconsider the matter *sua sponte*.

Review by Court of Appeals

A party may not appeal directly to the Court of Appeals from a magistrate judge's nondispositive pretrial order.[5]

RULE 72(b). DISPOSITIVE MOTIONS AND PRISONER PETITIONS

CORE CONCEPT

3. *See, e.g., Alpern v. Lieb,* 38 F.3d 933, 935 (7th Cir.1994) (citing conflicting cases; holding that Rule 72(a) does not confer such authority on magistrate judges). *But cf., Hutchinson v. Pfeil,* 208 F.3d 1180, 1184 n. 7 (10th Cir.2000) (refusing to decide issue).

4. *See, e.g., Gomez v. Martin Marietta Corp.,* 50 F.3d 1511 (10th Cir.1995)(decision not to impose dispositive sanction alters standard of review).

5. *See, e.g., United States v. Gonzalez–Ramirez,* 350 F.3d 731, 733 (8th Cir. 2003) (no right to appeal to circuit court unless district court has already reviewed magistrate judge's order after objection to order); *Simpson v. Lear Astronics Corp.,* 77 F.3d 1170, 1173–74 (9th Cir. 1996) (if party does not object to district court, and if district court does not therefore hear the issue, finding of magistrate judge under Rule 72(a) cannot be appealed to circuit court).

When a dispositive matter is referred to a magistrate judge, the magistrate judge will conduct evidentiary hearings and submit a recommendation, and when appropriate, submit proposed findings of fact to the district judge. If a party makes a timely written objection to the proposed findings and recommendation of the magistrate judge, the district judge must make a *de novo* review of the record.[6]

NOTE: A party must file specific, written objections to the magistrate judge's findings and recommendation within 10 days after being served with a copy of the recommended disposition. Failure to make timely objection constitutes a waiver of appellate review of the magistrate judge's findings and recommendation.[7]

APPLICATIONS

Matters Considered Dispositive

The following matters are deemed dispositive by statute:[8] (1) a motion for injunctive relief; (2) a motion for judgment on the pleadings; (3) a motion for summary judgment; (4) a motion to dismiss or permit maintenance of a class action; (5) a motion to dismiss for failure to state a claim upon which relief may be granted; or (6) a motion for involuntary dismissal.[9] The following matters may also be considered dispositive: (1) an application to proceed *in forma pauperis*;[10] (2) a motion to amend a pleading;[11] (3) a motion for attorney's fees;[12] and (4) an order remanding a removed case to state court.[13] It is unclear whether sanctions for violations of Rule 11 (governing pleadings, motions and other papers) is within a magistrate judge's authority under Rule 72(a), or whether the magistrate judge may only make a recommendation to the district judge under Rule 72(b).[14]

6. 28 U.S.C.A. § 636(b)(1)(C). *See also, Rajaratnam v. Moyer*, 47 F.3d 922, 925 n. 8 (7th Cir.1995)(de novo review does not require new trial; only a fresh look at issues to which objection has been raised). *But cf., Taylor v. Farrier*, 910 F.2d 518, 521 (8th Cir.1990)("in conducting [de novo] review, the district court must, at a minimum, listen to a tape recording or read a transcript of the evidentiary hearing.").

7. *See International Surplus Lines Insurance Co. v. Wyoming Coal Refining Systems, Inc.*, 52 F.3d 901, 904 (10th Cir.1995)(failure to make timely objection constitutes waiver).

8. 28 U.S.C.A. § 636(b)(1)(A).

9. *See, e.g., Bennett v. General Caster Service of N. Gordon Co.*, 976 F.2d 995, 997 (6th Cir. 1992)(identifying similar list and noting that list is "nonexhaustive").

10. *See, e.g., Woods v. Dahlberg*, 894 F.2d 187, 187 (6th Cir.1990) (per curiam)(motion to proceed in forma pauperis is dispositive, and therefore magistrate judge may only make recommendation).

11. *Lundy v. Adamar of New Jersey, Inc.*, 34 F.3d 1173, 1183 (3d Cir.1994)(motion to amend is dispositive of statute of limitations defense).

12. *See, e.g., Massey v. City of Ferndale,* 7 F.3d 506 (6th Cir.1993)(motion for attorney's fees is dispositive); *but see Merritt v. International Brotherhood of Boilermakers,* 649 F.2d 1013, 1016–18 (5th Cir.1981)(post-judgment award of attorney's fees as sanction for misconduct in pre-trial discovery is non-dispositive; held, pre-trial discovery issues are inherently non-dispositive matters).

13. *Vogel v. United States Office Products Co.*, 258 F.3d 509, 515 (6th Cir.2001) (also collecting other examples of dispositive motions); *First Union Mortgage Corp. v. Smith,* 229 F.3d 992, 996 (10th Cir.2000).

14. *See, e.g., Alpern v. Lieb,* 38 F.3d 933, 935 (7th Cir.1994) (citing conflicting cases; holding that Rule 72(a) does not confer such authority on magistrate judges). *But cf., Hutchinson v. Pfeil,* 208 F.3d 1180, 1184 n. 7 (10th Cir.2000) (refusing to decide issue).

Dispositive Sanction Not Imposed

If a motion seeks a sanction that would be dispositive, but the magistrate judge denies the motion, the matter is not considered dispositive. Instead, the standard of review is provided by Rule 72(a) (clearly erroneous or contrary to law), rather than Rule 72(b)(de novo review upon the record).[15]

Habeas Corpus

Rule 72(b) does not extend to habeas corpus petitions. Habeas corpus petitions are governed by specific statutes.[16]

Procedure for Dispositive Pretrial Matters

A magistrate judge has substantial discretion to conduct hearings on dispositive matters. The magistrate judge shall make a record of all evidentiary proceedings, but has discretion whether to keep a record of non-evidentiary proceedings. The magistrate judge shall submit a recommendation for disposition of the matter to the district judge who assigned the case to the magistrate judge. When appropriate, the magistrate judge shall submit proposed findings of fact with the recommendation. The clerk of the court is required to mail copies of the magistrate judge's recommendation and findings of fact to all parties.

Obligation to Order Transcript

A party objecting to the magistrate judge's recommended disposition should promptly arrange for the transcription of the record or portions of the record agreed upon by the parties or as directed by the magistrate judge, unless directed otherwise by the district judge.

Response to Objections

A party may respond to another party's objections within 10 days after service of a copy of the objections.[17]

De Novo Review of Dispositive Motions by District Judge

Upon proper objection, the district judge who assigned the motion to the magistrate judge shall make a *de novo* determination. After making a *de novo* review of the ruling, a district judge may accept, reject, or modify the recommended disposition or recommit the matter to the magistrate judge with instructions.

A district judge, under the *de novo* review standard, is not required to conduct a new hearing, but is required to make a new examination of the issues upon which specific, written objections were based, either on the record, through the recall of witnesses, or by receiving additional testimony.[18]

15. *See, e.g., Gomez v. Martin Marietta Corp.,* 50 F.3d 1511 (10th Cir.1995)(decision not to impose dispositive sanction alters standard of review).

16. 28 U.S.C.A. §§ 2254, 2255.

17. *See, e.g., United States v. Mora,* 135 F.3d 1351, 1357 (10th Cir.1998).

18. *See, e.g., Taylor v. Farrier,* 910 F.2d 518, 520 (8th Cir.1990) (de novo review of record requires study of transcript or tape recording).

Failure to Object and Untimely Objections

The courts are split on whether and to what extent the district judge is obligated to review a magistrate judge's recommendation absent a timely objection.[19]

Waiver of Right to Appeal

A party who fails to file a timely objection to the district judge regarding the magistrate judge's findings or recommendations waives the party's right to appeal the issue to the court of appeals.[20]

ADDITIONAL RESEARCH REFERENCES

Wright & Miller, *Federal Practice and Procedure* §§ 3076.1–3076.9.

C.J.S. United States Commissioners § 3.

West's Key No. Digests, United States Magistrates ⚷15–31.

But cf., Garcia v. City of Albuquerque, 232 F.3d 760, 766 (10th Cir.2000) (Rule 72(b) does not require district court to make specific findings, only a de novo review of record); *Carpet Group International v. Oriental Rug Importers Association, Inc.,* 227 F.3d 62, 72 (3d Cir.2000) (district judge has discretion to consider additional evidence not presented to magistrate judge).

19. *See, e.g., Conetta v. National Hair Care Centers, Inc.,* 236 F.3d 67, 73 (1st Cir.2001) (even in absence of timely objection to final action by magistrate judge, Rule 72(b) requires district court to "adapt, reject, or modify the recommendation before there is any final judgment"); *Federal Deposit Insurance Corp. v. Hillcrest Associates,* 66 F.3d 566, 569 (2d Cir.1995) (failure to make timely objection acts as waiver; very narrow exception to that general rule in pro se cases); *Douglass v. United Services Automobile Association,* 79 F.3d 1415 (5th Cir.1996) (court need only determine absence of clear error); *Park Motor Mart, Inc. v. Ford Motor Co.,* 616 F.2d 603 (1st Cir.1980) (no obligation); *Chamblee v. Schweiker,* 518 F.Supp. 519, 520 (N.D.Ga.1981) (The court is under no obligation to give de novo review but must review.).

20. *See, e.g., Phillips v. General Motors Corp.,* 307 F.3d 1206, 1210 (9th Cir.2002) (failure to file timely appeal is waiver of right to appeal to appellate court).

RULE 73

MAGISTRATE JUDGES; TRIAL BY CONSENT AND APPEAL

(a) Powers; Procedure. When specially designated to exercise such jurisdiction by local rule or order of the district court and when all parties consent thereto, a magistrate judge may exercise the authority provided by Title 28, U.S.C. § 636(c) and may conduct any or all proceedings, including a jury or nonjury trial, in a civil case. A record of the proceedings shall be made in accordance with the requirements of Title 28, U.S.C. § 636(c)(5).

(b) Consent. When a magistrate judge has been designated to exercise civil trial jurisdiction, the clerk shall give written notice to the parties of their opportunity to consent to the exercise by a magistrate judge of civil jurisdiction over the case, as authorized by Title 28, U.S.C. § 636(c). If, within the period specified by local rule, the parties agree to a magistrate judge's exercise of such authority, they shall execute and file a joint form of consent or separate forms of consent setting forth such election.

A district judge, magistrate judge, or other court official may again advise the parties of the availability of the magistrate judge, but, in so doing, shall also advise the parties that they are free to withhold consent without adverse substantive consequences. A district judge or magistrate judge shall not be informed of a party's response to the clerk's notification, unless all parties have consented to the referral of the matter to a magistrate judge.

The district judge, for good cause shown on the judge's own initiative, or under extraordinary circumstances shown by a party, may vacate a reference of a civil matter to a magistrate judge under this subdivision.

(c) Appeal. In accordance with Title 28, U.S.C. § 636(c)(3), appeal from a judgment entered upon direction of a magistrate judge in proceedings under this rule will lie to the court of appeals as it would from a judgment of the district court.

(d) Optional Appeal Route. [Abrogated].

[Former Rule 73 abrogated December 4, 1967, effective July 1, 1968; new Rule 73 adopted April 28, 1983, effective August 1, 1983; amended March 2, 1987, effective August 1, 1987; April 22, 1993, effective December 1, 1993, April 11, 1997, effective December 1, 1997.]

AUTHORS' COMMENTARY ON RULE 73

PURPOSE AND SCOPE

Rule 73 provides that, upon consent of the parties, a district judge may refer cases to a magistrate judge for trial or final disposition. Rule 73 also provides for the district judge to vacate the reference to the magistrate judge's ruling.

RULE 73(a). POWERS; PROCEDURE

CORE CONCEPT

By local rule or by order of court, and with the consent of the parties, a magistrate judge may be designated with case-dispositive or final judgment authority to conduct any or all of the proceedings in a jury or non-jury case. In such cases, the magistrate judge has all of the powers of a district judge, except the power of contempt. A local rule providing that magistrate judges may hear case-dispositive proceedings may not restrict the types of cases a magistrate judge may hear.

APPLICATIONS

Preserving the Record

The magistrate judge must decide by what means the record should be preserved, such as verbatim by a court reporter, by electronic sound, or by shorthand. When deciding the means of preservation of the record, the magistrate judge may consider the complexity of the case, the likelihood of appeal, the costs of the record, and time constraints.

Contempt

Magistrate judges may not hold contempt hearings. Instead, the magistrate judge will certify the facts of the contempt to the district judge and serve an order to show cause why a contempt citation should not be issued upon the alleged disobedient party. Subsequently, the district judge in a summary proceeding will hear the evidence of the contemptuous act and may punish the disobedient party.[1]

RULE 73(b). CONSENT

CORE CONCEPT

The clerk of court handles the procedures for obtaining the parties' consent to trial before a magistrate judge, isolating the district judge from the consenting process. All parties must make a free and voluntary consent to having a magistrate judge preside over their trial.[2]

APPLICATIONS

Consent Procedure

To prevent the district judge from exercising any influence over the decision by the parties and to prevent the district judge from knowing

1. 28 U.S.C.A. § 636(e).

2. 28 U.S.C.A. § 636(c)(2).

who may have opposed the reference, the clerk of court administers the complete consent procedure.

Notification

At the time the action is filed, the clerk of court notifies the parties in writing of their option to proceed before a magistrate judge.[3]

Time for Consent

The time for indicating a party's consent or lack of consent is set generally by local rule or court order.[4]

Acceptance

Parties indicate their consent by submitting completed consent forms supplied by the clerk of court.[5]

Voluntariness of Consent

Most courts have local rules to ensure the voluntariness and willingness of consent, such as preventing the clerk of court from notifying litigants that their case will be heard sooner by a magistrate judge or that they will receive an experienced magistrate judge. Neither the district judge, the magistrate judge, nor the clerk of court may attempt to persuade the parties to consent to a trial before a magistrate judge. The parties must clearly and unambiguously consent to a magistrate judge.[6] A mere acquiesence or failure to object does not constitute consent.[7]

3. 28 U.S.C.A. § 636(c)(2).

4. *See, e.g., Rembert v. Apfel,* 213 F.3d 1331, 1335 n. 1 (11th Cir.2000) ("Parties can consent even after judgment."); *Drake v. Minnesota Mineral & Manufacturing Co.,* 134 F.3d 878, 883 (7th Cir.1998) (good consent even after appellate oral argument). *But see Hajek v. Burlington Northern Railroad Co.,* 186 F.3d 1105, 1108 (9th Cir.1999) (consent in appellate brief is ineffective); *Archie v. Christian,* 808 F.2d 1132 (5th Cir.1987)(en banc)(consent must be given before trial begins—rule of 5th Circuit).

5. *But see Roell v. Withrow,* 538 U.S. 580, 581, 123 S.Ct. 1696, 1699, 155 L.Ed.2d 775 (2003) (noting normal requirement of written consent, but holding that where non-consenting parties appear before magistrate without making further objection, magistrate has jurisdiction; fact of inferred consent satisfies requirement of Rule 73(b)).

6. *See, e.g., Hajek v. Burlington Northern Railroad,* 186 F.3d 1105, 1108 (9th Cir.1999) (party's response to proposed referral to magistrate judge that " 'at this time the Defendant does not believe any special procedures are required or are appropriate' " is "far from 'clear and unambiguous' "). *Alaniz v. California Processors, Inc.,* 690 F.2d 717, 720 (9th Cir. 1982)(per curiam)(holding that consent must be clear and unambiguous). *Cf., Aldrich v. Bowen,* 130 F.3d 1364, 1365 (9th Cir.1997) (in the absence of written consent in the record, magistrate judge lacked jurisdiction to hear case). *But see Kadonsky v. United States,* 216 F.3d 499, 502 (5th Cir.2000), *cert. denied,* 531 U.S. 1176, 121 S.Ct. 1151, 148 L.Ed.2d 1013 (2001) (sufficient consent where party signed document "evincing his willingness to proceed before a magistrate judge;" use of particular written form is not required for consent); *Rembert v. Apfel,* 213 F.3d 1331, 1335 (11th Cir.2000) ("Although consent must be 'express and on the record,' it need not necessarily be written.").

7. *See, e.g., Hajek v. Burlington Northern Railroad,* 186 F.3d 1105, 1108 (9th Cir.1999) (local rule provided that failure to object to referral to magistrate judge was consent to referral; held, local rule is invalid); *In re Marriage of Nasca,* 160 F.3d 578, 579 (9th Cir.1998) (" 'consent by failure to object' " does not provide magistrate judge with authority under Rule 73(b); appellate court raised issue *sua sponte*); *Caprera v. Jacobs,* 790 F.2d 442, 444 (5th Cir. 1986)(consent cannot be inferred from parties' conduct; "consent to proceed before a magistrate [must] be explicit").

Consequence of Failure to Consent

If a magistrate judge hears a case without the consent of the parties, the resulting judgment is a "nullity."[8]

Additional Parties and Consent

In general, local rules will control the time within which new parties must exercise their right to consent. The clerk of court will notify new parties of their right to consent in the same manner as the original parties. When an additional party is joined who does not consent to the participation of the magistrate judge, the district judge must hear the case.[9]

Vacating the Reference to a Magistrate by the District Judge

The court may, for good cause shown on its own motion, or under extraordinary circumstances shown by any party, vacate its reference of a civil matter to a magistrate judge.[10] For example, it has been held that a district judge may vacate a proceeding from a magistrate judge when the magistrate judge is faced with extraordinary questions of law with possibly wide precedential effect.[11] This power may not be used routinely to vacate certain categories of cases from a magistrate judge.[12] The court retains this power, notwithstanding the consent of all parties to trial before a magistrate judge.

RULE 73(c). APPEAL

CORE CONCEPT

The appeal procedure provides that a party make a direct appeal of a magistrate judge's final judgment to the Court of Appeals in the same manner as a judgment from the district court.[13]

RULE 73(d). OPTIONAL APPEAL ROUTE

[Abrogated].

Note: Rule 73(a) and (b) identify the circumstances in which a magistrate judge may be authorized to conduct a civil trial. Rules 73(d) and 74–76 provided that when a magistrate judge hears a case, the parties could choose to appeal to either the district court or the court of appeals. However, effective in 1997 the so-called "optional appeal

8. *Binder v. Gillespie,* 184 F.3d 1059, 1063 (9th Cir.1999), *cert. denied,* 528 U.S. 1154, 120 S.Ct. 1158, 145 L.Ed.2d 1070 (2000).

9. *See, e.g., New York Chinese TV Programs, Inc. v. U.E. Enterprises, Inc.,* 996 F.2d 21, 24 (2d Cir.1993)(intervenors must also consent, even when joined after magistrate judge begins to hear case).

10. 28 U.S.C.A. § 636(c)(6).

11. *Gomez v. Harris,* 504 F.Supp. 1342, 1345 (D.Alaska 1981)(reference vacated in case with "controlling question of law and a thicket of procedural difficulties").

12. *See,* S.Report No. 74, 96th Cong., 1st Sess. 14 (1979) (WESTLAW: LH database, **ti(senate + 5 96–74)**).

13. *See, e.g., Dluhos v. Floating & Abandoned Vessel, Known as "New York,"* 162 F.3d 63, 67 (2d Cir.1998) (consent to trial before magistrate judge waives any appeal to district judge; appeal is to circuit court).

route'' to the district court was abolished by Congress. Accordingly, the Supreme Court abrogated Rules 73(d) and 74–76, effective in December, 1997. Henceforth appeals from trials conducted by magistrate judges shall be made only to the appropriate court of appeals.

ADDITIONAL RESEARCH REFERENCES

Wright & Miller, *Federal Practice and Procedure* §§ 3077.1–3077.5.

C.J.S. United States Commissioners § 3.

West's Key No. Digests, United States Magistrates ⚷12–13, 24–31.

RULE 74*

METHOD OF APPEAL FROM MAGISTRATE TO DISTRICT JUDGE UNDER TITLE 28, U.S.C. § 636(c)(4) AND RULE 73(d)

[ABROGATED]

RULE 75*

PROCEEDINGS ON APPEAL FROM MAGISTRATE TO DISTRICT JUDGE UNDER RULE 73(d)

[ABROGATED]

RULE 76*

JUDGMENT OF THE DISTRICT JUDGE ON THE APPEAL UNDER RULE 73(d) AND COSTS

[ABROGATED]

* Rules 73(d) and 74–76 provided that when a magistrate judge hears a case, the parties could choose to appeal to either the district court or the court of appeals. However, in 1997 the so-called "optional appeal route" to the district court was abolished by Congress. Accordingly, the Supreme Court abrogated Rules 73(d) and 74–76 effective in December, 1997. Henceforth appeals from trials conducted by magistrate judges shall be made only to the appropriate court of appeals.

X. DISTRICT COURTS AND CLERKS

RULE 77

DISTRICT COURTS AND CLERKS

(a) District Courts Always Open. The district courts shall be deemed always open for the purpose of filing any pleading or other proper paper, of issuing and returning mesne and final process, and of making and directing all interlocutory motions, orders, and rules.

(b) Trials and Hearings; Orders in Chambers. All trials upon the merits shall be conducted in open court and so far as convenient in a regular court room. All other acts or proceedings may be done or conducted by a judge in chambers, without the attendance of the clerk or other court officials and at any place either within or without the district; but no hearing, other than one ex parte, shall be conducted outside the district without the consent of all parties affected thereby.

(c) Clerk's Office and Orders by Clerk. The clerk's office with the clerk or a deputy in attendance shall be open during business hours on all days except Saturdays, Sundays, and legal holidays, but a district court may provide by local rule or order that its clerk's office shall be open for specified hours on Saturdays or particular legal holidays other than New Year's Day, Birthday of Martin Luther King, Jr., Washington's Birthday, Memorial Day, Independence Day, Labor Day, Columbus Day, Veterans Day, Thanksgiving Day, and Christmas Day. All motions and applications in the clerk's office for issuing mesne process, for issuing final process to enforce and execute judgments, for entering defaults or judgments by default, and for other proceedings which do not require allowance or order of the court are grantable of course by the clerk; but the clerk's action may be suspended or altered or rescinded by the court upon cause shown.

(d) Notice of Orders or Judgments. Immediately upon the entry of an order or judgment the clerk shall serve a notice of the entry in the manner provided for in Rule 5(b) upon each party who is not in default for failure to appear, and shall make a note in the docket of the service. Any party may in addition serve a notice of such entry in the manner provided in Rule 5(b) for the service of papers. Lack of notice of the entry by the Clerk does not affect the time to appeal or relieve or authorize the court to relieve a party for failure to appeal within the time allowed, except as permitted in Rule 4(a) of the Federal Rules of Appellate Procedure.

[Amended effective March 19, 1948; July 1, 1963; July 1, 1968; July 1, 1971; August 1, 1987; December 1, 1991; April 23, 2001, effective December 1, 2001.]

AUTHORS' COMMENTARY ON RULE 77

PURPOSE AND SCOPE

Rule 77 contains a variety of provisions pertaining to the operations of the district court and the clerk's office. It provides that the court is always "open," and sets forth the times that the clerk's office is open. It also states that trials and hearings shall be conducted in the courtroom. Finally, Rule 77 controls notice of judgments and orders.

RULE 77(a). DISTRICT COURTS ALWAYS OPEN

CORE CONCEPT

The district courts are deemed open at all times for the purposes of filing papers, issuing process, and the like.[1] This does not mean that the clerk's office will be manned and open at all times.[2] Rather, papers may be filed after hours by delivering them to the clerk or a deputy clerk, depositing them in a designated receptacle provided by the clerk and authorized by local rule,[3] or even leaving them with a judge under exceptional circumstances.[4] However, filing is not accomplished merely by delivery to the clerk's office without delivering the paper to a proper officer or otherwise using an established method of after-hours filing.[5]

RULE 77(b). TRIALS AND HEARINGS; ORDERS IN CHAMBERS

CORE CONCEPT

All trials must be conducted in open court, and in a regular courtroom to the extent practicable. Other proceedings, such as status

1. *In re Bradshaw*, 283 B.R. 814, 817 (1st Cir.BAP 2002) (the guiding principle is that clerks of court must be available in some fashion twenty-four hours a day).

2. *Stone Street Capital, Inc. v. McDonald's Corp.*, 300 F.Supp.2d 345, 348, n.4 (D.Md. 2003); *In re Bradshaw*, 283 B.R. 814, 818 (1st Cir.BAP 2002); *McIntosh v. Antonino*, 71 F.3d 29, 35 (1st Cir.1995).

3. *Ticketmaster Corp. v. Tickets.Com, Inc.*, 2000 WL 525390, 2000 (C.D.Cal.2000) (a drop box is one method to accommodate the fact that the court shall be deemed always open).

4. *Turner v. City of Newport*, 887 F.Supp. 149 (E.D.Ky.1995)(deposit in post office box of clerk deemed filing).

5. *McIntosh v. Antonino*, 71 F.3d 29, 35 (1st Cir.1995); *In the Matter of the Complaint of Fisherman's Wharf Fillet, Inc.*, 83 F.Supp.2d 651, 657 (E.D.Va.1999) (after hours facsimile is not adequate filing).

conferences, pretrial conferences, etc., may be conducted in chambers or some other location.[6] However, no hearing, other than one *ex parte,* may be held outside the district without consent of all parties.

RULE 77(c). CLERK'S OFFICE AND ORDERS BY CLERK

CORE CONCEPT

The clerk's office must be open at minimum during working hours on all days except weekends and holidays. The hours may be expanded by local rule. The clerk's office has the power to take certain acts, such as entering default judgments and process to execute judgments. Such actions by the clerk's office are reviewable by the court and may be suspended, altered, or rescinded upon cause shown.[7]

RULE 77(d). NOTICE OF ORDERS OF JUDGMENT

CORE CONCEPT

The clerk's office must send notice of the entry of judgment to all parties who have entered appearances in the manner set forth in Rule 5(b).[8] However, the failure of the clerk to do so does not necessarily increase the time for appeal[9] (but note that the appellate courts may extend the time for appeal and may consider the failure of the clerk to send notice).[10] A party who wants to insure that all parties have notice of the judgment (and thus that the time for appeal has commenced running) may serve the notice by mail[11] as provided in Rule 5.[12]

ADDITIONAL RESEARCH REFERENCES

Wright & Miller, *Federal Practice and Procedure* §§ 3081–3084.

C.J.S. Courts § 236; Federal Civil Procedure §§ 915 et seq., 1213; Federal Courts §§ 302 et seq.

West's Key No. Digests, Clerk of Courts ⚷1; Federal Civil Procedure ⚷1951, 2628; Federal Courts ⚷971.

6. *B.H. v. McDonald*, 49 F.3d 294 (7th Cir. 1995); *Crumrine v. NEG Micon USA, Inc.*, 104 F.Supp.2d 1123, 1126 (N.D.Iowa 2000) (court could be held at any courthouse within the district even without the consent of the parties).

7. *Brady v. United States*, 211 F.3d 499 (9th Cir.2000), *cert. denied*, 531 U.S. 1037, 121 S.Ct. 627, 148 L.Ed.2d 536 (2000) (clerk's entry of default may be set aside for cause shown).

8. *Poole v. Family Court of New Castle County*, 368 F.3d 263 (3rd Cir. 2004); *Arai v. American Bryce Ranches Inc.*, 316 F.3d 1066, 1068 (9th Cir.2003); *Nguyen v. Southwest Leasing and Rental Inc.*, 282 F.3d 1061, 1064–65 (9th Cir.2002) (Rule 77(d) contemplates that the notice will be in writing).

9. *Poole v. Family Court of New Castle County*, 368 F.3d 263 (3rd Cir. 2004); *United States v. Fiorelli*, 337 F.3d 282 (3rd Cir.2003); *In re City of Memphis*, 293 F.3d 345 (6th Cir.2002).

10. *Nguyen v. Southwest Leasing and Rental Inc.*, 282 F.3d 1061, 1065–66 (9th Cir.2002) (Rule 77(d) must be read in conjunction with Rule 4(a)(6) of the Federal Rules of Appellate Procedure); *In re Stein*, 197 F.3d 421, 424–25 (9th Cir.1999).

11. *Ryan v. First Unum Life Ins. Co.*, 174 F.3d 302, 304–05 (2d Cir.1999) (service must be by mail, not by hand delivery).

12. *Bass v. United States Dept. Of Agriculture,* 211 F.3d 959 (5th Cir.2000); *Nunley v. City of Los Angeles*, 52 F.3d 792 (9th Cir.1995).

RULE 78

MOTION DAY

Unless local conditions make it impracticable, each district court shall establish regular times and places, at intervals sufficiently frequent for the prompt dispatch of business, at which motions requiring notice and hearing may be heard and disposed of; but the judge at any time or place and on such notice, if any, as the judge considers reasonable may make orders for the advancement, conduct, and hearing of actions.

To expedite its business, the court may make provision by rule or order for the submission and determination of motions without oral hearing upon brief written statements of reasons in support and opposition.

[Amended effective August 1, 1987.]

AUTHORS' COMMENTARY ON RULE 78

SCOPE AND PURPOSE

Rule 78 requires each district to enact local rules establishing regular motion days for the presentation of motions requiring a hearing. However, judges may conduct oral arguments on motions at other times. Furthermore, the districts or individual judges may also provide that motions are to be determined on briefs only, without oral argument.[1]

ADDITIONAL RESEARCH REFERENCES

Wright & Miller, *Federal Practice and Procedure* §§ 3091.

C.J.S. Federal Civil Procedure § 933.

West's Key No. Digests, Federal Civil Procedure 1991.

1. *United States v. Peninsula Communications, Inc.*, 287 F.3d 832, 839 (9th Cir.2002); *Willis v. Pacific Maritime Association*, 244 F.3d 675, 684, n.2 (9th Cir.2001); *Jetton v. McDonnell Douglas Corp.*, 121 F.3d 423, 427 (8th Cir.1997); *Pipko v. C.I.A.*, 312 F.Supp.2d 669 (D.N.J. 2004).

RULE 79

BOOKS AND RECORDS KEPT BY THE CLERK AND ENTRIES THEREIN

(a) Civil Docket. The clerk shall keep a book known as "civil docket" of such form and style as may be prescribed by the Director of the Administrative Office of the United States Courts with the approval of the Judicial Conference of the United States, and shall enter therein each civil action to which these rules are made applicable. Actions shall be assigned consecutive file numbers. The file number of each action shall be noted on the folio of the docket whereon the first entry of the action is made. All papers filed with the clerk, all process issued and returns made thereon, all appearances, orders, verdicts, and judgments shall be entered chronologically in the civil docket on the folio assigned to the action and shall be marked with its file number. These entries shall be brief but shall show the nature of each paper filed or writ issued and the substance of each order or judgment of the court and of the returns showing execution of process. The entry of an order or judgment shall show the date the entry is made. When in an action trial by jury has been properly demanded or ordered the clerk shall enter the word "jury" on the folio assigned to that action.

(b) Civil Judgments and Orders. The clerk shall keep, in such form and manner as the Director of the Administrative Office of the United States Courts with the approval of the Judicial Conference of the United States may prescribe, a correct copy of every final judgment or appealable order, or order affecting title to or lien upon real or personal property, and any other order which the court may direct to be kept.

(c) Indices; Calendars. Suitable indices of the civil docket and of every civil judgment and order referred to in subdivision (b) of this rule shall be kept by the clerk under the direction of the court. There shall be prepared under the direction of the court calendars of all actions ready for trial, which shall distinguish "jury actions" from "court actions."

(d) Other Books and Records of the Clerk. The clerk shall also keep such other books and records as may be required from time to time by the Director of the Administrative Office of the United States Courts with the approval of the Judicial Conference of the United States.

[Amended effective March 19, 1948; October 20, 1949; July 1, 1963.]

AUTHORS' COMMENTARY ON RULE 79

PURPOSE AND SCOPE

Rule 79 governs the record keeping duties of the district court clerk's office.

RULE 79(a). CIVIL DOCKET

CORE CONCEPT

The clerk shall keep a civil docket, which is a descriptive, chronological[1] listing of each pleading, motion, order, etc., filed in the case. The docket may be maintained manually or electronically.[2]

APPLICATIONS

Description

The docket should contain a brief description of each entry. Entries should be entered chronologically and should show the dates on which orders or judgments are entered.[3]

Jury vs. Non-jury

The docket should indicate if the case is to be tried before a jury.

Judgments

Judgments are not effective until entered on the docket.[4] Under Rule 58, a judgment must be a separate document.[5]

Briefs

In general, briefs are not part of the record, so they are not filed and are not entered on the docket.

1. *Goode v. Winkler*, 252 F.3d 242 (2d Cir. 2001) (criticizing the district court for not arranging the docket strictly chronologically).

2. *Active Products Corp. v. A.H. Choitz & Co. Inc.*, 163 F.R.D. 274, 280–81 (N.D.Ind.1995).

3. *Connecticut ex rel. Blumenthal v. Crotty*, 346 F.3d 84, 92 (2nd Cir. 2003) (the operative date is the date the order is entered onto the docket, not the date the order is signed or dated); *Houston v. Greiner*, 174 F.3d 287 (2d Cir. 1999), *cert. denied*, 531 U.S. 926, 121 S.Ct. 323, 148 L.Ed.2d 260 (2000) (computerized docketing system that did not list a date for each entry violates Rule 79).

4. *Local Union No. 1992 of Intern. Broth. of Elec. Workers v. Okonite Co.*, 358 F.3d 278, 284, n.10 (3rd Cir. 2004); *United States v. Fiorelli*, 337 F.3d 282 (3d Cir.2003) (although an order may be signed by the district court, received by the clerk, and entered in the docket on different days, the entry date controls).

5. *Silivanch v. Celebrity Cruises, Inc.*, 333 F.3d 355, 363 (2d Cir.2003), *cert. denied*, 540 U.S. 1105, 124 S.Ct. 1047, 157 L.Ed.2d 890 (2004); *United States v. Johnson*, 254 F.3d 279, 286 (D.C.Cir.2001).

Time of Entry

Rule 79 does not specify the time for making entries in the docket. However, the parties' rights will not be prejudiced by a delay in entry on the docket.

RULE 79(b). CIVIL JUDGMENTS AND ORDERS

CORE CONCEPT

Rule 79(b) requires the clerk's office to retain a copy of every final judgment, appealable order, order creating a lien on property, and any other order as directed by the court.

RULE 79(c). INDICES; CALENDARS

CORE CONCEPT

Rule 79(c) requires the clerk's office to maintain an index or indices of the civil docket and of every civil judgment, appealable order, order creating a lien on property, and other order as directed by the court. The clerk's office must also maintain a calendar of all actions ready for trial. This calendar will indicate whether the matter is to be tried jury or non-jury.

RULE 79(d). OTHER BOOKS AND RECORDS OF THE CLERK

CORE CONCEPT

The Administrative Office of the United States may direct that the clerk's offices maintain other books and records.

ADDITIONAL RESEARCH REFERENCES

Wright & Miller, *Federal Practice and Procedure* §§ 3101–3107.

C.J.S. Federal Civil Procedure §§ 933, 1227 et seq.

West's Key No. Digests, Federal Civil Procedure ⚷1991, 2621.

RULE 80

STENOGRAPHER; STENOGRAPHIC REPORT OR TRANSCRIPT AS EVIDENCE

(a) [Abrogated].

(b) [Abrogated].

(c) Stenographic Report or Transcript as Evidence. Whenever the testimony of a witness at a trial or hearing which was stenographically reported is admissible in evidence at a later trial, it may be proved by the transcript thereof duly certified by the person who reported the testimony.

[Amended effective March 19, 1948.]

AUTHORS' COMMENTARY ON RULE 80

PURPOSE AND SCOPE

Rule 80 now addresses use of the transcript from a hearing or trial. In the past, it also discussed stenographers, but official stenographers are now appointed pursuant to statute.

RULE 80(a)-(b). ABROGATED

RULE 80(c). STENOGRAPHIC REPORT OR TRANSCRIPT AS EVIDENCE

CORE CONCEPT

Rule 80(c) pertains to the use of testimony at one trial or hearing as evidence at a subsequent hearing or trial. The rule provides that a transcript certified by an official court reporter is proof of the prior testimony.[1]

ADDITIONAL RESEARCH REFERENCES

Wright & Miller, *Federal Practice and Procedure* §§ 3121–3122.

C.J.S. Evidence §§ 629–633 et seq., 652 et seq.

West's Key No. Digests, Evidence ⚷332(1, 4), 340.

1. *Orr v. Bank of America, NT & SA*, 285 F.3d 764, 776 (9th Cir.2002) (transcripts not properly certified not admitted).

XI. GENERAL PROVISIONS

RULE 81

APPLICABILITY IN GENERAL

(a) To What Proceedings Applicable.

(1) These rules do not apply to prize proceedings in admiralty governed by Title 10, U.S.C. §§ 7651–7681. They do apply to proceedings in bankruptcy to the extent provided by the Federal Rules of Bankruptcy Procedure.

(2) These rules are applicable to proceedings for admission to citizenship, habeas corpus, and quo warranto, to the extent that the practice in such proceedings is not set forth in statutes of the United States, the Rules Governing Section 2254 Cases, or the Rules Governing Section 2255 Proceedings, and has heretofore conformed to the practice in civil actions.

(3) In proceedings under Title 9, U.S.C., relating to arbitration, or under the Act of May 20, 1926, ch. 347, § 9 (44 Stat. 585), U.S.C., Title 45, § 159, relating to boards of arbitration of railway labor disputes, these rules apply only to the extent that matters of procedure are not provided for in those statutes. These rules apply to proceedings to compel the giving of testimony or production of documents in accordance with a subpoena issued by an officer or agency of the United States under any statute of the United States except as otherwise provided by statute or by rules of the district court or by order of the court in the proceedings.

(4) These rules do not alter the method prescribed by the Act of February 18, 1922, c. 57, § 2 (42 Stat. 388), U.S.C., Title 7, § 292; or by the Act of June 10, 1930, c. 436, § 7 (46 Stat. 534), as amended, U.S.C., Title 7, § 499g(c), for instituting proceedings in the United States district courts to review orders of the Secretary of Agriculture; or prescribed by the Act of June 25, 1934, c. 742, § 2 (48 Stat. 1214), U.S.C., Title 15, § 522, for instituting proceedings to review orders of the Secretary of the Interior; or prescribed by the Act of February 22, 1935, c. 18, § 5 (49 Stat. 31), U.S.C., Title 15, § 715d(c), as extended, for instituting proceedings to review orders of petroleum control boards; but the conduct of such proceedings in the district courts shall be made to conform to these rules as far as applicable.

(5) These rules do not alter the practice in the United States district courts prescribed in the Act of July 5, 1935, c. 372, §§ 9

and 10 (49 Stat. 453), as amended, U.S.C., Title 29, §§ 159 and 160, for beginning and conducting proceedings to enforce orders of the National Labor Relations Board; and in respects not covered by those statutes, the practice in the district courts shall conform to these rules so far as applicable.

(6) These rules apply to proceedings for enforcement or review of compensation orders under the Longshoremen's and Harbor Workers' Compensation Act, Act of March 4, 1927, c. 509, §§ 18, 21 (44 Stat. 1434, 1436), as amended, U.S.C., Title 33, §§ 918, 921, except to the extent that matters of procedure are provided for in that Act. The provisions for service by publication and for answer in proceedings to cancel certificates of citizenship under the Act of June 27, 1952, c. 477, Title III, c. 2, § 340 (66 Stat. 260), U.S.C., Title 8, § 1451, remain in effect.

(7) [Abrogated].

(b) Scire Facias and Mandamus. The writs of scire facias and mandamus are abolished. Relief heretofore available by mandamus or scire facias may be obtained by appropriate action or by appropriate motion under the practice prescribed in these rules.

(c) Removed Actions. These rules apply to civil actions removed to the United States district courts from the state courts and govern procedure after removal. Repleading is not necessary unless the court so orders. In a removed action in which the defendant has not answered, the defendant shall answer or present the other defenses or objections available under these rules within 20 days after the receipt through service or otherwise of a copy of the initial pleading setting forth the claim for relief upon which the action or proceeding is based, or within 20 days after the service of summons upon such initial pleading, then filed, or within 5 days after the filing of the petition for removal, whichever period is longest. If at the time of removal all necessary pleadings have been served, a party entitled to trial by jury under Rule 38 shall be accorded it, if the party's demand therefor is served within 10 days after the petition for removal is filed if the party is the petitioner, or if not the petitioner within 10 days after service on the party of the notice of filing the petition. A party who, prior to removal, has made an express demand for trial by jury in accordance with state law, need not make a demand after removal. If state law applicable in the court from which the case is removed does not require the parties to make express demands in order to claim trial by jury, they need not make demands after removal unless the court directs that they do so within a specified time if they desire to claim trial by jury. The court may make this direction on its own motion and shall do so as a matter of course at the request of any party. The failure of a party to make demand as directed constitutes a waiver by that party of trial by jury.

(d) [Abrogated].

(e) Law Applicable. Whenever in these rules the law of the state which the district court is held is made applicable, the law applied in the District of Columbia governs proceedings in the United States District Court for the District of Columbia. When the word "state" is used, it includes, if appropriate, the District of Columbia. When the term "statute of the United States" is used, it includes, so far as concerns proceedings in the United States District Court for the District of Columbia, any Act of Congress locally applicable to and in force in the District of Columbia. When the law of a state is referred to, the word "law" includes the statutes of that state and the state judicial decisions construing them.

(f) References to Officer of the United States. Under any rule in which reference is made to an officer or agency of the United States, the term "officer" includes a district director of internal revenue, a former district director or collector of internal revenue, or the personal representative of a deceased district director or collector of internal revenue.

[Amended effective December 28, 1939; March 19, 1948; October 20, 1949; August 1, 1951; July 1, 1963; July 1, 1966; July 1, 1968; July 1, 1971; August 1, 1987; April 23, 2001, effective December 1, 2001; April 29, 2002, effective December 1, 2002.]

AUTHORS' COMMENTARY ON RULE 81

PURPOSE AND SCOPE

Rule 81 specifies whether the Federal Rules of Civil Procedure apply in various proceedings. It also specifies how the Rules operate in the District of Columbia, contains some provisions governing removed actions, abolishes the Writs of Mandamus and Scire Facias, and defines "Officer of the United States."

RULE 81(a). TO WHAT PROCEEDINGS APPLICABLE

CORE CONCEPT

Rule 81(a) lists specific proceedings to which the Rules apply and identifies specific proceedings to which the Rules do not apply.

APPLICATIONS

Not Applicable[1]

Rule 81(a) provides that the Rules do not apply to:

- Prize Proceedings in Admiralty;
- Proceedings to Review Orders of the Secretary of Agriculture;[2]
- Proceedings to Review Orders of the Secretary of the Interior;
- Proceedings to Review Orders of the Petroleum Control Boards; and
- Proceedings to Enforce Orders of the National Labor Relations Board.

Applicable

The Rules supplement the statutory procedures for the following:

- Bankruptcy Proceedings, to the extent provided by the Bankruptcy Rules;[3]
- Admission to Citizenship Proceedings;[4]
- Habeas Corpus Proceedings;[5]
- Quo Warranto Proceedings;
- Proceedings for Enforcement or Review of Compensation Orders under the Longshoremen's and Harbor Workers' Compensation Act;[6] and
- Proceedings to enforce subpoenas to testify or to produce documents issued by agencies of the United States.[7]

Arbitrations

In proceedings arbitrated under federal statute, the Rules generally act as default provisions, applying when no arbitration rule addresses the procedural issue.[8]

1. Rule 81(a) exempted copyright proceedings and mental health proceedings in the United States District Court for the District of Columbia from the Rules. These exemptions were removed by the 2001 amendments to Rule 81(a).

2. Riccelli's Produce, Inc. v. Horton Tomato Co., Inc., 155 F.R.D. 411 (N.D.N.Y.1994).

3. *Chrysler Financial Corp. v. Powe*, 312 F.3d 1241, 1243, n.1 (11th Cir.2002), *cert. denied*, 538 U.S. 998, 123 S.Ct. 1901, 155 L.Ed.2d 825 (2003).

4. *Alvear v. Kirk*, 87 F.Supp.2d 1241, 1243 (D.N.M.2000).

5. *Gonzalez v. Secretary for Dept. of Corrections*, 366 F.3d 1253, 1270 (11th Cir. 2004); *Miranda v. Bennett*, 322 F.3d 171, 175 (2nd Cir.2003); *Jordan v. Lefevre*, 293 F.3d 587 (2d Cir.2002).

6. *Galle v. Director, Office of Workers' Compensation Programs*, 246 F.3d 440, 447 (5th Cir. 2001), *cert. denied*, 534 U.S. 1002, 122 S.Ct. 479, 151 L.Ed.2d 392 (2001); *Pleasant-El v. Oil Recovery Co., Inc.*, 148 F.3d 1300, 1302 (11th Cir. 1998).

7. *Martin v. Bally's Park Place Hotel & Casino*, 983 F.2d 1252 (3d Cir.1993); *N.L.R.B. v. Cable Car Advertisers, Inc.*, 319 F.Supp.2d 991 (N.D.Cal. 2004).

8. *Deiulemar Compagnia Di Navigazione v. Allegra*, 198 F.3d 473, 481–82 (4th Cir.1999), *cert. denied*, 529 U.S. 1109, 120 S.Ct. 1962, 146 L.Ed.2d 794 (2000); *Champ v. Siegel Trading Co., Inc.*, 55 F.3d 269 (7th Cir.1995).

Habeas Corpus

Prior to the 2002 Amendments, Rule 81(a)(2) contained specific procedures relating to writs of habeas corpus. Those procedures were eliminated by the 2002 Amendments to eliminate the inconsistency between the procedures in Rule 81(a)(2) and in Sections 2254 and 2255.[9]

RULE 81(b). SCIRE FACIAS AND MANDAMUS

CORE CONCEPT

Rule 81(b) abolishes the Writs of Scire Facias (a writ with a variety of functions such as reviving a judgment[10] or effecting execution) and Mandamus (a writ compelling an official to take an action).[11]

APPLICATIONS

District Court Only

Rule 81(b) abolishes the Writs in the district court only. Thus, a Court of Appeals, under appropriate circumstances, may issue a Writ of Mandamus to a district judge under Rule 21 of the Federal Rules of Appellate Procedure.[12]

Relief Not Abolished

Only the Writs themselves are abolished. The relief sought may be available through some other motion or proceeding.[13]

RULE 81(c). REMOVED ACTIONS

CORE CONCEPT

Rule 81(c) provides that the Rules apply to actions commenced in state court and removed to federal court.[14] It also contains procedures governing removed actions.

9. The Advisory Committee Note to the 2002 Amendment to Rule 81.

10. *TDK Electronics Corp. v. Draiman*, 321 F.3d 677, 680 (7th Cir.2003)(although the writ of *scire facias* is abolished, revival or reentry of a judgment is obtainable by a more modern motion).

11. *SBA Communications, Inc. v. Zoning Commission of Town of Brookfield*, 96 F.Supp.2d 139 (D.Conn.2000).

12. *In re Nagy*, 89 F.3d 115, 116–17 (2d Cir.1996). *But see In re Campbell*, 264 F.3d 730, 731 (7th Cir.2001) (declining to issue writ of mandamus to state court).

13. *TDK Electronics Corp. v. Draiman*, 321 F.3d 677, 680 (7th Cir.2003)(although the writ of *scire facias* is abolished, revival or reentry of a judgment is obtainable by a more modern motion); *Hamil v. Vertrees*, 2001 WL 135716 (M.D.Ala.2001) (the court shall construe Plaintiff's request for a writ of mandamus as a request for mandatory injunctive relief).

14. *S. Wallace Edwards & Sons, Inc. v. Cincinnati Ins. Co.*, 353 F.3d 367, 374, n.4 (4th Cir. 2003); *Lee v. City of Beaumont*, 12 F.3d 933 (9th Cir.1993); *Tehan v. Disability Management Services, Inc.*, 111 F.Supp.2d 542 (D.N.J.2000).

APPLICATIONS

Rules Apply After Removal

The Rules apply to pleadings or motions filed after the removal.[15] Thus, Rules governing the form and service of pleadings would not apply to the complaint filed in state court prior to removal.[16]

Time to Answer

If the defendant has not yet answered at the time of removal, the defendant may file an answer either by the latest of 5 days (excluding weekends and holidays) from the date of removal,[17] or 20 days from service of the original pleading, if the pleading has been filed, whichever is later.[18] Note, however, that the act of removal alone does not trigger an obligation to answer a complaint that has not yet been properly served.[19]

Repleading Unnecessary

Unless the court orders otherwise, pleadings filed while the action was in state court do not need to be repleaded after removal to federal court.[20]

Jury Demand

If a jury trial demand has been properly made in state court, no new demand is necessary.[21] If no jury trial demand was made in state court and if all pleadings were filed in state court, the parties may nonetheless make a jury trial demand within 10 days of removal to federal court.[22] The 10 days are measured from filing the removal petition in the case of the petitioner and from service of the petition for all other parties. If no express jury trial demand is required under state law, none will be required in the removed action unless the court

15. *Pacific Employers Ins. Co. v. Sav-a-Lot of Winchester*, 291 F.3d 392 (6th Cir.2002); *Romo v. Gulf Stream Coach, Inc.*, 250 F.3d 1119 (7th Cir.2001) ("The Federal Rules make clear that they do not apply to filings in state court, even if the case is later removed to federal court.").

16. *See Prazak v. Local 1 Intern. Union of Bricklayers & Allied Crafts*, 233 F.3d 1149, 1152–53 (9th Cir.2000); *Griffen v. City of Oklahoma City*, 3 F.3d 336, (10th Cir.1993)(holding that Rule 11 sanctions do not apply to a complaint filed in state court and removed to federal court); *but see Levine v. McLeskey*, 881 F.Supp. 1030, 1048 (E.D.Va.1995), *affirmed in part, vacated in part*, 164 F.3d 210 (4th Cir.1998).

17. *Norsyn, Inc. v. Desai*, 351 F.3d 825, 828 (8th Cir. 2003); *Veryfine Products, Inc. v. Phlo Corp.*, 124 F.Supp.2d 16, 21 (D.Mass.2000) (discussing the counting of the 5 day period).

18. *Murphy Bros., Inc. v. Michetti Pipe Stringing, Inc.*, 526 U.S. 344, 346, 119 S.Ct. 1322, 1325, 143 L.Ed.2d 448 (1999); *Silva v. City of Madison*, 69 F.3d 1368, 1371 (7th Cir. 1995)(only proper service triggers the 20 day period to answer), *cert. denied*, 517 U.S. 1121, 116 S.Ct. 1354, 134 L.Ed.2d 522 (1996).

19. *Norsyn, Inc. v. Desai*, 351 F.3d 825, 829 (8th Cir. 2003).

20. *Kuehl v. Federal Deposit Insurance Corp.*, 8 F.3d 905 (1st Cir.1993), *cert. denied*, 511 U.S. 1034, 114 S.Ct. 1545, 128 L.Ed.2d 196 (1994); *Sapiro v. Encompass Ins.*, 221 F.R.D. 513 (N.D.Cal. 2004).

21. *Winter v. Minnesota Mutual Life Ins. Co.*, 199 F.3d 399, 406 (7th Cir.1999); *Marcella v. Brandywine Hospital*, 47 F.3d 618 (3d Cir.1995).

22. *Dunning v. Henry Flack Intern., Inc.*, 2002 WL 1046712 (W.D.Va.2002); *Reliance Electric Co. v. Exxon Capital Corp.*, 932 F.Supp. 101 (S.D.N.Y.1996).

so directs.[23] If a jury demand was made in the state court proceedings that does not meet the state requirements but does satisfy federal requirements, it can be accepted by the federal court.[24] There remain some scenarios that are not covered by Rule 81(c). In New York, jury demands may be made shortly before trial. In such cases, the court will have discretion to allow a late jury demand.[25]

RULE 81(e). LAW APPLICABLE

CORE CONCEPT

Rule 81(e) provides that, in general, when the Rules refer to "states," they include the District of Columbia.[26] Thus, when the Rules refer to the law of the state in which the court sits, the United States District Court for the District of Columbia uses the law applied in the District of Columbia. Rule 81(e) also defines the phrase "law of a state" as including statutes and judicial decisions construing the statutes.

RULE 81(f). REFERENCES TO OFFICER OF THE UNITED STATES

CORE CONCEPT

Rule 81(f) defines "officer of the United States" as including:

- District directors of internal revenue;
- Former district directors or collectors of internal revenue; and
- The personal representatives of a deceased district director or collector of internal revenue.

ADDITIONAL RESEARCH REFERENCES

Wright & Miller, *Federal Practice and Procedure* §§ 3131–3134.

C.J.S. Federal Civil Procedure §§ 7–23 et seq.

West's Key No. Digests, Federal Civil Procedure ⚷31–44.

23. *Bruns v. Amana,* 131 F.3d 761, 762 (8th Cir.1997).

24. *Wyatt v. Hunt Plywood Co., Inc.,* 297 F.3d 405, 415 (5th Cir.2002).

25. *See Rule 38(b); Breedlove v. Cabou,* 296 F.Supp.2d 253, 278 (N.D.N.Y. 2003); *Vincent v. AST Research, Inc.,* 199 F.R.D. 95, 96–7 (N.D.N.Y.2001) (describing the problem under New York law and listing three factors in determining whether to permit the late filing of a jury demand).

26. *Pharmachemie B.V. v. Pharmacia S.p.A.,* 934 F.Supp. 484 (D.Mass.1996).

RULE 82

JURISDICTION AND VENUE UNAFFECTED

These rules shall not be construed to extend or limit the jurisdiction of the United States district courts or the venue of actions therein. An admiralty or maritime claim within the meaning of Rule 9(h) shall not be treated as a civil action for the purposes of Title 28, U.S.C. §§ 1391–92.

[Amended effective October 20, 1949; July 1, 1966; April 23, 2001, effective December 1, 2001.]

AUTHORS' COMMENTARY ON RULE 82

PURPOSE AND SCOPE

Jurisdiction and venue are determined by statute (as discussed in separate sections of this book) and are not affected by the Rules.[1]

APPLICATIONS

Subject Matter Jurisdiction Only

Rule 82 refers to subject matter only (*i.e.,* the type of case a district court can hear), not personal jurisdiction (*i.e.,* which parties must appear and defend themselves). Likewise, the Rules contain timing requirements that are often described as "jurisdictional."[2]

Joinder

The Rules actually do affect subject matter jurisdiction in that they govern the joinder of ancillary claims and parties.[3]

Admiralty and Maritime Cases

Rule 82 also provides that admiralty and maritime cases are not considered civil actions for purposes of the venue statutes.[4] Admiralty

1. *Henderson v. United States*, 517 U.S. 654, 116 S.Ct. 1638, 134 L.Ed.2d 880 (1996); *United States v. Eleven Vehicles, Their Equipment and Accessories*, 200 F.3d 203, 216 (3d Cir.2000).

2. *Kontrick v. Ryan*, 540 U.S. 443, 124 S.Ct. 906, 157 L.Ed.2d 867 (U.S. 2004) ("the filing deadlines prescribed in Bankruptcy Rules 4004 and 9006(b)(3) are claim-processing rules that do not delineate what cases bankruptcy courts are competent to adjudicate"); *Brickwood Contractors, Inc. v. Datanet Engineering, Inc.*, 369 F.3d 385 (4th Cir. 2004) (courts are said to be without jurisdiction to consider an untimely motion under Rule 59); *American Canoe Ass'n, Inc. v. City Of Attalla*, 363 F.3d 1085, 1088 (11th Cir. 2004) (application of Rule 6(a)'s computational rules presents no offense to Rule 82).

3. *See Lunney v. U.S.*, 319 F.3d 550, 556–57 (2nd Cir.2003).

4. *See Sunbelt Corp. v. Noble, Denton & Associates, Inc.*, 5 F.3d 28 (3d Cir.1993); *Holmes v. Energy Catering Services, LLC*, 270 F.Supp.2d 882 (S.D.Tex.2003).

and maritime cases generally have separate venue provisions to facilitate suing seamen wherever they may be found.[5]

ADDITIONAL RESEARCH REFERENCES

Wright & Miller, *Federal Practice and Procedure* §§ 3141–3142.

C.J.S. Federal Civil Procedure § 19.

West's Key No. Digests, Federal Civil Procedure ⚷40.

5. *See Holmes v. Energy Catering Services, LLC*, 270 F.Supp.2d 882, 885 (S.D.Tex. 2003); *Denson v. United States*, 99 F.Supp.2d 792, 793 (S.D.Tex.2000).

RULE 83

RULES BY DISTRICT COURTS; JUDGE'S DIRECTIVES

(a) Local Rules.

(1) Each district court, acting by a majority of its district judges, may, after giving appropriate public notice and an opportunity for comment, make and amend rules governing its practice. A local rule shall be consistent with—but not duplicative of—Acts of Congress and rules adopted under 28 U.S.C. §§ 2072 and 2075, and shall conform to any uniform numbering system prescribed by the Judicial Conference of the United States. A local rule takes effect on the date specified by the district court and remains in effect unless amended by the court or abrogated by the judicial council of the circuit. Copies of rules and amendments shall, upon their promulgation, be furnished to the judicial council and the Administrative Office of the United States Courts and be made available to the public.

(2) A local rule imposing a requirement of form shall not be enforced in a manner that causes a party to lose rights because of a nonwillful failure to comply with the requirement.

(b) Procedures When There Is No Controlling Law. A judge may regulate practice in any manner consistent with federal law, rules adopted under 28 U.S.C. §§ 2072 and 2075, and local rules of the district. No sanction or other disadvantage may be imposed for noncompliance with any requirement not in federal law, federal rules, or the local district rules unless the alleged violator has been furnished in the particular case with actual notice of the requirement.

[Amended effective August 1, 1985; April 27, 1995, effective December 1, 1995.]

AUTHORS' COMMENTARY ON RULE 83

PURPOSE AND SCOPE

Rule 83 authorizes the districts to develop local rules that are "consistent" with the Federal Rules.

RULE 83(a). LOCAL RULES

CORE CONCEPT

Rule 83(a) provides that each district court can develop local rules. These local rules must be consistent with the federal rules, both in substance and in numbering. Local rules pertaining to matters of form cannot be enforced in a manner that prejudices the substantive rights of a party.

APPLICATIONS

Consistent with Federal Rules

Local rule must be consistent with, and not duplicative of,[1] Acts of Congress[2] and the Federal Rules.[3] Additionally, numbering must be consistent with the Federal Rules.

Typical Local Rules

Local rules can cover a wide variety of topics, and vary greatly in number and scope from district to district. Some typical local rules address:

- Admission to practice before the district courts;[4]
- Admission *Pro Hac Vice;*
- Procedures for disbarment;
- Security for court costs;
- Creation of divisions within the district;
- Form and number of copies of pleadings and briefs;
- Period of time for process;
- Manner for presentation of motions;[5]
- Notice for constitutional challenges to acts of Congress;
- Continuances;
- Discovery procedures;
- Pretrial and status conferences, including pretrial statements;

1. *United States v. Galiczynski*, 44 F.Supp.2d 707 (E.D.Pa.1999).

2. *D'Iorio v. Majestic Lanes, Inc.*, 370 F.3d 354 (3d Cir. 2004); *Weibrecht v. Southern Illinois Transfer, Inc.*, 241 F.3d 875, 879 (7th Cir. 2001)(to the extent a local rule conflicts with a federal statute, the local rule must be held invalid).

3. *NEPSK, Inc. v. Town of Houlton*, 283 F.3d 1, 7 (1st Cir.2002) (a district court cannot enforce its local rules in a way that conflicts with the Federal Rules of Civil Procedure); *Stern v. United States District Court for the District of Massachusetts*, 214 F.3d 4 (1st Cir.2000), *cert. denied*, 531 U.S. 1143, 121 S.Ct. 1077, 148 L.Ed.2d 954 (2001) ("Even if a local rule does not contravene the text of a national rule, the former cannot survive if it subverts the latter's purpose.").

4. *See In re Poole*, 222 F.3d 618, 621 (9th Cir.2000)

5. *Jetton v. McDonnell Douglas Corp.*, 121 F.3d 423, 426 (8th Cir.1997); *Goltz v. Univ. of Notre Dame*, 177 F.R.D. 638 (N.D.Ind.1997) (one purpose of local rules is to further the administration of justice by mandating that motions for summary judgment be properly briefed).

- Impartial medical examinations;
- Courtroom rules and regulations, including the use of cameras and recording equipment;
- Size, selection, and instruction of the jury;
- Handling and marking of exhibits;
- Entry of judgment; and
- Motions for new trials.

Effect of Local Rule

A valid local rule has the effect of law,[6] and must be obeyed.[7] The court has authority to impose sanctions when a party violates the court's local rules.[8] However, a local rule imposing a requirement of form (as opposed to substance) may not be enforced in a manner that causes a party to lose rights for a "nonwillful" violation.[9] Thus, a party should not be deprived of a right to a jury trial because it is unaware of or forgets a local rule requiring jury demands to be noted in the caption of pleadings.[10]

Promulgation of Local Rules

Local rules are adopted pursuant to the procedures in the Rules Enabling Act.[11]

Public Comment

Before a local rule may be enacted, it must be published for comment by the public.[12]

Copies

Local rules are included in West's court rules pamphlets for most states. A copy of the local rules can also be obtained from the clerk's office for a nominal fee. Additionally, Rule 83 provides that the district must submit a copy of the local rules to the Administrative Office of the United States Courts.[13]

Bankruptcy

Local rules do not apply to proceedings in Bankruptcy.[14]

6. *Jetton v. McDonnell Douglas Corp.*, 121 F.3d 423, 426 (8th Cir.1997) (local rule has "the force of law" and the parties are charged with knowledge of the district court's rules the same as with knowledge of the Federal Rules and all federal law); *Broussard v. Oryx Energy Co.*, 110 F.Supp.2d 532, 536–37 (E.D.Tex.2000) (a valid local rule has the force of law, and litigants are presumed to have notice of the local rules).

7. *Weil v. Neary,* 278 U.S. 160, 169, 49 S.Ct. 144, 148, 73 L.Ed. 243 (1929).

8. *Nick v. Morgan's Foods, Inc.*, 99 F.Supp.2d 1056, 1061 (E.D.Mo.2000).

9. The Advisory Committee Note to the 1995 Amendment to Rule 83.

10. The Advisory Committee Note to the 1995 amendment to Rule 83.

11. 28 U.S.C. § 2071(b); *In re Dorner*, 343 F.3d 910, 913 (7th Cir. 2003).

12. *In re Dorner*, 343 F.3d 910, 913 (7th Cir. 2003). *Antoine v. Atlas Turner, Inc.*, 66 F.3d 105, 108 (6th Cir.1995).

13. *Dais v. Lane Bryant, Inc.*, 2000 WL 869489 (S.D.N.Y.2000).

14. *In re Flanagan*, 999 F.2d 753 (3d Cir. 1993).

RULE 83(b). PROCEDURE WHEN THERE IS NO CONTROLLING LAW

CORE CONCEPT

The judges may regulate proceedings before them as they see fit, so long the court's rules are consistent with federal law, the Federal Rules, and local rules.[15]

APPLICATIONS

Orders Consistent with Other Rules

Individual judges' standing orders or requirements must be consistent with Acts of Congress, the Federal Rules, and local rules.[16]

Parties Must have Actual Notice of Court Requirements

The court may not sanction or "disadvantage" a party for noncompliance with a requirement not found in federal law, federal rules, or local rules unless that party has been furnished in the particular case with actual notice of the requirement.[17] Actual notice can be provided with a copy of the judge's requirements or by an order referencing the judge's standing order and indicating how copies can be obtained.[18]

ADDITIONAL RESEARCH REFERENCES

Wright & Miller, *Federal Practice and Procedure* §§ 3151–3155.

C.J.S. Federal Civil Procedure § 21.

West's Key No. Digests, Federal Civil Procedure ⚷25.

15. *Amnesty America v. Town of West Hartford*, 288 F.3d 467, 470–71 (2d Cir.2002) (district court may regulate motion practice in any manner consistent with federal law and the federal rules); *STMicroelectronics, Inc. v. Motorola, Inc.*, 307 F.Supp.2d 845, 848–49 (E.D.Tex. 2004).

16. *In re Dorner*, 343 F.3d 910, 913 (7th Cir. 2003).

17. *Amnesty America v. Town of West Hartford*, 288 F.3d 467, 471 (2d Cir.2002); *Carroll v. Jaques Admiralty Law Firm*, 110 F.3d 290, 293 (5th Cir.1997)(but, the rule does not eliminate a court's inherent power to sanction for intentional disruption of the discovery process); *STMicroelectronics, Inc. v. Motorola, Inc.*, 307 F.Supp.2d 845, 849, n.4 (E.D.Tex. 2004).

18. The Advisory Committee Note to the 1995 amendment to Rule 83.

RULE 84

FORMS

The forms contained in the Appendix of Forms are sufficient under the rules and are intended to indicate the simplicity and brevity of statement which the rules contemplate.

[Amended effective March 19, 1948.]

AUTHORS' COMMENTARY ON RULE 84

PURPOSE AND SCOPE

The Rules contain an Appendix of Forms that contains 35 forms, including complaints, answers, motions, discovery requests, and notices of appeal. The forms are intended to indicate the simplicity and brevity that are acceptable under in federal court.[1] The official forms cannot be challenged under the Rules[2] (although they can be challenged with substantive legal defenses, such as immunities).[3]

ADDITIONAL RESEARCH REFERENCES

Wright & Miller, *Federal Practice and Procedure* §§ 3161–3162.

C.J.S. Federal Civil Procedure § 251.

West's Key No. Digests, Federal Civil Procedure ⚷625–627.

1. *Educadores Puertorriquenos en Accion v. Hernandez*, 367 F.3d 61, 68 (1st Cir. 2004); *Hutton v. Priddy's Auction Galleries, Inc.*, 275 F.Supp.2d 428 (S.D.N.Y.2003).

2. *Guidry v. United States Tobacco Co., Inc.*, 188 F.3d 619, 632 (5th Cir.1999) (the forms in the Appendix of Forms are sufficient under the Rules); *Kirch v. Health Care Service Corp.*, 1997 WL 538683 (N.D.Ill.1997) (none of the forms spell out a legal theory).

3. *See Atchinson v. District of Columbia*, 73 F.3d 418, 423 (D.C.Cir.1996).

RULE 85

TITLE

These rules may be known and cited as the Federal Rules of Civil Procedure.

AUTHORS' COMMENTARY ON RULE 85

PURPOSE AND SCOPE

The full title of the Rules is the "Federal Rules of Civil Procedure." The Rules should be cited as "Fed.R.Civ.P. ___."

ADDITIONAL RESEARCH REFERENCES

Wright & Miller, *Federal Practice and Procedure* § 3171.

C.J.S. Federal Civil Procedure §§ 7 et seq.

West's Key No. Digests, Federal Civil Procedure ⚷31.

RULE 86

EFFECTIVE DATE

(a) Effective Date of Original Rules.* These rules will take effect on the day which is 3 months subsequent to the adjournment of the second regular session of the 75th Congress, but if that day is prior to September 1, 1938, then these rules will take effect on September 1, 1938. They govern all proceedings in actions brought after they take effect and also all further proceedings in actions then pending, except to the extent that in the opinion of the court their application in a particular action pending when the rules take effect would not be feasible or would work injustice, in which event the former procedure applies.

(b) Effective Date of Amendments. The amendments adopted by the Supreme Court on December 27, 1946, and transmitted to the Attorney General on January 2, 1947, shall take effect on the day which is three months subsequent to the adjournment of the first regular session of the 80th Congress, but, if that day is prior to September 1, 1947, then these amendments shall take effect on September 1, 1947. They govern all proceedings in actions brought after they take effect and also all further proceedings in actions then pending, except to the extent that in the opinion of the court their application in a particular action pending when the amendments take effect would not be feasible or would work injustice, in which event the former procedure applies.

(c) Effective Date of Amendments. The amendments adopted by the Supreme Court on December 29, 1948, and transmitted to the Attorney General on December 31, 1948, shall take effect on the day following the adjournment of the first regular session of the 81st Congress.

(d) Effective Date of Amendments. The amendments adopted by the Supreme Court on April 17, 1961, and transmitted to the Congress on April 18, 1961, shall take effect on July 19, 1961. They govern all proceedings in actions brought after they take effect and also all further proceedings in actions then pending, except to the extent that in the opinion of the court their application in a particular action pending when the amendments take effect would not be feasible or would work injustice, in which event the former procedure applies.

(e) Effective Date of Amendments. The amendments adopted by the Supreme Court on January 21, 1963, and transmitted to the Congress on January 21, 1963, shall take effect on July 1, 1963. They govern all proceedings in actions brought after they take effect and also all further proceedings in actions then pending, except to the extent that in the opinion of the court their application in a particular action pending when the amendments take effect would not be feasible or would work injustice, in which event the former procedure applies.

[Amended effective March 19, 1948; October 20, 1949; July 19, 1961; July 1, 1963.]

* Suggested title added by Publisher.

AUTHORS' COMMENTARY ON RULE 86

PURPOSE AND SCOPE

Rule 86 lists the effective dates of the Rules and certain of the amendments. Amendments typically become effective 90 days after transmittal to Congress.

APPLICATIONS

Pending Actions

In general, after their effective date, amendments to the Rules will be applied to all pending actions regardless of when the action was filed. However, if application of an amended Rule would not be feasible or would work an injustice, then the court can apply the old Rule.[1]

ADDITIONAL RESEARCH REFERENCES

Wright & Miller, *Federal Practice and Procedure* §§ 3181–3182.

C.J.S. Federal Civil Procedure §§ 7 et seq.

West's Key No. Digests, Federal Civil Procedure ⚷31.

1. *Ultra-Temp Corp. v. Advanced Vacuum Systems, Inc.*, 194 F.R.D. 378, 380, n.5 (D.Mass. 2000); *Eastman Kodak Co. v. Knight*, 1994 WL 258538 (D.N.H.1994).

SUPPLEMENTAL RULES FOR CERTAIN ADMIRALTY AND MARITIME CLAIMS

Adopted February 28, 1966, effective July 1, 1966

The former Rules of Practice in Admiralty and Maritime Cases, promulgated by the Supreme Court on December 6, 1920, effective March 7, 1921, as revised, amended and supplemented, were rescinded, effective July 1, 1966.

Including Amendments effective December 1, 2002

RULE A

SCOPE OF RULES

These Supplemental Rules apply to the procedure in admiralty and maritime claims within the meaning of Rule 9(h) with respect to the following remedies:

(1) Maritime attachment and garnishment;

(2) Actions in rem;

(3) Possessory, petitory, and partition actions;

(4) Actions for exoneration from or limitation of liability.

These rules also apply to the procedure in statutory condemnation proceedings analogous to maritime actions in rem, whether within the admiralty and maritime jurisdiction or not. Except as otherwise provided, references in these Supplemental Rules to actions in rem include such analogous statutory condemnation proceedings.

The general Rules of Civil Procedure for the United States District Courts are also applicable to the foregoing proceedings except to the extent that they are inconsistent with these Supplemental Rules.

[Added Feb. 28, 1966, eff. July 1, 1966.]

RULE B

IN PERSONAM ACTIONS: ATTACHMENT AND GARNISHMENT

(1) When Available; Complaint, Affidavit, Judicial Authorization, and Process. In an in personam action:

(a) If a defendant is not found within the district, a verified complaint may contain a prayer for process to attach the defendant's tangible or intangible personal property—up to the amount sued for—in the hands of garnishees named in the process.

(b) The plaintiff or the plaintiff's attorney must sign and file with the complaint an affidavit stating that, to the affiant's knowledge, or on information and belief, the defendant cannot be found within the district. The court must review the complaint and affidavit and, if the conditions of this Rule B appear to exist, enter an order so stating and authorizing process of attachment and garnishment. The clerk may issue supplemental process enforcing the court's order upon application without further court order.

(c) If the plaintiff or the plaintiff's attorney certifies that exigent circumstances make court review impracticable, the clerk must issue the summons and process of attachment and garnishment. The plaintiff has the burden in any post-attachment hearing under Rule E(4)(f) to show that exigent circumstances existed.

(d)(i) If the property is a vessel or tangible property on board a vessel, the summons, process, and any supplemental process must be delivered to the marshal for service.

(ii) If the property is other tangible or intangible property, the summons, process, and any supplemental process must be delivered to a person or organization authorized to serve it, who may be (A) a marshal; (B) someone under contract with the United States; (C) someone specially appointed by the court for that purpose; or, (D) in an action brought by the United States, any officer or employee of the United States.

(e) The plaintiff may invoke state-law remedies under Rule 64 for seizure of person or property for the purpose of securing satisfaction of the judgment.

(2) Notice to Defendant. No default judgment may be entered except upon proof—which may be by affidavit—that:

(a) the complaint, summons, and process of attachment or garnishment have been served on the defendant in a manner authorized by Rule 4;

(b) the plaintiff or the garnishee has mailed to the defendant the complaint, summons, and process of attachment or garnishment, using any form of mail requiring a return receipt; or

(c) the plaintiff or the garnishee has tried diligently to give notice of the action to the defendant but could not do so.

(3) Answer.

(a) By Garnishee. The garnishee shall serve an answer, together with answers to any interrogatories served with the complaint, within 20 days after service of process upon the garnishee. Interrogatories to the garnishee may be served with the complaint without leave of court. If the garnishee refuses or neglects to answer on oath as to the debts, credits, or effects of the defendant in the garnishee's hands, or any interrogatories concerning such debts, credits, and effects that may be propounded by the plaintiff, the court may award compulsory process against the garnishee. If the garnishee admits any debts, credits, or effects, they shall be held in the garnishee's hands or paid into the registry of the court, and shall be held in either case subject to the further order of the court.

(b) By Defendant. The defendant shall serve an answer within 30 days after process has been executed, whether by attachment of property or service on the garnishee.

[Added Feb. 28, 1966, eff. July 1, 1966, and amended Apr. 29, 1985, effective Aug. 1, 1985; Mar. 2, 1987, effective Aug. 1, 1987; April 17, 2000, effective December 1, 2000.]

RULE C

IN REM ACTIONS: SPECIAL PROVISIONS

(1) When Available. An action in rem may be brought:

(a) To enforce any maritime lien;

(b) Whenever a statute of the United States provides for a maritime action in rem or a proceeding analogous thereto.

Except as otherwise provided by law a party who may proceed in rem may also, or in the alternative, proceed in personam against any person who may be liable.

Statutory provisions exempting vessels or other property owned or possessed by or operated by or for the United States from arrest or seizure are not affected by this rule. When a statute so provides, an action against the United States or an instrumentality thereof may proceed on in rem principles.

(2) Complaint. In an action in rem the complaint must:

(a) be verified;

(b) describe with reasonable particularity the property that is the subject of the action;

(c) in an admiralty and maritime proceeding, state that the property is within the district or will be within the district while the action is pending;

(d) in a forfeiture proceeding for violation of a federal statute, state:

(i) the place of seizure and whether it was on land or on navigable waters;

(ii) whether the property is within the district, and if the property is not within the district the statutory basis for the court's exercise of jurisdiction over the property; and

(iii) all allegations required by the statute under which the action is brought.

(3) Judicial Authorization and Process.

(a) Arrest Warrant.

(i) When the United States files a complaint demanding a forfeiture for violation of a federal statute, the clerk must promptly issue a summons and a warrant for the arrest of the vessel or other property without requiring a certification of exigent circumstances, but if the property is real property the United States must proceed under applicable statutory procedures.

(ii)(A) In other actions, the court must review the complaint and any supporting papers. If the conditions for an in rem action appear to exist, the court must issue an order directing the clerk to issue a warrant for the arrest of the vessel or other property that is the subject of the action.

(B) If the plaintiff or the plaintiff's attorney certifies that exigent circumstances make court review impracticable, the clerk must promptly issue a summons and a warrant for the arrest of the vessel or other property that is the subject of the action. The plaintiff has the burden in any post-arrest hearing under Rule E(4)(f) to show that exigent circumstances existed.

(b) Service.

(i) If the property that is the subject of the action is a vessel or tangible property on board a vessel, the warrant and any supplemental process must be delivered to the marshal for service.

(ii) If the property that is the subject of the action is other property, tangible or intangible, the warrant and any supplemental process must be delivered to a person or organization authorized to enforce it, who may be: (A) a marshal; (B) someone under contract with the United States; (C) someone specially appointed by the court for that purpose; or, (D) in an action brought by the United States, any officer or employee of the United States.

(c) Deposit in Court. If the property that is the subject of the action consists in whole or in part of freight, the proceeds of property sold, or other intangible property, the clerk must issue—in addition to the warrant—a summons directing any person controlling the property to show cause why it should not be deposited in court to abide the judgment.

(d) Supplemental Process. The clerk may upon application issue supplemental process to enforce the court's order without further court order.

(4) Notice. No notice other than execution of process is required when the property that is the subject of the action has been released under Rule E(5). If the property is not released within 10 days after execution, the plaintiff must promptly—or within the time that the court allows—give public notice of the action and arrest in a newspaper designated by court order and having general circulation in the district, but publication may be terminated if the property is released before publication is completed. The notice must specify the time under Rule C(6) to file a statement of interest in or right against the seized property and to answer. This rule does not affect the notice requirements in an action to foreclose a preferred ship mortgage under 46 U.S.C. §§ 31301 et seq., as amended.

(5) Ancillary Process. In any action in rem in which process has been served as provided by this rule, if any part of the property that is the subject of the action has not been brought within the control of the court because it has been removed or sold, or because it is intangible property in the hands of a person who has not been served with process, the court may, on motion, order any person having possession or control of such property or its proceeds to show cause why it should not be delivered into the custody of the marshal or other person or organization having a warrant for the arrest of the property, or paid into court to abide the judgment; and, after hearing, the court may enter such judgment as law and justice may require.

(6) Responsive Pleading; Interrogatories.

(a) Civil Forfeiture. In an in rem forfeiture action for violation of a federal statute:

(i) a person who asserts an interest in or right against the property that is the subject of the action must file a verified statement identifying the interest or right:

(A) within 30 days after the earlier of (1) the date of service of the Government's complaint or (2) completed publication of notice under Rule C(4), or

(B) within the time that the court allows:

(ii) an agent, bailee, or attorney must state the authority to file a statement of interest in or right against the property on behalf of another; and

(iii) a person who files a statement of interest in or right against the property must serve and file an answer within 20 days after filing the statement.

(b) Maritime Arrests and Other Proceedings. In an in rem action not governed by Rule C(6)(a):

(i) A person who asserts a right of possession or any ownership interest in the property that is the subject of the action must file a verified statement of right or interest:

(A) within 10 days after the earlier of (1) the execution of process, or (2) completed publication of notice under Rule C(4), or

(B) within the time that the court allows:

(ii) the statement of right or interest must describe the interest in the property that supports the person's demand for its restitution or right to defend the action;

(iii) an agent, bailee, or attorney must state the authority to file a statement of right or interest on behalf of another; and

(iv) a person who asserts a right of possession or any ownership interest must serve an answer within 20 days after filing the statement of interest or right.

(c) Interrogatories. Interrogatories may be served with the complaint in an in rem action without leave of court. Answers to the interrogatories must be served with the answer to the complaint.

[Added Feb. 28, 1966, eff. Jul. 1, 1966, and amended Apr. 29, 1985, effective Aug. 1, 1985; Mar. 2, 1987, effective Aug. 1, 1987; Apr. 30, 1991, effective Dec. 1, 1991; April 17, 2000, effective December 1, 2000; April 29, 2002, effective December 1, 2002.]

RULE D

POSSESSORY, PETITORY, AND PARTITION ACTIONS

In all actions for possession, partition, and to try title maintainable according to the course of the admiralty practice with respect to a vessel, in all actions so maintainable with respect to the possession of cargo or other maritime property, and in all actions by one or more part owners against the others to obtain security for the return of the vessel from any voyage undertaken without their consent, or by one or more part owners against the others to obtain possession of the vessel for any voyage on giving security for its safe return, the process shall be by a warrant of arrest of the vessel, cargo, or other property, and by notice in the manner provided by Rule B(2) to the adverse party or parties.

[Added Feb. 28, 1966, eff. Jul. 1, 1966.]

RULE E

ACTIONS IN REM AND QUASI IN REM: GENERAL PROVISIONS

(1) Applicability. Except as otherwise provided, this rule applies to actions in personam with process of maritime attachment and garnishment, actions in rem, and petitory, possessory, and partition actions, supplementing Rules B, C, and D.

(2) Complaint; Security.

(a) *Complaint.* In actions to which this rule is applicable the complaint shall state the circumstances from which the claim arises with such particularity that the defendant or claimant will be able, without moving for a more definite statement, to commence an investigation of the facts and to frame a responsive pleading.

(b) *Security for Costs.* Subject to the provisions of Rule 54(d) and of relevant statutes, the court may, on the filing of the complaint or on the appearance of any defendant, claimant, or any other party, or at any later time, require the plaintiff, defendant, claimant, or other party to give security, or additional security, in such sum as the court shall direct to pay all costs and expenses that shall be awarded against the party by any interlocutory order or by the final judgment, or on appeal by any appellate court.

(3) Process.

(a) In admiralty and maritime proceedings process in rem or of maritime attachment and garnishment may be served only within the district.

(b) In forfeiture cases process in rem may be served within the district or outside the district when authorized by statute.

(c) Issuance and Delivery. Issuance and delivery of process in rem, or of maritime attachment and garnishment, shall be held in abeyance if the plaintiff so requests.

(4) Execution of Process; Marshal's Return; Custody of Property; Procedures for Release.

(a) *In General.* Upon issuance and delivery of the process, or, in the case of summons with process of attachment and garnishment, when it appears that the defendant cannot be found within the district, the marshal or other person or organization having a warrant shall forthwith execute the process in accordance with this subdivision (4), making due and prompt return.

(b) *Tangible Property.* If tangible property is to be attached or arrested, the marshal or other person or organization having the warrant shall take it into the marshal's possession for safe custody. If the character or situation of the property is such that the taking of actual possession is impracticable, the marshal or other person executing the process shall affix a copy thereof to the property in a conspicuous place and leave a copy of the complaint and process with the person having possession or the person's agent. In furtherance of the marshal's custody of any vessel the marshal is authorized to make a written request to the collector of customs not to grant clearance to such vessel until notified by the marshal or deputy marshal or by the clerk that the vessel has been released in accordance with these rules.

(c) *Intangible Property.* If intangible property is to be attached or arrested the marshal or other person or organization having the warrant shall execute the process by leaving with the garnishee or other obligor a copy of the complaint and process requiring the garnishee or other obligor to answer as provided in Rules B(3)(a) and C(6); or the marshal may accept for payment into the registry of the court the amount owed to the extent of the amount claimed by the plaintiff with interest and costs, in which event the garnishee or other obligor shall not be required to answer unless alias process shall be served.

(d) *Directions With Respect to Property in Custody.* The marshal or other person or organization having the warrant may at any time apply to the court for directions with respect to property that has been attached or arrested, and shall give notice of such application to any or all of the parties as the court may direct.

(e) *Expenses of Seizing and Keeping Property; Deposit.* These rules do not alter the provisions of Title 28, U.S.C., § 1921, as amended, relative to the expenses of seizing and keeping property attached or arrested and to the requirement of deposits to cover such expenses.

(f) *Procedure for Release From Arrest or Attachment.* Whenever property is arrested or attached, any person claiming an interest in it shall be entitled to a prompt hearing at which the plaintiff shall be required to show why the arrest or attachment should not be vacated or other relief granted consistent with these rules. This subdivision shall have no application to suits for seamen's wages when process is issued upon a certification of sufficient cause filed pursuant to Title 46, U.S.C. §§ 603 and 604 or to actions by the United States for forfeitures for violation of any statute of the United States.

(5) Release of Property.

(a) *Special Bond.* Except in cases of seizures for forfeiture under any law of the United States, whenever process of maritime attachment and garnishment or process in rem is issued the execution of such process shall be stayed, or the property released, on the giving of security, to be approved by the court or clerk, or by stipulation of the parties, conditioned to answer the judgment of the court or of any appellate court. The parties may stipulate the amount and nature of such security. In the event of the inability or refusal of the parties so to stipulate the court shall fix the principal sum of the bond or stipulation at an amount sufficient to cover the amount of the plaintiff's claim fairly stated with accrued interest and costs; but the principal sum shall in no event exceed (i) twice the amount of the plaintiff's claim or (ii) the value of the property on due appraisement, whichever is smaller. The bond or stipulation shall be conditioned for the payment of the principal sum and interest thereon at 6 per cent per annum.

(b) *General Bond.* The owner of any vessel may file a general bond or stipulation, with sufficient surety, to be approved by the court, conditioned to answer the judgment of such court in all or any actions that may be brought thereafter in such court in which the vessel is attached or arrested. Thereupon the execution of all such process against such vessel shall be stayed so long as the amount secured by such bond or stipulation is at least double the aggregate amount claimed by plaintiffs in all actions begun and pending in which such vessel has been attached or arrested. Judgments and remedies may be had on such bond or stipulation as if a special bond or stipulation had been filed in each of such actions. The district court may make necessary orders to carry this rule into effect, particularly as to the giving of proper notice of any action against or attachment of a vessel for which a general bond has been filed. Such bond or stipulation shall be indorsed by the clerk with a minute of the actions wherein process is so stayed. Further security may be required by the court at any time.

If a special bond or stipulation is given in a particular case, the liability on the general bond or stipulation shall cease as to that case.

(c) *Release by Consent or Stipulation; Order of Court or Clerk; Costs.* Any vessel, cargo, or other property in the custody of the marshal or other person or organization having the warrant may be released forthwith upon the marshal's acceptance and approval of a stipulation, bond, or other security, signed by the party on whose behalf the property is detained or the party's attorney and expressly authorizing such release, if all costs and charges of the court and its officers shall have first been paid. Otherwise no property in the custody of the marshal, other person or organization having the warrant, or other officer of the court shall be released without an order of the court; but such order may be entered as of course by the clerk, upon the giving of approved security as provided by law and these rules, or upon the dismissal or discontinuance of the action; but the marshal or other person or organization having the warrant shall not deliver any property so released until the costs and charges of the officers of the court shall first have been paid.

(d) *Possessory, Petitory, and Partition Actions.* The foregoing provisions of this subdivision (5) do not apply to petitory, possessory, and partition actions. In such cases the property arrested shall be released only by order of the court, on such terms and conditions and on the giving of such security as the court may require.

(6) Reduction or Impairment of Security. Whenever security is taken the court may, on motion and hearing, for good cause shown, reduce the amount of security given; and if the surety shall be or become insufficient, new or additional sureties may be required on motion and hearing.

(7) Security on Counterclaim.

(a) When a person who has given security for damages in the original action asserts a counterclaim that arises from the transaction or occurrence that is the subject of the original action, a plaintiff for whose benefit the security has been given must give security for damages demanded in the counterclaim unless the court for cause shown, directs otherwise. Proceedings on the original claim must be stayed until this security is given unless the court directs otherwise.

(b) The plaintiff is required to give security under Rule E(7)(a) when the United States or its corporate instrumentality counterclaims and would have been required to give security to respond in damages if a private party but is relieved by law from giving security.

(8) Restricted Appearance. An appearance to defend against an admiralty and maritime claim with respect to which there has issued process in rem, or process of attachment and garnishment, may be expressly restricted to the defense of such claim, and in that event is not an appearance for the purposes of any other claim with respect to which such process is not available or has not been served.

(9) Disposition of Property; Sales.

(a) *Actions for Forfeitures.* In any action in rem to enforce a forfeiture for violation of a statute of the United States the property shall be disposed of as provided by statute.

(b) ***Interlocutory Sales; Delivery.***

(i) On application of a party, the marshal, or other person having custody of the property, the court may order all or part of the property sold—with the sales proceeds, or as much of them as will satisfy the judgment, paid into court to await further orders of the court—if:

(A) the attached or arrested property is perishable, or liable to deterioration, decay, or injury by being detained in custody pending the action;

(B) the expense of keeping the property is excessive or disproportionate; or

(C) there is an unreasonable delay in securing release of the property.

(ii) In the circumstances described in Rule E(9)(b)(i), the court, on motion by a defendant or a person filing a statement of interest or right under Rule C(6), may order that the property, rather than being sold, be delivered to the movant upon giving security under these rules.

(c) *Sales, Proceeds.* All sales of property shall be made by the marshal or a deputy marshal, or by other person or organization having the warrant, or by any other person assigned by the court where the marshal or other person or organization having the warrant is a party in interest; and the proceeds of sale shall be forthwith paid into the registry of the court to be disposed of according to law.

(10) Preservation of Property. When the owner or another person remains in possession of property attached or arrested under the provisions of Rule E(4)(b) that permit execution of process without taking actual possession, the court, on a party's motion or on its own, may enter any order necessary to preserve the property and to prevent its removal.

[Added Feb. 28, 1966, eff. Jul. 1, 1966, and amended Apr. 29, 1985, effective Aug. 1, 1985; Mar. 2, 1987, effective Aug. 1, 1987; Apr. 30, 1991, effective Dec. 1, 1991; April 17, 2000, effective December 1, 2000.]

RULE F

LIMITATION OF LIABILITY

(1) Time for Filing Complaint; Security. Not later than six months after receipt of a claim in writing, any vessel owner may file a complaint in the appropriate district court, as provided in subdivision (9) of this rule, for limitation of liability pursuant to statute. The owner (a) shall deposit with the court, for the benefit of claimants, a sum equal to the amount or value of the owner's interest in the vessel and pending freight, or approved security therefor, and in addition such sums, or approved security therefor, as the court may from time to time fix as necessary to carry out the provisions of the statutes as amended; or (b) at the owner's option shall transfer to a trustee to be appointed by the court, for the benefit of claimants, the owner's interest in the vessel and pending freight, together with such sums, or approved security therefor, as the court may from time to time fix as necessary to carry out the provisions of the statutes as amended. The plaintiff shall also give security for costs and, if the plaintiff elects to give security, for interest at the rate of 6 percent per annum from the date of the security.

(2) Complaint. The complaint shall set forth the facts on the basis of which the right to limit liability is asserted and all facts necessary to enable the court to determine the amount to which the owner's liability shall be limited. The complaint may demand exoneration from as well as limitation of liability. It shall state the voyage if any, on which the demands sought to be limited arose, with the date and place of its termination; the amount of all demands including all unsatisfied liens or claims of lien, in contract or in tort or otherwise, arising on that voyage, so far as known to the plaintiff, and what actions and proceedings, if any, are pending thereon; whether the vessel was damaged, lost, or abandoned, and, if so, when and where; the value of the vessel at the close of the voyage or, in case of wreck, the value of her wreckage, strippings, or proceeds, if any, and where and in whose possession they are; and the amount of any pending freight recovered or recoverable. If the plaintiff elects to transfer the plaintiff's interest in the vessel to a trustee, the complaint must further show any prior paramount liens thereon, and what voyages or trips, if any, she has made since the voyage or trip on which the claims sought to be limited arose, and any existing liens arising upon any such subsequent voyage or trip, with the amounts and causes thereof, and the names and addresses of the lienors, so far as known; and whether the vessel sustained any injury upon or by reason of such subsequent voyage or trip.

(3) Claims Against Owner; Injunction. Upon compliance by the owner with the requirements of subdivision (1) of this rule all claims and proceedings against the owner or the owner's property with respect to the matter in question shall cease. On application of the plaintiff the court shall enjoin the further prosecution of any action or proceeding against the plaintiff or the plaintiff's property with respect to any claim subject to limitation in the action.

(4) Notice to Claimants. Upon the owner's compliance with subdivision (1) of this rule the court shall issue a notice to all persons asserting claims with respect to which the complaint seeks limitation, admonishing them to file their respective claims with the clerk of the court and to serve on the attorneys for the plaintiff a copy thereof on or before a date to be named in the notice. The date so fixed shall not be less than 30 days after issuance of the notice. For cause shown, the court may enlarge the time within which claims may be filed. The notice shall be published in such newspaper or newspapers as the court may direct once a week for four successive weeks prior to the date fixed for the filing of claims. The plaintiff not later than the day of second publication shall also mail a copy of the notice to every person known to have made any claim against the vessel or the plaintiff arising out of the voyage or trip on which the claims sought to be limited arose. In cases involving death a copy of such notice shall be mailed to the decedent at the decedent's last known address, and also to any person who shall be known to have made any claim on account of such death.

(5) Claims and Answer. Claims shall be filed and served on or before the date specified in the notice provided for in subdivision (4) of this rule. Each claim shall specify the facts upon which the claimant relies in support of the claim, the items thereof, and the dates on which the same accrued. If a claimant desires to contest either the right to exoneration from or the right to limitation of liability the claimant shall file and serve an answer to the complaint unless the claim has included an answer.

(6) Information to Be Given Claimants. Within 30 days after the date specified in the notice for filing claims, or within such time as the court thereafter may allow, the plaintiff shall mail to the attorney for each claimant (or if the claimant has no attorney to the claimant) a list setting forth (a) the name of each claimant, (b) the name and address of the claimant's attorney (if the claimant is known to have one), (c) the nature of the claim, i.e., whether property loss, property damage, death, personal injury etc., and (d) the amount thereof.

(7) Insufficiency of Fund or Security. Any claimant may by motion demand that the funds deposited in court or the security given by the plaintiff be increased on the ground that they are less than the value of the plaintiff's interest in the vessel and pending freight. Thereupon the court shall cause due appraisement to be made of the value of the plaintiff's interest in the vessel and pending freight; and if the court finds that the deposit or security is either insufficient or excessive it shall order its increase or reduction. In like manner any claimant may demand that the deposit or security be increased on the ground that it is insufficient to carry out the provisions of the statutes relating to claims in respect of loss of life or bodily injury; and, after notice and hearing, the court may similarly order that the deposit or security be increased or reduced.

(8) Objections to Claims: Distribution of Fund. Any interested party may question or controvert any claim without filing an objection thereto. Upon determination of liability the fund deposited or secured, or the proceeds of the vessel and pending freight, shall be divided pro rata, subject to all relevant provisions of law, among the several claimants in proportion to the amounts of their respective claims, duly proved, saving, however, to all parties any priority to which they may be legally entitled.

(9) Venue; Transfer. The complaint shall be filed in any district in which the vessel has been attached or arrested to answer for any claim with respect to which the plaintiff seeks to limit liability; or, if the vessel has not been attached or arrested, then in any district in which the owner has been sued with respect to any such claim. When the vessel has not been attached or arrested to answer the matters aforesaid, and suit has not been commenced against the owner, the proceedings may be had in the district in which the vessel may be, but if the vessel is not within any district and no suit has been commenced in any district, then the complaint may be filed in any district. For the convenience of parties and witnesses, in the interest of justice, the court may transfer the action to any district; if venue is wrongly laid the court shall dismiss or, if it be in the interest of justice, transfer the action to any district in which it could have been brought. If the vessel shall have been sold, the proceeds shall represent the vessel for the purposes of these rules.

[Added Feb. 28, 1966, eff. Jul. 1, 1966, and amended Mar. 2, 1987, effective Aug. 1, 1987.]

*

PART V

APPENDIX OF FORMS

(See Rule 84)

Table of Forms

INTRODUCTORY STATEMENT

1. The following forms are intended for illustration only. They are limited in number. No attempt is made to furnish a manual of forms. Each form assumes the action to be brought in the Southern District of New York. If the district in which an action is brought has divisions, the division should be indicated in the caption.

2. Except where otherwise indicated each pleading, motion, and other paper should have a caption similar to that of the summons, with the designation of the particular paper substituted for the word "Summons". In the caption of the summons and in the caption of the complaint all parties must be named but in other pleadings and papers, it is sufficient to state the name of the first party on either side, with an appropriate indication of other parties. See Rules 4(b), 7(b)(2), and 10(a).

3. In Form 3 and the forms following, the words, "Allegation of jurisdiction," are used to indicate the appropriate allegation in Form 2.

4. Each pleading, motion, and other paper is to be signed in his individual name by at least one attorney of record (Rule 11). The attorney's name is to be followed by his address as indicated in Form 3. In forms following Form 3 the signature and address are not indicated.

5. If a party is not represented by an attorney, the signature and address of the party are required in place of those of the attorney.

FORM 1
SUMMONS

United States District Court for the Southern District of New York

Civil Action, File Number ______

A. B., Plaintiff)
v.) *Summons*
C. D., Defendant)

To the above-named Defendant:

You are hereby summoned and required to serve upon ______, plaintiff's attorney, whose address is ______, an answer to the complaint which is herewith served upon you, within 20[1] days after service of this summons upon you, exclusive of the day of service. If you fail to do so, judgment by default will be taken against you for the relief demanded in the complaint.

____
Clerk of Court.

[Seal of the U.S. District Court]

Dated ______

(This summons is issued pursuant to Rule 4 of
the Federal Rules of Civil Procedure.)

1. If the United States or an officer or agency thereof is a defendant, the time to be inserted as to it is 60 days.

[Amended December 29, 1948, effective October 20, 1949.]

FORM 1A

NOTICE OF LAWSUIT AND REQUEST FOR WAIVER OF SERVICE OF SUMMONS

TO: (A)
____
[as (B) of (C)]
______________ ______________

A lawsuit has been commenced against you (or the entity on whose behalf you are addressed). A copy of the complaint is attached to this notice. It has been filed in the United States District Court for the (D) and has been assigned docket number (E) .

This is not a formal summons or notification from the court, but rather my request that you sign and return the enclosed waiver of service in order to save the cost of serving you with a judicial summons and an additional copy of the complaint. The cost of service will be avoided if I receive a signed copy of the waiver within (F) days after the date designated below as the date on which this Notice and Request is sent. I enclose a stamped and addressed envelope (or other means of cost-free return) for your use. An extra copy of the waiver is also attached for your records.

If you comply with this request and return the signed waiver, it will be filed with the court and no summons will be served on you. The action will then proceed as if you had been served on the date the waiver is filed, except that you will not be obligated to answer the complaint before 60 days from the date designated below as the date on which this notice is sent (or before 90 days from that date if your address is not in any judicial district of the United States).

If you do not return the signed waiver within the time indicated, I will take appropriate steps to effect formal service in a manner authorized by the Federal Rules of Civil Procedure and will then, to the extent authorized by those Rules, ask the court to require you (or the party on whose behalf you are addressed) to pay the full costs of such service. In that connection, please read the statement concerning the duty of parties to waive the service of the summons, which is set forth on the reverse side (or at the foot) of the waiver form.

I affirm that this request is being sent to you on behalf of the plaintiff, this ___ day of ______, ___.

____
Signature of Plaintiff's Attorney or
Unrepresented Plaintiff

Notes:

A—Name of individual defendant (or name of officer or agent of corporate defendant)

B—Title, or other relationship of individual to corporate defendant

C—Name of corporate defendant, if any

D—District

E—Docket number of action

F—Addressee must be given at least 30 days (60 days if located in foreign country) in which to return waiver

[Adopted April 22, 1993, effective December 1, 1993.]

FORM 1B
WAIVER OF SERVICE OF SUMMONS

TO: (name of plaintiff's attorney or unrepresented plaintiff)

I acknowledge receipt of your request that I waive service of a summons in the action of (caption of action), which is case number (docket number) in the United States District Court for the (district). I have also received a copy of the complaint in the action, two copies of this instrument, and a means by which I can return the signed waiver to you without cost to me.

I agree to save the cost of service of a summons and an additional copy of the complaint in this lawsuit by not requiring that I (or the entity on whose behalf I am acting) be served with judicial process in the manner provided by Rule 4.

I (or the entity on whose behalf I am acting) will retain all defenses or objections to the lawsuit or to the jurisdiction or venue of the court except for objections based on a defect in the summons or in the service of the summons.

I understand that a judgment may be entered against me (or the party on whose behalf I am acting) if an answer or motion under Rule 12 is not served upon you within 60 days after (date request was sent), or within 90 days after that date if the request was sent outside the United States.

____________________ ____________________

Date Signature

Printed/typed name: __________

[as _______________]

[of _______________]

To be printed on reverse side of the waiver form or set forth at the foot of the form:

Duty to Avoid Unnecessary Costs of Service of Summons

Rule 4 of the Federal Rules of Civil Procedure requires certain parties to cooperate in saving unnecessary costs of service of the summons and complaint. A defendant located in the United States who, after being notified of an action and asked by a plaintiff located in the United States to waive service of a summons, fails to do so will be required to bear the cost of such service unless good cause be shown for its failure to sign and return the waiver.

It is not good cause for a failure to waive service that a party believes that the complaint is unfounded, or that the action has been brought in an improper place or in a court that lacks jurisdiction over the subject matter of the action or over its person or property. A party who waives service of the summons retains all defenses and objections (except any relating to the summons or to the service of the summons), and may later object to the jurisdiction of the court or to the place where the action has been brought.

A defendant who waives service must within the time specified on the waiver form serve on the plaintiff's attorney (or unrepresented plaintiff) a response to the complaint and must also file a signed copy of the response with the court. If the answer or motion is not served within this time, a default judgment may be taken against that defendant. By waiving service, a defendant is allowed more time to answer than if the summons had been actually served when the request for waiver of service was received.

[Adopted April 22, 1993, effective December 1, 1993.]

FORM 2
ALLEGATION OF JURISDICTION

(a) Jurisdiction Founded on Diversity of Citizenship and Amount.

Plaintiff is a [citizen of the State of Connecticut] [1] [corporation incorporated under the laws of the State of Connecticut having its principal place of business in the State of Connecticut] and defendant is a corporation incorporated under the laws of the State of New York having its principal place of business in a State other than the State of Connecticut. The matter in controversy exceeds, exclusive of interest and costs, the sum specified by 28 U.S.C. § 1332.

(b) Jurisdiction Founded on the Existence of a Federal Question.

The action arises under [the Constitution of the United States, Article _______, Section _______]; [the _______ Amendment to the Constitution of the United States, Section _______]; [the Act of _______, _______ Stat. _______; U.S.C., Title _______, § _______]; [the Treaty of the United States (here describe the treaty)] [2] as hereinafter more fully appears.

(c) Jurisdiction Founded on the Existence of a Question Arising Under Particular Statutes.

The action arises under the Act of _______, _______ Stat. _______; U.S.C., Title _______, § _______, as hereinafter more fully appears.

(d) Jurisdiction Founded on the Admiralty or Maritime Character of the Claim.

This is a case of admiralty and maritime jurisdiction, as hereinafter more fully appears. [If the pleader wishes to invoke the distinctively maritime procedures referred to in Rule 9(h), add the following or its substantial equivalent: This is an admiralty or maritime claim within the meaning of Rule 9(h).]

1. Form for natural person.

2. Use the appropriate phrase or phrases. The general allegation of the existence of a Federal question is ineffective unless the matters constituting the claim for relief as set forth in the complaint raise a Federal question.

Notes of Advisory Committee

1. Diversity of citizenship. U.S.C., Title 28, § 1332 (Diversity of citizenship; amount in controversy; costs), as amended by PL 85–554, 72 Stat. 415, July 25, 1958, states in subsection (c) that "For the purposes of this section and section 1441 of this

title [removable actions], a corporation shall be deemed a citizen of any State by which it has been incorporated and of the State where it has its principal place of business.'' Thus if the defendant corporation in Form 2(a) had its principal place of business in Connecticut, diversity of citizenship would not exist. An allegation regarding the principal place of business of each corporate party must be made in addition to an allegation regarding its place of incorporation.

2. Jurisdictional amount. U.S.C., Title 28, § 1331 (Federal question; amount in controversy; costs) and § 1332 (Diversity of citizenship; amount in controversy; costs), as amended by PL 85–554, 72 Stat. 415, July 25, 1958, require that the amount in controversy, exclusive of interest and costs, be in excess of $10,000. The allegation as to the amount in controversy may be omitted in any case where by law no jurisdictional amount is required. See, for example, (Patents, copyrights, trademarks, and unfair competition), § 1343 (Civil rights and elective franchise).

3. Pleading venue. Since improper venue is a matter of defense, it is not necessary for plaintiff to include allegations showing the venue to be proper. See 1 Moore's Federal Practice, par. 0.140[1–4] (2d ed. 1959).

(As amended Apr. 17, 1961, eff. July 19, 1961; Feb. 28, 1966, eff. July 1, 1966; Apr. 22, 1993, eff. Dec. 1, 1993; Apr. 29, 1999, eff. Dec. 1, 1999.)

FORM 3

COMPLAINT ON A PROMISSORY NOTE

1. Allegation of jurisdiction.

2. Defendant on or about June 1, 1935, executed and delivered to plaintiff a promissory note [in the following words and figures: (here set out the note verbatim)]; [a copy of which is hereto annexed as Exhibit A]; [whereby defendant promised to pay to plaintiff or order on June 1, 1936 the sum of _______ dollars with interest thereon at the rate of six percent. per annum].

3. Defendant owes to plaintiff the amount of said note and interest.

Wherefore plaintiff demands judgment against defendant for the sum of ______ dollars, interest, and costs.

Signed: ____________________________
Attorney for Plaintiff.

Address: ___________________________

[Amended January 21, 1963, effective July 1, 1963.]

Notes of Advisory Committee

1. The pleader may use the material in one of the three sets of brackets. His choice will depend upon whether he desires to plead the document verbatim, or by exhibit, or according to its legal effect.

2. Under the rules free joinder of claims is permitted. See Rules 8(e) and 18. Consequently the claims set forth in each and all of the following forms may be joined with this complaint or with each other. Ordinarily each claim should be stated in a separate division of the complaint, and the divisions should be designated as counts successively numbered. In particular the rules permit alternative and inconsistent pleading. See Form 10.

FORM 4

COMPLAINT ON AN ACCOUNT

1. Allegation of jurisdiction.

2. Defendant owes plaintiff _______ dollars according to the account hereto annexed as Exhibit A.

Wherefore (etc. as in Form 3).

[Amended January 21, 1963, effective July 1, 1963.]

FORM 5

COMPLAINT FOR GOODS SOLD AND DELIVERED

1. Allegation of jurisdiction.

2. Defendant owes plaintiff _______ dollars for goods sold and delivered by plaintiff to defendant between June 1, 1936 and December 1, 1936.

Wherefore (etc. as in Form 3).

[Amended January 21, 1963, effective July 1, 1963.]

Notes of Advisory Committee

This form may be used where the action is for an agreed price or for the reasonable value of the goods.

FORM 6

COMPLAINT FOR MONEY LENT

1. Allegation of jurisdiction.

2. Defendant owes plaintiff ______ dollars for money lent by plaintiff to defendant on June 1, 1936.

Wherefore (etc. as in Form 3).

[Amended January 21, 1963, effective July 1, 1963.]

FORM 7

COMPLAINT FOR MONEY PAID BY MISTAKE

1. Allegation of jurisdiction.

2. Defendant owes plaintiff ______ dollars for money paid by plaintiff to defendant by mistake on June 1, 1936, under the following circumstances: [here state the circumstances with particularity—see Rule 9(b)].

Wherefore (etc. as in Form 3).

[Amended January 21, 1963, effective July 1, 1963.]

FORM 8

COMPLAINT FOR MONEY HAD AND RECEIVED

1. Allegation of jurisdiction.

2. Defendant owes plaintiff ______ dollars for money had and received from one G. H. on June 1, 1936, to be paid by defendant to plaintiff.

Wherefore (etc. as in Form 3).

[Amended January 21, 1963, effective July 1, 1963.]

FORM 9

COMPLAINT FOR NEGLIGENCE

1. Allegation of jurisdiction.

2. On June 1, 1936, in a public highway called Boylston Street in Boston, Massachusetts, defendant negligently drove a motor vehicle against plaintiff who was then crossing said highway.

3. As a result plaintiff was thrown down and had his leg broken and was otherwise injured, was prevented from transacting his business, suffered great pain of body and mind, and incurred expenses for medical attention and hospitalization in the sum of one thousand dollars.

Wherefore plaintiff demands judgment against defendant in the sum of ______ dollars and costs.

[Amended January 21, 1963, effective July 1, 1963.]

Notes of Advisory Committee

Since contributory negligence is an affirmative defense, the complaint need contain no allegation of due care of plaintiff.

FORM 10

COMPLAINT FOR NEGLIGENCE WHERE PLAINTIFF IS UNABLE TO DETERMINE DEFINITELY WHETHER THE PERSON RESPONSIBLE IS C. D. OR E. F. OR WHETHER BOTH ARE RESPONSIBLE AND WHERE HIS EVIDENCE MAY JUSTIFY A FINDING OF WILFULNESS OR OF RECKLESSNESS OR OF NEGLIGENCE

A. B., Plaintiff)
v.) *Complaint*
C. D. and E. F., Defendants)

1. Allegation of jurisdiction.

2. On June 1, 1936, in a public highway called Boylston Street in Boston, Massachusetts, defendant C. D. or defendant E. F., or both defendants C. D. and E. F. wilfully or recklessly or negligently drove or caused to be driven a motor vehicle against plaintiff who was then crossing said highway.

3. As a result plaintiff was thrown down and had his leg broken and was otherwise injured, was prevented from transacting his business, suffered great pain of body and mind, and incurred expenses for medical attention and hospitalization in the sum of one thousand dollars.

Wherefore plaintiff demands judgment against C. D. or against E. F. or against both in the sum of ______ dollars and costs.

[Amended January 21, 1963, effective July 1, 1963.]

FORM 11

COMPLAINT FOR CONVERSION

1. Allegation of jurisdiction.

2. On or about December 1, 1936, defendant converted to his own use ten bonds of the ______ Company (here insert brief identification as by number and issue) of the value of ______ dollars, the property of plaintiff.

Wherefore plaintiff demands judgment against defendant in the sum of ______ dollars, interest, and costs.

[Amended January 21, 1963, effective July 1, 1963.]

FORM 12

COMPLAINT FOR SPECIFIC PERFORMANCE OF CONTRACT TO CONVEY LAND

1. Allegation of jurisdiction.

2. On or about December 1, 1936, plaintiff and defendant entered into an agreement in writing a copy of which is hereto annexed as Exhibit A.

3. In accord with the provisions of said agreement plaintiff tendered to defendant the purchase price and requested a conveyance of the land, but defendant refused to accept the tender and refused to make the conveyance.

4. Plaintiff now offers to pay the purchase price.

Wherefore plaintiff demands (1) that defendant be required specifically to perform said agreement, (2) damages in the sum of one thousand dollars, and (3) that if specific performance is not granted plaintiff have judgment against defendant in the sum of ______ dollars.

[Amended January 21, 1963, effective July 1, 1963.]

Notes of Advisory Committee

Here, as in Form 3, plaintiff may set forth the contract verbatim in the complaint or plead it, as indicated, by exhibit, or plead it according to its legal effect. Furthermore, plaintiff may seek legal or equitable relief or both even though this was impossible under the system in operation before these rules.

FORM 13

COMPLAINT ON CLAIM FOR DEBT AND TO SET ASIDE FRAUDULENT CONVEYANCE UNDER RULE 18(b)

A. B., Plaintiff)
v.) *Complaint*
C. D. and E. F., Defendants)

1. Allegation of jurisdiction.

2. Defendant C. D. on or about ______ executed and delivered to plaintiff a promissory note [in the following words and figures: (here set out the note verbatim)]; [a copy of which is hereto annexed as Exhibit A]; [whereby defendant C. D. promised to pay to plaintiff or order on ______ the sum of five thousand dollars with interest thereon at the rate of ______ percent. per annum].

3. Defendant C. D. owes to plaintiff the amount of said note and interest.

4. Defendant C. D. on or about ______ conveyed all his property, real and personal [or specify and describe] to defendant E. F. for the purpose of defrauding plaintiff and hindering and delaying the collection of the indebtedness evidenced by the note above referred to.

Wherefore plaintiff demands:

(1) That plaintiff have judgment against defendant C. D. for ______ dollars and interest; (2) that the aforesaid conveyance to defendant E. F. be declared void and the judgment herein be declared a lien on said property; (3) that plaintiff have judgment against the defendants for costs.

[Amended January 21, 1963, effective July 1, 1963.]

FORM 14

COMPLAINT FOR NEGLIGENCE UNDER FEDERAL EMPLOYERS' LIABILITY ACT

1. Allegation of jurisdiction.

2. During all the times herein mentioned defendant owned and operated in interstate commerce a railroad which passed through a tunnel located at ______ and known as Tunnel No. ______.

3. On or about June 1, 1936, defendant was repairing and enlarging the tunnel in order to protect interstate trains and passengers and freight from

injury and in order to make the tunnel more conveniently usable for interstate commerce.

4. In the course of thus repairing and enlarging the tunnel on said day defendant employed plaintiff as one of its workmen, and negligently put plaintiff to work in a portion of the tunnel which defendant had left unprotected and unsupported.

5. By reason of defendant's negligence in thus putting plaintiff to work in that portion of the tunnel, plaintiff was, while so working pursuant to defendant's orders, struck and crushed by a rock, which fell from the unsupported portion of the tunnel, and was (here describe plaintiff's injuries).

6. Prior to these injuries, plaintiff was a strong, able-bodied man, capable of earning and actually earning ______ dollars per day. By these injuries he has been made incapable of any gainful activity, has suffered great physical and mental pain, and has incurred expense in the amount of ______ dollars for medicine, medical attendance, and hospitalization.

Wherefore plaintiff demands judgment against defendant in the sum of ______ dollars and costs.

FORM 15

COMPLAINT FOR DAMAGES UNDER MERCHANT MARINE ACT

1. Allegation of jurisdiction. [If the pleader wishes to invoke the distinctively maritime procedures referred to in Rule 9(h), add the following or its substantial equivalent: This is an admiralty or maritime claim within the meaning of Rule 9(h).]

2. During all the times herein mentioned defendant was the owner of the steamship ______ and used it in the transportation of freight for hire by water in interstate and foreign commerce.

3. During the first part of (month and year) at ______ plaintiff entered the employ of defendant as an able seaman on said steamship under seamen's articles of customary form for a voyage from ______ ports to the Orient and return at a wage of ______ dollars per month and found, which is equal to a wage of ______ dollars per month as a shore worker.

4. On June 1, 1936, said steamship was about ______ days out of the port of ______ and was being navigated by the master and crew on the return voyage to ______ ports. (Here describe weather conditions and the condition of the ship and state as in an ordinary complaint for personal injuries the negligent conduct of defendant.)

5. By reason of defendant's negligence in thus (brief statement of defendant's negligent conduct) and the unseaworthiness of said steamship, plaintiff was (here describe plaintiff's injuries).

6. Prior to these injuries, plaintiff was a strong, able-bodied man, capable of earning and actually earning ______ dollars per day. By these injuries he has been made incapable of any gainful activity; has suffered great physical and mental pain, and has incurred expense in the amount of ______ dollars for medicine, medical attendance, and hospitalization.

Wherefore plaintiff demands judgment against defendant in the sum of ______ dollars and costs.

[Amended February 28, 1966, effective July 1, 1966.]

FORM 16

COMPLAINT FOR INFRINGEMENT OF PATENT

1. Allegation of jurisdiction.

2. On May 16, 1934, United States Letters Patent No. ______ were duly and legally issued to plaintiff for an invention in an electric motor; and since that date plaintiff has been and still is the owner of those Letters Patent.

3. Defendant has for a long time past been and still is infringing those Letters Patent by making, selling, and using electric motors embodying the patented invention, and will continue to do so unless enjoined by this court.

4. Plaintiff has placed the required statutory notice on all electric motors manufactured and sold by him under said Letters Patent, and has given written notice to defendant of his said infringement.

Wherefore plaintiff demands a preliminary and final injunction against continued infringement, an accounting for damages, and an assessment of interest and costs against defendant.

[Amended January 21, 1963, effective July 1, 1963.]

FORM 17

COMPLAINT FOR INFRINGEMENT OF COPYRIGHT AND UNFAIR COMPETITION

1. Allegation of jurisdiction.

2. Prior to March, 1936, plaintiff, who then was and ever since has been a citizen of the United States, created and wrote an original book, entitled ______.

3. This book contains a large amount of material wholly original with plaintiff and is copyrightable subject matter under the laws of the United States.

4. Between March 2, 1936, and March 10, 1936, plaintiff complied in all respects with the Act of (give citation) and all other laws governing copyright, and secured the exclusive rights and privileges in and to the copyright of said book, and received from the Register of Copyrights a certificate of registration, dated and identified as follows: "March 10, 1936, Class ______, No. ______."

5. Since March 10, 1936, said book has been published by plaintiff and all copies of it made by plaintiff or under his authority or license have been printed, bound, and published in strict conformity with the provisions of the Act of ______ and all other laws governing copyright.

6. Since March 10, 1936, plaintiff has been and still is the sole proprietor of all rights, title, and interest in and to the copyright in said book.

7. After March 10, 1936, defendant infringed said copyright by publishing and placing upon the market a book entitled ______, which was copied largely from plaintiff's copyrighted book, entitled ______.

8. A copy of plaintiff's copyrighted book is hereto attached as "Exhibit 1"; and a copy of defendant's infringing book is hereto attached as "Exhibit 2."

9. Plaintiff has notified defendant that defendant has infringed the copyright of plaintiff, and defendant has continued to infringe the copyright.

10. After March 10, 1936, and continuously since about ______, defendant has been publishing, selling and otherwise marketing the book entitled ______, and has thereby been engaging in unfair trade practices and unfair competition against plaintiff to plaintiff's irreparable damage.

Wherefore plaintiff demands:

(1) That defendant, his agents, and servants be enjoined during the pendency of this action and permanently from infringing said copyright of said plaintiff in any manner, and from publishing, selling, marketing or otherwise disposing of any copies of the book entitled ______.

(2) That defendant be required to pay to plaintiff such damages as plaintiff has sustained in consequence of defendant's infringement of said copyright and said unfair trade practices and unfair competition and to account for

(a) all gains, profits and advantages derived by defendant by said trade practices and unfair competition and

(b) all gains, profits, and advantages derived by defendant by his infringement of plaintiff's copyright or such damages as to the court shall appear proper within the provisions of the copyright statutes, but not less than two hundred and fifty dollars.

(3) That defendant be required to deliver up to be impounded during the pendency of this action all copies of said book entitled ______ in his possession or under his control and to deliver up for destruction all infringing copies and all plates, molds, and other matter for making such infringing copies.

(4) That defendant pay to plaintiff the costs of this action and reasonable attorney's fees to be allowed to the plaintiff by the court.

(5) That plaintiff have such other and further relief as is just.

[Amended December 27, 1946, effective March 19, 1948.]

FORM 18

COMPLAINT FOR INTERPLEADER AND DECLARATORY RELIEF

1. Allegation of jurisdiction.

2. On or about June 1, 1935, plaintiff issued to G. H. a policy of life insurance whereby plaintiff promised to pay to K. L. as beneficiary the sum of ______ dollars upon the death of G. H. The policy required the payment by G. H. of a stipulated premium on June 1, 1936, and annually thereafter as a condition precedent to its continuance in force.

3. No part of the premium due June 1, 1936, was ever paid and the policy ceased to have any force or effect on July 1, 1936.

4. Thereafter, on September 1, 1936, G. H. and K. L. died as the result of a collision between a locomotive and the automobile in which G. H. and K. L. were riding.

5. Defendant C. D. is the duly appointed and acting executor of the will of G. H.; defendant E. F. is the duly appointed and acting executor of the will of K. L.; defendant X. Y. claims to have been duly designated as beneficiary of said policy in place of K. L.

6. Each of defendants, C. D., E. F., and X. Y. is claiming that the above-mentioned policy was in full force and effect at the time of the death of G. H.;

each of them is claiming to be the only person entitled to receive payment of the amount of the policy and has made demand for payment thereof.

7. By reason of these conflicting claims of the defendants, plaintiff is in great doubt as to which defendant is entitled to be paid the amount of the policy, if it was in force at the death of G. H.

Wherefore plaintiff demands that the court adjudge:

(1) That none of the defendants is entitled to recover from plaintiff the amount of said policy or any part thereof.

(2) That each of the defendants be restrained from instituting any action against plaintiff for the recovery of the amount of said policy or any part thereof.

(3) That, if the court shall determine that said policy was in force at the death of G. H., the defendants be required to interplead and settle between themselves their rights to the money due under said policy, and that plaintiff be discharged from all liability in the premises except to the person whom the court shall adjudge entitled to the amount of said policy.

(4) That plaintiff recover its costs.

[Amended January 21, 1963, effective July 1, 1963.]

FORM 18–A

NOTICE AND ACKNOWLEDGMENT FOR SERVICE BY MAIL [ABROGATED]

[Abrogated April 22, 1993, effective December 1, 1993.]

FORM 19

MOTION TO DISMISS, PRESENTING DEFENSES OF FAILURE TO STATE A CLAIM, OF LACK OF SERVICE OF PROCESS, OF IMPROPER VENUE, AND OF LACK OF JURISDICTION UNDER RULE 12(b)

The defendant moves the court as follows:

1. To dismiss the action because the complaint fails to state a claim against defendant upon which relief can be granted.

2. To dismiss the action or in lieu thereof to quash the return of service of summons on the grounds (a) that the defendant is a corporation organized under the laws of Delaware and was not and is not subject to service of process within the Southern District of New York, and (b) that the defendant has not been properly served with process in this action, all of which more clearly appears in the affidavits of M. N. and X. Y. hereto annexed as Exhibit A and Exhibit B respectively.

3. To dismiss the action on the ground that it is in the wrong district because (a) the jurisdiction of this court is invoked solely on the ground that the action arises under the Constitution and laws of the United States and (b) the defendant is a corporation incorporated under the laws of the State of Delaware and is not licensed to do or doing business in the Southern District of New York, all of which more clearly appears in the affidavits of K. L. and V. W. hereto annexed as Exhibits C and D respectively.

4. To dismiss the action on the ground that the court lacks jurisdiction because the amount actually in controversy is less than ten thousand dollars exclusive of interest and costs.*

Signed: ______________________
Attorney for Defendant.

Address: ______________________

Notice of Motion

To: ______________________
Attorney for Plaintiff.

____

Please take notice, that the undersigned will bring the above motion on for hearing before this Court at Room ______, United States Court House, Foley Square, City of New York, on the ______ day of ______, 20__, at 10 o'clock in the forenoon of that day or as soon thereafter as counsel can be heard.

Signed: ______________________
Attorney for Defendant.

Address: ______________________

[Amended December 29, 1948, effective October 20, 1949; April 17, 1961, effective July 19, 1961; March 27, 2003, effective December 1, 2003.]

Notes of Advisory Committee

1. The above motion and notice of motion may be combined and denominated Notice of Motion. See Rule 7(b).

2. As to paragraph 3, see U.S.C., Title 28, § 1391 (Venue generally), subsections (b) and (c).

3. As to paragraph 4, see U.S.C., Title 28, § 1331 (Federal question; amount in controversy; costs), as amended by P.L. 85–554, 72 Stat. 415, July 25, 1958, requiring that the amount in controversy, exclusive of interest and costs, be in excess of $10,000.*

* Pub. Note: The $10,000 minimum amount in controversy requirement of the federal question jurisdiction statute was repealed in 1980. 28 U.S.C.A. § 1331, as amended by Pub.L. 96–486, § 2(a), December 1, 1980, 94 Stat. 2369. Also note that the amount in controversy required in diversity of citizenship suits under 28 U.S.C.A. § 1332(a) was increased to $50,000 by Pub.L. 100–702, Title II, §§ 201 to 203, November 19, 1988, 102 Stat. 4646.

FORM 20
ANSWER PRESENTING DEFENSES UNDER RULE 12(b)

First Defense

The complaint fails to state a claim against defendant upon which relief can be granted.

Second Defense

If defendant is indebted to plaintiffs for the goods mentioned in the complaint, he is indebted to them jointly with G. H. G. H. is alive; is a citizen of the State of New York and a resident of this district, is subject to the jurisdiction of this court, as to both service of process and venue; can be made a party without depriving this court of jurisdiction of the present parties, and has not been made a party.

Third Defense

Defendant admits the allegation contained in paragraphs 1 and 4 of the complaint; alleges that he is without knowledge or information sufficient to form a belief as to the truth of the allegations contained in paragraph 2 of the complaint; and denies each and every other allegation contained in the complaint.

Fourth Defense

The right of action set forth in the complaint did not accrue within six years next before the commencement of this action.

Counterclaim

(Here set forth any claim as a counterclaim in the manner in which a claim is pleaded in a complaint. No statement of the grounds on which the court's jurisdiction depends need be made unless the counterclaim requires independent grounds of jurisdiction.)

Cross-Claim Against Defendant M. N.

(Here set forth the claim constituting a cross-claim against defendant M. N. in the manner in which a claim is pleaded in a complaint. The statement of grounds upon which the court's jurisdiction depends need not be made unless the cross-claim requires independent grounds of jurisdiction.)

Notes of Advisory Committee

The above form contains examples of certain defenses provided for in Rule 12(b). The first defense challenges the legal sufficiency of the complaint. It is a substitute for a general demurrer or a motion to dismiss.

The second defense embodies the old plea in abatement; the decision thereon, however, may well provide under Rules 19 and 21 for the citing in of the party rather than an abatement of the action.

The third defense is an answer on the merits.

The fourth defense is one of the affirmative defenses provided for in Rule 8(c).

The answer also includes a counterclaim and a cross-claim.

[The Notes incorporate revisions made by the Advisory Committee at the same time amendments to certain other rules were made by Order dated December 27, 1946, effective March 19, 1948.]

FORM 21

ANSWER TO COMPLAINT SET FORTH IN FORM 8, WITH COUNTERCLAIM FOR INTERPLEADER

Defense

Defendant admits the allegations stated in paragraph 1 of the complaint; and denies the allegations stated in paragraph 2 to the extent set forth in the counterclaim herein.

Counterclaim for Interpleader

1. Defendant received the sum of ______ dollars as a deposit from E. F.

2. Plaintiff has demanded the payment of such deposit to him by virtue of an assignment of it which he claims to have received from E. F.

3. E. F. has notified the defendant that he claims such deposit, that the purported assignment is not valid, and that he holds the defendant responsible for the deposit.

Wherefore defendant demands:

(1) That the court order E. F. to be made a party defendant to respond to the complaint and to this counterclaim.[1]

(2) That the court order the plaintiff and E. F. to interplead their respective claims.

(3) That the court adjudge whether the plaintiff or E. F. is entitled to the sum of money.

(4) That the court discharge defendant from all liability in the premises except to the person it shall adjudge entitled to the sum of money.

(5) That the court award to the defendant its costs and attorney's fees.

1. Rule 13(h) provides for the court ordering parties to a counterclaim, but who are not parties to the original action, to be brought in as defendants.

[Amended January 21, 1963, effective July 1, 1963.]

FORM 22

MOTION TO BRING IN THIRD–PARTY DEFENDANT [SUPERSEDED]

[Superseded by Forms 22–A and 22–B January 21, 1963, effective July 1, 1963.]

FORM 22–A

SUMMONS AND COMPLAINT AGAINST THIRD–PARTY DEFENDANT

United States District Court for the Southern District of New York

Civil Action, File Number ______

A. B., Plaintiff)
v.)
C. D., Defendant and)
Third-Party Plaintiff) Summons
v.)
E. F., Third-Party)
Defendant)

To the above-named Third-Party Defendant:

You are hereby summoned and required to serve upon ______, plaintiff's attorney whose address is ______, and upon ______, who is attorney for C. D., defendant and third-party plaintiff, and whose address is ______, an answer to the third-party complaint which is herewith served upon you within 20 days after the service of this summons upon you exclusive of the day of service. If you fail to do so, judgment by default will be taken against you for the relief demanded in the third-party complaint. There is also served upon you herewith a copy of the complaint of the plaintiff which you may but are not required to answer.

____
Clerk of Court.

[Seal of District Court]

Dated ______

United States District Court for the Southern District of New York

Civil Action, File Number ______

A. B., Plaintiff)
v.)
C. D., Defendant and)
Third-Party Plaintiff) Third-Party Complaint
v.)
E. F., Third-Party)
Defendant)

1. Plaintiff A. B. has filed against defendant C. D. a complaint, a copy of which is hereto attached as "Exhibit A."

2. (Here state the grounds upon which C. D. is entitled to recover from E. F., all or part of what A. B. may recover from C. D. The statement should be framed as in an original complaint.)

Wherefore C. D. demands judgment against third-party defendant E. F. for all sums [1] that may be adjudged against defendant C. D. in favor of plaintiff A. B.

Signed: ____________________
Attorney for C. D.,
Third-Party
Plaintiff.

Address: ____________________

1. Make appropriate change where C. D. is entitled to only partial recovery-over against E. F.

[Adopted January 21, 1963, effective July 1, 1963.]

FORM 22–B

MOTION TO BRING IN THIRD–PARTY DEFENDANT

Defendant moves for leave, as third-party plaintiff, to cause to be served upon E. F. a summons and third-party complaint, copies of which are hereto attached as Exhibit X.

Signed: ____________________
Attorney for
Defendant
C. D.

Address: ____________________

Notice of Motion

(Contents the same as in Form 19. The notice should be addressed to all parties to the action.)

Exhibit X

(Contents the same as in Form 22–A.)

[Adopted January 21, 1963, effective July 1, 1963.]

FORM 23
MOTION TO INTERVENE AS A DEFENDANT UNDER RULE 24

(Based upon the complaint, Form 16)

United States District Court for the Southern District of New York

Civil Action, File Number ______

A. B., Plaintiff)
v.) *Motion to intervene as*
C. D., Defendant) *a defendant*
E. F., Applicant for)
Intervention)

E. F. moves for leave to intervene as a defendant in this action, in order to assert the defenses set forth in his proposed answer, of which a copy is hereto attached, on the ground that he is the manufacturer and vendor to the defendant, as well as to others, of the articles alleged in the complaint to be an infringement of plaintiff's patent, and as such has a defense to plaintiff's claim presenting both questions of law and of fact which are common to the main action.[1]

Signed: ______________________,
Attorney for E. F.,
Applicant for
Intervention.

Address: ______________________

Notice of Motion

(Contents the same as in Form 19)

United States District Court for the Southern District of New York

Civil Action, File Number ______

A. B., Plaintiff)
v.) *Intervener's Answer*
C. D., Defendant)
E. F., Intervener)

First Defense

Intervener admits the allegations stated in paragraphs 1 and 4 of the complaint; denies the allegations in paragraph 3, and denies the allegations in paragraph 2 in so far as they assert the legality of the issuance of the Letters Patent to plaintiff.

Second Defense

Plaintiff is not the first inventor of the articles covered by the Letters Patent specified in his complaint, since articles substantially identical in character were previously patented in Letters Patent granted to intervener on January 5, 1920.

Signed: ____________________________,
Attorney for E. F.,
Intervener.

Address: ____________________________

1. For other grounds of intervention, either of right or in the discretion of the court, see Rule 24(a) and (b).

[Amended December 29, 1948, effective October 20, 1949.]

FORM 24

REQUEST FOR PRODUCTION OF DOCUMENTS, ETC., UNDER RULE 34

Plaintiff A. B. requests defendant C. D. to respond within ______ days to the following requests:

(1) That defendant produce and permit plaintiff to inspect and to copy each of the following documents:

(Here list the documents either individually or by category and describe each of them.)

(Here state the time, place, and manner of making the inspection and performance of any related acts.)

(2) That defendant produce and permit plaintiff to inspect and to copy, test, or sample each of the following objects:

(Here list the objects either individually or by category and describe each of them.)

(Here state the time, place, and manner of making the inspection and performance of any related acts.)

(3) That defendant permit plaintiff to enter (here describe property to be entered) and to inspect and to photograph, test or sample (here describe the portion of the real property and the objects to be inspected).

(Here state the time, place, and manner of making the inspection and performance of any related acts.)

Signed: ____________________________,
Attorney for
Plaintiff.

Address: ____________________________

[Amended March 30, 1970, effective July 1, 1970.]

FORM 25

REQUEST FOR ADMISSION UNDER RULE 36

Plaintiff A. B. requests defendant C. D. within ______ days after service of this request to make the following admissions for the purpose of this action only and subject to all pertinent objections to admissibility which may be interposed at the trial:

1. That each of the following documents, exhibited with this request, is genuine.

(Here list the documents and describe each document.)

2. That each of the following statements is true.

(Here list the statements.)

Signed: __________________________________,
Attorney for Plaintiff.

Address: __________________________________

[Amended December 27, 1946, effective March 19, 1948.]

FORM 26

ALLEGATION OF REASON FOR OMITTING PARTY

When it is necessary, under Rule 19(c), for the pleader to set forth in his pleading the names of persons who ought to be made parties, but who are not so made, there should be an allegation such as the one set out below:

John Doe named in this complaint is not made a party to this action [because he is not subject to the jurisdiction of this court]; [because he cannot be made a party to this action without depriving this court of jurisdiction].

FORM 27

NOTICE OF APPEAL TO COURT OF APPEALS UNDER [FORMER] RULE 73(b) [ABROGATED]

[Abrogated December 4, 1967, effective July 1, 1968.]

Notes of Advisory Committee

The form of notice of appeal is transferred to the Federal Rules of Appellate Procedure as Form 1.

FORM 28

NOTICE: CONDEMNATION

United States District Court for the Southern District of New York

CIVIL ACTION, FILE NUMBER _______

UNITED STATES OF AMERICA,)
PLAINTIFF)
v.)
1,000 ACRES OF LAND IN [here insert)
a general location as "City of) *Notice*
_______" or "County of _______"],)
JOHN DOE ET AL., AND UNKNOWN)
OWNERS, DEFENDANTS)

To (here insert the names of the defendants to whom the notice is directed):

You are hereby notified that a complaint in condemnation has heretofore been filed in the office of the clerk of the United States District Court for the Southern District of New York, in the United States Court House in New York City, New York, for the taking (here state the interest to be acquired, as "an estate in fee simple") for use (here state briefly the use, "as a site for a post-office building") of the following described property in which you have or claim an interest.

(Here insert brief description of the property in which the defendants, to whom the notice is directed, have or claim an interest.)

The authority for the taking is (here state briefly, as "the Act of ______, ______ Stat. ______, U.S.C., Title ______, § ______".) [1]

You are further notified that if you desire to present any objection or defense to the taking of your property you are required to serve your answer on the plaintiff's attorney at the address herein designated within twenty days after ______.[2]

Your answer shall identify the property in which you claim to have an interest, state the nature and extent of the interest you claim, and state all of your objections and defenses to the taking of your property. All defenses and objections not so presented are waived. And in case of your failure so to answer the complaint, judgment of condemnation of that part of the above-described property in which you have or claim an interest will be rendered.

But without answering, you may serve on the plaintiff's attorney a notice of appearance designating the property in which you claim to be interested. Thereafter you will receive notice of all proceedings affecting it. At the trial of the issue of just compensation, whether or not you have previously appeared or answered, you may present evidence as to the amount of the compensation to be paid for your property, and you may share in the distribution of the award.

____

United States Attorney.

Address ______________________

(Here state an address within the district where the United States Attorney may be served as "United States Court House, New York, N. Y.")

Dated ______

1. And where appropriate add a citation to any applicable Executive Order.

2. Here insert the words "personal service of this notice upon you," if personal service is to be made pursuant to subdivision (d)(3)(i) of this rule [Rule 71A]; or, insert the date of the last publication of notice, if service by publication is to be made pursuant to subdivision (d)(3)(ii) of this rule. [*Pub. Note: Subdivisions (d)(3)(i) and (d)(3)(ii) were renumbered as (d)(3)(A) and (d)(3)(B), effective December 1, 1993.*]

[Adopted April 30, 1951, effective August 1, 1951.]

FORM 29

COMPLAINT: CONDEMNATION

United States District Court for the Southern District of New York

CIVIL ACTION, FILE NUMBER ______

UNITED STATES OF AMERICA, PLAINTIFF *v.* 1,000 ACRES OF LAND IN [here insert a general location as "City of ______" or "County of ______"], JOHN DOE ET AL., AND UNKNOWN OWNERS, DEFENDANTS	*Complaint*

1. This is an action of a civil nature brought by the United States of America for the taking of property under the power of eminent domain and for the ascertainment and award of just compensation to the owners and parties in interest.[1]

2. The authority for the taking is (here state briefly, as "the Act of ______, ______ Stat. ______, U.S.C., Title ______, § ______").[2]

3. The use for which the property is to be taken is (here state briefly the use, "as a site for a post-office building").

4. The interest to be acquired in the property is (here state the interest as "an estate in fee simple").

5. The property so to be taken is (here set forth a description of the property sufficient for its identification) or (described in Exhibit A hereto attached and made a part hereof).

6. The persons known to the plaintiff to have or claim an interest in the property [3] are:

(Here set forth the names of such persons and the interests claimed.) [4]

7. In addition to the persons named, there are or may be others who have or may claim some interest in the property to be taken, whose names are unknown to the plaintiff and on diligent inquiry have not been ascertained. They are made parties to the action under the designation "Unknown Owners."

Wherefore the plaintiff demands judgment that the property be condemned and that just compensation for the taking be ascertained and awarded and for such other relief as may be lawful and proper.

____

United States Attorney.

Address ______________________

(Here state an address within the district where the United States Attorney may be served, as "United States Court House, New York, N. Y.")

1. If the plaintiff is not the United States, but is, for example, a corporation invoking the power of eminent domain delegated to it by the state, then this paragraph 1 of the complaint should be appropriately modified and should be preceded by a paragraph appropriately alleging federal jurisdiction for the action, such as diversity. See Form 2.

2. And where appropriate add a citation to any applicable Executive Order.

3. At the commencement of the action the plaintiff need name as defendants only the persons having or claiming an interest in the property whose names are then known, but prior to any hearing involving the compensation to be paid for a particular piece of property the plaintiff must add as defendants all persons having or claiming an interest in that property whose names can be ascertained by an appropriate search of the records and also those whose names have otherwise been learned. See Rule 71A(c)(2).

4. The plaintiff should designate, as to each separate piece of property, the defendants who have been joined as owners thereof or of some interest therein. See Rule 71A(c)(2).

[Adopted April 30, 1951, effective August 1, 1951.]

FORM 30

SUGGESTION OF DEATH UPON THE RECORD UNDER RULE 25(a)(1)

A. B. [describe as a party, or as executor, administrator, or other representative or successor of C. D., the deceased party] suggests upon the record, pursuant to Rule 25(a)(1), the death of C. D. [describe as party] during the pendency of this action.

[Adopted January 21, 1963, effective July 1, 1963.]

FORM 31

JUDGMENT ON JURY VERDICT

United States District Court for the Southern District of New York

Civil Action, File Number ______

A. B., Plaintiff)
v.) *Judgment*
C. D., Defendant)

This action came on for trial before the Court and a jury, Honorable John Marshall, District Judge, presiding, and the issues having been duly tried and the jury having duly rendered its verdict,

It is Ordered and Adjudged

[that the plaintiff A. B. recover of the defendant C. D. the sum of ______, with interest thereon at the rate of ______ per cent as provided by law, and his costs of action.]

[that the plaintiff take nothing, that the action be dismissed on the merits, and that the defendant C. D. recover of the plaintiff A. B. his costs of action.]

Dated at New York, New York, this ______ day of ______, 20__.

____

Clerk of Court.

[Adopted January 21, 1963, effective July 1, 1963; March 27, 2003, effective December 1, 2003.]

Notes of Advisory Committee

1. This Form is illustrative of the judgment to be entered upon the general verdict of a jury. It deals with the cases where there is a general jury verdict awarding the plaintiff money damages or finding for the defendant, but is adaptable to other situations of jury verdicts.

2. The clerk, unless the court otherwise orders, is required forthwith to prepare, sign, and enter the judgment upon a general jury verdict without awaiting any direction by the court. The form of the judgment upon a special verdict or a general verdict accompanied by answers to interrogatories shall be promptly approved by the court, and the clerk shall thereupon enter it. See Rule 58, as amended.

3. The Rules contemplate a simple judgment promptly entered. See Rule 54(a). Every judgment shall be set forth on a separate document. See Rule 58, as amended.

4. Attorneys are not to submit forms of judgment unless directed in exceptional cases to do so by the court. See Rule 58, as amended.

FORM 32

JUDGMENT ON DECISION BY THE COURT

United States District Court for the Southern District of New York

Civil Action, File Number ______

A. B., Plaintiff)
v.) *Judgment*
C. D., Defendant)

This action came on for [trial] [hearing] before the Court, Honorable John Marshall, District Judge, presiding, and the issues having been duly [tried] [heard] and a decision having been duly rendered,

It is Ordered and Adjudged

[that the plaintiff A. B. recover of the defendant C. D. the sum of ______, with interest thereon at the rate of ______ per cent as provided by law, and his costs of action.]

[that the plaintiff take nothing, that the action be dismissed on the merits, and that the defendant C. D. recover of the plaintiff A. B. his costs of action.]

Dated at New York, New York, this ______ day of ______, 20__.

____

Clerk of Court.

[Adopted January 21, 1963, effective July 1, 1963; March 27, 2003, effective December 1, 2003.]

Notes of Advisory Committee

1. This Form is illustrative of the judgment to be entered upon a decision of the court. It deals with the cases of decisions by the court awarding a party only money damages or costs, but is adaptable to other decisions by the court.

2. The clerk, unless the court otherwise orders, is required forthwith, without awaiting any direction by the court, to prepare, sign, and enter the judgment upon a decision by the court that a party shall recover only a sum certain or costs or that all relief shall be denied. The form of the judgment upon a decision by the court granting other relief shall be promptly approved by the court, and the clerk shall thereupon enter it. See Rule 58, as amended.

3. See also paragraphs 3–4 of the Explanatory Note to Form 31.

FORM 33

NOTICE OF AVAILABILITY OF A MAGISTRATE JUDGE TO EXERCISE JURISDICTION AND APPEAL OPTION

In accordance with the provisions of Title 28, U.S.C. § 636(c), you are hereby notified that a United States magistrate judge of this district court is available to exercise the court's jurisdiction and to conduct any or all proceedings in this case including a jury or nonjury trial, and entry of a final judgment. Exercise of this jurisdiction by a magistrate judge is, however, permitted only if all parties voluntarily consent.

You may, without adverse substantive consequences, withhold your consent, but this will prevent the court's jurisdiction from being exercised by a magistrate judge. If any party withholds consent, the identity of the parties consenting or withholding consent will not be communicated to any magistrate judge or to the district judge to whom the case has been assigned.

An appeal from a judgment entered by a magistrate judge may be taken directly to the United States court of appeals for this judicial circuit in the same manner as an appeal from any other judgment of a district court.

Copies of the Form for the "Consent to Jurisdiction by a United States Magistrate Judge" are available from the clerk of the court.

[Adopted April 28, 1983, effective August 1, 1983; amended April 22, 1993, effective December 1, 1993, April 11, 1997, effective December 1, 1997.]

FORM 34

CONSENT TO EXERCISE OF JURISDICTION BY A UNITED STATES MAGISTRATE JUDGE

UNITED STATES DISTRICT COURT
______ DISTRICT OF ______

)
Plaintiff,)
)
vs.) Docket No. ______
)
Defendant.)

CONSENT TO JURISDICTION BY A UNITED STATES MAGISTRATE JUDGE

In accordance with the provisions of Title 28, U.S.C. § 636(c), the undersigned party or parties to the above-captioned civil matter hereby voluntarily consent to have a United States magistrate judge conduct any and all further proceedings in the case, including trial, and order the entry of a final judgment.

____________________ ____________________
Date Signature

Note: Return this form to the Clerk of the Court if you consent to jurisdiction by a magistrate judge. Do not send a copy of this form to any district judge or magistrate judge.

[Adopted April 28, 1983, effective August 1, 1983; amended April 22, 1993, effective December 1, 1993, April 11, 1997, effective December 1, 1997.]

FORM 34A

ORDER OF REFERENCE

UNITED STATES DISTRICT COURT
______ DISTRICT OF ______

)
Plaintiff,)
)
vs.) Docket No. _______
)
Defendant.)

ORDER OF REFERENCE

IT IS HEREBY ORDERED that the above-captioned matter be referred to United States Magistrate Judge ______ for all further proceedings and entry of judgment in accordance with Title 28, U.S.C. § 636(c) and the consent of the parties.

____
U. S. District Judge

[Adopted April 22, 1993, effective December 1, 1993.]

FORM 35

REPORT OF PARTIES' PLANNING MEETING

[Caption and Names of Parties]

1. Pursuant to Fed.R.Civ.P. 26(f), a meeting was held on (date) at (place) and was attended by:

(name) for plaintiff(s)

(name) for defendant(s) (party name)

(name) for defendant(s) (party name)

2. Pre-discovery Disclosures. The parties [have exchanged] [will exchange by (date)] the information required by [Fed.R.Civ.P. 26(a)(1)] [local rule ___].

3. Discovery Plan. The parties jointly propose to the court the following discovery plan: [Use separate paragraphs or subparagraphs as necessary if parties disagree.]

Discovery will be needed on the following subjects: (brief description of subjects on which discovery will be needed)

All discovery commenced in time to be completed by (date) . [Discovery on (issue for early discovery) to be completed by (date) .]

Maximum of ___ interrogatories by each party to any other party. [Responses due ___ days after service.]

Maximum of ___ requests for admission by each party to any other party. [Responses due ___ days after service.]

Maximum of ___ depositions by plaintiff(s) and ___ by defendant(s).

Each deposition [other than of ______] limited to maximum of ___ hours unless extended by agreement of parties.

Reports from retained experts under Rule 26(a)(2) due:

from plaintiff(s) by (date)

from defendant(s) by (date)

Supplementations under Rule 26(e) due (time(s) or interval(s)).

4. Other Items. [Use separate paragraphs or subparagraphs as necessary if parties disagree.]

The parties [request] [do not request] a conference with the court before entry of the scheduling order.

The parties request a pretrial conference in (month and year).

Plaintiff(s) should be allowed until (date) to join additional parties and until (date) to amend the pleadings.

Defendant(s) should be allowed until (date) to join additional parties and until (date) to amend the pleadings.

All potentially dispositive motions should be filed by (date).

Settlement [is likely] [is unlikely] [cannot be evaluated prior to (date)] [* may be enhanced by use of the following alternative dispute resolution procedure: [__________]].

Final lists of witnesses and exhibits under Rule 26(a)(3) should be due

from plaintiff(s) by (date)

from defendant(s) by (date)

Parties should have ___ days after service of final lists of witnesses and exhibits to list objections under Rule 26(a)(3).

The case should be ready for trial by (date) [and at this time is expected to take approximately (length of time)].

[Other matters.]

Date: ______

* Pub. Note: So in original, without closed bracket.

[Adopted April 22, 1993, effective December 1, 1993.]

PART VI

FEDERAL APPEALS—OVERVIEW

Table of Sections

---

§ 6.1 Introduction

The rules and procedures for appealing a district court's judgment or order are no longer included in the Federal Rules of Civil Procedure, as they once were. Since 1968, these rules and procedures have been set forth in the "Federal Rules of Appellate Procedure", as supplemented by the local rules adopted by each of the various courts of appeals.

In-depth, rule-by-rule commentary regarding the federal appeals rules is beyond the scope of this text. However, the following preview of federal appellate procedure is included for the practitioner's reference. This preview is intended only to orient the practitioner to the general procedures governing appeals in the federal courts; this section is *not* a substitute for careful study of both the Federal Rules of Appellate Procedure and the local rules applicable to the pertinent court of appeals.

§ 6.2 Step One: Appealability

CORE CONCEPT

Not every order entered by a federal district judge is immediately appealable to the courts of appeals. Instead, litigants are generally required to wait until the lawsuit is completed in the district court—until there is a "final order" in the case—before an appeal from any of the district court's rulings may be taken.[1] This "finality" doctrine was designed to limit the expense, delays, burdens, and inefficiencies of repeated, successive appeals in a single case.[2] Important exceptions to this finality or "final order" doctrine exist, however.

1. *See Digital Equip. Corp. v. Desktop Direct, Inc.*, 511 U.S. 863, 868, 114 S.Ct. 1992, 1996, 128 L.Ed.2d 842 (1994)(noting federal court practice that litigants are entitled to only a single appeal in their case, that this single appeal is deferred until the district court enters its final judgment, and that the appeal may include claims of trial error from every stage of the litigation).

2. The finality, or "final order", doctrine has several objectives. It codifies the deference the appellate courts owe to the trial courts as fo-

NOTE: Practitioners must exercise great care in determining an order's immediate appealability. When an order is immediately appealable, the failure to take such an appeal may forever foreclose the right of appeal. When an order is not immediately appealable, the premature filing of an appeal may be dismissed summarily.

APPLICATIONS

Threshold Nature of Appellate Jurisdiction

Federal appellate jurisdiction is not assumed, nor can it be waived by the parties' failure to assert the absence of jurisdiction. Instead, the courts of appeals have a separate, special obligation to confirm the presence of appellate jurisdiction, even where the parties to the appeal are prepared to concede it.[3] Moreover, if the appellate court independently determines that the trial court lacked subject matter jurisdiction over the dispute, the court of appeals has jurisdiction over the appeal for the limited purpose of correcting the jurisdictional error only.[4]

Final Orders

Congress has vested the courts of appeals with jurisdiction to hear appeals from all "final orders" of the district courts.[5] Final orders are, thus, immediately appealable to the courts of appeals. A final order is a ruling that "ends the litigation on the merits and leaves nothing for the court to do but execute the judgment."[6]

Interlocutory Orders

Interlocutory orders are all other interim rulings by the district courts—rulings that do not end the litigation and that contemplate some type of further action by the trial judge. Interlocutory orders are generally not appealable immediately to the courts of appeals. Review of interlocutory orders must ordinarily wait until the district court enters its final order on the merits of the litigation. Under well-settled

rums that are obligated to first decide the many questions of law and fact arising at trial. The doctrine thus protects the independence of the district judges. The doctrine also avoids the obstruction to proper appellate review that would come from permitting successive appeals from the many rulings issued in a litigation, from the date the complaint is served until final judgment is entered. The doctrine thus promotes judicial efficiency. *See Firestone Tire & Rubber Co. v. Risjord*, 449 U.S. 368, 374, 101 S.Ct. 669, 673, 66 L.Ed.2d 571 (1981). *See also Cobbledick v. United States*, 309 U.S. 323, 325, 60 S.Ct. 540, 541, 84 L.Ed. 783 (1940)(judicial administration's "momentum would be arrested by permitting separate reviews of the component elements in a unified cause").

3. *See Bender v. Williamsport Area Sch. Dist.*, 475 U.S. 534, 541, 106 S.Ct. 1326, 1331, 89 L.Ed.2d 501 (1986).

4. *See Bender v. Williamsport Area Sch. Dist.*, 475 U.S. 534, 541, 106 S.Ct. 1326, 1331, 89 L.Ed.2d 501 (1986).

5. *See* 28 U.S.C.A. § 1291.

6. *See Van Cauwenberghe v. Biard,* 486 U.S. 517, 521–22, 108 S.Ct. 1945, 1949, 100 L.Ed.2d 517 (1988)(quoting *Catlin v. United States,* 324 U.S. 229, 233, 65 S.Ct. 631, 633, 89 L.Ed. 911 (1945)). *Accord Cunningham v. Hamilton County*, 527 U.S. 198, 201–03, 119 S.Ct. 1915, 1919–20, 144 L.Ed.2d 184 (1999) (same, holding that order imposing sanctions on attorney for discovery abuses (under Federal Rules of Civil Procedure) was not a final order from which appeal would lie). *See Behrens v. Pelletier*, 516 U.S. 299, 304, 116 S.Ct. 834, 838, 133 L.Ed.2d 773 (1996)(commenting that finality prevents consideration of rulings that remain subject to revision).

appellate tenets, litigants may, while appealing a final order, challenge all the preceding rulings previously entered by the trial court.[7]

There are statutory and case law exceptions to and "constructions" of the final order rule.

Partial Final Orders (Rule 54(b))

Ordinarily, a judgment as to less than all claims in a lawsuit, or as to less than all parties in a lawsuit, is not immediately appealable until all other claims affecting all other parties are finally resolved. However, the district court may, in the exercise of its discretion, convert such "partial" judgments into immediately appealable final orders by (a) finally resolving at least one claim or the rights and liabilities of at least one party, (b) expressly declaring that no just cause exists to delay the appeal from such a ruling, and (c) directing the entry of judgment on the ruling.[8] The purpose, prerequisites, and procedure for such immediately appealable "partial" judgments are discussed earlier in this text.[9]

Permitted Interlocutory Appeals (28 U.S.C. § 1292(a))

Certain rulings involving federal injunctions, receiverships, and admiralty orders are immediately appealable to the courts of appeals, notwithstanding that the rulings do not qualify as "final orders":

Injunctions: Interlocutory orders that grant, continue, modify, refuse, or dissolve injunctions, or that refuse to dissolve or modify injunctions are appealable immediately.[10]

Receivers: Interlocutory orders that appoint receivers, or refuse orders to wind up receiverships or take steps to accomplish those purposes (*i.e.,* directing disposals of property) are appealable immediately.[11]

Admiralty: Decrees that determine the rights and liabilities of parties to admiralty cases in which appeals from final decrees are allowed, are appealable immediately.[12]

Discretionary Interlocutory Appeals (28 U.S.C. § 1292(b))

The district court may, in the exercise of its discretion,[13] choose to certify certain non-final, interlocutory orders as eligible for immediate appellate review.[14] The district court's certification does *not* require the court of appeals to immediately hear the appeal; instead, whether to entertain an immediate appeal from a certified interlocutory order remains subject to the court of appeals' discretion.[15] In fact, the court of

7. *See Exxon Corp. v. St. Paul Fire & Marine Ins. Co.,* 129 F.3d 781, 784 (5th Cir.1997).

8. *See* Rule 54(b).

9. *See supra* **Authors' Commentary** to Rule 54(b).

10. 28 U.S.C.A. § 1292(a)(1).

11. 28 U.S.C.A. § 1292(a)(2).

12. 28 U.S.C.A. § 1292(a)(3).

13. *See Swint v. Chambers County Comm'n,* 514 U.S. 35, 47, 115 S.Ct. 1203, 1210, 131 L.Ed.2d 60 (1995) (noting that Congress conferred upon district courts the "first line discretion to allow interlocutory appeals").

14. *See* 28 U.S.C.A. § 1292(b).

15. *See* 28 U.S.C.A. § 1292(b). *See also Van Cauwenberghe v. Biard,* 486 U.S. 517, 530, 108 S.Ct. 1945, 1953, 100 L.Ed.2d 517 (1988) (noting that Court of Appeals may, in its discretion,

appeals may deny the certified appeal "for any reason, including docket congestion".[16]

Certification by the district judge is not routinely granted, and such certified immediate appeals are reserved for "exceptional" cases,[17] and are "hen's teeth rare".[18] Liberal grants of interlocutory appeals are "bad policy", and threaten the appropriate division of responsibility between federal trial and appellate courts.[19] To qualify for certification, the district court must state in writing:

(1) That the order in question involves a "controlling question of law" (which generally means a question of "pure law", which the appellate court can resolve "quickly and cleanly" without laboring over the record[20]—such as the meaning of a regulatory, statutory, or constitutional provision or common law doctrine,[21] the resolution of which is *likely* (although not necessarily certain) to affect the future course of the litigation[22]); and

(2) There is "substantial ground for difference of opinion" on the legal issue the order resolves (which generally means either that there is conflicting legal authority on the disputed issue or that the

determine that certified order warrants immediate review); *Coopers & Lybrand v. Livesay*, 437 U.S. 463, 475, 98 S.Ct. 2454, 2461, 57 L.Ed.2d 351 (1978) (noting that even if the district court certifies the order, the appellant must still persuade the Court of Appeals that "exceptional circumstances" justify hearing the appeal immediately); *Tidewater Oil Co. v. United States*, 409 U.S. 151, 173 n. 50, 93 S.Ct. 408, 421 n. 50, 34 L.Ed.2d 375 (1972) (noting Court of Appeals' discretion); *McFarlin v. Conseco Servs., LLC*, 381 F.3d 1251, 1255 (11th Cir. 2004) (same); *Nystrom v. TREX Co.*, 339 F.3d 1347, 1351 (Fed. Cir.2003) (same).

16. *Coopers & Lybrand v. Livesay*, 437 U.S. 463, 475, 98 S.Ct. 2454, 2461, 57 L.Ed.2d 351 (1978).

17. *See Caterpillar Inc. v. Lewis*, 519 U.S. 61, 74, 117 S.Ct. 467, 475, 136 L.Ed.2d 437 (1996) (commenting that "[r]outine resort to § 1292(b) requests would hardly comport with Congress' design to reserve interlocutory review for 'exceptional' cases while generally retaining for the federal courts a firm final judgment rule"); *Coopers & Lybrand v. Livesay*, 437 U.S. 463, 475, 98 S.Ct. 2454, 2461, 57 L.Ed.2d 351 (1978) ("exceptional circumstances" must exist).

18. *See Camacho v. Puerto Rico Ports Auth.*, 369 F.3d 570, 573 (1st Cir. 2004).

19. *See McFarlin v. Conseco Servs., LLC*, 381 F.3d 1251, 1259 (11th Cir. 2004)

20. *See McFarlin v. Conseco Servs., LLC*, 381 F.3d 1251, 1258 (11th Cir. 2004); *id.* at 1259 ("The legal question must be stated at a high enough level of abstraction to lift the question out of the details of the evidence or facts of a particular case and give it general relevance to other cases in the same area of law.").

21. *See Ahrenholz v. Board of Trustees of Univ. of Ill.*, 219 F.3d 674, 676 (7th Cir.2000).

22. *See Sokaogon Gaming Enter. Corp. v. Tushie–Montgomery Assocs., Inc.*, 86 F.3d 656, 659 (7th Cir.1996) ("controlling" if issue's resolution is "quite likely" to affect further course of litigation); *In re Baker & Getty Fin. Servs., Inc.*, 954 F.2d 1169, 1172 n. 8 (6th Cir.1992) (to be "controlling", all that must be shown is that issue's resolution on appeal could materially affect outcome of litigation in trial court); *Klinghoffer v. S.N.C. Achille Lauro Ed Altri–Gestione Motonave Achille Lauro in Amministrazione Straordinaria*, 921 F.2d 21, 24 (2d Cir.1990) ("controlling" if reversal on appeal would terminate lawsuit); *In re Cement Antitrust Litig. (MDL No. 296)*, 673 F.2d 1020, 1026 (9th Cir. 1981) ("controlling"if resolution on appeal could materially affect outcome of litigation in trial court); *Katz v. Carte Blanche Corp.*, 496 F.2d 747, 755 (3d Cir.1974) ("controlling" if trial court's error would require reversal). *See also Katz v. Carte Blanche Corp.*, 496 F.2d 747, 755 (3d Cir.1974) ("controlling" means "serious to the conduct of the litigation, either practically or legally", and saving of district court's time and litigants' money are "highly relevant" factors).

issue is a particularly difficult or uncertain one of first impression);[23] and

(3) An immediate appeal from the interlocutory order may "materially advance" the ultimate termination of the litigation (which generally means that immediate appeal may avoid expensive and protracted litigation).[24]

The moving party must satisfy *all* of these criteria; unless each criterion is meet, the trial judge cannot grant the Rule 1292(b) certification.[25] If certification is granted, the trial judge generally should specify what question of law it finds to be "controlling"–although a failure to do so is not necessarily dispositive.[26] Certification is jurisdictional; if certification is not granted, the court of appeals lacks authority to hear the appeal under Section 1292(b).[27]

A party may move the district court for such a certification. There is no express time limit for seeking the trial judge to grant a Section 1292(b) certification, although unreasonably dilatory requests may be denied by the trial judge or refused by the courts of appeals.[28] If granted by the district judge, the party may petition the court of appeals within 10 days thereafter for permission to immediately appeal the certified question.[29] The scope of the appellate review is limited to the certified

23. *See McFarlin v. Conseco Servs., LLC*, 381 F.3d 1251, 1255 (11th Cir. 2004) (same); *White v. Nix*, 43 F.3d 374, 378 (8th Cir.1994) ("substantial ground for disagreement" could be shown by sufficient number of conflicting and contradictory opinions); *In re Baker & Getty Fin. Servs., Inc.*, 954 F.2d 1169, 1172 (6th Cir.1992) (split among Circuits on issue); *Klinghoffer v. S.N.C. Achille Lauro Ed Altri–Gestione Motonave Achille Lauro in Amministrazione Straordinaria*, 921 F.2d 21, 25 (2d Cir.1990) (difficult issues of first impression). *But cf. In re Flor*, 79 F.3d 281, 284 (2d Cir.1996) (holding that mere presence of disputed issue of first impression is not, by itself, sufficient to show substantial ground for difference of opinion).

24. *See McFarlin v. Conseco Servs., LLC*, 381 F.3d 1251, 1259 and 1262 (11th Cir. 2004) (resolution would "avoid a trial or otherwise substantially shorten the litigation").. *See also White v. Nix*, 43 F.3d 374, 378–79 (8th Cir.1994) (when case will proceed in substantially similar manner regardless of decision on appeal, Court of Appeals' review will not "materially advance" termination of litigation); *People Who Care v. Rockford Bd. of Educ. Dist. No. 205*, 921 F.2d 132, 134 (7th Cir.1991) (commenting that it was "hard to see how resolving the dispute one way or the other could 'materially advance the ultimate termination of the litigation' "); *Klinghoffer v. S.N.C. Achille Lauro Ed Altri–Gestione Motonave Achille Lauro in Amministrazione Straordinaria*, 921 F.2d 21, 25 (2d Cir.1990) (if Court of Appeals rules that jurisdiction is absent over one defendant, ruling would greatly assist litigation's ultimate termination).

25. *See Ahrenholz v. Board of Trustees of Univ. of Ill.*, 219 F.3d 674, 676 (7th Cir.2000).

26. *See McFarlin v. Conseco Servs., LLC*, 381 F.3d 1251, 1264 (11th Cir. 2004) ("Given our caseload, when the district court hands us an entire case to sort through for ourselves we are likely to hand it right back. If the district court is unsure about which of the questions, if any, that are answered by its order qualify for certification under § 1292(b), it should not certify the order for review. If convinced that a particular question does qualify, the district court should tell us which question it is.").

27. *See In re Ford Motor Co., Bridgestone/Firestone North American Tire, LLC*, 344 F.3d 648, 654–55 (7th Cir. 2003) (noting jurisdictional nature, and how most courts hold that mandamus is not proper to compel district court to certify).

28. *See Richardson Elecs., Ltd. v. Panache Broad. of Pa., Inc.*, 202 F.3d 957, 958 (7th Cir. 2000). *See also Ahrenholz v. Board of Trustees of Univ. of Ill.*, 219 F.3d 674, 675–76 (7th Cir.2000) (commenting that petitions for certification must be filed in the district court within a "reasonable time" after the contested order is entered).

29. *See* 28 U.S.C.A. § 1292(b); Fed. R. App. P. 5. The district court may, in certain circum-

order. The court may not reach beyond that order to consider other, uncertified rulings by the trial judge.[30] But the court of appeals may address any issue that is "fairly included" within the certified order itself; review is limited by the order that is certified, not by the precise question found to be controlling.[31]

Collateral Order Doctrine

In addition to the Rule and statutory exceptions to the "final order" limitation, the Supreme Court has developed the common law "collateral order" doctrine, which recognizes that certain important legal rulings—concededly collateral to the litigation's underlying merits—may nevertheless be deemed "final" and eligible for immediate appellate review. To qualify under the collateral order Doctrine, the district court's order must:

(1) Be conclusive on the issue sought to be immediately appealed; and

(2) Resolve an "important question" that is completely separate from the underlying merits; and

(3) Be effectively unreviewable if the appeal were to await a final order on the merits.[32]

This collateral order exception represents a narrow, common law construction of the final order doctrine; it is applied stringently and is never permitted to "swallow" the federal courts' general prohibition against piecemeal appeals.[33]

Other Exceptions

Orders may be deemed immediately appealable for other special, common law reasons. For example, certain interlocutory orders may also be appealable immediately where they resolve the rights of one party to the potentially irreparable injury of another party.[34] The

stances, rescue a party's failure to petition within 10 days by vacating and re-entering the certification order. Generally, this is permitted when the moving party is blameless and the delay is caused by the court itself or by a failure to timely receive the certification order. *See In re City of Memphis*, 293 F.3d 345, 348–50 (6th Cir.2002) (discussing process and National case law on point).

30. *See Yamaha Motor Corp., U.S.A. v. Calhoun*, 516 U.S. 199, 205, 116 S.Ct. 619, 623, 133 L.Ed.2d 578 (1996); *Rosado v. Ford Motor Co.*, 337 F.3d 291, 296 (3d Cir.2003).

31. *See Yamaha Motor Corp. v. Calhoun*, 516 U.S. 199, 205, 116 S.Ct. 619, 623, 133 L.Ed.2d 578 (1996) ("it is the order that is appealable, and not the controlling question identified by the district court"). *Accord McFarlin v. Conseco Servs., LLC*, 381 F.3d 1251, 1255 (11th Cir. 2004); *California Public Employees' Retirement Sys. v. WorldCom, Inc.*, 368 F.3d 86, 95 (2d Cir. 2004); *Egervary v. Young*, 366 F.3d 238, 245 (3d Cir. 2004); *Rivera v. Nibco, Inc.*, 364 F.3d 1057, 1063 (9th Cir. 2004).

32. *See Coopers & Lybrand v. Livesay*, 437 U.S. 463, 468–69, 98 S.Ct. 2454, 2457–58, 57 L.Ed.2d 351 (1978); *Cohen v. Beneficial Indus. Loan Corp.*, 337 U.S. 541, 546, 69 S.Ct. 1221, 1226, 93 L.Ed. 1528 (1949). *Accord Sell v. United States*, 539 U.S. 166, 176, 123 S.Ct. 2174, 2182, 156 L.Ed.2d 197 (2003); *Cunningham v. Hamilton County*, 527 U.S. 198, 201–203, 119 S.Ct. 1915, 1919–20, 144 L.Ed.2d 184 (1999).

33. *See Digital Equip. Corp. v. Desktop Direct, Inc.*, 511 U.S. 863, 868, 114 S.Ct. 1992, 1996, 128 L.Ed.2d 842 (1994).

34. *See Forgay v. Conrad*, 47 U.S. (6 How.) 201, 201, 12 L.Ed. 404 (1848)(allowing immediate appeal from order directing delivery of property to appellee).

extensive case law that explains and defines the precise reach of these other, common law exceptions to the final order doctrine is beyond the scope of this text. When in doubt, practitioners should carefully research whether a particular district court ruling qualifies for immediate appellate review.

ADDITIONAL RESEARCH REFERENCES

Federal Courts §§ 290(1)–291(5) et seq.

West's Key No. Digests, Federal Courts ⚷551–600.

§ 6.3 Step Two: Time for Taking an Appeal

CORE CONCEPT

In civil cases, an appeal generally must be taken within 30 days after the entry of the disputed judgment or order.[35] This time for appeal is mandatory and jurisdictional.[36] A failure to file a timely appeal will forfeit that party's right of appeal.

APPLICATIONS

Dated From "Entry" of Judgment or Order

For purposes of timeliness on appeal, a judgment or order is "entered" when the formal judgment is filed by the district court in accordance with Federal Rule of Civil Procedure 58 and entered by the district court on its docket in accordance with Federal Rule of Civil Procedure 79(a).[37]

Note: The "separate document" requirement of Rule 58 was significantly amended in 2002, and case law precedent decided before that amendment must be cited with great care.[38] When the "separate document" requirement applies, the time for appeal will not begin to run until the "separate document" prerequisite is satisfied or the 150–day period expires.[39]

When United States Is a Party

When the United States or a federal officer or agency is a party to the litigation, the parties have 60 days after the entry of the disputed judgment or order in which to take an appeal.[40] This 60–day period

35. Fed. R. App. P. 4(a)(1)(A). *See Selkridge v. United of Omaha Life Ins. Co.*, 360 F.3d 155, 160–61 (3d Cir. 2004).

36. *See Browder v. Director, Dep't of Corrections*, 434 U.S. 257, 264, 98 S.Ct. 556, 560, 54 L.Ed.2d 521 (1978); *Fruit of the Loom, Inc. v. American Marketing Enters., Inc.*, 192 F.3d 73, 75 (2d Cir.1999).

37. Fed. R. App. P. 4(a)(7). *Cf. Selletti v. Carey*, 173 F.3d 104, 109 (2d Cir.1999) (although appeal was taken more than 30 days after order was entered, appeal was nevertheless proper where district court had never entered separate judgment on the docket, as Rule 58 requires).

38. *See* **Authors' Commentary** to Rule 58 (discussing text and effect of 2002 amendments to Rule 58's "separate document" requirement).

39. *See* Rule 58. *See also Freudensprung v. Offshore Tech. Servs., Inc.*, 379 F.3d 327, 337 (5th Cir. 2004);

40. Fed. R. App. P. 4(a)(1)(B).

applies to all parties in the case—the federal parties as well as all others.

When United States Is *Not* a Party

In all other cases, the parties have 30 days after the entry of the disputed judgment or order in which to take an appeal.[41]

When Opponent Appeals

After one party takes an appeal, all other parties to the litigation have at least 14 days thereafter in which to take their own appeals.[42] The parties receive the benefit of this 14–day "extension" period even if the original notice of appeal is defective or otherwise is dismissed.[43]

Some courts of appeals have ruled that this 14–day period is mandatory and jurisdictional—if the time period lapses, the right to cross-appeal is irretrievably lost.[44] Other courts of appeals take a different view. These courts conclude that the 14–day period is simply "proper procedure", but not jurisdictional; they reason that appellate jurisdiction was already properly invoked with the filing of the *original* notice of appeal (*i.e.*, the one to which the cross-notice would be filed) and, thus, the court enjoys the authority to adjudicate fully the entire appeal before it.[45] These courts would permit the 14–day period to be excused in a proper circumstance.

Computing Time For Taking Appeal

The period within which an appeal must be taken is calculated according to the counting method set in the federal appellate rules. The period[46] is calculated: (1) by *excluding* the day of the event that triggers the period; and (2) by *including* the last day of the period *unless* the last day is a Saturday, Sunday, legal holiday, or day on which weather or other conditions make the clerk's office inaccessible.[47]

41. Fed. R. App. P. 4(a)(1)(A).

42. Fed. R. App. P. 4(a)(3)(party may file notice of appeal within 14 days after first notice of appeal was filed or within the 30 or 60 day period prescribed in Rule 4(a), whichever period is longer).

43. *See In re Julien Co.*, 146 F.3d 420, 423 (6th Cir.1998) (applying 14–day extension rule even where first appeal was dismissed for lack of standing).

44. *See Johnson v. Teamsters Local 559*, 102 F.3d 21, 29 (1st Cir.1996); *EF Operating Corp. v. American Bldgs.*, 993 F.2d 1046, 1049 n. 1 (3d Cir.), *cert. denied*, 510 U.S. 868, 114 S.Ct. 193, 126 L.Ed.2d 151 (1993) (same); *Francis v. Clark Equip. Co.*, 993 F.2d 545, 552–53 (6th Cir.1993); *Rollins v. Metro. Life Ins. Co.*, 912 F.2d 911, 917 (7th Cir.1990); *Memorial Hosp. Sys. v. Northbrook Life Ins. Co.*, 904 F.2d 236, 239 n. 2 (5th Cir.1990); *Savage v. Cache Valley Dairy Ass'n*, 737 F.2d 887 (10th Cir.1984).

45. *See Mendocino Env'l Ctr. v. Mendocino County*, 192 F.3d 1283, 1297 (9th Cir.1999); *Texport Oil Co. v. M/V Amolyntos*, 11 F.3d 361, 366 (2d Cir.1993); *Spann v. Colonial Village, Inc.*, 899 F.2d 24, 33 (D.C.Cir.1990); *LaFaut v. Smith*, 834 F.2d 389, 394 n. 9 (4th Cir.1987).

46. If any appeal period is ever 6 days or less, the period is further modified by the federal appellate rules by *excluding* all intermediate Saturdays, Sundays, and legal holidays. *See* Fed. R. App. P. 26(a)(2).

47. *See* Fed. R. App. P. 26(a). *See also Keyser v. Sacramento City Unified Sch. Dist.*, 238 F.3d 1132, 1135 (9th Cir.) (ruling that 30th day of appeal period, which would have been Friday, November 26, 1999, was deemed extended until Monday, November 29, because the California clerk's office was officially closed on Friday (day after Thanksgiving), and appeal period cannot expire on a Saturday or Sunday), *amended and superseded on other grounds*, 265 F.3d 741 (9th Cir. 2001).

Suspending Time For Appeal by Filing Post–Trial Motions

The timely filing of certain post-trial motions will suspend the time for appeal.[48] The post-trial motions that qualify for this suspension effect are:

- Motions for judgment as a matter of law, under Federal Rule of Civil Procedure 50(b);
- Motions to alter or supplement findings of fact, under Federal Rule of Civil Procedure 52(b);
- Motions for attorney's fees, under Federal Rule of Civil Procedure 54(d), but only if the district court extends the time for appeal in accordance with Federal Rule of Civil Procedure 58; and
- Motions to alter or amend the judgment, under Federal Rule of Civil Procedure 59;
- Motions for a new trial, under Federal Rule of Civil Procedure 59; and
- Motions for relief from a judgment or order, under Federal Rule of Civil Procedure 60, but only if such motion is served within 10 days after entry of judgment.

These motions need not be successful in order to extend the appeal period.[49] But the motions must be filed timely; an untimely filed post-trial motion will *not* suspend the appeal time.[50] Once the district court grants or denies the post-trial motion, the time for appeal begins to run.

Explicit or Implicit Post–Trial Rulings as Appellate Trigger

The courts of appeals are divided on the issue of whether the district court must *expressly* rule on all pending post-trial motions before the appeal clock resumes ticking. The majority rule holds that the appeal time remains tolled until the trial court explicitly grants or denies the pending post-trial motions.[51] The minority view holds that the appeal period begins to run as soon as the district court enters the judgment (interpreting the entry as an implicit denial of the post-trial motions).[52]

Successive Post–Trial Motions

Most courts of appeals have ruled that after the time for appeal has been *once* extended by the filing of a tolling post-trial motion, the appeal period can not be suspended *again* by the filing of a *subsequent* post-trial motion.[53]

48. *See* Fed. R. App. P. 4(a)(4)(A).

49. *See Urso v. United States*, 72 F.3d 59, 61 (7th Cir.1995).

50. *See Panhorst v. United States*, 241 F.3d 367, 370 (4th Cir.2001).

51. *See Havird Oil Co. v. Marathon Oil Co.*, 149 F.3d 283 (4th Cir.1998) (holding that district court must explicitly dispose of all outstanding post-trial motions before appeal period resumes).

52. *See Dunn v. Truck World, Inc.*, 929 F.2d 311, 313 (7th Cir.1991) (holding that entry of judgment is implicitly the order denying a post-trial motion).

53. *See Johnson v. Teamsters Local 559*, 102 F.3d 21, 29–30 (1st Cir.1996); *Glinka v. Maytag*

Extensions of Time by District Court for Filing an Appeal

The district court may extend the time for appeal only in two narrow circumstances–(1) for excusable neglect/good cause or (2) when there is a failure to receive the order.

- *Excusable Neglect* or *Good Cause:* Upon a showing of either excusable neglect or good cause, the district court may briefly extend the time for appeal.[54] To obtain such an extension, the movant *must* seek the extension within the original 30–day appeal period itself or within 30 days after the original appeal period expires.[55] The district court may only extend the time for appeal for 30 days after the original appeal period expires, or for 10 days after the order granting the motion for extension is granted, whichever time is later.[56]
- *Excusable Neglect* or *Good Cause:* The presence of *either* excusable neglect or good cause can justify an extension by the district court.[57]
- *Excusable Neglect Defined:* Excusable neglect applies in circumstances involving fault, and seeks an extension typically made necessary by something that should have been within the movant's control.[58] Whether the neglect is "excusable" is a determination vested to the district court's discretion.[59] In evaluating whether "excusable neglect" exists, the courts will assess the risk of prejudice to the non-moving party, the length of the delay, the delay's potential impact on the proceedings, the reason for the delay and (especially whether that reason was within the reasonable control of the moving party), and the

Corp., 90 F.3d 72 (2d Cir.1996); *In re Stangel*, 68 F.3d 857, 859 (5th Cir.1995)(per curiam); *Moody v. Pepsi–Cola Metropolitan Bottling Co.*, 915 F.2d 201, 206 (6th Cir.1990); *Stark v. Lambert*, 750 F.2d 45, 47 (8th Cir.1984) (per curiam); *Turner v. Evers*, 726 F.2d 112, 114 (3d Cir.1984); *United States v. Marsh*, 700 F.2d 1322, 1327–28 (10th Cir.1983); *American Sec. Bank, N.A. v. John Y. Harrison Realty, Inc.*, 670 F.2d 317, 320 (D.C.Cir.1982); *Needham v. White Labs., Inc.*, 639 F.2d 394, 397 (7th Cir.), *cert. denied*, 454 U.S. 927, 102 S.Ct. 427, 70 L.Ed.2d 237 (1981).

54. *See* Fed. R. App. P. 4(a)(5).

55. *See* Fed.R.App.P. 4(a)(5). *See also Cohen v. Empire Blue Cross & Blue Shield*, 142 F.3d 116, 118 (2d Cir.1998) (holding that district court lacks jurisdiction to grant extension that is not filed within 30–day grace period).

56. Fed.R.App.P. 4(a)(5)(C). *Cf. Harris v. Ballard*, 158 F.3d 1164, 1166 (11th Cir.1998) (holding that 30–day extension runs from date original appeal expires, *not* 30 days from date extension motion is granted), *cert. denied*, 527 U.S. 1041, 119 S.Ct. 2406, 144 L.Ed.2d 804 (1999).

57. *See* Fed. R. App. P. 4(a)(5)(A). *See also id.* advisory committee notes to 2002 amendments. *See also Gibbons v. United States*, 317 F.3d 852, 854 n.3 (8th Cir.2003) (noting that either is sufficient, and observing that the recent Rule amendment corrected an earlier, contrary interpretation that "good cause" applied to motions filed before original deadline expired and "excusable neglect" applied during the 30 days thereafter).

58. *See* Fed. R. App. P. 4(a)(5)(A) advisory committee notes to 2002 amendments.

59. *See Gibbons v. United States*, 317 F.3d 852, 853–54 (8th Cir.2003); *Farthing v. City of Shawnee*, 39 F.3d 1131, 1134 n. 1 (10th Cir. 1994). The courts of appeals are divided on the standard to be applied to Rule 4(a)(5) motions for extensions. The majority view holds that "good cause" is required to justify extension motions filed before the expiration of the original timely appeal period, and "excusable neglect" is required to warrant an extension sought after the expiration of the time period. *See Virella–Nieves v. Briggs & Stratton Corp.*, 53 F.3d 451, 453 (1st Cir.1995)(summarizing majority view).

moving party's good faith.[60] These factors are not given equal weight–the excuse offered for the delay often has the greatest impact.[61] The "excusable neglect" analysis thus generally requires something more than an attorney's busy caseload or an oversight in consulting or a misreading of the procedural rules to justify an extension of the time for appeal.[62]

- *Good Cause Defined:* Good cause applies in circumstances where there is no fault (excusable or otherwise), and seeks an extension typically made necessary by something that was not within the movant's control.[63]
- *Failure to Receive Order:* If the district court determines that a party entitled to notice of the entry of a judgment or order did not receive such notice within 21 days of the entry of the judgment or order, the district court may extend the time for appeal for 14 days, but only if: (a) no party would be prejudiced by the requested extension *and* (b) the party's motion for such an extension is filed either within 180 days of the entry of the judgment or order, or within 7 days after receipt of the untimely notice of the judgment or order.[64] (Some courts date this "receipt of notice" from the date the party receives *written* notice of the judgment or order; however, other courts hold that this 180–day/7–day extension period runs from the date of "actual" notice, whether in writing or otherwise.)[65] The burden of

60. *See Pioneer Investment Servs. Co. v. Brunswick Assocs. Ltd. Partnership*, 507 U.S. 380, 395, 113 S.Ct. 1489, 1498, 123 L.Ed.2d 74 (1993)(assessing "excusable neglect" in bankruptcy rules context). *See also Bishop v. Corsentino*, 371 F.3d 1203, 1206–07 (10th Cir. 2004) (listing factors); *Gibbons v. United States*, 317 F.3d 852, 854 (8th Cir.2003)(same).

61. *See Gibbons v. United States*, 317 F.3d 852, 854 (8th Cir.2003).

62. *See Midwest Employers Cas. Co. v. Williams*, 161 F.3d 877, 879–80 (5th Cir.1998) (holding that misinterpretations of the Federal Rules could constitute excusable neglect in a "rare case", where the Rule at issue is unambiguous, district court's determination that neglect was inexcusable is "virtually unassailable"); *Advanced Estimating Sys., Inc. v. Riney*, 130 F.3d 996, 998 (11th Cir.1997) (holding that counsel's misunderstanding of a procedural rule's plain language cannot qualify as such excusable neglect); *United States v. Vaccaro*, 51 F.3d 189, 191 (9th Cir.1995) (commenting that inadvertence or mistake by counsel will not qualify as excusable neglect); *Weinstock v. Cleary, Gottlieb, Steen & Hamilton*, 16 F.3d 501, 503 (2d Cir.1994)(noting that "excusable neglect" is never satisfied by a showing of an inability or refusal to read and comprehend the plain language of the Federal Rules); *Gochis v. Allstate Ins. Co.*, 16 F.3d 12, 14 (1st Cir.1994)(to constitute "excusable neglect", the moving party must demonstrate unique or extraordinary circumstances warranting an extension). *Cf. Zipperer v. School Bd. of Seminole County*, 111 F.3d 847, 849–50 (11th Cir.1997) (finding excusable neglect where notice was filed one-day late, having been mailed to the Court, by in-State mailing, six days before filing, noting that normal mail delivery is three days).

63. *See* Fed. R. App. P. 4(a)(5)(A) advisory committee notes to 2002 amendments. *See also Bishop v. Corsentino*, 371 F.3d 1203, 1207 (10th Cir. 2004).

64. Fed. R. App. P. 4(a)(6). *See In re Marchiando*, 13 F.3d 1111, 1114 (7th Cir.1994) (holding that district court must make express findings that Rule 4(a)(6) conditions are satisfied), *cert. denied*, 512 U.S. 1205, 114 S.Ct. 2675, 129 L.Ed.2d 810 (1994).

65. *Compare Scott–Harris v. City of Fall River*, 134 F.3d 427 (1st Cir.1997) (written notice required), *rev'd on other grounds*, 523 U.S. 44, 118 S.Ct. 966, 140 L.Ed.2d 79 (1998), *cert. denied*, 523 U.S. 1003, 118 S.Ct. 1184, 140 L.Ed.2d 315 (1998) and *Avolio v. County of Suffolk*, 29 F.3d 50, 53 (2d Cir.1994) (same) with *Nguyen v. Southwest Leasing & Rental Inc.*, 282 F.3d 1061, 1061–67 (9th Cir.2002) (notice must either be written or by specific, reliable, and unequivocal communication that rises to the functional

demonstrating non-receipt rests with the moving party.[66] Evidence that the order was properly mailed creates a presumption of receipt, but this presumption is defeated by the moving party's specific factual denial of receipt; the district court, in such cases, will assess the proof and make a considered factual determination on the question of receipt or non-receipt.[67] Motions for extensions due to non-receipt are committed to the district court's discretion.[68] In exercising that discretion, the district court may deny this extension even where the litigant otherwise satisfies the technical elements of the extension rule (provided, of course, that the basis for the court's denial is something other than the district court's own assessment of the merits of the appeal).[69] The moving party is ordinarily not required to demonstrate "excusable neglect" in order to justify such relief.[70]

Note: This 180–day extension rule provides the *exclusive* method for extensions based on a party's failure to receive notice of the judgment or order. Seeking relief from orders under other rules, such as Rule 60(b), cannot be used to circumvent this 180–day limitation.[71]

Extensions of Time by Court of Appeals for Filing an Appeal

The courts of appeals may not grant litigants an extension of the time for appeal under any circumstances.[72]

Premature Appeals

A notice of appeal is *not* fatally defective merely because it is filed too quickly. If the notice is filed after the district court announces its decision, but before the judgment or order is formally entered, the notice of appeal will be held in abeyance and deemed "filed" on the day the district court formally enters the judgment or order.[73]

equivalent of written notice) *and Nunley v. City of Los Angeles*, 52 F.3d 792, 794 (9th Cir.1995) (actual notice suffices) *and Zimmer St. Louis, Inc. v. Zimmer Co.*, 32 F.3d 357, 359 (8th Cir. 1994) (same).

66. *See Nunley v. City of Los Angeles*, 52 F.3d 792, 795 (9th Cir.1995).

67. *See Nunley v. City of Los Angeles*, 52 F.3d 792, 796 (9th Cir.1995)(noting that, once specific factual denial of receipt is made, district court can give no further weight to presumption of receipt). *Cf. Benavides v. Bureau of Prisons*, 79 F.3d 1211, 1214 (D.C.Cir.1996)(holding that 7–day period does not begin to run until party receives notice of the judgment's or order's entry "directly 'from the clerk or any party'"; inquiry notice of an order, from a second-hand source not connected with the dispute, does not begin the 7–day period).

68. *See* Fed. R. App. P. 4(a)(6)("The district court . . . *may* extend the time for filing a notice of appeal . . .")(emphasis added).

69. *See Arai v. American Bryce Ranches Inc.*, 316 F.3d 1066, 1069–71 (9th Cir.2003).

70. *See Benavides v. Bureau of Prisons*, 79 F.3d 1211, 1214 (D.C.Cir.1996)(showings of excusable neglect and good cause are not required because the court supposes that the party's tardiness is not his or her fault; if the party is at fault (e.g., by negligently failing to notify the clerk of a change of address), the court may deny relief); *Nunley v. City of Los Angeles*, 52 F.3d 792, 798 (9th Cir.1995).

71. *See Vencor Hosps., Inc. v. Standard Life & Acc. Ins. Co.*, 279 F.3d 1306, 1310 (11th Cir.2002).

72. Fed. R. App. P. 26(b). *See Delta Airlines v. Butler*, 383 F.3d 1143, 1145 (10th Cir. 2004).

73. Fed. R. App. P. 4(a)(2).

If the notice of appeal is filed after the district court formally enters the judgment or order, but before the district court rules upon those types of post-trial motions that suspend the time for appeal, the notice is deemed to lie dormant. The notice will become effective on the date the trial court rules on the outstanding post-trial motions.[74]

ADDITIONAL RESEARCH REFERENCES

C.J.S. Federal Courts §§ 293(5–17) et seq.

West's Key No. Digests, Federal Courts ⚷652–660.40.

§ 6.4 Step Three: Procedure for Taking an Appeal

CORE CONCEPT

A federal appeal is taken by filing a notice of appeal with the district court.

APPLICATIONS

Contents of Notice of Appeal

A notice of appeal is typically a simple, one-page form that contains the case caption, specifies the party or parties taking the appeal, designates the challenged judgment or order, and identifies the court to which the appeal is taken.[75] The notice of appeal need not identify the appellees[76] nor should it contain the appealing party's assignment of errors or legal arguments.

- *Naming All Parties:* The parties to the appeal should each be individually named.[77] The failure to name each appealing party is dangerous practice.[78] The courts of appeals will only permit appeals from parties actually named on the

74. Fed. R. App. P. 4(a)(4)(B). *See Schroeder v. McDonald*, 55 F.3d 454, 458 (9th Cir. 1995)(noting that prematurely filed notice of appeal is held in abeyance and become effective upon date of entry of order resolving Rule 59(e) post-trial motion); *United States v. One Hundred Twenty–Four Thousand Eight Hundred Thirteen Dollars ($124,813) in United States Currency*, 53 F.3d 108, 110 (5th Cir.1995)(ruling that claimant's notice of appeal would be treated as dormant until date post-judgment motion was decided), *cert. denied*, 516 U.S. 1171, 116 S.Ct. 1260, 134 L.Ed.2d 209 (1996). This Rule represents a change in earlier practice, which before 1993 held that a notice of appeal was a "nullity" if prematurely filed while post-trial motions remained pending. *See also Leader Nat'l Ins. Co. v. Industrial Indem. Ins. Co.*, 19 F.3d 444, 445 (9th Cir.1994)(noting 1993 amendment's change to practice); *Burt v. Ware*, 14 F.3d 256, 258 (5th Cir.1994)(same).

75. Fed. R. App. P. 3(c)(1). *See* Fed. R. App. P. Appendix, Form 1.

76. *See MIF Realty L.P. v. Rochester Assocs.*, 92 F.3d 752, 758 (8th Cir.1996) (Rules do not require specific listing of all appellees called upon to respond to the appeal); *Crawford v. Roane*, 53 F.3d 750, 752 (6th Cir.1995)(same), *cert. denied*, 517 U.S. 1121, 116 S.Ct. 1354, 134 L.Ed.2d 522 (1996).

77. *See* Fed. R. App. P. 3(c)(1)(A).

78. *See Agee v. Paramount Communications, Inc.*, 114 F.3d 395 (2d Cir.1997) (following entry of award of attorney's fees and costs against *both* party and party's attorney, party's attorney lost right to appeal where the notice of appeal listed only party as appellant).

notice and from parties whose intent to appeal is "objectively clear" from the notice.[79] Thus, for example, using the phrase "*et al.*" to describe the members of a certified class action should be adequate to appeal on behalf of all class members.[80] Even in that instance, however, the courts prefer a clearer designation of the identities of the appealing parties.[81]

- *Naming All Parts of Order Appealed From:* Each part of a separable judgment or separable order appealed from must be named.[82] Ordinarily, an appeal taken from the final judgment itself will support appellate review of all earlier interlocutory orders in the case,[83] so long as the intent to appeal from each particular interlocutory order is clear.[84] However, if a party chooses to state in the Notice of Appeal an intention to appeal from a particular order or ruling (*e.g.*, appealing from the order of November 10 granting summary judgment), the court of appeals may rule that the party has *not* also appealed from other rulings in the same case.[85] To

79. Fed. R. App. P. 3(c)(4) & 1993 advisory committee note. *See Pugh v. Goord*, 345 F.3d 121, 124 n.2 (2d Cir. 2003) (although names of all appellants did not appear in caption, their names did appear in notice and, thus, were "objectively clear"); *Garcia v. Wash*, 20 F.3d 608 (5th Cir.1994)(noting that appellant's references were sufficiently clear to show that appellant intended to appeal). This provision marks a change from earlier practice, which held that the failure to specifically name all appealing parties (for example, with the use of grouping phrases such as "et al.") precluded those parties' rights to appeal. *See also Spain v. Board of Educ. of Meridian Community Unit Sch. Dist. No. 101*, 214 F.3d 925, 929 (7th Cir.2000) (permitting appeal by "Mr. Spain" because, although not named in body of notice of appeal, his intent to appeal was otherwise clear from notice). *Cf. Torres v. Oakland Scavenger Co.*, 487 U.S. 312, 108 S.Ct. 2405, 101 L.Ed.2d 285 (1988).

80. *See Air Line Pilots Ass'n v. Continental Airlines*, 125 F.3d 120 (3d Cir.1997) (finding term "the LPP Claimants" sufficient to adequately identify appellants), *cert. denied*, 522 U.S. 1114, 118 S.Ct. 1049, 140 L.Ed.2d 113 (1998); *Olenhouse v. Commodity Credit Corp.*, 42 F.3d 1560, 1572 (10th Cir.1994)(commenting that use of phrase "et al." to identify group of appellants is discouraged, but where class has been certified, phrase provides ample notice for appeal on behalf of class). *Cf. Murphy v. Keystone Steel & Wire Co.*, 61 F.3d 560 (7th Cir. 1995)(in class action, court had appellate jurisdiction only over named plaintiffs because only they were listed in the notice of appeal, and no other objective notice existed that the appeal was intended to be taken on behalf of the entire class).

81. *See Olenhouse v. Commodity Credit Corp.*, 42 F.3d 1560, 1572 n. 19 (10th Cir. 1994)(observing that the preferred means of identifying a class of appellants is by naming a designated member "as representative of the class").

82. *See* Fed. R. App. P. 3(c)(1)(B).

83. *See Newman v. Federal Exp. Corp.*, 266 F.3d 401, 404 (6th Cir.2001) (noting that appeal from final judgment draws into question all prior non-final rulings and orders); *Trust Co. of La. v. N.N.P. Inc.*, 104 F.3d 1478, 1485–86 (5th Cir.1997) (commenting that appeal from final judgment preserves all prior orders intertwined with final judgment).

84. *See Lolli v. County of Orange*, 351 F.3d 410, 414–15 (9th Cir. 2003) (appellant presumed to appeal from merits of summary judgment motion, and not just denial of reconsideration). *Cf. C & S Acquisitions Corp. v. Northwest Aircraft, Inc.*, 153 F.3d 622 (8th Cir.1998) (principle did not apply where notice failed to give sufficient notice of intent to appeal separate, distinct issues).

85. *See Parkhill v. Minnesota Mut. Life Ins. Co.*, 286 F.3d 1051, 1058 (8th Cir.2002) (appeals from one order do not inherently imply intent to appeal from all other orders in case, and notice that manifests appeal from specific district court order precludes appellant from challenging other unlisted orders); *Newman v. Federal Exp. Corp.*, 266 F.3d 401, 404 (6th Cir.2001) (if appellant chooses to designate specific orders in Notice,

ease the harsh effect of this application, some courts of appeals will allow added information supplied in the party's "Docketing Statement" to supplement (and, perhaps, rescue) an otherwise insufficiently detailed Notice of Appeal.[86]

- *Naming Court of Appeals:* The notice of appeal must identify the specific court to which the appeal is being taken.[87]

Errors in Notice of Appeal

The appellate rules prescribing the contents of a notice of appeal are jurisdictional in nature,[88] although these rules are construed liberally. Thus, appeal papers that are "technically at variance with the letter of Rule 3" may be excused if the appellant's actions are otherwise the functional equivalent of what the rules require.[89] The courts will apply an "intent" rule, testing whether the litigant's intention to seek appellate review is objectively clear; a litigant's subjective motivation is not dispositive.[90] Nevertheless, whether the litigants comply literally or functionally, the rules must be satisfied before a court of appeals may entertain the appeal.[91]

Notice Must Be *Filed* Timely

The notice of appeal must be actually filed with the clerk of court within the time allotted under the Rules for taking an appeal. Mailing the notice to the court or serving the notice on other parties is not sufficient.

Filing by Pro Se Prisoners: A notice of appeal is deemed to be "filed" when a *pro se* prisoner deposits the notice into the prison's

only those determinations are appealed); *Trust Co. of La. v. N.N.P. Inc.*, 104 F.3d 1478, 1485–86 (5th Cir.1997) (court may not hear challenges to other rulings or orders not specified in notice, if party designates particular orders only and not final judgment); *MCI Telecommunications Corp. v. Teleconcepts, Inc.*, 71 F.3d 1086, 1092 (3d Cir.1995) (noting that court does not acquire jurisdiction over issues not designated in appeal), *cert. denied*, 519 U.S. 815, 117 S.Ct. 64, 136 L.Ed.2d 25 (1996).

86. *See Trotter v. Regents of Univ. of N.M.*, 219 F.3d 1179, 1184 (10th Cir.2000) (holding that timely filed docketing statement that "clearly" describes the appellate issues will be accepted as the "functional equivalent" of a proper notice of appeal).

87. *See* Fed. R. App. P. 3(c)(1)(C). *Bradley v. Work*, 154 F.3d 704 (7th Cir.1998). *But cf. United States v. Treto–Haro*, 287 F.3d 1000, 1002 n.1 (10th Cir.2002) (failure to name correct court will not warrant dismissal where intention to appeal to a certain court of appeals may be reasonably inferred from notice and where defect did not materially mislead appellee); *Dillon v. United States*, 184 F.3d 556 (6th Cir.1999) (holding that where appeal may only be taken to one court, appeal is not defective merely because Notice of Appeal fails to name particular appellate court).

88. *See Smith v. Barry*, 502 U.S. 244, 248, 112 S.Ct. 678, 681, 116 L.Ed.2d 678 (1992).

89. *See Smith v. Barry*, 502 U.S. 244, 248, 112 S.Ct. 678, 681, 116 L.Ed.2d 678 (1992); *Torres v. Oakland Scavenger Co.*, 487 U.S. 312, 316–17, 108 S.Ct. 2405, 2408, 101 L.Ed.2d 285 (1988). *See also Becker v. Montgomery*, 532 U.S. 757, 121 S.Ct. 1801, 149 L.Ed.2d 983 (2001) (holding that failure to timely sign the notice of appeal did not compel dismissal of the appeal; the error was curable and a timely signature was not a jurisdictional failing); *Remer v. Burlington Area Sch. Dist.*, 205 F.3d 990, 995 (7th Cir.2000) (holding that litigant's petition for interlocutory appeal was sufficient "notice of appeal" to vest appellate jurisdiction).

90. *See Rinaldo v. Corbett*, 256 F.3d 1276, 1278–79 (11th Cir.2001).

91. *See Smith v. Barry*, 502 U.S. 244, 248, 112 S.Ct. 678, 681, 116 L.Ed.2d 678 (1992).

internal mail system.[92]

Place of Filing

A notice of appeal is filed with the clerk of the district court from which the appeal is taken.[93] However, mistakenly filing the notice with the court of appeals will *not* defeat the appeal. If the notice is filed with the court of appeals within the permitted time for taking an appeal, the appeals court clerk will note the date of filing and send the notice to the clerk of the district court.[94]

Service Not Required

The appealing party need not serve the notice of appeal on all other parties; this service is made by the clerk of court.[95] The clerk's failure to serve the notice, however, does not defeat the appeal.[96]

> *Service Copies to the Court:* Although the appellant does not actually serve the notice of appeal on the other parties, the appellant is required to provide the clerk's office with sufficient copies of the notice for service.[97]

Joint Appeals

Joint appeals may be taken by two or more parties whose similar interests make such joinder practicable.[98] Each plaintiff, however, must file a timely notice of appeal. The fact that some similarly situated plaintiffs timely appealed is immaterial; the appeal of each plaintiff must be appropriately noticed to the court.[99]

Consolidated Appeals

Upon its own motion or by motion of a party, the court of appeals may consolidate the appeals of different parties.[100]

Fees

The appealing party must pay to the district court both the district court fee for appeal and the court of appeals' docket fee.[101]

ADDITIONAL RESEARCH REFERENCES

Federal Courts §§ 282–301(48) et seq.

West's Key No. Digests, Federal Courts ⚷521–956.

92. Fed. R. App. P. 4(c)(requiring accompanying notarized statement or declaration).

93. Fed. R. App. P. 3(a).

94. Fed. R. App. P. 4(d).

95. Fed. R. App. P. 3(d)(1).

96. Fed. R. App. P. 3(d)(3).

97. Fed. R. App. P. 3(a)(1).

98. Fed. R. App. P. 3(b)(1).

99. *See Wooden v. Board of Regents of Univ. Sys. of Ga.*, 247 F.3d 1262, 1273 (11th Cir.2001).

100. Fed. R. App. P. 3(b)(2).

101. Fed. R. App. P. 3(e).

§ 6.5 Step Four: Stays Pending Appeal

CORE CONCEPT

A party may seek a stay of judgment by filing such an application with the district court. In applications *not* involving stays of injunctions, receiverships, or accountings in patent infringement actions, a party may request a stay pending appeal by filing a supersedeas bond. Stay applications must be filed timely and, generally, initially in the district court.

APPLICATIONS

10–Day "Automatic" Stay

For a period of 10 days after a judgment is entered, the parties are barred from executing upon the judgment or pursuing further proceedings for its enforcement.[102] This automatic stay does *not* apply to judgments involving injunctions, judgments in receivership actions, or judgments or orders directing accountings in patent infringement actions.

Time to Apply for Stay

Applications for stay generally should be filed at the earliest possible opportunity. Because the automatic stay does not apply in certain injunction, receivership, and patent infringement circumstances, appellants in those cases do not enjoy the automatic 10–day stay period and the time for execution and enforcement will immediately arrive. Even in automatic stay cases, supersedeas bonds must first be approved by the court before any stay is effective.[103] Consequently, a delay in seeking a stay will expose the defeated party to execution and enforcement of the judgment.

Where to Apply for Stay

Ordinarily, stays pending appeal must be filed first with the district court.[104] Only in those circumstances where applying in the district court is not practicable, or where the district court has denied the request or failed to grant all the relief requested, may a party request a stay in the court of appeals.[105]

Procedure for Stay Applications in the District Court

In cases that do not involve injunctions, receivers, or accountings in patent infringement cases, the posting of a supersedeas bond—after it has been approved by the court—will stay execution and enforcement of the judgment.[106]

In cases involving injunctions, the district court may, in its discretion, grant a stay of the injunction pending appeal.[107] To obtain such a stay, the moving party must generally make the traditional showing

102. *See* Rule 62(a).
103. *See* Rule 62(d).
104. *See* Fed. R. App. P. 8(a)(1).
105. *See* Fed. R. App. P. 8(a)(2).
106. *See* Rule 62(d).
107. *See* Rule 62(c).

required for any injunction: strong likelihood of success on the merits, irreparable injury, no substantial harm to others, and no damage to the public interest.[108] The court may condition such a stay upon the posting of a bond or other appropriate security.[109]

Procedure for Stay Applications in the Court of Appeals

In applying for a stay in the court of appeals, the moving party must make several showings in the motion papers:[110]

a. *Proceedings Before Trial Court:* The motion must show why a stay application cannot be practicably directed to the district judge, or that the district judge has denied a stay or failed to grant all the relief requested (the district court's reasons must be set forth); *and*

b. *Reasons for Relief:* The motion must show the reasons for the relief requested, and set forth the facts relied upon in support of that showing. Relevant parts of the record shall be included and, where the facts relied upon are subject to dispute, supporting affidavits or other sworn statements shall also be included; *and*

c. *Reasonable Notice:* Reasonable notice of the motion shall be given to the non-moving party; *and*

d. *Disposition:* The motion will ordinarily be resolved by a panel or division of the court, unless exceptional circumstances justify submitting the motion to a single judge; *and*

e. *Bond or Security:* If the motion is granted, the court of appeals can condition the stay upon the filing in the district court of a bond or other appropriate security.[111]

§ 6.6 Step Five: The Appeal Process

CORE CONCEPT

Once the appeal is timely filed, the court of appeals will mail to each party a briefing notice that will schedule the filing of an Appellant's Brief, an Appellee's Brief, and an Appellant's Reply Brief. Thereafter, the court of appeals may schedule oral argument, the case will be submitted, and a written disposition on appeal will be filed.

APPLICATIONS

Effect of Appeal

Once the appeal is taken, jurisdiction over the case passes from the district court to the court of appeals.[112] The district court thereafter

108. *See* **Author's Commentary** to Rule 62(c).

109. *See* Rule 62(c).

110. *See* Fed. R. App. P. 8(a)(2)(A)–(2)(D).

111. *See* Fed. R. App. P. 8(a)(2)(E).

112. *See Griggs v. Provident Consumer Discount Co.*, 459 U.S. 56, 58, 103 S.Ct. 400, 402, 74 L.Ed.2d 225 (1982)(noting that notice of appeal is an event of jurisdictional significance, conferring jurisdiction on the Court of Appeals and divesting the district court of control over those aspects of the litigation involved in the appeal).

enjoys only the narrow power to perform ministerial functions, issue stays and injunctions pending appeal, and, in certain instances, award counsel fees.

Compliance With Schedule and Procedures

Failure to comply with the court of appeals' schedule and procedures is ground for such action as the court of appeals deems appropriate, including denial of right to participate in oral argument or even dismissal of the appeal itself.[113]

Designation of the Record and Statement of Issues

The "record" on appeal consists of (1) the original papers and exhibits filed in the trial court, (2) the transcript, and (3) a certified copy of docket entries.[114] The "record" encompasses not just those exhibits admitted into evidence, but may include items presented for admission and denied by the district court.[115] Within 10 days after filing the notice of appeal, the appealing party must order those portions of the transcript that are necessary for the appeal. Unless the appellant orders the entire transcript, the appellant must, during this same 10–day period, file a statement of the issues for appeal and a list of the intended contents of the Appendix. The appellee may thereafter serve a counter-designation of additional portions of the transcript to be included.[116]

Note: Some districts have promulgated Local Rules requiring the appellant to transcribe the entire proceedings.[117] Practitioners should be diligent in consulting their local rules for guidance on this point.

Briefing Procedures

Briefing procedures are generally set in the Federal Rules of Appellate Procedure, but additional provisions vary by Local Rules among the different courts of appeals. The practitioner should always consult the Local Rules for these additional procedures.

Content of Appellate Briefs:	Rule 28
Filing/Service of Briefs:	Rules 25 & 31
Form of Briefs/Appendix:	Rule 32
Appendix to the Briefs:	Rule 30

Briefing Reminders

The "Do's" and "Don't's" of effective appellate briefing could fill volumes. Several common oversights, however, are worth special mention:

113. *See* Fed. R. App. P. 3(a)(2).

114. *See Morton Int'l, Inc. v. A.E. Staley Mfg. Co.*, 343 F.3d 669, 682 (3d Cir. 2003).

115. *See Morton Int'l, Inc. v. A.E. Staley Mfg. Co.*, 343 F.3d 669, 682 (3d Cir. 2003).

116. *See* Fed. R. App. P. 10, 11, & 30.

117. *See* E.D.Pa. Loc. R. 7.1(e)(requiring moving party to order "a transcript of the trial"); *Bongard v. Korn*, 1993 WL 39267 (E.D.Pa. 1993)("the whole transcript is to be ordered rather than a mere portion of the trial transcript as the particular party requesting post-trial relief unilaterally deems necessary").

Corporate Disclosure Statement: The Appellate Rules require each non-governmental corporate party in every civil case to file a statement identifying each of its parent corporations and all publicly-held companies that own 10% or more of the party's stock, and to supplement that statement whenever the necessary information changes.[118] The Rules require that this Statement be reprinted in front of the Table of Contents in that party's opening brief, even if the Statement has already been filed with the Court of Appeals.[119]

Footnote Restrictions: Some courts of appeals have adopted local rules that severely limit the use of footnotes in appellate briefs.[120] Practitioners should be careful to consult their court of appeals' local rules to be certain their briefs comply with these restrictions.

Oral Argument

Oral argument is permitted generally unless the appeal is frivolous, the dispositive issues were authoritatively decided, or the decisional process would not be significantly aided by argument because the facts and legal arguments are adequately set forth in the briefs.[121] The length, scheduling, and location of argument is set by the particular court of appeals.

> *Note:* The parties cannot postpone oral argument by stipulation; postponement can occur only upon court order.

§ 6.7 Step Six: Appeals To The United States Supreme Court

CORE CONCEPT

A party enjoys an appeal as of right to the United States Supreme Court in only very few circumstances. In all other cases, the Supreme Court has the discretion whether to permit or refuse appeals to the Court. In practice, only a small handful of the many thousands of requests for Supreme Court review are granted each year.

APPLICATIONS

Appeals As Of Right; Time to File

Whenever a specially convened three-judge district court panel declares any Act of Congress to be unconstitutional, a direct appeal may be taken to the Supreme Court.[122] Such appeals must be filed within 30 days of the date the district court's order is entered.[123] Congress may permit other direct appeals from the district courts, and such appeals must also be filed within 30 days of the district court's action.[124]

Discretionary Appeals; Time to File

The Supreme Court may, in its discretion, grant a party appellate review from other federal and State court rulings. Supreme Court

118. Fed. R. App. P. 26.1(a).

119. Fed. R. App. P. 26.1(b).

120. *See* 3d Cir. Loc. App. R. 32.2(a)("Excessive footnotes in briefs are discouraged. Footnotes shall be printed in the same size type utilized in the text.").

121. Fed. R. App. P. 34(a)(2).

122. *See* 28 U.S.C.A. § 1253.

123. *See* 28 U.S.C.A. § 2102(a).

124. *See* 28 U.S.C.A. § 2102(b).

review of federal appellate court decisions may be sought by petitioning for a Writ of Certiorari[125] or by seeking a certification from the court of appeals.[126] The Supreme Court may, in its discretion, also grant a Writ of Certiorari to review of decisions from the highest court of any State, but only where (a) a federal treaty or statute is drawn into question, (b) a State statute is drawn into question on federal grounds, or (c) any title, right, privilege, or immunity is specially set up or claimed under federal law.[127]

Petitions for Writs of Certiorari from federal court of appeals rulings must be filed with the Supreme Court within 90 days after the entry of the disputed judgment or decree.[128] Petitions for Writs from qualifying State court rulings must also be filed with the Supreme Court within 90 days after the entry of the disputed judgment or decree.[129]

Considerations in Granting Writs of Certiorari

The Supreme Court Rules provide a non-controlling, non-exhaustive list of the types of "compelling reasons" that may prompt the Supreme Court to grant a Writ of Certiorari:

(1) A conflict among the federal Circuits on an "important matter";

(2) A conflict between a federal court of appeals and the highest court of a State on an "important federal question";

(3) A ruling by a court of appeals that "so far departed from the accepted and usual course of judicial proceedings" (or that sanctions such a departure by a lower court) that the Supreme Court's "supervisory power" is called for;

(4) A ruling by the highest court of a State that conflicts with the decision of another State's highest court or a federal court of appeals on an "important federal question"; or

(5) A ruling by a State court or a federal court of appeals that decides "an important question of federal law that has not been, but should be," settled by the Supreme Court, or that decides "an important federal question in a way that conflicts with relevant decisions" of the Supreme Court.[130]

125. *See* 28 U.S.C.A. § 1254(1). In Latin, "certiorari" means "to be informed of"; such writs of certiorari are of common law origin, and were (and are) issued by a higher court to a lower court requiring that the certified record in a case be delivered for review. *See Black's Law Dictionary* 207 (5th ed. 1979).

126. *See* 28 U.S.C.A. § 1254(2).

127. *See* 28 U.S.C.A. § 1257.

128. *See* 28 U.S.C.A. § 2101(c); U.S. S. Ct. R. 13(1), (3). *See also id.* (permitting Supreme Court, for good cause shown, to extend this 90–day period for another 60 days); U.S. S. Ct. R. 13(5) (same).

129. *See* 28 U.S.C. § 2101(d); U.S. S. Ct. R. 13(1), (3).

130. *See* U.S. S. Ct. R. 10(a)-(c).

*

PART VII

JUDICIAL RULEMAKING

A. THE FEDERAL RULES OF PRACTICE AND PROCEDURE *

The federal rules govern procedure, practice, and evidence in the federal courts. They set forth the procedures for the conduct of court proceedings and serve as a pattern for the procedural rules adopted by many state court systems.

Authority

The Congress has authorized the federal judiciary to prescribe the rules of practice, procedure, and evidence for the federal courts, subject to the ultimate legislative right of the Congress to reject, modify, or defer any of the rules. The authority and procedures for promulgating rules are set forth in the Rules Enabling Act. 28 U.S.C. §§ 2071–2077.

The Judicial Conference of the United States is also required by statute to "carry on a continuous study of the operation and effect of the general rules of practice and procedure." 28 U.S.C. § 331. As part of this continuing obligation, the Conference is authorized to recommend amendments and additions to the rules to promote

- simplicity in procedure,
- fairness in administration,
- the just determination of litigation, and
- the elimination of unjustifiable expense and delay.

The Rules Committees

The Judicial Conference's responsibilities as to rules are coordinated by its Committee on Rules of Practice and Procedure, commonly referred to as the "Standing Committee." 28 U.S.C. § 2073(b). The Standing Committee has five advisory committees, dealing respectively with the appellate, bankruptcy, civil, criminal, and evidence rules. 28 U.S.C. § 2073(a)(2). The Standing Committee reviews and coordinates the recommendations of the five advisory committees, and it recommends to the Judicial Conference proposed rules changes "as may be necessary to maintain consistency and otherwise promote the interests of justice." 28 U.S.C. § 2073(b).

The Standing Committee and the advisory committees are composed of federal judges, practicing lawyers, law professors, state chief justices, and representatives of the Department of Justice. Each committee has a reporter, a prominent law professor, who is responsible for coordinating the committee's agenda and drafting appropriate amendments to the rules and explanatory committee notes.

The Assistant Director for Judges Programs of the Administrative Office of the United States Courts currently serves as secretary to the Standing Committee, coordinates the operational aspects of the rules process, and maintains the

* This description of current procedures for federal judicial rulemaking is a summary prepared for the bench and bar by the Administrative Office of the U.S. Courts.

records of the committees. The Rules Committee Support Office of the Administrative Office provides the day to day administrative and legal support for the secretary and the committees.

Open Meetings and Records

Meetings of the rules committees are open to the public and are widely announced. All records of the committees, including minutes of committee meetings, suggestions and comments submitted by the public, statements of witnesses, transcripts of public hearings, and memoranda prepared by the reporters, are public and are maintained by the secretary. Copies of the rules and proposed amendments are available from the Rules Committee Support Office. The proposed amendments are also published on the Judiciary's website <http:\\www.uscourts.gov>.

B. HOW THE RULES ARE AMENDED

The pervasive and substantial impact of the rules on the practice of law in the federal courts demands exacting and meticulous care in drafting rule changes. The rulemaking process is time-consuming and involves a minimum of seven stages of formal comment and review. From beginning to end, it usually takes two to three years for a suggestion to be enacted as a rule.

The process, however, may be expedited when there is an urgent need to enact an amendment to the rules.

All interested individuals and organizations are provided an opportunity to comment on proposed rules amendments and to recommend alternative proposals. The comments received from this extensive and thorough public examination are studied very carefully by the committees and generally improve the amendments. The committees actively encourage the submission of comments, both positive and negative, to ensure that proposed amendments have been considered by a broad segment of the bench and bar.

STEP 1. INITIAL CONSIDERATION BY THE ADVISORY COMMITTEE

Making suggestions for changes

Proposed changes in the rules are suggested by judges, clerks of court, lawyers, professors, government agencies, or other individuals and organizations. They are considered in the first instance by the appropriate advisory committees (appellate, bankruptcy, civil, criminal, or evidence). Suggestions for changes, additions, or deletions must be submitted in writing to the secretary, who acknowledges each letter and distributes it to the chair of the Standing Committee and the chair and reporter of the advisory committee.

The reporter normally analyzes the suggestions and makes appropriate recommendations to the advisory committee. The suggestions from the public and the recommendations of the reporter are placed on the advisory committee's agenda and are normally discussed at its next meeting. The advisory committees usually meet twice a year, and they also conduct business by telephone and correspondence.

Consideration of suggestions

In considering a suggestion for a change in the rules, the advisory committee may take several courses of action, including:

1. Accepting the suggestion, either completely or with modifications or limitations:
2. Deferring action on the suggestion or seeking additional information regarding its operation and impact;
3. Rejecting a suggestion because it does not have merit or would be inconsistent with other rules or a statute; or
4. Rejecting a suggestion because, although it may be meritorious, it simply is not necessary or important enough to warrant the significant step of an amendment to the federal rules.

The secretary is required, to the extent feasible, to advise the person making a suggestion of the action taken on it by the advisory committee.

Drafting Rules Changes

When an advisory committee decides initially that a particular change in the rules would be appropriate, it normally asks its reporter to prepare a draft amendment to the rules and an explanatory committee note. The draft amendment and committee note are discussed and voted upon at a committee meeting.

The Standing Committee has a style subcommittee that works with the respective advisory committees in reviewing proposed amendments to ensure that the rules are written in clear and consistent language. In addition, the reporter of the Standing Committee and the reporters of the five advisory committees are encouraged to work together to promote clarity and consistency among the various sets of federal rules.

Step 2. Publication and Public Comment

Once an advisory committee votes initially to recommend an amendment to the rules, it must obtain the approval of the Standing Committee, or its chair, to publish the proposed amendment for public comment. In seeking publication, the advisory committee must explain to the Standing Committee the reasons for its proposal, including any minority or separate views.

After publication is approved, the secretary arranges for printing and distribution of the proposed amendment to the bench and bar, to publishers, and to the general public. More than 10,000 persons and organizations are on the mailing list, including

- federal judges and other federal court officers,
- United States attorneys,
- other federal government agencies and officials,
- state chief justices,
- state attorneys general,
- legal publications,
- law schools,
- bar associations, and
- interested lawyers, individuals, and organizations requesting distribution.

The public is normally given 6 months to comment in writing to the secretary regarding the proposed amendment.

In an emergency, a shorter time period may be authorized by the Standing Committee.

During the 6–month comment period, the advisory committee schedules one or more public hearings on the proposed amendments. Persons who wish to appear and testify at the hearings are required to contact the secretary at least 30 days before the hearings.

Step 3. Consideration of the Public Comments and Final Approval by the Advisory Committee

At the conclusion of the public comment period, the reporter is required to prepare a summary of the written comments received from the public and the testimony presented at the hearings. The advisory committee then takes a fresh look at the proposed rule changes in light of the written comments and testimony.

If the advisory committee decides to make a substantial change in its proposal, it will provide a period for additional public notice and comment.

Once the advisory committee decides to proceed in final form, it submits the proposed amendment to the Standing Committee for approval. Each proposed amendment must be accompanied by a separate report summarizing the comments received from the public and explaining any changes made by the advisory committee following the original publication. The advisory committee's report must also include minority views of any members who wish to have their separate views recorded.

Step 4. Approval by the Standing Committee

The Standing Committee considers the final recommendations of the advisory committee and may accept, reject, or modify them. If the Standing Committee approves a proposed rule change, it will transmit it to the Judicial Conference with a recommendation for approval, accompanied by the advisory committee's reports and the Standing Committee's own report explaining any modifications it made. If the Standing Committee makes a modification that constitutes a substantial change from the recommendation of the advisory committee, the proposal will normally be returned to the advisory committee with appropriate instructions.

Step 5. Judicial Conference Approval

The Judicial Conference normally considers proposed amendments to the rules at its September session each year. If approved by the Conference, the amendments are transmitted promptly to the Supreme Court.

Step 6. Supreme Court Approval

The Supreme Court has the authority to prescribe the federal rules, subject to a statutory waiting period. 28 U.S.C. § 2072, 2075. The Court normally transmits proposed rules amendments to the Congress by May 1 of each year. 28 U.S.C. § 2074.

Step 7. Congressional Review

The Congress has a statutory period of at least 7 months to act on any rules prescribed by the Supreme Court. If the Congress does not enact legislation to reject, modify, or defer the rules, they take effect as a matter of law on December 1. 28 U.S.C. §§ 2074, 2075.

C. SUMMARY OF PROCEDURES

Action	Date
STEP 1	
• Suggestion for a change in the rules. (*Submitted in writing to the secretary.*)	At any time.
• Referred by the secretary to the appropriate advisory committee.	Promptly after receipt.
• Considered by the advisory committee.	Normally at the next committee meeting.
• If approved, the advisory committee seeks authority from the Standing Committee to circulate to bench and bar for comment.	Normally at the same meeting or the next committee meeting.
STEP 2	
• Public comment period.	6 months.
• Public hearings.	During the public comment period.
STEP 3	
• Advisory committee considers the amendment afresh in light of public comments and testimony at the hearings.	About one or two months after the close of the comment period.
• Advisory committee approves amendment in final form and transmits to the Standing Committee.	About one or two months after the close of the comment period.
STEP 4	
• Standing Committee approves amendment, with or without revisions, and recommends approval by the Judicial Conference.	Normally at its June meeting.
STEP 5	
• Judicial Conference approves amendment and transmits to the Supreme Court.	Normally at its September meeting.
STEP 6	
• The Supreme Court prescribes the amendment.	By May 1.
STEP 7	
• Congress has statutory time period in which to enact legislation to reject, modify, or defer the amendment.	By December 1.
• Absent Congressional action, the amendment becomes law.	December 1.

D. 2005 CIVIL RULE DEVELOPMENTS

During 2005 the following judicial rulemaking developments should be noted.

1. RULES BEFORE THE SUPREME COURT AND CONGRESS

Under the proposed schedule, amendments to several federal civil rules would become effective on December 1, 2005, if they are approved by the Supreme Court, and if they are not altered by Congress.

Proposed Amendments to the Federal Rules of Civil Procedure

[Editorial Note: Following its September 2004 meeting, the Advisory Committee did not include among its recommendations for Judicial Conference approval either new Rule 5.1 or conforming amendments to Rule 24(c), temporarily tabling discussion of that particular proposal for further work. It was recommended that the Conference transmit to the Supreme Court for 2005 consideration proposed amendments to Civil Rules 6, 27, and 45, and to Supplemental Rules B and C. Among the following, then, the fate of new Rule 5.1 is speculative.]

New **Rule 5.1** (Constitutional Challenge to Statute—Notice and Certification) would require that a party who files a paper that draws into question the constitutionality of an Act of Congress or a state statute must file and serve notice of such challenge on the United States Attorney General or state attorney general. Such notice ensures that the appropriate government official is informed of a constitutional challenge and can intervene at the earliest possible stage in the litigation. The new rule replaces the final three sentences of Rule 24(c), which set out the court's notification duty.

Rule 6 (Time) would be amended to clarify the method of counting the additional three days provided to respond if service is by mail or one of the methods prescribed in Rule 5(b)(2)(C) or (D). Under the proposed amendments, three additional days would be added after the prescribed period expires. All other time-counting rules remain unchanged.

The proposed amendment to **Rule 27** (Depositions Before Action or Pending Appeal) corrects the outdated cross-reference to former Civil Rule 4(d). The amendment makes clear that all methods of service authorized under Rule 4 can be used to serve a petition to perpetuate testimony.

Amended **Rule 45** (Subpoena) would require that a deposition subpoena state the manner for recording testimony. Under the present rules, a non-party deponent may not be notified of how the deposition will be recorded. Providing early notice of how testimony will be recorded enables a deponent to raise any objections to the deposition in a timely and efficient manner.

Rule B, Supplemental Rules for Certain Admiralty and Maritime Claims (In Personam Actions: Attachment and Garnishment) would be amended by fixing the time for determining whether a defendant is "found" in the district at the time when the verified complaint and the accompanying affidavit are filed. The proposed amendments are intended to prevent a defendant from defeating attachment and evading a security device by waiting until a complaint is filed before appointing an agent to receive service of process.

The proposed amendments to **Rule C**, Supplemental Rules for Certain Admiralty and Maritime Claims (In Rem Actions: Special Provisions) are technical in nature and correct amendments made in 2000.

2. RECENT RULES PROPOSALS DEFERRED OR REJECTED

The proposed amendments to **Rule 26(c)** (*General Provisions Governing Discovery; Duty of Disclosure*) dealing with protective orders were originally published for comment in October 1993, but were later revised and republished in September 1995 after being returned to the rules committees by the Judicial Conference. In 1996 the advisory committee decided not to proceed with the amendments, but to defer further consideration to coincide with future study of the American College of Trial Lawyers' request to narrow the general scope of discovery.

The proposed amendments to **Rule 47** (*Selection of Jurors*) would have given the parties a right to supplement the court's examination and orally question prospective jurors under reasonable limits on time, manner, and subject matter determined by the trial court in its discretion. The proposed amendments were circulated to the bench and bar for comment in September 1995. The advisory committee decided not to go forward with the proposal in 1996. Instead, the advisory committee urged the Federal Judicial Center to include presentations of experienced practitioners and judges on voir dire at future judicial programs and orientations.

Controversial proposed amendments to **Rule 48** (*Number of Jurors—Participation in Verdict*) would have required the initial empaneling of a jury of twelve persons in all civil cases, in the absence of stipulation by counsel to a lesser number. The jury might have been reduced to fewer members if some were excused under Rule 47(c). A jury might have been reduced to fewer than six members, however, only if the parties stipulated to a lower number before the verdict was returned. The proposed amendments would not have altered the requirement of unanimity, nor required alternate jurors. The Standing Committee noted the substantial public comment on the proposed amendments, much of it adverse from the bench, while positive from practitioners, including national bar associations and the Department of Justice. In the end, despite the ultimately affirmative recommendations of the Standing Committee and its advisory committee, at its September 1996 session the Judicial Conference did not approve the proposed amendments to Civil Rule 48.

In many class action cases, the decision to certify is the single most important judicial event, which often sets into motion a series of actions inexorably leading to settlement. The advisory committee heard much testimony about the intense pressure placed on the defendant to settle once a class action had been certified, rather than risk any chance of losing. The proposed amendment of **Rule 23(c)(1)** would amend the requirement that the class action certification determination be made "as soon as practicable." The advisory committee's proposed change to "when practicable" was designed to conform present practice, which permits a ruling on a motion to dismiss or for summary judgment before addressing certification questions. The Standing Rules Committee recognized that in most class action cases a judge needs sufficient information, which often requires adequate time for discovery, before making the critical class action certification decision. But concern was expressed that a delay in the certification decision might as a practical matter eliminate any real relief to some injured parties under certain circumstances, particularly when their claims may become moot if not acted on expeditiously. In addition, the advisory committee continues to study proposed revisions to other parts of the rule and could further consider the change to (c)(1) at the same time. Accordingly, the Standing Committee voted in late 1997 to recommit the proposed amendments to **Rule 23(c)(1)** to the advisory committee for further consideration.

*

PART VIII

TITLE 28, JUDICIARY AND JUDICIAL PROCEDURE—SELECTED PROVISIONS

Including Amendments Received to March 2005

Table of Sections

§ 41. Number and composition of circuits

The thirteen judicial circuits of the United States are constituted as follows:

Circuits and Composition

District of Columbia: District of Columbia

First: Maine, Massachusetts, New Hampshire, Puerto Rico, Rhode Island

Second: Connecticut, New York, Vermont

Third: Delaware, New Jersey, Pennsylvania, Virgin Islands

Fourth: Maryland, North Carolina, South Carolina, Virginia, West Virginia

Fifth: District of the Canal Zone, Louisiana, Mississippi, Texas

Sixth: Kentucky, Michigan, Ohio, Tennessee

Seventh: Illinois, Indiana, Wisconsin

Eighth: Arkansas, Iowa, Minnesota, Missouri, Nebraska, North Dakota, South Dakota

Ninth: Alaska, Arizona, California, Idaho, Montana, Nevada, Oregon, Washington, Guam, Hawaii

Tenth: Colorado, Kansas, New Mexico, Oklahoma, Utah, Wyoming

Eleventh: Alabama, Florida, Georgia

Federal: All Federal judicial districts

(June 25, 1948, c. 646, 62 Stat. 870; Oct. 31, 1951, c. 655, § 34, 65 Stat. 723; Oct. 14, 1980, Pub.L. 96–452, § 2, 94 Stat. 1994; Apr. 2,1982, Pub.L. 97–164, Title I, § 101, 96 Stat. 25.)

§ 144. Bias or prejudice of judge

Whenever a party to any proceeding in a district court makes and files a timely and sufficient affidavit that the judge before whom the matter is pending has a personal bias or prejudice either against him or in favor of any adverse party, such judge shall proceed no further therein, but another judge shall be assigned to hear such proceeding.

The affidavit shall state the facts and the reasons for the belief that bias or prejudice exists, and shall be filed not less than ten days before the beginning of the term at which the proceeding is to be heard, or good cause shall be shown for failure to file it within such time. A party may file only one such affidavit in any case. It shall be accompanied by a certificate of counsel of record stating that it is made in good faith.

(June 25, 1948, c. 646, 62 Stat. 898; May 24, 1949, c. 139, § 65, 63 Stat. 99.)

§ 451. Definitions

As used in this title:

The term "court of the United States" includes the Supreme Court of the United States, courts of appeals, district courts constituted by chapter 5 of this title, including the Court of International Trade and any court created by Act of Congress the judges of which are entitled to hold office during good behavior.

The terms "district court" and "district court of the United States" mean the courts constituted by chapter 5 of this title.

The term "judge of the United States" includes judges of the courts of appeals, district courts, Court of International Trade and any court created by Act of Congress, the judges of which are entitled to hold office during good behavior.

The term "justice of the United States" includes the Chief Justice of the United States and the associate justices of the Supreme Court.

The term "district" and "judicial district" mean the districts enumerated in Chapter 5 of this title.

The term "department" means one of the executive departments enumerated in section 1 of Title 5, unless the context shows that such term was intended to describe the executive, legislative, or judicial branches of the government.

The term "agency" includes any department, independent establishment, commission, administration, authority, board or bureau of the United States or any corporation in which the United States has a proprietary interest, unless the context shows that such term was intended to be used in a more limited sense.

(As amended Mar. 18, 1959, Pub.L. 86–3, § 10, 73 Stat. 9; Sept. 12, 1966, Pub.L. 89–571, § 3, 80 Stat. 764; Oct. 10, 1980, 96–417, Title V, § 501(10), 94 Stat. 1742; Apr. 2, 1982, Pub.L. 97–164, Title I, § 114, 96 Stat. 29.)

§ 452. Courts always open; powers unrestricted by expiration of sessions

All courts of the United States shall be deemed always open for the purpose of filing proper papers, issuing and returning process, and making motions and orders.

The continued existence or expiration of a session of court in no way affects the power of the court to do any act or take any proceeding.

(As amended Oct. 16, 1963, Pub.L. 88–139, § 2, 77 Stat. 248.)

§ 455. Disqualification of justice, judge, or magistrate

(a) Any justice, judge, or magistrate of the United States shall disqualify himself in any proceeding in which his impartiality might reasonably be questioned.

(b) He shall also disqualify himself in the following circumstances:

(1) Where he has a personal bias or prejudice concerning a party, or personal knowledge of disputed evidentiary facts concerning the proceeding;

(2) Where in private practice he served as lawyer in the matter in controversy, or a lawyer with whom he previously practiced law served during such association as a lawyer concerning the matter, or the judge or such lawyer has been a material witness concerning it;

(3) Where he has served in governmental employment and in such capacity participated as counsel, adviser or material witness concerning the proceeding or expressed an opinion concerning the merits of the particular case in controversy;

(4) He knows that he, individually or as a fiduciary, or his spouse or minor child residing in his household, has a financial interest in the subject matter in controversy or in a party to the proceeding, or any other interest that could be substantially affected by the outcome of the proceeding;

(5) He or his spouse, or a person within the third degree of relationship to either of them, or the spouse of such a person:

(i) Is a party to the proceeding, or an officer, director, or trustee of a party;

(ii) Is acting as a lawyer in the proceeding;

(iii) Is known by the judge to have an interest that could be substantially affected by the outcome of the proceeding;

(iv) Is to the judge's knowledge likely to be a material witness in the proceeding.

(c) A judge should inform himself about his personal and fiduciary financial interests, and make a reasonable effort to inform himself about the personal financial interests of his spouse and minor children residing in his household.

(d) For the purposes of this section the following words or phrases shall have the meaning indicated:

(1) "proceeding" includes pretrial, trial, appellate review, or other stages of litigation;

(2) the degree of relationship is calculated according to the civil law system;

(3) "fiduciary" includes such relationships as executor, administrator, trustee, and guardian;

(4) "financial interest" means ownership of a legal or equitable interest, however small, or a relationship as director, adviser, or other active participant in the affairs of a party, except that:

(i) Ownership in a mutual or common investment fund that holds securities is not a "financial interest" in such securities unless the judge participates in the management of the fund;

(ii) An office in an educational, religious, charitable, fraternal, or civic organization is not a "financial interest" in securities held by the organization;

(iii) The proprietary interest of a policyholder in a mutual insurance company, of a depositor in a mutual savings association, or a similar proprietary interest, is a "financial interest" in the organization only if the outcome of the proceeding could substantially affect the value of the interest;

(iv) Ownership of government securities is a "financial interest" in the issuer only if the outcome of the proceeding could substantially affect the value of the securities.

(e) No justice, judge, or magistrate shall accept from the parties to the proceeding a waiver of any ground for disqualification enumerated in subsection (b). Where the ground for disqualification arises only under subsection (a), waiver may be accepted provided it is preceded by a full disclosure on the record of the basis for disqualification.

(f) Notwithstanding the preceding provisions of this section, if any justice, judge, magistrate, or bankruptcy judge to whom a matter has been assigned would be disqualified, after substantial judicial time has been devoted to the matter, because of the appearance or discovery, after the matter was assigned to him or her, that he or she individually or as a fiduciary, or his or her spouse or minor child residing in his or her household, has a financial interest in a party (other than an interest that could be substantially affected by the outcome), disqualification is not required if the justice, judge, magistrate, bankruptcy judge, spouse or minor child, as the case may be, divests himself or herself of the interest that provides the grounds for the disqualification.

(June 25, 1948, c. 646, 62 Stat. 908; Dec. 5, 1974, Pub.L. 93–512, § 1, 88 Stat. 1609; Nov. 6, 1978, Pub.L. 95–598, Title II, § 214(a), (b), 92 Stat. 2661; Nov. 19, 1988, Pub.L. 100–702, Title X, § 1007, 102 Stat. 4667.)

§ 631. Appointment and Tenure

(a) The judges of each United States district court and the district courts of the Virgin Islands, Guam, and the Northern Mariana Islands shall appoint United States magistrate judges in such numbers and to serve at such locations within the judicial districts as the Judicial Conference may determine under this chapter. In the case of a magistrate judge appointed by the district court of the Virgin Islands, Guam, or the Northern Mariana Islands, this chapter shall apply as though the court appointing such a magistrate judge were a United States district court. Where there is more than one judge of a district court, the appointment, whether an original appointment or a reappointment, shall be by the concurrence of a majority of all the judges of such district court, and when there is no such concurrence, then by the chief judge. Where the conference deems it desirable, a magistrate may be designated to serve in one or more districts adjoining the district for which he is appointed. Such a designation shall be made by the concurrence of a majority of the judges of each of the district courts involved and shall specify the duties to be performed by the magistrate in the adjoining district or districts.

(b) No individual may be appointed or reappointed to serve as a magistrate under this chapter unless:

(1) He has been for at least five years a member in good standing of the bar of the highest court of a State, the District of Columbia, the Commonwealth of Puerto Rico, the Territory of Guam, the Commonwealth of the Northern Mariana Islands, or the Virgin Islands of the United States, except that an individual who does not meet the bar membership requirements of this paragraph may be appointed and serve as a part-time magistrate if the appointing court or courts and the conference find that no qualified individual who is a member of the bar is available to serve at a specific location;

(2) He is determined by the appointing district court or courts to be competent to perform the duties of the office;

(3) In the case of an individual appointed to serve in a national park, he resides within the exterior boundaries of that park, or at some place reasonably adjacent thereto;

(4) He is not related by blood or marriage to a judge of the appointing court or courts at the time of his initial appointment; and

(5) He is selected pursuant to standards and procedures promulgated by the Judicial Conference of the United States. Such standards and procedures shall contain provision for public notice of all vacancies in magistrate positions and for the establishment by the district courts of merit selection panels, composed of residents of the individual judicial districts, to assist the courts in identifying and recommending persons who are best qualified to fill such positions.

(c) A magistrate may hold no other civil or military office or employment under the United States: Provided, however, That, with the approval of the conference, a part-time referee in bankruptcy or a clerk or deputy clerk of a court of the United States may be appointed and serve as a part-time United States magistrate, but the conference shall fix the aggregate amount of compensation to be received for performing the duties of part-time magistrate and part-time referee in bankruptcy, clerk or deputy clerk: And provided further, That retired officers and retired enlisted personnel of the Regular and Reserve components of the Army, Navy, Air Force, Marine Corps, and Coast Guard, members of the Reserve components of the Army, Navy, Air Force, Marine Corps, and Coast Guard, and members of the Army National Guard of the United States, the Air National Guard of the United States, and the Naval Militia and of the National Guard of a State, territory, or the District of Columbia, except the National Guard disbursing officers who are on a full-time salary basis, may be appointed and serve as United States magistrates.

(d) Except as otherwise provided in sections 375 and 636(h) of this title, no individual may serve under this chapter after having attained the age of seventy years: Provided, however, That upon a majority vote of all the judges of the appointing court or courts, which is taken upon the magistrate's attaining age seventy and upon each subsequent anniversary thereof, a magistrate who has attained the age of seventy years may continue to serve and may be reappointed under this chapter.

(e) The appointment of any individual as a full-time magistrate shall be for a term of eight years, and the appointment of any individuals as a part-time magistrate shall be for a term of four years, except that the term of a full-time or part-time magistrate appointed under subsection (k) shall expire upon—

(1) the expiration of the absent magistrate's term,

(2) the reinstatement of the absent magistrate in regular service in office as a magistrate,

(3) the failure of the absent magistrate to make timely application under subsection (j) of this section for reinstatement in regular service in office as a magistrate after discharge or release from military service,

(4) the death or resignation of the absent magistrate, or

(5) the removal from office of the absent magistrate pursuant to subsection (i) of this section,

whichever may first occur.

(f) Upon the expiration of his term, a magistrate may, by a majority vote of the judges of the appointing district court or courts and with the approval of the judicial council of the circuit, continue to perform the duties of his office until his successor is appointed, or for 180 days after the date of the expiration of the magistrate's term, whichever is earlier.

(g) Each individual appointed as a magistrate under this section shall take the oath or affirmation prescribed by section 453 of this title before performing the duties of his office.

(h) Each appointment made by a judge or judges of a district court shall be entered of record in such court, and notice of such appointment shall be given at once by the clerk of that court to the Director.

(i) Removal of a magistrate during the term for which he is appointed shall be only for incompetency, misconduct, neglect of duty, or physical or mental disability, but a magistrate's office shall be terminated if the conference determines that the services performed by his office are no longer needed. Removal shall be by the judges of the district court for the judicial district in which the magistrate serves; where there is more than one judge of a district court, removal shall not occur unless a majority of all the judges of such court concur in the order of removal; and when there is a tie vote of the judges of the district court on the question of the removal or retention in office of a magistrate, then removal shall be only by a concurrence of a majority of all the judges of the council. In the case of a magistrate appointed under the third sentence of subsection (a) of this section, removal shall not occur unless a majority of all the judges of the appointing district courts concur in the order of removal; and where there is a tie vote on the question of the removal or retention in office of a magistrate, then removal shall be only by a concurrence of a majority of all the judges of the council or councils. Before any order or removal shall be entered, a full specification of the charges shall be furnished to the magistrate, and he shall be accorded by the judge or judges of the removing court, courts, council, or councils an opportunity to be heard on the charges.

(j) Upon the grant by the appropriate district court or courts of a leave of absence to a magistrate entitled to such relief under chapter 43 of title 38, such court or courts may proceed to appoint, in the manner specified in subsection (a) of this section, another magistrate, qualified for appointment and service under subsections (b), (c), and (d) of this section, who shall serve for the period specified in subsection (e) of this section.

(k) A United States magistrate appointed under this chapter shall be exempt from the provisions of subchapter I of chapter 63 of title 5.

[***(l)*** Redesignated (k)]

(June 25, 1948, c. 646, 62 Stat. 915; May 24, 1949, c. 139, § 73, 63 Stat. 100; July 9, 1952, c. 609, § 1, 66 Stat. 509; July 25, 1956, c. 722, 70 Stat. 642; Oct. 17, 1968, Pub.L. 90–578, Title I, § 101, 82 Stat. 1108; Oct. 17, 1976, Pub.L. 94–520, § 2, 90 Stat. 2458; Nov. 6, 1978, Pub.L. 95–598, Title II, § 231, 92 Stat. 2665; Oct. 10, 1979, Pub.L. 96–82, § 3(a)-(d), 93 Stat. 644, 645; Aug. 6, 1982, Pub.L. 97–230, 96 Stat. 255; Nov. 14, 1986, Pub.L. 99–651, Title II, § 201(a)(1), 100 Stat. 3646; Nov. 15, 1988, Pub.L. 100–659, § 5, 102 Stat. 3918; Nov. 19, 1988, Pub.L. 100–702, Title X, § 1003(a)(2), 102 Stat. 4665; June 30, 1989, Pub.L. 101–45, Title II, § 104, 103 Stat. 122; Dec. 1, 1990, Pub.L. 101–650, Title III, § 308(b), 104 Stat. 5112; Oct. 13, 1994, Pub.L. 103–353, § 2(c), 108 Stat. 3169; Nov. 13, 2000, Pub.L. 106–518, Title II, § 201, 114 Stat. 2412.)

§ 632. Character of Service

(a) Full-time United States magistrates may not engage in the practice of law, and may not engage in any other business, occupation, or employment inconsistent with the expeditious, proper, and impartial performance of their duties as judicial officers.

(b) Part-time United States magistrates shall render such service as judicial officers as is required by law. While so serving they may engage in the practice of law, but may not serve as counsel in any criminal action in any court of the United States, nor act in any capacity that is, under such regulations as the conference may establish, inconsistent with the proper discharge of their office. Within such restrictions, they may engage in any other business, occupation, or employment which is not inconsistent with the expeditious, proper, and impartial performance of their duties as judicial officers.

(June 25, 1948, c. 646, 62 Stat. 916; Oct. 17, 1968, Pub.L. 90–578, Title I, § 101, 82 Stat. 1110.)

§ 633. Determination of Number, Locations, and Salaries of Magistrates

(a) Surveys by the Director.—

(1) The Director shall, within one year immediately following the date of the enactment of the Federal Magistrates Act, make a careful survey of conditions in judicial districts to determine (A) the number of appointments of full-time magistrates and part-time magistrates required to be made under this chapter to provide for the expeditious and effective administration of justice, (B) the locations at which such officers shall serve, and (C) their respective salaries under section 634 of this title. Thereafter, the Director shall, from time to time, make such surveys, general or local, as the conference shall deem expedient.

(2) In the course of any survey, the Director shall take into account local conditions in each judicial district, including the areas and the populations to be served, the transportation and communications facilities available, the amount and distribution of business of the type expected to arise before officers appointed under this chapter (including such matters as may be assigned under section 636(b) of this chapter), and any other material factors. The Director shall give consideration to suggestions from any interested parties, including district judges, United States commissioners or officers appointed under this chapter, United States attorneys, bar associations, and other parties having relevant experience or information.

(3) The surveys shall be made with a view toward creating and maintaining a system of full-time United States magistrates. However, should the Director find, as a result of any such surveys, areas in which the employment of a full-time magistrate would not be feasible or desirable, he shall recommend the appointment of part-time United States magistrates in such numbers and at such locations as may be required to permit prompt and efficient issuance of process and to permit individuals charged with criminal offenses against the United States to be brought before a judicial officer of the United States promptly after arrest.

(b) Determination by the conference.—Upon the completion of the initial surveys required by subsection (a) of this section, the Director shall report to the district courts, the councils, and the conference his recommendations concerning the number of full-time magistrates and part-time magistrates, their respective locations, and the amount of their respective salaries under section 634 of this title. The district courts shall advise their respective councils, stating their recommendations and the reasons therefor; the councils shall advise the conference, stating their recommendations and the reasons therefor, and shall also report to the conference the recommendations of the district courts. The conference shall determine, in the light of the recommendations of the Director, the district courts, and the councils, the number of full-time United States magistrates and part-time United States magistrates, the locations at which they shall serve, and their respective salaries. Such determinations shall take effect in each judicial district at such time as the district court for such judicial district shall determine, but in no event later than one year after they are promulgated.

(c) Changes in number, locations, and salaries.—Except as otherwise provided in this chapter, the conference may, from time to time, in the light of the recommendations of the Director, the district courts, and the councils, change the number, locations, and salaries of full-time and part-time magistrates, as the expeditious administration of justice may require.

(June 25, 1948, c. 646, 62 Stat. 916; Aug. 13, 1954, c. 728, § 1(a), (b), 68 Stat. 703, 704; Sept. 2, 1957, Pub.L. 85–276, §§ 1, 2, 71 Stat. 600; Oct. 17, 1968, Pub.L. 90–578, Title I, § 101, 82 Stat. 1111; Oct. 10, 1979, Pub.L. 96–82, § 4, 93 Stat. 645; Nov. 14, 1986, Pub.L. 99–651, Title II, § 202(d), 100 Stat. 3648.)

§ 636. Jurisdiction, Powers, and Temporary Assignment

(a) Each United States magistrate judge serving under this chapter shall have within the territorial jurisdiction prescribed by his appointment—

(1) all powers and duties conferred or imposed upon United States commissioners by law or by the Rules of Criminal Procedure for the United States District Courts;

(2) the power to administer oaths and affirmations, issue orders pursuant to section 3142 of title 18 concerning release or detention of persons pending trial, and take acknowledgements, affidavits, and depositions;

(3) the power to conduct trials under *section 3401, title 18, United States Code*, in conformity with and subject to the limitations of that section;

(4) the power to enter a sentence for a petty offense; and

(5) the power to enter a sentence for a class A misdemeanor in a case in which the parties have consented.

(b)(1) Notwithstanding any provision of law to the contrary—

(A) a judge may designate a magistrate judge to hear and determine any pretrial matter pending before the court, except a motion for injunctive relief, for judgment on the pleadings, for summary judgment, to dismiss or quash an indictment or information made by the defendant, to suppress evidence in a criminal case, to dismiss or to permit maintenance of a class action, to dismiss for failure to state a claim upon which relief can be granted, and to involuntarily dismiss an action. A judge of the court may reconsider any pretrial matter under this subparagraph (A) where it has been shown that the magistrate judge's order is clearly erroneous or contrary to law.

(B) a judge may also designate a magistrate judge to conduct hearings, including evidentiary hearings, and to submit to a judge of the court proposed findings of fact and recommendations for the disposition, by a judge of the court, of any motion excepted in subparagraph (A), of applications for posttrial [1] relief made by individuals convicted of criminal offenses and of prisoner petitions challenging conditions of confinement.

(C) the magistrate judge shall file his proposed findings and recommendations under subparagraph (B) with the court and a copy shall forthwith be mailed to all parties.

Within ten days after being served with a copy, any party may serve and file written objections to such proposed findings and recommendations as provided by rules of court. A judge of the court shall make a de novo determination of those portions of the report or specified proposed findings or recommendations to which objection is made. A judge of the court may accept, reject, or modify, in whole or in part, the findings or recommendations made by the magistrate judge.

1. So in original. Probably should be "post-trial".

The judge may also receive further evidence or recommit the matter to the magistrate judge with instructions.

(2) A judge may designate a magistrate judge to serve as a special master pursuant to the applicable provisions of this title and the Federal Rules of Civil Procedure for the United States district courts. A judge may designate a magistrate judge to serve as a special master in any civil case, upon consent of the parties, without regard to the provisions of *rule 53(b) of the Federal Rules of Civil Procedure* for the United States district courts.

(3) A magistrate judge may be assigned such additional duties as are not inconsistent with the Constitution and laws of the United States.

(4) Each district court shall establish rules pursuant to which the magistrate judges shall discharge their duties.

(c) Notwithstanding any provision of law to the contrary—

(1) Upon the consent of the parties, a full-time United States magistrate judge or a part-time United States magistrate judge who serves as a full-time judicial officer may conduct any or all proceedings in a jury or nonjury civil matter and order the entry of judgment in the case, when specially designated to exercise such jurisdiction by the district court or courts he serves. Upon the consent of the parties, pursuant to their specific written request, any other part-time magistrate judge may exercise such jurisdiction, if such magistrate judge meets the bar membership requirements set forth in section 631(b)(1) and the chief judge of the district court certifies that a full-time magistrate judge is not reasonably available in accordance with guidelines established by the judicial council of the circuit. When there is more than one judge of a district court, designation under this paragraph shall be by the concurrence of a majority of all the judges of such district court, and when there is no such concurrence, then by the chief judge.

(2) If a magistrate judge is designated to exercise civil jurisdiction under paragraph (1) of this subsection, the clerk of court shall, at the time the action is filed, notify the parties of the availability of a magistrate judge to exercise such jurisdiction. The decision of the parties shall be communicated to the clerk of court. Thereafter, either the district court judge or the magistrate judge may again advise the parties of the availability of the magistrate judge, but in so doing, shall also advise the parties that they are free to withhold consent without adverse substantive consequences. Rules of court for the reference of civil matters to magistrate judges shall include procedures to protect the voluntariness of the parties' consent.

(3) Upon entry of judgment in any case referred under paragraph (1) of this subsection, an aggrieved party may appeal directly to the appropriate United States court of appeals from the judgment of the magistrate judge in the same manner as an appeal from any other judgment of a district court. The consent of the parties allows a magistrate judge designated to exercise civil jurisdiction under paragraph (1) of this subsection to direct the entry of a judgment of the district court in accordance with the Federal Rules of Civil Procedure. Nothing in this paragraph shall be construed as a limitation of any party's right to seek review by the Supreme Court of the United States.

(4) The court may, for good cause shown on its own motion, or under extraordinary circumstances shown by any party, vacate a reference of a civil matter to a magistrate judge under this subsection.

(5) The magistrate judge shall, subject to guidelines of the Judicial Conference, determine whether the record taken pursuant to this section shall be taken by electronic sound recording, by a court reporter, or by other means.

[**(6), (7)** Redesignated (4), (5)]

(d) The practice and procedure for the trial of cases before officers serving under this chapter shall conform to rules promulgated by the Supreme Court pursuant to section 2072 of this title.

(e) Contempt authority.—

(1) In general.—A United States magistrate judge serving under this chapter shall have within the territorial jurisdiction prescribed by the appointment of such magistrate judge the power to exercise contempt authority as set forth in this subsection.

(2) Summary criminal contempt authority.—A magistrate judge shall have the power to punish summarily by fine or imprisonment, or both, such contempt of the authority of such magistrate judge constituting misbehavior of any person in the magistrate judge's presence so as to obstruct the administration of justice. The order of contempt shall be issued under the Federal Rules of Criminal Procedure.

(3) Additional criminal contempt authority in civil consent and misdemeanor cases.—In any case in which a United States magistrate judge presides with the consent of the parties under subsection (c) of this section, and in any misdemeanor case proceeding before a magistrate judge under *section 3401 of title 18*, the magistrate judge shall have the power to punish, by fine or imprisonment, or both, criminal contempt constituting disobedience or resistance to the magistrate judge's lawful writ, process, order, rule, decree, or command. Disposition of such contempt shall be conducted upon notice and hearing under the Federal Rules of Criminal Procedure.

(4) Civil contempt authority in civil consent and misdemeanor cases.—In any case in which a United States magistrate judge presides with the consent of the parties under subsection (c) of this section, and in any misdemeanor case proceeding before a magistrate judge under *section 3401 of title 18*, the magistrate judge may exercise the civil contempt authority of the district court. This paragraph shall not be construed to limit the authority of a magistrate judge to order sanctions under any other statute, the Federal Rules of Civil Procedure, or the Federal Rules of Criminal Procedure.

(5) Criminal contempt penalties.—The sentence imposed by a magistrate judge for any criminal contempt provided for in paragraphs (2) and (3) shall not exceed the penalties for a Class C misdemeanor as set forth in *sections 3581(b)(8)* and *3571(b)(6) of title 18*.

(6) Certification of other contempts to the district court.—Upon the commission of any such act—

(A) in any case in which a United States magistrate judge presides with the consent of the parties under subsection (c) of this section, or in any misdemeanor case proceeding before a magistrate judge under *section 3401 of title 18*, that may, in the opinion of the magistrate judge, constitute a serious criminal contempt punishable by penalties exceeding those set forth in paragraph (5) of this subsection, or

(B) in any other case or proceeding under subsection (a) or (b) of this section, or any other statute, where—

(i) the act committed in the magistrate judge's presence may, in the opinion of the magistrate judge, constitute a serious criminal contempt punishable by penalties exceeding those set forth in paragraph (5) of this subsection,

(ii) the act that constitutes a criminal contempt occurs outside the presence of the magistrate judge, or

(iii) the act constitutes a civil contempt,

the magistrate judge shall forthwith certify the facts to a district judge and may serve or cause to be served, upon any person whose behavior is brought into question under this paragraph, an order requiring such person to appear before a district judge upon a day certain to show cause why that person should not be adjudged in contempt by reason of the facts so certified. The district judge shall thereupon hear the evidence as to the act or conduct complained of and, if it is such as to warrant punishment, punish such person in the same manner and to the same extent as for a contempt committed before a district judge.

(7) Appeals of magistrate judge contempt orders.—The appeal of an order of contempt under this subsection shall be made to the court of appeals in cases proceeding under subsection (c) of this section. The appeal of any other order of contempt issued under this section shall be made to the district court.

(f) In an emergency and upon the concurrence of the chief judges of the districts involved, a United States magistrate judge may be temporarily assigned to perform any of the duties specified in subsection (a), (b), or (c) of this section in a judicial district other than the judicial district for which he has been appointed. No magistrate judge shall perform any of such duties in a district to which he has been temporarily assigned until an order has been issued by the chief judge of such district specifying (1) the emergency by reason of which he has been transferred, (2) the duration of his assignment, and (3) the duties which he is authorized to perform. A magistrate judge so assigned shall not be entitled to additional compensation but shall be reimbursed for actual and necessary expenses incurred in the performance of his duties in accordance with section 635.

(g) A United States magistrate judge may perform the verification function required by *section 4107 of title 18, United States Code*. A magistrate judge may be assigned by a judge of any United States district court to perform the verification required by section 4108 and the appointment of counsel authorized by *section 4109 of title 18, United States Code*, and may perform such functions beyond the territorial limits of the United States. A magistrate judge assigned such functions shall have no authority to perform any other function within the territory of a foreign country.

(h) A United States magistrate judge who has retired may, upon the consent of the chief judge of the district involved, be recalled to serve as a magistrate judge in any judicial district by the judicial council of the circuit within which such district is located. Upon recall, a magistrate judge may receive a salary for such service in accordance with regulations promulgated by the Judicial Conference, subject to the restrictions on the payment of an annuity set forth in section 377 of this title or in subchapter III of chapter 83, and chapter 84, of title 5 which are applicable to such magistrate judge. The requirements set forth in subsections (a), (b)(3), and (d) of section 631, and paragraph (1) of subsection (b) of such section to the extent such paragraph requires membership of the bar of the location in which an individual is to serve as a magistrate judge, shall not apply to the recall of a retired magistrate judge under this subsection or section 375 of this title. Any other requirement set forth in section 631(b) shall apply to the recall of a retired magistrate judge under this subsection or section 375 of this title unless such retired magistrate judge met such requirement upon appointment or reappointment as a magistrate judge under section 361.

(June 25, 1948, c. 646, 62 Stat. 917; Oct. 17, 1968, Pub.L. 90–578, Title I, § 101, 82 Stat. 1113; Mar. 1, 1972, Pub.L. 92–239, § § 1, 2, 86 Stat. 47; Oct. 21, 1976, Pub.L. 94–577, § 1, 90 Stat. 2729; Oct. 28, 1977, Pub.L. 95–144, § 2, 91 Stat. 1220; Oct. 10, 1979, Pub.L. 96–82, § 2, 93 Stat. 643; Oct. 12, 1984, Pub.L. 98–473, Title II, § 208, 98 Stat. 1986; Nov. 8, 1984, Pub.L. 98–620, Title IV, § 402(29)(B), 98 Stat. 3359; Nov. 14, 1986, Pub.L. 99–651, Title II, § 201(a)(2), 100 Stat. 3647; Nov. 15, 1988, Pub.L. 100–659, § 4(c), 102 Stat. 3918; Nov. 18, 1988, Pub.L. 100–690, Title VII, § 7322, 102 Stat. 4467; Nov. 19, 1988, Pub.L. 100–702, Title IV, § 404(b)(1), Title X, § 1014, 102 Stat. 4651, 4669; Dec. 1, 1990, Pub.L. 101–650, Title III, § § 308(a), 321, 104 Stat. 5112, 5117; Oct. 19, 1996, Pub.L. 104–317, Title II, § § 201, 202(b), 207, 110 Stat. 3848, 3849, 3851; Nov. 13, 2000, Pub.L. 106–518, Title II, § § 202, 203(b), 114 Stat. 2412, 2414; Nov. 2, 2002, Pub.L. 107–273, Div. B, Title III, § 3002(b), 116 Stat. 1805.)

§ 639. Definitions

As used in this chapter—

(1) "Conference" shall mean the Judicial Conference of the United States;

(2) "Council" shall mean the Judicial Council of the Circuit;

(3) "Director" shall mean the Director of the Administrative Office of the United States Courts;

(4) "Full-time magistrate" shall mean a full-time United States magistrate;

(5) "Part-time magistrate" shall mean a part-time United States magistrate; and

(6) "United States magistrate" and "magistrate" shall mean both full-time and part-time United States magistrates.

(June 25, 1948, c. 646, 62 Stat. 917; Oct. 17, 1968, Pub.L. 90–578, Title I, § 101, 82 Stat. 1114.)

§ 1251. Original jurisdiction

(a) The Supreme Court shall have original and exclusive jurisdiction of all controversies between two or more States.

(b) The Supreme Court shall have original but not exclusive jurisdiction of:

(1) All actions or proceedings to which ambassadors, other public ministers, consuls, or vice consuls of foreign states are parties;

(2) All controversies between the United States and a State;

(3) All actions or proceedings by a State against the citizens of another State or against aliens.

(As amended Sept. 30, 1978, Pub.L. 95–393, § 8(b), 92 Stat. 810.)

§ 1253. Direct appeals from decisions of three-judge courts

Except as otherwise provided by law, any party may appeal to the Supreme Court from an order granting or denying, after notice and hearing, an interlocutory or permanent injunction in any civil action, suit or proceeding required by any Act of Congress to be heard and determined by a district court of three judges.

§ 1254. Courts of appeals; certiorari; certified questions

Cases in the courts of appeals may be reviewed by the Supreme Court by the following methods:

(1) By writ of certiorari granted upon the petition of any party to any civil or criminal case, before or after rendition of judgment or decree;

(2) By certification at any time by a court of appeals of any question of law in any civil or criminal case as to which instructions are desired, and upon such certification the Supreme Court may give binding instructions or require the entire record to be sent up for decision of the entire matter in controversy.

(As amended June 27, 1988, Pub.L. 100–352, § 2(a), (b), 102 Stat. 662.)

§ 1257. State courts; certiorari

(a) Final judgments or decrees rendered by the highest court of a State in which a decision could be had, may be reviewed by the Supreme Court by writ of certiorari where the validity of a treaty or statute of the United States is drawn in question or where the validity of a statute of any State is drawn in question on the ground of its being repugnant to the Constitution, treaties, or laws of the United States, or where any title, right, privilege, or immunity is specially set up or claimed under the Constitution or the treaties or statutes of, or any commission held or authority exercised under, the United States.

(b) For the purposes of this section, the term "highest court of a State" includes the District of Columbia Court of Appeals.

(As amended July 29, 1970, Pub.L. 91–358, Title I, § 172(a)(1), 84 Stat. 590; June 27, 1988, Pub.L. 100–352, § 3, 102 Stat. 662.)

§ 1291. Final decisions of district courts

The courts of appeals (other than the United States Court of Appeals for the Federal Circuit) shall have jurisdiction of appeals from all final decisions of the district courts of the United States, the United States District Court for the District of the Canal Zone, the District Court of Guam, and the District Court of the Virgin Islands, except where a direct review may be had in the Supreme Court. The jurisdiction of the United States Court of Appeals for the Federal Circuit shall be limited to the jurisdiction described in sections 1292(c) and (d) and 1295 of this title.

(As amended Oct. 31, 1951, c. 655, § 48, 65 Stat. 726; July 7, 1958, Pub.L. 85–508, § 12(e), 72 Stat. 348; Apr. 2, 1982, Pub.L. 97–164, Title I, § 124, 96 Stat. 36.)

§ 1292. Interlocutory decisions

(a) Except as provided in subsections (c) and (d) of this section, the courts of appeals shall have jurisdiction of appeals from:

(1) Interlocutory orders of the district courts of the United States, the United States District Court for the District of the Canal Zone, the District Court of Guam, and the District Court of the Virgin Islands, or of the judges thereof, granting, continuing, modifying, refusing or dissolving injunctions, or refusing to dissolve or modify injunctions, except where a direct review may be had in the Supreme Court;

(2) Interlocutory orders appointing receivers, or refusing orders to wind up receiverships or to take steps to accomplish the purposes thereof, such as directing sales or other disposals of property;

(3) Interlocutory decrees of such district courts or the judges thereof determining the rights and liabilities of the parties to admiralty cases in which appeals from final decrees are allowed.

(b) When a district judge, in making in a civil action an order not otherwise appealable under this section, shall be of the opinion that such order involves a controlling question of law as to which there is substantial ground for difference of opinion and that an immediate appeal from the order may materially advance the ultimate termination of the litigation, he shall so state in writing in such order. The Court of Appeals which would have jurisdiction of an appeal of such action may thereupon, in its discretion, permit an appeal to be taken from such order, if application is made to it within ten days after the entry of the order: *Provided, however,* that application for an appeal hereunder shall not stay proceedings in the district court unless the district judge or the Court of Appeals or a judge thereof shall so order.

(c) The United States Court of Appeals for the Federal Circuit shall have exclusive jurisdiction—

(1) of an appeal from an interlocutory order or decree described in subsection (a) or (b) of this section in any case over which the court would have jurisdiction of an appeal under section 1295 of this title; and

(2) of an appeal from a judgment in a civil action for patent infringement which would otherwise be appealable to the United States Court of Appeals for the Federal Circuit and is final except for an accounting.

(d)(1) When the chief judge of the Court of International Trade issues an order under the provisions of section 256(b) of this title, or when any judge of the Court of International Trade, in issuing any other interlocutory order, includes in the order a statement that a controlling question of law is involved with respect to which there is a substantial ground for difference of opinion and that an immediate appeal from that order may materially advance the ultimate termination of the litigation, the United States Court of Appeals for the Federal Circuit may, in its discretion, permit an appeal to be taken from such order, if application is made to that Court within ten days after the entry of such order.

(2) When the chief judge of the United States Court of Federal Claims issues an order under section 798(b) of this title, or when any judge of the United States Court of Federal Claims, in issuing an interlocutory order, includes in the order a statement that a controlling question of law is involved with respect to which there is a substantial ground for difference of opinion and that an immediate appeal from that order may materially advance the ultimate termination of the litigation, the United States Court of Appeals for the Federal Circuit may, in its discretion, permit an appeal to be taken from such order, if application is made to that Court within ten days after the entry of such order.

(3) Neither the application for nor the granting of an appeal under this subsection shall stay proceedings in the Court of International Trade or in the Court of Federal Claims, as the case may be, unless a stay is ordered by a judge of the Court of International Trade or of the Court of Federal Claims or by the United States Court of Appeals for the Federal Circuit or a judge of that court.

(4)(A) The United States Court of Appeals for the Federal Circuit shall have exclusive jurisdiction of an appeal from an interlocutory order of a district court of the United States, the District Court of Guam, the District Court of the Virgin Islands, or the District Court for the Northern Mariana Islands, granting or denying, in whole or in part, a motion to transfer an action to the United States Court of Federal Claims under section 1631 of this title.

(B) When a motion to transfer an action to the Court of Federal Claims is filed in a district court, no further proceedings shall be taken in the district court until 60 days after the court has ruled upon the motion. If an appeal is taken from the district court's grant or denial of the motion, proceedings shall be further stayed until the appeal has been decided by the Court of Appeals for the Federal Circuit. The stay of proceedings in the district court shall not bar the granting of preliminary or injunctive relief, where appropriate and where expedition is reasonably necessary. However, during the period in which proceedings are stayed as provided in this subparagraph, no transfer to the Court of Federal Claims pursuant to the motion shall be carried out.

(e) The Supreme Court may prescribe rules, in accordance with section 2072 of this title, to provide for an appeal of an interlocutory decision to the courts of appeals that is not otherwise provided for under subsection (a), (b), (c), or (d).

(As amended Oct. 31, 1951, c. 655, § 49, 65 Stat. 726; July 7, 1958, Pub.L. 85–508, § 12(e), 72 Stat. 348; Sept. 2, 1958, Pub.L. 85–919, 72 Stat. 1770; Apr. 2, 1982, Pub. L. 97–164, Title I, § 125, 96 Stat. 36; Nov. 8, 1984, Pub.L. 98–620, Title IV, § 412, 98 Stat. 3362; Nov. 19, 1988, Pub.L. 100–702, Title V, § 501, 102 Stat. 4652; Oct. 29, 1992, Pub.L. 102–572, Title I, § 101, Title IX, §§ 902(b), 906(c), 106 Stat. 4506, 4516, 4518.)

§ 1330. Actions against foreign states

(a) The district courts shall have original jurisdiction without regard to amount in controversy of any nonjury civil action against a foreign state as defined in section 1603(a) of this title as to any claim for relief in personam with respect to which the foreign state is not entitled to immunity either under sections 1605–1607 of this title or under any applicable international agreement.

(b) Personal jurisdiction over a foreign state shall exist as to every claim for relief over which the district courts have jurisdiction under subsection (a) where service has been made under section 1608 of this title.

(c) For purposes of subsection (b), an appearance by a foreign state does not confer personal jurisdiction with respect to any claim for relief not arising out of any transaction or occurrence enumerated in sections 1605–1607 of this title.

(Added Pub.L. 94–583, § 2(a), Oct. 21, 1976, 90 Stat. 2891.)

§ 1331. Federal question

The district courts shall have original jurisdiction of all civil actions arising under the Constitution, laws, or treaties of the United States.

(As amended July 25, 1958, Pub.L. 85–554, § 1, 72 Stat. 415; Oct. 21, 1976, Pub.L. 94–574, § 2, 90 Stat. 2721; Dec. 1, 1980, Pub. L. 96–486, § 2(a), 94 Stat. 2369.)

§ 1332. Diversity of citizenship; amount in controversy; costs

(a) The district courts shall have original jurisdiction of all civil actions where the matter in controversy exceeds the sum or value of $75,000, exclusive of interest and costs, and is between—

(1) citizens of different States;

(2) citizens of a State and citizens or subjects of a foreign state;

(3) citizens of different States and in which citizens or subjects of a foreign state are additional parties; and

(4) a foreign state, defined in section 1603(a) of this title, as plaintiff and citizens of a State or of different States.

For the purposes of this section, section 1335, and section 1441, an alien admitted to the United States for permanent residence shall be deemed a citizen of the State in which such alien is domiciled.

(b) Except when express provision therefor is otherwise made in a statute of the United States, where the plaintiff who files the case originally in the Federal courts is finally adjudged to be entitled to recover less than the sum or value of $75,000, computed without regard to any setoff or counterclaim to which the defendant may be adjudged to be entitled, and exclusive of interest and costs, the district court may deny costs to the plaintiff and, in addition, may impose costs on the plaintiff.

(c) For the purposes of this section and section 1441 of this title—

(1) a corporation shall be deemed to be a citizen of any State by which it has been incorporated and of the State where it has its principal place of business, except that in any direct action against the insurer of a policy or contract of liability insurance, whether incorporated or unincorporated, to which action the insured is not joined as a party-defendant, such insurer shall be deemed a citizen of the State of which the insured is a citizen, as well as of any State by which the insurer has been incorporated and of the State where it has its principal place of business; and

(2) the legal representative of the estate of a decedent shall be deemed to be a citizen only of the same State as the decedent, and the legal representative of an infant or incompetent shall be deemed to be a citizen only of the same State as the infant or incompetent.

(d)(1) In this subsection—

(A) the term "class" means all of the class members in a class action;

(B) the term "class action" means any civil action filed under rule 23 of the Federal Rules of Civil Procedure or similar State statute or rule of judicial procedure authorizing an action to be brought by 1 or more representative persons as a class action;

(C) the term "class certification order" means an order issued by a court approving the treatment of some or all aspects of a civil action as a class action; and

(D) the term "class members" means the persons (named or unnamed) who fall within the definition of the proposed or certified class in a class action.

(2) The district courts shall have original jurisdiction of any civil action in which the matter in controversy exceeds the sum or value of $5,000,000, exclusive of interest and costs, and is a class action in which—

(A) any member of a class of plaintiffs is a citizen of a State different from any defendant;

(B) any member of a class of plaintiffs is a foreign state or a citizen or subject of a foreign state and any defendant is a citizen of a State; or

(C) any member of a class of plaintiffs is a citizen of a State and any defendant is a foreign state or a citizen or subject of a foreign state.

(3) A district court may, in the interests of justice and looking at the totality of the circumstances, decline to exercise jurisdiction under paragraph (2) over a class action in which greater than one-third but less than two-thirds of the members of all proposed plaintiff classes in the aggregate and the primary defendants are citizens of the State in which the action was originally filed based on consideration of—

(A) whether the claims asserted involve matters of national or interstate interest;

(B) whether the claims asserted will be governed by laws of the State in which the action was originally filed or by the laws of other States;

(C) whether the class action has been pleaded in a manner that seeks to avoid Federal jurisdiction;

(D) whether the action was brought in a forum with a distinct nexus with the class members, the alleged harm, or the defendants;

(E) whether the number of citizens of the State in which the action was originally filed in all proposed plaintiff classes in the aggregate is substantially larger than the number of citizens from any other State, and the citizenship of the other members of the proposed class is dispersed among a substantial number of States; and

(F) whether, during the 3–year period preceding the filing of that class action, 1 or more other class actions asserting the same or similar claims on behalf of the same or other persons have been filed.

(4) A district court shall decline to exercise jurisdiction under paragraph (2)—

(A)(i) over a class action in which—

(I) greater than two-thirds of the members of all proposed plaintiff classes in the aggregate are citizens of the State in which the action was originally filed;

(II) at least 1 defendant is a defendant—

(aa) from whom significant relief is sought by members of the plaintiff class;

(bb) whose alleged conduct forms a significant basis for the claims asserted by the proposed plaintiff class; and

(cc) who is a citizen of the State in which the action was originally filed; and

(III) principal injuries resulting from the alleged conduct or any related conduct of each defendant were incurred in the State in which the action was originally filed; and

(ii) during the 3-year period preceding the filing of that class action, no other class action has been filed asserting the same or similar factual allegations against any of the defendants on behalf of the same or other persons; or

(B) two-thirds or more of the members of all proposed plaintiff classes in the aggregate, and the primary defendants, are citizens of the State in which the action was originally filed.

(5) Paragraphs (2) through (4) shall not apply to any class action in which—

(A) the primary defendants are States, State officials, or other governmental entities against whom the district court may be foreclosed from ordering relief; or

(B) the number of members of all proposed plaintiff classes in the aggregate is less than 100.

(6) In any class action, the claims of the individual class members shall be aggregated to determine whether the matter in controversy exceeds the sum or value of $5,000,000, exclusive of interest and costs.

(7) Citizenship of the members of the proposed plaintiff classes shall be determined for purposes of paragraphs (2) through (6) as of the date of filing of the complaint or amended complaint, or, if the case stated by the initial pleading is not subject to Federal jurisdiction, as of the date of service by plaintiffs of an amended pleading, motion, or other paper, indicating the existence of Federal jurisdiction.

(8) This subsection shall apply to any class action before or after the entry of a class certification order by the court with respect to that action.

(9) Paragraph (2) shall not apply to any class action that solely involves a claim—

(A) concerning a covered security as defined under 16(f)(3)[1] of the Securities Act of 1933 (15 U.S.C. 78p(f)(3)) and section 28(f)(5)(E) of the Securities Exchange Act of 1934 (15 U.S.C. 78bb(f)(5)(E));

(B) that relates to the internal affairs or governance of a corporation or other form of business enterprise and that arises under or by virtue of the laws of the State in which such corporation or business enterprise is incorporated or organized; or

(C) that relates to the rights, duties (including fiduciary duties), and obligations relating to or created by or pursuant to any security (as defined under section 2(a)(1) of the Securities Act of 1933 (15 U.S.C. 77b(a)(1)) and the regulations issued thereunder).

(10) For purposes of this subsection and section 1453, an unincorporated association shall be deemed to be a citizen of the State where it has its principal place of business and the State under whose laws it is organized.

(11)(A) For purposes of this subsection and section 1453, a mass action shall be deemed to be a class action removable under paragraphs (2) through (10) if it otherwise meets the provisions of those paragraphs.

(B)(i) As used in subparagraph (A), the term "mass action" means any civil action (except a civil action within the scope of section 1711(2)) in which monetary relief claims of 100 or more persons are proposed to be tried jointly on the ground that the plaintiffs' claims involve common questions of law or fact, except that jurisdiction shall exist only over those plaintiffs whose claims in a mass action satisfy the jurisdictional amount requirements under subsection (a).

(ii) As used in subparagraph (A), the term "mass action" shall not include any civil action in which—

(I) all of the claims in the action arise from an event or occurrence in the State in which the action was filed, and that allegedly resulted in injuries in that State or in States contiguous to that State;

(II) the claims are joined upon motion of a defendant;

(III) all of the claims in the action are asserted on behalf of the general public (and not on behalf of individual claimants or members of a purported class) pursuant to a State statute specifically authorizing such action; or

(IV) the claims have been consolidated or coordinated solely for pretrial proceedings.

(C)(i) Any action(s) removed to Federal court pursuant to this subsection shall not thereafter be transferred to any other court pursuant to section 1407, or the rules promulgated thereunder, unless a majority of the plaintiffs in the action request transfer pursuant to section 1407.

(ii) This subparagraph will not apply—

(I) to cases certified pursuant to rule 23 of the Federal Rules of Civil Procedure; or

(II) if plaintiffs propose that the action proceed as a class action pursuant to rule 23 of the Federal Rules of Civil Procedure.

(D) The limitations periods on any claims asserted in a mass action that is removed to Federal court pursuant to this subsection shall be deemed tolled during the period that the action is pending in Federal court.

(e) The word "States", as used in this section, includes the Territories, the District of Columbia, and the Commonwealth of Puerto Rico.

(June 25, 1948, c. 646, 62 Stat. 930; July 26, 1956, c. 740, 70 Stat. 658; July 25, 1958, Pub.L. 85–554, § 2, 72 Stat. 415; Aug. 14, 1964, Pub.L. 88–439, § 1, 78 Stat. 445; Oct. 21, 1976, Pub.L. 94–583, § 3, 90 Stat. 2891; Nov. 19, 1988, Pub.L. 100–702, Title II, §§ 201(a), 202(a), 203(a), 102 Stat. 4646; Oct. 19, 1996, Pub.L. 104–317, Title II, § 205(a), 110 Stat. 3850; Feb. 18, 2005, Pub.L. 109–2, § 4(a), 119 Stat. 9.)

§ 1333. Admiralty, maritime and prize cases

The district courts shall have original jurisdiction, exclusive of the courts of the States, of:

(1) Any civil case of admiralty or maritime jurisdiction, saving to suitors in all cases all other remedies to which they are otherwise entitled.

(2) Any prize brought into the United States and all proceedings for the condemnation of property taken as prize.

(June 25, 1948, c. 646, 62 Stat. 931; May 24, 1949, c. 139, § 79, 63 Stat. 101.)

§ 1334. Bankruptcy cases and proceedings

(a) Except as provided in subsection (b) of this section, the district court shall have original and exclusive jurisdiction of all cases under title 11.

(b) Notwithstanding any Act of Congress that confers exclusive jurisdiction on a court or courts other than the district courts, the district courts shall have original but not exclusive jurisdiction of all civil proceedings arising under title 11, or arising in or related to cases under title 11.

(c)(1) Nothing in this section prevents a district court in the interest of justice, or in the interest of comity with State courts or respect for State law, from abstaining from hearing a particular proceeding arising under title 11 or arising in or related to a case under title 11.

(2) Upon timely motion of a party in a proceeding based upon a State law claim or State law cause of action, related to a case under title 11 but not arising under title 11 or arising in a case under title 11, with respect to which an action could not have been commenced in a court of the United States absent jurisdiction under this section, the district court shall abstain from hearing such proceeding if an action is commenced, and can be timely adjudicated, in a State forum of appropriate jurisdiction.

(d) Any decision to abstain or not to abstain made under this subsection (other than a decision not to abstain in a proceeding described in subsection (c)(2)) is not reviewable by appeal or otherwise by the court of appeals under section 158(d), 1291, or 1292 of this title or by the Supreme Court of the United States under section 1254 of this title. This subsection shall not be construed to limit the applicability of the stay provided for by section 362 of title 11, United States Code, as such section applies to an action affecting the property of the estate in bankruptcy.

(e) The district court in which a case under title 11 is commenced or is pending shall have exclusive jurisdiction of all of the property, wherever located, of the debtor as of the commencement of such case, and of property of the estate.

(June 25, 1948, c. 646, 62 Stat. 931; Nov. 6, 1978, Pub.L. 95–598, Title II, § 238(a), 92 Stat. 2667; July 10, 1984, Pub.L. 98–353, Title I, § 101(a), 98 Stat. 333; Oct. 27, 1986, Pub.L. 99–554, Title I,

§ 144(e), 100 Stat. 3096; Dec. 1, 1990, Pub.L. 101–650, Title III, § 309(b), 104 Stat. 5113; Oct. 22, 1994, Pub.L. 103–394, Title I, § 104(b), 108 Stat. 4109.)

§ 1335. Interpleader

(a) The district courts shall have original jurisdiction of any civil action of interpleader or in the nature of interpleader filed by any person, firm, or corporation, association, or society having in his or its custody or possession money or property of the value of $500 or more, or having issued a note, bond, certificate, policy of insurance, or other instrument of value or amount of $500 or more, or providing for the delivery or payment or the loan of money or property of such amount or value, or being under any obligation written or unwritten to the amount of $500 or more, if

(1) Two or more adverse claimants, of diverse citizenship as defined in section 1332 of this title, are claiming or may claim to be entitled to such money or property, or to any one or more of the benefits arising by virtue of any note, bond, certificate, policy or other instrument, or arising by virtue of any such obligation; and if (2) the plaintiff has deposited such money or property or has paid the amount of or the loan or other value of such instrument or the amount due under such obligation into the registry of the court, there to abide the judgment of the court, or has given bond payable to the clerk of the court in such amount and with such surety as the court or judge may deem proper, conditioned upon the compliance by the plaintiff with the future order or judgment of the court with respect to the subject matter of the controversy.

(b) Such an action may be entertained although the titles or claims of the conflicting claimants do not have a common origin, or are not identical, but are adverse to and independent of one another.

§ 1337. Commerce and antitrust regulations; amount in controversy, costs

(a) The district courts shall have original jurisdiction of any civil action or proceeding arising under any Act of Congress regulating commerce or protecting trade and commerce against restraints and monopolies: Provided, however, That the district courts shall have original jurisdiction of an action brought under section 11706 or 14706 of title 49, only if the matter in controversy for each receipt or bill of lading exceeds $10,000, exclusive of interest and costs.

(b) Except when express provision therefor is otherwise made in a statute of the United States, where a plaintiff who files the case under section 11706 or 14706 of title 49, originally in the Federal courts is finally adjudged to be entitled to recover less than the sum or value of $10,000, computed without regard to any setoff or counterclaim to which the defendant may be adjudged to be entitled, and exclusive of any interest and costs, the district court may deny costs to the plaintiff and, in addition, may impose costs on the plaintiff.

(c) The district courts shall not have jurisdiction under this section of any matter within the exclusive jurisdiction of the Court of International Trade under chapter 95 of this title.

(June 25, 1948, c. 646, 62 Stat. 931; Oct. 20, 1978, Pub.L. 95–486, § 9(a), 92 Stat. 1633; Oct. 10, 1980, Pub.L. 96–417, Title V, § 505, 94 Stat. 1743; Jan. 12, 1983, Pub.L. 97–449, § 5(f), 96 Stat. 2442; Dec. 29, 1995, Pub.L. 104–88, Title III, § 305(a)(3), 109 Stat. 944.)

§ 1338. Patents, plant variety protection, copyrights, mask works, designs, trademarks, and unfair competition

(a) The district courts shall have original jurisdiction of any civil action arising under any Act of Congress relating to patents, plant variety protection, copyrights and trademarks. Such jurisdiction shall be exclusive of the courts of the states in patent, plant variety protection and copyright cases.

(b) The district courts shall have original jurisdiction of any civil action asserting a claim of unfair competition when joined with a substantial and related claim under the copyright, patent, plant variety protection or trademark laws.

(c) Subsections (a) and (b) apply to exclusive rights in mask works under chapter 9 of title 17, and to exclusive rights in designs under chapter 13 of title 17, to the same extent as such subsections apply to copyrights.

(June 25, 1948, c. 646, 62 Stat. 931; Dec. 24, 1970, Pub.L. 91–577, Title III, § 143(b), 84 Stat. 1559; Nov. 19, 1988, Pub.L. 100–702, Title X, § 1020(a)(4), 102 Stat. 4671; Oct. 28, 1998, Pub.L 105–304, Title V, § 503(b)(1), (2)(A), 112 Stat. 2917; Nov. 29, 1999, Pub.L. 106–113, Div. B, § 1000(a)(9) [S. 1948, Title III, § 3009(1)], 113 Stat. 1536, 1537–____.)

§ 1339. Postal matters

The district courts shall have original jurisdiction of any civil action arising under any Act of Congress relating to the postal service.

(June 25, 1948, c. 646, 62 Stat. 932.)

§ 1340. Internal revenue; customs duties

The district courts shall have original jurisdiction of any civil action arising under any Act of Congress providing for internal revenue, or revenue from imports or tonnage except matters within the jurisdiction of the Court of International Trade.

(June 25, 1948, c. 646, 62 Stat. 932; Oct. 10, 1980, Pub.L. 96–417, Title V, § 501(21), 94 Stat. 1742.)

§ 1343. Civil rights and elective franchise

(a) The district courts shall have original jurisdiction of any civil action authorized by law to be commenced by any person:

(1) To recover damages for injury to his person or property, or because of the deprivation of any right or privilege of a citizen of the United States, by any act done in furtherance of any conspiracy mentioned in section 1985 of Title 42;

(2) To recover damages from any person who fails to prevent or to aid in preventing any wrongs mentioned in section 1985 of Title 42 which he had knowledge were about to occur and power to prevent;

(3) To redress the deprivation, under color of any State law, statute, ordinance, regulation, custom or usage, of any right, privilege or immunity secured by the Constitution of the United States or by any Act of Congress providing for equal rights of citizens or of all persons within the jurisdiction of the United States;

(4) To recover damages or to secure equitable or other relief under any Act of Congress providing for the protection of civil rights, including the right to vote.

(b) For purposes of this section—

(1) the District of Columbia shall be considered to be a State; and

(2) any Act of Congress applicable exclusively to the District of Columbia shall be considered to be a statute of the District of Columbia.

(As amended Sept. 3, 1954, c. 1263, § 42, 68 Stat. 1241; Sept. 9, 1957, Pub.L. 85–315, Part III, § 121, 71 Stat. 637; Dec. 29, 1979, Pub.L. 96–170, § 2, 93 Stat. 1284.)

§ 1345. United States as plaintiff

Except as otherwise provided by Act of Congress, the district courts shall have original jurisdiction of all civil actions, suits or proceedings commenced by the United States, or by any agency or officer thereof expressly authorized to sue by Act of Congress.

§ 1346. United States as defendant

(a) The district courts shall have original jurisdiction, concurrent with the United States Court of Federal Claims, of:

(1) Any civil action against the United States for the recovery of any internal-revenue tax alleged to have been erroneously or illegally assessed or collected, or any penalty claimed to have been collected without authority or any sum alleged to have been excessive or in any manner wrongfully collected under the internal-revenue laws;

(2) Any other civil action or claim against the United States, not exceeding $10,000 in amount, founded either upon the Constitution, or any Act of Congress, or any regulation of an executive department, or upon any express or implied contract with the United States, or for liquidated or unliquidated damages in cases not sounding in tort, except that the district courts shall not have jurisdiction of any civil action or claim against the United States founded upon any express or implied contract with the United States or for liquidated or unliquidated damages in cases not sounding in tort which are subject to sections 8(g)(1) and 10(a)(1) of the Contract Disputes Act of 1978. For the purpose of this paragraph, an express or implied contract with the Army and Air Force Exchange Service, Navy Exchanges, Marine Corps Exchanges, Coast Guard Exchanges, or Exchange Councils of the National Aeronautics and Space Administration shall be considered an express or implied contract with the United States.

(b)(1) Subject to the provisions of chapter 171 of this title, the district courts, together with the United States District Court for the District of the Canal Zone and the District Court of the Virgin Islands, shall have exclusive jurisdiction of civil actions on claims against the United States, for money damages, accruing on and after January 1, 1945, for injury or loss of property, or personal injury or death caused by the negligent or wrongful act or omission of any employee of the Government while acting within the scope of his office or employment, under circumstances where the United States, if a private person, would be liable to the claimant in accordance with the law of the place where the act or omission occurred.

(2) No person convicted of a felony who is incarcerated while awaiting sentencing or while serving a sentence may bring a civil action against the United States or an agency, officer, or employee of the Government, for mental or emotional injury suffered while in custody without a prior showing of physical injury.

(c) The jurisdiction conferred by this section includes jurisdiction of any set-off, counterclaim, or other claim or demand whatever on the part of the United States against any plaintiff commencing an action under this section.

(d) The district courts shall not have jurisdiction under this section of any civil action or claim for a pension.

(e) The district courts shall have original jurisdiction of any civil action against the United States provided in section 6226, 6228(a), 7426, or 7428 (in the case of the United States district court for the District of Columbia) or section 7429 of the Internal Revenue Code of 1986.

(f) The district courts shall have exclusive original jurisdiction of civil actions under section 2409a to quiet title to an estate or interest in real property in which an interest is claimed by the United States.

(g) Subject to the provisions of chapter 179, the district courts of the United States shall have exclusive jurisdiction over any civil action commenced under section 453(2) of title 3, by a covered employee under chapter 5 of such title.

(June 25, 1948, c. 646, 62 Stat. 933; Apr. 25, 1949, c. 92, § 2(a), 63 Stat. 62; May 24, 1949, c. 139, s 80(a), (b), 63 Stat. 101; Oct. 31, 1951, c. 655, § 50(b), 65 Stat. 727; July 30, 1954, c. 648, § 1, 68 Stat. 589; July 7, 1958, Pub.L. 85–508, § 12(e), 72 Stat. 348; Aug. 30, 1964, Pub.L. 88–519, 78 Stat. 699; Nov. 2, 1966, Pub.L. 89–719, Title II, § 202(a), 80 Stat. 1148; July 23, 1970, Pub.L. 91–350, § 1(a), 84 Stat. 449; Oct. 25, 1972, Pub.L. 92–562, s 1, 86 Stat. 1176; Oct. 4, 1976, Pub.L. 94–455, Title XII, § 1204(c)(1), Title XIII, § 1306(b)(7), 90 Stat. 1697, 1719; Nov. 1, 1978, Pub.L. 95–563, § 14(a), 92 Stat. 2389; Apr. 2, 1982, Pub.L. 97–164, Title I, § 129, 96 Stat. 39; Sept. 3, 1982, Pub.L. 97–248, Title IV, § 402(c)(17), 96 Stat. 669; Oct. 22, 1986, Pub.L. 99–514, § 2, 100 Stat. 2095; Oct. 29, 1992, Pub.L. 102–572, Title IX, § 902(b)(1), 106 Stat. 4516; Apr. 26, 1996, Pub.L. 104–134, Title I, § 101[(a)][Title VIII, § 806], 110 Stat. 1321–75; renumbered Title I May 2, 1996, Pub.L. 104–140, § 1(a), 110 Stat. 1327; Oct. 26, 1996, Pub.L 104–331, § 3(b)(1), 110 Stat. 4069.)

§ 1349. Corporation organized under federal law as party

The district courts shall not have jurisdiction of any civil action by or against any corporation upon the ground that it was incorporated by or under an Act of Congress, unless the United States is the owner of more than one-half of its capital stock.

§ 1357. Injuries under Federal laws

The district courts shall have original jurisdiction of any civil action commenced by any person to recover damages for any injury to his person or property on account of any act done by him, under any Act of Congress, for the protection or collection of any of the revenues, or to enforce the right of citizens of the United States to vote in any State.

§ 1359. Parties collusively joined or made

A district court shall not have jurisdiction of a civil action in which any party, by assignment or otherwise, has been improperly or collusively made or joined to invoke the jurisdiction of such court.

§ 1361. Action to compel an officer of the United States to perform his duty

The district courts shall have original jurisdiction of any action in the nature of mandamus to compel an officer or employee of the United States or any agency thereof to perform a duty owed to the plaintiff.

(Added Pub.L. 87–748, § 1(a), Oct. 5, 1962, 76 Stat. 744.)

§ 1367. Supplemental jurisdiction

(a) Except as provided in subsections (b) and (c) or as expressly provided otherwise by Federal statute, in any civil action of which the district courts have original jurisdiction, the district courts shall have supplemental jurisdiction over all other claims that are so related to claims in the action within such original jurisdiction that they form part of the same case or controversy under Article III of the United States Constitution. Such supplemental jurisdiction shall include claims that involve the joinder or intervention of additional parties.

(b) In any civil action of which the district courts have original jurisdiction founded solely on section 1332 of this title, the district courts shall not have supplemental jurisdiction under subsection (a) over claims by plaintiffs against persons made parties under Rule 14, 19, 20, or 24 of the Federal Rules of Civil Procedure, or over claims by persons proposed to be joined as plaintiffs under Rule 19 of such rules, or seeking to intervene as plaintiffs under Rule 24 of such rules, when exercising supplemental jurisdiction over such claims would be inconsistent with the jurisdictional requirements of section 1332.

(c) The district courts may decline to exercise supplemental jurisdiction over a claim under subsection (a) if—

(1) the claim raises a novel or complex issue of State law,

(2) the claim substantially predominates over the claim or claims over which the district court has original jurisdiction,

(3) the district court has dismissed all claims over which it has original jurisdiction, or

(4) in exceptional circumstances, there are other compelling reasons for declining jurisdiction.

(d) The period of limitations for any claim asserted under subsection (a), and for any other claim in the same action that is voluntarily dismissed at the same time as or after the dismissal of the claim under subsection (a), shall be tolled while the claim is pending and for a period of 30 days after it is dismissed unless State law provides for a longer tolling period.

(e) As used in this section, the term "State" includes the District of Columbia, the Commonwealth of Puerto Rico, and any territory or possession of the United States.

(Added Pub.L. 101–650, Title III, § 310(a), Dec. 1, 1990, 104 Stat. 5113.)

§ 1369. Multiparty, multiforum jurisdiction

(a) In general.—The district courts shall have original jurisdiction of any civil action involving minimal diversity between adverse parties that arises from a single accident, where at least 75 natural persons have died in the accident at a discrete location, if—

(1) a defendant resides in a State and a substantial part of the accident took place in another State or other location, regardless of whether that defendant is also a resident of the State where a substantial part of the accident took place;

(2) any two defendants reside in different States, regardless of whether such defendants are also residents of the same State or States; or

(3) substantial parts of the accident took place in different States.

(b) Limitation of jurisdiction of district courts.—The district court shall abstain from hearing any civil action described in subsection (a) in which—

(1) the substantial majority of all plaintiffs are citizens of a single State of which the primary defendants are also citizens; and

(2) the claims asserted will be governed primarily by the laws of that State.

(c) Special rules and definitions.—For purposes of this section—

(1) minimal diversity exists between adverse parties if any party is a citizen of a State and any adverse party is a citizen of another State, a citizen or subject of a foreign state, or a foreign state as defined in section 1603(a) of this title;

(2) a corporation is deemed to be a citizen of any State, and a citizen or subject of any foreign state, in which it is incorporated or has its principal place of business, and is deemed to be a resident of any State in which it is incorporated or licensed to do business or is doing business;

(3) the term "injury" means—

(A) physical harm to a natural person; and

(B) physical damage to or destruction of tangible property, but only if physical harm described in subparagraph (A) exists;

(4) the term "accident" means a sudden accident, or a natural event culminating in an accident, that results in death incurred at a discrete location by at least 75 natural persons; and

(5) the term "State" includes the District of Columbia, the Commonwealth of Puerto Rico, and any territory or possession of the United States.

(d) Intervening parties.—In any action in a district court which is or could have been brought, in whole or in part, under this section, any person with a claim arising from the accident described in subsection (a) shall be permitted to intervene as a party plaintiff in the action, even if that person could not have brought an action in a district court as an original matter.

(e) Notification of judicial panel on multidistrict litigation.—A district court in which an action under this section is pending shall promptly notify the judicial panel on multidistrict litigation of the pendency of the action.

(Added Pub.L. 107–273, Div. C, Title I, § 11020(b)(1)(A), Nov. 2, 2002, 116 Stat. 1826.)

§ 1391. Venue generally

(a) A civil action wherein jurisdiction is founded only on diversity of citizenship may, except as otherwise provided by law, be brought only in (1) a judicial district where any defendant resides, if all defendants reside in the same State, (2) a judicial district in which a substantial part of the events or omissions giving rise to the claim occurred, or a substantial part of property that is the subject of the action is situated, or (3) a judicial district in which any defendant is subject to personal jurisdiction at the time the action is commenced, if there is no district in which the action may otherwise be brought.

(b) A civil action wherein jurisdiction is not founded solely on diversity of citizenship may, except as otherwise provided by law, be brought only in (1) a judicial district where any defendant resides, if all defendants reside in the same State, (2) a judicial district in which a substantial part of the events or omissions giving rise to the claim occurred, or a substantial part of property that is the subject of the action is situated, or (3) a judicial district in which any defendant may be found, if there is no district in which the action may otherwise be brought.

(c) For purposes of venue under this chapter, a defendant that is a corporation shall be deemed to reside in any judicial district in which it is subject to personal jurisdiction at the time the action is commenced. In a State which has more than one judicial district and in which a defendant that is a corporation is subject to personal jurisdiction at the time an action is commenced, such corporation shall be deemed to reside in any district in that State within which its contacts would be sufficient to subject it to personal jurisdiction if that district were a separate State, and, if there is no such district, the corporation shall be deemed to reside in the district within which it has the most significant contacts.

(d) An alien may be sued in any district.

(e) A civil action in which a defendant is an officer or employee of the United States or any agency thereof acting in his official capacity or under color of legal authority, or an agency of the United States, or the United States, may, except as otherwise provided by law, be brought in any judicial district in which (1) a defendant in the action resides, (2) a substantial part of the events or omissions giving rise to the claim occurred, or a substantial part of property that is the subject of the action is situated, or (3) the plaintiff resides if no real property is involved in the action. Additional persons may be joined as parties to any such action in accordance with the Federal Rules of Civil Procedure and with such other venue requirements as would be applicable if the United States or one of its officers, employees, or agencies were not a party.

The summons and complaint in such an action shall be served as provided by the Federal Rules of Civil Procedure except that the delivery of the summons and complaint to the officer or agency as required by the rules may be made by certified mail beyond the territorial limits of the district in which the action is brought.

(f) A civil action against a foreign state as defined in section 1603(a) of this title may be brought—

(1) in any judicial district in which a substantial part of the events or omissions giving rise to the claim occurred, or a substantial part of property that is the subject of the action is situated;

(2) in any judicial district in which the vessel or cargo of a foreign state is situated, if the claim is asserted under section 1605(b) of this title;

(3) in any judicial district in which the agency or instrumentality is licensed to do business or is doing business, if the action is brought against an agency or instrumentality of a foreign state as defined in section 1603(b) of this title; or

(4) in the United States District Court for the District of Columbia if the action is brought against a foreign state or political subdivision thereof.

(g) A civil action in which jurisdiction of the district court is based upon section 1369 of this title may be brought in any district in which any defendant resides or in which a substantial part of the accident giving rise to the action took place.

(June 25, 1948, c. 646, 62 Stat. 935; Oct. 5, 1962, Pub.L. 87–748, § 2, 76 Stat. 744; Dec. 23, 1963, Pub.L. 88–234, 77 Stat. 473; Nov. 2, 1966, Pub.L. 89–714, § § 1, 2, 80 Stat. 1111; Oct. 21, 1976, Pub.L. 94–574, § 3, 90 Stat. 2721; Oct. 21, 1976, Pub.L. 94–583, § 5, 90 Stat. 2897; Nov. 19, 1988, Pub.L. 100–702, Title X, § 1013(a), 102 Stat. 4669; Dec. 1, 1990, Pub.L. 101–650, Title III, § 311, 104 Stat. 5114; Dec. 9, 1991, Pub.L. 102–198, § 3, 105 Stat. 1623; Oct. 29, 1992, Pub.L. 102–572, Title V, § 504, 106 Stat. 4513; Oct. 3, 1995, Pub.L. 104–34, § 1, 109 Stat. 293; Nov. 2, 2002, Pub.L. 107–273, Div. C, Title I, § 11020(b)(2), 116 Stat. 1827.)

§ 1392. Defendants or property in different districts in same State

Any civil action, of a local nature, involving property located in different districts in the same State, may be brought in any of such districts.

(June 25, 1948, c. 646, 62 Stat. 935; Oct. 1, 1996, Pub.L. 104–220, § 1, 110 Stat. 3023.)

§ 1397. Interpleader

Any civil action of interpleader or in the nature of interpleader under section 1335 of this title may be brought in the judicial district in which one or more of the claimants reside.

§ 1401. Stockholder's derivative action

Any civil action by a stockholder on behalf of his corporation may be prosecuted in any judicial district where the corporation might have sued the same defendants.

§ 1402. United States as defendant

(a) Any civil action in a district court against the United States under subsection (a) of section 1346 of this title may be prosecuted only:

(1) Except as provided in paragraph (2), in the judicial district where the plaintiff resides;

(2) In the case of a civil action in a district court by a corporation under paragraph (1) of subsection (a) of section 1346, in the judicial district in which is located the principal place of business or principal office or agency of the corporation; or if it has no principal place of business or principal office or agency in any judicial district (A) in the judicial district in which is located the office to which was made the return of the tax in respect of which the claim is made, or (B) if no return was made, in the judicial district in which lies the District of Columbia. Notwithstanding the foregoing provisions of this paragraph a district court, for the convenience of the parties and witnesses, in the interest of justice, may transfer any such action to any other district or division.

(b) Any civil action on a tort claim against the United States under subsection (b) of section 1346 of this title may be prosecuted only in the judicial district where the plaintiff resides or wherein the act or omission complained of occurred.

(c) Any civil action against the United States under subsection (e) of section 1346 of this title may be prosecuted only in the judicial district where the property is situated at the time of levy, or if no levy is made, in the judicial district in which the event occurred which gave rise to the cause of action.

(d) Any civil action under section 2409a to quiet title to an estate or interest in real property in which an interest is claimed by the United States shall be brought in the district court of the district where the property is located or, if located in different districts, in any of such districts.

(As amended Sept. 2, 1958, Pub.L. 85–920, 72 Stat. 1770; Nov. 2, 1966, Pub.L. 89–719, Title II, § 202(b), 80 Stat. 1149; Oct. 25, 1972, Pub.L. 92–562, § 2, 86 Stat. 1176; Apr. 2, 1982, Pub.L. 97–164, Title I, § 131, 96 Stat. 39.)

§ 1404. Change of venue

(a) For the convenience of parties and witnesses, in the interest of justice, a district court may transfer any civil action to any other district or division where it might have been brought.

(b) Upon motion, consent or stipulation of all parties, any action, suit or proceeding of a civil nature or any motion or hearing thereof, may be transferred, in the discretion of the court, from the division in which pending to any other division in the same district. Transfer of proceedings in rem brought by or on behalf of the United States may be transferred under this section without the consent of the United States where all other parties request transfer.

(c) A district court may order any civil action to be tried at any place within the division in which it is pending.

(d) As used in this section, "district court" includes the District Court of Guam, the District Court for the Northern Mariana Islands, and the District Court of the Virgin Islands, and the term "district" includes the territorial jurisdiction of that court.

(As amended Oct. 18, 1962, Pub.L. 87–845, § 9, 76A Stat. 699; Oct. 19, 1996, Pub.L. 104–317, Title VI, § 610, 110 Stat. 3860.)

§ 1406. Cure or waiver of defects

(a) The district court of a district in which is filed a case laying venue in the wrong division or district shall dismiss, or if it be in the interest of justice, transfer such case to any district or division in which it could have been brought.

(b) Nothing in this chapter shall impair the jurisdiction of a district court of any matter involving a party who does not interpose timely and sufficient objection to the venue.

(c) As used in this section, "district court" includes the District Court of Guam, the District Court for the Northern Mariana Islands, and the District Court of the Virgin Islands, and the term "district" includes the territorial jurisdiction of that court.

(As amended May 24, 1949, c. 139, § 81, 63 Stat. 101; Sept. 13, 1960, Pub.L. 86–770, § 1, 74 Stat. 912; Oct. 18, 1962, Pub.L. 87–845, § 10, 76A Stat. 699; Apr. 2, 1982, Pub.L. 97–164, Title I, § 132, 96 Stat. 39; Oct. 19, 1996, Pub.L. 104–317, Title VI, § 610, 110 Stat. 3860.)

§ 1407. Multidistrict litigation

(a) When civil actions involving one or more common questions of fact are pending in different districts, such actions may be transferred to any district for coordinated or consolidated pretrial proceedings. Such transfers shall be made by the judicial panel on multidistrict litigation authorized by this section upon its determination that transfers for such proceedings will be for the convenience of parties and witnesses and will promote the just and efficient conduct of such actions. Each action so transferred shall be remanded by the panel at or before the conclusion of such pretrial proceedings to the district from which it was transferred unless it shall have been previously terminated: *Provided, however*, That the panel may separate any claim, cross-claim, counter-claim, or third-party claim and remand any of such claims before the remainder of the action is remanded.

(b) Such coordinated or consolidated pretrial proceedings shall be conducted by a judge or judges to whom such actions are assigned by the judicial panel on multidistrict litigation. For this purpose, upon request of the panel, a circuit judge or a district judge may be designated and assigned temporarily for service in the transferee district by the Chief Justice of the United States or the chief judge of the circuit, as may be required, in accordance with the provisions of chapter 13 of this title. With the consent of the transferee district court, such actions may be assigned by the panel to a judge or judges of such district. The judge or judges to whom such actions are assigned, the members of the judicial panel on multidistrict litigation, and other circuit and district judges designated when needed by the panel may exercise the powers of a district judge in any district for the purpose of conducting pretrial depositions in such coordinated or consolidated pretrial proceedings.

(c) Proceedings for the transfer of an action under this section may be initiated by—

(i) the judicial panel on multidistrict litigation upon its own initiative, or

(ii) motion filed with the panel by a party in any action in which transfer for coordinated or consolidated pretrial proceedings under this section may be appropriate. A copy of such motion shall be filed in the district court in which the moving party's action is pending.

The panel shall give notice to the parties in all actions in which transfers for coordinated or consolidated pretrial proceedings are contemplated, and such notice shall specify the time and place of any hearing to determine whether such transfer shall be made. Orders of the panel to set a hearing and other orders of the panel issued prior to the order either directing or denying transfer shall be filed in the office of the clerk of the district court in which a transfer hearing is to be or has been held. The panel's order of transfer shall be based upon a record of such hearing at which material evidence may be offered by any party to an action pending in any district that would be affected by the proceedings under this section, and shall be supported by findings of fact and conclusions of law based upon such record. Orders of transfer and such other orders as the panel may make thereafter shall be filed in the office of the clerk of the district court of the transferee district and shall be effective when thus filed. The clerk of the transferee district court shall forthwith transmit a certified copy of the panel's order to transfer to the clerk of the district court from which the action is being transferred. An order denying transfer shall be filed in each district wherein there is a case pending in which the motion for transfer has been made.

(d) The judicial panel on multidistrict litigation shall consist of seven circuit and district judges designated from time to time by the Chief Justice of the United States, no two of whom shall be from the same circuit. The concurrence of four members shall be necessary to any action by the panel.

(e) No proceedings for review of any order of the panel may be permitted except by extraordinary writ pursuant to the provisions of title 28, section 1651, United States Code. Petitions for an extraordinary writ to review an order of the panel to set a transfer hearing and other orders of the panel issued prior to the order either directing or denying transfer shall be filed only in the court of appeals having jurisdiction over the district in which a hearing is to be or has been held. Petitions for an extraordinary writ to review an order to transfer or orders subsequent to transfer shall be filed only in the court of appeals having jurisdiction over the transferee district. There shall be no appeal or review of an order of the panel denying a motion to transfer for consolidated or coordinated proceedings.

(f) The panel may prescribe rules for the conduct of its business not inconsistent with Acts of Congress and the Federal Rules of Civil Procedure.

(g) Nothing in this section shall apply to any action in which the United States is a complainant arising under the antitrust laws. "Antitrust laws" as used herein include those acts referred to in the Act of October 15, 1914, as amended (38 Stat. 730; 15 U.S.C. 12), and also include the Act of June 19, 1936 (49 Stat. 1526; 15 U.S.C. 13, 13a, and 13b) and the Act of September 26, 1914, as added March 21, 1938 (52 Stat. 116, 117; 15 U.S.C. 56); but shall not include section 4A of the Act of October 15, 1914, as added July 7, 1955 (69 Stat. 282; 15 U.S.C. 15a).

(h) Notwithstanding the provisions of section 1404 or subsection (f) of this section, the judicial panel on multidistrict litigation may consolidate and transfer with or without the consent of the parties, for both pretrial purposes and for trial, any action brought under section 4C of the Clayton Act.

(Added Pub.L. 90–296, § 1, Apr. 29, 1968, 82 Stat. 109, and amended Pub.L. 94–435, Title III, § 303, Sept. 30, 1976, 90 Stat. 1396.)

§ 1412. Change of venue

A district court may transfer a case or proceeding under title 11 to a district court for another district, in the interest of justice or for the convenience of the parties.

(Added Pub.L. 98–353, Title I, § 102(a), July 10, 1984, 98 Stat. 335.)

§ 1441. Actions removable generally

(a) Except as otherwise expressly provided by Act of Congress, any civil action brought in a State court of which the district courts of the United States have original jurisdiction, may be removed by the defendant or the defendants, to the district court of the United States for the district and division embracing the place where such action is pending. For purposes of removal under this chapter, the citizenship of defendants sued under fictitious names shall be disregarded.

(b) Any civil action of which the district courts have original jurisdiction founded on a claim or right arising under the Constitution, treaties or laws of the United States shall be removable without regard to the citizenship or residence of the parties. Any other such action shall be removable only if none of the parties in interest properly joined and served as defendants is a citizen of the State in which such action is brought.

(c) Whenever a separate and independent claim or cause of action within the jurisdiction conferred by section 1331 of this title is joined with one or more otherwise non-removable claims or causes of action, the entire case may be removed and the district court may determine all issues therein, or, in its discretion, may remand all matters in which State law predominates.

(d) Any civil action brought in a State court against a foreign state as defined in section 1603(a) of this title may be removed by the foreign state to the district court of the United States for the district and division embracing the place where such action is pending. Upon removal the action shall be tried by the court without jury. Where removal is based upon this subsection, the time limitations of section 1446(b) of this chapter may be enlarged at any time for cause shown.

(e)(1) Notwithstanding the provisions of subsection (b) of this section, a defendant in a civil action in a State court may remove the action to the district court of the United States for the district and division embracing the place where the action is pending if—

(A) the action could have been brought in a United States district court under section 1369 of this title; or

(B) the defendant is a party to an action which is or could have been brought, in whole or in part, under section 1369 in a United States district court and arises from the same accident as the action in State court, even if the action to be removed could not have been brought in a district court as an original matter.

The removal of an action under this subsection shall be made in accordance with section 1446 of this title, except that a notice of removal may also be filed before trial of the action in State court within 30 days after the date on which the defendant first becomes a party to an action under section 1369 in a United States district court that arises from the same accident as the action in State court, or at a later time with leave of the district court.

(2) Whenever an action is removed under this subsection and the district court to which it is removed or transferred under section 1407(j) has made a liability determination requiring further proceedings as to damages, the district court shall remand the action to the State court from which it had been removed for the determination of damages, unless the court finds that, for the convenience of parties and witnesses and in the interest of justice, the action should be retained for the determination of damages.

(3) Any remand under paragraph (2) shall not be effective until 60 days after the district court has issued an order determining liability and has certified its intention to remand the removed action for the determination of damages. An appeal with respect to the liability determination of the district court may be taken during that 60–day period to the court of appeals with appellate jurisdiction over the district court. In the event a party files such an appeal, the remand shall not be effective until the appeal has been finally disposed of. Once the remand has become effective, the liability determination shall not be subject to further review by appeal or otherwise.

(4) Any decision under this subsection concerning remand for the determination of damages shall not be reviewable by appeal or otherwise.

(5) An action removed under this subsection shall be deemed to be an action under section 1369 and an action in which jurisdiction is based on section 1369 of this title for purposes of this section and sections 1407, 1697, and 1785 of this title.

(6) Nothing in this subsection shall restrict the authority of the district court to transfer or dismiss an action on the ground of inconvenient forum.

(f) The court to which a civil action is removed under this section is not precluded from hearing and determining any claim in such civil action because the State court from which such civil action is removed did not have jurisdiction over that claim.

(June 25, 1948, c. 646, 62 Stat. 937; Oct. 21, 1976, Pub.L. 94–583, § 6, 90 Stat. 2898; June 19, 1986, Pub.L. 99–336, § 3(a), 100 Stat. 637; Nov. 19, 1988, Pub.L. 100–702, Title X, § 1016(a), 102 Stat. 4669; Dec. 1, 1990, Pub.L. 101–650, Title III, § 312, 104 Stat. 5114; Dec. 9, 1991, Pub.L. 102–198, § 4, 105 Stat. 1623; Nov. 2, 2002, Pub.L. 107–273, Div. C, Title I, § 11020(b)(3), 116 Stat. 1827.)

§ 1442. Federal officers or agencies sued or prosecuted

(a) A civil action or criminal prosecution commenced in a State court against any of the following may be removed by them to the district court of the United States for the district and division embracing the place wherein it is pending:

(1) The United States or any agency thereof or any officer (or any person acting under that officer) of the United States or of any agency thereof, sued in an official or individual capacity for any act under color of such office or on account of any right, title or authority claimed under any

Act of Congress for the apprehension or punishment of criminals or the collection of the revenue.

(2) A property holder whose title is derived from any such officer, where such action or prosecution affects the validity of any law of the United States.

(3) Any officer of the courts of the United States, for any act under color of office or in the performance of his duties;

(4) Any officer of either House of Congress, for any act in the discharge of his official duty under an order of such House.

(b) A personal action commenced in any State court by an alien against any citizen of a State who is, or at the time the alleged action accrued was, a civil officer of the United States and is a nonresident of such State, wherein jurisdiction is obtained by the State court by personal service of process, may be removed by the defendant to the district court of the United States for the district and division in which the defendant was served with process.

(As amended Oct. 19, 1996, Pub.L. 104–317, 110 Stat. 3847.)

§ 1442a. Members of armed forces sued or prosecuted

A civil or criminal prosecution in a court of a State of the United States against a member of the armed forces of the United States on account of an act done under color of his office or status, or in respect to which he claims any right, title, or authority under a law of the United States respecting the armed forces thereof, or under the law of war, may at any time before the trial or final hearing thereof be removed for trial into the district court of the United States for the district where it is pending in the manner prescribed by law, and it shall thereupon be entered on the docket of the district court, which shall proceed as if the cause had been originally commenced therein and shall have full power to hear and determine the cause.

(Added Aug. 10, 1956, c. 1041, § 19(a), 70A Stat. 626.)

§ 1443. Civil rights cases

Any of the following civil actions or criminal prosecutions, commenced in a State court may be removed by the defendant to the district court of the United States for the district and division embracing the place wherein it is pending:

(1) Against any person who is denied or cannot enforce in the courts of such State a right under any law providing for the equal civil rights of citizens of the United States, or of all persons within the jurisdiction thereof;

(2) For any act under color of authority derived from any law providing for equal rights, or for refusing to do any act on the ground that it would be inconsistent with such law.

§ 1445. Nonremovable actions

(a) A civil action in any State court against a railroad or its receivers or trustees, arising under sections 1–4 and 5–10 of the Act of April 22, 1908 (45

U.S.C. 51–54, 55–60), may not be removed to any district court of the United States.

(b) A civil action in any State court against a carrier or its receivers or trustees to recover damages for delay, loss, or injury of shipments, arising under section 11706 or 14706 of title 49, may not be removed to any district court of the United States unless the matter in controversy exceeds $10,000, exclusive of interest and costs.

(c) A civil action in any State court arising under the workmen's compensation laws of such State may not be removed to any district court of the United States.

(d) A civil action in any State court arising under section 40302 of the Violence Against Women Act of 1994 may not be removed to any district court of the United States.

(June 25, 1948, c. 646, 62 Stat. 939; July 25, 1958, Pub.L. 85–554, § 5, 72 Stat. 415; Oct. 17, 1978, Pub.L. 95–473, § 2(a)(3)(A), 92 Stat. 1465; Oct. 20, 1978, Pub.L. 95–486, § 9(b), 92 Stat. 1634; Sept. 13, 1994, Pub.L. 103–322, Title IV, § 40302(e)(5), 108 Stat. 1942; Dec. 29, 1995, Pub.L. 104–88, Title III, § 305(b), 109 Stat. 944; Oct. 11, 1996, Pub.L. 104–287, § 3, 110 Stat. 3388.)

§ 1446. Procedure for removal

(a) A defendant or defendants desiring to remove any civil action or criminal prosecution from a State court shall file in the district court of the United States for the district and division within which such action is pending a notice of removal signed pursuant to Rule 11 of the Federal Rules of Civil Procedure and containing a short and plain statement of the grounds for removal, together with a copy of all process, pleadings, and orders served upon such defendant or defendants in such action.

(b) The notice of removal of a civil action or proceeding shall be filed within thirty days after the receipt by the defendant, through service or otherwise, of a copy of the initial pleading setting forth the claim for relief upon which such action or proceeding is based, or within thirty days after the service of summons upon the defendant if such initial pleading has then been filed in court and is not required to be served on the defendant, whichever period is shorter.

If the case stated by the initial pleading is not removable, a notice of removal may be filed within thirty days after receipt by the defendant, through service or otherwise, of a copy of an amended pleading, motion, order or other paper from which it may first be ascertained that the case is one which is or has become removable, except that a case may not be removed on the basis of jurisdiction conferred by section 1332 of this title more than 1 year after commencement of the action.

(c)(1) A notice of removal of a criminal prosecution shall be filed not later than thirty days after the arraignment in the State court, or at any time before trial, whichever is earlier, except that for good cause shown the United States district court may enter an order granting the defendant or defendants leave to file the notice at a later time.

(2) A notice of removal of a criminal prosecution shall include all grounds for such removal. A failure to state grounds which exist at the time of the filing of the notice shall constitute a waiver of such grounds, and a second notice may be filed only on grounds not existing at the time of the original notice. For good cause shown, the United States district court may grant relief from the limitations of this paragraph.

(3) The filing of a notice of removal of a criminal prosecution shall not prevent the State court in which such prosecution is pending from proceeding further, except that a judgment of conviction shall not be entered unless the prosecution is first remanded.

(4) The United States district court in which such notice is filed shall examine the notice promptly. If it clearly appears on the face of the notice and any exhibits annexed thereto that removal should not be permitted, the court shall make an order for summary remand.

(5) If the United States district court does not order the summary remand of such prosecution, it shall order an evidentiary hearing to be held promptly and after such hearing shall make such disposition of the prosecution as justice shall require. If the United States district court determines that removal shall be permitted, it shall so notify the State court in which prosecution is pending, which shall proceed no further.

(d) Promptly after the filing of such notice of removal of a civil action the defendant or defendants shall give written notice thereof to all adverse parties and shall file a copy of the notice with the clerk of such State court, which shall effect the removal and the State court shall proceed no further unless and until the case is remanded.

(e) If the defendant or defendants are in actual custody on process issued by the State court, the district court shall issue its writ of habeas corpus, and the marshal shall thereupon take such defendant or defendants into his custody and deliver a copy of the writ to the clerk of such State court.

(f) With respect to any counterclaim removed to a district court pursuant to section 337(c) of the Tariff Act of 1930, the district court shall resolve such counterclaim in the same manner as an original complaint under the Federal Rules of Civil Procedure, except that the payment of a filing fee shall not be required in such cases and the counterclaim shall relate back to the date of the original complaint in the proceeding before the International Trade Commission under section 337 of that Act.

(As amended May 24, 1949, c. 139, § 83, 63 Stat. 101; Sept. 29, 1965, Pub.L. 89–215, 79 Stat. 887; July 30, 1977, Pub.L. 95–78, § 3, 91 Stat. 321; Nov. 19, 1988, Pub.L. 100–702, Title X, § 1016(b), 102 Stat. 4669; Dec. 9, 1991, Pub.L. 102–198, § 10(a), 105 Stat. 1626; Dec. 8, 1994, Pub.L. 103–465, Title III, § 321(b)(2), 108 Stat. 4946; Oct. 19, 1996, Pub.L. 104–317, 110 Stat. 3847.)

§ 1447. Procedure after removal generally

(a) In any case removed from a State court, the district court may issue all necessary orders and process to bring before it all proper parties whether served by process issued by the State court or otherwise.

(b) It may require the removing party to file with its clerk copies of all records and proceedings in such State court or may cause the same to be brought before it by writ of certiorari issued to such State court.

(c) A motion to remand the case on the basis of any defect other than lack of subject matter jurisdiction must be made within 30 days after the filing of the notice of removal under section 1446(a). If at any time before final judgment it appears that the district court lacks subject matter jurisdiction, the case shall be remanded. An order remanding the case may require payment of just costs and any actual expenses, including attorney fees, incurred as a result of the removal. A certified copy of the order of remand shall be mailed by the clerk to the clerk of the State court. The State court may thereupon proceed with such case.

(d) An order remanding a case to the State court from which it was removed is not reviewable on appeal or otherwise, except that an order remanding a case to the State court from which it was removed pursuant to section 1443 of this title shall be reviewable by appeal or otherwise.

(e) If after removal the plaintiff seeks to join additional defendants whose joinder would destroy subject matter jurisdiction, the court may deny joinder, or permit joinder and remand the action to the State court.

(As amended May 24, 1949, c. 139, § 84, 63 Stat. 102; July 2, 1964, Pub.L. 88–352, Title IX, § 901, 78 Stat. 266; Nov. 19, 1988, Pub.L. 100–702, Title X, § 1016(c), 102 Stat. 4670; Dec. 9, 1991, Pub.L. 102–198, § 10(b), 105 Stat. 1626; Oct. 1, 1996, Pub.L. 104–219, 110 Stat. 3022.)

§ 1448. Process after removal

In all cases removed from any State court to any district court of the United States in which any one or more of the defendants has not been served with process or in which the service has not been perfected prior to removal, or in which process served proves to be defective, such process or service may be completed or new process issued in the same manner as in cases originally filed in such district court.

This section shall not deprive any defendant upon whom process is served after removal of his right to move to remand the case.

§ 1449. State court record supplied

Where a party is entitled to copies of the records and proceedings in any suit or prosecution in a State court, to be used in any district court of the United States, and the clerk of such State court, upon demand, and the payment or tender of the legal fees, fails to deliver certified copies, the district court may, on affidavit reciting such facts, direct such record to be supplied by affidavit or otherwise. Thereupon such proceedings, trial, and judgment may be had in such district court, and all such process awarded, as if certified copies had been filed in the district court.

(As amended May 24, 1949, c. 139, § 85, 63 Stat. 102.)

§ 1451. Definitions

For purposes of this chapter—

(1) The term "State court" includes the Superior Court of the District of Columbia.

(2) The term "State" includes the District of Columbia.

(Added Pub.L. 91–358, Title I, § 172(d)(1), July 29, 1970, 84 Stat. 591.)

§ 1453. Removal of class actions

(a) Definitions.—In this section, the terms "class", "class action", "class certification order", and "class member" shall have the meanings given such terms under section 1332(d)(1).

(b) In general.—A class action may be removed to a district court of the United States in accordance with section 1446 (except that the 1–year limitation under section 1446(b) shall not apply), without regard to whether any defendant is a citizen of the State in which the action is brought, except that such action may be removed by any defendant without the consent of all defendants.

(c) Review of remand orders.—

(1) In general.—Section 1447 shall apply to any removal of a case under this section, except that notwithstanding section 1447(d), a court of appeals may accept an appeal from an order of a district court granting or denying a motion to remand a class action to the State court from which it was removed if application is made to the court of appeals not less than 7 days after entry of the order.

(2) Time period for judgment.—If the court of appeals accepts an appeal under paragraph (1), the court shall complete all action on such appeal, including rendering judgment, not later than 60 days after the date on which such appeal was filed, unless an extension is granted under paragraph (3).

(3) Extension of time period.—The court of appeals may grant an extension of the 60–day period described in paragraph (2) if—

(A) all parties to the proceeding agree to such extension, for any period of time; or

(B) such extension is for good cause shown and in the interests of justice, for a period not to exceed 10 days.

(4) Denial of appeal.—If a final judgment on the appeal under paragraph (1) is not issued before the end of the period described in paragraph (2), including any extension under paragraph (3), the appeal shall be denied.

(d) Exception.—This section shall not apply to any class action that solely involves—

(1) a claim concerning a covered security as defined under section 16(f)(3) of the Securities Act of 1933 (15 U.S.C. 78p(f)(3)) and section 28(f)(5)(E) of the Securities Exchange Act of 1934 (15 U.S.C. 78bb(f)(5)(E));

(2) a claim that relates to the internal affairs or governance of a corporation or other form of business enterprise and arises under or by virtue of the laws of the State in which such corporation or business enterprise is incorporated or organized; or

(3) a claim that relates to the rights, duties (including fiduciary duties), and obligations relating to or created by or pursuant to any security (as defined under section 2(a)(1) of the Securities Act of 1933 (15 U.S.C. 77b(a)(1)) and the regulations issued thereunder).

(Added Pub.L. 109–2, § 5(a), Feb. 18, 2005, 119 Stat. 12.)

§ 1631. Transfer to cure want of jurisdiction

Whenever a civil action is filed in a court as defined in section 610 of this title or an appeal, including a petition for review of administrative action, is noticed for or filed with such a court and that court finds that there is a want of jurisdiction, the court shall, if it is in the interest of justice, transfer such action or appeal to any other such court in which the action or appeal could have been brought at the time it was filed or noticed, and the action or appeal shall proceed as if it had been filed in or noticed for the court to which it is transferred on the date upon which it was actually filed in or noticed for the court from which it is transferred.

(Added Pub.L. 97–164, Title III, § 301(a), Apr. 2, 1982, 96 Stat. 55.)

§ 1651. Writs

(a) The Supreme Court and all courts established by Act of Congress may issue all writs necessary or appropriate in aid of their respective jurisdictions and agreeable to the usages and principles of law.

(b) An alternative writ or rule nisi may be issued by a justice or judge of a court which has jurisdiction.

(As amended May 24, 1949, c. 139, § 90, 63 Stat. 102.)

§ 1652. State laws as rules of decision

The laws of the several states, except where the Constitution or treaties of the United States or Acts of Congress otherwise require or provide, shall be regarded as rules of decision in civil actions in the courts of the United States, in cases where they apply.

§ 1653. Amendment of pleadings to show jurisdiction

Defective allegations of jurisdiction may be amended, upon terms, in the trial or appellate courts.

§ 1654. Appearance personally or by counsel

In all courts of the United States the parties may plead and conduct their own cases personally or by counsel as, by the rules of such courts, respectively, are permitted to manage and conduct causes therein.

(As amended May 24, 1949, c. 139, § 91, 63 Stat. 103.)

§ 1657. Priority of civil actions

(a) Notwithstanding any other provision of law, each court of the United States shall determine the order in which civil actions are heard and determined, except that the court shall expedite the consideration of any action brought under chapter 153 or section 1826 of this title, any action for temporary or preliminary injunctive relief, or any other action if good cause therefor is shown. For purposes of this subsection, "good cause" is shown if a right under the Constitution of the United States or a Federal Statute (including rights under section 552 of title 5) would be maintained in a factual context that indicates that a request for expedited consideration has merit.

(b) The Judicial Conference of the United States may modify the rules adopted by the courts to determine the order in which civil actions are heard and determined, in order to establish consistency among the judicial circuits.

(Added Pub.L. 98–620, Title IV, § 401(a), Nov. 8, 1984, 98 Stat. 3356.)

§ 1658. Time limitations on the commencement of civil actions arising under Acts of Congress

(a) Except as otherwise provided by law, a civil action arising under an Act of Congress enacted after the date of the enactment of this section may not be commenced later than 4 years after the cause of action accrues.

(b) Notwithstanding subsection (a), a private right of action that involves a claim of fraud, deceit, manipulation, or contrivance in contravention of a regulatory requirement concerning the securities laws, as defined in section 3(a)(47) of the Securities Exchange Act of 1934 *(15 U.S.C. 78c(a)(47))*, may be brought not later than the earlier of—

(1) 2 years after the discovery of the facts constituting the violation; or

(2) 5 years after such violation.

(Added *Pub.L. 101–650, Title III, 313(a)*, Dec. 1, 1990, 104 Stat. 5114; as amended *Pub.L. 107–204, Title VIII, 804(a)*, July 30, 2002, 116 Stat. 801.)

§ 1691. Seal and teste of process

All writs and process issuing from a court of the United States shall be under the seal of the court and signed by the clerk thereof.

§ 1692. Process and orders affecting property in different districts

In proceedings in a district court where a receiver is appointed for property, real, personal, or mixed, situated in different districts, process may issue and be executed in any such district as if the property lay wholly within one district, but orders affecting the property shall be entered of record in each of such districts.

§ 1695. Stockholder's derivative action

Process in a stockholder's action in behalf of his corporation may be served upon such corporation in any district where it is organized or licensed to do business or is doing business.

§ 1696. Service in foreign and international litigation

(a) The district court of the district in which a person resides or is found may order service upon him of any document issued in connection with a proceeding in a foreign or international tribunal. The order may be made pursuant to a letter rogatory issued, or request made, by a foreign or international tribunal or upon application of any interested person and shall direct the manner of service. Service pursuant to this subsection does not, of itself, require the recognition or enforcement in the United States of a judgment, decree, or order rendered by a foreign or international tribunal.

(b) This section does not preclude service of such a document without an order of court.

(Added Oct. 3, 1964, Pub.L. 88–619, § 4(a), 78 Stat. 995.)

§ 1697. Service in multiparty, multiforum actions

When the jurisdiction of the district court is based in whole or in part upon section 1369 of this title, process, other than subpoenas, may be served at any place within the United States, or anywhere outside the United States if otherwise permitted by law.

(Added Pub.L. 107–273, Div. C, Title I, § 11020(b)(4)(A)(i), Nov. 2, 2002, 116 Stat. 1828.)

§ 1711. Definitions

In this chapter:

(1) Class.—The term "class" means all of the class members in a class action.

(2) Class action.—The term "class action" means any civil action filed in a district court of the United States under rule 23 of the Federal Rules of Civil Procedure or any civil action that is removed to a district court of the United States that was originally filed under a State statute or rule of judicial procedure authorizing an action to be brought by 1 or more representatives as a class action.

(3) Class counsel.—The term "class counsel" means the persons who serve as the attorneys for the class members in a proposed or certified class action.

(4) Class members.—The term "class members" means the persons (named or unnamed) who fall within the definition of the proposed or certified class in a class action.

(5) Plaintiff class action.—The term "plaintiff class action" means a class action in which class members are plaintiffs.

(6) Proposed settlement.—The term "proposed settlement" means an agreement regarding a class action that is subject to court approval and that, if approved, would be binding on some or all class members.

(Added Pub.L. 109–2, § 3(a), Feb. 18, 2005, 119 Stat. 5.)

§ 1712. Coupon settlements

(a) Contingent fees in coupon settlements.—If a proposed settlement in a class action provides for a recovery of coupons to a class member, the portion of any attorney's fee award to class counsel that is attributable to the award of the coupons shall be based on the value to class members of the coupons that are redeemed.

(b) Other attorney's fee awards in coupon settlements.—

(1) In general.—If a proposed settlement in a class action provides for a recovery of coupons to class members, and a portion of the recovery of the coupons is not used to determine the attorney's fee to be paid to class counsel, any attorney's fee award shall be based upon the amount of time class counsel reasonably expended working on the action.

(2) Court approval.—Any attorney's fee under this subsection shall be subject to approval by the court and shall include an appropriate attorney's fee, if any, for obtaining equitable relief, including an injunction, if applicable. Nothing in this subsection shall be construed to prohibit application of a lodestar with a multiplier method of determining attorney's fees.

(c) Attorney's fee awards calculated on a mixed basis in coupon settlements.—If a proposed settlement in a class action provides for an award of coupons to class members and also provides for equitable relief, including injunctive relief—

(1) that portion of the attorney's fee to be paid to class counsel that is based upon a portion of the recovery of the coupons shall be calculated in accordance with subsection (a); and

(2) that portion of the attorney's fee to be paid to class counsel that is not based upon a portion of the recovery of the coupons shall be calculated in accordance with subsection (b).

(d) Settlement valuation expertise.—In a class action involving the awarding of coupons, the court may, in its discretion upon the motion of a party, receive expert testimony from a witness qualified to provide information on the actual value to the class members of the coupons that are redeemed.

(e) Judicial scrutiny of coupon settlements.—In a proposed settlement under which class members would be awarded coupons, the court may approve the proposed settlement only after a hearing to determine whether, and making a written finding that, the settlement is fair, reasonable, and adequate for class members. The court, in its discretion, may also require that a proposed settlement agreement provide for the distribution of a portion of the value of unclaimed coupons to 1 or more charitable or governmental organizations, as agreed to by the parties. The distribution and redemption of any proceeds under this subsection shall not be used to calculate attorneys' fees under this section.

(Added Pub.L. 109–2, § 3(a), Feb. 18, 2005, 119 Stat. 6.)

§ 1713. Protection against loss by class members

The court may approve a proposed settlement under which any class member is obligated to pay sums to class counsel that would result in a net loss to the class member only if the court makes a written finding that nonmonetary benefits to the class member substantially outweigh the monetary loss.

(Added Pub.L. 109–2, § 3(a), Feb. 18, 2005, 119 Stat. 7.)

§ 1714. Protection against discrimination based on geographic location

The court may not approve a proposed settlement that provides for the payment of greater sums to some class members than to others solely on the basis that the class members to whom the greater sums are to be paid are located in closer geographic proximity to the court.

(Added Pub.L. 109–2, § 3(a), Feb. 18, 2005, 119 Stat. 7.)

§ 1715. Notifications to appropriate Federal and State officials

(a) Definitions.—

(1) Appropriate Federal official.—In this section, the term "appropriate Federal official" means—

(A) the Attorney General of the United States; or

(B) in any case in which the defendant is a Federal depository institution, a State depository institution, a depository institution holding company, a foreign bank, or a nondepository institution subsidiary of the foregoing (as such terms are defined in section 3 of the Federal Deposit Insurance Act (12 U.S.C. 1813)), the person who has the primary Federal regulatory or supervisory responsibility with respect to the defendant, if some or all of the matters alleged in the class action are subject to regulation or supervision by that person.

(2) Appropriate State official.—In this section, the term "appropriate State official" means the person in the State who has the primary regulatory or supervisory responsibility with respect to the defendant, or who licenses or otherwise authorizes the defendant to conduct business in the State, if some or all of the matters alleged in the class action are subject to regulation by that person. If there is no primary regulator, supervisor, or licensing authority, or the matters alleged in the class action are not subject to regulation or supervision by that person, then the appropriate State official shall be the State attorney general.

(b) In general.—Not later than 10 days after a proposed settlement of a class action is filed in court, each defendant that is participating in the proposed settlement shall serve upon the appropriate State official of each State in which a class member resides and the appropriate Federal official, a notice of the proposed settlement consisting of—

(1) a copy of the complaint and any materials filed with the complaint and any amended complaints (except such materials shall not be required to be served if such materials are made electronically available through the Internet and such service includes notice of how to electronically access such material);

(2) notice of any scheduled judicial hearing in the class action;

(3) any proposed or final notification to class members of—

(A)(i) the members' rights to request exclusion from the class action; or

(ii) if no right to request exclusion exists, a statement that no such right exists; and

(B) a proposed settlement of a class action;

(4) any proposed or final class action settlement;

(5) any settlement or other agreement contemporaneously made between class counsel and counsel for the defendants;

(6) any final judgment or notice of dismissal;

(7)(A) if feasible, the names of class members who reside in each State and the estimated proportionate share of the claims of such members to the entire settlement to that State's appropriate State official; or

(B) if the provision of information under subparagraph (A) is not feasible, a reasonable estimate of the number of class members residing in each State and the estimated proportionate share of the claims of such members to the entire settlement; and

(8) any written judicial opinion relating to the materials described under subparagraphs (3) through (6).

(c) Depository institutions notification.—

(1) Federal and other depository institutions.—In any case in which the defendant is a Federal depository institution, a depository institution holding company, a foreign bank, or a non-depository institution subsidiary of the foregoing, the notice requirements of this section are satisfied by serving the notice required under subsection (b) upon the person who has the primary Federal regulatory or supervisory responsibility with respect to the defendant, if some or all of the matters alleged in the class action are subject to regulation or supervision by that person.

(2) State depository institutions.—In any case in which the defendant is a State depository institution (as that term is defined in section 3 of the Federal Deposit Insurance Act (12 U.S.C. 1813)), the notice requirements of this section are satisfied by serving the notice required under subsection (b) upon the State bank supervisor (as that term is defined in section 3 of the Federal Deposit Insurance Act (12 U.S.C. 1813)) of the State in which the defendant is incorporated or chartered, if some or all of the matters alleged in the class action are subject to regulation or supervision by that person, and upon the appropriate Federal official.

(d) Final approval.—An order giving final approval of a proposed settlement may not be issued earlier than 90 days after the later of the dates on which the appropriate Federal official and the appropriate State official are served with the notice required under subsection (b).

(e) Noncompliance if notice not provided.—

(1) In general.—A class member may refuse to comply with and may choose not to be bound by a settlement agreement or consent decree in a class action if the class member demonstrates that the notice required under subsection (b) has not been provided.

(2) Limitation.—A class member may not refuse to comply with or to be bound by a settlement agreement or consent decree under paragraph (1) if the notice required under subsection (b) was directed to the appropriate Federal official and to either the State attorney general or the person that has primary regulatory, supervisory, or licensing authority over the defendant.

(3) Application of rights.—The rights created by this subsection shall apply only to class members or any person acting on a class member's behalf, and shall not be construed to limit any other rights affecting a class member's participation in the settlement.

(f) Rule of construction.—Nothing in this section shall be construed to expand the authority of, or impose any obligations, duties, or responsibilities upon, Federal or State officials.

(Added Pub.L. 109–2, § 3(a), Feb. 18, 2005, 119 Stat. 7.)

§ 1731. Handwriting

The admitted or proved handwriting of any person shall be admissible, for purposes of comparison, to determine genuineness of other handwriting attributed to such person.

§ 1732. Record made in regular course of business; photographic copies

If any business, institution, member of a profession or calling, or any department or agency of government, in the regular course of business or activity has kept or recorded any memorandum, writing, entry, print, representation or combination thereof, of any act, transaction, occurrence, or event, and in the regular course of business has caused any or all of the same to be recorded, copied, or reproduced by any photographic, photostatic, microfilm, micro-card, miniature photographic, or other process which accurately reproduces or forms a durable medium for so reproducing the original, the original may be destroyed in the regular course of business unless its preservation is required by law. Such reproduction, when satisfactorily identified, is as admissible in evidence as the original itself in any judicial or administrative proceeding whether the original is in existence or not and an enlargement or facsimile of such reproduction is likewise admissible in evidence if the original reproduction is in existence and available for inspection under direction of court. The introduction of a reproduced record, enlargement, or facsimile does not preclude admission of the original. This subsection shall not be construed to exclude from evidence any document or copy thereof which is otherwise admissible under the rules of evidence.

(As amended Aug. 28, 1951, c. 351, §§ 1, 3, 65 Stat. 206; Aug. 30, 1961, Pub.L. 87–183, 75 Stat. 413; Jan. 2, 1975, Pub.L. 93–595, § 2(b), 88 Stat. 1949.)

§ 1733. Government records and papers; copies

(a) Books or records of account or minutes of proceedings of any department or agency of the United States shall be admissible to prove the act, transaction or occurrence as a memorandum of which the same were made or kept.

(b) Properly authenticated copies or transcripts of any books, records, papers or documents of any department or agency of the United States shall be admitted in evidence equally with the originals thereof.

(c) This section does not apply to cases, actions, and proceedings to which the Federal Rules of Evidence apply.

(As amended Jan. 2, 1975, Pub.L. 93–595, § 2(c), 88 Stat. 1949.)

§ 1734. Court record lost or destroyed, generally

(a) A lost or destroyed record of any proceeding in any court of the United States may be supplied on application of any interested party not at fault, by substituting a copy certified by the clerk of any court in which an authentic copy is lodged.

(b) Where a certified copy is not available, any interested person not at fault may file in such court a verified application for an order establishing the lost or destroyed record.

Every other interested person shall be served personally with a copy of the application and with notice of hearing on a day stated, not less than sixty days after service. Service may be made on any nonresident of the district anywhere within the jurisdiction of the United States or in any foreign country.

Proof of service in a foreign country shall be certified by a minister or consul of the United States in such country, under his official seal.

If, after the hearing, the court is satisfied that the statements contained in the application are true, it shall enter an order reciting the substance and effect of the lost or destroyed record. Such order, subject to intervening rights of third persons, shall have the same effect as the original record.

§ 1735. Court record lost or destroyed where United States interested

(a) When the record of any case or matter in any court of the United States to which the United States is a party, is lost or destroyed, a certified copy of any official paper of a United States attorney, United States marshal or clerk or other certifying or recording officer of any such court, made pursuant to law, on file in any department or agency of the United States and relating to such case or matter, shall, on being filed in the court to which it relates, have the same effect as an original paper filed in such court. If the copy so filed discloses the date and amount of a judgment or decree and the names of the parties thereto, the court may enforce the judgment or decree as though the original record had not been lost or destroyed.

(b) Whenever the United States is interested in any lost or destroyed records or files of a court of the United States, the clerk of such court and the United States attorney for the district shall take the steps necessary to restore such records or files, under the direction of the judges of such court.

§ 1736. Congressional Journals

Extracts from the Journals of the Senate and the House of Representatives, and from the Executive Journal of the Senate when the injunction of secrecy is removed, certified by the Secretary of the Senate or the Clerk of the House of Representatives shall be received in evidence with the same effect as the originals would have.

§ 1737. Copy of officer's bond

Any person to whose custody the bond of any officer of the United States has been committed shall, on proper request and payment of the fee allowed by any Act of Congress, furnish certified copies thereof, which shall be prima facie evidence in any court of the execution, filing and contents of the bond.

§ 1738. State and Territorial statutes and judicial proceedings; full faith and credit

The Acts of the legislature of any State, Territory, or Possession of the United States, or copies thereof, shall be authenticated by affixing the seal of such State, Territory or Possession thereto.

The records and judicial proceedings of any court of any such State, Territory or Possession, or copies thereof, shall be proved or admitted in other courts within the United States and its Territories and Possessions by the attestation of the clerk and seal of the court annexed, if a seal exists, together with a certificate of a judge of the court that the said attestation is in proper form.

Such Acts, records and judicial proceedings or copies thereof, so authenticated, shall have the same full faith and credit in every court within the United States and its Territories and Possessions as they have by law or usage in the courts of such State, Territory or Possession from which they are taken.

§ 1739. State and Territorial nonjudicial records; full faith and credit

All nonjudicial records or books kept in any public office of any State, Territory, or Possession of the United States, or copies thereof, shall be proved or admitted in any court or office in any other State, Territory, or Possession by the attestation of the custodian of such records or books, and the seal of his office annexed, if there be a seal, together with a certificate of a judge of a court of record of the county, parish, or district in which such office may be kept, or of the Governor, or secretary of state, the chancellor or keeper of the great seal, of the State, Territory, or Possession that the said attestation is in due form and by the proper officers.

If the certificate is given by a judge, it shall be further authenticated by the clerk or prothonotary of the court, who shall certify, under his hand and the seal of his office, that such judge is duly commissioned and qualified; or, if given by such Governor, secretary, chancellor, or keeper of the great seal, it shall be under the great seal of the State, Territory, or Possession in which it is made.

Such records or books, or copies thereof, so authenticated, shall have the same full faith and credit in every court and office within the United States and its Territories and Possessions as they have by law or usage in the courts or offices of the State, Territory, or Possession from which they are taken.

§ 1740. Copies of consular papers

Copies of all official documents and papers in the office of any consul or vice consul of the United States, and of all official entries in the books or records of any such office, authenticated by the consul or vice consul, shall be admissible equally with the originals.

§ 1741. Foreign official documents

An official record or document of a foreign country may be evidenced by a copy, summary, or excerpt authenticated as provided in the Federal Rules of Civil Procedure.

(As amended Oct. 3, 1964, Pub.L. 88–619, § 5(a), 78 Stat. 996.)

§ 1743. Demand on postmaster

The certificate of the Postmaster General or the General Accounting Office of the mailing to a postmaster of a statement of his account and that payment of the balance stated has not been received shall be sufficient evidence of a demand notwithstanding any allowances or credits subsequently made. A copy of such statement shall be attached to the certificate.

§ 1744. Copies of United States Patent and Trademark Office documents, generally

Copies of letters patent or of any records, books, papers, or drawings belonging to the United States Patent and Trademark Office and relating to patents, authenticated under the seal of the United States Patent and Trademark Office and certified by the Under Secretary of Commerce for Intellectual Property and Director of the United States Patent and Trademark Office, or by another officer of the United States Patent and Trademark Office authorized to do so by the Director, shall be admissible in evidence with the same effect as the originals.

Any person making application and paying the required fee may obtain such certified copies.

(As amended May 24, 1949, c. 139, § 92(c), 63 Stat. 103; Pub.L. 106–113, Div. B, § 1000(a)(9) [S. 1948, Title IV, § 4732(b)(15)(B), (C)], Nov. 29, 1999, 113 Stat. 1536–___.)

§ 1745. Copies of foreign patent documents

Copies of the specifications and drawings of foreign letters patent, or applications for foreign letters patent, and copies of excerpts of the official journals and other official publications of foreign patent offices belonging to the United States Patent and Trademark Office, certified in the manner provided by section 1744 of this title are prima facie evidence of their contents and of the dates indicated on their face.

(Formerly § 1746. Renumbered § 1745, May 24, 1949, c. 139, § 92(e), 63 Stat. 103, amended Oct. 3, 1964, Pub.L. 88–619, § 7(a), 78 Stat. 996; Pub.L. 106–113, Div. B, § 1000(a)(9) [S. 1948, Title IV, § 4732(b)(16)], Nov. 29, 1999, 113 Stat. 1537–___.)

§ 1746. Unsworn declarations under penalty of perjury

Wherever, under any law of the United States or under any rule, regulation, order, or requirement made pursuant to law, any matter is required or permitted to be supported, evidenced, established, or proved by the sworn declaration, verification, certificate, statement, oath, or affidavit, in writing of the person making the same (other than a deposition, or an oath of office, or an oath required to be taken before a specified official other than a notary public), such matter may, with like force and effect, be supported, evidenced, established, or proved by the unsworn declaration, certificate, verification, or statement, in writing of such person which is subscribed by him, as true under penalty of perjury, and dated, in substantially the following form:

(1) If executed without the United States: "I declare (or certify, verify, or state) under penalty of perjury under the laws of the United States of America that the foregoing is true and correct. Executed on (date).

(Signature)".

(2) If executed within the United States, its territories, possessions, or commonwealths: "I declare (or certify, verify, or state) under penalty of perjury that the foregoing is true and correct. Executed on (date).

(Signature)".

(Added Pub.L. 94–550, § 1(a), Oct. 18, 1976, 90 Stat. 2534.)

§ 1781. Transmittal of letter rogatory or request

(a) The Department of State has power, directly, or through suitable channels—

(1) to receive a letter rogatory issued, or request made, by a foreign or international tribunal, to transmit it to the tribunal, officer, or agency in the United States to whom it is addressed, and to receive and return it after execution; and

(2) to receive a letter rogatory issued, or request made, by a tribunal in the United States, to transmit it to the foreign or international tribunal, officer, or agency to whom it is addressed, and to receive and return it after execution.

(b) This section does not preclude—

(1) the transmittal of a letter rogatory or request directly from a foreign or international tribunal to the tribunal, officer, or agency in the United States to whom it is addressed and its return in the same manner; or

(2) the transmittal of a letter rogatory or request directly from a tribunal in the United States to the foreign or international tribunal, officer, or agency to whom it is addressed and its return in the same manner.

(As amended Oct. 3, 1964, Pub.L. 88–619, § 8(a), 78 Stat. 996.)

§ 1782. Assistance to foreign and international tribunals and to litigants before such tribunals

(a) The district court of the district in which a person resides or is found may order him to give his testimony or statement or to produce a document or other thing for use in a proceeding in a foreign or international tribunal, including criminal investigations conducted before formal accusation. The order may be made pursuant to a letter rogatory issued, or request made, by a foreign or international tribunal or upon the application of any interested person and may direct that the testimony or statement be given, or the document or other thing be produced, before a person appointed by the court. By virtue of his appointment, the person appointed has power to administer any necessary oath and take the testimony or statement. The order may prescribe the practice and procedure, which may be in whole or part the practice and procedure of the foreign country or the international tribunal, for taking the testimony or statement or producing the document or other thing. To the extent that the order does not prescribe otherwise, the testimony or statement shall be taken, and the document or other thing produced, in accordance with the Federal Rules of Civil Procedure.

A person may not be compelled to give his testimony or statement or to produce a document or other thing in violation of any legally applicable privilege.

(b) This chapter does not preclude a person within the United States from voluntarily giving his testimony or statement, or producing a document or other thing, for use in a proceeding in a foreign or international tribunal before any person and in any manner acceptable to him.

(June 25, 1948, c. 646, 62 Stat. 949; May 24, 1949, c. 139, § 93, 63 Stat. 103; Oct. 3, 1964, Pub.L. 88–619, § 9(a), 78 Stat. 997; Feb. 10, 1996, Pub.L. 104–106, Div. A, Title XIII, § 1342(b), 110 Stat. 486.)

§ 1783. Subpoena of person in foreign country

(a) A court of the United States may order the issuance of a subpoena requiring the appearance as a witness before it, or before a person or body designated by it, of a national or resident of the United States who is in a foreign country, or requiring the production of a specified document or other thing by him, if the court finds that particular testimony or the production of the document or other thing by him is necessary in the interest of justice, and, in other than a criminal action or proceeding, if the court finds, in addition, that it is not possible to obtain his testimony in admissible form without his personal appearance or to obtain the production of the document or other thing in any other manner.

(b) The subpoena shall designate the time and place for the appearance or for the production of the document or other thing. Service of the subpoena and any order to show cause, rule, judgment, or decree authorized by this section or by section 1784 of this title shall be effected in accordance with the provisions of the Federal Rules of Civil Procedure relating to service of process on a person in a foreign country. The person serving the subpoena shall tender to the person to whom the subpoena is addressed his estimated necessary travel and attendance expenses, the amount of which shall be determined by the court and stated in the order directing the issuance of the subpoena.

(As amended Oct. 3, 1964, Pub.L. 88–619, § 10(a), 78 Stat. 997.)

§ 1784. Contempt

(a) The court of the United States which has issued a subpoena served in a foreign country may order the person who has failed to appear or who has failed to produce a document or other thing as directed therein to show cause before it at a designated time why he should not be punished for contempt.

(b) The court, in the order to show cause, may direct that any of the person's property within the United States be levied upon or seized, in the manner provided by law or court rules governing levy or seizure under execution, and held to satisfy any judgment that may be rendered against him pursuant to subsection (d) of this section if adequate security, in such amount as the court may direct in the order, be given for any damage that he might suffer should he not be found in contempt. Security under this subsection may not be required of the United States.

(c) A copy of the order to show cause shall be served on the person in accordance with section 1783(b) of this title.

(d) On the return day of the order to show cause or any later day to which the hearing may be continued, proof shall be taken. If the person is found in contempt, the court, notwithstanding any limitation upon its power generally to punish for contempt, may fine him not more than $100,000 and direct that the fine and costs of the proceedings be satisfied by a sale of the property levied upon or seized, conducted upon the notice required and in the manner provided for sales upon execution.

(As amended Oct. 3, 1964, Pub.L. 88–619, § 11, 78 Stat. 998.)

§ 1785. Subpoenas in multiparty, multiforum actions

When the jurisdiction of the district court is based in whole or in part upon section 1369 of this title, a subpoena for attendance at a hearing or trial may, if authorized by the court upon motion for good cause shown, and upon such terms and conditions as the court may impose, be served at any place within the United States, or anywhere outside the United States if otherwise permitted by law.

(Added Pub.L. 107–273, Div. C, Title I, § 11020(b)(4)(B)(i), Nov. 2, 2002, 116 Stat. 1828.)

§ 1821. Per diem and mileage generally; subsistence

(a)(1) Except as otherwise provided by law, a witness in attendance at any court of the United States, or before a United States Magistrate, or before any person authorized to take his deposition pursuant to any rule or order of a court of the United States, shall be paid the fees and allowances provided by this section.

(2) As used in this section, the term "court of the United States" includes, in addition to the courts listed in section 451 of this title, any court created by Act of Congress in a territory which is invested with any jurisdiction of a district court of the United States.

(b) A witness shall be paid an attendance fee of $40 per day for each day's attendance. A witness shall also be paid the attendance fee for the time necessarily occupied in going to and returning from the place of attendance at the beginning and end of such attendance or at any time during such attendance.

(c)(1) A witness who travels by common carrier shall be paid for the actual expenses of travel on the basis of the means of transportation reasonably utilized and the distance necessarily traveled to and from such witness's residence by the shortest practical route in going to and returning from the place of attendance. Such a witness shall utilize a common carrier at the most economical rate reasonably available. A receipt or other evidence of actual cost shall be furnished.

(2) A travel allowance equal to the mileage allowance which the Administrator of General Services has prescribed, pursuant to section 5704 of title 5, for official travel of employees of the Federal Government shall be paid to each witness who travels by privately owned vehicle. Computation of mileage under this paragraph shall be made on the basis of a uniformed table of distances adopted by the Administrator of General Services.

(3) Toll charges for toll roads, bridges, tunnels, and ferries, taxicab fares between places of lodging and carrier terminals, and parking fees (upon presentation of a valid parking receipt), shall be paid in full to a witness incurring such expenses.

(4) All normal travel expenses within and outside the judicial district shall be taxable as costs pursuant to section 1920 of this title.

(d)(1) A subsistence allowance shall be paid to a witness when an overnight stay is required at the place of attendance because such place is so far removed from the residence of such witness as to prohibit return thereto from day to day.

(2) A subsistence allowance for a witness shall be paid in an amount not to exceed the maximum per diem allowance prescribed by the Administrator of General Services, pursuant to section 5702(a) of title 5, for official travel in the area of attendance by employees of the Federal Government.

(3) A subsistence allowance for a witness attending in an area designated by the Administrator of General Services as a high-cost area shall be paid in an amount not to exceed the maximum actual subsistence allowance prescribed by the Administrator, pursuant to section 5702(c)(B) of title 5, for official travel in such area by employees of the Federal Government.

(4) When a witness is detained pursuant to section 3144 of title 18 for want of security for his appearance, he shall be entitled for each day of detention when not in attendance at court, in addition to his subsistence, to the daily attendance fee provided by subsection (b) of this section.

(e) An alien who has been paroled into the United States for prosecution, pursuant to section 212(d)(5) of the Immigration and Nationality Act (8 U.S.C. 1182(d)(5)), or an alien who either has admitted belonging to a class of aliens who are deportable or has been determined pursuant to section 240 of such Act (8 U.S.C. 1252(b)) to be deportable, shall be ineligible to receive the fees or allowances provided by this section.

(f) Any witness who is incarcerated at the time that his or her testimony is given (except for a witness to whom the provisions of section 3144 of title 18 apply) may not receive fees or allowances under this section, regardless of whether such a witness is incarcerated at the time he or she makes a claim for fees or allowances under this section.

(As amended May 10, 1949, c. 96, 63 Stat. 65; May 24, 1949, c. 139, § 94, 63 Stat. 103; Oct. 31, 1951, c. 655, § 51(a), 65 Stat. 727; Sept. 3, 1954, c. 1263, § 45, 68 Stat. 1242; Aug. 1, 1956, c. 826, 70 Stat. 798; Mar. 27, 1968, Pub.L. 90–274, § 102(b), 82 Stat. 62; Oct. 27, 1978, Pub.L. 95–535, § 1, 92 Stat. 2033; Dec. 1, 1990, Pub.L. 101–650, Title III, § 314(a), 104 Stat. 5115; Oct. 14, 1992, Pub.L. 102–417, § 2(a)–(c), 106 Stat. 2138.)

Amendment of Subsec. (e)

Pub.L. 104–208, Div. C, Title III, §§ 308(g)(5)(E), 309, Sept. 30, 1996, 110 Stat. 3009–623, 3009–625, provided that, to take effect, with certain exceptions and subject to certain transitional rules, on the first day of the first month beginning more than 180 days after Sept. 30, 1996, subsec. (e) of this section is amended by striking "242(b)" and inserting "240".

§ 1826. Recalcitrant witnesses

(a) Whenever a witness in any proceeding before or ancillary to any court or grand jury of the United States refuses without just cause shown to comply with an order of the court to testify or provide other information, including any book, paper, document, record, recording or other material, the court, upon such refusal, or when such refusal is duly brought to its attention, may summarily order his confinement at a suitable place until such time as the witness is willing to give such testimony or provide such information. No period of such confinement shall exceed the life of—

(1) the court proceeding, or

(2) the term of the grand jury, including extensions,

before which such refusal to comply with the court order occurred, but in no event shall such confinement exceed eighteen months.

(b) No person confined pursuant to subsection (a) of this section shall be admitted to bail pending the determination of an appeal taken by him from the order for his confinement if it appears that the appeal is frivolous or taken for delay. Any appeal from an order of confinement under this section shall be disposed of as soon as practicable, but not later than thirty days from the filing of such appeal.

(c) Whoever escapes or attempts to escape from the custody of any facility or from any place in which or to which he is confined pursuant to this section or section 4243 of title 18, or whoever rescues or attempts to rescue or instigates, aids, or assists the escape or attempt to escape of such a person, shall be subject to imprisonment for not more than three years, or a fine of not more than $10,000, or both.

(Added Pub.L. 91–452, Title III, § 301(a), Oct. 15, 1970, 84 Stat. 932, and amended Pub.L. 98–473, Title II, § 1013, Oct. 12, 1984, 98 Stat. 2142.)

§ 1914. District court; filing and miscellaneous fees; rules of court

(a) The clerk of each district court shall require the parties instituting any civil action, suit or proceeding in such court, whether by original process, removal or otherwise, to pay a filing fee of $150, except that on application for a writ of habeas corpus the filing fee shall be $5.

(b) The clerk shall collect from the parties such additional fees only as are prescribed by the Judicial Conference of the United States.

(c) Each district court by rule or standing order may require advance payment of fees.

(As amended Nov. 6, 1978, Pub.L. 95–598, Title II, § 244, 92 Stat. 2671; June 14, 1986, Pub.L. 99–336, § 4(a), 100 Stat. 637; Oct. 18, 1986, Pub.L. 99–500, Title I, § 101(b), [Title IV, § 407(a)], 100 Stat. 1783–64; Oct. 30, 1986, Pub.L. 99–591, Title I, § 101(b), [Title IV, § 407(a)], 100 Stat. 3341–64; Oct. 19, 1996, Pub.L. 104–317, Title IV, § 401(a), 110 Stat. 3853.)

§ 1915. Proceedings in forma pauperis

(a)(1) Subject to subsection (b), any court of the United States may authorize the commencement, prosecution or defense of any suit, action or proceeding, civil or criminal, or appeal therein, without prepayment of fees or security therefor, by a person who submits an affidavit that includes a statement of all assets such prisoner possesses that the person is unable to pay such fees or give security therefor. Such affidavit shall state the nature of the action, defense or appeal and affiant's belief that the person is entitled to redress.

(2) A prisoner seeking to bring a civil action or appeal a judgment in a civil action or proceeding without prepayment of fees or security therefor, in addition to filing the affidavit filed under paragraph (1), shall submit a certified copy of the trust fund account statement (or institutional equivalent) for the prisoner for the 6-month period immediately preceding the filing of the complaint or notice of appeal, obtained from the appropriate official of each prison at which the prisoner is or was confined.

(3) An appeal may not be taken in forma pauperis if the trial court certifies in writing that it is not taken in good faith.

(b)(1) Notwithstanding subsection (a), if a prisoner brings a civil action or files an appeal in forma pauperis, the prisoner shall be required to pay the full amount of a filing fee. The court shall assess and, when funds exist, collect, as a partial payment of any court fees required by law, an initial partial filing fee of 20 percent of the greater of—

(A) the average monthly deposits to the prisoner's account; or

(B) the average monthly balance in the prisoner's account for the 6-month period immediately preceding the filing of the complaint or notice of appeal.

(2) After payment of the initial partial filing fee, the prisoner shall be required to make monthly payments of 20 percent of the preceding month's income credited to the prisoner's account. The agency having custody of the prisoner shall forward payments from the prisoner's account to the clerk of the court each time the amount in the account exceeds $10 until the filing fees are paid.

(3) In no event shall the filing fee collected exceed the amount of fees permitted by statute for the commencement of a civil action or an appeal of a civil action or criminal judgment.

(4) In no event shall a prisoner be prohibited from bringing a civil action or appealing a civil or criminal judgment for the reason that the prisoner has no assets and no means by which to pay the initial partial filing fee.

(c) Upon the filing of an affidavit in accordance with subsections (a) and (b) and the prepayment of any partial filing fee as may be required under subsection (b), the court may direct payment by the United States of the expenses of (1) printing the record on appeal in any civil or criminal case, if such printing is required by the appellate court; (2) preparing a transcript of proceedings before a United States magistrate in any civil or criminal case, if such transcript is required by the district court, in the case of proceedings conducted under section 636(b) of this title or under section 3401(b) of title 18, United States Code; and (3) printing the record on appeal if such printing is required by the appellate court, in the case of proceedings conducted pursuant to section 636(c) of this title. Such expenses shall be paid when authorized by the Director of the Administrative Office of the United States Courts.

(d) The officers of the court shall issue and serve all process, and perform all duties in such cases. Witnesses shall attend as in other cases, and the same remedies shall be available as are provided for by law in other cases.

(e)(1) The court may request an attorney to represent any person unable to afford counsel.

(2) Notwithstanding any filing fee, or any portion thereof, that may have been paid, the court shall dismiss the case at any time if the court determines that—

(A) the allegation of poverty is untrue; or

(B) the action or appeal—

(i) is frivolous or malicious;

(ii) fails to state a claim on which relief may be granted; or

(iii) seeks monetary relief against a defendant who is immune from such relief.

(f)(1) Judgment may be rendered for costs at the conclusion of the suit or action as in other proceedings, but the United States shall not be liable for any of the costs thus incurred. If the United States has paid the cost of a stenographic transcript or printed record for the prevailing party, the same shall be taxed in favor of the United States.

(2)(A) If the judgment against a prisoner includes the payment of costs under this subsection, the prisoner shall be required to pay the full amount of the costs ordered.

(B) The prisoner shall be required to make payments for costs under this subsection in the same manner as is provided for filing fees under subsection (a)(2).

(C) In no event shall the costs collected exceed the amount of the costs ordered by the court.

(g) In no event shall a prisoner bring a civil action or appeal a judgment in a civil action or proceeding under this section if the prisoner has, on 3 or more prior occasions, while incarcerated or detained in any facility, brought an action or appeal in a court of the United States that was dismissed on the grounds that it is frivolous, malicious, or fails to state a claim upon which relief may be granted, unless the prisoner is under imminent danger of serious physical injury.

(h) As used in this section, the term 'prisoner' means any person incarcerated or detained in any facility who is accused of, convicted of, sentenced for, or adjudicated delinquent for, violations of criminal law or the terms and conditions of parole, probation, pretrial release, or diversionary program.

(June 25, 1948, c. 646, 62 Stat. 954; May 24, 1949, c. 139, § 98, 63 Stat. 104; Oct. 31, 1951, c. 655, § 51(b), (c), 65 Stat. 727; Sept. 21, 1959, Pub.L. 86–320, 73 Stat. 590; Oct. 10, 1979, Pub.L. 96–82, § 6, 93 Stat. 645; Apr. 26, 1996, Pub.L. 104–134, Title I, § 101[(a)][Title VIII, § 804(a), (c) to (e)], 110 Stat. 1321–73, 1321–74; renumbered Title I May 2, 1996, Pub.L. 104–140, § 1(a), 110 Stat. 1327.)

§ 1917. District courts; fee on filing notice of or petition for appeal

Upon the filing of any separate or joint notice of appeal or application for appeal or upon the receipt of any order allowing, or notice of the allowance of, an appeal or of a writ of certiorari $5 shall be paid to the clerk of the district court, by the appellant or petitioner.

§ 1920. Taxation of costs

A judge or clerk of any court of the United States may tax as costs the following:

(1) Fees of the clerk and marshal;

(2) Fees of the court reporter for all or any part of the stenographic transcript necessarily obtained for use in the case;

(3) Fees and disbursements for printing and witnesses;

(4) Fees for exemplification and copies of papers necessarily obtained for use in the case;

(5) Docket fees under section 1923 of this title;

(6) Compensation of court appointed experts, compensation of interpreters, and salaries, fees, expenses, and costs of special interpretation services under section 1828 of this title.

A bill of costs shall be filed in the case and, upon allowance, included in the judgment or decree.

(As amended Oct. 28, 1978, Pub.L. 95–539, § 7, 92 Stat. 2044.)

§ 1921. United States marshal's fees

(a)(1) The United States marshals or deputy marshals shall routinely collect, and a court may tax as costs, fees for the following:

(A) Serving a writ of possession, partition, execution, attachment in rem, or libel in admiralty, warrant, attachment, summons, complaints, or any other writ, order or process in any case or proceeding.

(B) Serving a subpoena or summons for a witness or appraiser.

(C) Forwarding any writ, order, or process to another judicial district for service.

(D) The preparation of any notice of sale, proclamation in admiralty, or other public notice or bill of sale.

(E) The keeping of attached property (including boats, vessels, or other property attached or libeled), actual expenses incurred, such as storage, moving, boat hire, or other special transportation, watchmen's or keepers' fees, insurance, and an hourly rate, including overtime, for each deputy marshal required for special services, such as guarding, inventorying, and moving.

(F) Copies of writs or other papers furnished at the request of any party.

(G) Necessary travel in serving or endeavoring to serve any process, writ, or order, except in the District of Columbia, with mileage to be computed from the place where service is returnable to the place of service or endeavor.

(H) Overtime expenses incurred by deputy marshals in the course of serving or executing civil process.

(2) The marshals shall collect, in advance, a deposit to cover the initial expenses for special services required under paragraph (1)(E), and periodically thereafter such amounts as may be necessary to pay such expenses until the litigation is concluded. This paragraph applies to all private litigants, including seamen proceeding pursuant to section 1916 of this title.

(3) For purposes of paragraph (1)(G), if two or more services or endeavors, or if an endeavor and a service, are made in behalf of the same party in the same case on the same trip, mileage shall be computed to the place of service or endeavor which is most remote from the place where service is returnable, adding thereto any additional mileage traveled in serving or endeavoring to serve in behalf of the party. If two or more writs of any kind, required to be served in behalf of the same party on the same person in the same case or proceeding, may be served at the same time, mileage on only one such writ shall be collected.

(b) The Attorney General shall from time to time prescribe by regulation the fees to be taxed and collected under subsection (a). Such fees shall, to the extent practicable, reflect the actual and reasonable cost of the service provided.

(c)(1) The United States Marshals Service shall collect a commission of 3 percent of the first $1,000 collected and 1½ percent on the excess of any sum over $1,000, for seizing or levying on property (including seizures in admiralty), disposing of such property by sale, setoff, or otherwise, and receiving and paying over money, except that the amount of commission shall be within the range set by the Attorney General. if[1] the property is not disposed of by marshal's sale, commission shall be in such amount, within the range set by the Attorney General, as may be allowed by the court. In any case in which the vessel or other property is sold by a public auctioneer, or by some party other than a marshal or deputy marshal, the commission authorized under this subsection shall be reduced by the amount paid to such auctioneer or other party. This subsection applies to any judicially ordered sale or execution sale, without regard to whether the judicial order of sale constitutes a seizure or levy within the meaning of State law. This subsection shall not apply to any seizure, forfeiture, sale, or other disposition of property pursuant to the applicable provisions of law amended by the Comprehensive Forfeiture Act of 1984 (98 Stat. 2040).

(2) The Attorney General shall prescribe from time to time regulations which establish a minimum and maximum amount for the commission collected under paragraph (1).

(d) The United States marshals may require a deposit to cover the fees and expenses prescribed under this section.

(e) Notwithstanding section 3302 of title 31, the United States Marshals Service is authorized, to the extent provided in advance in appropriations Acts—

(1) to credit to such Service's appropriation all fees, commissions, and expenses collected by such Service for—

(A) the service of civil process, including complaints, summonses, subpoenas, and similar process; and

(B) seizures, levies, and sales associated with judicial orders of execution; and

(2) to use such credited amounts for the purpose of carrying out such activities.

1. So in original. Probably should be "If".

(As amended Sept. 9, 1950, c. 937, 64 Stat. 824; Aug. 31, 1962, Pub.L. 87–621, § 1, 76 Stat. 417; Nov. 10, 1986, Pub.L. 99–646, § 39(a), 100 Stat. 3600; Nov. 18, 1988, Pub.L. 100–690, Title VII, § 7608(c), 102 Stat. 4515; Nov. 29, 1990, Pub.L. 101–647, Title XII, § 1212, 104 Stat. 4833.)

§ 1924. Verification of bill of costs

Before any bill of costs is taxed, the party claiming any item of cost or disbursement shall attach thereto an affidavit, made by himself or by his duly authorized attorney or agent having knowledge of the facts, that such item is correct and has been necessarily incurred in the case and that the services for which fees have been charged were actually and necessarily performed.

§ 1927. Counsel's liability for excessive costs

Any attorney or other person admitted to conduct cases in any court of the United States or any Territory thereof who so multiplies the proceedings in any case unreasonably and vexatiously may be required by the court to satisfy personally the excess costs, expenses, and attorneys' fees reasonably incurred because of such conduct.

(As amended Sept. 12, 1980, Pub.L. 96–349, § 3, 94 Stat. 1156.)

§ 1961. Interest

(a) Interest shall be allowed on any money judgment in a civil case recovered in a district court. Execution therefor may be levied by the marshal, in any case where, by the law of the State in which such court is held, execution may be levied for interest on judgments recovered in the courts of the State. Such interest shall be calculated from the date of the entry of the judgment, at a rate equal to the weekly average 1–year constant maturity Treasury yield, as published by the Board of Governors of the Federal Reserve System, for the calendar week preceding the date of the judgment. The Director of the Administrative Office of the United States Courts shall distribute notice of that rate and any changes in it to all Federal judges.

(b) Interest shall be computed daily to the date of payment except as provided in section 2516(b) of this title and section 1304(b) of title 31, and shall be compounded annually.

(c)(1) This section shall not apply in any judgment of any court with respect to any internal revenue tax case. Interest shall be allowed in such cases at the underpayment rate or overpayment rate (whichever is appropriate) established under section 6621 of the Internal Revenue Code of 1986.

(2) Except as otherwise provided in paragraph (1) of this subsection, interest shall be allowed on all final judgments against the United States in the United States Court of Appeals for the Federal circuit,[1] at the rate provided in subsection (a) and as provided in subsection (b).

(3) Interest shall be allowed, computed, and paid on judgments of the United States Court of Federal Claims only as provided in paragraph (1) of this subsection or in any other provision of law.

(4) This section shall not be construed to affect the interest on any judgment of any court not specified in this section.

1. So in original. Probably should be "Circuit,".

(June 25, 1948, c. 646, 62 Stat. 957; Apr. 2, 1982, Pub.L. 97–164, Title III, § 302(a), 96 Stat. 55; Sept. 13, 1982, Pub.L. 97–258, § 2(m) (1), 96 Stat. 1062; Jan. 12, 1983, Pub.L. 97–452, § 2(d)(1), 96 Stat. 2478; Oct. 22, 1986, Pub.L. 99–514, § 2, Title XV, § 1511(c)(17), 100 Stat. 2095, 2745; Oct. 29, 1992, Pub.L. 102–572, Title IX, § 902(b)(1), 106 Stat. 4516; Dec. 21, 2000, Pub.L. 106–554, § 1(a)(7) [Title III, § 307(d)(1)], 114 Stat. 2763, 2763A–636.)

[Interest on any money judgment in a civil case recovered in a district court is calculated from the date of entry of the judgment at a rate equal to the equivalent coupon issue yield of the average accepted auction price for the last auction of fifty-two week United States Treasury bills settled immediately prior to the date of the judgment. 28 U.S.C.A. § 1961(a). For a listing of historical and current interest rates, consult West's annually revised **Federal Civil Judicial Procedure and Rules** (and supplements).]

§ 1963. Registration of judgments for enforcement in other districts

A judgment in an action for the recovery of money or property entered in any court of appeals, district court, bankruptcy court, or in the Court of International Trade may be registered by filing a certified copy of the judgment in any other district or, with respect to the Court of International Trade, in any judicial district, when the judgment has become final by appeal or expiration of the time for appeal or when ordered by the court that entered the judgment for good cause shown. Such a judgment entered in favor of the United States may be so registered any time after judgment is entered. A judgment so registered shall have the same effect as a judgment of the district court of the district where registered and may be enforced in like manner.

A certified copy of the satisfaction of any judgment in whole or in part may be registered in like manner in any district in which the judgment is a lien.

The procedure prescribed under this section is in addition to other procedures provided by law for the enforcement of judgments.

(As amended Aug. 23, 1954, c. 837, 68 Stat. 772; July 7, 1958, Pub.L. 85–508, § 12(*o*), 72 Stat. 349; Nov. 19, 1988, Pub.L. 100–702, Title X, § 1002(a), (b)(1), 102 Stat. 4664; Nov. 29, 1990, Pub.L. 101–647, Title XXXVI, § 3628, 104 Stat. 4965; Oct. 19, 1996, Pub.L. 104–317, 110 Stat. 3847.)

§ 1964. Constructive notice of pending actions

Where the law of a State requires a notice of an action concerning real property pending in a court of the State to be registered, recorded, docketed, or indexed in a particular manner, or in a certain office or county or parish in order to give constructive notice of the action as it relates to the real property, and such law authorizes a notice of an action concerning real property pending in a United States district court to be registered, recorded, docketed, or indexed in the same manner, or in the same place, those requirements of the State law must be complied with in order to give constructive notice of such an action pending in a United States district court as it relates to real property in such State.

(Added Aug. 20, 1958, Pub.L. 85–689, § 1(a), 72 Stat. 683.)

§ 2071. Rule-making power generally

(a) The Supreme Court and all courts established by Act of Congress may from time to time prescribe rules for the conduct of their business. Such rules shall be consistent with Acts of Congress and rules of practice and procedure prescribed under section 2072 of this title.

(b) Any rule prescribed by a court, other than the Supreme Court, under subsection (a) shall be prescribed only after giving appropriate public notice and an opportunity for comment. Such rule shall take effect upon the date specified by the prescribing court and shall have such effect on pending proceedings as the prescribing court may order.

(c)(1) A rule of a district court prescribed under subsection (a) shall remain in effect unless modified or abrogated by the judicial council of the relevant circuit.

(2) Any other rule prescribed by a court other than the Supreme Court under subsection (a) shall remain in effect unless modified or abrogated by the Judicial Conference.

(d) Copies of rules prescribed under subsection (a) by a district court shall be furnished to the judicial council, and copies of all rules prescribed by a court other than the Supreme Court under subsection (a) shall be furnished to the Director of the Administrative Office of the United States Courts and made available to the public.

(e) If the prescribing court determines that there is an immediate need for a rule, such court may proceed under this section without public notice and opportunity for comment, but such court shall promptly thereafter afford such notice and opportunity for comment.

(f) No rule may be prescribed by a district court other than under this section.

(As amended May 24, 1949, c. 139, § 102, 63 Stat. 104; Nov. 19, 1988, Pub.L. 100–702, Title IV, § 403(a)(1), 102 Stat. 4650.)

§ 2072. Rules of procedure and evidence; power to prescribe

(a) The Supreme Court shall have the power to prescribe general rules of practice and procedure and rules of evidence for cases in the United States district courts (including proceedings before magistrates thereof) and courts of appeals.

(b) Such rules shall not abridge, enlarge or modify any substantive right. All laws in conflict with such rules shall be of no further force or effect after such rules have taken effect.

(c) Such rules may define when a ruling of a district court is final for the purposes of appeal under section 1291 of this title.

(As amended Pub.L. 101–650, Title III, § 315, Dec. 1, 1990, 104 Stat. 5115.)

§ 2073. Rules of procedure and evidence; method of prescribing

(a)(1) The Judicial Conference shall prescribe and publish the procedures for the consideration of proposed rules under this section.

(2) The Judicial Conference may authorize the appointment of committees to assist the Conference by recommending rules to be prescribed under sections 2072 and 2075 of this title. Each such committee shall consist of members of the bench and the professional bar, and trial and appellate judges.

(b) The Judicial Conference shall authorize the appointment of a standing committee on rules of practice, procedure, and evidence under subsection (a) of this section. Such standing committee shall review each recommendation of any other committees so appointed and recommend to the Judicial Conference rules of practice, procedure, and evidence and such changes in rules proposed by a committee appointed under subsection (a)(2) of this section as may be necessary to maintain consistency and otherwise promote the interest of justice.

(c)(1) Each meeting for the transaction of business under this chapter by any committee appointed under this section shall be open to the public except when the committee is meeting, in open session and with a majority present, determines that it is in the public interest that all or part of the remainder of the meeting on that day shall be closed to the public, and states the reason for so closing the meeting. Minutes of each meeting for the transaction of business under this chapter shall be maintained by the committee and made available to the public, except that any portion of such minutes, relating to a closed meeting and made available to the public, may contain such deletions as may be necessary to avoid frustrating the purposes of closing the meeting.

(2) Any meeting for the transaction of business under this chapter, by a committee appointed under this section, shall be preceded by sufficient notice to enable all interested persons to attend.

(d) In making a recommendation under this section or under section 2072 or 2075, the body making that recommendation shall provide a proposed rule, an explanatory note on the rule, and a written report explaining the body's action, including any minority or other separate views.

(e) Failure to comply with this section does not invalidate a rule prescribed under section 2072 or 2075 of this title.

(As amended Pub.L. 103–394, Title I, § 104(e), Oct. 22, 1994, 108 Stat. 4110.)

§ 2074. Rules of procedure and evidence; submission to Congress; effective date

(a) The Supreme Court shall transmit to the Congress not later than May 1 of the year in which a rule prescribed under section 2072 is to become effective a copy of the proposed rule. Such rule shall take effect no earlier than December 1 of the year in which such rule is so transmitted unless otherwise provided by law. The Supreme Court may fix the extent such rule shall apply to proceedings then pending, except that the Supreme Court shall not require the application of such rule to further proceedings then pending to the extent that, in the opinion of the court in which such proceedings are pending, the application of such rule in such proceedings would not be feasible or would work injustice, in which event the former rule applies.

(b) Any such rule creating, abolishing, or modifying an evidentiary privilege shall have no force or effect unless approved by Act of Congress.

§ 2075. Bankruptcy rules

The Supreme Court shall have the power to prescribe by general rules, the forms of process, writs, pleadings, and motions, and the practice and procedure in cases under title 11.

Such rules shall not abridge, enlarge, or modify any substantive right.

The Supreme Court shall transmit to Congress not later than May 1 of the year in which a rule prescribed under this section is to become effective a copy of the proposed rule. The rule shall take effect no earlier than December 1 of the year in which it is transmitted to Congress unless otherwise provided by law.

(As amended Pub.L. 95–598, Title II, § 247, Nov. 6, 1978, 92 Stat. 2672; Pub.L. 103–394, Title I, § 104(f), Oct. 22, 1994, 108 Stat. 4110.)

§ 2077. Publication of rules; advisory committees

(a) The rules for the conduct of the business of each court of appeals, including the operating procedures of such court, shall be published. Each court of appeals shall print or cause to be printed necessary copies of the rules. The Judicial Conference shall prescribe the fees for sales of copies under section 1913 of this title, but the Judicial Conference may provide for free distribution of copies to members of the bar of each court and to other interested persons.

(b) Each court, except the Supreme Court, that is authorized to prescribe rules of the conduct of such court's business under section 2071 of this title shall appoint an advisory committee for the study of the rules of practice and internal operating procedures of such court and, in the case of an advisory committee appointed by a court of appeals, of the rules of the judicial council of the circuit. The advisory committee shall make recommendations to the court concerning such rules and procedures. Members of the committee shall serve without compensation, but the Director may pay travel and transportation expenses in accordance with section 5703 of title 5.

(As amended Pub.L. 100–702, Title IV, § 401(b), Nov. 19, 1988, 102 Stat. 4650; Pub.L. 101–650, Title IV, § 406, Dec. 1, 1990, 104 Stat. 5124.)

§ 2101. Supreme Court; time for appeal or certiorari; docketing; stay

(a) A direct appeal to the Supreme Court from any decision under section 1253 of this title, holding unconstitutional in whole or in part, any Act of Congress, shall be taken within thirty days after the entry of the interlocutory or final order, judgment or decree. The record shall be made up and the case docketed within sixty days from the time such appeal is taken under rules prescribed by the Supreme Court.

(b) Any other direct appeal to the Supreme Court which is authorized by law, from a decision of a district court in any civil action, suit or proceeding, shall be taken within thirty days from the judgment, order or decree, appealed from, if interlocutory, and within sixty days if final.

(c) Any other appeal or any writ of certiorari intended to bring any judgment or decree in a civil action, suit or proceeding before the Supreme Court for review shall be taken or applied for within ninety days after the entry of such judgment or decree. A justice of the Supreme Court, for good cause shown, may extend the time for applying for a writ of certiorari for a period not exceeding sixty days.

(d) The time for appeal or application for a writ of certiorari to review the judgment of a State court in a criminal case shall be as prescribed by rules of the Supreme Court.

(e) An application to the Supreme Court for a writ of certiorari to review a case before judgment has been rendered in the court of appeals may be made at any time before judgment.

(f) In any case in which the final judgment or decree of any court is subject to review by the Supreme Court on writ of certiorari, the execution and enforcement of such judgment or decree may be stayed for a reasonable time to enable the party aggrieved to obtain a writ of certiorari from the Supreme Court. The stay may be granted by a judge of the court rendering the judgment or decree or by a justice of the Supreme Court, and may be conditioned on the giving of security, approved by such judge or justice, that if the aggrieved party fails to make application for such writ within the period allotted therefor, or fails to obtain an order granting his application, or fails to make his plea good in the Supreme Court, he shall answer for all damages and costs which the other party may sustain by reason of the stay.

(g) The time for application for a writ of certiorari to review a decision of the United States Court of Appeals for the Armed Forces shall be as prescribed by rules of the Supreme Court.

(As amended May 24, 1949, c. 139, § 106, 63 Stat. 104; Dec. 6, 1983, Pub.L. 98–209, § 10(b), 97 Stat. 1406; June 27, 1988, Pub.L. 100–352, § 5(b), 102 Stat. 663; Oct. 5, 1994, Pub.L. 103–337, Div. A, Title IX, § 924(d)(1)(C), 108 Stat. 2832.)

§ 2104. Reviews of State court decisions

A review by the Supreme Court of a judgment or decree of a State court shall be conducted in the same manner and under the same regulations, and shall have the same effect, as if the judgment or decree reviewed had been rendered in a court of the United States.

(As amended June 27, 1988, Pub.L. 100–352, § 5(d)(1), 102 Stat. 663.)

§ 2105. Scope of review; abatement

There shall be no reversal in the Supreme Court or a court of appeals for error in ruling upon matters in abatement which do not involve jurisdiction.

§ 2106. Determination

The Supreme Court or any other court of appellate jurisdiction may affirm, modify, vacate, set aside or reverse any judgment, decree, or order of a court lawfully brought before it for review, and may remand the cause and direct the entry of such appropriate judgment, decree, or order, or require such further proceedings to be had as may be just under the circumstances.

§ 2107. Time for appeal to court of appeals

(a) Except as otherwise provided in this section, no appeal shall bring any judgment, order or decree in an action, suit or proceeding of a civil nature before a court of appeals for review unless notice of appeal is filed, within thirty days after the entry of such judgment, order or decree.

(b) In any such action, suit or proceeding in which the United States or an officer or agency thereof is a party, the time as to all parties shall be sixty days from such entry.

(c) The district court may, upon motion filed not later than 30 days after the expiration of the time otherwise set for bringing appeal, extend the time for appeal upon a showing of excusable neglect or good cause. In addition, if the district court finds—

(1) that a party entitled to notice of the entry of a judgment or order did not receive such notice from the clerk or any party within 21 days of its entry, and

(2) that no party would be prejudiced,

the district court may, upon motion filed within 180 days after entry of the judgment or order or within 7 days after receipt of such notice, whichever is earlier, reopen the time for appeal for a period of 14 days from the date of entry of the order reopening the time for appeal.

(d) This section shall not apply to bankruptcy matters or other proceedings under Title 11.

(As amended May 24, 1949, c. 139, §§ 107, 108, 63 Stat. 104; Dec. 9, 1991, Pub.L. 102–198, § 12, 105 Stat. 1627.)

§ 2111. Harmless error

On the hearing of any appeal or writ of certiorari in any case, the court shall give judgment after an examination of the record without regard to errors or defects which do not affect the substantial rights of the parties.

(Added May 24, 1949, c. 139, § 110, 63 Stat. 105.)

§ 2201. Creation of remedy

(a) In a case of actual controversy within its jurisdiction, except with respect to Federal taxes other than actions brought under section 7428 of the Internal Revenue Code of 1986, a proceeding under section 505 or 1146 of title 11, or in any civil action involving an antidumping or countervailing duty proceeding regarding a class or kind of merchandise of a free trade area country (as defined in section 516A(f)(10) of the Tariff Act of 1930), as determined by the administering authority, any court of the United States, upon the filing of an appropriate pleading, may declare the rights and other legal relations of any interested party seeking such declaration, whether or not further relief is or could be sought. Any such declaration shall have the force and effect of a final judgment or decree and shall be reviewable as such.

(b) For limitations on actions brought with respect to drug patents see section 505 or 512 of the Federal Food, Drug, and Cosmetic Act.

(As amended May 24, 1949, c. 139, § 111, 63 Stat. 105; Aug. 28, 1954, c. 1033, 68 Stat. 890; July 7, 1958, Pub.L. 85–508, § 12(p), 72 Stat. 349; Oct. 4, 1976, Pub.L. 94–455, Title XIII, § 1306(b)(8), 90 Stat. 1719; Nov. 6, 1978, Pub.L. 95–598, Title II, § 249, 92 Stat. 2672; Sept. 24, 1984, Pub.L. 98–417, Title I, § 106, 98 Stat. 1597; Sept. 28, 1988, Pub.L. 100–449, Title IV, § 402(c), 102 Stat. 1584; Nov. 16, 1988, Pub.L. 100–670, Title I, § 107(b), 102 Stat. 3984; Dec. 8, 1993, Pub.L. 103–182, Title IV, § 414(b), 107 Stat. 2147.)

§ 2202. Further relief

Further necessary or proper relief based on a declaratory judgment or decree may be granted, after reasonable notice and hearing, against any adverse party whose rights have been determined by such judgment.

§ 2283. Stay of State court proceedings

A court of the United States may not grant an injunction to stay proceedings in a State court except as expressly authorized by Act of Congress, or where necessary in aid of its jurisdiction, or to protect or effectuate its judgments.

§ 2284. Three-judge court; when required; composition; procedure

(a) A district court of three judges shall be convened when otherwise required by Act of Congress, or when an action is filed challenging the constitutionality of the apportionment of congressional districts or the apportionment of any statewide legislative body.

(b) In any action required to be heard and determined by a district court of three judges under subsection (a) of this section, the composition and procedure of the court shall be as follows:

(1) Upon the filing of a request for three judges, the judge to whom the request is presented shall, unless he determines that three judges are not required, immediately notify the chief judge of the circuit, who shall designate two other judges, at least one of whom shall be a circuit judge. The judges so designated, and the judge to whom the request was presented, shall serve as members of the court to hear and determine the action or proceeding.

(2) If the action is against a State, or officer or agency thereof, at least five days' notice of hearing of the action shall be given by registered or certified mail to the Governor and attorney general of the State.

(3) A single judge may conduct all proceedings except the trial, and enter all orders permitted by the rules of civil procedure except as provided in this subsection. He may grant a temporary restraining order on a specific finding, based on evidence submitted, that specified irreparable damage will result if the order is not granted, which order, unless previously revoked by the district judge, shall remain in force only until the hearing and determination by the district court of three judges of an application for a preliminary injunction. A single judge shall not appoint a master, or order a reference, or hear and determine any application for a preliminary or permanent injunction or motion to vacate such an injunction, or enter judgment on the merits. Any action of a single judge may be reviewed by the full court at any time before final judgment.

(As amended June 11, 1960, Pub.L. 86–507, § 1(19), 74 Stat. 201; Aug. 12, 1976, Pub.L. 94–381, § 3, 90 Stat. 1119; Nov. 8, 1984, Pub.L. 98–620, Title IV, § 402(29)(E), 98 Stat. 3359.)

§ 2361. Process and procedure

In any civil action of interpleader or in the nature of interpleader under section 1335 of this title, a district court may issue its process for all claimants and enter its order restraining them from instituting or prosecuting any proceeding in any State or United States court affecting the property, instrument or obligation involved in the interpleader action until further order of the court. Such process and order shall be returnable at such time as the court or judge thereof directs, and shall be addressed to and served by the United States marshals for the respective districts where the claimants reside or may be found.

Such district court shall hear and determine the case, and may discharge the plaintiff from further liability, make the injunction permanent, and make all appropriate orders to enforce its judgment.

(As amended May 24, 1949, c. 139, § 117, 63 Stat. 105.)

§ 2401. Time for commencing action against United States

(a) Except as provided by the Contract Disputes Act of 1978, every civil action commenced against the United States shall be barred unless the complaint is filed within six years after the right of action first accrues. The action of any person under legal disability or beyond the seas at the time the claim accrues may be commenced within three years after the disability ceases.

(b) A tort claim against the United States shall be forever barred unless it is presented in writing to the appropriate Federal agency within two years after such claim accrues or unless action is begun within six months after the date of mailing, by certified or registered mail, of notice of final denial of the claim by the agency to which it was presented.

(As amended Apr. 25, 1949, c. 92, § 1, 63 Stat. 62; Sept. 8, 1959, Pub.L. 86–238, § 1(3), 73 Stat. 472; July 18, 1966, Pub.L. 89–506, § 7, 80 Stat. 307; Nov. 1, 1978, Pub.L. 95–563, § 14(b), 92 Stat. 2389.)

§ 2402. Jury trial in actions against United States

Subject to chapter 179 of this title, any action against the United States under section 1346 shall be tried by the court without a jury, except that any action against the United States under section 1346(a)(1) shall, at the request of either party to such action, be tried by the court with a jury.

(As amended July 30, 1954, c. 648, § 2(a), 68 Stat. 589; Oct. 26, 1996, Pub.L. 104–331, § 3(b)(3), 110 Stat. 4069.)

§ 2403. Intervention by United States or a State; constitutional question

(a) In any action, suit or proceeding in a court of the United States to which the United States or any agency, officer or employee thereof is not a party, wherein the constitutionality of any Act of Congress affecting the public interest is drawn in question, the court shall certify such fact to the Attorney General, and shall permit the United States to intervene for presentation of evidence, if evidence is otherwise admissible in the case, and for argument on the question of constitutionality. The United States shall, subject to the applicable provisions of law, have all the rights of a party and be subject to all liabilities of a party as to court costs to the extent necessary for a proper presentation of the facts and law relating to the question of constitutionality.

(b) In any action, suit, or proceeding in a court of the United States to which a State or any agency, officer, or employee thereof is not a party, wherein the constitutionality of any statute of that State affecting the public interest is drawn in question, the court shall certify such fact to the attorney general of the State, and shall permit the State to intervene for presentation of evidence, if evidence is otherwise admissible in the case, and for argument on the question of constitutionality. The State shall, subject to the applicable provisions of law, have all the rights of a party and be subject to all liabilities of a party as to court costs to the extent necessary for a proper presentation of the facts and law relating to the question of constitutionality.

(As amended Aug. 12, 1976, Pub.L. 94–381, § 5, 90 Stat. 1120.)

§ 2404. Death of defendant in damage action

A civil action for damages commenced by or on behalf of the United States or in which it is interested shall not abate on the death of a defendant but shall survive and be enforceable against his estate as well as against surviving defendants.

§ 2408. Security not required of United States

Security for damages or costs shall not be required of the United States, any department or agency thereof or any party acting under the direction of any such department or agency on the issuance of process or the institution or prosecution of any proceeding.

Costs taxable, under other Acts of Congress, against the United States or any such department, agency or party shall be paid out of the contingent fund of the department or agency which directed the proceedings to be instituted.

§ 2411. Interest

In any judgment of any court rendered (whether against the United States, a collector or deputy collector of internal revenue, a former collector or deputy collector, or the personal representative in case of death) for any overpayment in respect of any internal-revenue tax, interest shall be allowed at the overpayment rate established under section 6621 of the Internal Revenue Code of 1986 upon the amount of the overpayment, from the date of the payment or collection thereof to a date preceding the date of the refund check by not more than thirty days, such date to be determined by the Commissioner of Internal Revenue. The Commissioner is authorized to tender by check payment of any such judgment, with interest as herein provided, at any time after such judgment becomes final, whether or not a claim for such payment has been duly filed, and such tender shall stop the running of interest, whether or not such refund check is accepted by the judgment creditor.

(As amended May 24, 1949, c. 139, § 120, 63 Stat. 106; Jan. 3, 1975, Pub.L. 93–625, § 7(a)(2), 88 Stat. 2115; Apr. 2, 1982, Pub.L. 97–164, Title III, § 302(b), 96 Stat. 56; Oct. 22, 1986, Pub.L. 99–514, § 2, Title XV, § 1511(c)(18), 100 Stat. 2095, 2746.)

§ 2412. Costs and fees

(a)(1) Except as otherwise specifically provided by statute, a judgment for costs, as enumerated in section 1920 of this title, but not including the fees and expenses of attorneys, may be awarded to the prevailing party in any civil action brought by or against the United States or any agency or any official of the United States acting in his or her official capacity in any court having jurisdiction of such action. A judgment for costs when taxed against the United States shall, in an amount established by statute, court rule, or order, be limited to reimbursing in whole or in part the prevailing party for the costs incurred by such party in the litigation.

(2) A judgment for costs, when awarded in favor of the United States in an action brought by the United States, may include an amount equal to the filing fee prescribed under section 1914(a) of this title. The preceding sentence shall not be construed as requiring the United States to pay any filing fee.

(b) Unless expressly prohibited by statute, a court may award reasonable fees and expenses of attorneys, in addition to the costs which may be awarded pursuant to subsection (a), to the prevailing party in any civil action brought by or against the United States or any agency or any official of the United States acting in his or her official capacity in any court having jurisdiction of such action. The United States shall be liable for such fees and expenses to the same extent that any other party would be liable under the common law or under the terms of any statute which specifically provides for such an award.

(c)(1) Any judgment against the United States or any agency and any official of the United States acting in his or her official capacity for costs pursuant to subsection (a) shall be paid as provided in sections 2414 and 2517 of this title and shall be in addition to any relief provided in the judgment.

(2) Any judgment against the United States or any agency and any official of the United States acting in his or her official capacity for fees and expenses of attorneys pursuant to subsection (b) shall be paid as provided in sections 2414 and 2517 of this title, except that if the basis for the award is a finding that the United States acted in bad faith, then the award shall be paid by any agency found to have acted in bad faith and shall be in addition to any relief provided in the judgment.

(d)(1)(A) Except as otherwise specifically provided by statute, a court shall award to a prevailing party other than the United States fees and other expenses, in addition to any costs awarded pursuant to subsection (a), incurred by that party in any civil action (other than cases sounding in tort), including proceedings for judicial review of agency action, brought by or against the United States in any court having jurisdiction of that action, unless the court finds that the position of the United States was substantially justified or that special circumstances make an award unjust.

(B) A party seeking an award of fees and other expenses shall, within thirty days of final judgment in the action, submit to the court an application for fees and other expenses which shows that the party is a prevailing party and is eligible to receive an award under this subsection, and the amount sought, including an itemized statement from any attorney or expert witness representing or appearing in behalf of the party stating the actual time expended and the rate at which fees and other expenses were computed. The party shall also allege that the position of the United States was not substantially justified. Whether or not the position of the United States was substantially justified shall be determined on the basis of the record (including the record with respect to the action or failure to act by the agency upon which the civil action is based) which is made in the civil action for which fees and other expenses are sought.

(C) The court, in its discretion, may reduce the amount to be awarded pursuant to this subsection, or deny an award, to the extent that the prevailing party during the course of the proceedings engaged in conduct which unduly and unreasonably protracted the final resolution of the matter in controversy.

(D) If, in a civil action brought by the United States or a proceeding for judicial review of an adversary adjudication described in section 504(a)(4) of title 5, the demand by the United States is substantially in excess of the judgment finally obtained by the United States and is unreasonable when compared with such judgment, under the facts and circumstances of the case, the court shall award to the party the fees and other expenses related to defending against the excessive demand, unless the party has committed a willful violation of law or otherwise acted in bad faith, or special circumstances make an award unjust. Fees and expenses awarded under this subparagraph shall be paid only as a consequence of appropriations provided in advance.

(2) For the purposes of this subsection—

(A) "fees and other expenses" includes the reasonable expenses of expert witnesses, the reasonable cost of any study, analysis, engineering report, test, or project which is found by the court to be necessary for the preparation of the party's case, and reasonable attorney fees (The amount of fees awarded under this subsection shall be based upon prevailing market rates for the kind and quality of the services furnished, except that (i) no expert witness shall be compensated at a rate in excess of the highest rate of compensation for expert witnesses paid by the United States; and (ii) attorney fees shall not be awarded in excess of $125 per hour unless the court determines that an increase in the cost of living or a special factor, such as the limited availability of qualified attorneys for the proceedings involved, justifies a higher fee.);

(B) "party" means (i) an individual whose net worth did not exceed $2,000,000 at the time the civil action was filed, or (ii) any owner of an unincorporated business, or any partnership, corporation, association, unit of local government, or organization, the net worth of which did not exceed $7,000,000 at the time the civil action was filed, and which had not more than 500 employees at the time the civil action was filed; except that an organization described in section 501(c)(3) of the Internal Revenue Code of 1986 (26 U.S.C. 501(c)(3)) exempt from taxation under section 501(a) of such Code, or a cooperative association as defined in section 15(a) of the Agricultural Marketing Act (12 U.S.C. 1141j(a)), may be a party regardless of the net worth of such organization or cooperative association or for purposes of subsection (d)(1)(D), a small entity as defined in section 601 of Title 5;

(C) "United States" includes any agency and any official of the United States acting in his or her official capacity;

(D) "position of the United States" means, in addition to the position taken by the United States in the civil action, the action or failure to act by the agency upon which the civil action is based; except that fees and expenses may not be awarded to a party for any portion of the litigation in which the party has unreasonably protracted the proceedings;

(E) "civil action brought by or against the United States" includes an appeal by a party, other than the United States, from a decision of a contracting officer rendered pursuant to a disputes clause in a contract with the Government or pursuant to the Contract Disputes Act of 1978;

(F) "court" includes the United States Court of Federal Claims and the United States Court of Appeals for Veterans Claims;

(G) "final judgment" means a judgment that is final and not appealable, and includes an order of settlement;

(H) "prevailing party", in the case of eminent domain proceedings, means a party who obtains a final judgment (other than by settlement), exclusive of interest, the amount of which is at least as close to the highest valuation of the property involved that is attested to at trial on behalf of the property owner as it is to the highest valuation of the property involved that is attested to at trial on behalf of the Government; and

(I) "demand" means the express demand of the United States which led to the adversary adjudication, but shall not include a recitation of the maximum statutory penalty (i) in the complaint, or (ii) elsewhere when accompanied by an express demand for a lesser amount.

(3) In awarding fees and other expenses under this subsection to a prevailing party in any action for judicial review of an adversary adjudication, as defined in subsection (b)(1)(C) of section 504 of title 5, United States Code, or an adversary adjudication subject to the Contract Disputes Act of 1978, the court shall include in that award fees and other expenses to the same extent authorized in subsection (a) of such section, unless the court finds that during such adversary adjudication the position of the United States was substantially justified, or that special circumstances make an award unjust.

(4) Fees and other expenses awarded under this subsection to a party shall be paid by any agency over which the party prevails from any funds made available to the agency by appropriation or otherwise.

[**(5)** Repealed. Pub.L. 104–66, Title I, § 1091(b), Dec. 21, 1995, 109 Stat. 722]

(e) The provisions of this section shall not apply to any costs, fees, and other expenses in connection with any proceeding to which section 7430 of the Internal Revenue Code of 1986 applies (determined without regard to subsections (b) and (f) of such section). Nothing in the preceding sentence shall prevent the awarding under subsection (a) of section 2412 of title 28, United States Code, of costs enumerated in section 1920 of such title (as in effect on October 1, 1981).

(f) If the United States appeals an award of costs or fees and other expenses made against the United States under this section and the award is affirmed in whole or in part, interest shall be paid on the amount of the award as affirmed. Such interest shall be computed at the rate determined under section 1961(a) of this title, and shall run from the date of the award through the day before the date of the mandate of affirmance.

(June 25, 1948, c. 646, 62 Stat. 973; July 18, 1966, Pub.L. 89–507, § 1, 80 Stat. 308; Oct. 21, 1980, Pub. L. 96–481, Title II, § 204(a), (c), 94 Stat. 2327, 2329; Sept. 3, 1982, Pub. L. 97–248, Title II, § 292(c), 96 Stat. 574; Aug. 5, 1985, Pub. L. 99–80, §§ 2, 6(a), (b)(2), 99 Stat. 184, 186; Oct. 22, 1986, Pub.L. 99–514, § 2, 100 Stat. 2095; Oct. 29, 1992, Pub.L. 102–572, Title III, § 301(a), Title V, §§ 502(b), 506(a), Title IX, § 902(b)(1), 106 Stat. 4511–4513, 4516; Dec. 21, 1995, Pub.L. 104–66, Title I, § 1091(b), 109 Stat. 722; Mar. 29, 1996, Pub.L. 104–121, Title II, § 232, 110 Stat. 863; Pub.L 105–368, Title V, § 521(b)(1)(B), Nov. 10, 1998, 112 Stat. 3342.)

§ 2413. Executions in favor of United States

A writ of execution on a judgment obtained for the use of the United States in any court thereof shall be issued from and made returnable to the court which rendered the judgment, but may be executed in any other State, in any Territory, or in the District of Columbia.

§ 2414. Payment of judgments and compromise settlements

Except as provided by the Contract Disputes Act of 1978, payment of final judgments rendered by a district court or the Court of International Trade against the United States shall be made on settlements by the Secretary of the Treasury. Payment of final judgments rendered by a State or foreign court or tribunal against the United States, or against its agencies or officials upon obligations or liabilities of the United States, shall be made on settlements by the Secretary of the Treasury after certification by the Attorney General that it is in the interest of the United States to pay the same.

Whenever the Attorney General determines that no appeal shall be taken from a judgment or that no further review will be sought from a decision affirming the same, he shall so certify and the judgment shall be deemed final.

Except as otherwise provided by law, compromise settlements of claims referred to the Attorney General for defense of imminent litigation or suits against the United States, or against its agencies or officials upon obligations or liabilities of the United States, made by the Attorney General or any person authorized by him, shall be settled and paid in a manner similar to judgments in like causes and appropriations or funds available for the payment of such judgments are hereby made available for the payment of such compromise settlements.

(As amended Aug. 30, 1961, Pub.L. 87–187, § 1, 75 Stat. 415; Nov. 1, 1978, Pub.L. 95–563, § 14(d), 92 Stat. 2390; Oct. 10, 1980, Pub.L. 96–417, Title V, § 512, 94 Stat. 1744; Oct. 19, 1996, Pub.L. 104–316, Title II, § 202(k), 110 Stat. 3843.)

§ 2415. Time for commencing actions brought by the United States

(a) Subject to the provisions of section 2416 of this title, and except as otherwise provided by Congress, every action for money damages brought by the United States or an officer or agency thereof which is founded upon any contract express or implied in law or fact, shall be barred unless the complaint is filed within six years after the right of action accrues or within one year after final decisions have been rendered in applicable administrative proceedings required by contract or by law, whichever is later: *Provided,* That in the event of later partial payment or written acknowledgment of debt, the right of action shall be deemed to accrue again at the time of each such payment or acknowledgment: *Provided further,* That an action for money damages brought by the United

States for or on behalf of a recognized tribe, band or group of American Indians shall not be barred unless the complaint is filed more than six years and ninety days after the right of action accrued: *Provided further,* That an action for money damages which accrued on the date of enactment of this Act in accordance with subsection (g) brought by the United States for or on behalf of a recognized tribe, band, or group of American Indians, or on behalf of an individual Indian whose land is held in trust or restricted status, shall not be barred unless the complaint is filed sixty days after the date of publication of the list required by section 4(c) of the Indian Claims Limitation Act of 1982: *Provided,* That, for those claims that are on either of the two lists published pursuant to the Indian Claims Limitation Act of 1982, any right of action shall be barred unless the complaint is filed within (1) one year after the Secretary of the Interior has published in the Federal Register a notice rejecting such claim or (2) three years after the date the Secretary of the Interior has submitted legislation or legislative report to Congress to resolve such claim or more than two years after a final decision has been rendered in applicable administrative proceedings required by contract or by law, whichever is later.

(b) Subject to the provisions of section 2416 of this title, and except as otherwise provided by Congress, every action for money damages brought by the United States or an officer or agency thereof which is founded upon a tort shall be barred unless the complaint is filed within three years after the right of action first accrues: *Provided,* That an action to recover damages resulting from a trespass on lands of the United States; an action to recover damages resulting from fire to such lands; an action to recover for diversion of money paid under a grant program; and an action for conversion of property of the United States may be brought within six years after the right of action accrues, except that such actions for or on behalf of a recognized tribe, band or group of American Indians, including actions relating to allotted trust or restricted Indian lands, may be brought within six years and ninety days after the right of action accrues, except that such actions for or on behalf of a recognized tribe, band or group of American Indians, including actions relating to allotted trust or restricted Indian lands, or on behalf of an individual Indian whose land is held in trust or restricted status which accrued on the date of enactment of this Act in accordance with subsection (g) may be brought on or before sixty days after the date of the publication of the list required by section 4(c) of the Indian Claims Limitation Act of 1982: *Provided,* That, for those claims that are on either of the two lists published pursuant to the Indian Claims Limitation Act of 1982, any right of action shall be barred unless the complaint is filed within (1) one year after the Secretary of the Interior has published in the Federal Register a notice rejecting such claim or (2) three years after the Secretary of the Interior has submitted legislation or legislative report to Congress to resolve such claim.

(c) Nothing herein shall be deemed to limit the time for bringing an action to establish the title to, or right of possession of, real or personal property.

(d) Subject to the provisions of section 2416 of this title and except as otherwise provided by Congress, every action for the recovery of money erroneously paid to or on behalf of any civilian employee of any agency of the United States or to or on behalf of any member or dependent of any member of the uniformed services of the United States, incident to the employment or services of such employee or member, shall be barred unless the complaint is filed within six years after the right of action accrues: *Provided,* That in the event of later partial payment or written acknowledgment of debt, the right of action shall be deemed to accrue again at the time of each such payment or acknowledgment.

(e) In the event that any action to which this section applies is timely brought and is thereafter dismissed without prejudice, the action may be recommenced within one year after such dismissal, regardless of whether the action would otherwise then be barred by this section. In any action so recommenced the defendant shall not be barred from interposing any claim which would not have been barred in the original action.

(f) The provisions of this section shall not prevent the assertion, in an action against the United States or an officer or agency thereof, of any claim of the United States or an officer or agency thereof against an opposing party, a co-party, or a third party that arises out of the transaction or occurrence that is the subject matter of the opposing party's claim. A claim of the United States or an officer or agency thereof that does not arise out of the transaction or occurrence that is the subject matter of the opposing party's claim may, if time-barred, be asserted only by way of offset and may be allowed in an amount not to exceed the amount of the opposing party's recovery.

(g) Any right of action subject to the provisions of this section which accrued prior to the date of enactment of this Act shall, for purposes of this section, be deemed to have accrued on the date of enactment of this Act.

(h) Nothing in this Act shall apply to actions brought under the Internal Revenue Code or incidental to the collection of taxes imposed by the United States.

(i) The provisions of this section shall not prevent the United States or an officer or agency thereof from collecting any claim of the United States by means of administrative offset, in accordance with section 3716 of title 31.

(Added Pub.L. 89–505, § 1, July 18, 1966, 80 Stat. 304, and amended Pub.L. 92–353, July 18, 1972, 86 Stat. 499; Pub.L. 92–485, Oct. 13, 1972, 86 Stat. 803; Pub.L. 95–64, July 11, 1977, 91 Stat. 268; Pub.L. 95–103, Aug. 15, 1977, 91 Stat. 842; Pub.L. 96–217, § 1, Mar. 27, 1980, 94 Stat. 126; Pub.L. 97–365, § 9, Oct. 25, 1982, 96 Stat. 1754; Pub.L. 97–394, Title I, § 2, Dec. 30, 1982, 96 Stat. 1976; Pub.L. 97–452, § 2(d)(2), Jan. 12, 1983, 96 Stat. 2478; Pub.L. 98–250, § 4(a), Apr. 3, 1984, 98 Stat. 118.)

§ 2416. Time for commencing actions brought by the United States—Exclusions

For the purpose of computing the limitations periods established in section 2415, there shall be excluded all periods during which—

(a) the defendant or the res is outside the United States, its territories and possessions, the District of Columbia, or the Commonwealth of Puerto Rico; or

(b) the defendant is exempt from legal process because of infancy, mental incompetence, diplomatic immunity, or for any other reason; or

(c) facts material to the right of action are not known and reasonably could not be known by an official of the United States charged with the responsibility to act in the circumstances; or

(d) the United States is in a state of war declared pursuant to article I, section 8, of the Constitution of the United States.

(Added Pub.L. 89–505, § 1, July 18, 1966, 80 Stat. 305.)

PART IX

CONSTITUTION OF THE UNITED STATES

Preamble

We the People of the United States, in Order to form a more perfect Union, establish Justice, insure domestic Tranquility, provide for the common defence, promote the general Welfare, and secure the Blessings of Liberty to ourselves and our Posterity, do ordain and establish this Constitution for the United States of America.

Article I

Section 1. All legislative Powers herein granted shall be vested in a Congress of the United States, which shall consist of a Senate and House of Representatives.

Section 2. [1] The House of Representatives shall be composed of Members chosen every second Year by the People of the several States, and the Electors in each State shall have the Qualifications requisite for Electors of the most numerous Branch of the State Legislature.

[2] No Person shall be a Representative who shall not have attained to the Age of twenty five Years, and been seven Years a Citizen of the United States, and who shall not, when elected, be an Inhabitant of that State in which he shall be chosen.

[3] Representatives and direct Taxes shall be apportioned among the several States which may be included within this Union, according to their respective Numbers, which shall be determined by adding to the whole Number of free Persons, including those bound to Service for a Term of Years, and excluding Indians not taxed, three fifths of all other Persons. The actual Enumeration shall be made within three Years after the first Meeting of the Congress of the United States, and within every subsequent Term of ten Years, in such Manner as they shall by Law direct. The Number of Representatives shall not exceed one for every thirty Thousand, but each State shall have at Least one Representative; and until such enumeration shall be made, the State of New Hampshire shall be entitled to chuse three, Massachusetts eight, Rhode Island and Providence Plantations one, Connecticut five, New York six, New Jersey four, Pennsylvania eight, Delaware one, Maryland six, Virginia ten, North Carolina five, South Carolina five, and Georgia three.

[4] When vacancies happen in the Representation from any State, the Executive Authority thereof shall issue Writs of Election to fill such Vacancies.

[5] The House of Representatives shall chuse their Speaker and other Officers; and shall have the sole Power of Impeachment.

Section 3. [1] The Senate of the United States shall be composed of two Senators from each State, chosen by the Legislature thereof, for six Years; and each Senator shall have one Vote.

[2] Immediately after they shall be assembled in Consequence of the first Election, they shall be divided as equally as may be into three Classes. The Seats of the Senators of the first Class shall be vacated at the Expiration of the Second Year, of the second Class at the Expiration of the fourth Year, and of the third Class at the Expiration of the sixth Year, so that one third may be chosen every second Year; and if Vacancies happen by Resignation, or otherwise, during the Recess of the Legislature of any State, the Executive thereof may make temporary Appointments until the next Meeting of the Legislature, which shall then fill such Vacancies.

[3] No Person shall be a Senator who shall not have attained to the Age of thirty Years, and been nine Years a Citizen of the United States, and who shall not, when elected, by an Inhabitant of that State for which he shall be chosen.

[4] The Vice President of the United States shall be President of the Senate, but shall have no Vote, unless they be equally divided.

[5] The Senate shall chuse their other Officers, and also a President pro tempore, in the Absence of the Vice President, or when he shall exercise the Office of President of the United States.

[6] The Senate shall have the sole Power to try all Impeachments. When sitting for that Purpose, they shall be on Oath or Affirmation. When the President of the United States is tried, the Chief Justice shall preside: And no Person shall be convicted without the Concurrence of two thirds of the Members present.

[7] Judgment in Cases of Impeachment shall not extend further than to removal from Office, and disqualification to hold and enjoy any Office of honor, Trust, or Profit under the United States: but the Party convicted shall nevertheless be liable and subject to Indictment, Trial, Judgment, and Punishment, according to Law.

Section 4. [1] The Times, Places and Manner of holding Elections for Senators and Representatives, shall be prescribed in each State by the Legislature thereof; but the Congress may at any time by Law make or alter such Regulations, except as to the Places of chusing Senators.

[2] The Congress shall assemble at least once in every Year, and such Meeting shall be on the first Monday in December, unless they shall by Law appoint a different Day.

Section 5. [1] Each House shall be the Judge of the Elections, Returns, and Qualifications of its own Members, and a Majority of each shall constitute a Quorum to do Business; but a smaller Number may adjourn from day to day, and may be authorized to compel the Attendance of absent Members, in such Manner, and under such Penalties as each House may provide.

[2] Each House may determine the Rules of its Proceedings, punish its Members for disorderly Behavior, and, with the Concurrence of two thirds, expel a Member.

[3] Each House shall keep a Journal of its Proceedings, and from time to time publish the same, excepting such Parts as may in their Judgment require Secrecy; and the Yeas and Nays of the Members of either House on any question shall, at the Desire of one fifth of those Present, be entered on the Journal.

[4] Neither House, during the Session of Congress, shall without the Consent of the other, adjourn for more than three days, nor to any other Place than that in which the two Houses shall be sitting.

Section 6. [1] The Senators and Representatives shall receive a Compensation for their Services, to be ascertained by Law, and paid out of the Treasury of the United States. They shall in all Cases, except Treason, Felony and Breach of the Peace, be privileged from Arrest during their Attendance at the Session of their respective Houses, and in going to and returning from the same; and for any Speech or Debate in either House, they shall not be questioned in any other Place.

[2] No Senator or Representative shall, during the Time for which he was elected, be appointed to any civil Office under the Authority of the United States, which shall have been created, or the Emoluments whereof shall have been increased during such time; and no Person holding any Office under the United States, shall be a Member of either House during his Continuance in Office.

Section 7. [1] All Bills for raising Revenue shall originate in the House of Representatives; but the Senate may propose or concur with Amendments as on other Bills.

[2] Every Bill which shall have passed the House of Representatives and the Senate, shall, before it become a Law, be presented to the President of the United States; If he approve he shall sign it, but if not he shall return it, with his Objections to the House in which it shall have originated, who shall enter the Objections at large on their Journal, and proceed to reconsider it. If after such Reconsideration two thirds of that House shall agree to pass the Bill, it shall be sent together with the Objections, to the other House, by which it shall likewise be reconsidered, and if approved by two thirds of that House, it shall become a Law. But in all such Cases the Votes of both Houses shall be determined by yeas and Nays, and the Names of the Persons voting for and against the Bill shall be entered on the Journal of each House respectively. If any Bill shall not be returned by the President within ten Days (Sundays excepted) after it shall have been presented to him, the Same shall be a Law, in like Manner as if he had signed it, unless the Congress by their Adjournment prevent its Return in which Case it shall not be a Law.

[3] Every Order, Resolution, or Vote, to Which the Concurrence of the Senate and House of Representatives may be necessary (except on a question of Adjournment) shall be presented to the President of the United States; and before the Same shall take Effect, shall be approved by him, or being disapproved by him, shall be repassed by two thirds of the Senate and House of Representatives, according to the Rules and Limitations prescribed in the Case of a Bill.

Section 8. [1] The Congress shall have Power To lay and collect Taxes, Duties, Imposts and Excises, to pay the Debts and provide for the common Defence and general Welfare of the United States; but all Duties, Imposts and Excises shall be uniform throughout the United States;

[2] To borrow money on the credit of the United States;

[3] To regulate Commerce with foreign Nations, and among the several States, and with the Indian Tribes;

[4] To establish an uniform Rule of Naturalization, and uniform Laws on the subject of Bankruptcies throughout the United States;

[5] To coin Money, regulate the Value thereof, and of foreign Coin, and fix the Standard of Weights and Measures;

[6] To provide for the Punishment of counterfeiting the Securities and current Coin of the United States;

[7] To Establish Post Offices and Post Roads;

[8] To promote the Progress of Science and useful Arts, by securing for limited Times to Authors and Inventors the exclusive Right to their respective Writings and Discoveries;

[9] To constitute Tribunals inferior to the supreme Court;

[10] To define and punish Piracies and Felonies committed on the high Seas, and Offenses against the Law of Nations;

[11] To declare War, grant Letters of Marque and Reprisal, and make Rules concerning Captures on Land and Water;

[12] To raise and support Armies, but no Appropriation of Money to that Use shall be for a longer Term than two Years;

[13] To provide and maintain a Navy;

[14] To make Rules for the Government and Regulation of the land and naval Forces;

[15] To provide for calling forth the Militia to execute the Laws of the Union, suppress Insurrections and repel Invasions;

[16] To provide for organizing, arming, and disciplining, the Militia, and for governing such Part of them as may be employed in the Service of the United States, reserving to the States respectively, the Appointment of the Officers, and the Authority of training the Militia according to the discipline prescribed by Congress;

[17] To exercise exclusive Legislation in all Cases whatsoever, over such District (not exceeding ten Miles square) as may, by Cession of particular States, and the Acceptance of Congress, become the Seat of the Government of the United States, and to exercise like Authority over all Places purchased by the Consent of the Legislature of the State in which the Same shall be, for the Erection of Forts, Magazines, Arsenals, dock-Yards, and other needful Buildings;—And

[18] To make all Laws which shall be necessary and proper for carrying into Execution the foregoing Powers, and all other Powers vested by this Constitution in the Government of the United States, or in any Department or Officer thereof.

Section 9. [1] The Migration or Importation of Such Persons as any of the States now existing shall think proper to admit, shall not be prohibited by the Congress prior to the Year one thousand eight hundred and eight, but a Tax or duty may be imposed on such Importation, not exceeding ten dollars for each Person.

[2] The privilege of the Writ of Habeas Corpus shall not be suspended, unless when in Cases of Rebellion or Invasion the public Safety may require it.

[3] No Bill of Attainder or ex post facto Law shall be passed.

[4] No Capitation, or other direct, Tax shall be laid, unless in Proportion to the Census or Enumeration herein before directed to be taken.

[5] No Tax or Duty shall be laid on Articles exported from any State.

[6] No Preference shall be given by any Regulation of Commerce or Revenue to the Ports of one State over those of another: nor shall Vessels bound to, or from, one State be obliged to enter, clear, or pay Duties in another.

[7] No money shall be drawn from the Treasury, but in Consequence of Appropriations made by Law; and a regular Statement and Account of the Receipts and Expenditures of all public Money shall be published from time to time.

[8] No Title of Nobility shall be granted by the United States: And no Person holding any Office of Profit or Trust under them, shall, without the Consent of the Congress, accept of any present, Emolument, Office, or Title, of any kind whatever, from any King, Prince, or foreign State.

Section 10. [1] No State shall enter into any Treaty, Alliance, or Confederation; grant Letters of Marque and Reprisal; coin Money; emit Bills of Credit; make any Thing but gold and silver Coin a Tender in Payment of Debts; pass any Bill of Attainder, ex post facto Law, or Law impairing the Obligation of Contracts, or grant any Title of Nobility.

[2] No State shall, without the Consent of the Congress, lay any Imposts or Duties on Imports or Exports, except what may be absolutely necessary for executing it's inspection Laws: and the net Produce of all Duties and Imposts, laid by any State on Imports or Exports, shall be for the Use of the Treasury of the United States; and all such Laws shall be subject to the Revision and Controul of the Congress.

[3] No State shall, without the Consent of Congress, lay any Duty of Tonnage, keep Troops, or Ships of War in time of Peace, enter into any Agreement or Compact with another State, or with a foreign Power, or engage in War, unless actually invaded, or in such imminent Danger as will not admit of delay.

ARTICLE II

Section 1. [1] The executive Power shall be vested in a President of the United States of America. He shall hold his Office during the Term of four Years, and, together with the Vice President, chosen for the same Term, be elected, as follows:

[2] Each State shall appoint, in such Manner as the Legislature thereof may direct, a Number of Electors, equal to the whole Number of Senators and Representatives to which the State may be entitled in the Congress; but no Senator or Representative, or Person holding an Office of Trust or Profit under the United States, shall be appointed an Elector.

[3] The Electors shall meet in their respective States, and vote by Ballot for two Persons, of whom one at least shall not be an Inhabitant of the same State with themselves. And they shall make a List of all the Persons voted for, and of the Number of Votes for each; which List they shall sign and certify, and transmit sealed to the Seat of the Government of the United States, directed to the President of the Senate. The President of the Senate shall, in the Presence of the Senate and House of Representatives, open all the Certificates, and the Votes shall then be counted. The Person having the greatest Number of Votes shall be the President, if such Number be a Majority of the whole Number of Electors appointed; and if there be more than one who have such Majority, and have an equal Number of Votes, then the House of Representatives shall immediately chuse by Ballot one of them for President; and if no Person have a Majority, then from the five highest on the List the said House shall in like Manner chuse the President. But in chusing the President, the Votes shall be taken by States the Representation from each State having one Vote; A quorum for this Purpose shall consist of a Member or Members from two thirds of the States, and a Majority of all the States shall be necessary to a Choice. In every Case, after the Choice of the President, the Person having the greater Number of Votes of the Electors shall be the Vice President. But if there should remain two or more who have equal Votes, the Senate shall chuse from them by Ballot the Vice President.

[4] The Congress may determine the Time of chusing the Electors, and the Day on which they shall give their Votes; which Day shall be the same throughout the United States.

[5] No person except a natural born Citizen, or a Citizen of the United States, at the time of the Adoption of this Constitution, shall be eligible to the Office of President; neither shall any Person be eligible to that Office who shall not have attained to the Age of thirty five Years, and been fourteen Years a Resident within the United States.

[6] In case of the removal of the President from Office, or of his Death, Resignation or Inability to discharge the Powers and Duties of the said Office, the Same shall devolve on the Vice President, and the Congress may by Law provide for the Case of Removal, Death, Resignation or Inability, both of the President and Vice President, declaring what Officer shall then act as President, and such Officer shall act accordingly, until the Disability be removed, or a President shall be elected.

[7] The President shall, at stated Times, receive for his Services, a Compensation, which shall neither be increased nor diminished during the Period for which he shall have been elected, and he shall not receive within that Period any other Emolument from the United States, or any of them.

[8] Before he enter on the Execution of his Office, he shall take the following Oath or Affirmation: "I do solemnly swear (or affirm) that I will faithfully execute the Office of President of the United States, and will to the best of my Ability, preserve, protect and defend the Constitution of the United States."

Section 2. [1] The President shall be Commander in Chief of the Army and Navy of the United States, and of the militia of the several States, when called into the actual Service of the United States; he may require the Opinion, in writing, of the principal

Officer in each of the Executive Departments, upon any Subject relating to the Duties of their respective Offices, and he shall have Power to grant Reprieves and Pardons for Offenses against the United States, except in Cases of Impeachment.

[2] He shall have Power, by and with the Advice and Consent of the Senate to make Treaties, provided two thirds of the Senators present concur; and he shall nominate, and by and with the Advice and Consent of the Senate, shall appoint Ambassadors, other public Ministers and Consuls, Judges of the supreme Court, and all other Officers of the United States, whose Appointments are not herein otherwise provided for, and which shall be established by Law; but the Congress may by Law vest the Appointment of such inferior Officers, as they think proper, in the President alone, in the Courts of Law, or in the Heads of Departments.

[3] The President shall have Power to fill up all Vacancies that may happen during the Recess of the Senate, by granting Commissions which shall expire at the End of their next Session.

Section 3. He shall from time to time give to the Congress Information of the State of the Union, and recommend to their Consideration such Measures as he shall judge necessary and expedient; he may, on extraordinary Occasions, convene both Houses, or either of them, and in Case of Disagreement between them, with Respect to the Time of Adjournment, he may adjourn them to such Time as he shall think proper; he shall receive Ambassadors and other public Ministers; he shall take Care that the Laws be faithfully executed, and shall Commission all the Officers of the United States.

Section 4. The President, Vice President and all civil Officers of the United States, shall be removed from Office on Impeachment for, and Conviction of, Treason, Bribery, or other high Crimes and Misdemeanors.

Article III

Section 1. The judicial Power of the United States, shall be vested in one supreme Court, and in such inferior Courts as the Congress may from time to time ordain and establish. The Judges, both of the supreme and inferior Courts, shall hold their Offices during good Behaviour, and shall, at stated Times, receive for their Services a Compensation, which shall not be diminished during their Continuance in Office.

Section 2. [1] The judicial Power shall extend to all Cases, in Law and Equity, arising under this Constitution, the Laws of the United States, and Treaties made, or which shall be made, under their Authority;—to all Cases affecting Ambassadors, other public Ministers and Consuls;—to all Cases of admiralty and maritime Jurisdiction;—to Controversies to which the United States shall be a Party;—to Controversies between two or more States;—between a State and Citizens of another State;—between Citizens of different States;—between Citizens of the same State claiming Lands under the Grants of different States, and between a State, or the Citizens thereof, and foreign States, Citizens or Subjects.

[2] In all Cases affecting Ambassadors, other public Ministers and Consuls, and those in which a State shall be a Party, the supreme Court shall have original Jurisdiction. In all the other Cases before mentioned, the supreme Court shall have appellate Jurisdiction, both as to Law and Fact, with such Exceptions, and under such Regulations as the Congress shall make.

[3] The trial of all Crimes, except in Cases of Impeachment, shall be by Jury; and such Trial shall be held in the State where the said Crimes shall have been committed; but when not committed within any State, the Trial shall be at such Place or Places as the Congress may by Law have directed.

Section 3. [1] Treason against the United States, shall consist only in levying War against them, or, in adhering to their Enemies, giving them Aid and Comfort. No Person shall be convicted of Treason unless on the Testimony of two Witnesses to the same overt Act, or on Confession in open Court.

[2] The Congress shall have Power to declare the Punishment of Treason, but no Attainder of Treason shall work Corruption of Blood, or Forfeiture except during the Life of the Person attainted.

Article IV

Section 1. Full Faith and Credit shall be given in each State to the public Acts, Records, and judicial Proceedings of every other State. And the Congress may by general Laws prescribe the Manner in which such Acts, Records and Proceedings shall be proved, and the Effect thereof.

Section 2. [1] The Citizens of each State shall be entitled to all Privileges and Immunities of Citizens in the several States.

[2] A Person charged in any State with Treason, Felony, or other Crime, who shall flee from Justice, and be found in another State, shall on demand of the executive Authority of the State from which he fled, be delivered up, to be removed to the State having Jurisdiction of the Crime.

[3] No Person held to Service or Labour in one State, under the Laws thereof, escaping into another, shall, in Consequence of any Law or Regulation therein, be discharged from such Service or Labour, but shall be delivered up on Claim of the Party to whom such Service or Labour may be due.

Section 3. [1] New States may be admitted by the Congress into this Union; but no new State shall be formed or erected within the Jurisdiction of any other State; nor any State be formed by the Junction of two or more States, or Parts of States, without the Consent of the Legislatures of the States concerned as well as of the Congress.

[2] The Congress shall have Power to dispose of and make all needful Rules and Regulations respecting the Territory or other Property belonging to the United States; and nothing in this Constitution shall be so construed as to Prejudice any Claims of the United States, or of any particular State.

Section 4. The United States shall guarantee to every State in this Union a Republican Form of Government, and shall protect each of them against Invasion; and on Application of the Legislature, or of the Executive (when the Legislature cannot be convened) against domestic Violence.

Article V

The Congress, whenever two thirds of both Houses shall deem it necessary, shall propose Amendments to this Constitution, or, on the Application of the Legislatures of two thirds of the several States, shall call a Convention for proposing Amendments, which, in either Case, shall be valid to all Intents and Purposes, as part of this Constitution, when ratified by the Legislatures of three fourths of the several States, or by Conventions in three fourths thereof, as the one or the other Mode of Ratification may be proposed by the Congress; Provided that no Amendment which may be made prior to the Year One thousand eight hundred and eight shall in any Manner affect the first and fourth Clauses in the Ninth Section of the first Article; and that no State, without its Consent, shall be deprived of its equal Suffrage in the Senate.

Article VI

[1] All Debts contracted and Engagements entered into, before the Adoption of this Constitution shall be as valid against the United States under this Constitution, as under the Confederation.

[2] This Constitution, and the Laws of the United States which shall be made in Pursuance thereof; and all Treaties made, or which shall be made, under the Authority of the United States, shall be the supreme Law of the Land; and the Judges in every State shall be bound thereby, any Thing in the Constitution or Laws of any State to the Contrary notwithstanding.

[3] The Senators and Representatives before mentioned, and the Members of the several State Legislatures, and all executive and judicial Officers, both of the United States and of the several States, shall be bound by Oath or Affirmation, to support this Constitution; but no religious Test shall ever be required as a Qualification to any Office or public Trust under the United States.

Article VII

The Ratification of the Conventions of nine States shall be sufficient for the Establishment of this Constitution between the States so ratifying the Same.

AMENDMENTS OF THE CONSTITUTION OF THE UNITED STATES OF AMERICA, PROPOSED BY CONGRESS AND RATIFIED BY THE LEGISLATURES OF THE SEVERAL STATES PURSUANT TO THE FIFTH ARTICLE OF THE ORIGINAL CONSTITUTION.

Amendment I [1791]

Congress shall make no law respecting an establishment of religion, or prohibiting the free exercise thereof; or abridging the freedom of speech, or of the press; or the right of the people peaceably to assemble, and to petition the Government for a redress of grievances.

Amendment II [1791]

A well regulated Militia, being necessary to the security of a free State, the right of the people to keep and bear Arms, shall not be infringed.

Amendment III [1791]

No Soldier shall, in time of peace be quartered in any house, without the consent of the Owner, nor in time of war, but in a manner to be prescribed by law.

Amendment IV [1791]

The right of the people to be secure in their persons, houses, papers, and effects, against unreasonable searches and seizures, shall not be violated, and no Warrants shall issue, but upon probable cause, supported by Oath or affirmation and particularly describing the place to be searched, and the persons or things to be seized.

Amendment V [1791]

No person shall be held to answer for a capital, or otherwise infamous crime, unless on a presentment or indictment of a Grand Jury, except in cases arising in the land or naval forces, or in the Militia, when in actual service in time of War or public danger; nor shall any person be subject for the same offence to be twice put in jeopardy of life or limb; nor shall be compelled in any criminal case to be a witness against himself, nor be deprived of life, liberty, or property, without due process of law; nor shall private property be taken for public use, without just compensation.

Amendment VI [1791]

In all criminal prosecutions, the accused shall enjoy the right to a speedy and public trial, by an impartial jury of the State and district wherein the crime shall have been committed, which district shall have been previously ascertained by law, and to be informed of the nature and cause of the accusation; to be confronted with the witnesses against him; to have compulsory process for obtaining witnesses in his favor, and to have the Assistance of Counsel for his defence.

AMENDMENT VII [1791]

In Suits at common law, where the value in controversy shall exceed twenty dollars, the right of trial by jury shall be preserved, and no fact tried by jury, shall be otherwise re-examined in any Court of the United States, than according to the rules of the common law.

AMENDMENT VIII [1791]

Excessive bail shall not be required, nor excessive fines imposed, nor cruel and unusual punishments inflicted.

AMENDMENT IX [1791]

The enumeration in the Constitution, of certain rights, shall not be construed to deny or disparage others retained by the people.

AMENDMENT X [1791]

The powers not delegated to the United States by the Constitution, nor prohibited by it to the States, are reserved to the States respectively, or to the people.

AMENDMENT XI [1798]

The Judicial power of the United States shall not be construed to extend to any suit in law or equity, commenced or prosecuted against one of the United States by Citizens of another State, or by Citizens or Subjects of any Foreign State.

AMENDMENT XII [1804]

The Electors shall meet in their respective states and vote by ballot for President and Vice-President, one of whom, at least, shall not be an inhabitant of the same state with themselves; they shall name in their ballots the person voted for as President, and in distinct ballots the person voted for as Vice-President, and they shall make distinct lists of all persons voted for as President, and of all persons voted for as Vice-President, and of the number of votes for each, which lists they shall sign and certify, and transmit sealed to the seat of the government of the United States, directed to the President of the Senate;—The President of the Senate shall, in the presence of the Senate and House of Representatives, open all the certificates and the votes shall then be counted;—The person having the greatest number of votes for President, shall be the President, if such number be a majority of the whole number of Electors appointed; and if no person have such majority, then from the persons having the highest numbers not exceeding three on the list of those voted for as President, the House of Representatives shall choose immediately, by ballot, the President. But in choosing the President, the votes shall be taken by states, the representation from each state having one vote; a quorum for this purpose shall consist of a member or members from two-thirds of the states, and a majority of all the states shall be necessary to a choice. And if the House of Representatives shall not choose a President whenever the right of choice shall devolve upon them before the fourth day of March next following, then the Vice-President shall act as President, as in the case of the death or other constitutional disability of the President.—The person having the greatest number of votes as Vice-President, shall be the Vice-President, if such number be a majority of the whole number of Electors appointed, and if no person have a majority, then from the two highest numbers on the list, the Senate shall choose the Vice-President; a quorum for the purpose shall consist of two-thirds of the whole number of Senators, and a majority of the whole number shall be necessary to a choice. But no person constitutionally ineligible to the office of President shall be eligible to that of Vice-President of the United States.

AMENDMENT XIII [1865]

Section 1. Neither slavery nor involuntary servitude, except as a punishment for crime whereof the party shall have been duly convicted, shall exist within the United States, or any place subject to their jurisdiction.

Section 2. Congress shall have power to enforce this article by appropriate legislation.

AMENDMENT XIV [1868]

Section 1. All persons born or naturalized in the United States, and subject to the jurisdiction thereof, are citizens of the United States and of the State wherein they reside. No State shall make or enforce any law which shall abridge the privileges or immunities of citizens of the United States; nor shall any State deprive any person of life, liberty, or property, without due process of law; nor deny to any person within its jurisdiction the equal protection of the laws.

Section 2. Representatives shall be apportioned among the several States according to their respective numbers, counting the whole number of persons in each State, excluding Indians not taxed. But when the right to vote at any election for the choice of electors for President and Vice President of the United States, Representatives in Congress, the Executive and Judicial officers of a State, or the members of the Legislature thereof, is denied to any of the male inhabitants of such State, being twenty-one years of age, and citizens of the United States, or in any way abridged, except for participation in rebellion, or other crime, the basis of representation therein shall be reduced in the proportion which the number of such male citizens shall bear to the whole number of male citizens twenty-one years of age in such State.

Section 3. No person shall be a Senator or Representative in Congress, or elector of President and Vice President, or hold any office, civil or military, under the United States, or under any State, who having previously taken an oath, as a member of Congress, or as an officer of the United States, or as a member of any State legislature, or as an executive or judicial officer of any State, to support the Constitution of the United States, shall have engaged in insurrection or rebellion against the same, or given aid or comfort to the enemies thereof. But Congress may by a vote of two-thirds of each House, remove such disability.

Section 4. The validity of the public debt of the United States, authorized by law, including debts incurred for payment of pensions and bounties for services in suppressing insurrection or rebellion, shall not be questioned. But neither the United States nor any State shall assume or pay any debt or obligation incurred in aid of insurrection or rebellion against the United States, or any claim for the loss or emancipation of any slave; but all such debts, obligations and claims shall be held illegal and void.

Section 5. The Congress shall have power to enforce, by appropriate legislation, the provisions of this article.

AMENDMENT XV [1870]

Section 1. The right of citizens of the United States to vote shall not be denied or abridged by the United States or by any State on account of race, color, or previous condition of servitude.

Section 2. The Congress shall have power to enforce this article by appropriate legislation.

AMENDMENT XVI [1913]

The Congress shall have power to lay and collect taxes on incomes, from whatever source derived, without apportionment among the several States, and without regard to any census or enumeration.

Amendment XVII [1913]

[1] The Senate of the United States shall be composed of two Senators from each State, elected by the people thereof, for six years; and each Senator shall have one vote. The electors in each State shall have the qualifications requisite for electors of the most numerous branch of the State legislatures.

[2] When vacancies happen in the representation of any State in the Senate, the executive authority of such State shall issue writs of election to fill such vacancies: *Provided,* That the legislature of any State may empower the executive thereof to make temporary appointments until the people fill the vacancies by election as the legislature may direct.

[3] This amendment shall not be so construed as to affect the election or term of any Senator chosen before it becomes valid as part of the Constitution.

Amendment XVIII [1919]

Section 1. After one year from the ratification of this article the manufacture, sale, or transportation of intoxicating liquors within, the importation thereof into, or the exportation thereof from the United States and all territory subject to the jurisdiction thereof for beverage purposes is hereby prohibited.

Section 2. The Congress and the several States shall have concurrent power to enforce this article by appropriate legislation.

Section 3. This article shall be inoperative unless it shall have been ratified as an amendment to the Constitution by the legislatures of the several States, as provided in the Constitution, within seven years from the date of the submission hereof to the States by the Congress.

Amendment XIX [1920]

[1] The right of citizens of the United States to vote shall not be denied or abridged by the United States or by any State on account of sex.

[2] Congress shall have power to enforce this article by appropriate legislation.

Amendment XX [1933]

Section 1. The terms of the President and Vice President shall end at noon on the 20th day of January, and the terms of Senators and Representatives at noon on the 3d day of January, of the years in which such terms would have ended if this article had not been ratified; and the terms of their successors shall then begin.

Section 2. The Congress shall assemble at least once in every year, and such meeting shall begin at noon on the 3d day of January, unless they shall by law appoint a different day.

Section 3. If, at the time fixed for the beginning of the term of the President, the President elect shall have died, the Vice President elect shall become President. If the President shall not have been chosen before the time fixed for the beginning of his term, or if the President elect shall have failed to qualify, then the Vice President elect shall act as President until a President shall have qualified; and the Congress may by law provide for the case wherein neither a President elect nor a Vice President elect shall have qualified, declaring who shall then act as President, or the manner in which one who is to act shall be selected, and such person shall act accordingly until a President or Vice President shall have qualified.

Section 4. The Congress may by law provide for the case of the death of any of the persons from whom the House of Representatives may choose a President whenever the right of choice shall have devolved upon them, and for the case of the death of any of the persons from whom the Senate may choose a Vice President whenever the right of choice shall have devolved upon them.

Section 5. Sections 1 and 2 shall take effect on the 15th day of October following the ratification of this article.

Section 6. This article shall be inoperative unless it shall have been ratified as an amendment to the Constitution by the legislatures of three-fourths of the several States within seven years from the date of its submission.

Amendment XXI [1933]

Section 1. The eighteenth article of amendment to the Constitution of the United States is hereby repealed.

Section 2. The transportation or importation into any State, Territory, or possession of the United States for delivery or use therein of intoxicating liquors, in violation of the laws thereof, is hereby prohibited.

Section 3. This article shall be inoperative unless it shall have been ratified as an amendment to the Constitution by conventions in the several States, as provided in the Constitution, within seven years from the date of the submission hereof to the States by the Congress.

Amendment XXII [1951]

Section 1. No person shall be elected to the office of the President more than twice, and no person who has held the office of President, or acted as President, for more than two years of a term to which some other person was elected President shall be elected to the office of President more than once. But this Article shall not apply to any person holding the office of President when this Article was proposed by the Congress, and shall not prevent any person who may be holding the office of President, or acting as President, during the term within which this Article becomes operative from holding the office of President or acting as President during the remainder of such term.

Section 2. This article shall be inoperative unless it shall have been ratified as an amendment to the Constitution by the legislatures of three-fourths of the several States within seven years from the date of its submission to the States by the Congress.

Amendment XXIII [1961]

Section 1. The District constituting the seat of Government of the United States shall appoint in such manner as the Congress may direct:

A number of electors of President and Vice President equal to the whole number of Senators and Representatives in Congress to which the District would be entitled if it were a State, but in no event more than the least populous state; they shall be in addition to those appointed by the states, but they shall be considered, for the purposes of the election of President and Vice President, to be electors appointed by a state; and they shall meet in the District and perform such duties as provided by the twelfth article of amendment.

Section 2. The Congress shall have power to enforce this article by appropriate legislation.

Amendment XXIV [1964]

Section 1. The right of citizens of the United States to vote in any primary or other election for President or Vice President, for electors for President or Vice President, or for Senator or Representative in Congress, shall not be denied or abridged by the United States or any State by reason of failure to pay any poll tax or other tax.

Section 2. The Congress shall have power to enforce this article by appropriate legislation.

AMENDMENT XXV [1967]

Section 1. In case of the removal of the President from office or of his death or resignation, the Vice President shall become President.

Section 2. Whenever there is a vacancy in the office of the Vice President, the President shall nominate a Vice President who shall take office upon confirmation by a majority vote of both Houses of Congress.

Section 3. Whenever the President transmits to the President pro tempore of the Senate and the Speaker of the House of Representatives his written declaration that he is unable to discharge the powers and duties of his office, and until he transmits to them a written declaration to the contrary, such powers and duties shall be discharged by the Vice President as Acting President.

Section 4. Whenever the Vice President and a majority of either the principal officers of the executive departments or of such other body as Congress may by law provide, transmit to the President pro tempore of the Senate and the Speaker of the House of Representatives their written declaration that the President is unable to discharge the powers and duties of his office, the Vice President shall immediately assume the powers and duties of the office as Acting President.

Thereafter, when the President transmits to the President pro tempore of the Senate and the Speaker of the House of Representatives his written declaration that no inability exists, he shall resume the powers and duties of his office unless the Vice President and a majority of either the principal officers of the executive department or of such other body as Congress may by law provide, transmit within four days to the President pro tempore of the Senate and the Speaker of the House of Representatives their written declaration that the President is unable to discharge the powers and duties of his office. Thereupon Congress shall decide the issue, assembling within forty-eight hours for that purpose if not in session. If the Congress, within twenty-one days after receipt of the latter written declaration, or, if Congress is not in session, within twenty-one days after Congress is required to assemble, determines by two-thirds vote of both Houses that the President is unable to discharge the powers and duties of his office, the Vice President shall continue to discharge the same as Acting President; otherwise, the President shall resume the powers and duties of his office.

AMENDMENT XXVI [1971]

Section 1. The right of citizens of the United States, who are eighteen years of age or older, to vote shall not be denied or abridged by the United States or by any State on account of age.

Section 2. The Congress shall have power to enforce this article by appropriate legislation.

AMENDMENT XXVII [1992] *

No law, varying compensation for the services of Senators and Representatives, shall take effect, until an election of Representatives shall have intervened.

* On May 7, 1992, more than 200 years after it was first proposed by James Madison, the Twenty–Seventh Amendment was ratified by a 38th State (Michigan). Although Congress set no time limit for ratification of this amendment, ten of the *other* amendments proposed at the same time (1789)—now known as the Bill of Rights—were ratified in a little more than two years. After all this time, is the ratification of the Twenty–Seventh Amendment valid? Does it matter that many of the states that ratified the amendment did not exist at the time it was first proposed?

†